DRAGON BALL

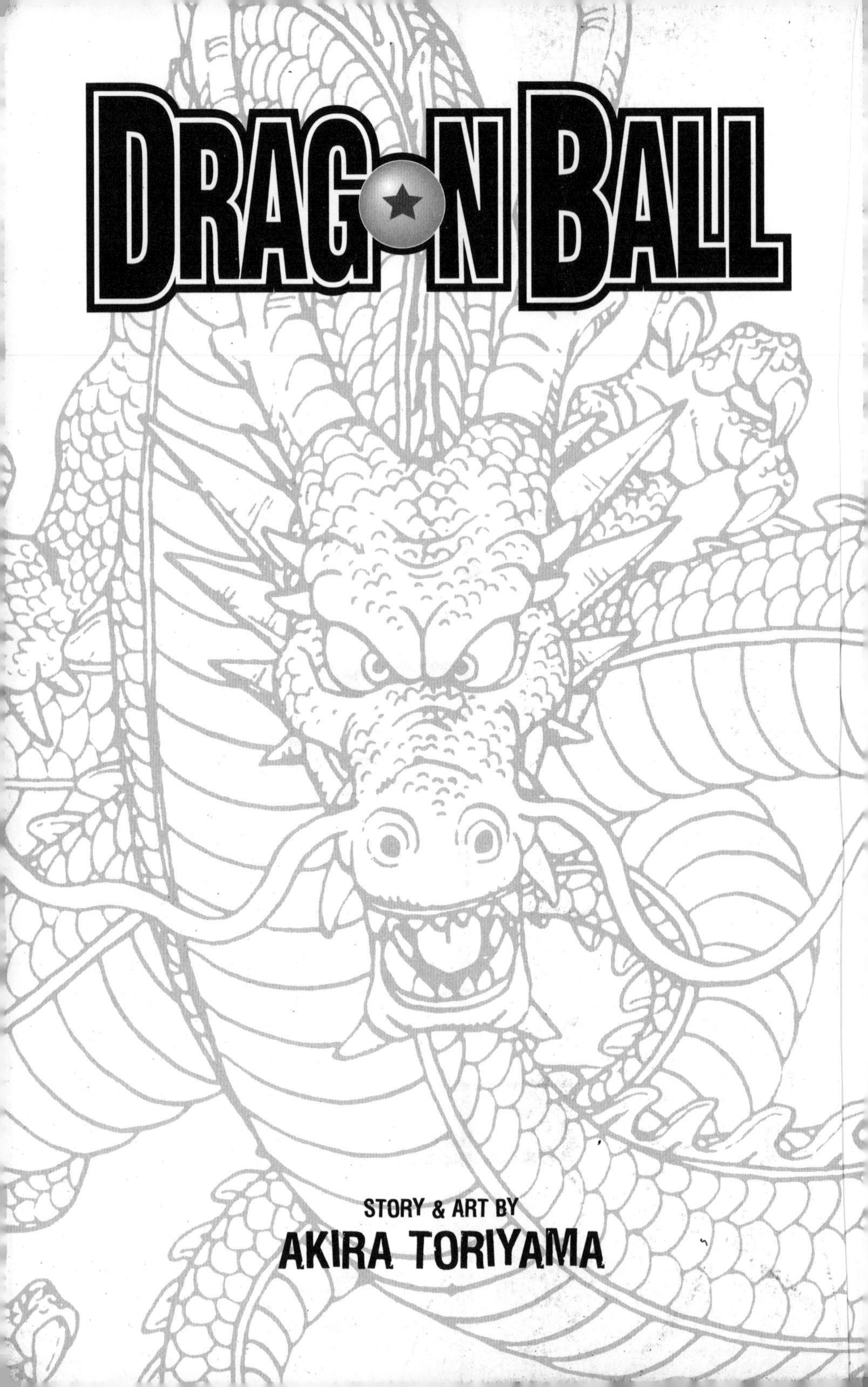

STORY & ART BY

AKIRA TORIYAMA

Dragon Ball
Volume 2
VIZBIG Edition

STORY AND ART BY
AKIRA TORIYAMA

English Adaptation **Gerard Jones**
Translation **Mari Morimoto**
Touch-up Art & Lettering **Wayne Truman**
Shonen Jump Series Design **Sean Lee**
VIZBIG Edition Design **Courtney Utt**
Shonen Jump Series Editor **Jason Thompson**
VIZBIG Edition Editor **Amy Yu**

Printed in China

Published by VIZ Media, LLC
P.O. Box 77010
San Francisco, CA 94107

10 9 8 7 6 5 4 3 2
First printing, September 2008
Second printing, September 2015

www.viz.com

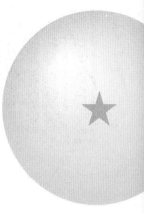

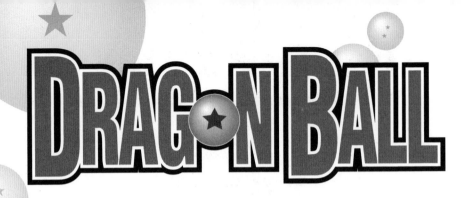

DRAGON BALL

VOLUME 4
STRONGEST UNDER THE HEAVENS

VOLUME 5
THE RED RIBBON ARMY

VOLUME 6
BULMA RETURNS

STORY & ART BY
AKIRA TORIYAMA

SHONEN JUMP MANGA . VIZBIG EDITION

CONTENTS

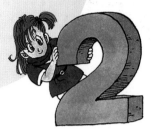

VOLUME 5
THE RED RIBBON ARMY

VOLUME 6
BULMA RETURNS

CAST OF CHARACTERS

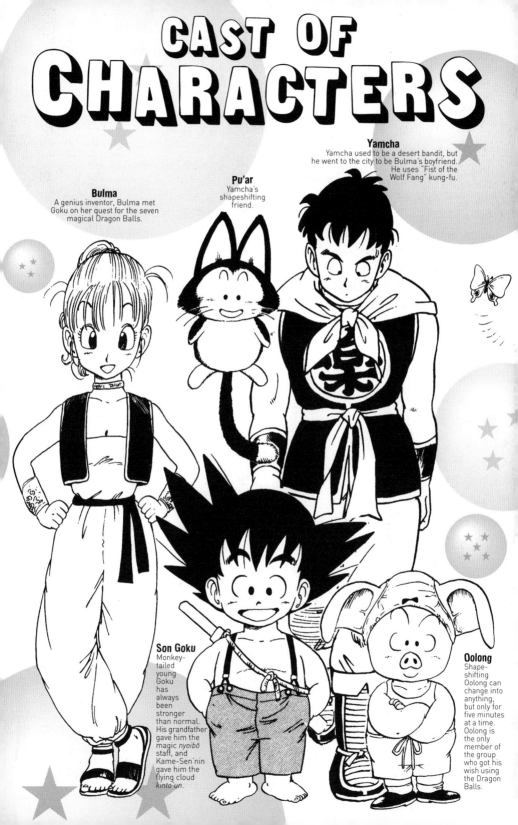

Yamcha
Yamcha used to be a desert bandit, but he went to the city to be Bulma's boyfriend. He uses "Fist of the Wolf Fang" kung-fu.

Pu'ar
Yamcha's shapeshifting friend.

Bulma
A genius inventor, Bulma met Goku on her quest for the seven magical Dragon Balls.

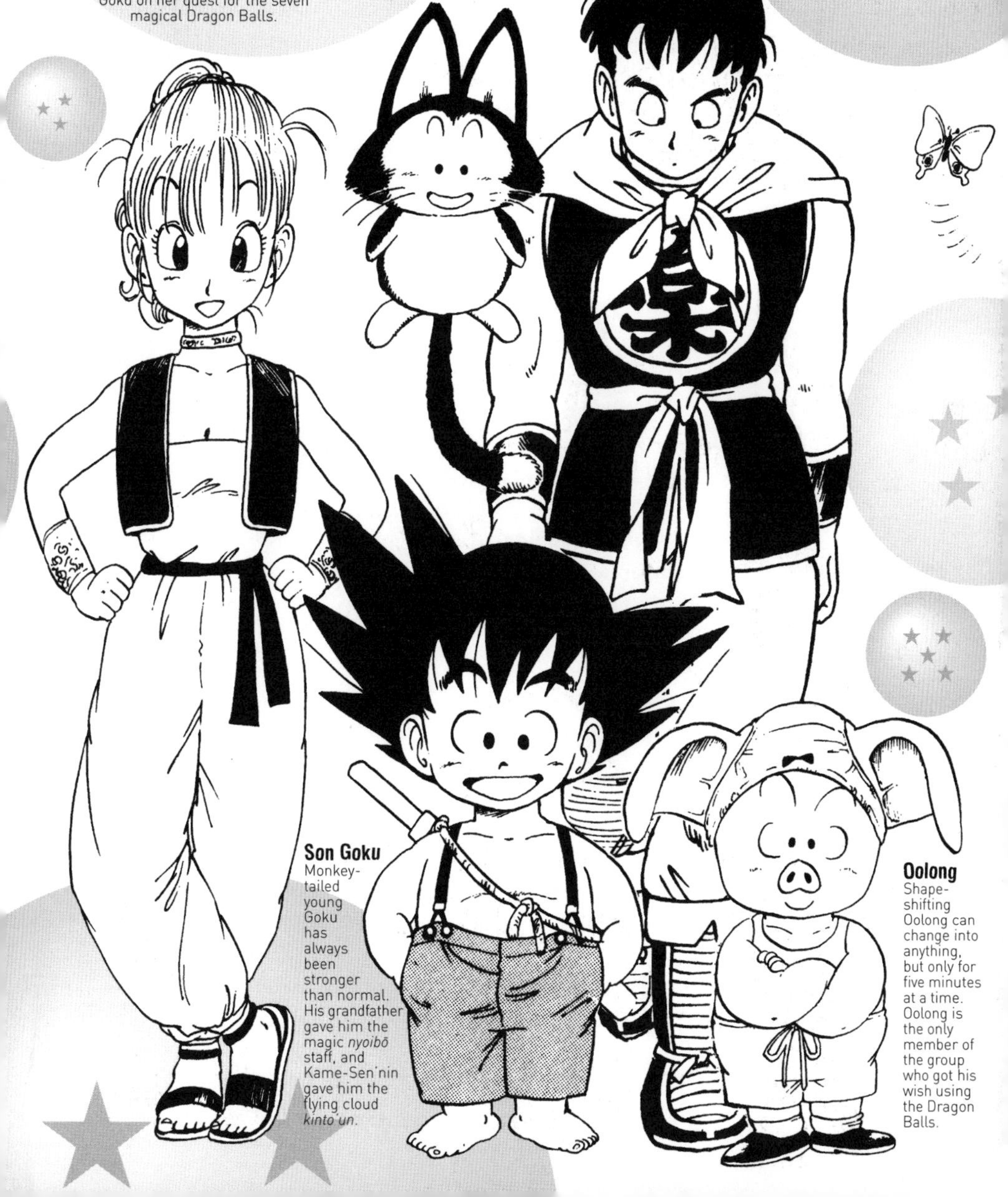

Son Goku
Monkey-tailed young Goku has always been stronger than normal. His grandfather gave him the magic *nyoibō* staff, and Kame-Sen'nin gave him the flying cloud *kinto'un*.

Oolong
Shape-shifting Oolong can change into anything, but only for five minutes at a time. Oolong is the only member of the group who got his wish using the Dragon Balls.

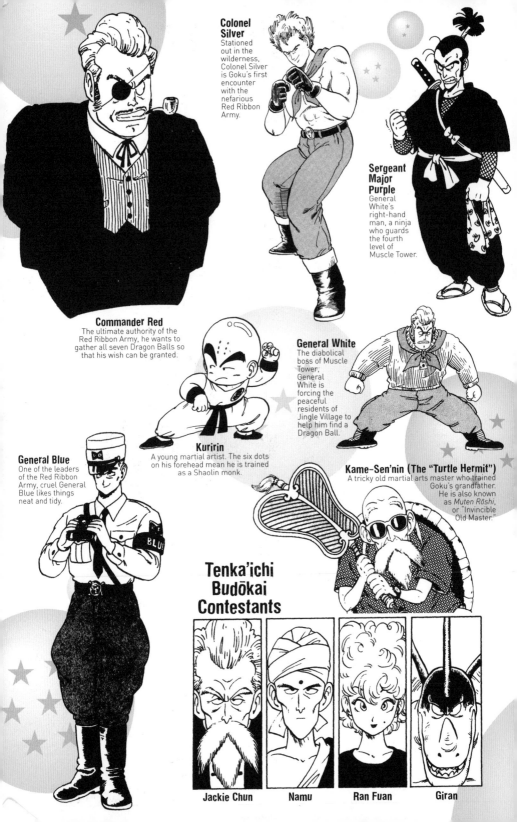

Colonel Silver
Stationed out in the wilderness, Colonel Silver is Goku's first encounter with the nefarious Red Ribbon Army.

Sergeant Major Purple
General White's right-hand man, a ninja who guards the fourth level of Muscle Tower.

Commander Red
The ultimate authority of the Red Ribbon Army, he wants to gather all seven Dragon Balls so that his wish can be granted.

General White
The diabolical boss of Muscle Tower, General White is forcing the peaceful residents of Jingle Village to help him find a Dragon Ball.

Kuririn
A young martial artist. The six dots on his forehead mean he is trained as a Shaolin monk.

General Blue
One of the leaders of the Red Ribbon Army, cruel General Blue likes things neat and tidy.

Kame-Sen'nin (The "Turtle Hermit")
A tricky old martial arts master who trained Goku's grandfather. He is also known as *Muten Rōshi*, or "Invincible Old Master."

Tenka'ichi Budōkai Contestants

Jackie Chun

Namu

Ran Fuan

Giran

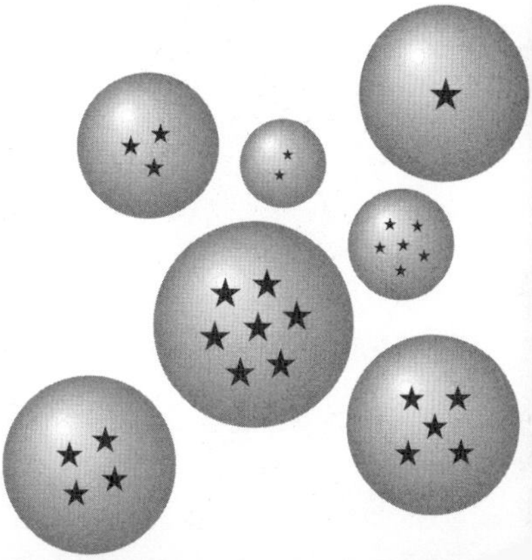

DragonBall

VOLUME 4

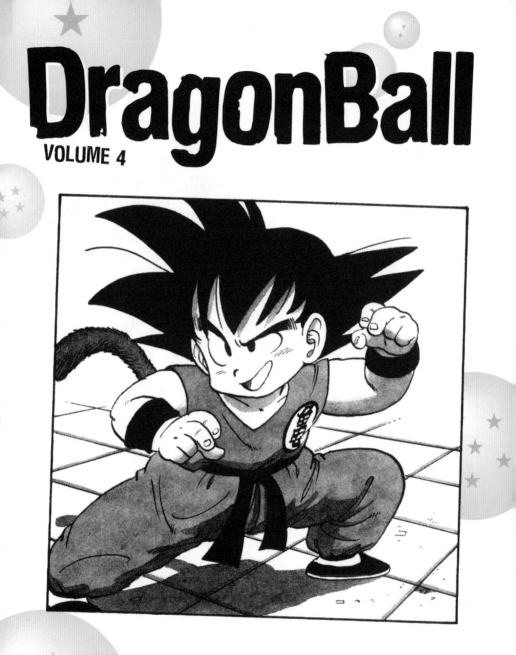

STRONGEST UNDER THE HEAVENS

Tale 37
Match No. 2

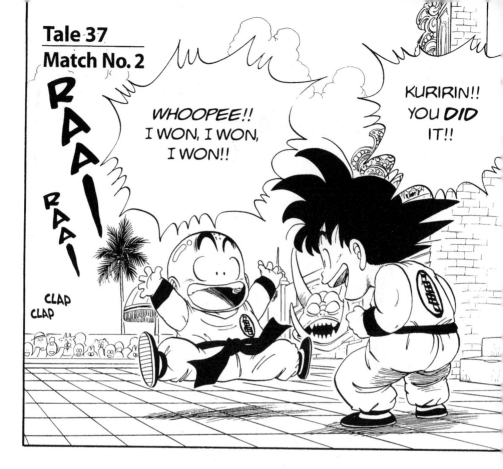

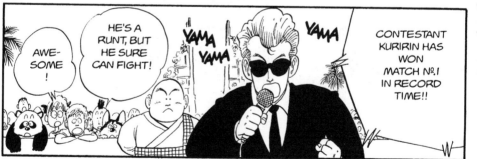

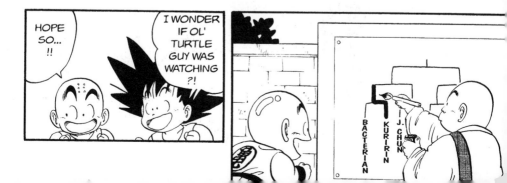

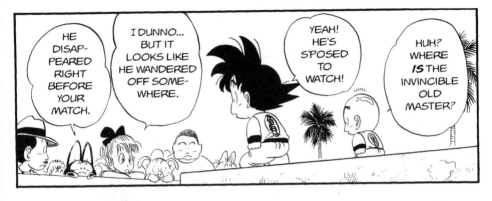

HE DISAPPEARED RIGHT BEFORE YOUR MATCH.

I DUNNO... BUT IT LOOKS LIKE HE WANDERED OFF SOMEWHERE.

YEAH! HE'S S'POSED TO WATCH!

HUH? WHERE *IS* THE INVINCIBLE OLD MASTER?

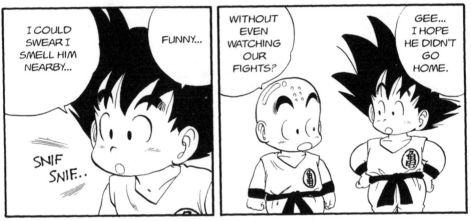

I COULD SWEAR I SMELL HIM NEARBY...

FUNNY...

SNIF SNIF...

WITHOUT EVEN WATCHING OUR FIGHTS?

GEE... I HOPE HE DIDN'T GO HOME.

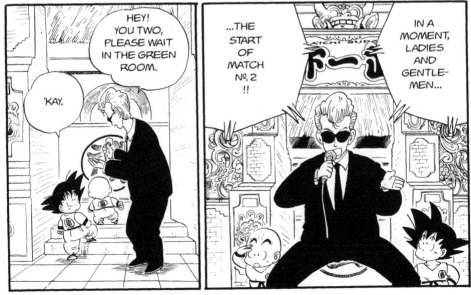

HEY! YOU TWO, PLEASE WAIT IN THE GREEN ROOM.

'KAY.

...THE START OF MATCH № 2 !!

IN A MOMENT, LADIES AND GENTLEMEN...

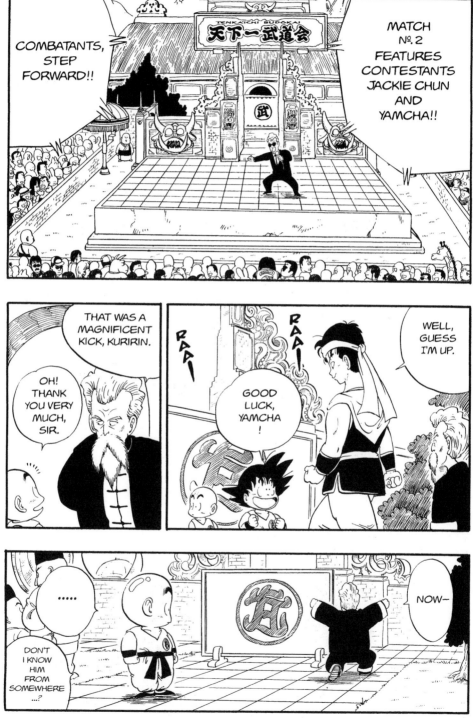

COMBATANTS, STEP FORWARD!!

MATCH Nº 2 FEATURES CONTESTANTS JACKIE CHUN AND YAMCHA!!

THAT WAS A MAGNIFICENT KICK, KURIRIN.

OH! THANK YOU VERY MUCH, SIR.

RAA!

RAA!

GOOD LUCK, YAMCHA!

WELL, GUESS I'M UP.

.....

DON'T I KNOW HIM FROM SOMEWHERE ...?

NOW—

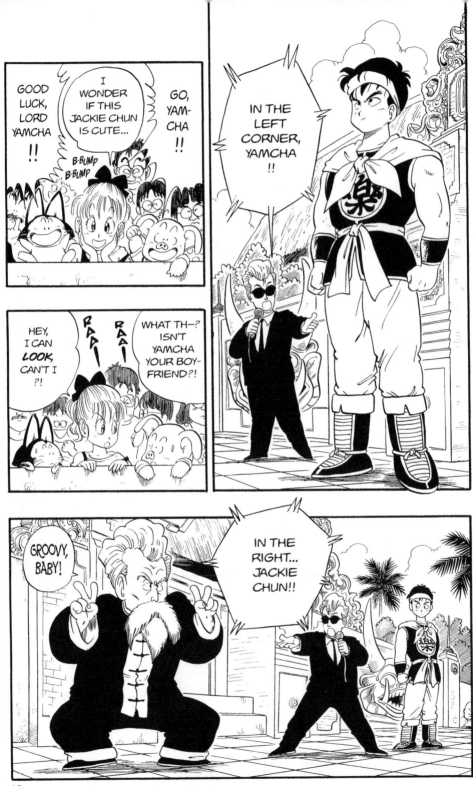

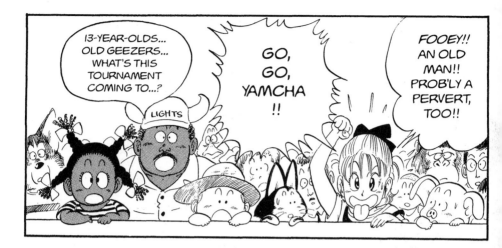

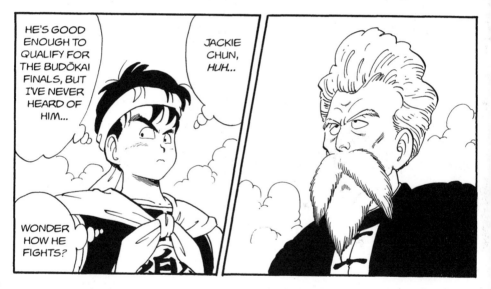

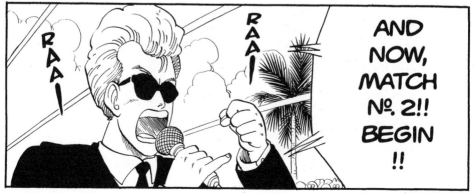

14

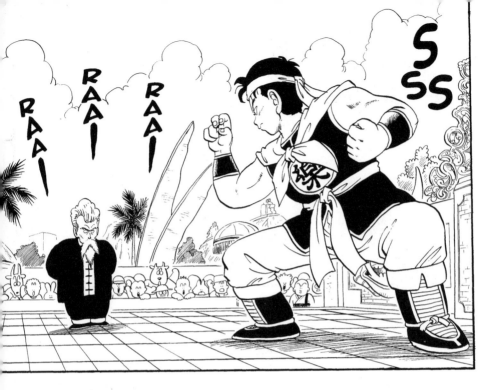

HE'S LEAVING HIMSELF OPEN ALL OVER THE PLACE. AND I DON'T FEEL AN OUNCE OF BATTLE-SPIRIT IN HIM, EITHER...

WH-WHAT THE—? HE'S NOT TAKING A STANCE?

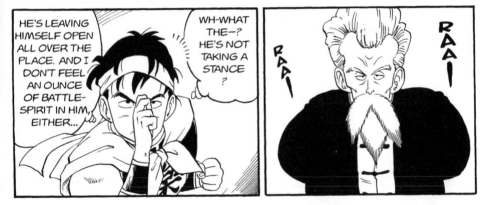

COME TO THINK OF IT, DURING THE QUALIFYING ROUNDS, IT SEEMED LIKE THIS OLD GUY WAS ENDING HIS FIGHTS AWFUL QUICK... I GUESS I SHOULD MAKE THE FIRST MOVE AND SEE HOW HE COUNTERS!

HE MUST HAVE OVER-WHELMING CONFIDENCE...

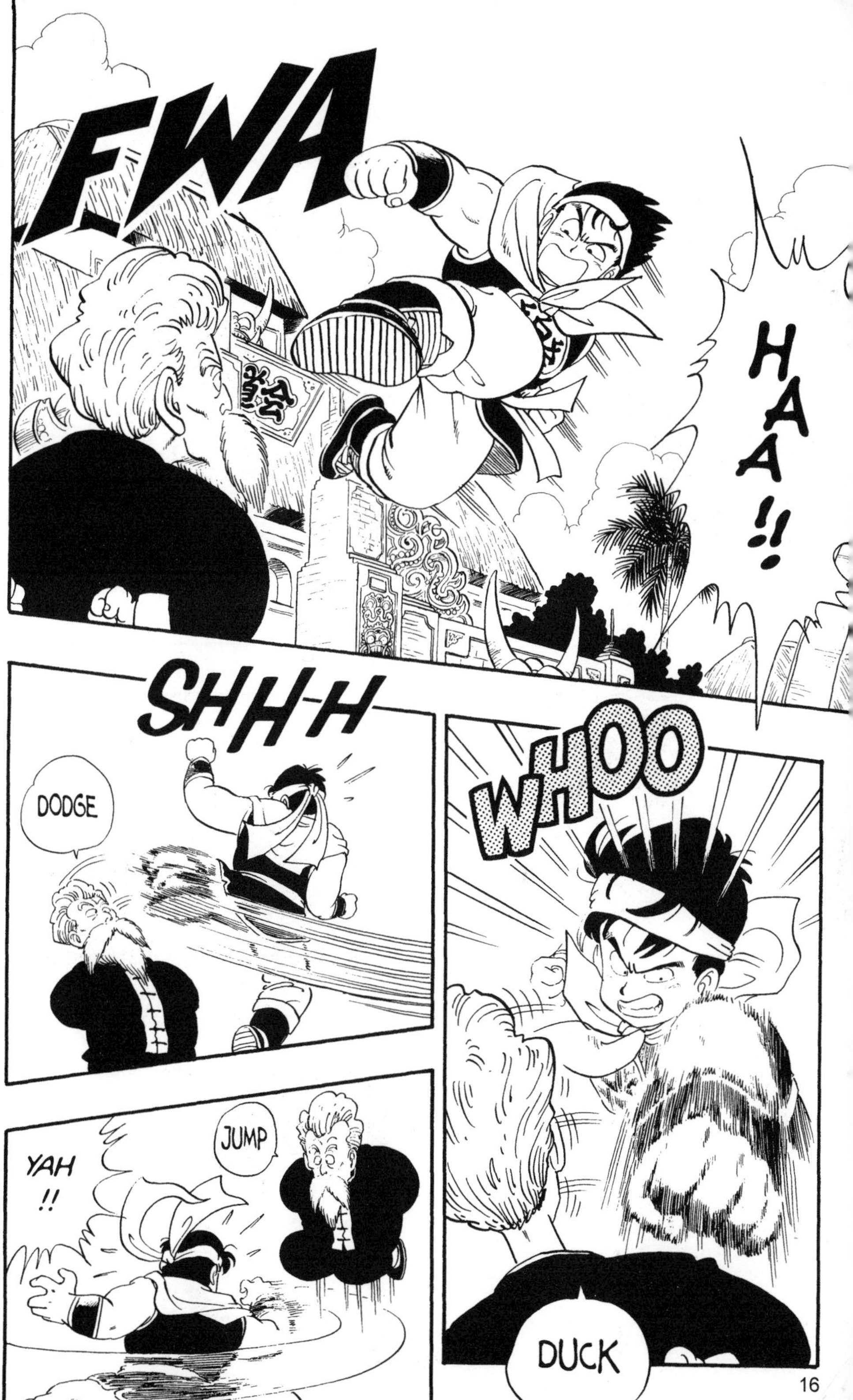
HAA!!
FWA
WHOO
DUCK
SHH-H
DODGE
JUMP
YAH!!

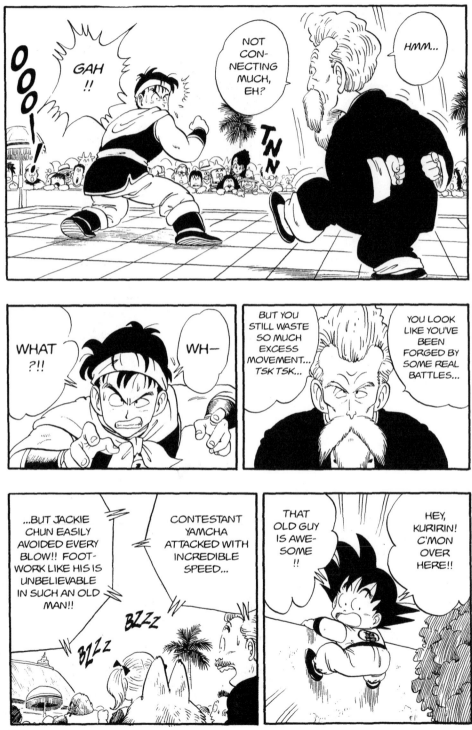

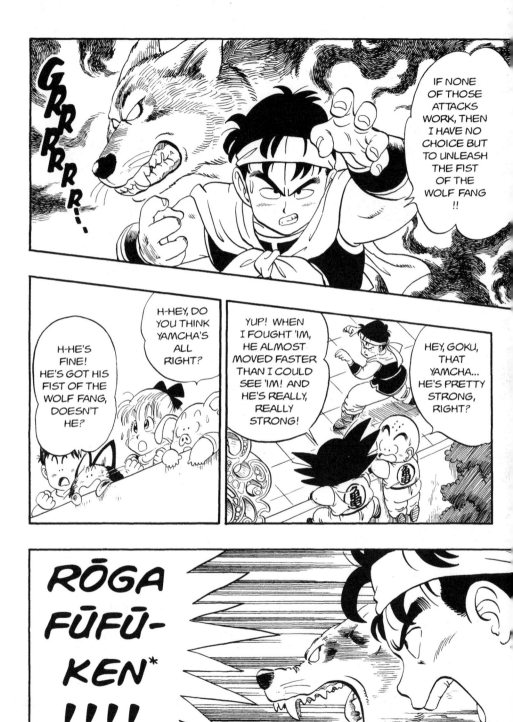

GRRRRR...

IF NONE OF THOSE ATTACKS WORK, THEN I HAVE NO CHOICE BUT TO UNLEASH THE FIST OF THE WOLF FANG!!

H-HE'S FINE! HE'S GOT HIS FIST OF THE WOLF FANG, DOESN'T HE?

H-HEY, DO YOU THINK YAMCHA'S ALL RIGHT?

YUP! WHEN I FOUGHT 'IM, HE ALMOST MOVED FASTER THAN I COULD SEE 'IM! AND HE'S REALLY, REALLY STRONG!

HEY, GOKU, THAT YAMCHA... HE'S PRETTY STRONG, RIGHT?

RŌGA FŪFŪ- KEN*!!!!

*FIST OF THE WOLF FANG GALE

18

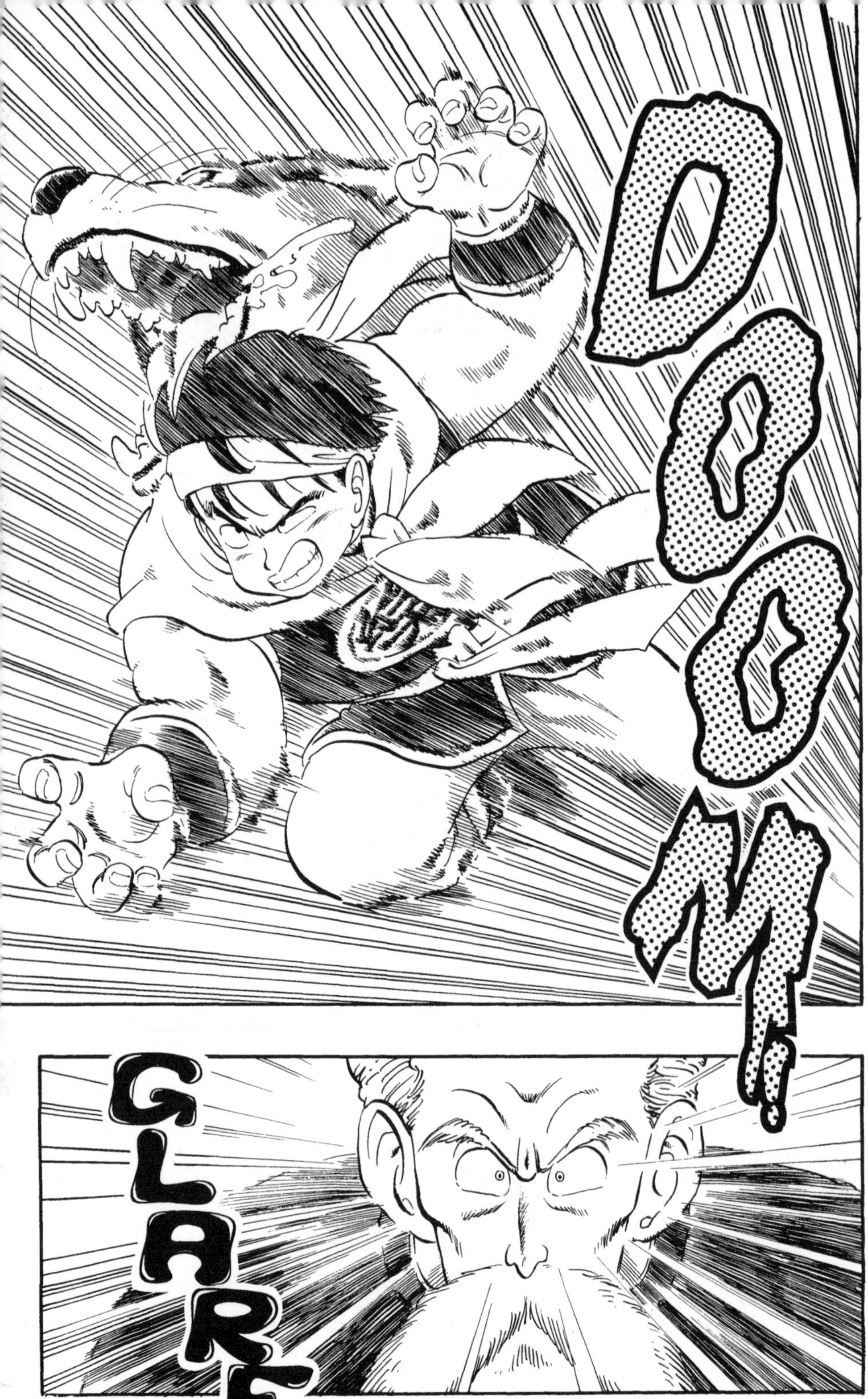
DOOOM!
GLARE

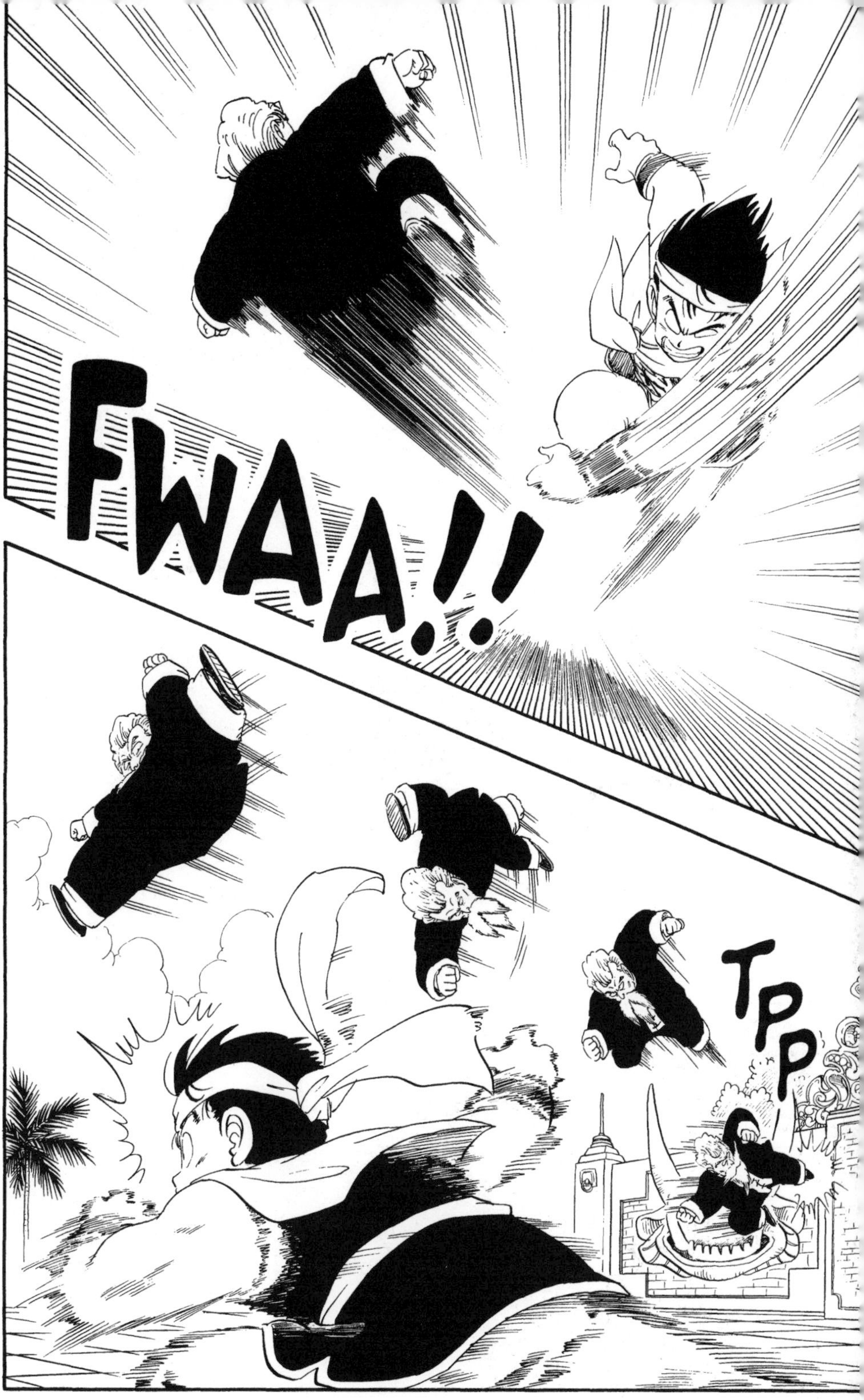
FWAA!!
TPP

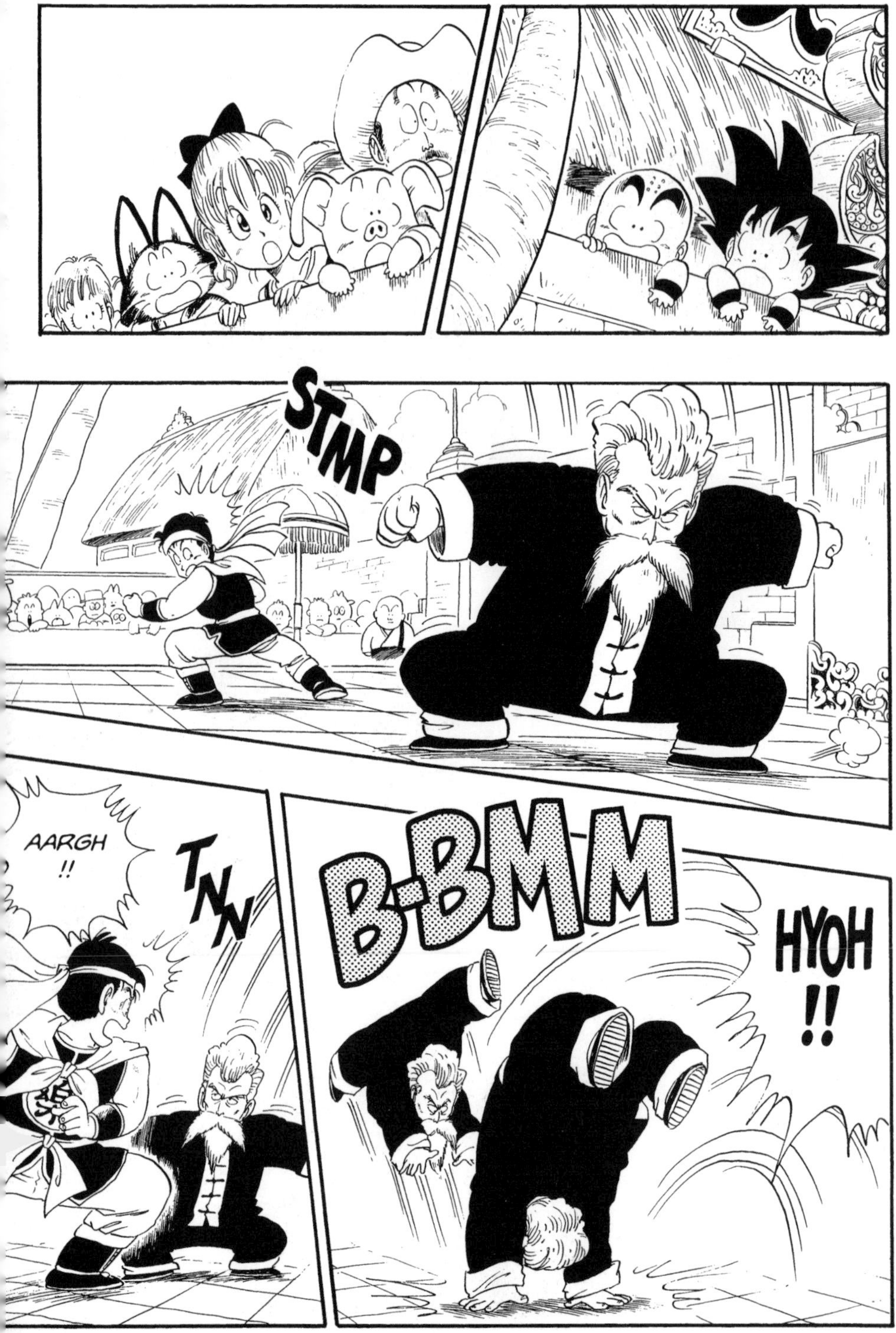
STMP
B-BMM
HYOH !!
AARGH !!
TNN

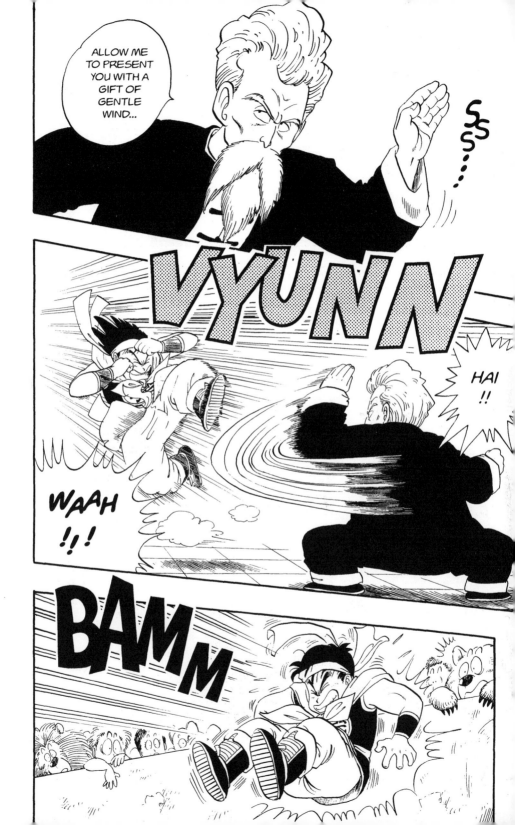

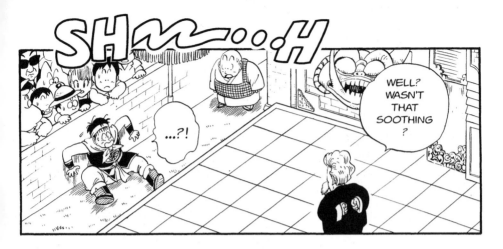

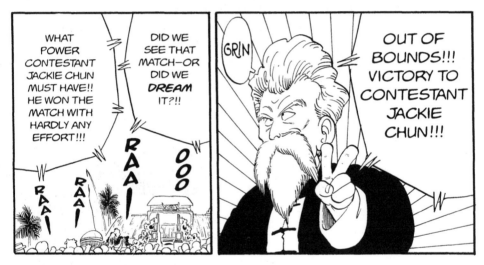

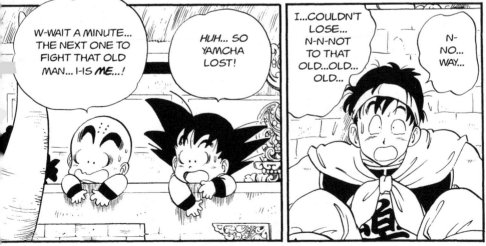

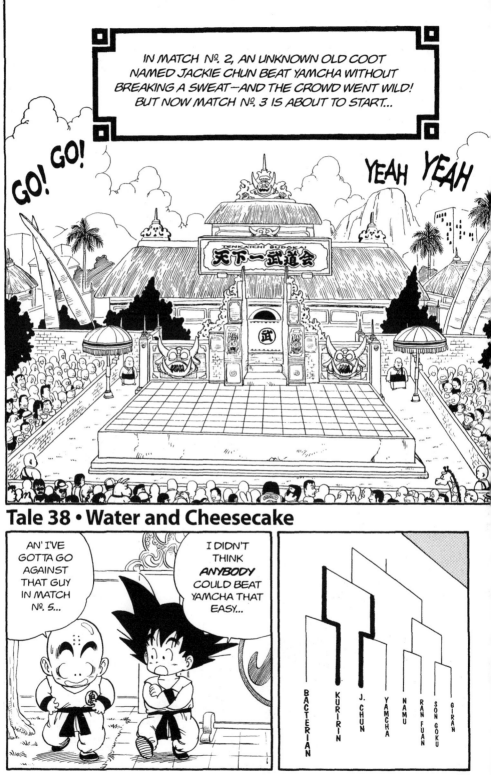

IN MATCH Nº. 2, AN UNKNOWN OLD COOT NAMED JACKIE CHUN BEAT YAMCHA WITHOUT BREAKING A SWEAT—AND THE CROWD WENT WILD! BUT NOW MATCH Nº. 3 IS ABOUT TO START...

GO! GO!

YEAH YEAH

Tale 38 • Water and Cheesecake

AN' I'VE GOTTA GO AGAINST THAT GUY IN MATCH Nº. 5...

I DIDN'T THINK *ANYBODY* COULD BEAT YAMCHA THAT EASY...

BACTERIAN · KURIRIN · J. CHUN · YAMCHA · NAMU · RAN FUAN · SON GOKU · GIRAN

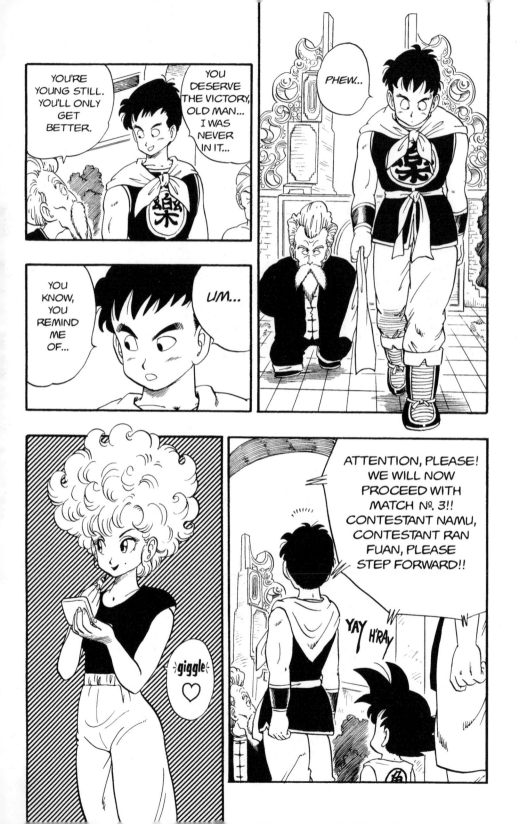

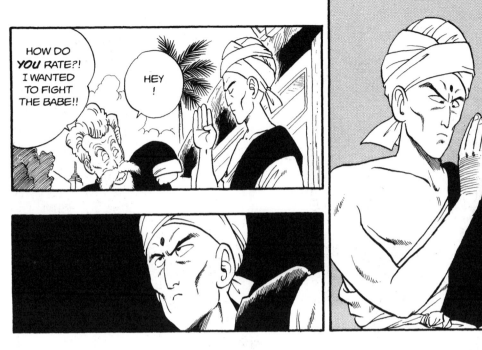

HOW DO **YOU** RATE?!
I WANTED
TO FIGHT
THE BABE!!

HEY
!

HOW CAN HE BE
EMANATING SUCH
INTENSITY OF WILL...
IN A GLORIFIED
CARNIVAL LIKE **THIS**?!

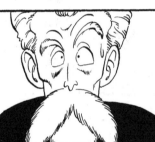

WHAT...?
THAT GAZE...
POWERFUL...
IMPLACABLE...
STRAIGHT OUT
OF A COMIC
BOOK!

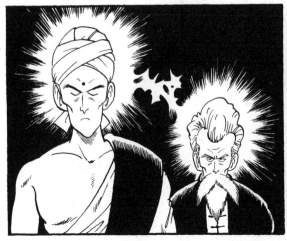

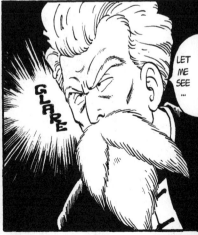

GLARE

LET
ME
SEE
...

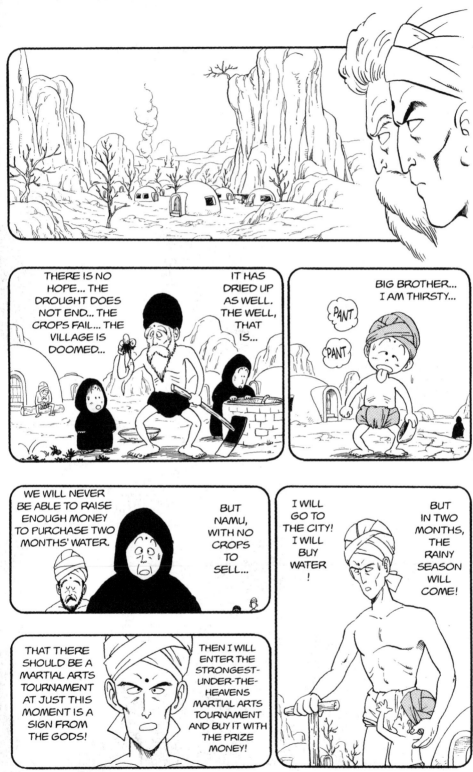

27

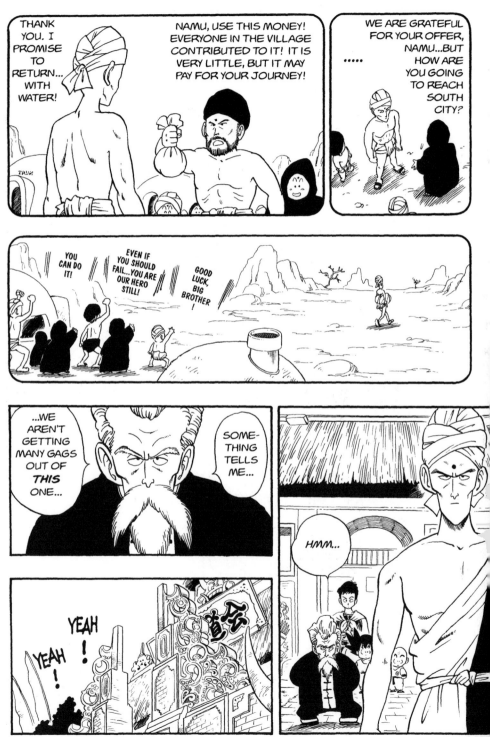

28

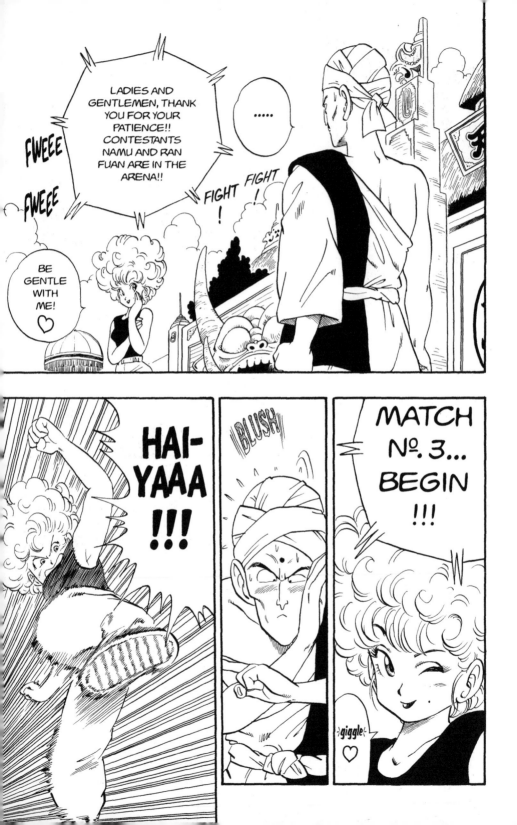

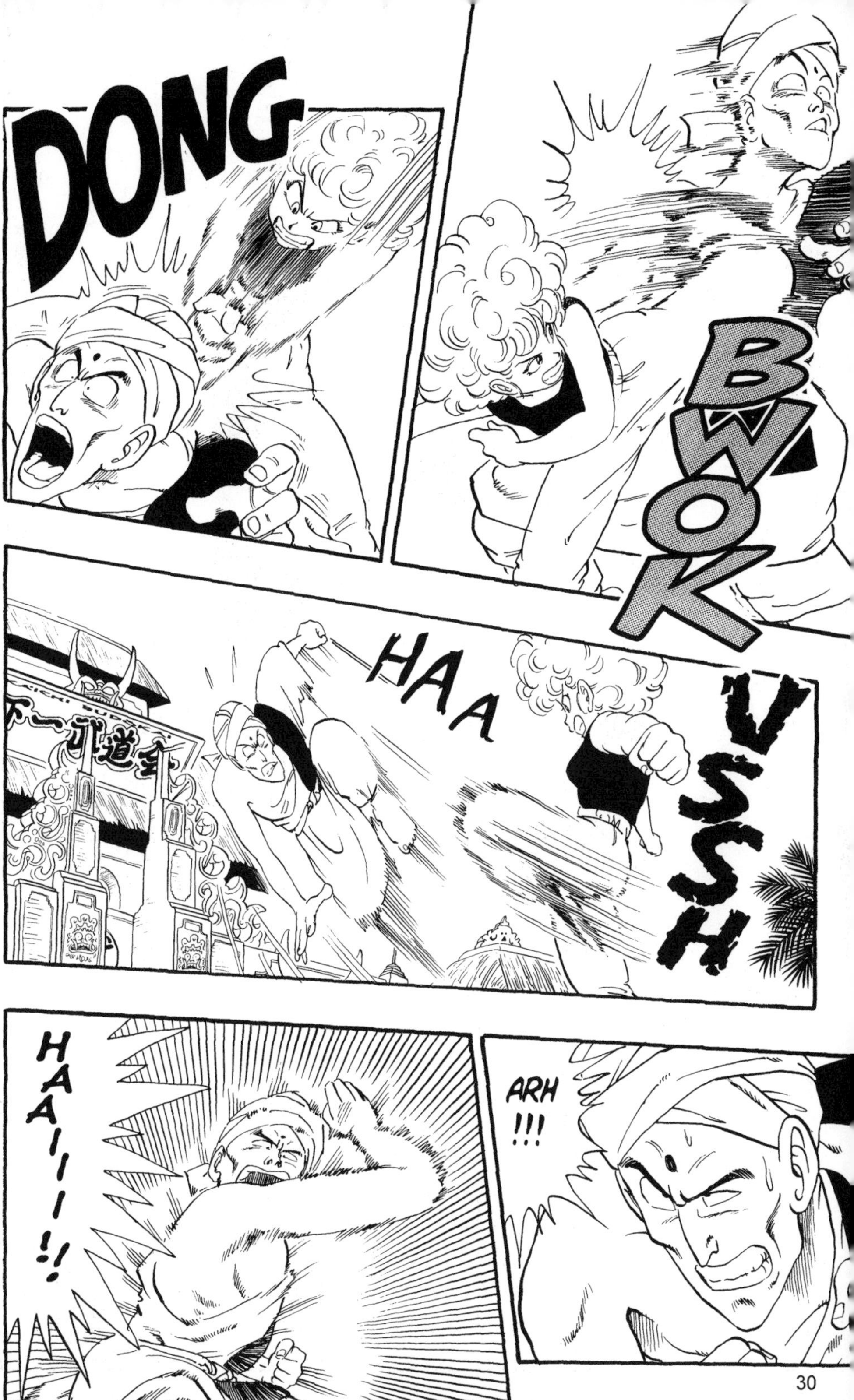
BWOK
DONG
VSSH
HAA
ARH !!!
HAAIIII!!

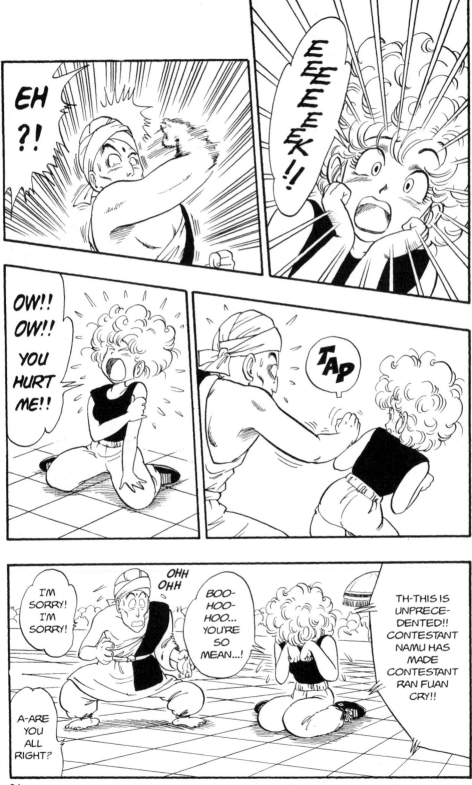

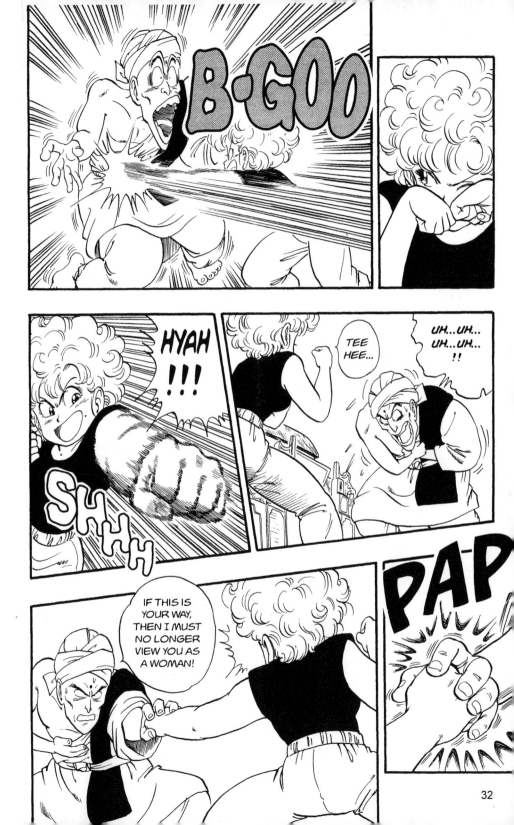

32

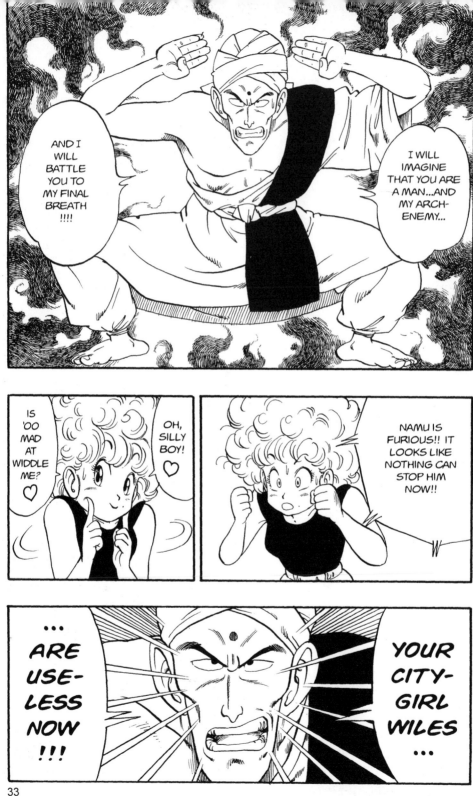

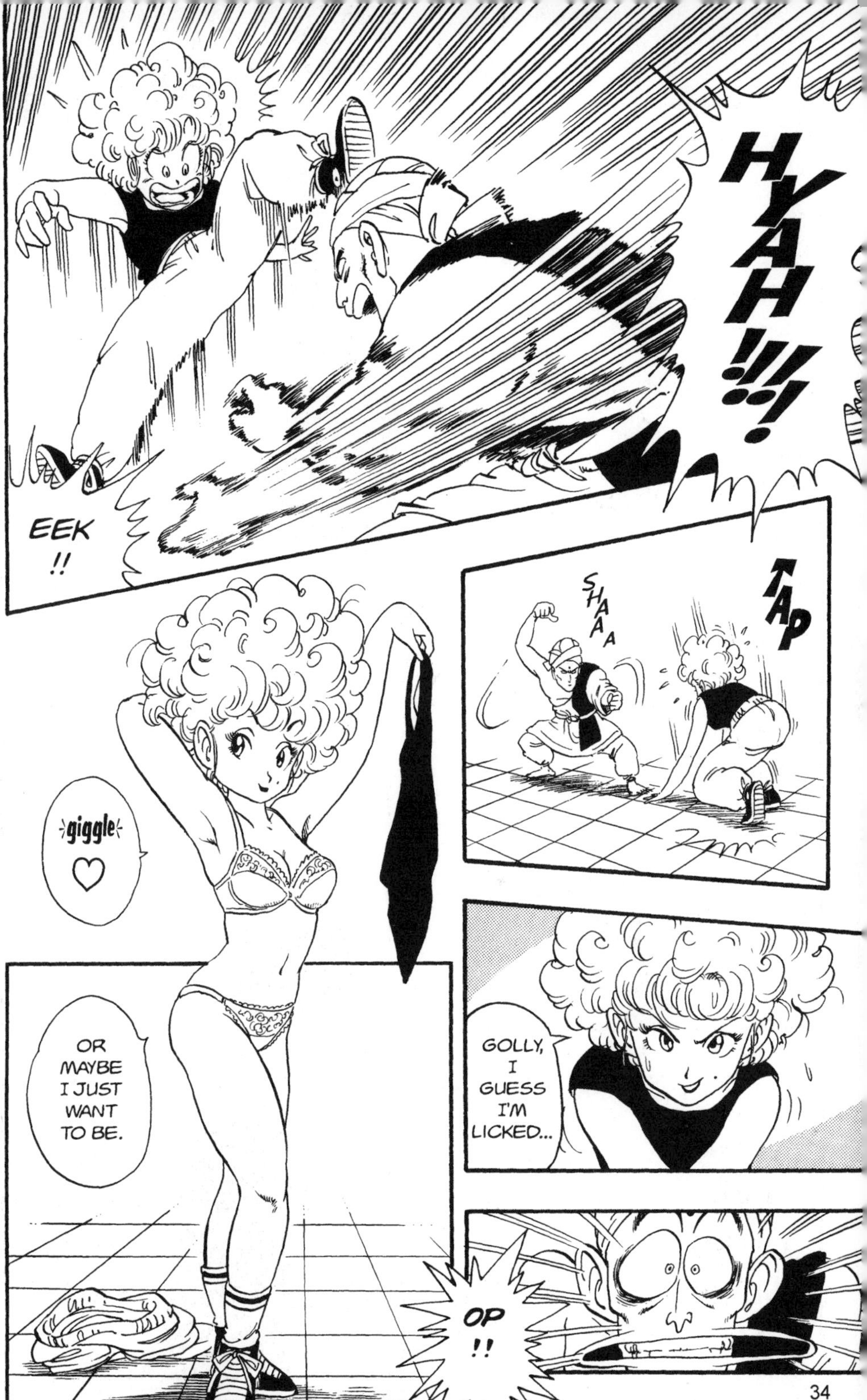
HYAH!!!!
EEK !!
TAP
SHAAA
GOLLY, I GUESS I'M LICKED...
OP !!
giggle ♡
OR MAYBE I JUST WANT TO BE.

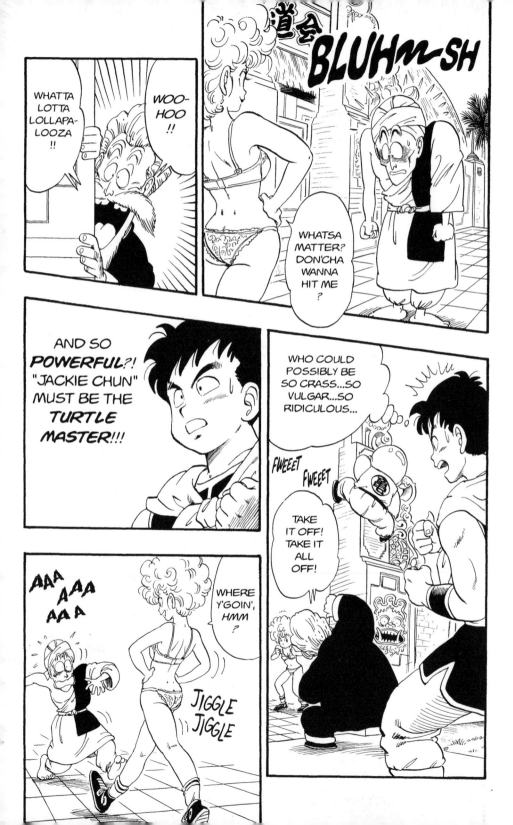

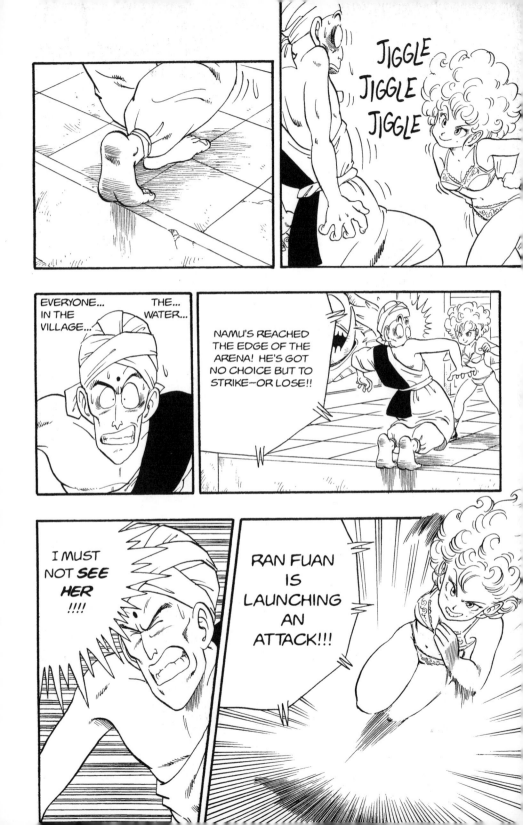

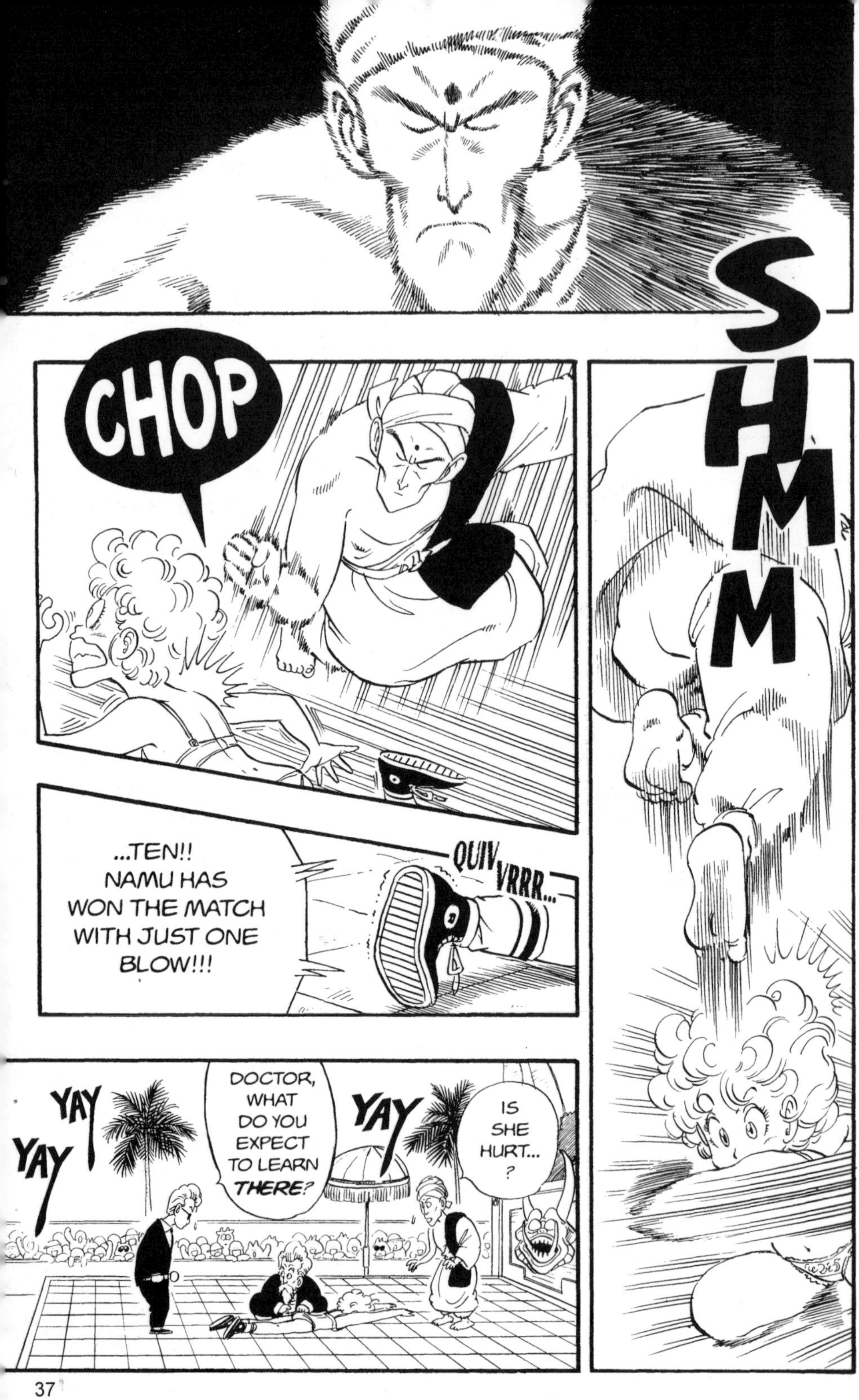
SHMMM
CHOP
...TEN!! NAMU HAS WON THE MATCH WITH JUST ONE BLOW!!!
QUIV VRRR...
IS SHE HURT...?
YAY
DOCTOR, WHAT DO YOU EXPECT TO LEARN *THERE?*
YAY
YAY

Tale 39
Monster Smash!

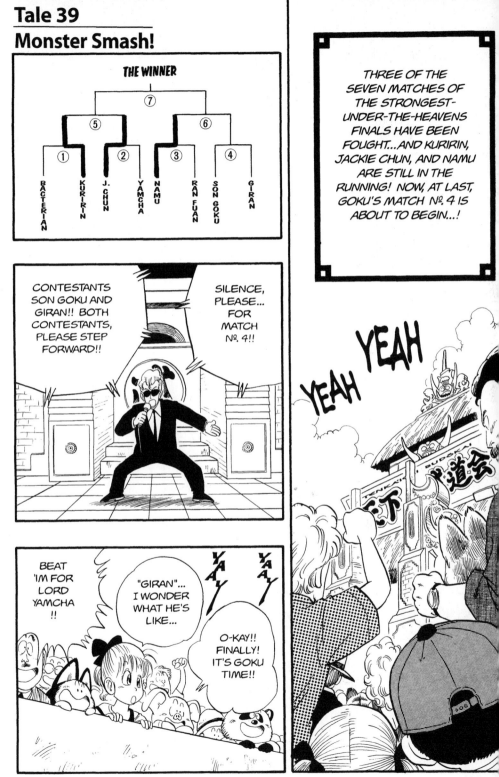

THE WINNER

⑦

⑤　　　　⑥

①　②　　③　④

BACTERIAN　KURIRIN　J. CHUN　YAMCHA　NAMU　RAN FUAN　SON GOKU　GIRAN

THREE OF THE SEVEN MATCHES OF THE STRONGEST-UNDER-THE-HEAVENS FINALS HAVE BEEN FOUGHT...AND KURIRIN, JACKIE CHUN, AND NAMU ARE STILL IN THE RUNNING! NOW, AT LAST, GOKU'S MATCH No. 4 IS ABOUT TO BEGIN...!

CONTESTANTS SON GOKU AND GIRAN!! BOTH CONTESTANTS, PLEASE STEP FORWARD!!

SILENCE, PLEASE... FOR MATCH No. 4!!

YEAH YEAH

BEAT 'IM FOR LORD YAMCHA !!

"GIRAN"... I WONDER WHAT HE'S LIKE...

YAAY YAAY

O-KAY!! FINALLY! IT'S GOKU TIME!!

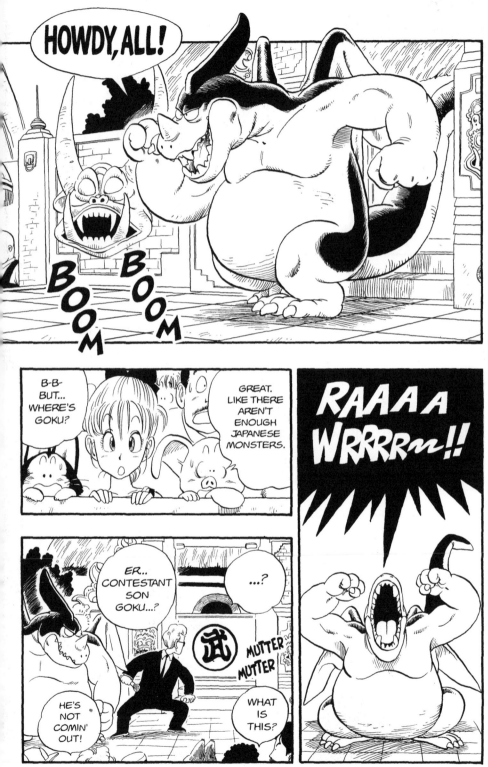

39

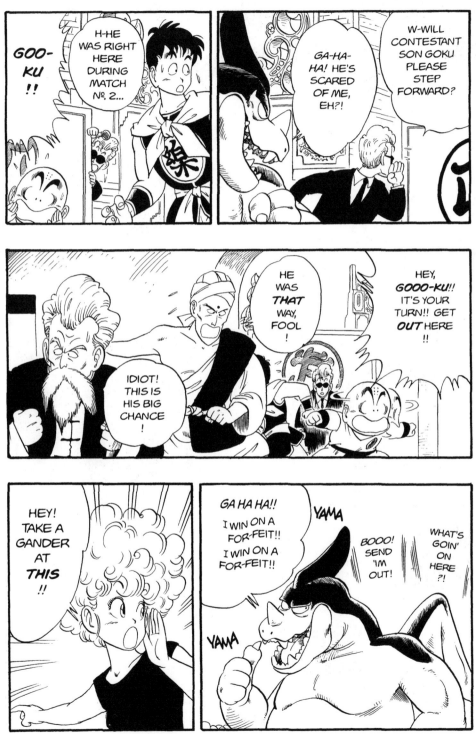

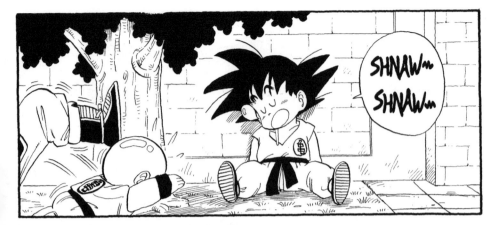

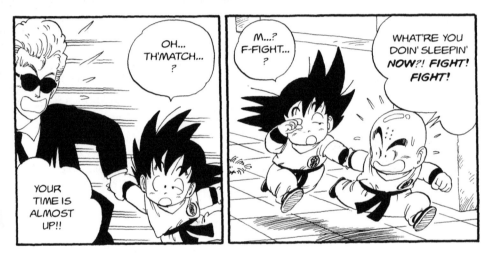

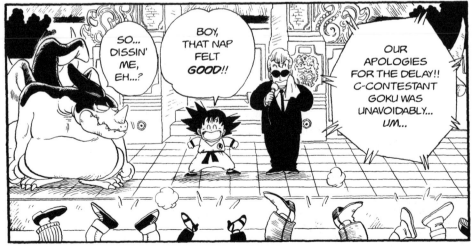

41

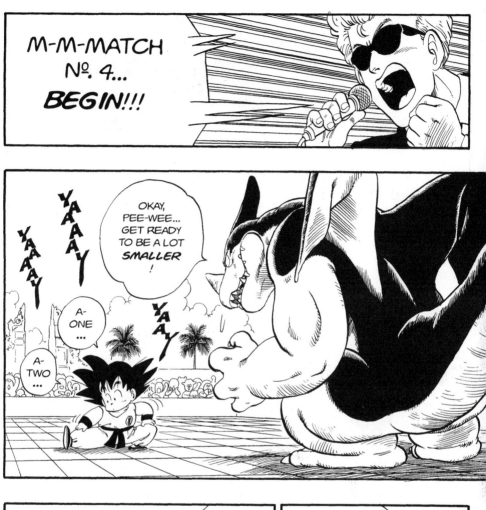

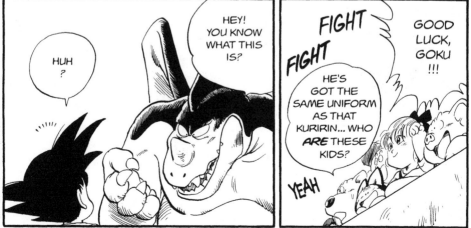

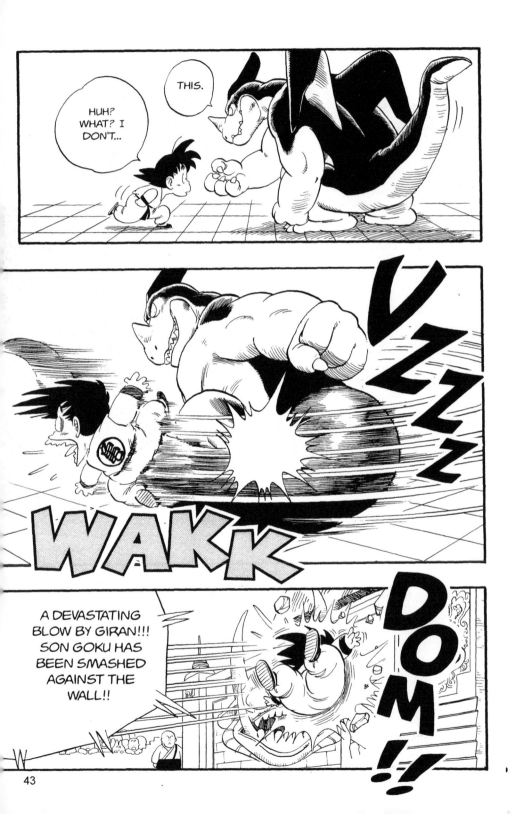

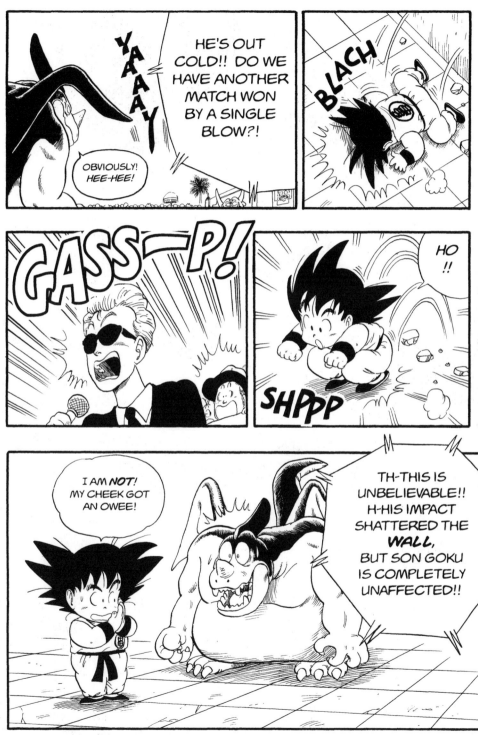

44

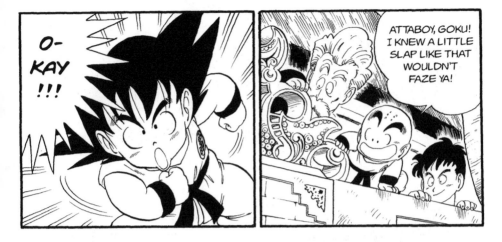

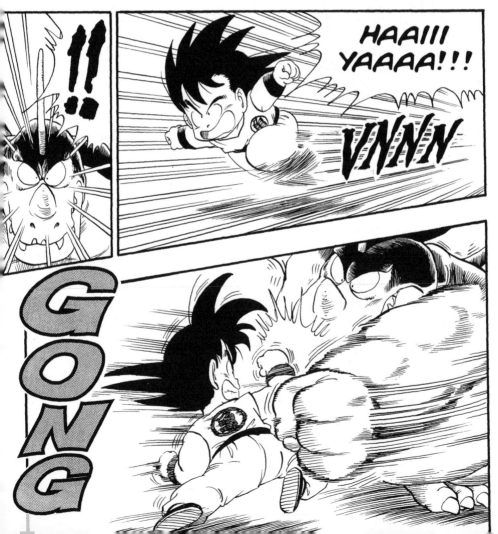

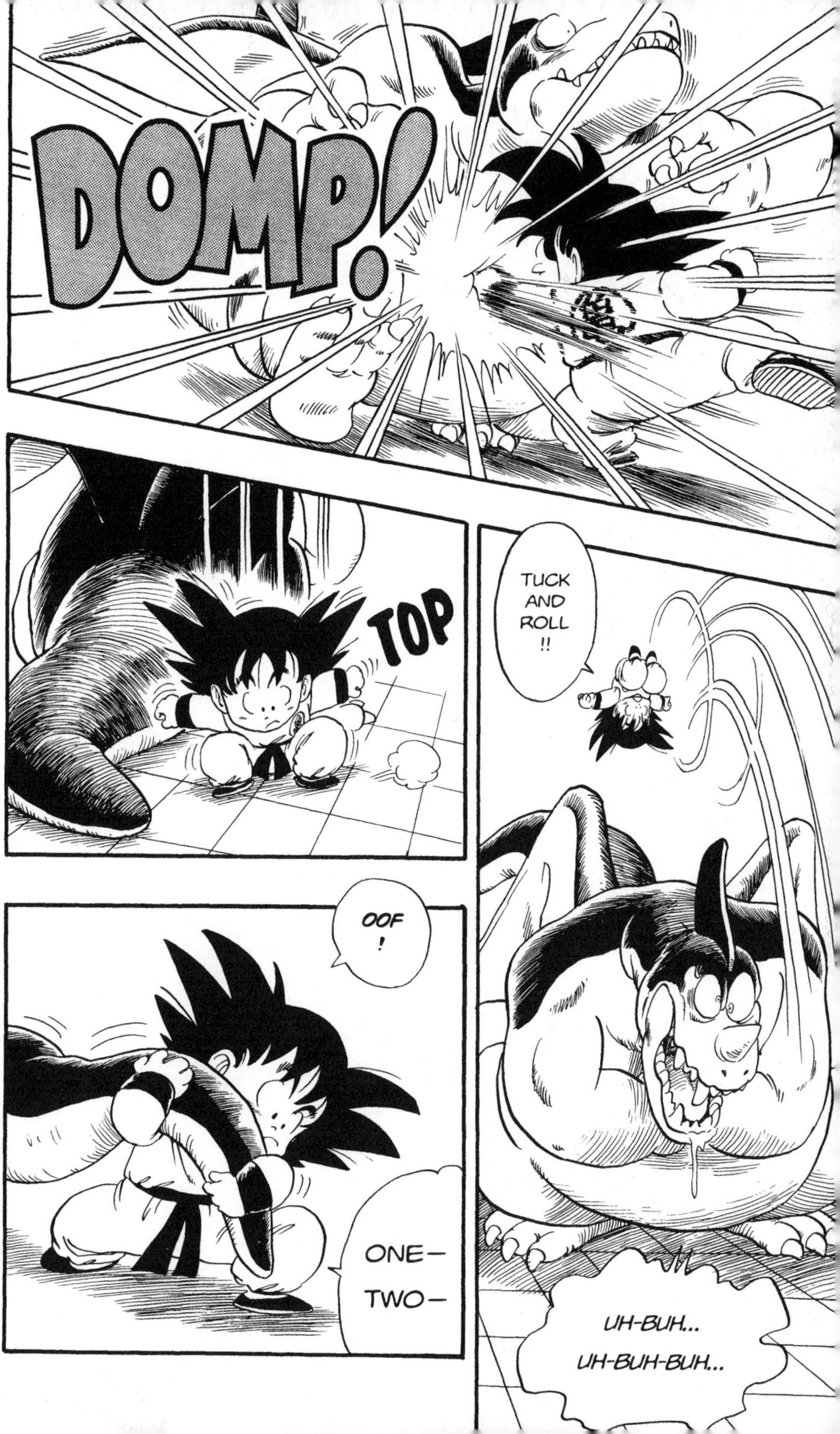
DOMP!
TUCK AND ROLL !!
UH-BUH... UH-BUH-BUH...
TOP
OOF !
ONE- TWO-

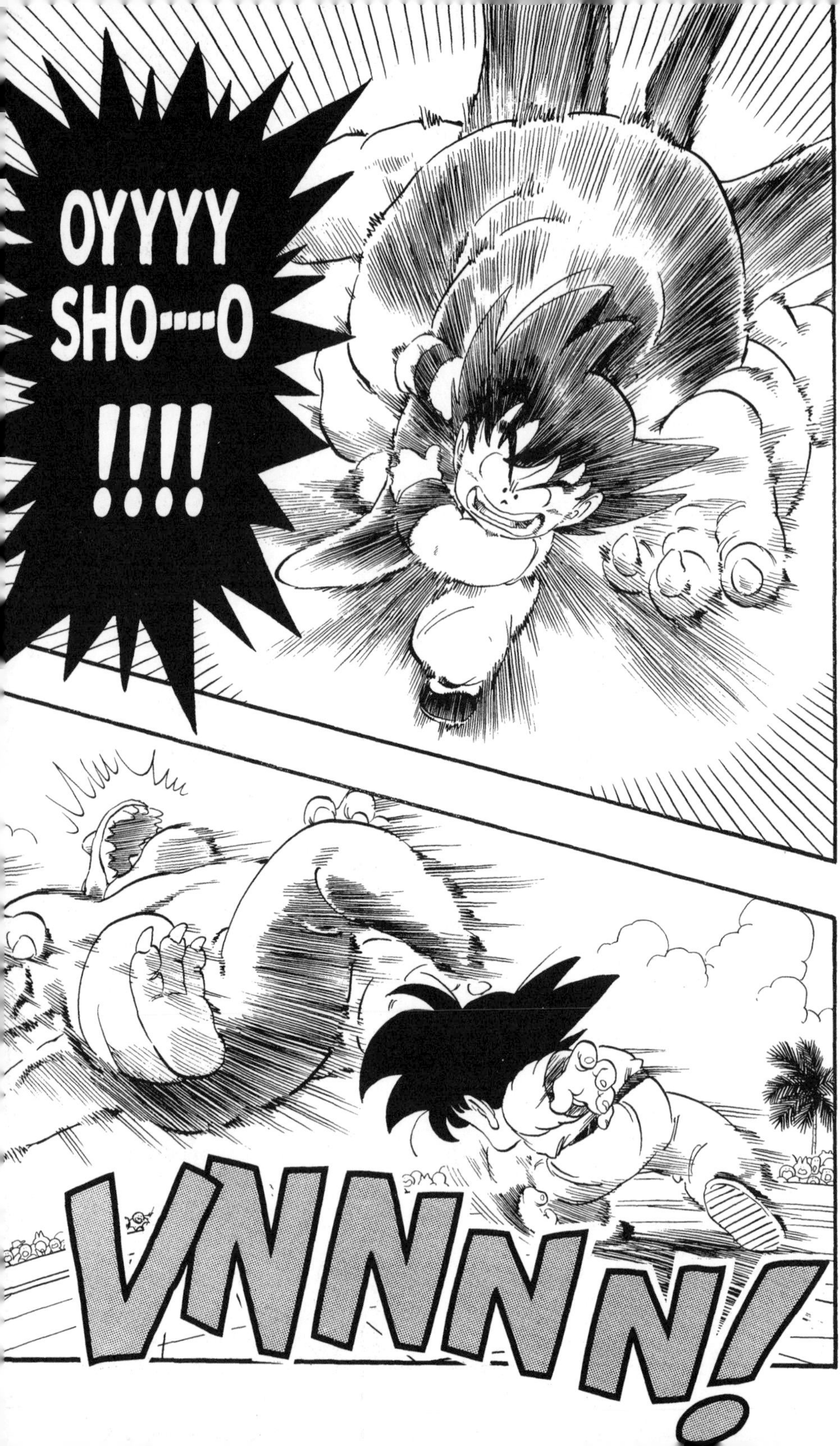
OYYYY SHO----O !!!!
VNNNN!

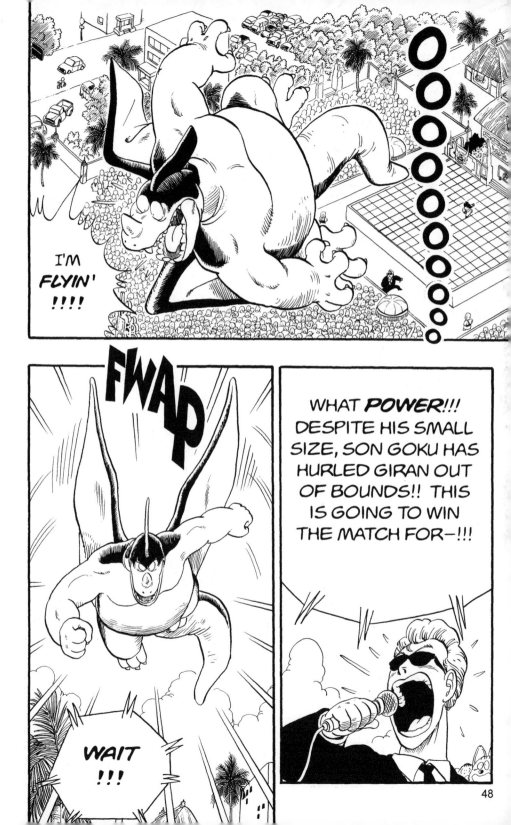

48

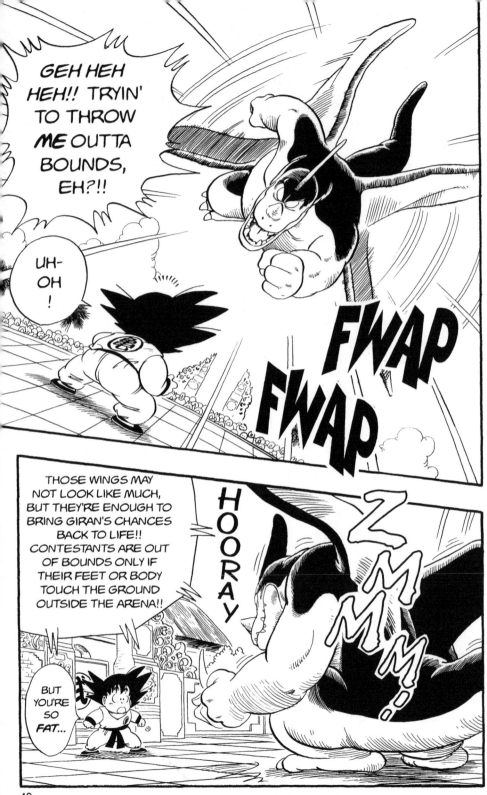

49

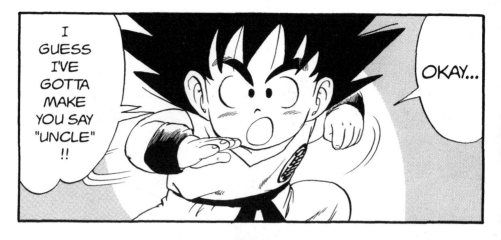

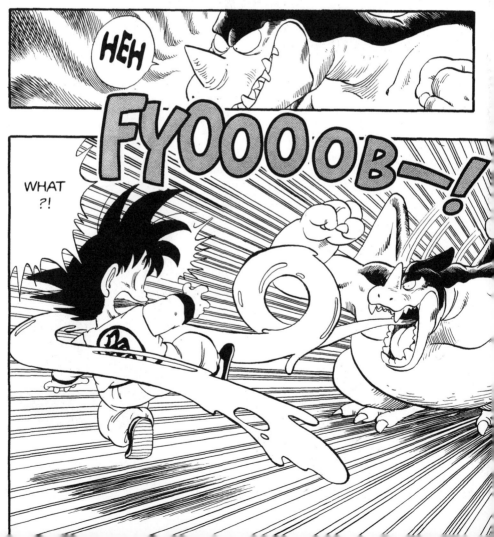

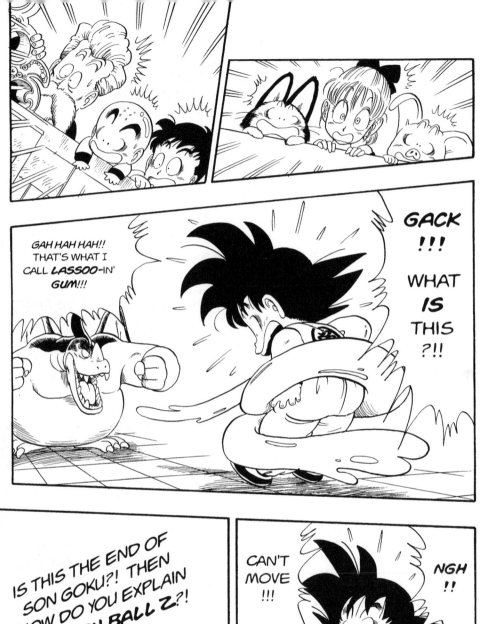

GAH HAH HAH!! THAT'S WHAT I CALL *LASSOO*-IN' *GUM!!!*

GACK!!!

WHAT **IS** THIS?!!

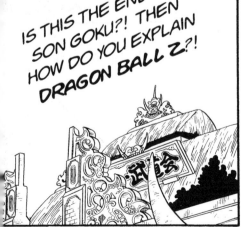

IS THIS THE END OF SON GOKU?! THEN HOW DO YOU EXPLAIN **DRAGON BALL Z?!**

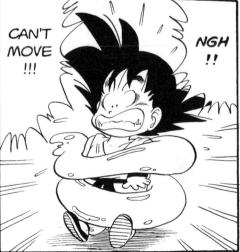

CAN'T MOVE!!!

NGH!!

Tale 40 • The Tail of Goku

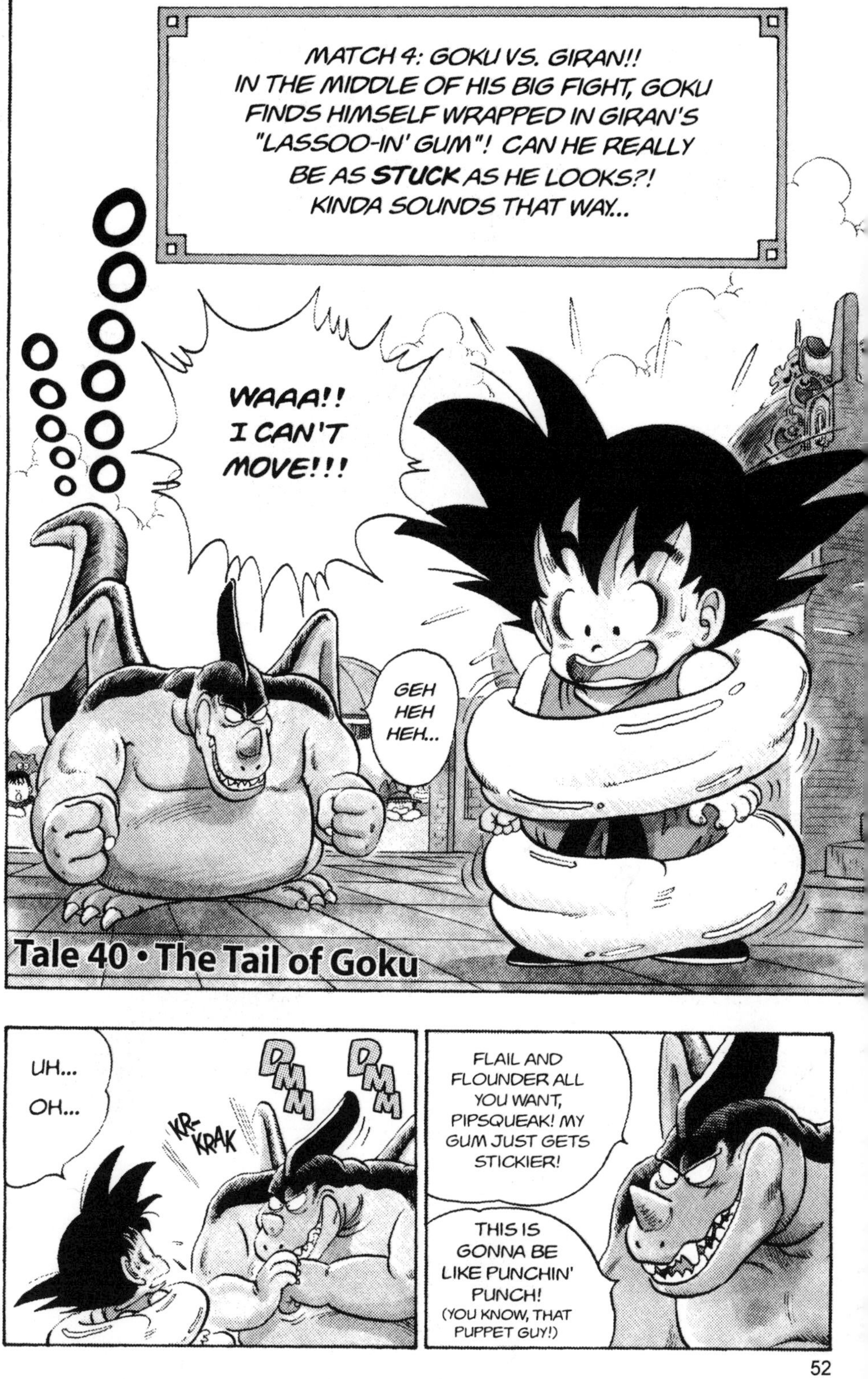
MATCH 4: GOKU VS. GIRAN!! IN THE MIDDLE OF HIS BIG FIGHT, GOKU FINDS HIMSELF WRAPPED IN GIRAN'S "LASSOO-IN' GUM"! CAN HE REALLY BE AS **STUCK** AS HE LOOKS?! KINDA SOUNDS THAT WAY...
WAAA!! I CAN'T MOVE!!!
GEH HEH HEH...
FLAIL AND FLOUNDER ALL YOU WANT, PIPSQUEAK! MY GUM JUST GETS STICKIER!
THIS IS GONNA BE LIKE PUNCHIN' PUNCH! (YOU KNOW, THAT PUPPET GUY!)
DMM DMM
KR-KRAK
UH... OH...

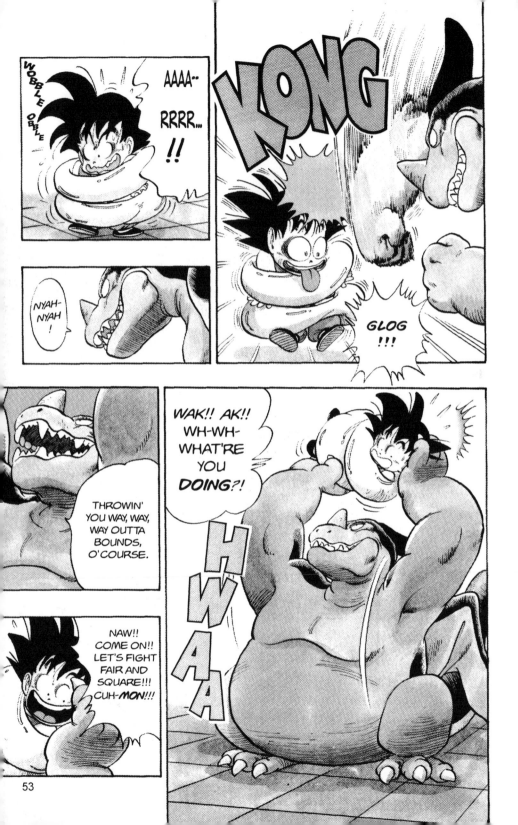

53

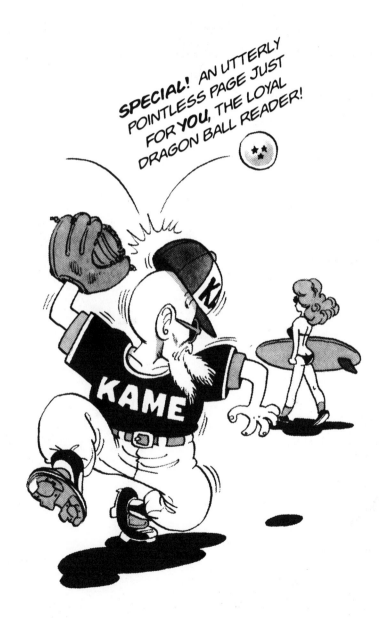

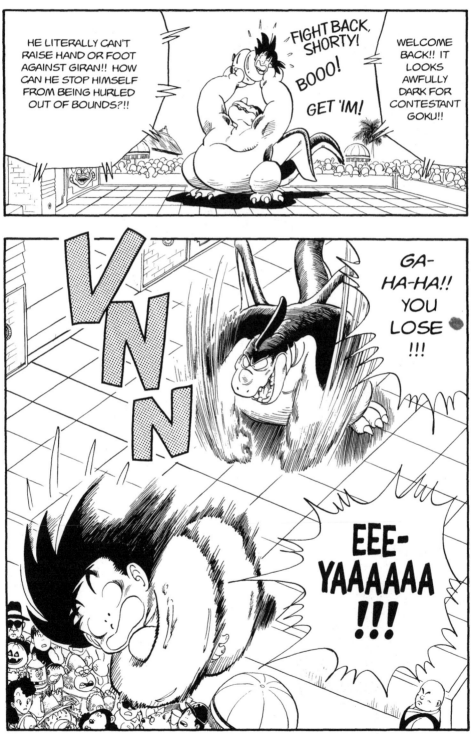

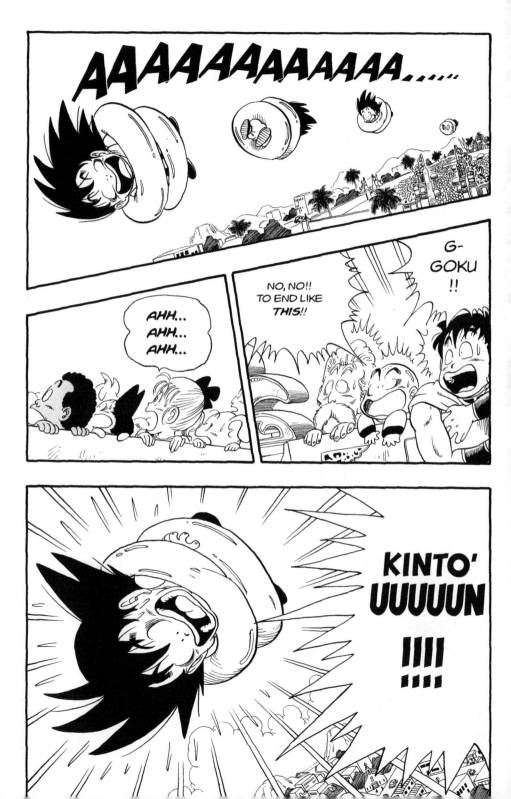

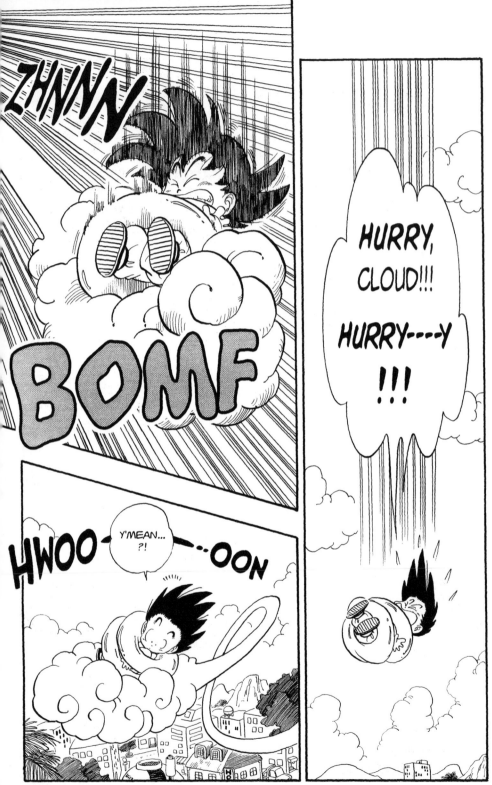

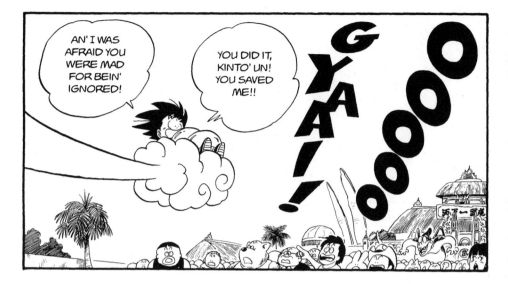

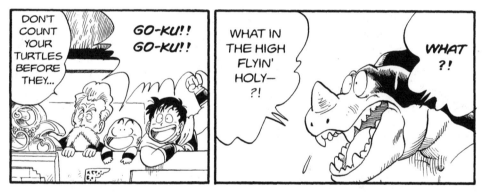

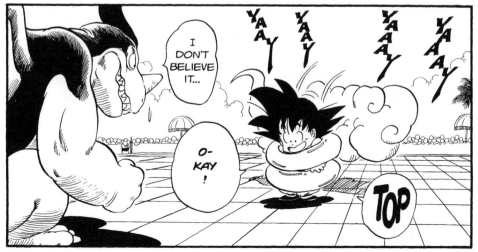

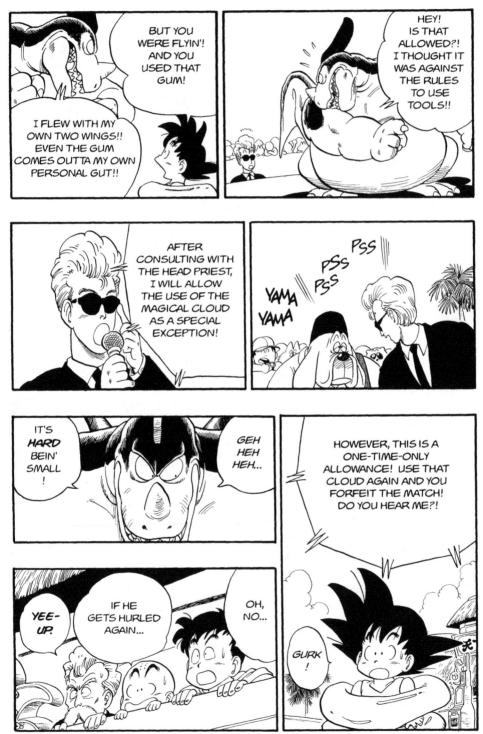

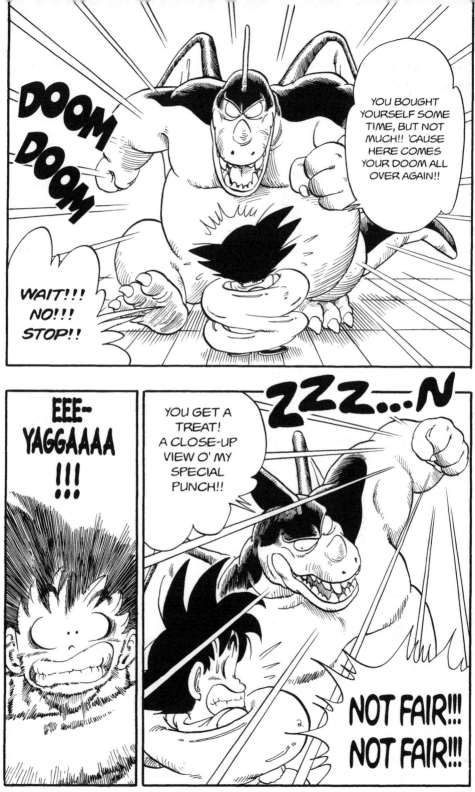

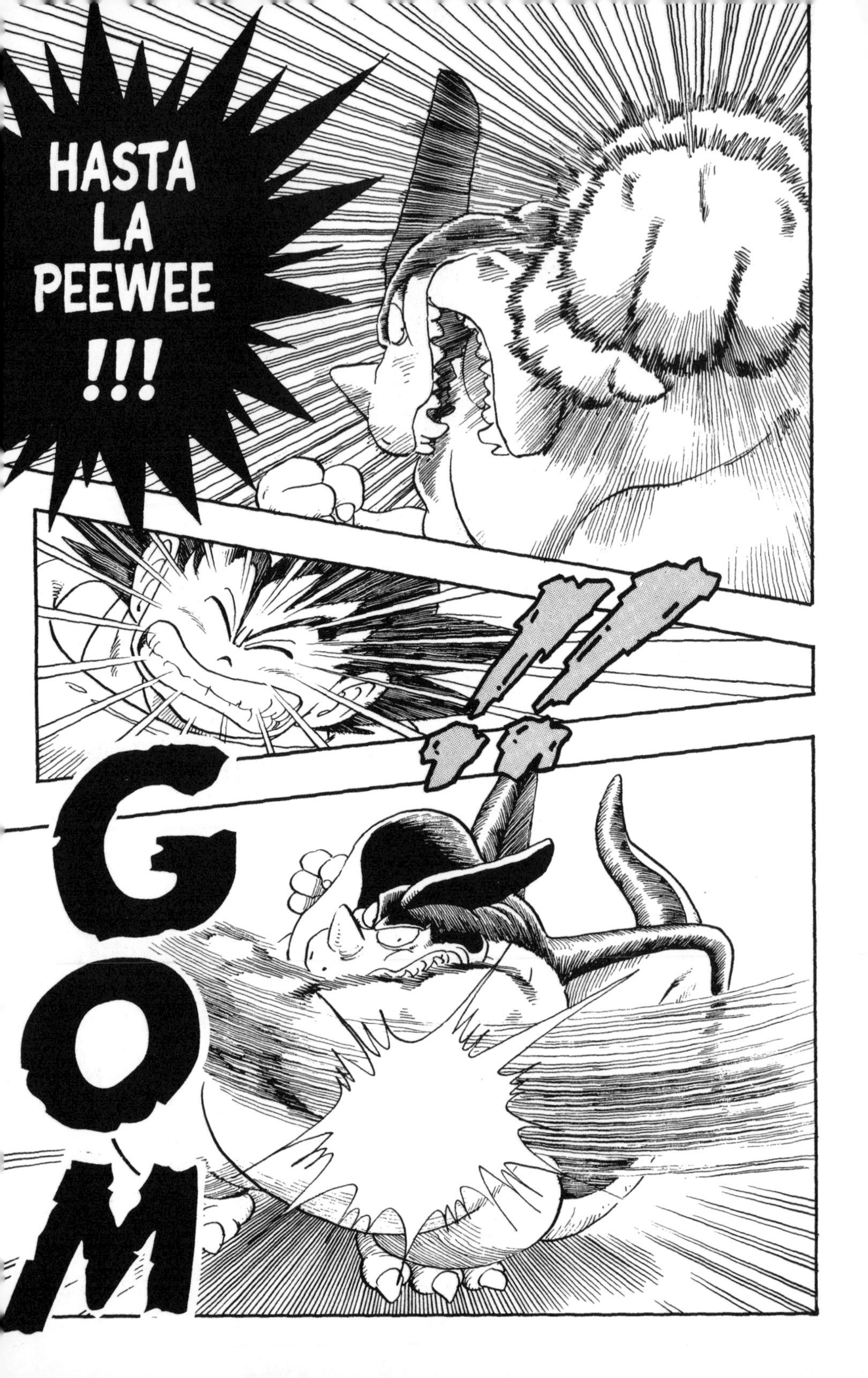
HASTA LA PEEWEE !!!
GOOM

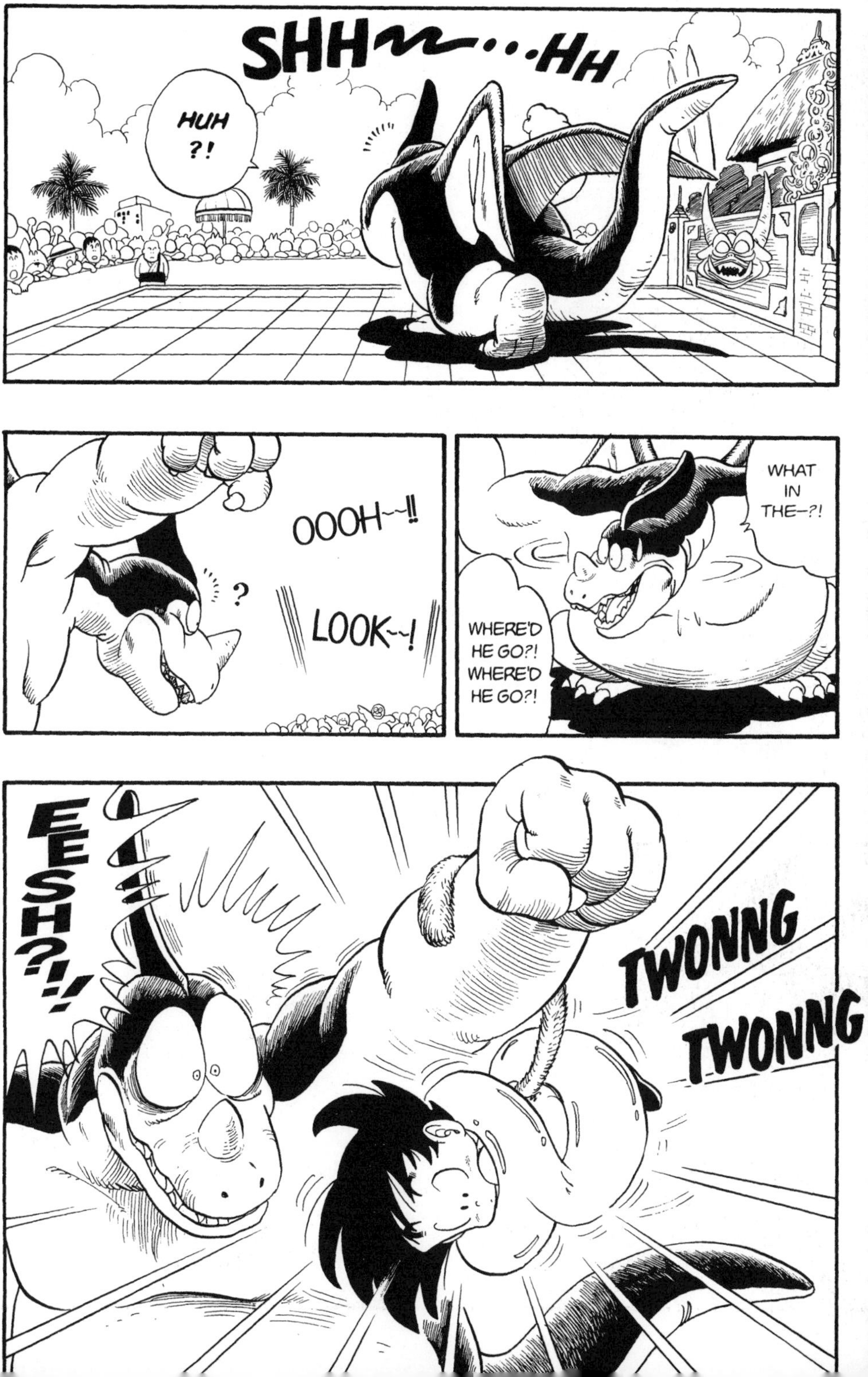
SHH~~...HH
HUH ?!
WHAT IN THE--?!
WHERE'D HE GO?! WHERE'D HE GO?!
OOOH~~!!
?
LOOK~~!
TWONNG
TWONNG
EESH?!!

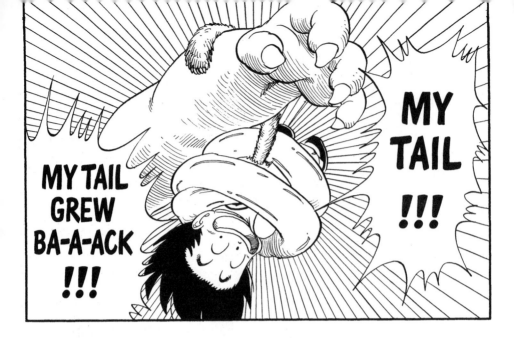

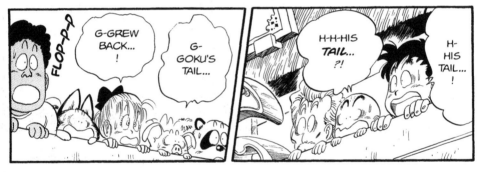

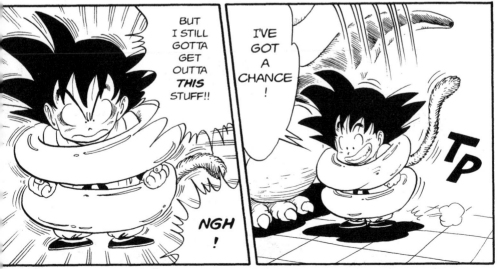

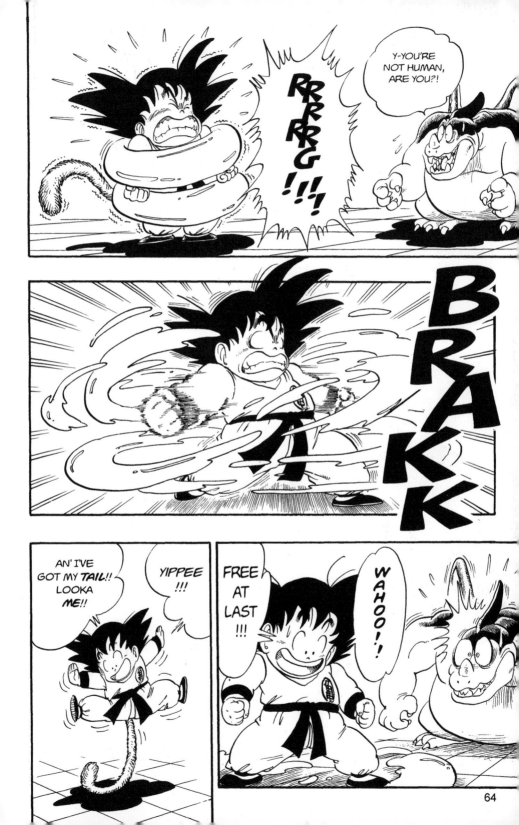

64

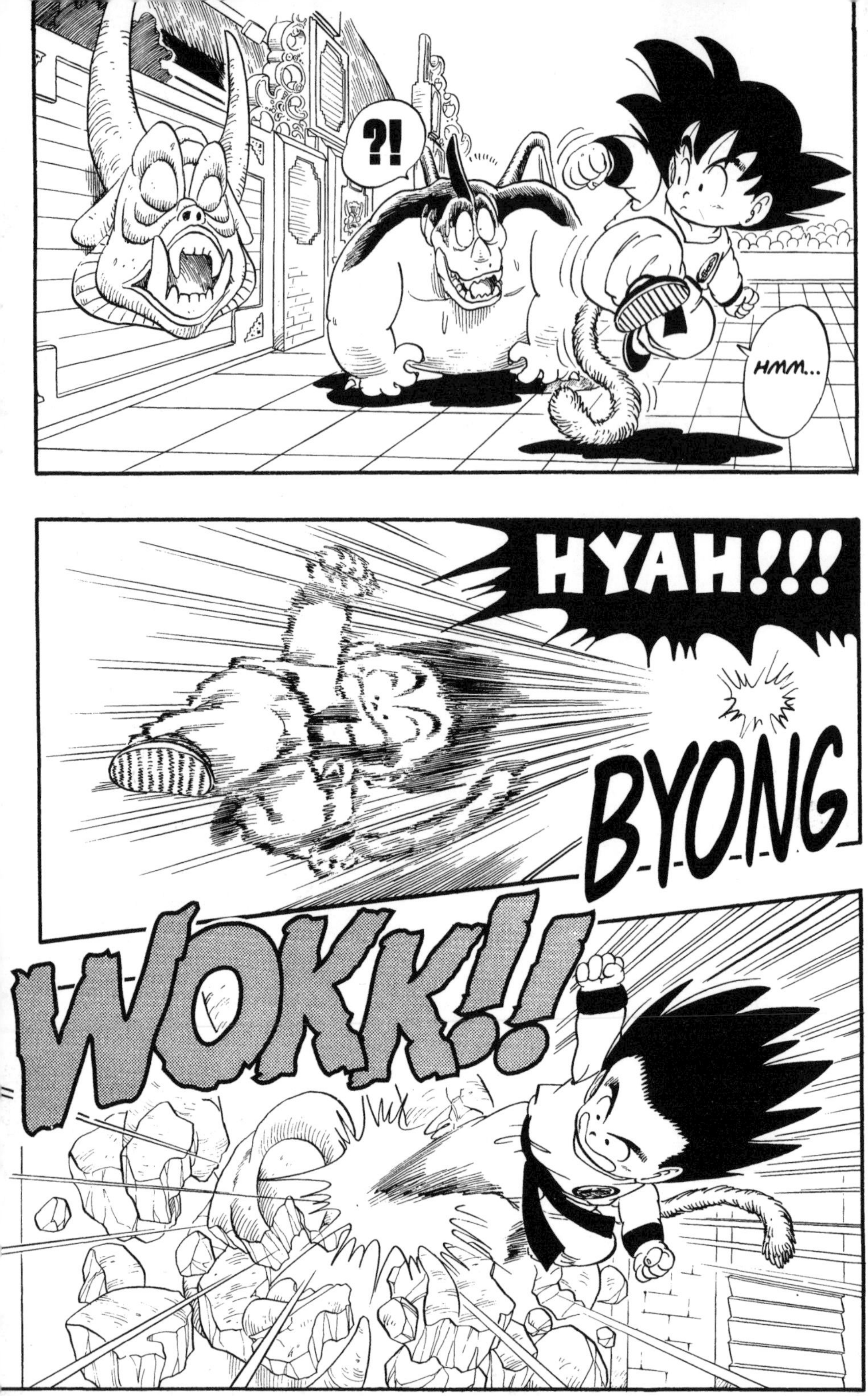
?!
HMM...
HYAH!!!
BYONG
WOKK!!

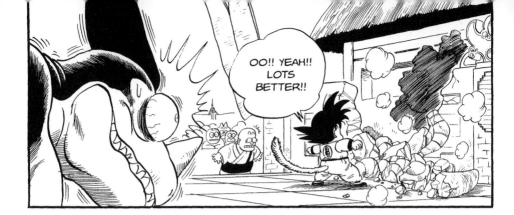

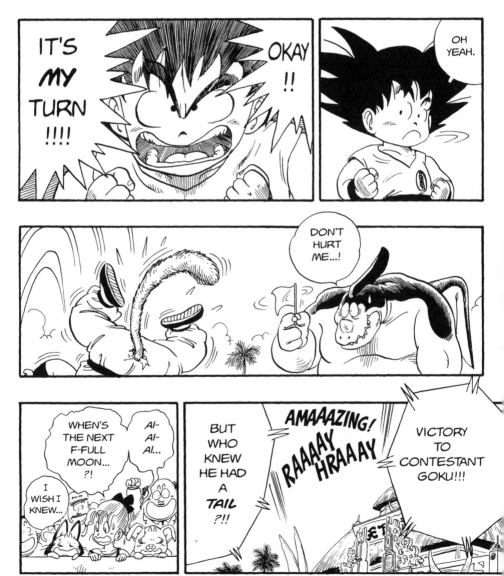

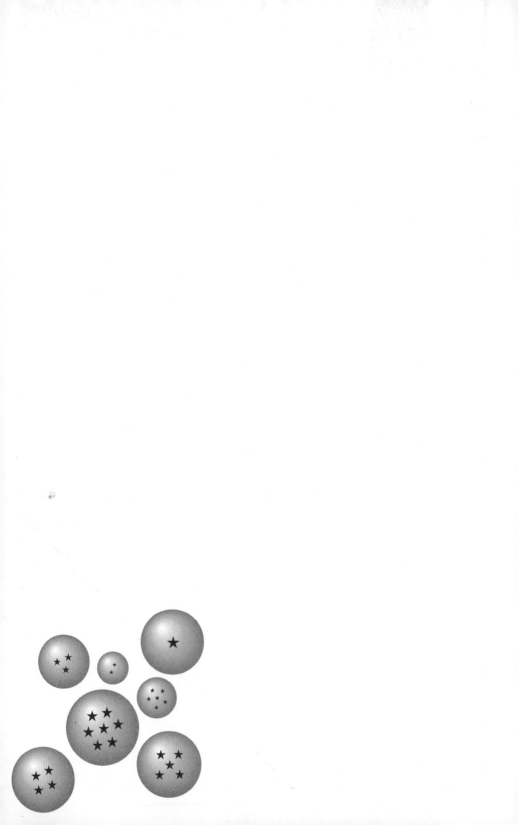

Tale 41
Kuririn vs. Jackie Chun

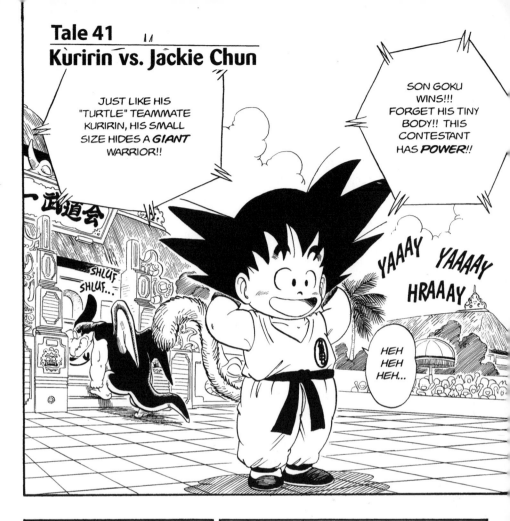

JUST LIKE HIS "TURTLE" TEAMMATE KURIRIN, HIS SMALL SIZE HIDES A *GIANT* WARRIOR!!

SON GOKU WINS!!! FORGET HIS TINY BODY!! THIS CONTESTANT HAS *POWER*!!

SHLUF SHLUF...

YAAAY YAAAAY HRAAAY

HEH HEH HEH...

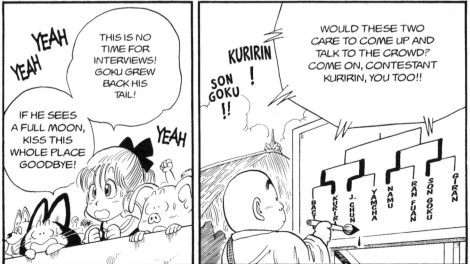

YEAH YEAH YEAH

THIS IS NO TIME FOR INTERVIEWS! GOKU GREW BACK HIS TAIL!

IF HE SEES A FULL MOON, KISS THIS WHOLE PLACE GOODBYE!

YEAH

KURIRIN

SON GOKU !!

WOULD THESE TWO CARE TO COME UP AND TALK TO THE CROWD? COME ON, CONTESTANT KURIRIN, YOU TOO!!

BACT KURIRIN J. CHUN YAMCHA NAMU RAN FUAN SON GOKU GIRAN

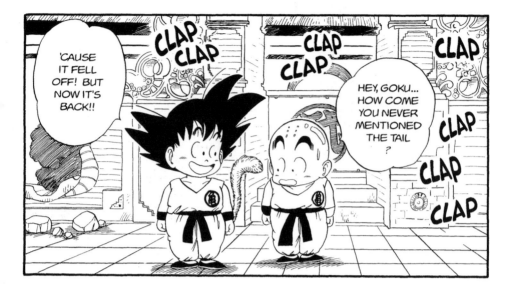

'CAUSE IT FELL OFF! BUT NOW IT'S BACK!!

CLAP CLAP CLAP CLAP CLAP CLAP CLAP CLAP

HEY, GOKU... HOW COME YOU NEVER MENTIONED THE TAIL?

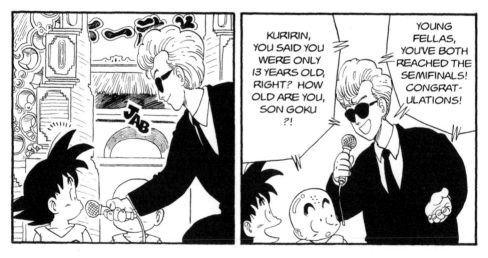

KURIRIN, YOU SAID YOU WERE ONLY 13 YEARS OLD, RIGHT? HOW OLD ARE YOU, SON GOKU?!

JAB

YOUNG FELLAS, YOU'VE BOTH REACHED THE SEMIFINALS! CONGRATULATIONS!

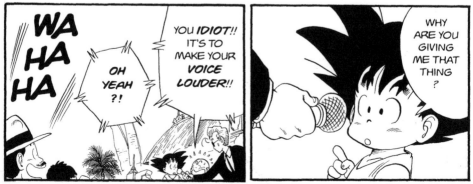

WA HA HA

OH YEAH?!

YOU *IDIOT*!! IT'S TO MAKE YOUR *VOICE LOUDER*!!

WHY ARE YOU GIVING ME THAT THING?

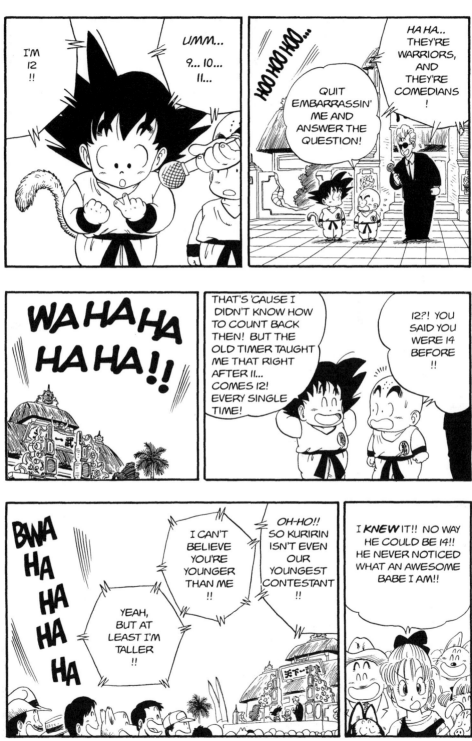

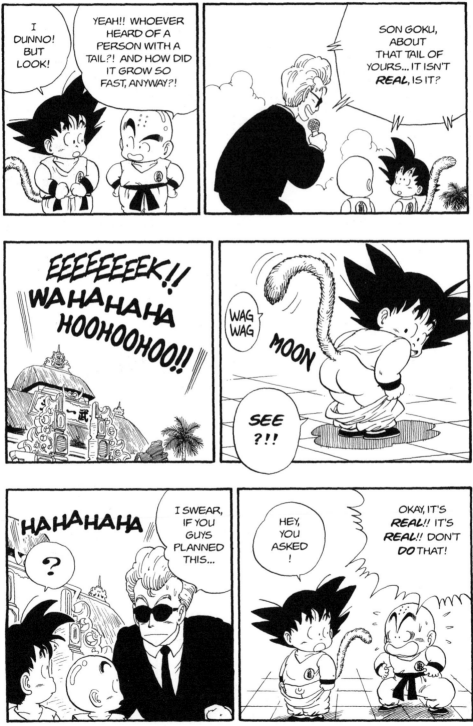

71

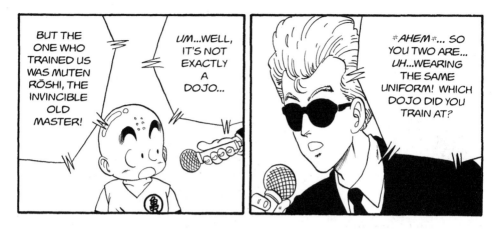

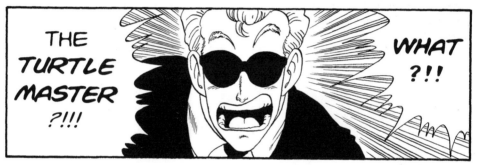

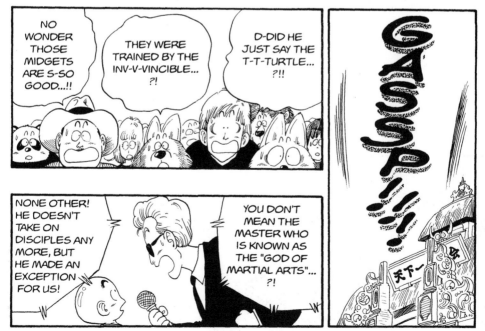

72

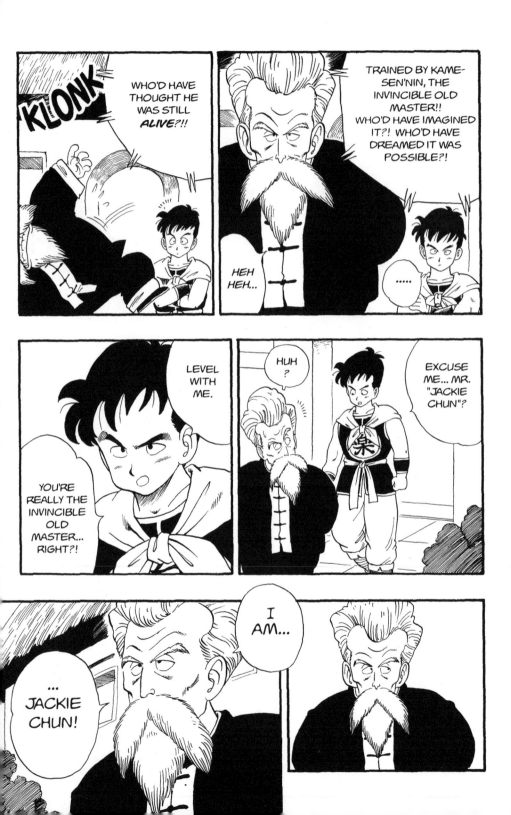

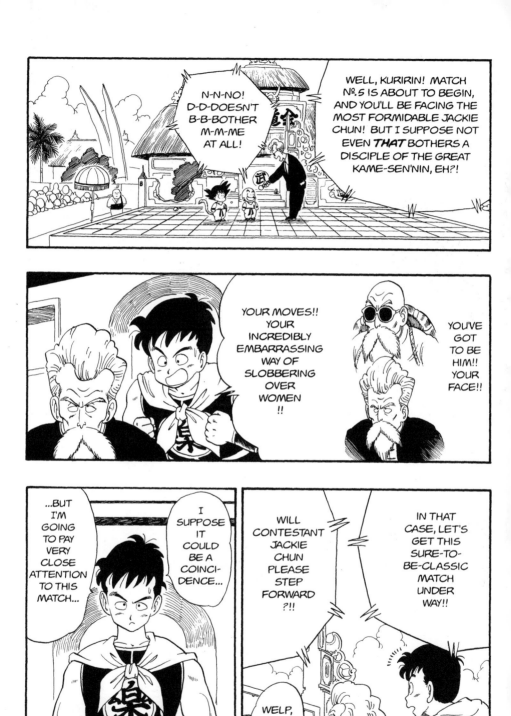

74

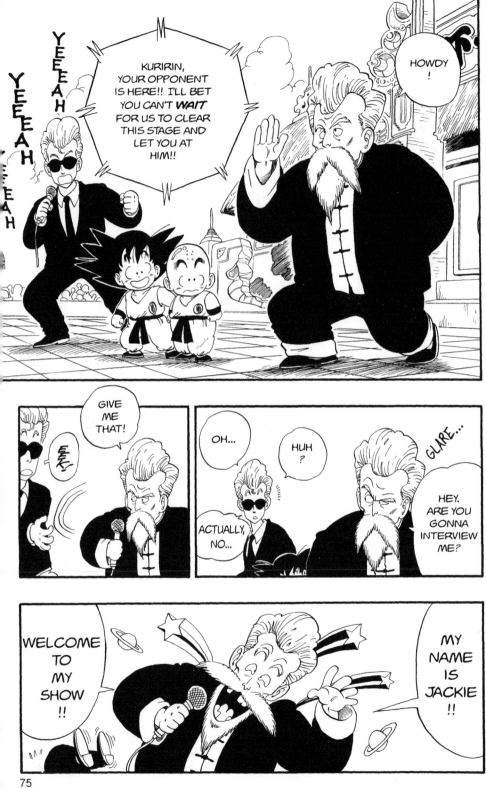

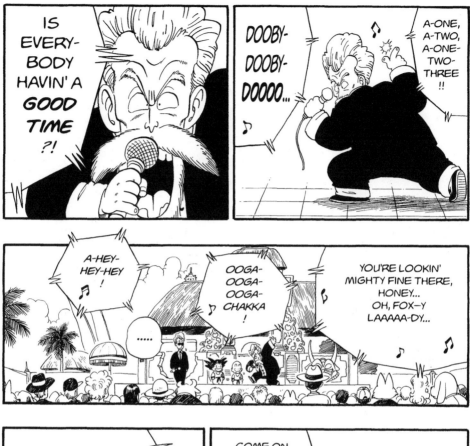

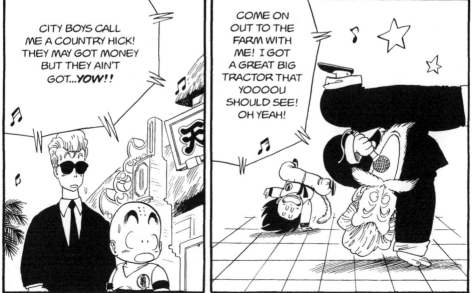

76

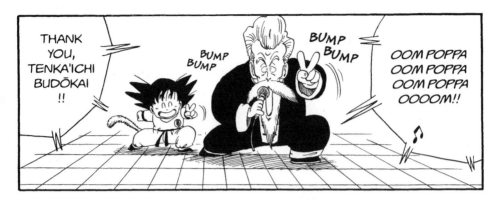

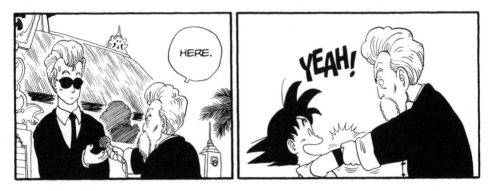

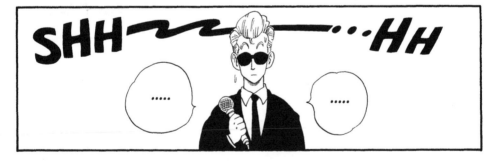

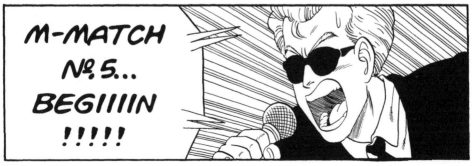

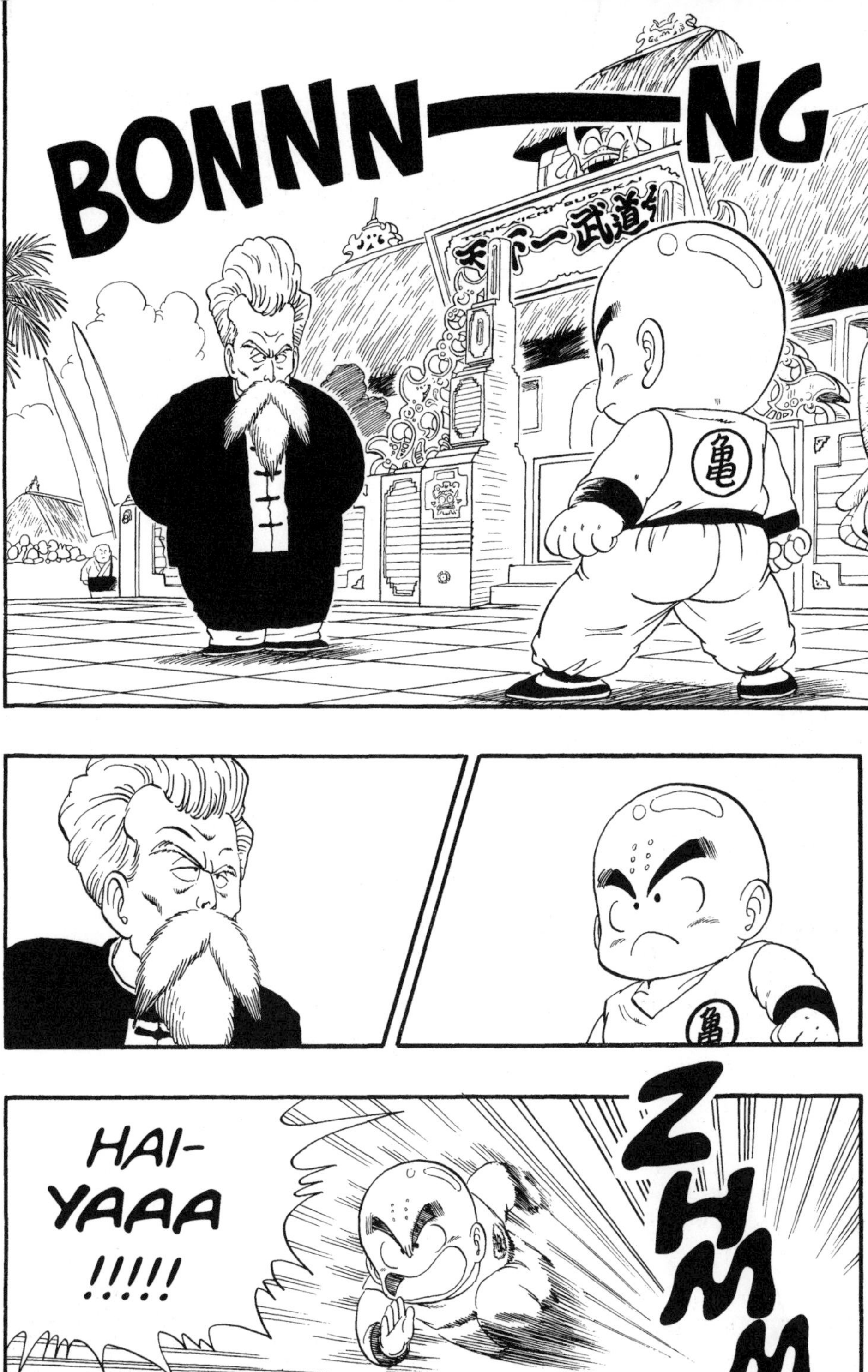
BONNN——NG
ZHMM
HAI-
YAAA
!!!!!

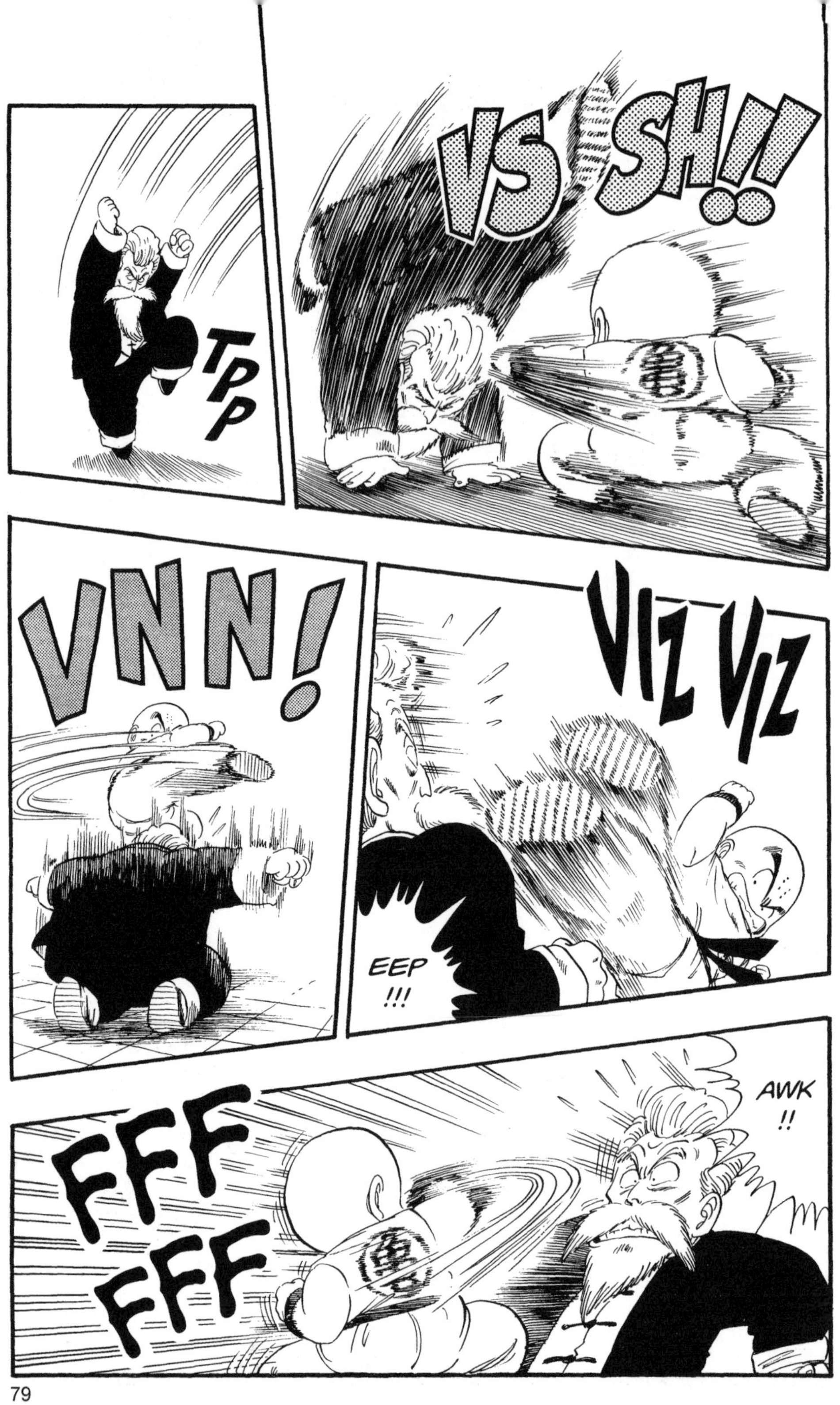
VS SH!!
TPP
VIZ VIZ
EEP !!!
VNN!
AWK !!
FFF FFF

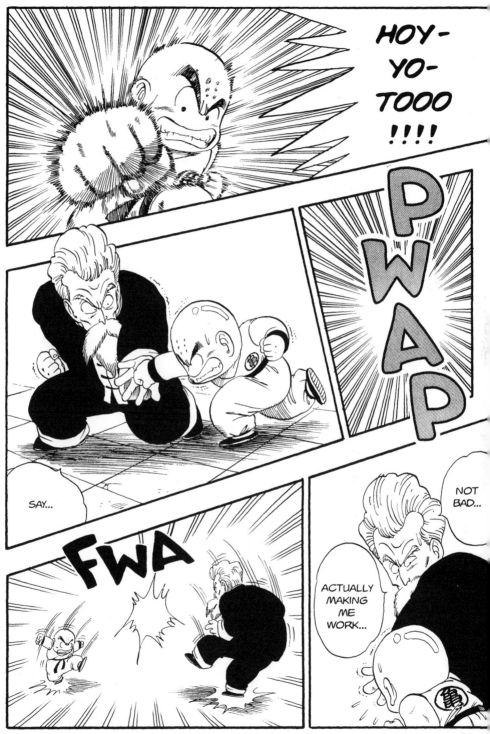

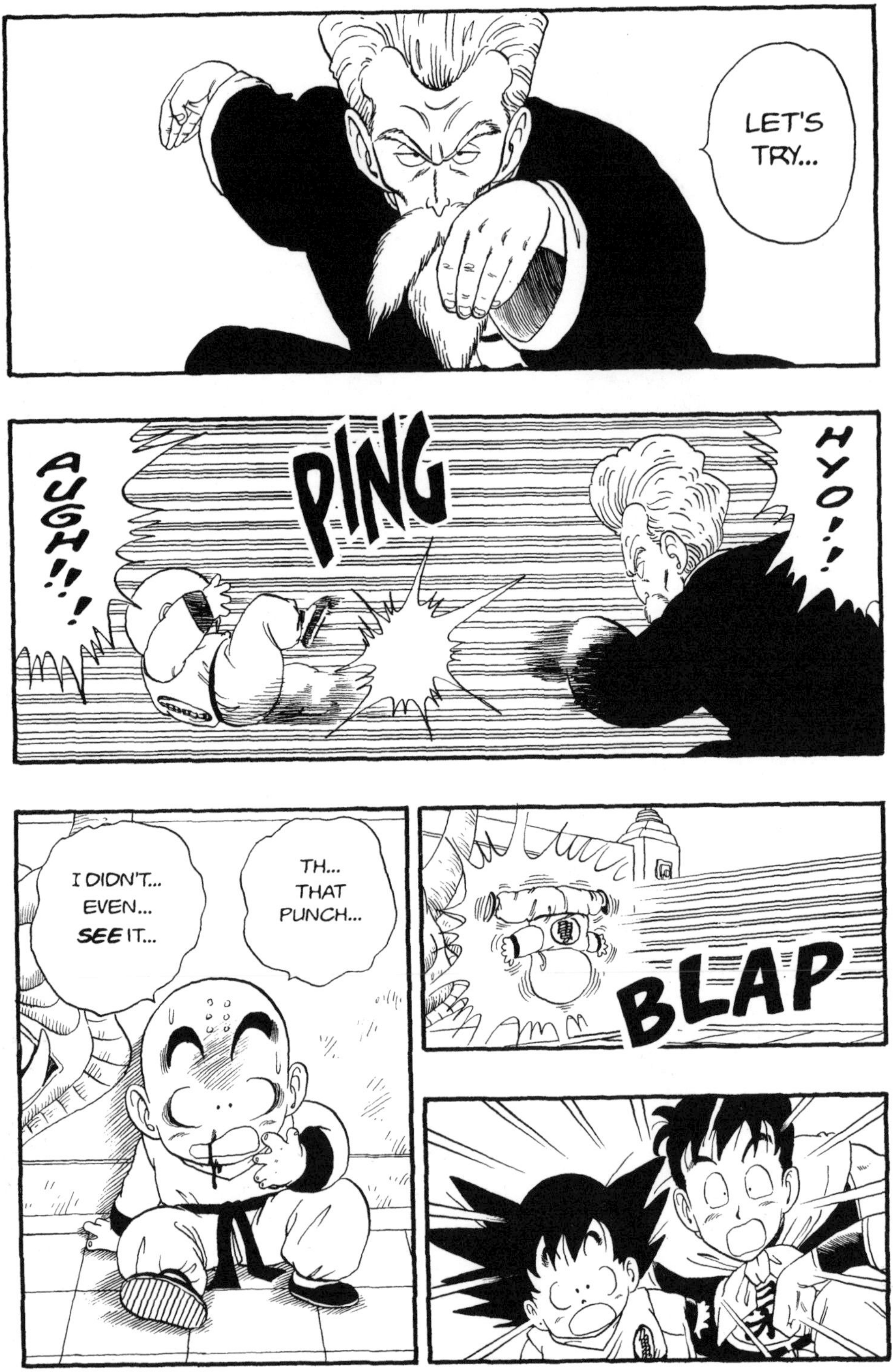
LET'S TRY...
HYO!!
PING
AUGH!!!
BLAP
TH... THAT PUNCH...
I DIDN'T... EVEN... SEE IT...

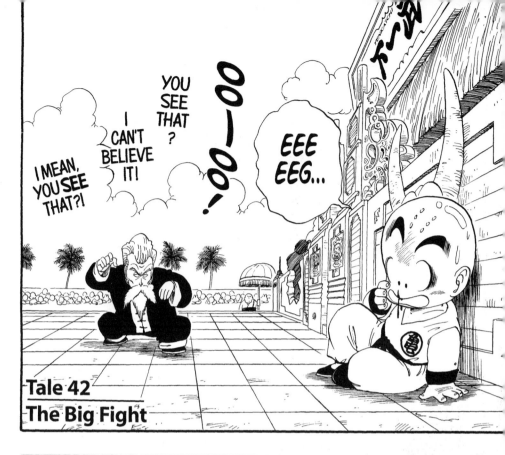

Tale 42
The Big Fight

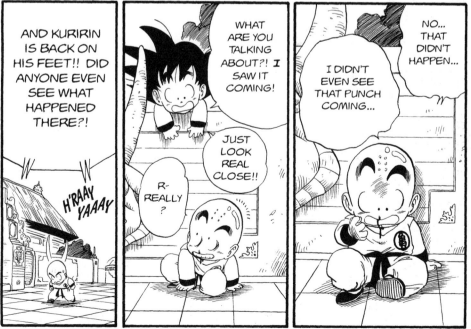

82

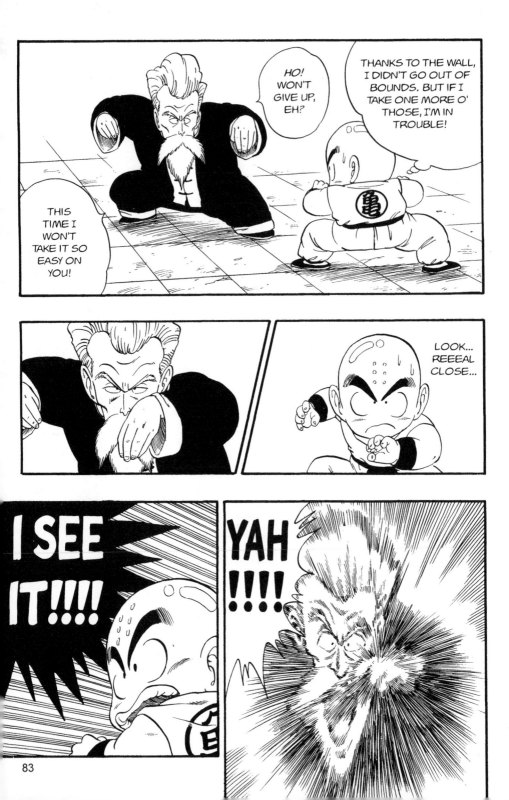

83

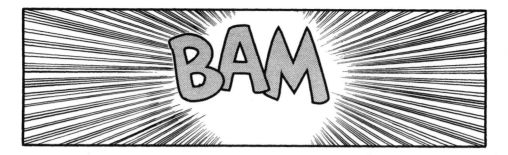

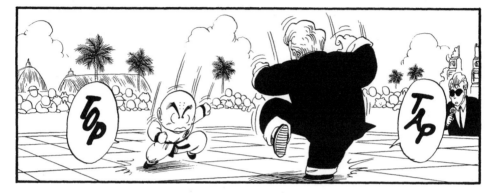

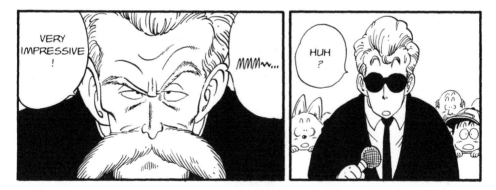

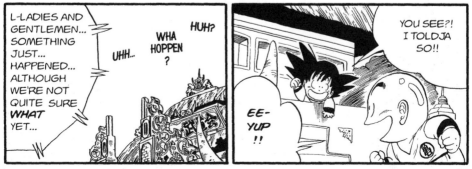

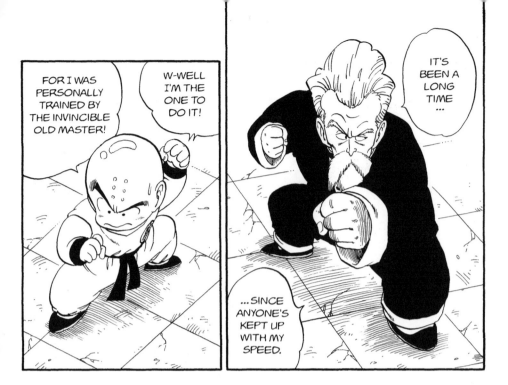

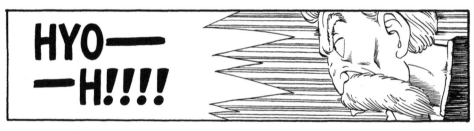

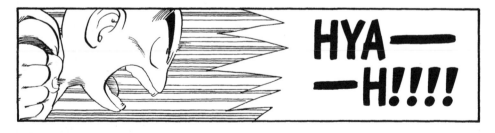

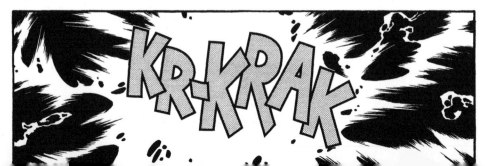

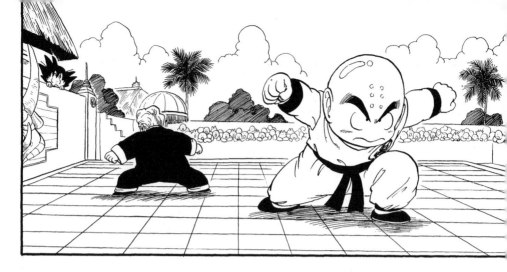

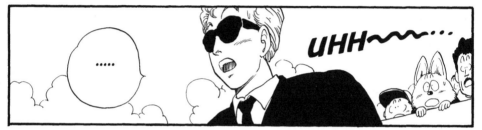

.....

UHH~~~....

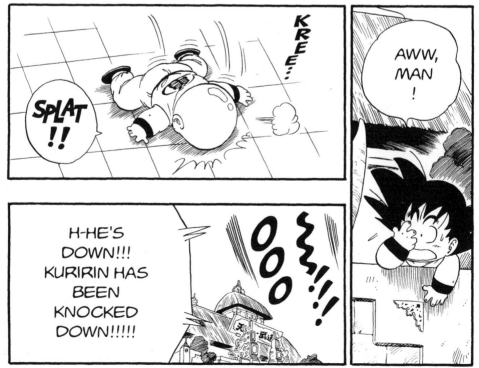

SPLAT
!!

KREE..

AWW,
MAN
!

H-HE'S
DOWN!!!
KURIRIN HAS
BEEN
KNOCKED
DOWN!!!!!

OOO
!!!

86

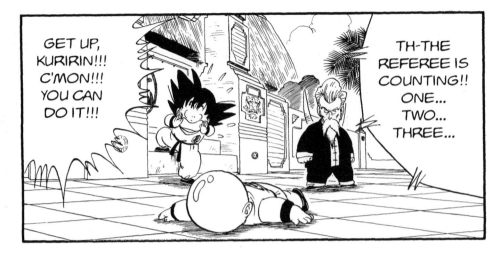

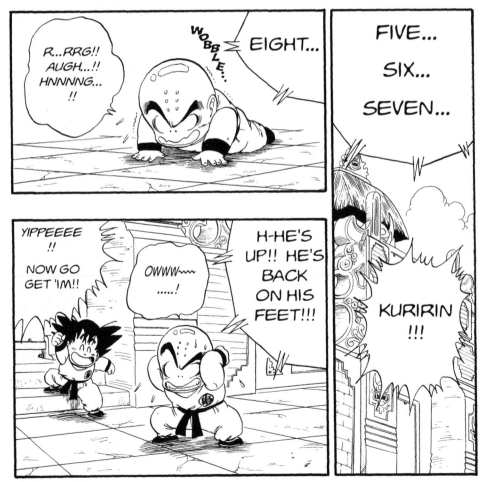

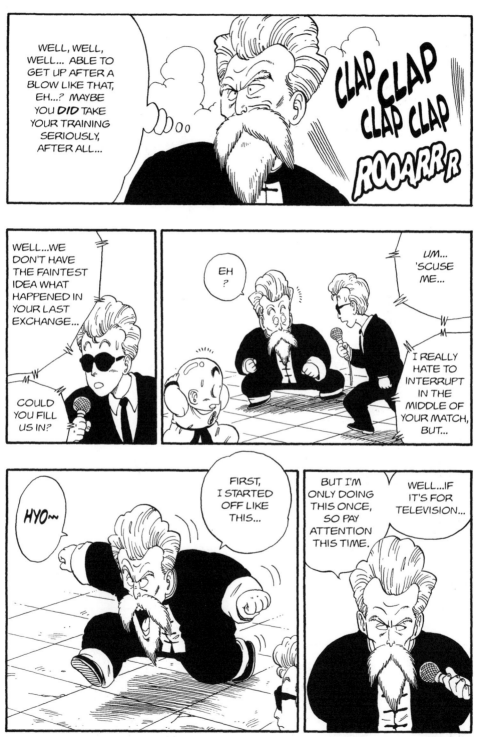

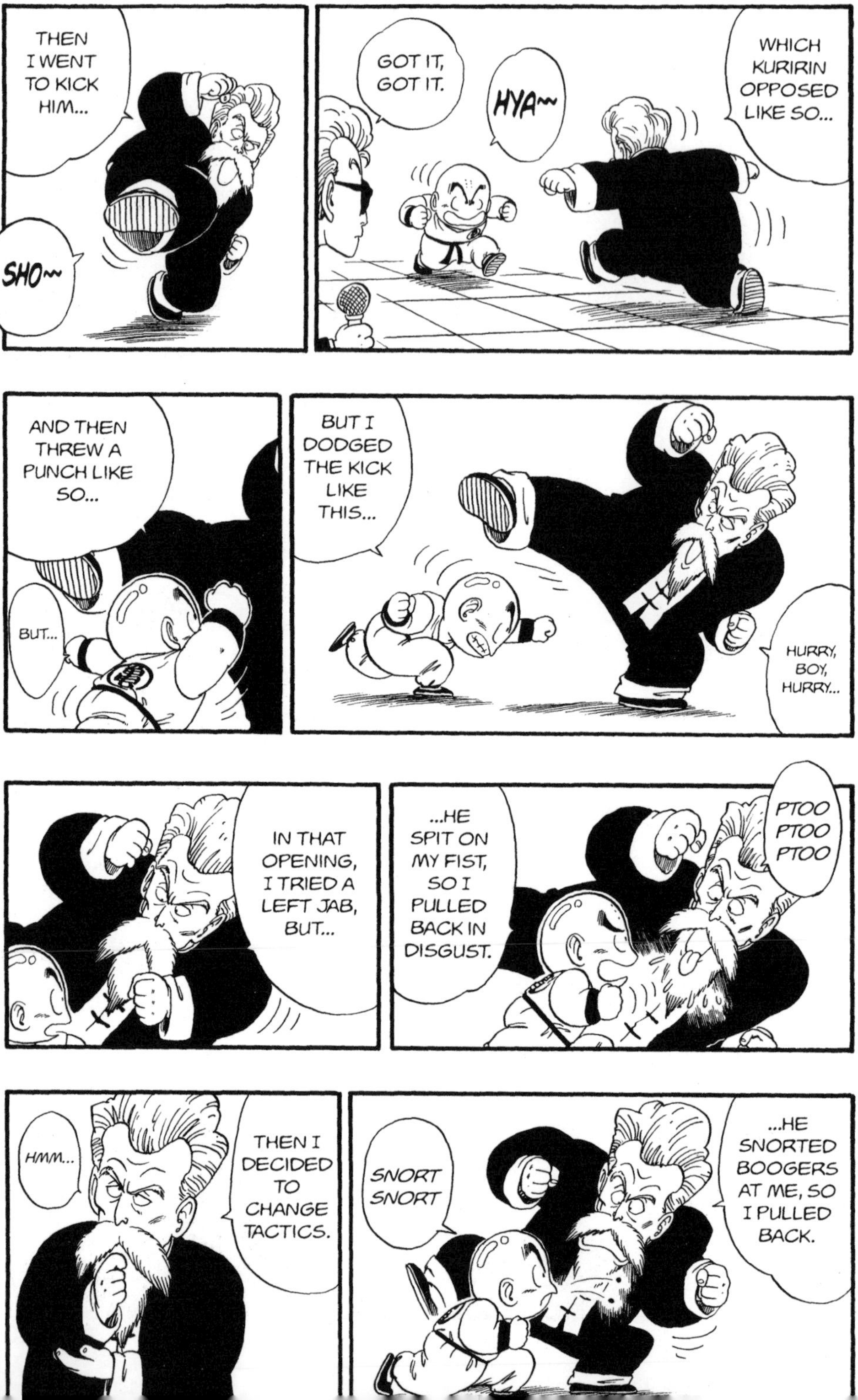
THEN I WENT TO KICK HIM...
SHO~~
GOT IT, GOT IT.
HYA~~
WHICH KURIRIN OPPOSED LIKE SO...
AND THEN THREW A PUNCH LIKE SO...
BUT...
BUT I DODGED THE KICK LIKE THIS...
HURRY, BOY, HURRY...
IN THAT OPENING, I TRIED A LEFT JAB, BUT...
...HE SPIT ON MY FIST, SO I PULLED BACK IN DISGUST.
PTOO PTOO PTOO
HMM...
THEN I DECIDED TO CHANGE TACTICS.
SNORT SNORT
...HE SNORTED BOOGERS AT ME, SO I PULLED BACK.

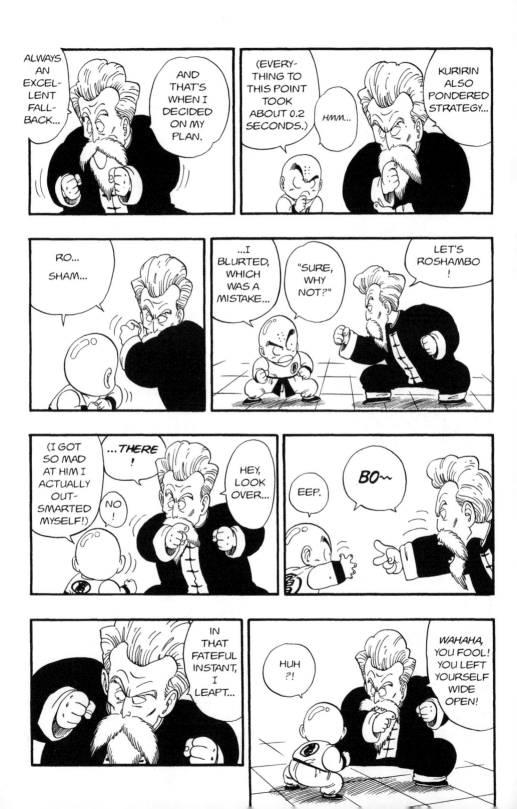

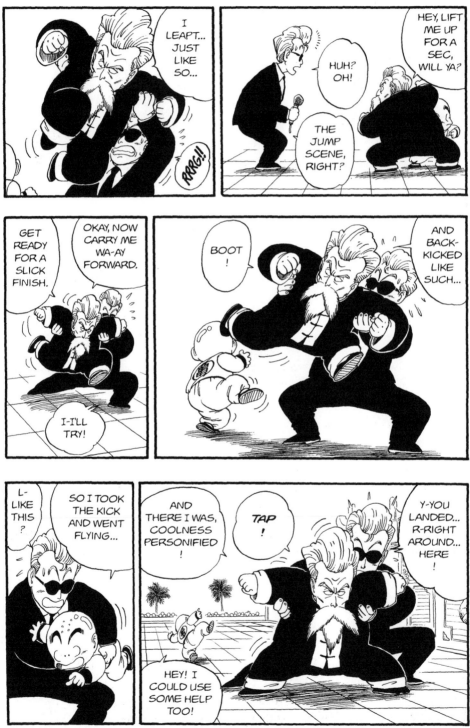

91

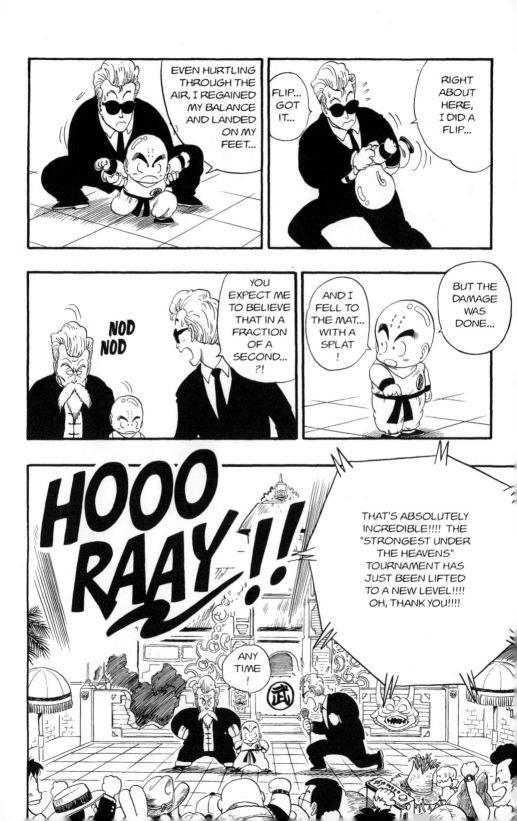

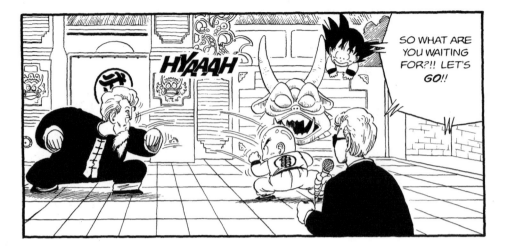

HYAAAH

SO WHAT ARE YOU WAITING FOR?!! LET'S *GO!!*

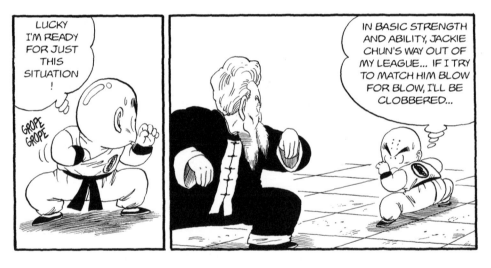

LUCKY I'M READY FOR JUST THIS SITUATION !

GROPE GROPE

IN BASIC STRENGTH AND ABILITY, JACKIE CHUN'S WAY OUT OF MY LEAGUE... IF I TRY TO MATCH HIM BLOW FOR BLOW, I'LL BE CLOBBERED...

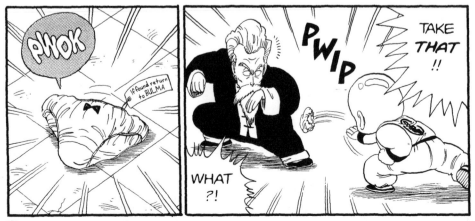

PWOK

If found return to BULMA

PWIP

TAKE *THAT* !!

WHAT ?!

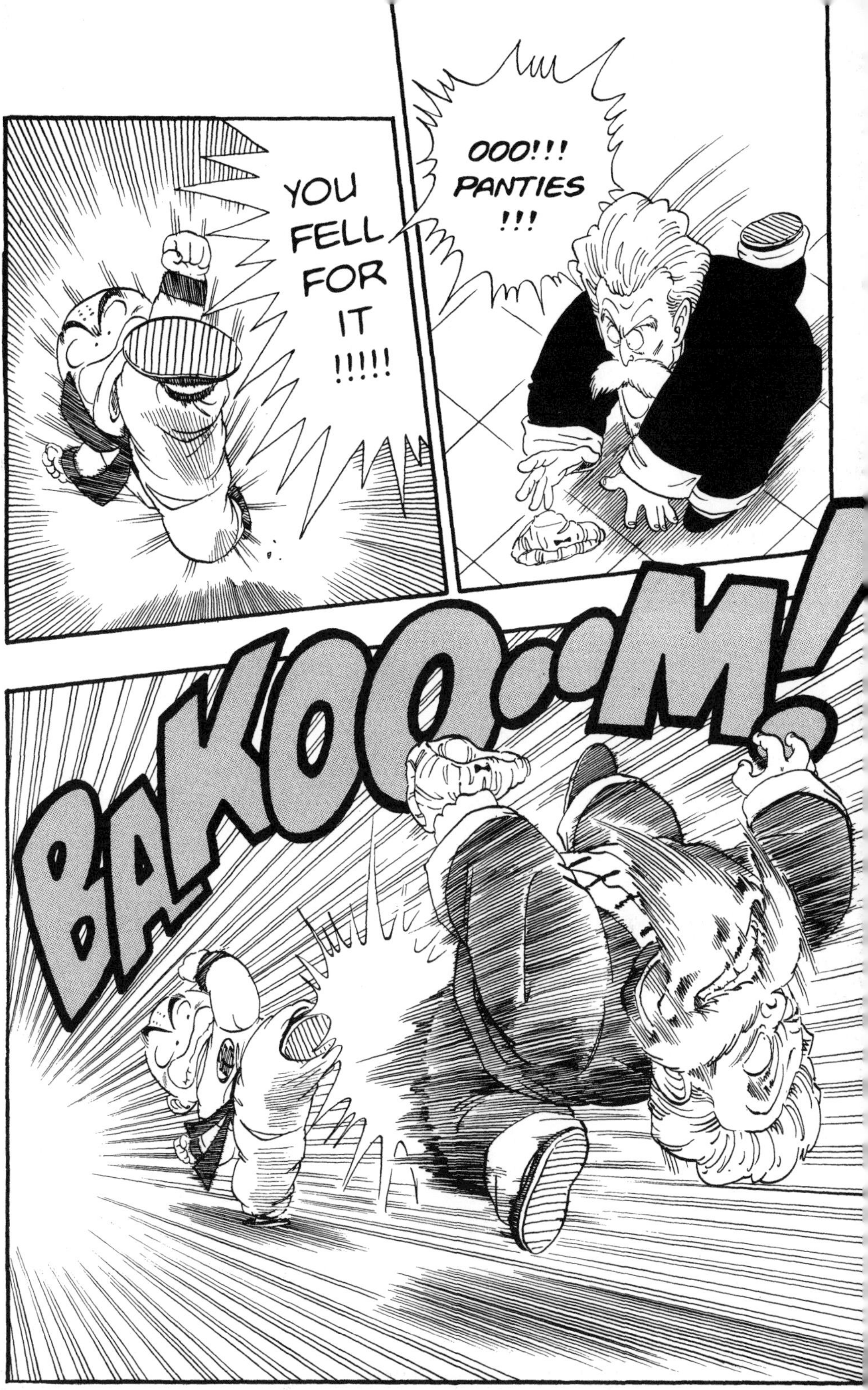
OOO!!! PANTIES !!!
YOU FELL FOR IT !!!!!
BAKOO...M!

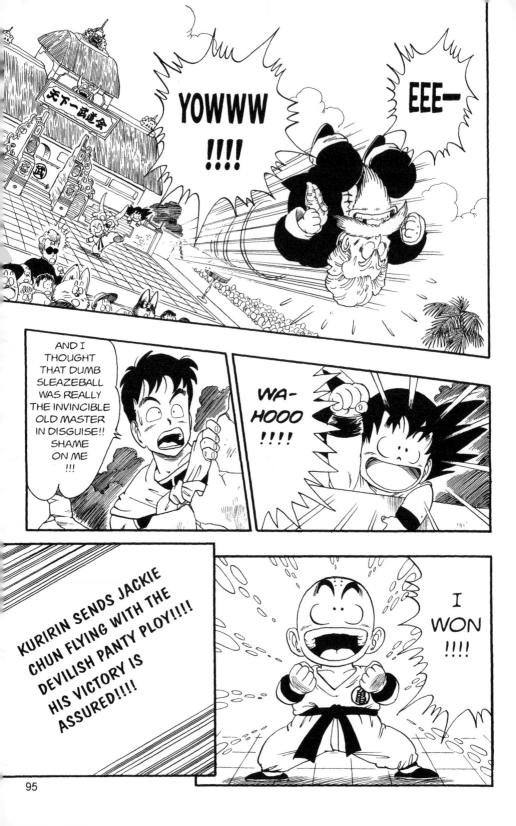

Tale 43 • The Mysterious Jackie Chun

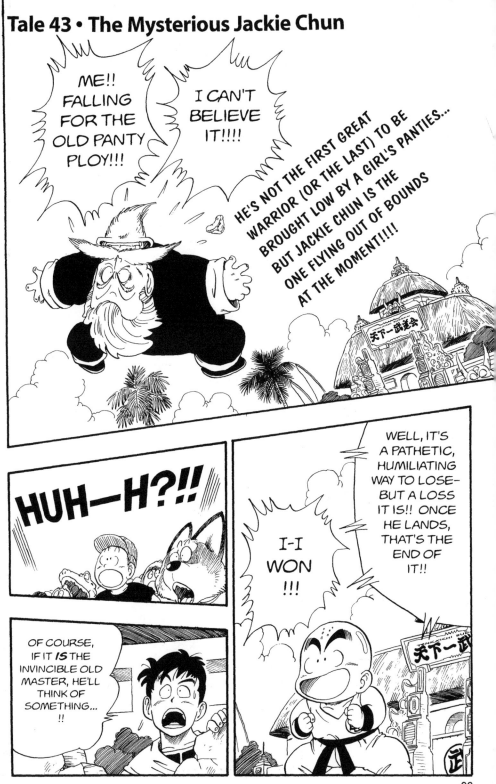

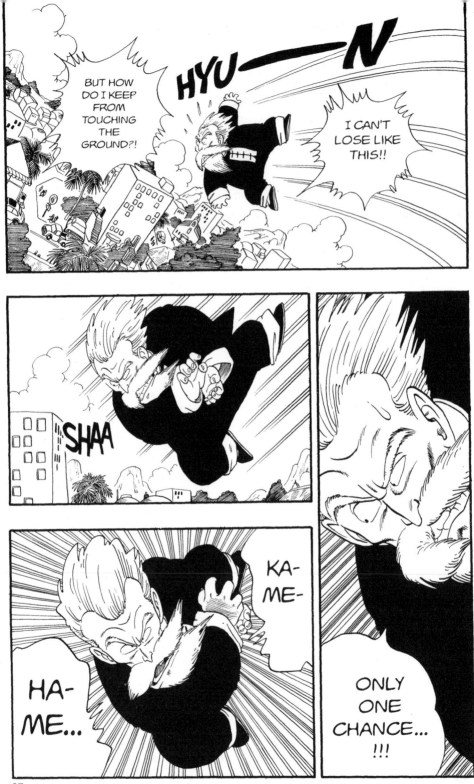

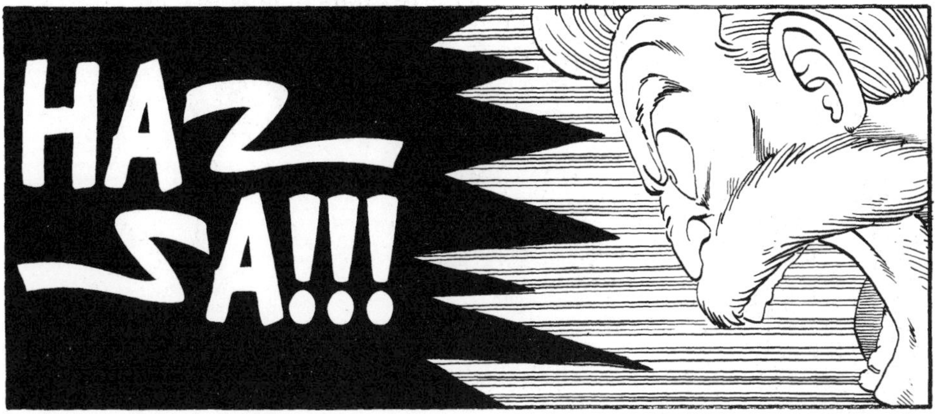
HAA SA!!!

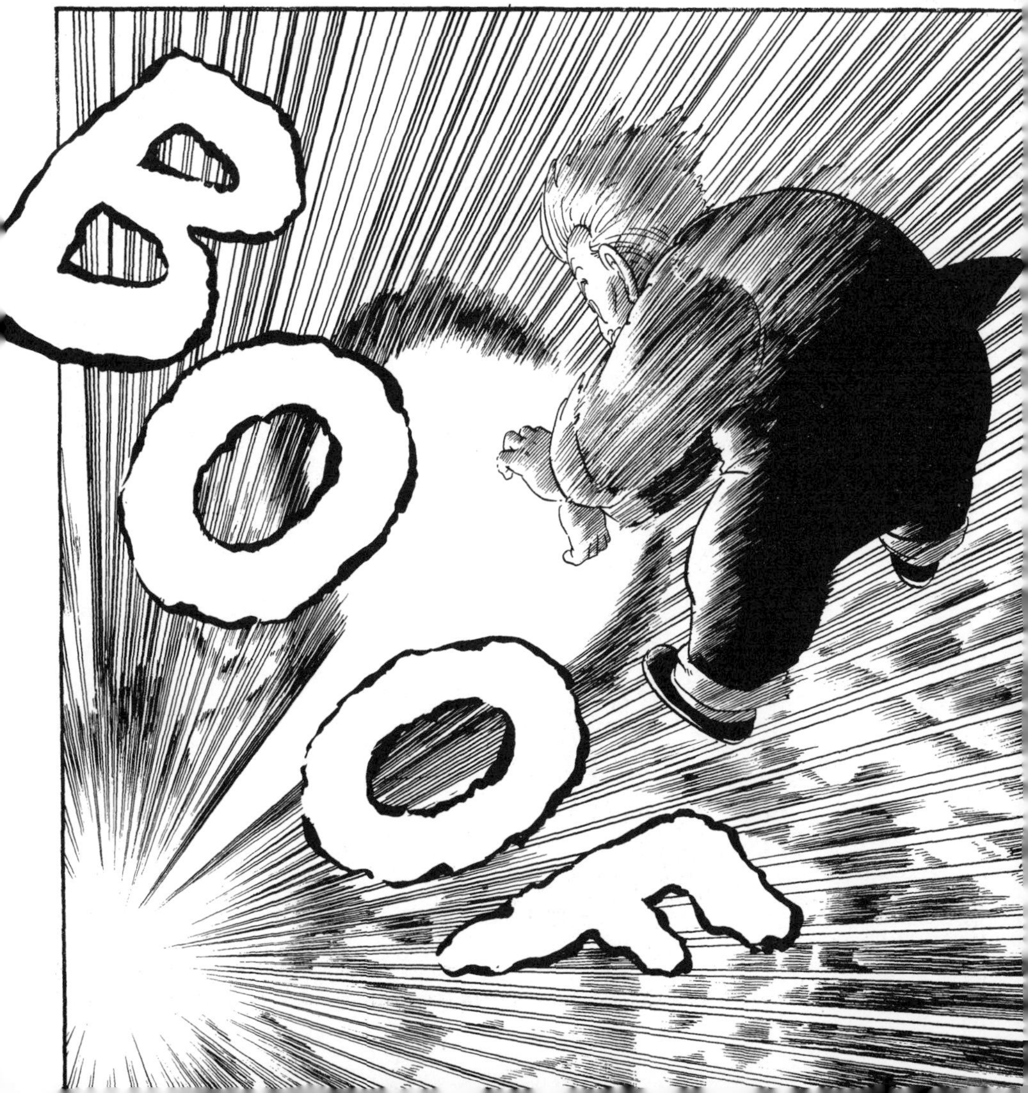
BOOF

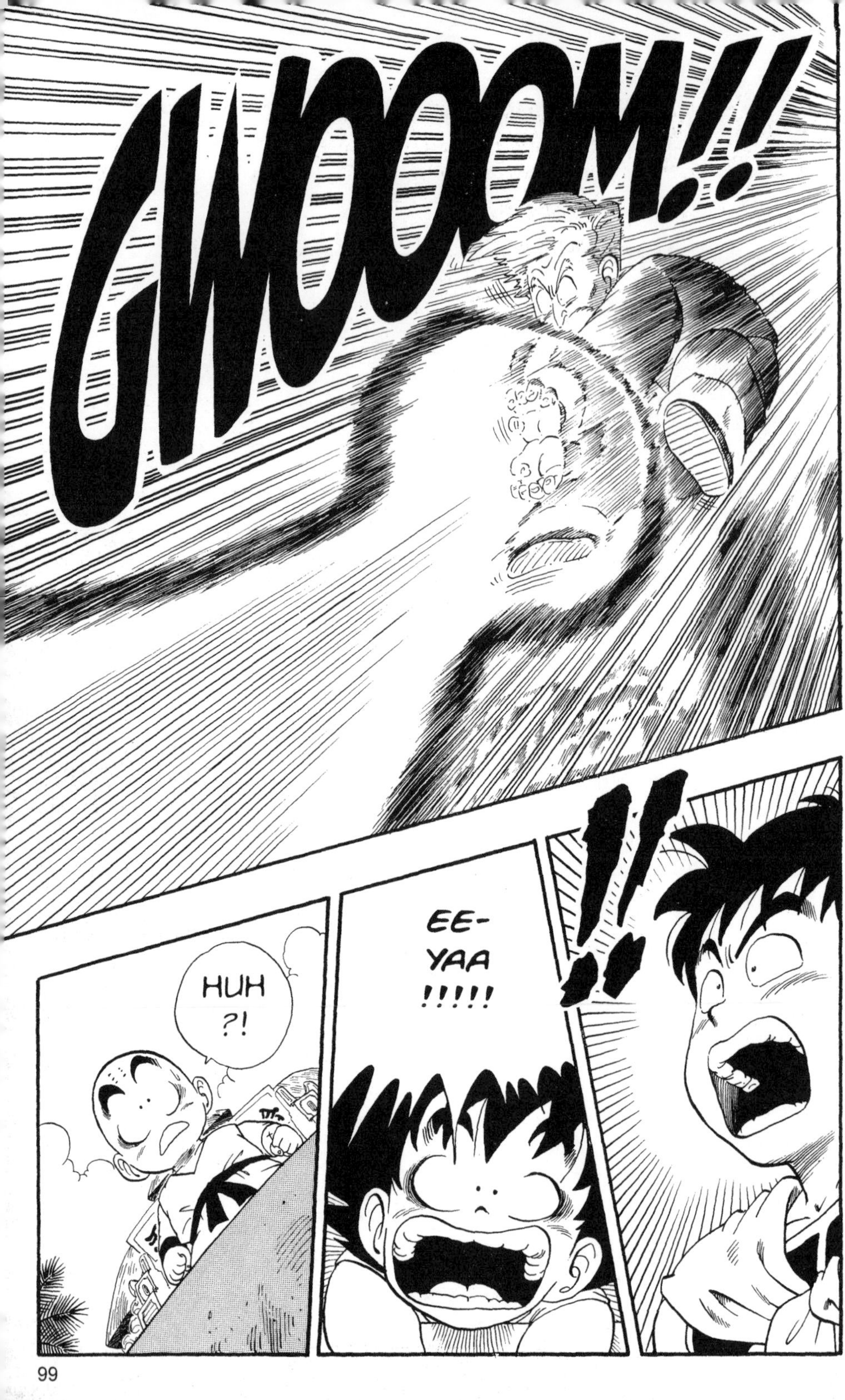
GWOOOM!!
!!
EE-YAA!!!!!
HUH ?!

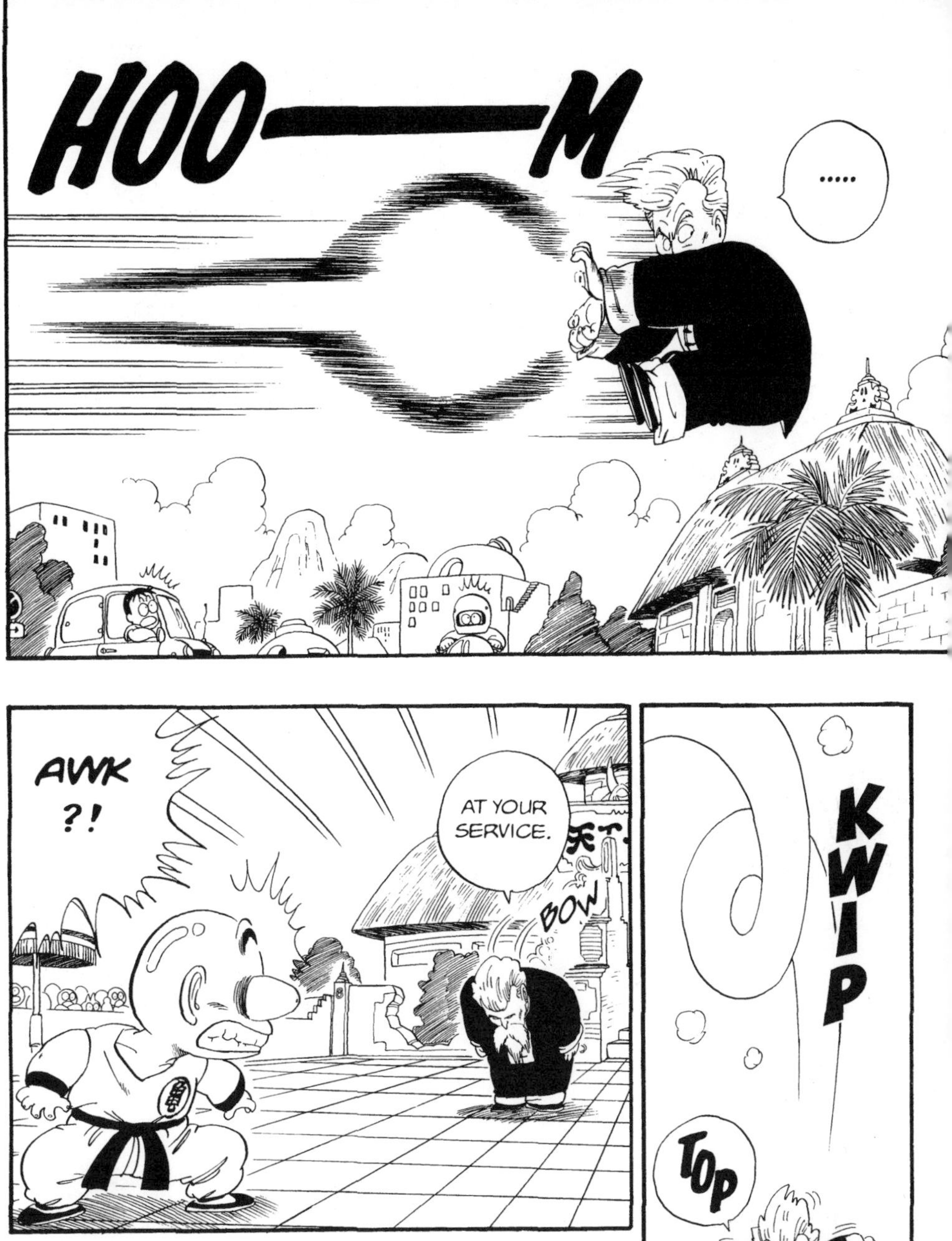
HOO—M
......
KWIP
TOP
AWK ?!
AT YOUR SERVICE.
BOW
WH-WH-WH-WH-WH-
WHAT THE... WHAT THE... WHAT THE–?!!!

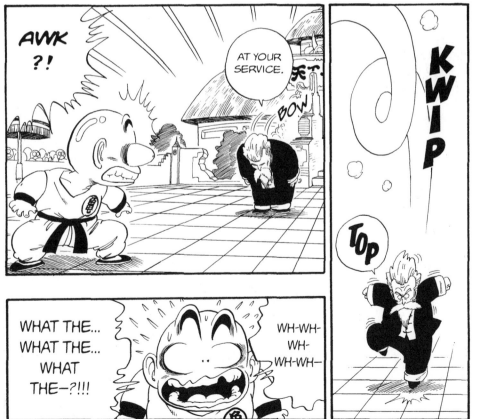

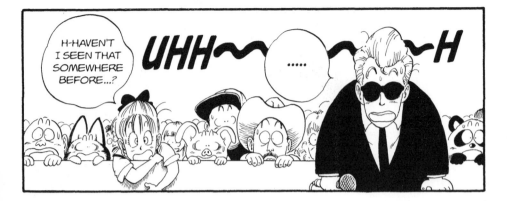

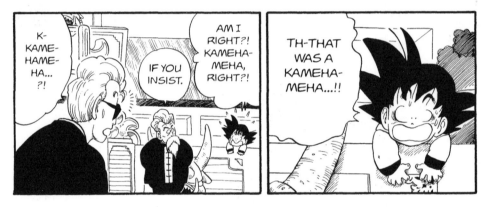

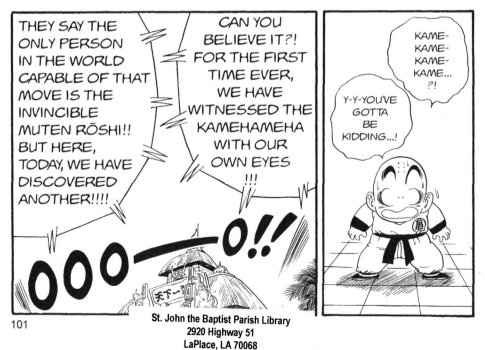

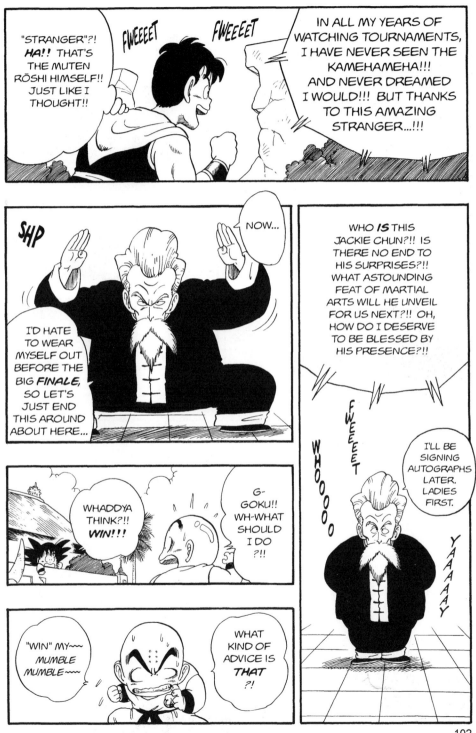

102

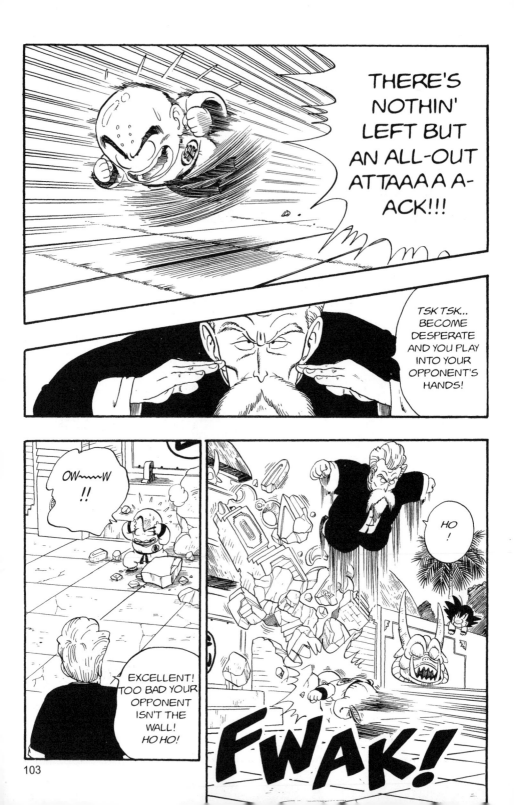

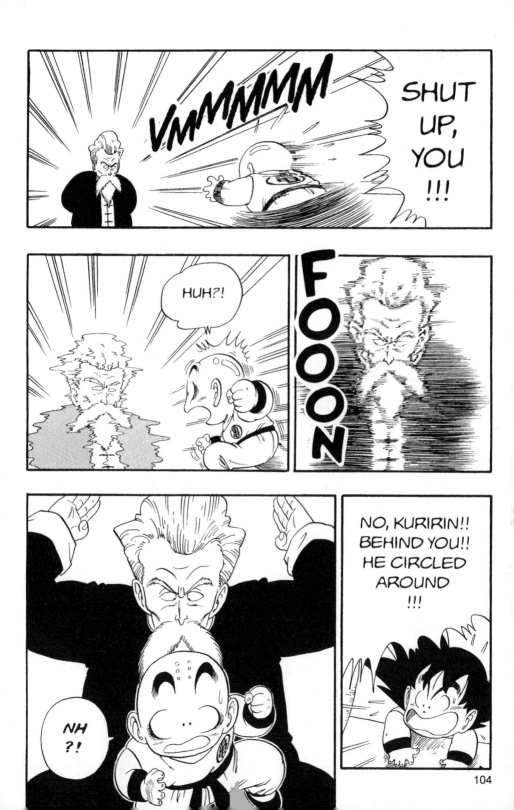

104

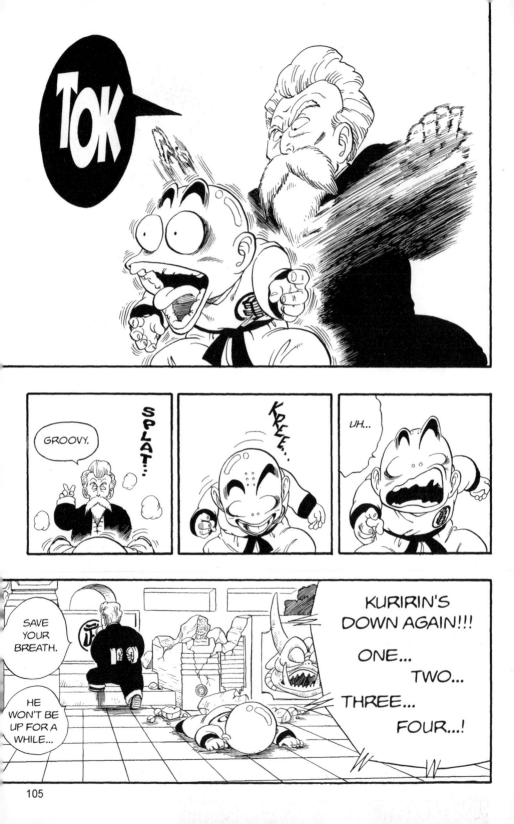

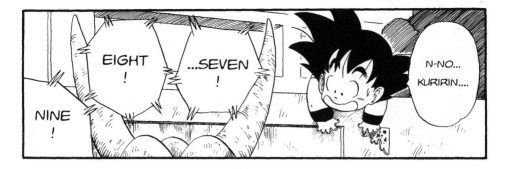

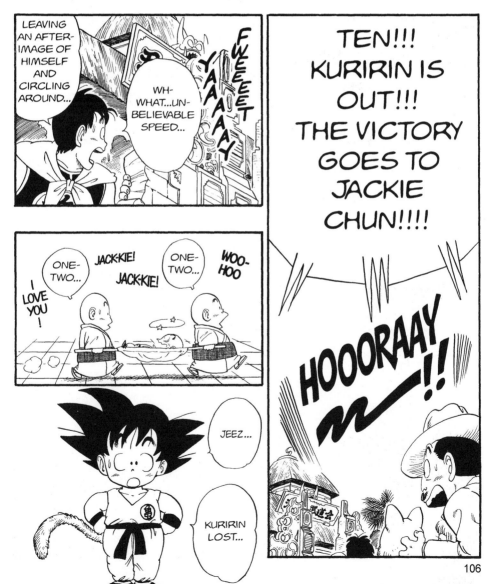

WITH THAT VICTORY, CONTESTANT JACKIE CHUN ADVANCES TO THE FINAL ROUND, WHERE HE WILL FACE THE WINNER OF THE UPCOMING MATCH Nº. 6!!!

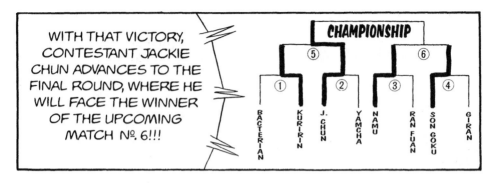

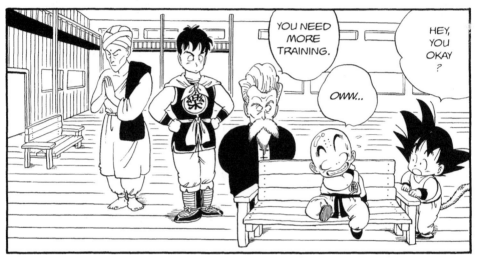

YOU NEED MORE TRAINING.

OWW...

HEY, YOU OKAY?

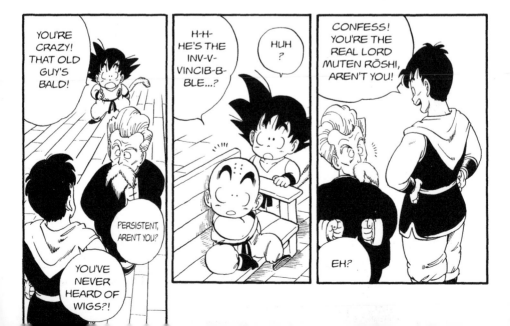

YOU'RE CRAZY! THAT OLD GUY'S BALD!

PERSISTENT, AREN'T YOU?

YOU'VE NEVER HEARD OF WIGS?!

H-H-HE'S THE INV-V-VINCIB-B-BLE...?

HUH?

CONFESS! YOU'RE THE REAL LORD MUTEN RŌSHI, AREN'T YOU!

EH?

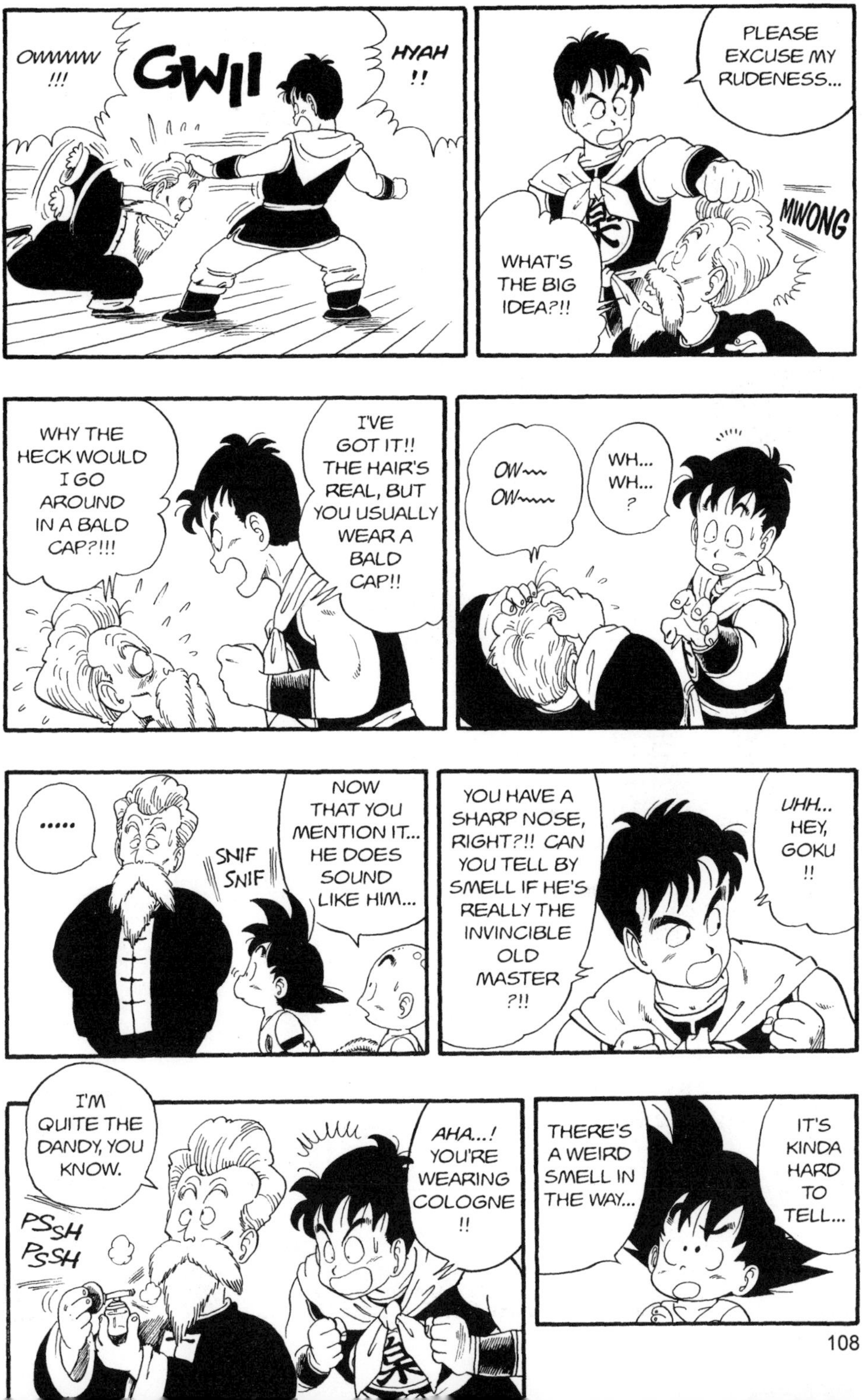
OWWWW !!!
GWII
HYAH !!
PLEASE EXCUSE MY RUDENESS...
MWONG
WHAT'S THE BIG IDEA?!!
WHY THE HECK WOULD I GO AROUND IN A BALD CAP?!!!
I'VE GOT IT!! THE HAIR'S REAL, BUT YOU USUALLY WEAR A BALD CAP!!
OW~~ OW~~~
WH... WH... ?
.....
SNIF SNIF
NOW THAT YOU MENTION IT... HE DOES SOUND LIKE HIM...
YOU HAVE A SHARP NOSE, RIGHT?!! CAN YOU TELL BY SMELL IF HE'S REALLY THE INVINCIBLE OLD MASTER ?!!
UHH... HEY, GOKU !!
I'M QUITE THE DANDY, YOU KNOW.
PSSH PSSH
AHA...! YOU'RE WEARING COLOGNE !!
THERE'S A WEIRD SMELL IN THE WAY...
IT'S KINDA HARD TO TELL...

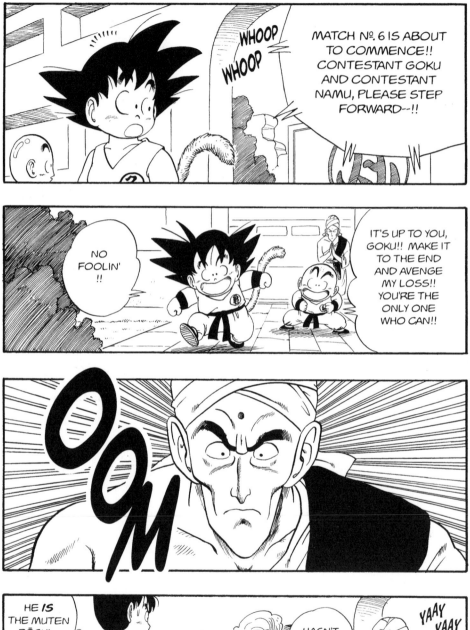

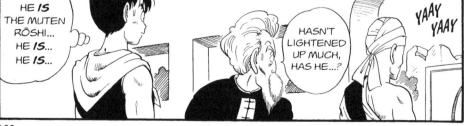

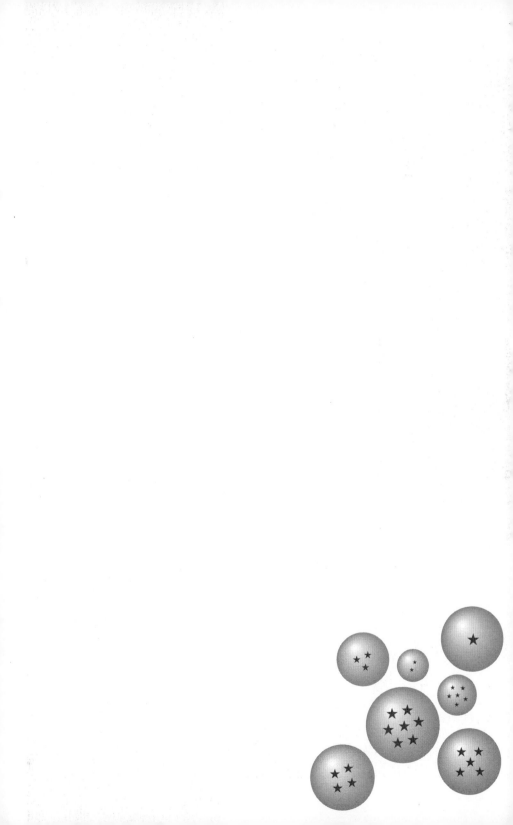

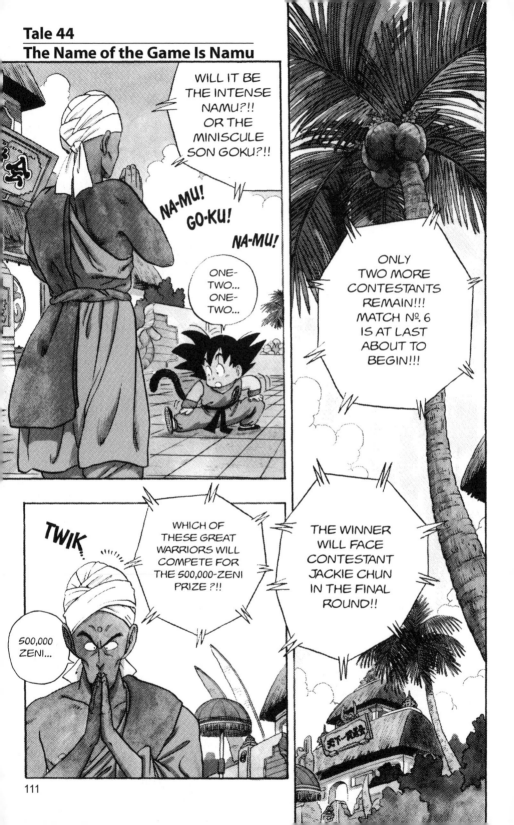

WILL IT BE THE INTENSE NAMU?!! OR THE MINISCULE SON GOKU?!!

NA-MU!

GO-KU!

NA-MU!

ONE-TWO... ONE-TWO...

ONLY TWO MORE CONTESTANTS REMAIN!!! MATCH Nº 6 IS AT LAST ABOUT TO BEGIN!!!

TWIK...

WHICH OF THESE GREAT WARRIORS WILL COMPETE FOR THE 500,000-ZENI PRIZE?!!

THE WINNER WILL FACE CONTESTANT JACKIE CHUN IN THE FINAL ROUND!!

500,000 ZENI...

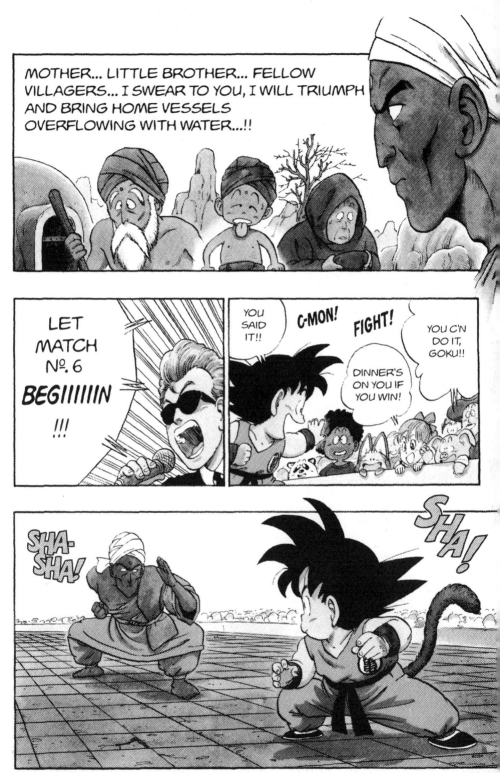

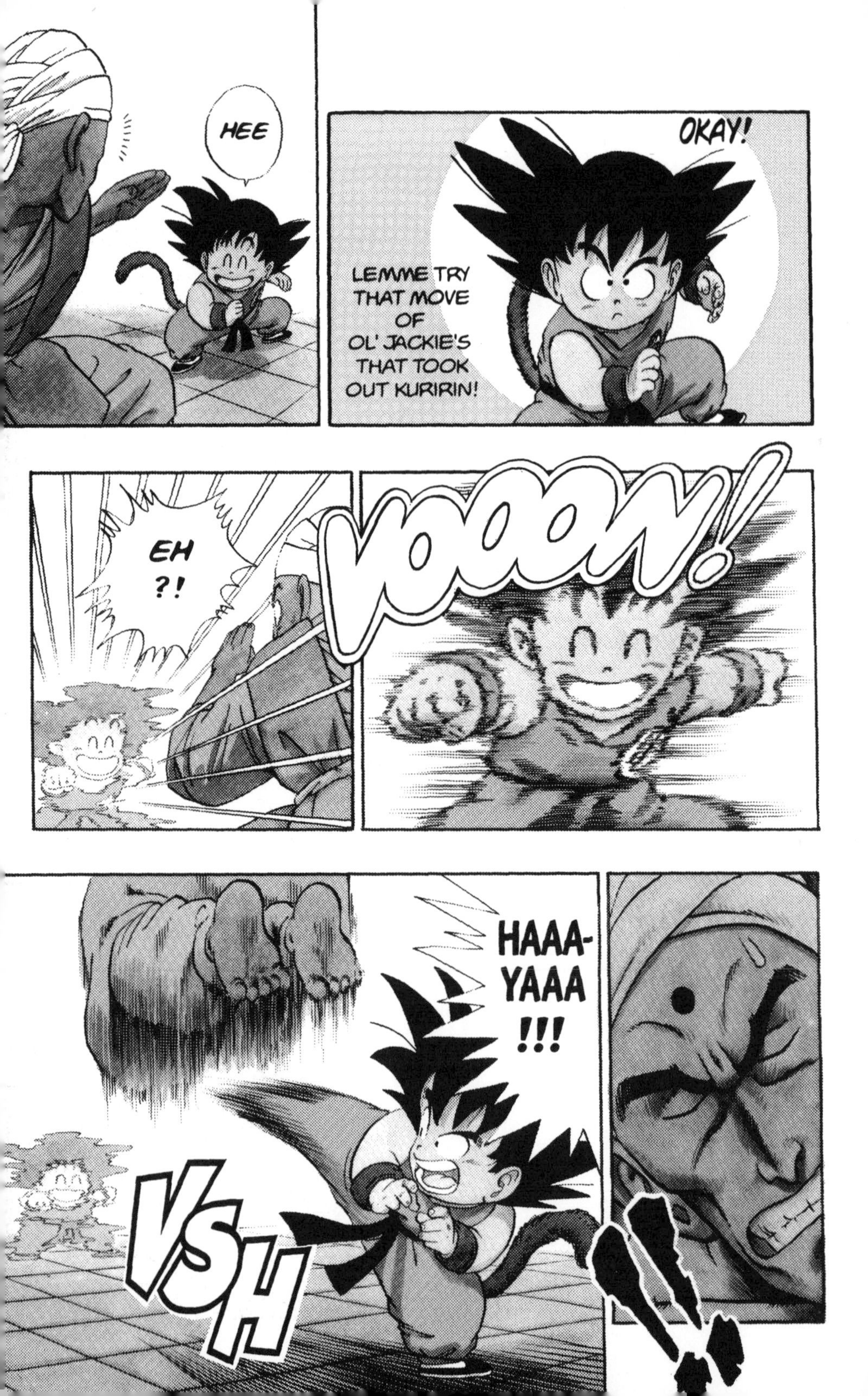
OKAY!
LEMME TRY THAT MOVE OF OL' JACKIE'S THAT TOOK OUT KURIRIN!
HEE
VOOON!
EH ?!
!!
HAAA-YAAA !!!
VSH

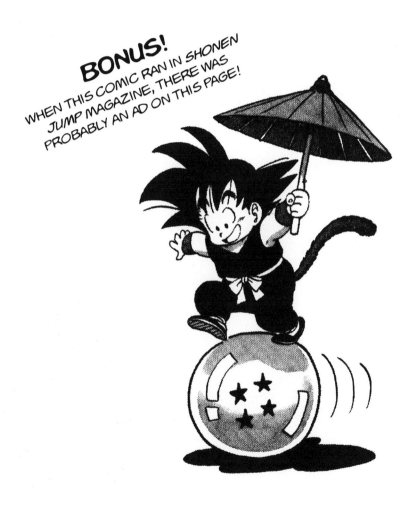

BONUS!
WHEN THIS COMIC RAN IN SHONEN
JUMP MAGAZINE, THERE WAS
PROBABLY AN AD ON THIS PAGE!

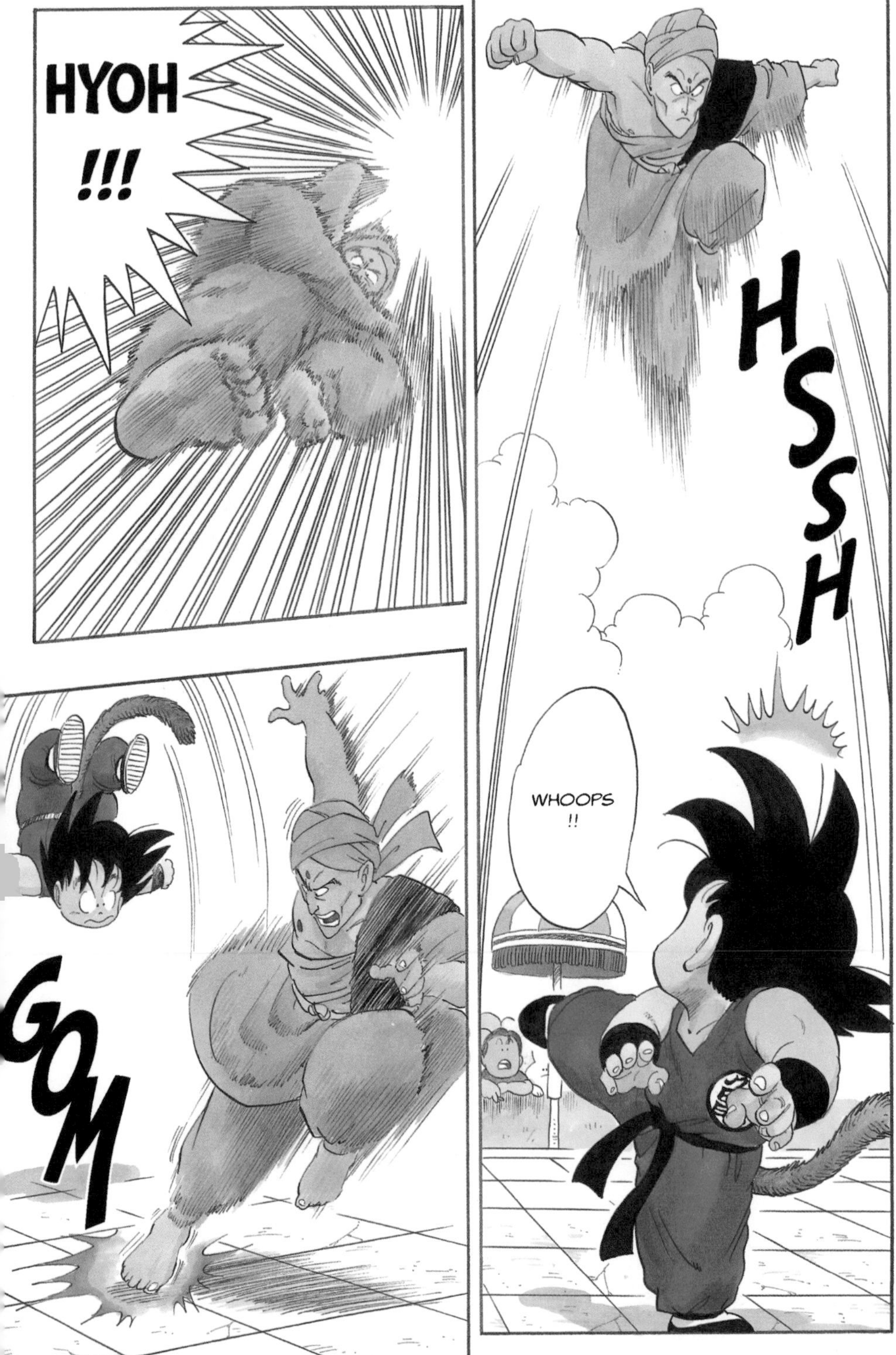
HSSH
WHOOPS !!
HYOH !!!
GOM

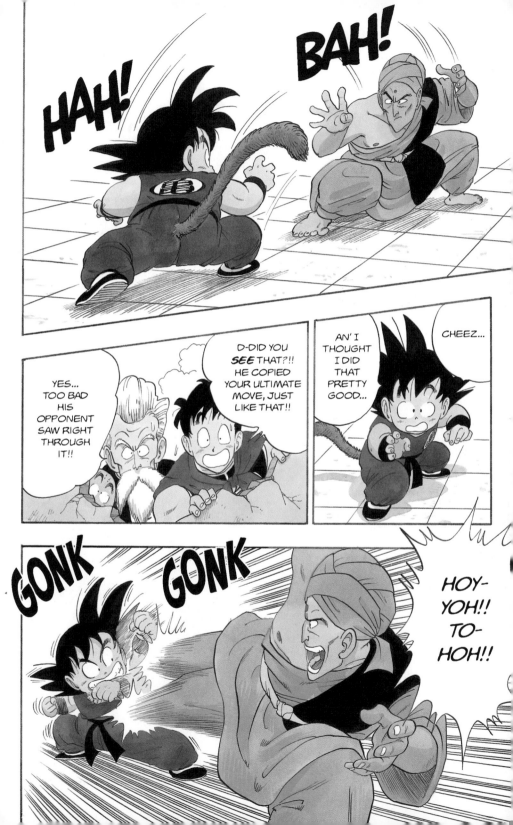

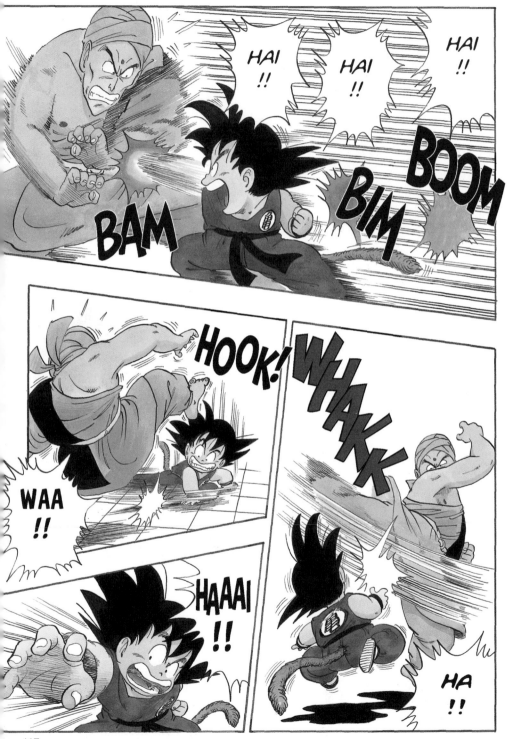

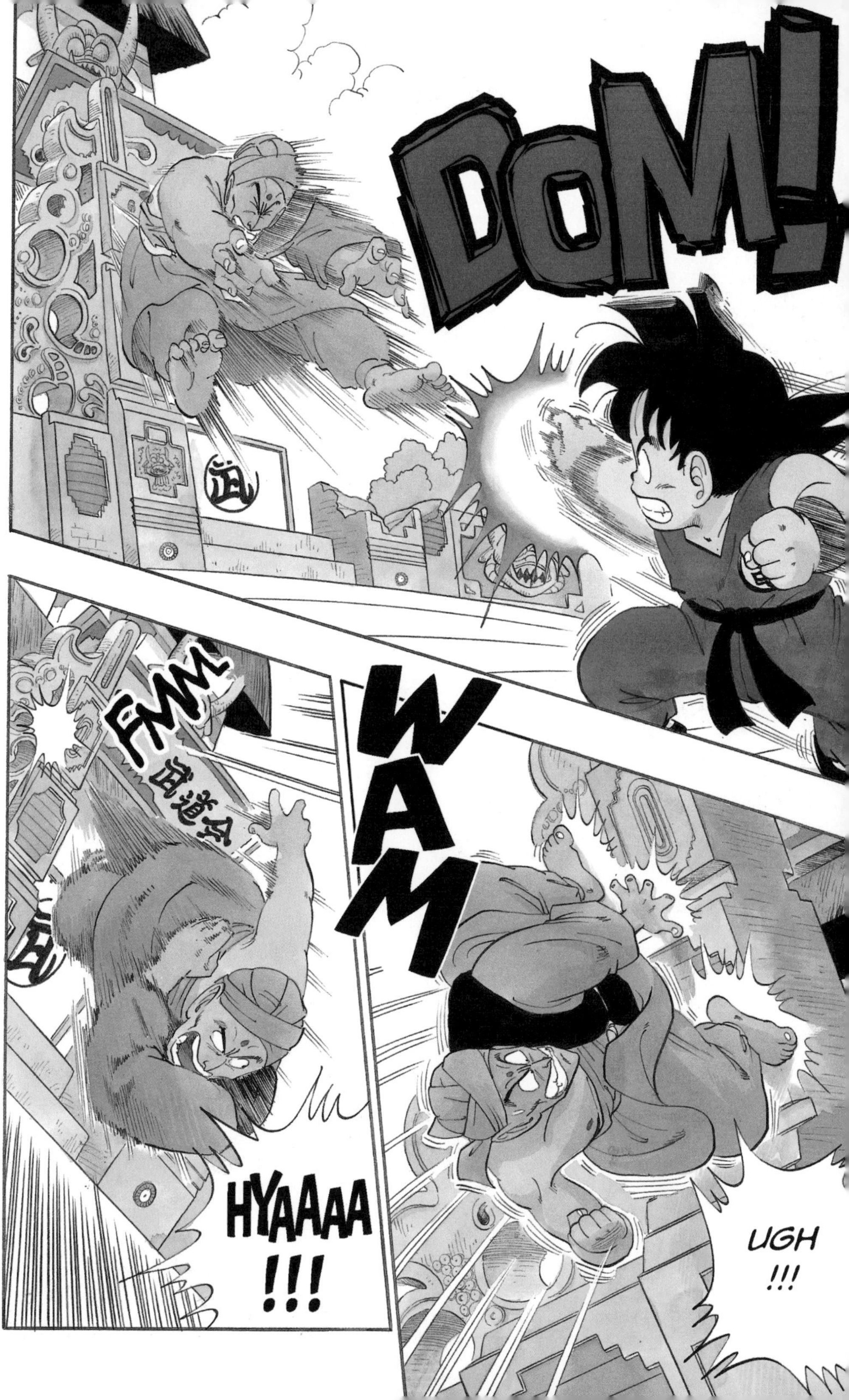
DOM!
WAM
UGH !!!
FWM
武道会
HYAAAA !!!

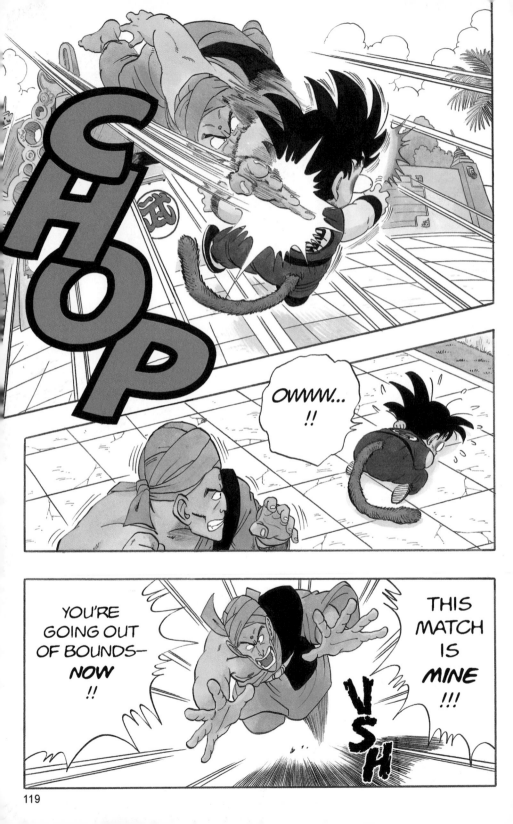

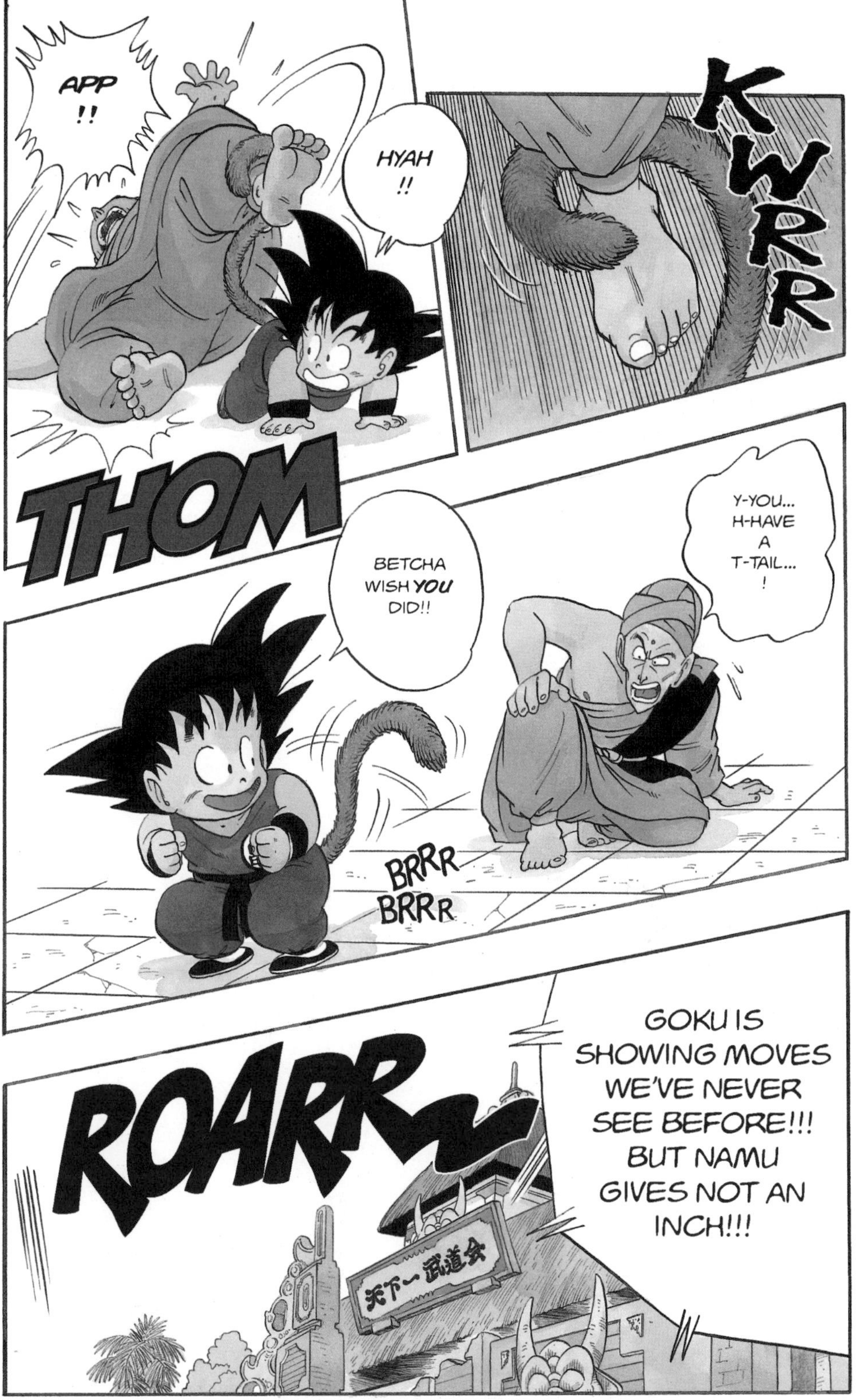
KWRR
APP !!
HYAH !!
THOM
Y-YOU... H-HAVE A T-TAIL... !
BETCHA WISH YOU DID!!
BRRR BRRR
GOKU IS SHOWING MOVES WE'VE NEVER SEE BEFORE!!! BUT NAMU GIVES NOT AN INCH!!!
ROARR
天下一武道会

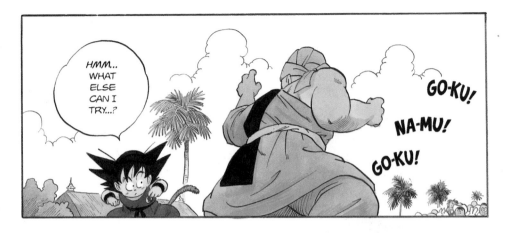

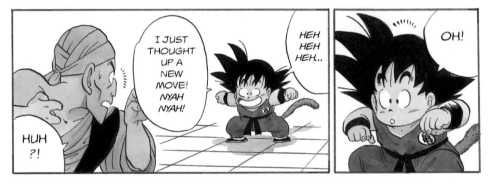

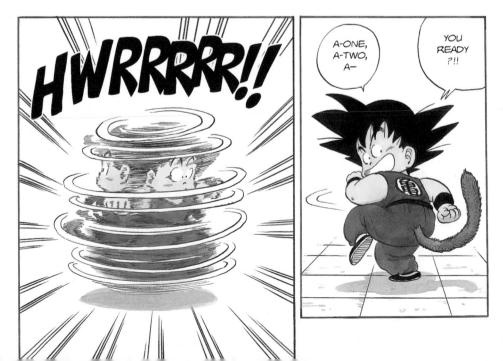

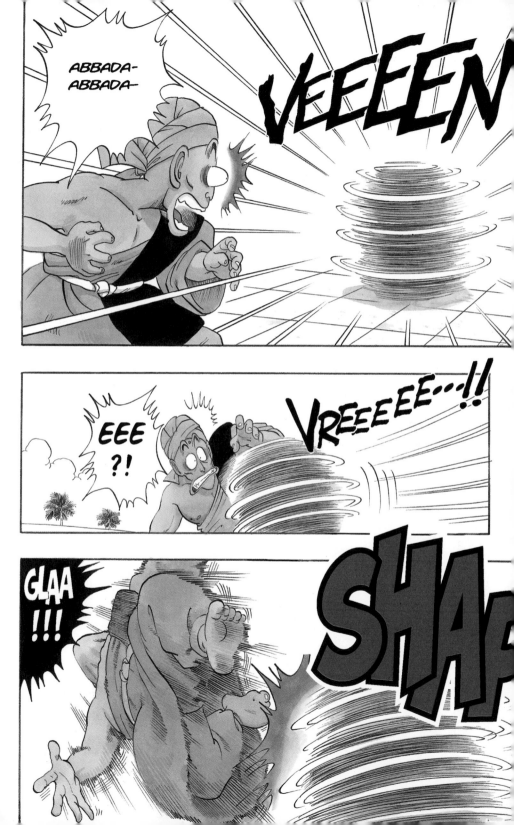

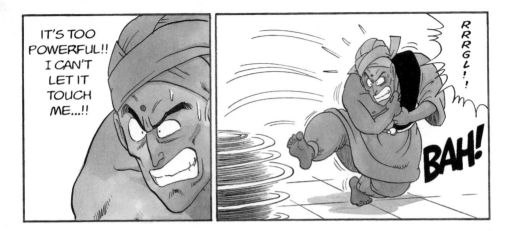

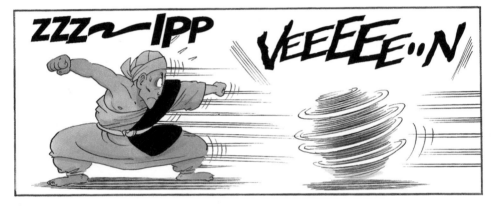

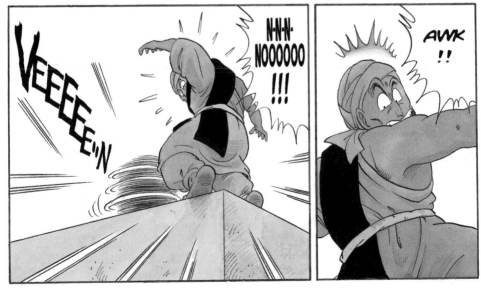

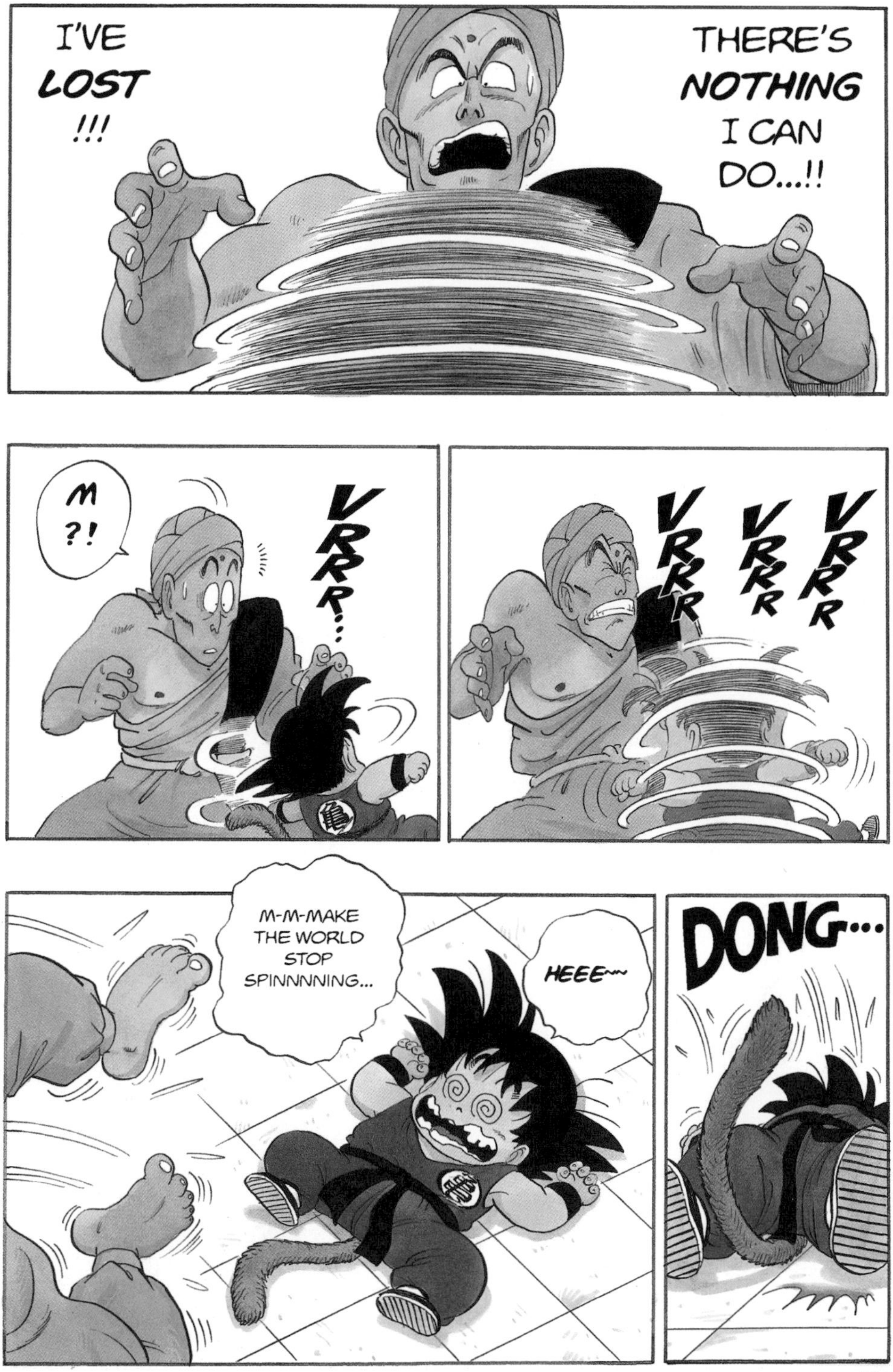
THERE'S NOTHING I CAN DO...!!
I'VE LOST!!!
VRRR VRRR VRRR
VRRR...
M?!
DONG...
HEEE~~
M-M-MAKE THE WORLD STOP SPINNNNING...

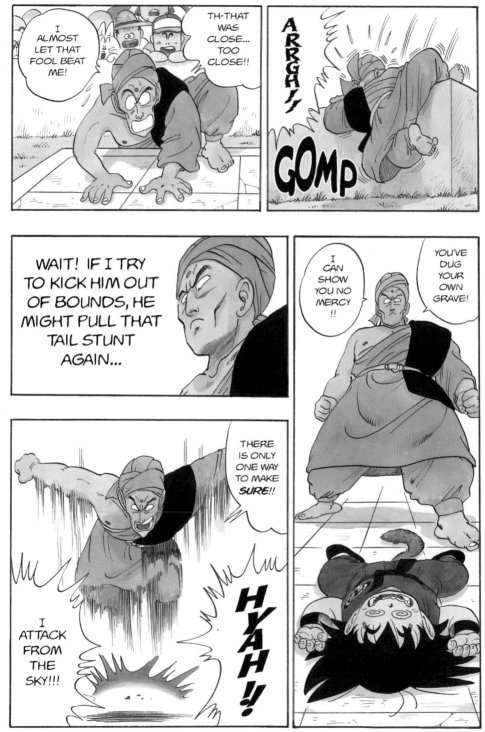

125

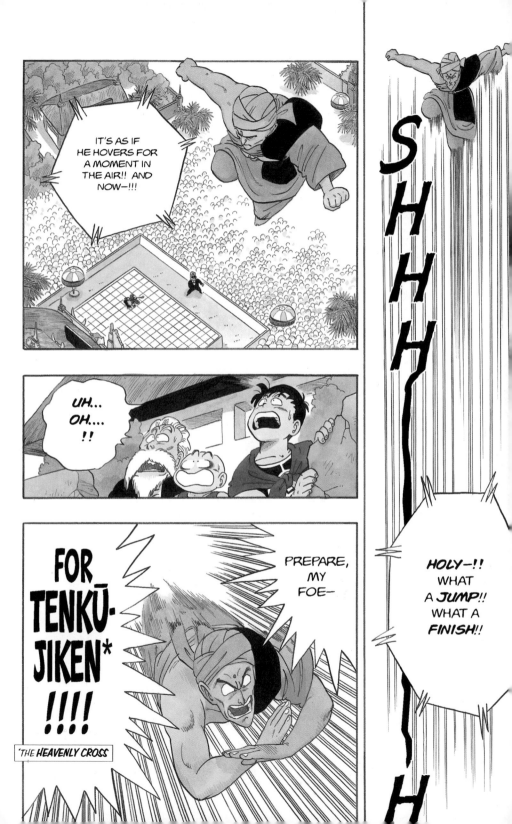

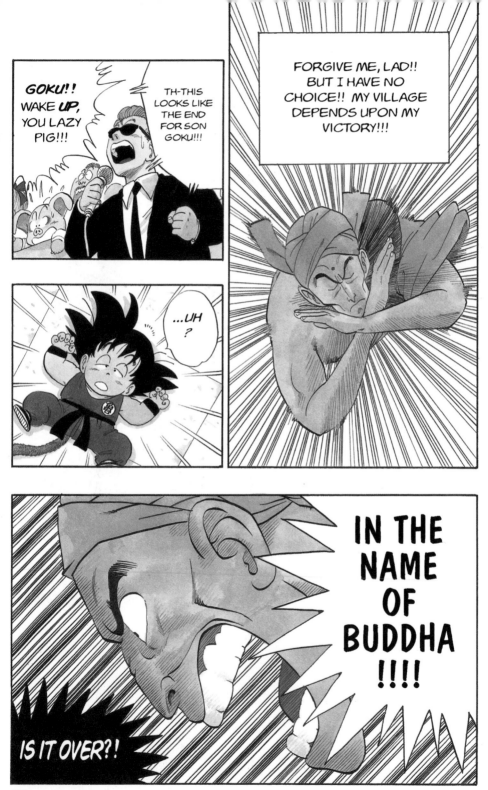

127

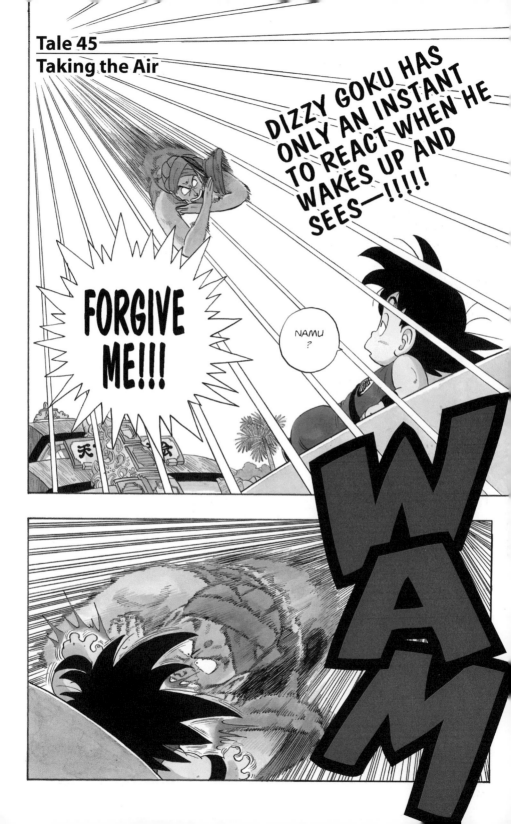

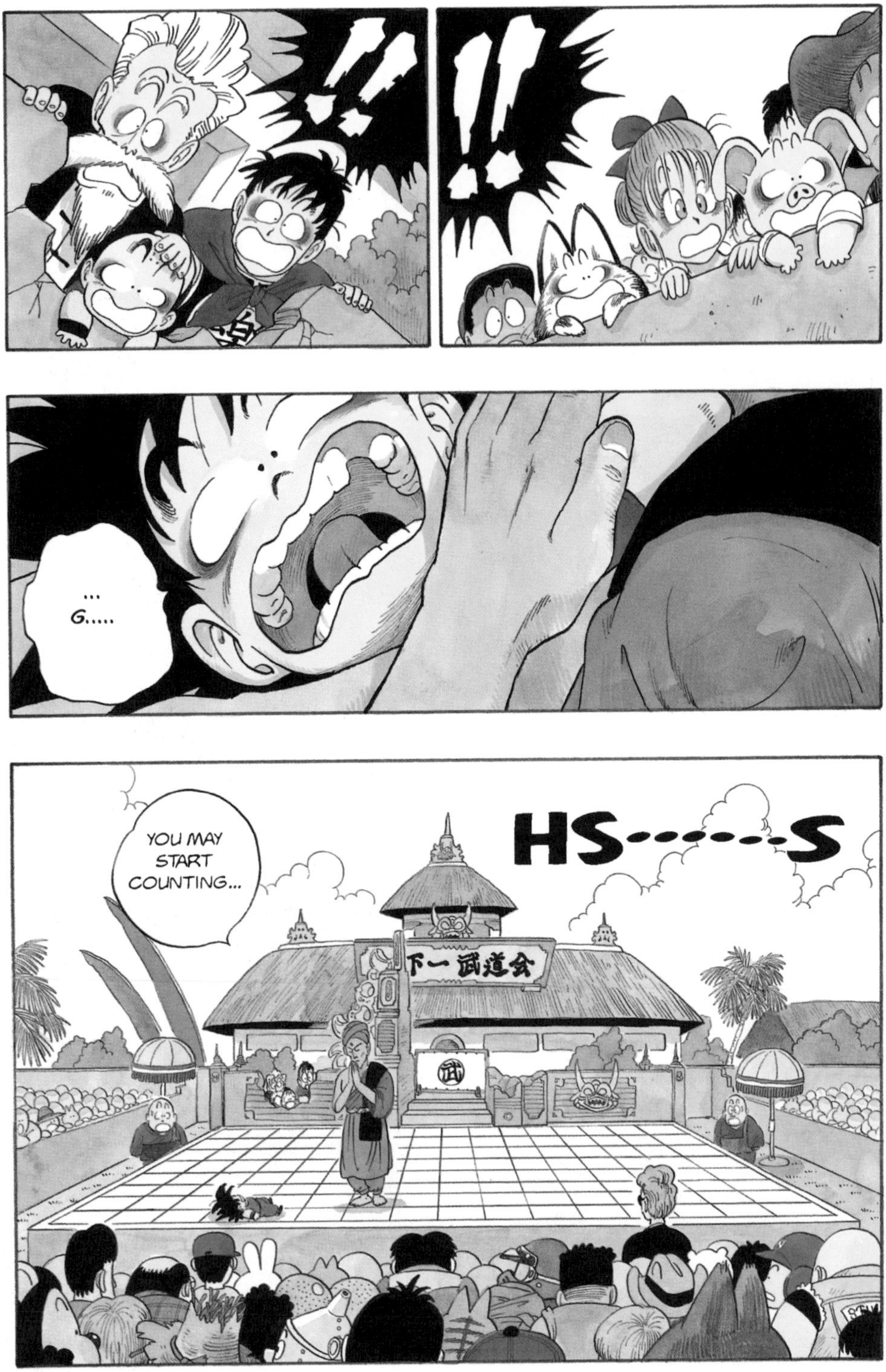
!!
!!
...
G.....
HS------S
YOU MAY START COUNTING...
下一武道会

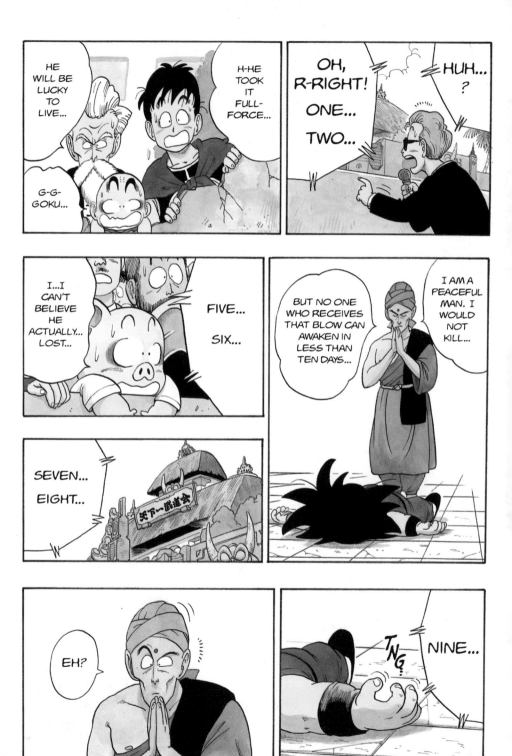

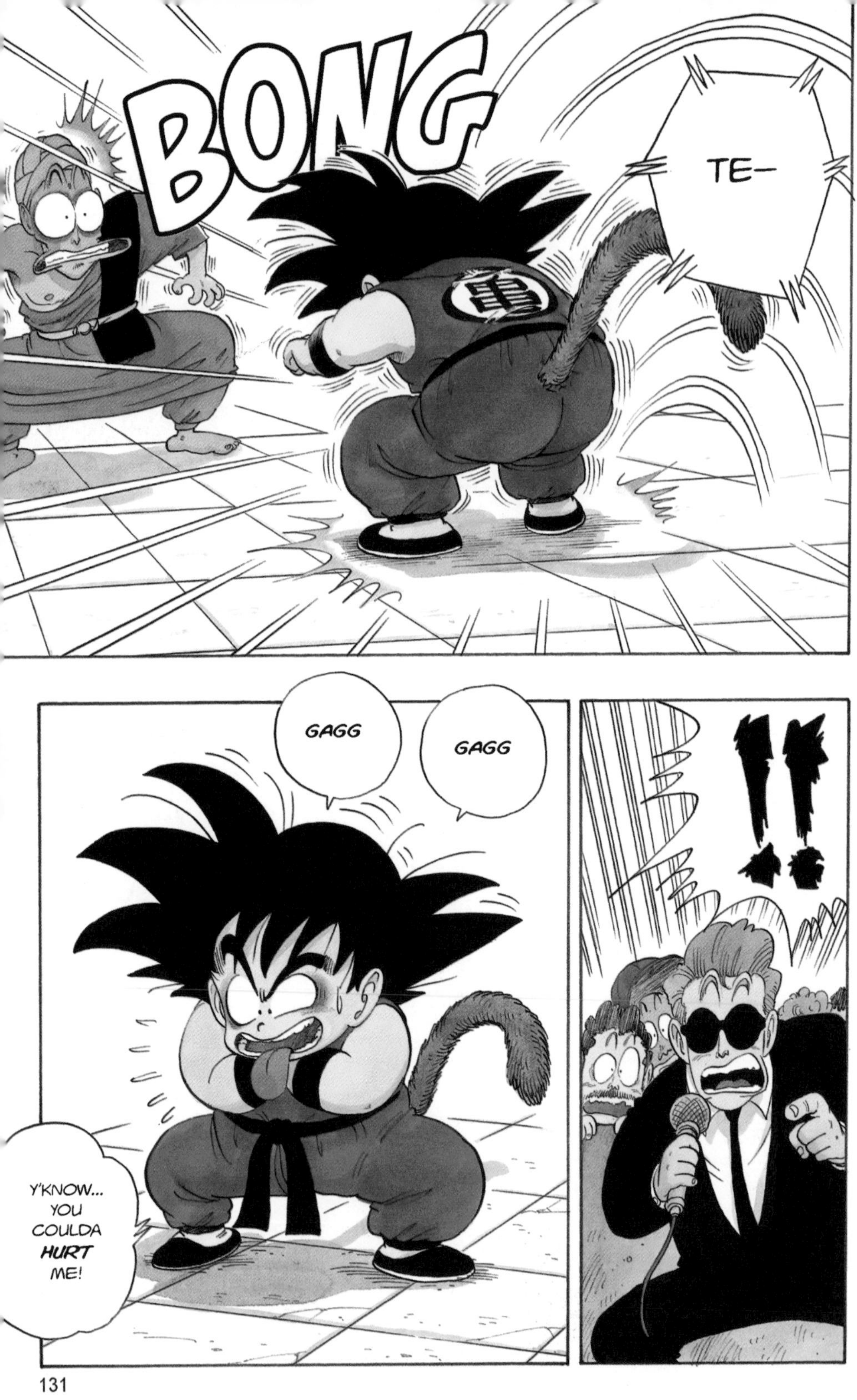
TE—
BONG
!!
GAGG
GAGG
Y'KNOW... YOU COULDA HURT ME!

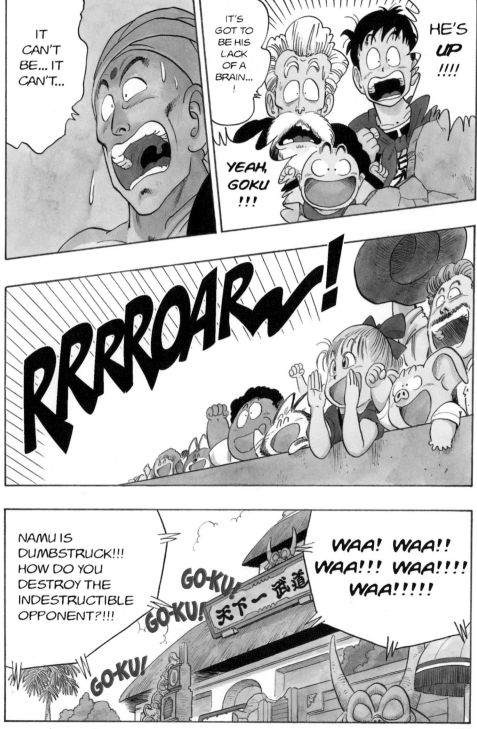

132

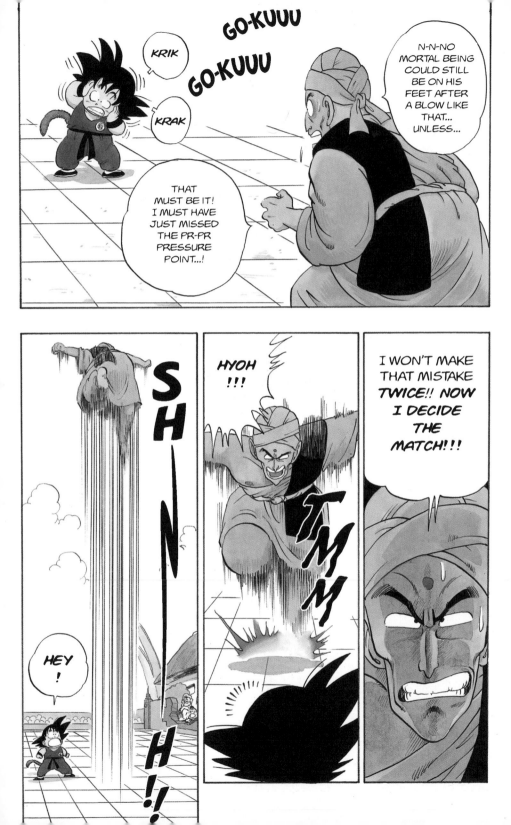

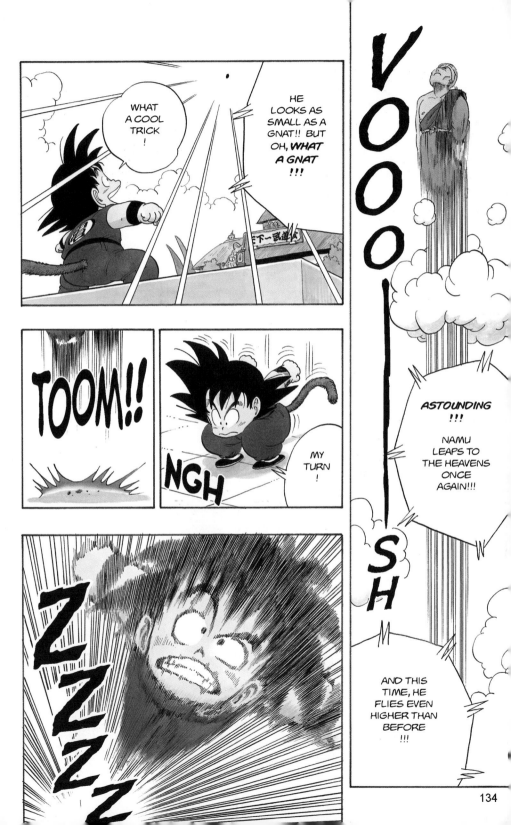

134

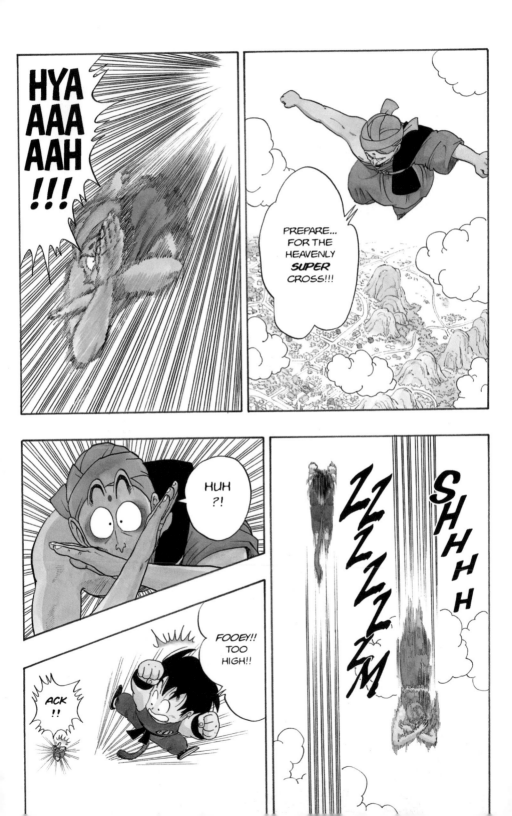

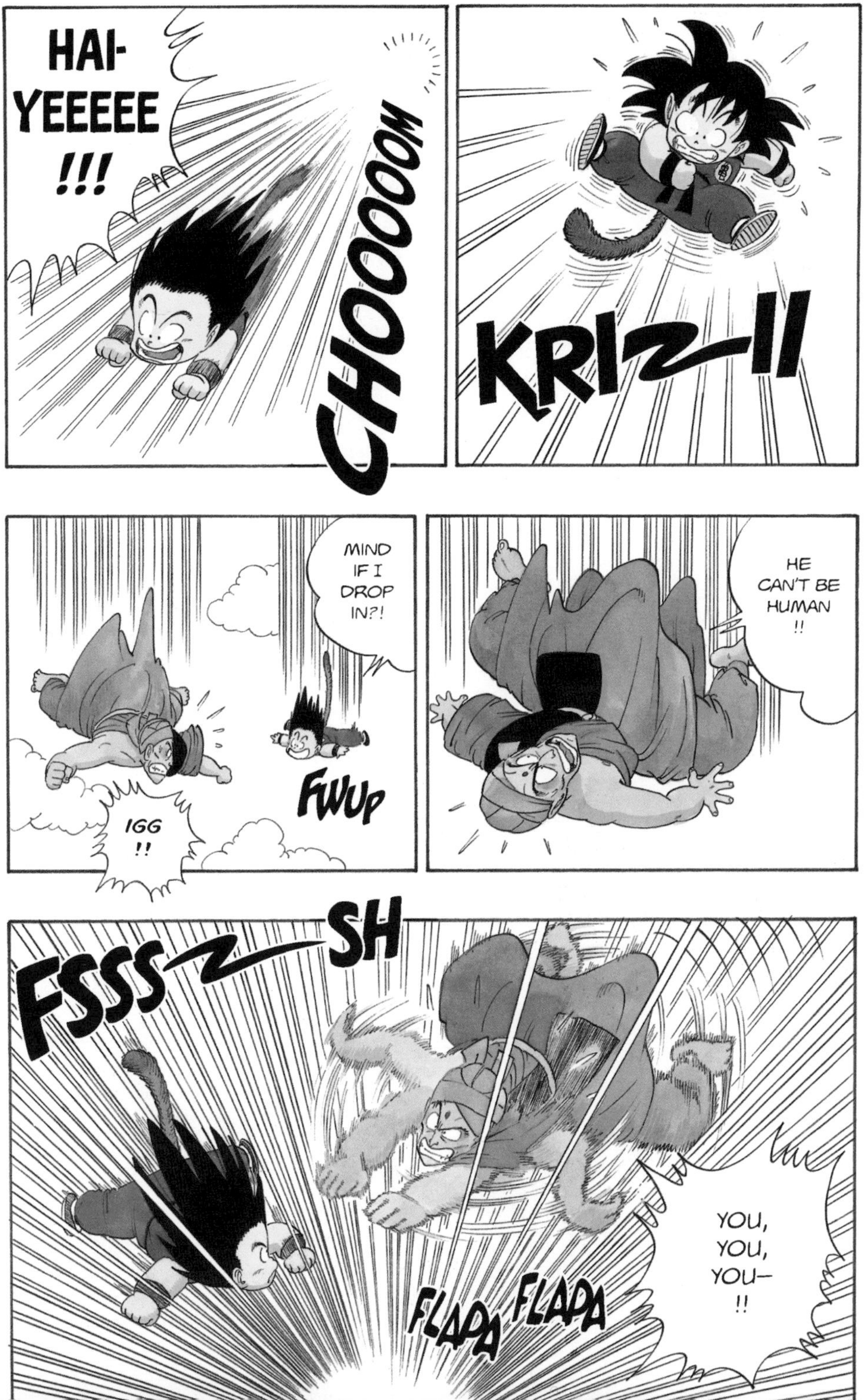
KRIZ—II
HAI-YEEEEE!!!
CHOOOOM
HE CAN'T BE HUMAN!!
MIND IF I DROP IN?!
FWUP
IGG!!
YOU, YOU, YOU—!!
FSSS—SH
FLAPA FLAPA

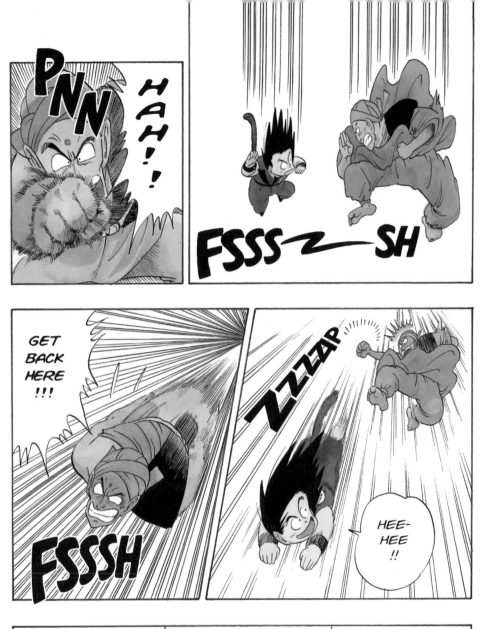

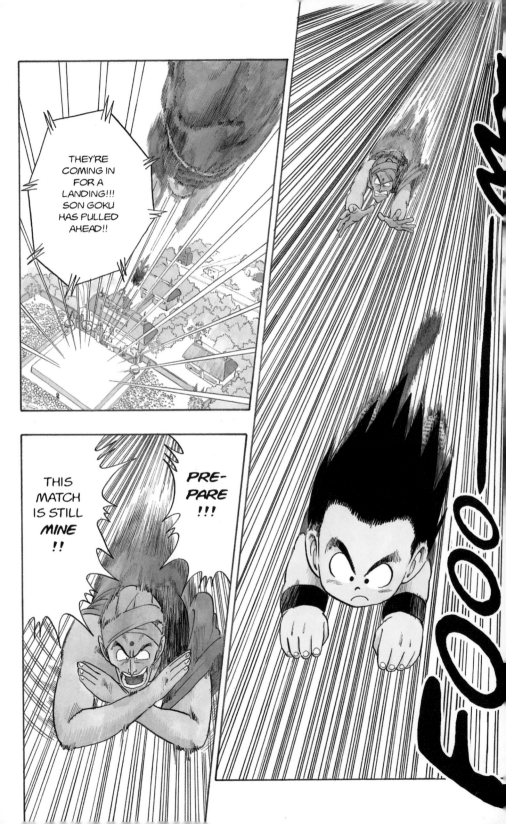

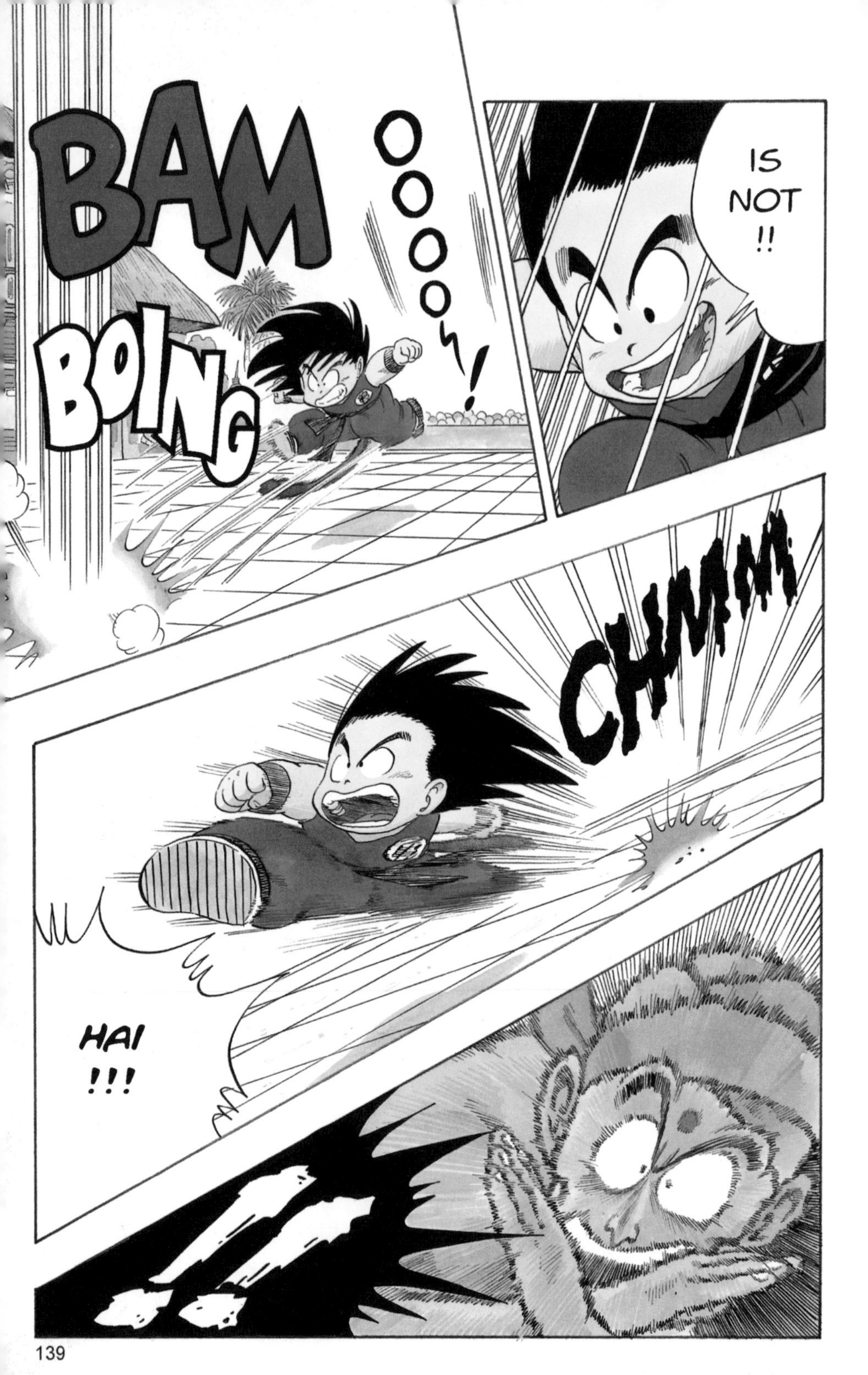
IS NOT !!
BAM
OOOOh!
BOING
CHMM
HAI !!!

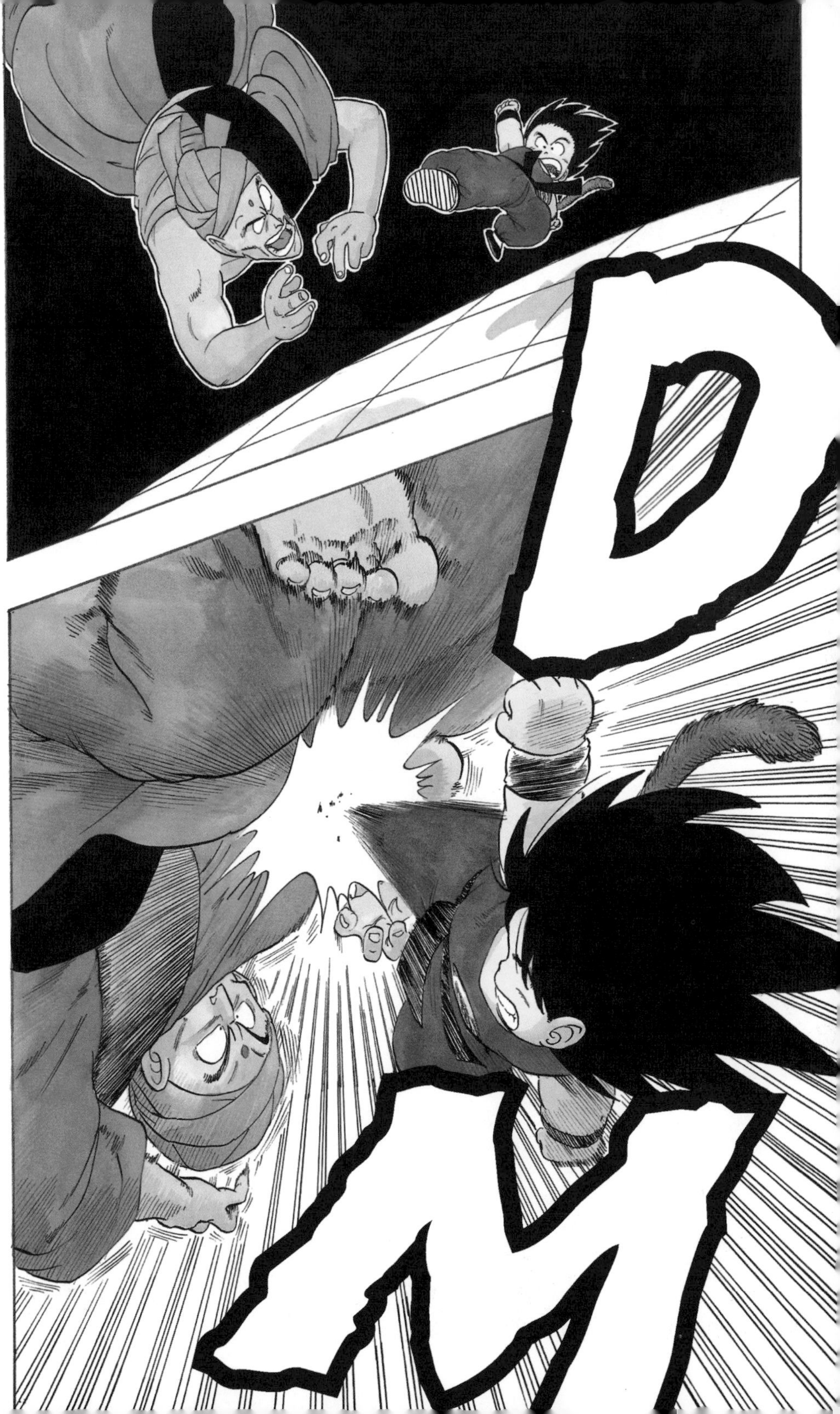
DM

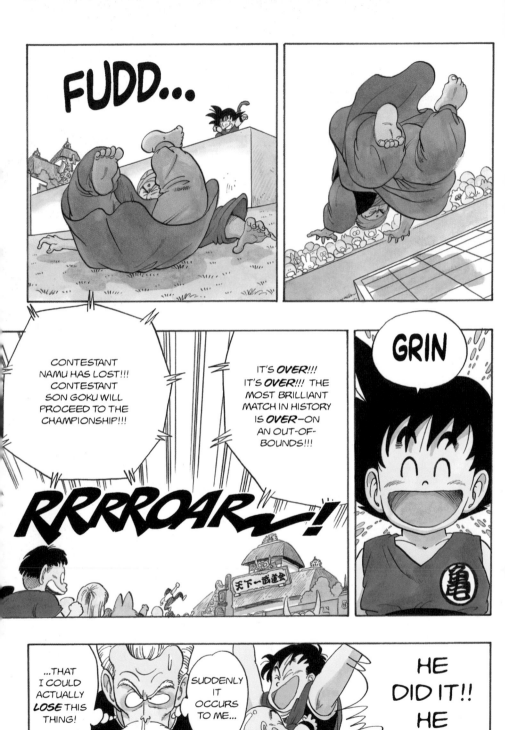

FUDD...

CONTESTANT NAMU HAS LOST!!! CONTESTANT SON GOKU WILL PROCEED TO THE CHAMPIONSHIP!!!

IT'S *OVER*!!! IT'S *OVER*!!! THE MOST BRILLIANT MATCH IN HISTORY IS *OVER*—ON AN OUT-OF-BOUNDS!!!

GRIN

RRRROARゝ!

...THAT I COULD ACTUALLY *LOSE* THIS THING!

SUDDENLY IT OCCURS TO ME...

HE DID IT!! HE DID IT!!

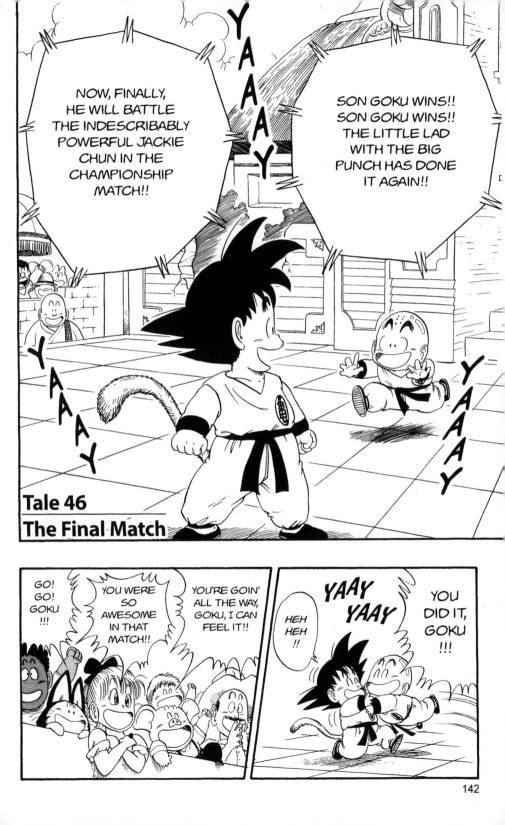

Tale 46
The Final Match

142

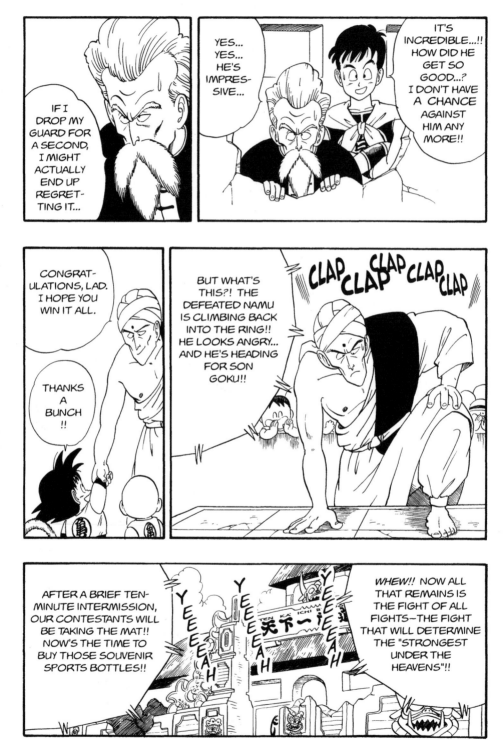

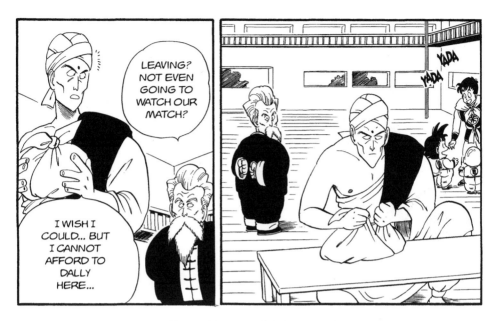

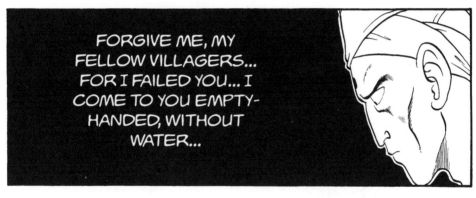

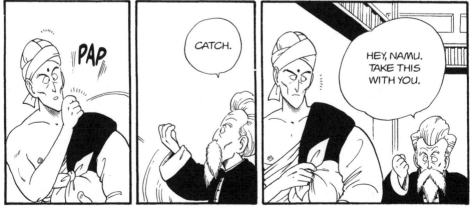

144

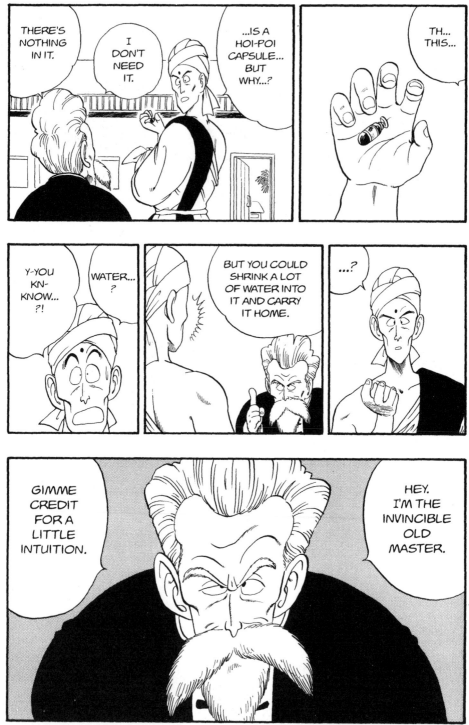

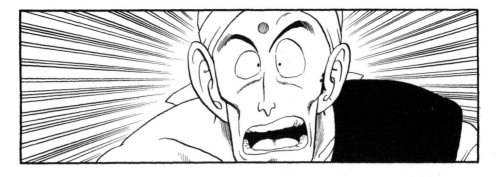

B-BUT I DON'T UNDER-STAND... WHY?

I DON'T WANT THEM TO KNOW!

SHH! SHH!!

TH- THEN YOU REALLY *ARE* THE MUTEN RŌ—

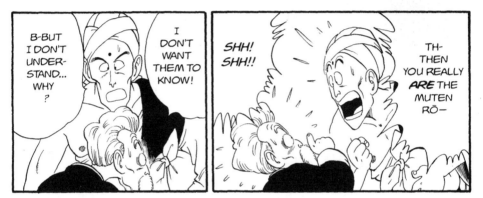

THEY'VE FAR SURPASSED MY EXPECTATIONS IN THEIR TRAINING, AND JUST KEEP GETTING BETTER AND BETTER...

AS YOU KNOW, MY TWO DISCIPLES, KURIRIN AND GOKU, ENTERED THIS MARTIAL ARTS TOURNAMENT...

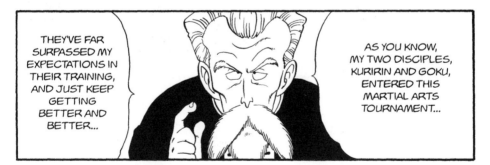

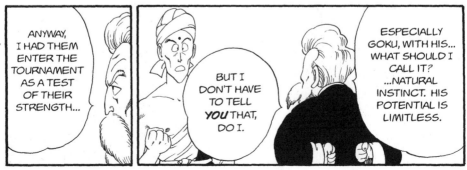

ANYWAY, I HAD THEM ENTER THE TOURNAMENT AS A TEST OF THEIR STRENGTH...

BUT I DON'T HAVE TO TELL *YOU* THAT, DO I.

ESPECIALLY GOKU, WITH HIS... WHAT SHOULD I CALL IT? ...NATURAL INSTINCT. HIS POTENTIAL IS LIMITLESS.

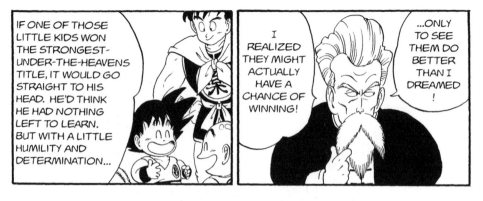

IF ONE OF THOSE LITTLE KIDS WON THE STRONGEST-UNDER-THE-HEAVENS TITLE, IT WOULD GO STRAIGHT TO HIS HEAD. HE'D THINK HE HAD NOTHING LEFT TO LEARN. BUT WITH A LITTLE HUMILITY AND DETERMINATION...

I REALIZED THEY MIGHT ACTUALLY HAVE A CHANCE OF WINNING!

...ONLY TO SEE THEM DO BETTER THAN I DREAMED!

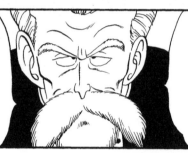

SO I DECIDED TO ENTER AS WELL, IN DISGUISE, TO TEACH THEM THAT NO MATTER HOW GREAT YOU ARE, THERE IS ALWAYS SOMEONE EVEN BETTER.

I COULD TURN THEM BOTH INTO THE GREATEST FIGHTERS EVER!

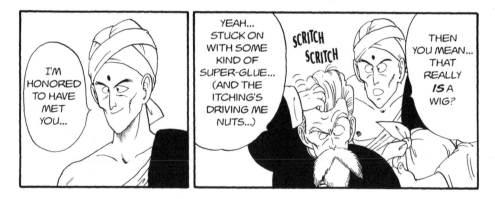

I'M HONORED TO HAVE MET YOU...

YEAH... STUCK ON WITH SOME KIND OF SUPER-GLUE... (AND THE ITCHING'S DRIVING ME NUTS...)

SCRITCH SCRITCH

THEN YOU MEAN... THAT REALLY *IS* A WIG?

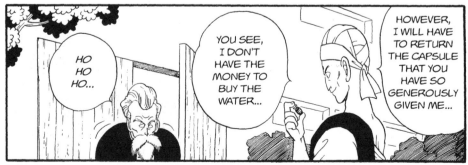

HO HO HO...

YOU SEE, I DON'T HAVE THE MONEY TO BUY THE WATER...

HOWEVER, I WILL HAVE TO RETURN THE CAPSULE THAT YOU HAVE SO GENEROUSLY GIVEN ME...

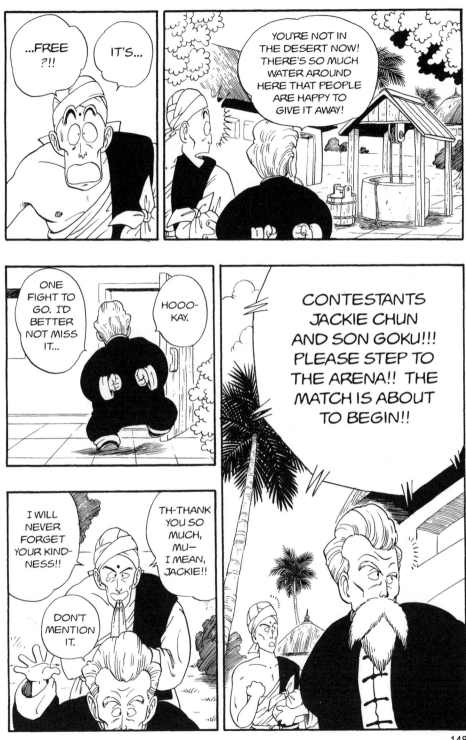

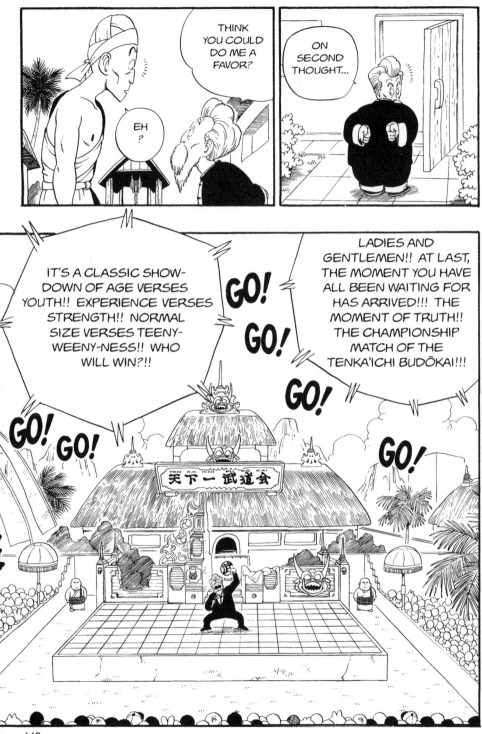

149

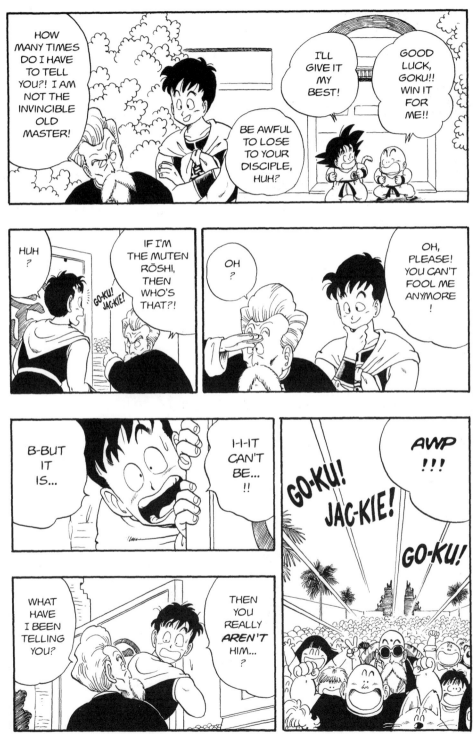

150

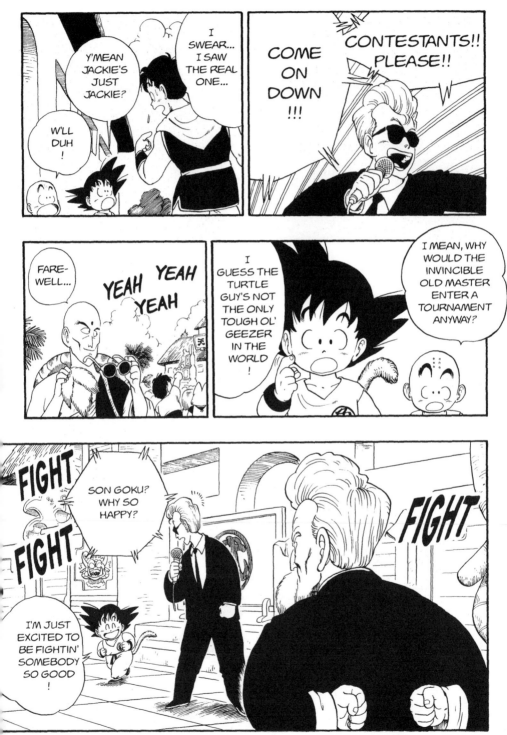

151

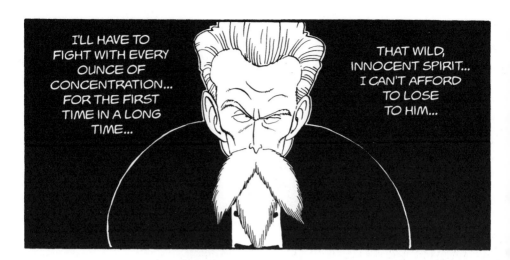

I'LL HAVE TO FIGHT WITH EVERY OUNCE OF CONCENTRATION... FOR THE FIRST TIME IN A LONG TIME...

THAT WILD, INNOCENT SPIRIT... I CAN'T AFFORD TO LOSE TO HIM...

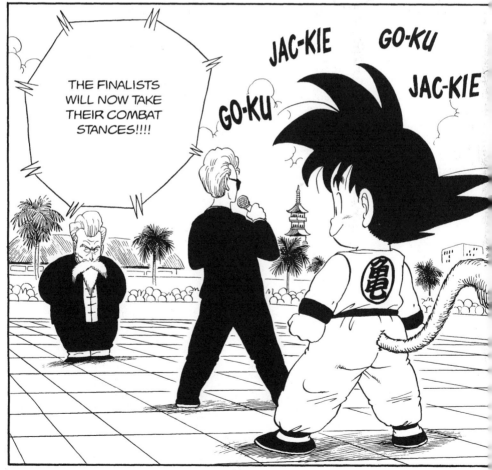

THE FINALISTS WILL NOW TAKE THEIR COMBAT STANCES!!!!

JAC-KIE

GO-KU

GO-KU

JAC-KIE

GO-KU

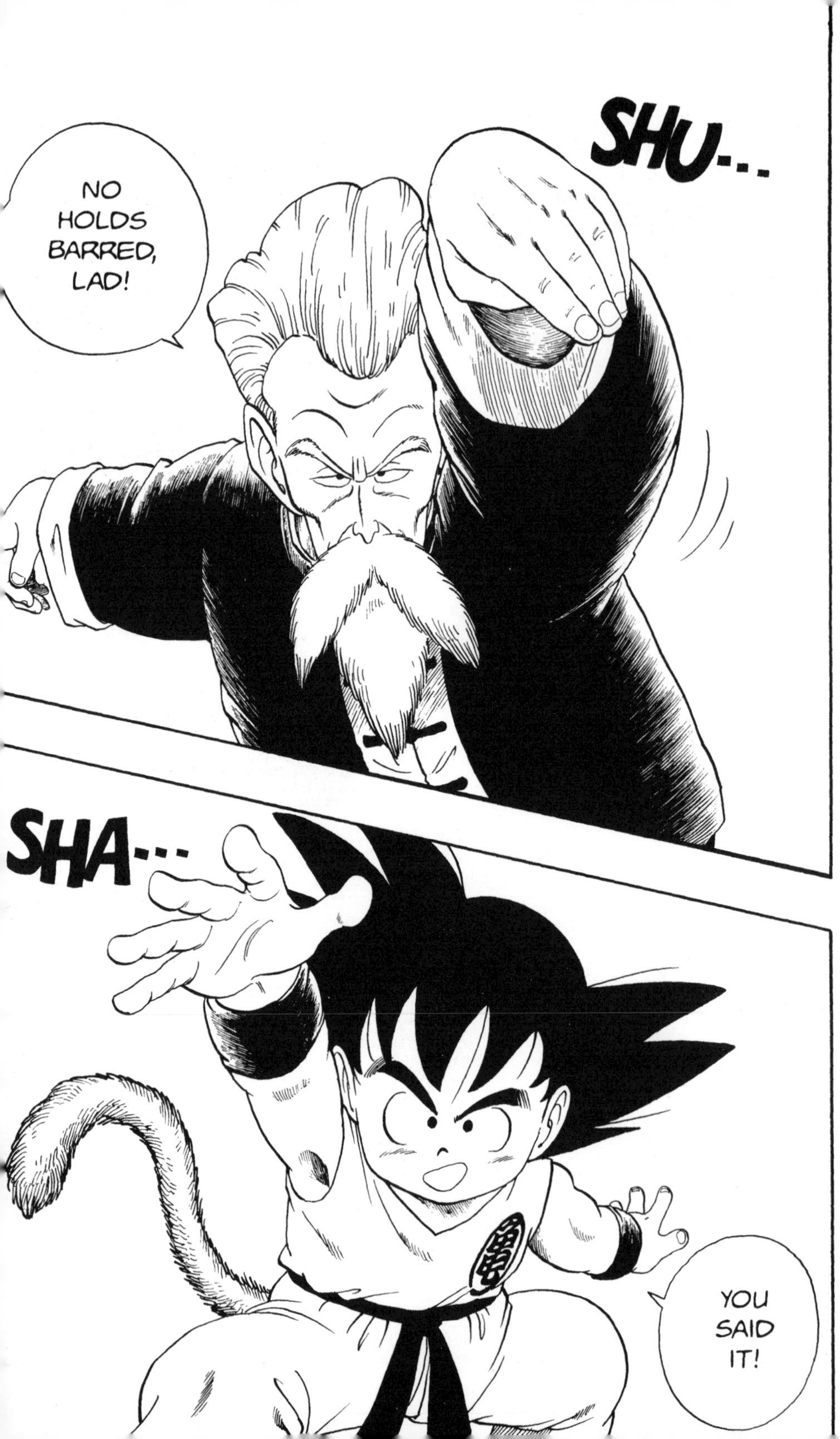
SHU...
NO HOLDS BARRED, LAD!
SHA...
YOU SAID IT!

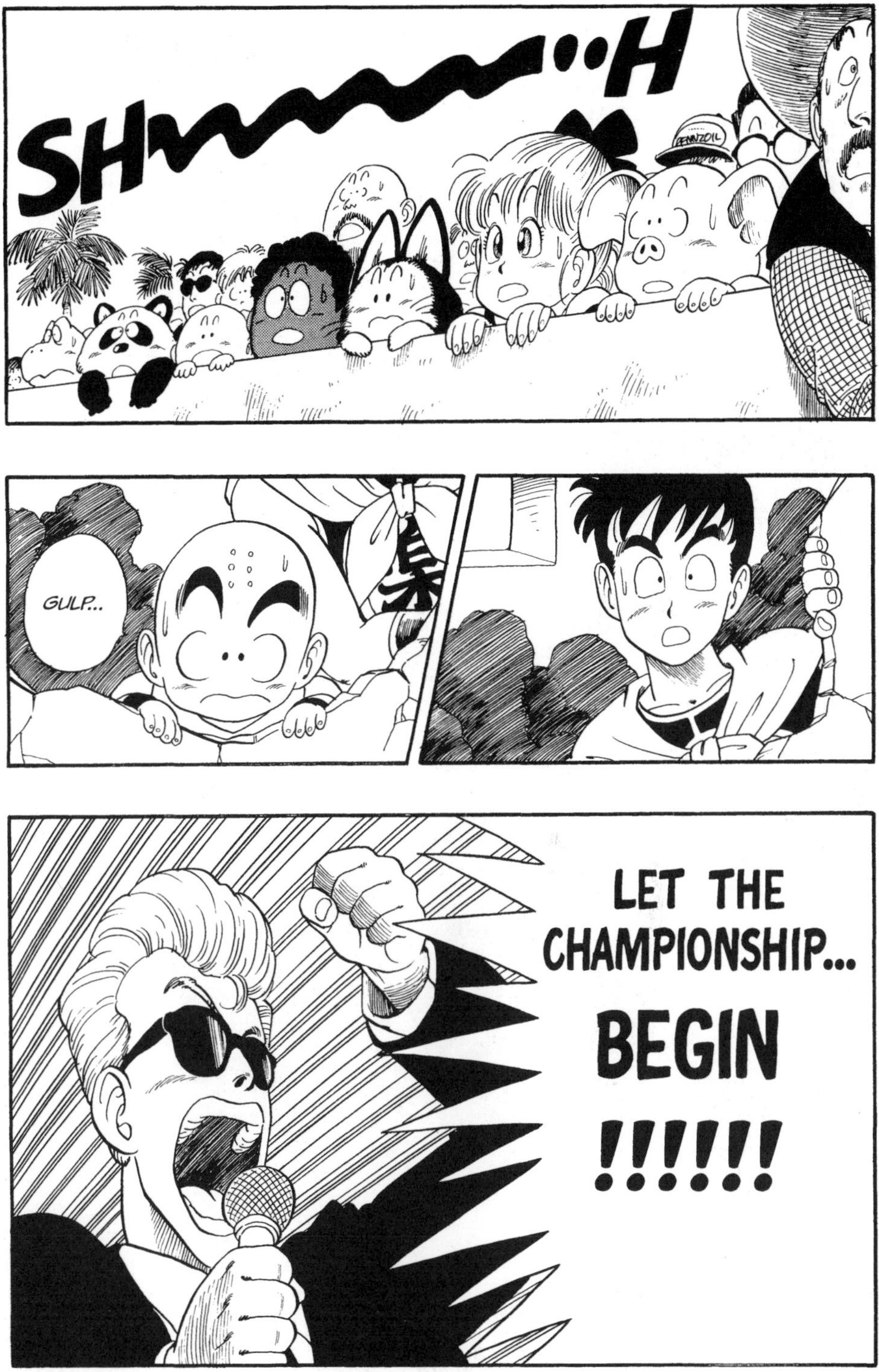
SH...H
GULP...
LET THE CHAMPIONSHIP... BEGIN !!!!!!

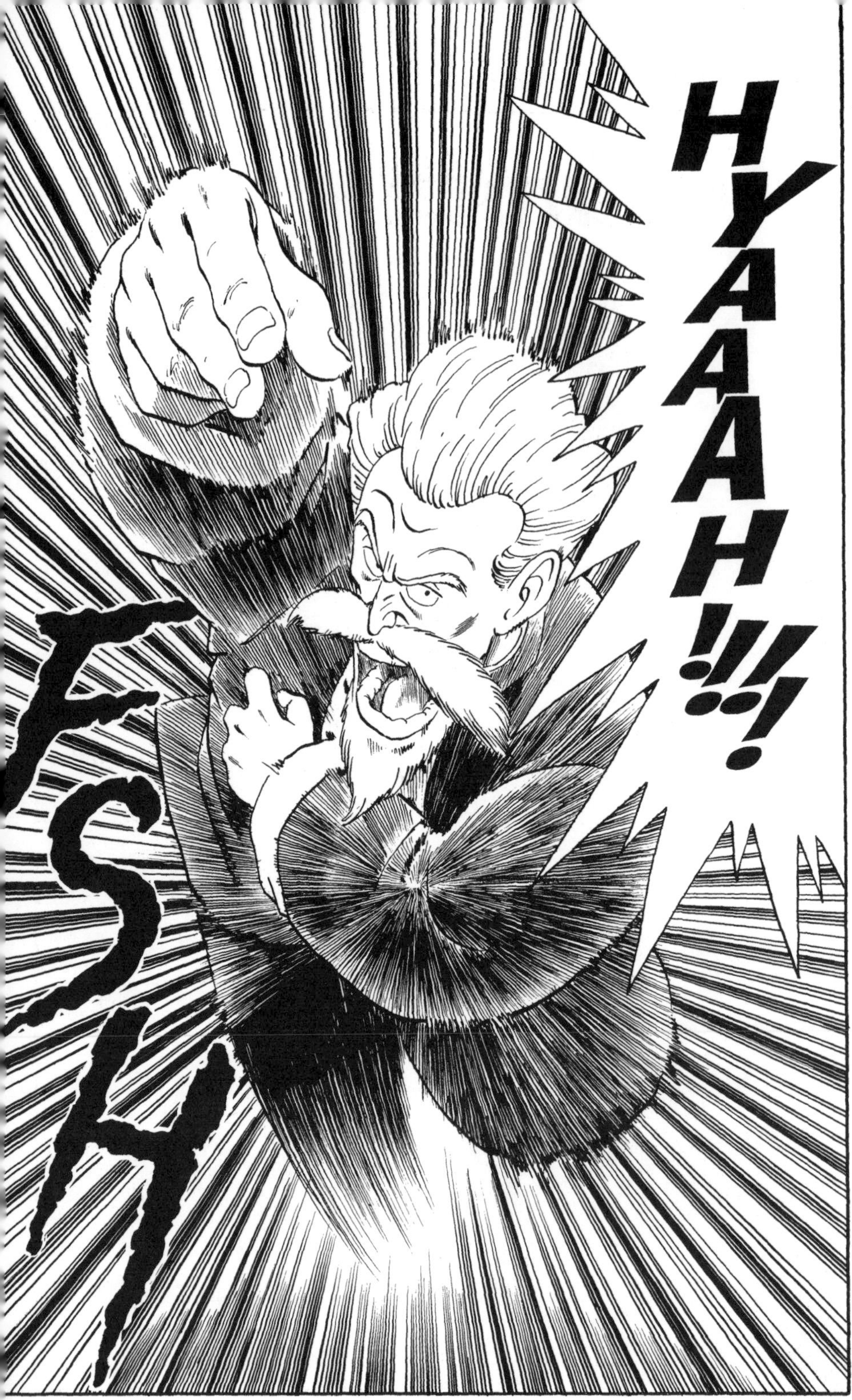
HYAAAAH!!!!
FSH

Tale 47 • The Kamehameha

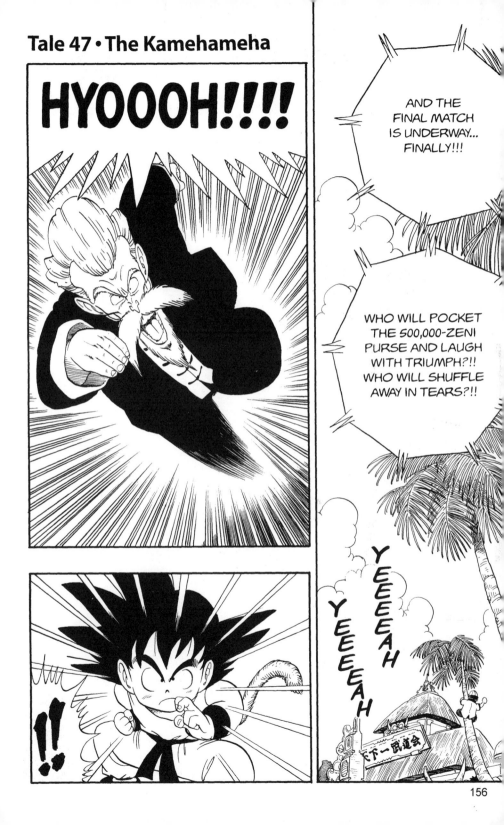

156

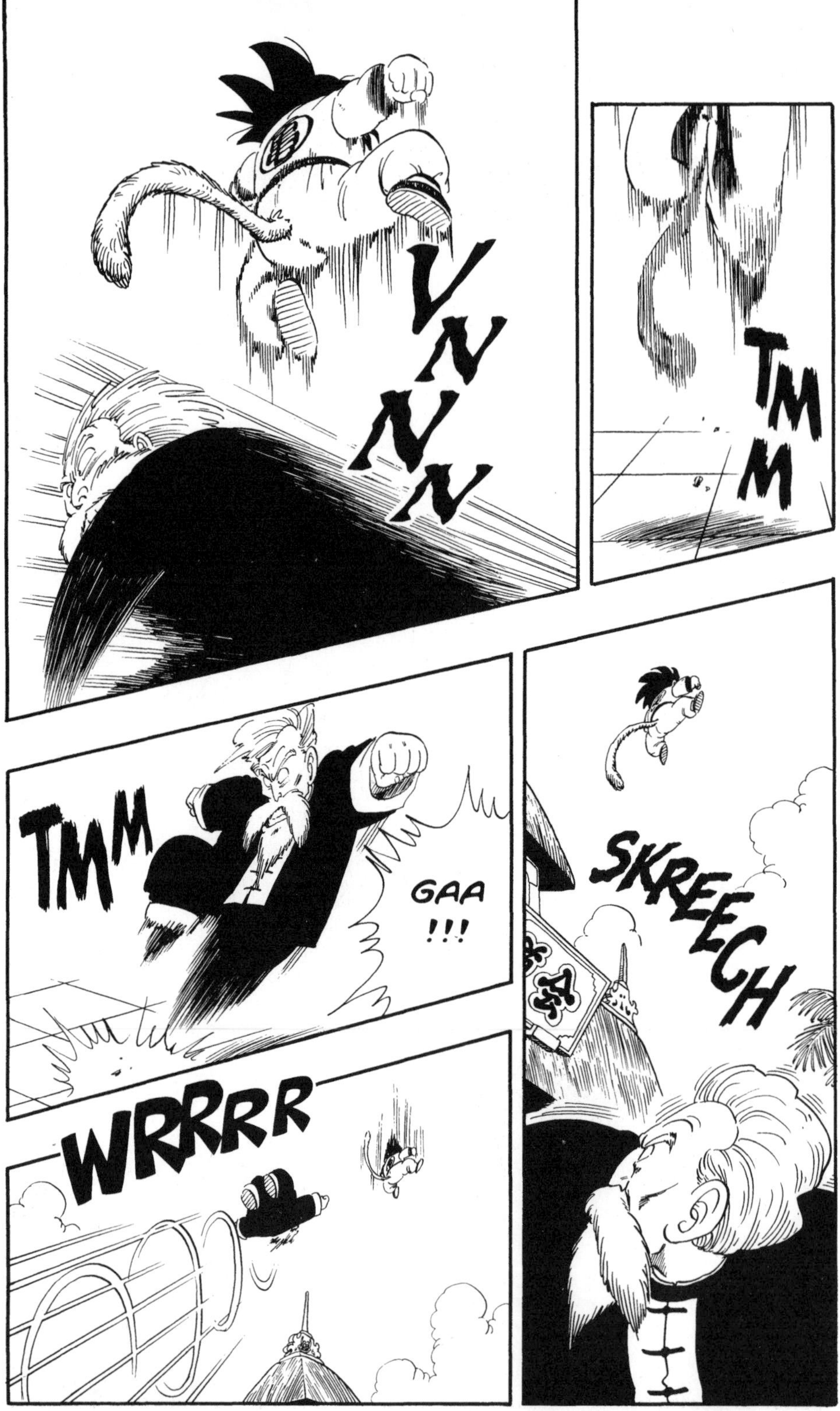
TMM
VNNN
SKREECH
TMM
GAA!!!
WRRRR

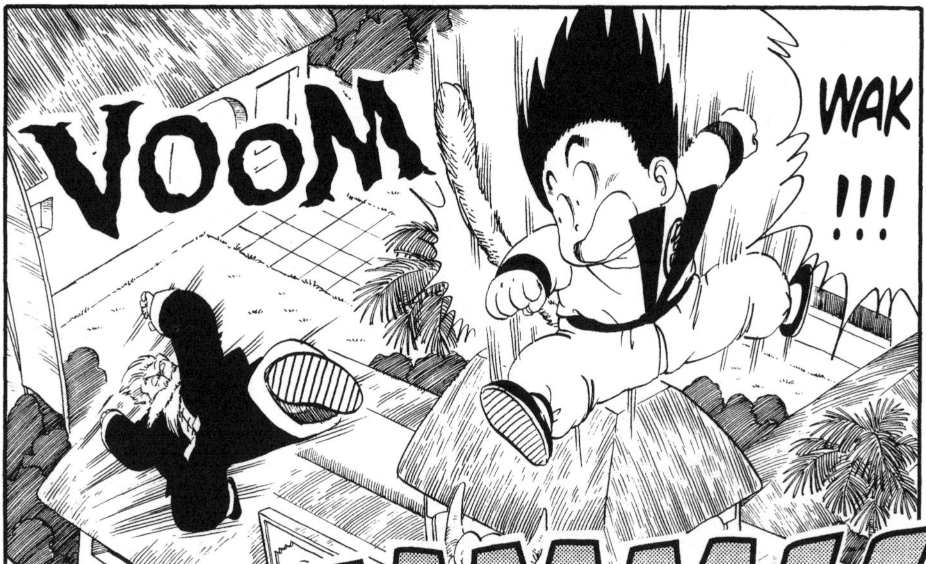
WAK !!!
VOOM
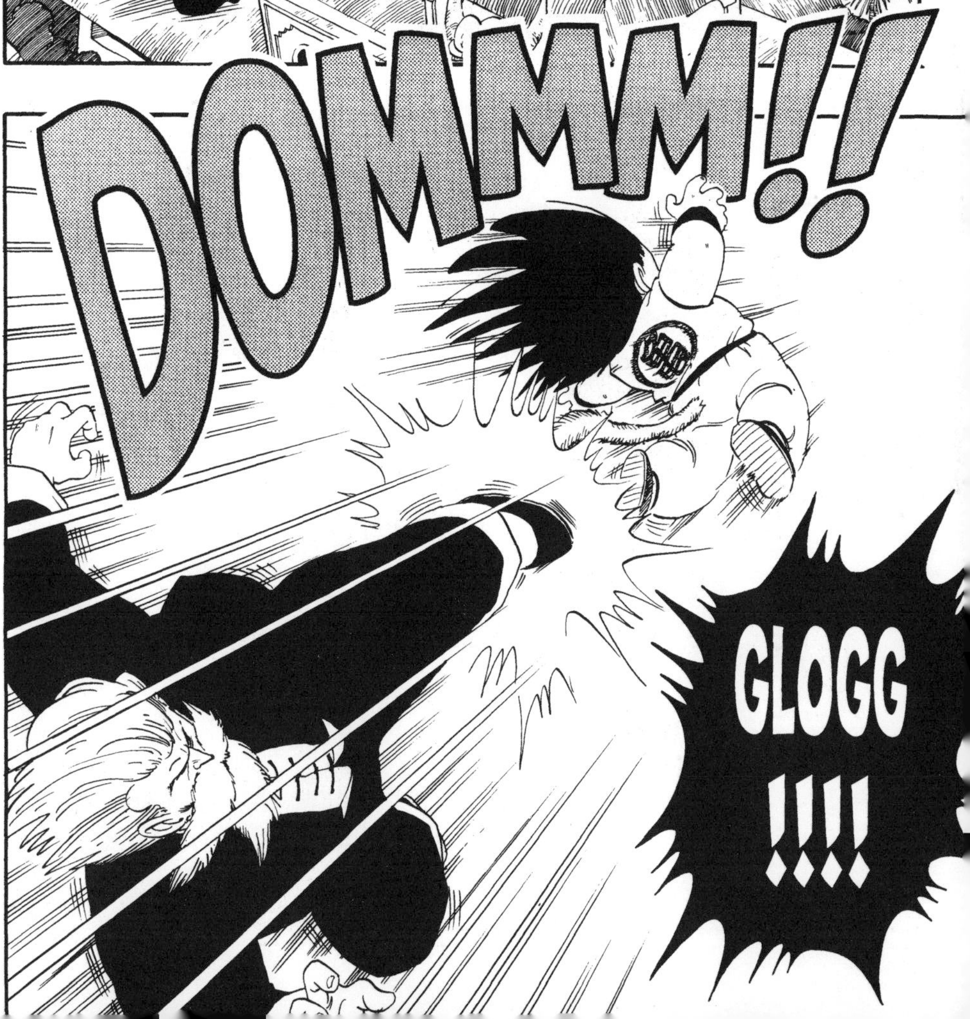
DOMMMM!!
GLOGG !!!!

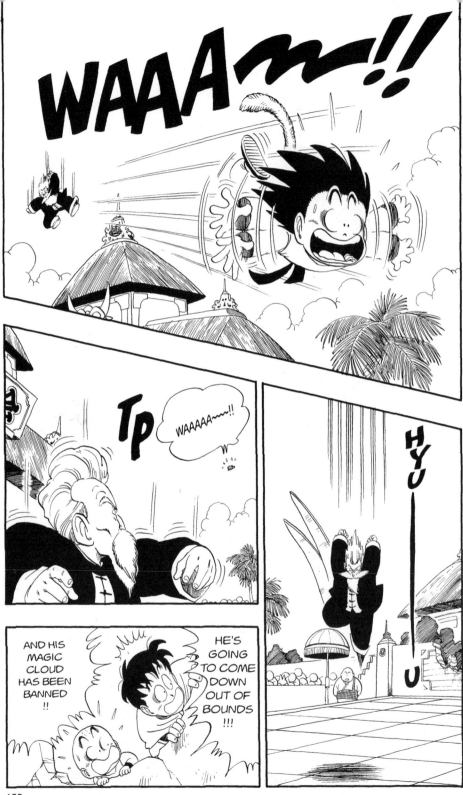

159

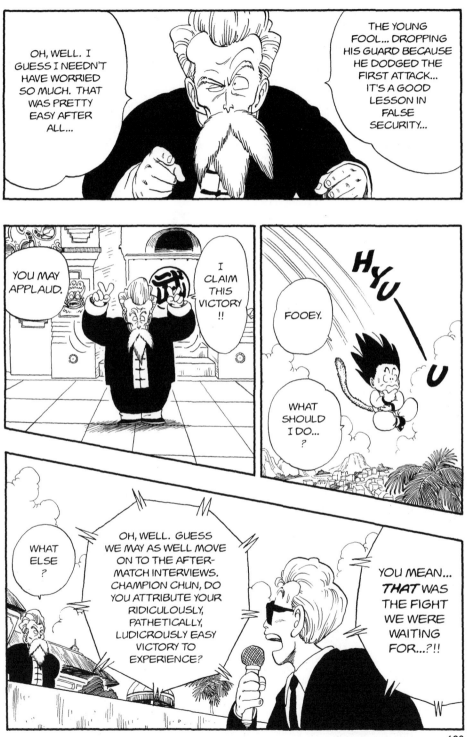

160

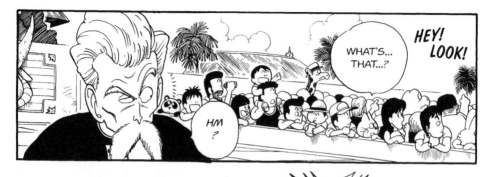

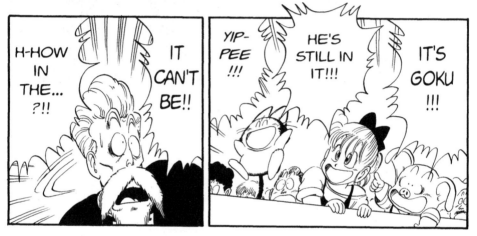

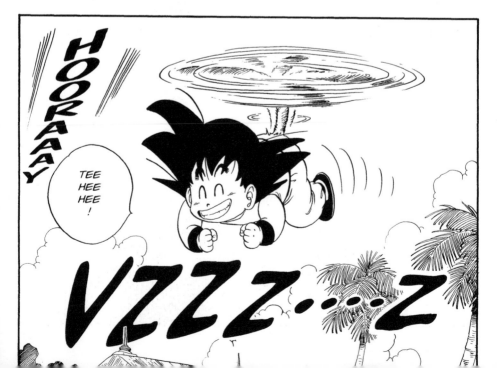

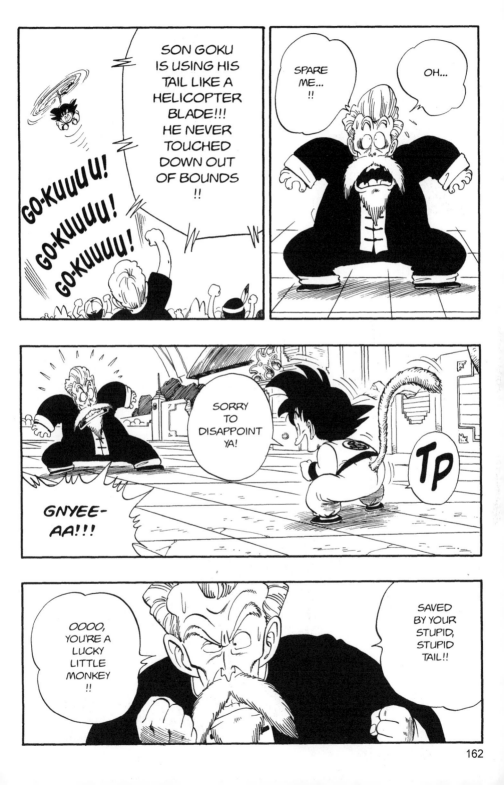

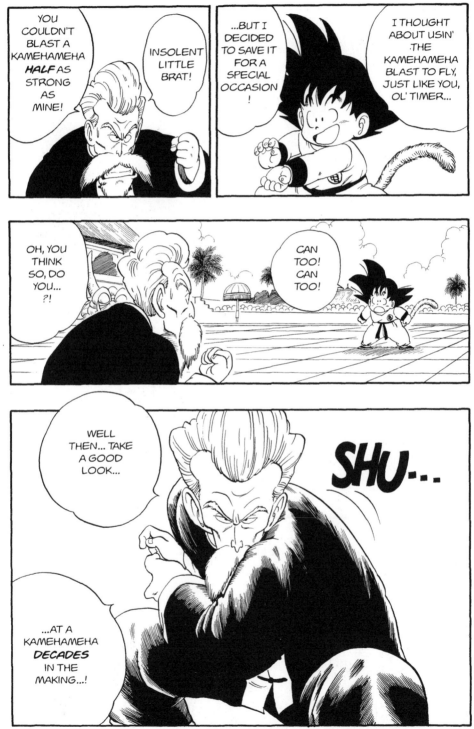

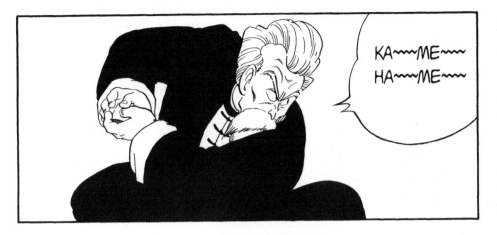

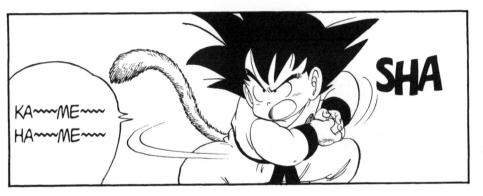

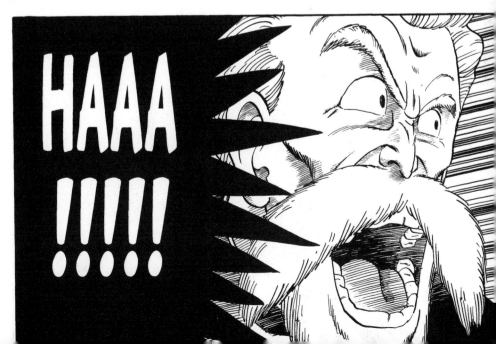

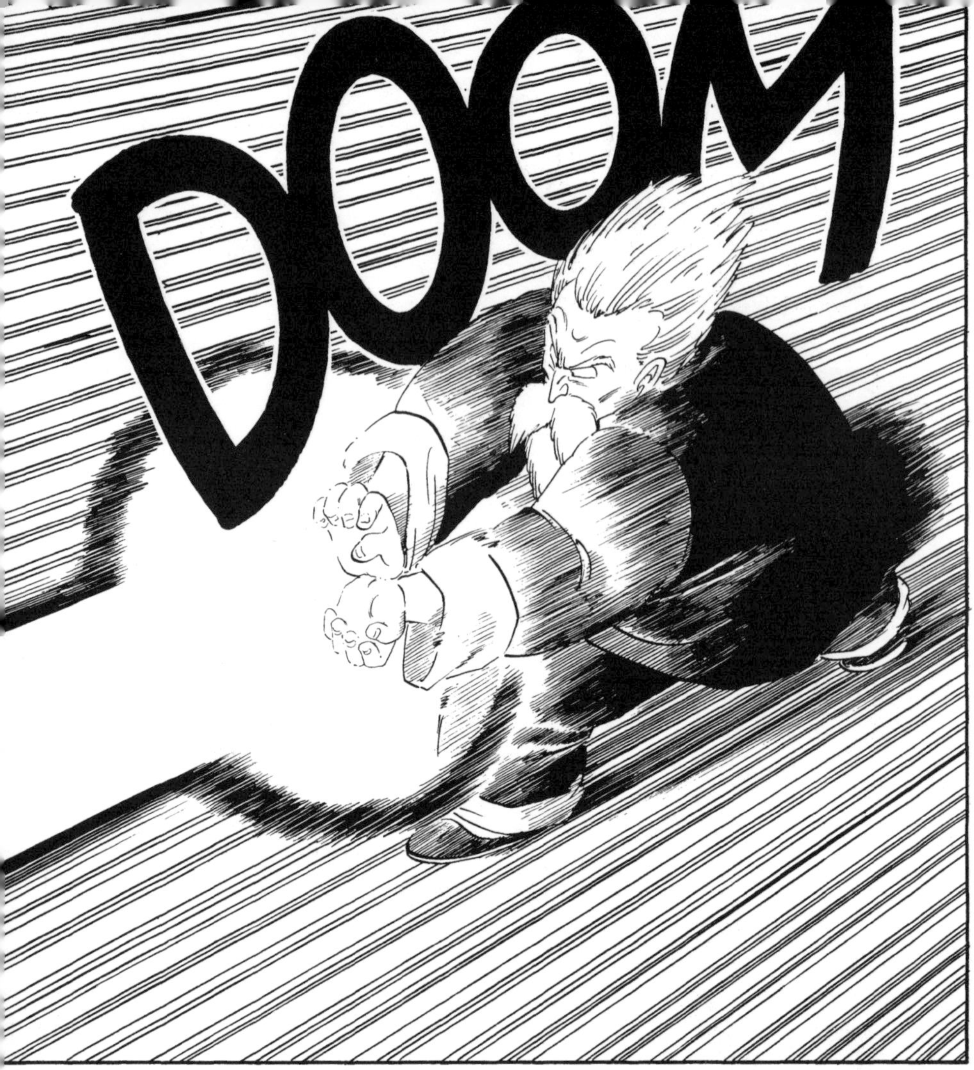
DOOM
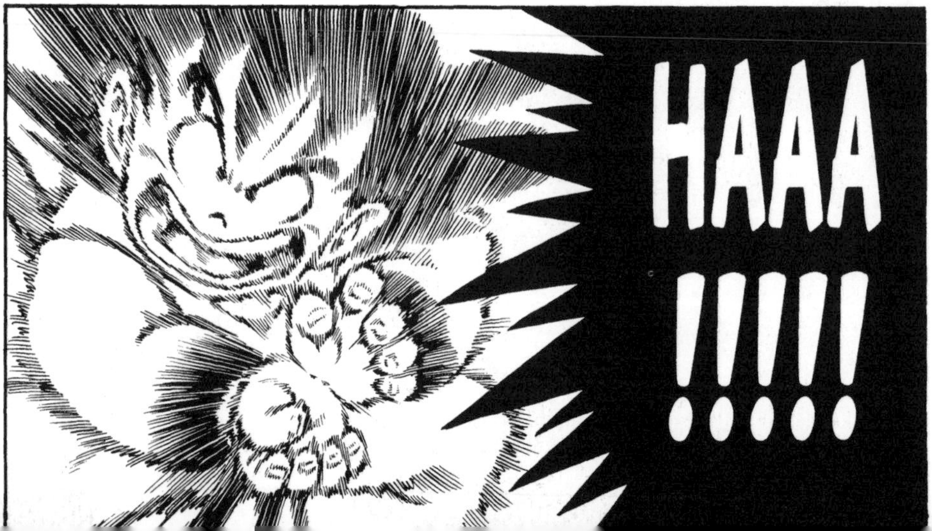
HAAA
!!!!!

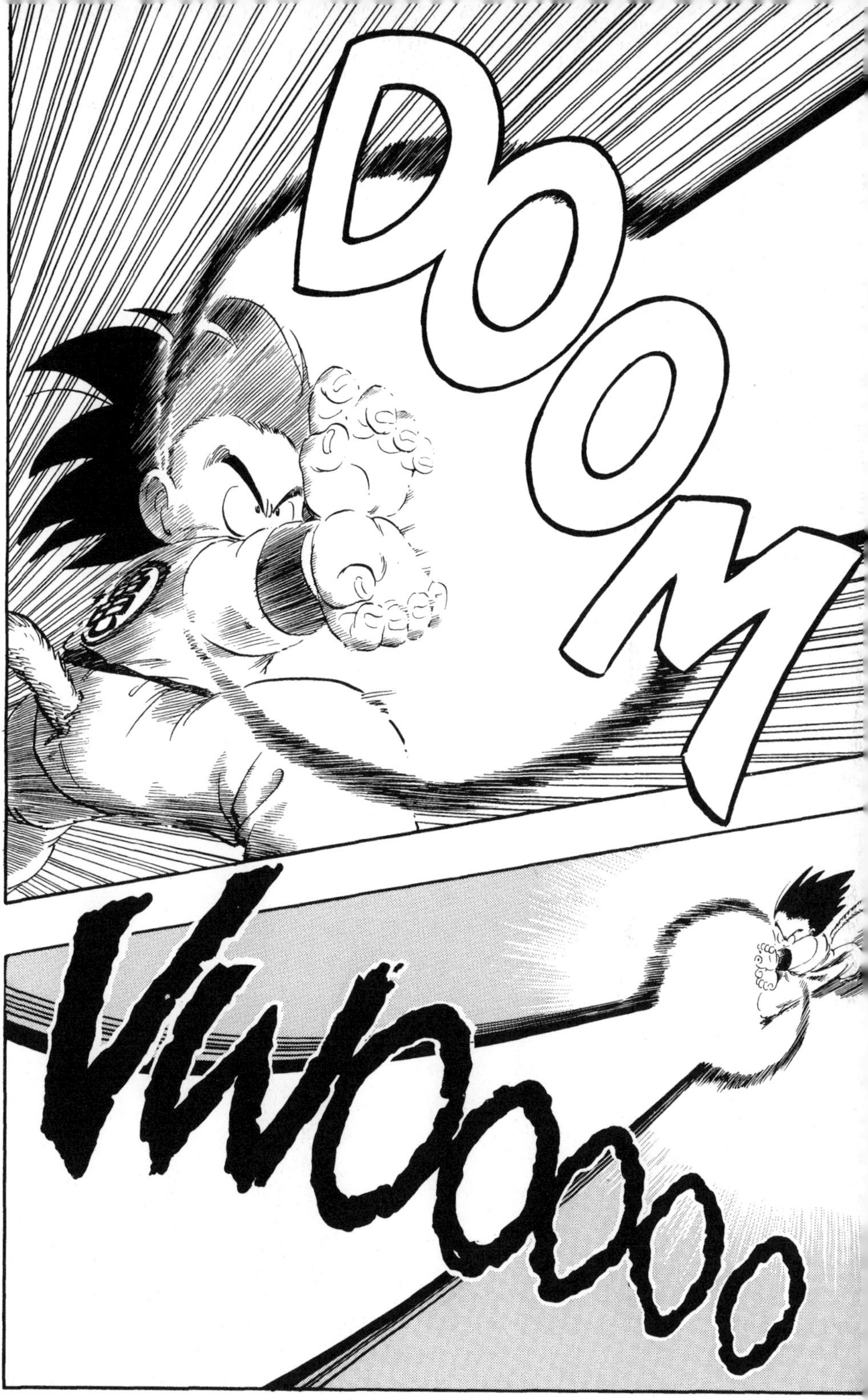
DOOOM
VWOOOOOOO

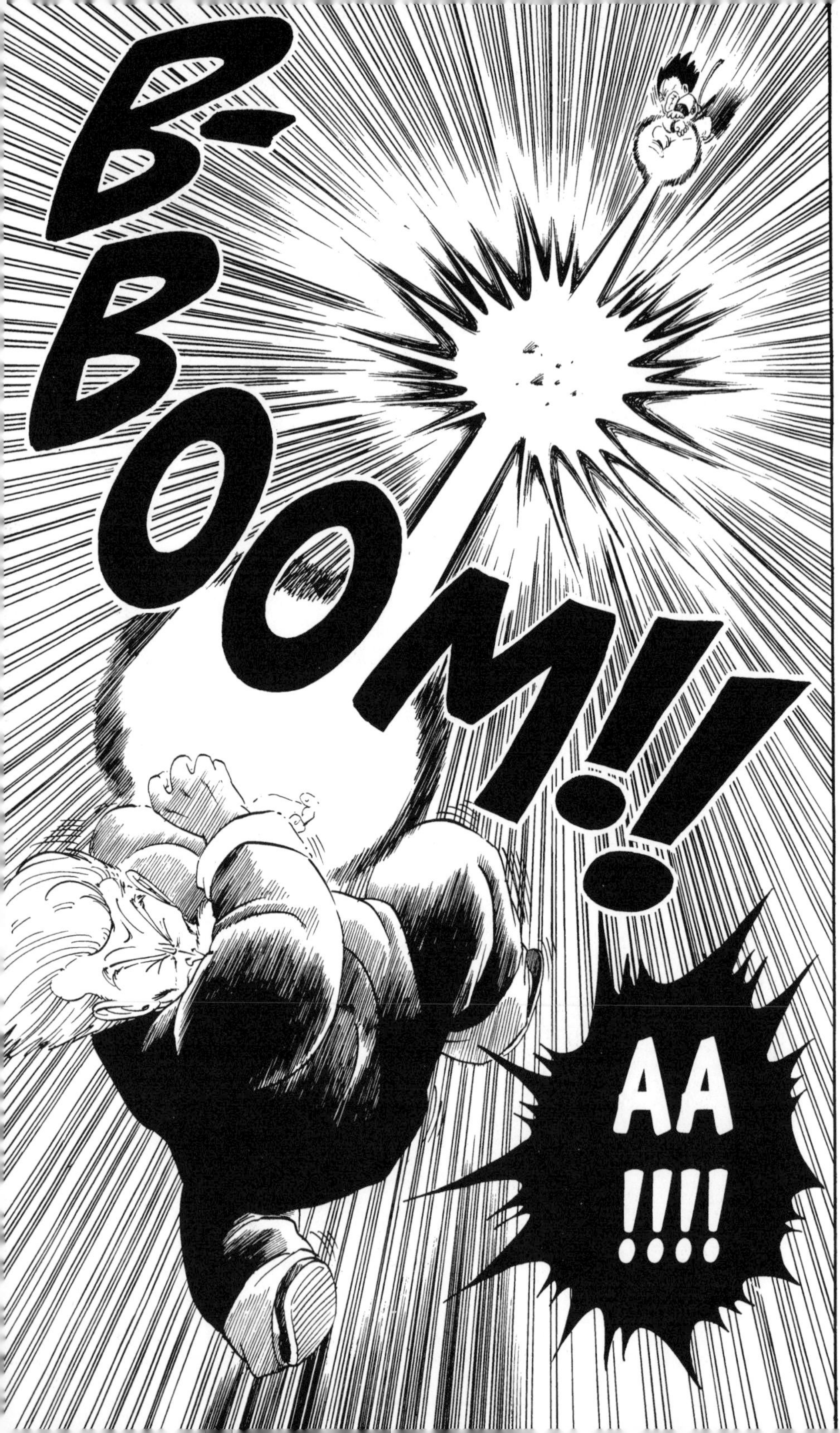
B-BOOM!!
AA!!!!

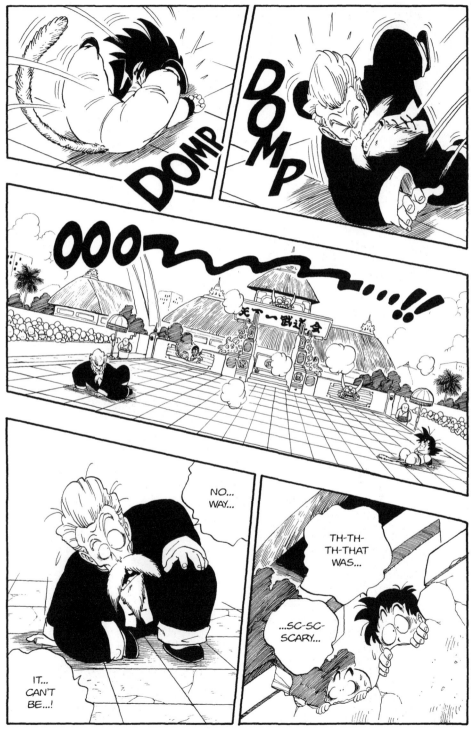

168

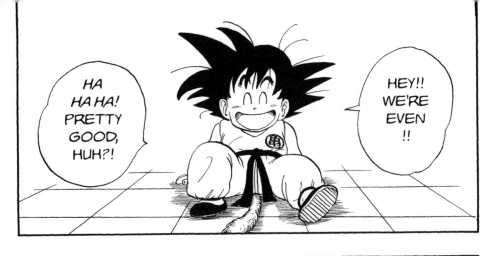

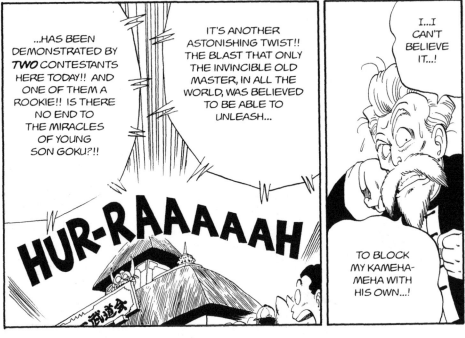

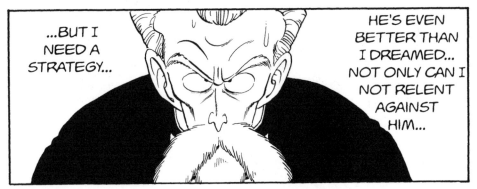

169

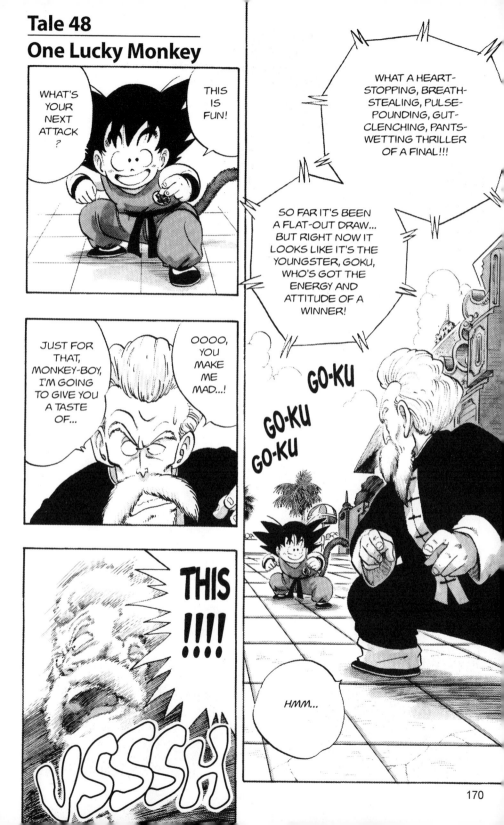

Tale 48
One Lucky Monkey

WHAT'S YOUR NEXT ATTACK?

THIS IS FUN!

WHAT A HEART-STOPPING, BREATH-STEALING, PULSE-POUNDING, GUT-CLENCHING, PANTS-WETTING THRILLER OF A FINAL!!!

SO FAR IT'S BEEN A FLAT-OUT DRAW... BUT RIGHT NOW IT LOOKS LIKE IT'S THE YOUNGSTER, GOKU, WHO'S GOT THE ENERGY AND ATTITUDE OF A WINNER!

JUST FOR THAT, MONKEY-BOY, I'M GOING TO GIVE YOU A TASTE OF...

OOOO, YOU MAKE ME MAD...!

GO-KU

GO-KU

GO-KU GO-KU

HMM...

THIS!!!!

VSSSH

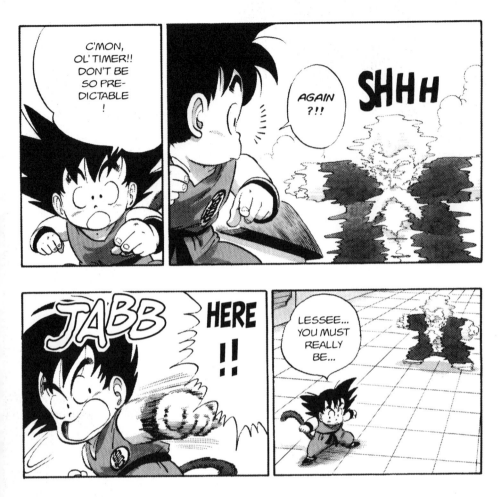

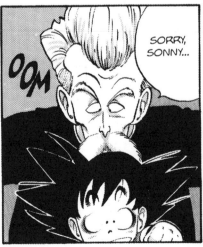

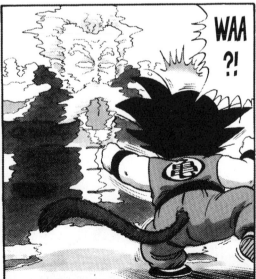

171

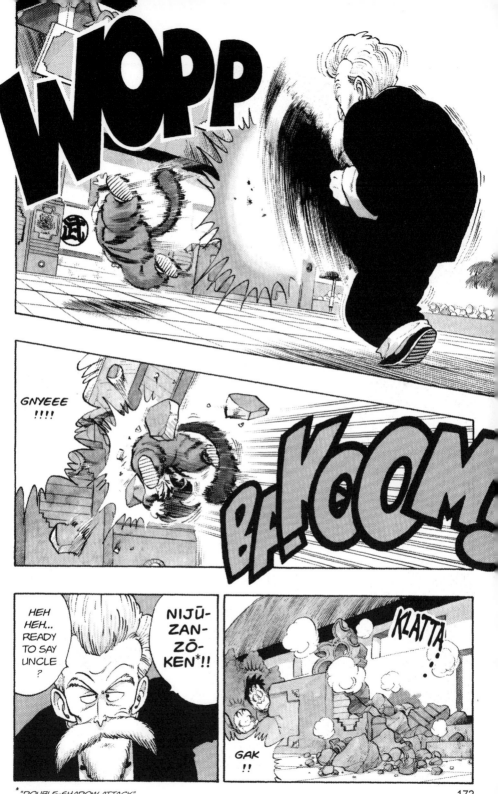

*"DOUBLE-SHADOW ATTACK"

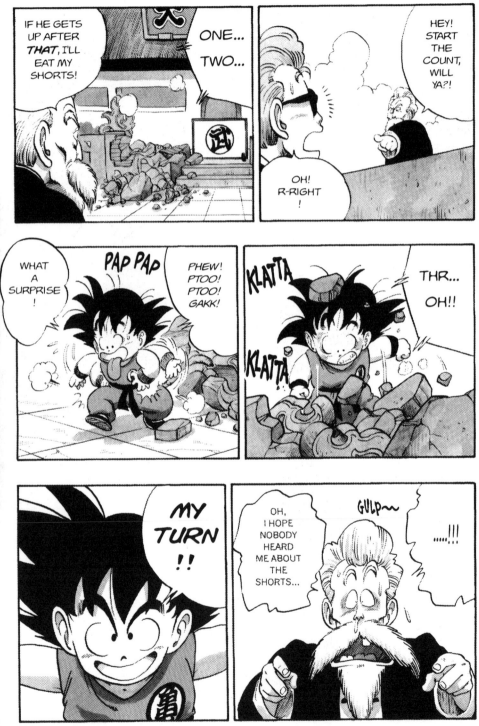

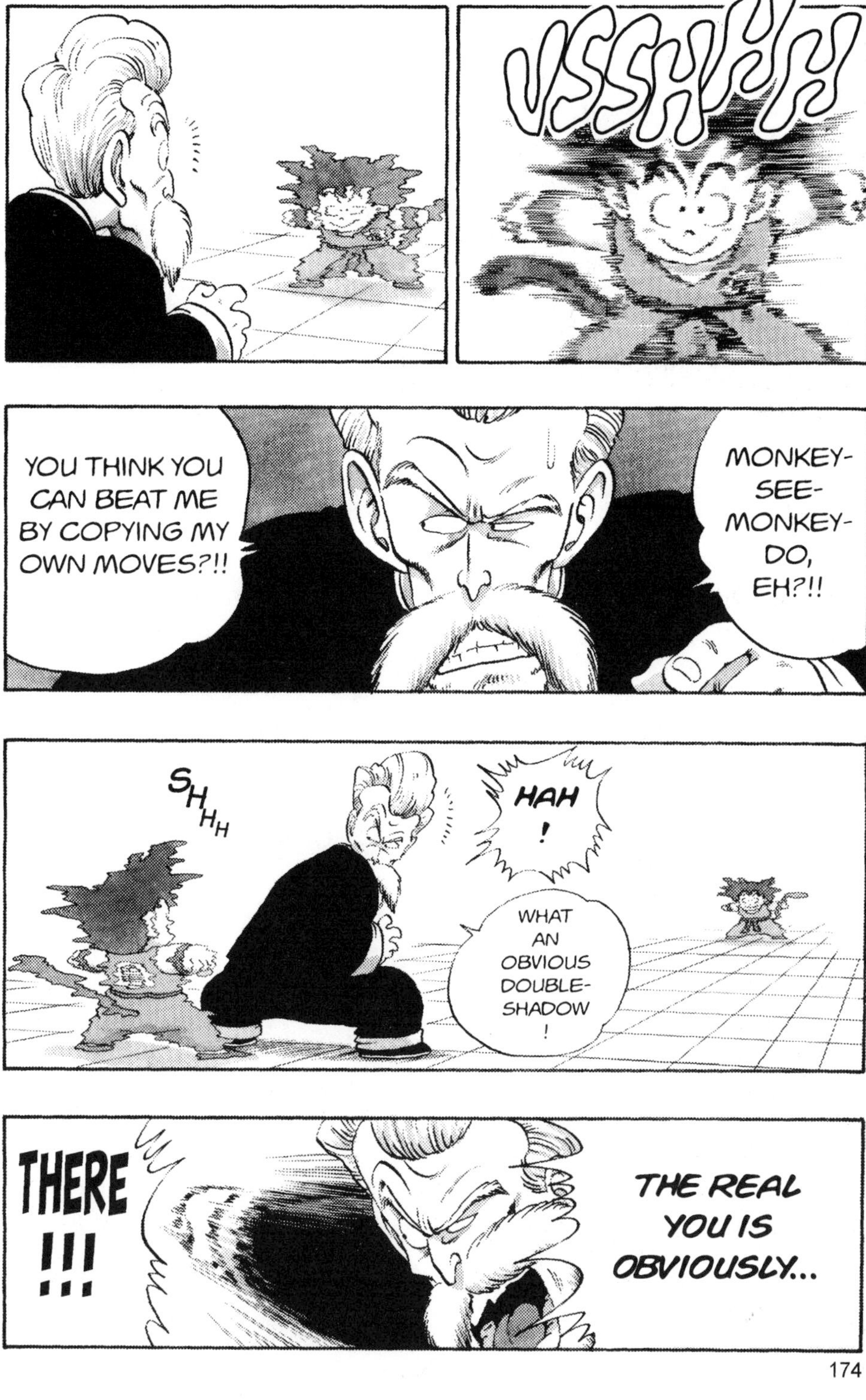
VSSHHH
MONKEY-SEE-MONKEY-DO, EH?!!
YOU THINK YOU CAN BEAT ME BY COPYING MY OWN MOVES?!!
HAH!
WHAT AN OBVIOUS DOUBLE-SHADOW!
SHHH
THE REAL YOU IS OBVIOUSLY...
THERE!!!

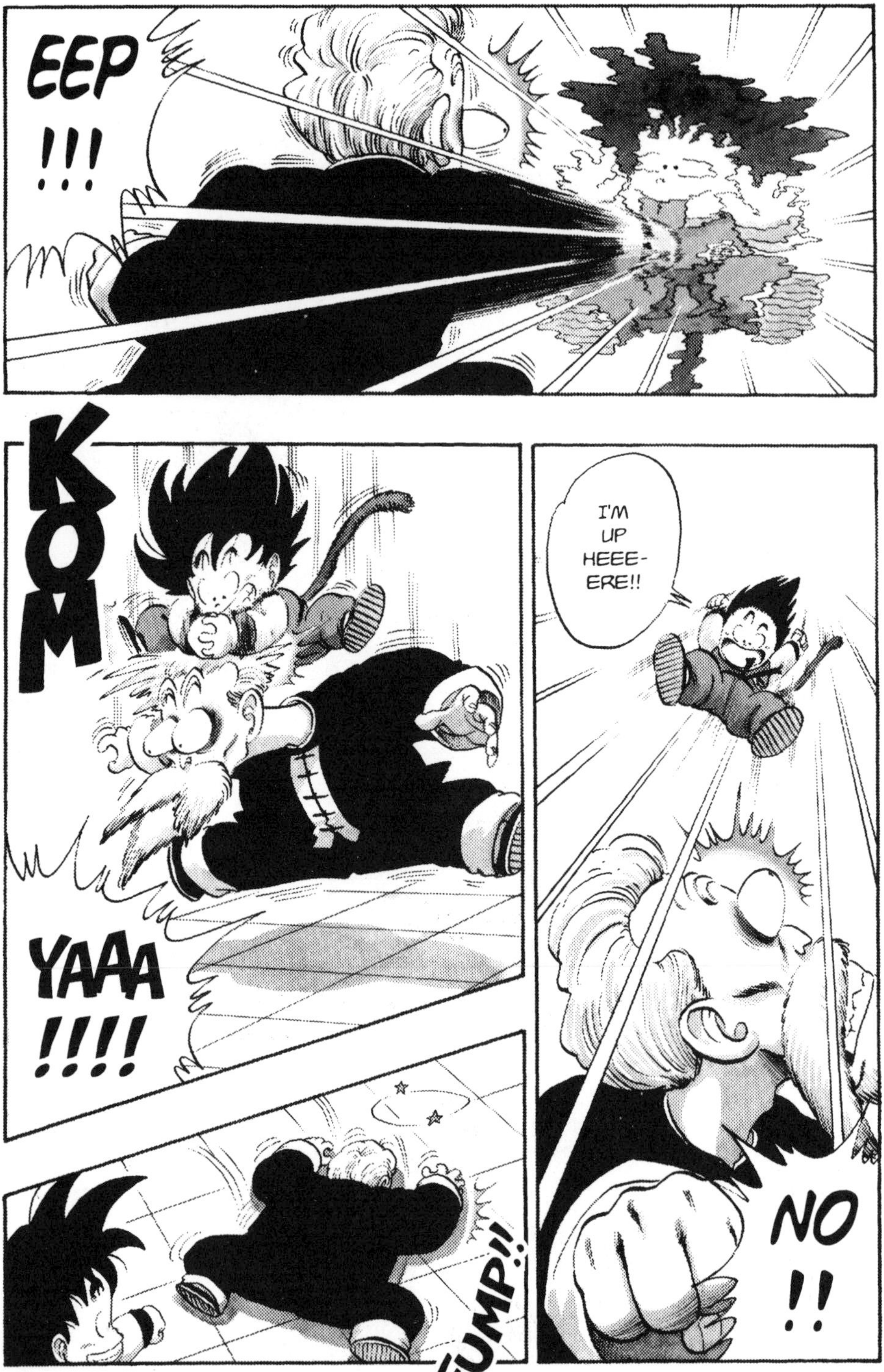
EEP!!!
I'M UP HEEEE-ERE!!
NO!!
KOM
YAAA!!!!
FUMP!!

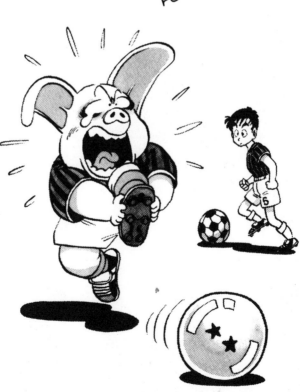

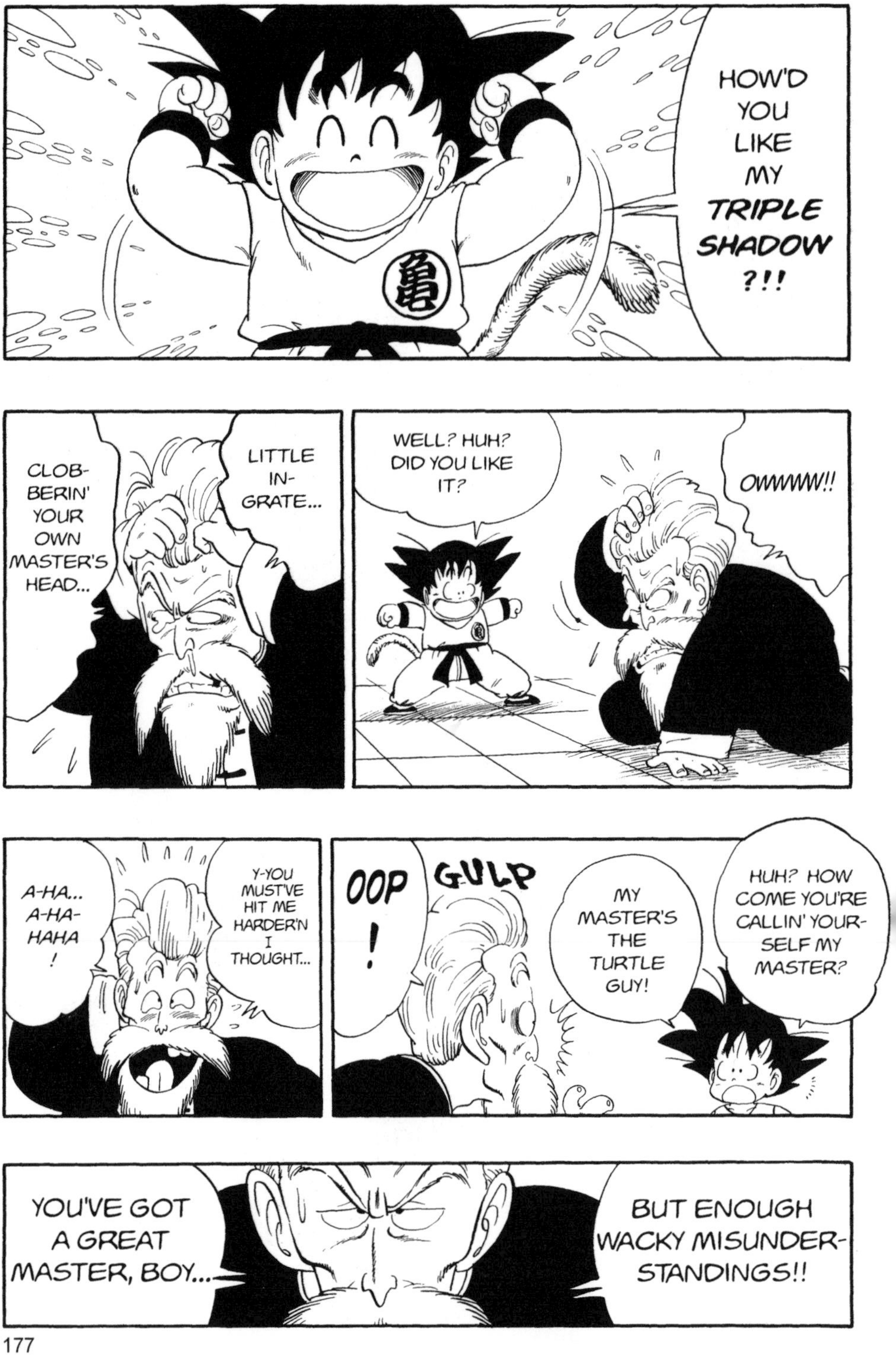
HOW'D YOU LIKE MY TRIPLE SHADOW ?!!
OWWWW!!
WELL? HUH? DID YOU LIKE IT?
LITTLE INGRATE...
CLOBBERIN' YOUR OWN MASTER'S HEAD...
HUH? HOW COME YOU'RE CALLIN' YOURSELF MY MASTER?
MY MASTER'S THE TURTLE GUY!
GULP
OOP!
Y-YOU MUST'VE HIT ME HARDER'N I THOUGHT...
A-HA... A-HA-HAHA!
BUT ENOUGH WACKY MISUNDERSTANDINGS!!
YOU'VE GOT A GREAT MASTER, BOY...

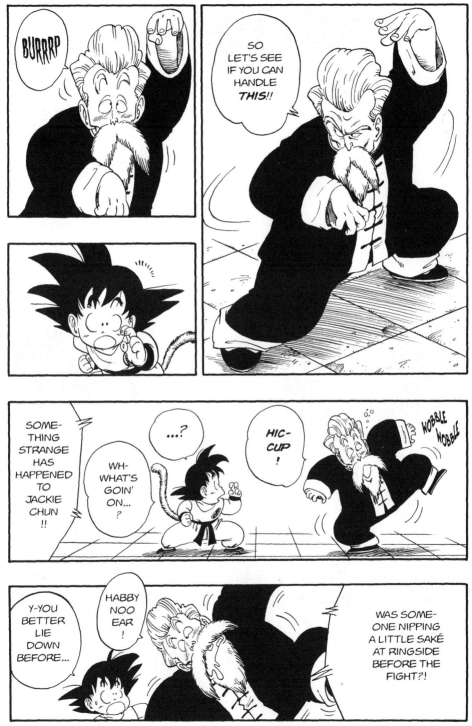

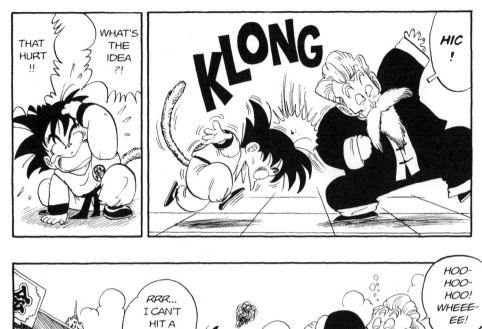

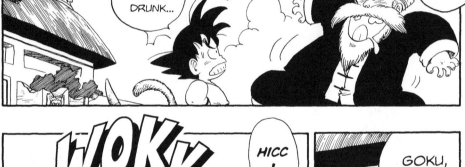

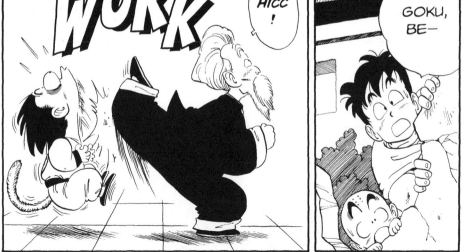

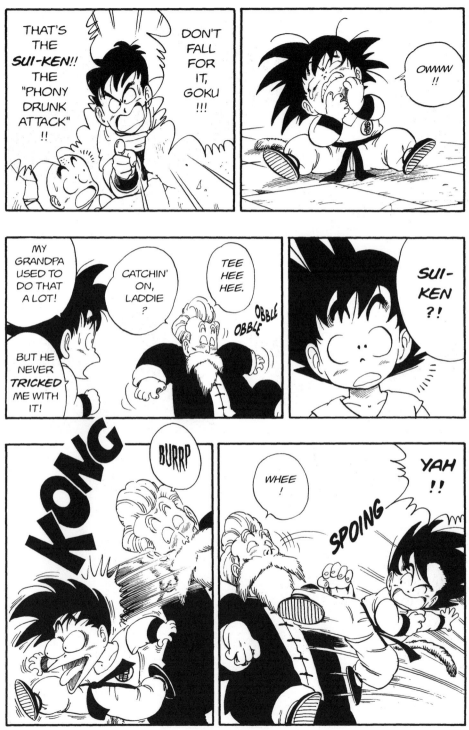

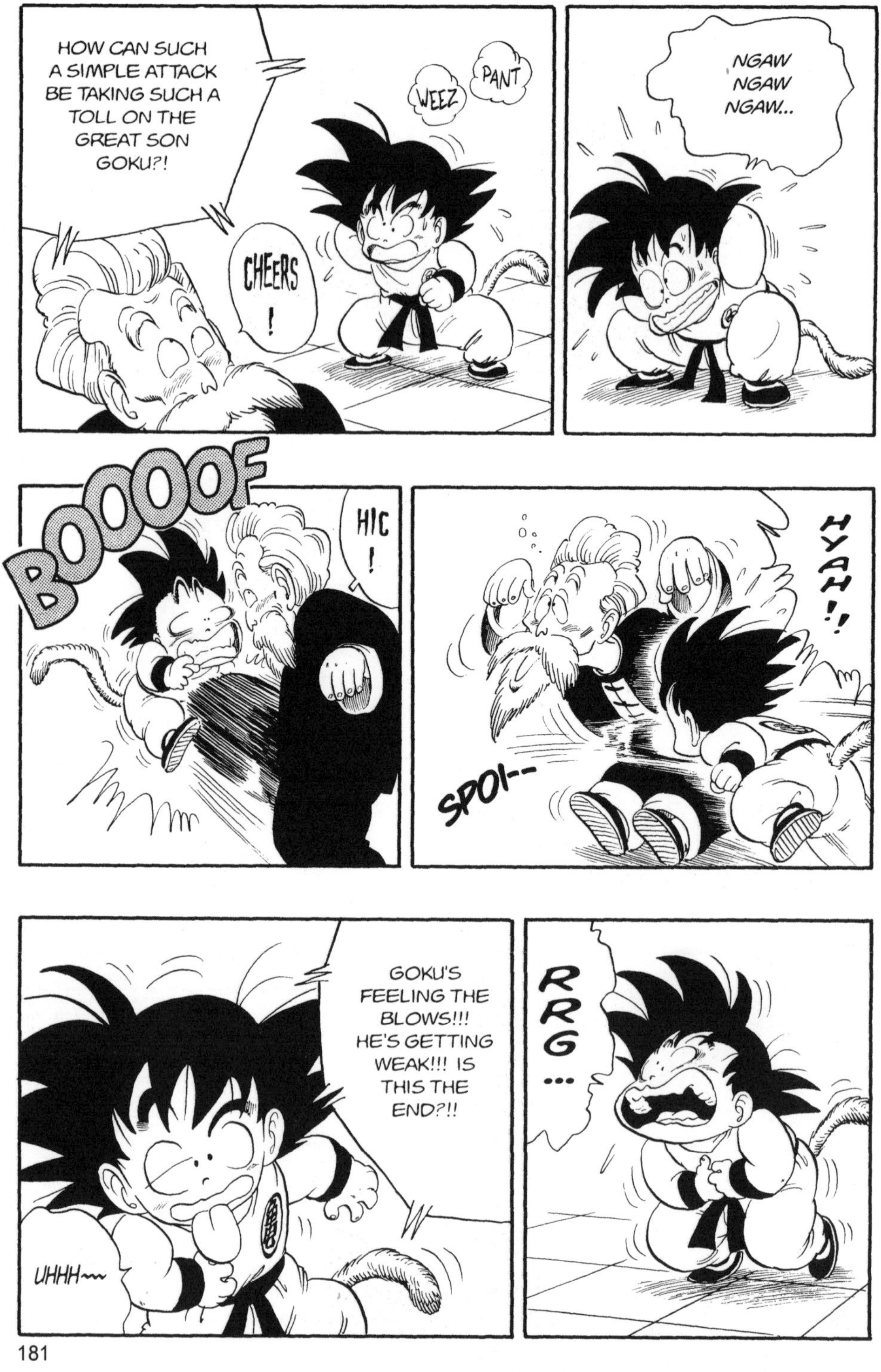
NGAW NGAW NGAW...
PANT
WEEZ
HOW CAN SUCH A SIMPLE ATTACK BE TAKING SUCH A TOLL ON THE GREAT SON GOKU?!
CHEERS !
HYAH!!
SPOI--
HIC !
BOOOOF
RRG...
GOKU'S FEELING THE BLOWS!!! HE'S GETTING WEAK!!! IS THIS THE END?!!
UHHH~~

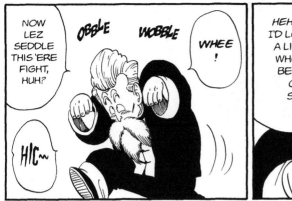
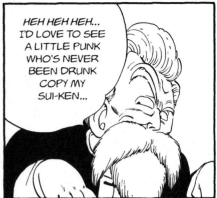
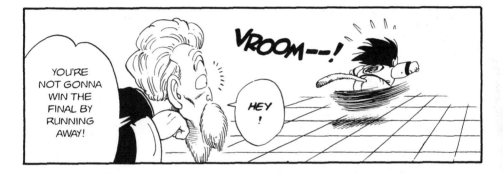
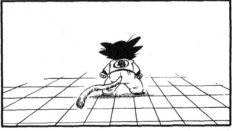
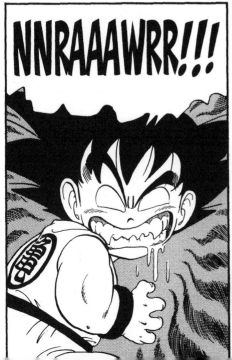
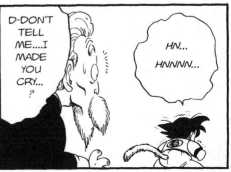

182

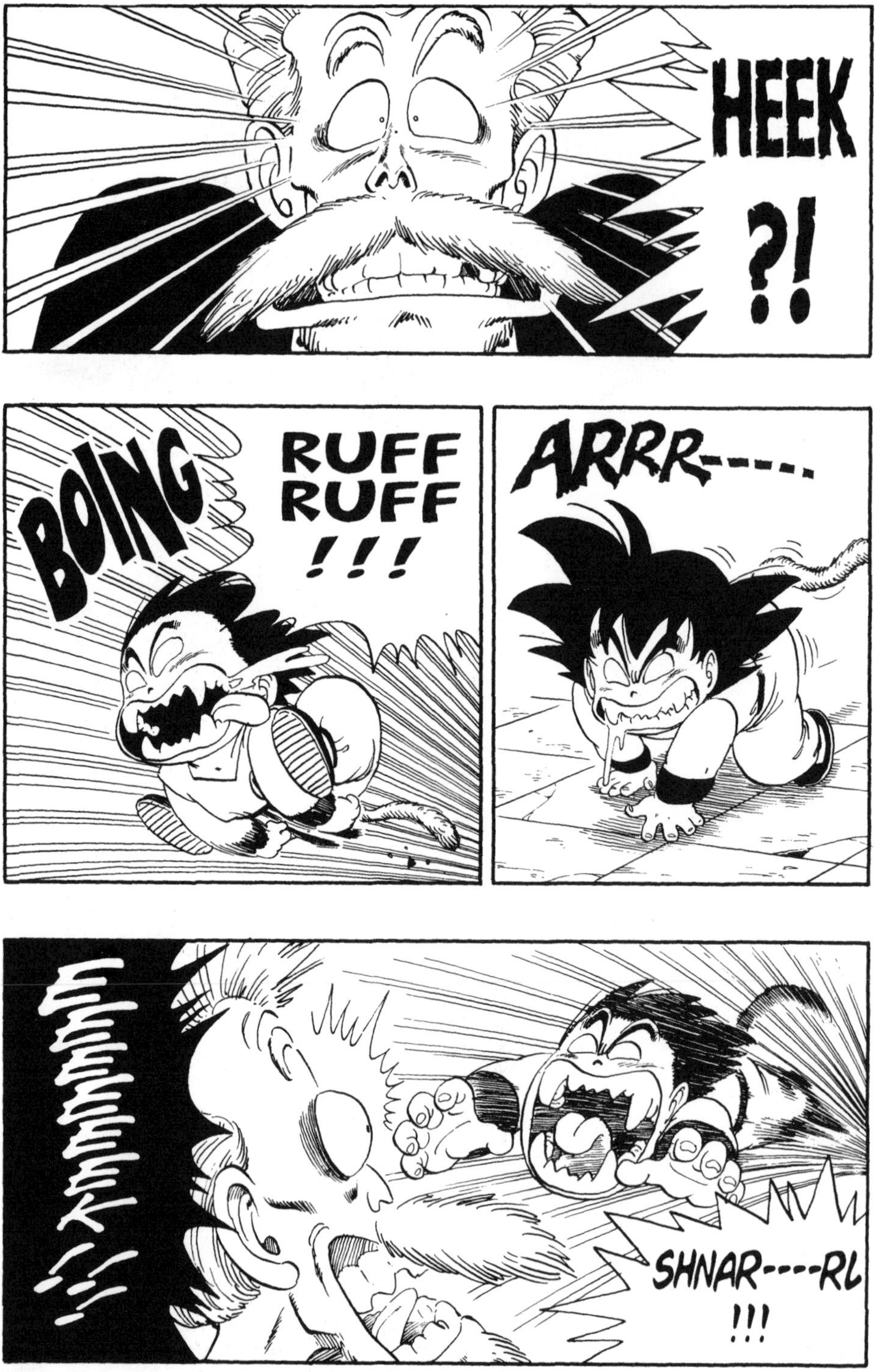
HEEK ?!
ARRR-----
BOING
RUFF RUFF !!!
SHNAR----RL !!!
EEEEEEEK!!!

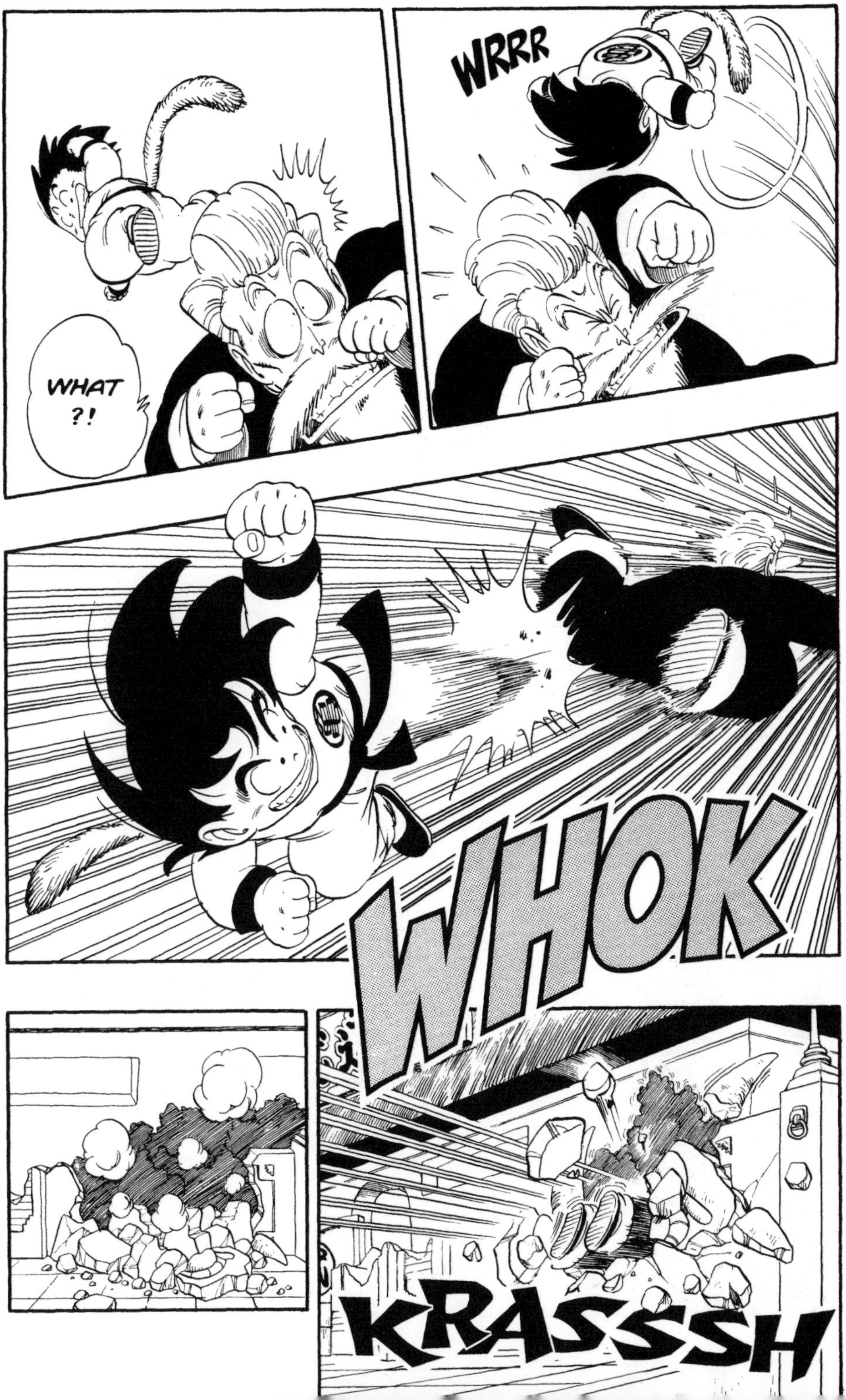
WRRR
WHAT ?!
WHOK
KRASSSH

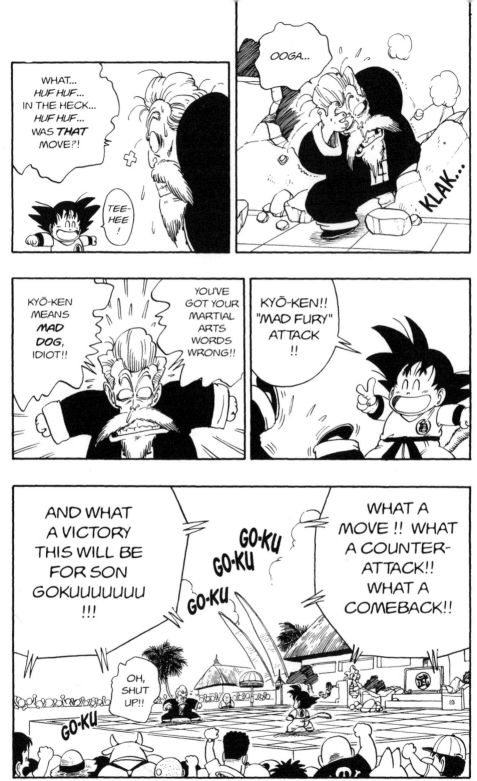

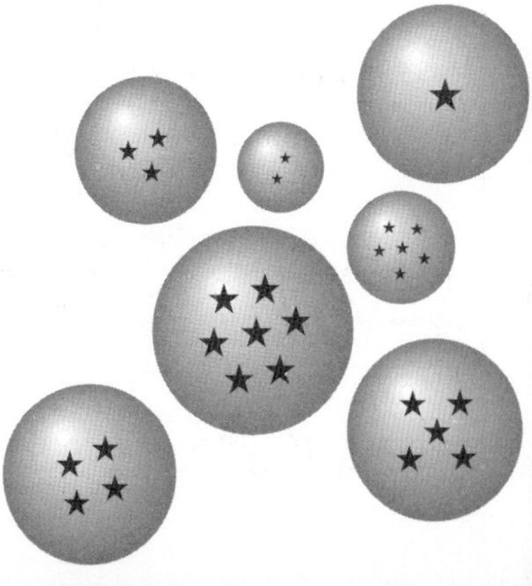

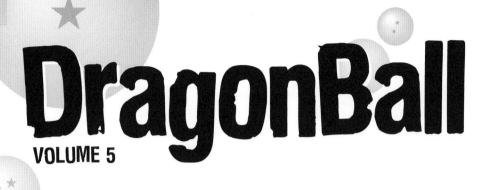

DragonBall

VOLUME 5

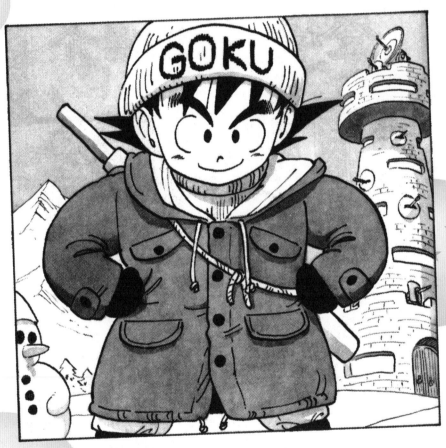

THE RED RIBBON ARMY

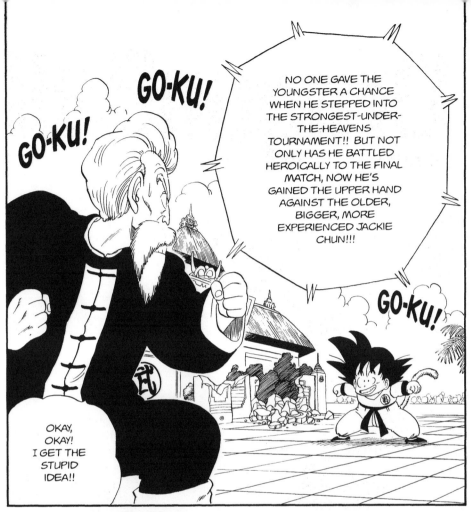

Tale 49 · The Big Sleep

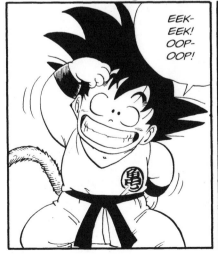

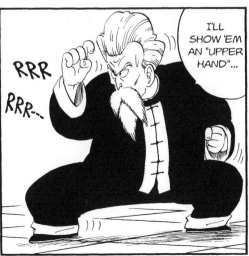

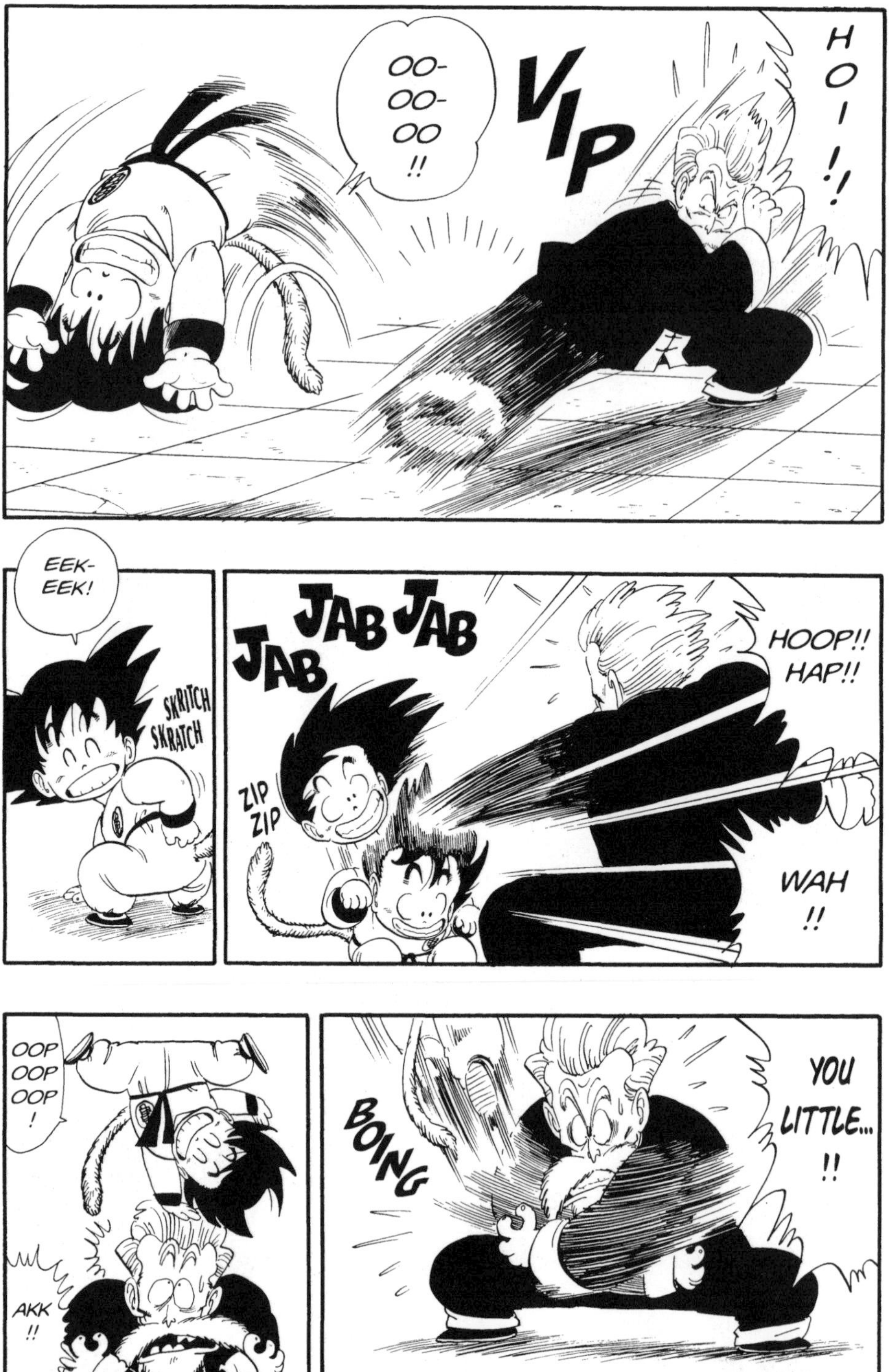

HO-!!
VIP
OO-OO-OO!!
EEK-EEK!
SKRITCH SKRATCH
HOOP!! HAP!!
JAB JAB JAB
ZIP ZIP
WAH!!
OOP OOP OOP!
AKK!!
YOU LITTLE...!!
BOING

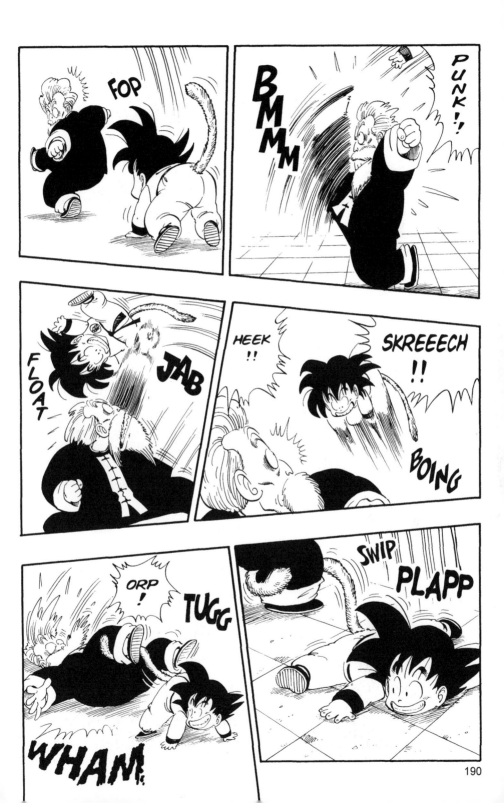

190

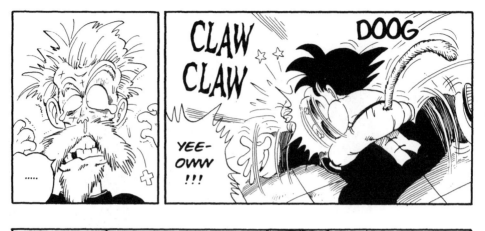

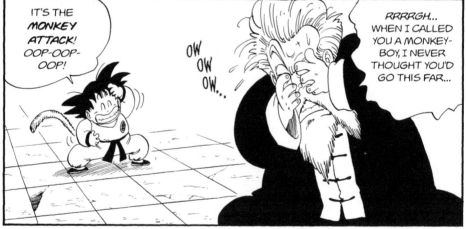

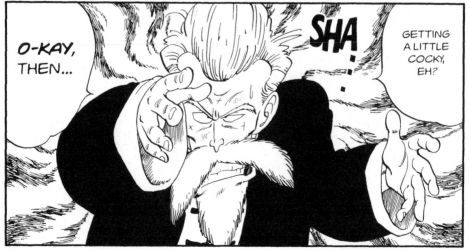

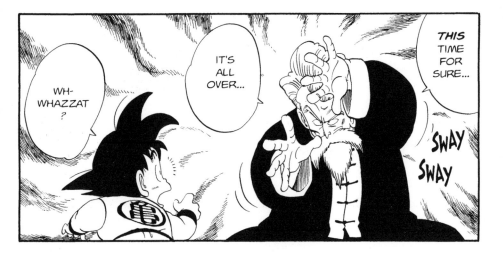

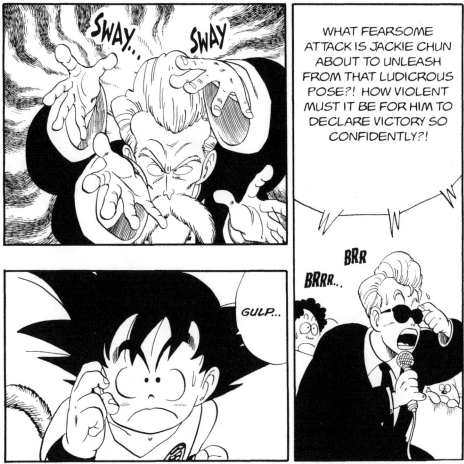

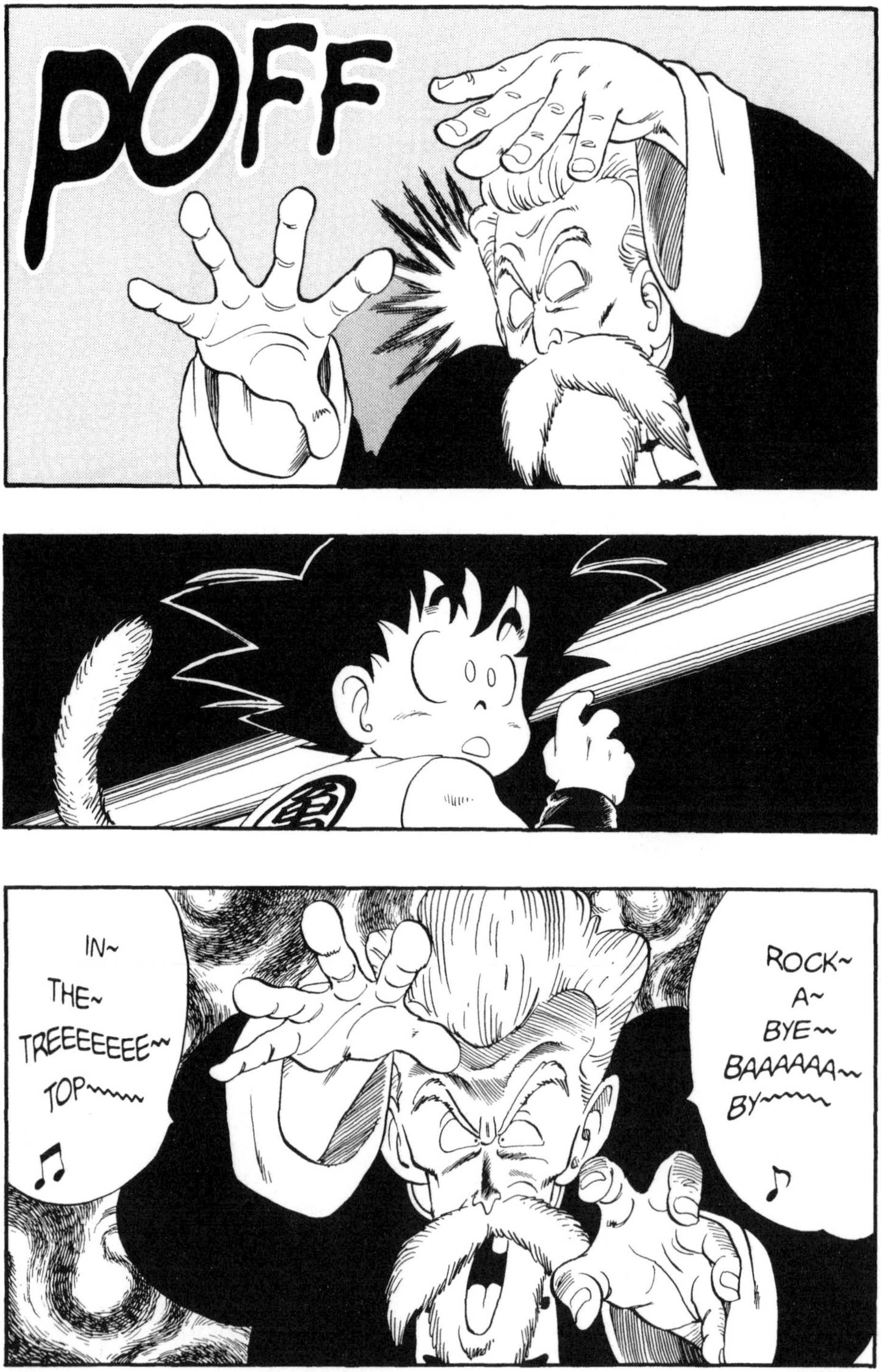
POFF
ROCK~ A~ BYE~ BAAAAAA~ BY~~~ ♪
IN~ THE~ TREEEEEEE~ TOP~~~ ♫

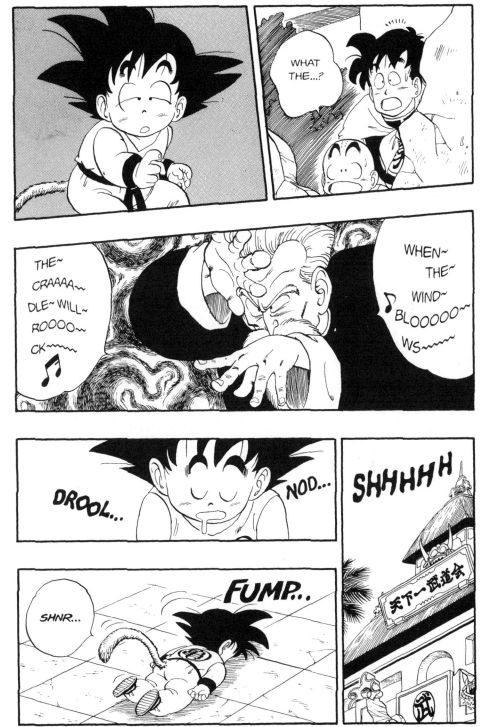

194

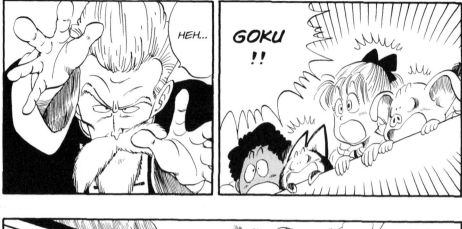

HEH...

GOKU!!

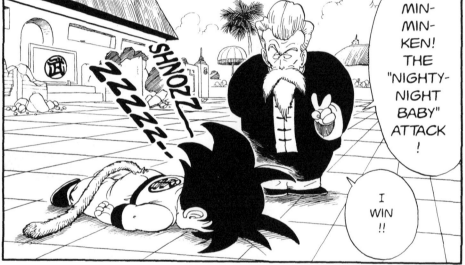

SHNOZZ

ZZZZZZ...

MIN-MIN-KEN! THE "NIGHTY-NIGHT BABY" ATTACK!

I WIN!!

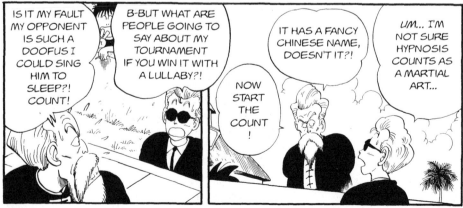

IS IT MY FAULT MY OPPONENT IS SUCH A DOOFUS I COULD SING HIM TO SLEEP?! COUNT!

B-BUT WHAT ARE PEOPLE GOING TO SAY ABOUT MY TOURNAMENT IF YOU WIN IT WITH A LULLABY?!

NOW START THE COUNT!

IT HAS A FANCY CHINESE NAME, DOESN'T IT?!

UM... I'M NOT SURE HYPNOSIS COUNTS AS A MARTIAL ART...

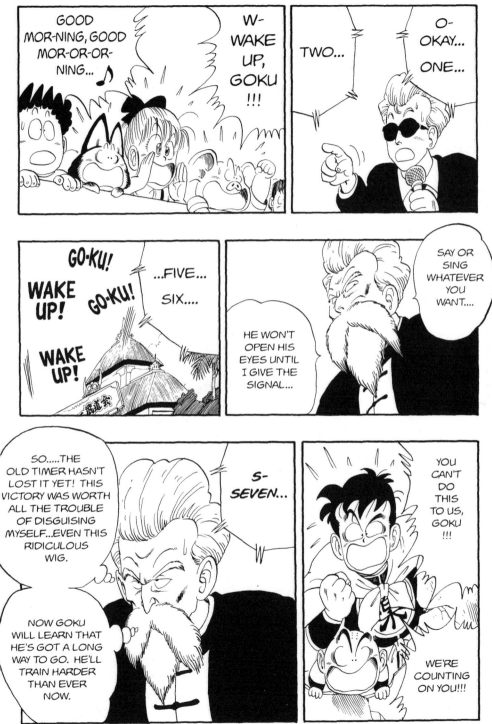

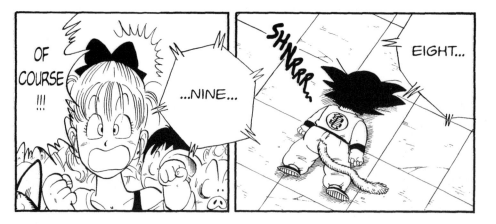

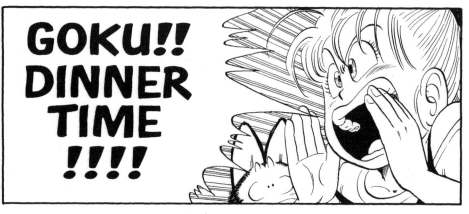

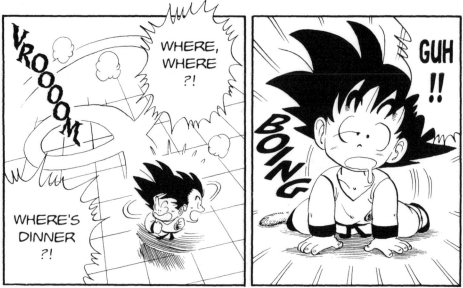

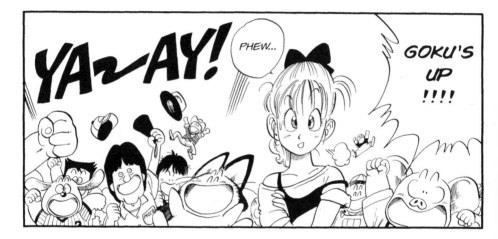

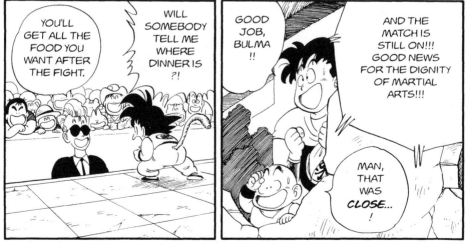

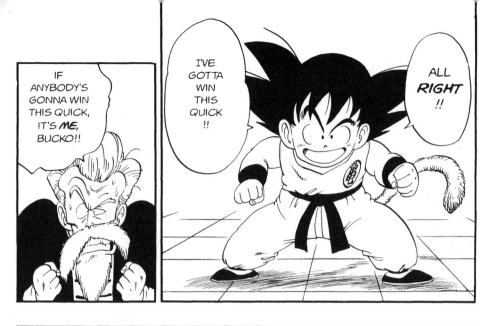

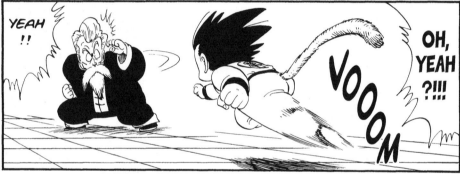

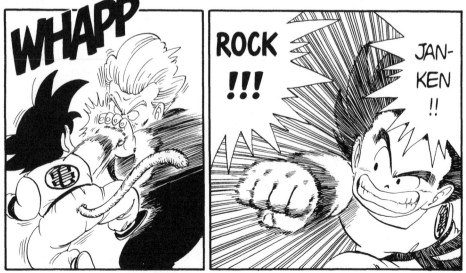

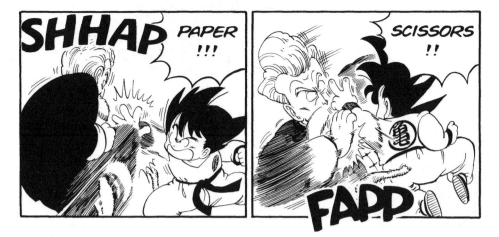

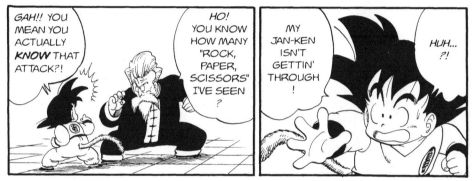

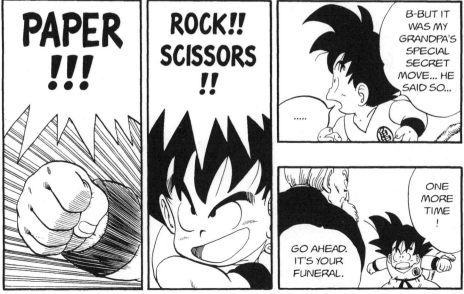

200

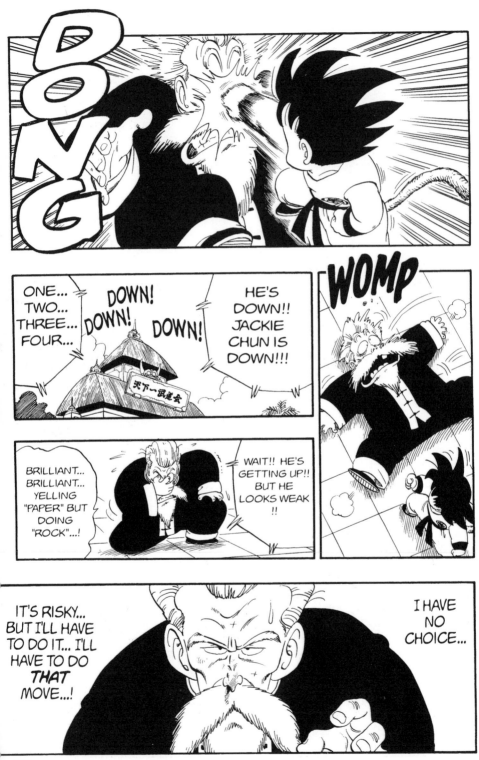

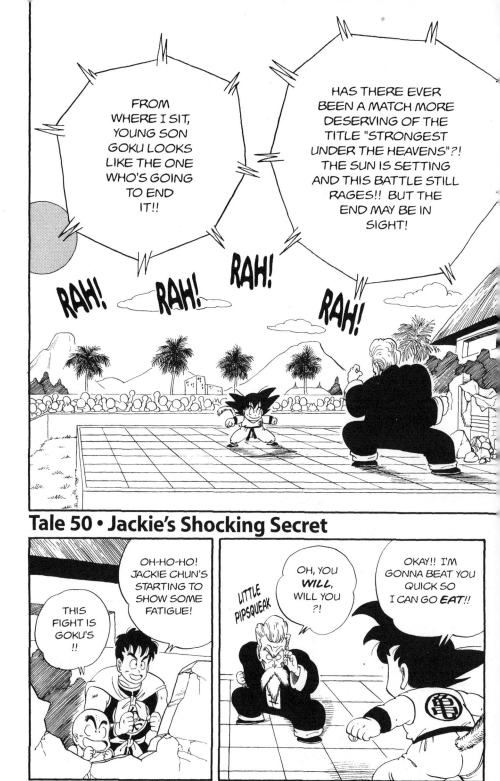

Tale 50 • Jackie's Shocking Secret

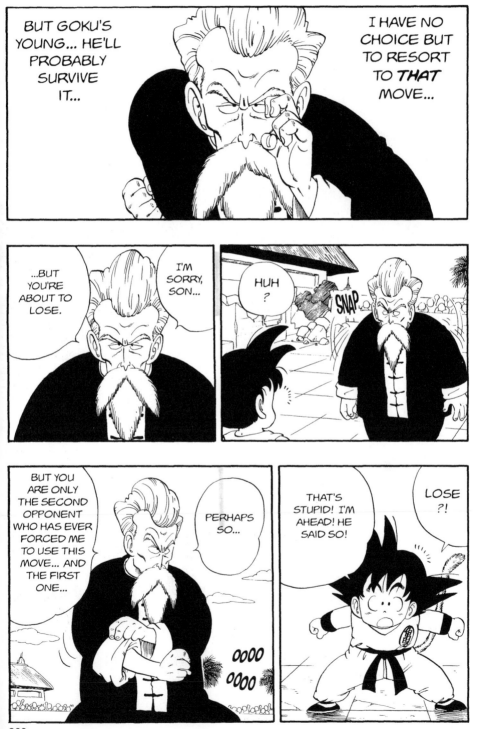

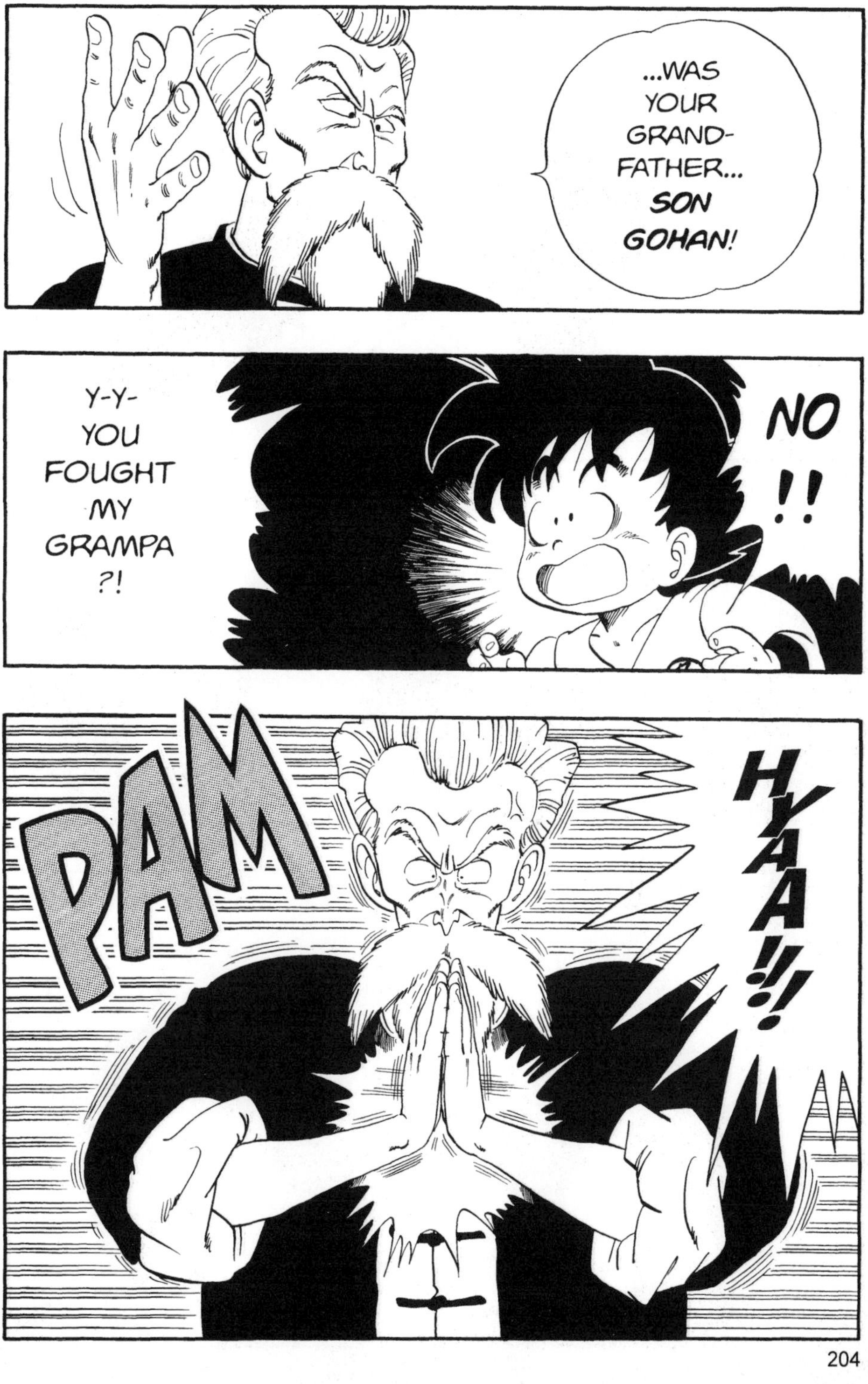
...WAS YOUR GRAND-FATHER... **SON GOHAN!**
NO !!
Y-Y-YOU FOUGHT MY GRAMPA ?!
HYAA!!!
PAM

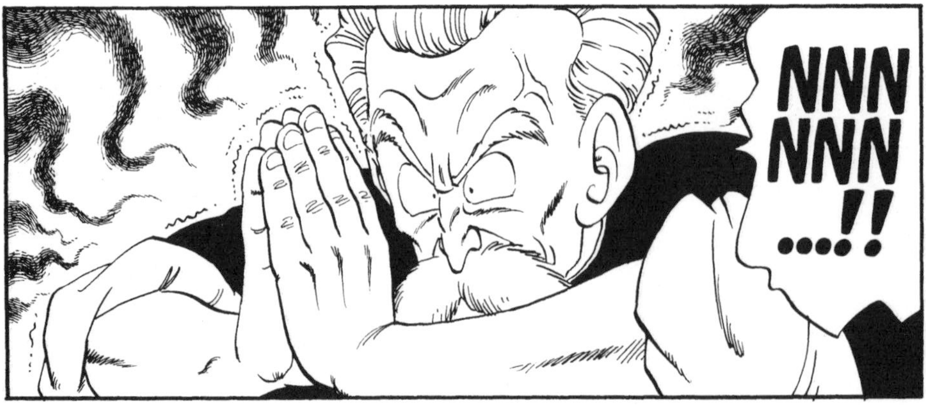
NNN
NNN
....!!
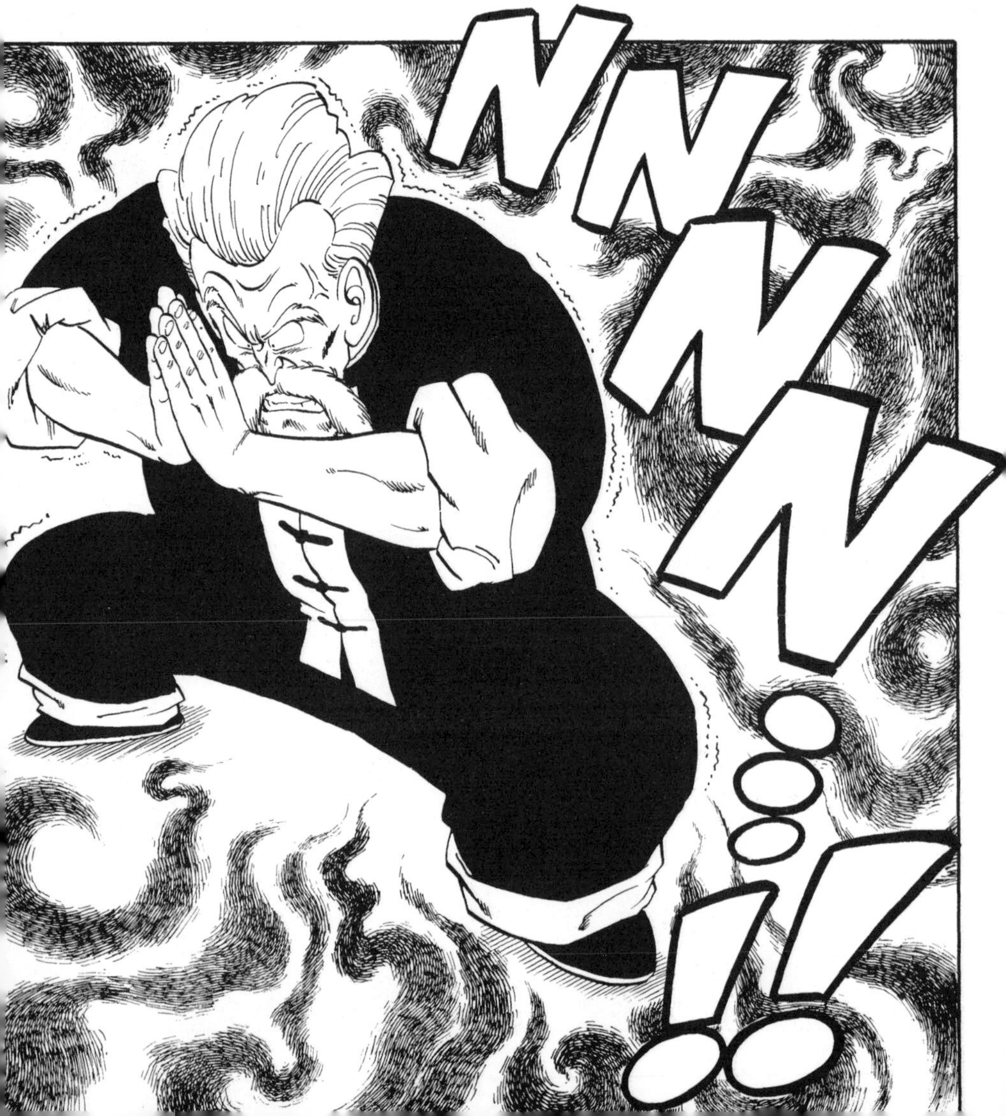
NNNNN....!!

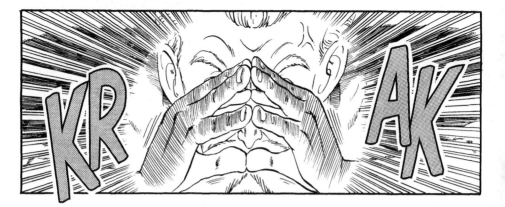

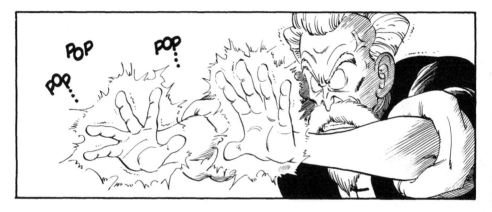

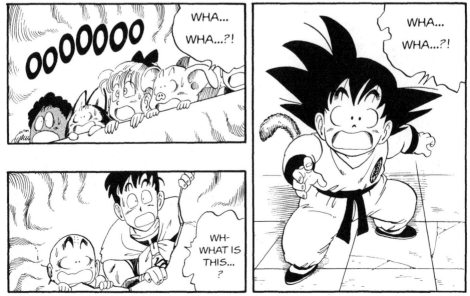

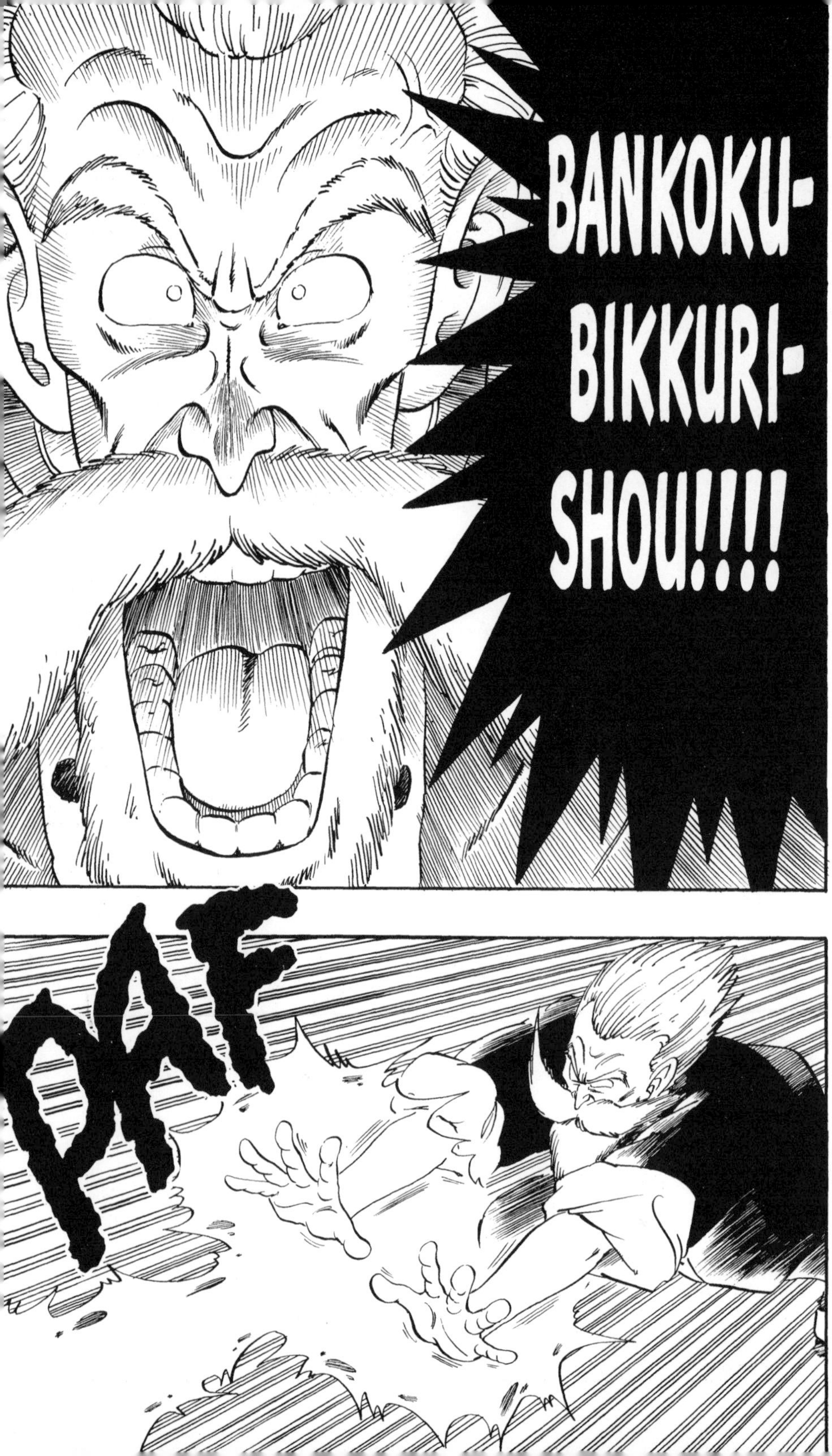
BANKOKU-BIKKURI-SHOU!!!!
PAF

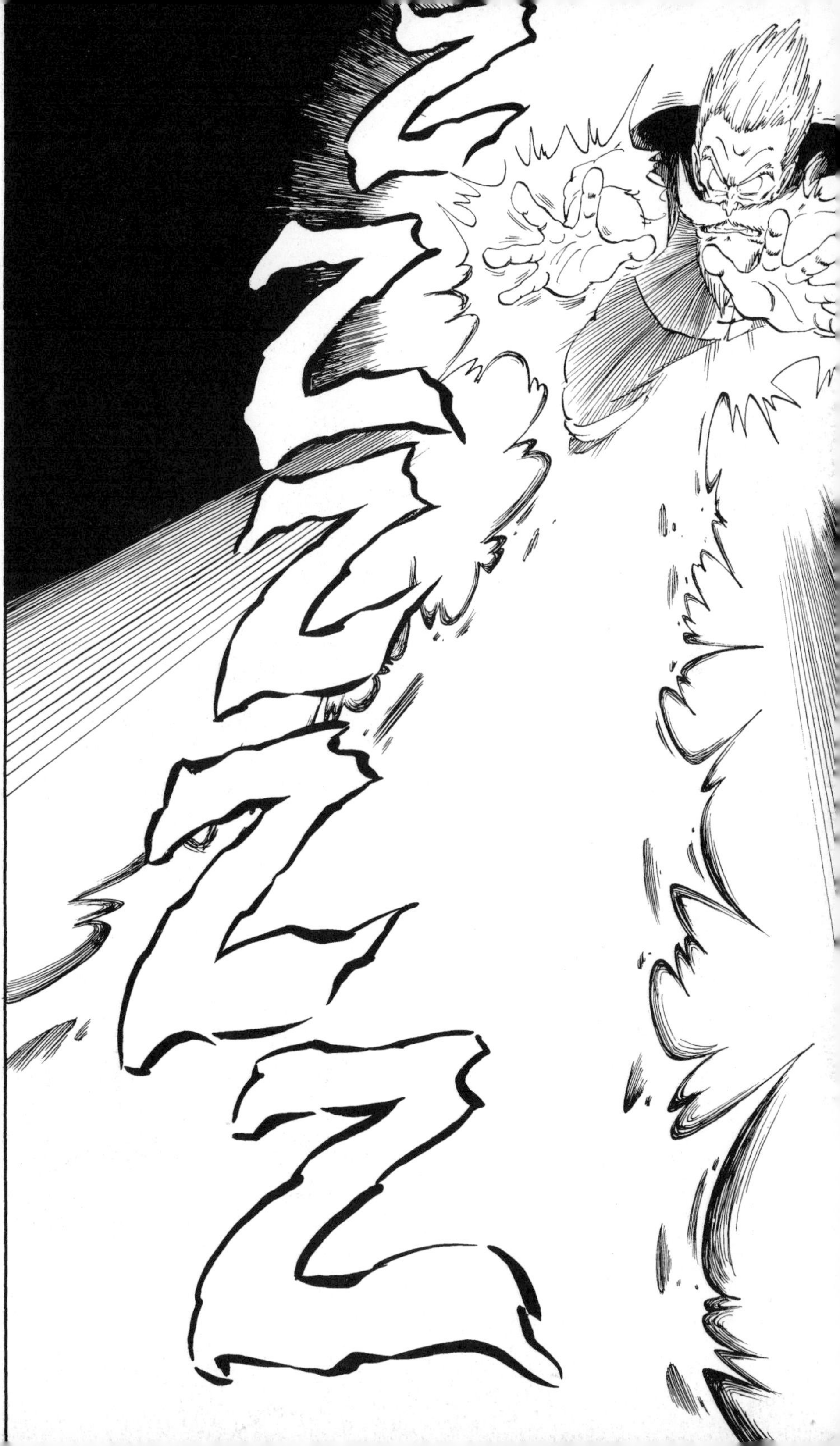

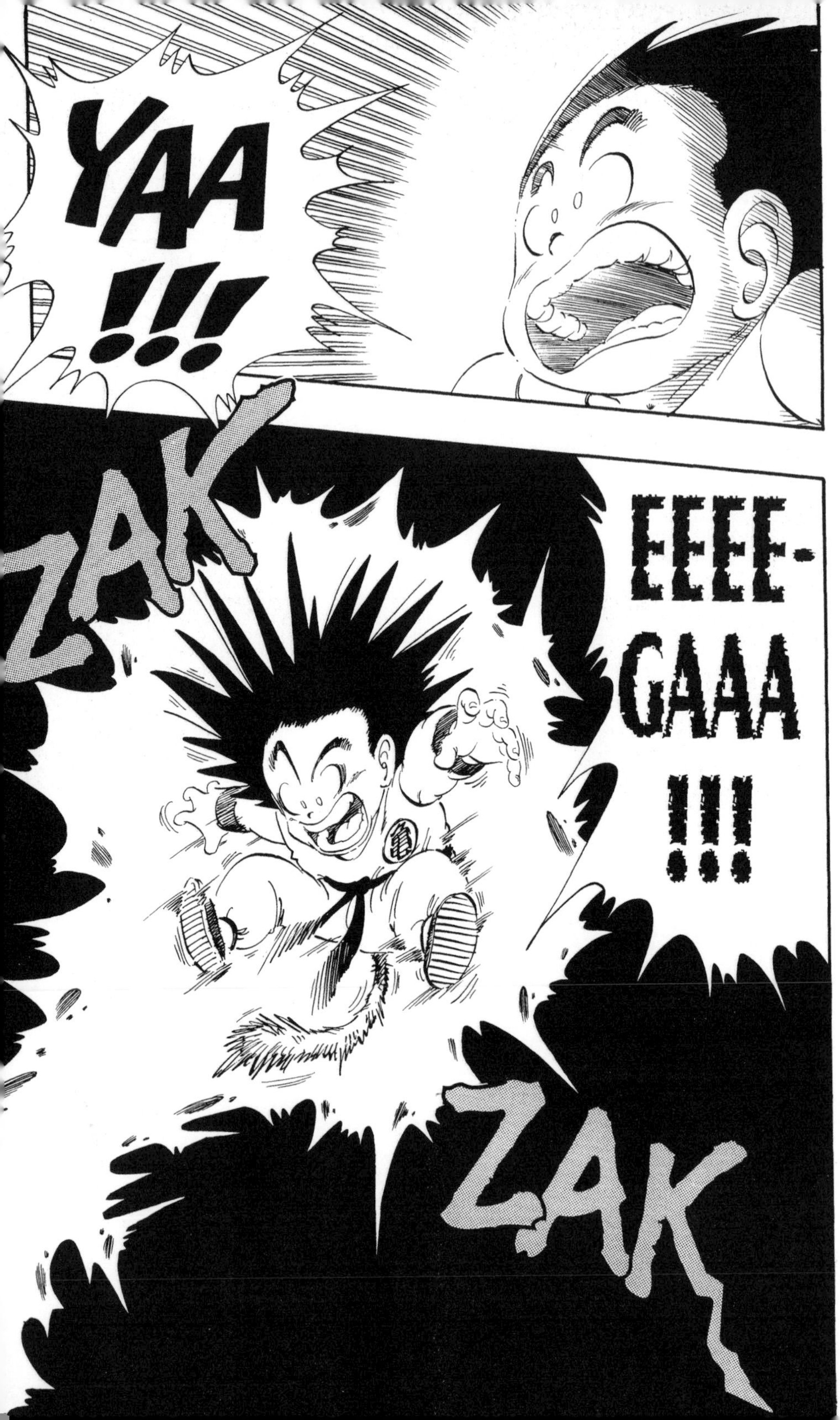
YAA!!!
EEEE-GAAA!!!
ZAK
ZAK

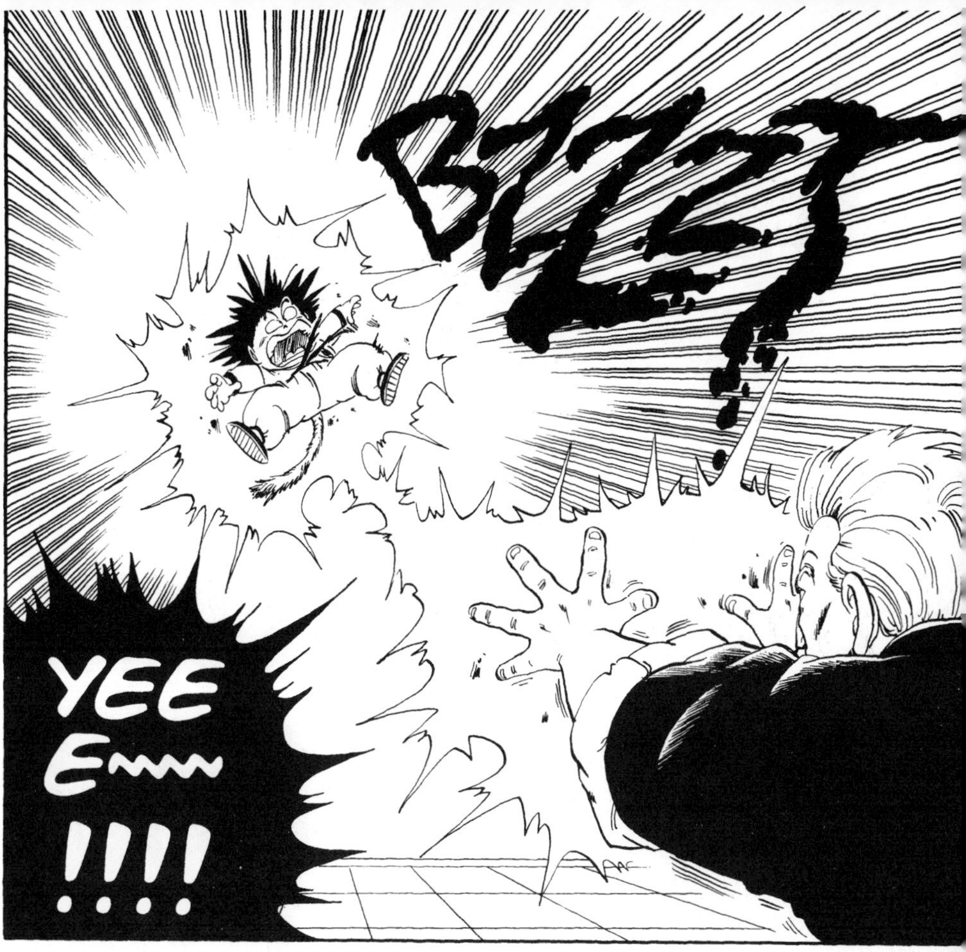
BZZZT
YEEE~~~!!!!

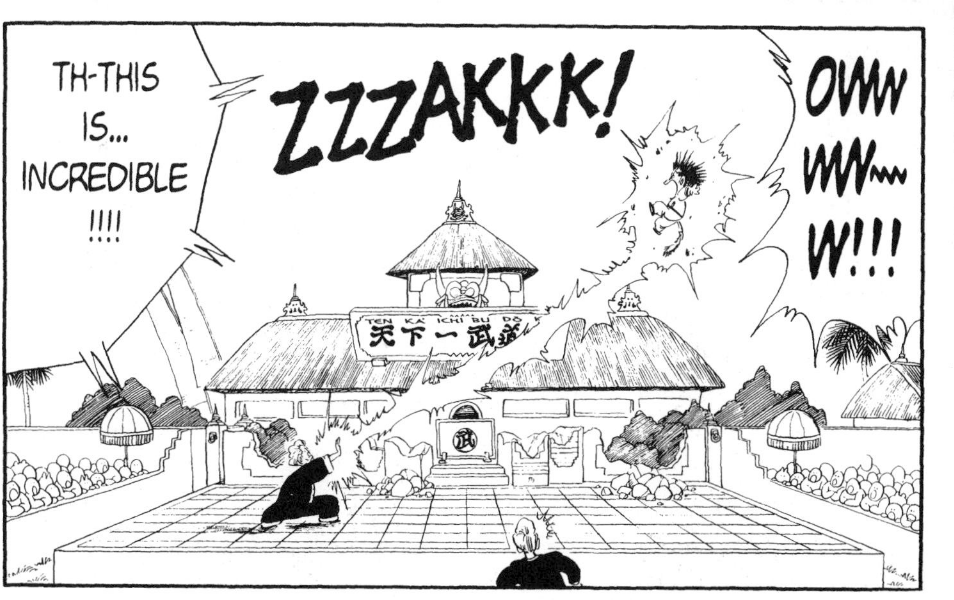
OWWWW~~W!!!
ZZZAKKK!
TH-THIS IS... INCREDIBLE!!!!
TEN KA ICHI BU DŌ

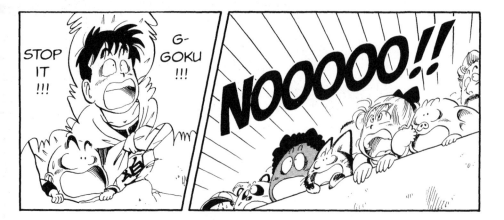

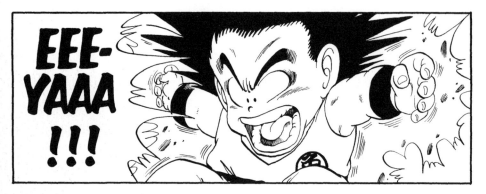

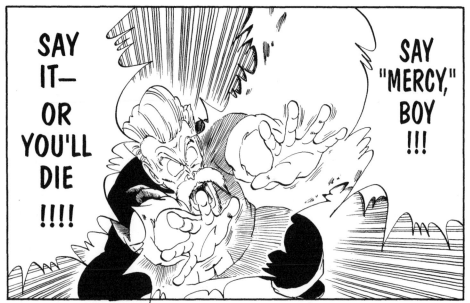

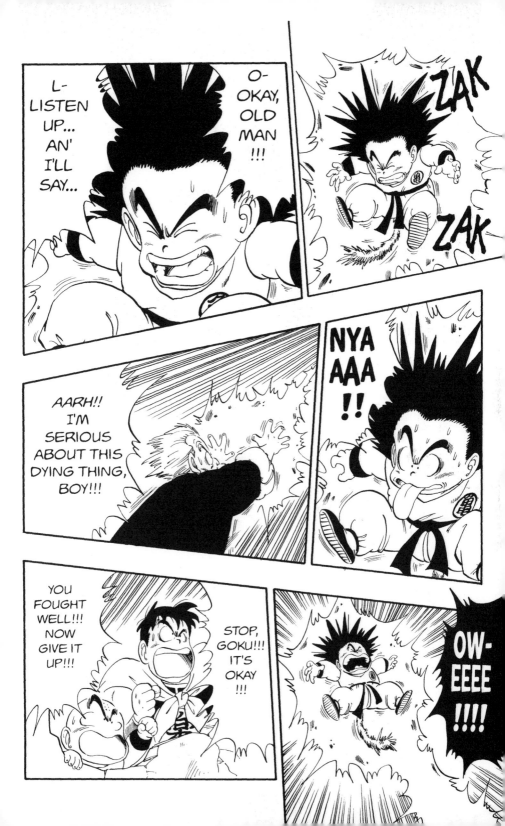

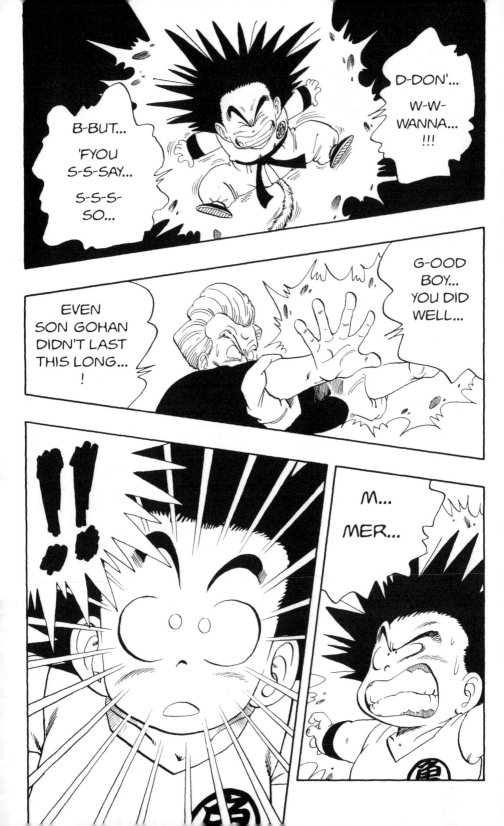

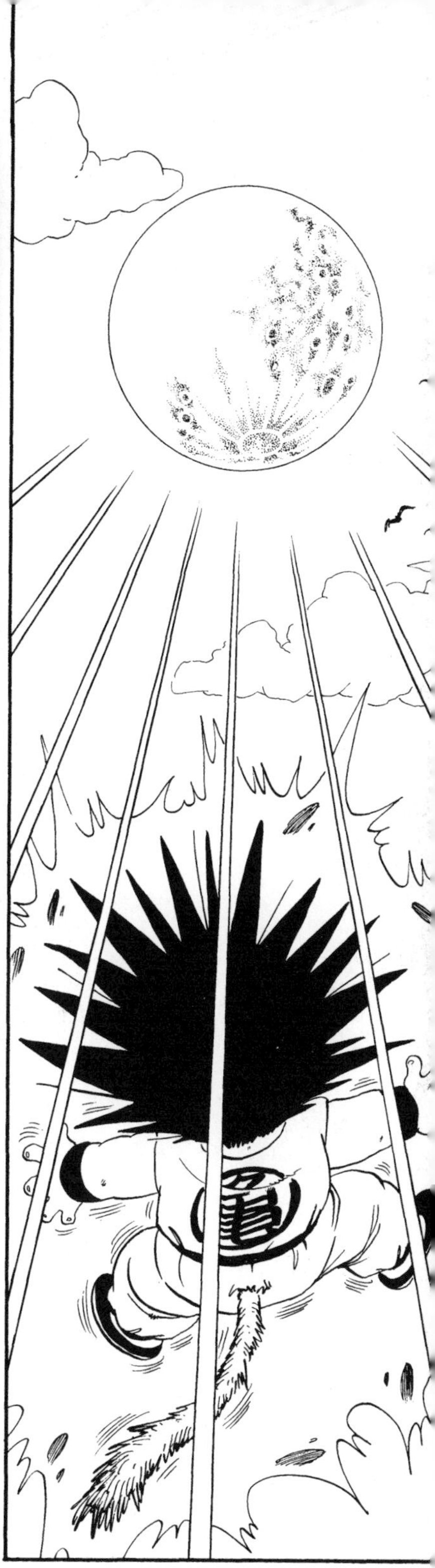

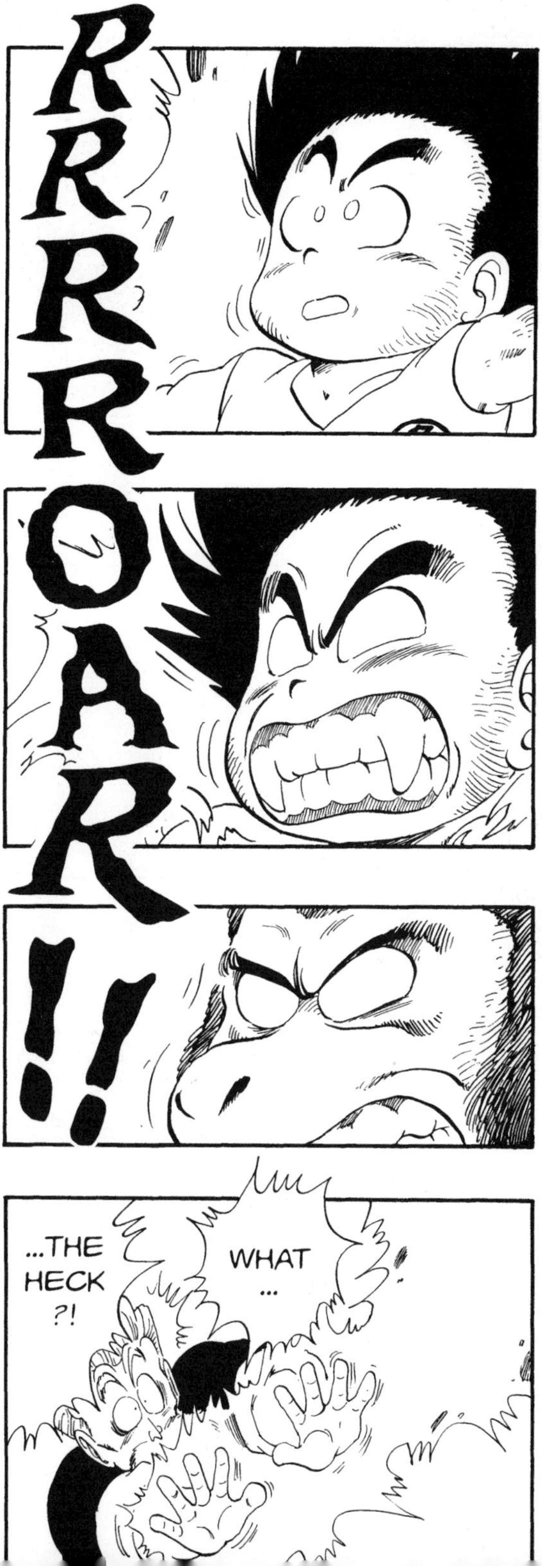
RRRROAR!!
WHAT ...
...THE HECK ?!

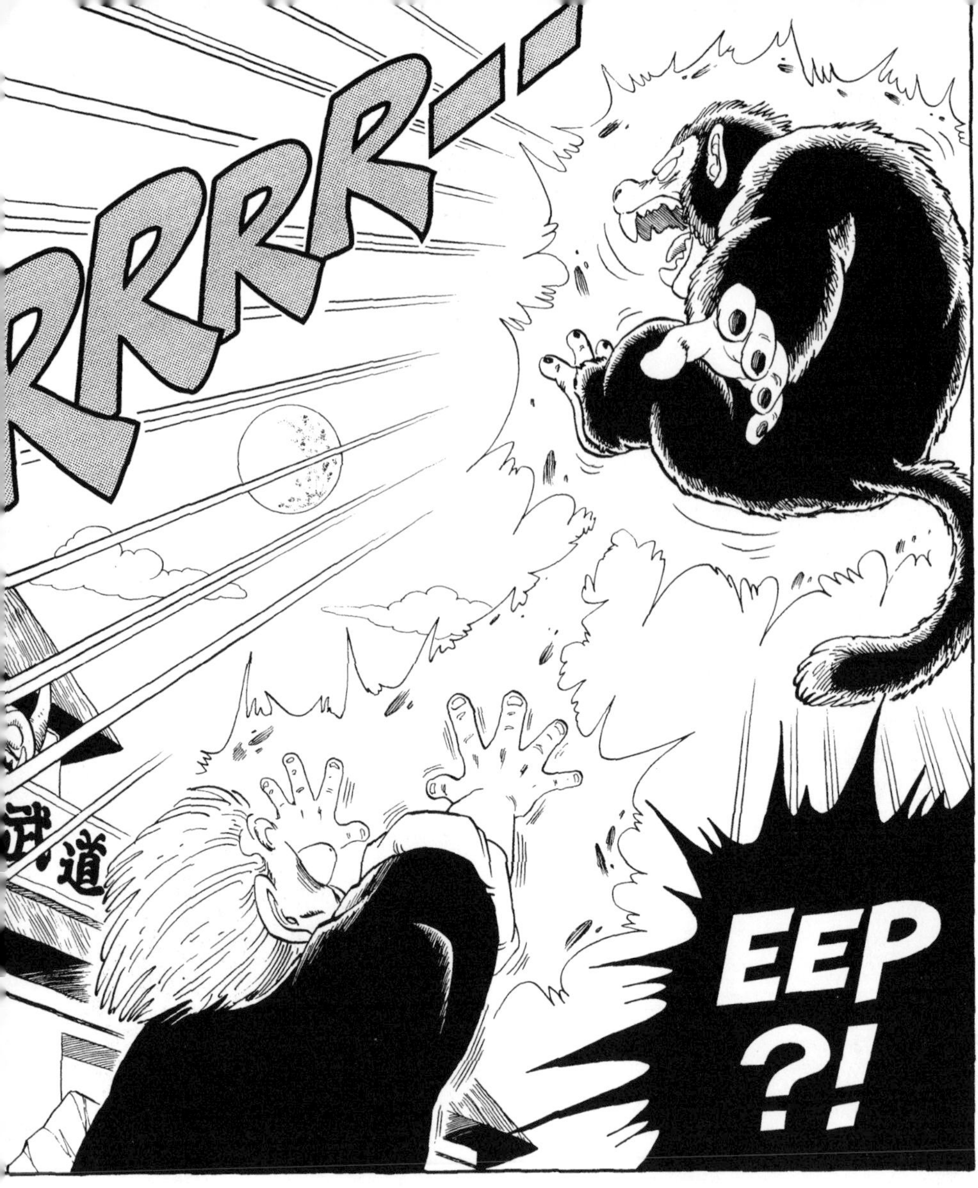
RRRR--
EEP ?!
武道

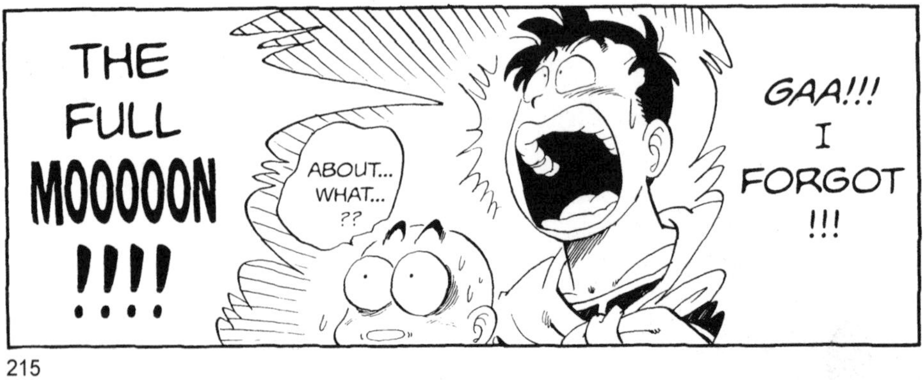
GAA!!! I FORGOT !!!
ABOUT... WHAT... ??
THE FULL MOOOOON !!!!

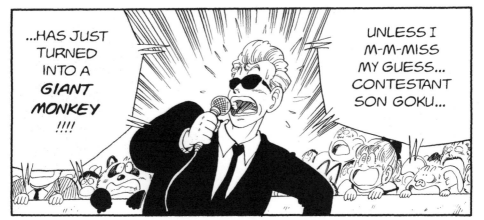

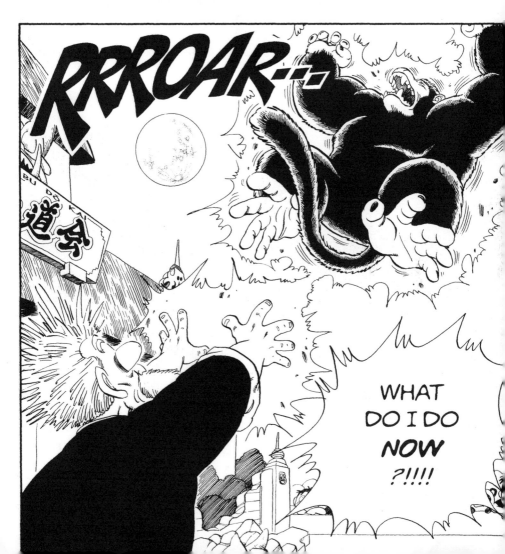

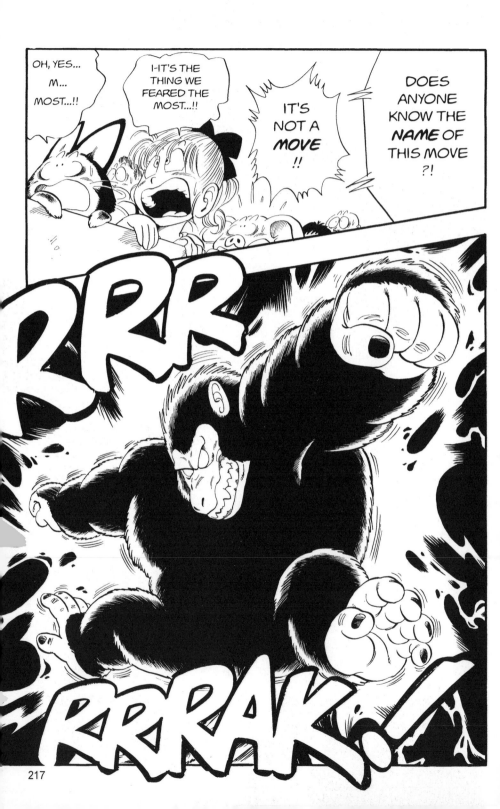

217

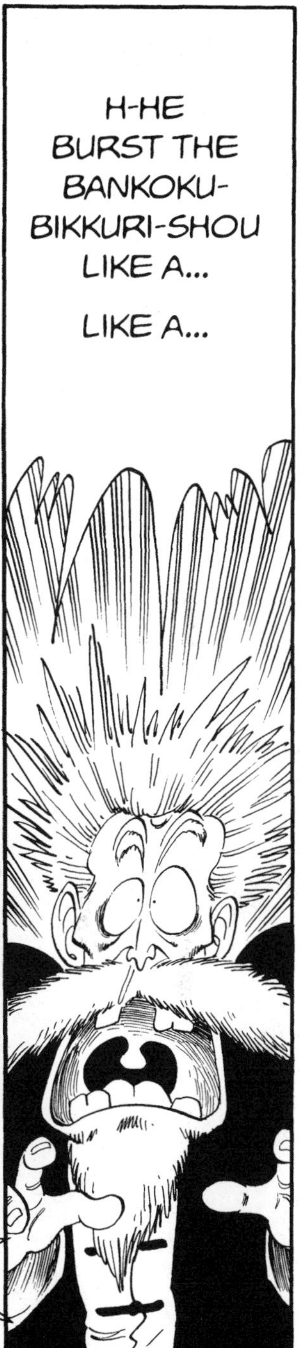
H-HE
BURST THE
BANKOKU-
BIKKURI-SHOU
LIKE A...
LIKE A...

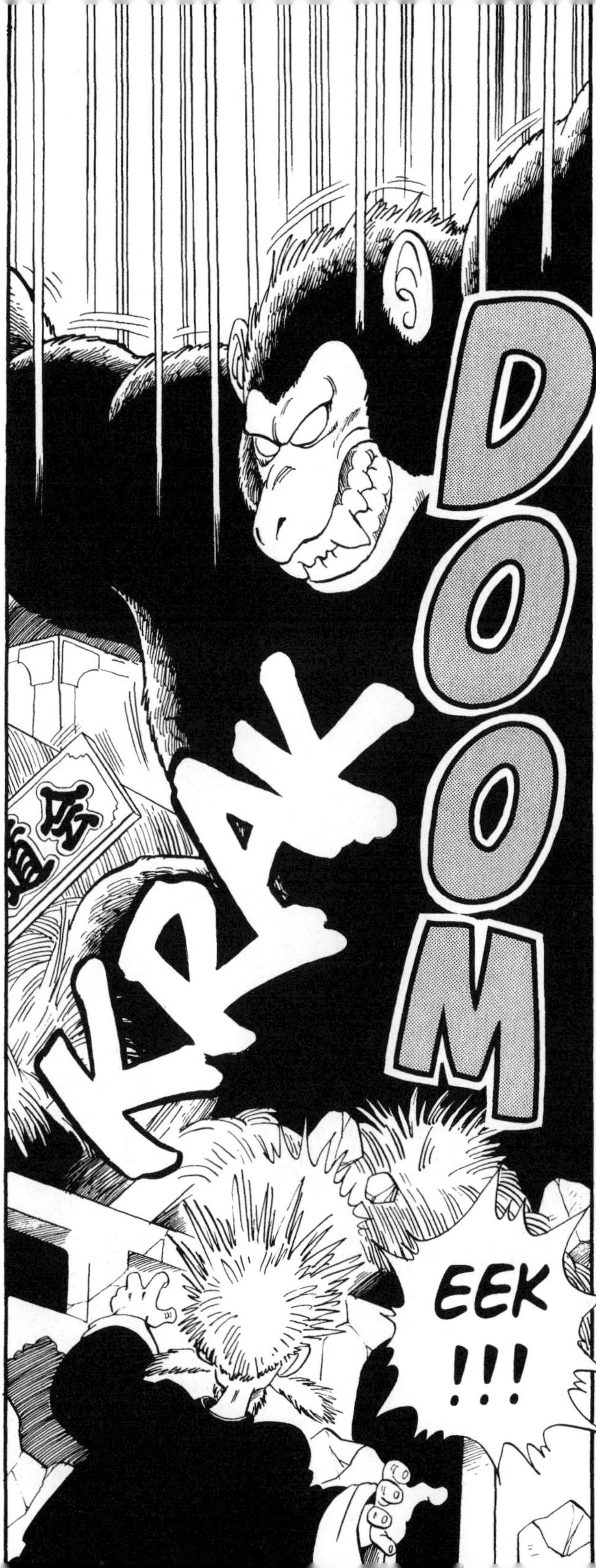
DOOM
KRAK
EEK
!!!

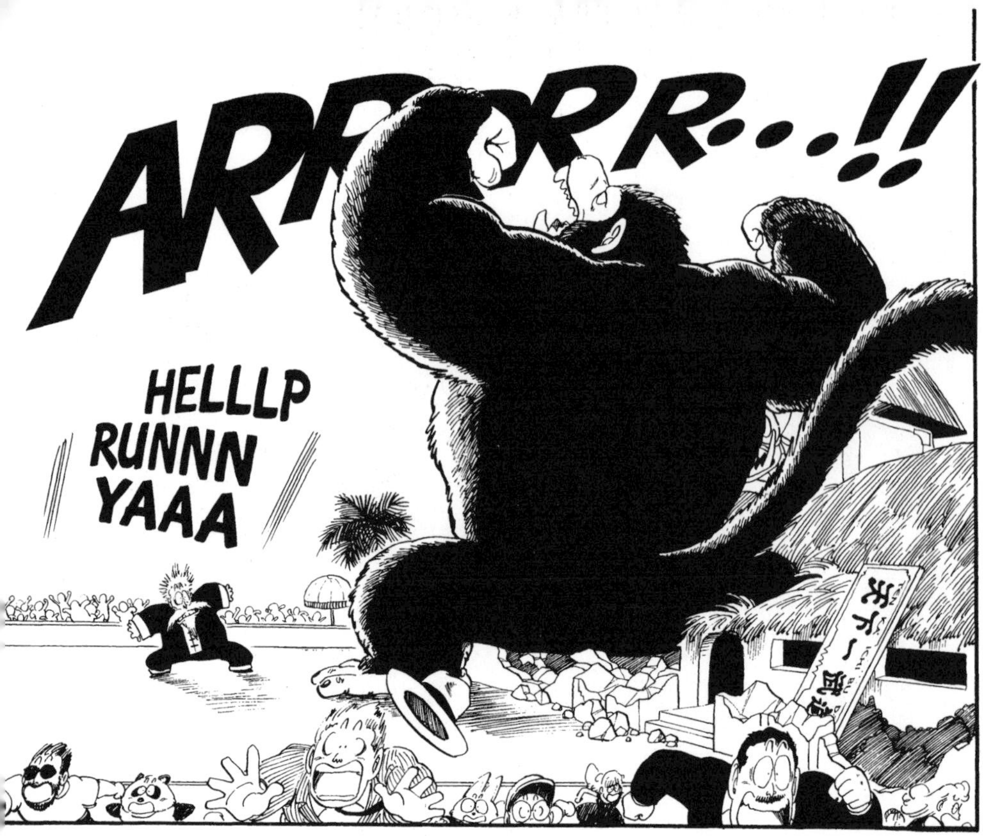
ARRRR...!!
HELLLP
RUNNN
YAAA
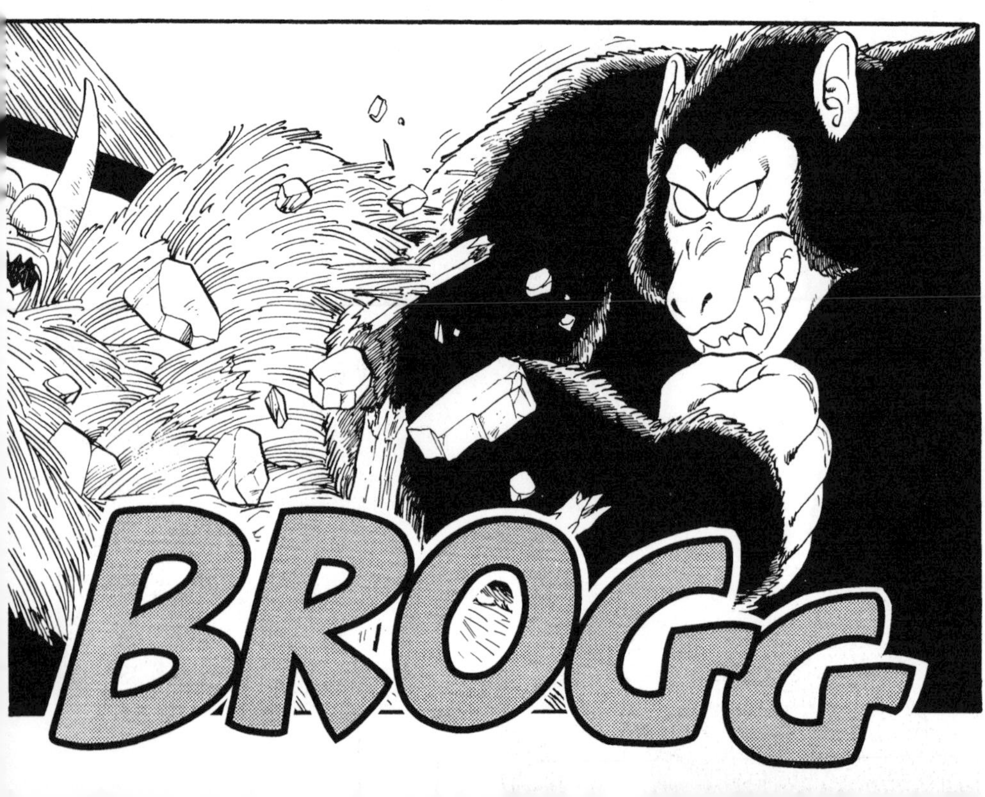
BROGG

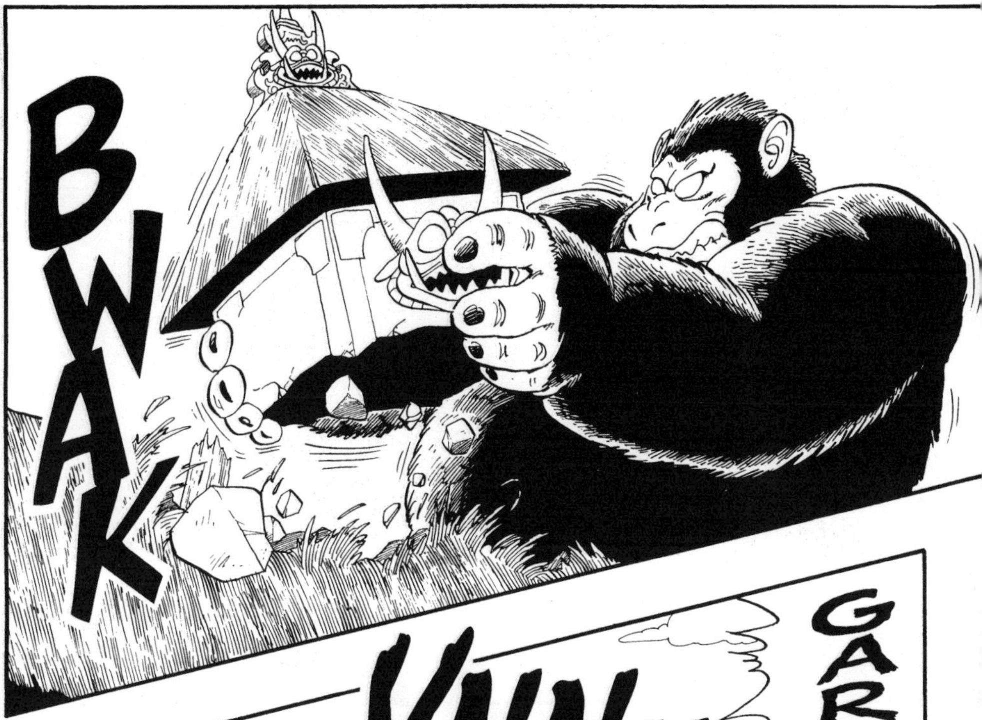
BWAK
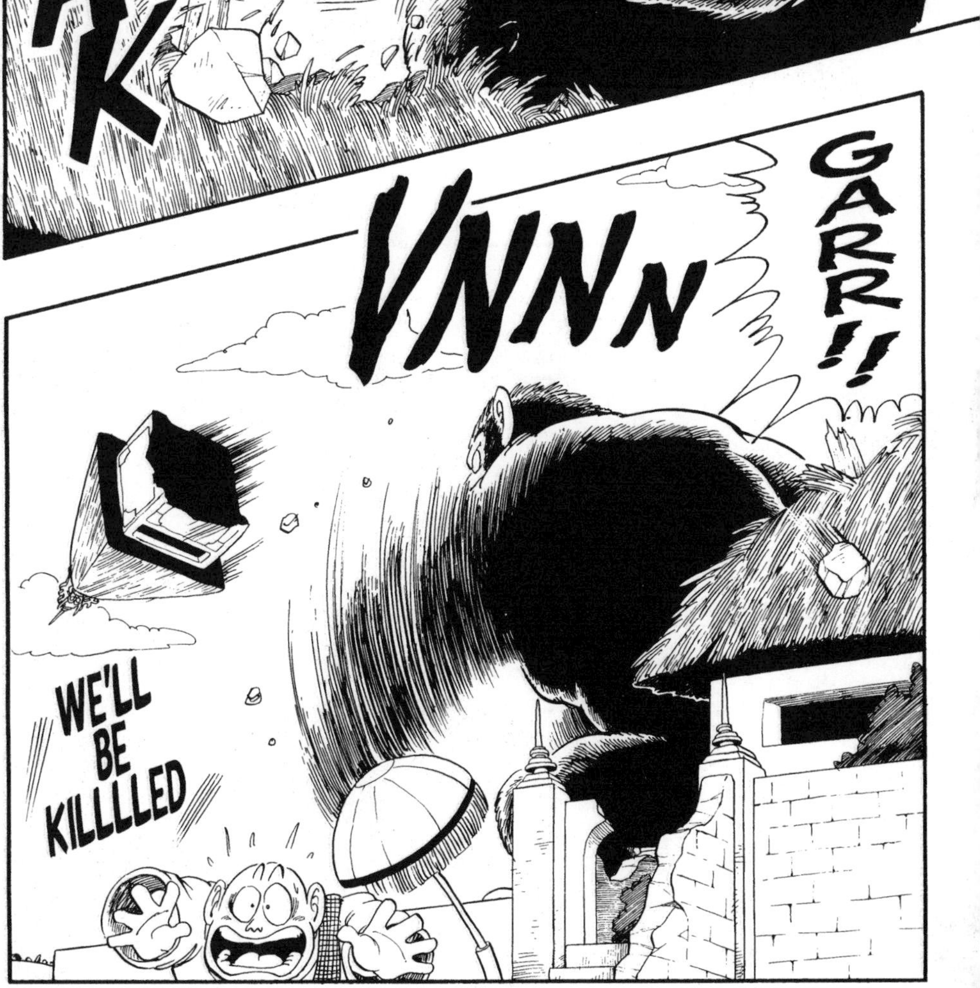
GARR!!
VNNN
WE'LL BE KILLLLED

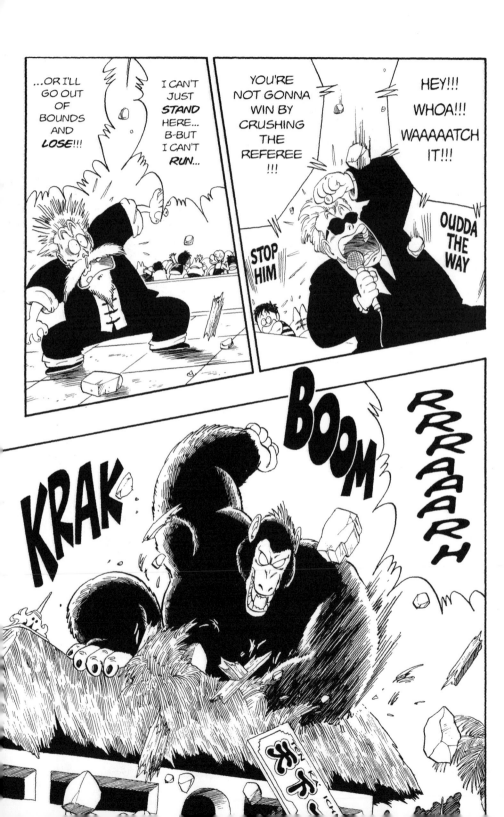

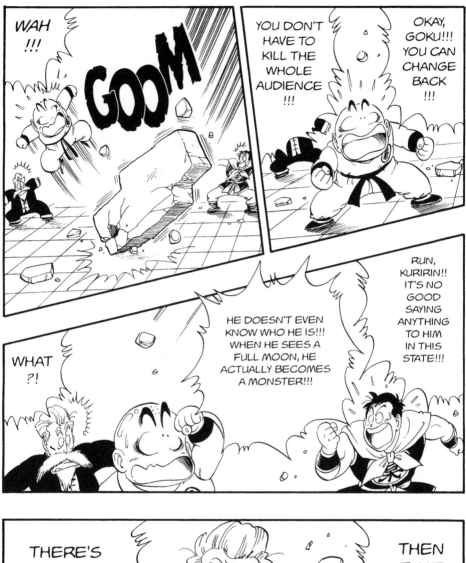

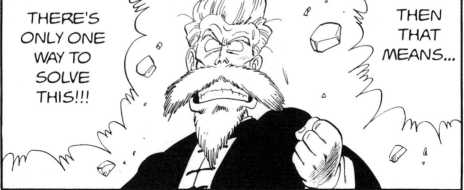

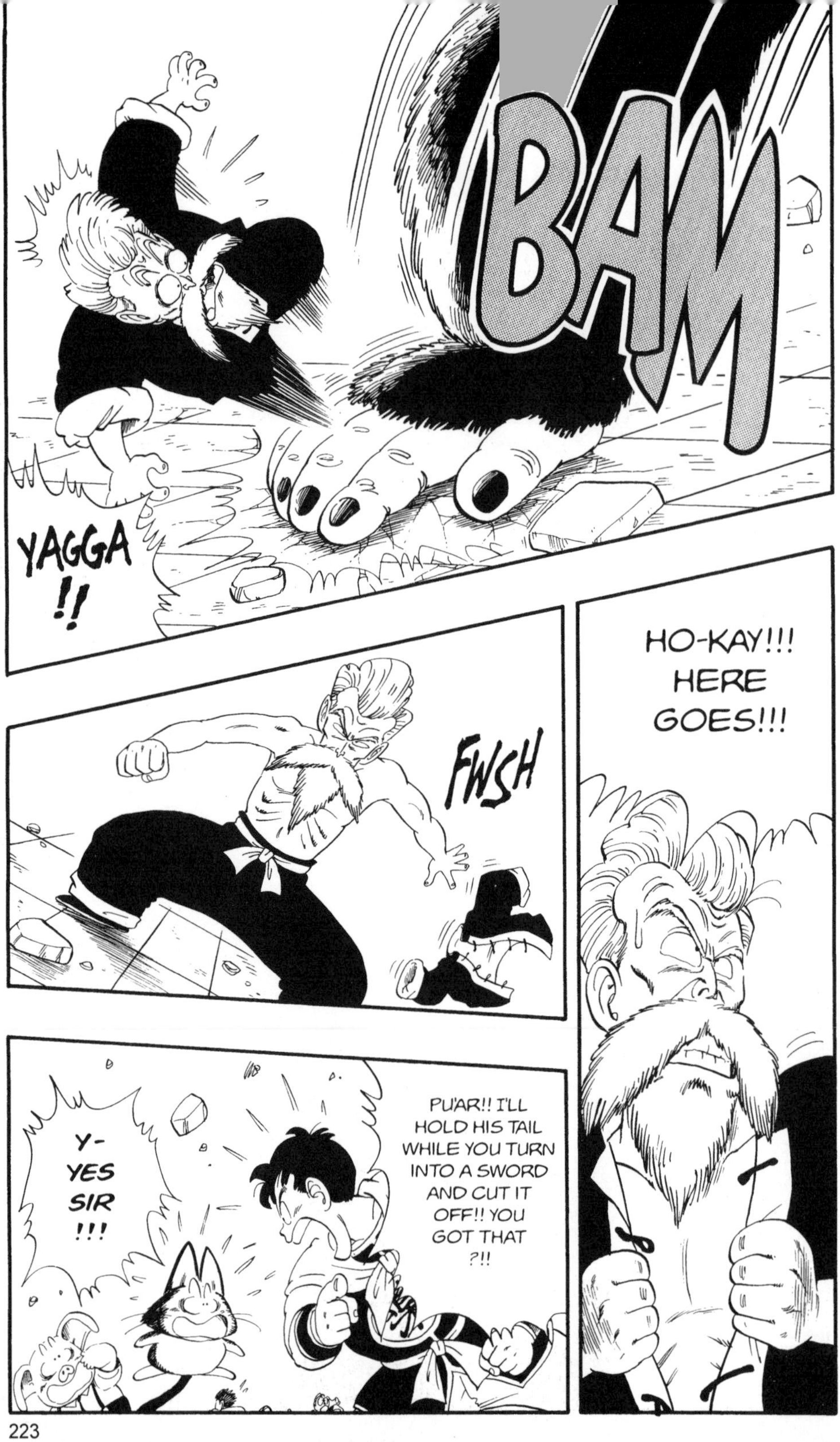
BAM
YAGGA!!
HO-KAY!!! HERE GOES!!!
FWSH
PU'AR!! I'LL HOLD HIS TAIL WHILE YOU TURN INTO A SWORD AND CUT IT OFF!! YOU GOT THAT?!!
Y-YES SIR!!!

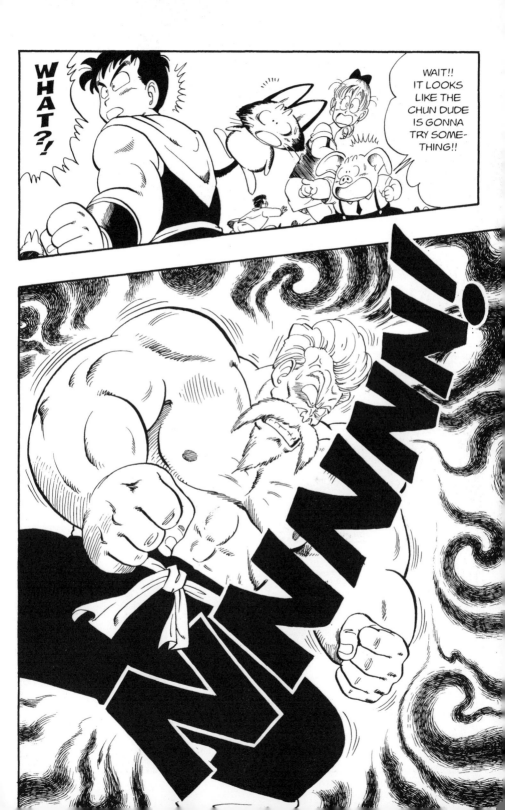

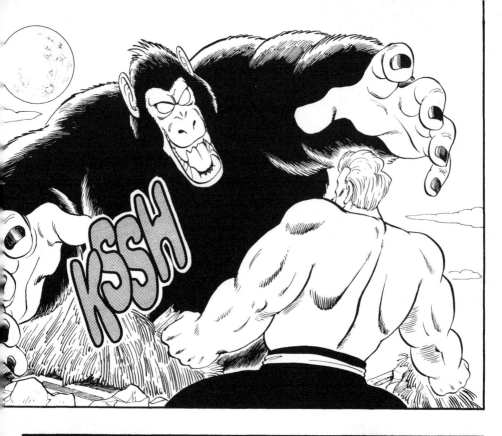

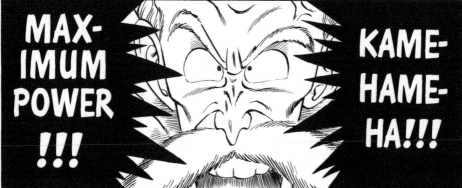

MAX-IMUM POWER!!!

KAME-HAME-HA!!!

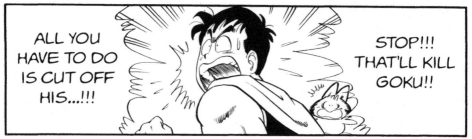

ALL YOU HAVE TO DO IS CUT OFF HIS...!!!

STOP!!! THAT'LL KILL GOKU!!

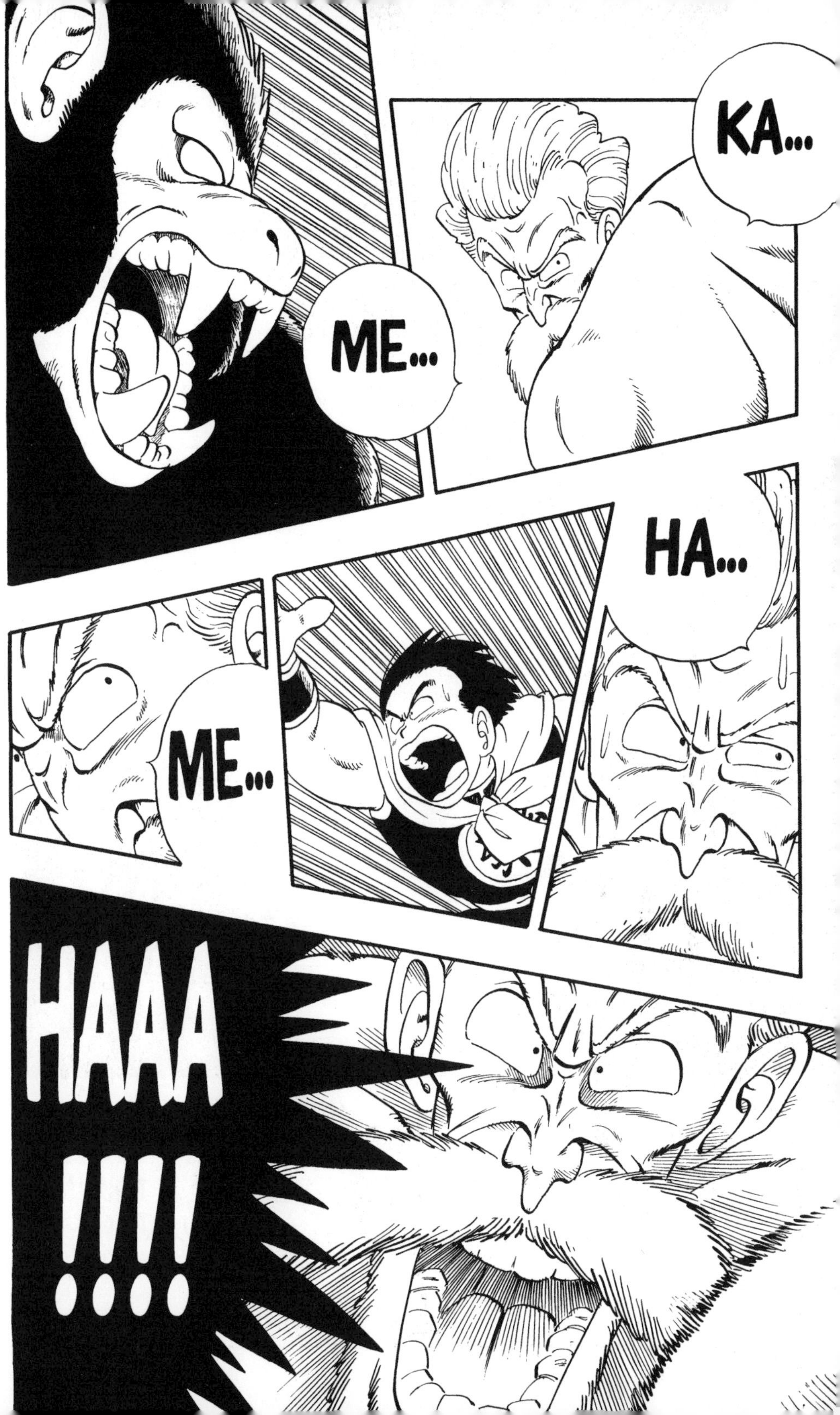
KA...
ME...
HA...
ME...
HAAA !!!!

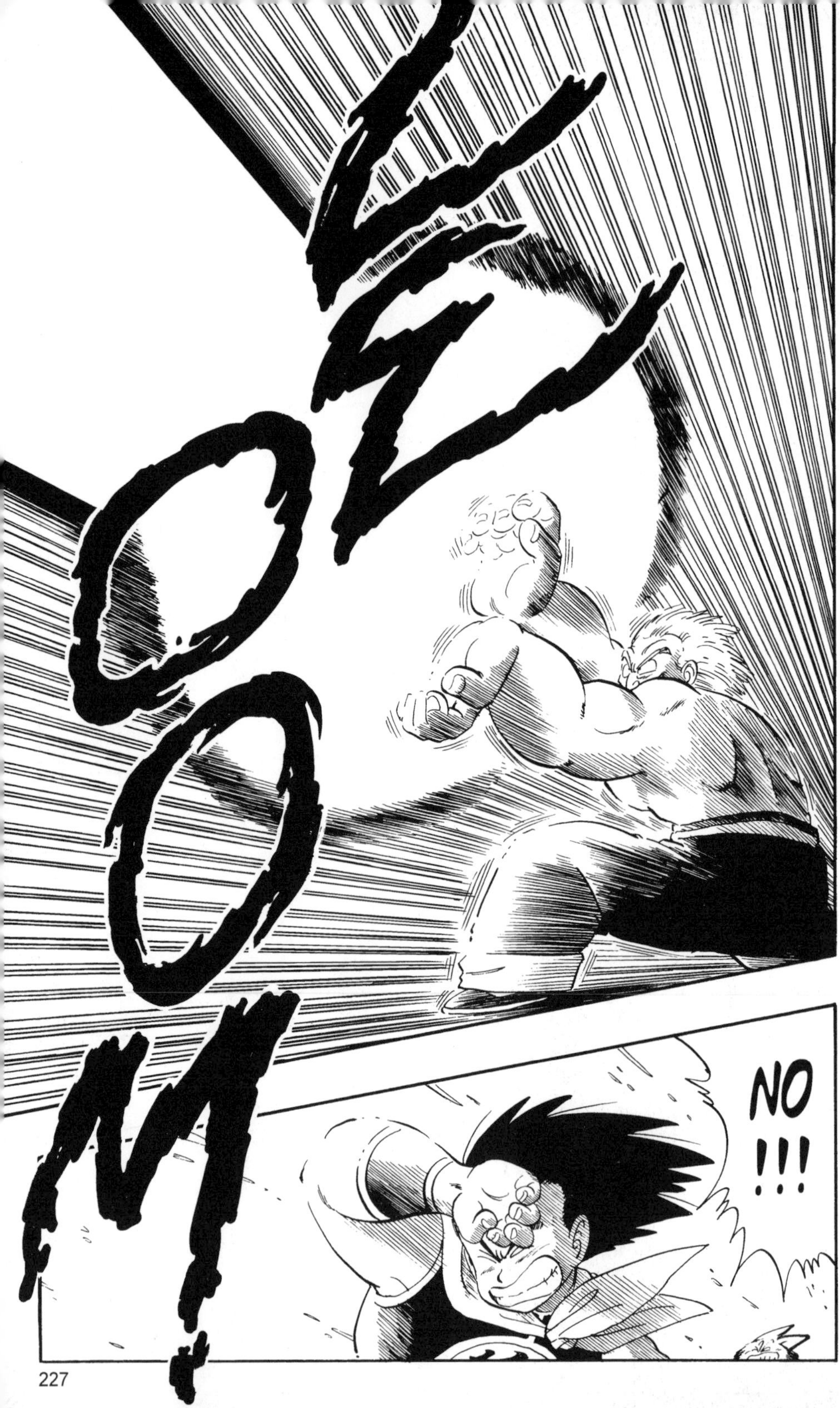
NO
!!!

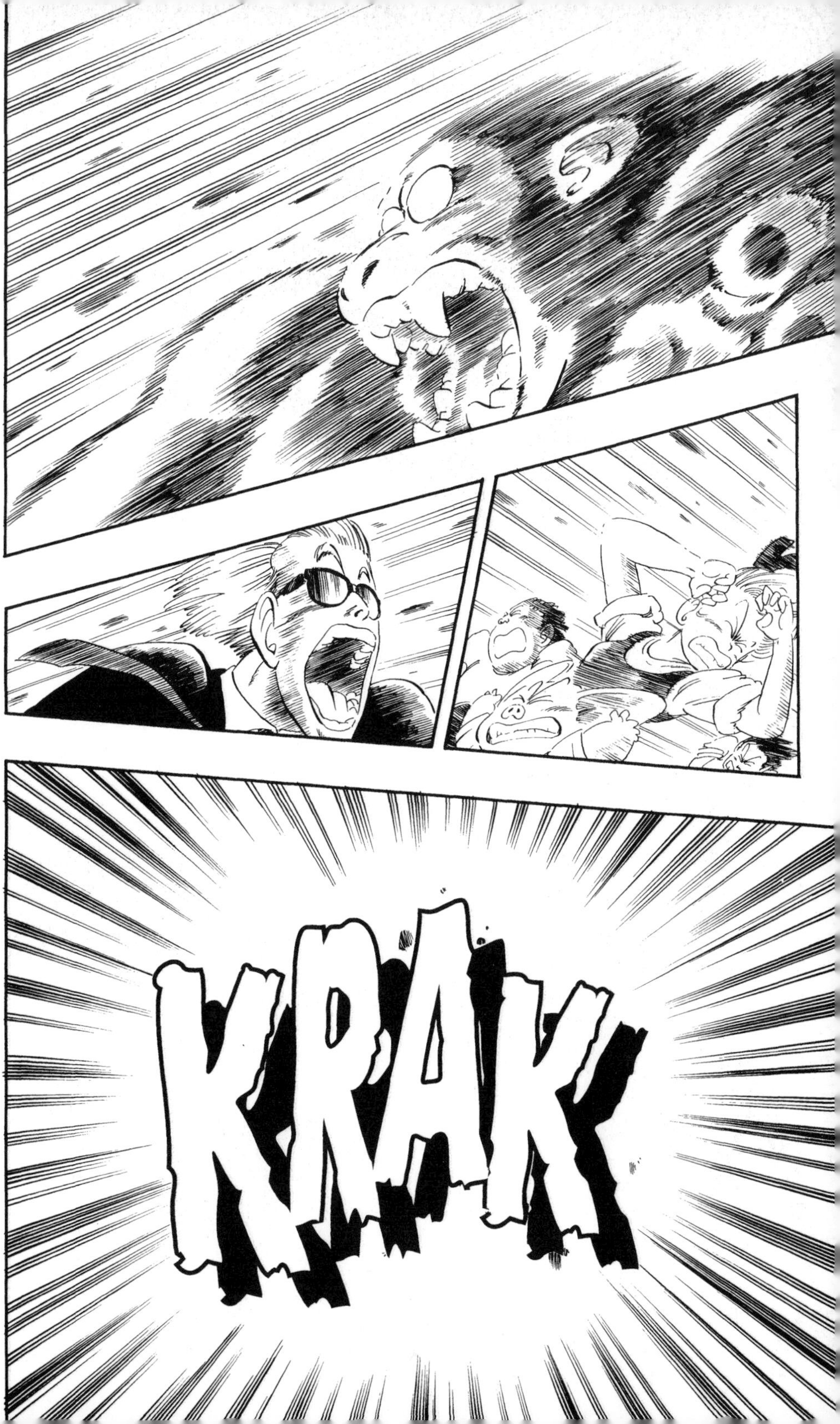
KRAK

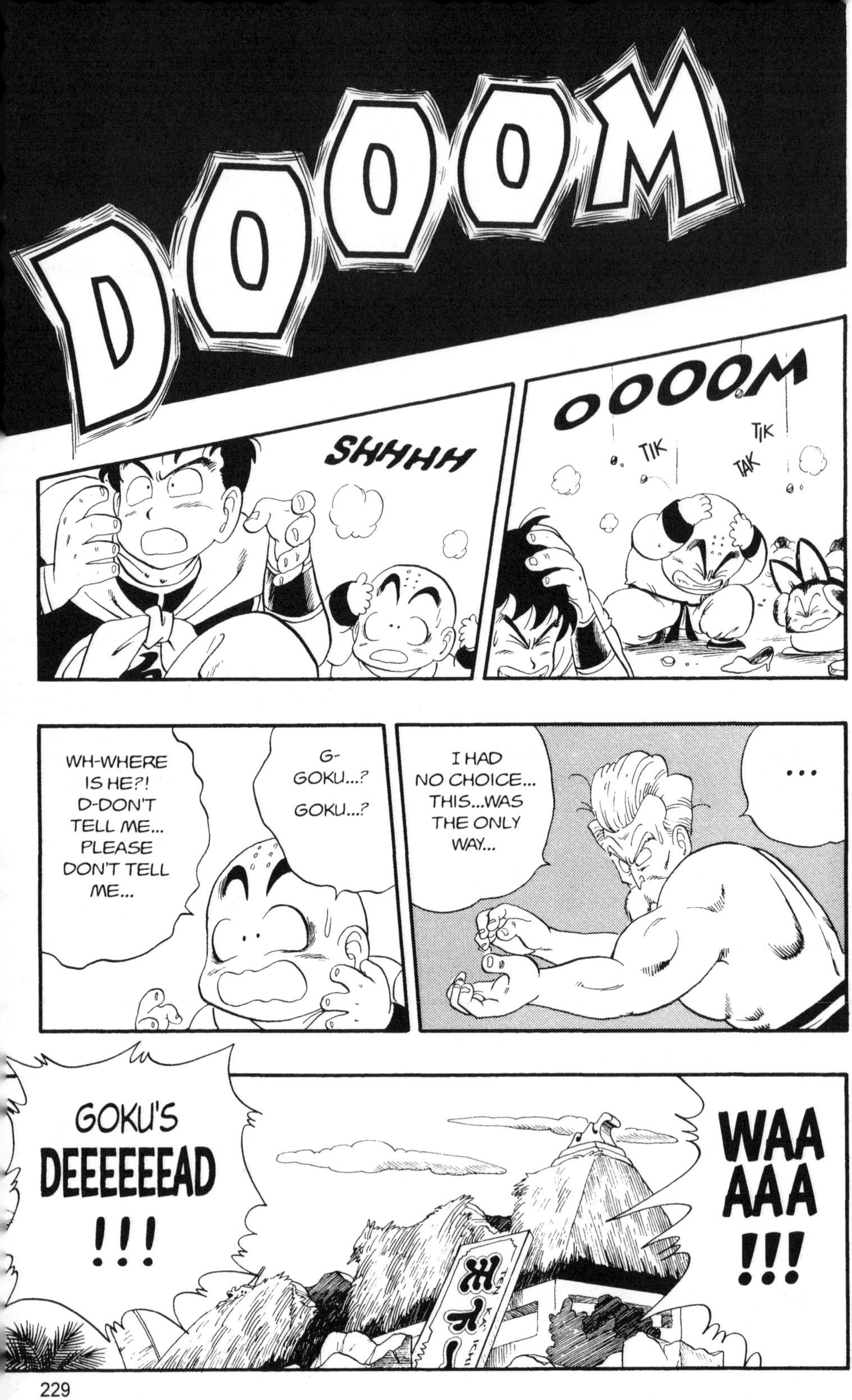
DOOOM
OOOOM
TIK
TIK
TAK
SHHHH
...
I HAD NO CHOICE... THIS...WAS THE ONLY WAY...
G- GOKU...? GOKU...?
WH-WHERE IS HE?! D-DON'T TELL ME... PLEASE DON'T TELL ME...
WAA AAA !!!
GOKU'S DEEEEEEAD !!!

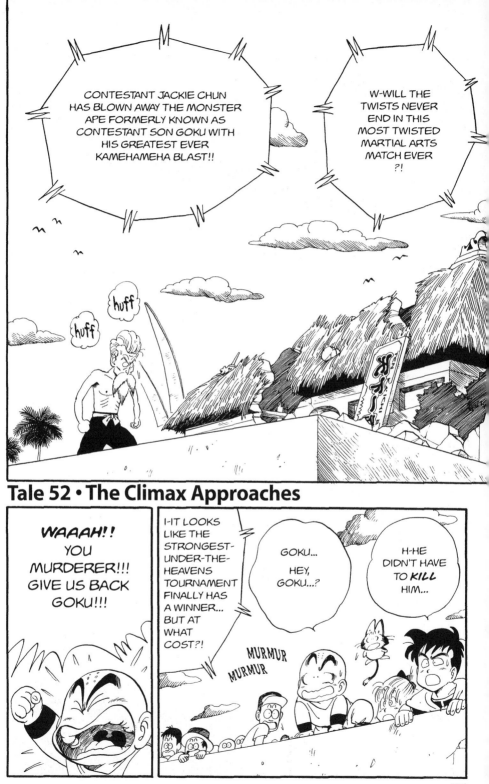

Tale 52 • The Climax Approaches

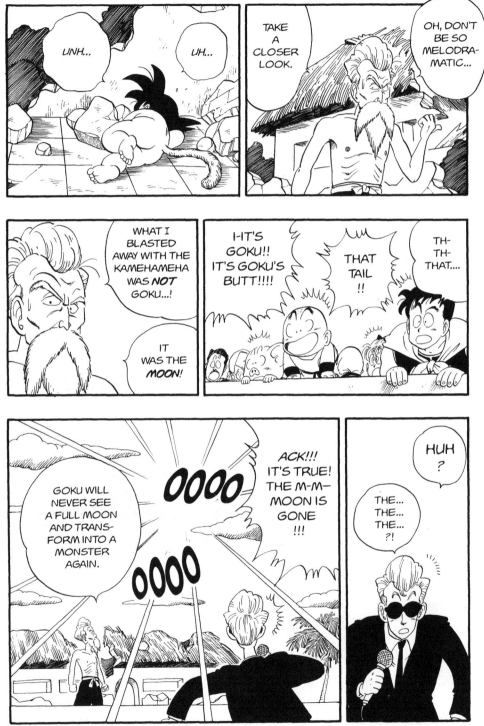

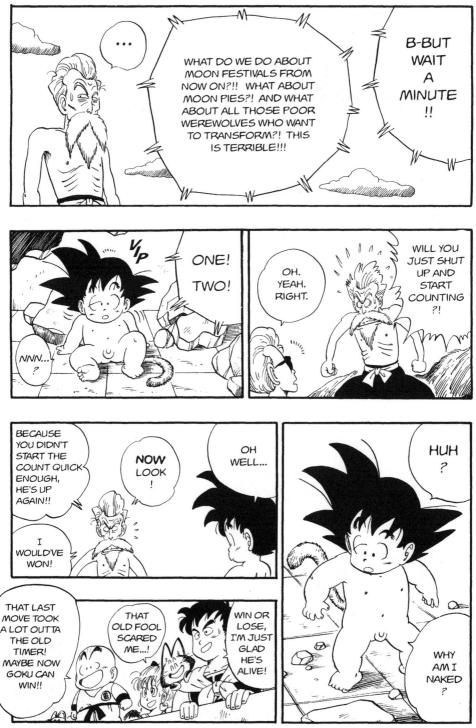

232

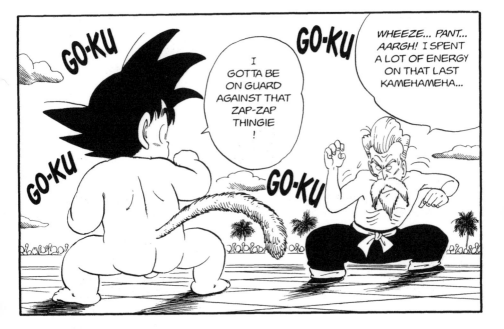

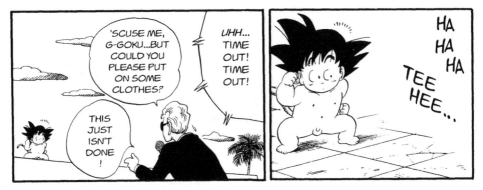

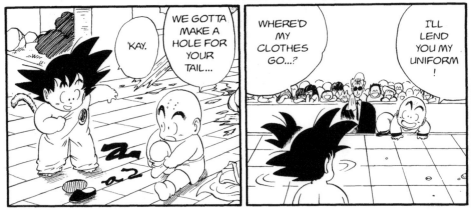

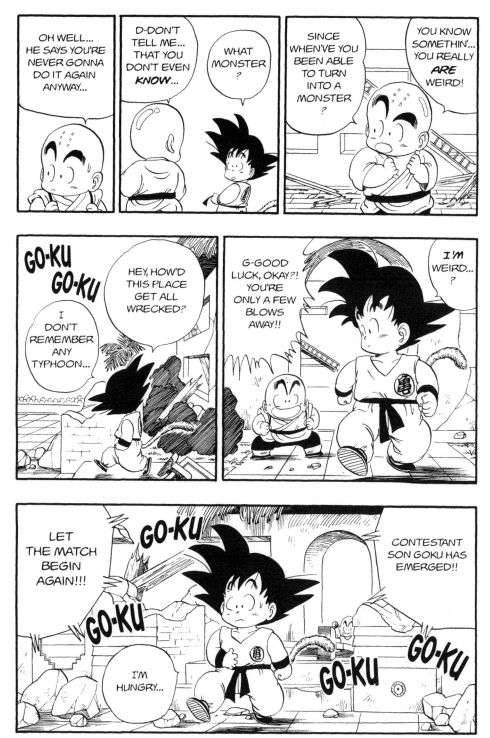

234

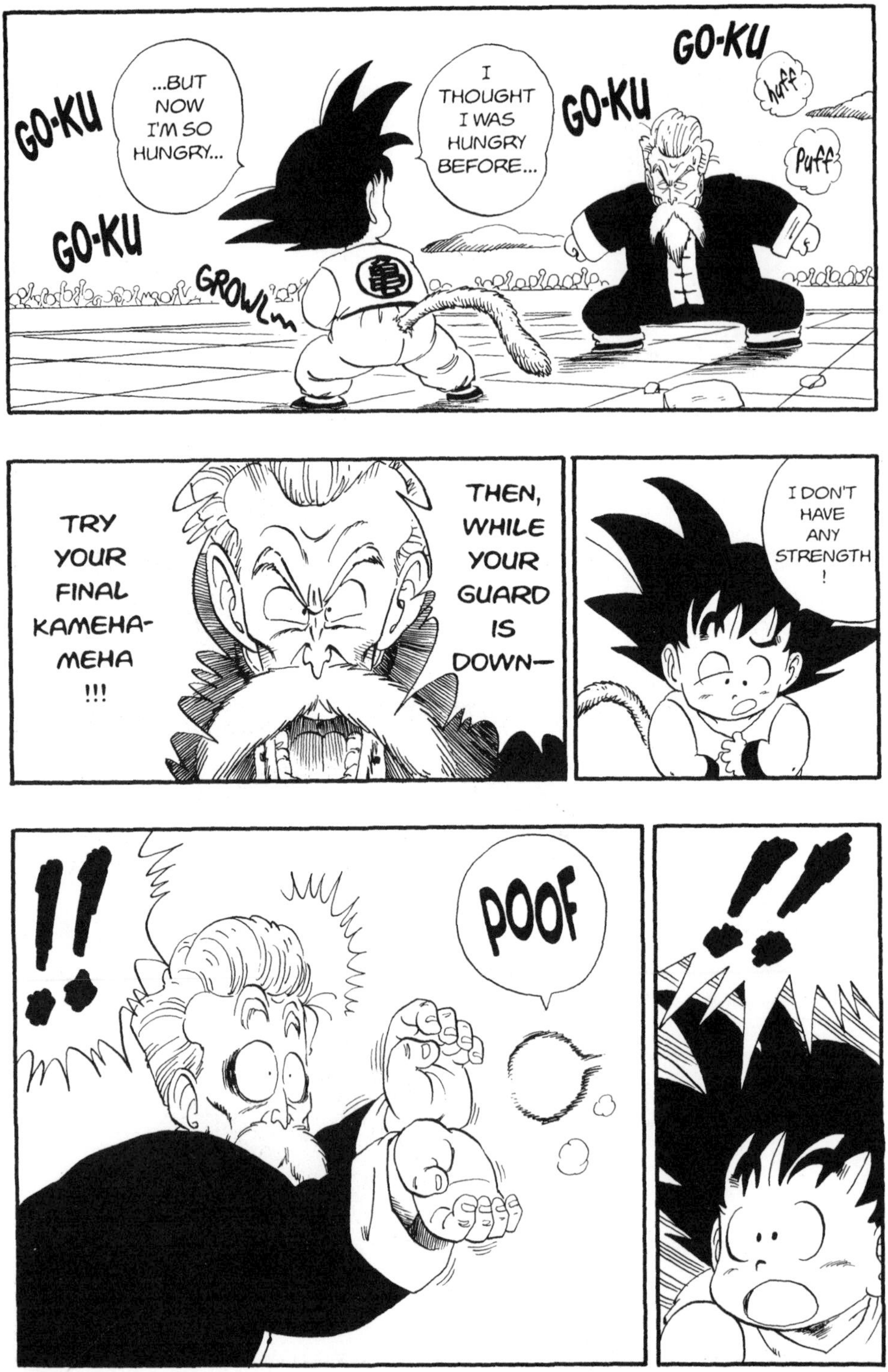
GO-KU
huff
Puff
GO-KU
I THOUGHT I WAS HUNGRY BEFORE...
...BUT NOW I'M SO HUNGRY...
GO-KU
GO-KU
GROWL
I DON'T HAVE ANY STRENGTH!
THEN, WHILE YOUR GUARD IS DOWN—
TRY YOUR FINAL KAMEHAMEHA!!!
!!
POOF
!!

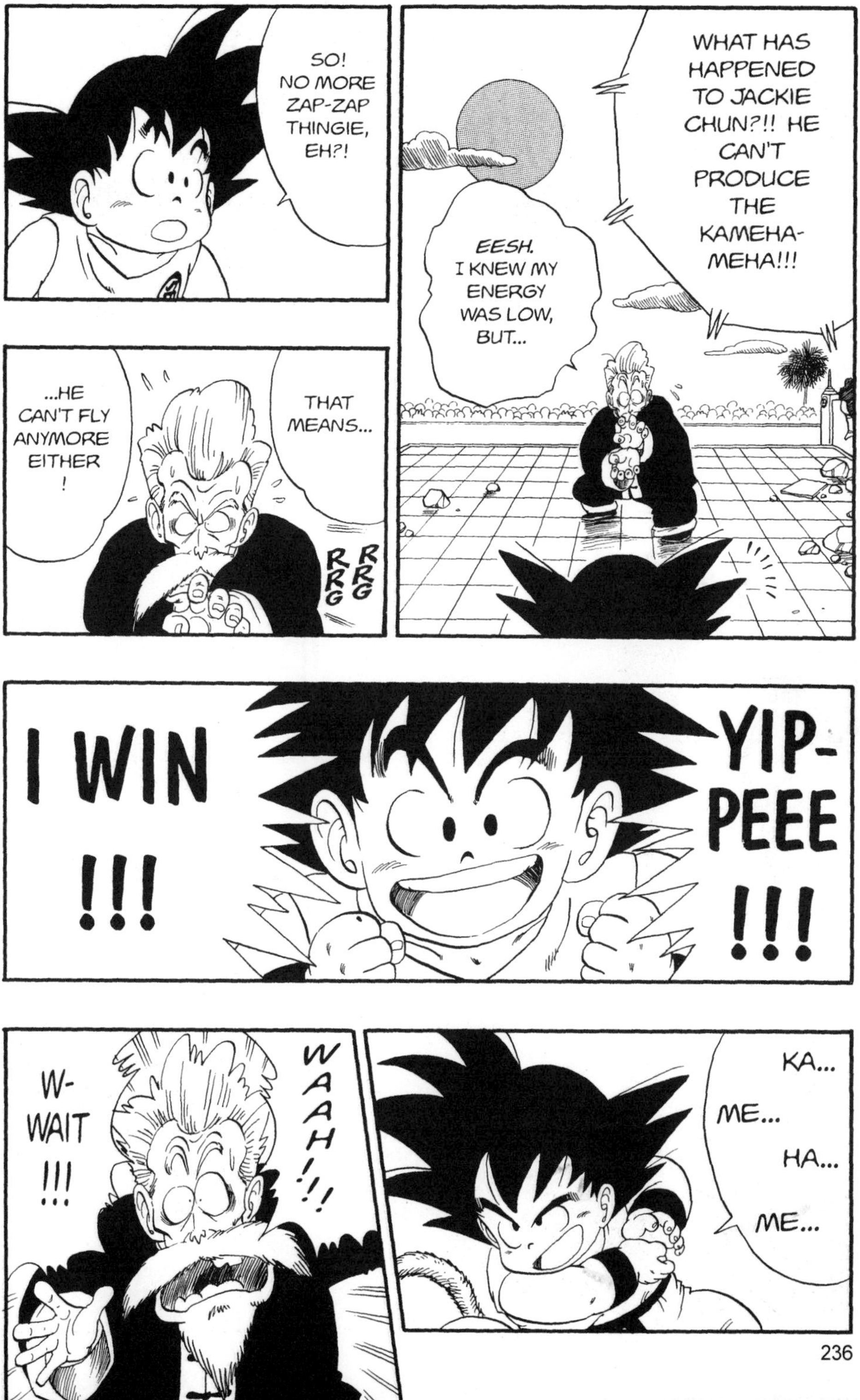

WHAT HAS HAPPENED TO JACKIE CHUN?!! HE CAN'T PRODUCE THE KAMEHA-MEHA!!!
EESH. I KNEW MY ENERGY WAS LOW, BUT...
SO! NO MORE ZAP-ZAP THINGIE, EH?!
THAT MEANS...
...HE CAN'T FLY ANYMORE EITHER!
RRRG RRRG
YIP-PEEE!!!
I WIN!!!
KA... ME... HA... ME...
WAAAH!!!
W-WAIT!!!

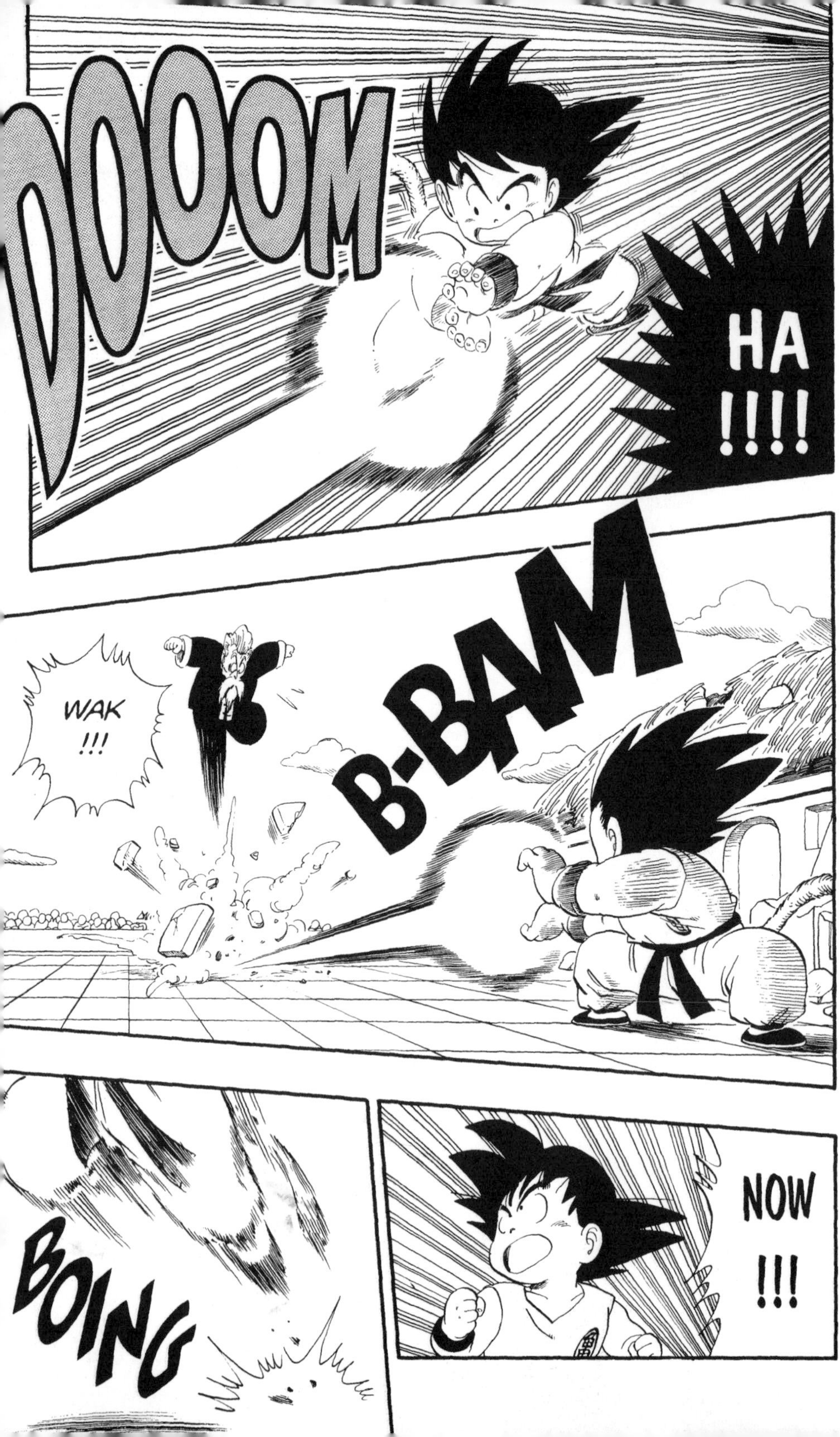
HA !!!!
DOOOM
B-BAM
WAK !!!
NOW !!!
BOING

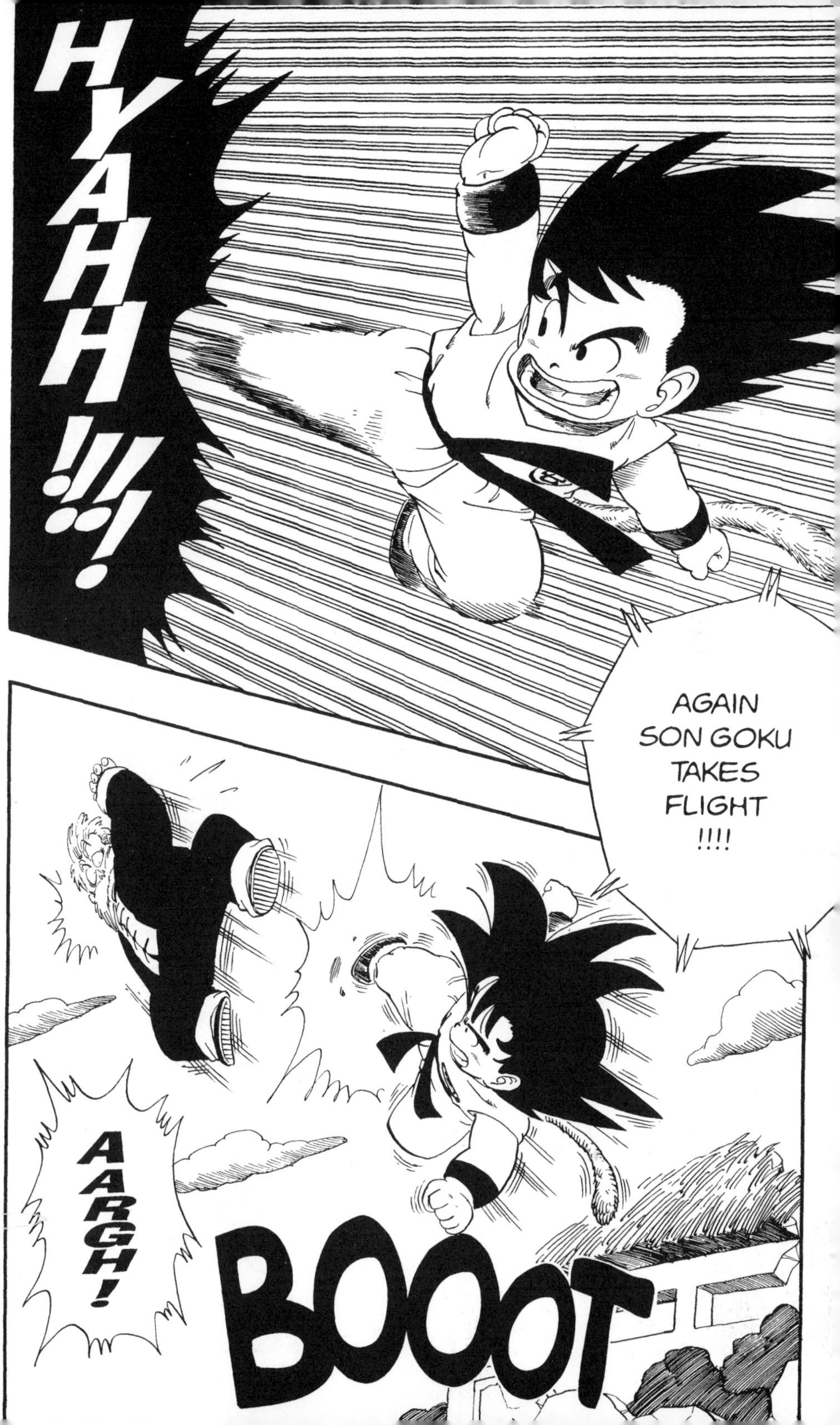
HYAHH!!!!
AGAIN SON GOKU TAKES FLIGHT !!!!
AARGH!
BOOOT

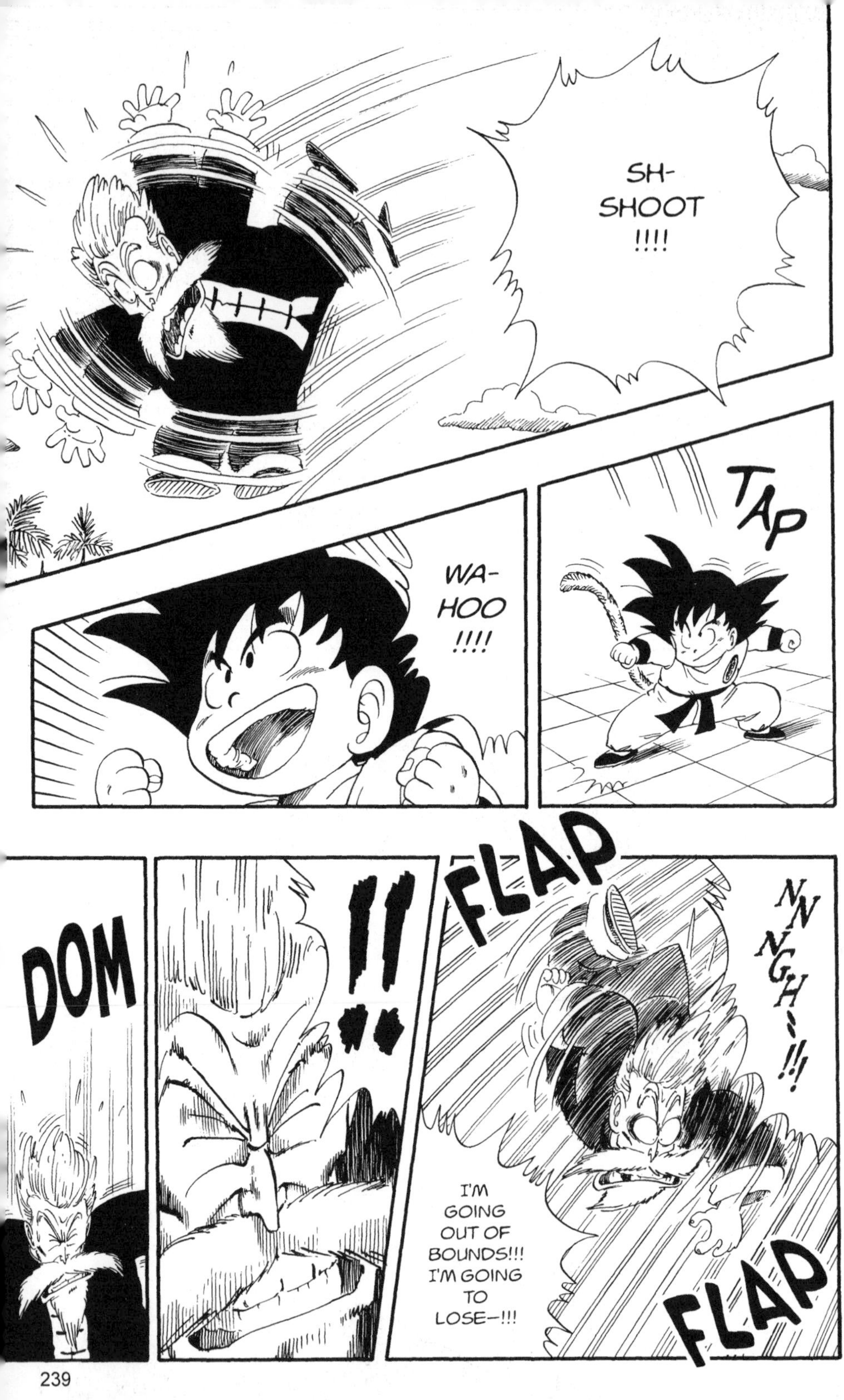
SH-SHOOT!!!!
TAP
WA-HOO!!!!
FLAP
NNNGH—!!!
I'M GOING OUT OF BOUNDS!!! I'M GOING TO LOSE—!!!
FLAP
!!
DOM

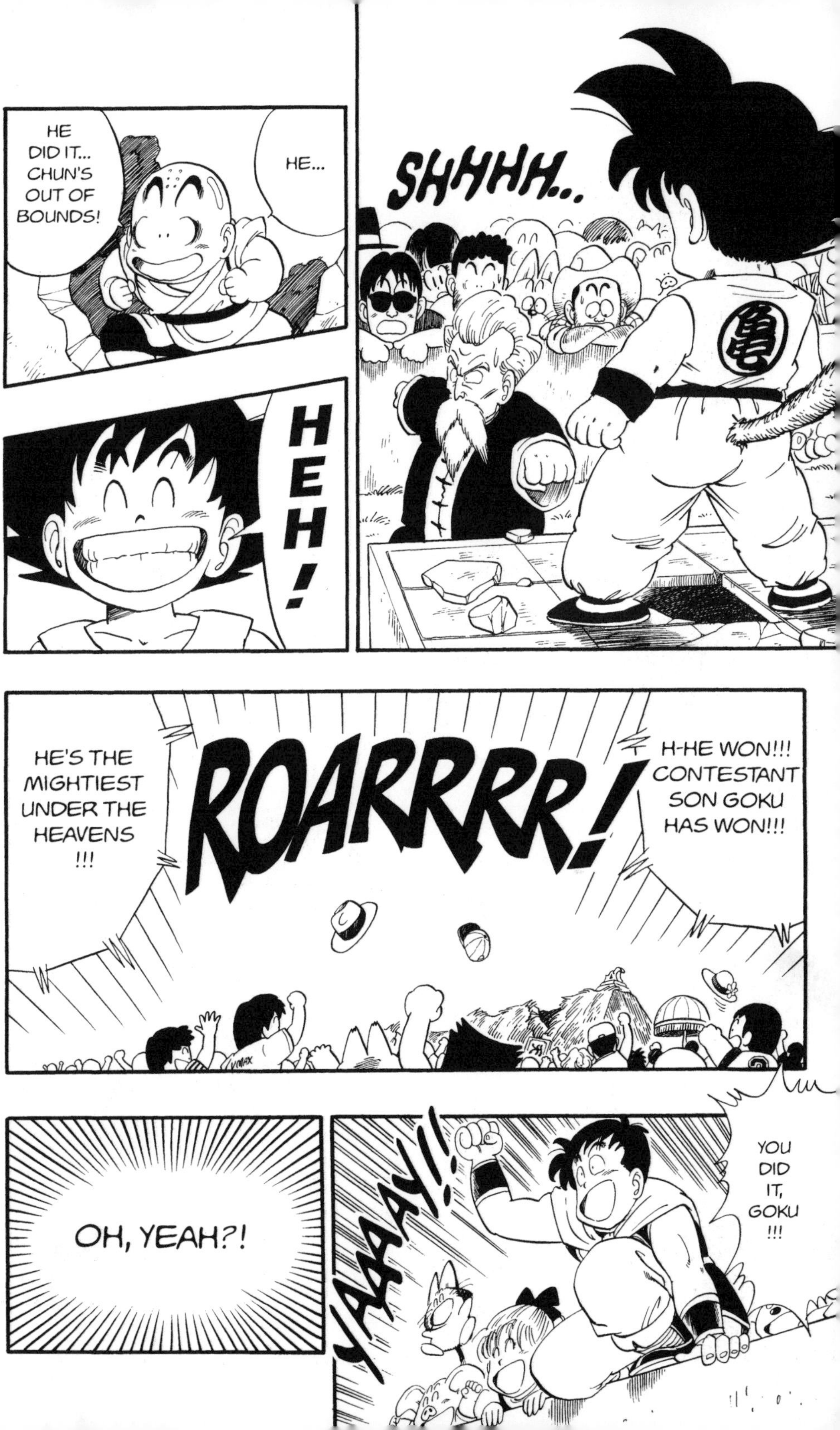
SHHHH...
HE...
HE DID IT... CHUN'S OUT OF BOUNDS!
HEH!
H-HE WON!!! CONTESTANT SON GOKU HAS WON!!!
ROARRRR!
HE'S THE MIGHTIEST UNDER THE HEAVENS !!!
YOU DID IT, GOKU !!!
YAAAAY!!
OH, YEAH?!

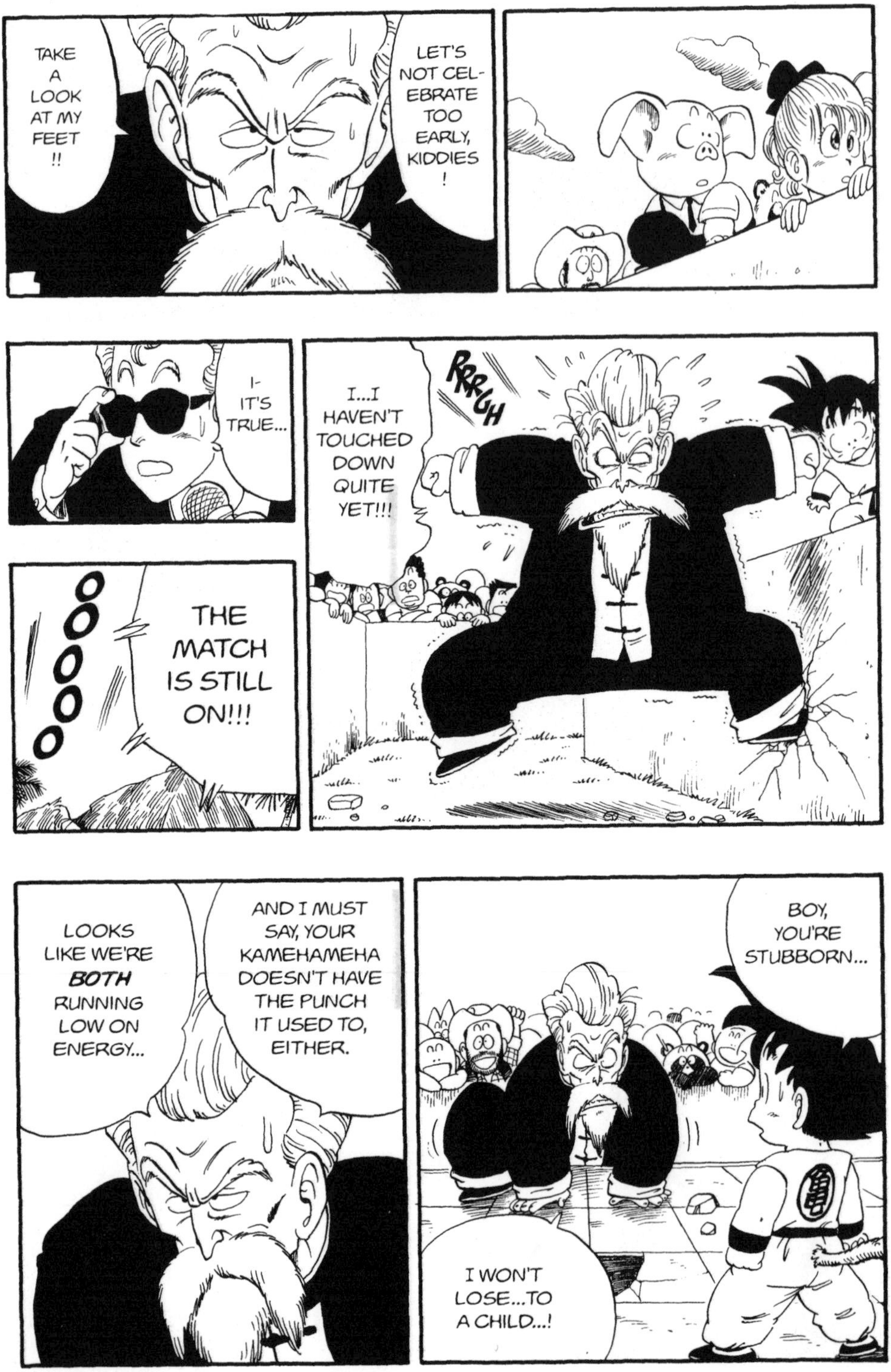
LET'S NOT CELEBRATE TOO EARLY, KIDDIES!
TAKE A LOOK AT MY FEET!!
RRRGH
I...I HAVEN'T TOUCHED DOWN QUITE YET!!!
I- IT'S TRUE...
OOOOOO
THE MATCH IS STILL ON!!!
BOY, YOU'RE STUBBORN...
I WON'T LOSE...TO A CHILD...!
AND I MUST SAY, YOUR KAMEHAMEHA DOESN'T HAVE THE PUNCH IT USED TO, EITHER.
LOOKS LIKE WE'RE **BOTH** RUNNING LOW ON ENERGY...

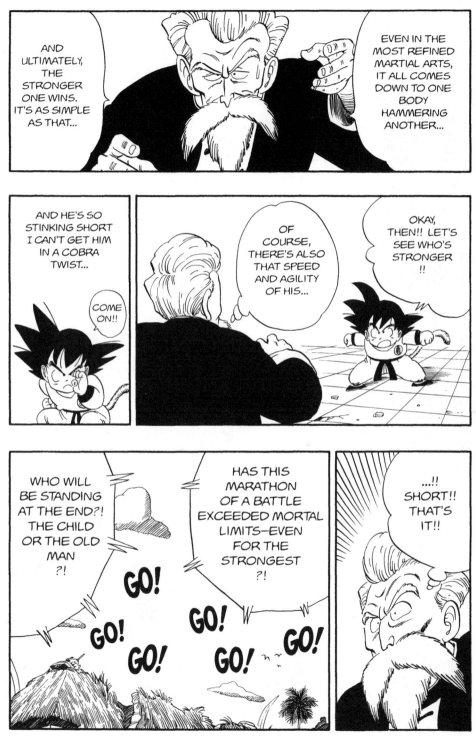

AND ULTIMATELY, THE STRONGER ONE WINS. IT'S AS SIMPLE AS THAT...

EVEN IN THE MOST REFINED MARTIAL ARTS, IT ALL COMES DOWN TO ONE BODY HAMMERING ANOTHER...

AND HE'S SO STINKING SHORT I CAN'T GET HIM IN A COBRA TWIST...

COME ON!!

OF COURSE, THERE'S ALSO THAT SPEED AND AGILITY OF HIS...

OKAY, THEN!! LET'S SEE WHO'S STRONGER !!

WHO WILL BE STANDING AT THE END?! THE CHILD OR THE OLD MAN ?!

HAS THIS MARATHON OF A BATTLE EXCEEDED MORTAL LIMITS—EVEN FOR THE STRONGEST ?!

GO! GO! GO! GO! GO! GO!

...!! SHORT!! THAT'S IT!!

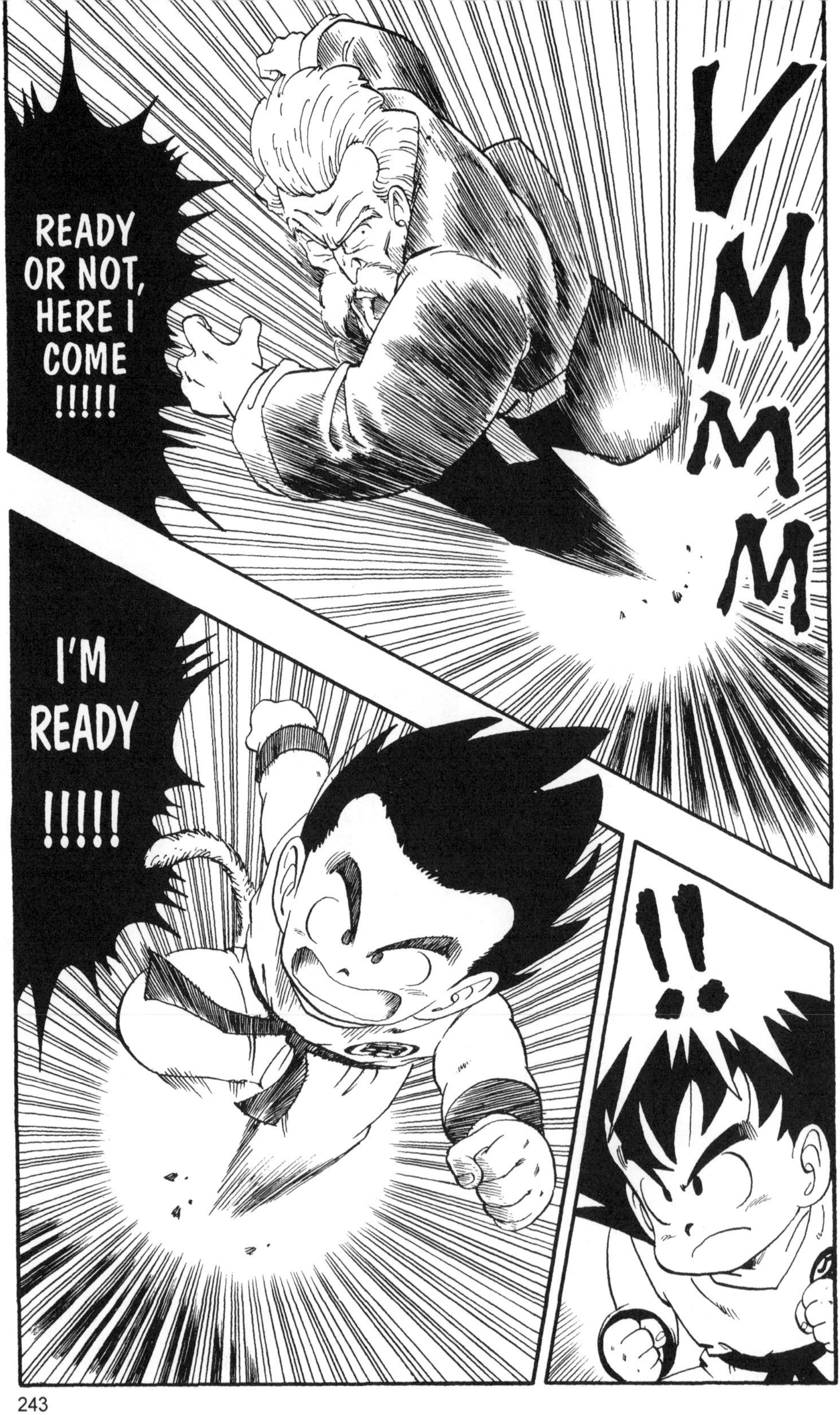
VMMM
READY OR NOT, HERE I COME !!!!!
I'M READY !!!!!
!!

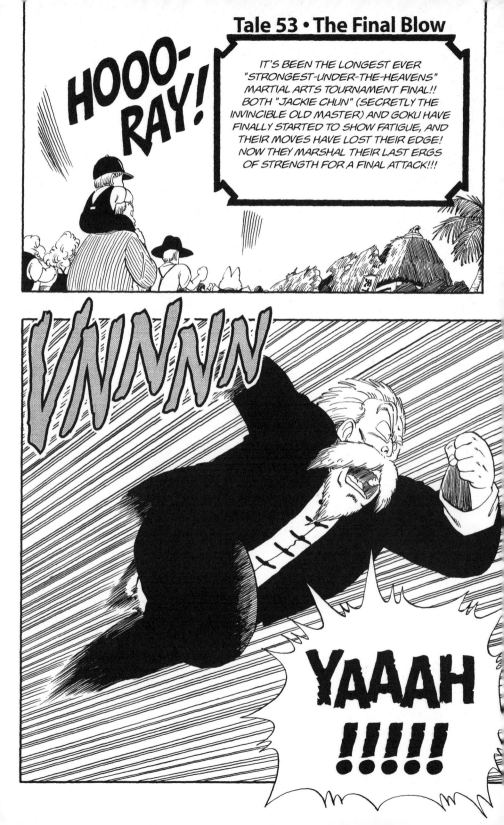

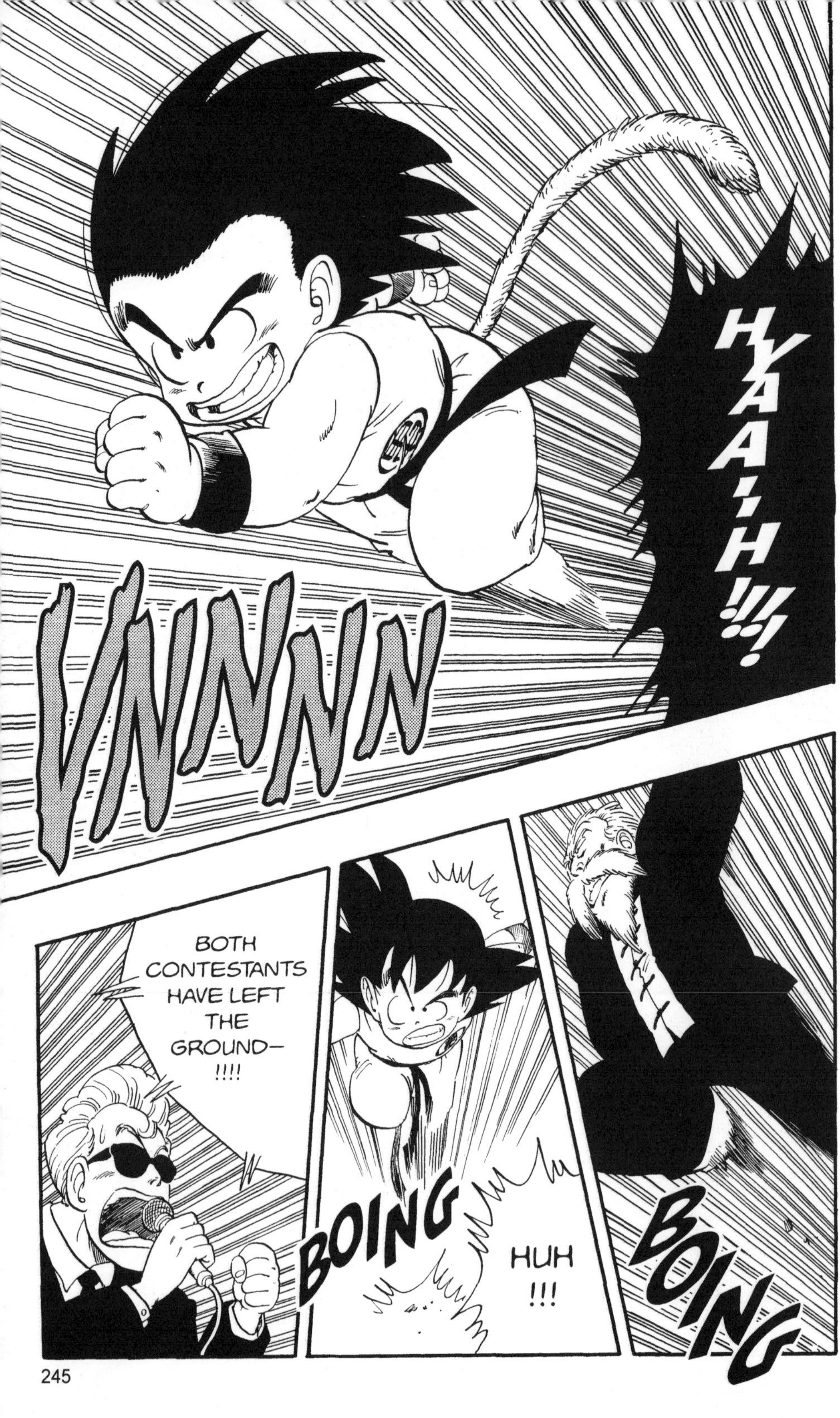
HYAAAH!!!!
VNNNN
BOING
BOING
HUH
!!!
BOTH CONTESTANTS HAVE LEFT THE GROUND—
!!!!

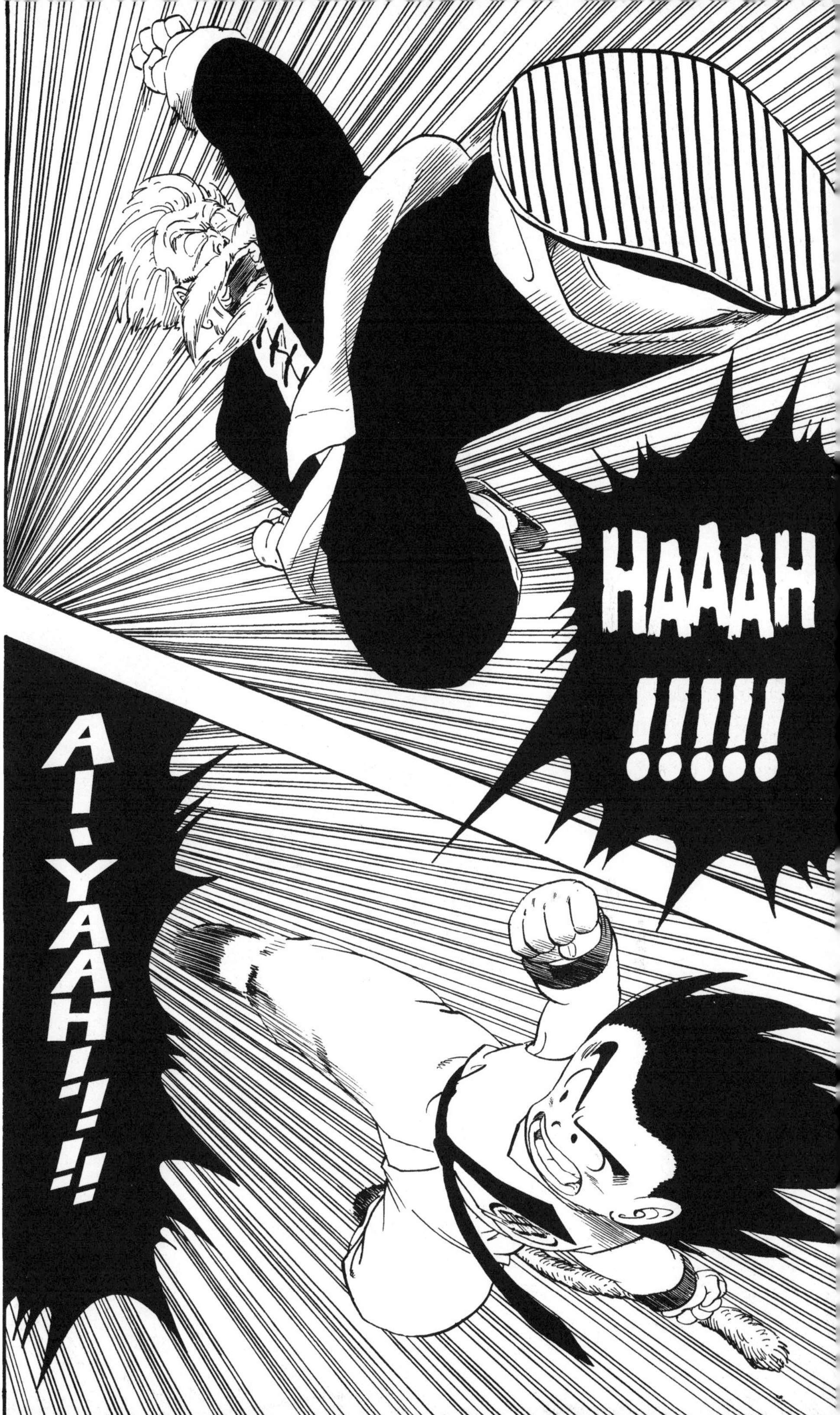
HAAAH!!!!!!
AI-YAAAH!!!!!

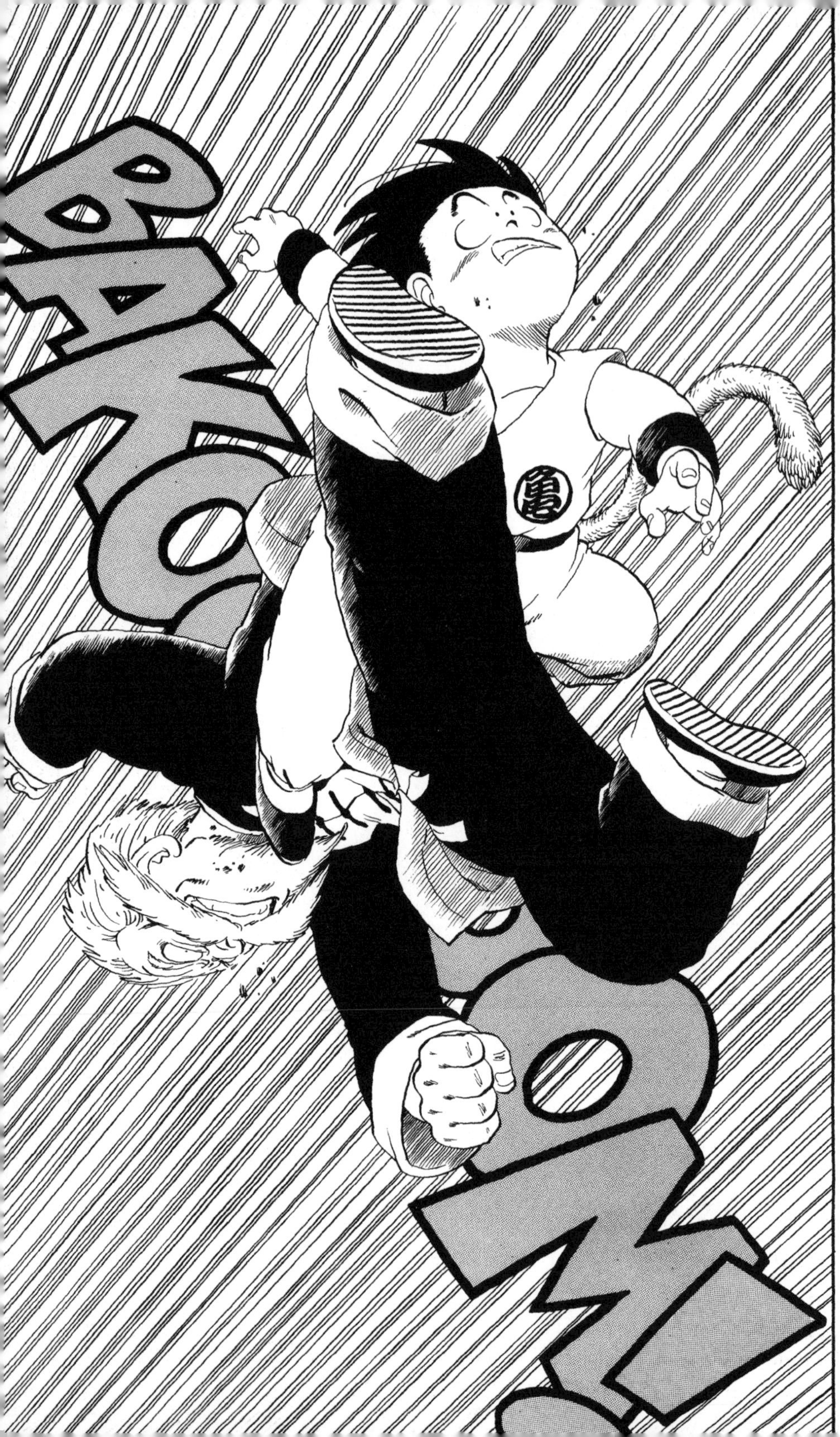
BAKOOM!

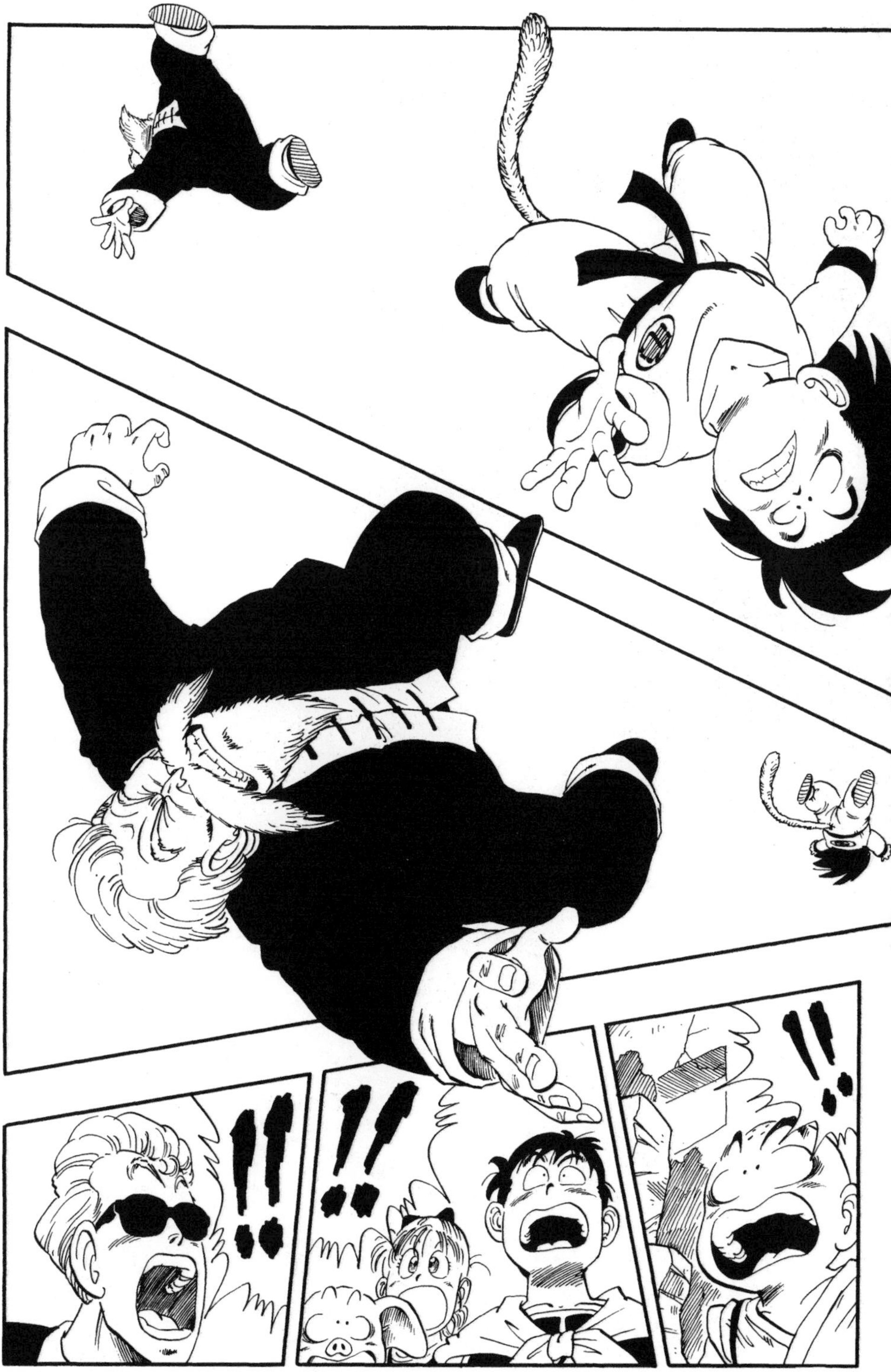
!!
!!
!!

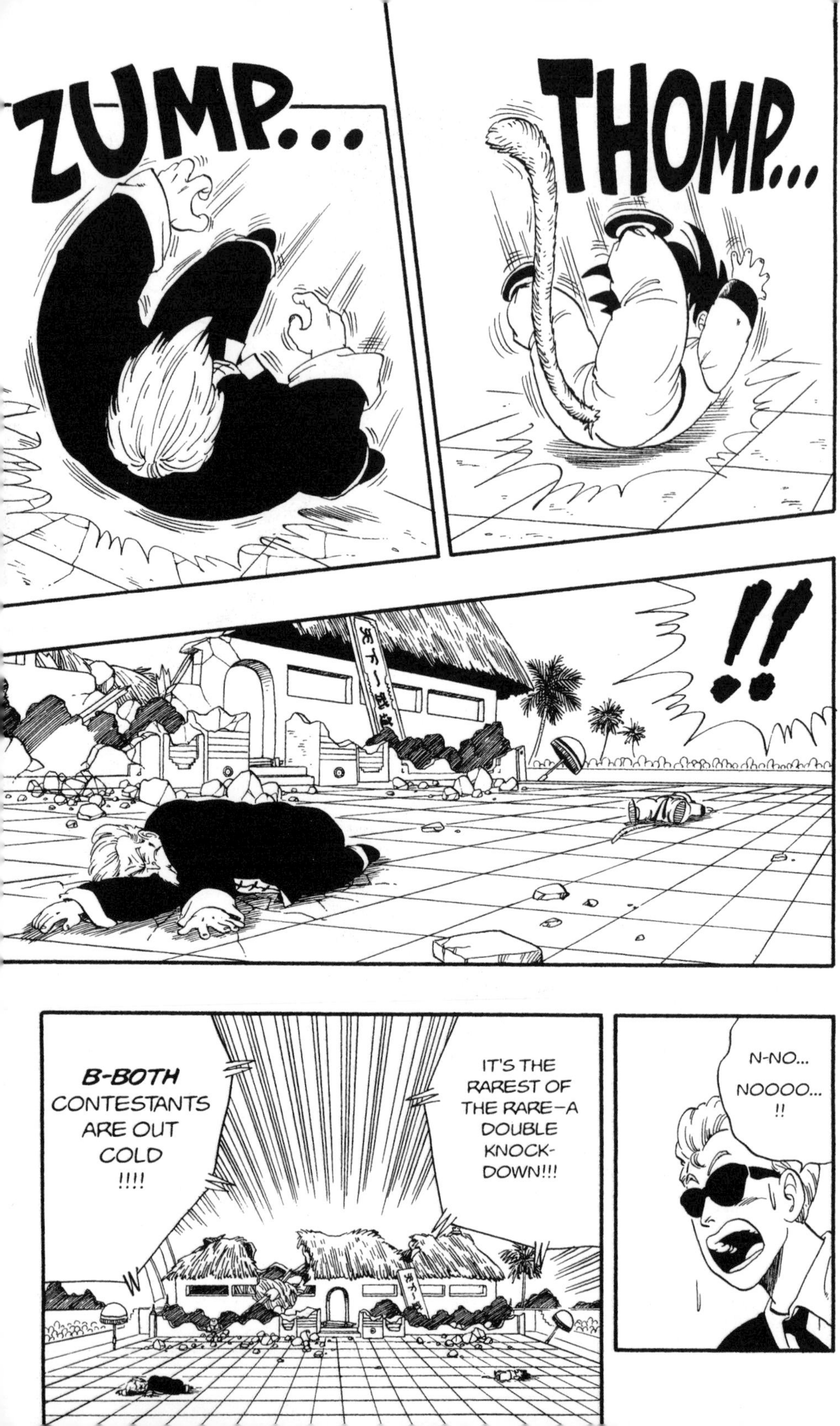
THOMP...
ZUMP...
!!
N-NO...
NOOOO...
!!
IT'S THE RAREST OF THE RARE—A DOUBLE KNOCK-DOWN!!!
B-BOTH CONTESTANTS ARE OUT COLD !!!!

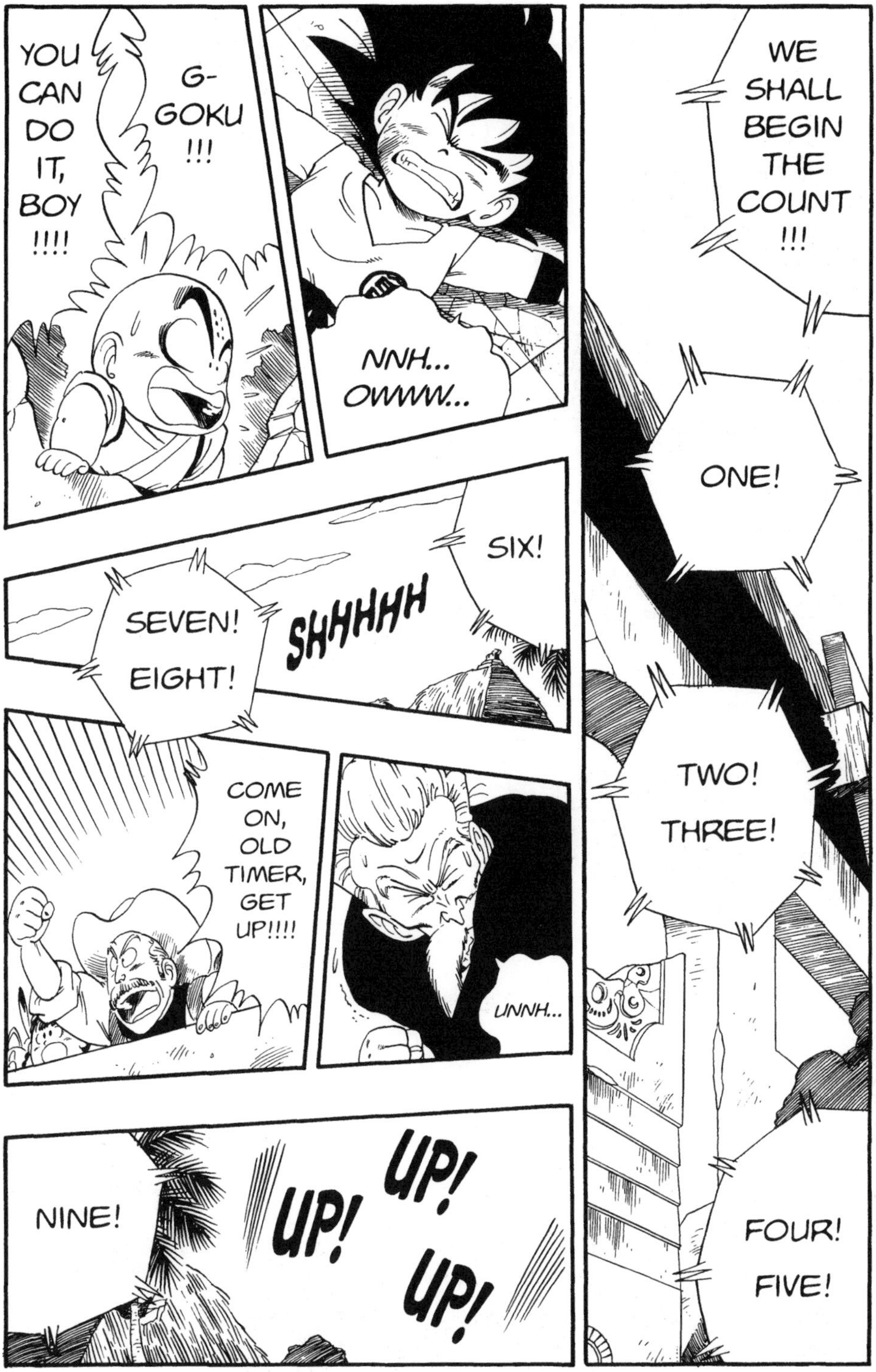
WE SHALL BEGIN THE COUNT!!!
ONE!
TWO! THREE!
FOUR! FIVE!
NNH... OWWW...
G-GOKU!!!
YOU CAN DO IT, BOY!!!!
SIX!
SHHHHH
SEVEN! EIGHT!
UNNH...
COME ON, OLD TIMER, GET UP!!!!
UP!
UP!
UP!
NINE!

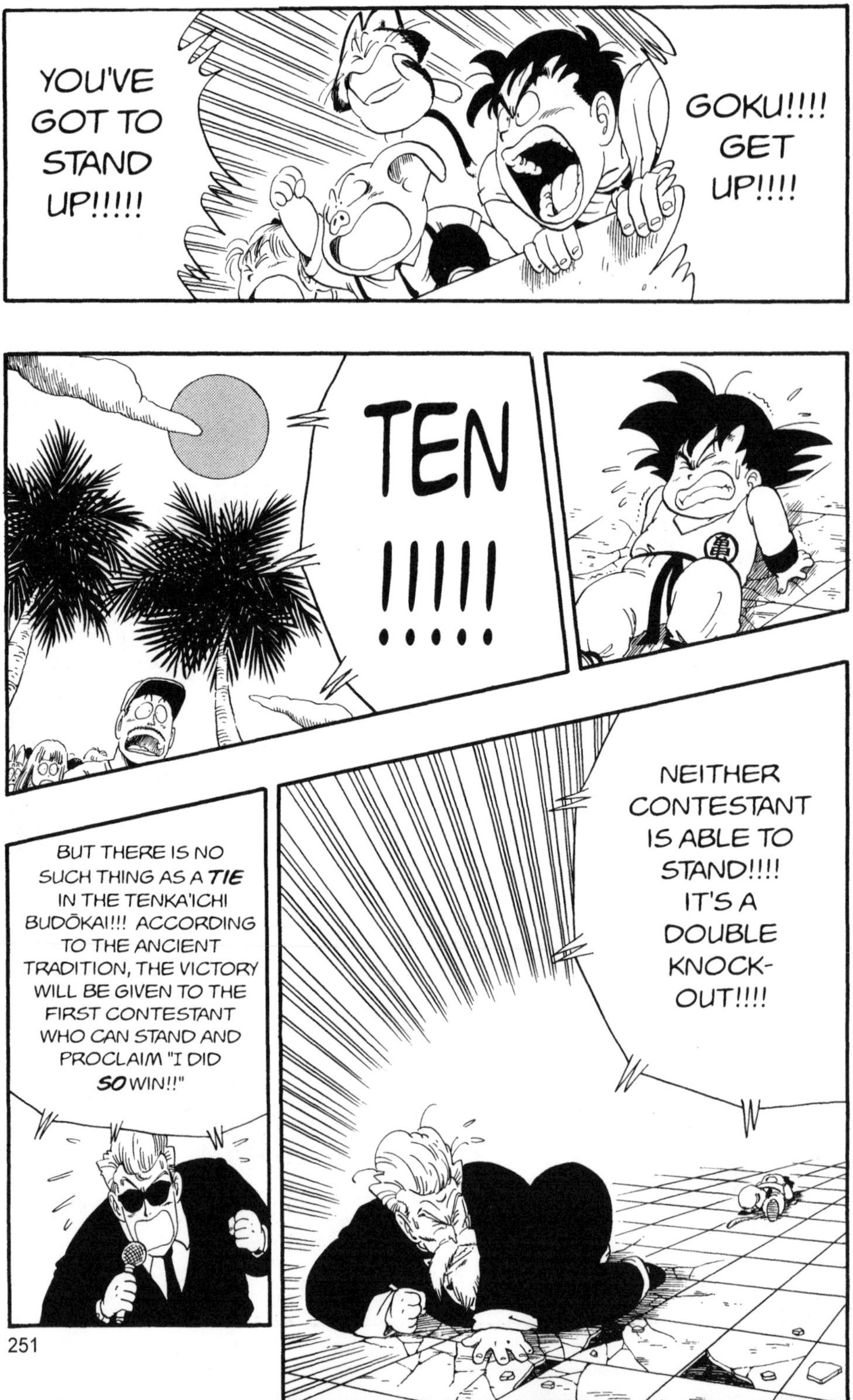
GOKU!!!! GET UP!!!!
YOU'VE GOT TO STAND UP!!!!!
TEN!!!!!
NEITHER CONTESTANT IS ABLE TO STAND!!!! IT'S A DOUBLE KNOCK-OUT!!!!
BUT THERE IS NO SUCH THING AS A ***TIE*** IN THE TENKA'ICHI BUDŌKAI!!! ACCORDING TO THE ANCIENT TRADITION, THE VICTORY WILL BE GIVEN TO THE FIRST CONTESTANT WHO CAN STAND AND PROCLAIM "I DID ***SO*** WIN!!"

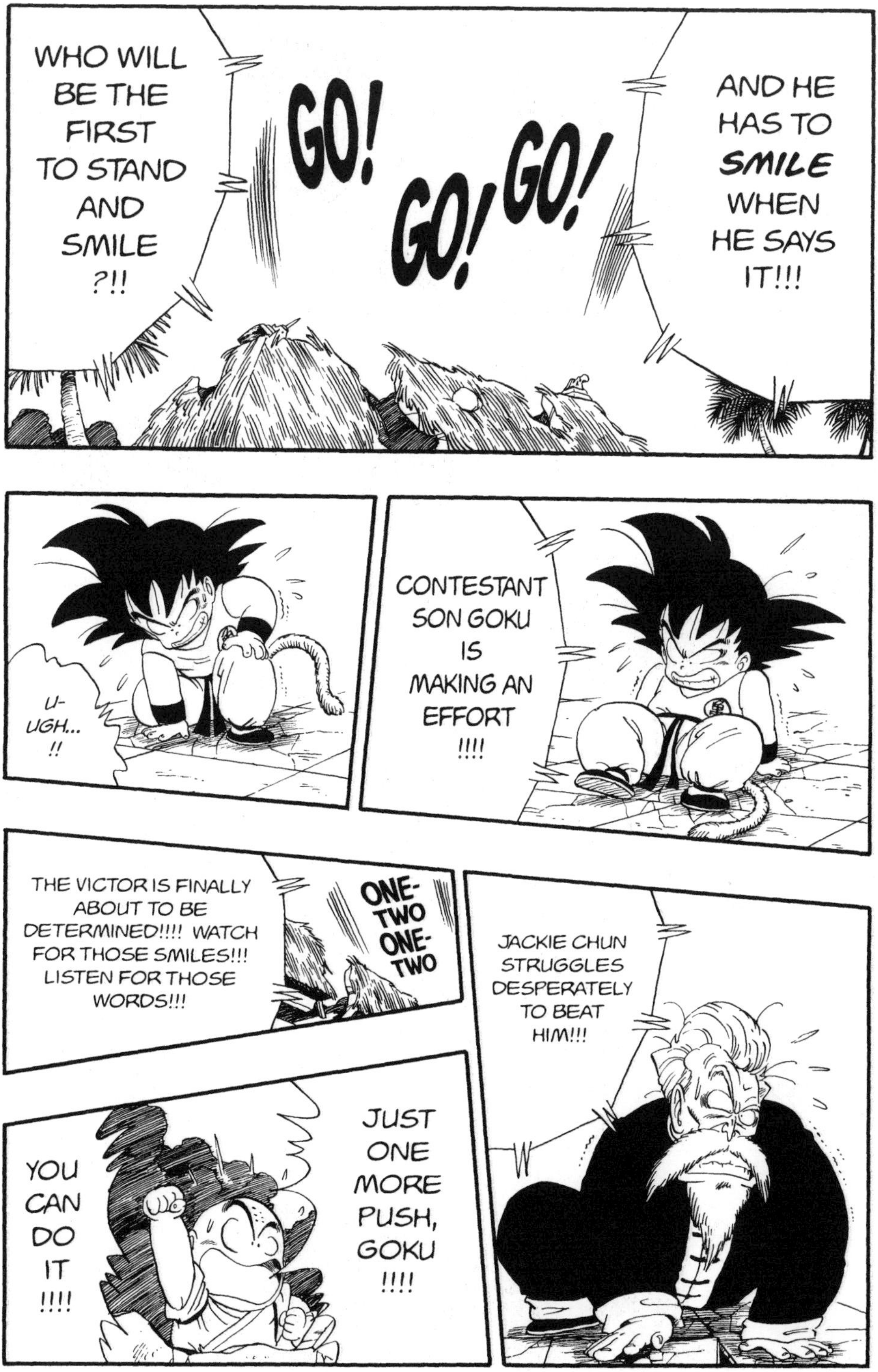
AND HE HAS TO SMILE WHEN HE SAYS IT!!!
GO! GO! GO!
WHO WILL BE THE FIRST TO STAND AND SMILE ?!!
CONTESTANT SON GOKU IS MAKING AN EFFORT !!!!
U-UGH... !!
JACKIE CHUN STRUGGLES DESPERATELY TO BEAT HIM!!!
ONE-TWO ONE-TWO
THE VICTOR IS FINALLY ABOUT TO BE DETERMINED!!!! WATCH FOR THOSE SMILES!!! LISTEN FOR THOSE WORDS!!!
JUST ONE MORE PUSH, GOKU !!!!
YOU CAN DO IT !!!!

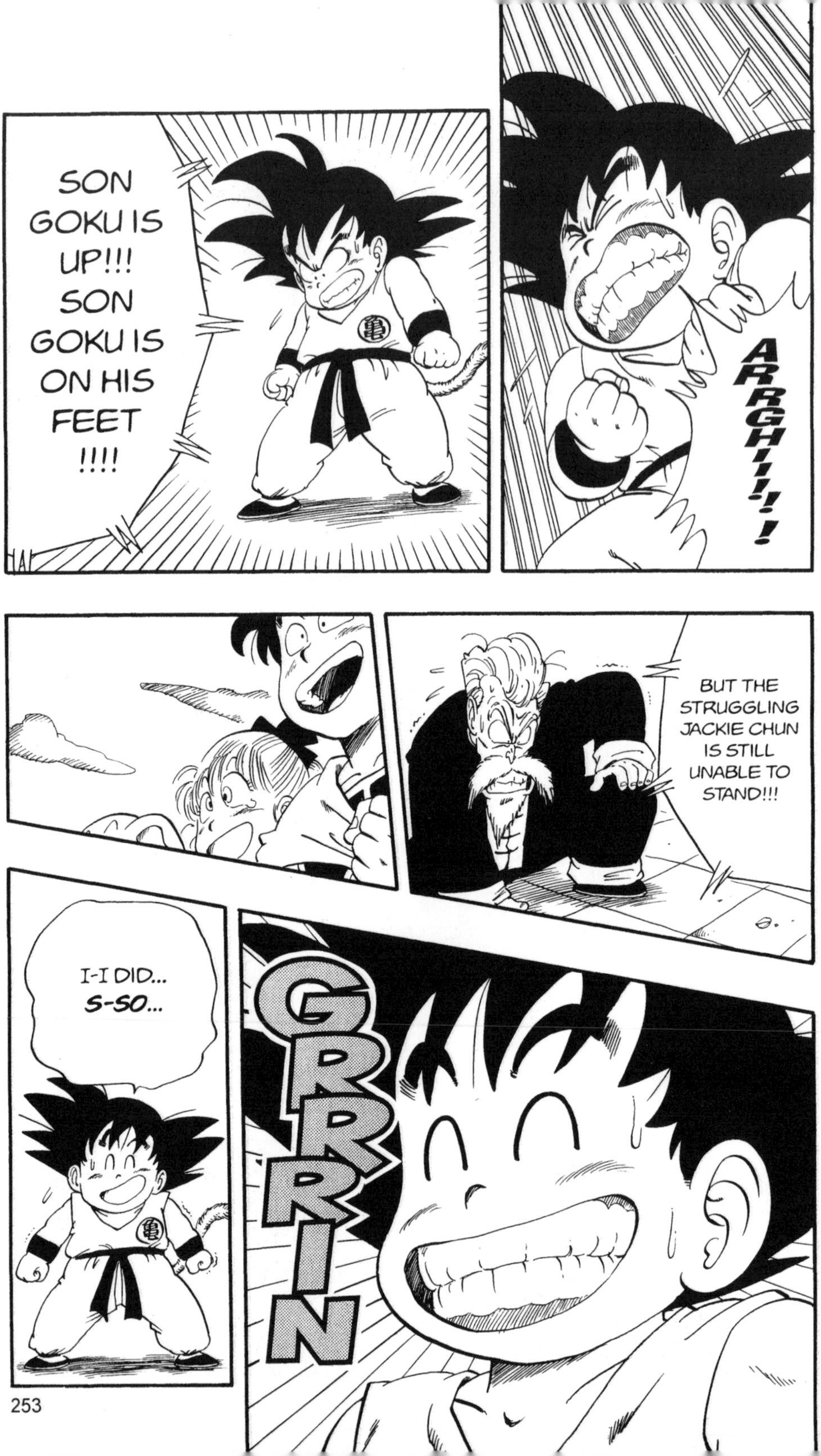
ARRGH!!!!!
SON GOKU IS UP!!! SON GOKU IS ON HIS FEET !!!!
BUT THE STRUGGLING JACKIE CHUN IS STILL UNABLE TO STAND!!!
GRRRIN
I-I DID... *S-SO*...

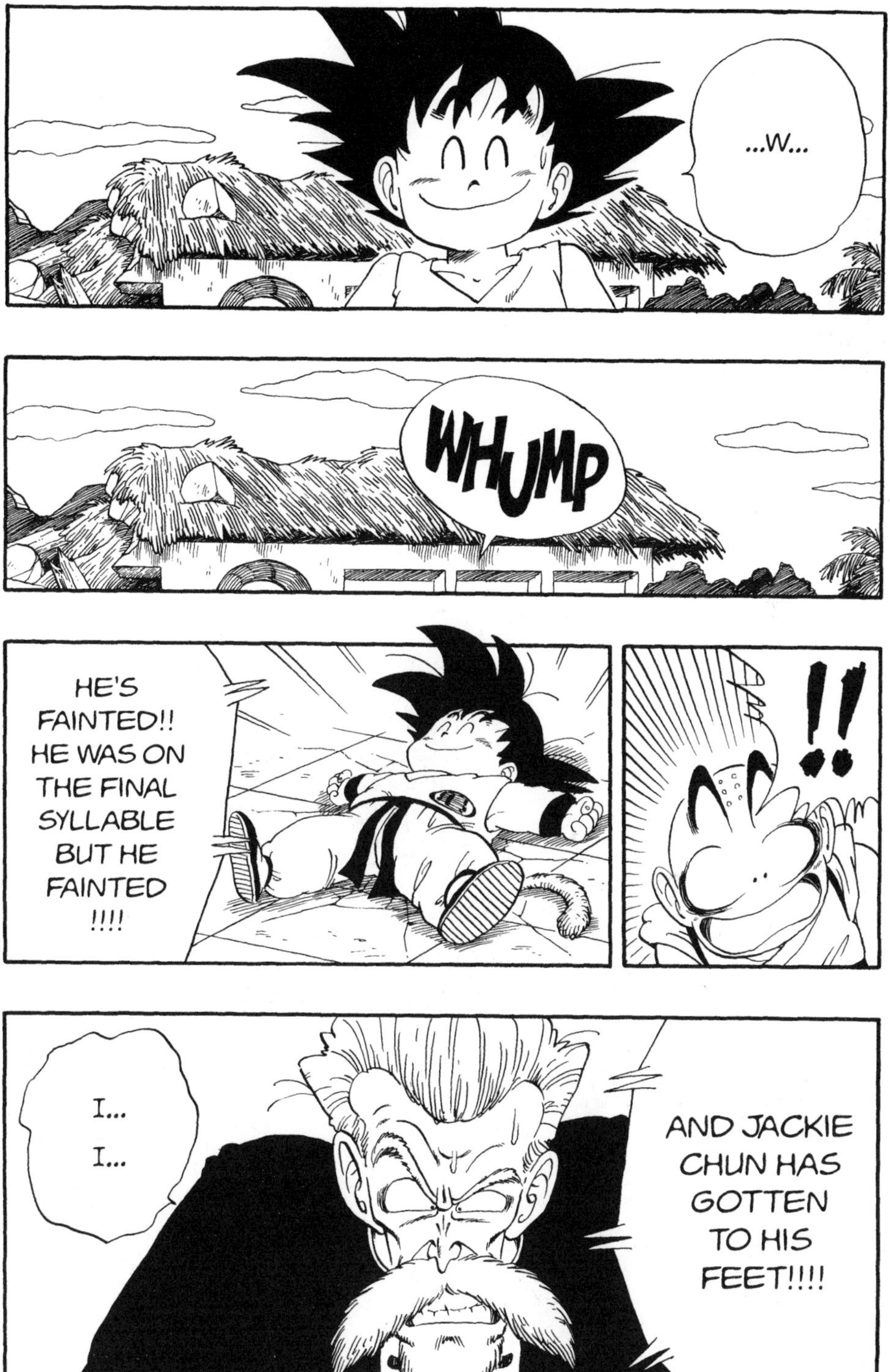
...W...
WHUMP
!!
HE'S FAINTED!! HE WAS ON THE FINAL SYLLABLE BUT HE FAINTED !!!!
AND JACKIE CHUN HAS GOTTEN TO HIS FEET!!!!
I... I...

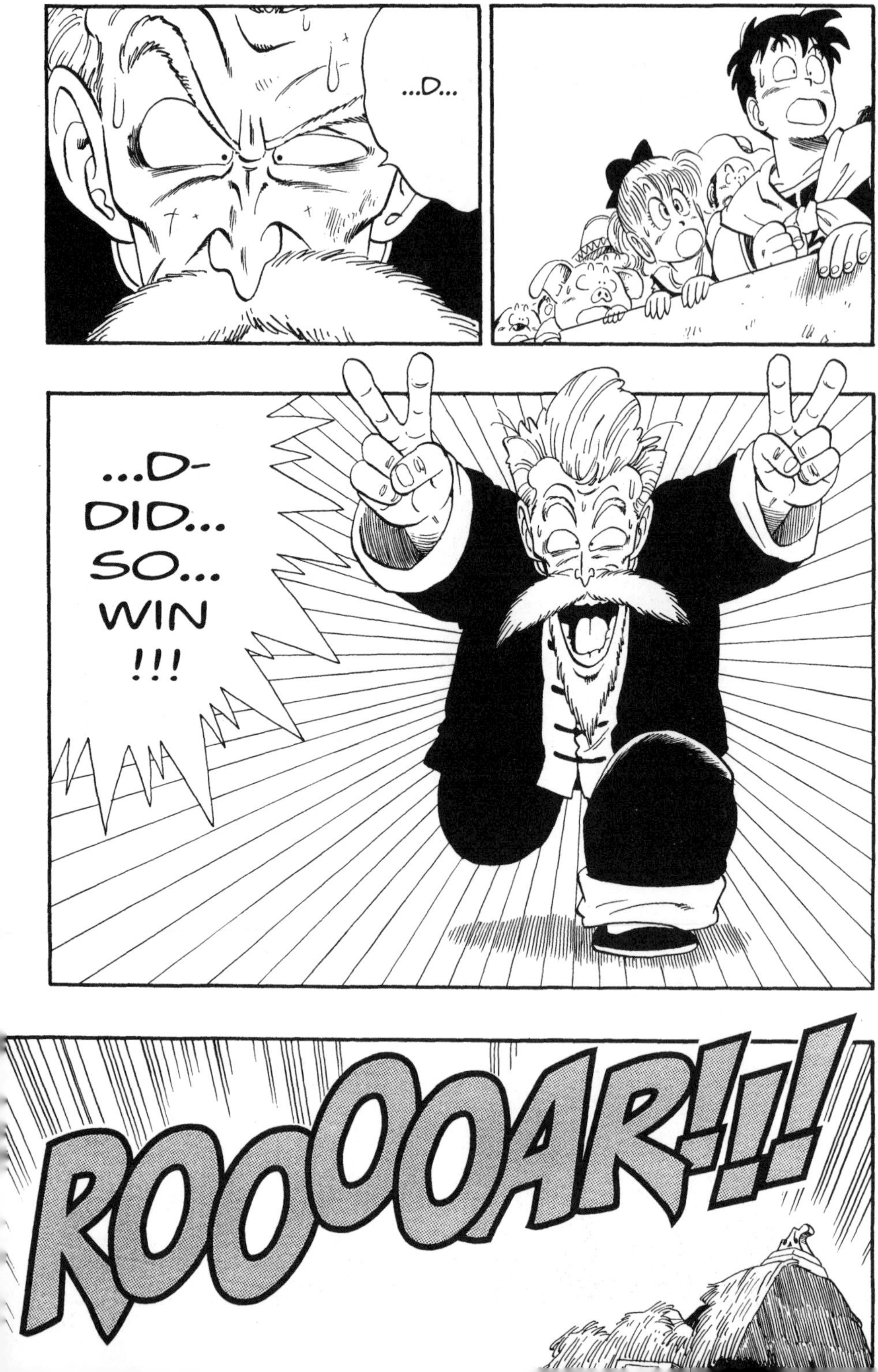
...D...
...D-
DID...
SO...
WIN
!!!
ROOOOAR!!!

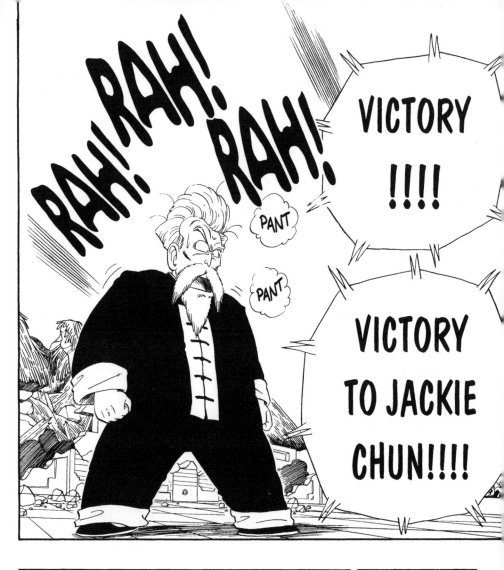

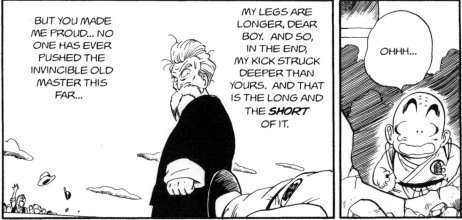

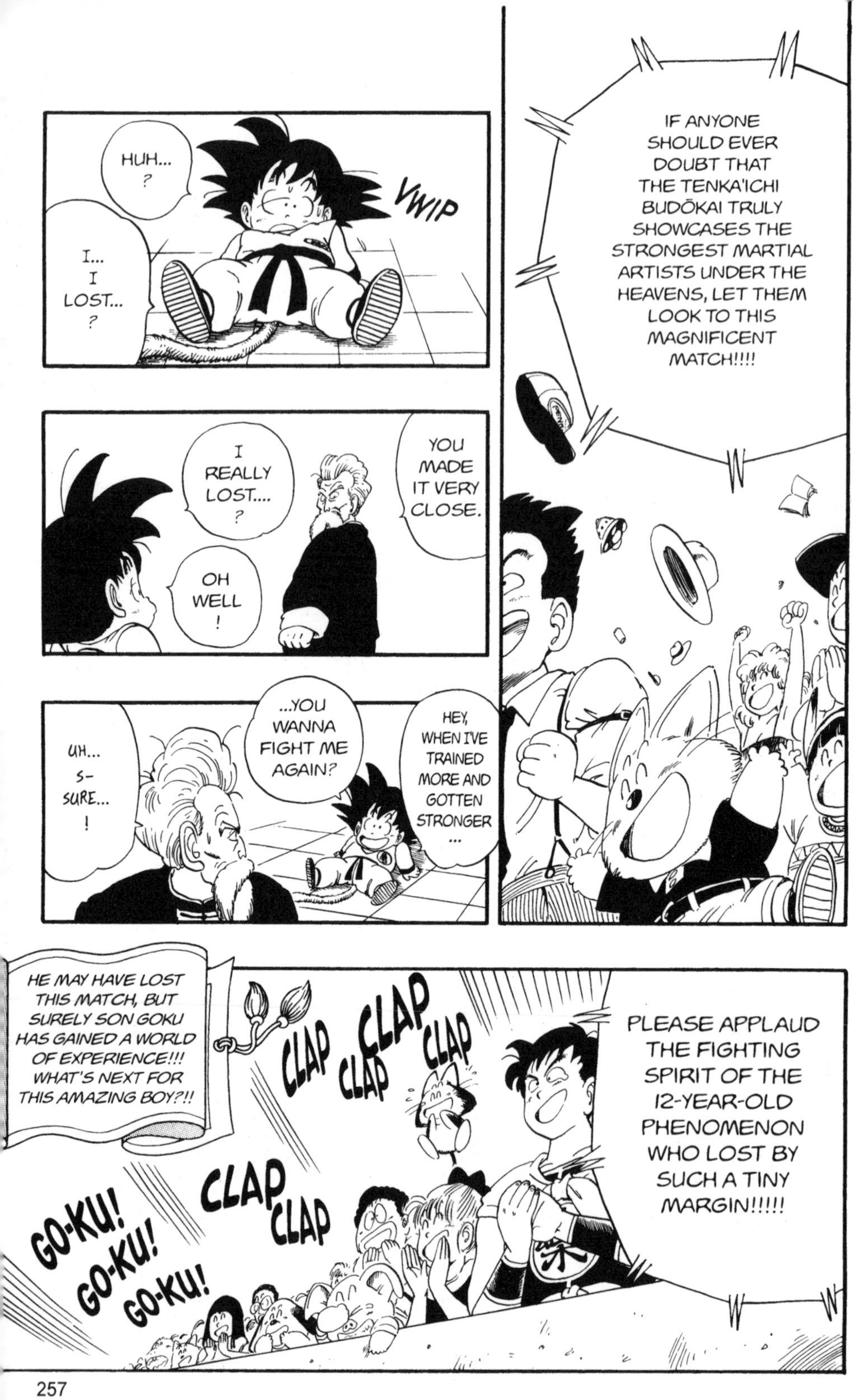
IF ANYONE SHOULD EVER DOUBT THAT THE TENKA'ICHI BUDŌKAI TRULY SHOWCASES THE STRONGEST MARTIAL ARTISTS UNDER THE HEAVENS, LET THEM LOOK TO THIS MAGNIFICENT MATCH!!!!
VWIP
HUH...?
I... I LOST...?
YOU MADE IT VERY CLOSE.
I REALLY LOST....?
OH WELL!
HEY, WHEN I'VE TRAINED MORE AND GOTTEN STRONGER...
...YOU WANNA FIGHT ME AGAIN?
UH... S-SURE...!
PLEASE APPLAUD THE FIGHTING SPIRIT OF THE 12-YEAR-OLD PHENOMENON WHO LOST BY SUCH A TINY MARGIN!!!!!
CLAP CLAP CLAP CLAP
HE MAY HAVE LOST THIS MATCH, BUT SURELY SON GOKU HAS GAINED A WORLD OF EXPERIENCE!!! WHAT'S NEXT FOR THIS AMAZING BOY?!!
CLAP CLAP
GO-KU! GO-KU! GO-KU!

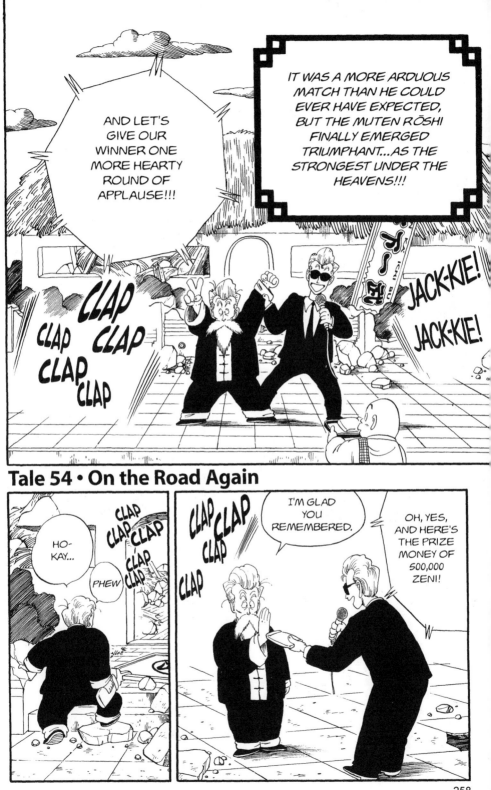

Tale 54 • On the Road Again

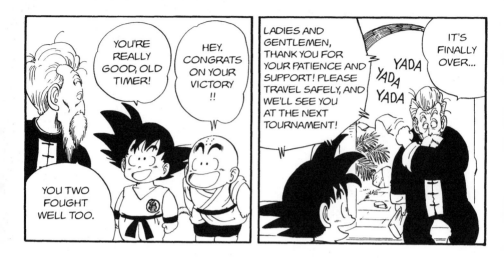

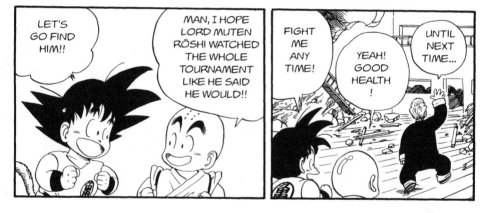

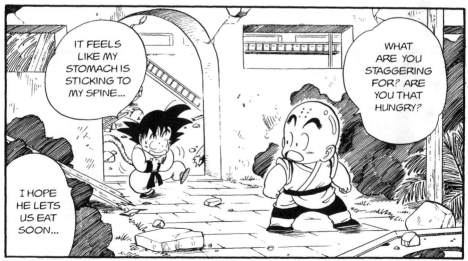

259

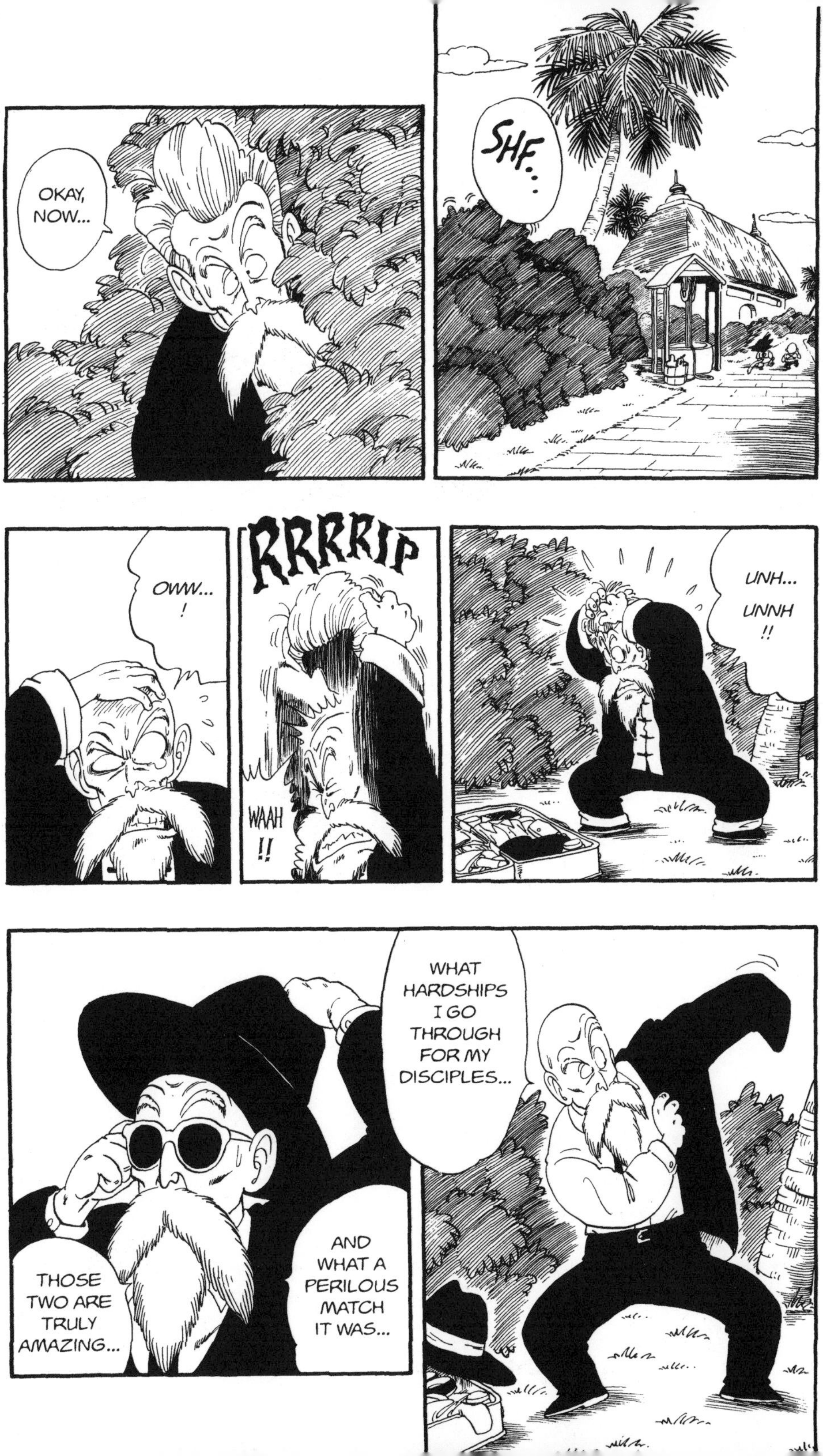
SHF...
OKAY, NOW...
UNH... UNNH!!
RRRRIP
WAAH!!
OWW...!
WHAT HARDSHIPS I GO THROUGH FOR MY DISCIPLES...
AND WHAT A PERILOUS MATCH IT WAS...
THOSE TWO ARE TRULY AMAZING...

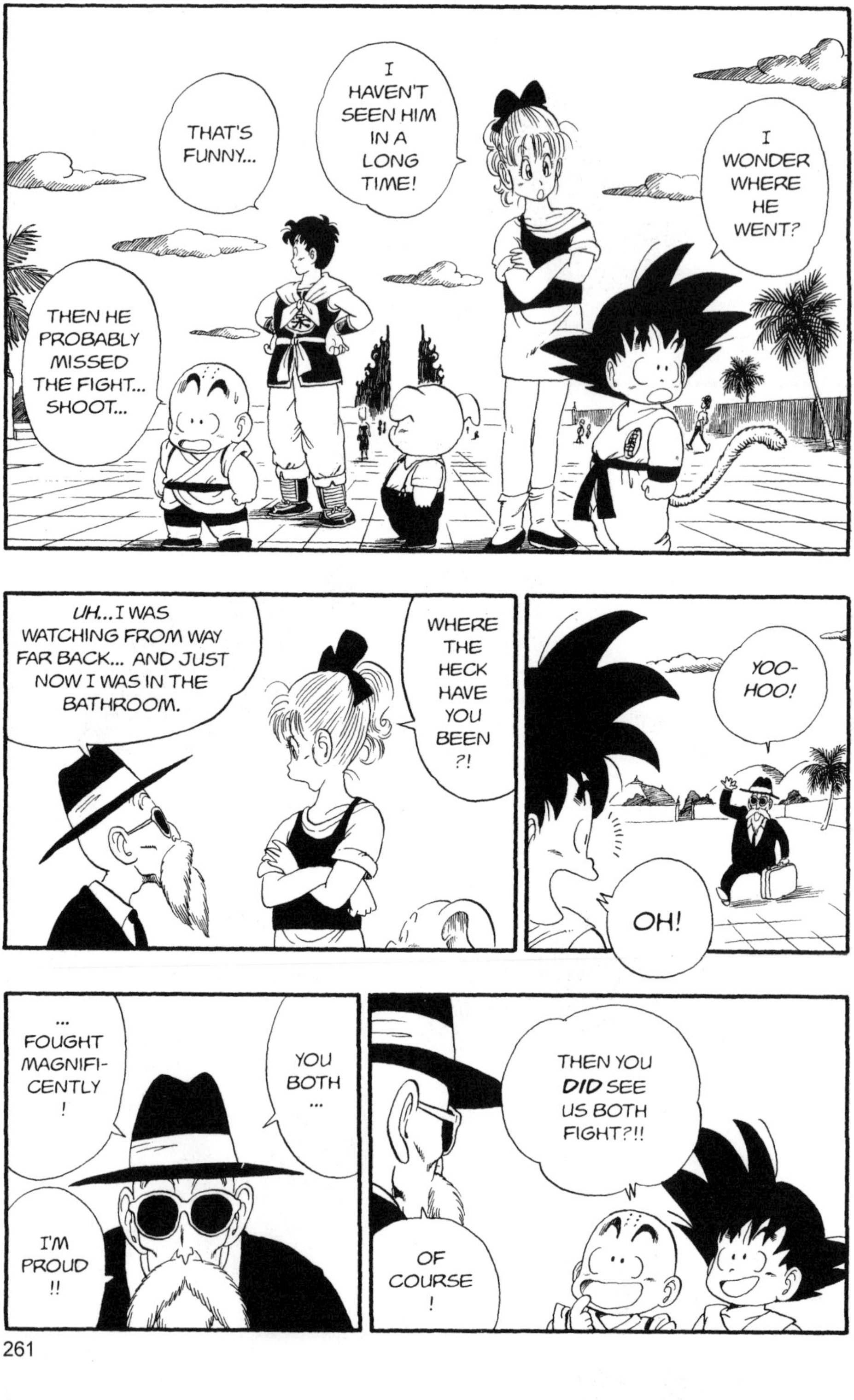
I WONDER WHERE HE WENT?
I HAVEN'T SEEN HIM IN A LONG TIME!
THAT'S FUNNY...
THEN HE PROBABLY MISSED THE FIGHT... SHOOT...
YOO-HOO!
OH!
WHERE THE HECK HAVE YOU BEEN ?!
UH...I WAS WATCHING FROM WAY FAR BACK... AND JUST NOW I WAS IN THE BATHROOM.
THEN YOU DID SEE US BOTH FIGHT?!!
OF COURSE !
YOU BOTH ...
... FOUGHT MAGNIFI-CENTLY !
I'M PROUD !!

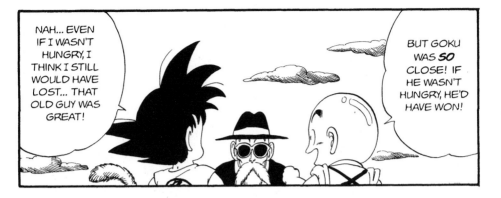

NAH... EVEN IF I WASN'T HUNGRY, I THINK I STILL WOULD HAVE LOST... THAT OLD GUY WAS GREAT!

BUT GOKU WAS **SO** CLOSE! IF HE WASN'T HUNGRY, HE'D HAVE WON!

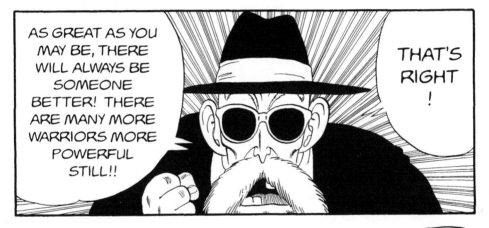

AS GREAT AS YOU MAY BE, THERE WILL ALWAYS BE SOMEONE BETTER! THERE ARE MANY MORE WARRIORS MORE POWERFUL STILL!!

THAT'S RIGHT!

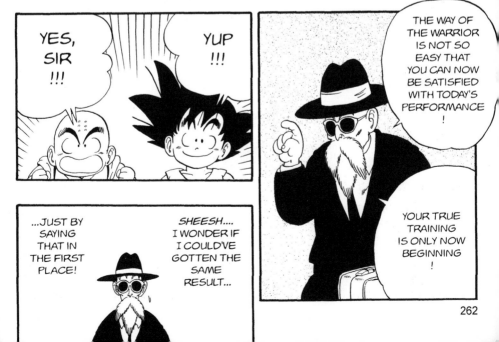

YES, SIR !!!

YUP !!!

THE WAY OF THE WARRIOR IS NOT SO EASY THAT YOU CAN NOW BE SATISFIED WITH TODAY'S PERFORMANCE !

...JUST BY SAYING THAT IN THE FIRST PLACE!

SHEESH.... I WONDER IF I COULD'VE GOTTEN THE SAME RESULT...

YOUR TRUE TRAINING IS ONLY NOW BEGINNING !

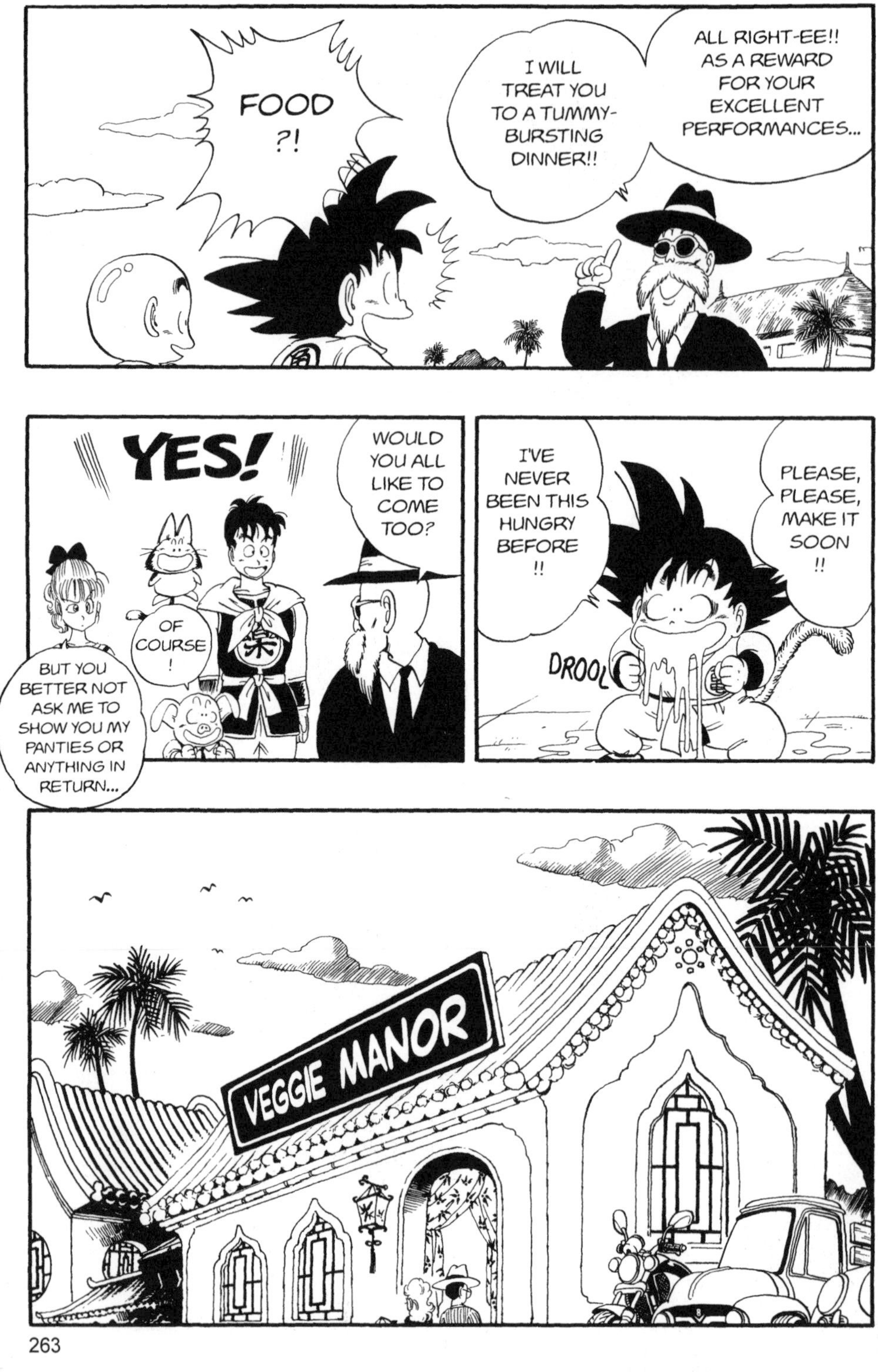
ALL RIGHT-EE!! AS A REWARD FOR YOUR EXCELLENT PERFORMANCES...
I WILL TREAT YOU TO A TUMMY-BURSTING DINNER!!
FOOD ?!
PLEASE, PLEASE, MAKE IT SOON !!
I'VE NEVER BEEN THIS HUNGRY BEFORE !!
DROOL
WOULD YOU ALL LIKE TO COME TOO?
YES!
OF COURSE !
BUT YOU BETTER NOT ASK ME TO SHOW YOU MY PANTIES OR ANYTHING IN RETURN...
VEGGIE MANOR

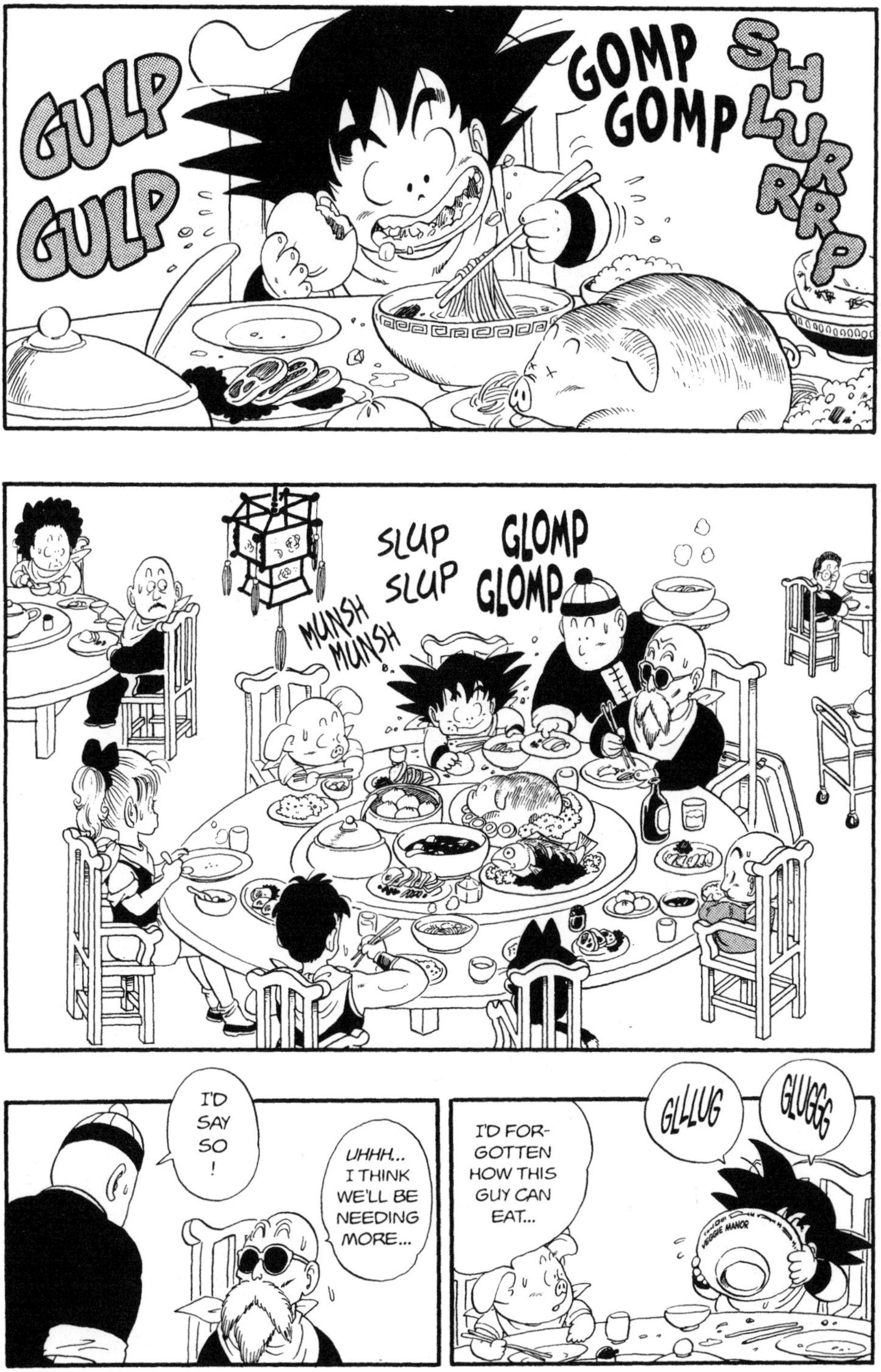
SHLURRRP
GOMP GOMP
GULP GULP
GLOMP GLOMP
SLUP SLUP
MUNSH MUNSH
GLUGGG
GLLLUG
I'D FOR-GOTTEN HOW THIS GUY CAN EAT...
VEGGIE MANOR
I'D SAY SO!
UHHH... I THINK WE'LL BE NEEDING MORE...

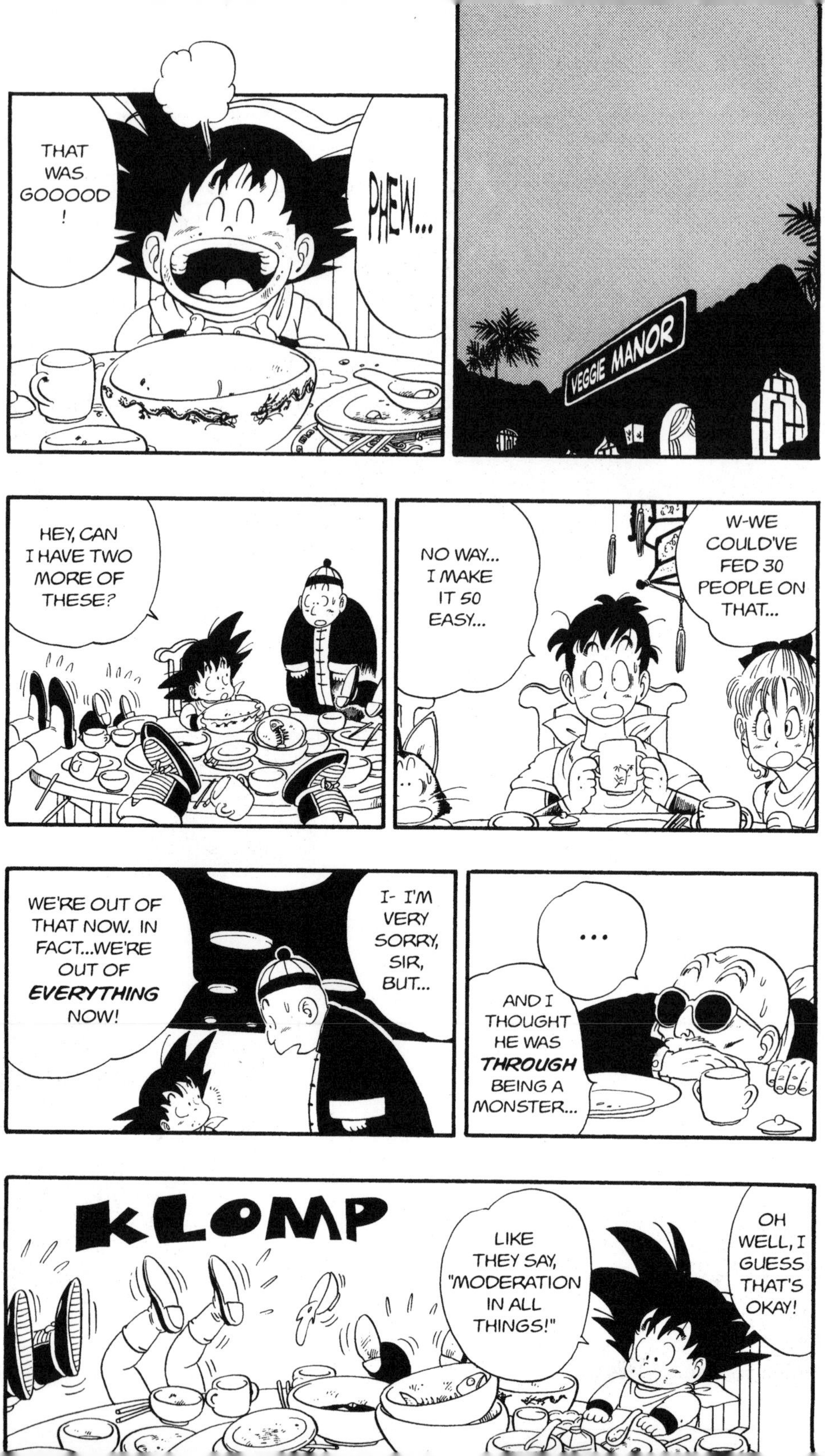
VEGGIE MANOR
PHEW...
THAT WAS GOOOOD!
W-WE COULD'VE FED 30 PEOPLE ON THAT...
NO WAY... I MAKE IT 50 EASY...
HEY, CAN I HAVE TWO MORE OF THESE?
...
AND I THOUGHT HE WAS **THROUGH** BEING A MONSTER...
I- I'M VERY SORRY, SIR, BUT...
WE'RE OUT OF THAT NOW. IN FACT...WE'RE OUT OF ***EVERYTHING*** NOW!
OH WELL, I GUESS THAT'S OKAY!
LIKE THEY SAY, "MODERATION IN ALL THINGS!"
KLOMP

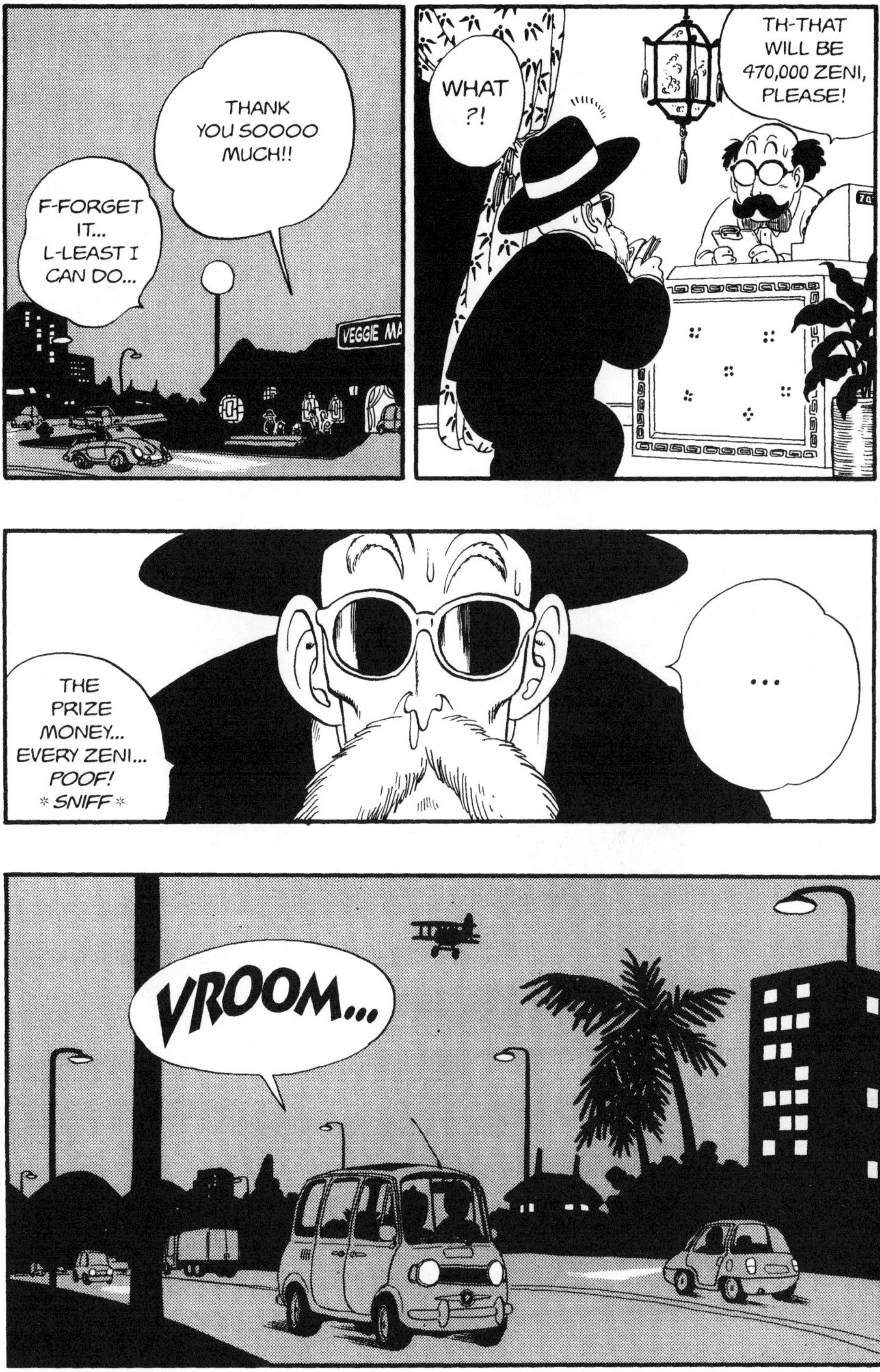
TH-THAT WILL BE 470,000 ZENI, PLEASE!
WHAT?!
THANK YOU SOOOO MUCH!!
F-FORGET IT... L-LEAST I CAN DO...
VEGGIE MA
...
THE PRIZE MONEY... EVERY ZENI... POOF! *SNIFF*
VROOM...

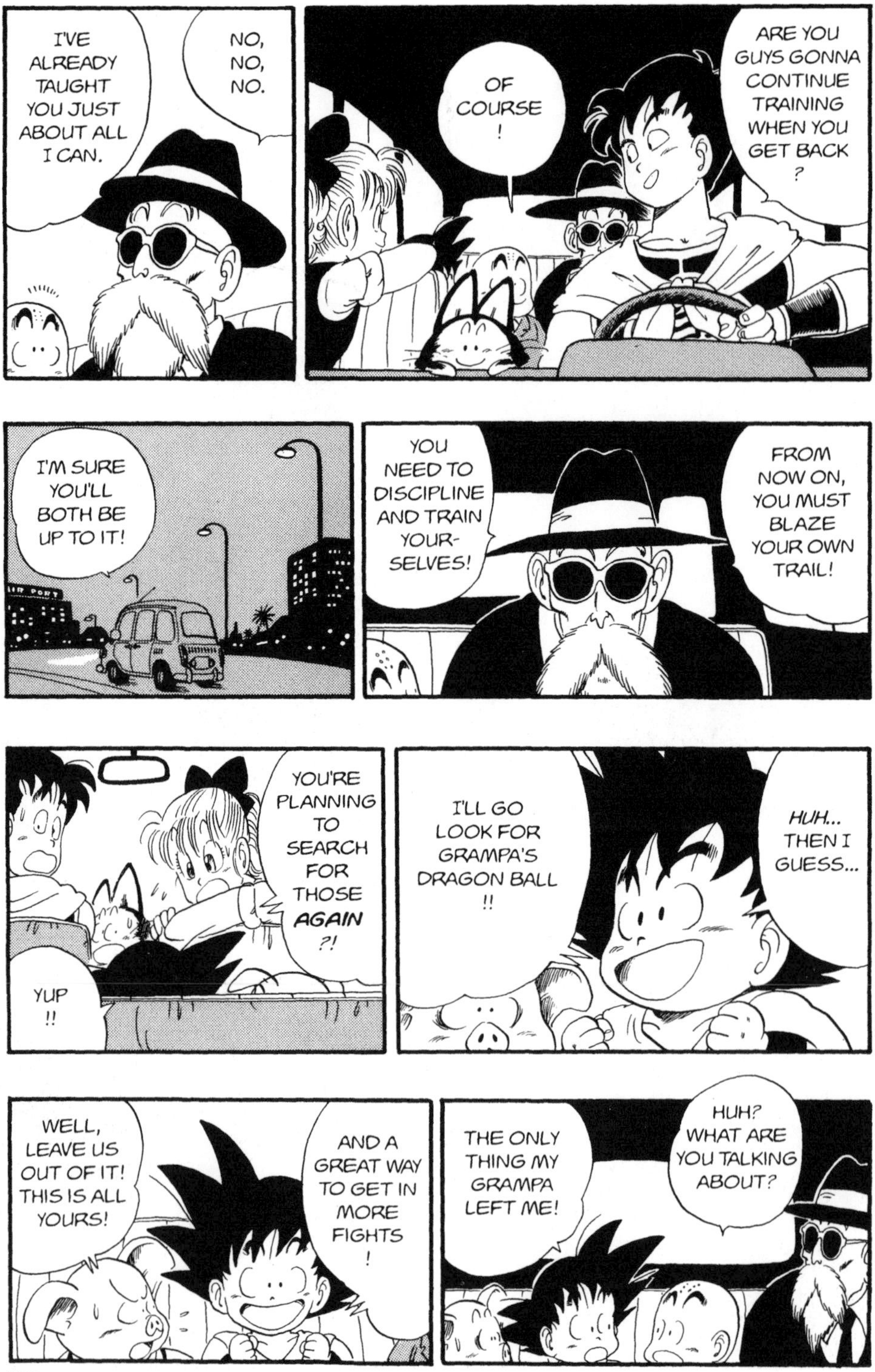
ARE YOU GUYS GONNA CONTINUE TRAINING WHEN YOU GET BACK?
OF COURSE!
NO, NO, NO.
I'VE ALREADY TAUGHT YOU JUST ABOUT ALL I CAN.
FROM NOW ON, YOU MUST BLAZE YOUR OWN TRAIL!
YOU NEED TO DISCIPLINE AND TRAIN YOURSELVES!
I'M SURE YOU'LL BOTH BE UP TO IT!
HUH... THEN I GUESS...
I'LL GO LOOK FOR GRAMPA'S DRAGON BALL!!
YOU'RE PLANNING TO SEARCH FOR THOSE AGAIN?!
YUP!!
HUH? WHAT ARE YOU TALKING ABOUT?
THE ONLY THING MY GRAMPA LEFT ME!
AND A GREAT WAY TO GET IN MORE FIGHTS!
WELL, LEAVE US OUT OF IT! THIS IS ALL YOURS!

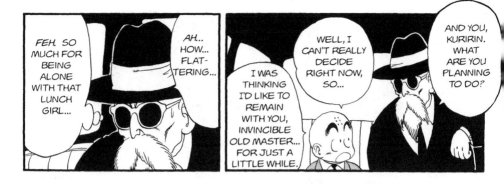

FEH. SO MUCH FOR BEING ALONE WITH THAT LUNCH GIRL...

AH... HOW... FLATTERING...

I WAS THINKING I'D LIKE TO REMAIN WITH YOU, INVINCIBLE OLD MASTER... FOR JUST A LITTLE WHILE.

WELL, I CAN'T REALLY DECIDE RIGHT NOW, SO...

AND YOU, KURIRIN. WHAT ARE YOU PLANNING TO DO?

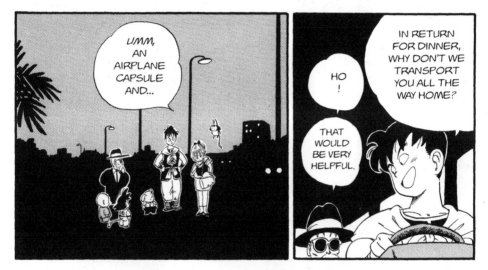

UMM, AN AIRPLANE CAPSULE AND...

HO!

THAT WOULD BE VERY HELPFUL.

IN RETURN FOR DINNER, WHY DON'T WE TRANSPORT YOU ALL THE WAY HOME?

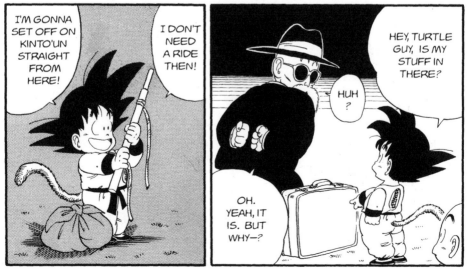

I'M GONNA SET OFF ON KINTO'UN STRAIGHT FROM HERE!

I DON'T NEED A RIDE THEN!

HEY, TURTLE GUY, IS MY STUFF IN THERE?

HUH?

OH. YEAH, IT IS. BUT WHY—?

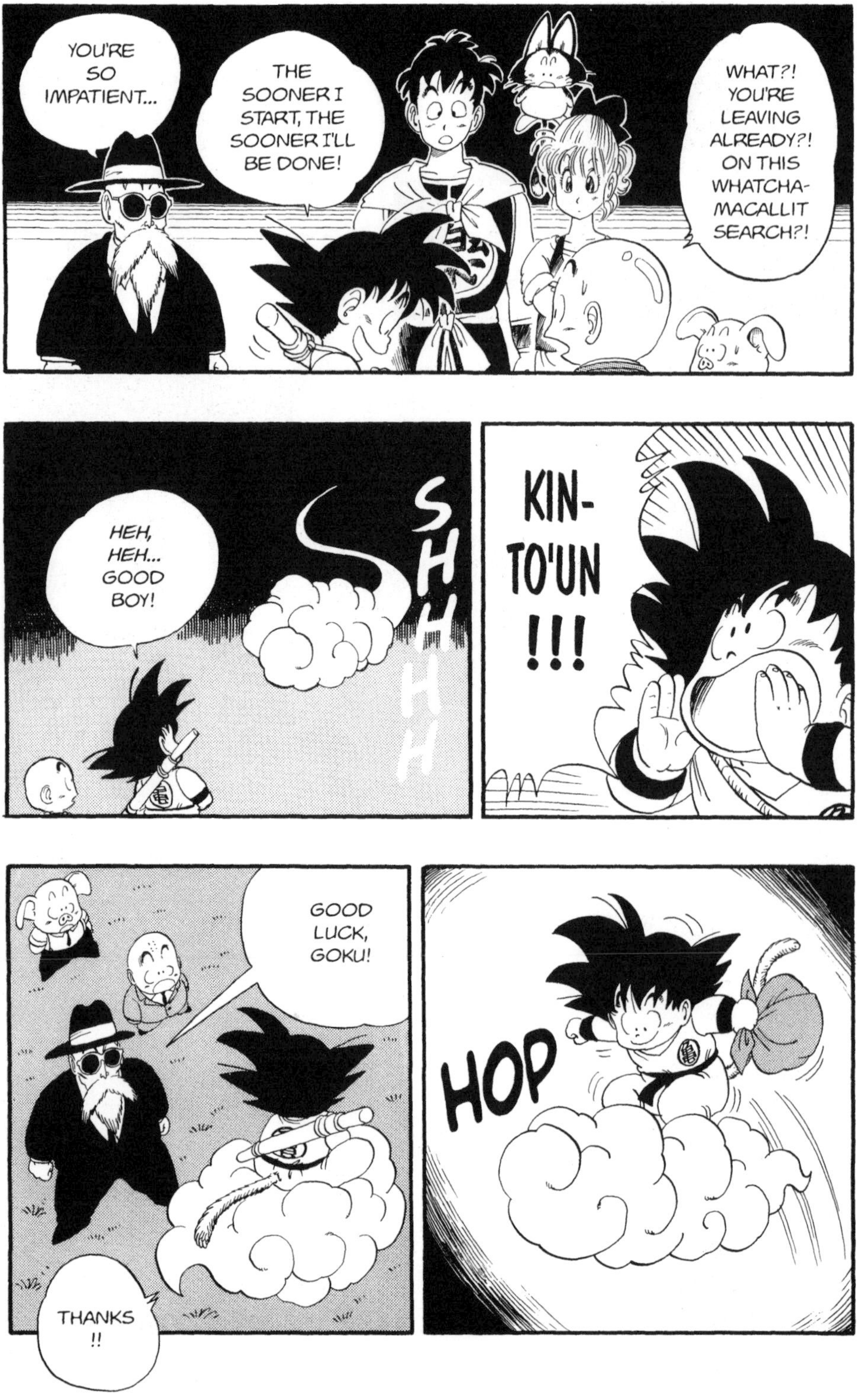
WHAT?! YOU'RE LEAVING ALREADY?! ON THIS WHATCHA-MACALLIT SEARCH?!
THE SOONER I START, THE SOONER I'LL BE DONE!
YOU'RE SO IMPATIENT...
KIN-TO'UN!!!
SHHHHHH
HEH, HEH... GOOD BOY!
HOP
GOOD LUCK, GOKU!
THANKS!!

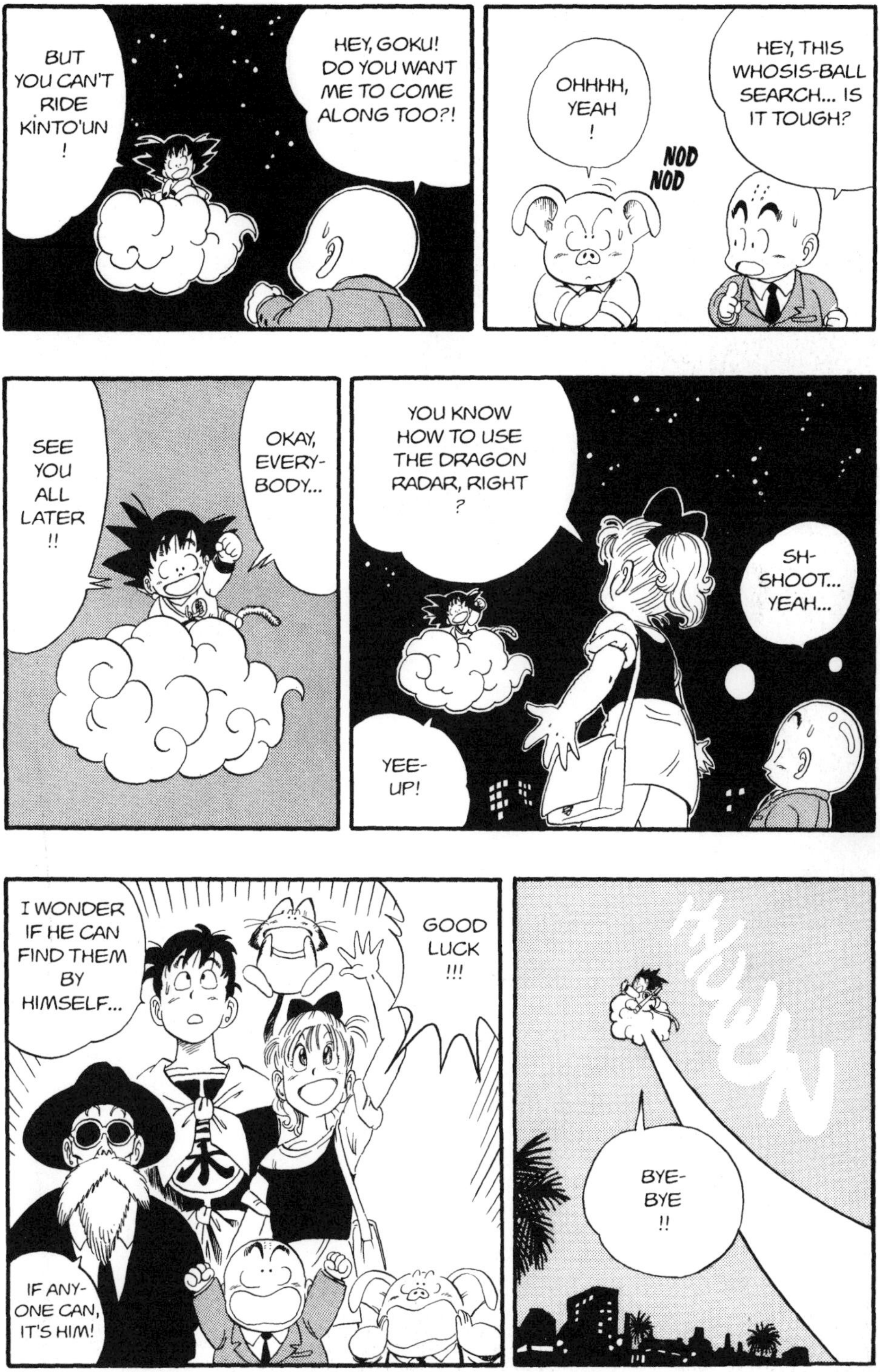
HEY, THIS WHOSIS-BALL SEARCH... IS IT TOUGH?
OHHHH, YEAH !
NOD NOD
HEY, GOKU! DO YOU WANT ME TO COME ALONG TOO?!
BUT YOU CAN'T RIDE KINTO'UN !
YOU KNOW HOW TO USE THE DRAGON RADAR, RIGHT ?
SH-SHOOT... YEAH...
YEE-UP!
OKAY, EVERY-BODY...
SEE YOU ALL LATER !!
HWUUN
BYE-BYE !!
GOOD LUCK !!!
I WONDER IF HE CAN FIND THEM BY HIMSELF...
IF ANY-ONE CAN, IT'S HIM!

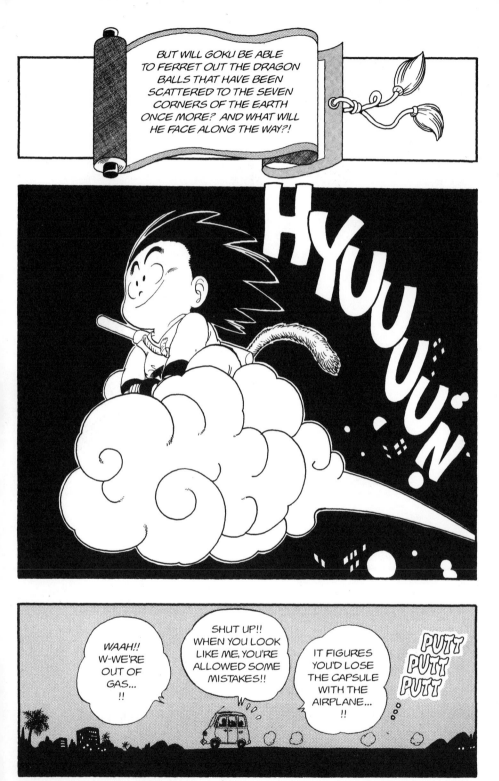

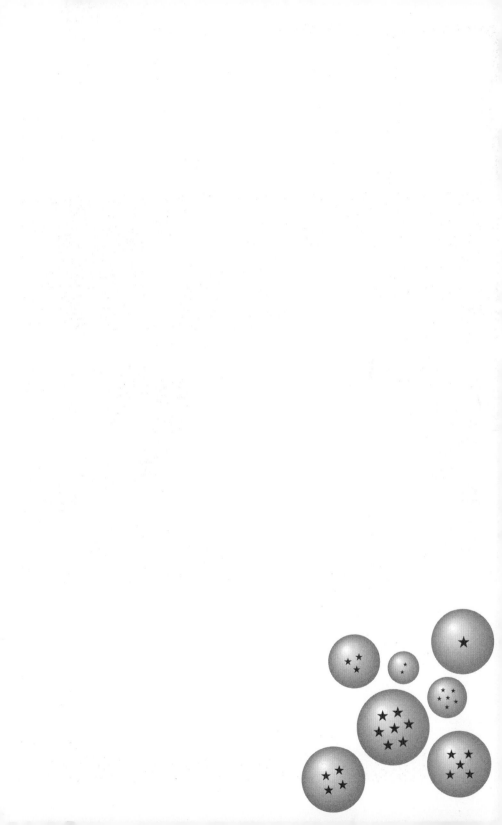

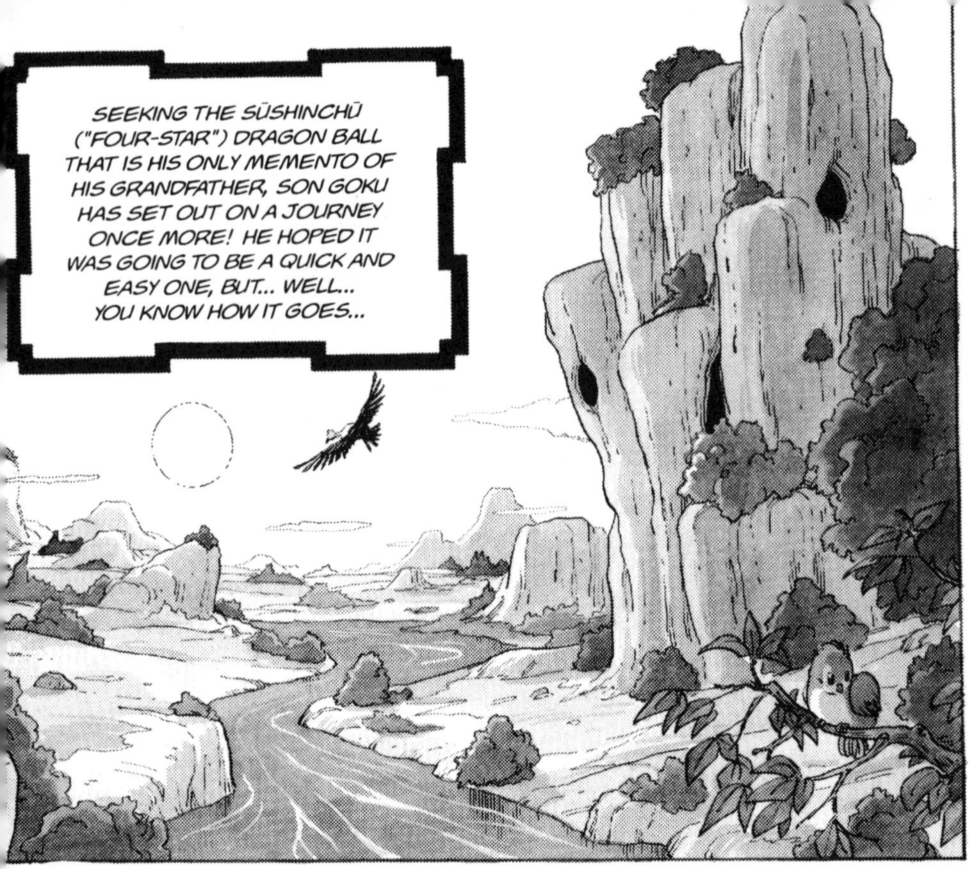
SEEKING THE SŪSHINCHŪ ("FOUR-STAR") DRAGON BALL THAT IS HIS ONLY MEMENTO OF HIS GRANDFATHER, SON GOKU HAS SET OUT ON A JOURNEY ONCE MORE! HE HOPED IT WAS GOING TO BE A QUICK AND EASY ONE, BUT... WELL... YOU KNOW HOW IT GOES...

Tale 55 · The Red Ribbon

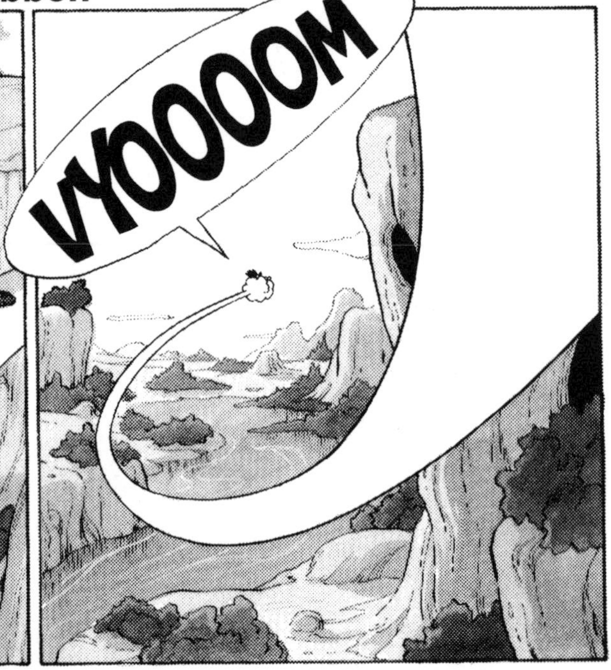
VYOOOOM

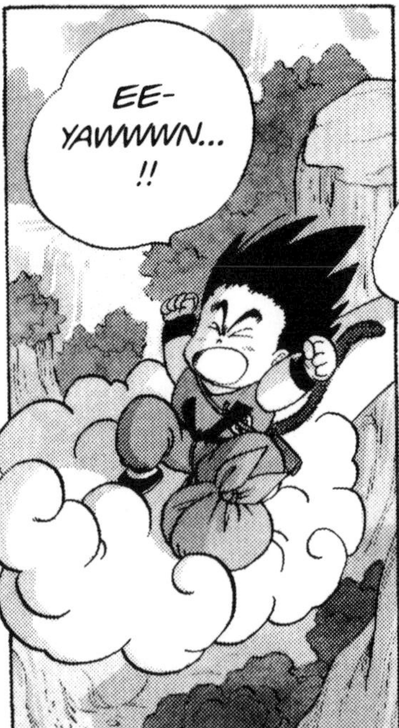
EE-YAWWWN... !!

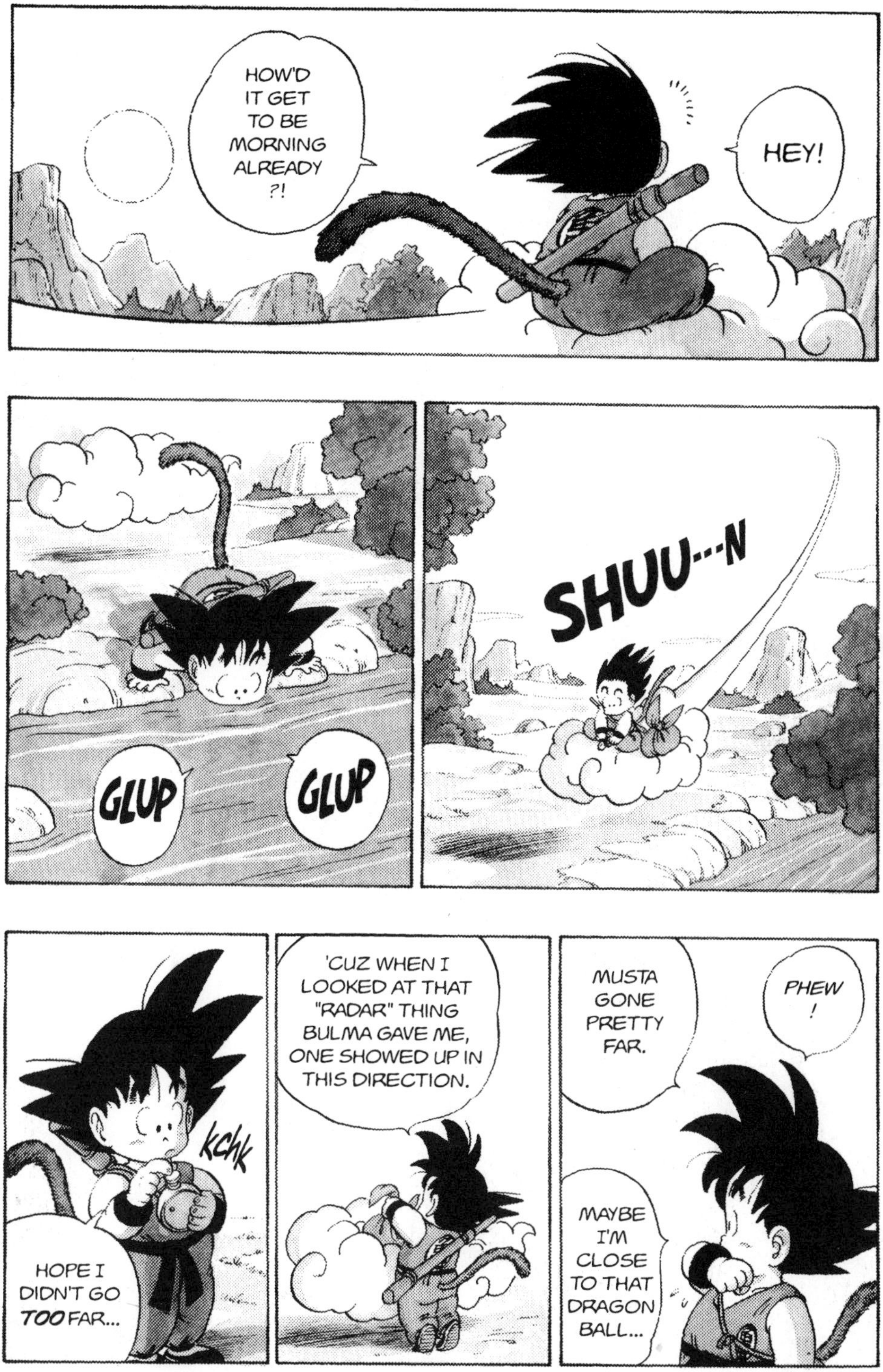
HEY!
HOW'D IT GET TO BE MORNING ALREADY ?!
SHUU···N
GLUP
GLUP
PHEW!
MUSTA GONE PRETTY FAR.
MAYBE I'M CLOSE TO THAT DRAGON BALL...
'CUZ WHEN I LOOKED AT THAT "RADAR" THING BULMA GAVE ME, ONE SHOWED UP IN THIS DIRECTION.
KCHK
HOPE I DIDN'T GO TOO FAR...

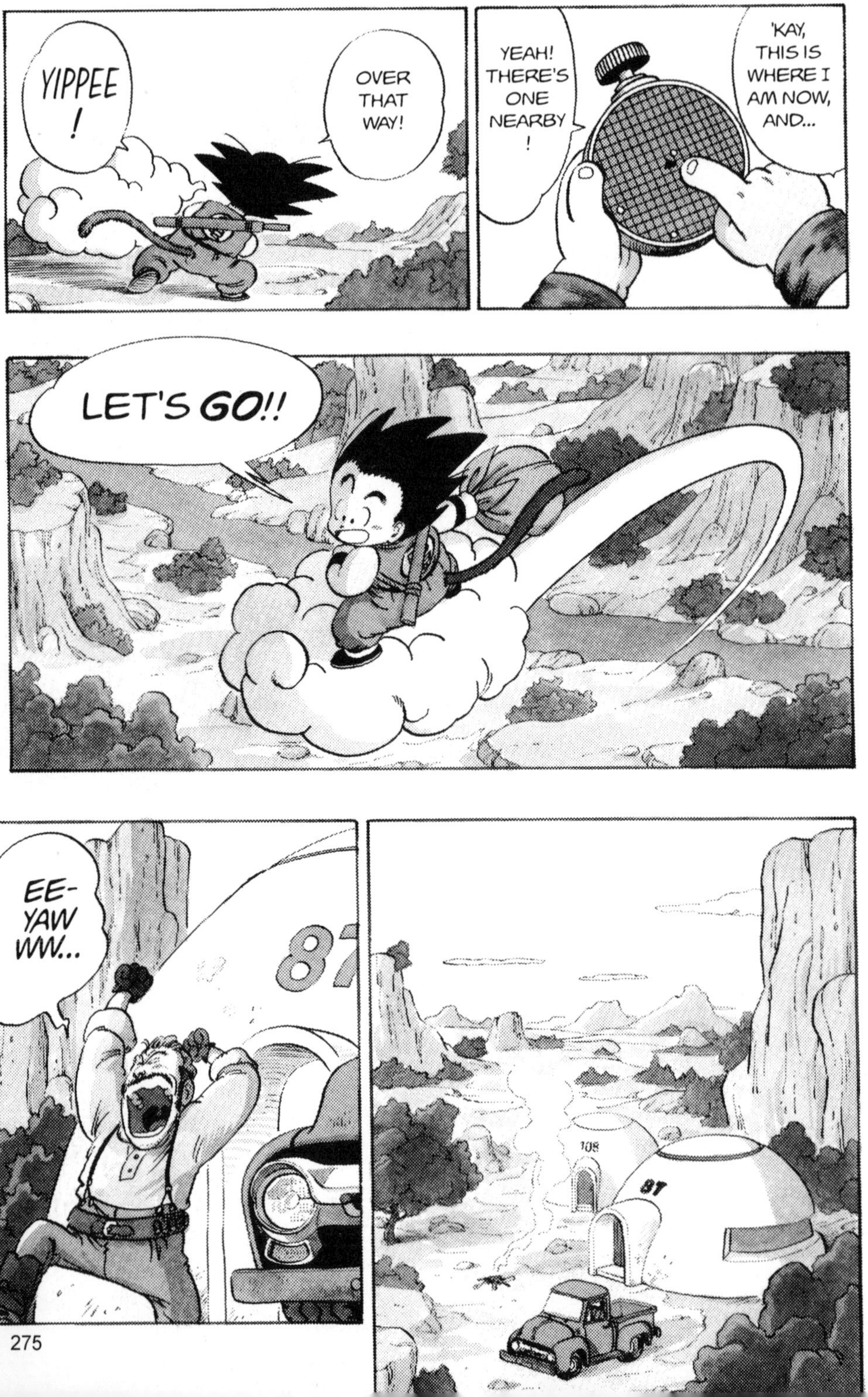
'KAY, THIS IS WHERE I AM NOW, AND...
YEAH! THERE'S ONE NEARBY!
OVER THAT WAY!
YIPPEE!
LET'S GO!!
EE-YAWWW...

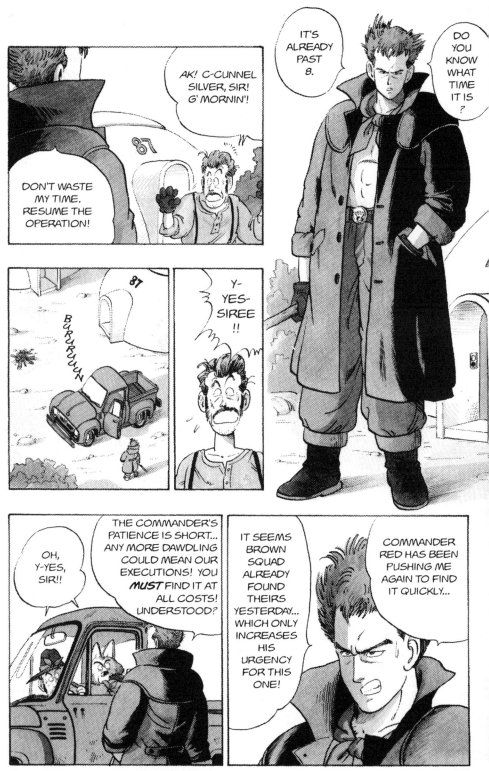

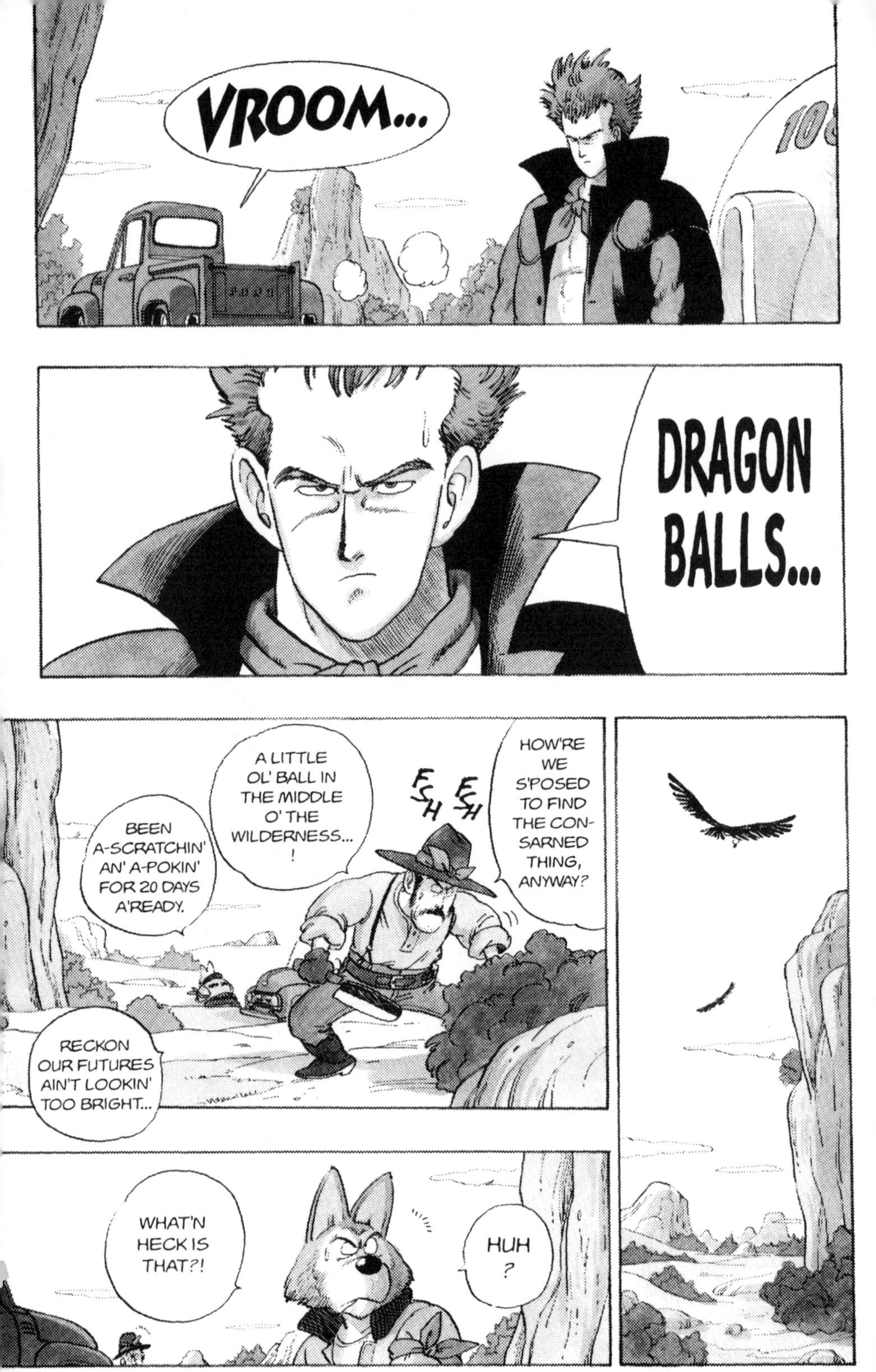
VROOM...
DRAGON BALLS...
HOW'RE WE S'POSED TO FIND THE CON-SARNED THING, ANYWAY?
FSH FSH
A LITTLE OL' BALL IN THE MIDDLE O' THE WILDERNESS... !
BEEN A-SCRATCHIN' AN' A-POKIN' FOR 20 DAYS A'READY.
RECKON OUR FUTURES AIN'T LOOKIN' TOO BRIGHT...
HUH ?
WHAT'N HECK IS THAT?!

BREAK TIME!

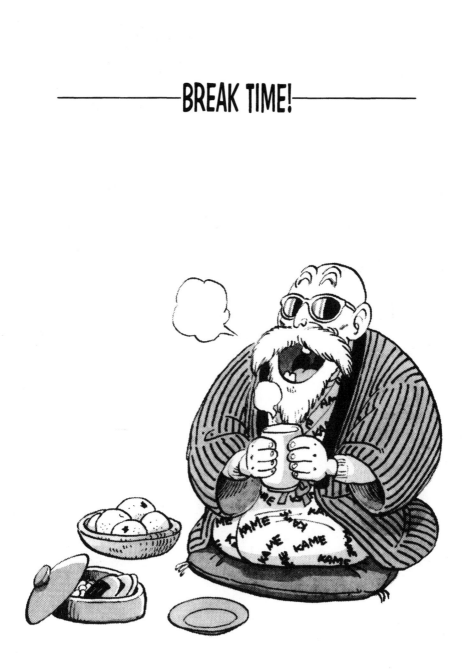

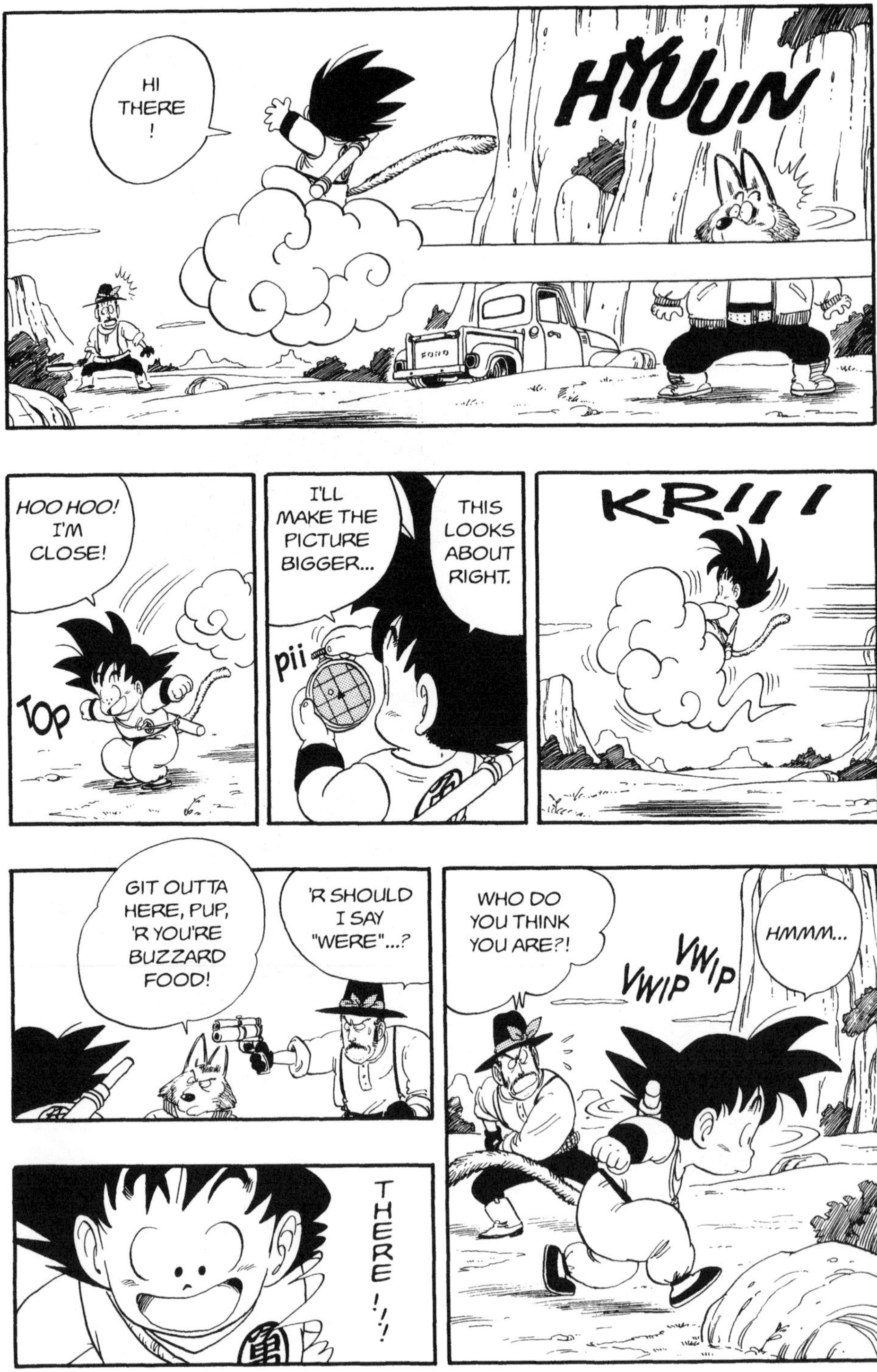
HI THERE !
HYUUN
HOO HOO! I'M CLOSE!
TOP
I'LL MAKE THE PICTURE BIGGER...
pii
THIS LOOKS ABOUT RIGHT.
KRIII
GIT OUTTA HERE, PUP, 'R YOU'RE BUZZARD FOOD!
'R SHOULD I SAY "WERE"...?
THERE !!!
WHO DO YOU THINK YOU ARE?!
VWIP VWIP
HMMM...

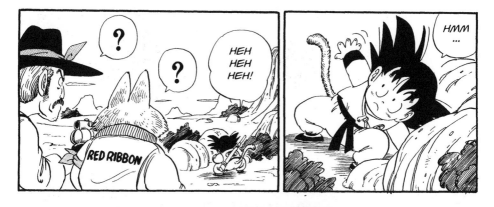

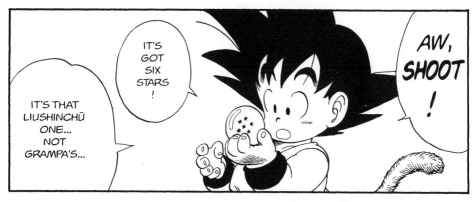

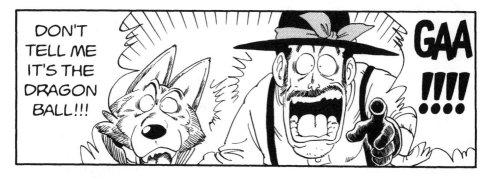

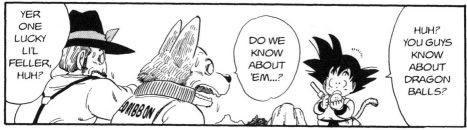

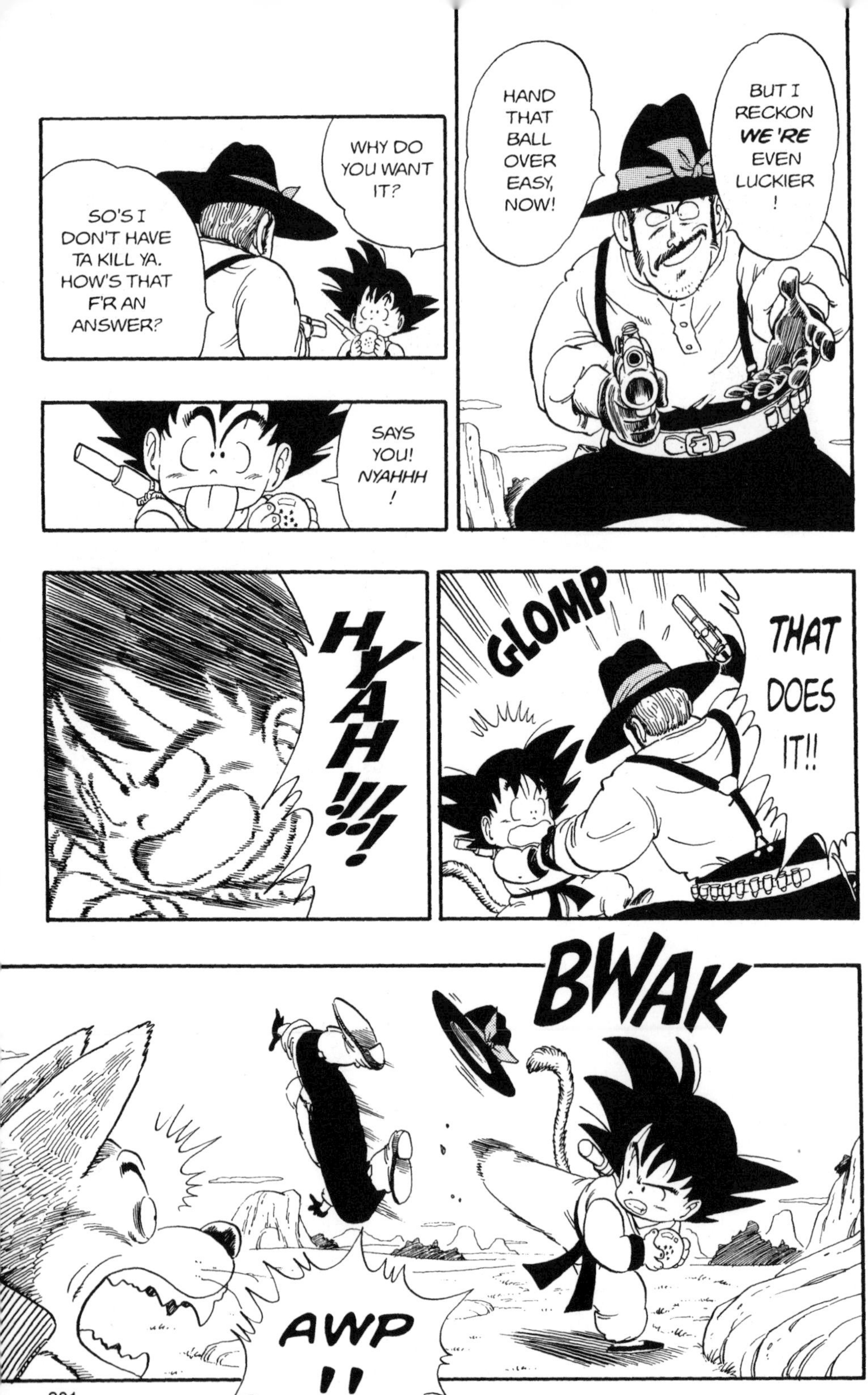

BUT I RECKON WE'RE EVEN LUCKIER!
HAND THAT BALL OVER EASY, NOW!
WHY DO YOU WANT IT?
SO'S I DON'T HAVE TA KILL YA. HOW'S THAT F'R AN ANSWER?
SAYS YOU! NYAHHH!
THAT DOES IT!!
GLOMP
HYAH!!!!
BWAK
AWP!!

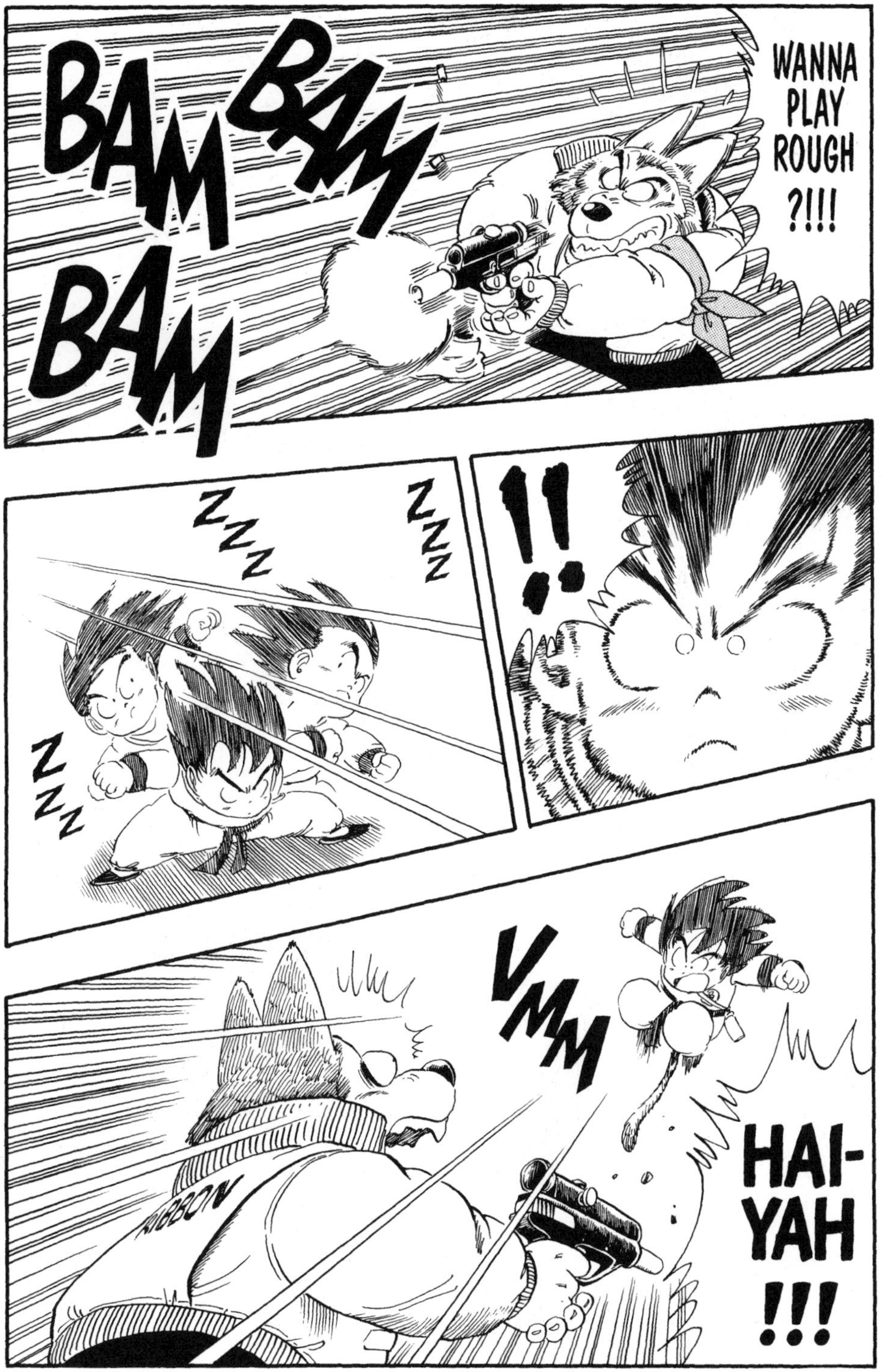
WANNA PLAY ROUGH ?!!!
BAM BAM
BAM
!!
ZZZ
ZZZ
ZZZ
HAI-YAH !!!
VMM
RIBBON

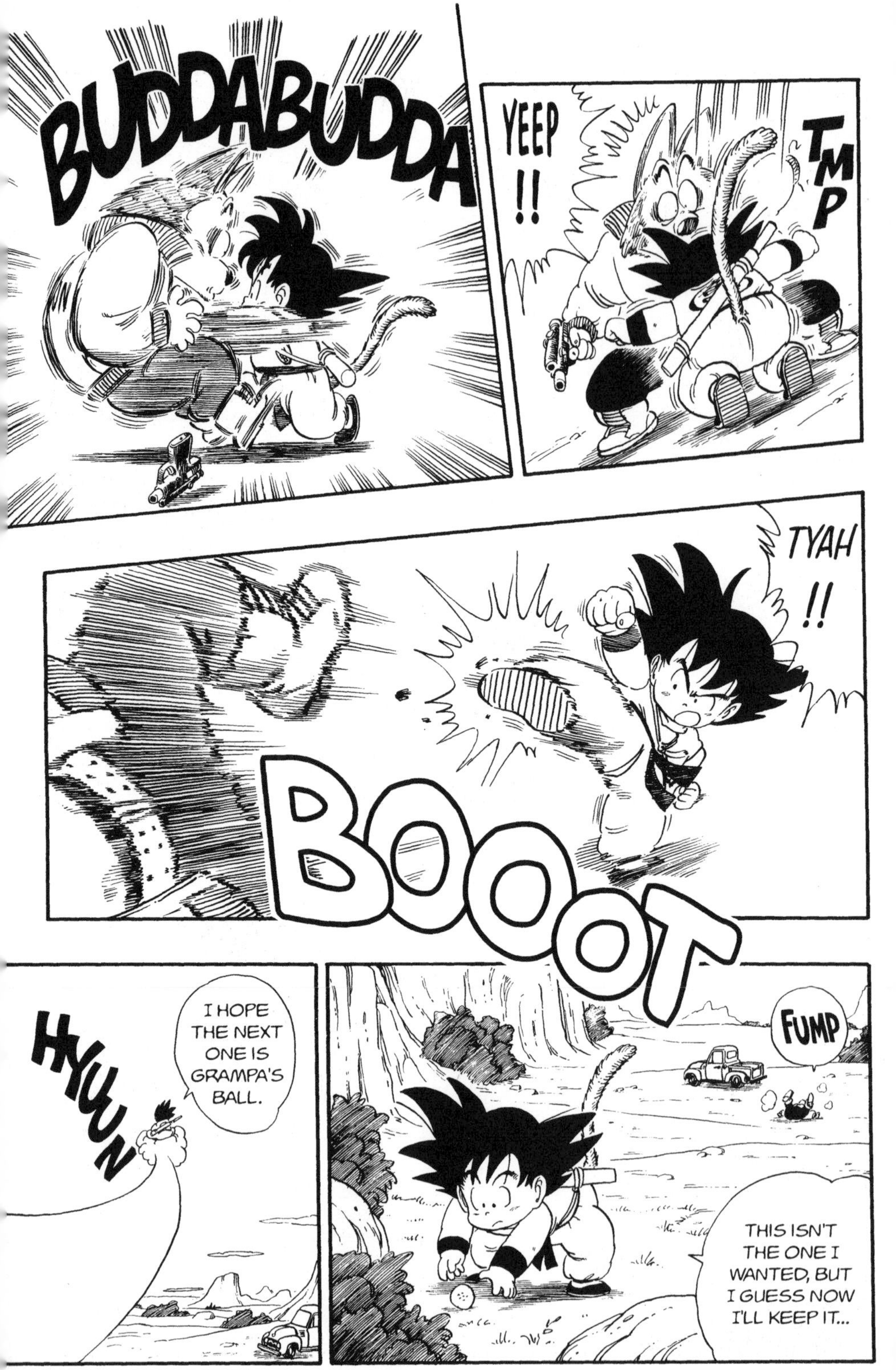
YEEP!!
TMP
BUDDABUDDA
TYAH!!
BOOOT
FUMP
THIS ISN'T THE ONE I WANTED, BUT I GUESS NOW I'LL KEEP IT...
HYUUN
I HOPE THE NEXT ONE IS GRAMPA'S BALL.

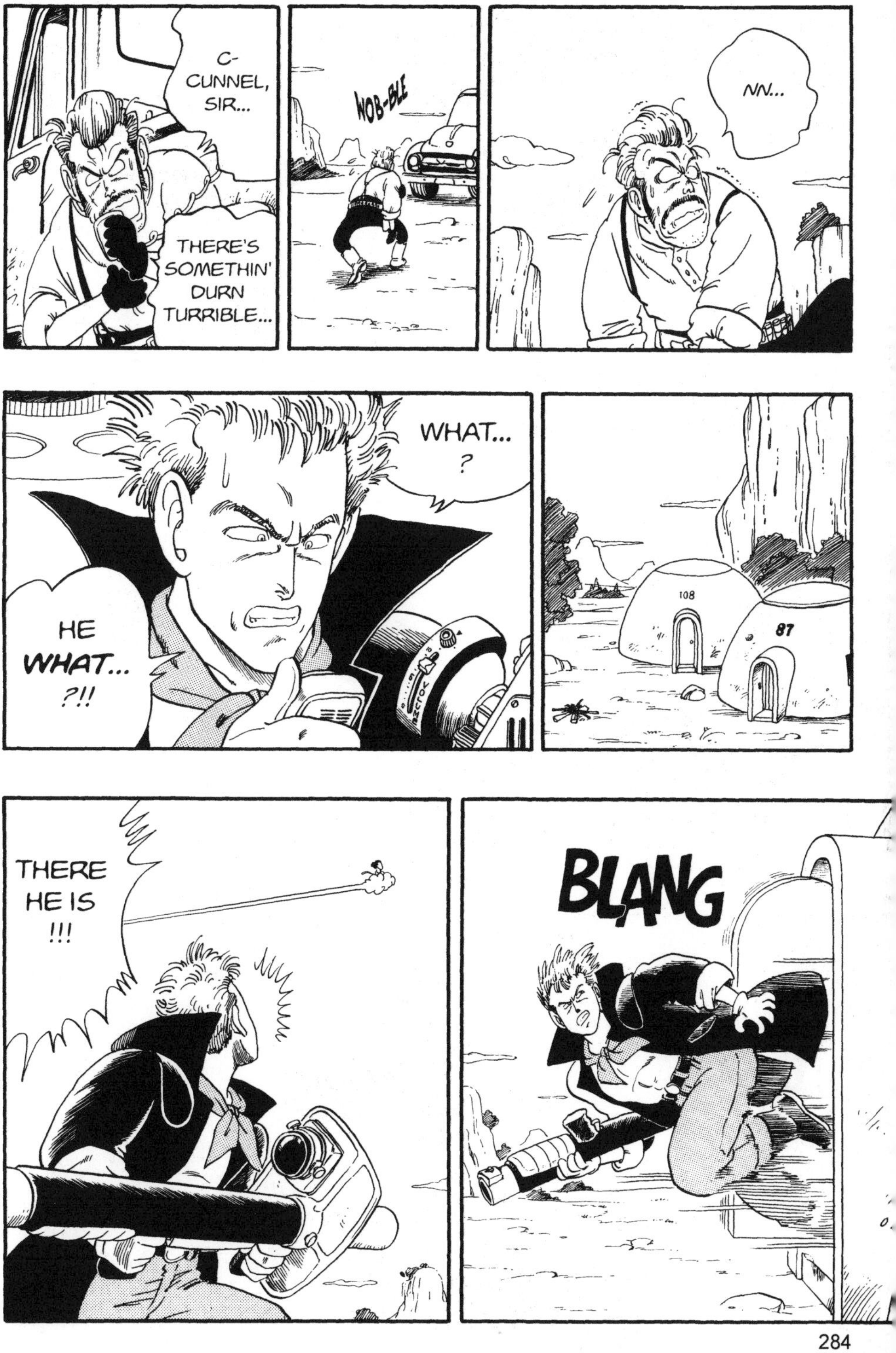
NN...
WOB-BLE
C-CUNNEL, SIR...
THERE'S SOMETHIN' DURN TURRIBLE...
WHAT...?
HE WHAT...?!!
BLANG
THERE HE IS!!!

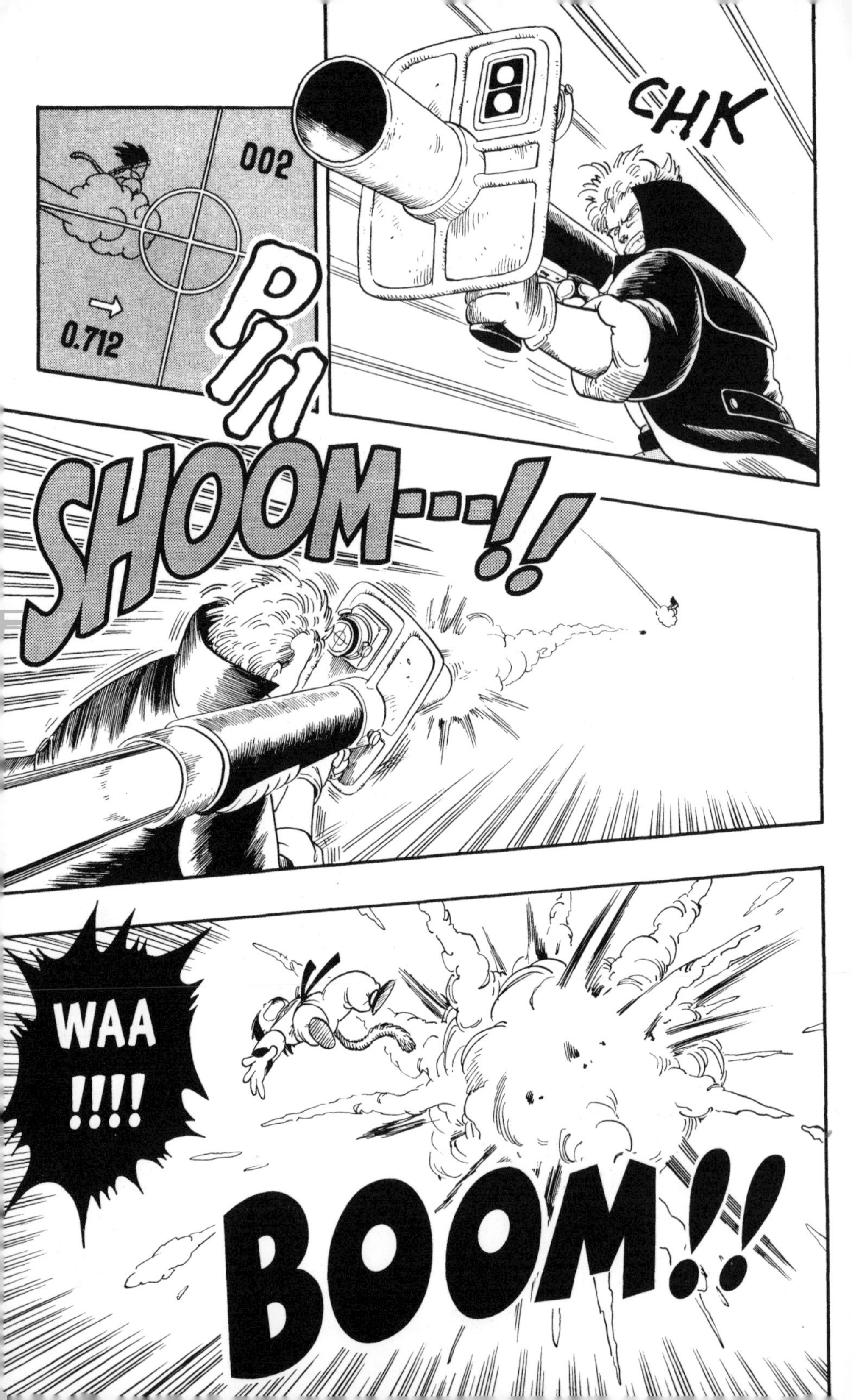
CHK
002
0.712
PIN
SHOOM---!!
WAA !!!!
BOOM!!

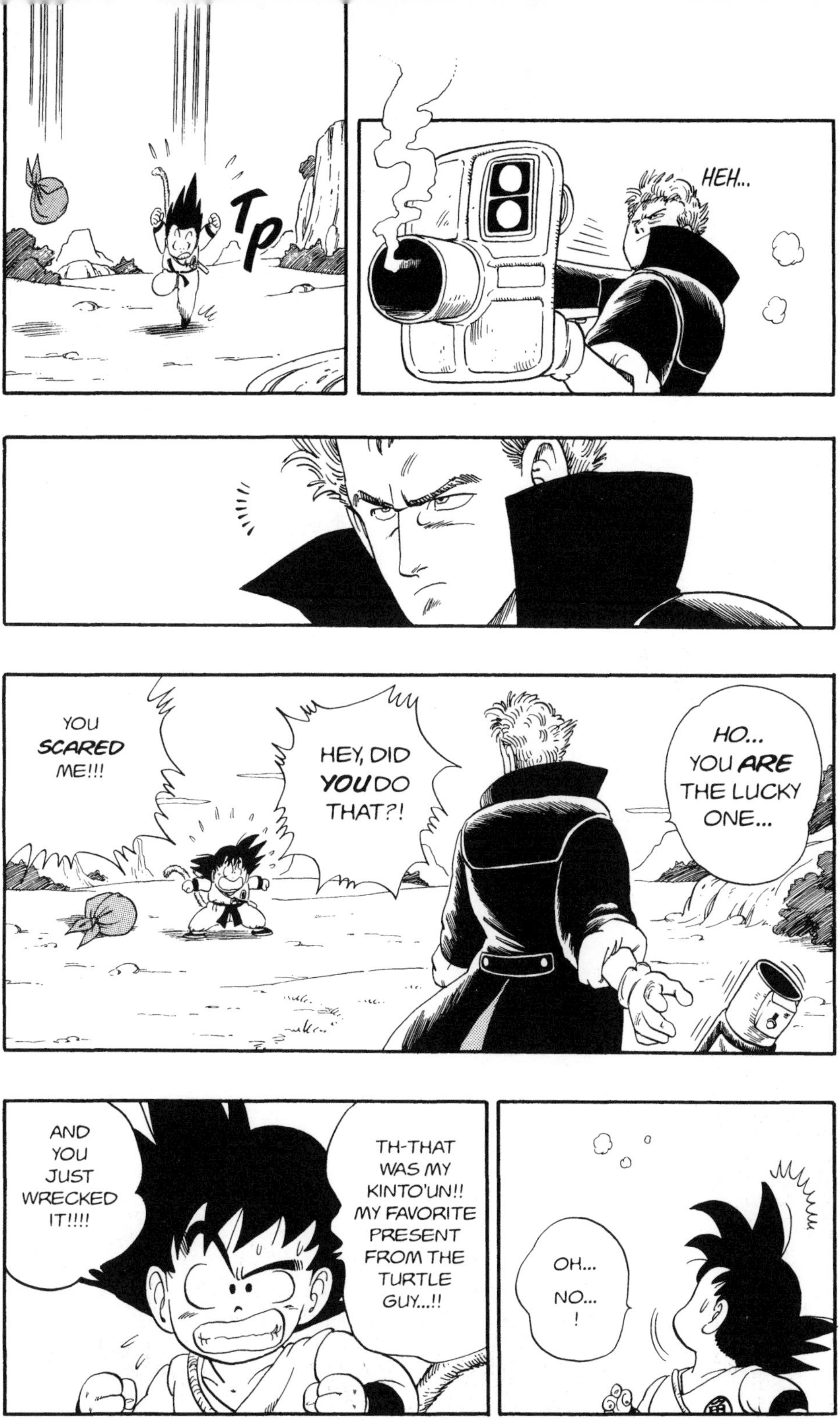
HEH...
TP
HO... YOU ARE THE LUCKY ONE...
HEY, DID YOU DO THAT?!
YOU SCARED ME!!!
OH... NO... !
TH-THAT WAS MY KINTO'UN!! MY FAVORITE PRESENT FROM THE TURTLE GUY...!!
AND YOU JUST WRECKED IT!!!!

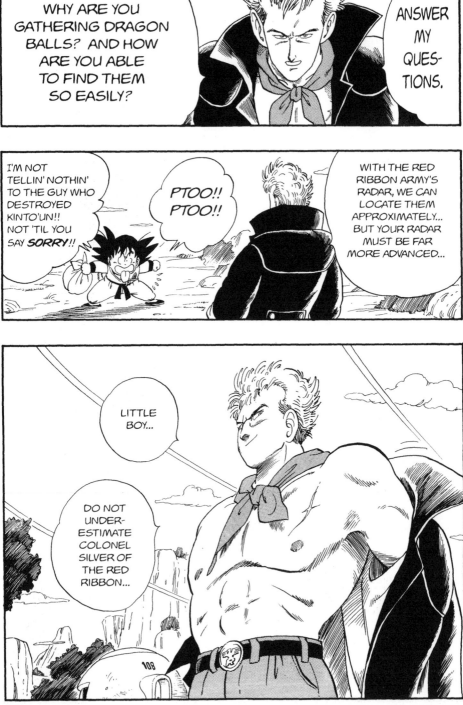

Tale 56 • The Dragon Ball Scramble

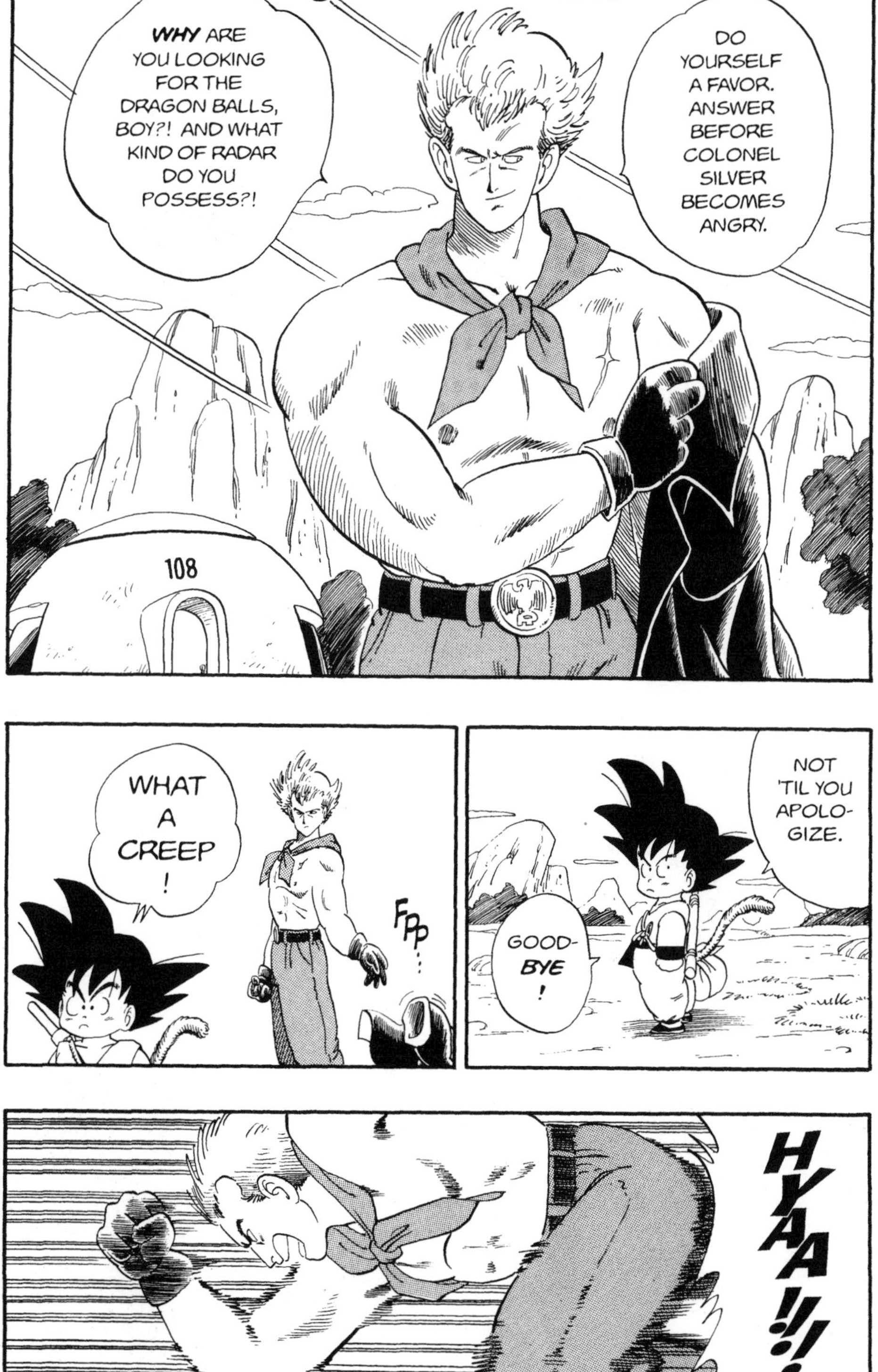
DO YOURSELF A FAVOR. ANSWER BEFORE COLONEL SILVER BECOMES ANGRY.
WHY ARE YOU LOOKING FOR THE DRAGON BALLS, BOY?! AND WHAT KIND OF RADAR DO YOU POSSESS?!
108
NOT 'TIL YOU APOLOGIZE.
GOOD-*BYE*!
WHAT A CREEP!
FPP...
HYAA!!!

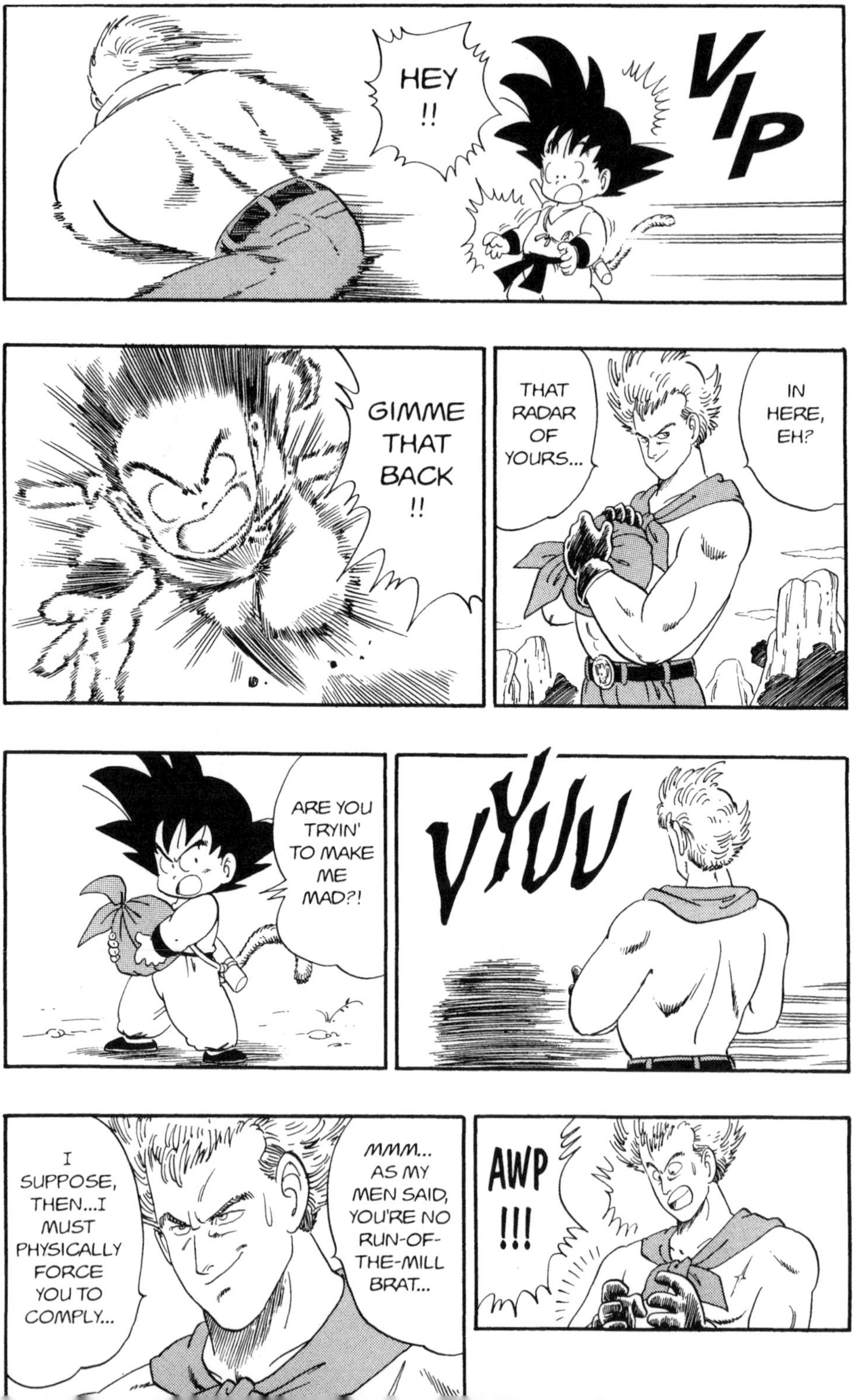
VIP
HEY !!
IN HERE, EH?
THAT RADAR OF YOURS...
GIMME THAT BACK !!
VYUU
ARE YOU TRYIN' TO MAKE ME MAD?!
AWP !!!
MMM... AS MY MEN SAID, YOU'RE NO RUN-OF-THE-MILL BRAT...
I SUPPOSE, THEN...I MUST PHYSICALLY FORCE YOU TO COMPLY...

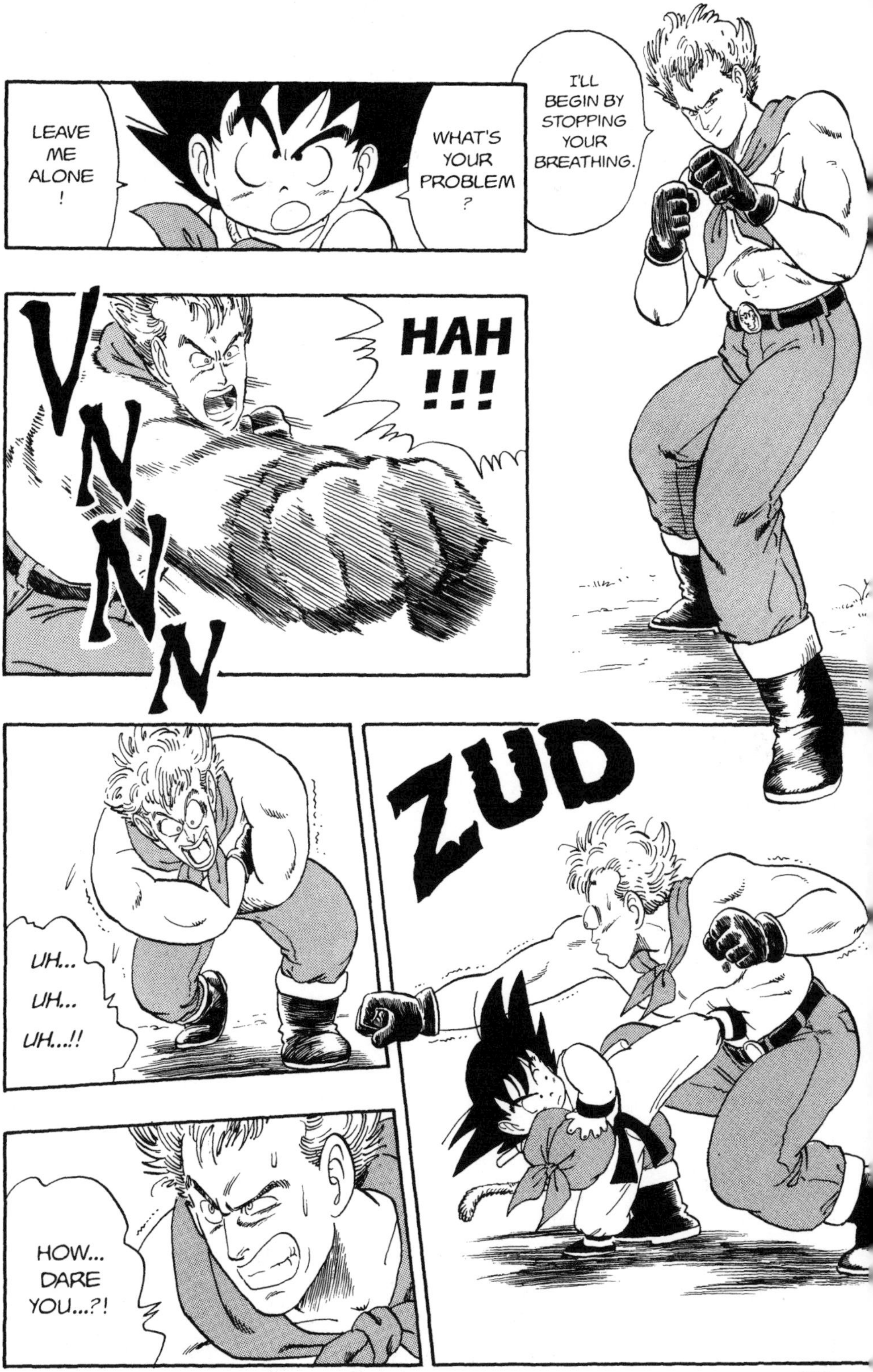
I'LL BEGIN BY STOPPING YOUR BREATHING.
WHAT'S YOUR PROBLEM ?
LEAVE ME ALONE !
HAH !!!
VNNNN
ZUD
UH... UH... UH...!!
HOW... DARE YOU...?!

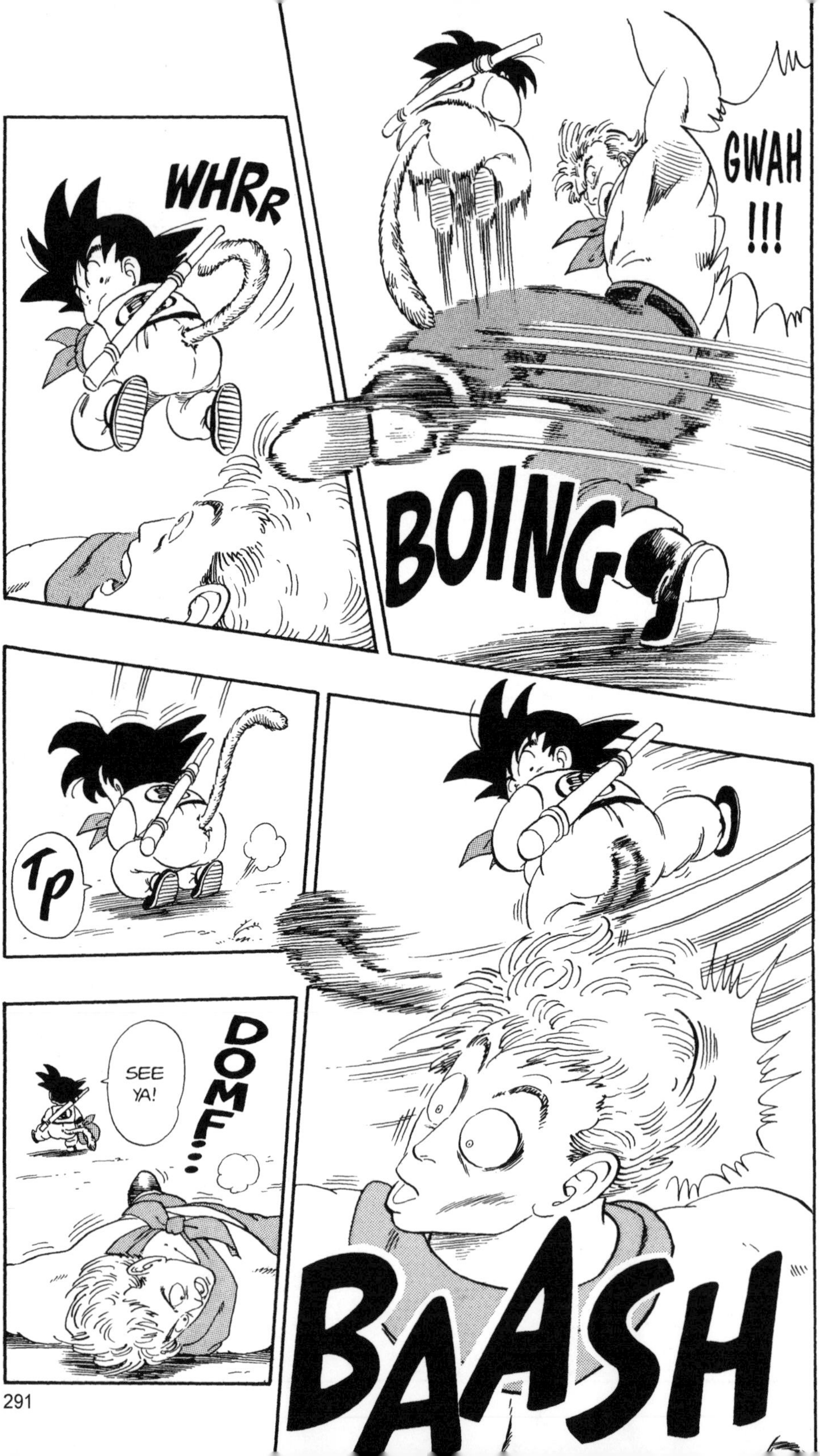
GWAH !!!
BOING
WHRR
BAASH
TP
SEE YA!
DOMF...

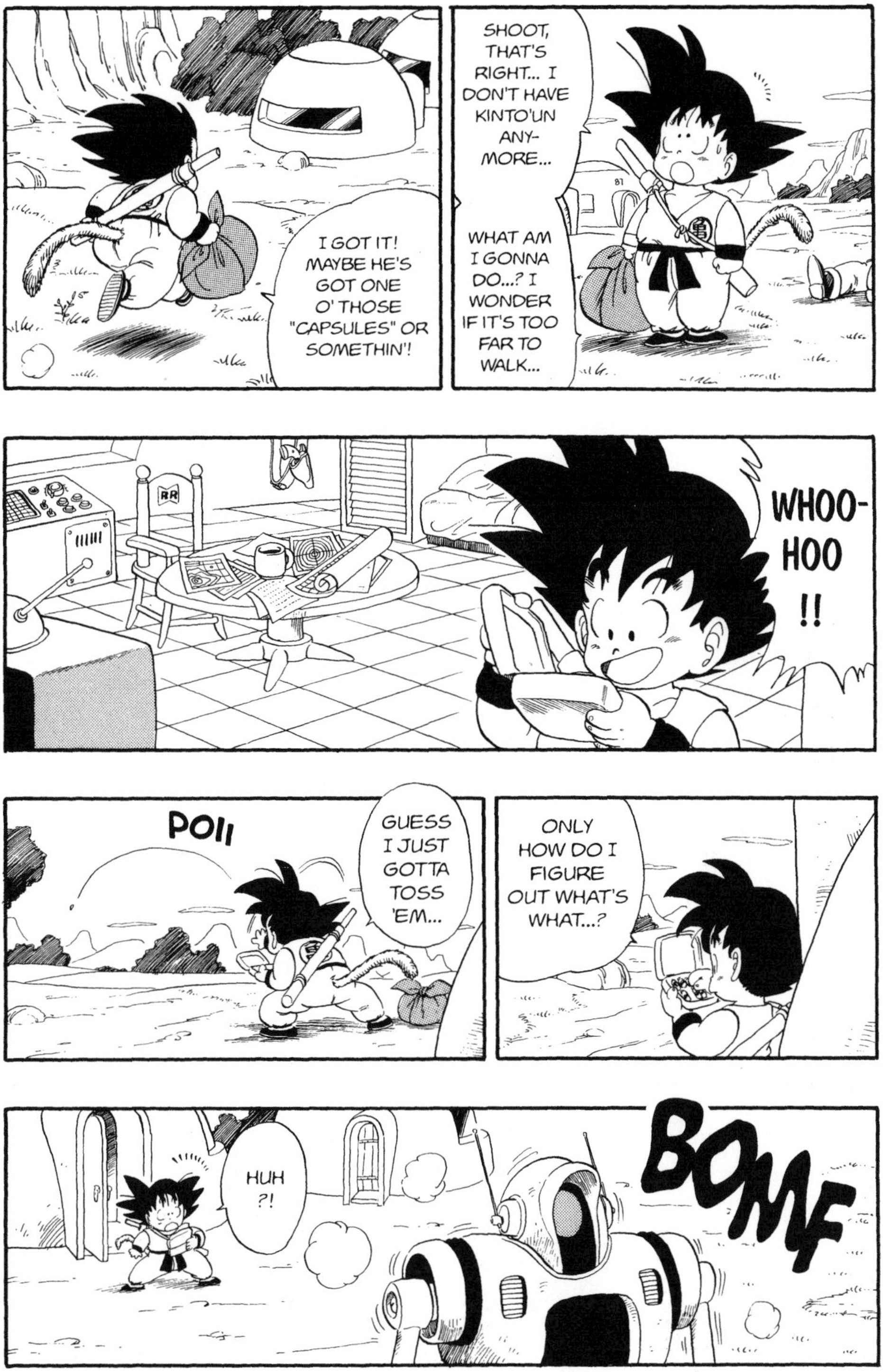
SHOOT, THAT'S RIGHT... I DON'T HAVE KINTO'UN ANY-MORE...
WHAT AM I GONNA DO...? I WONDER IF IT'S TOO FAR TO WALK...
I GOT IT! MAYBE HE'S GOT ONE O' THOSE "CAPSULES" OR SOMETHIN'!
WHOO-HOO !!
ONLY HOW DO I FIGURE OUT WHAT'S WHAT...?
GUESS I JUST GOTTA TOSS 'EM...
POI
BOMF
HUH ?!

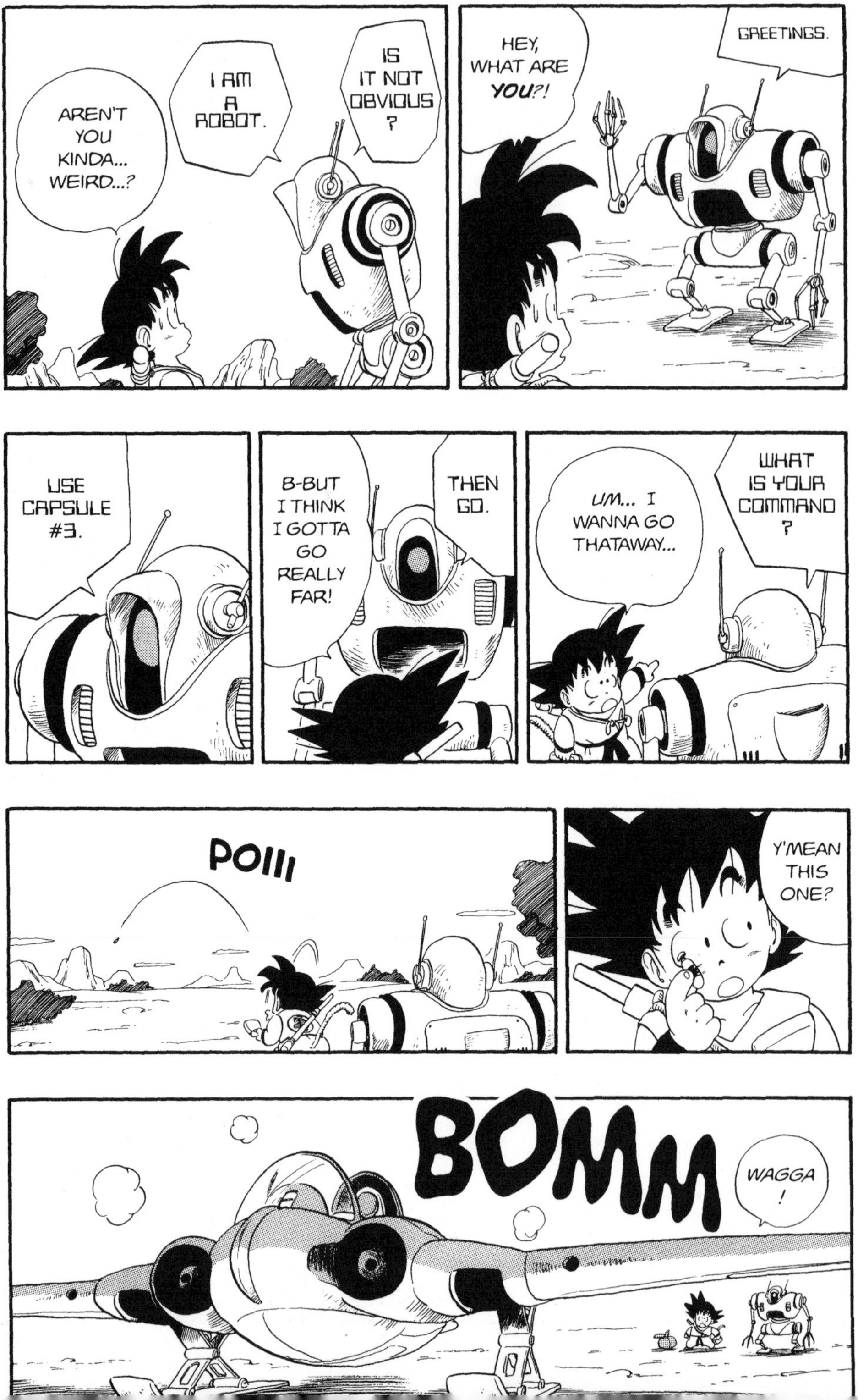
GREETINGS.
HEY, WHAT ARE *YOU*?!
IS IT NOT OBVIOUS ?
I AM A ROBOT.
AREN'T YOU KINDA... WEIRD...?
WHAT IS YOUR COMMAND ?
UM... I WANNA GO THATAWAY...
THEN GO.
B-BUT I THINK I GOTTA GO REALLY FAR!
USE CAPSULE #3.
Y'MEAN THIS ONE?
POIII
BOMM
WAGGA !

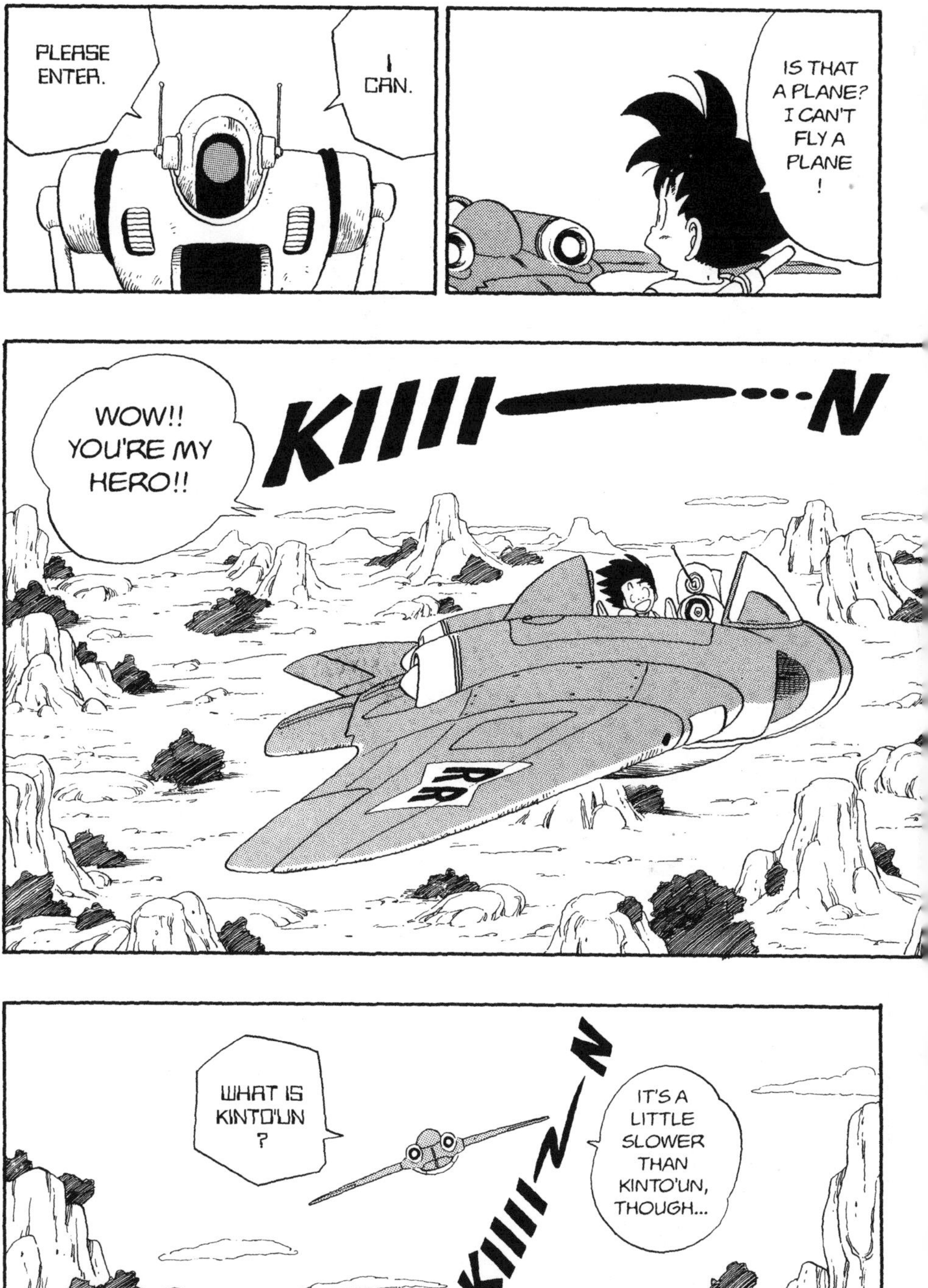
IS THAT A PLANE? I CAN'T FLY A PLANE !
I CAN.
PLEASE ENTER.
KIIII——…N
WOW!! YOU'RE MY HERO!!
IT'S A LITTLE SLOWER THAN KINTO'UN, THOUGH...
KIIII~N
WHAT IS KINTO'UN ?

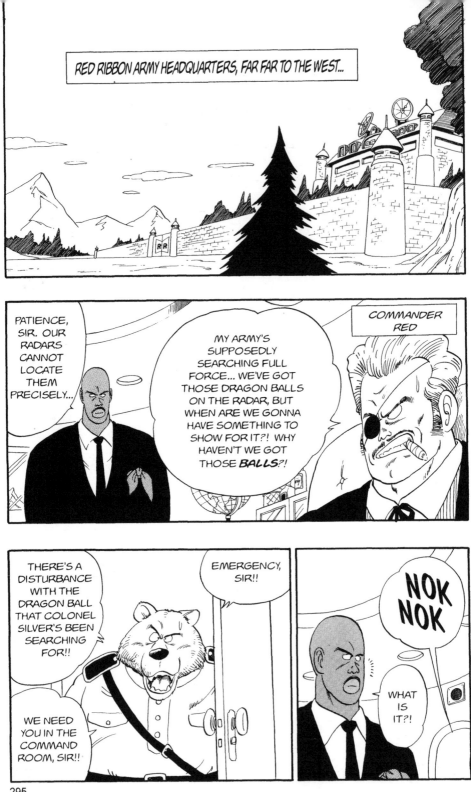

RED RIBBON ARMY HEADQUARTERS, FAR FAR TO THE WEST...

PATIENCE, SIR. OUR RADARS CANNOT LOCATE THEM PRECISELY...

MY ARMY'S SUPPOSEDLY SEARCHING FULL FORCE... WE'VE GOT THOSE DRAGON BALLS ON THE RADAR, BUT WHEN ARE WE GONNA HAVE SOMETHING TO SHOW FOR IT?! WHY HAVEN'T WE GOT THOSE **BALLS**?!

COMMANDER RED

THERE'S A DISTURBANCE WITH THE DRAGON BALL THAT COLONEL SILVER'S BEEN SEARCHING FOR!!

WE NEED YOU IN THE COMMAND ROOM, SIR!!

EMERGENCY, SIR!!

NOK NOK

WHAT IS IT?!

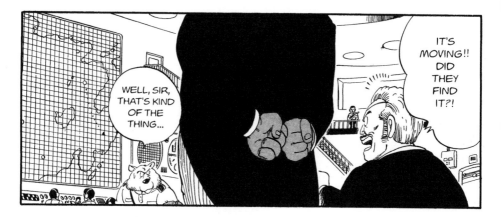

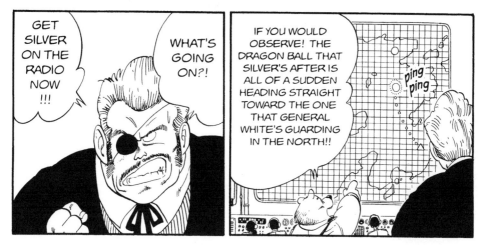

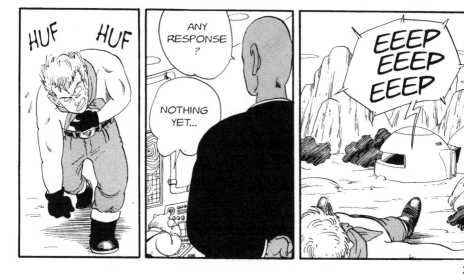

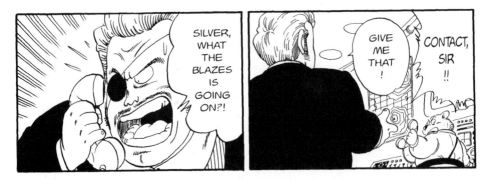

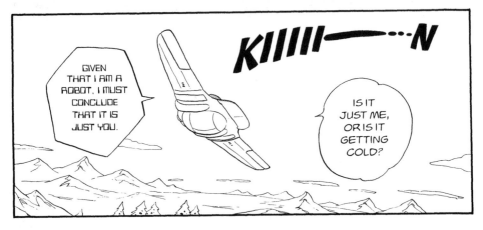

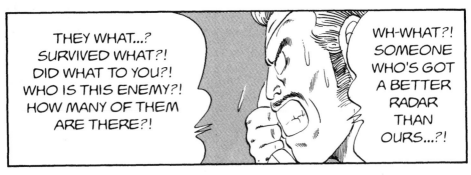

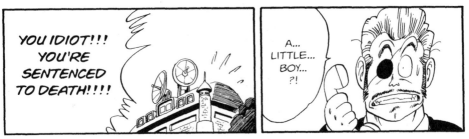

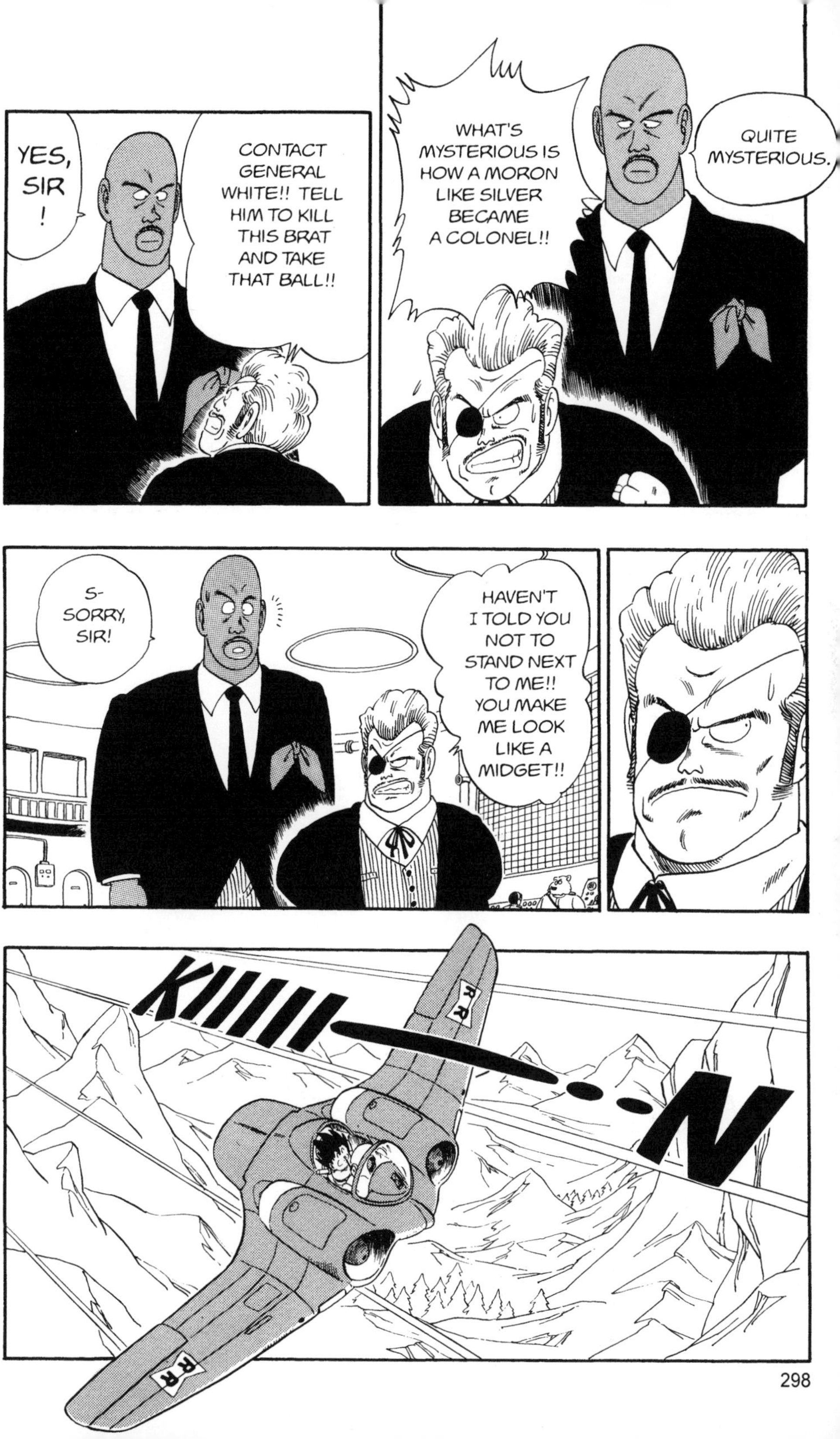
QUITE MYSTERIOUS.
WHAT'S MYSTERIOUS IS HOW A MORON LIKE SILVER BECAME A COLONEL!!
CONTACT GENERAL WHITE!! TELL HIM TO KILL THIS BRAT AND TAKE THAT BALL!!
YES, SIR!
HAVEN'T I TOLD YOU NOT TO STAND NEXT TO ME!! YOU MAKE ME LOOK LIKE A MIDGET!!
S-SORRY, SIR!
KIIIII--N

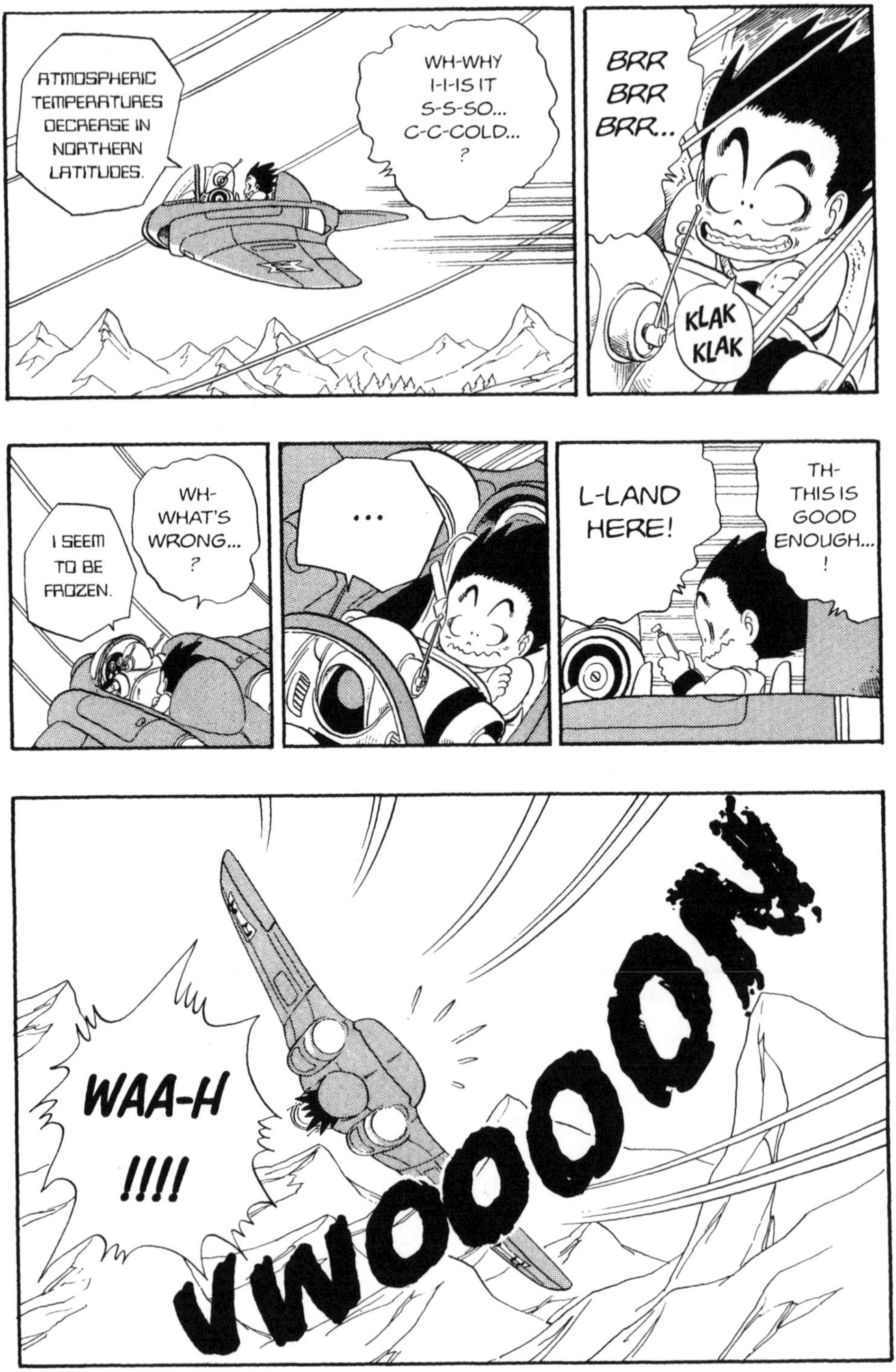
BRR
BRR
BRR...
KLAK
KLAK
WH-WHY I-I-IS IT S-S-SO... C-C-COLD...?
ATMOSPHERIC TEMPERATURES DECREASE IN NORTHERN LATITUDES.
TH-THIS IS GOOD ENOUGH...!
L-LAND HERE!
...
WH-WHAT'S WRONG...?
I SEEM TO BE FROZEN.
VWOOOOOM
WAA-H!!!!

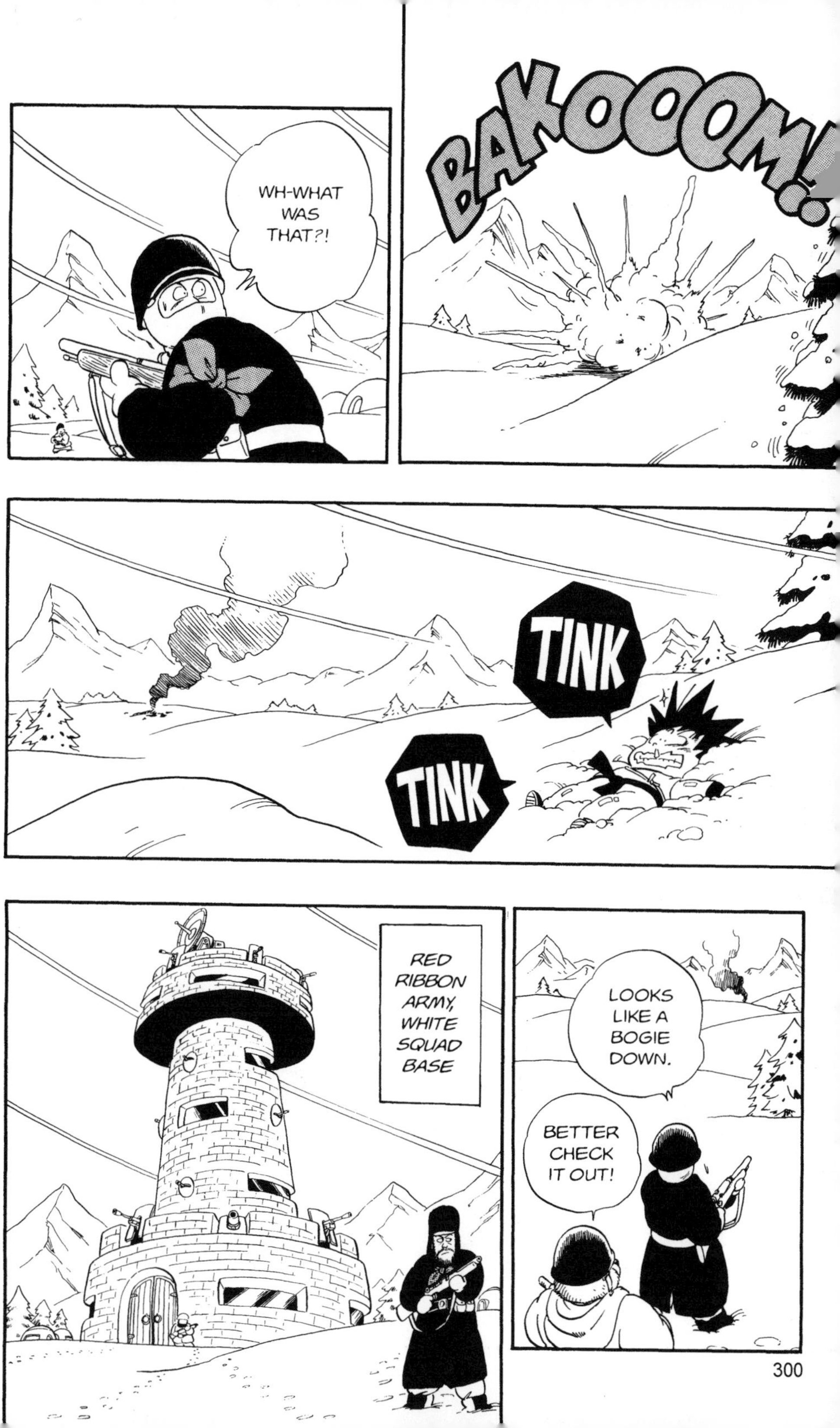
BAKOOOM!!
WH-WHAT WAS THAT?!
TINK
TINK
LOOKS LIKE A BOGIE DOWN.
BETTER CHECK IT OUT!
RED RIBBON ARMY, WHITE SQUAD BASE

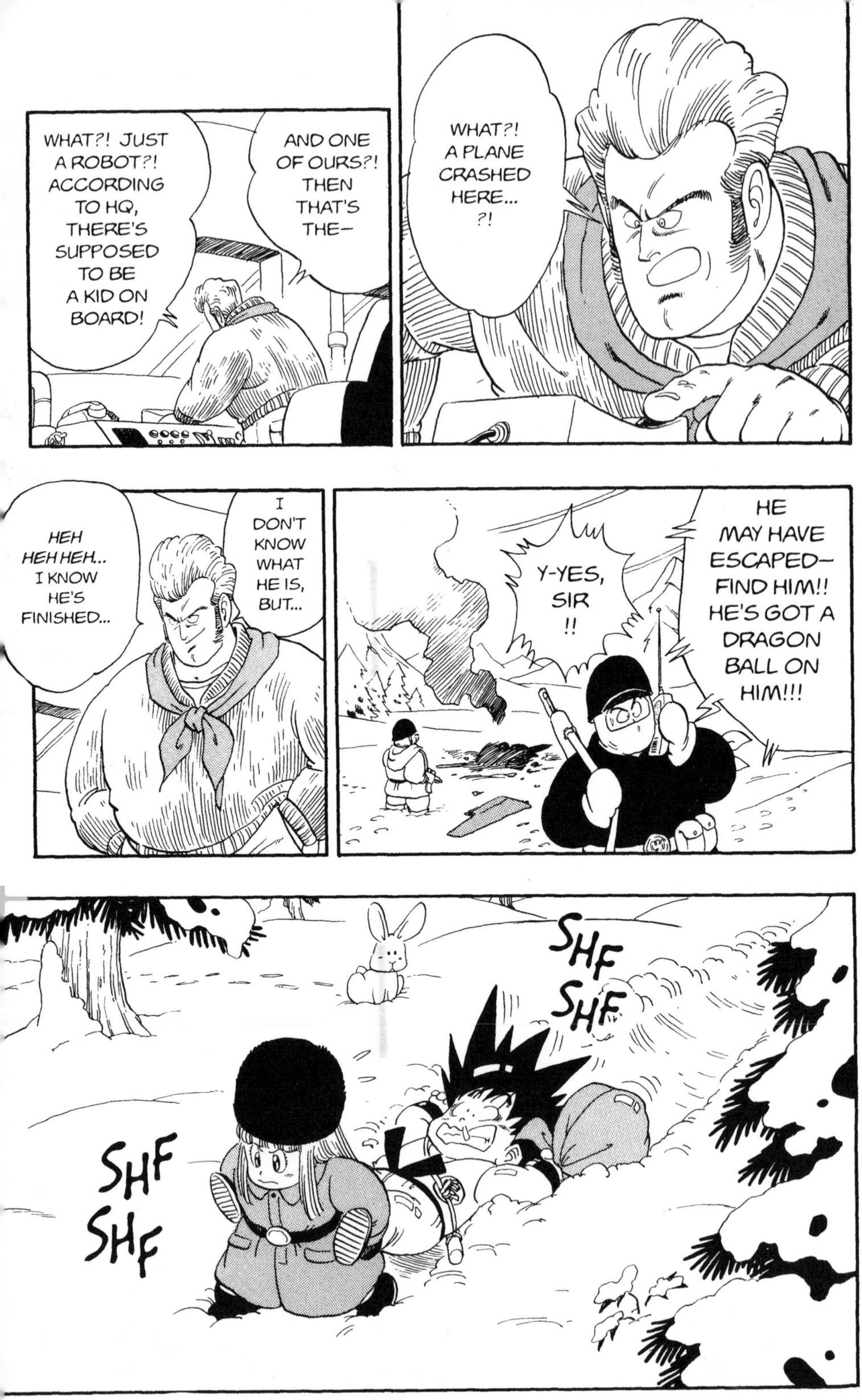
WHAT?! A PLANE CRASHED HERE... ?!
AND ONE OF OURS?! THEN THAT'S THE—
WHAT?! JUST A ROBOT?! ACCORDING TO HQ, THERE'S SUPPOSED TO BE A KID ON BOARD!
HE MAY HAVE ESCAPED— FIND HIM!! HE'S GOT A DRAGON BALL ON HIM!!!
Y-YES, SIR !!
I DON'T KNOW WHAT HE IS, BUT...
HEH HEH HEH... I KNOW HE'S FINISHED...
SHF SHF
SHF SHF

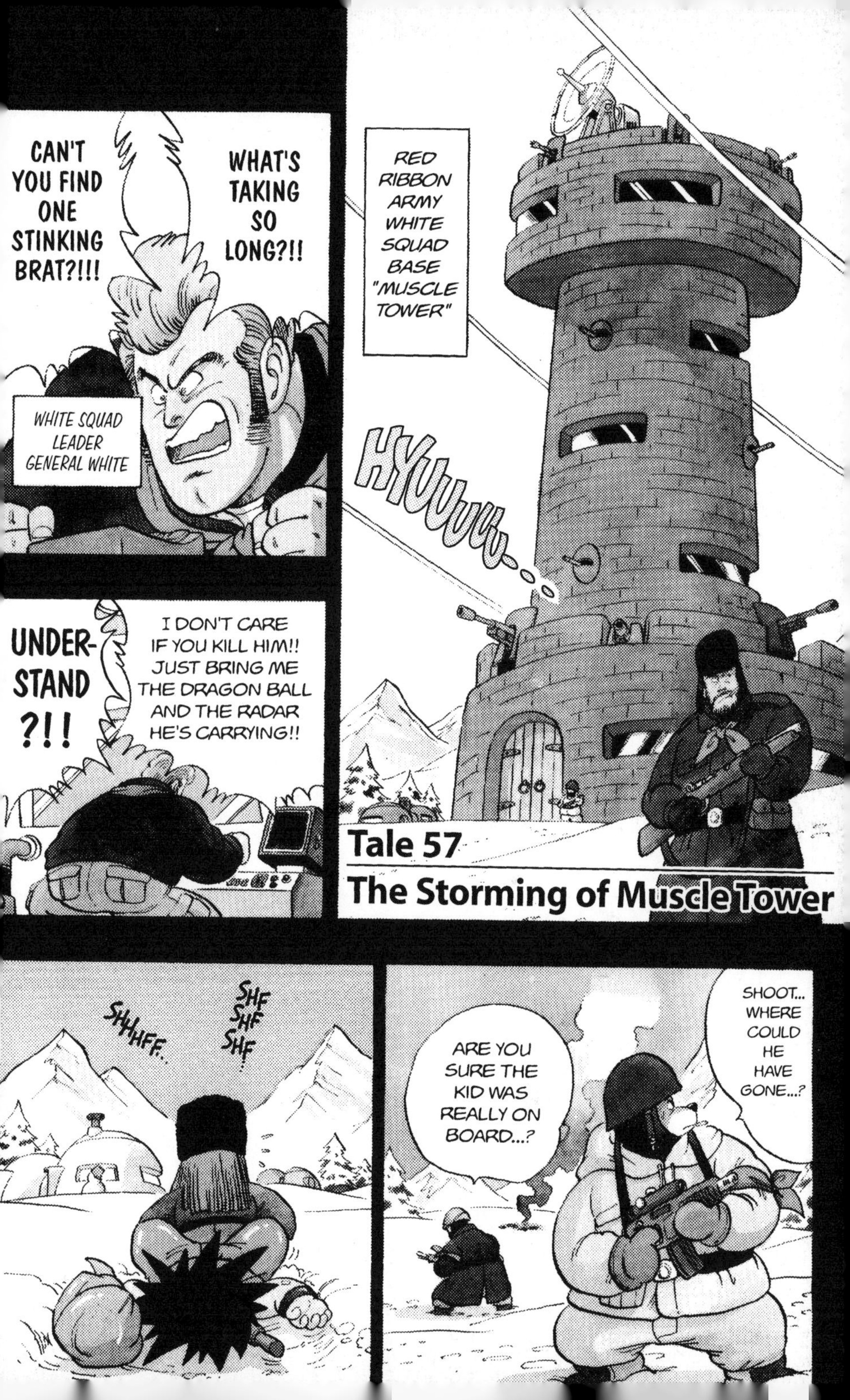
RED RIBBON ARMY WHITE SQUAD BASE "MUSCLE TOWER"
HYUUUUU...
Tale 57
The Storming of Muscle Tower
WHAT'S TAKING SO LONG?!!
CAN'T YOU FIND ONE STINKING BRAT?!!!
WHITE SQUAD LEADER GENERAL WHITE
I DON'T CARE IF YOU KILL HIM!! JUST BRING ME THE DRAGON BALL AND THE RADAR HE'S CARRYING!!
UNDER-STAND?!!
SHOOT... WHERE COULD HE HAVE GONE...?
ARE YOU SURE THE KID WAS REALLY ON BOARD...?
SHF SHF SHF
SHHHFF...

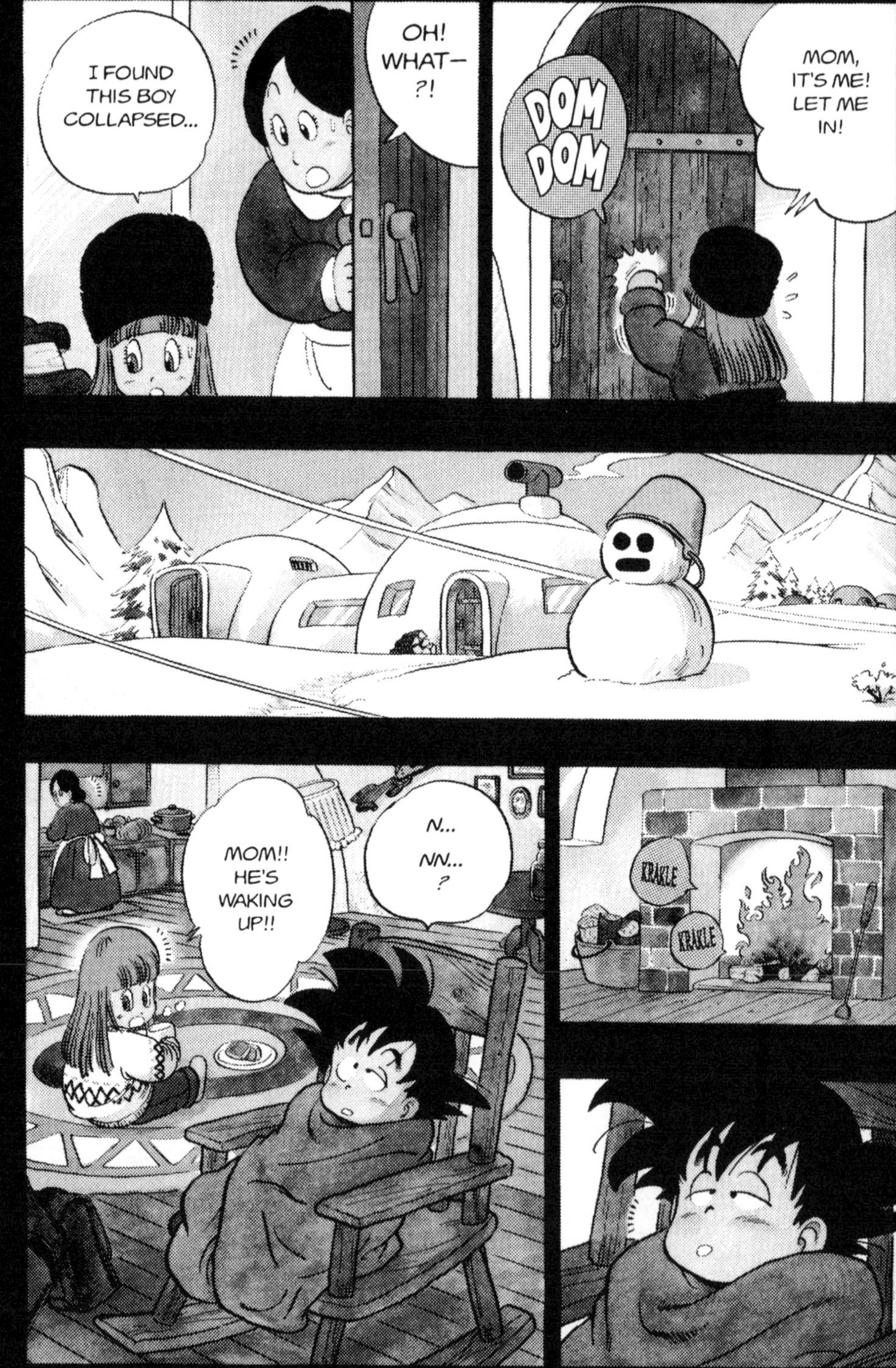

MOM, IT'S ME! LET ME IN!
DOM DOM
OH! WHAT— ?!
I FOUND THIS BOY COLLAPSED...
KRAKLE
KRAKLE
N... NN... ?
MOM!! HE'S WAKING UP!!

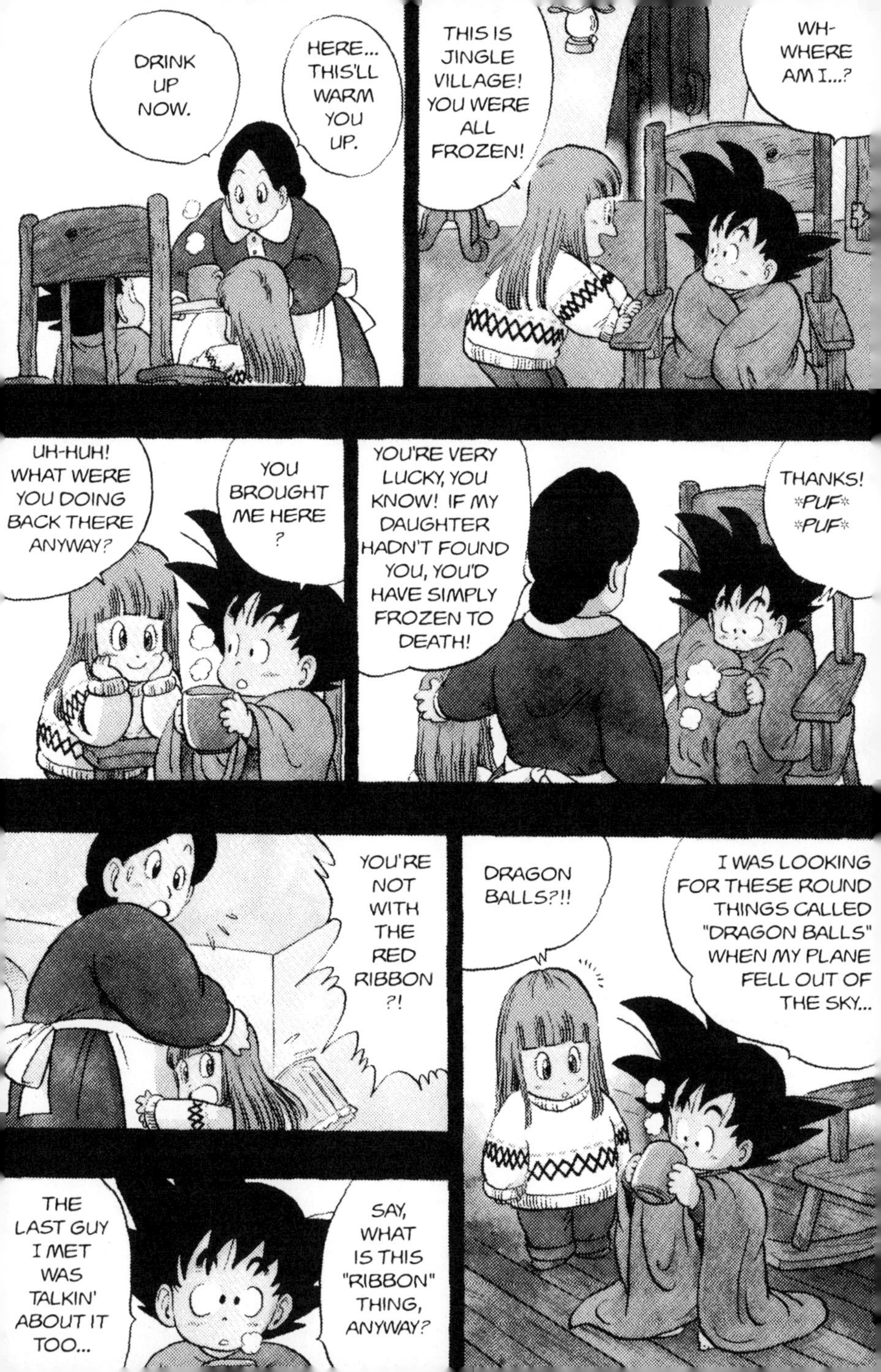
WH- WHERE AM I...?
THIS IS JINGLE VILLAGE! YOU WERE ALL FROZEN!
HERE... THIS'LL WARM YOU UP.
DRINK UP NOW.
THANKS! *PUF* *PUF*
YOU'RE VERY LUCKY, YOU KNOW! IF MY DAUGHTER HADN'T FOUND YOU, YOU'D HAVE SIMPLY FROZEN TO DEATH!
YOU BROUGHT ME HERE?
UH-HUH! WHAT WERE YOU DOING BACK THERE ANYWAY?
I WAS LOOKING FOR THESE ROUND THINGS CALLED "DRAGON BALLS" WHEN MY PLANE FELL OUT OF THE SKY...
DRAGON BALLS?!!
YOU'RE NOT WITH THE RED RIBBON?!
SAY, WHAT IS THIS "RIBBON" THING, ANYWAY?
THE LAST GUY I MET WAS TALKIN' ABOUT IT TOO...

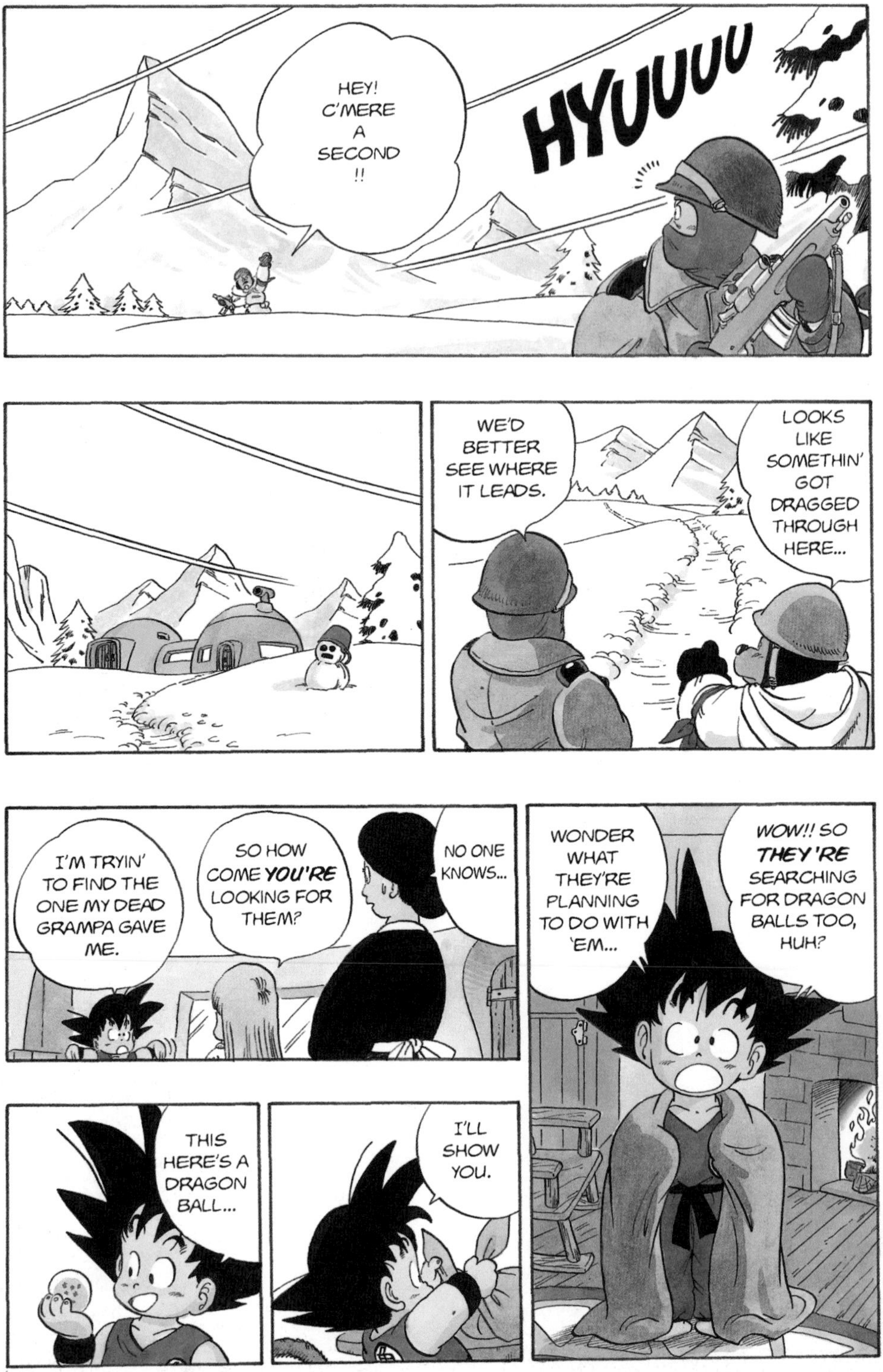
HYUUUU
HEY! C'MERE A SECOND!!
LOOKS LIKE SOMETHIN' GOT DRAGGED THROUGH HERE...
WE'D BETTER SEE WHERE IT LEADS.
WOW!! SO *THEY'RE* SEARCHING FOR DRAGON BALLS TOO, HUH?
WONDER WHAT THEY'RE PLANNING TO DO WITH 'EM...
NO ONE KNOWS...
SO HOW COME *YOU'RE* LOOKING FOR THEM?
I'M TRYIN' TO FIND THE ONE MY DEAD GRAMPA GAVE ME.
I'LL SHOW YOU.
THIS HERE'S A DRAGON BALL...

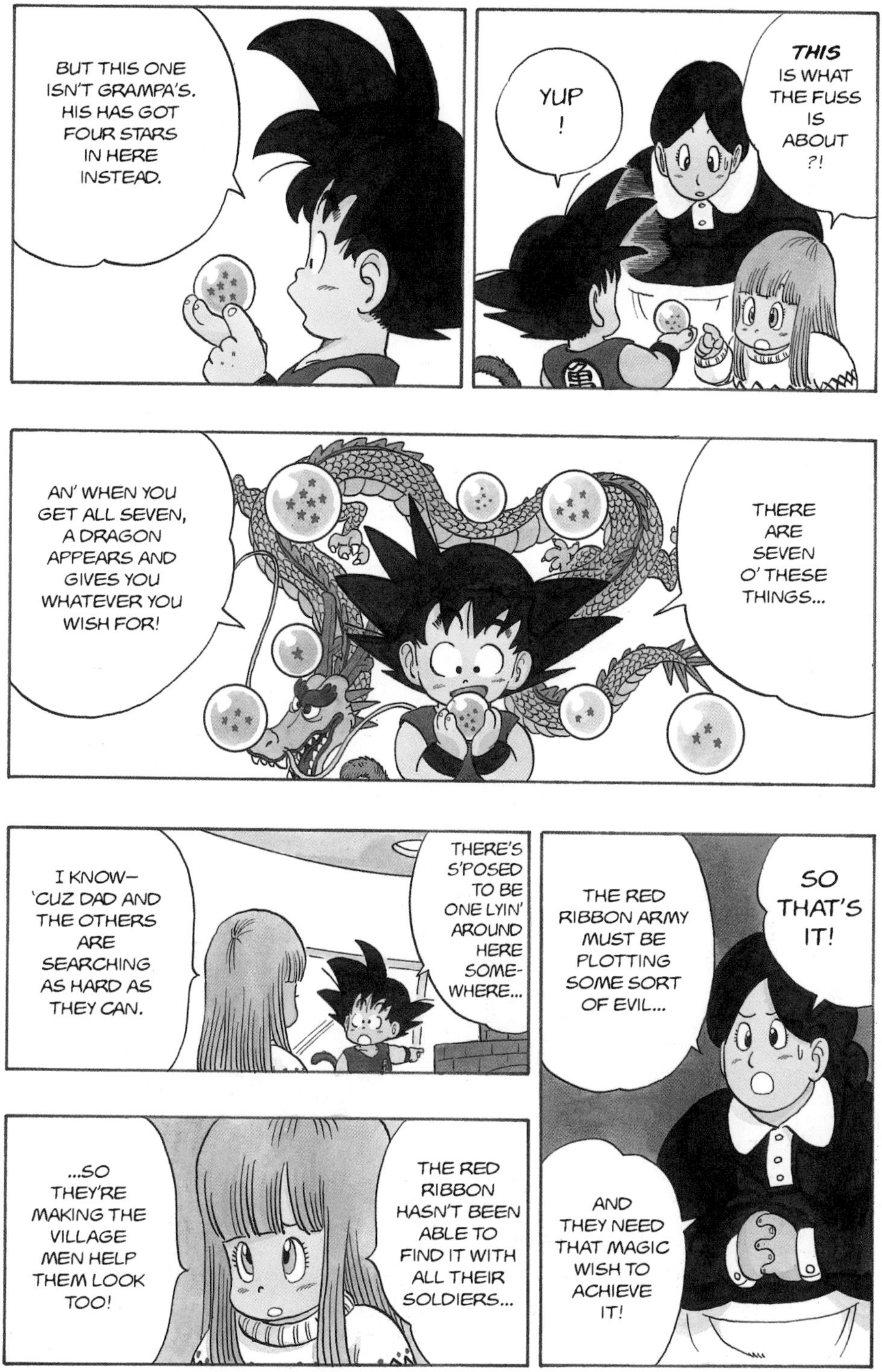
THIS IS WHAT THE FUSS IS ABOUT ?!
YUP !
BUT THIS ONE ISN'T GRAMPA'S. HIS HAS GOT FOUR STARS IN HERE INSTEAD.
THERE ARE SEVEN O' THESE THINGS...
AN' WHEN YOU GET ALL SEVEN, A DRAGON APPEARS AND GIVES YOU WHATEVER YOU WISH FOR!
SO THAT'S IT!
THE RED RIBBON ARMY MUST BE PLOTTING SOME SORT OF EVIL...
AND THEY NEED THAT MAGIC WISH TO ACHIEVE IT!
THERE'S S'POSED TO BE ONE LYIN' AROUND HERE SOME-WHERE...
I KNOW— 'CUZ DAD AND THE OTHERS ARE SEARCHING AS HARD AS THEY CAN.
THE RED RIBBON HASN'T BEEN ABLE TO FIND IT WITH ALL THEIR SOLDIERS...
...SO THEY'RE MAKING THE VILLAGE MEN HELP THEM LOOK TOO!

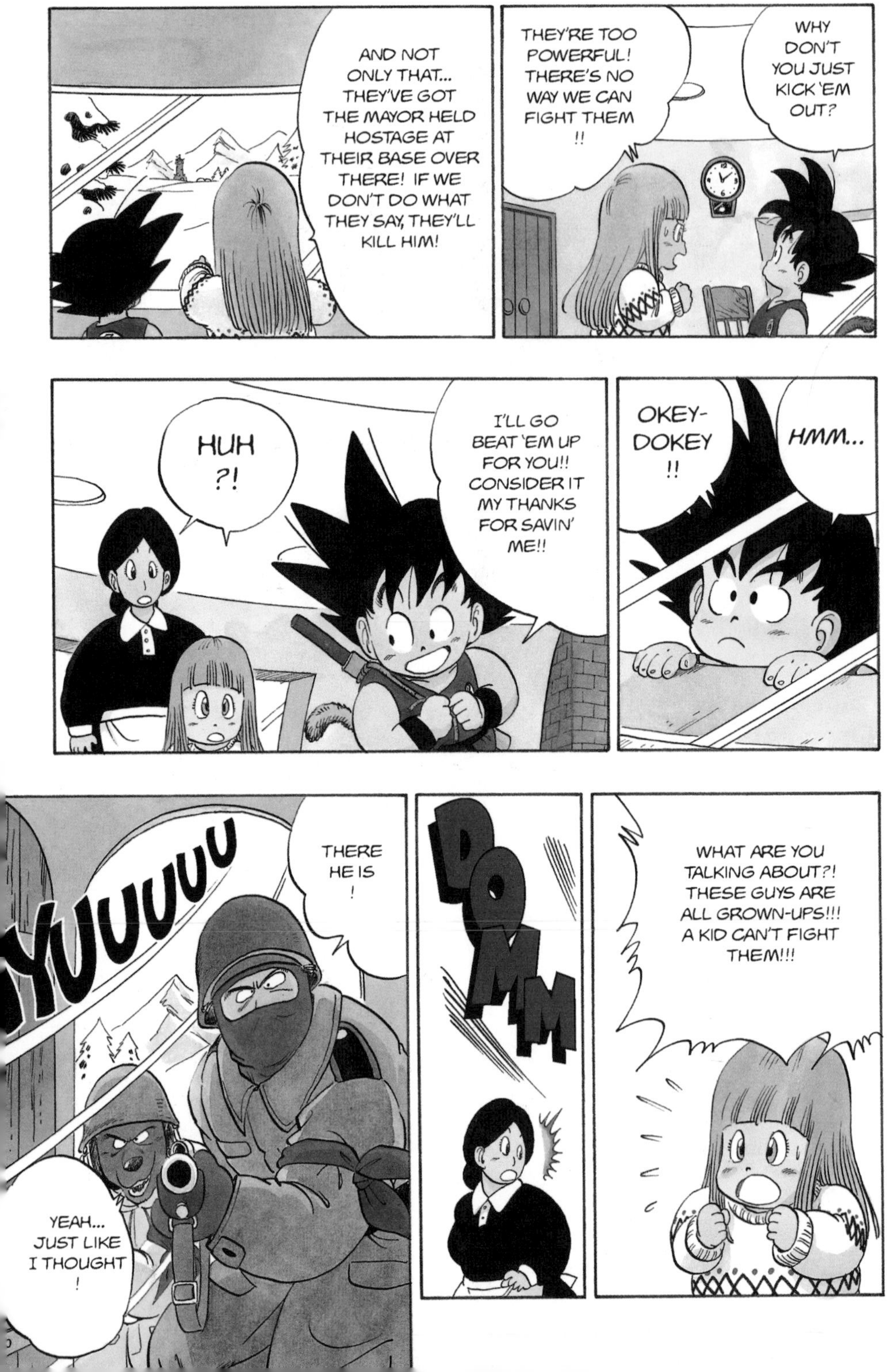
WHY DON'T YOU JUST KICK 'EM OUT?
THEY'RE TOO POWERFUL! THERE'S NO WAY WE CAN FIGHT THEM !!
AND NOT ONLY THAT... THEY'VE GOT THE MAYOR HELD HOSTAGE AT THEIR BASE OVER THERE! IF WE DON'T DO WHAT THEY SAY, THEY'LL KILL HIM!
HMM...
OKEY-DOKEY !!
I'LL GO BEAT 'EM UP FOR YOU!! CONSIDER IT MY THANKS FOR SAVIN' ME!!
HUH ?!
WHAT ARE YOU TALKING ABOUT?! THESE GUYS ARE ALL GROWN-UPS!!! A KID CAN'T FIGHT THEM!!!
DOMMM
THERE HE IS !
YUUUUU
YEAH... JUST LIKE I THOUGHT !

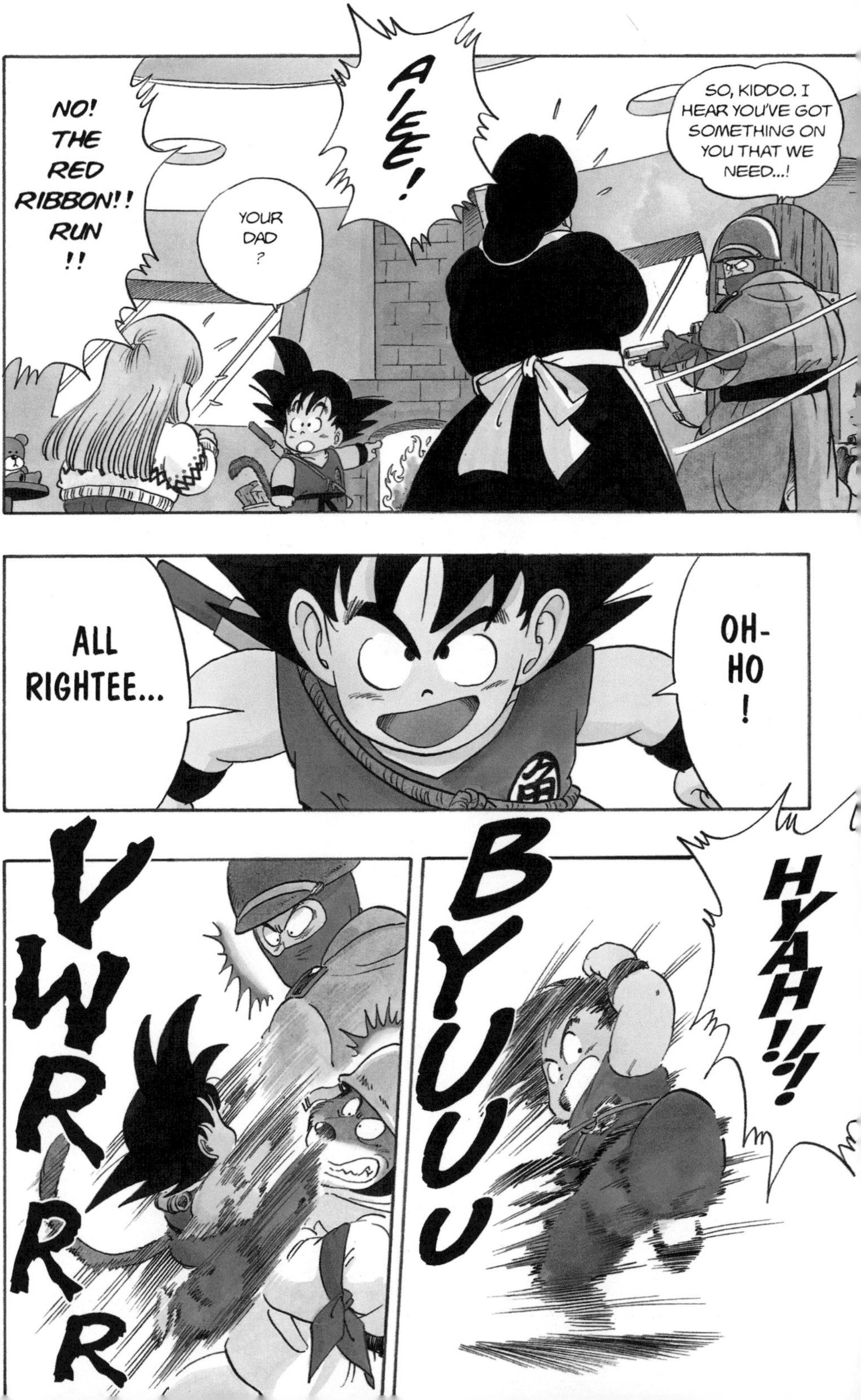
SO, KIDDO. I HEAR YOU'VE GOT SOMETHING ON YOU THAT WE NEED...!
AIEE!
YOUR DAD ?
NO! THE RED RIBBON!! RUN !!
OH-HO !
ALL RIGHTEE...
HYAH!!!
BYUUU
VWRRRR

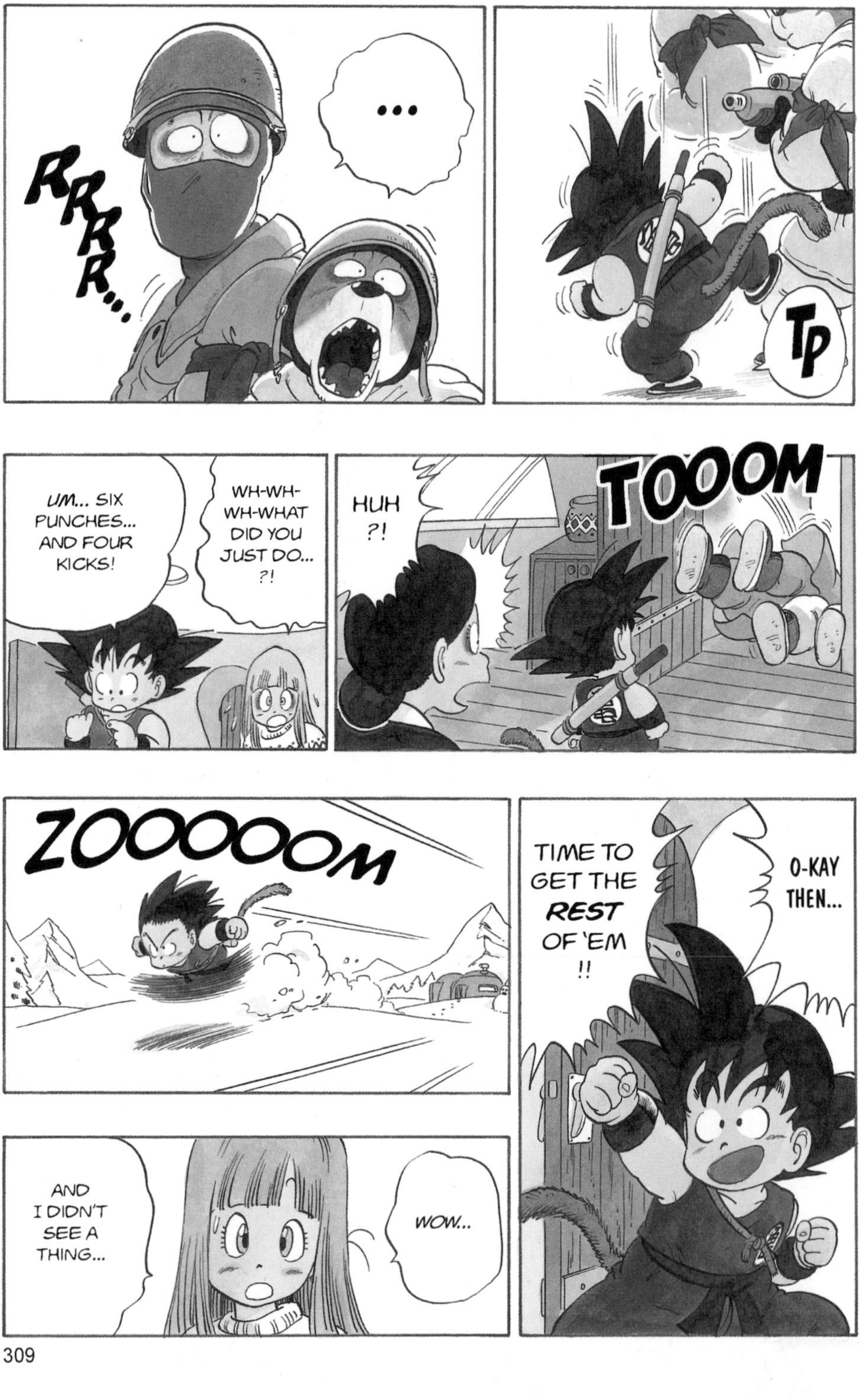
Tp
...
RRRR...
TOOOM
HUH ?!
WH-WH-WH-WHAT DID YOU JUST DO... ?!
UM... SIX PUNCHES... AND FOUR KICKS!
O-KAY THEN...
TIME TO GET THE REST OF 'EM !!
ZOOOOOM
WOW...
AND I DIDN'T SEE A THING...

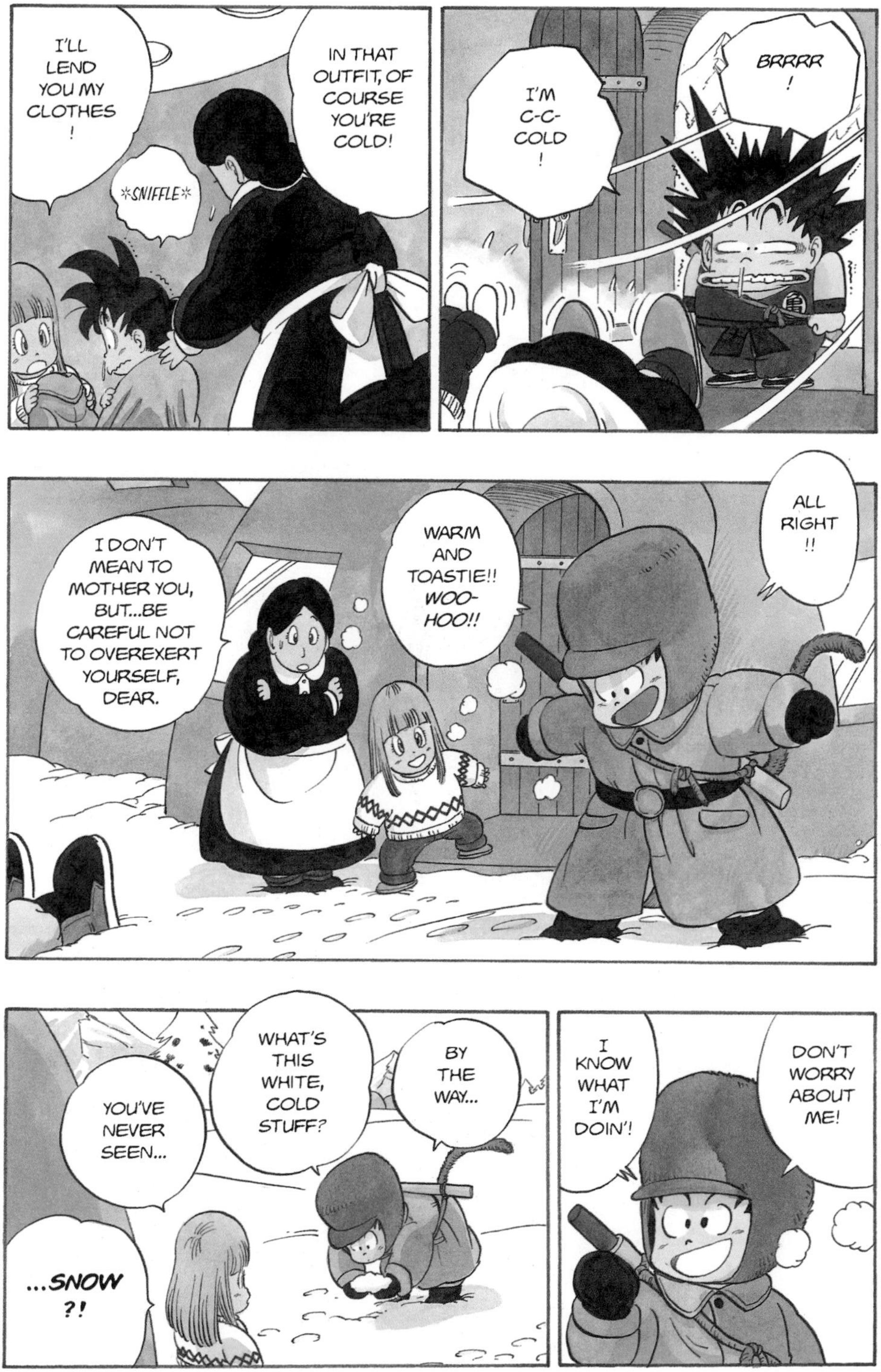
BRRRR!
I'M C-C-COLD!
IN THAT OUTFIT, OF COURSE YOU'RE COLD!
I'LL LEND YOU MY CLOTHES!
SNIFFLE
ALL RIGHT!!
WARM AND TOASTIE!! WOO-HOO!!
I DON'T MEAN TO MOTHER YOU, BUT...BE CAREFUL NOT TO OVEREXERT YOURSELF, DEAR.
DON'T WORRY ABOUT ME!
I KNOW WHAT I'M DOIN'!
BY THE WAY...
WHAT'S THIS WHITE, COLD STUFF?
YOU'VE NEVER SEEN...
...SNOW?!

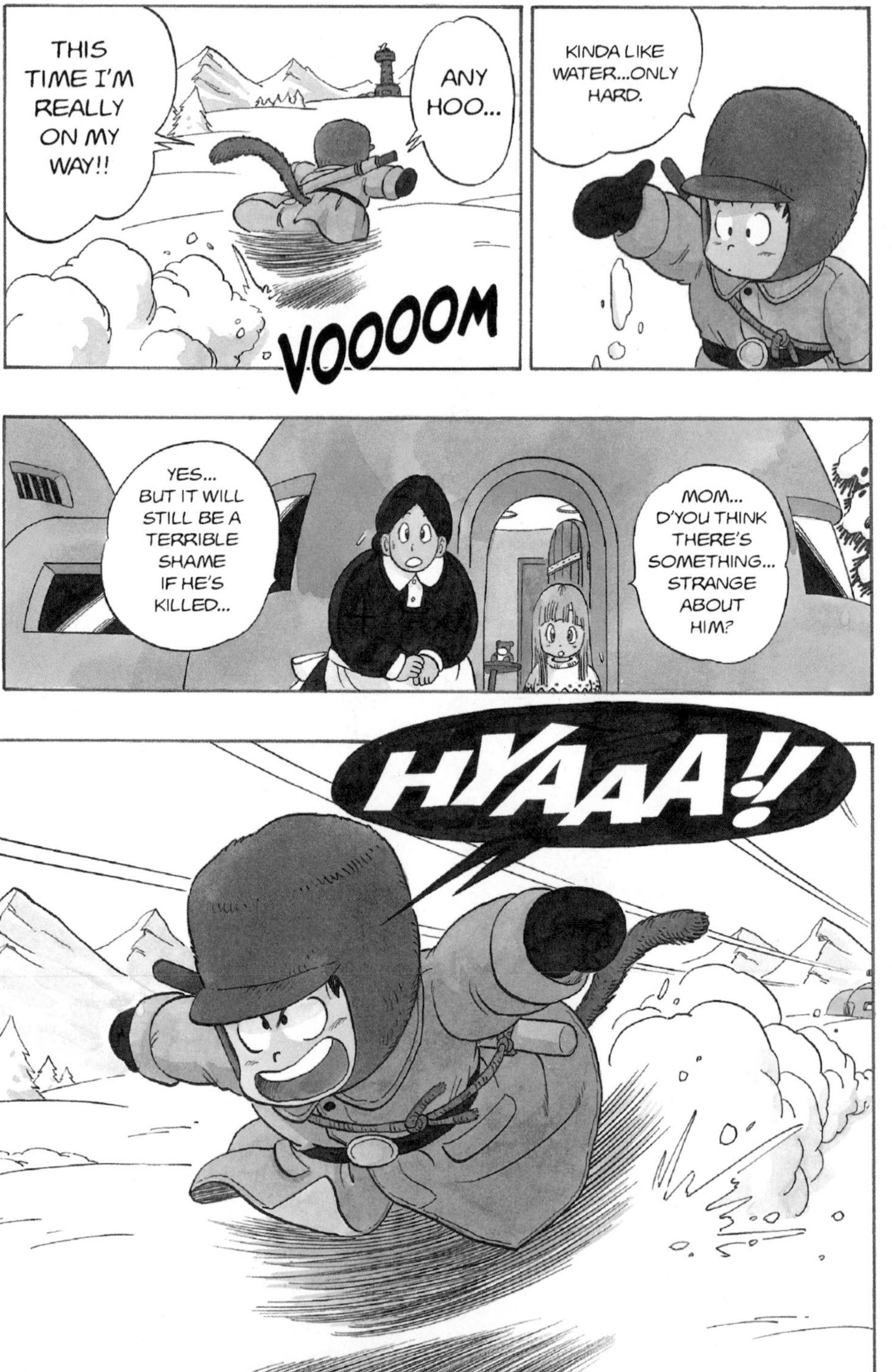
KINDA LIKE WATER...ONLY HARD.
ANY HOO...
THIS TIME I'M REALLY ON MY WAY!!
VOOOOM
MOM... D'YOU THINK THERE'S SOMETHING... STRANGE ABOUT HIM?
YES... BUT IT WILL STILL BE A TERRIBLE SHAME IF HE'S KILLED...
HYAAA!!

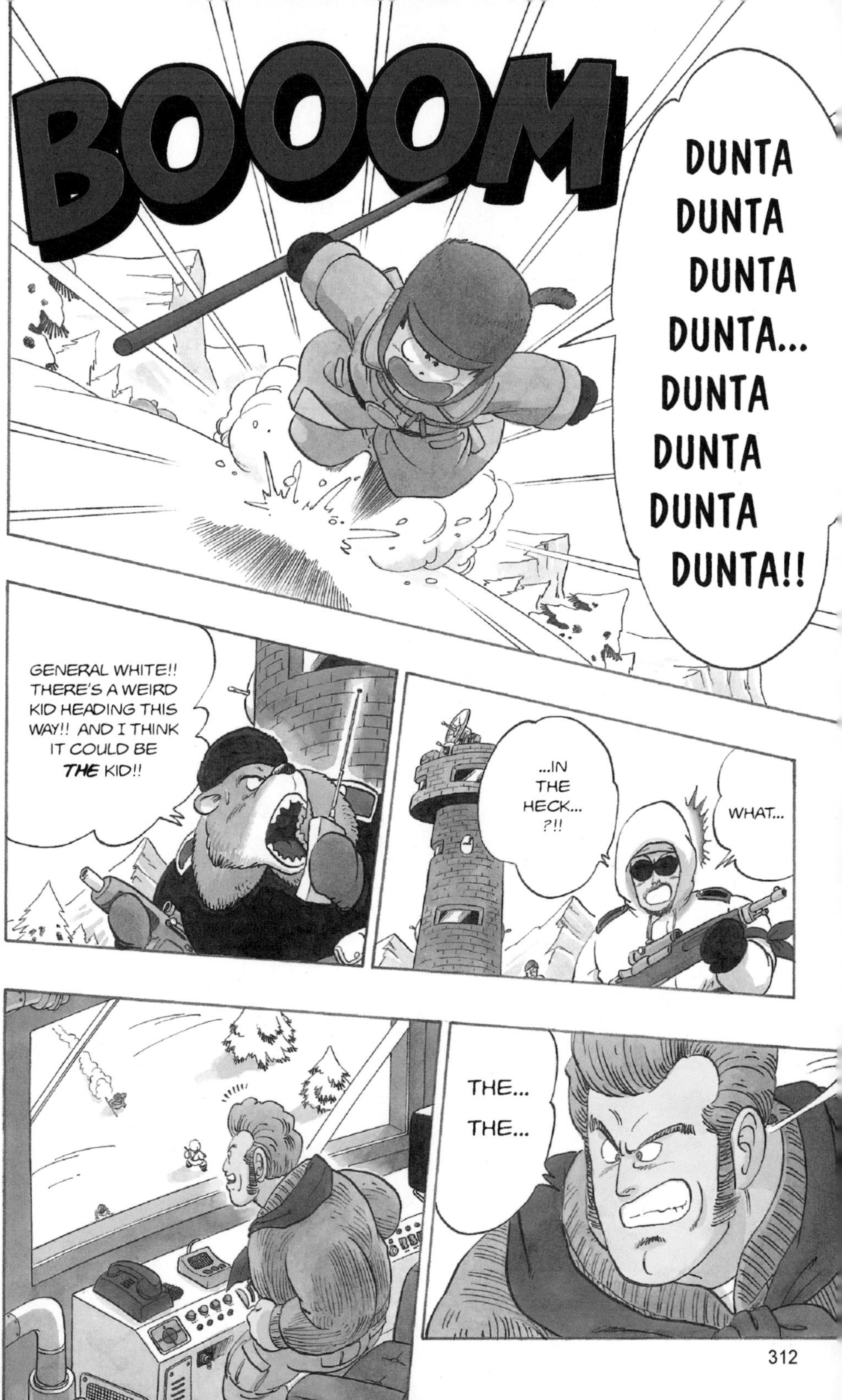
DUNTA DUNTA DUNTA DUNTA... DUNTA DUNTA DUNTA DUNTA!!
BOOOM
WHAT...
...IN THE HECK...?!!
GENERAL WHITE!! THERE'S A WEIRD KID HEADING THIS WAY!! AND I THINK IT COULD BE ***THE*** KID!!
THE... THE...

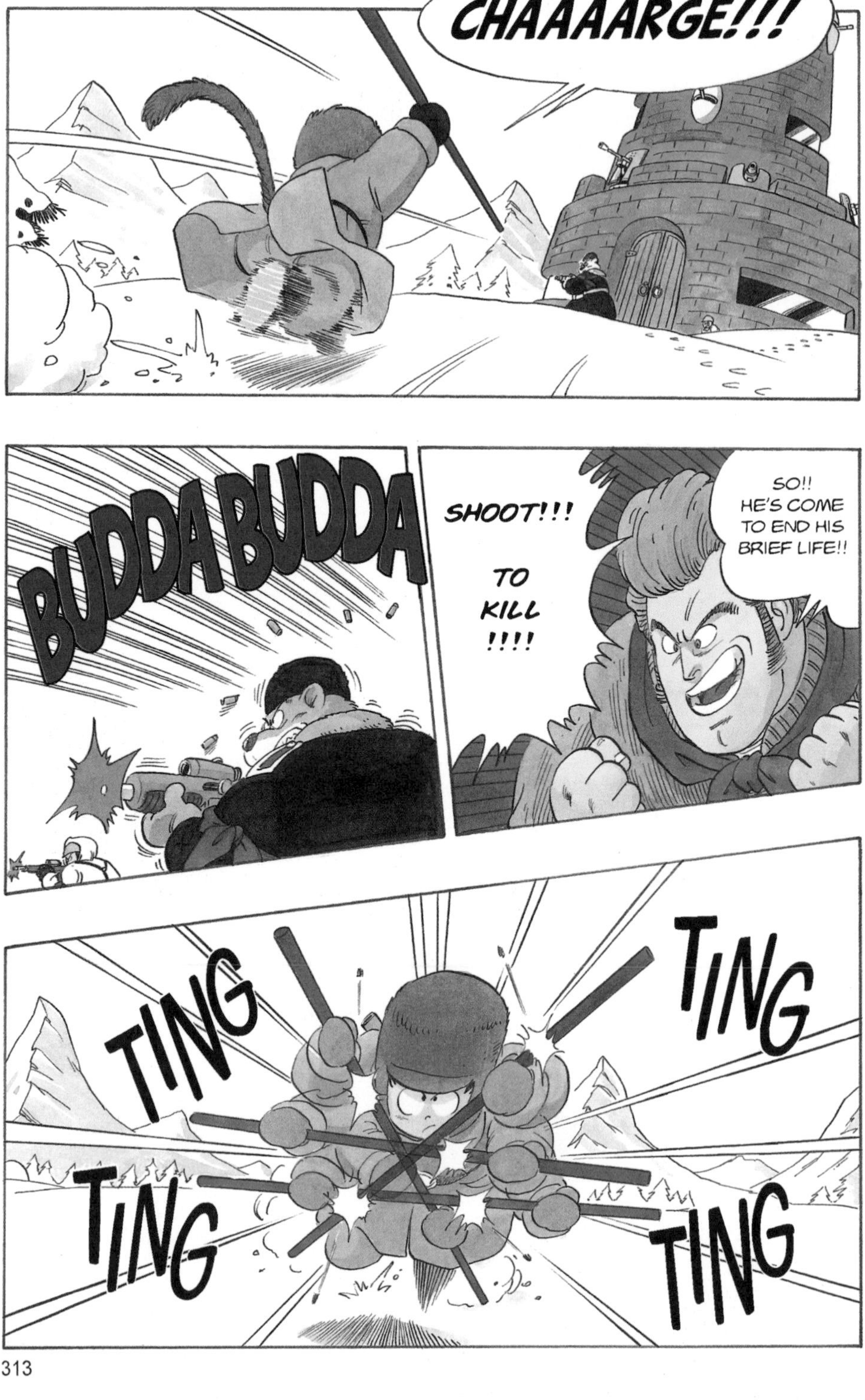
CHAAAARGE!!!
SO!! HE'S COME TO END HIS BRIEF LIFE!!
SHOOT!!!
TO KILL !!!!
BUDDA BUDDA
TING
TING
TING
TING

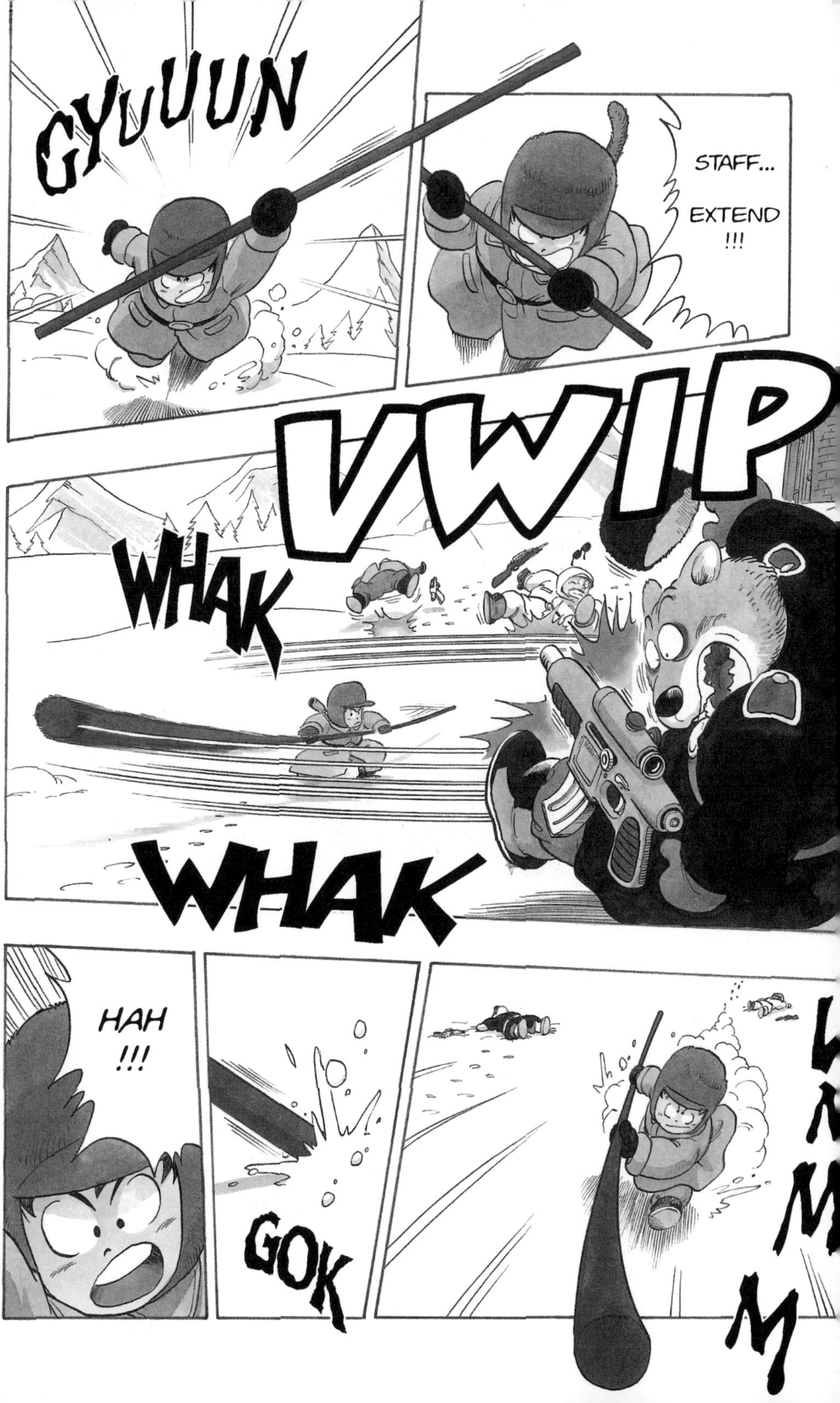
STAFF...
EXTEND !!!
GYUUUN
VWIP
WHAK
WHAK
GOK
HAH !!!

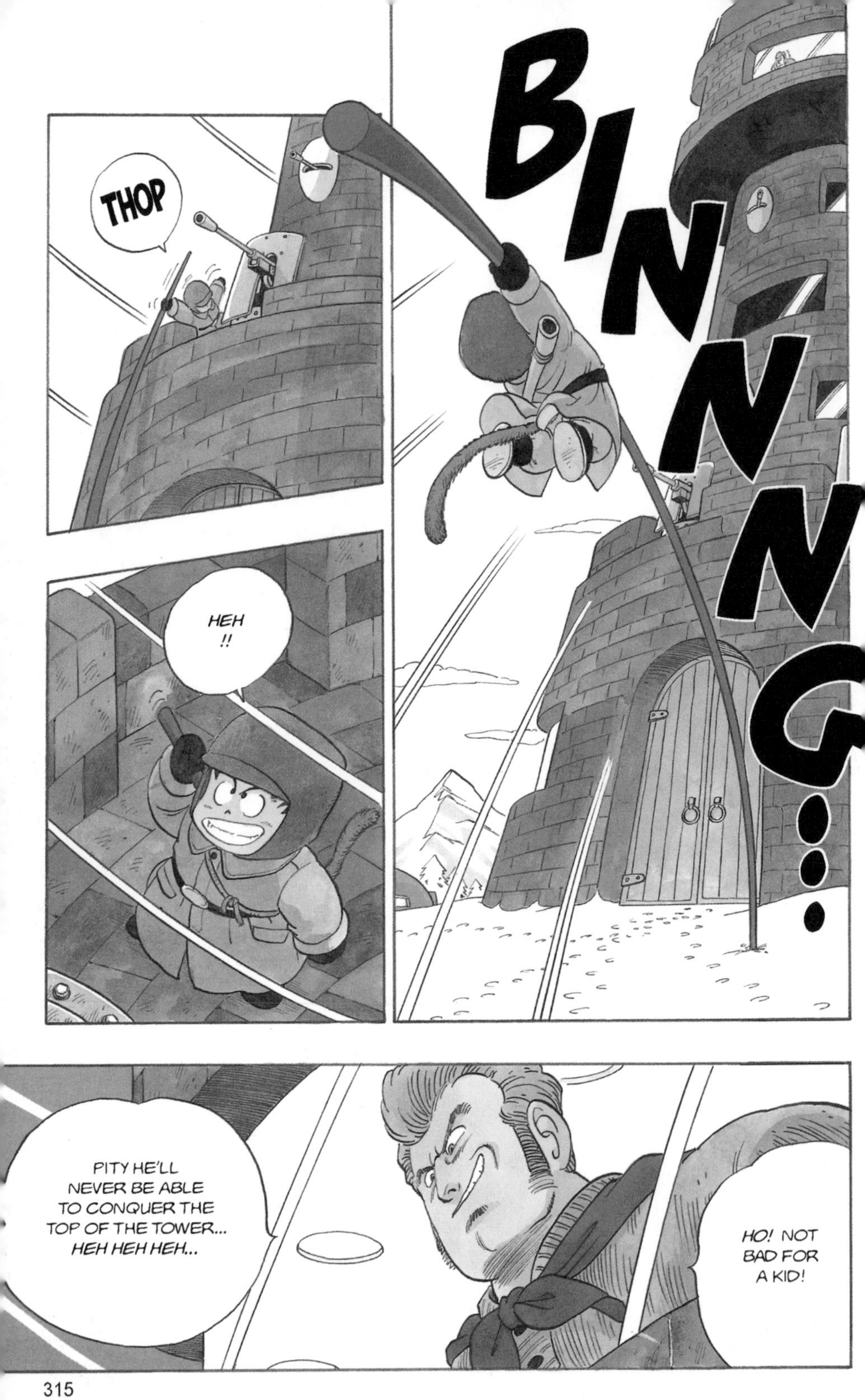
BINNNG...
THOP
HEH !!
HO! NOT BAD FOR A KID!
PITY HE'LL NEVER BE ABLE TO CONQUER THE TOP OF THE TOWER... HEH HEH HEH...

Tale 58 • The Flexing of Muscle Tower

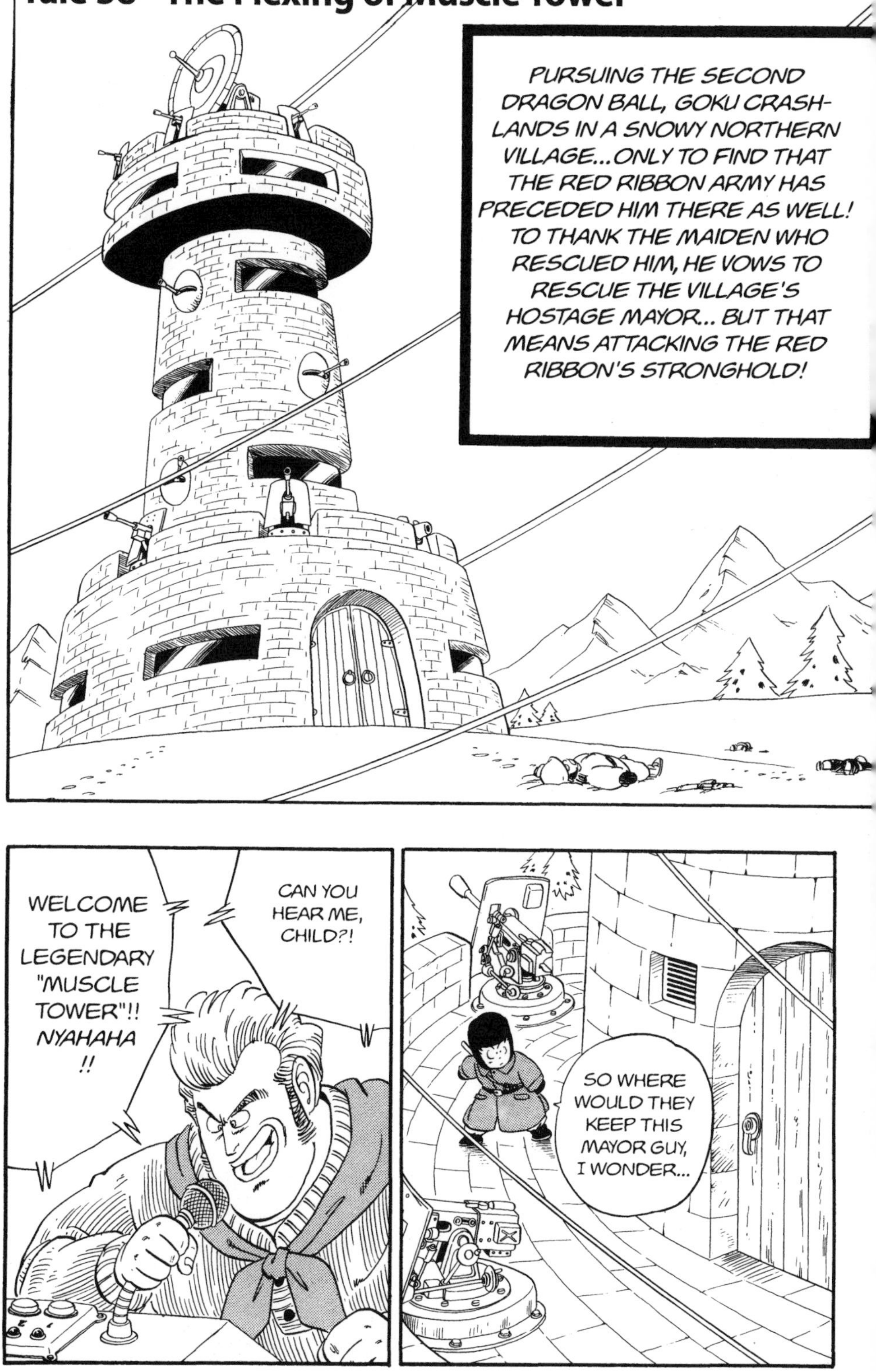
PURSUING THE SECOND DRAGON BALL, GOKU CRASH-LANDS IN A SNOWY NORTHERN VILLAGE...ONLY TO FIND THAT THE RED RIBBON ARMY HAS PRECEDED HIM THERE AS WELL! TO THANK THE MAIDEN WHO RESCUED HIM, HE VOWS TO RESCUE THE VILLAGE'S HOSTAGE MAYOR... BUT THAT MEANS ATTACKING THE RED RIBBON'S STRONGHOLD!
SO WHERE WOULD THEY KEEP THIS MAYOR GUY, I WONDER...
CAN YOU HEAR ME, CHILD?!
WELCOME TO THE LEGENDARY "MUSCLE TOWER"!! NYAHAHA !!

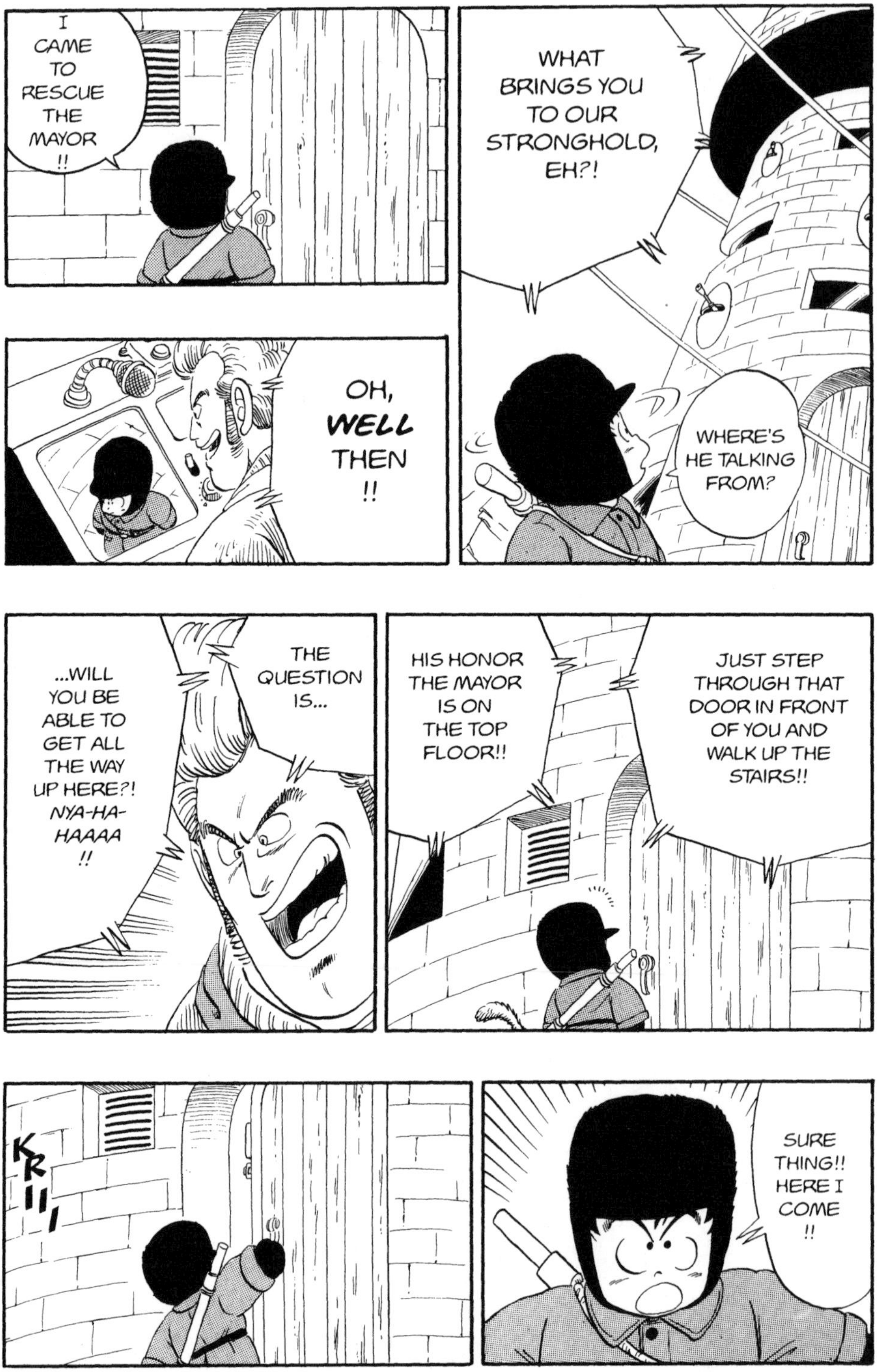
WHAT BRINGS YOU TO OUR STRONGHOLD, EH?!
WHERE'S HE TALKING FROM?
I CAME TO RESCUE THE MAYOR!!
OH, WELL THEN!!
JUST STEP THROUGH THAT DOOR IN FRONT OF YOU AND WALK UP THE STAIRS!!
HIS HONOR THE MAYOR IS ON THE TOP FLOOR!!
THE QUESTION IS...
...WILL YOU BE ABLE TO GET ALL THE WAY UP HERE?! NYA-HA-HAAAA!!
SURE THING!! HERE I COME!!
KRIII

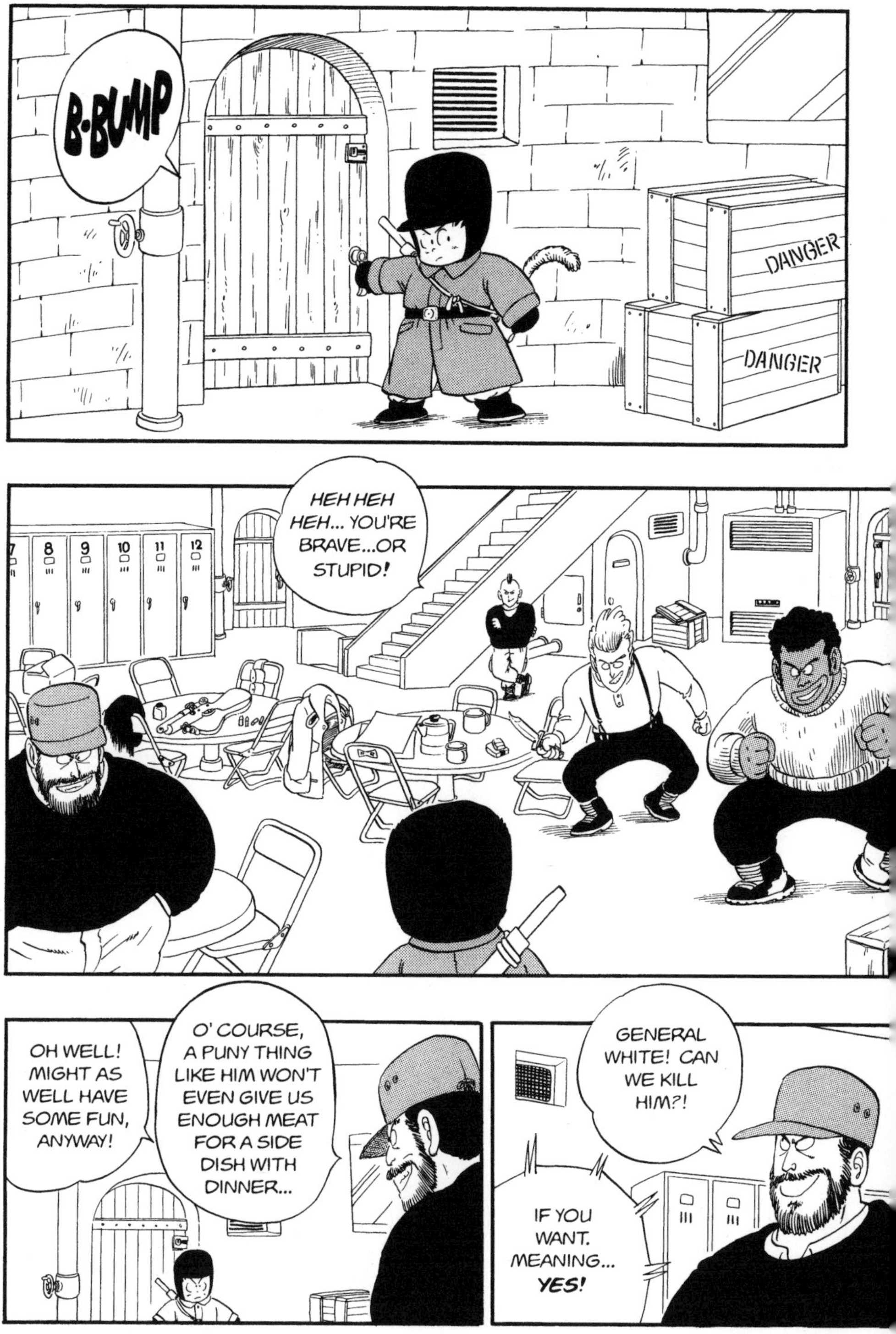
B-BUMP
DANGER
DANGER
HEH HEH HEH... YOU'RE BRAVE...OR STUPID!
GENERAL WHITE! CAN WE KILL HIM?!
IF YOU WANT. MEANING... ***YES!***
O' COURSE, A PUNY THING LIKE HIM WON'T EVEN GIVE US ENOUGH MEAT FOR A SIDE DISH WITH DINNER...
OH WELL! MIGHT AS WELL HAVE SOME FUN, ANYWAY!

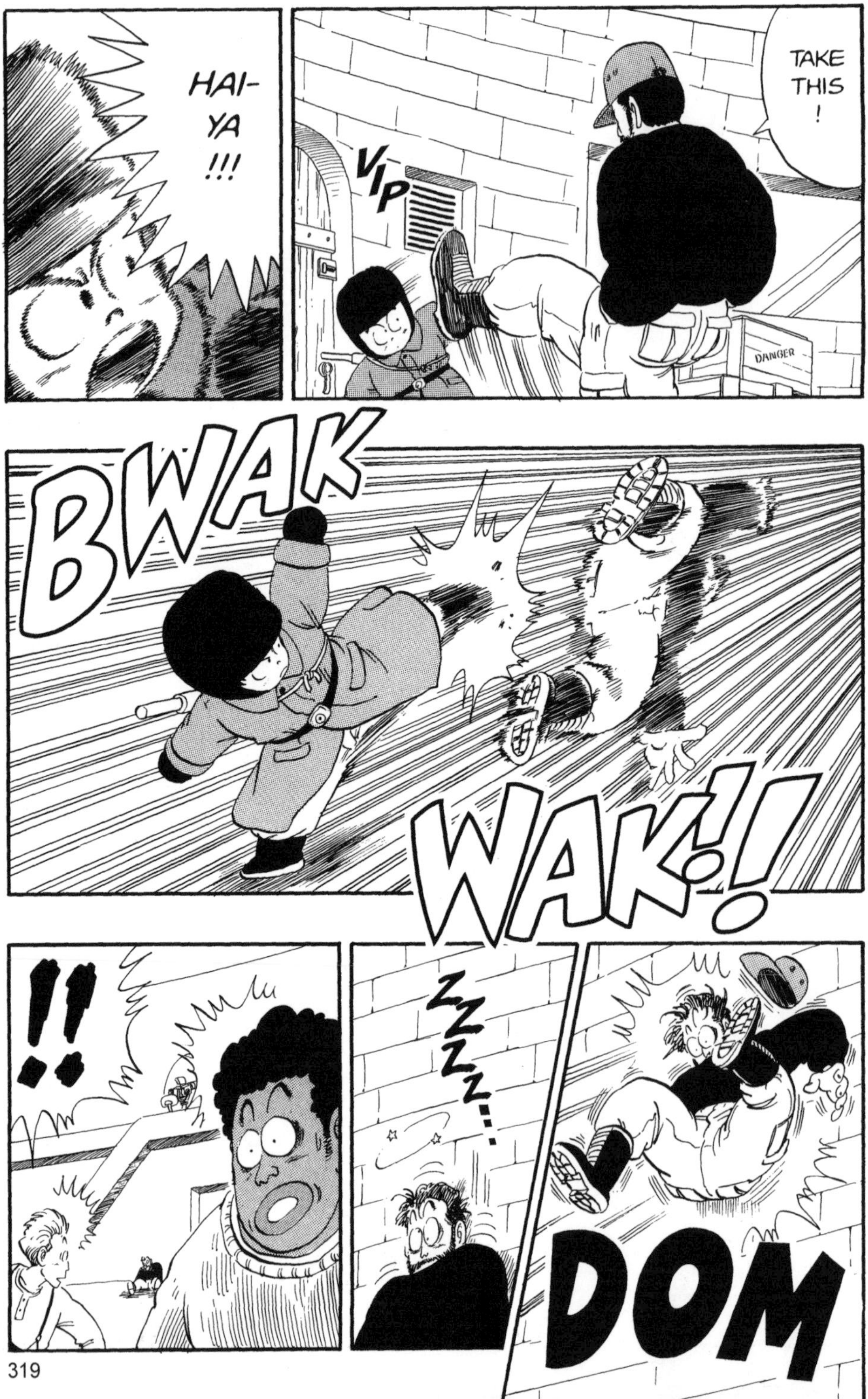
TAKE THIS !
VIP
DANGER
HAI-YA !!!
BWAK
WAK!!
DOM
ZZZZ...
!!

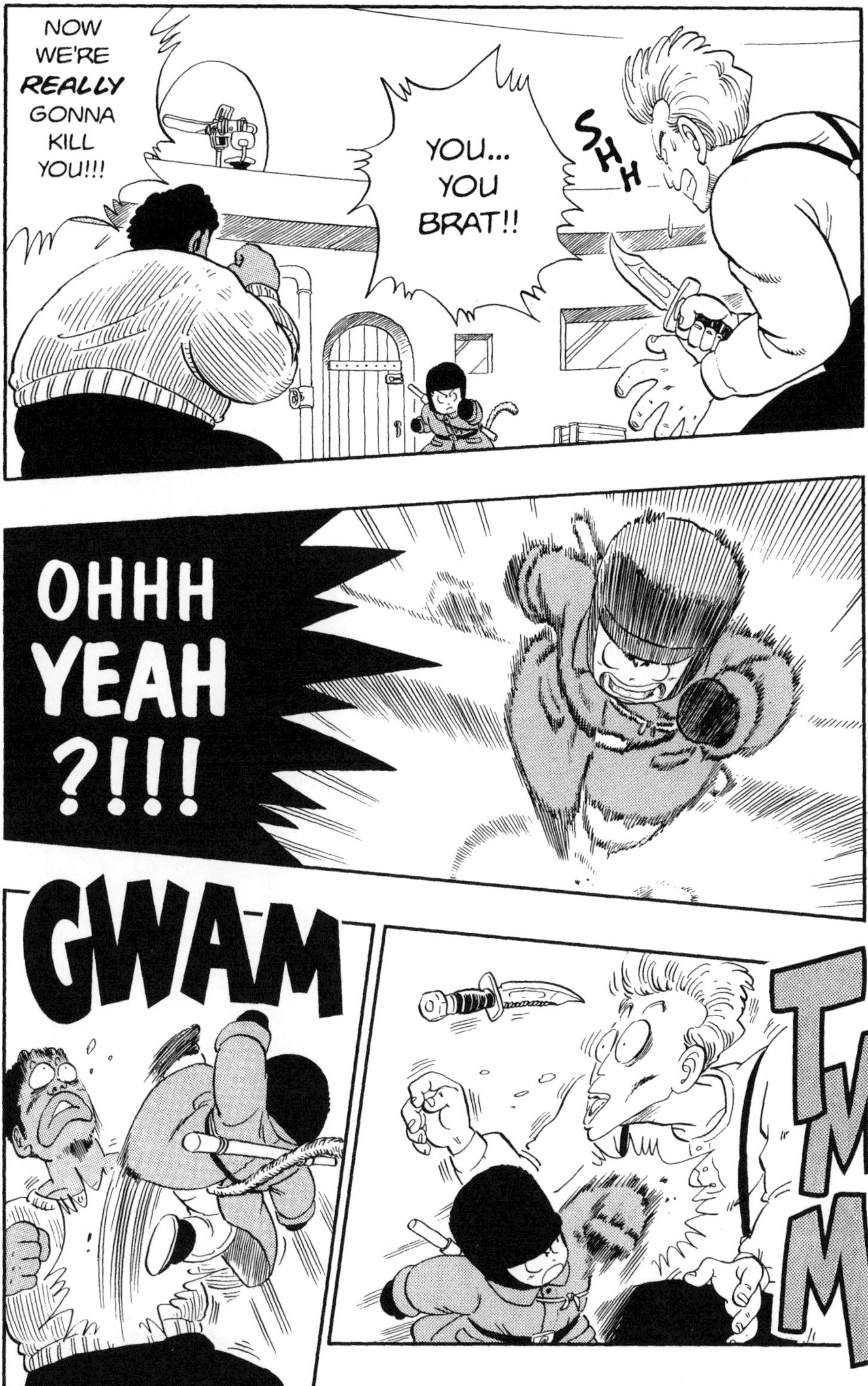
SHH
YOU... YOU BRAT!!
NOW WE'RE REALLY GONNA KILL YOU!!!
OHHH YEAH?!!!
TMM
GWAM

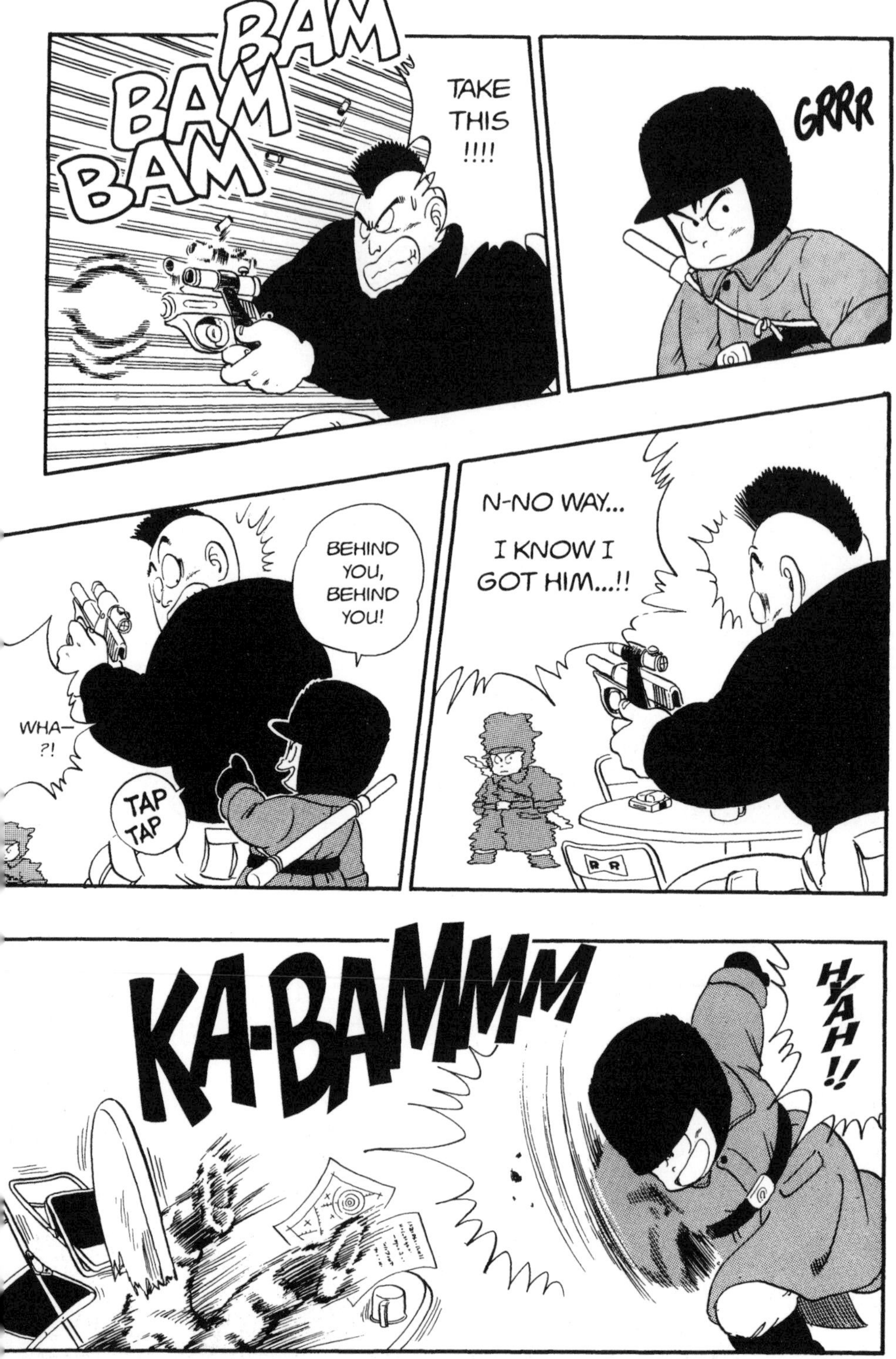
GRRR
BAM
BAM
BAM
TAKE THIS !!!!
N-NO WAY...
I KNOW I GOT HIM...!!
BEHIND YOU, BEHIND YOU!
WHA— ?!
TAP TAP
HYAH!!
KA-BAMMMM

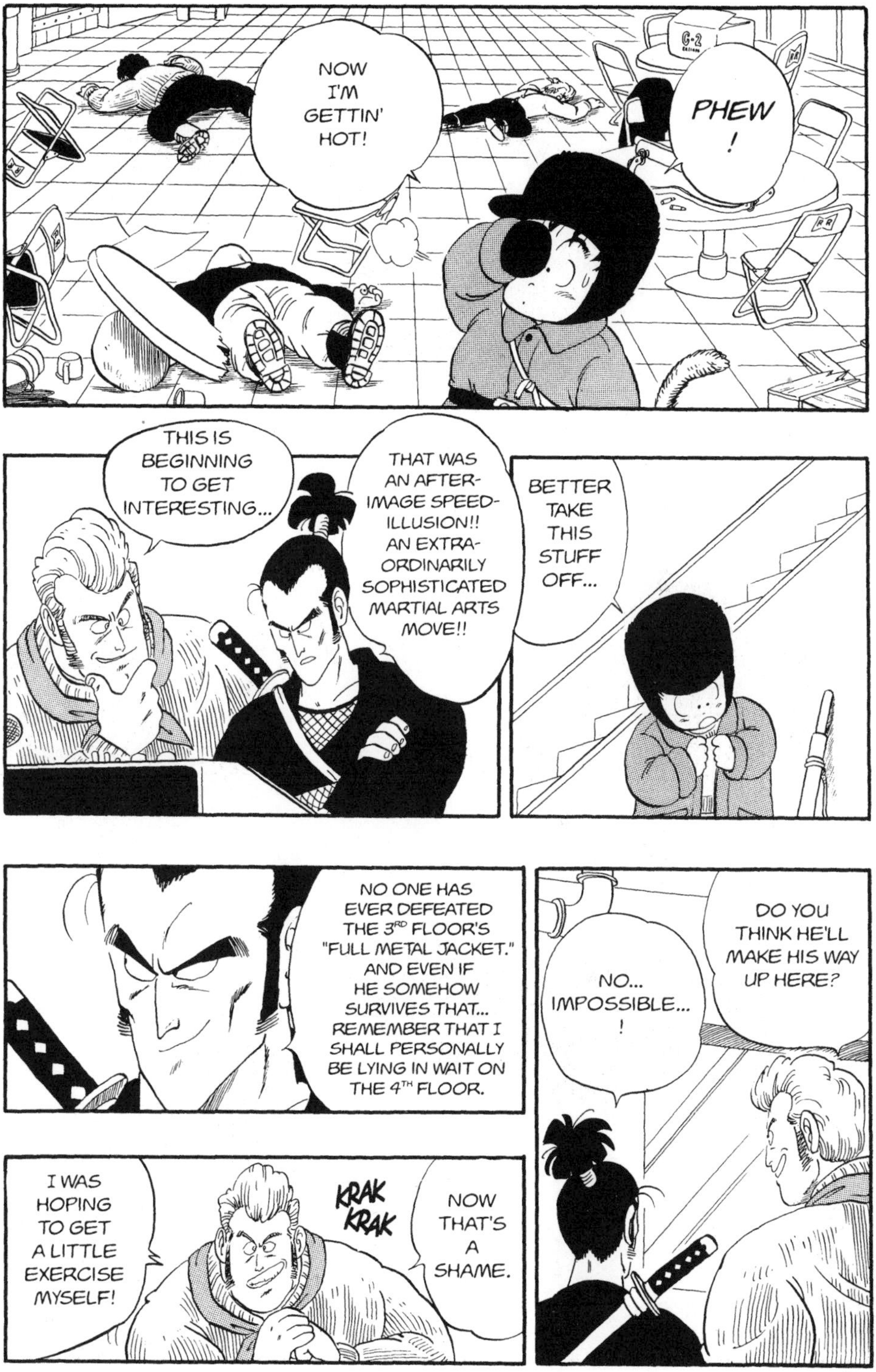
PHEW !
NOW I'M GETTIN' HOT!
BETTER TAKE THIS STUFF OFF...
THAT WAS AN AFTER-IMAGE SPEED-ILLUSION!! AN EXTRA-ORDINARILY SOPHISTICATED MARTIAL ARTS MOVE!!
THIS IS BEGINNING TO GET INTERESTING...
DO YOU THINK HE'LL MAKE HIS WAY UP HERE?
NO... IMPOSSIBLE... !
NO ONE HAS EVER DEFEATED THE 3RD FLOOR'S "FULL METAL JACKET." AND EVEN IF HE SOMEHOW SURVIVES THAT... REMEMBER THAT I SHALL PERSONALLY BE LYING IN WAIT ON THE 4TH FLOOR.
NOW THAT'S A SHAME.
KRAK KRAK
I WAS HOPING TO GET A LITTLE EXERCISE MYSELF!

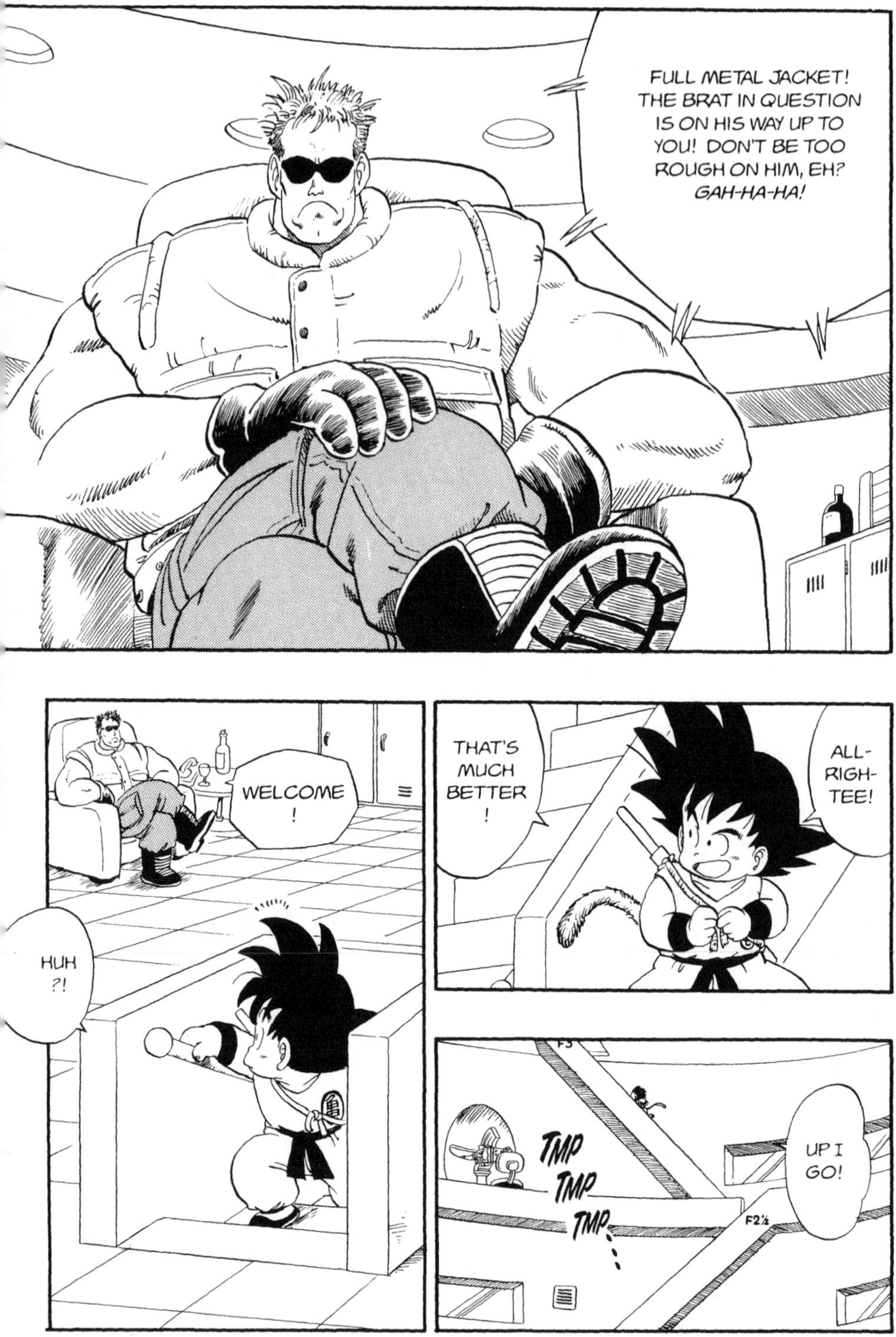
FULL METAL JACKET! THE BRAT IN QUESTION IS ON HIS WAY UP TO YOU! DON'T BE TOO ROUGH ON HIM, EH? GAH-HA-HA!
ALL-RIGHTEE!
THAT'S MUCH BETTER!
F3
UP I GO!
TMP TMP TMP...
F2½
WELCOME!
HUH?!

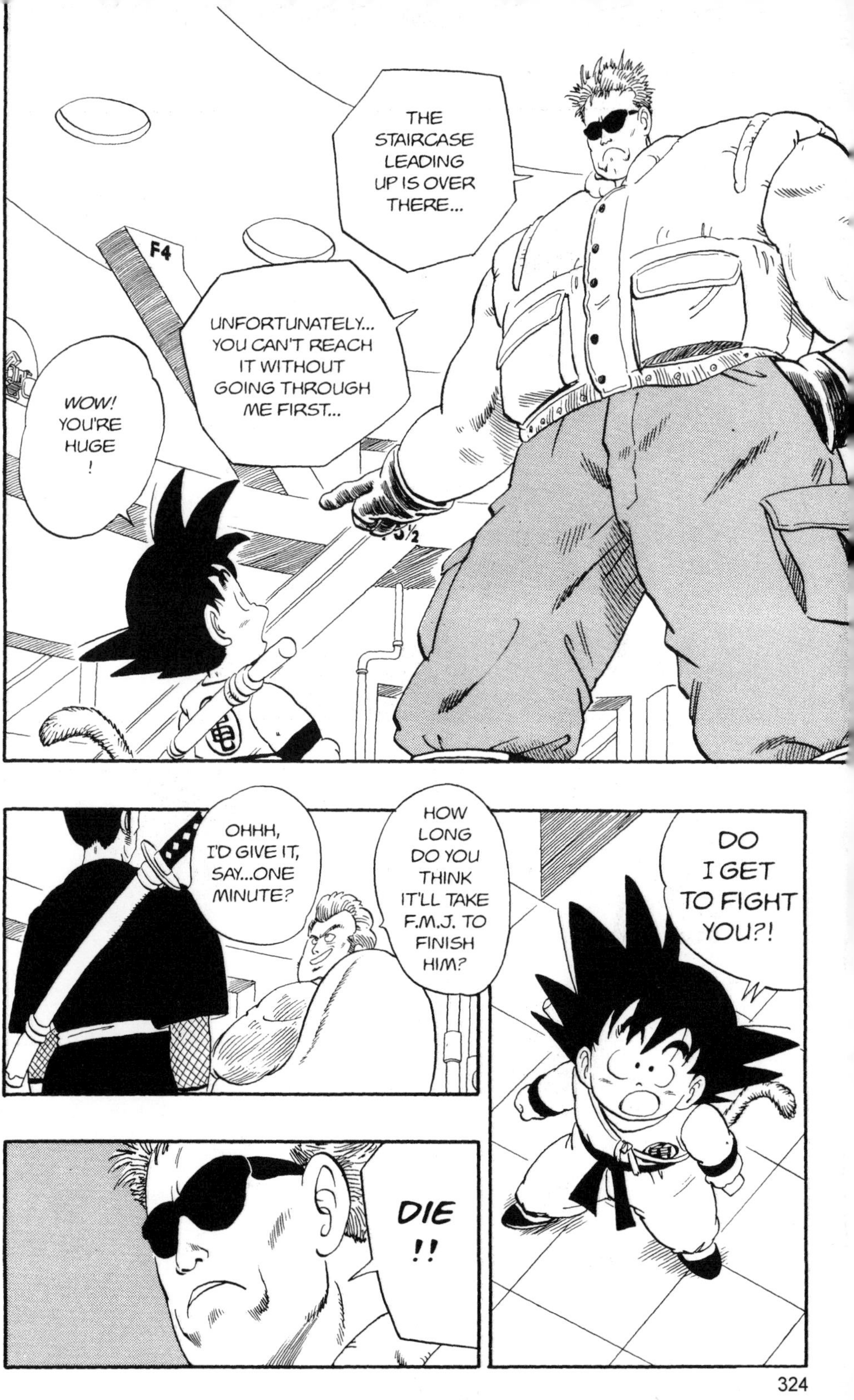
THE STAIRCASE LEADING UP IS OVER THERE...
F4
UNFORTUNATELY... YOU CAN'T REACH IT WITHOUT GOING THROUGH ME FIRST...
WOW! YOU'RE HUGE!
DO I GET TO FIGHT YOU?!
HOW LONG DO YOU THINK IT'LL TAKE F.M.J. TO FINISH HIM?
OHHH, I'D GIVE IT, SAY...ONE MINUTE?
DIE!!

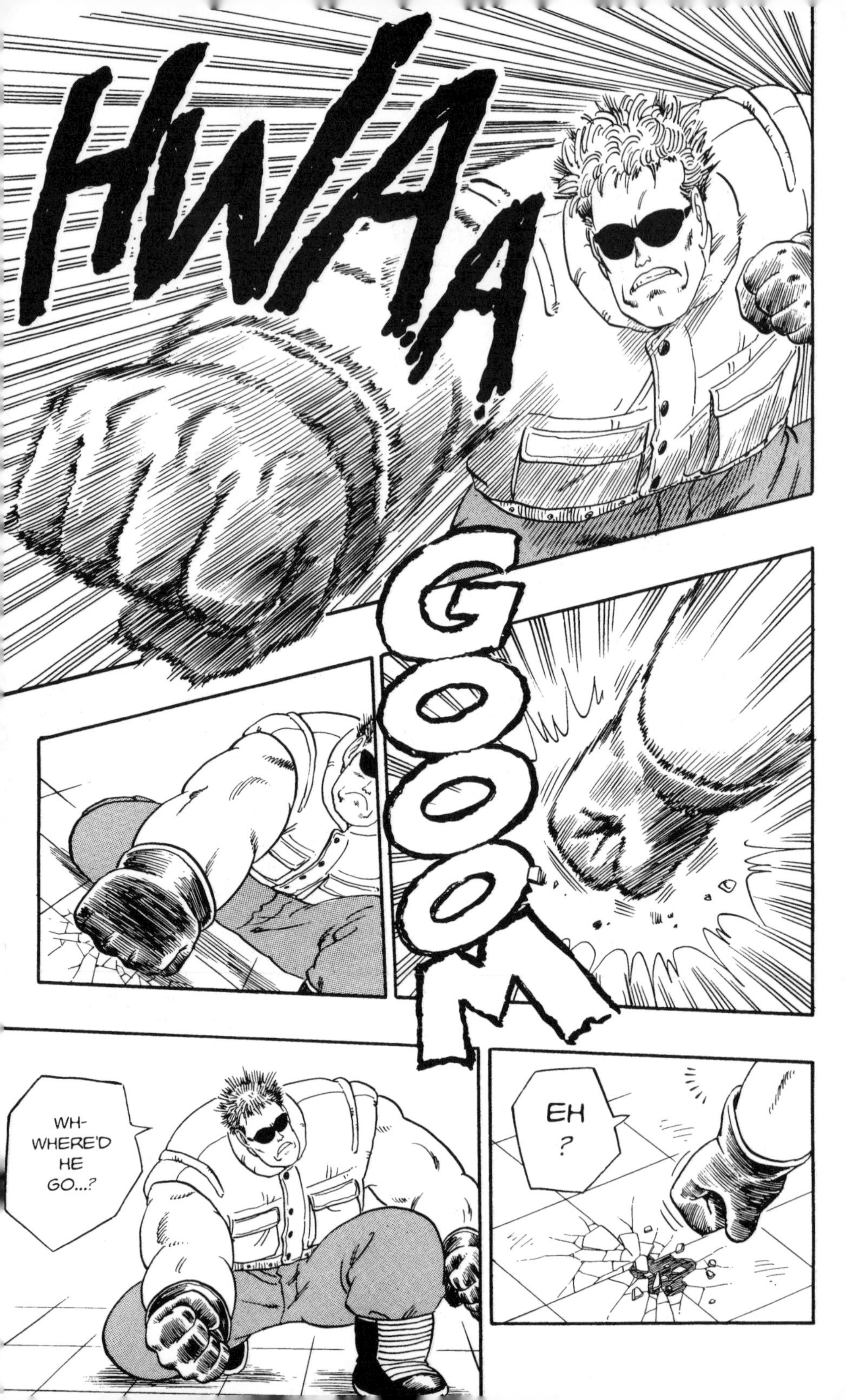
HWAA
GOOOOM
EH ?
WH- WHERE'D HE GO...?

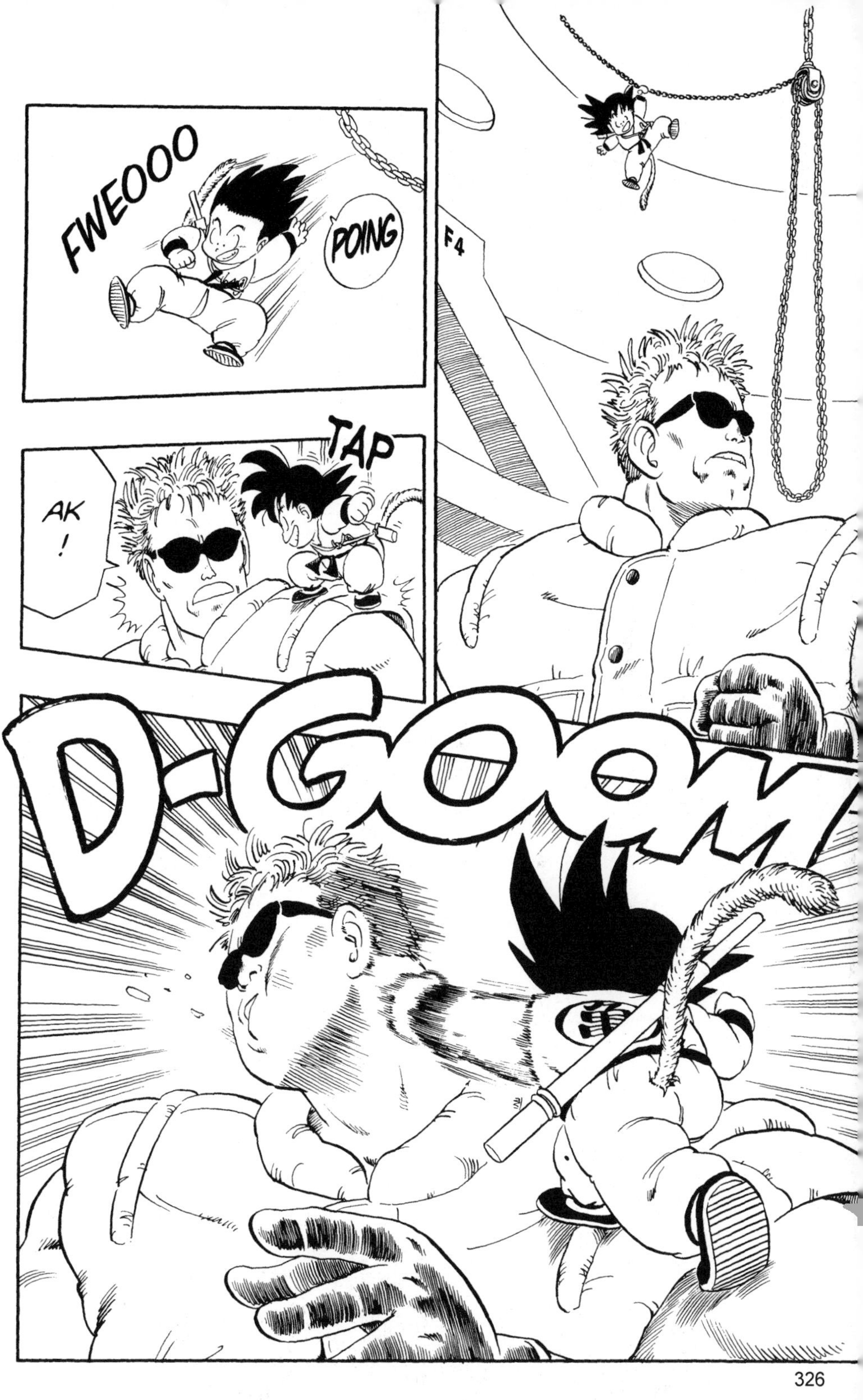
F4
FWEOOO
POING
TAP
AK!
D-GOOM

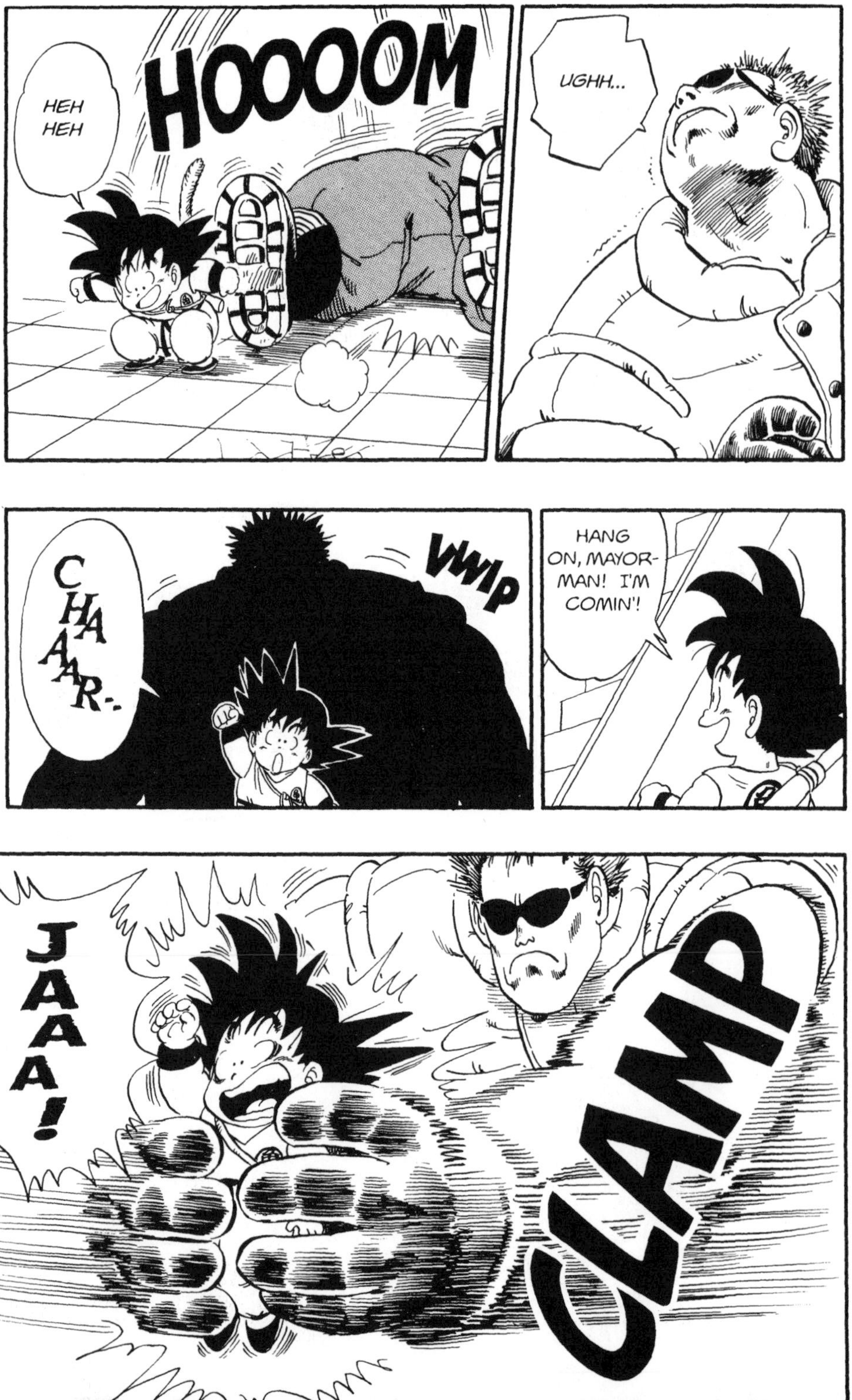
UGHH...
HOOOOM
HEH HEH
HANG ON, MAYOR-MAN! I'M COMIN'!
VWIP
CHAAAAR-.
JAAAA!
CLAMP

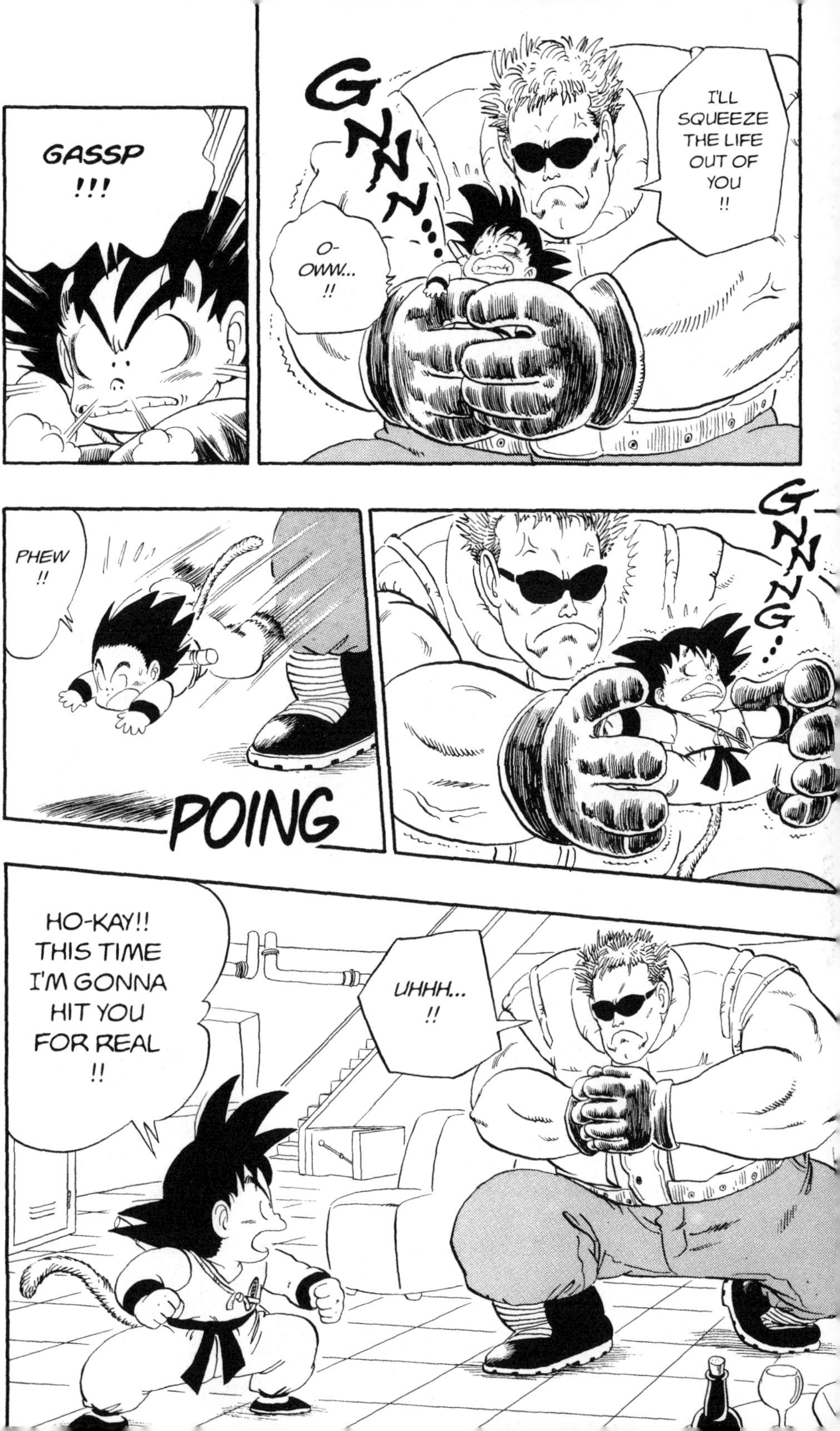
I'LL SQUEEZE THE LIFE OUT OF YOU !!
GNN...
O-OWW... !!
GASSP !!!
GNNNG...
PHEW !!
POING
HO-KAY!! THIS TIME I'M GONNA HIT YOU FOR REAL !!
UHHH... !!

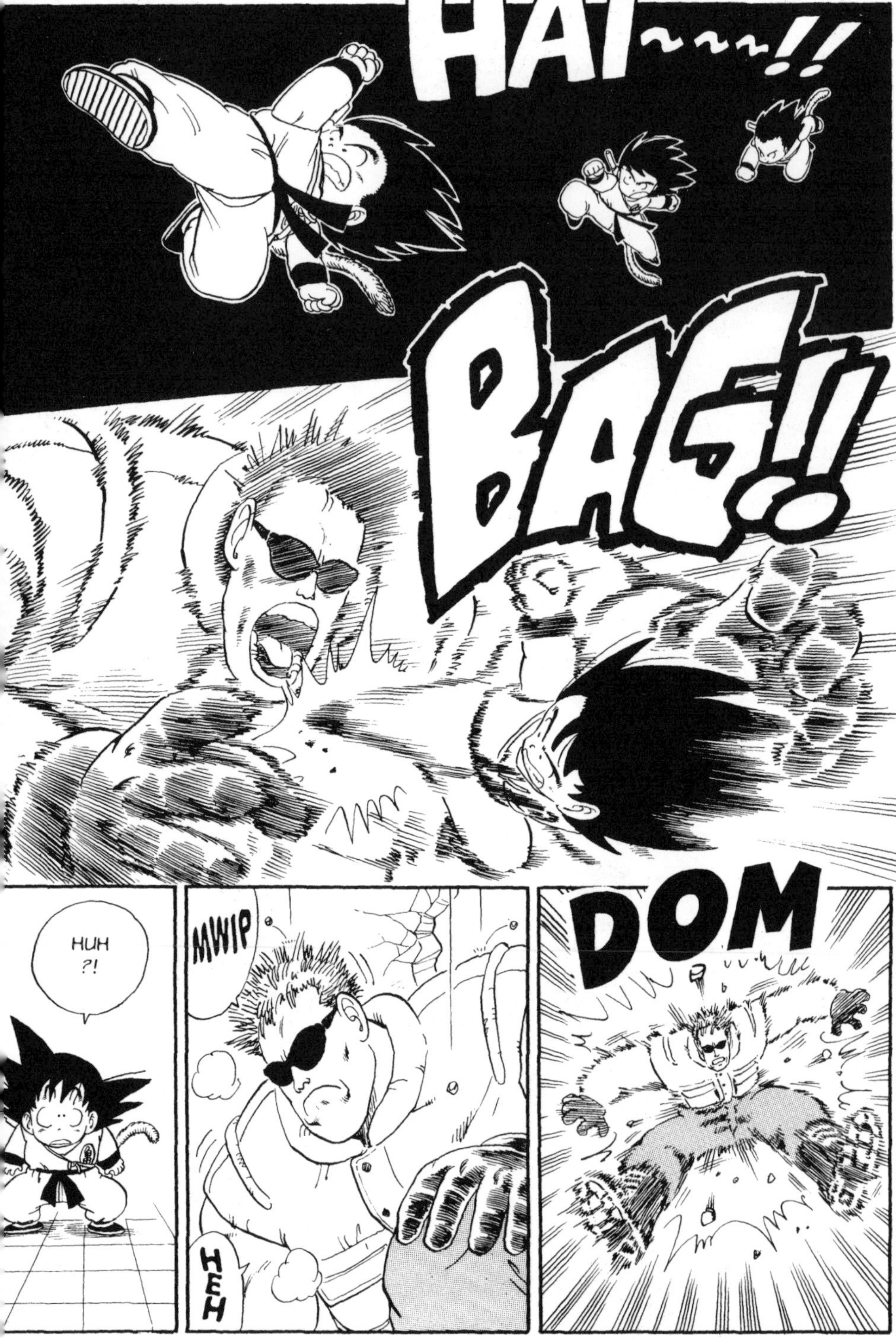
HAI~~~!!
BAG!!
DOM
MWIP
HEH
HUH ?!

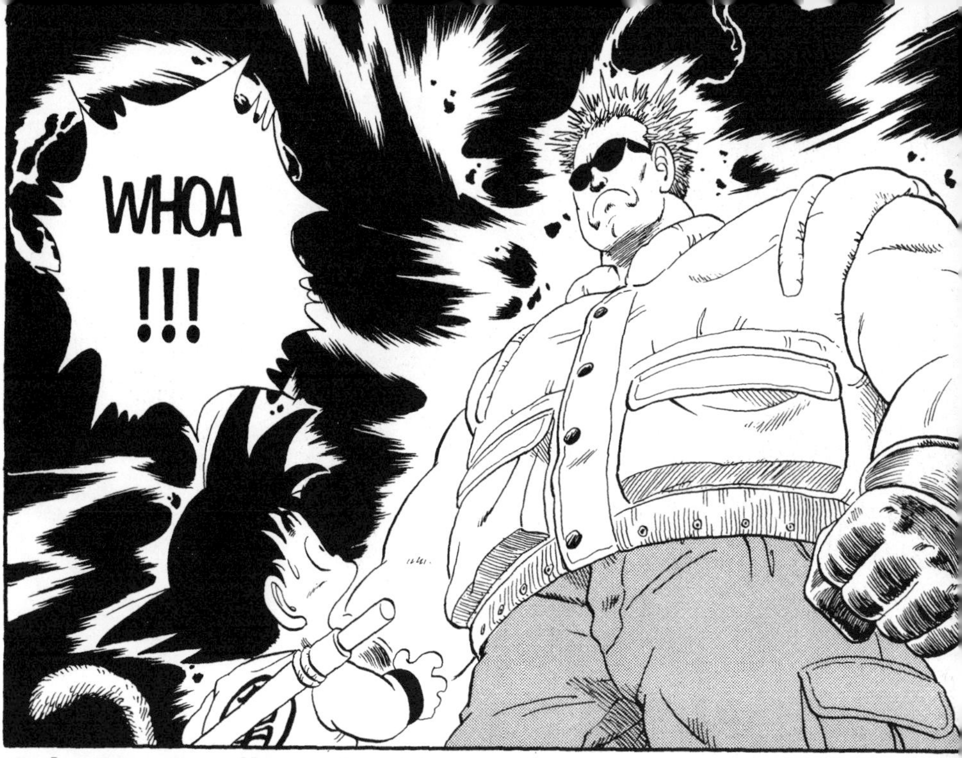
WHOA !!!

Tale 59 • Devil on the Third Floor

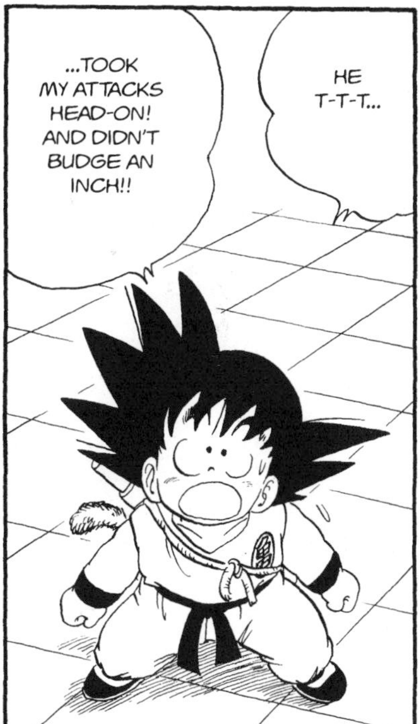
HE T-T-T...
...TOOK MY ATTACKS HEAD-ON! AND DIDN'T BUDGE AN INCH!!

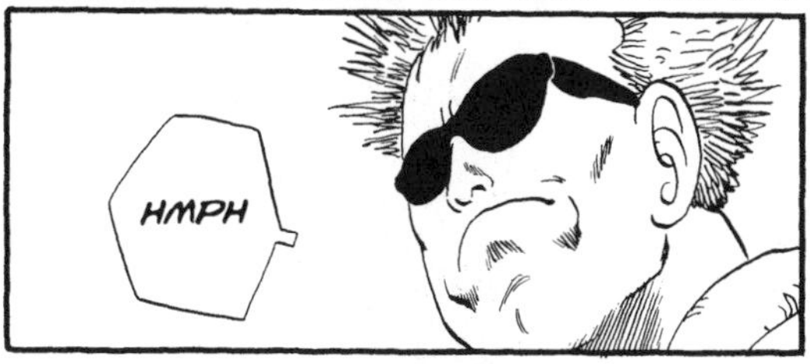
HMPH

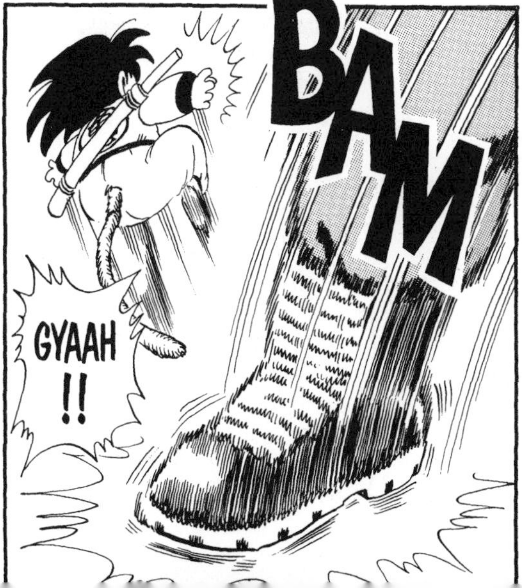
BAM
GYAAH !!

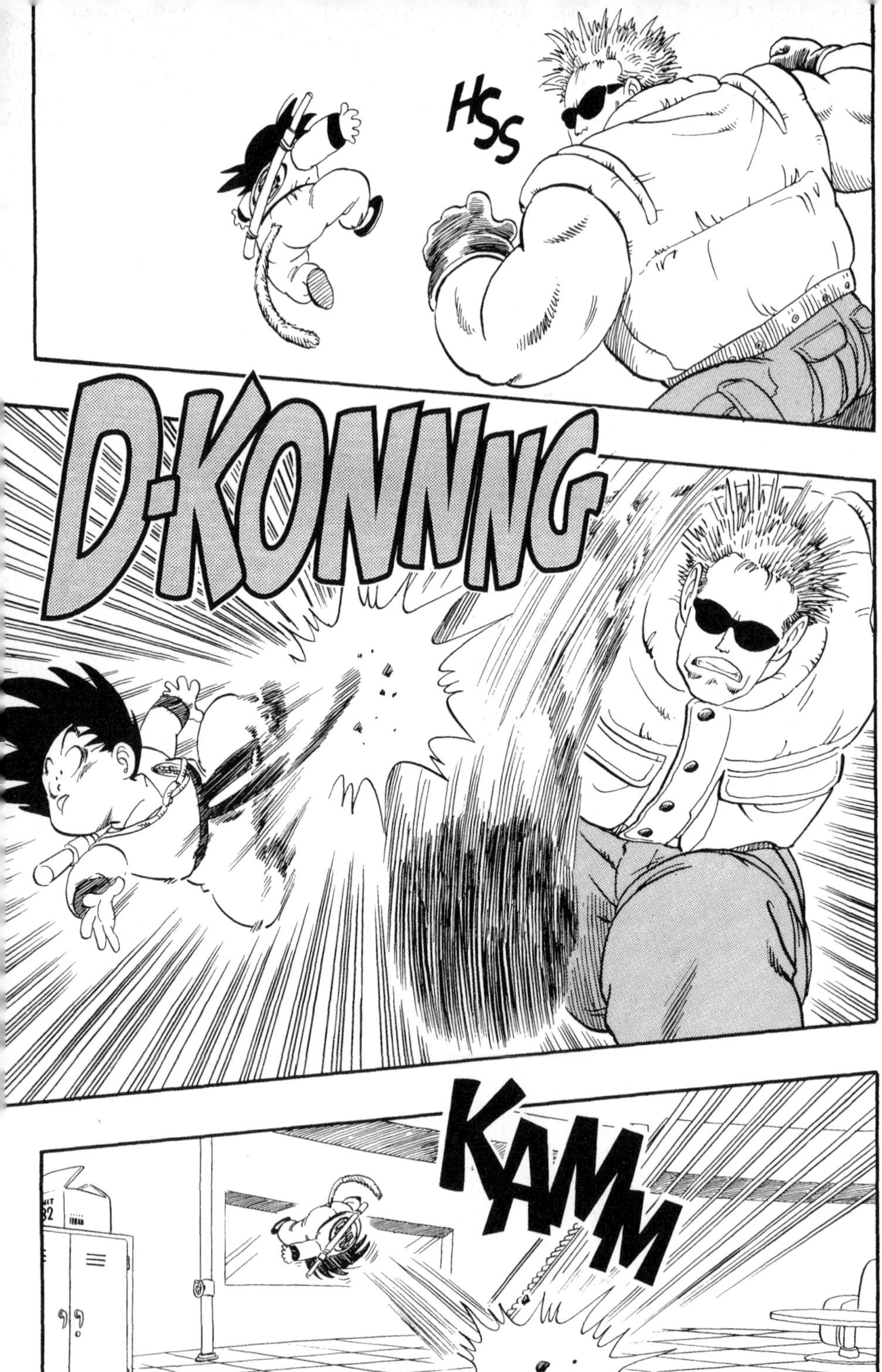
HSS
D-KONNNG
KAMM

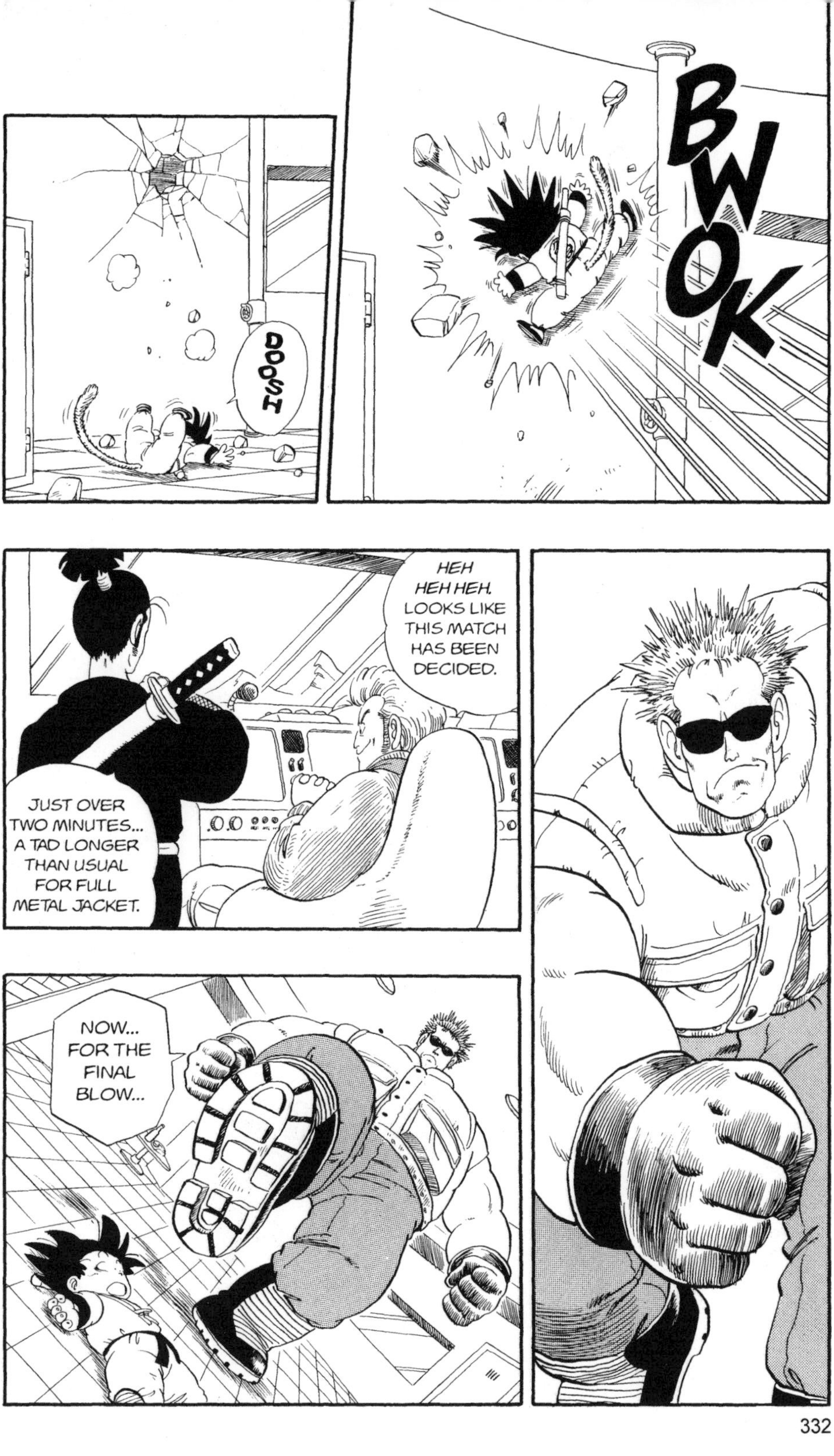
BWOK
DOOSH
HEH HEH HEH. LOOKS LIKE THIS MATCH HAS BEEN DECIDED.
JUST OVER TWO MINUTES... A TAD LONGER THAN USUAL FOR FULL METAL JACKET.
NOW... FOR THE FINAL BLOW...

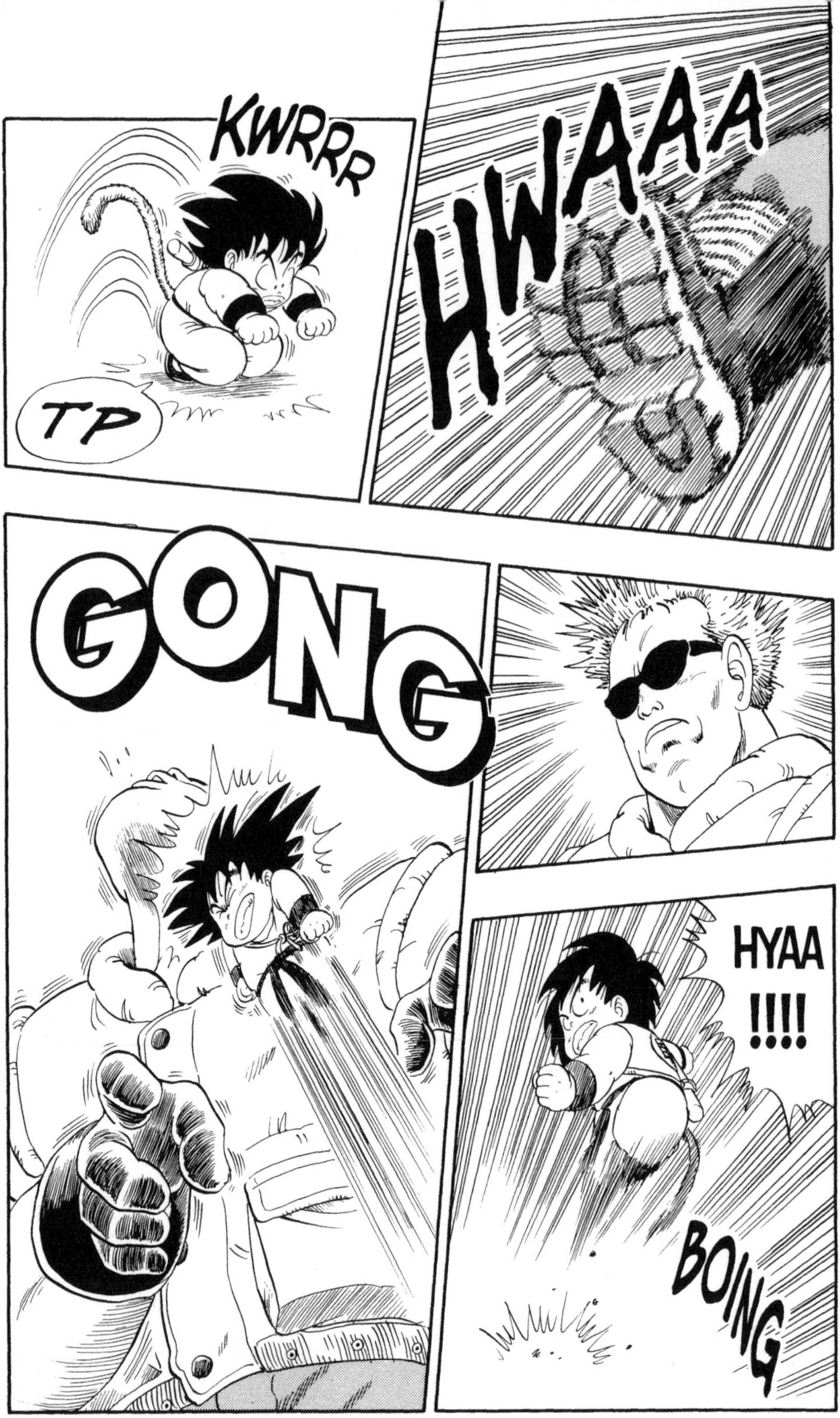
HWAAAA
KWRRR
TP
HYAA
!!!!
BOING
GONG

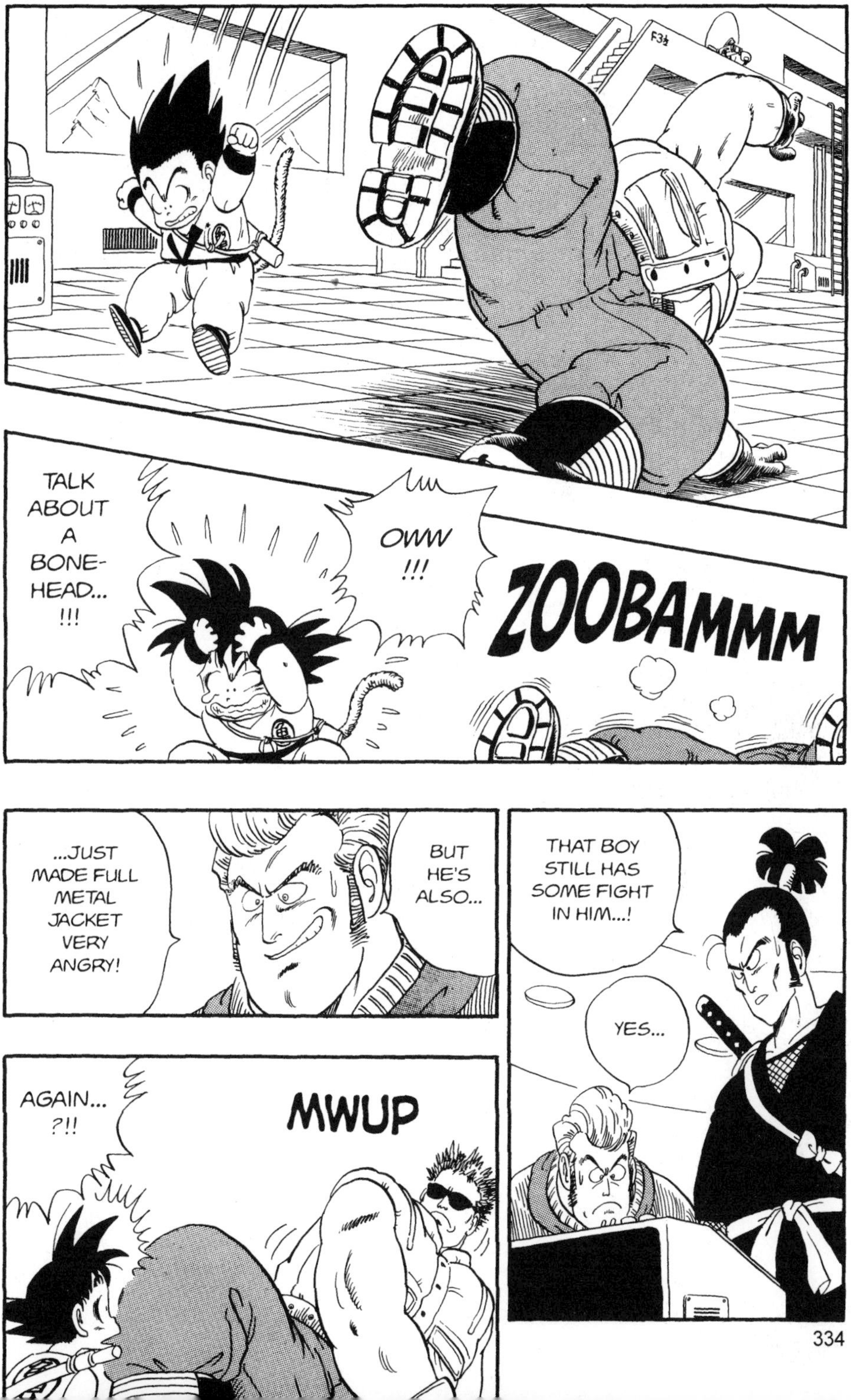
ZOOBAMMM
OWW !!!
TALK ABOUT A BONE-HEAD... !!!
THAT BOY STILL HAS SOME FIGHT IN HIM...!
YES...
BUT HE'S ALSO...
...JUST MADE FULL METAL JACKET VERY ANGRY!
MWUP
AGAIN... ?!!

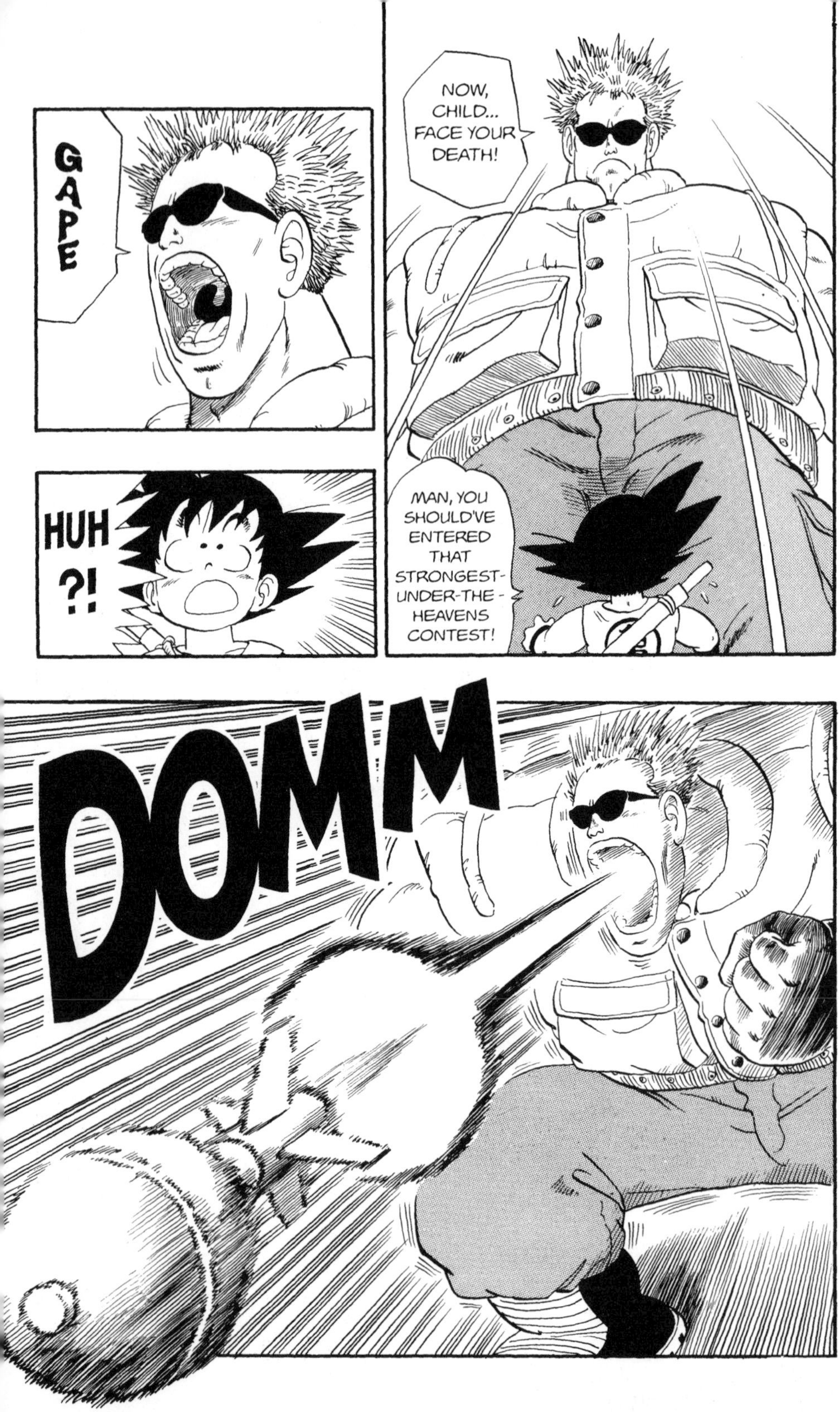
NOW, CHILD... FACE YOUR DEATH!
MAN, YOU SHOULD'VE ENTERED THAT STRONGEST-UNDER-THE-HEAVENS CONTEST!
GAPE
HUH ?!
DOMM

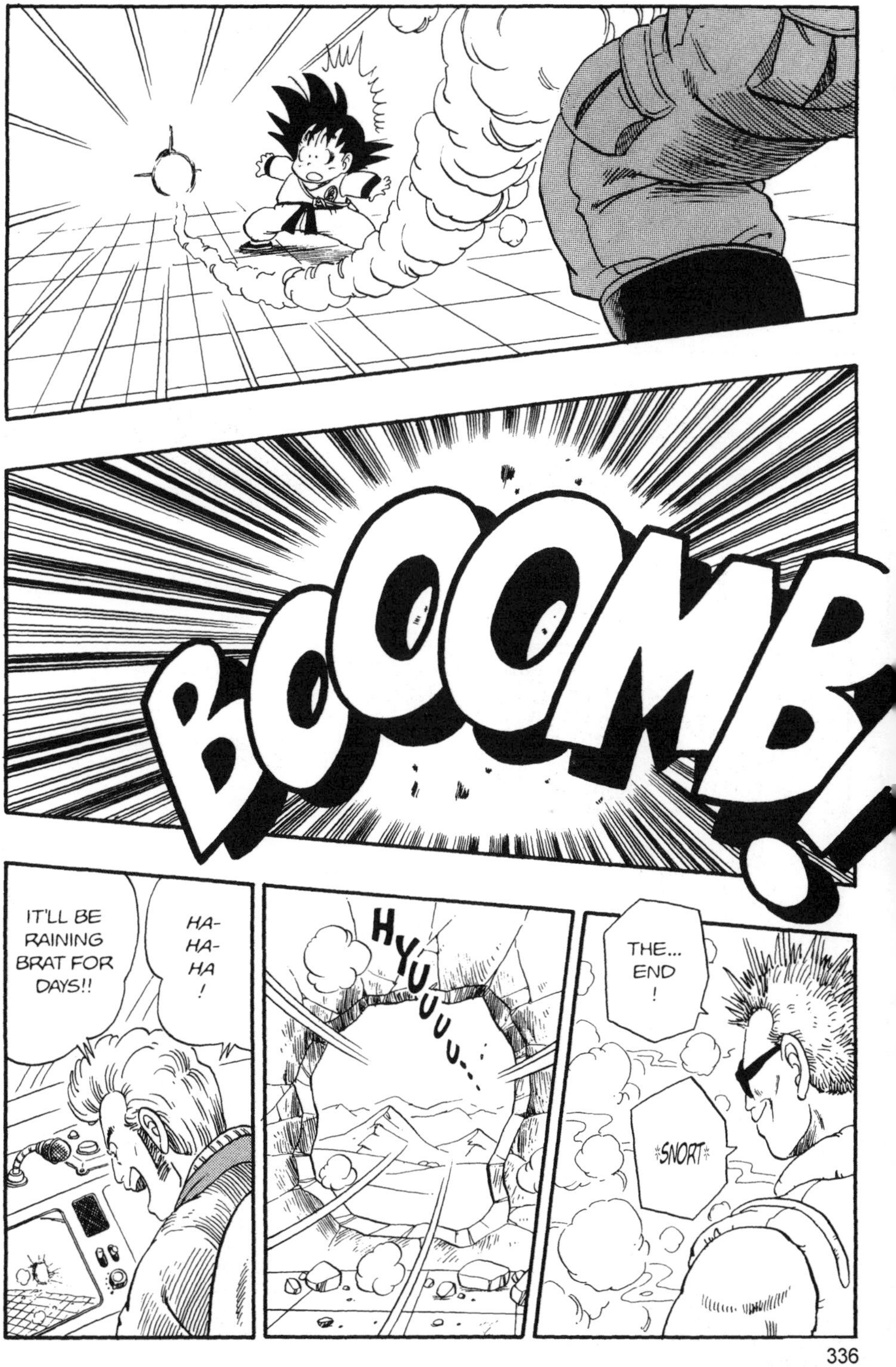
BOOOMB!
THE... END !
SNORT
HYUUUUU...
HA-HA-HA !
IT'LL BE RAINING BRAT FOR DAYS!!

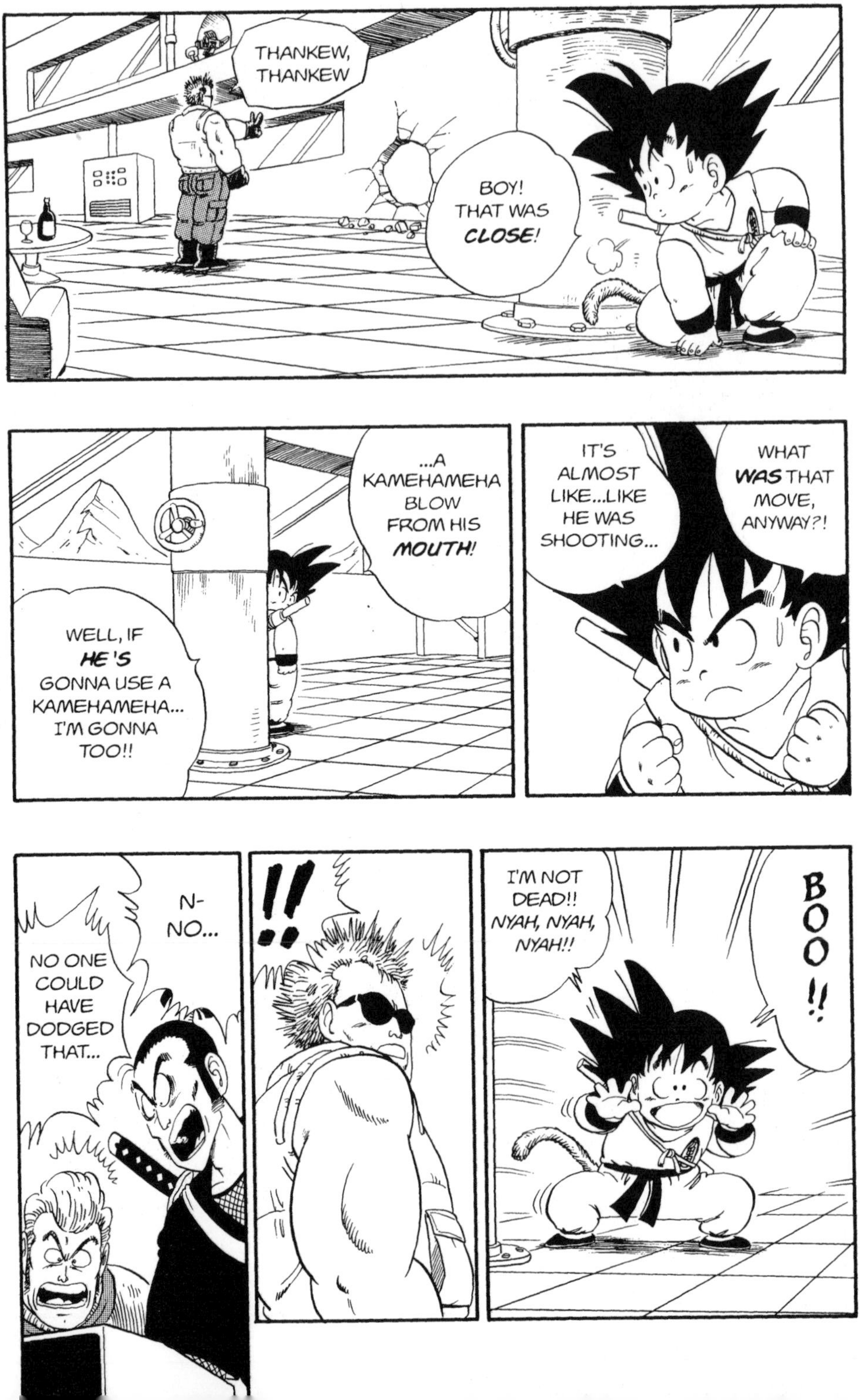
THANKEW, THANKEW
BOY! THAT WAS **CLOSE**!
WHAT **WAS** THAT MOVE, ANYWAY?!
IT'S ALMOST LIKE...LIKE HE WAS SHOOTING...
...A KAMEHAMEHA BLOW FROM HIS **MOUTH**!
WELL, IF **HE'S** GONNA USE A KAMEHAMEHA... I'M GONNA TOO!!
BOO!!
I'M NOT DEAD!! *NYAH, NYAH, NYAH!!*
!!
N- NO...
NO ONE COULD HAVE DODGED THAT...

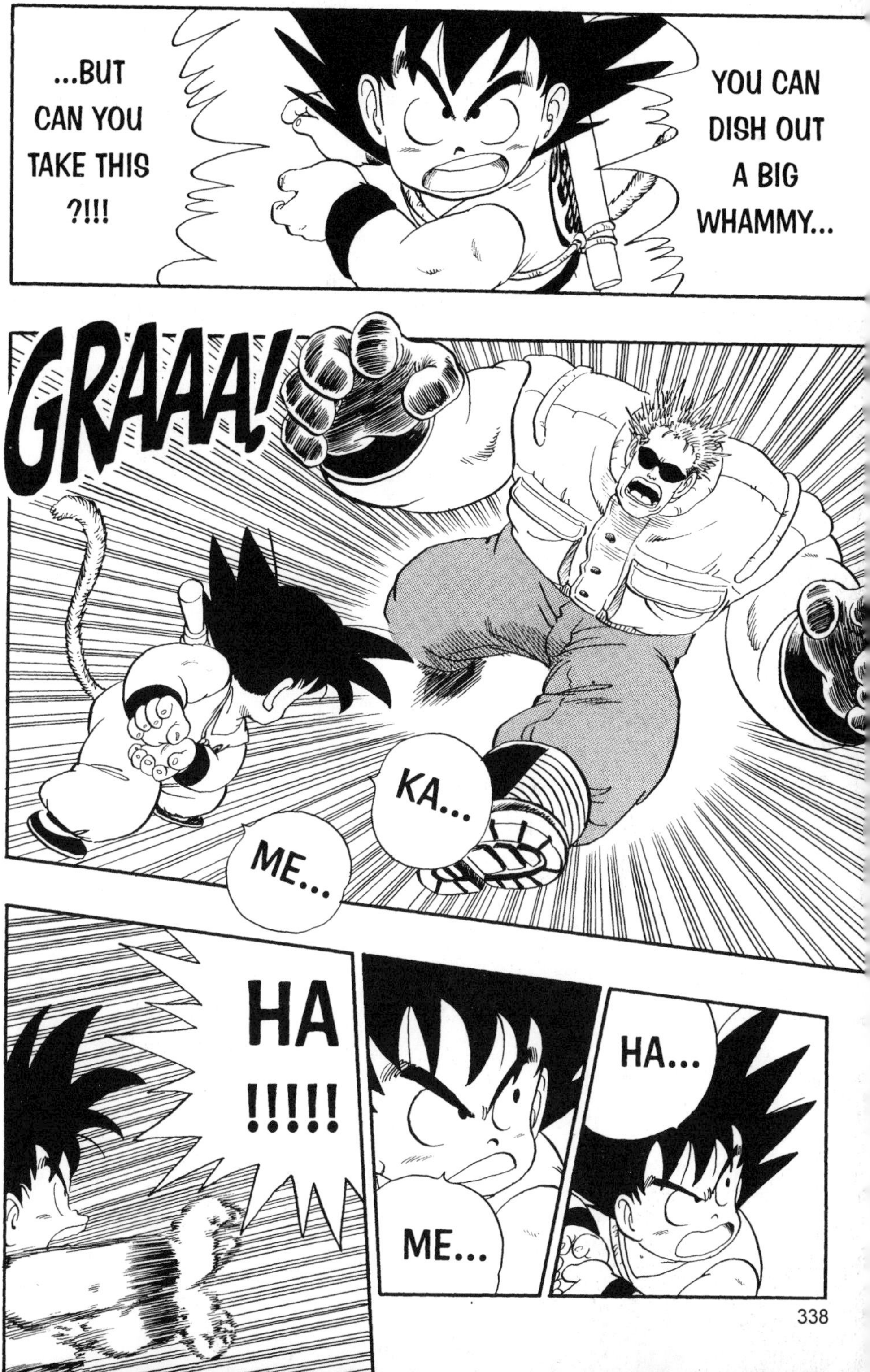
YOU CAN DISH OUT A BIG WHAMMY...
...BUT CAN YOU TAKE THIS ?!!!
GRAAA!
KA...
ME...
HA...
ME...
HA !!!!!

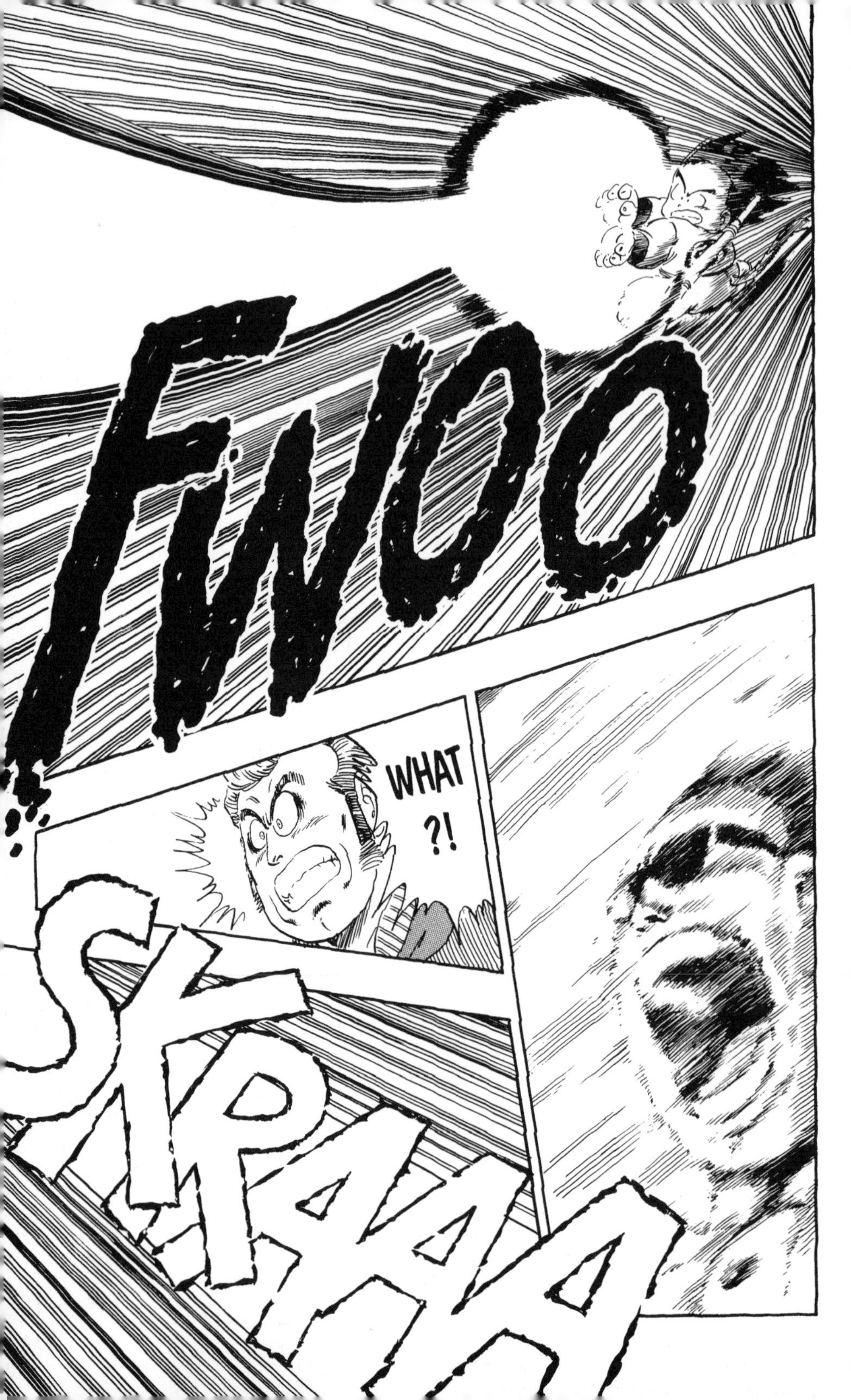
FWOO
WHAT ?!
SKRAAA

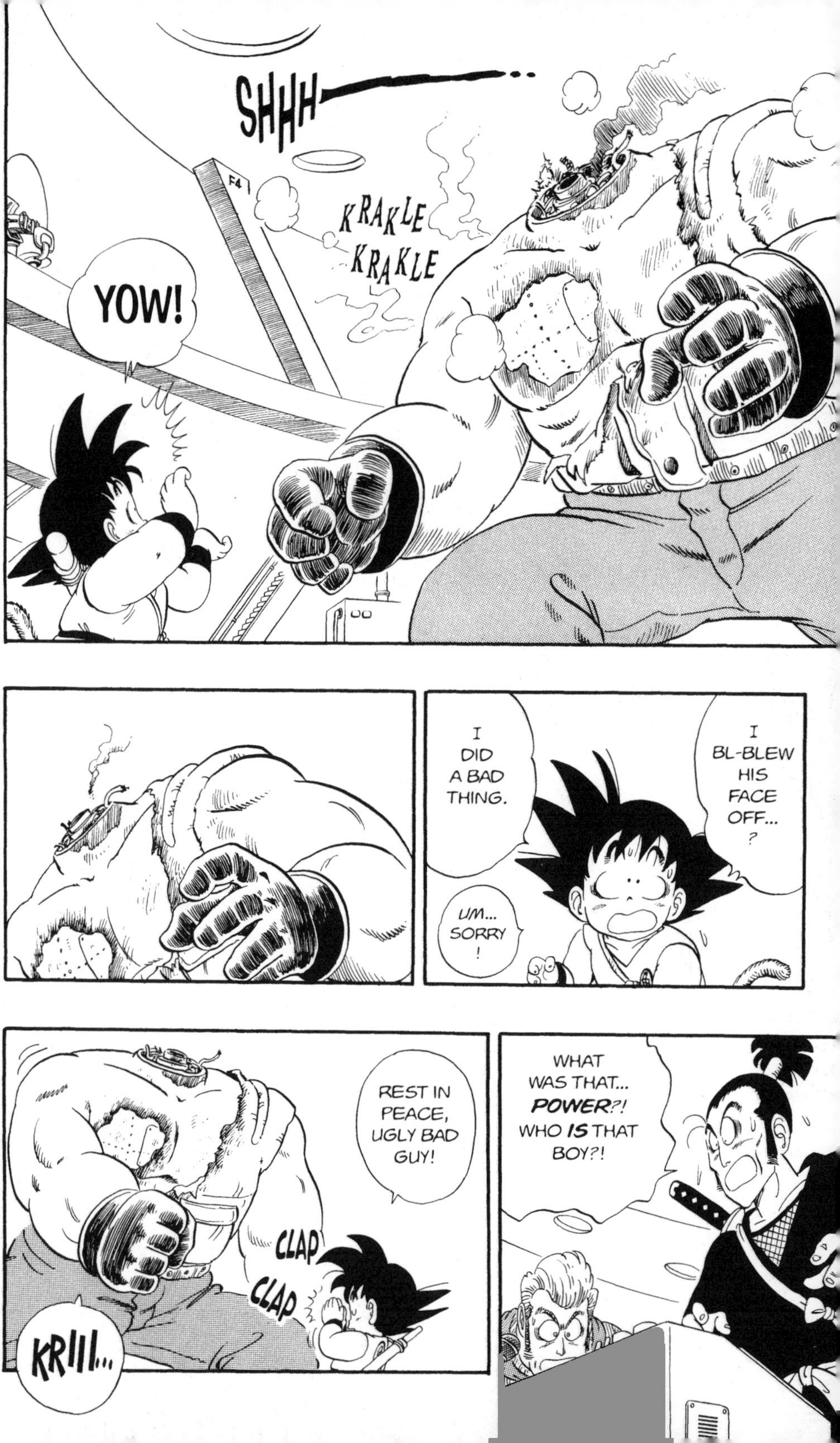
SHHH
KRAKLE KRAKLE
YOW!
I BL-BLEW HIS FACE OFF...?
I DID A BAD THING.
UM... SORRY!
WHAT WAS THAT... **POWER**?! WHO **IS** THAT BOY?!
REST IN PEACE, UGLY BAD GUY!
CLAP
CLAP
KRIII...

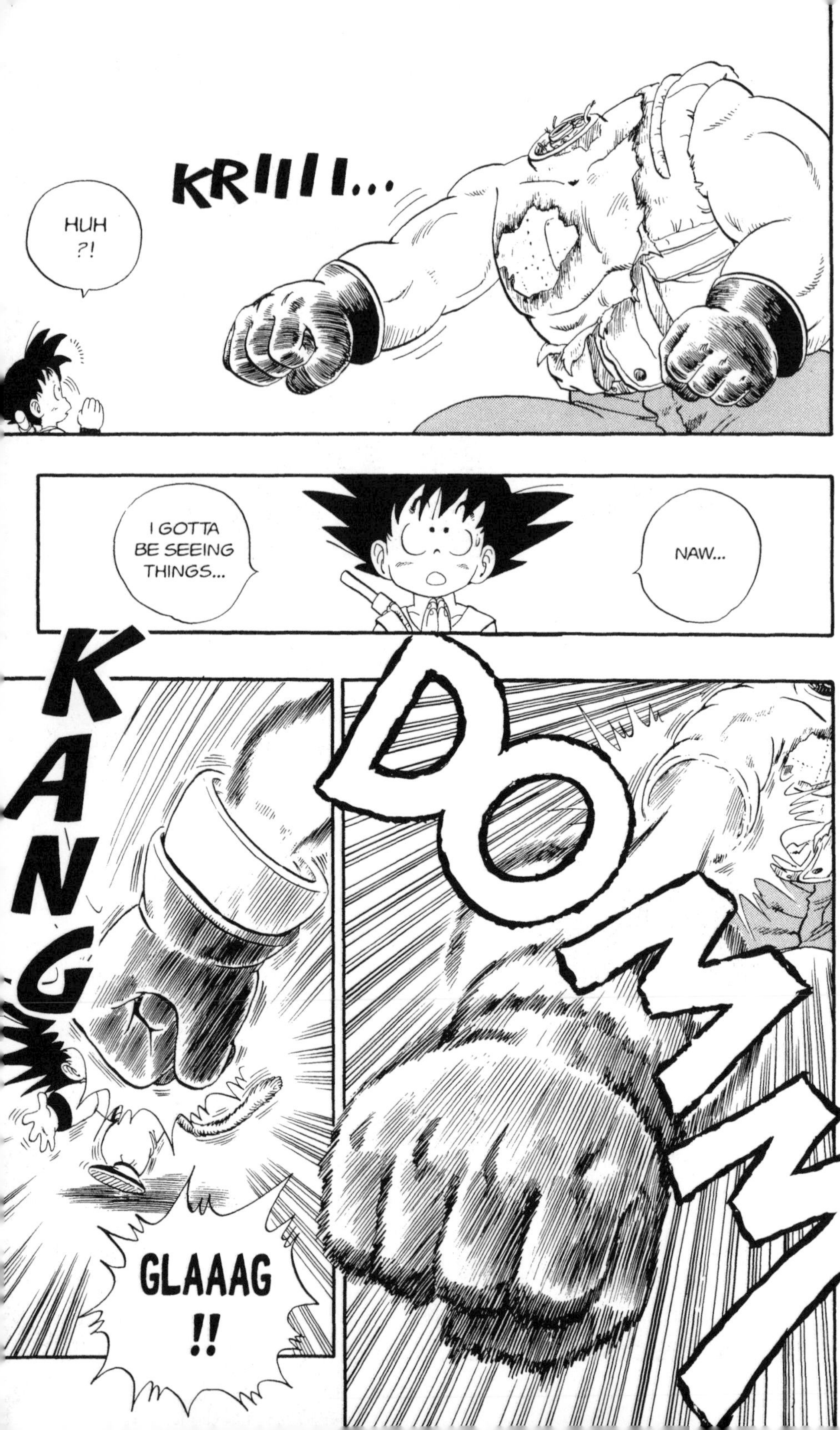
KRIIII...
HUH ?!
NAW...
I GOTTA BE SEEING THINGS...
DOOMM
KANG
GLAAAG !!

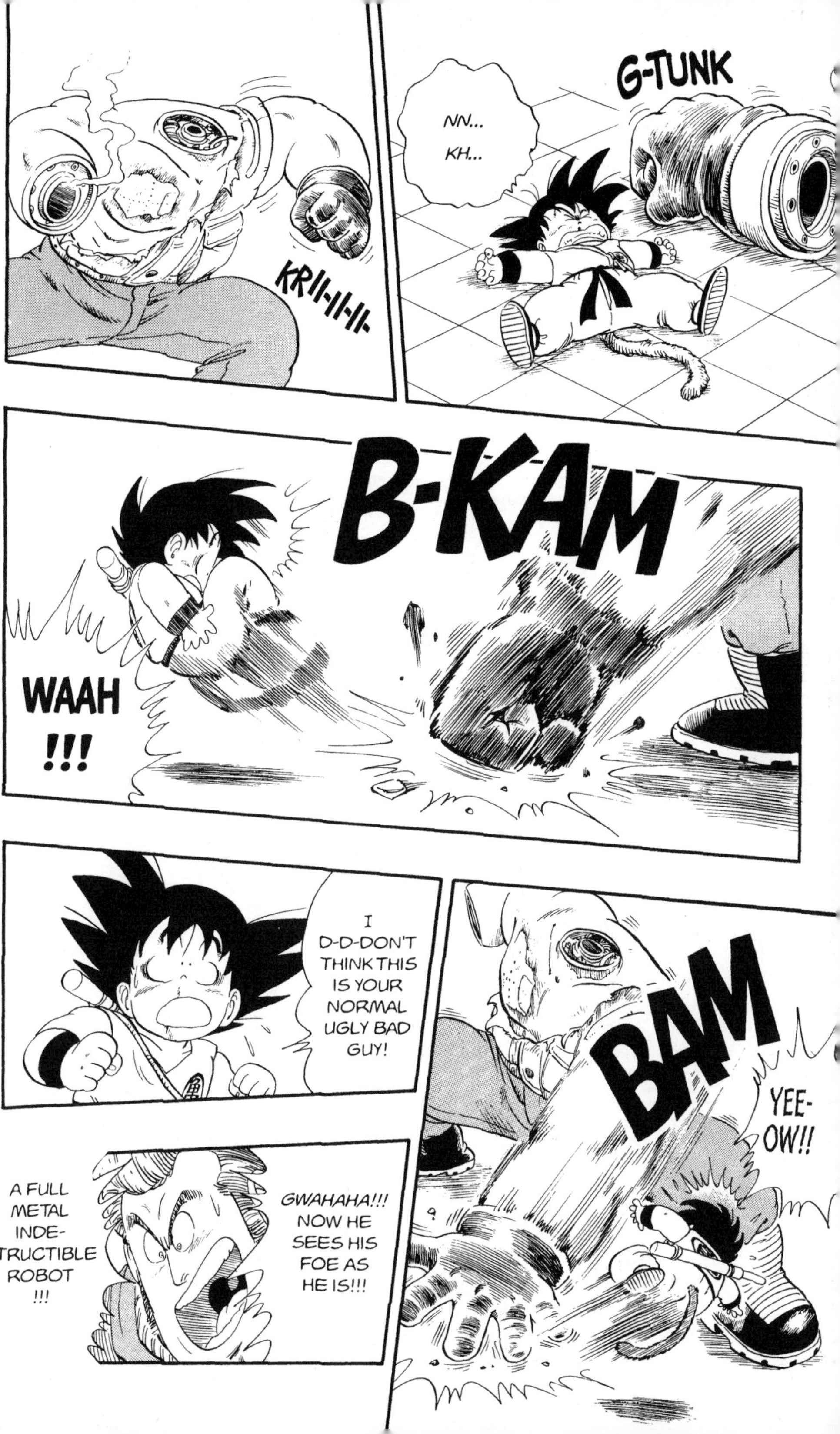
G-TUNK
NN... KH...
KRI-I-I-I-I-I
B-KAM
WAAH !!!
BAM
YEE-OW!!
I D-D-DON'T THINK THIS IS YOUR NORMAL UGLY BAD GUY!
GWAHAHA!!! NOW HE SEES HIS FOE AS HE IS!!!
A FULL METAL INDE-STRUCTIBLE ROBOT !!!

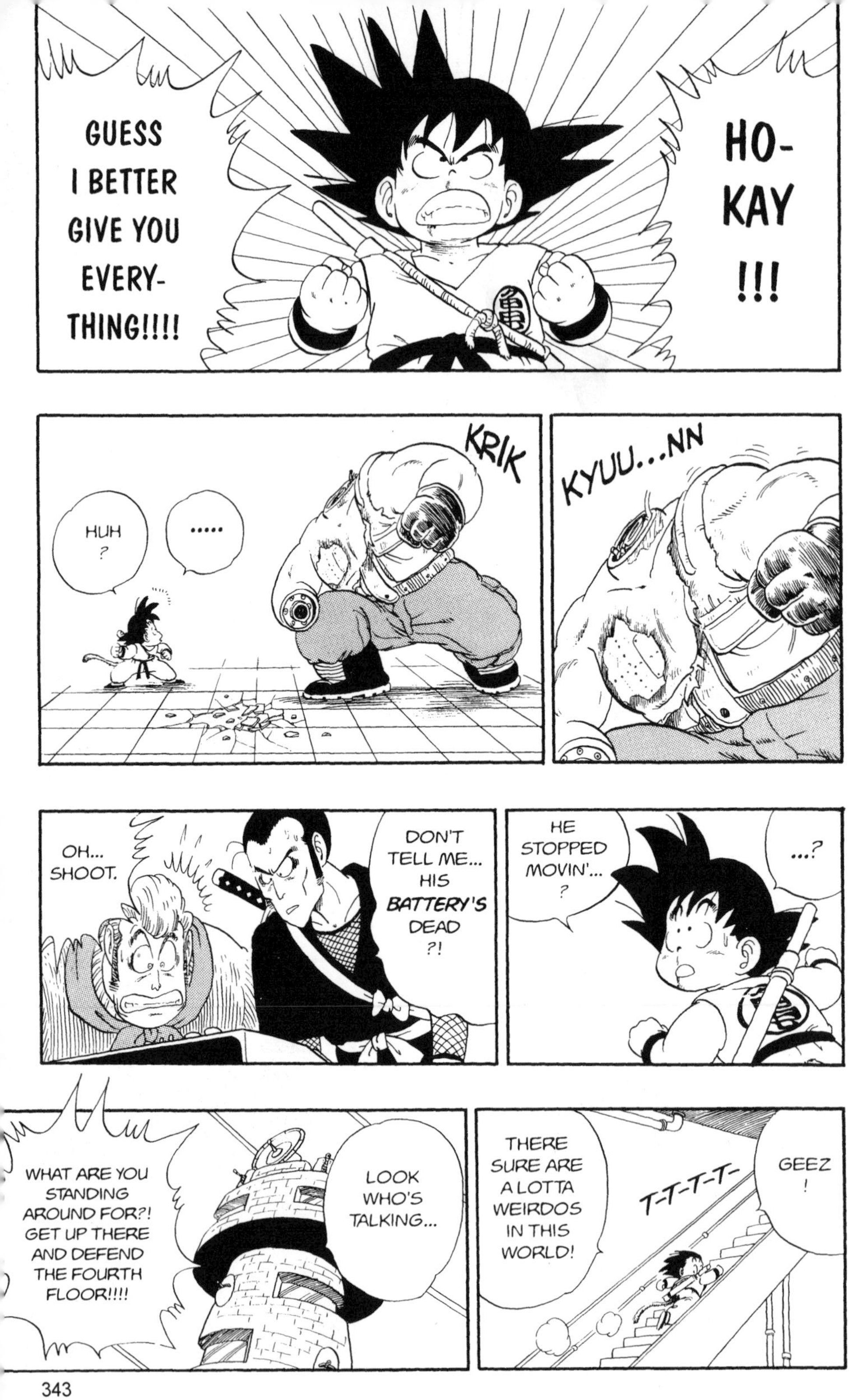
HO-KAY!!!
GUESS I BETTER GIVE YOU EVERY-THING!!!!
KYUU...NN
KRIK
HUH?
.....
...?
HE STOPPED MOVIN'...?
DON'T TELL ME... HIS *BATTERY'S* DEAD?!
OH... SHOOT.
GEEZ!
T-T-T-T-
THERE SURE ARE A LOTTA WEIRDOS IN THIS WORLD!
LOOK WHO'S TALKING...
WHAT ARE YOU STANDING AROUND FOR?! GET UP THERE AND DEFEND THE FOURTH FLOOR!!!!

Tale 60 • Purple People Beater

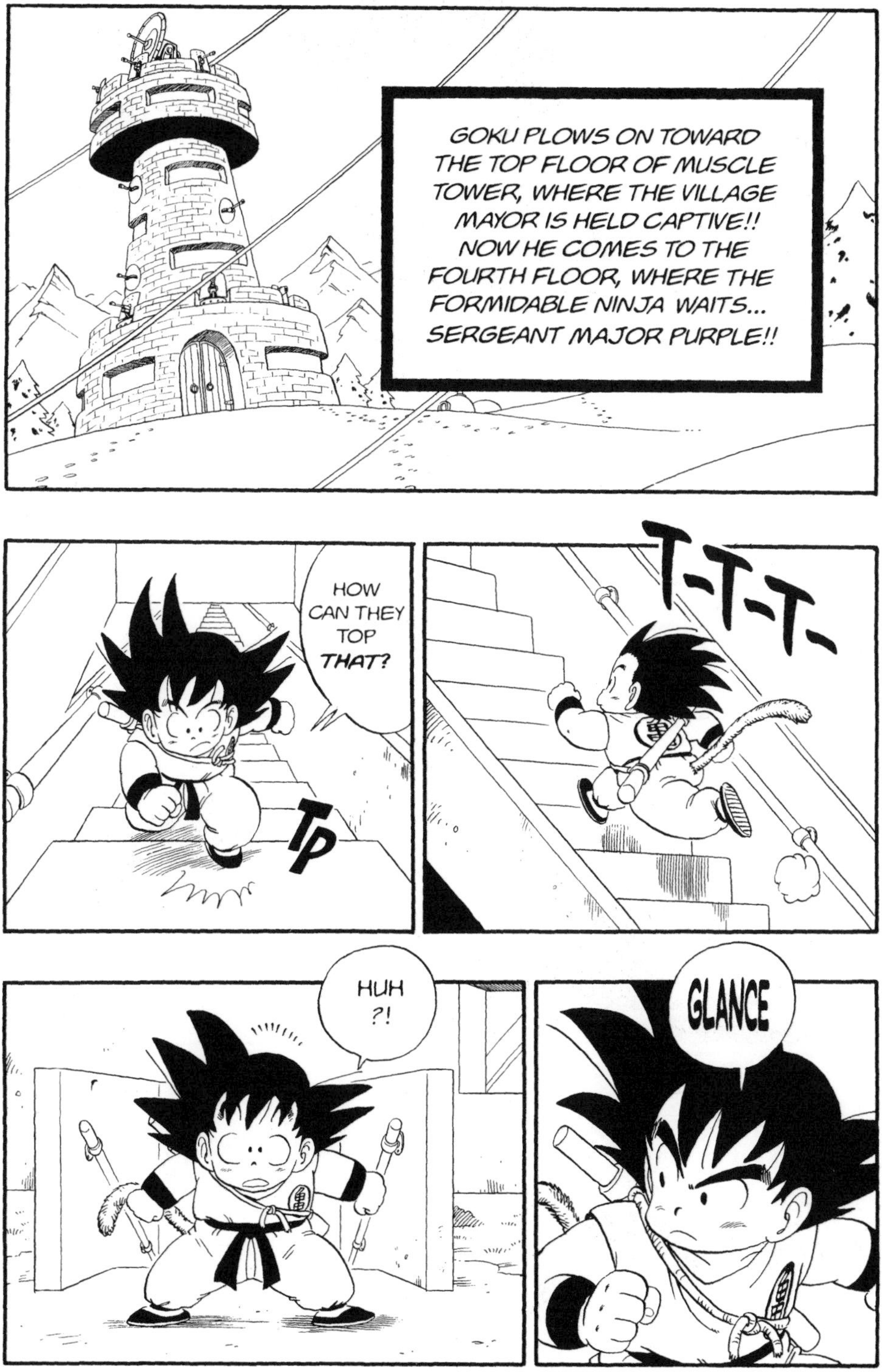
GOKU PLOWS ON TOWARD THE TOP FLOOR OF MUSCLE TOWER, WHERE THE VILLAGE MAYOR IS HELD CAPTIVE!! NOW HE COMES TO THE FOURTH FLOOR, WHERE THE FORMIDABLE NINJA WAITS... SERGEANT MAJOR PURPLE!!
T-T-T-
HOW CAN THEY TOP *THAT?*
TP
GLANCE
HUH ?!

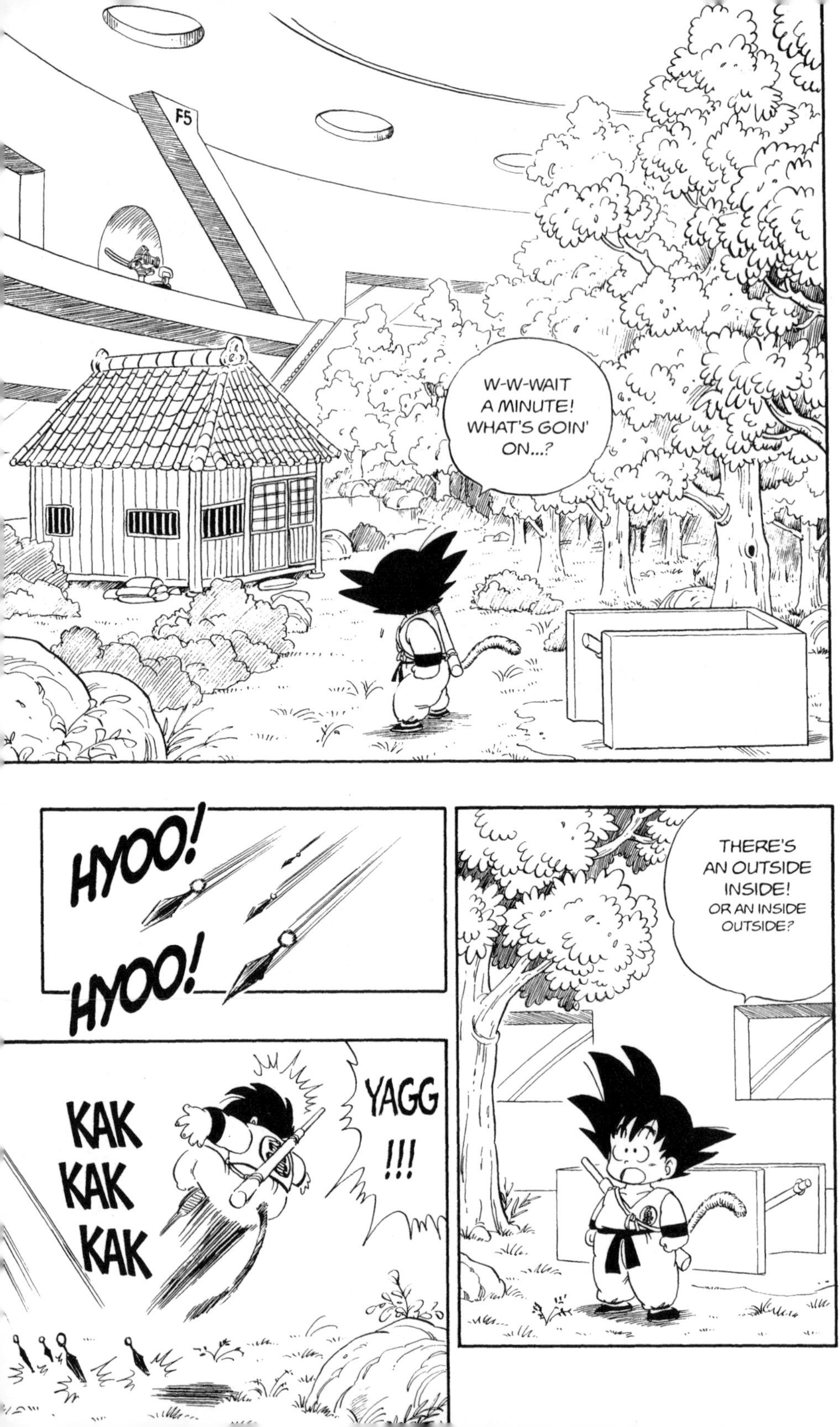
F5
W-W-WAIT A MINUTE! WHAT'S GOIN' ON...?
THERE'S AN OUTSIDE INSIDE! OR AN INSIDE OUTSIDE?
HYOO!
HYOO!
KAK KAK KAK
YAGG !!!

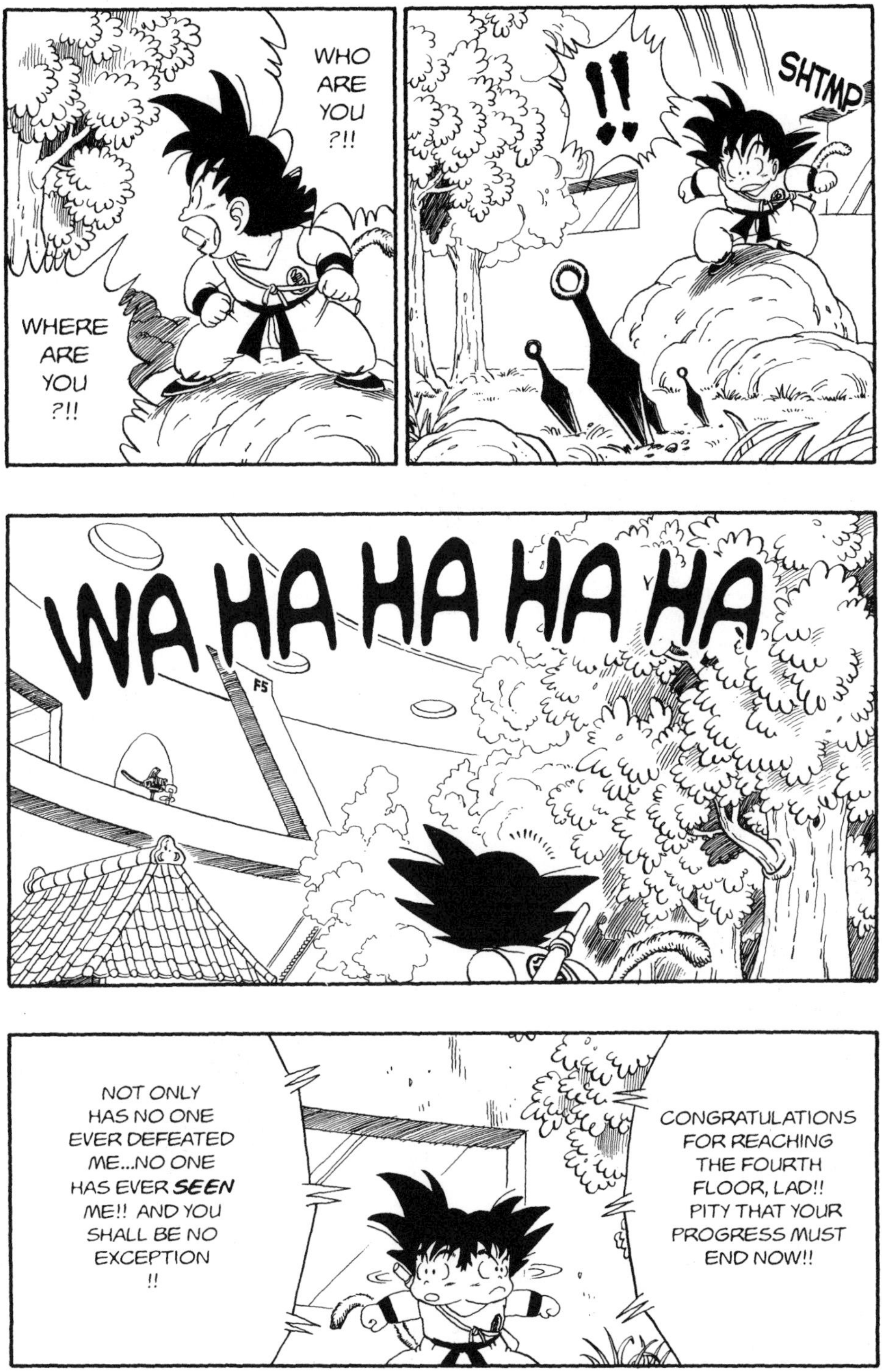
!!
SHTMP
WHO ARE YOU ?!!
WHERE ARE YOU ?!!
WA HA HA HA HA HA
CONGRATULATIONS FOR REACHING THE FOURTH FLOOR, LAD!! PITY THAT YOUR PROGRESS MUST END NOW!!
NOT ONLY HAS NO ONE EVER DEFEATED ME...NO ONE HAS EVER *SEEN* ME!! AND YOU SHALL BE NO EXCEPTION !!

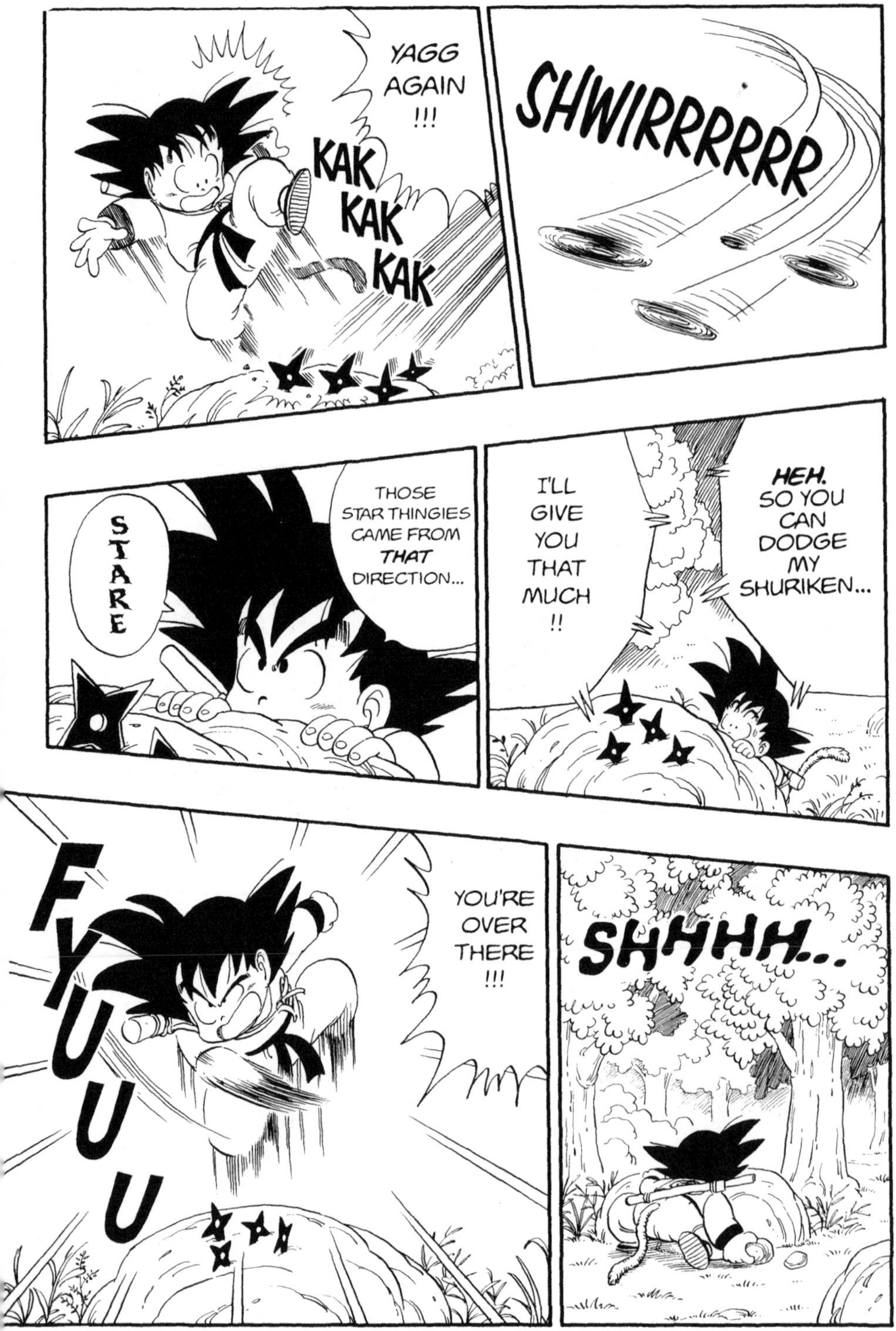
SHWIRRRRRRR
YAGG AGAIN!!!
KAK KAK KAK
HEH. SO YOU CAN DODGE MY SHURIKEN...
I'LL GIVE YOU THAT MUCH!!
THOSE STAR THINGIES CAME FROM ***THAT*** DIRECTION...
STARE
SHHHH...
YOU'RE OVER THERE!!!
FYUUUU

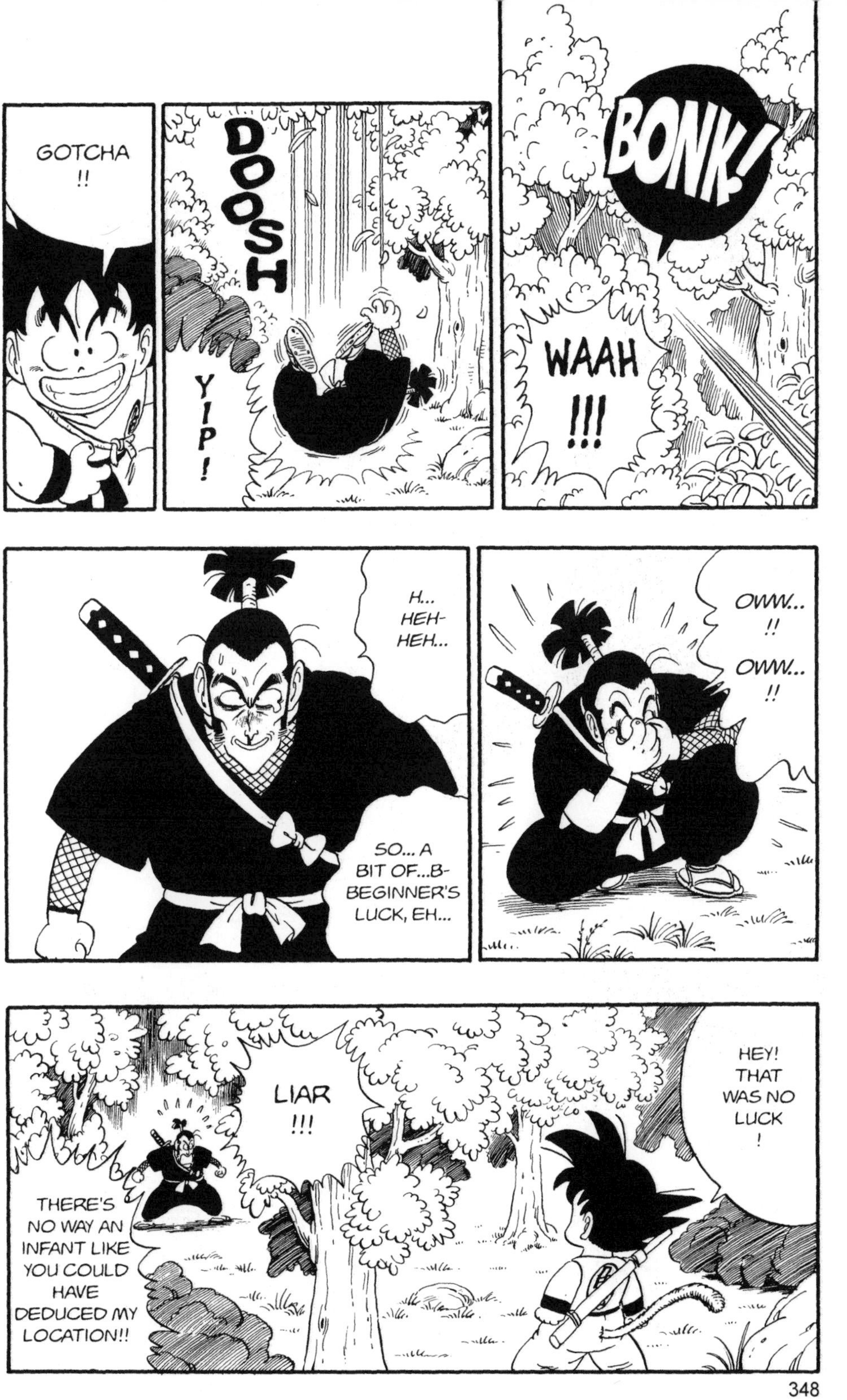
BONK!
WAAH!!!
DOOSH
YIP!
GOTCHA!!
OWW...!!
OWW...!!
H... HEH-HEH...
SO... A BIT OF...B-BEGINNER'S LUCK, EH...
HEY! THAT WAS NO LUCK!
LIAR!!!
THERE'S NO WAY AN INFANT LIKE YOU COULD HAVE DEDUCED MY LOCATION!!

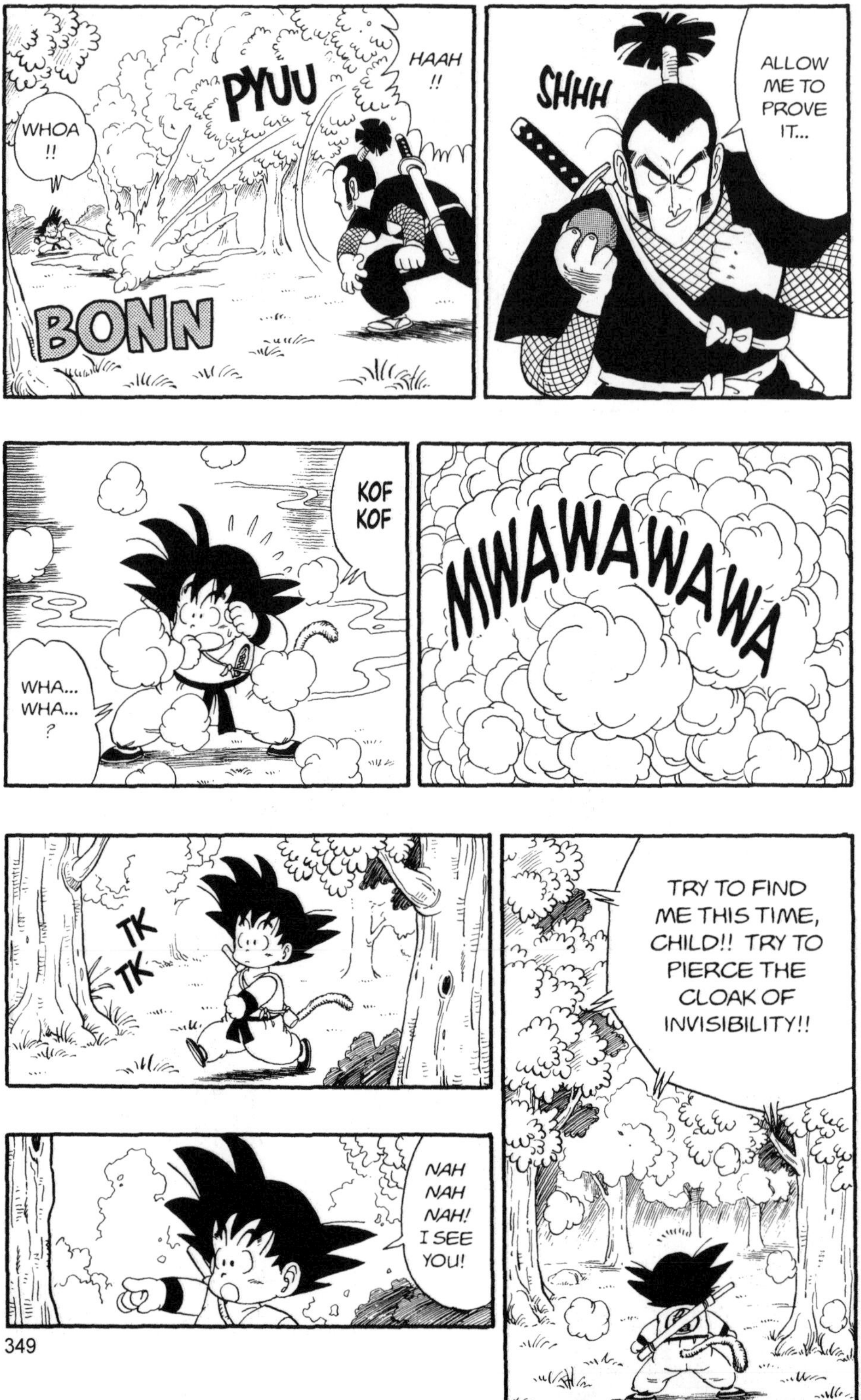
SHHH
ALLOW ME TO PROVE IT...
HAAH!!
PYUU
WHOA!!
BONN
MWAWAWAWA
KOF KOF
WHA... WHA...?
TRY TO FIND ME THIS TIME, CHILD!! TRY TO PIERCE THE CLOAK OF INVISIBILITY!!
TK TK
NAH NAH NAH! I SEE YOU!

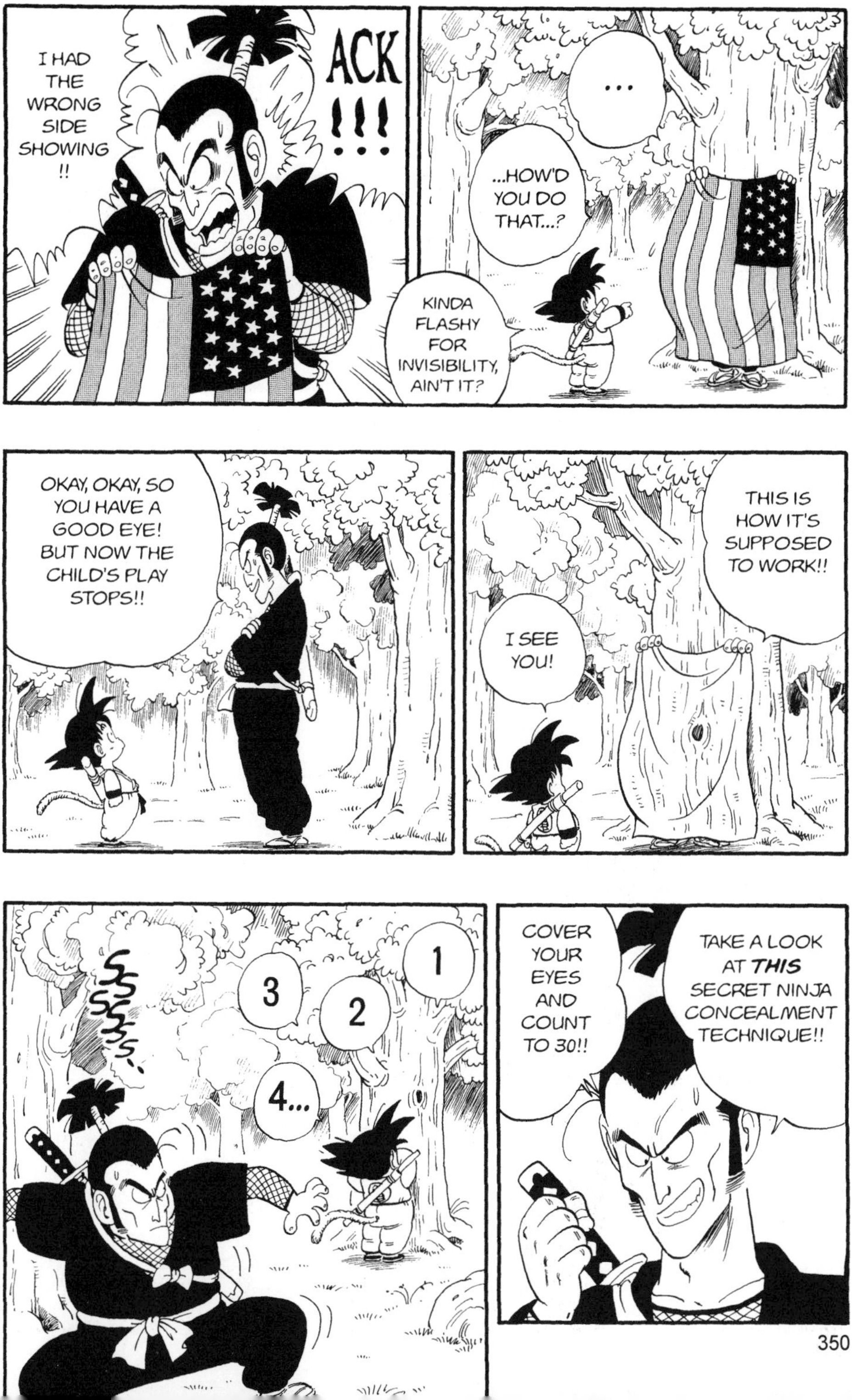
...
...HOW'D YOU DO THAT...?
KINDA FLASHY FOR INVISIBILITY, AIN'T IT?
ACK!!!
I HAD THE WRONG SIDE SHOWING!!
THIS IS HOW IT'S SUPPOSED TO WORK!!
I SEE YOU!
OKAY, OKAY, SO YOU HAVE A GOOD EYE! BUT NOW THE CHILD'S PLAY STOPS!!
TAKE A LOOK AT **THIS** SECRET NINJA CONCEALMENT TECHNIQUE!!
COVER YOUR EYES AND COUNT TO 30!!
1
2
3
4...
SSSSSS

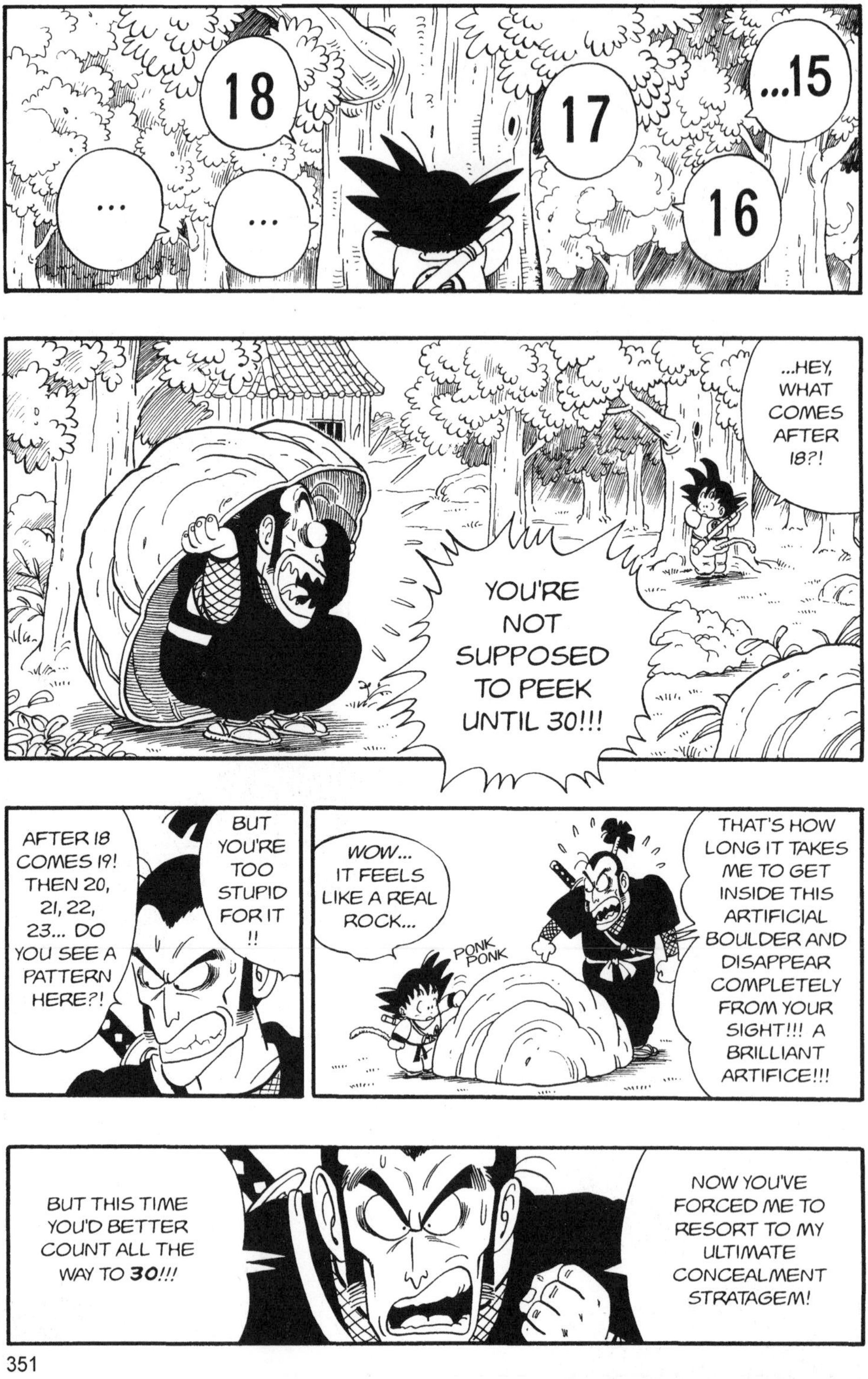
...15
16
17
18
...
...
...HEY, WHAT COMES AFTER 18?!
YOU'RE NOT SUPPOSED TO PEEK UNTIL 30!!!
THAT'S HOW LONG IT TAKES ME TO GET INSIDE THIS ARTIFICIAL BOULDER AND DISAPPEAR COMPLETELY FROM YOUR SIGHT!!! A BRILLIANT ARTIFICE!!!
WOW... IT FEELS LIKE A REAL ROCK...
PONK PONK
BUT YOU'RE TOO STUPID FOR IT!!
AFTER 18 COMES 19! THEN 20, 21, 22, 23... DO YOU SEE A PATTERN HERE?!
NOW YOU'VE FORCED ME TO RESORT TO MY ULTIMATE CONCEALMENT STRATAGEM!
BUT THIS TIME YOU'D BETTER COUNT ALL THE WAY TO 30!!!

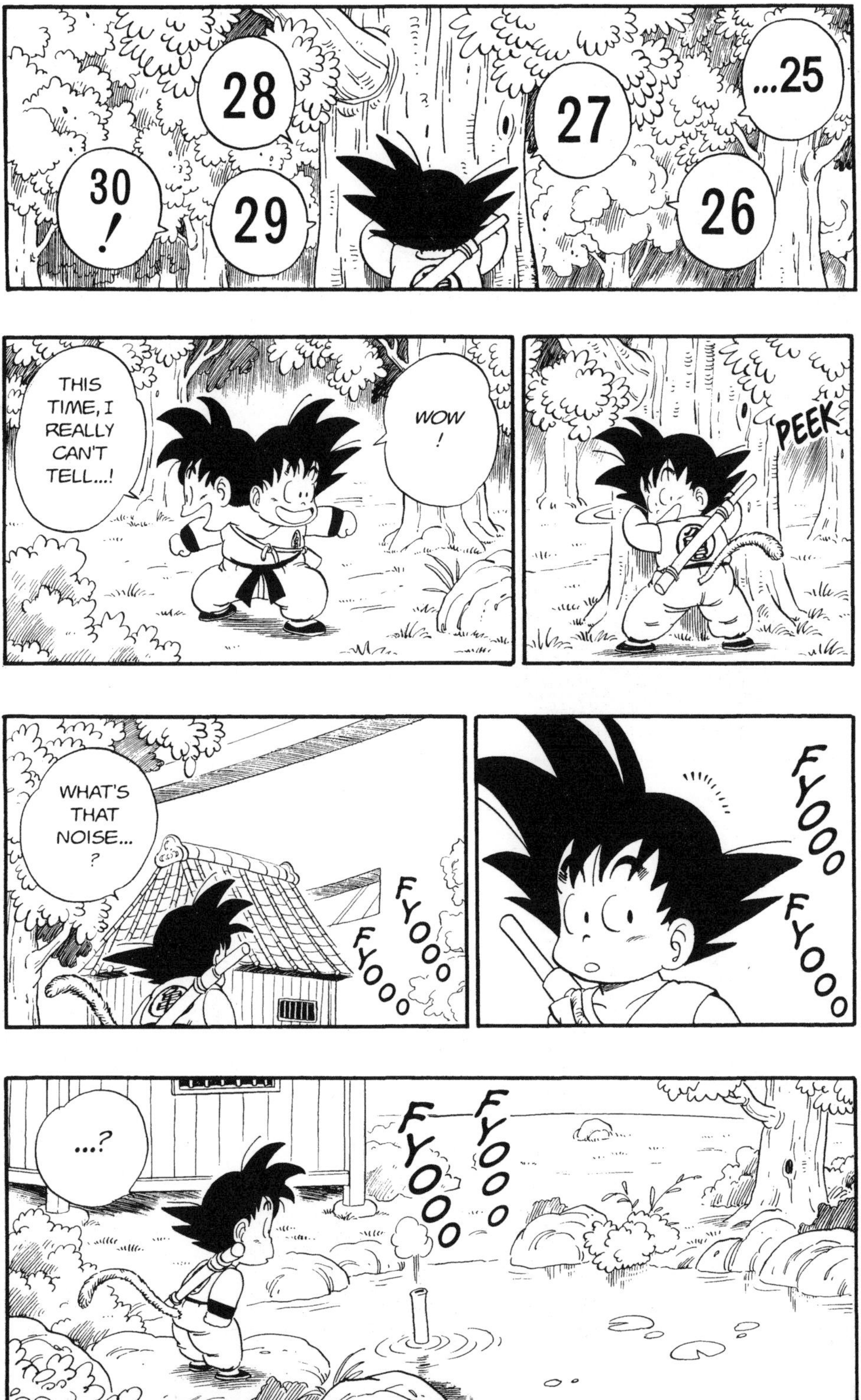
...25
26
27
28
29
30!
PEEK
WOW!
THIS TIME, I REALLY CAN'T TELL...!
FYOOO
FYOOO
WHAT'S THAT NOISE...?
FYOOO
FYOOO
FYOOO
FYOOO
...?

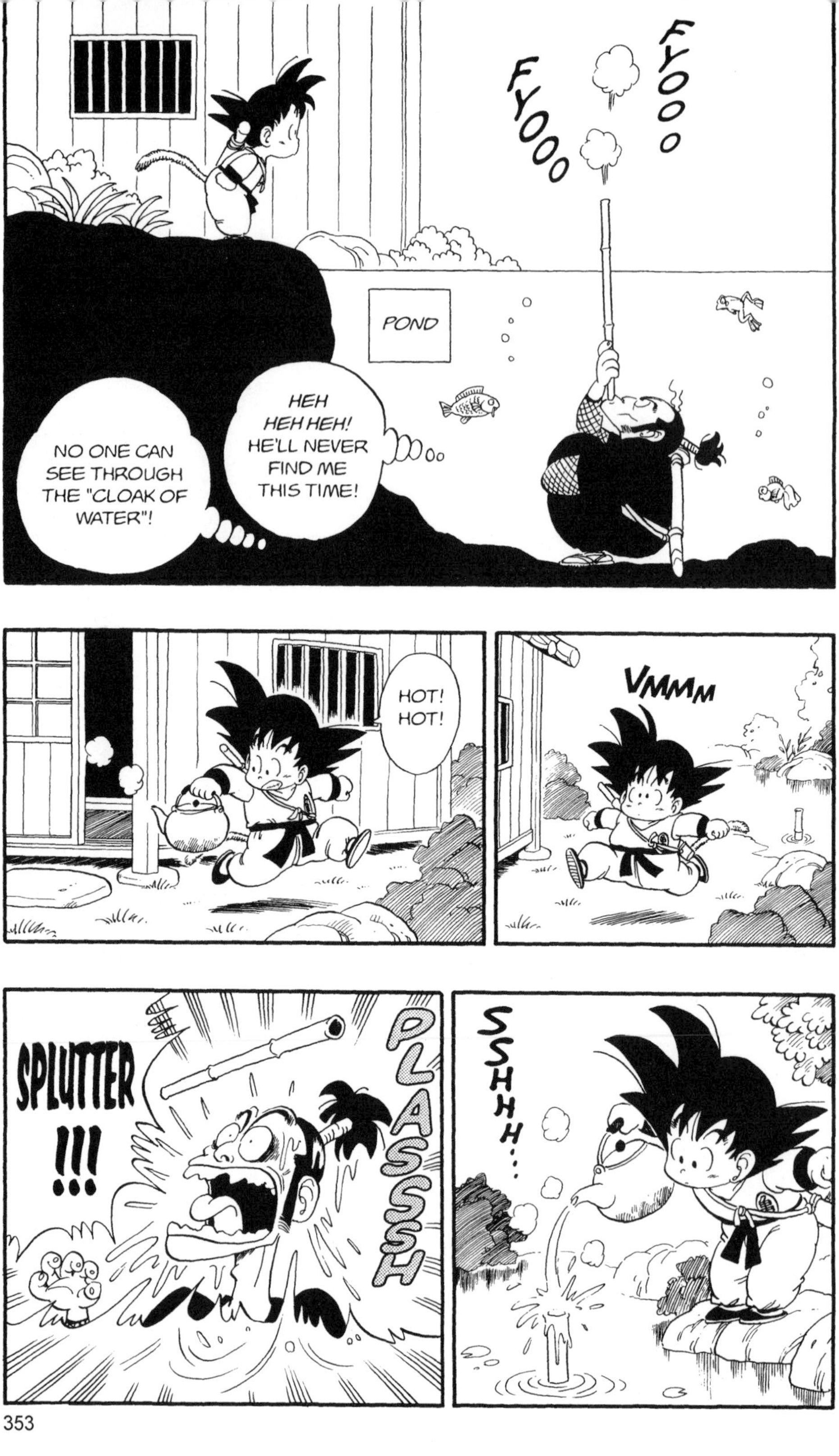
FYOOOO
FYOOOO
POND
HEH HEH HEH! HE'LL NEVER FIND ME THIS TIME!
NO ONE CAN SEE THROUGH THE "CLOAK OF WATER"!
VMMM
HOT! HOT!
SSHHH...
PLASSSH
SPLUTTER !!!

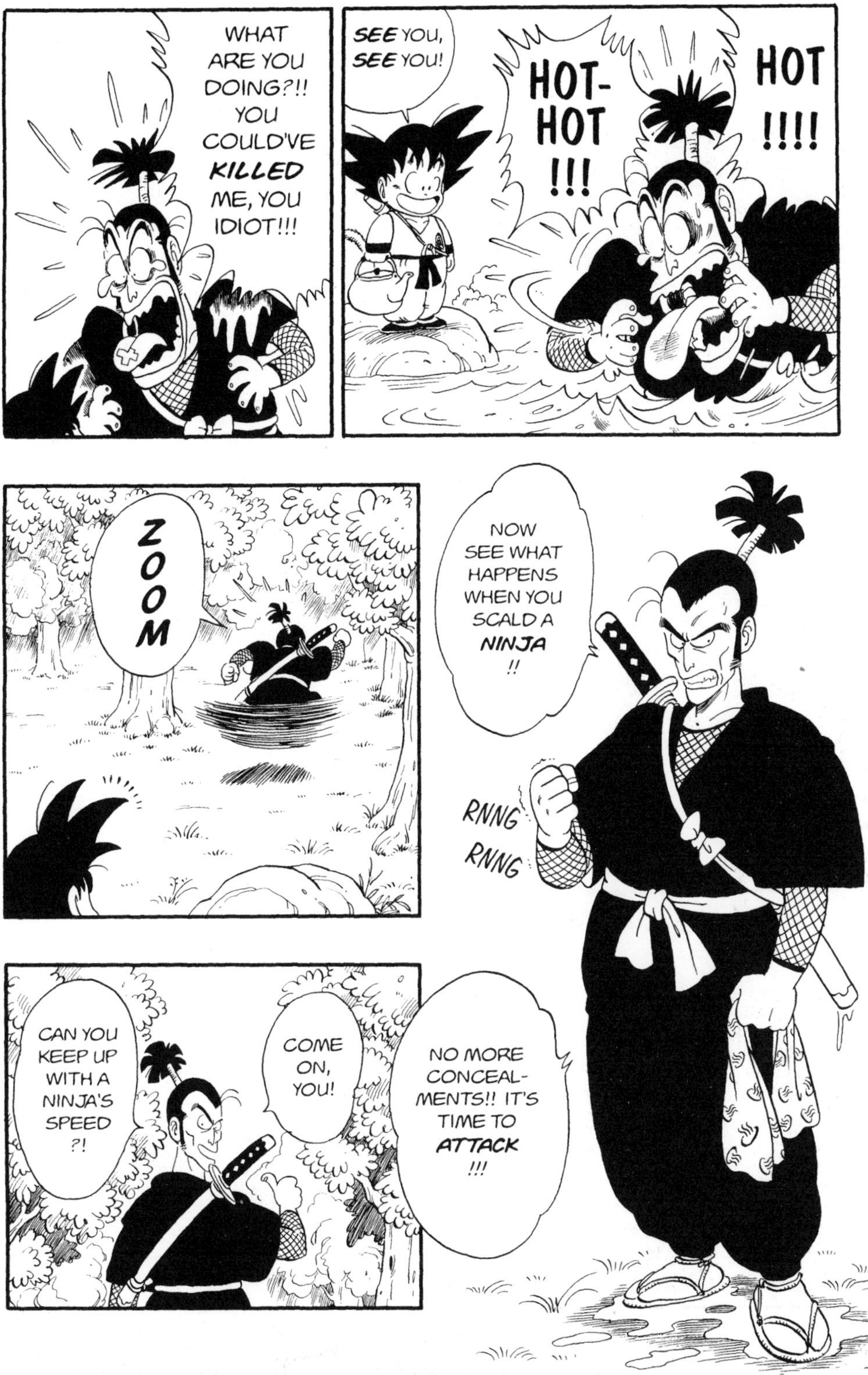
HOT !!!!
HOT-HOT !!!
SEE YOU, SEE YOU!
WHAT ARE YOU DOING?!! YOU COULD'VE KILLED ME, YOU IDIOT!!!
NOW SEE WHAT HAPPENS WHEN YOU SCALD A NINJA !!
RNNG RNNG
NO MORE CONCEAL-MENTS!! IT'S TIME TO ATTACK !!!
ZOOM
COME ON, YOU!
CAN YOU KEEP UP WITH A NINJA'S SPEED ?!

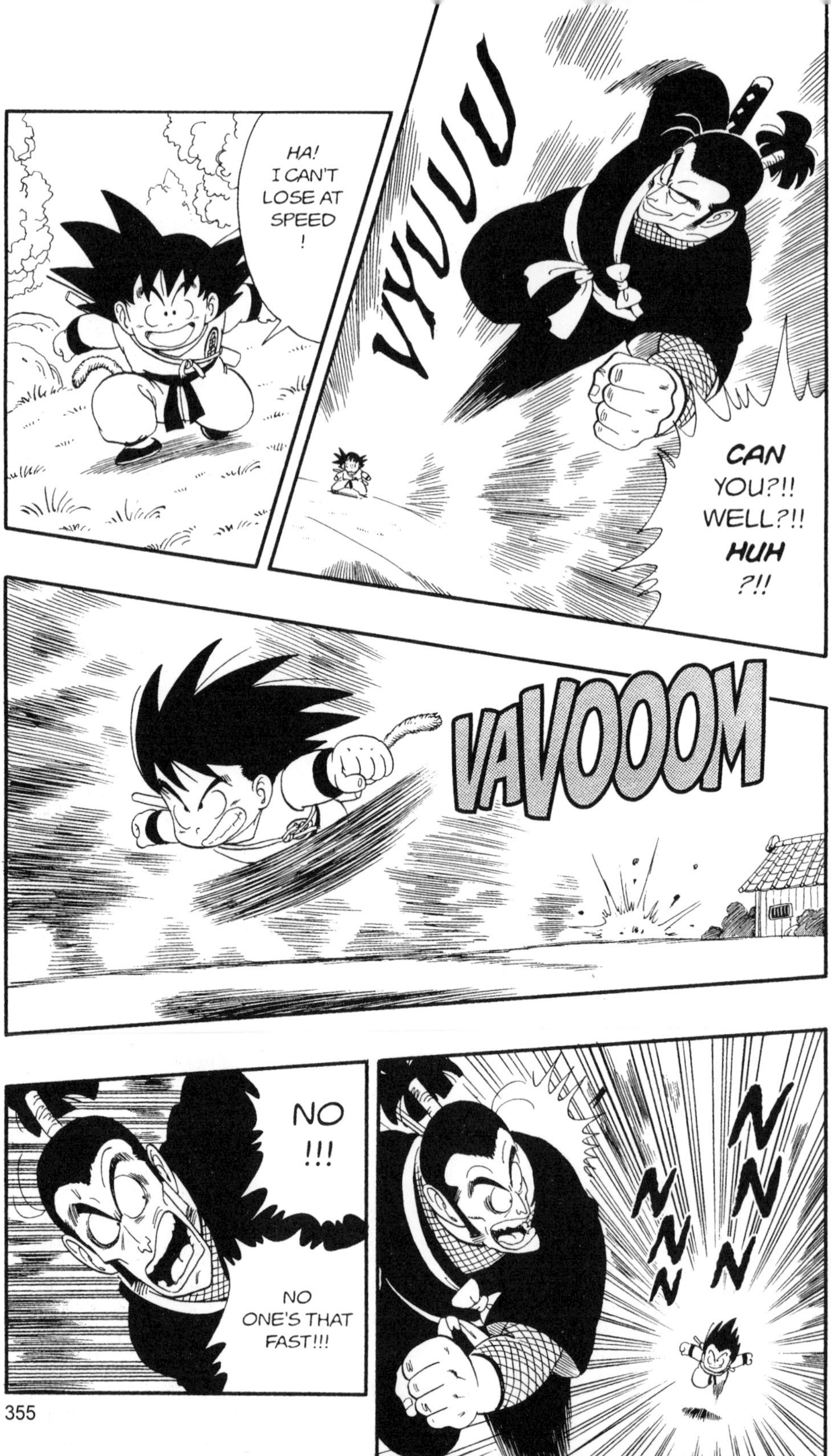

VYUUU
CAN YOU?!! WELL?!! HUH ?!!
HA! I CAN'T LOSE AT SPEED !
VAVOOOM
NNNNN
NNNNN
NO !!!
NO ONE'S THAT FAST!!!

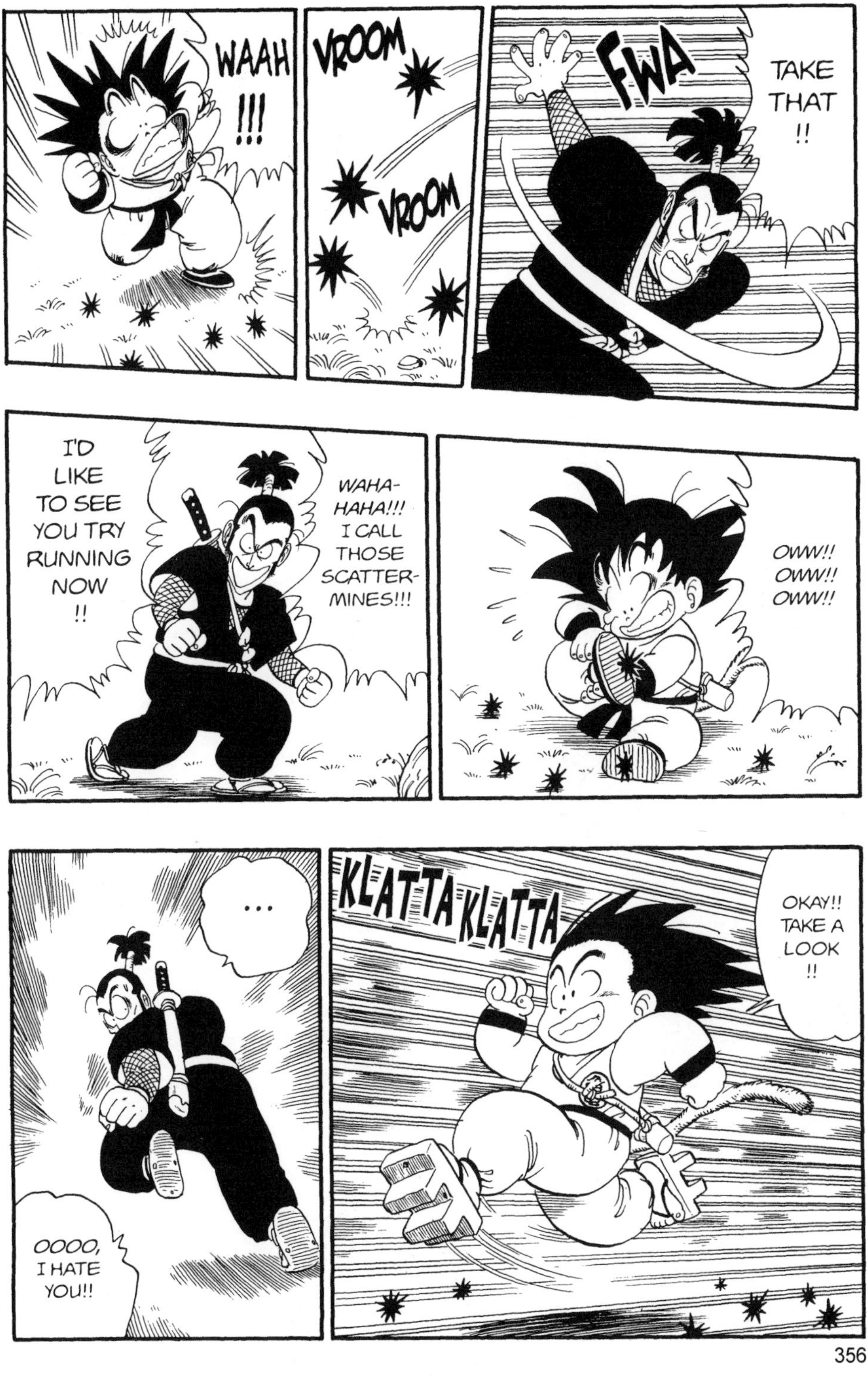
TAKE THAT!!
FWA
VROOM
VROOM
WAAH!!!
OWW!! OWW!! OWW!!
WAHA-HAHA!!! I CALL THOSE SCATTER-MINES!!!
I'D LIKE TO SEE YOU TRY RUNNING NOW!!
OKAY!! TAKE A LOOK!!
KLATTA KLATTA
...
OOOO, I HATE YOU!!

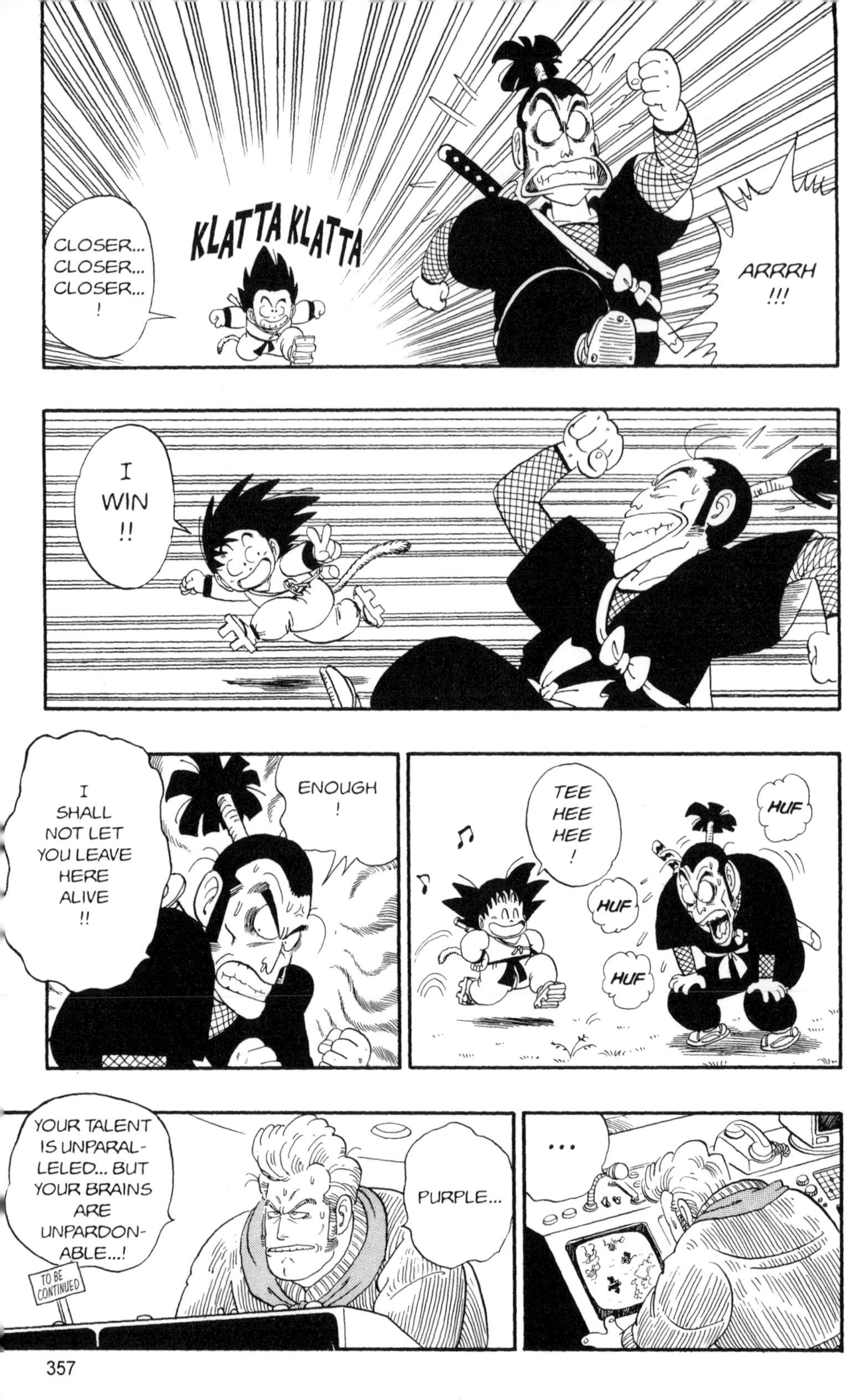
ARRRH !!!
KLATTA KLATTA
CLOSER... CLOSER... CLOSER... !
I WIN !!
HUF
TEE HEE HEE !
HUF
HUF
ENOUGH !
I SHALL NOT LET YOU LEAVE HERE ALIVE !!
...
PURPLE...
YOUR TALENT IS UNPARAL-LELED... BUT YOUR BRAINS ARE UNPARDON-ABLE...!
TO BE CONTINUED

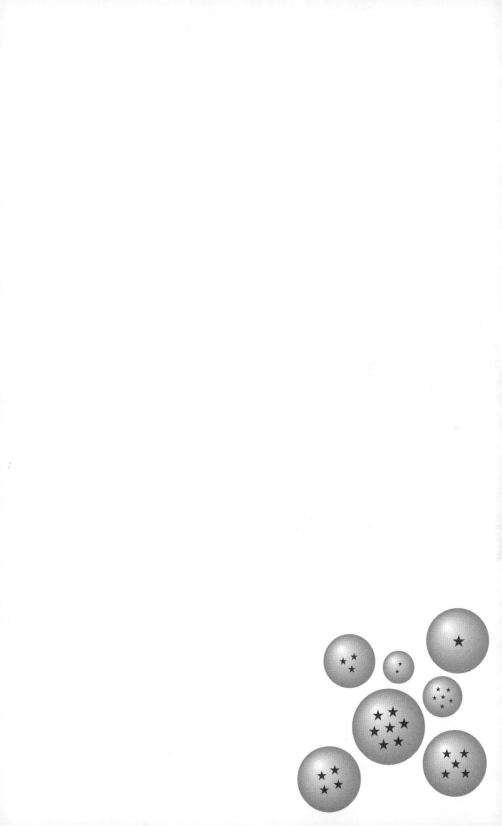

DragonBall

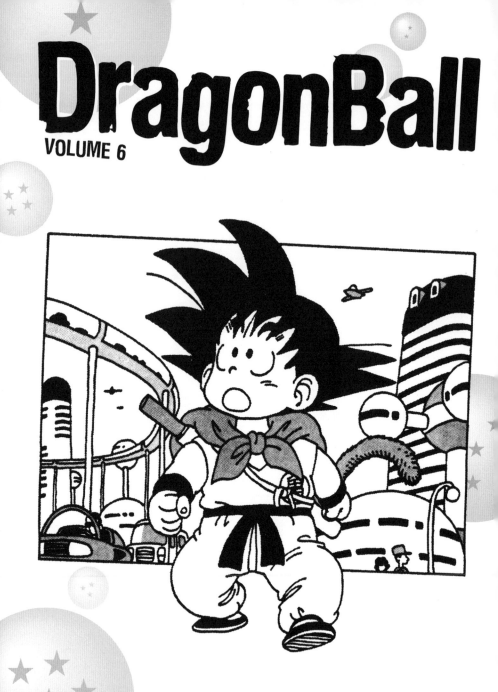

BULMA RETURNS

Tale 61 · The 4 ½ Tatami Mat Flip

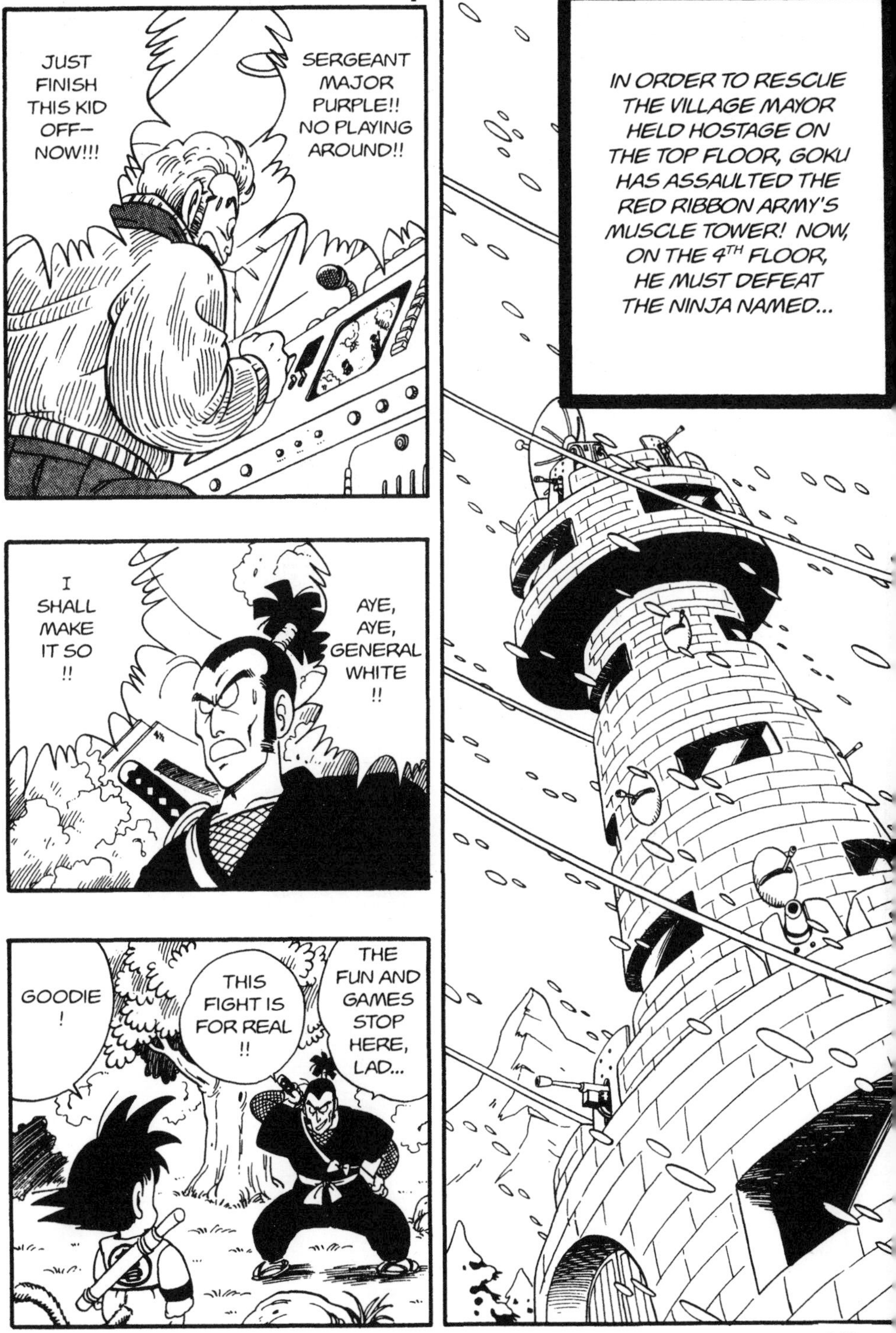

JUST FINISH THIS KID OFF— NOW!!!

SERGEANT MAJOR PURPLE!! NO PLAYING AROUND!!

IN ORDER TO RESCUE THE VILLAGE MAYOR HELD HOSTAGE ON THE TOP FLOOR, GOKU HAS ASSAULTED THE RED RIBBON ARMY'S MUSCLE TOWER! NOW, ON THE 4TH FLOOR, HE MUST DEFEAT THE NINJA NAMED...

I SHALL MAKE IT SO !!

AYE, AYE, GENERAL WHITE !!

GOODIE !

THIS FIGHT IS FOR REAL !!

THE FUN AND GAMES STOP HERE, LAD...

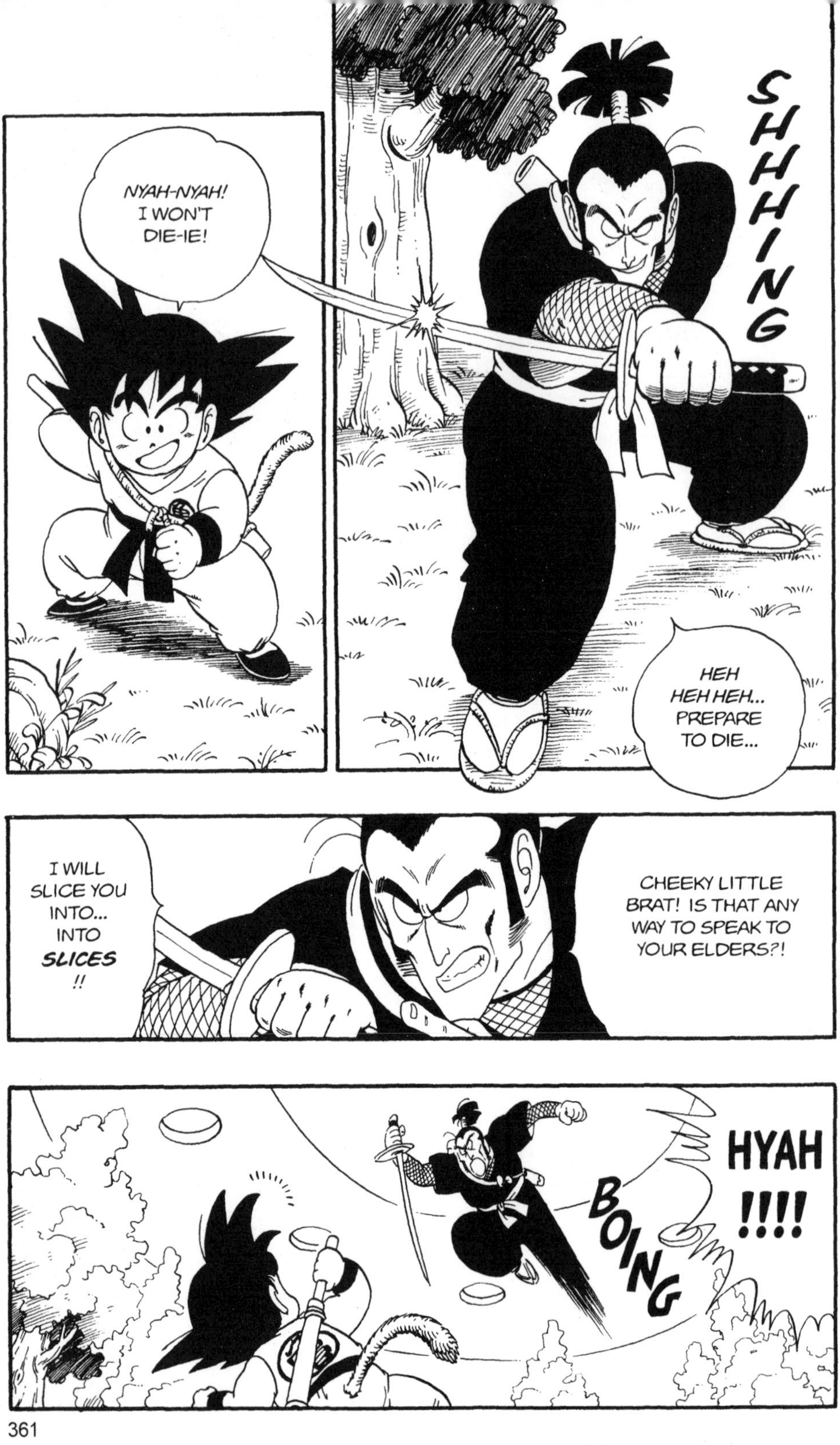
SHHHING
HEH HEH HEH... PREPARE TO DIE...
NYAH-NYAH! I WON'T DIE-IE!
CHEEKY LITTLE BRAT! IS THAT ANY WAY TO SPEAK TO YOUR ELDERS?!
I WILL SLICE YOU INTO... INTO SLICES !!
HYAH !!!!
BOING

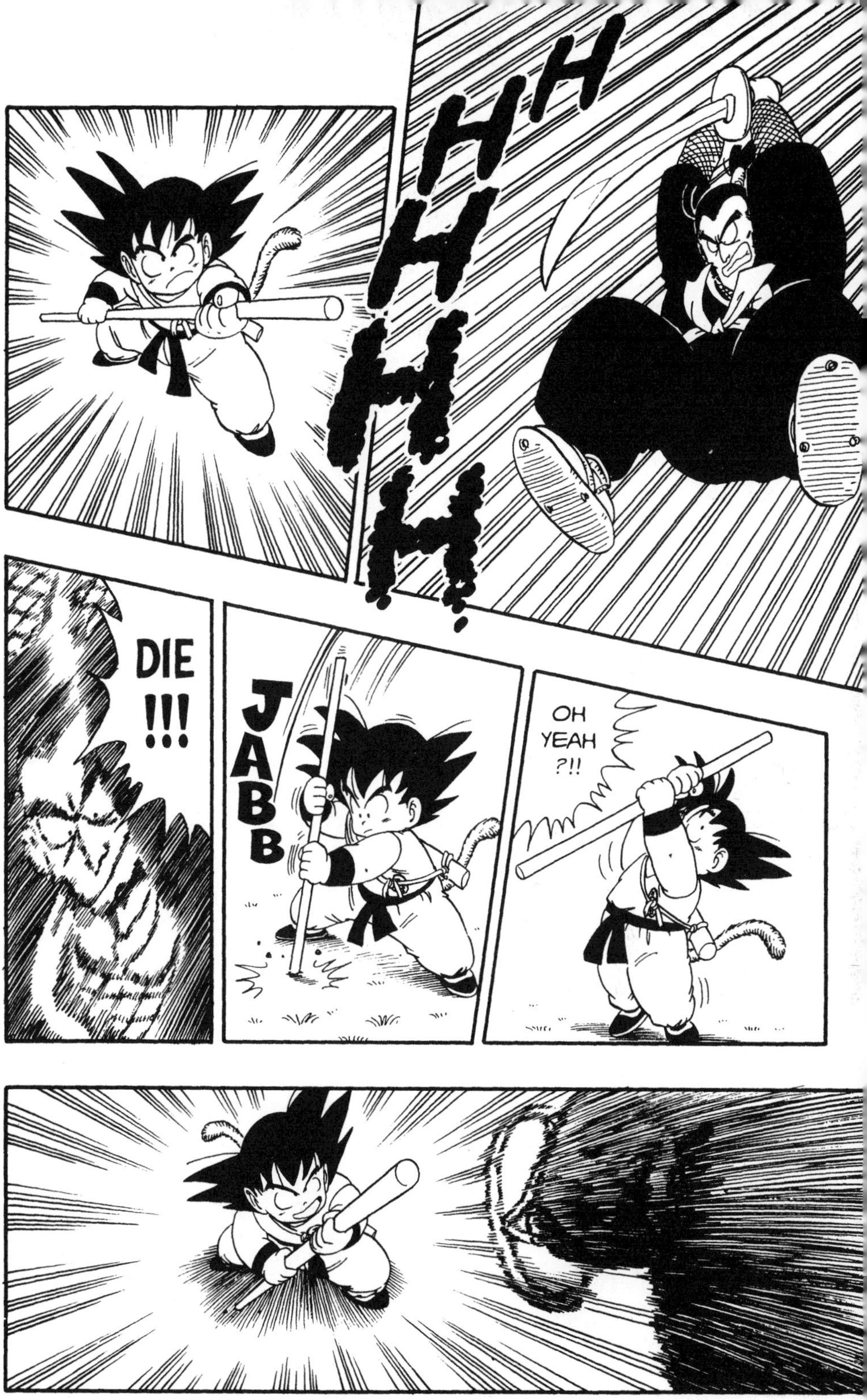
HHHHH!
OH YEAH ?!!
JABB
DIE !!!

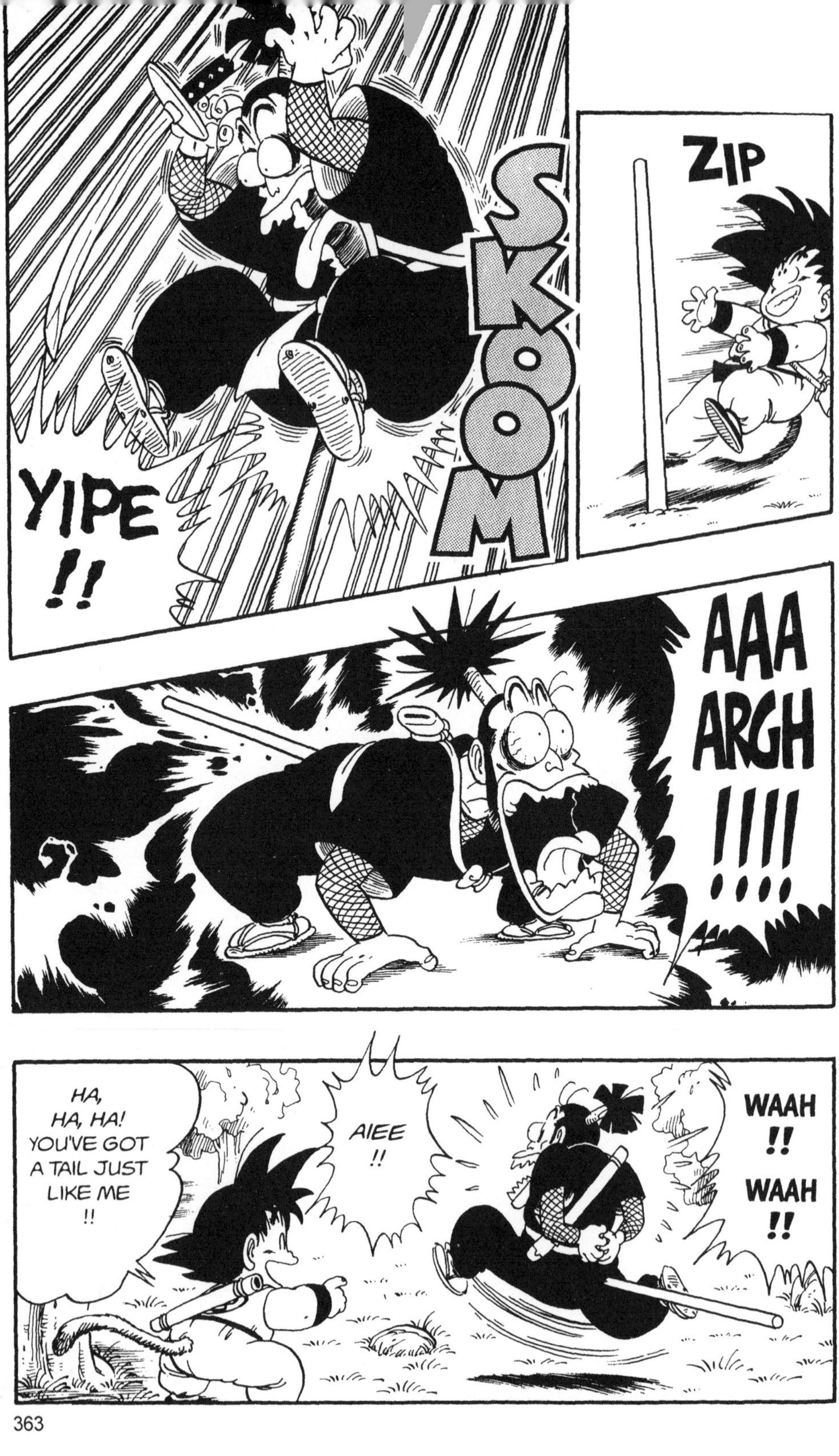
ZIP
SKOOM
YIPE !!
AAA ARGH !!!!
WAAH !! WAAH !!
AIEE !!
HA, HA, HA! YOU'VE GOT A TAIL JUST LIKE ME !!

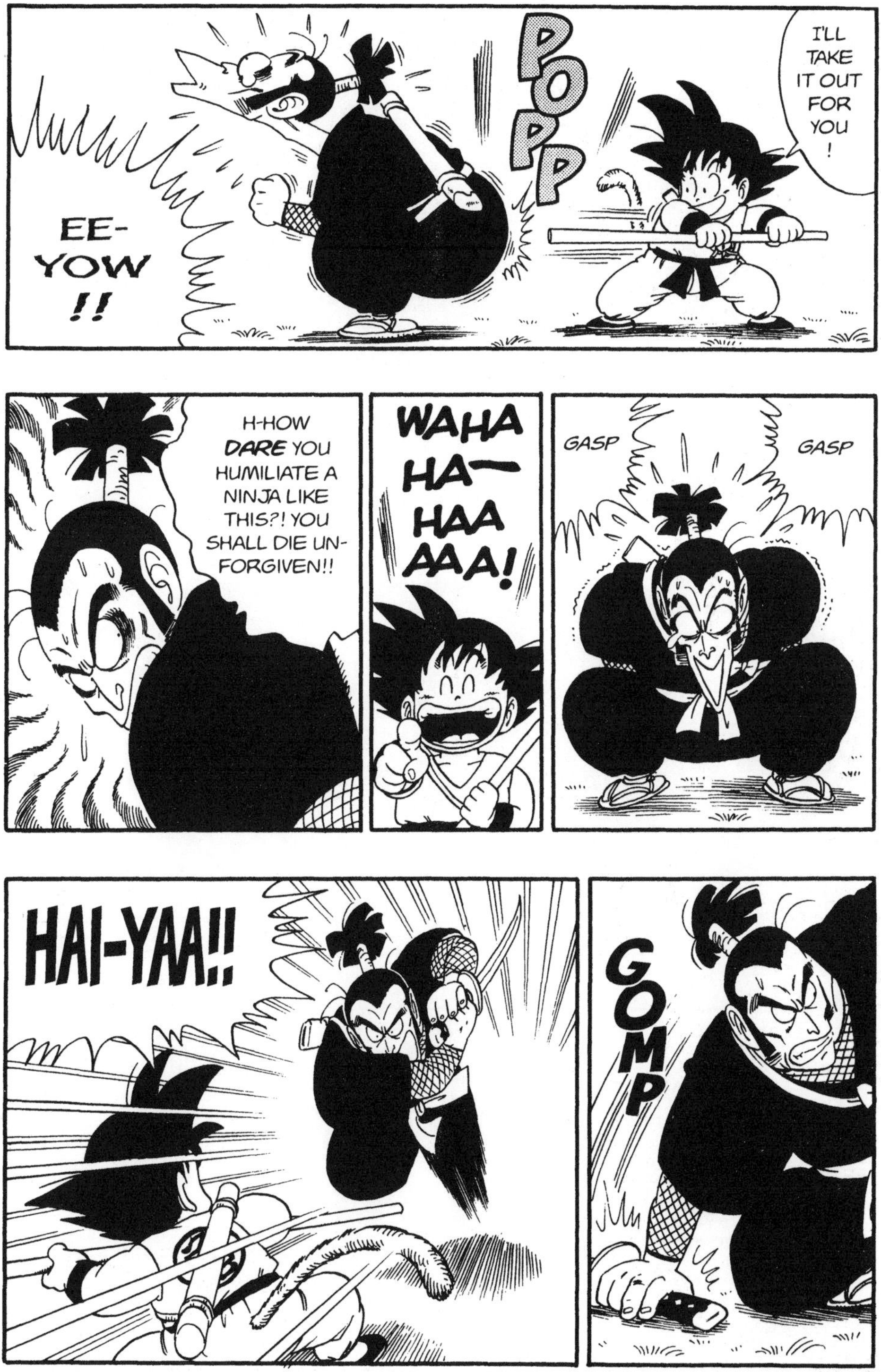
I'LL TAKE IT OUT FOR YOU!
POPP
EE-YOW!!
GASP
GASP
WAHA HA— HAA AAA!
H-HOW DARE YOU HUMILIATE A NINJA LIKE THIS?! YOU SHALL DIE UN-FORGIVEN!!
GOMP
HAI-YAA!!

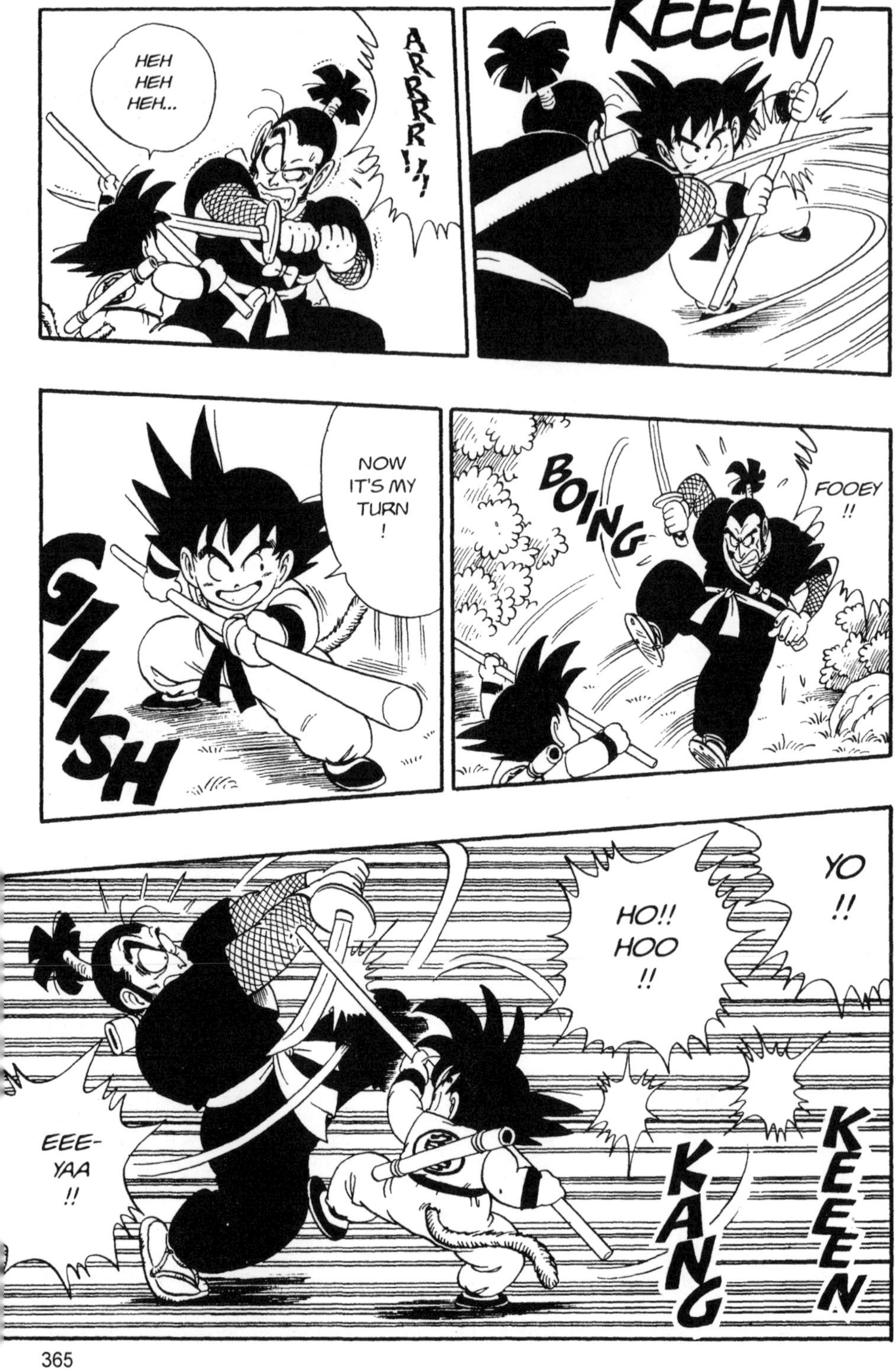
KEEEN
ARRRR!!!
HEH HEH HEH...
BOING
FOOEY!!
NOW IT'S MY TURN!
GIIISH
YO!!
HO!! HOO!!
KEEEEN
KANG
EEE-YAA!!

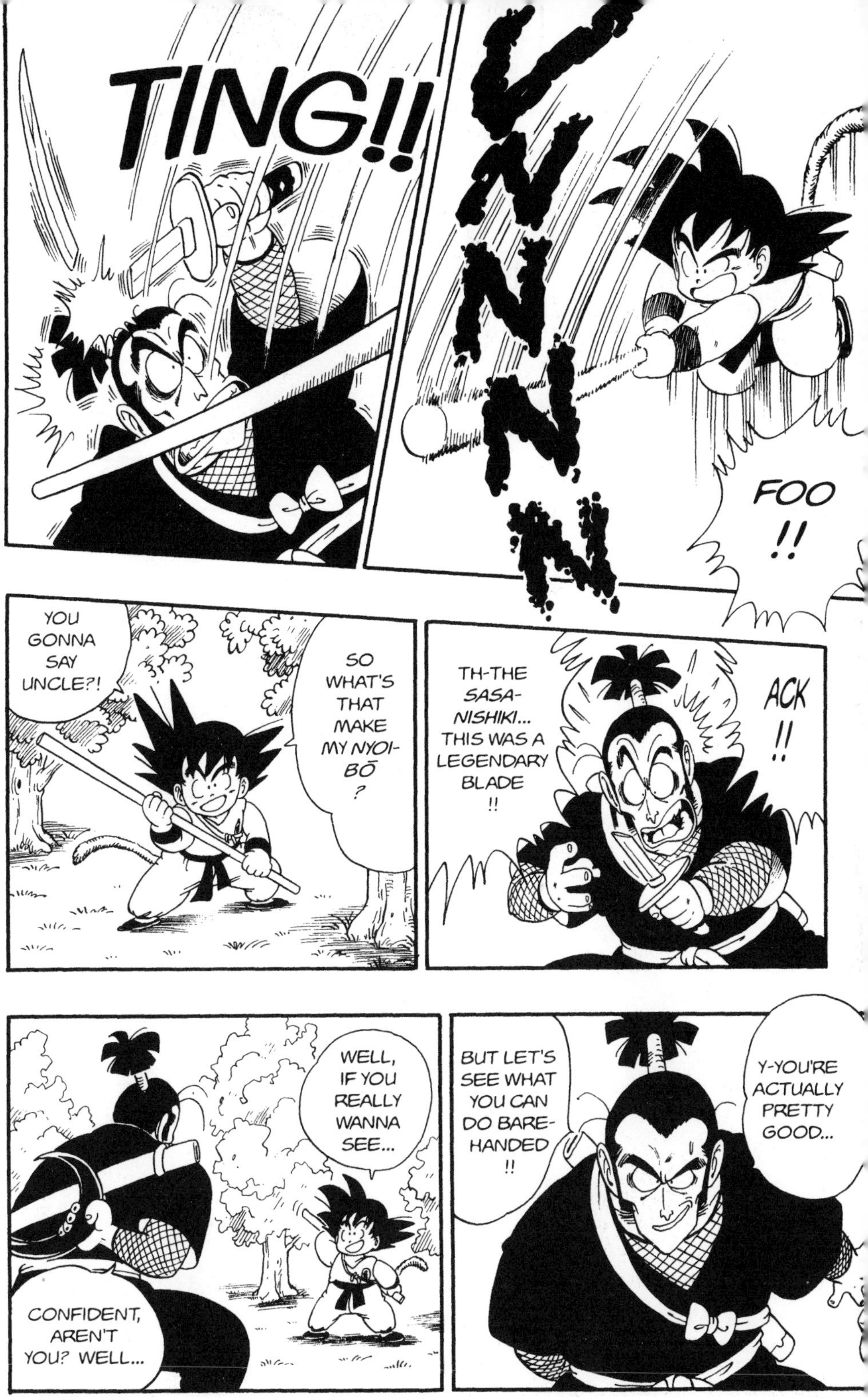
VNNNN
FOO!!
TING!!
ACK!!
TH-THE *SASANISHIKI*... THIS WAS A LEGENDARY BLADE!!
SO WHAT'S THAT MAKE MY *NYOI-BŌ*?
YOU GONNA SAY UNCLE?!
Y-YOU'RE ACTUALLY PRETTY GOOD...
BUT LET'S SEE WHAT YOU CAN DO BARE-HANDED!!
WELL, IF YOU REALLY WANNA SEE...
CONFIDENT, AREN'T YOU? WELL...

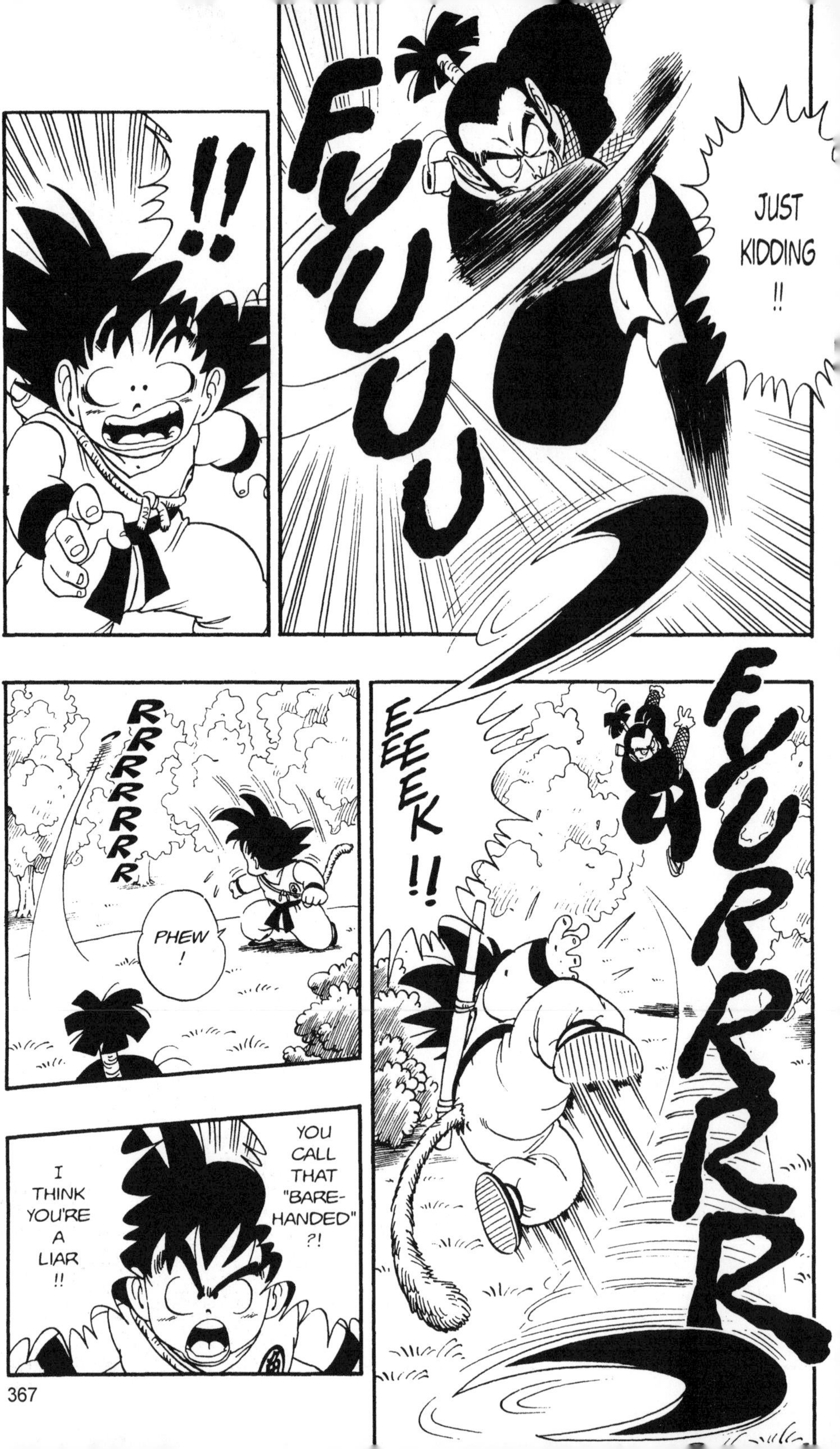
FUUUU
JUST KIDDING !!
!!
EEEEK !!
FURRRR
RRRRRRR
PHEW !
YOU CALL THAT "BARE-HANDED" ?!
I THINK YOU'RE A LIAR !!

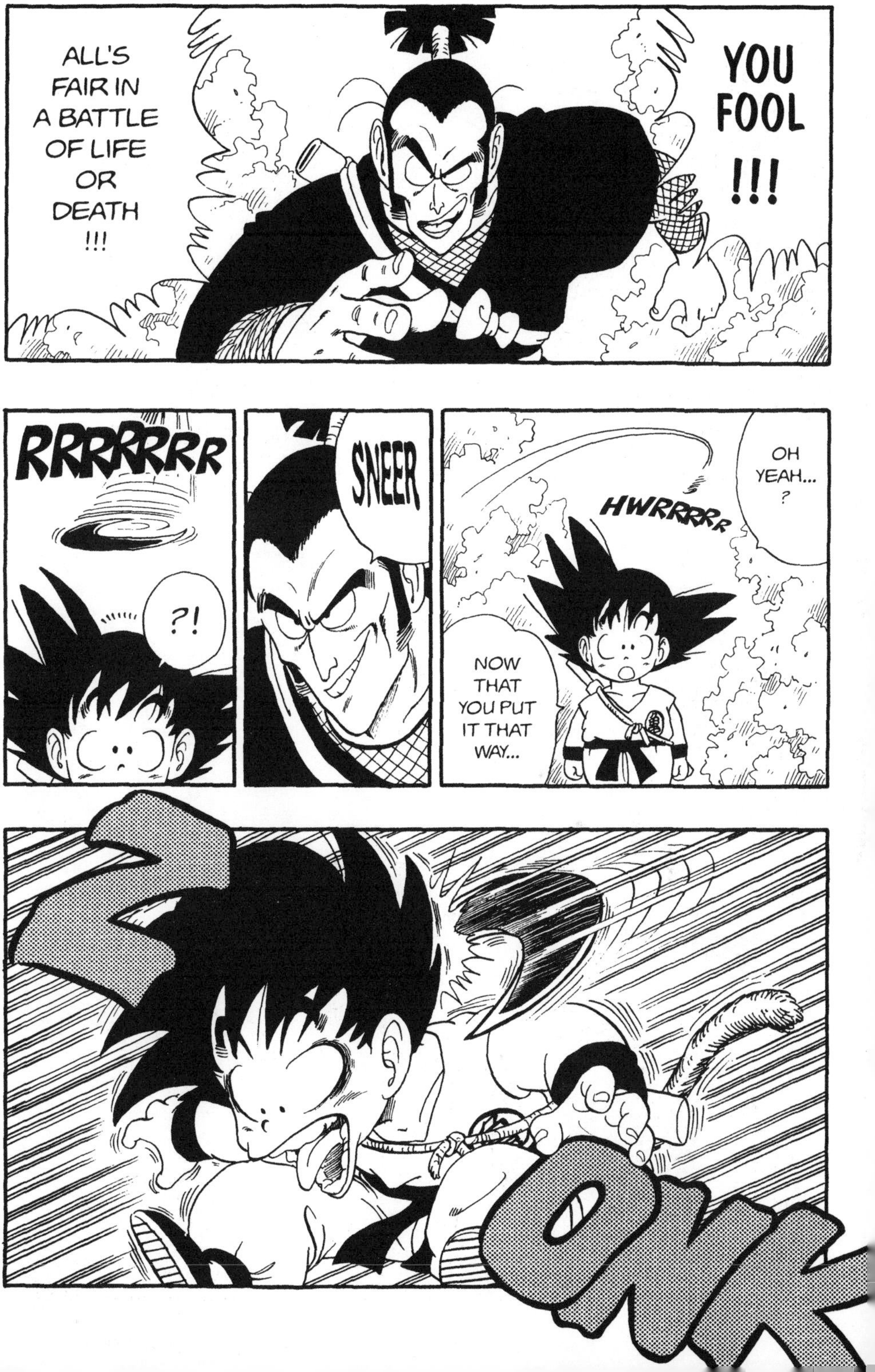
YOU FOOL !!!
ALL'S FAIR IN A BATTLE OF LIFE OR DEATH !!!
OH YEAH...?
HWRRRRRR
NOW THAT YOU PUT IT THAT WAY...
SNEER
RRRRRRR
?!
ONK

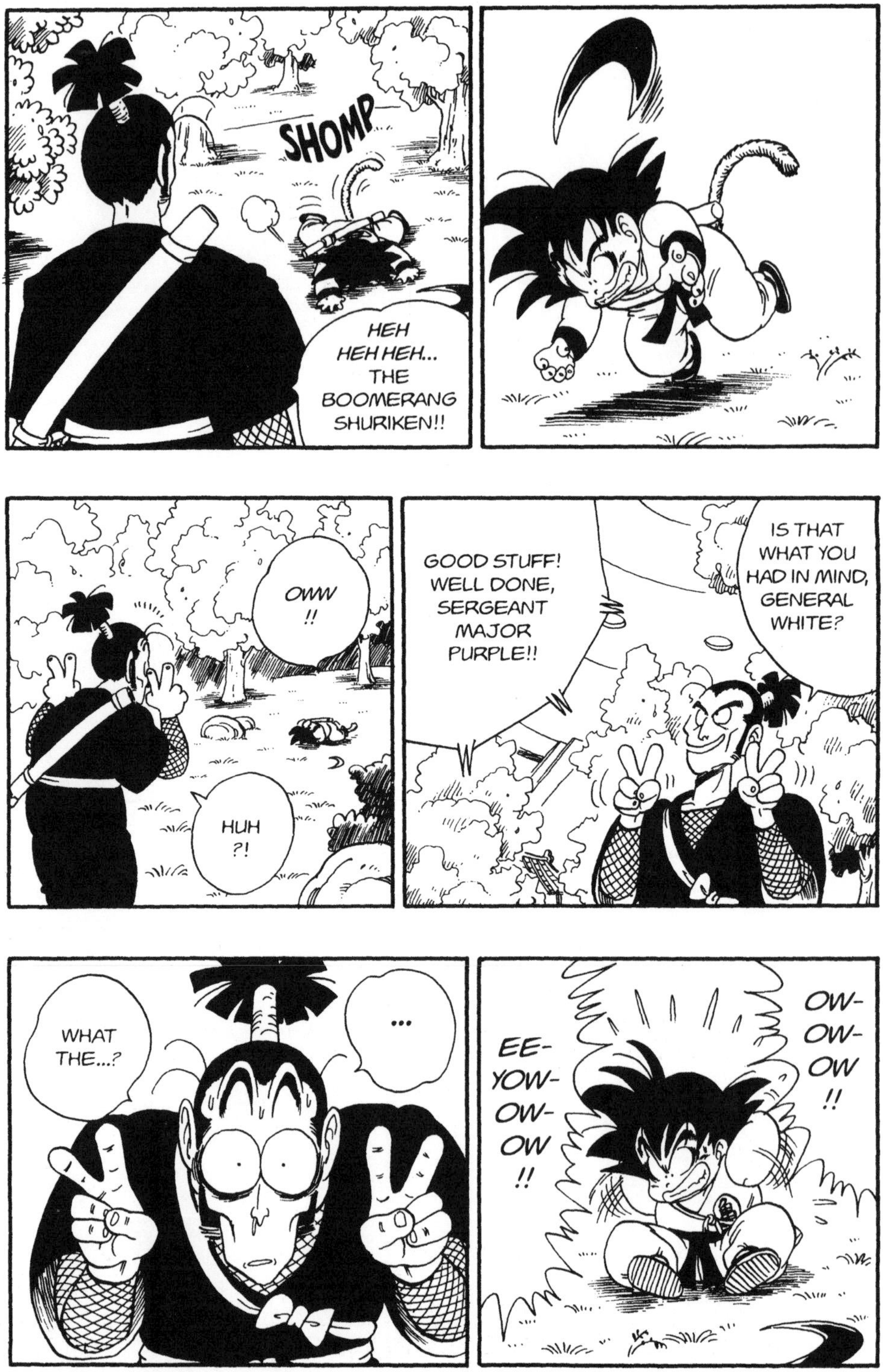
SHOMP
HEH HEH HEH... THE BOOMERANG SHURIKEN!!
IS THAT WHAT YOU HAD IN MIND, GENERAL WHITE?
GOOD STUFF! WELL DONE, SERGEANT MAJOR PURPLE!!
OWW !!
HUH ?!
OW-OW-OW !!
EE-YOW-OW-OW !!
...
WHAT THE...?

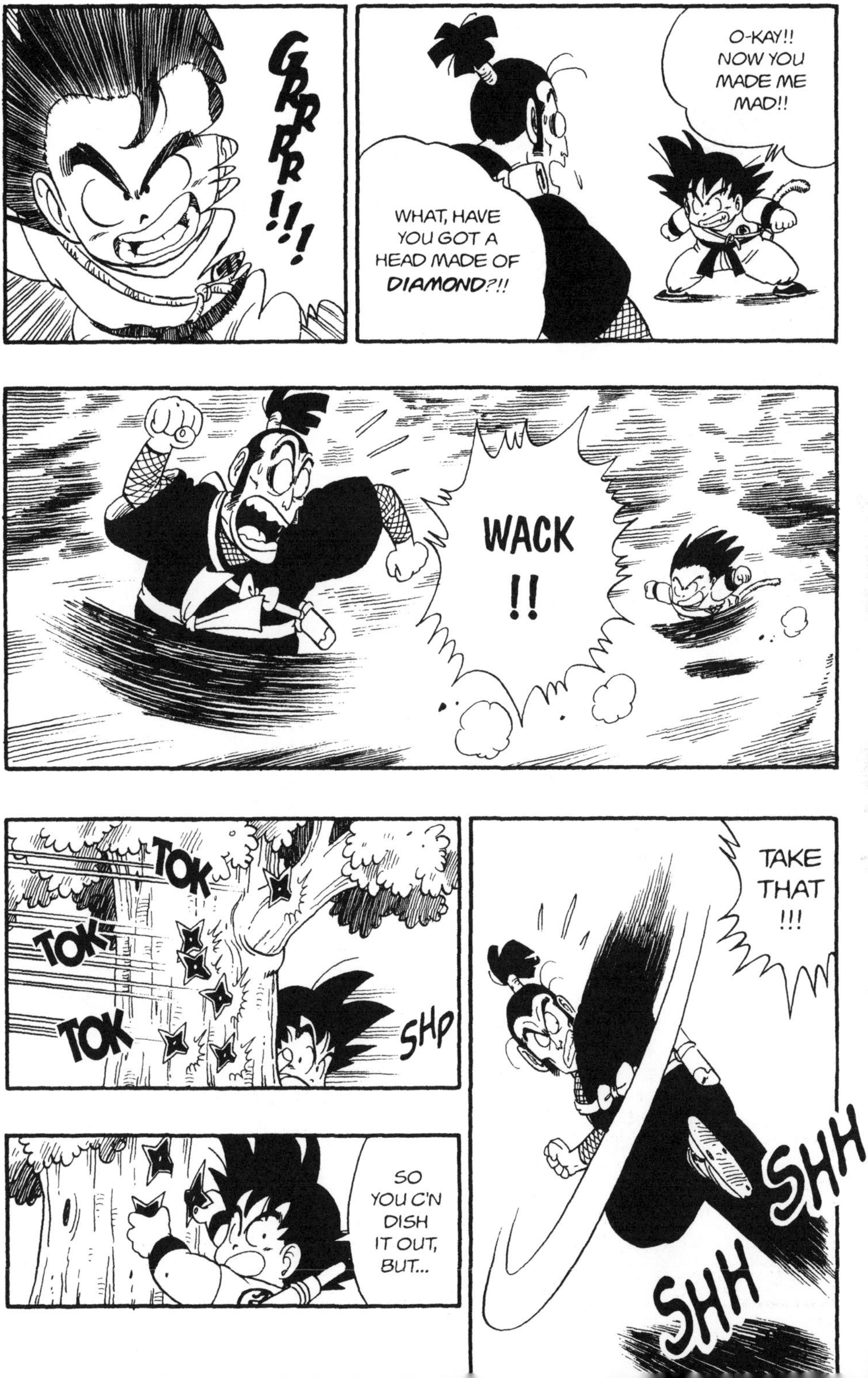
O-KAY!! NOW YOU MADE ME MAD!!
WHAT, HAVE YOU GOT A HEAD MADE OF DIAMOND?!!
GRRRR!!!
WACK!!
TAKE THAT!!!
SHH
SHH
TOK
TOK
TOK
SHP
SO YOU C'N DISH IT OUT, BUT...

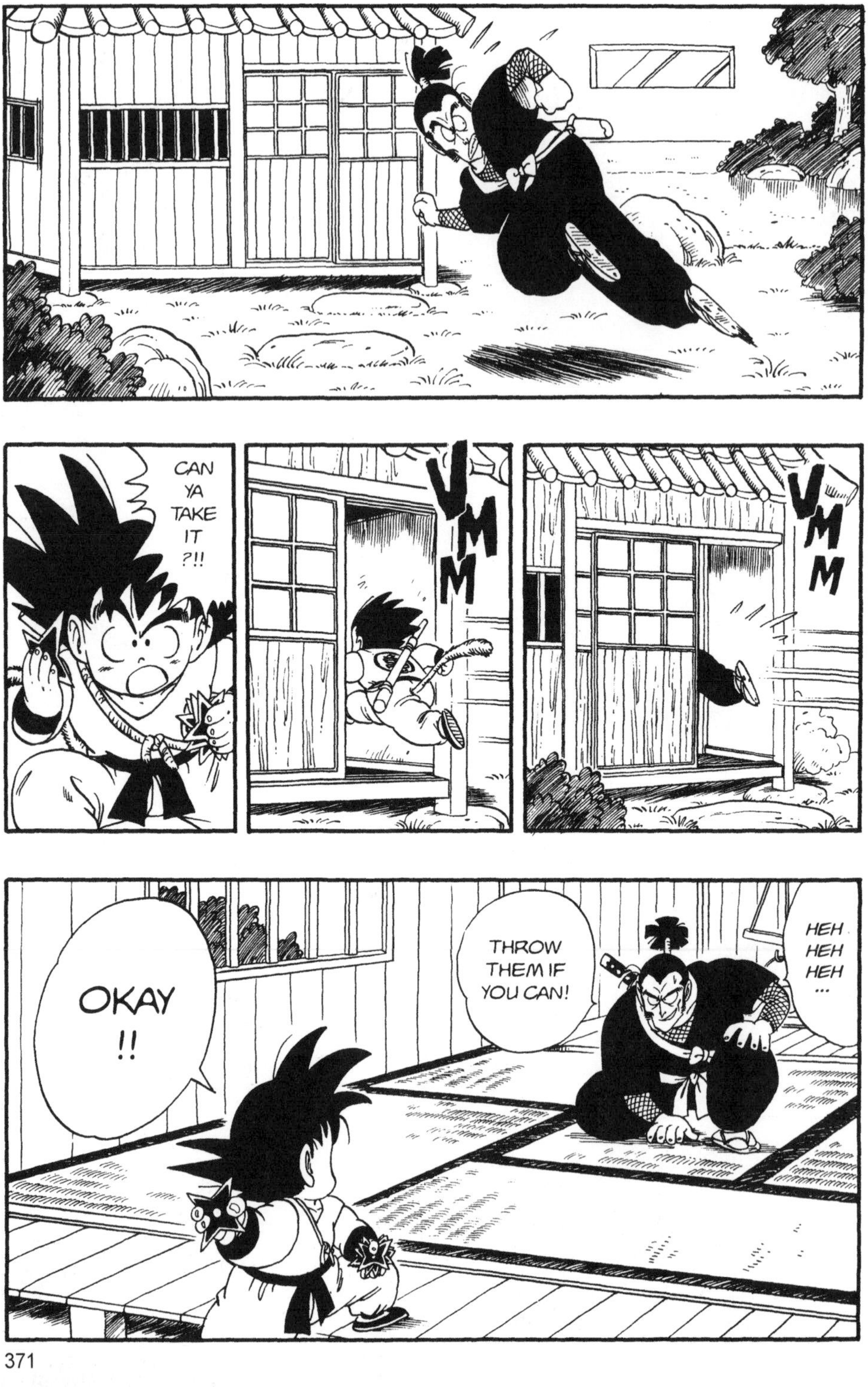
VMM
VMM
CAN YA TAKE IT ?!!
HEH HEH HEH ...
THROW THEM IF YOU CAN!
OKAY !!

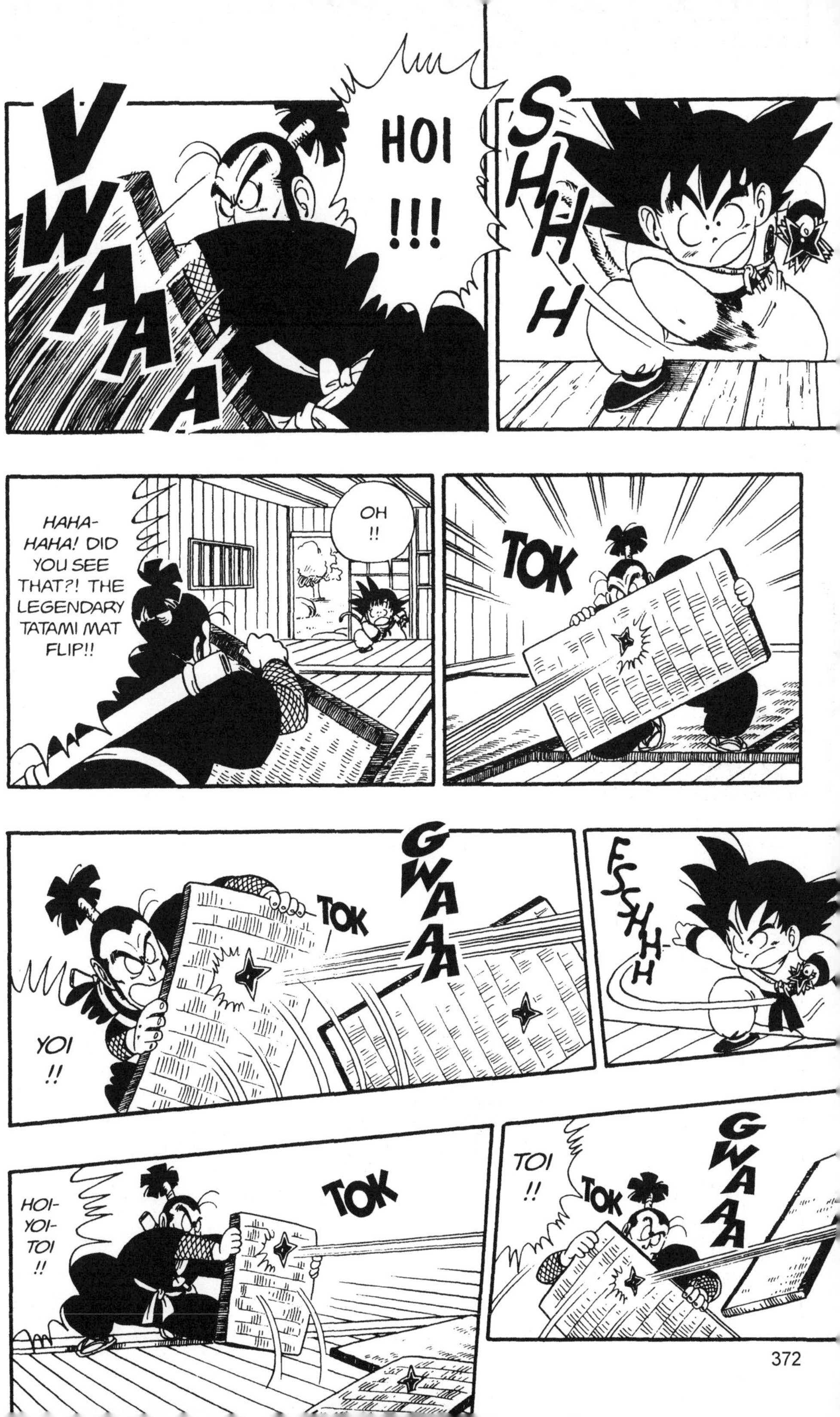
SHHHH
VWAAAA
HOI !!!
TOK
OH !!
HAHA-HAHA! DID YOU SEE THAT?! THE LEGENDARY TATAMI MAT FLIP!!
FSSHHH
GWAAAA
TOK
YOI !!
GWAAA
TOI !!
TOK
TOK
HOI-YOI-TOI !!

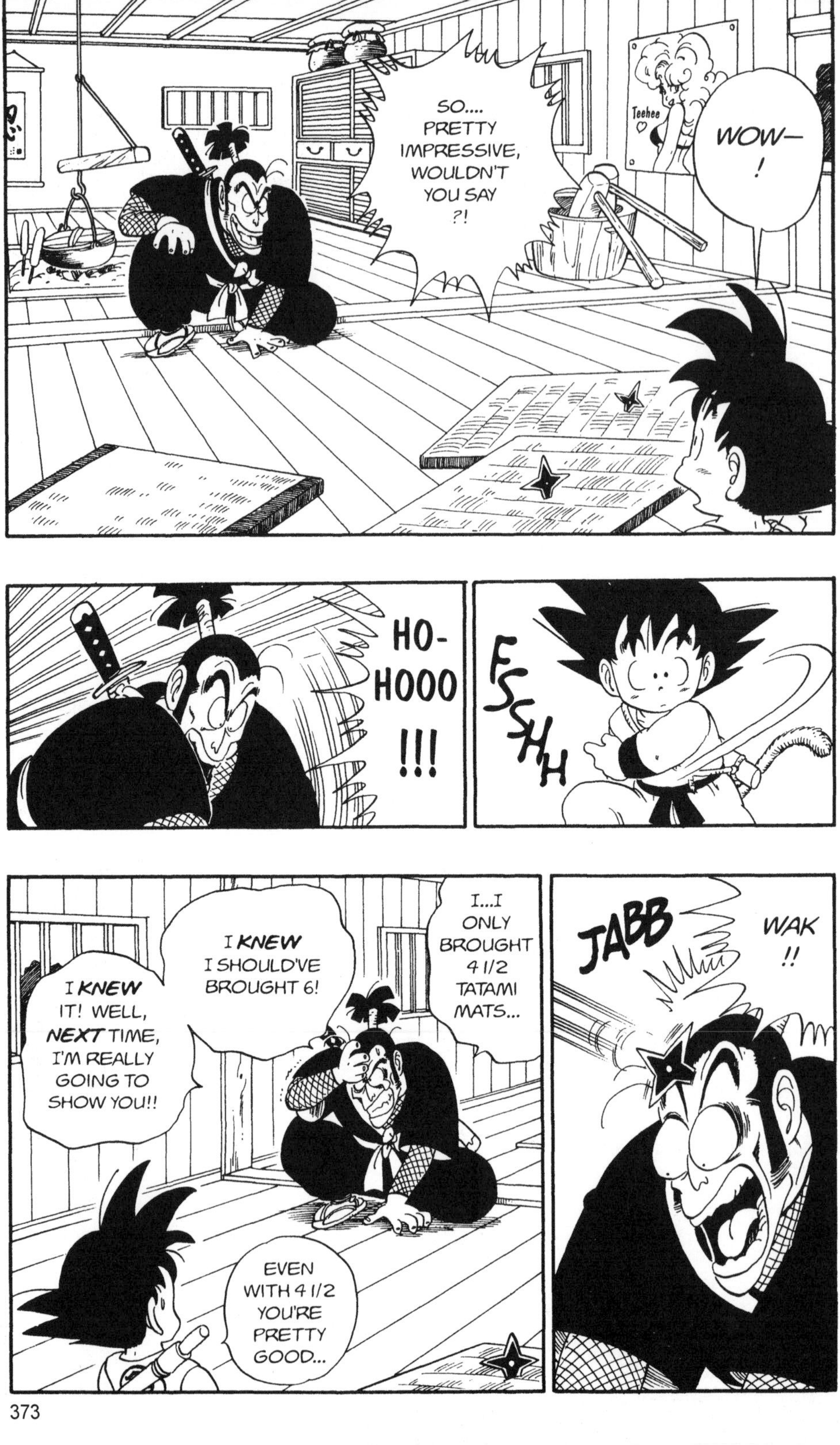
Teehee ♡
WOW—!
SO.... PRETTY IMPRESSIVE, WOULDN'T YOU SAY ?!
FSSHH
HO-HOOO !!!
JABB
WAK !!
I...I ONLY BROUGHT 4 1/2 TATAMI MATS...
I **KNEW** I SHOULD'VE BROUGHT 6!
I **KNEW** IT! WELL, **NEXT** TIME, I'M REALLY GOING TO SHOW YOU!!
EVEN WITH 4 1/2 YOU'RE PRETTY GOOD...

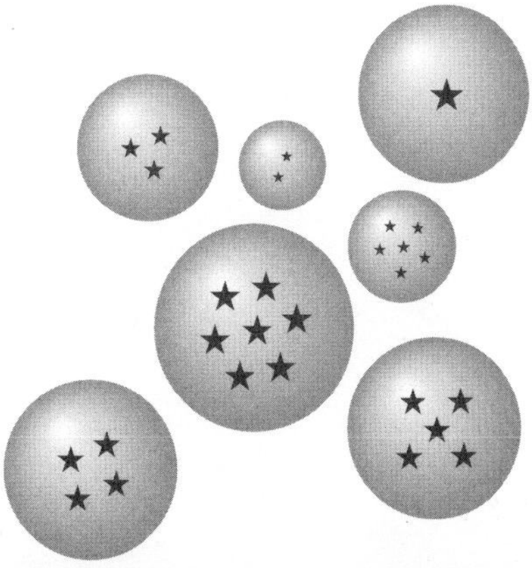

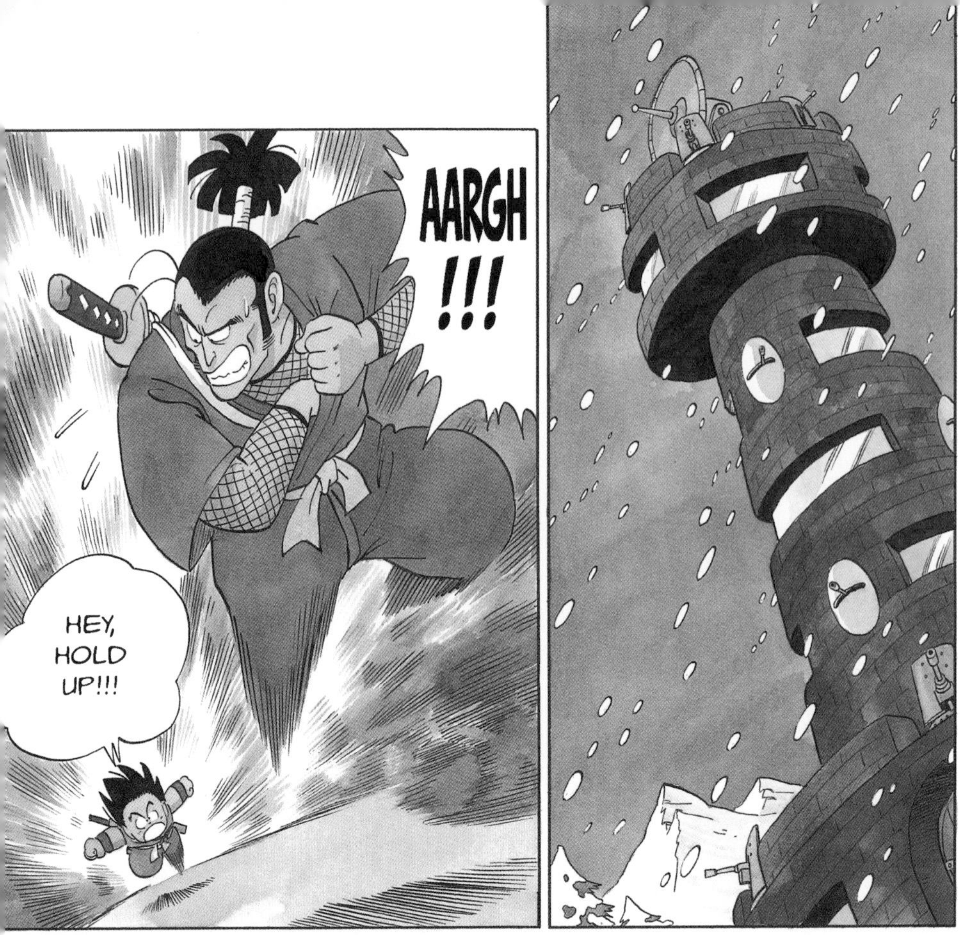
AARGH!!!
HEY, HOLD UP!!!

Tale 62 · The Ninja Split!

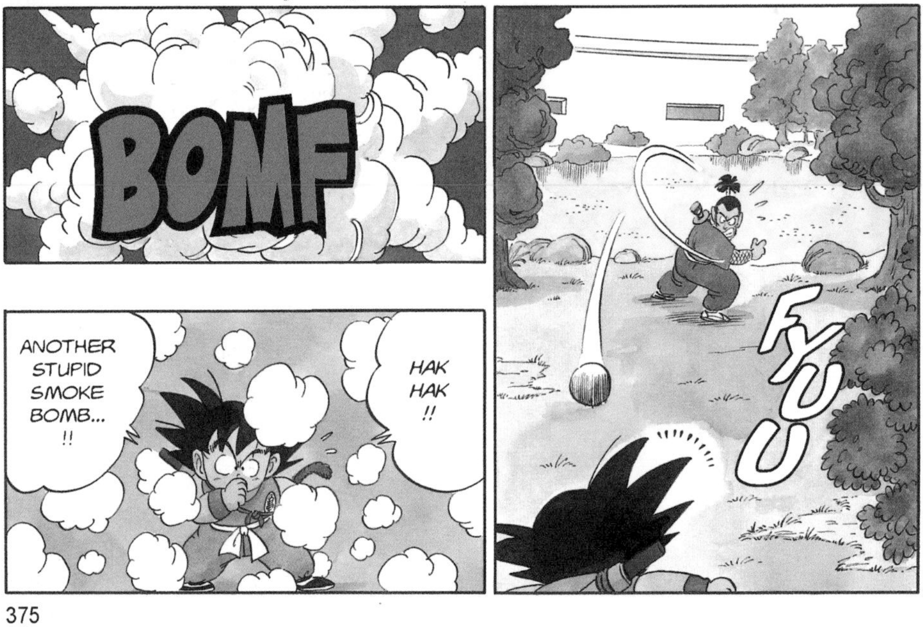
FYUU
BOMF
HAK HAK !!
ANOTHER STUPID SMOKE BOMB... !!

SON GOKU

HERO OF THE
ANCIENT CHINESE
FABLE **SAIYŪKI**
("JOURNEY TO THE WEST")

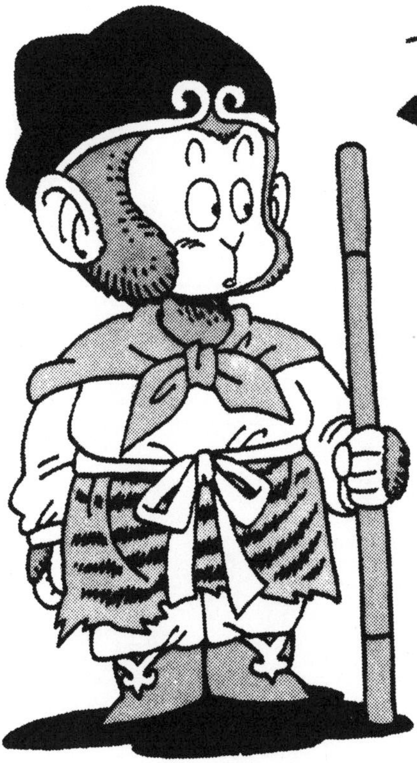

SON GOKU

HERO OF
DRAGON BALL

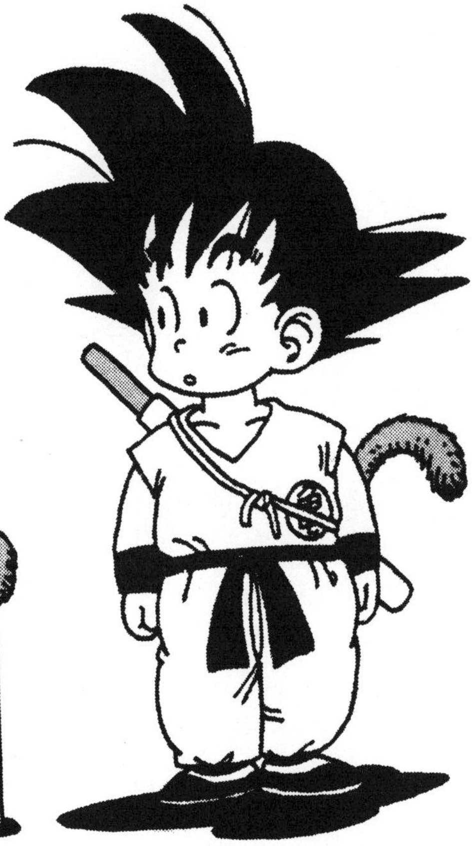

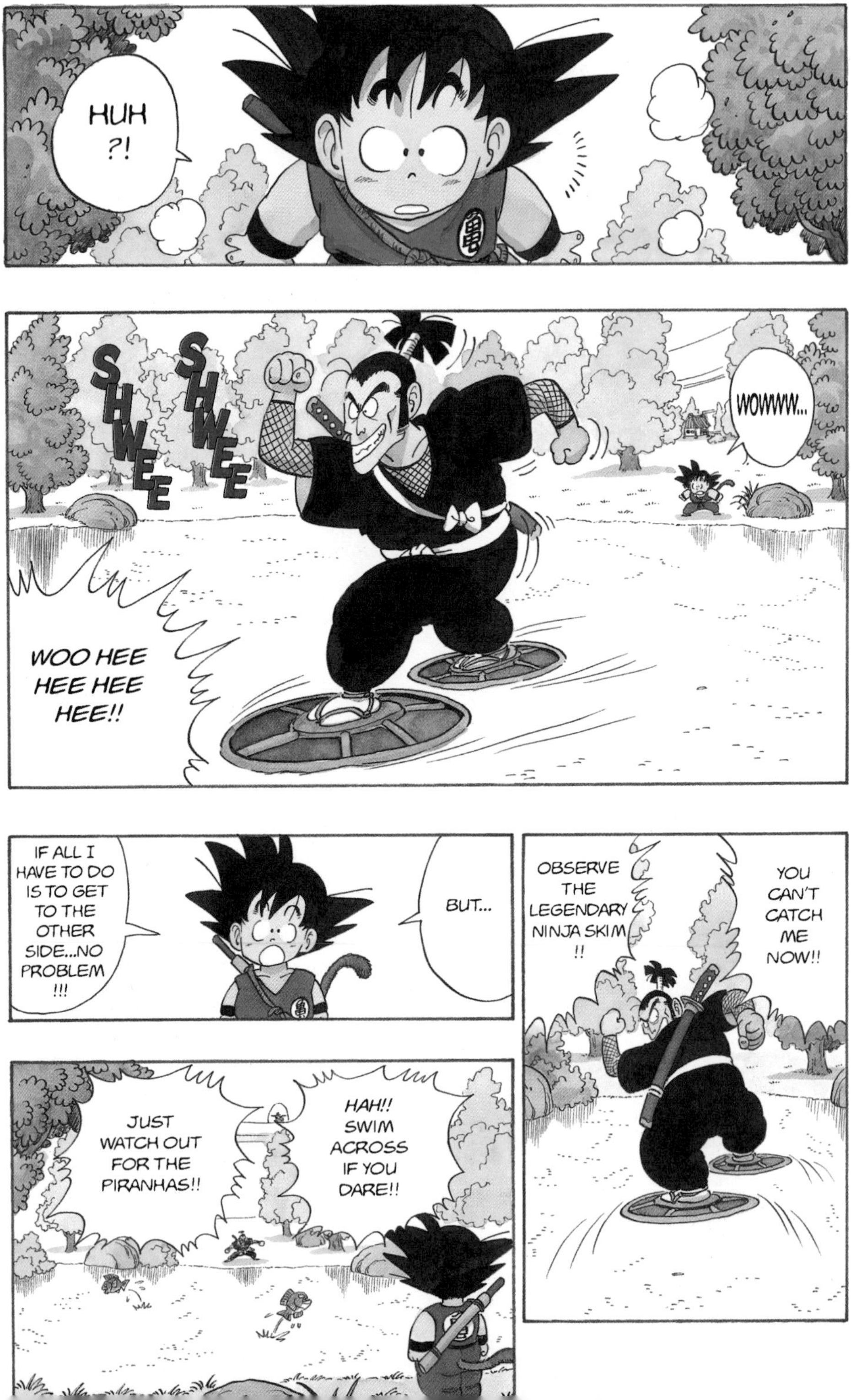
HUH ?!
WOWWW...
SHWEE
SHWEE
WOO HEE HEE HEE HEE!!
YOU CAN'T CATCH ME NOW!!
OBSERVE THE LEGENDARY NINJA SKIM !!
BUT...
IF ALL I HAVE TO DO IS TO GET TO THE OTHER SIDE...NO PROBLEM !!!
HAH!! SWIM ACROSS IF YOU DARE!!
JUST WATCH OUT FOR THE PIRANHAS!!

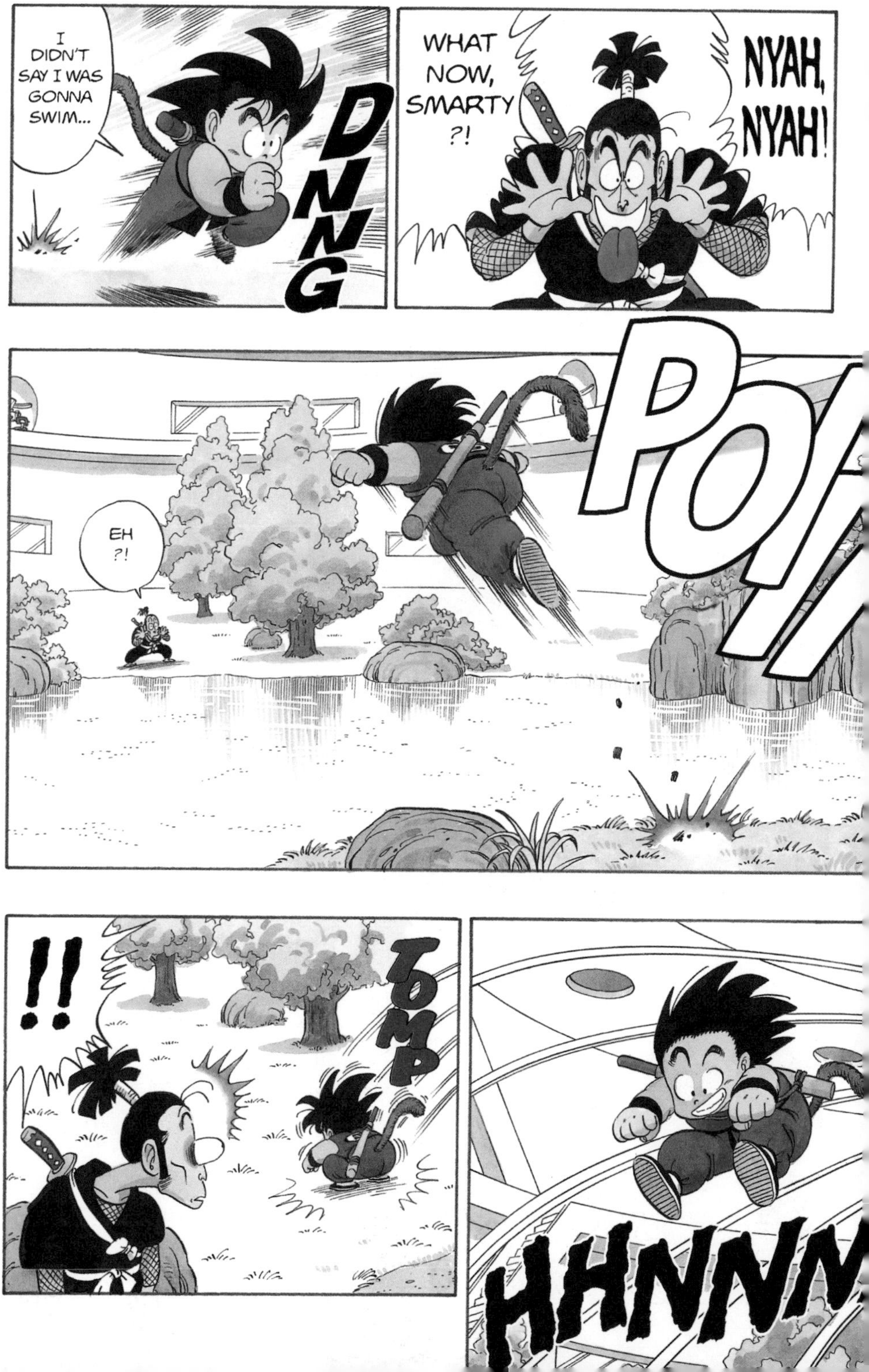
WHAT NOW, SMARTY?!
NYAH, NYAH!
I DIDN'T SAY I WAS GONNA SWIM...
DNNG
EH?!
POI
HHNNN
!!
TOMP

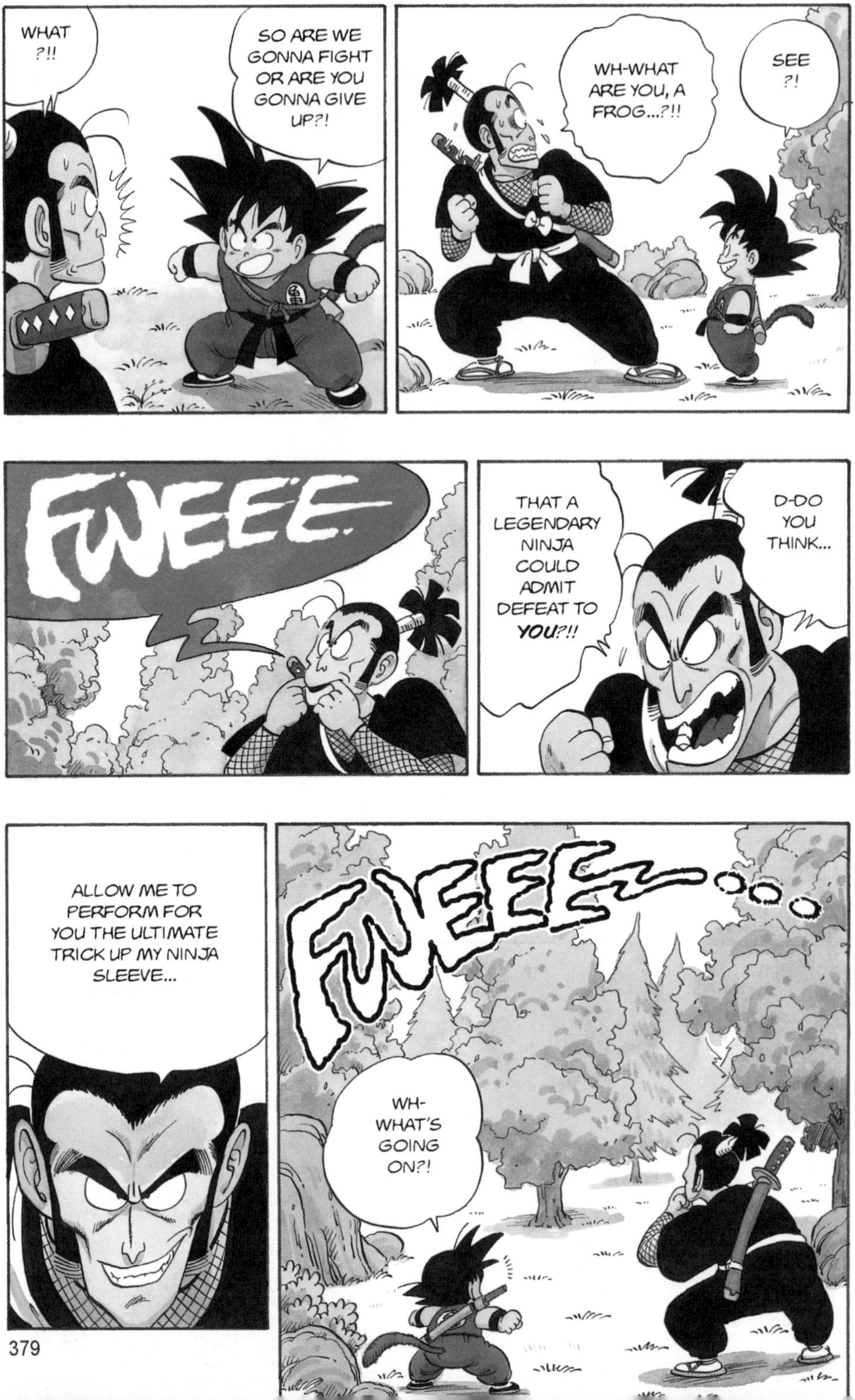
SEE ?!
WH-WHAT ARE YOU, A FROG...?!!
SO ARE WE GONNA FIGHT OR ARE YOU GONNA GIVE UP?!
WHAT ?!!
D-DO YOU THINK...
THAT A LEGENDARY NINJA COULD ADMIT DEFEAT TO ***YOU***?!!
FWEEE
FWEEE...
WH- WHAT'S GOING ON?!
ALLOW ME TO PERFORM FOR YOU THE ULTIMATE TRICK UP MY NINJA SLEEVE...

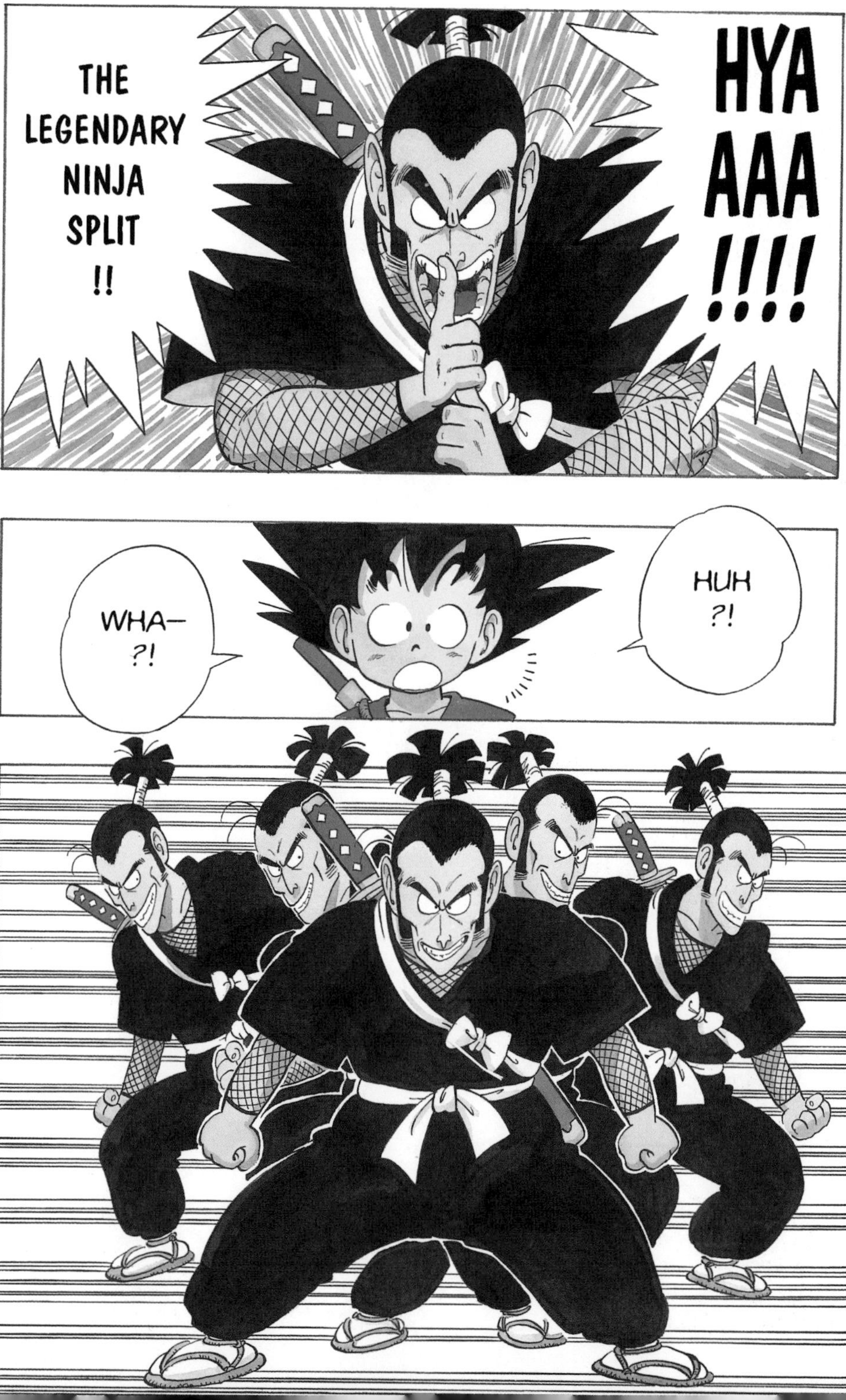
HYA AAA !!!!
THE LEGENDARY NINJA SPLIT !!
HUH ?!
WHA- ?!

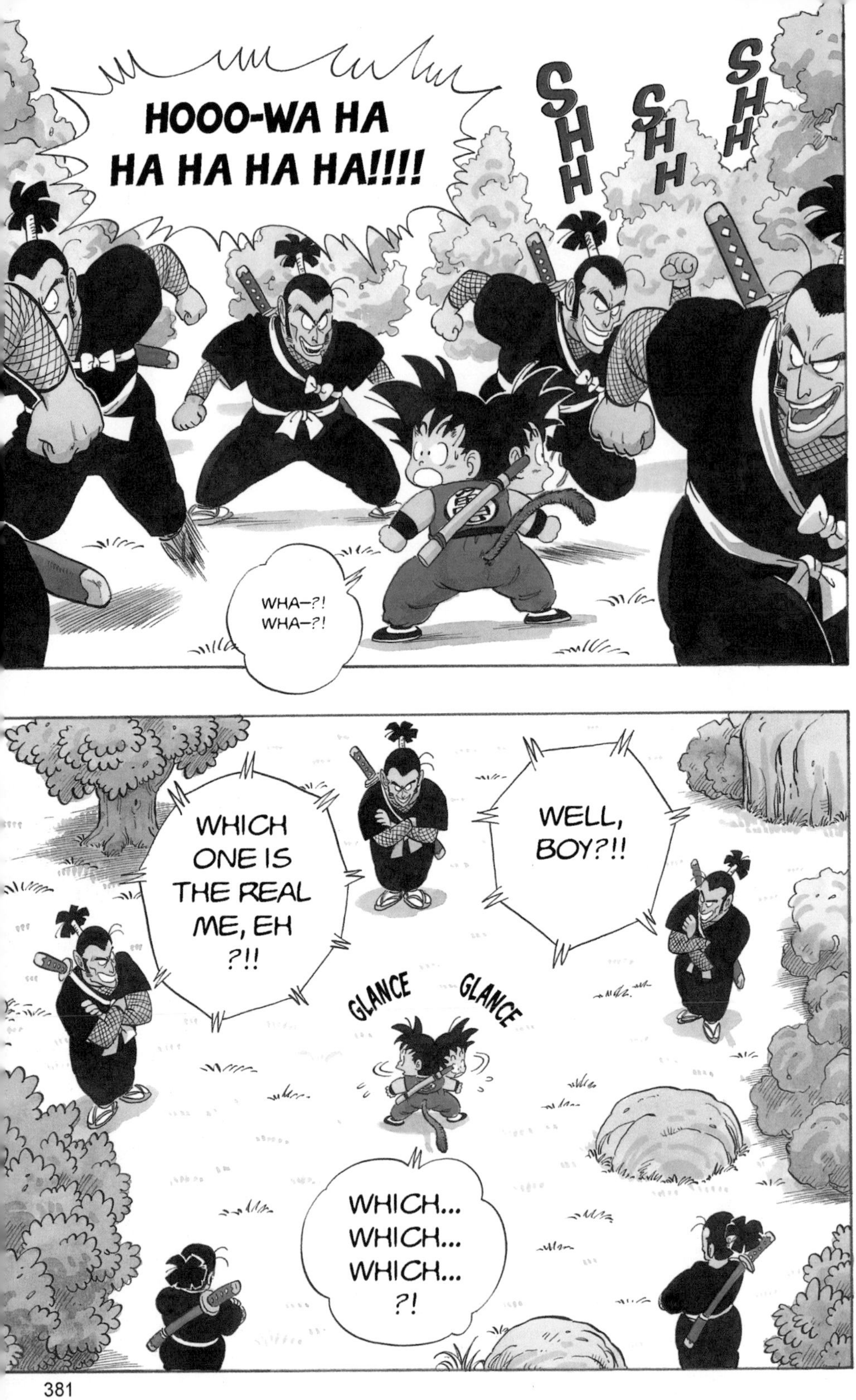
SHH SHH SHH
HOOOO-WA HA HA HA HA HA!!!!
WHA-?! WHA-?!
WELL, BOY?!!
WHICH ONE IS THE REAL ME, EH ?!!
GLANCE GLANCE
WHICH... WHICH... WHICH... ?!

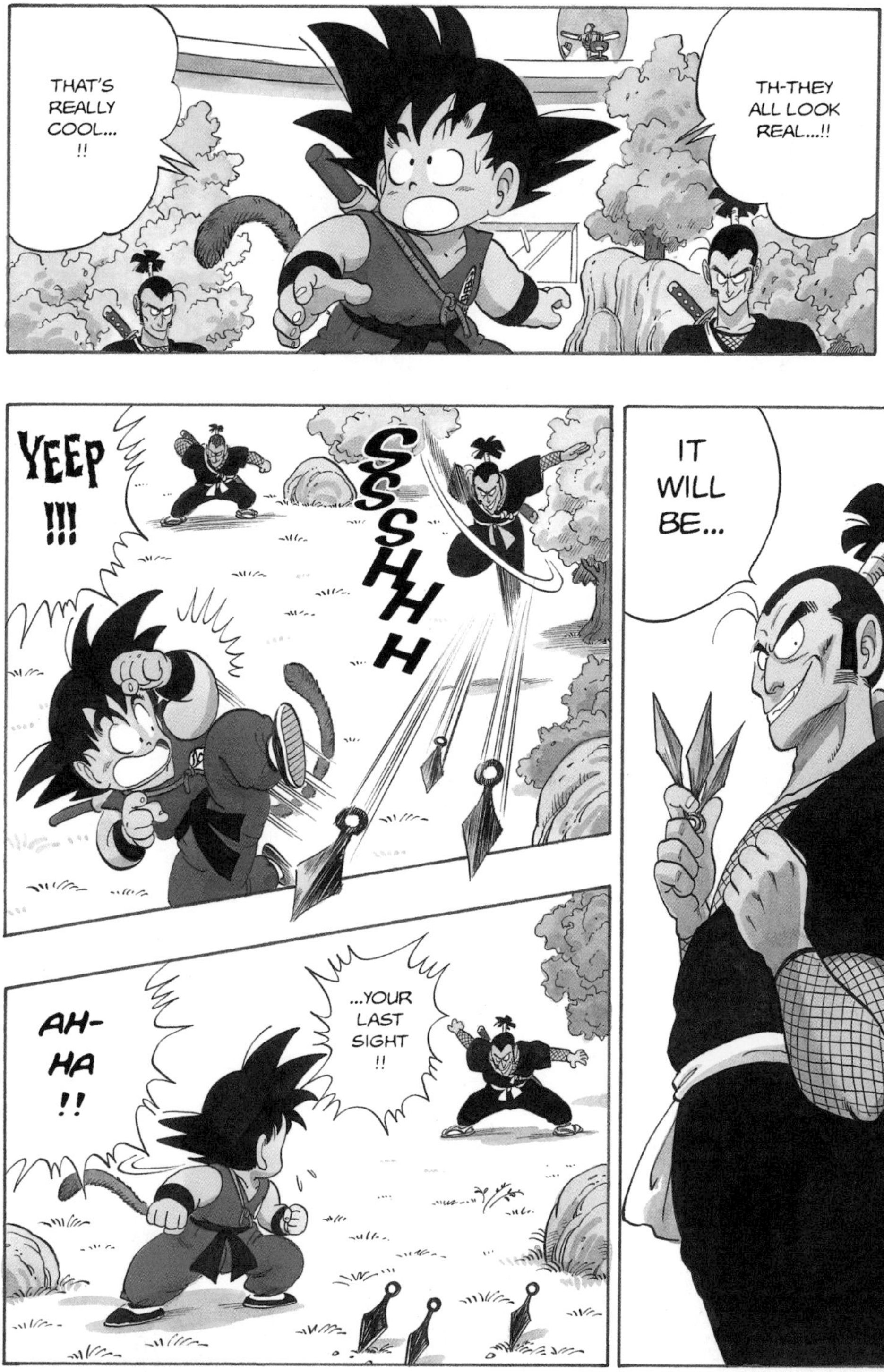
TH-THEY ALL LOOK REAL...!!
THAT'S REALLY COOL... !!
IT WILL BE...
SSHHHH
YEEP !!!
...YOUR LAST SIGHT !!
AH-HA !!

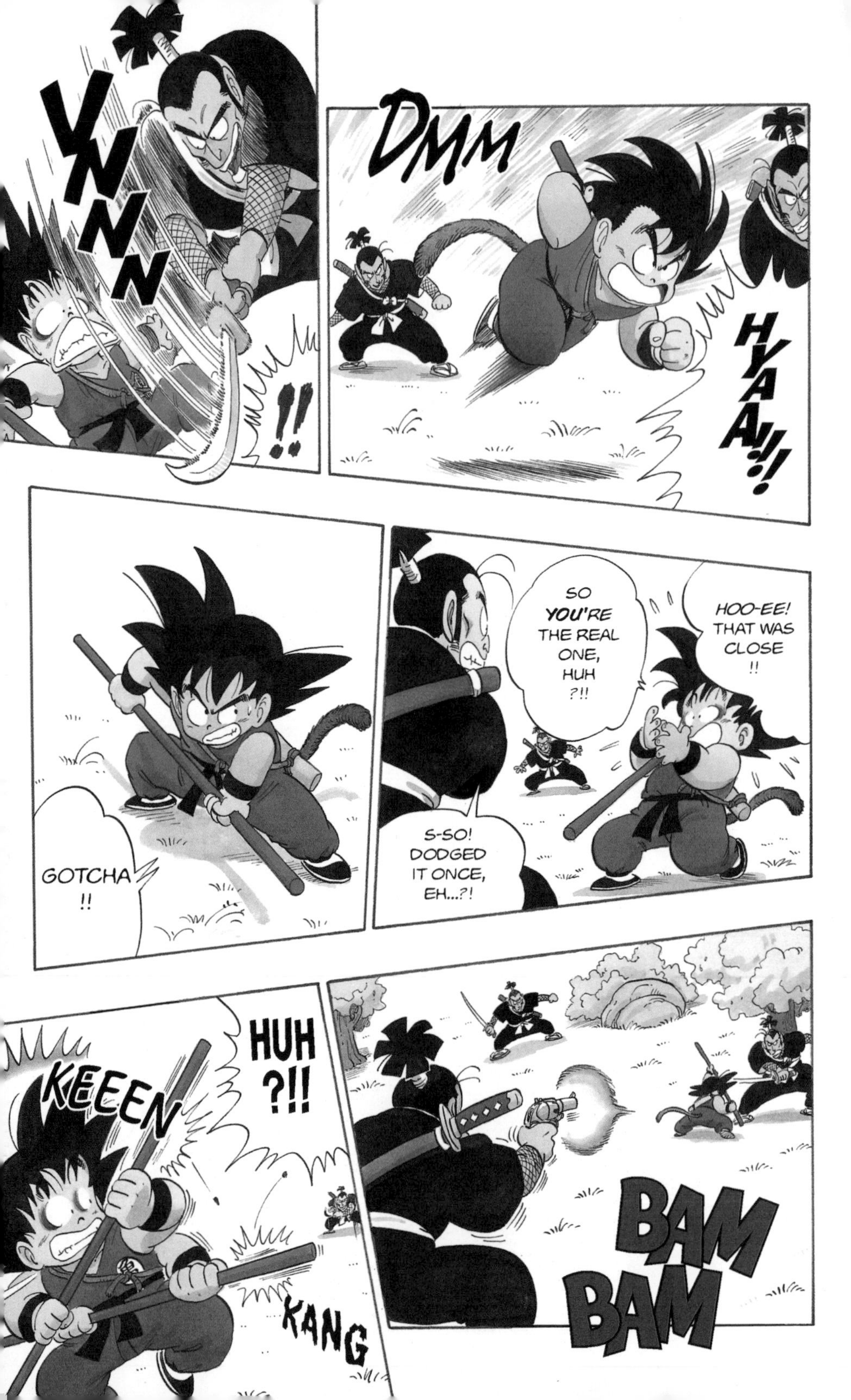

DMM
HYAA!!
VNNN
!!
HOO-EE! THAT WAS CLOSE !!
SO YOU'RE THE REAL ONE, HUH ?!!
S-SO! DODGED IT ONCE, EH...?!
GOTCHA !!
BAM BAM
HUH ?!!
KEEEN
KANG

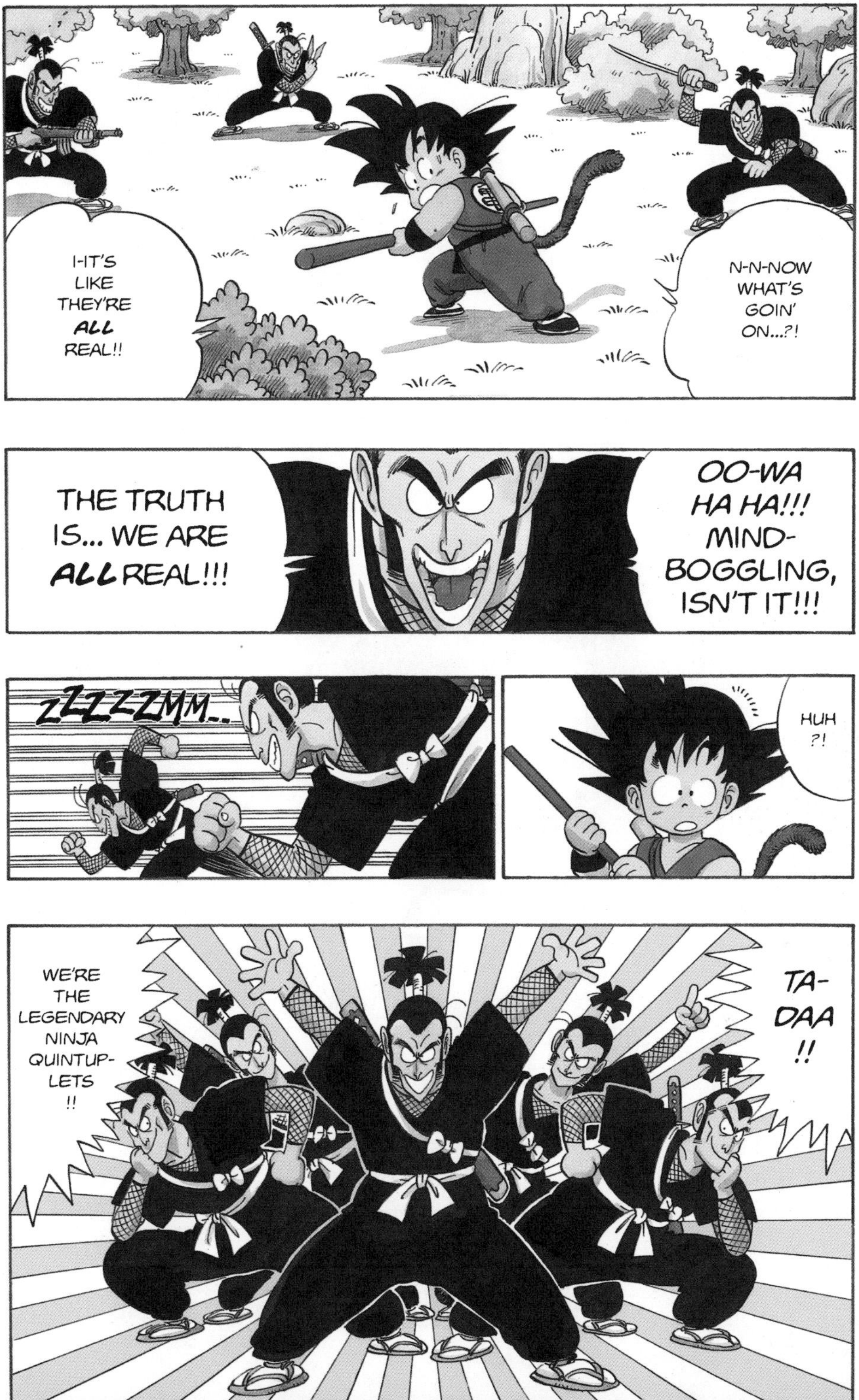
N-N-NOW WHAT'S GOIN' ON...?!
I-IT'S LIKE THEY'RE ALL REAL!!
OO-WA HA HA!!! MIND-BOGGLING, ISN'T IT!!!
THE TRUTH IS... WE ARE ALL REAL!!!
HUH ?!
ZZZZZMM..
TA-DAA !!
WE'RE THE LEGENDARY NINJA QUINTUPLETS !!

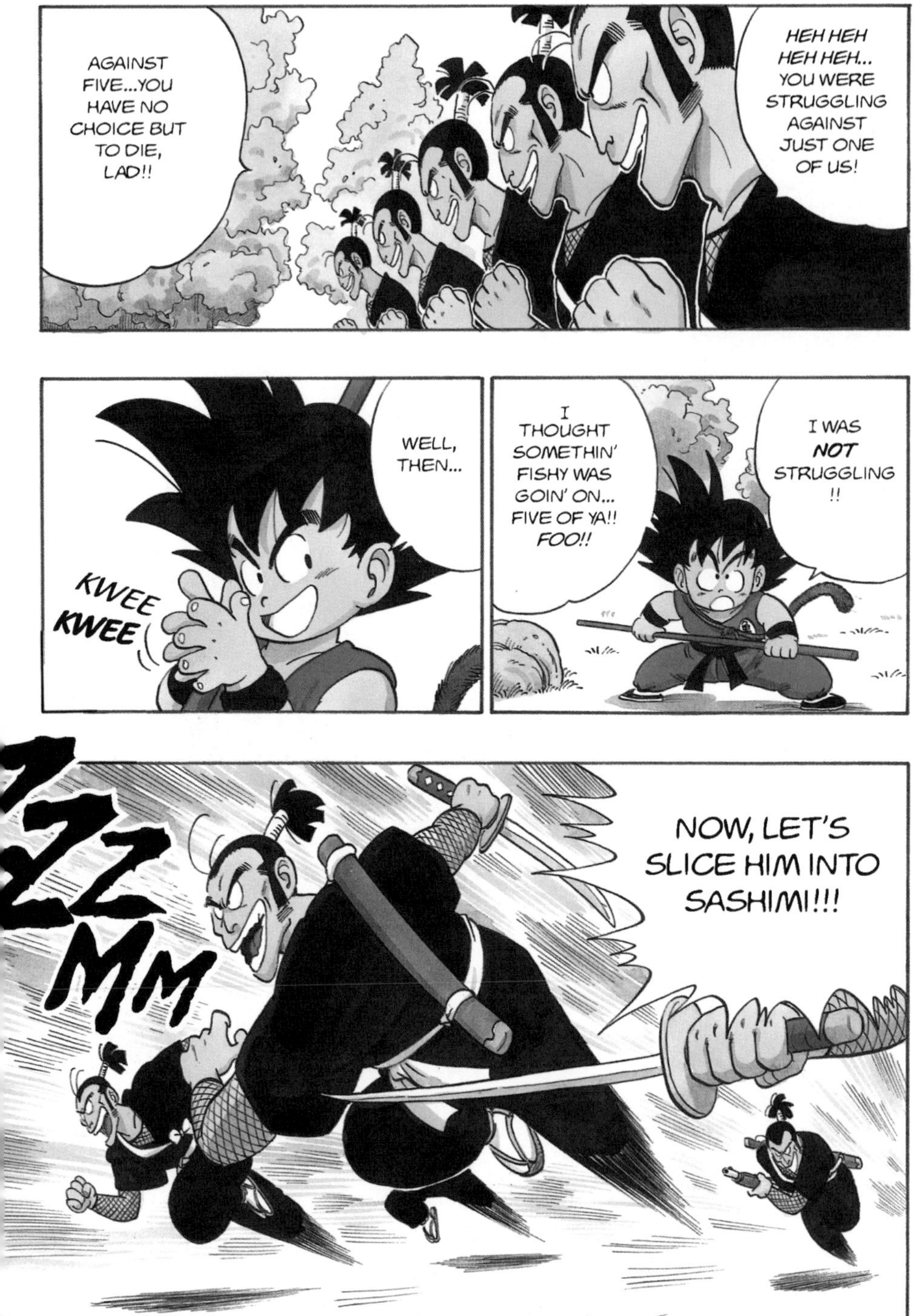
HEH HEH HEH HEH... YOU WERE STRUGGLING AGAINST JUST ONE OF US!
AGAINST FIVE...YOU HAVE NO CHOICE BUT TO DIE, LAD!!
I WAS NOT STRUGGLING !!
I THOUGHT SOMETHIN' FISHY WAS GOIN' ON... FIVE OF YA!! FOO!!
WELL, THEN...
KWEE KWEE
NOW, LET'S SLICE HIM INTO SASHIMI!!!
ZZMM

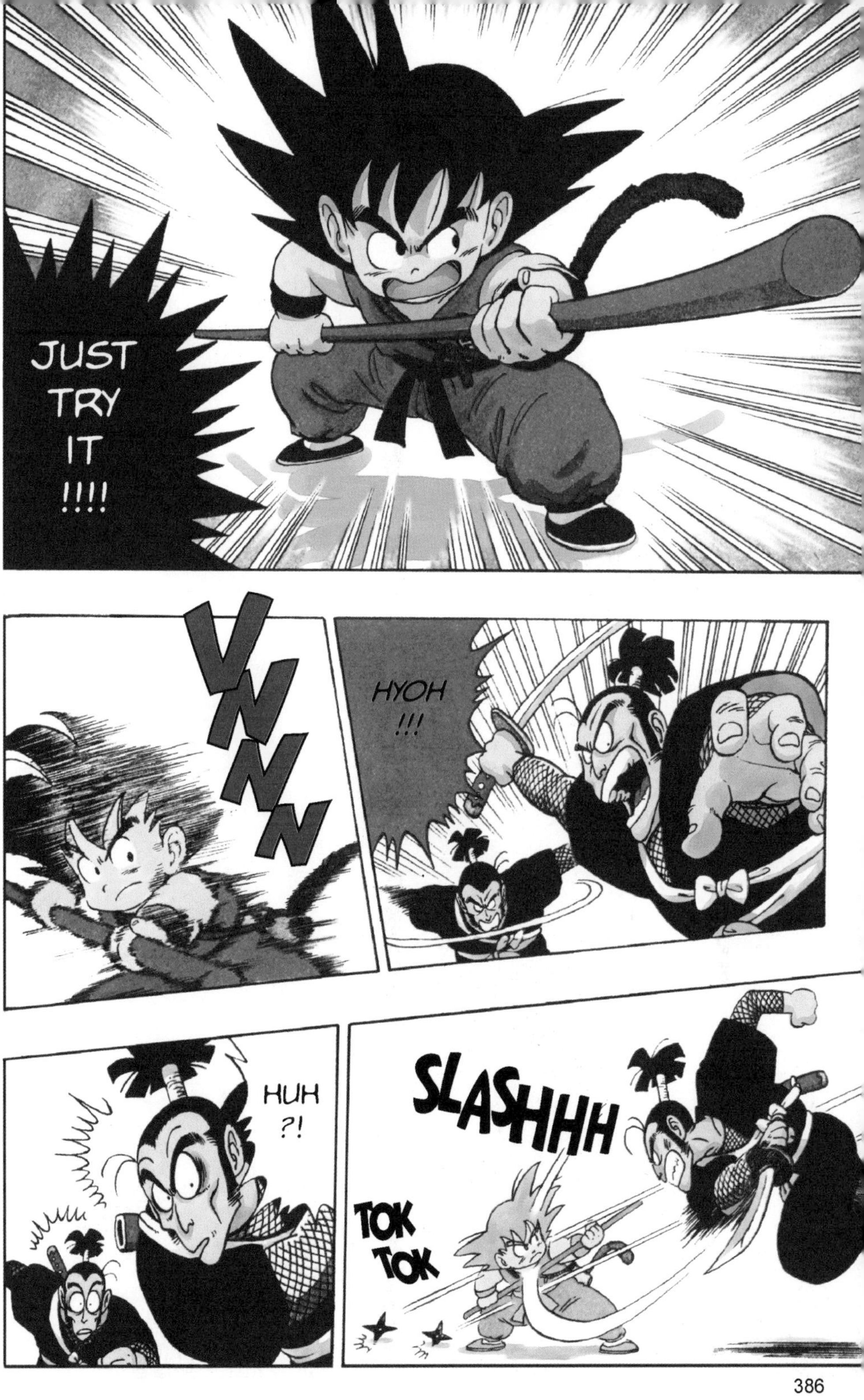
JUST TRY IT !!!!
HYOH !!!
VNNN
SLASHHH
TOK TOK
HUH ?!

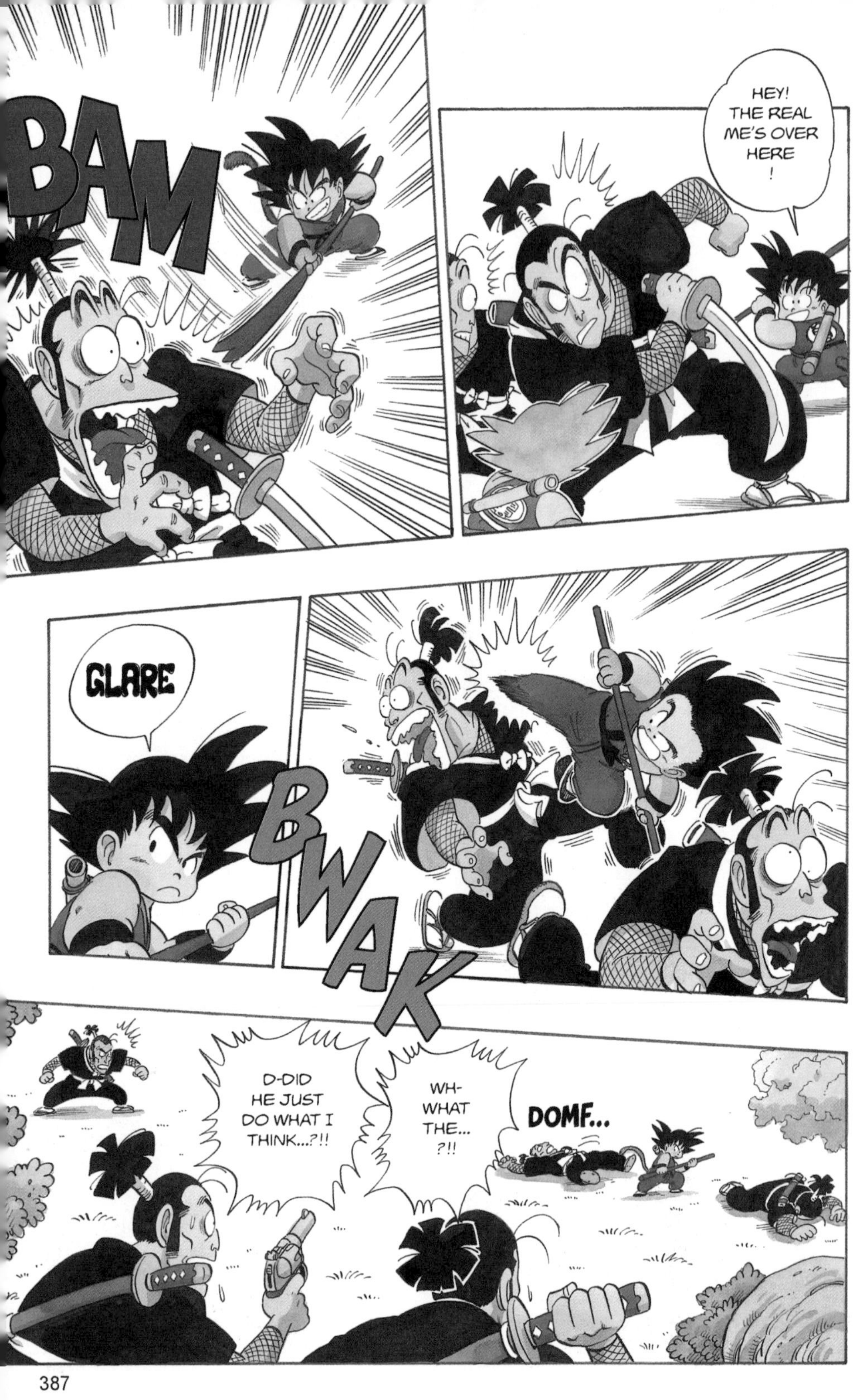
HEY! THE REAL ME'S OVER HERE !
BAM
BWAK
GLARE
DOMF...
WH- WHAT THE... ?!!
D-DID HE JUST DO WHAT I THINK...?!!

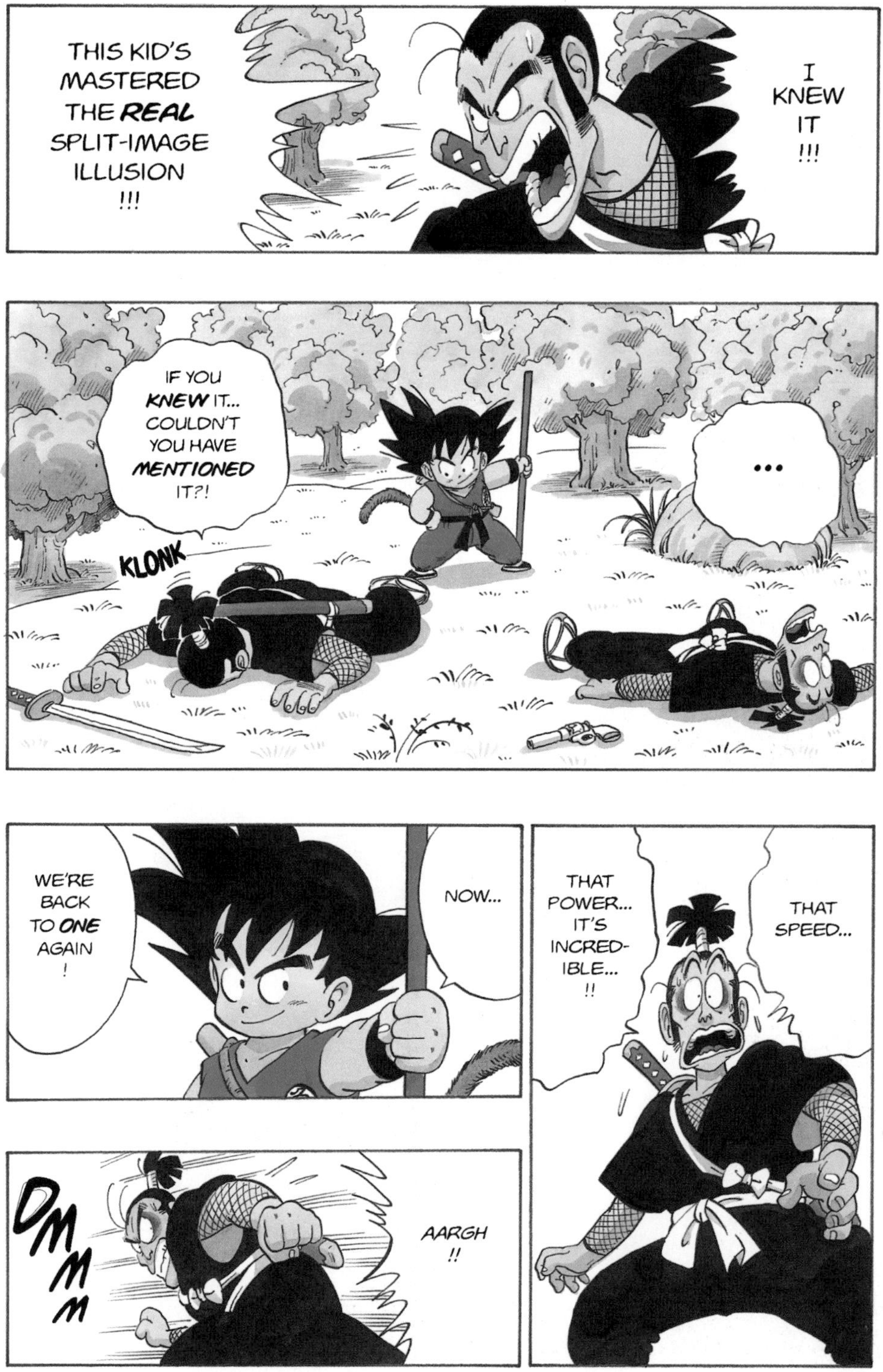
I KNEW IT !!!
THIS KID'S MASTERED THE REAL SPLIT-IMAGE ILLUSION !!!
...
IF YOU KNEW IT... COULDN'T YOU HAVE MENTIONED IT?!
KLONK
THAT SPEED...
THAT POWER... IT'S INCRED-IBLE... !!
NOW...
WE'RE BACK TO ONE AGAIN !
AARGH !!
DMMM

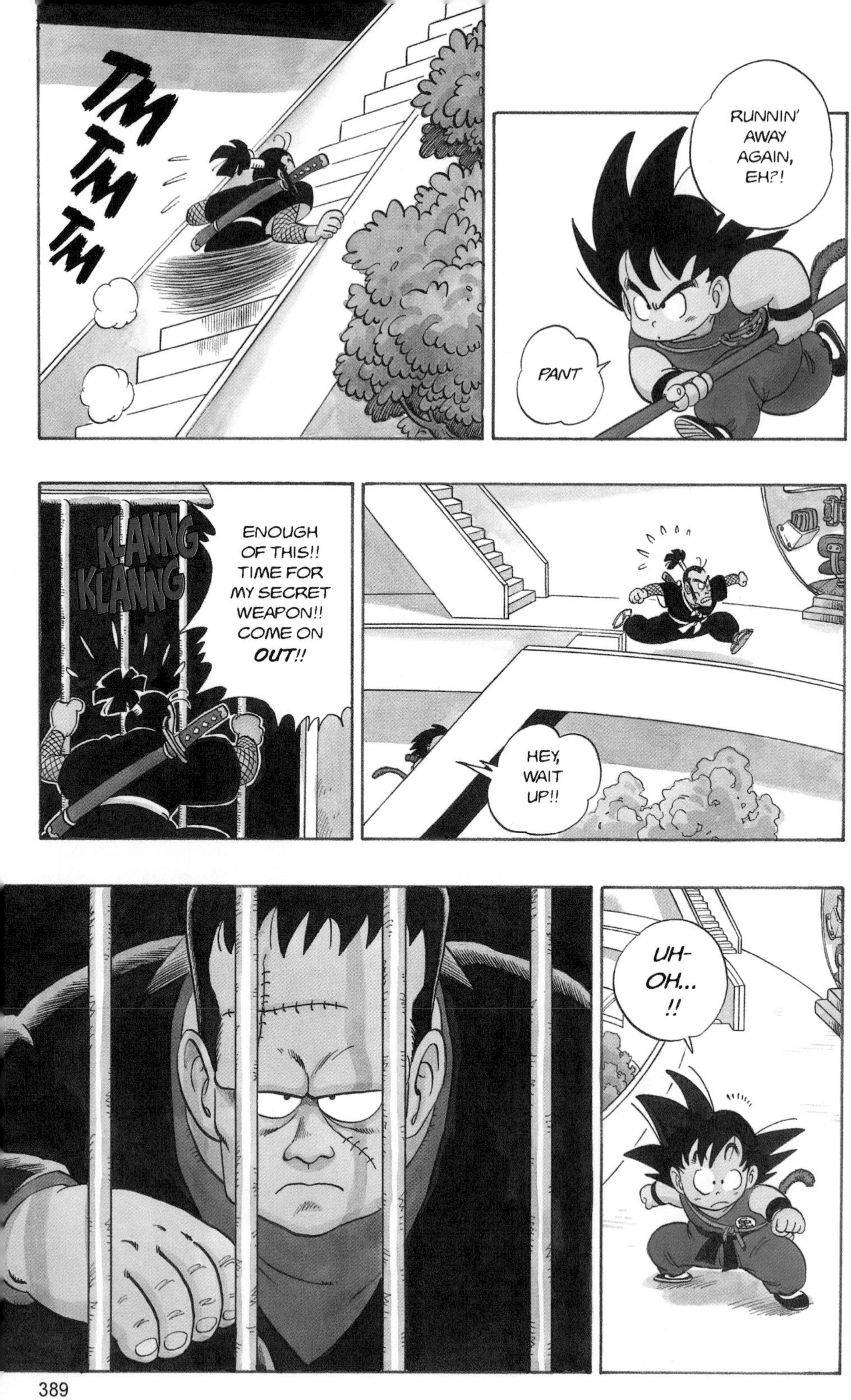
RUNNIN' AWAY AGAIN, EH?!
PANT
TM TM TM
HEY, WAIT UP!!
ENOUGH OF THIS!! TIME FOR MY SECRET WEAPON!! COME ON OUT!!
KLANNG KLANNG
UH-OH... !!

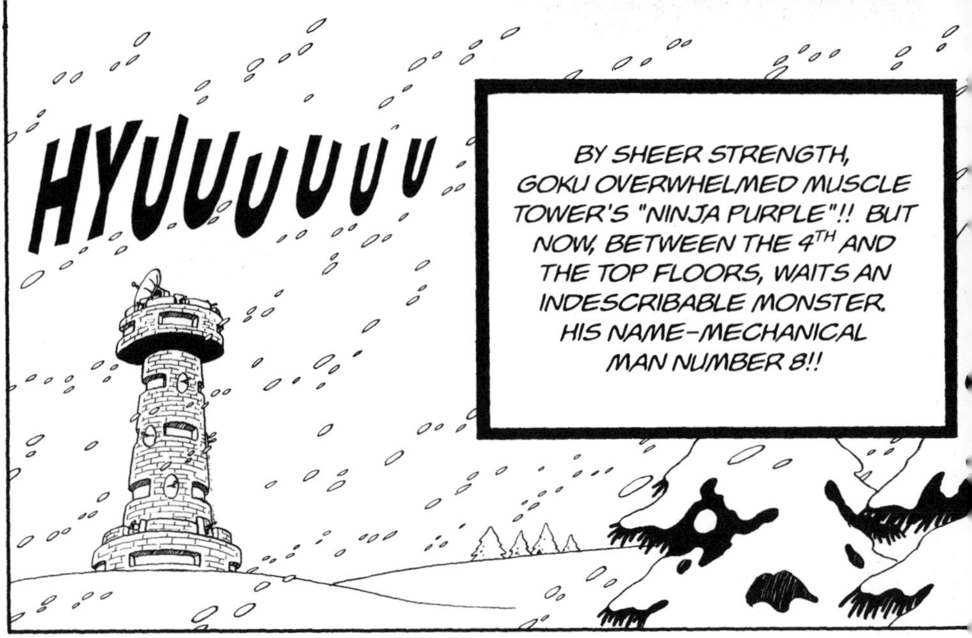
HYUUUUUUU
BY SHEER STRENGTH, GOKU OVERWHELMED MUSCLE TOWER'S "NINJA PURPLE"!! BUT NOW, BETWEEN THE 4TH AND THE TOP FLOORS, WAITS AN INDESCRIBABLE MONSTER. HIS NAME–MECHANICAL MAN NUMBER 8!!

Tale 63 • Mechanical Man No. 8

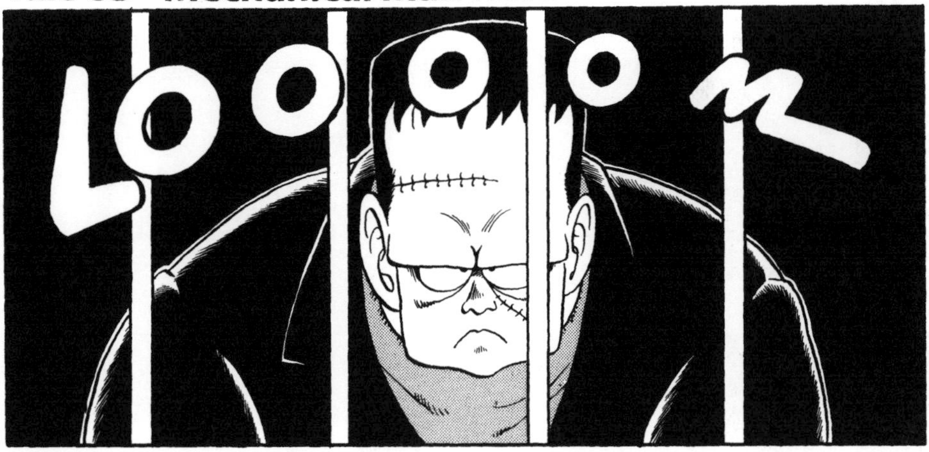
LOOOOM

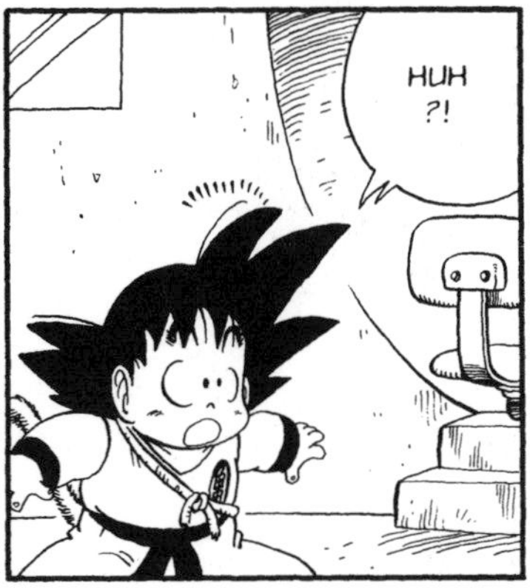
HUH ?!

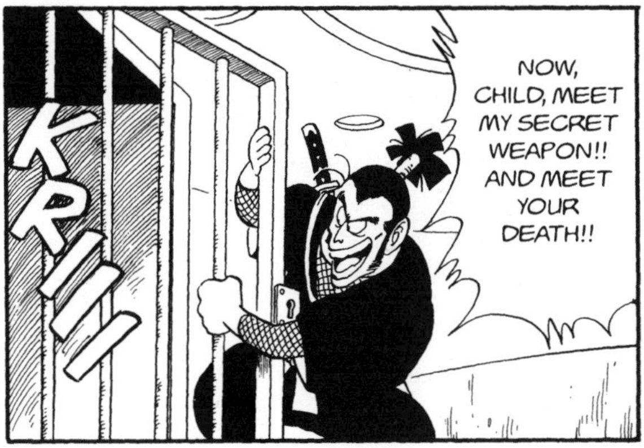
KRIII
NOW, CHILD, MEET MY SECRET WEAPON!! AND MEET YOUR DEATH!!

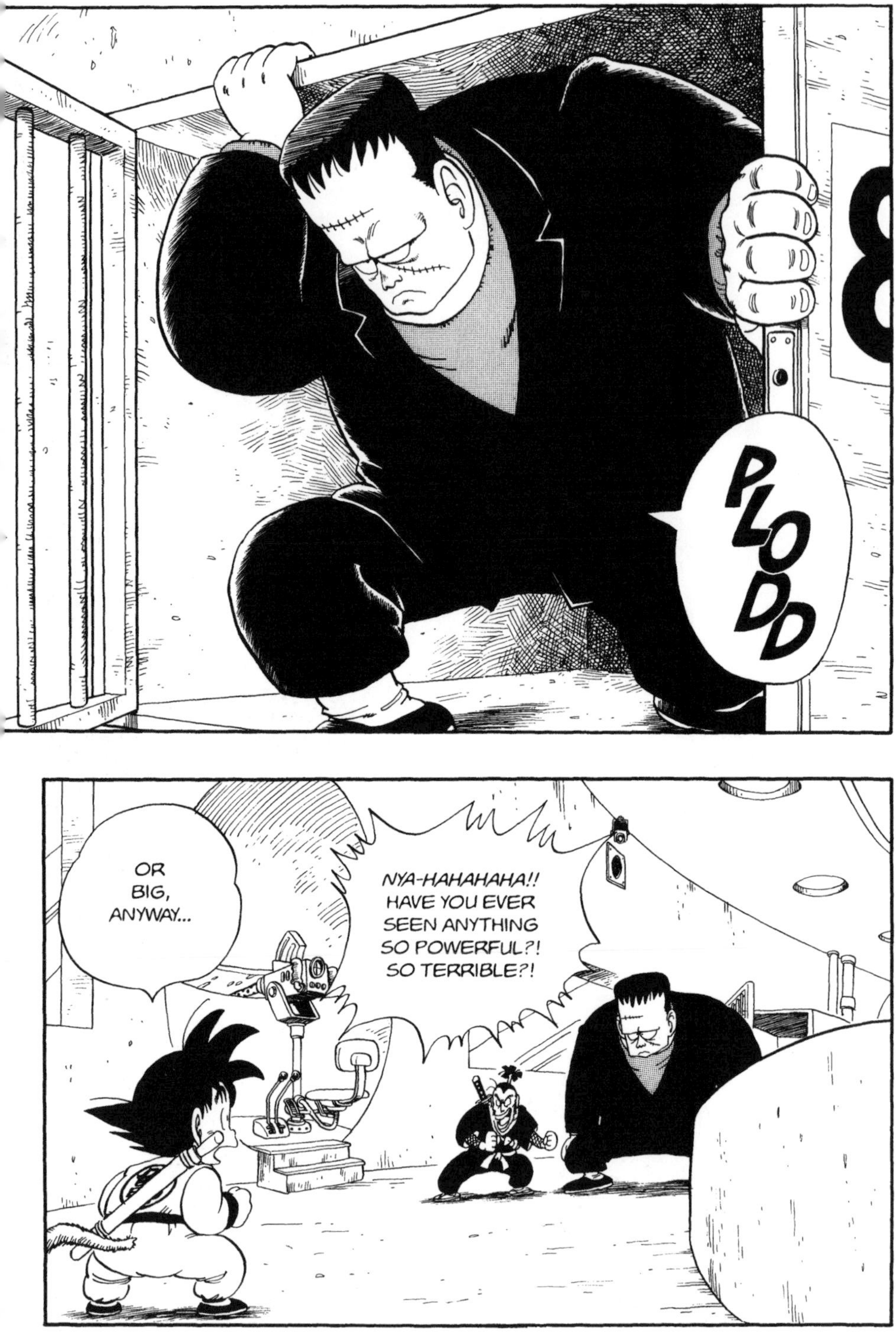
PLODD
NYA-HAHAHAHA!! HAVE YOU EVER SEEN ANYTHING SO POWERFUL?! SO TERRIBLE?!
OR BIG, ANYWAY...

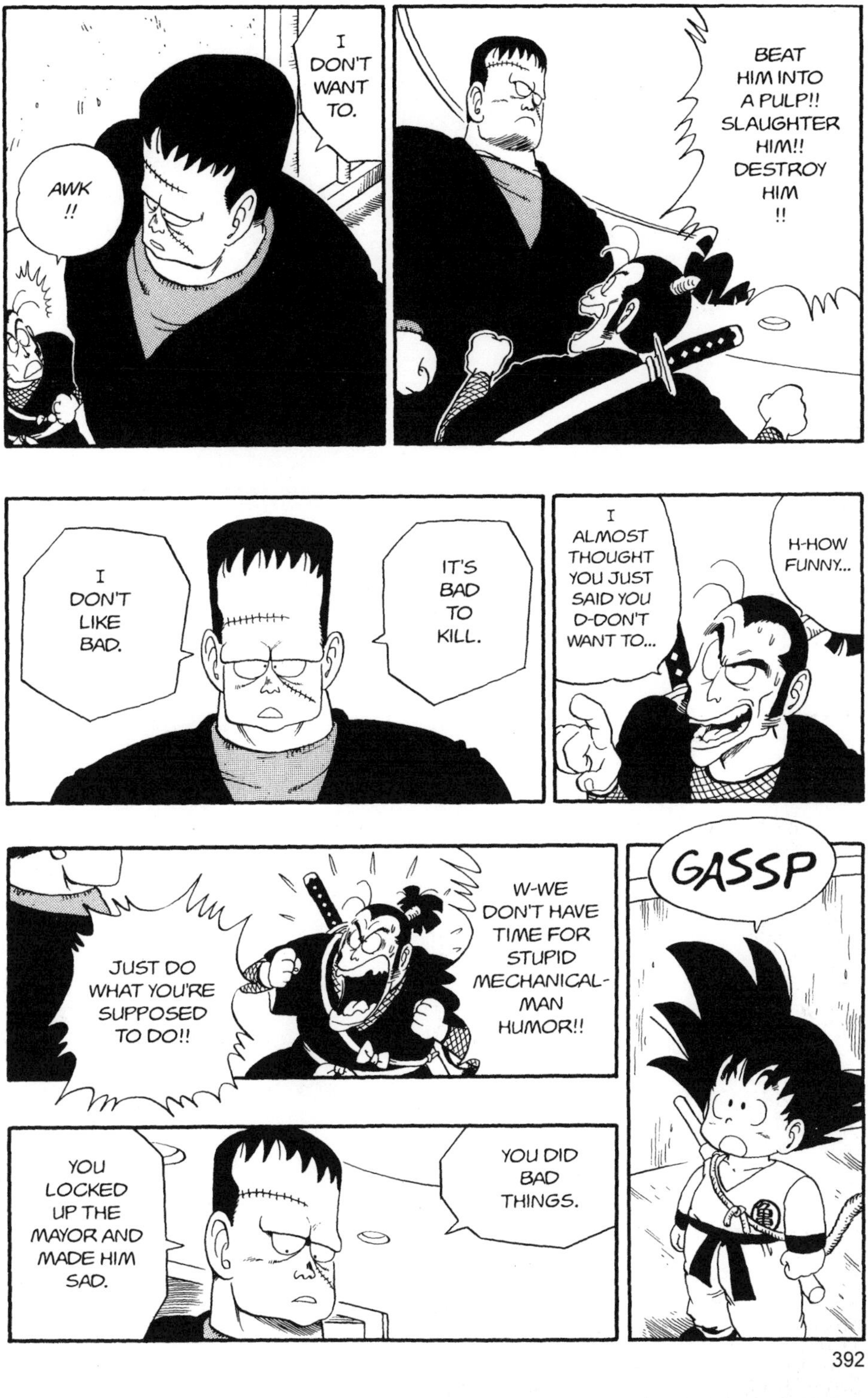
BEAT HIM INTO A PULP!! SLAUGHTER HIM!! DESTROY HIM !!
I DON'T WANT TO.
AWK !!
H-HOW FUNNY...
I ALMOST THOUGHT YOU JUST SAID YOU D-DON'T WANT TO...
IT'S BAD TO KILL.
I DON'T LIKE BAD.
GASSP
W-WE DON'T HAVE TIME FOR STUPID MECHANICAL-MAN HUMOR!!
JUST DO WHAT YOU'RE SUPPOSED TO DO!!
YOU DID BAD THINGS.
YOU LOCKED UP THE MAYOR AND MADE HIM SAD.

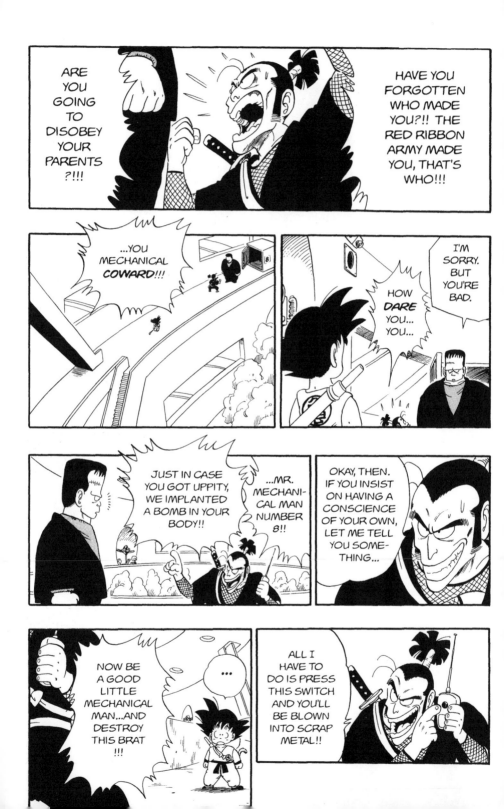

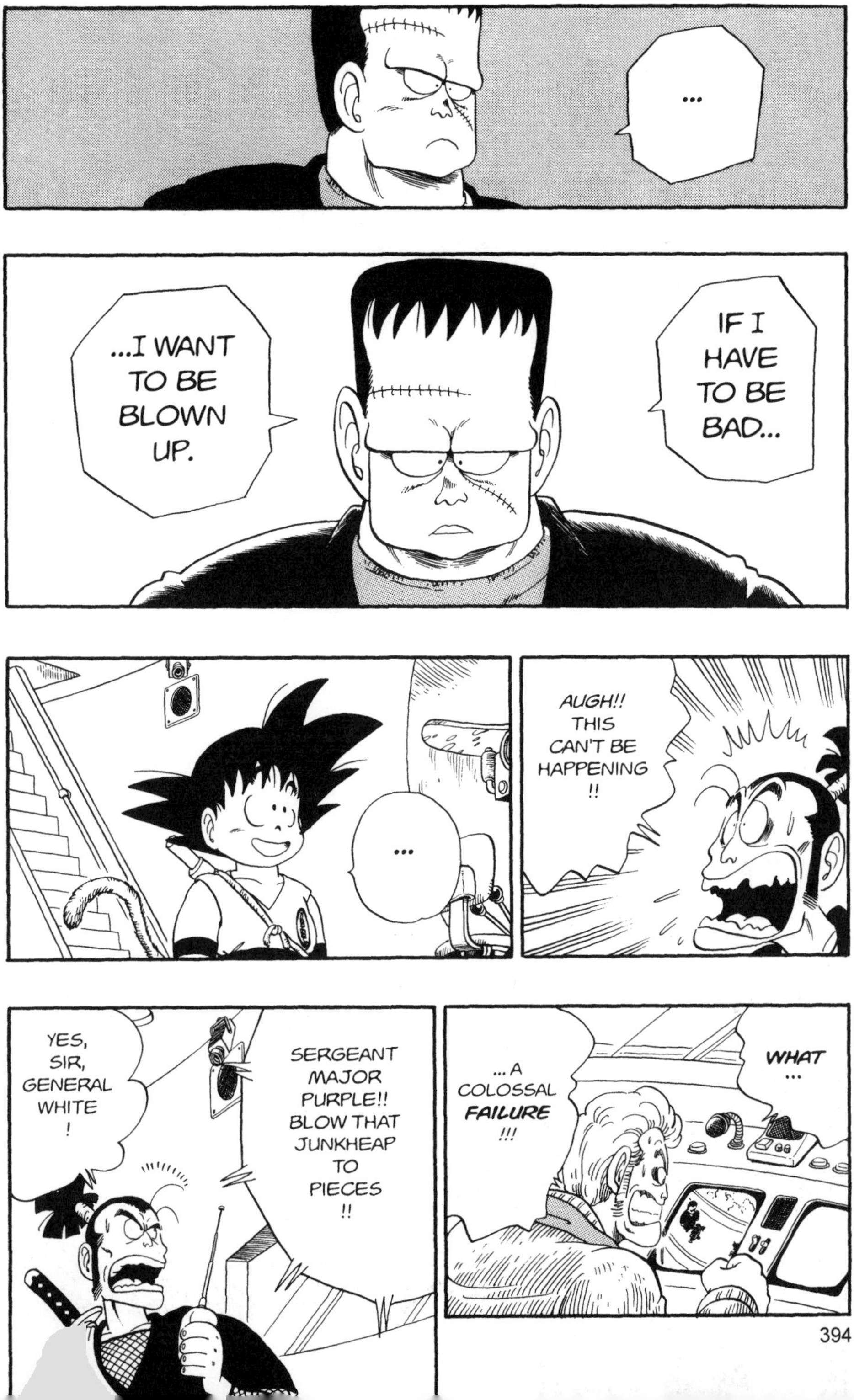
...
IF I HAVE TO BE BAD...
...I WANT TO BE BLOWN UP.
AUGH!! THIS CAN'T BE HAPPENING!!
...
WHAT...
... A COLOSSAL FAILURE!!!
SERGEANT MAJOR PURPLE!! BLOW THAT JUNKHEAP TO PIECES!!
YES, SIR, GENERAL WHITE!

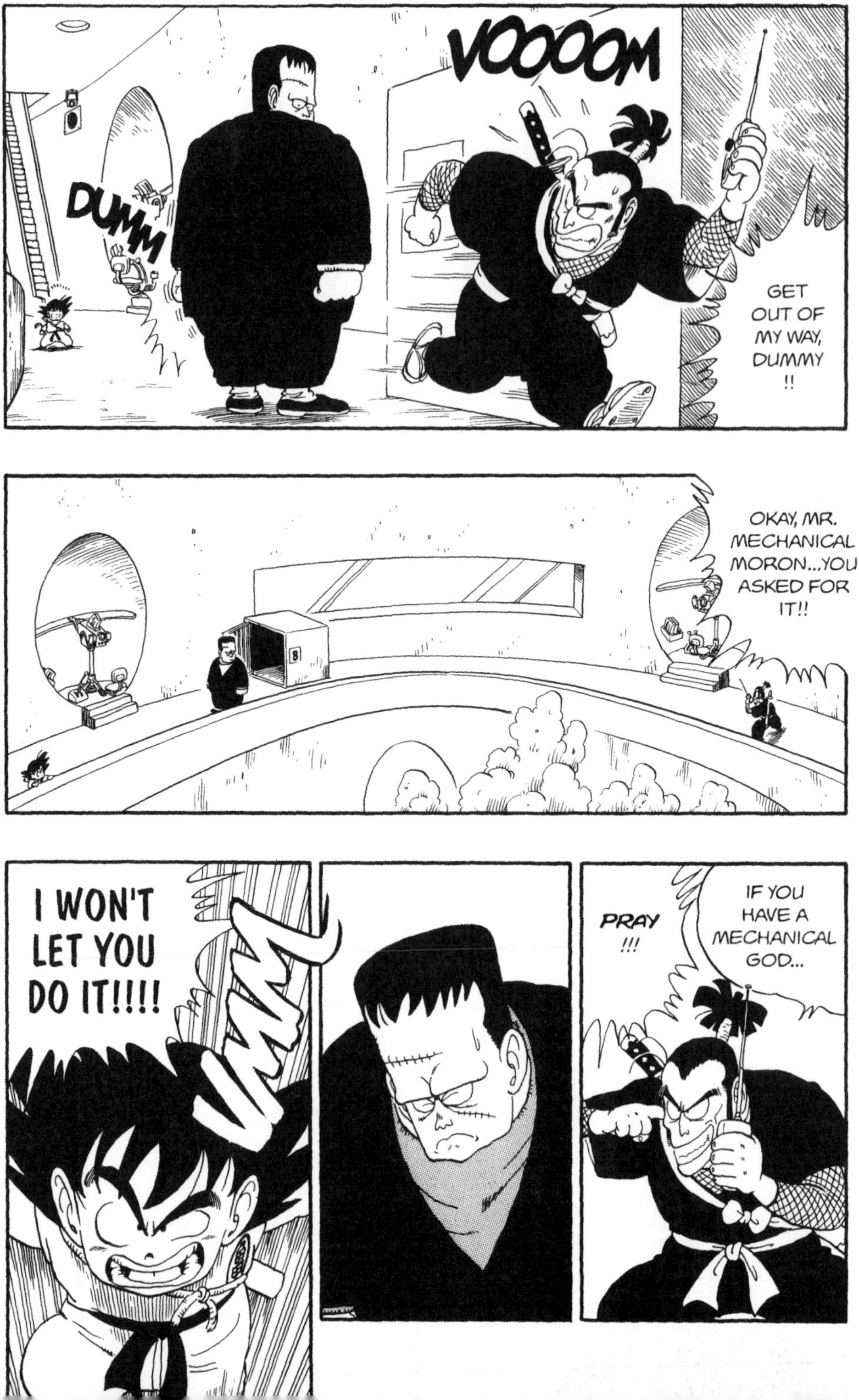
VOOOOM
GET OUT OF MY WAY, DUMMY !!
DUMM
OKAY, MR. MECHANICAL MORON...YOU ASKED FOR IT!!
IF YOU HAVE A MECHANICAL GOD...
PRAY !!!
I WON'T LET YOU DO IT!!!!
VMM

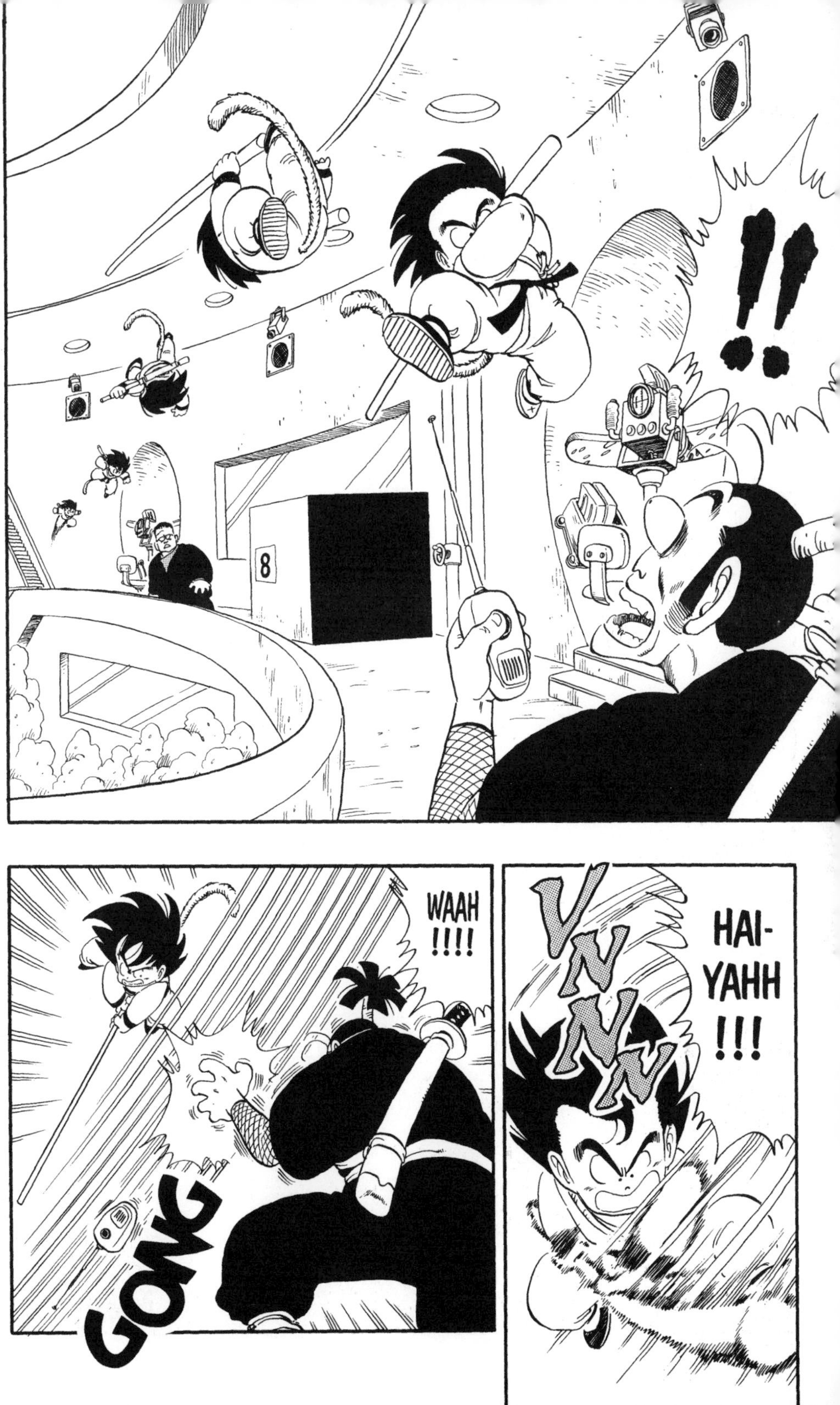
!!
VNNN
HAI-YAHH!!!
WAAH!!!!
GONG

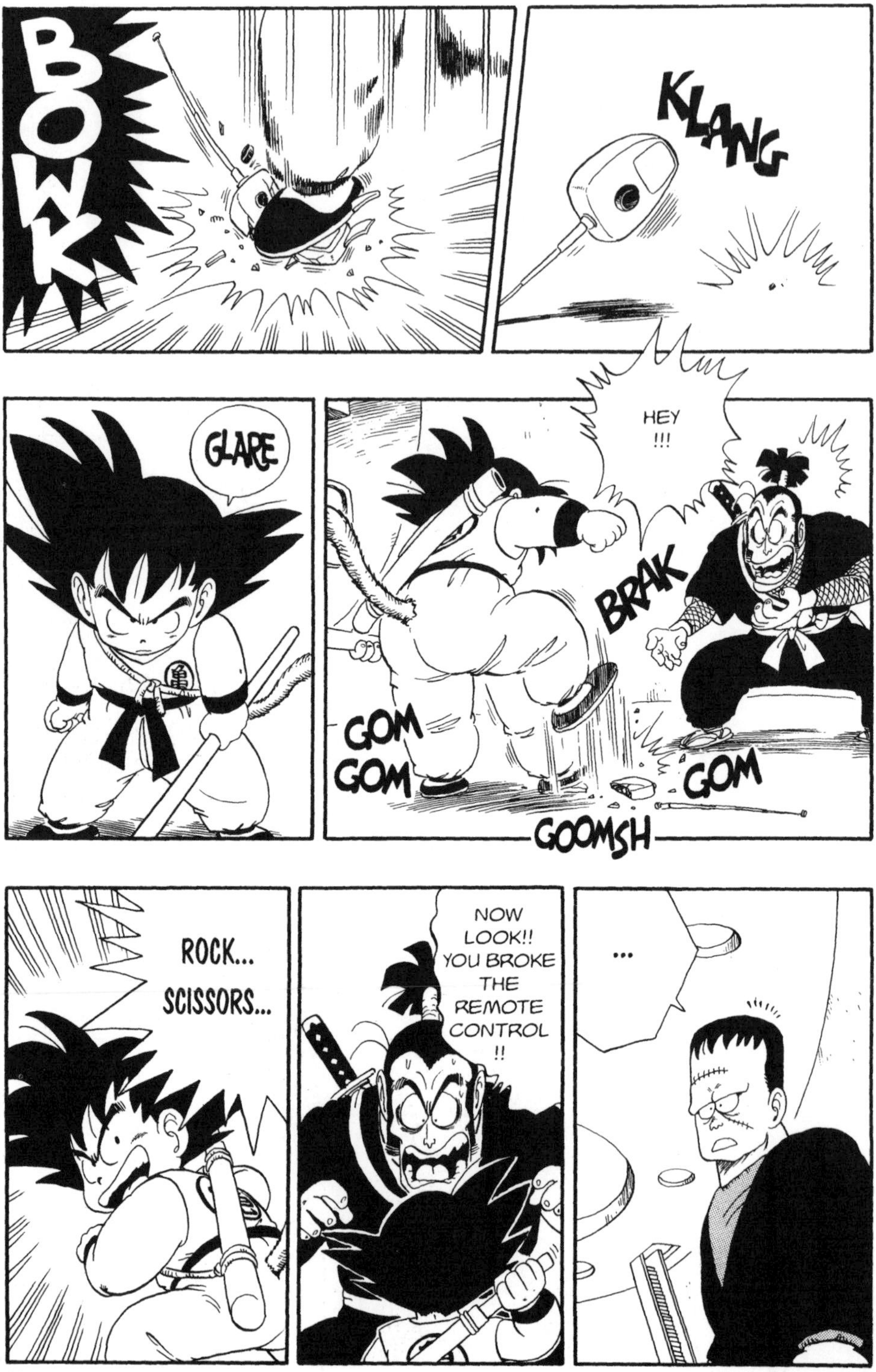
KLANG
BOWK
HEY !!!
BRAK
GOM
GOM GOM
GOOMSH
GLARE
...
NOW LOOK!! YOU BROKE THE REMOTE CONTROL !!
ROCK... SCISSORS...

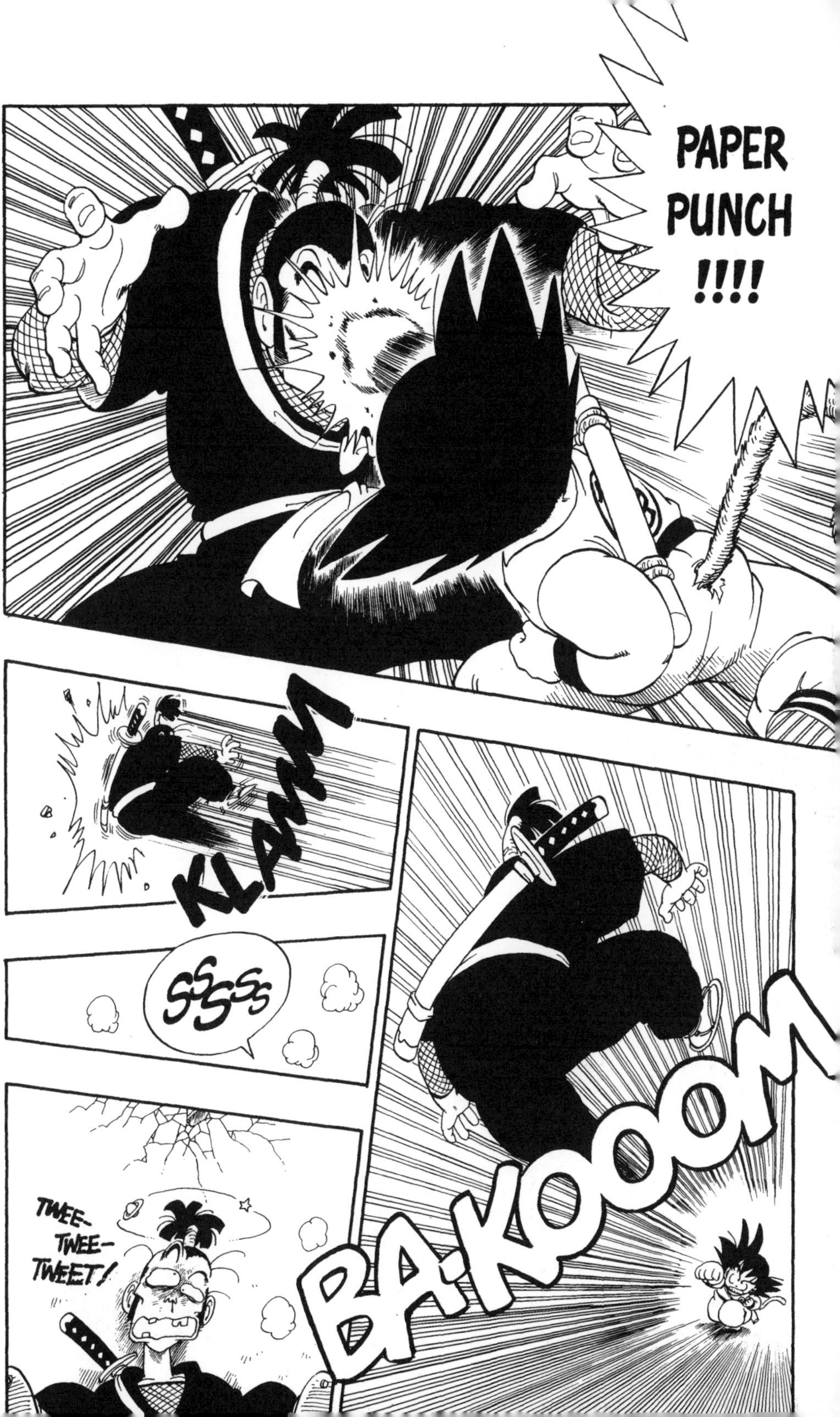
PAPER PUNCH !!!!
BA-KOOOOM
KLAMM
SSSSS
TWEE-TWEE-TWEET!

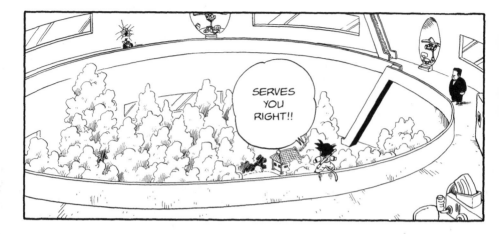

SERVES YOU RIGHT!!

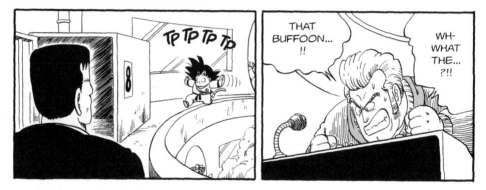

TP TP TP TP

THAT BUFFOON...!!

WH-WHAT THE...?!!

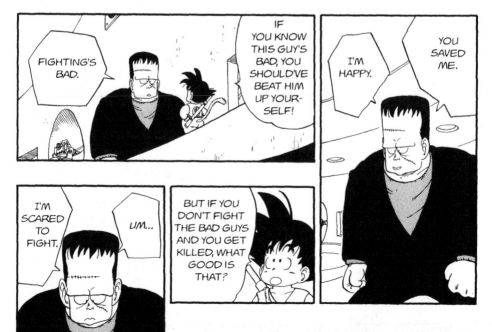

FIGHTING'S BAD.

IF YOU KNOW THIS GUY'S BAD, YOU SHOULD'VE BEAT HIM UP YOUR-SELF!

I'M HAPPY.

YOU SAVED ME.

I'M SCARED TO FIGHT.

UM...

BUT IF YOU DON'T FIGHT THE BAD GUYS AND YOU GET KILLED, WHAT GOOD IS THAT?

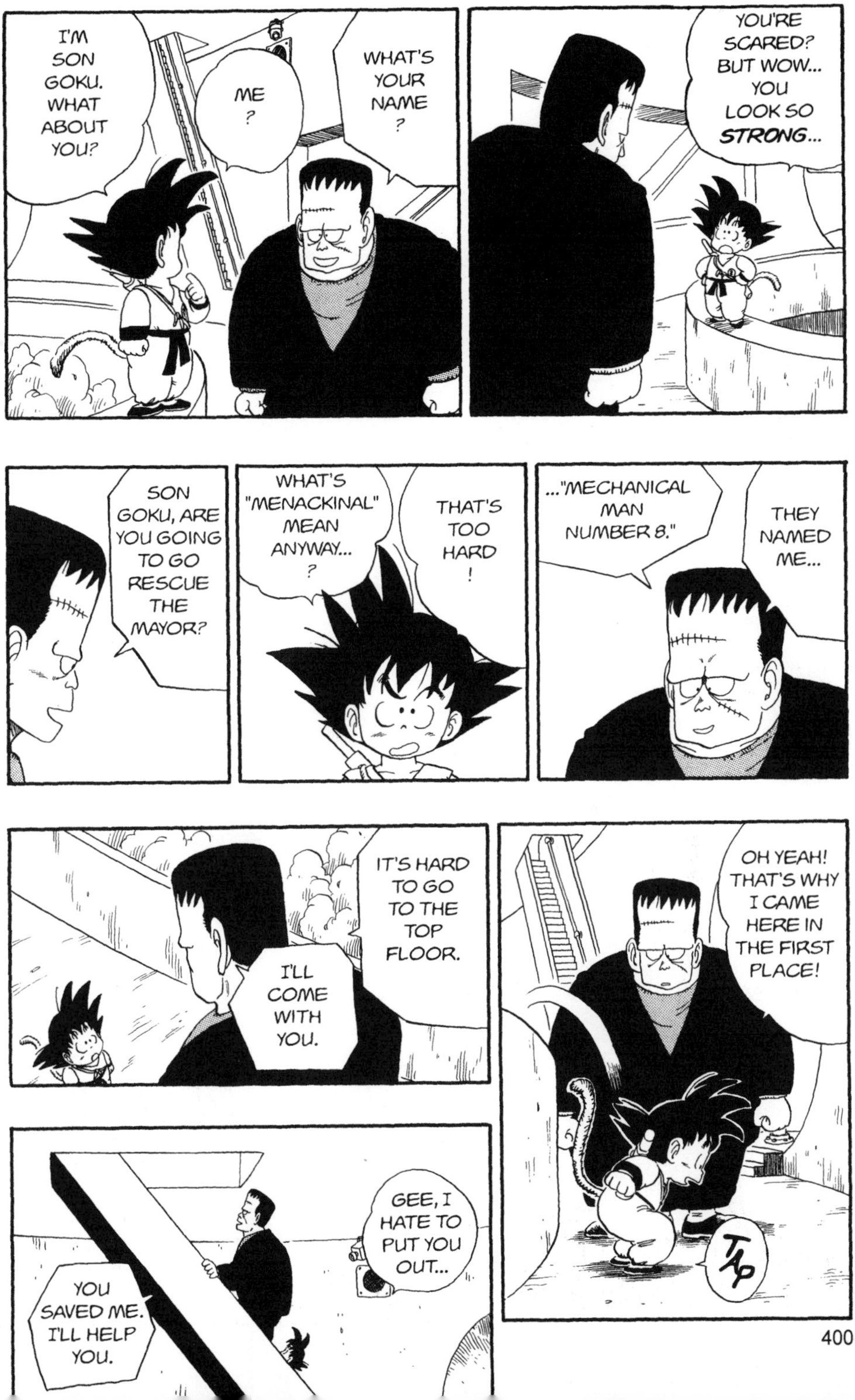
YOU'RE SCARED? BUT WOW... YOU LOOK SO **STRONG**...
WHAT'S YOUR NAME ?
ME ?
I'M SON GOKU. WHAT ABOUT YOU?
THEY NAMED ME...
..."MECHANICAL MAN NUMBER 8."
THAT'S TOO HARD !
WHAT'S "MENACKINAL" MEAN ANYWAY... ?
SON GOKU, ARE YOU GOING TO GO RESCUE THE MAYOR?
OH YEAH! THAT'S WHY I CAME HERE IN THE FIRST PLACE!
TAP
IT'S HARD TO GO TO THE TOP FLOOR.
I'LL COME WITH YOU.
GEE, I HATE TO PUT YOU OUT...
YOU SAVED ME. I'LL HELP YOU.

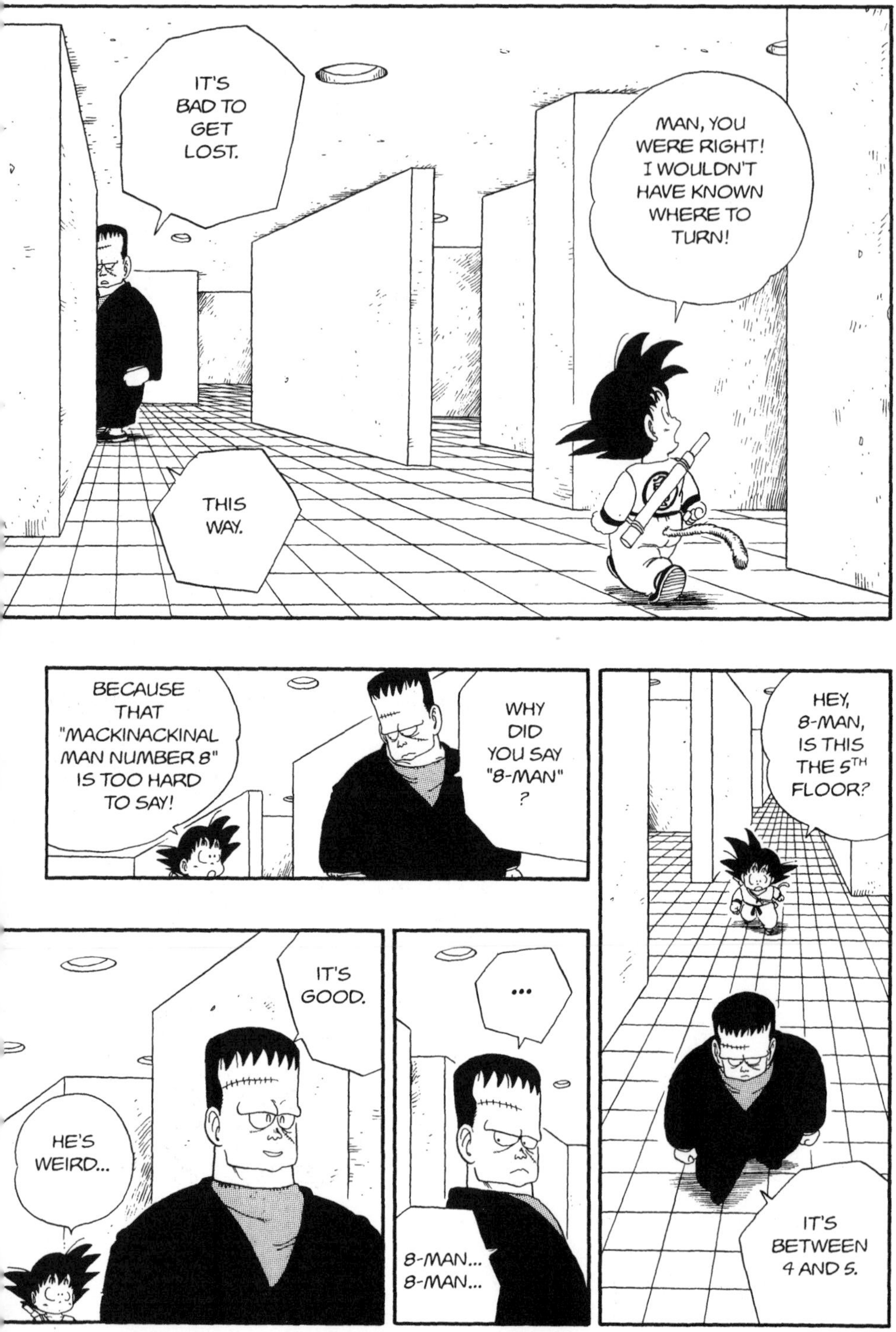
MAN, YOU WERE RIGHT! I WOULDN'T HAVE KNOWN WHERE TO TURN!
IT'S BAD TO GET LOST.
THIS WAY.
HEY, 8-MAN, IS THIS THE 5TH FLOOR?
IT'S BETWEEN 4 AND 5.
WHY DID YOU SAY "8-MAN"?
BECAUSE THAT "MACKINACKINAL MAN NUMBER 8" IS TOO HARD TO SAY!
...
8-MAN... 8-MAN...
IT'S GOOD.
HE'S WEIRD...

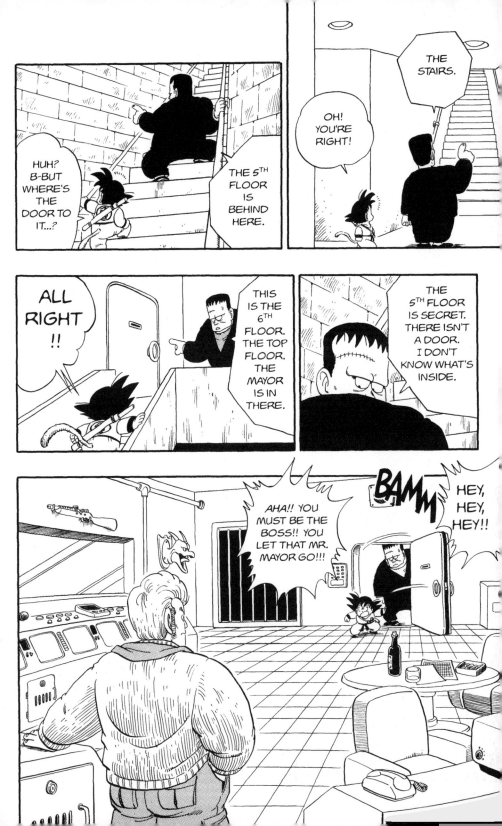

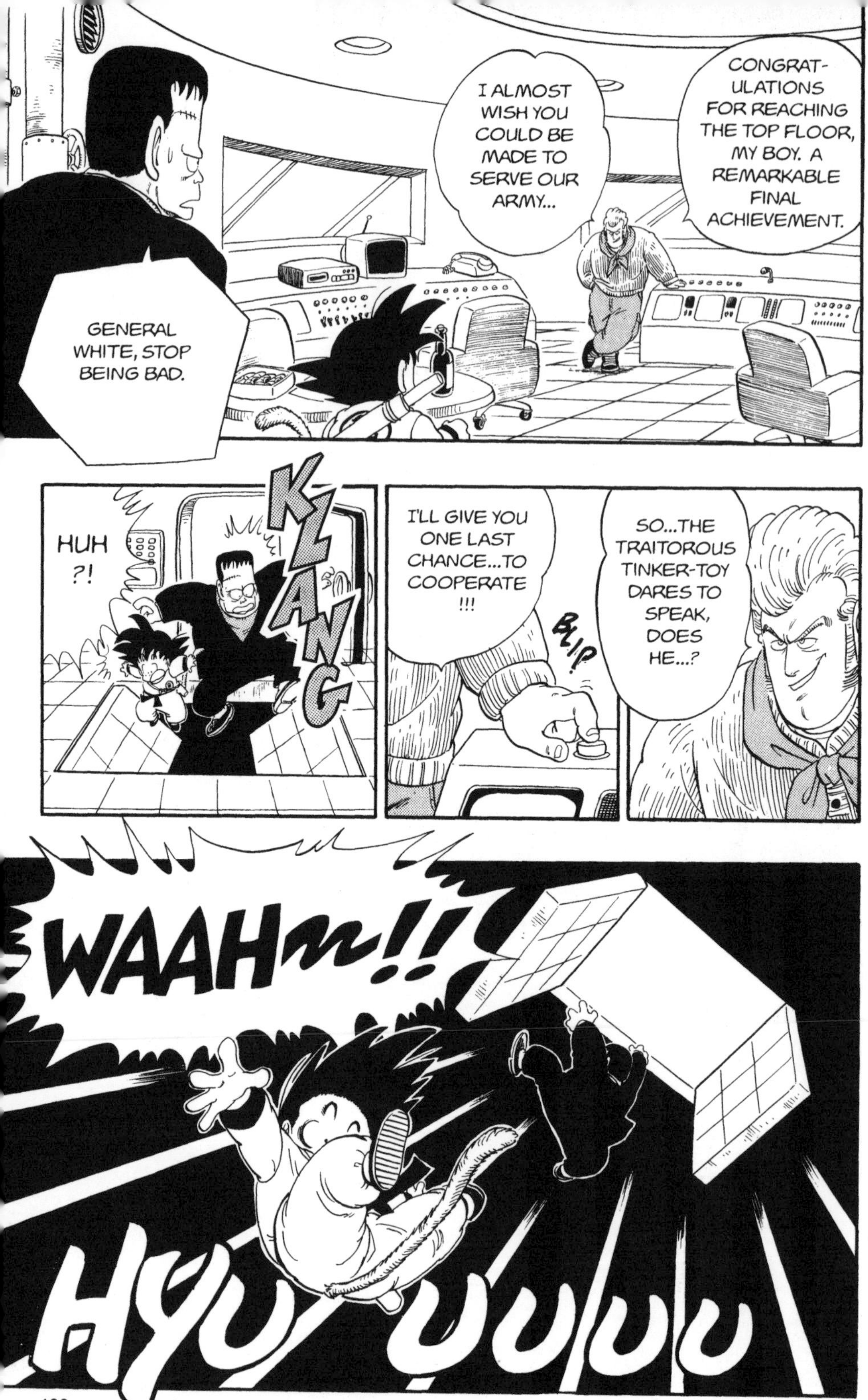
CONGRAT-ULATIONS FOR REACHING THE TOP FLOOR, MY BOY. A REMARKABLE FINAL ACHIEVEMENT.
I ALMOST WISH YOU COULD BE MADE TO SERVE OUR ARMY...
GENERAL WHITE, STOP BEING BAD.
SO...THE TRAITOROUS TINKER-TOY DARES TO SPEAK, DOES HE...?
I'LL GIVE YOU ONE LAST CHANCE...TO COOPERATE !!!
BLIP
KLANG
HUH ?!
WAAHH!!
HYUUUUUU

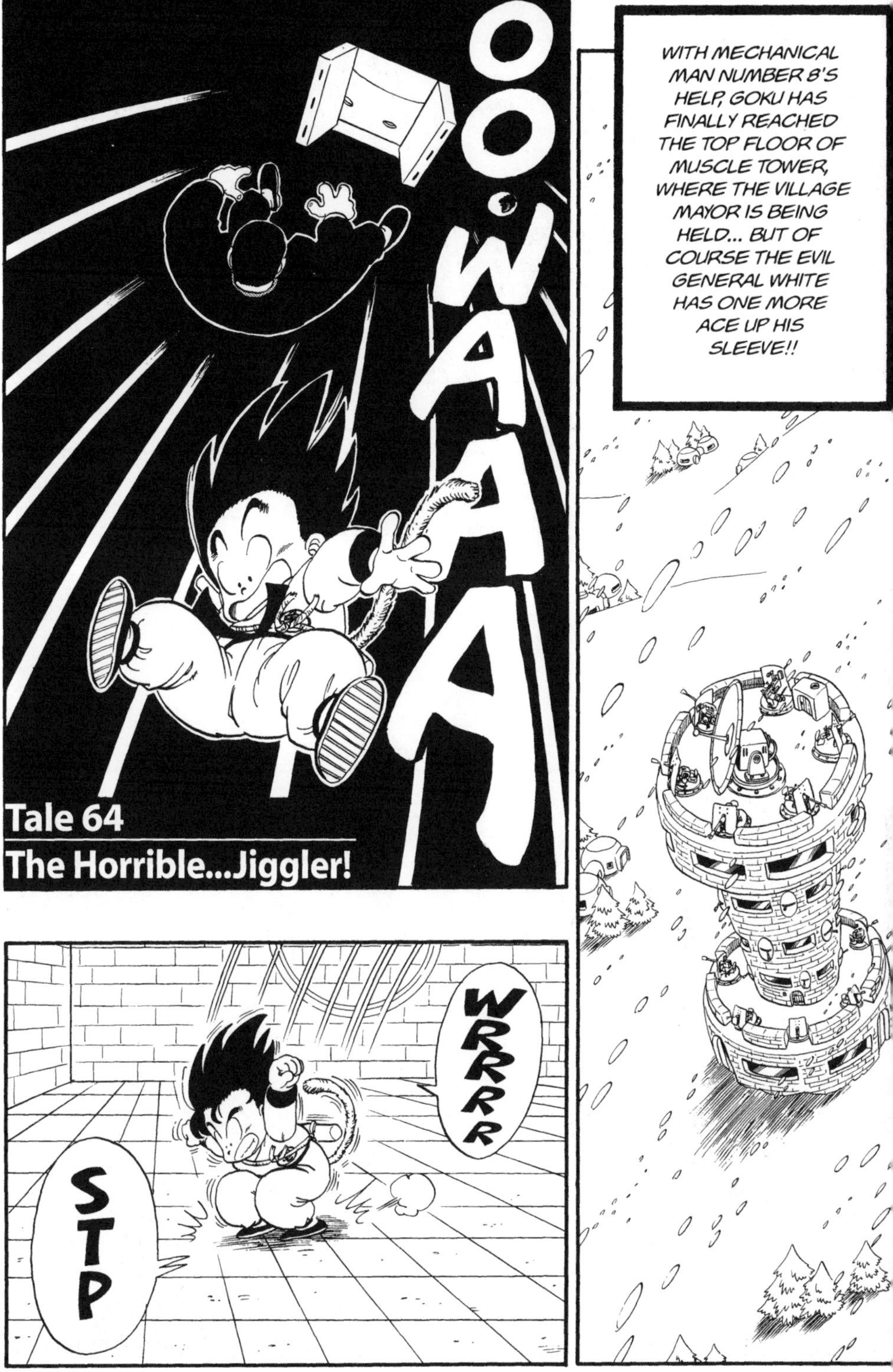
WITH MECHANICAL MAN NUMBER 8'S HELP, GOKU HAS FINALLY REACHED THE TOP FLOOR OF MUSCLE TOWER, WHERE THE VILLAGE MAYOR IS BEING HELD... BUT OF COURSE THE EVIL GENERAL WHITE HAS ONE MORE ACE UP HIS SLEEVE!!
OOWAAAA
Tale 64
The Horrible...Jiggler!
WRRRR
STP

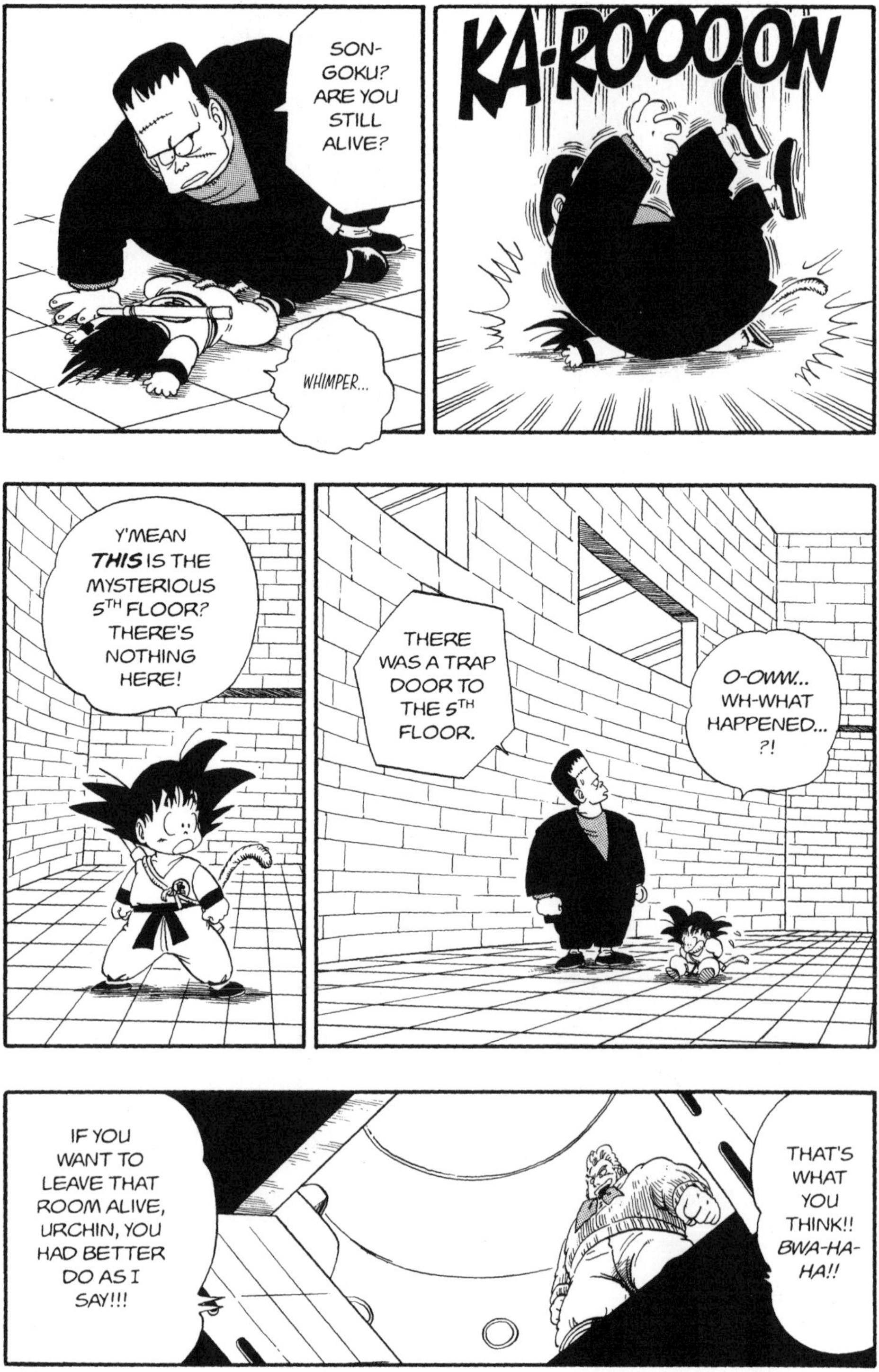

KA-ROOOON
SON-GOKU? ARE YOU STILL ALIVE?
WHIMPER...
O-OWW... WH-WHAT HAPPENED...?!
THERE WAS A TRAP DOOR TO THE 5TH FLOOR.
Y'MEAN **THIS** IS THE MYSTERIOUS 5TH FLOOR? THERE'S NOTHING HERE!
THAT'S WHAT YOU THINK!! *BWA-HA-HA!!*
IF YOU WANT TO LEAVE THAT ROOM ALIVE, URCHIN, YOU HAD BETTER DO AS I SAY!!!

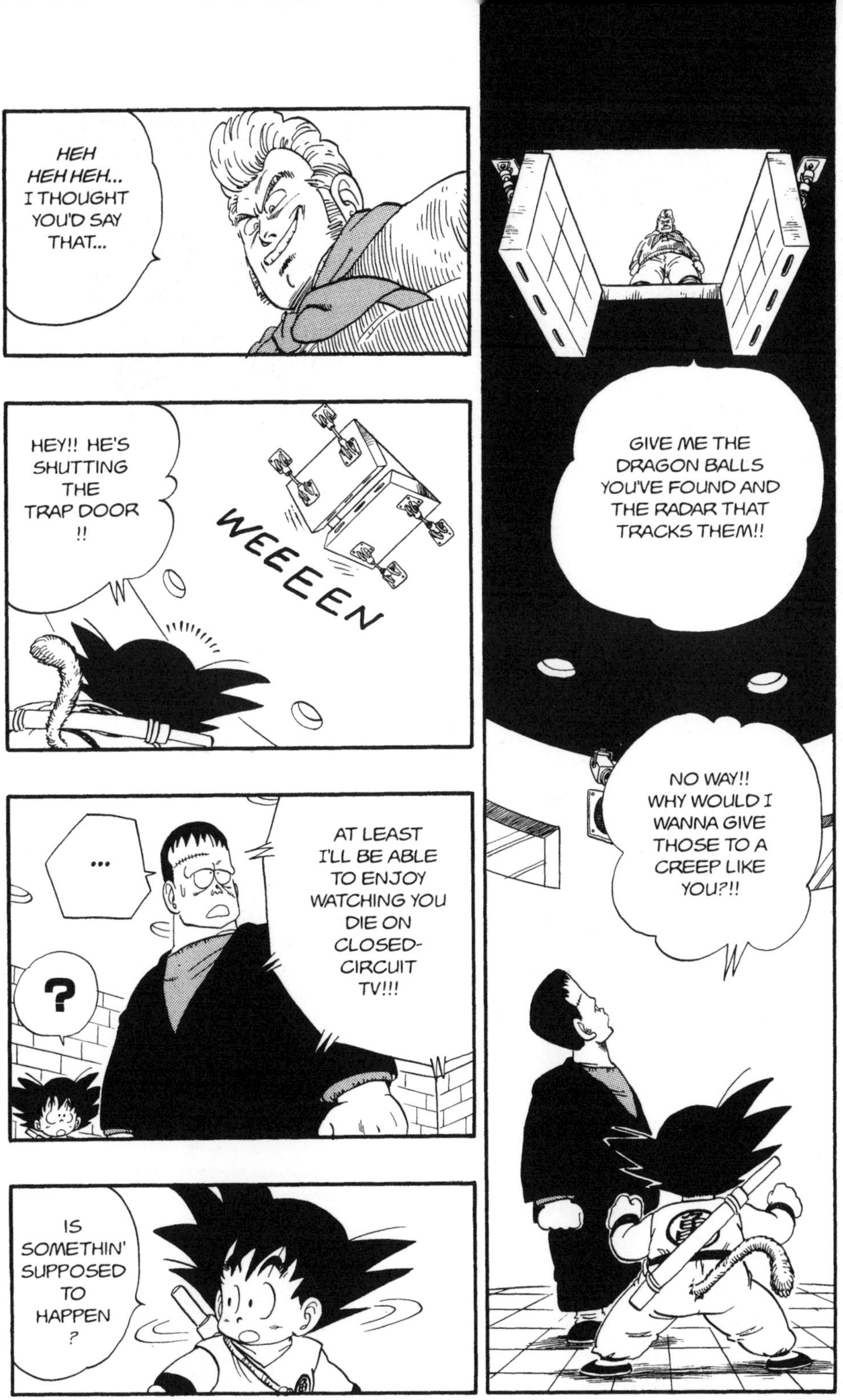
GIVE ME THE DRAGON BALLS YOU'VE FOUND AND THE RADAR THAT TRACKS THEM!!
NO WAY!! WHY WOULD I WANNA GIVE THOSE TO A CREEP LIKE YOU?!!
HEH HEH HEH... I THOUGHT YOU'D SAY THAT...
HEY!! HE'S SHUTTING THE TRAP DOOR !!
WEEEEN
AT LEAST I'LL BE ABLE TO ENJOY WATCHING YOU DIE ON CLOSED-CIRCUIT TV!!!
...
?
IS SOMETHIN' SUPPOSED TO HAPPEN ?

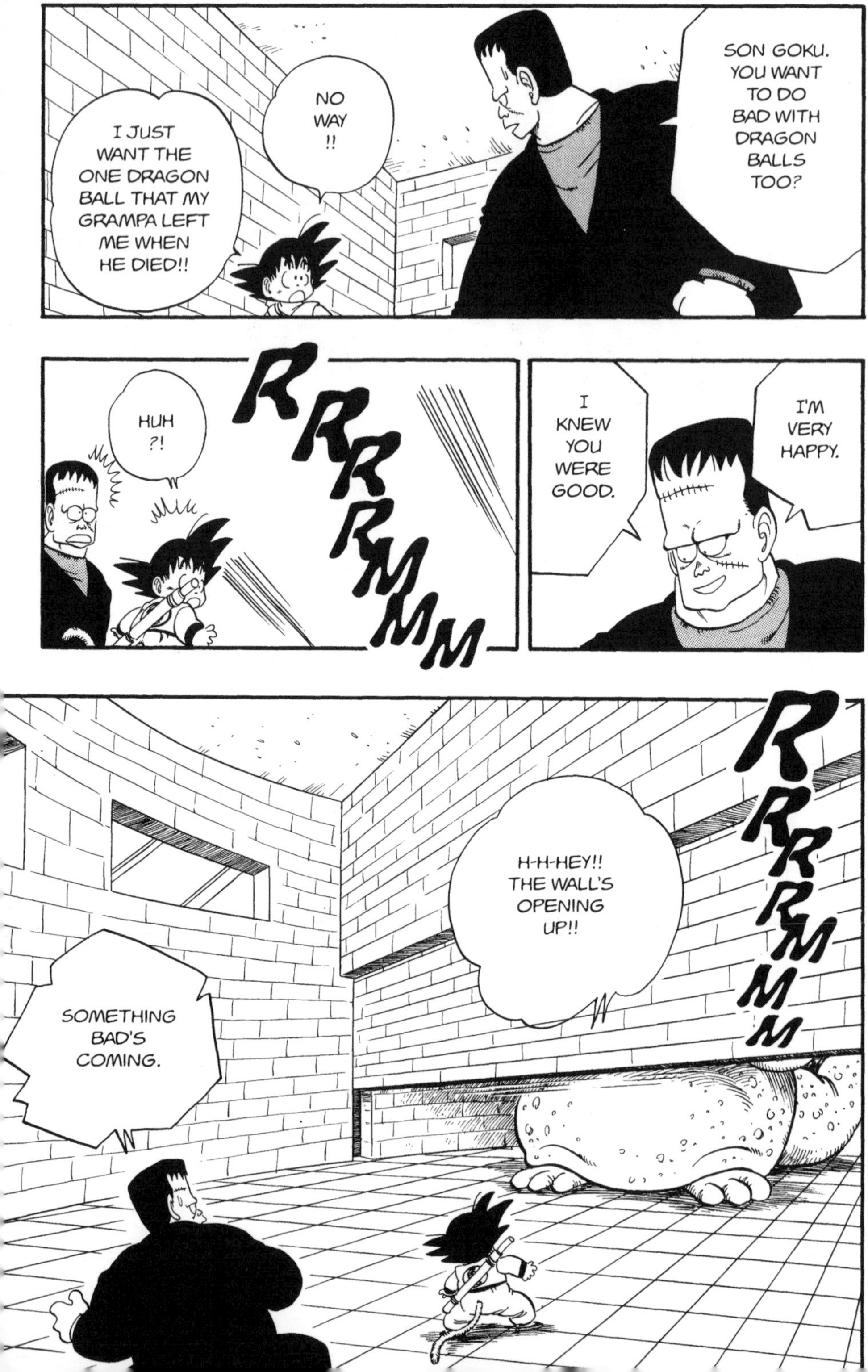
SON GOKU. YOU WANT TO DO BAD WITH DRAGON BALLS TOO?
NO WAY!!
I JUST WANT THE ONE DRAGON BALL THAT MY GRAMPA LEFT ME WHEN HE DIED!!
I'M VERY HAPPY.
I KNEW YOU WERE GOOD.
RRRRMMM
HUH?!
RRRRMMM
H-H-HEY!! THE WALL'S OPENING UP!!
SOMETHING BAD'S COMING.

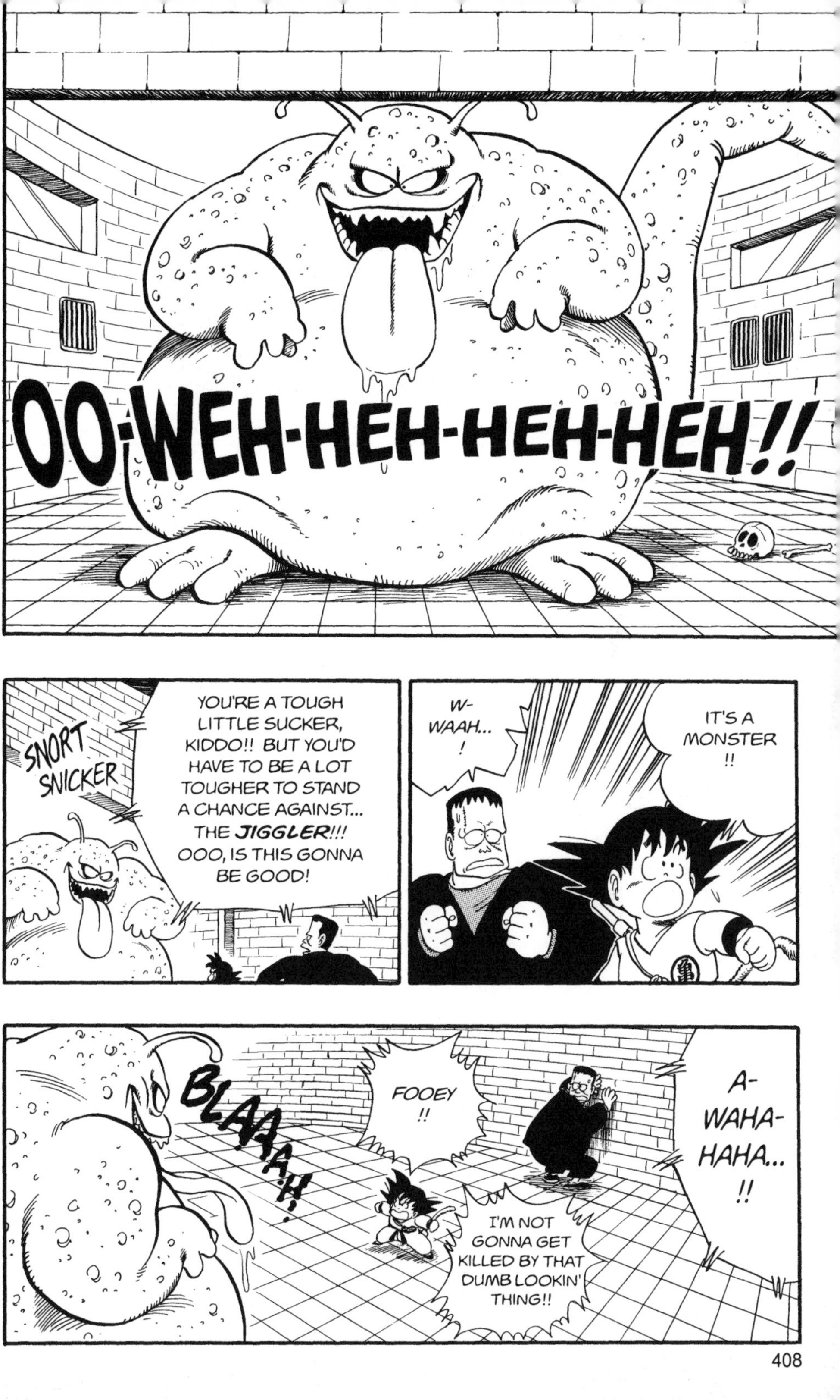
OO-WEH-HEH-HEH-HEH!!
IT'S A MONSTER!!
W-WAAH...!
YOU'RE A TOUGH LITTLE SUCKER, KIDDO!! BUT YOU'D HAVE TO BE A LOT TOUGHER TO STAND A CHANCE AGAINST... THE *JIGGLER*!!! OOO, IS THIS GONNA BE GOOD!
SNORT SNICKER
A-WAHA-HAHA...!!
FOOEY!!
BLAAAAH!!
I'M NOT GONNA GET KILLED BY THAT DUMB LOOKIN' THING!!

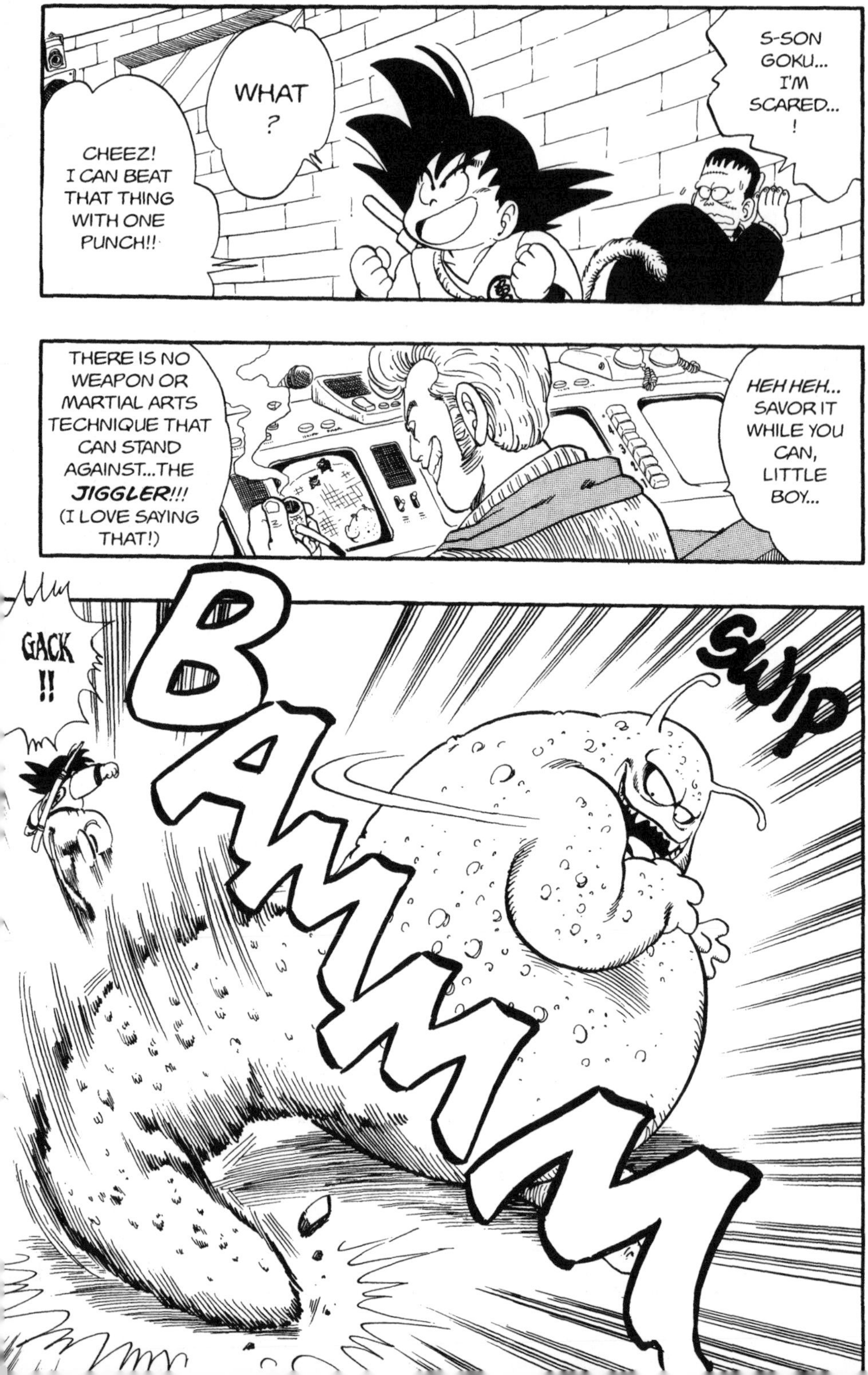
S-SON GOKU... I'M SCARED... !
WHAT ?
CHEEZ! I CAN BEAT THAT THING WITH ONE PUNCH!!
HEH HEH... SAVOR IT WHILE YOU CAN, LITTLE BOY...
THERE IS NO WEAPON OR MARTIAL ARTS TECHNIQUE THAT CAN STAND AGAINST...THE ***JIGGLER***!!! (I LOVE SAYING THAT!)
SWIP
BAMMMMM
GACK !!

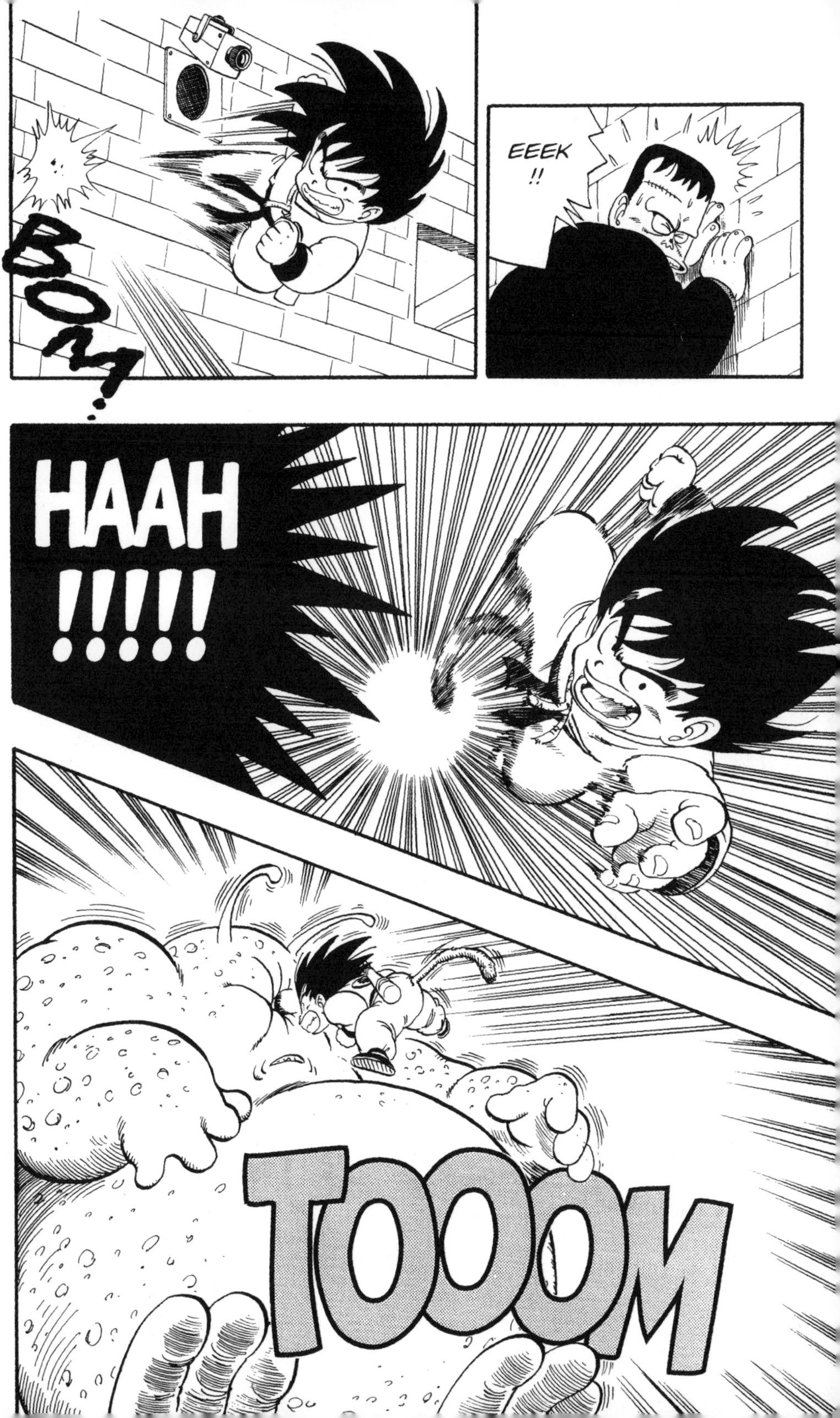
EEEK !!
BOM!
HAAH !!!!!
TOOOM

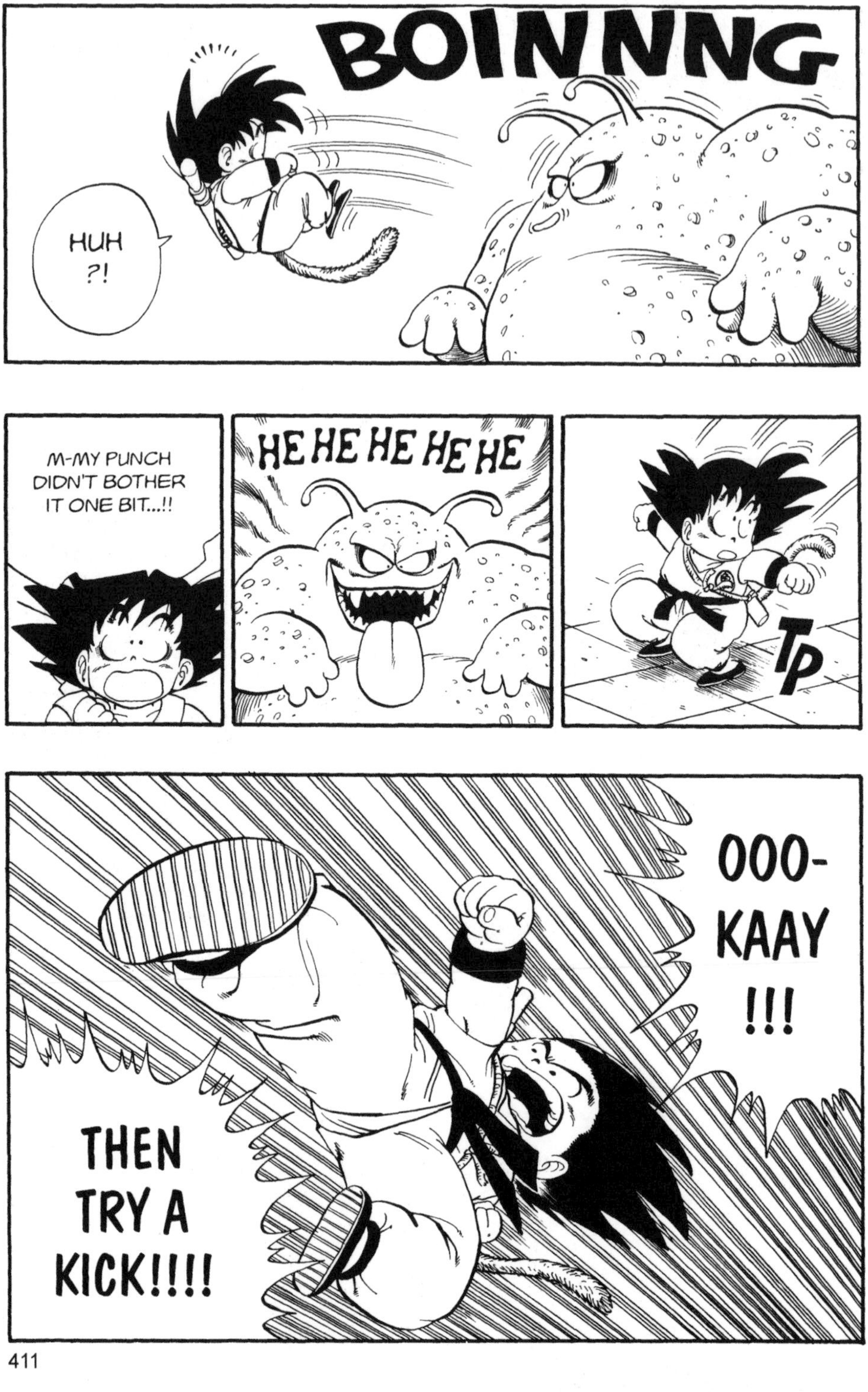
BOINNNG
HUH ?!
TP
HE HE HE HE HE
M-MY PUNCH DIDN'T BOTHER IT ONE BIT...!!
OOO-KAAY !!!
THEN TRY A KICK!!!!

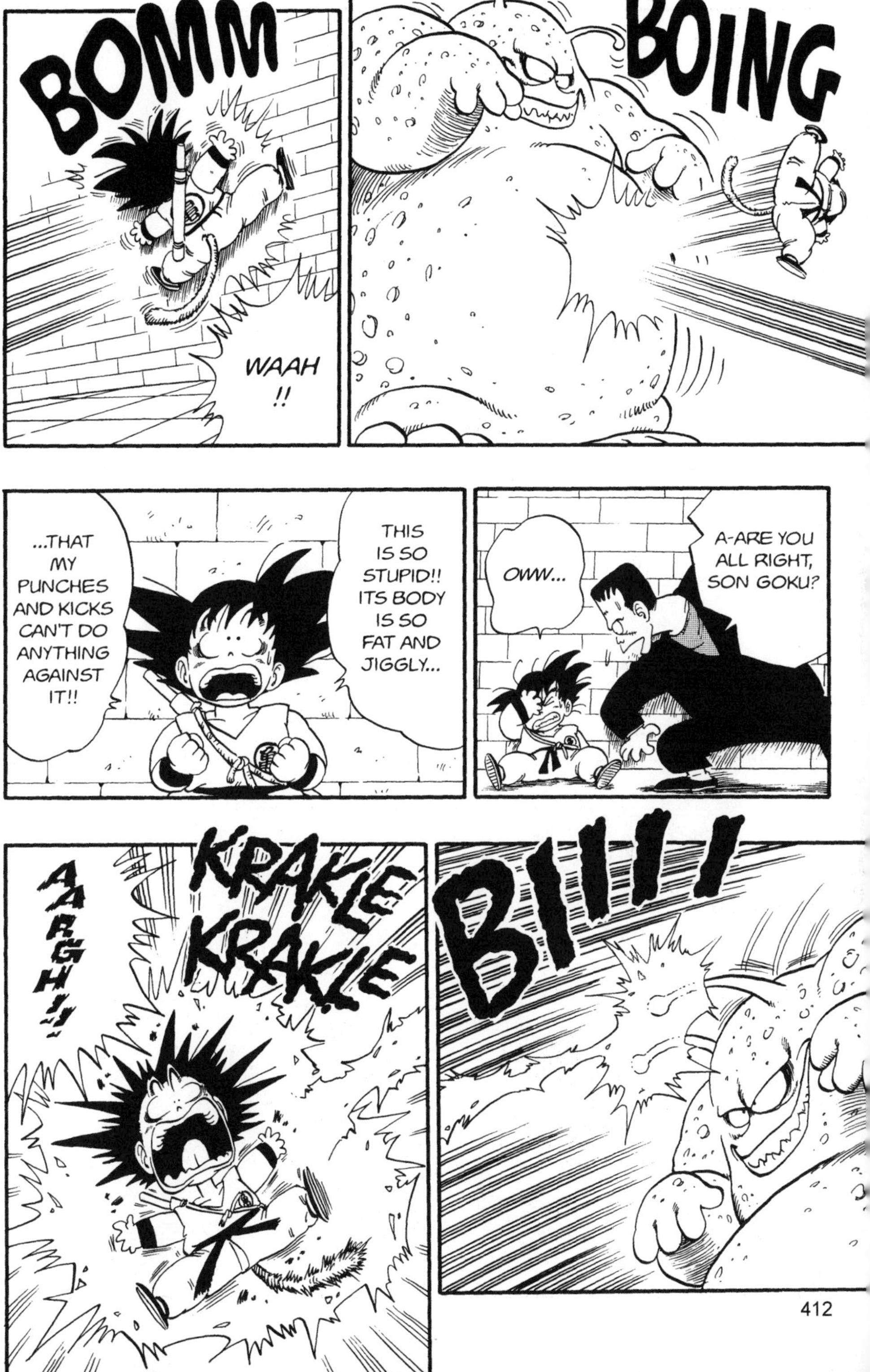
BOING
BOMM
WAAH !!
A-ARE YOU ALL RIGHT, SON GOKU?
OWW...
THIS IS SO STUPID!! ITS BODY IS SO FAT AND JIGGLY...
...THAT MY PUNCHES AND KICKS CAN'T DO ANYTHING AGAINST IT!!
BIIIII
KRAKLE KRAKLE
AARGH!!!

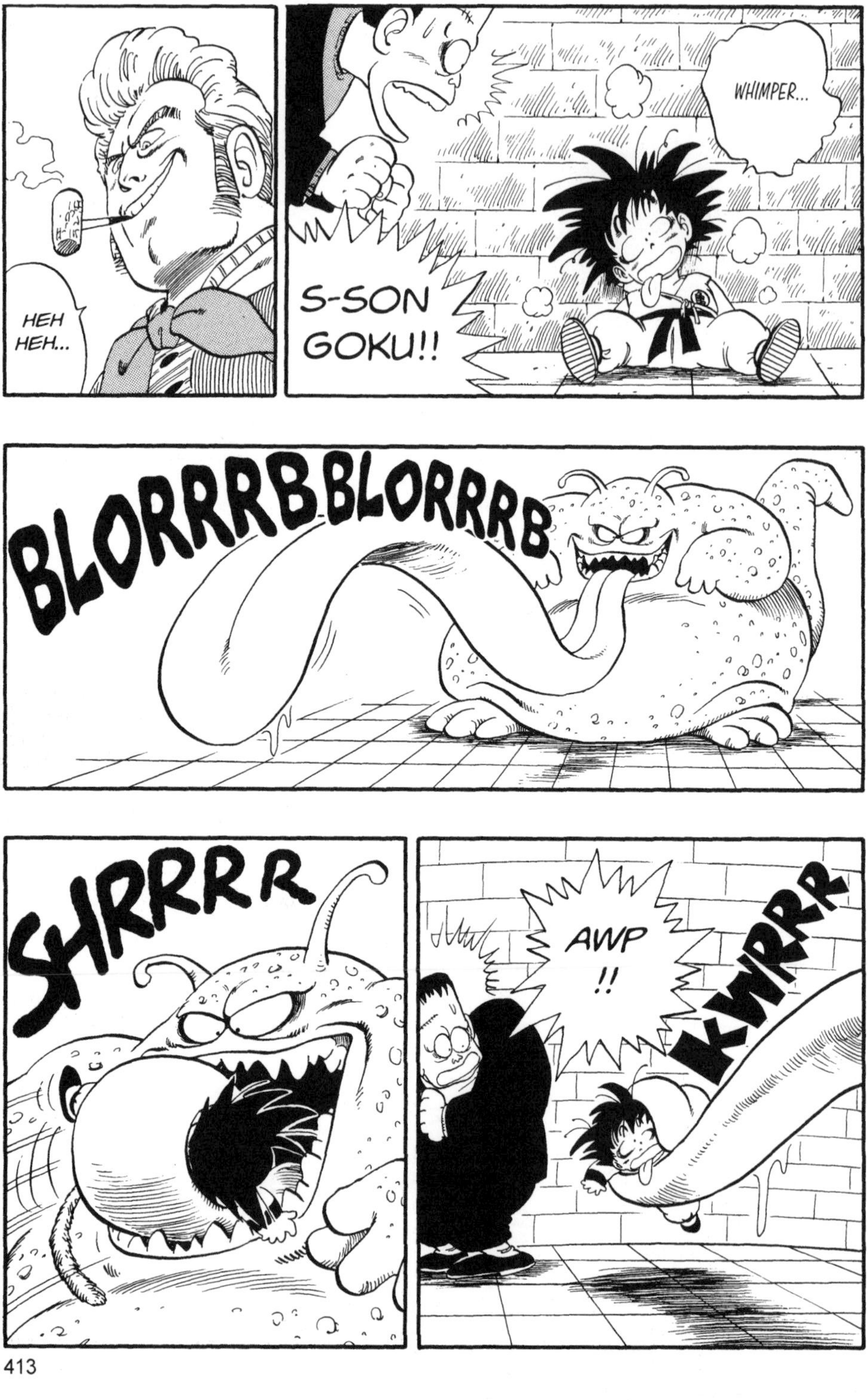
WHIMPER...
S-SON GOKU!!
HEH HEH...
BLORRRB BLORRRB
KWRRR
AWP !!
SHRRRR

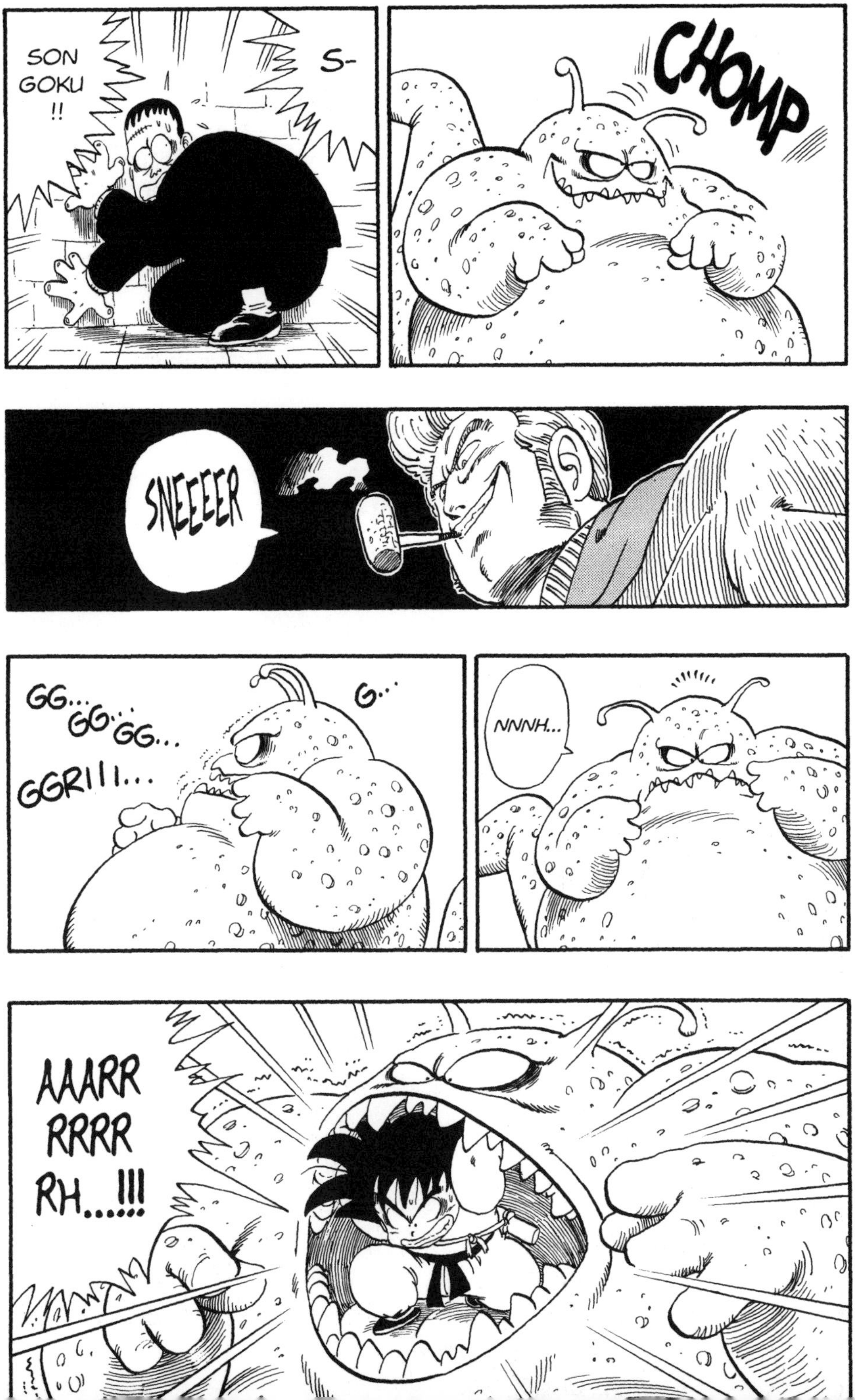
CHOMP
S-
SON GOKU !!
SNEEEER
NNNH...
G...
GG... GG... GG...
GGRIII...
AAARR RRRR RH...!!!

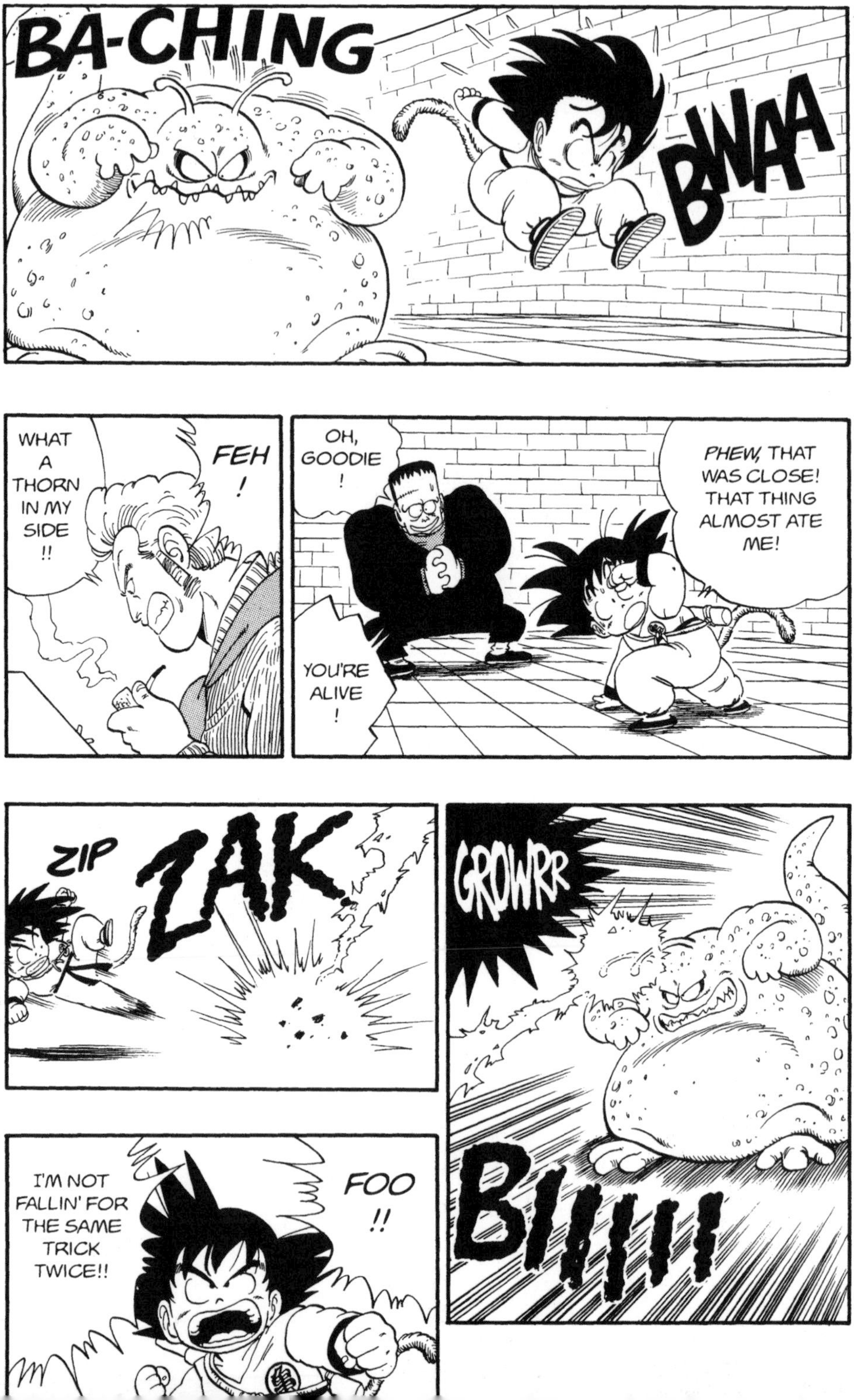
BA-CHING
BWAA
PHEW, THAT WAS CLOSE! THAT THING ALMOST ATE ME!
OH, GOODIE!
YOU'RE ALIVE!
FEH!
WHAT A THORN IN MY SIDE!!
GROWRR
BIIIII
ZAK
ZIP
FOO!!
I'M NOT FALLIN' FOR THE SAME TRICK TWICE!!

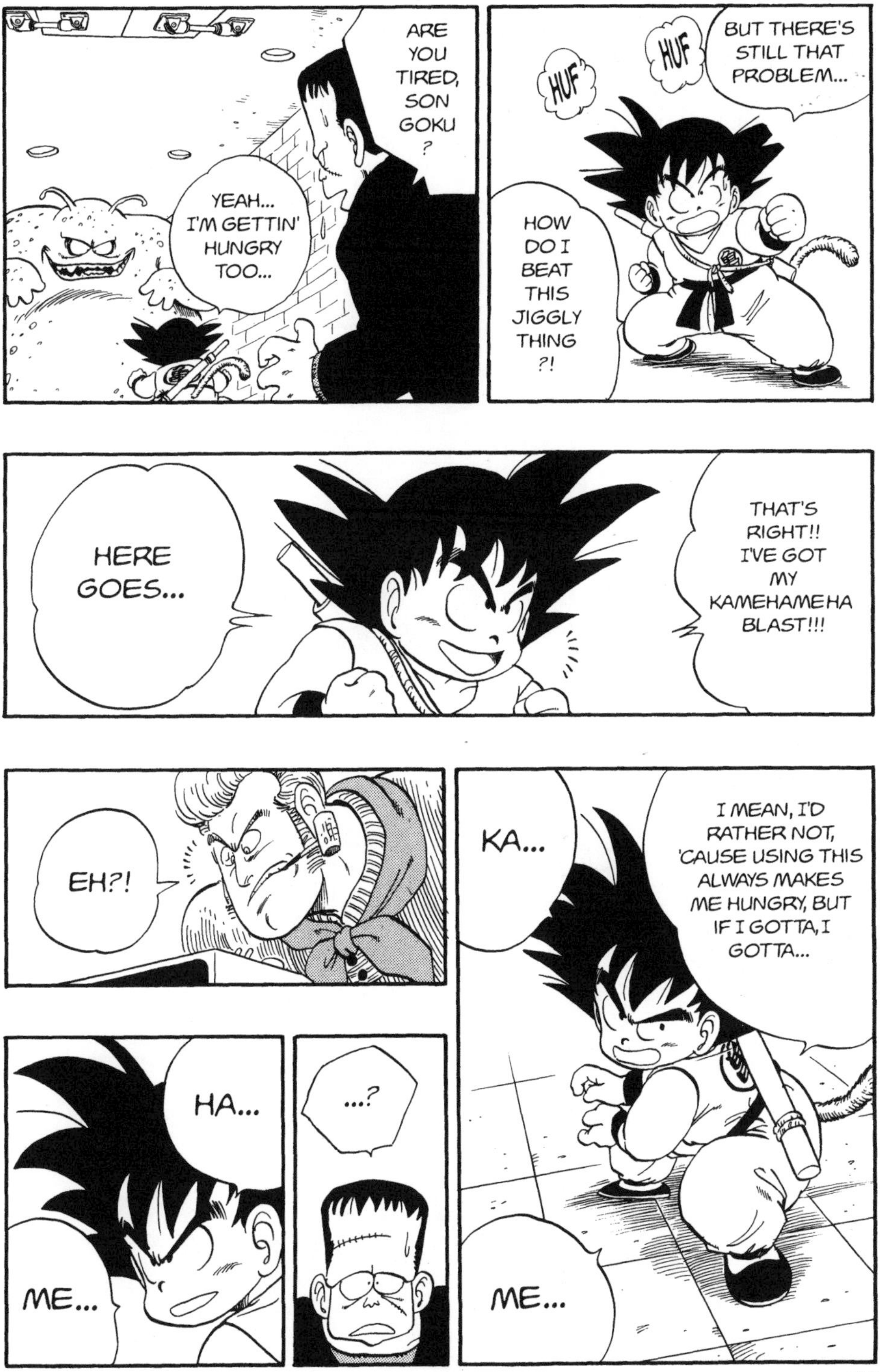
HUF
HUF
BUT THERE'S STILL THAT PROBLEM...
HOW DO I BEAT THIS JIGGLY THING ?!
ARE YOU TIRED, SON GOKU ?
YEAH... I'M GETTIN' HUNGRY TOO...
THAT'S RIGHT!! I'VE GOT MY KAMEHAMEHA BLAST!!!
HERE GOES...
I MEAN, I'D RATHER NOT, 'CAUSE USING THIS ALWAYS MAKES ME HUNGRY, BUT IF I GOTTA, I GOTTA...
KA...
ME...
EH?!
...?
HA...
ME...

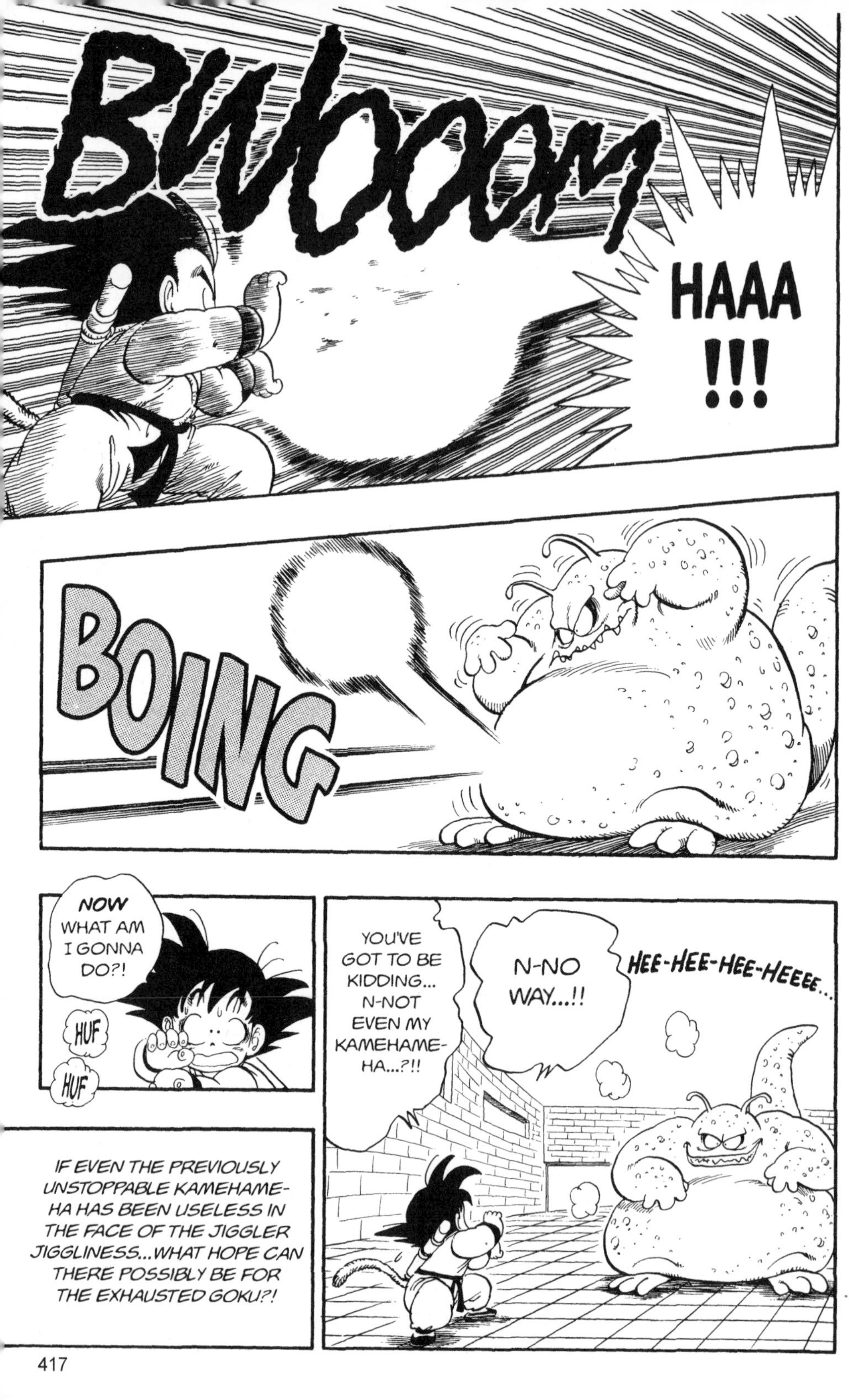
BUBOOM
HAAA!!!
BOING
HEE-HEE-HEE-HEEEE...
N-NO WAY...!!
YOU'VE GOT TO BE KIDDING... N-NOT EVEN MY KAMEHAME-HA...?!!
NOW WHAT AM I GONNA DO?!
HUF
HUF
IF EVEN THE PREVIOUSLY UNSTOPPABLE KAMEHAME-HA HAS BEEN USELESS IN THE FACE OF THE JIGGLER JIGGLINESS...WHAT HOPE CAN THERE POSSIBLY BE FOR THE EXHAUSTED GOKU?!

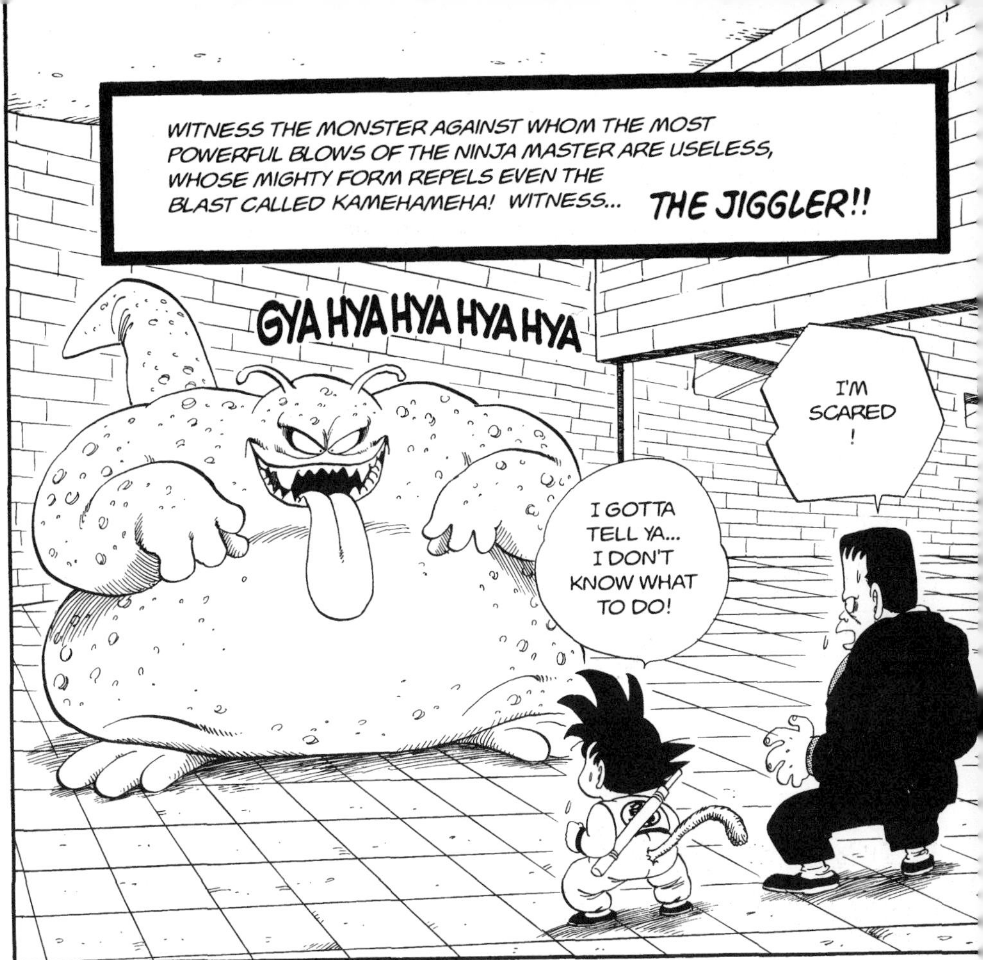
WITNESS THE MONSTER AGAINST WHOM THE MOST POWERFUL BLOWS OF THE NINJA MASTER ARE USELESS, WHOSE MIGHTY FORM REPELS EVEN THE BLAST CALLED KAMEHAMEHA! WITNESS... THE JIGGLER!!
GYA HYA HYA HYA HYA
I'M SCARED !
I GOTTA TELL YA... I DON'T KNOW WHAT TO DO!

Tale 65 • How to Unjiggle a Jiggler

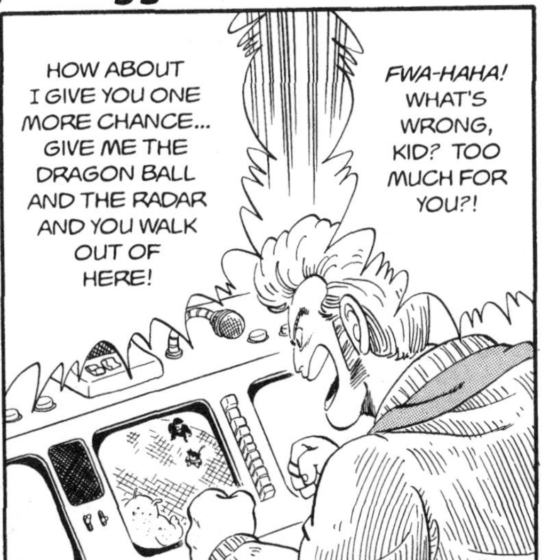
FWA-HAHA! WHAT'S WRONG, KID? TOO MUCH FOR YOU?!
HOW ABOUT I GIVE YOU ONE MORE CHANCE... GIVE ME THE DRAGON BALL AND THE RADAR AND YOU WALK OUT OF HERE!

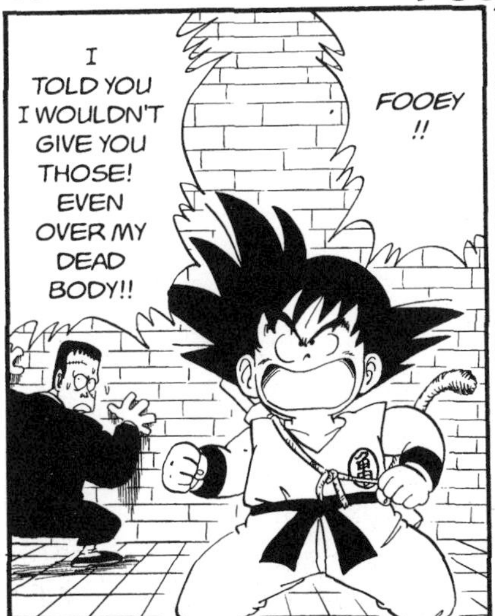
FOOEY !!
I TOLD YOU I WOULDN'T GIVE YOU THOSE! EVEN OVER MY DEAD BODY!!

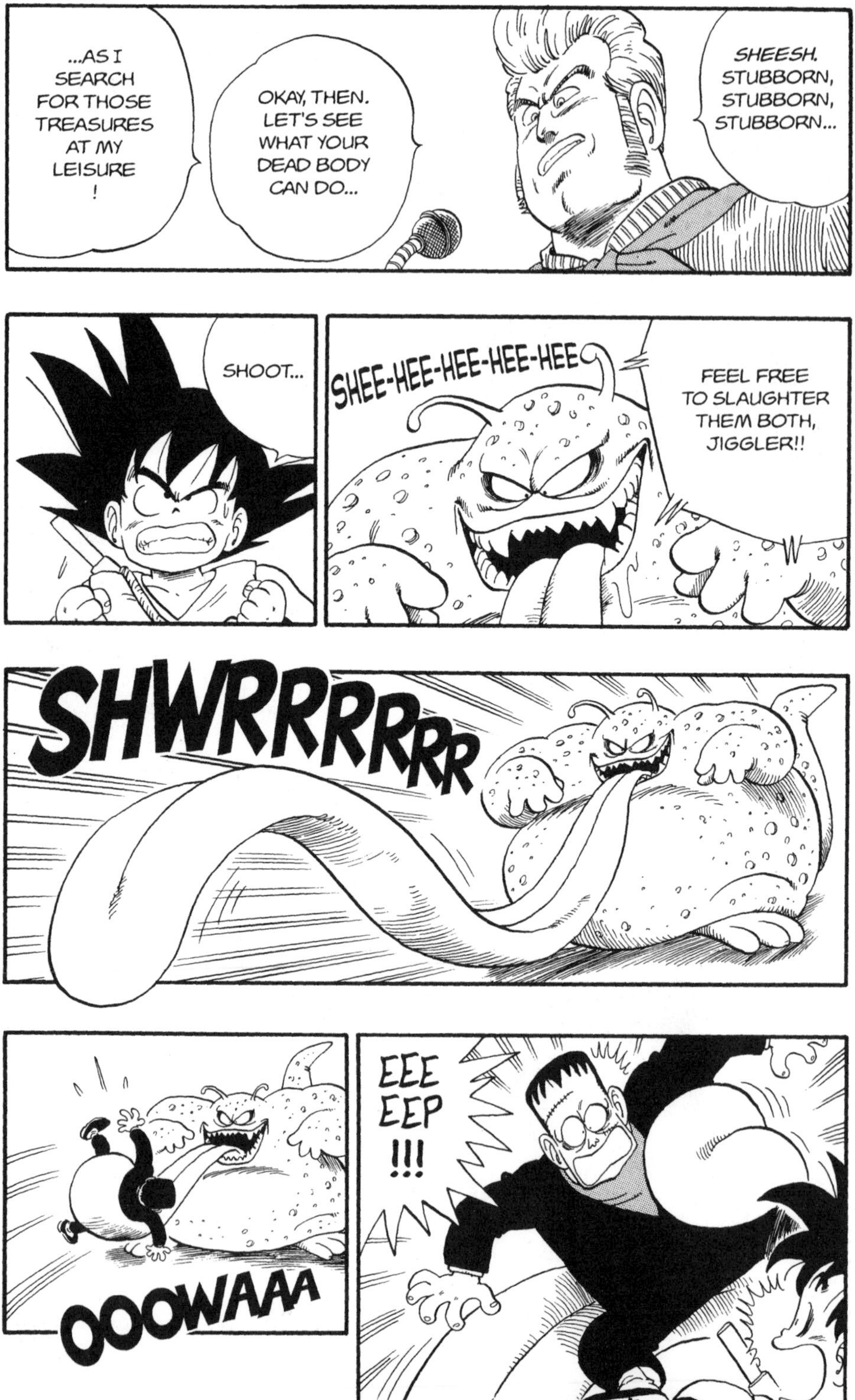
SHEESH. STUBBORN, STUBBORN, STUBBORN...
OKAY, THEN. LET'S SEE WHAT YOUR DEAD BODY CAN DO...
...AS I SEARCH FOR THOSE TREASURES AT MY LEISURE !
FEEL FREE TO SLAUGHTER THEM BOTH, JIGGLER!!
SHEE-HEE-HEE-HEE-HEE
SHOOT...
SHWRRRRRRR
EEE EEP !!!
OOOWAAA

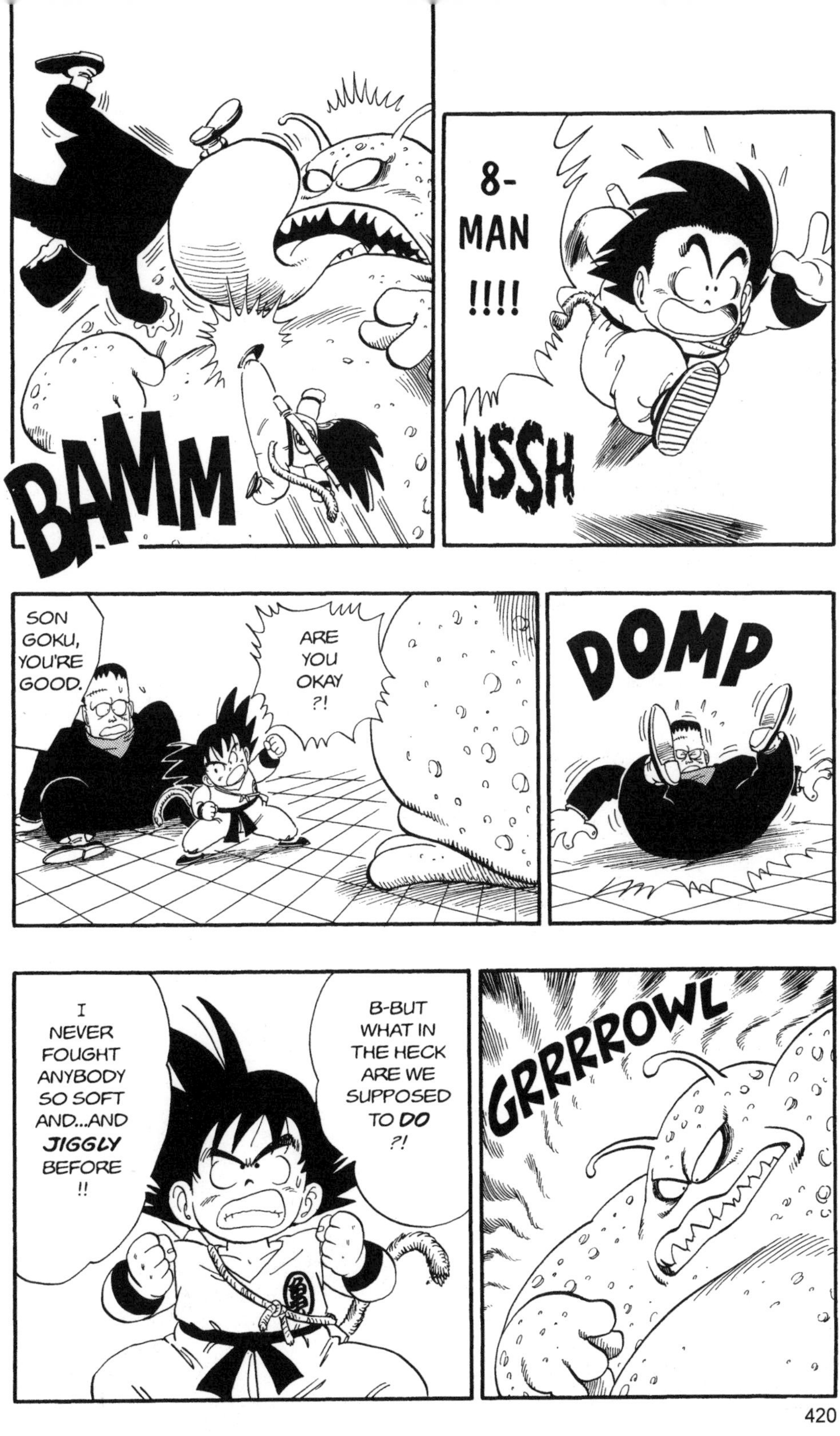
8-MAN!!!!
VSSH
BAMM
DOMP
ARE YOU OKAY?!
SON GOKU, YOU'RE GOOD.
GRRRROWL
B-BUT WHAT IN THE HECK ARE WE SUPPOSED TO *DO*?!
I NEVER FOUGHT ANYBODY SO SOFT AND...AND *JIGGLY* BEFORE!!

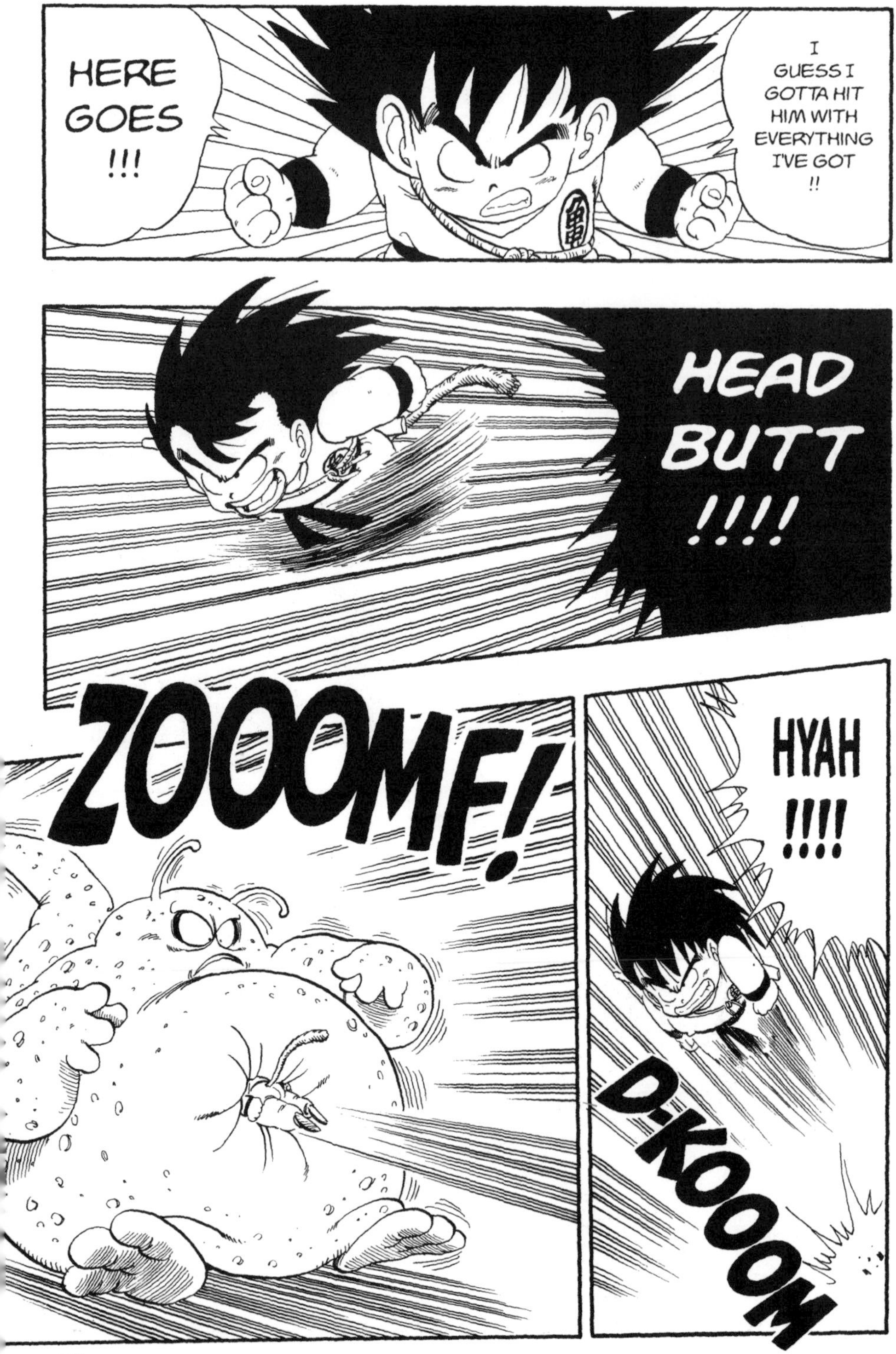
I GUESS I GOTTA HIT HIM WITH EVERYTHING I'VE GOT !!
HERE GOES !!!
HEAD BUTT !!!!
HYAH !!!!
D-KOOOM
ZOOOMF!

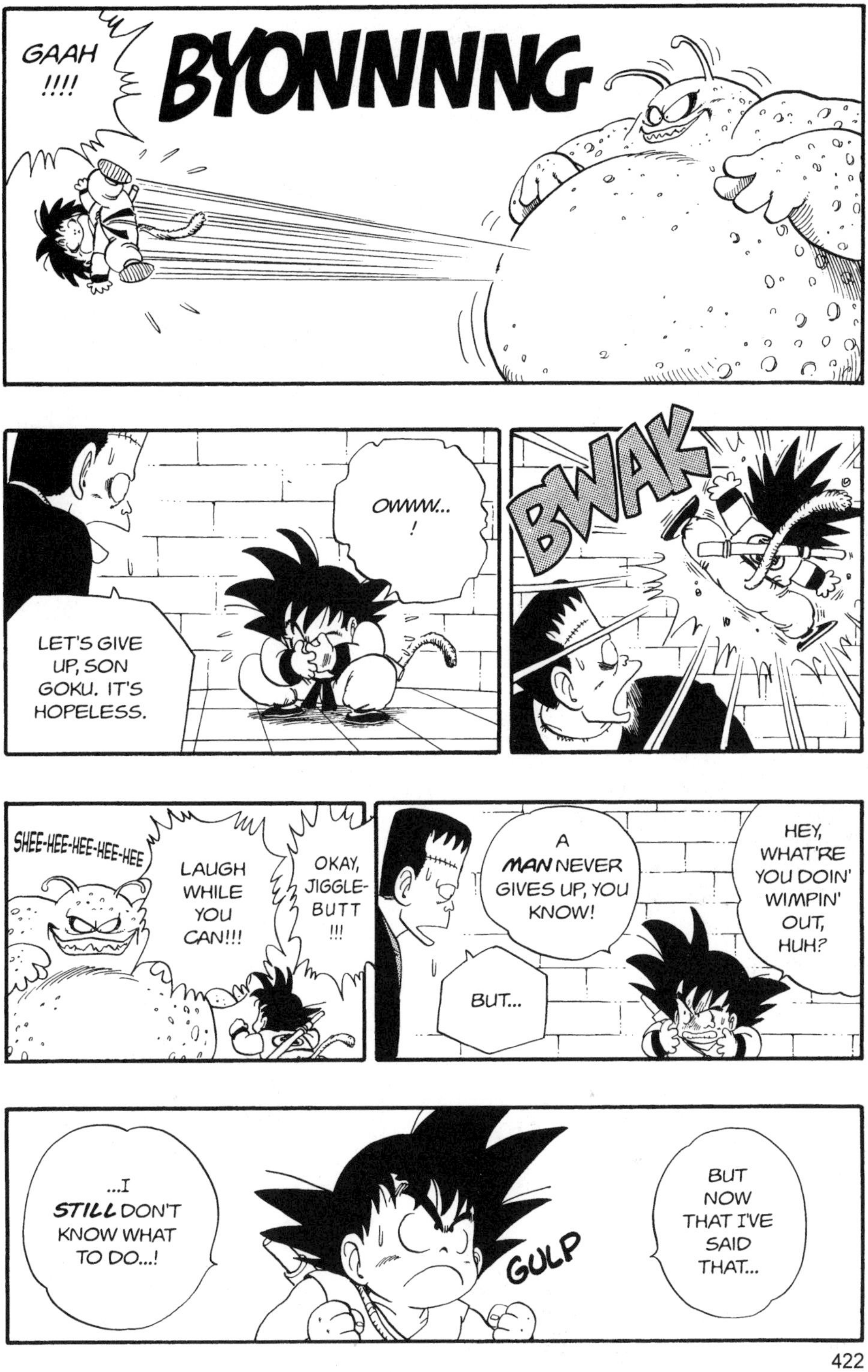
BYONNNNG
GAAH !!!!
BWAK
OWWW... !
LET'S GIVE UP, SON GOKU. IT'S HOPELESS.
HEY, WHAT'RE YOU DOIN' WIMPIN' OUT, HUH?
A MAN NEVER GIVES UP, YOU KNOW!
BUT...
OKAY, JIGGLE-BUTT !!!
LAUGH WHILE YOU CAN!!!
SHEE-HEE-HEE-HEE-HEE
BUT NOW THAT I'VE SAID THAT...
GULP
...I STILL DON'T KNOW WHAT TO DO...!

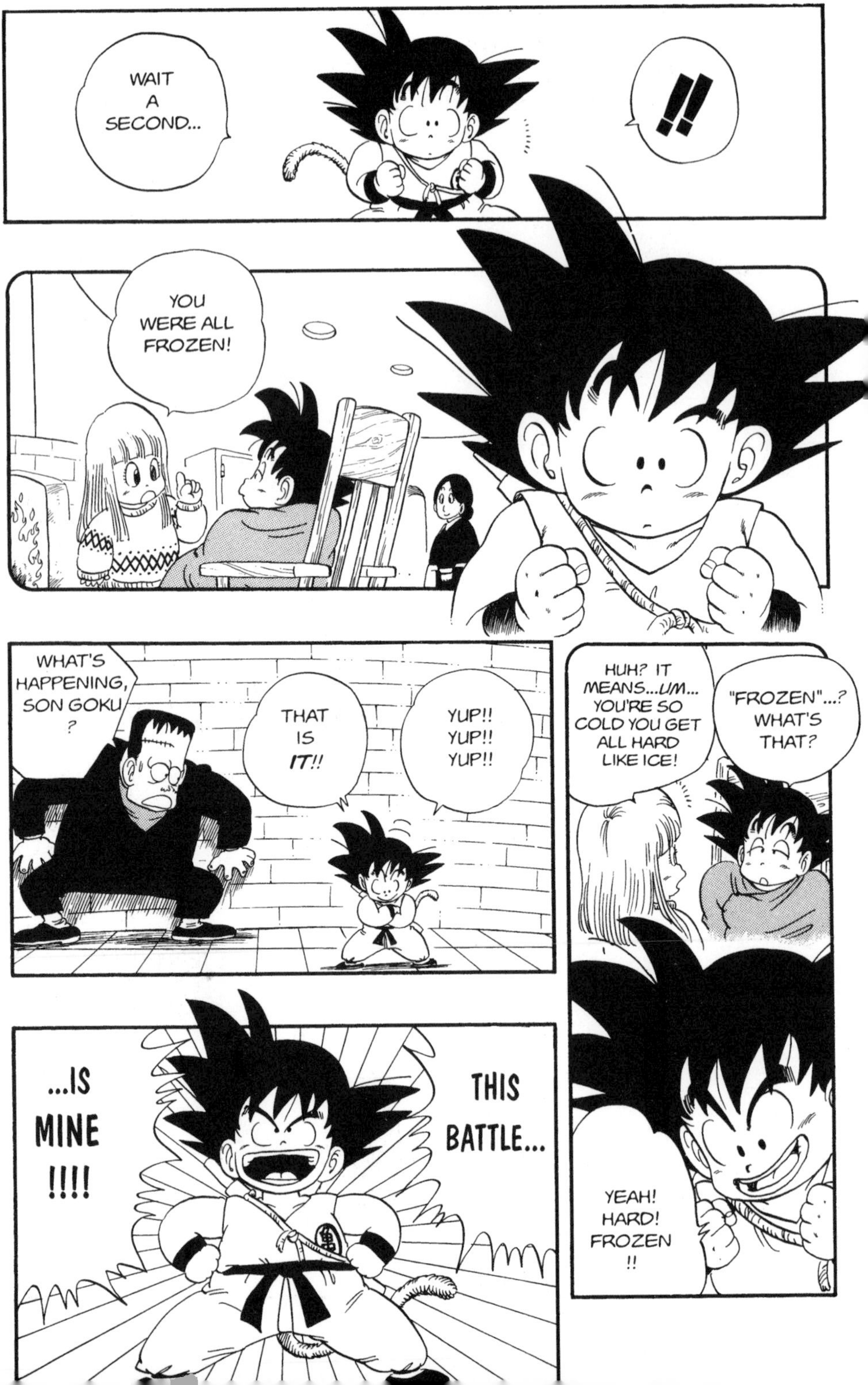
!!
WAIT A SECOND...
YOU WERE ALL FROZEN!
"FROZEN"...? WHAT'S THAT?
HUH? IT MEANS...UM... YOU'RE SO COLD YOU GET ALL HARD LIKE ICE!
YEAH! HARD! FROZEN!!
YUP!! YUP!! YUP!!
THAT IS *IT*!!
WHAT'S HAPPENING, SON GOKU?
THIS BATTLE...
...IS MINE!!!!

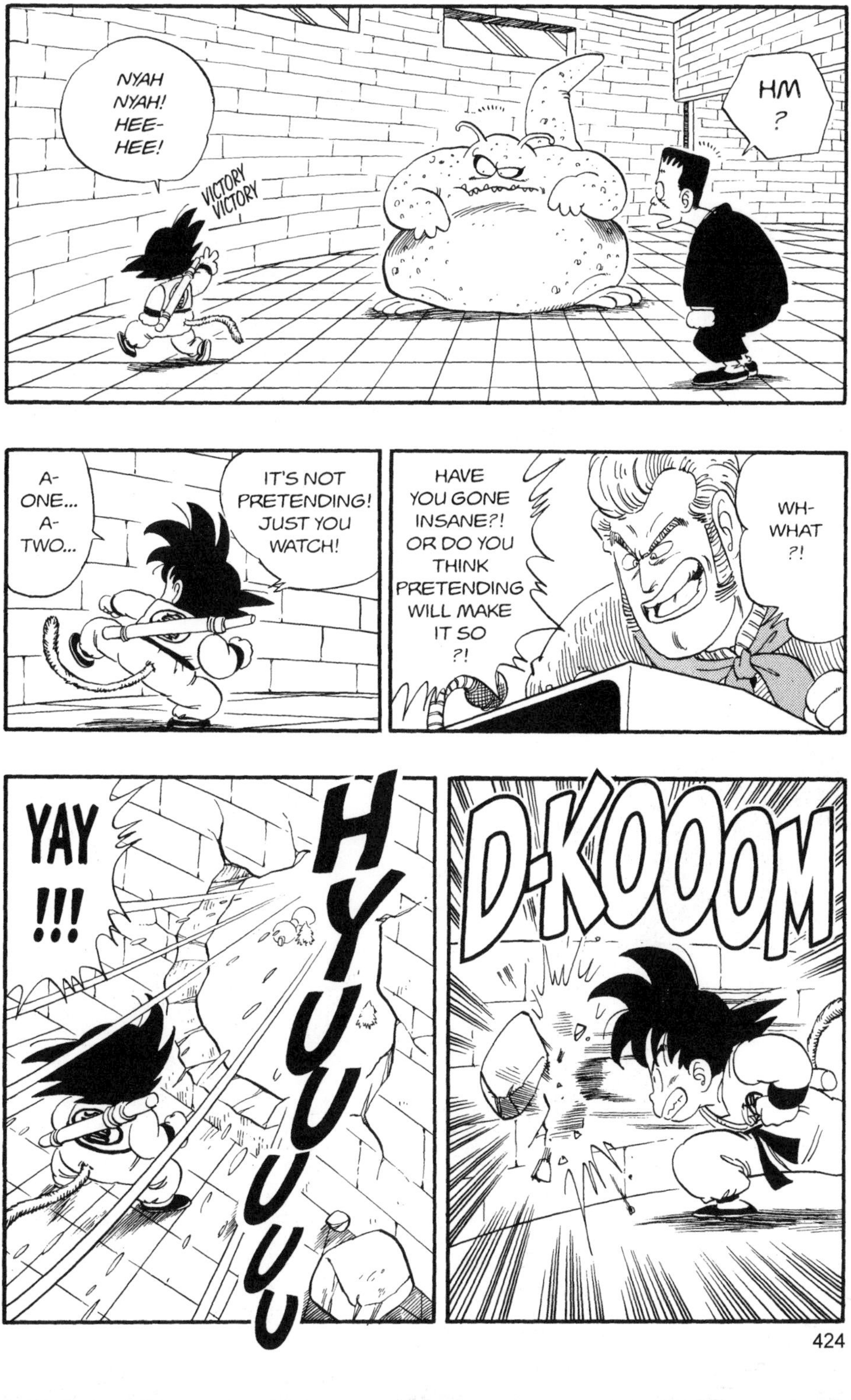
HM ?
NYAH NYAH! HEE-HEE!
VICTORY VICTORY
WH-WHAT ?!
HAVE YOU GONE INSANE?! OR DO YOU THINK PRETENDING WILL MAKE IT SO ?!
IT'S NOT PRETENDING! JUST YOU WATCH!
A-ONE... A-TWO...
D-KOOOM
HYUUUUUU
YAY !!!

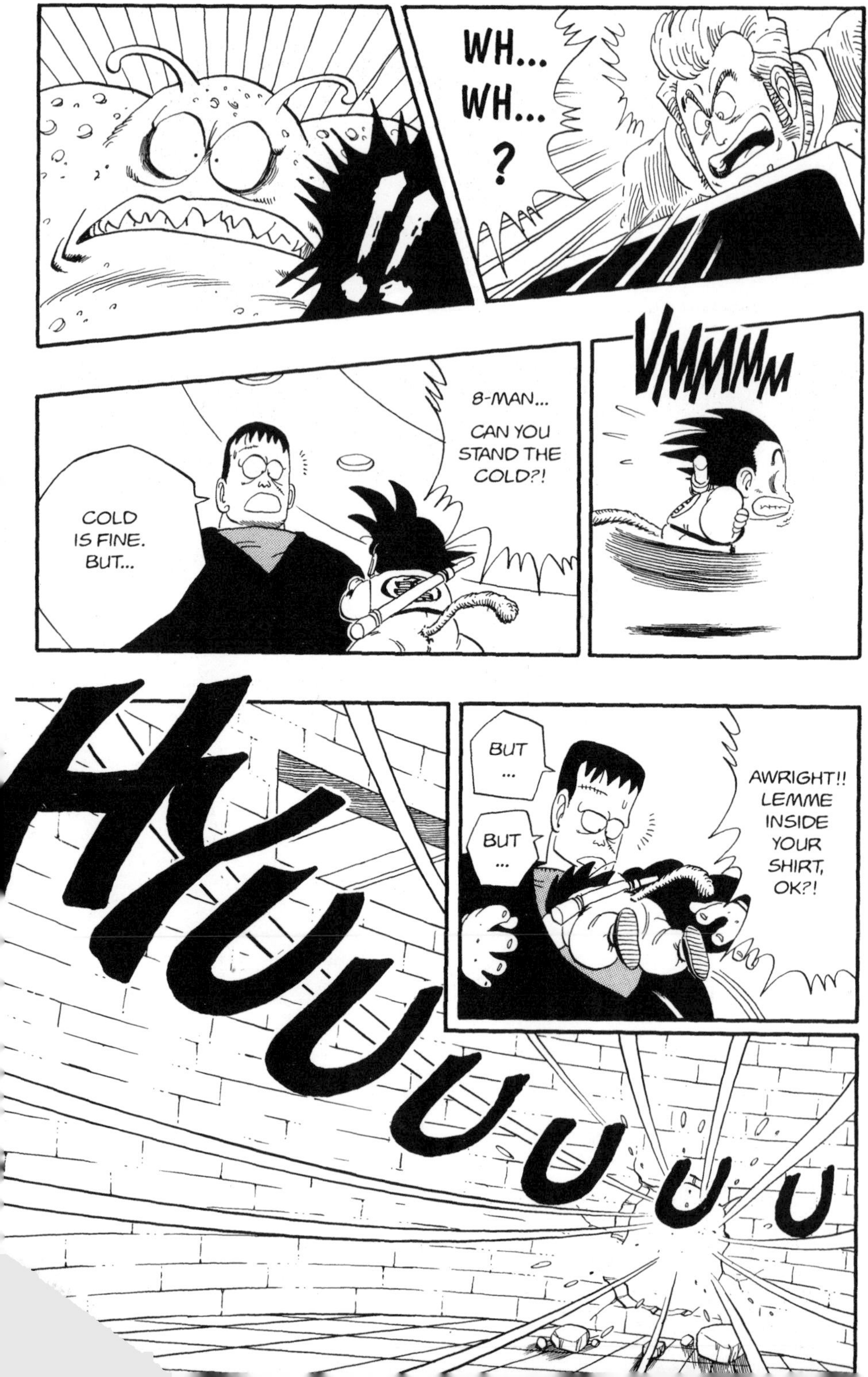
WH... WH... ?
VMMMM
8-MAN... CAN YOU STAND THE COLD?!
COLD IS FINE. BUT...
AWRIGHT!! LEMME INSIDE YOUR SHIRT, OK?!
BUT ...
BUT ...
HYUUUUUUUU

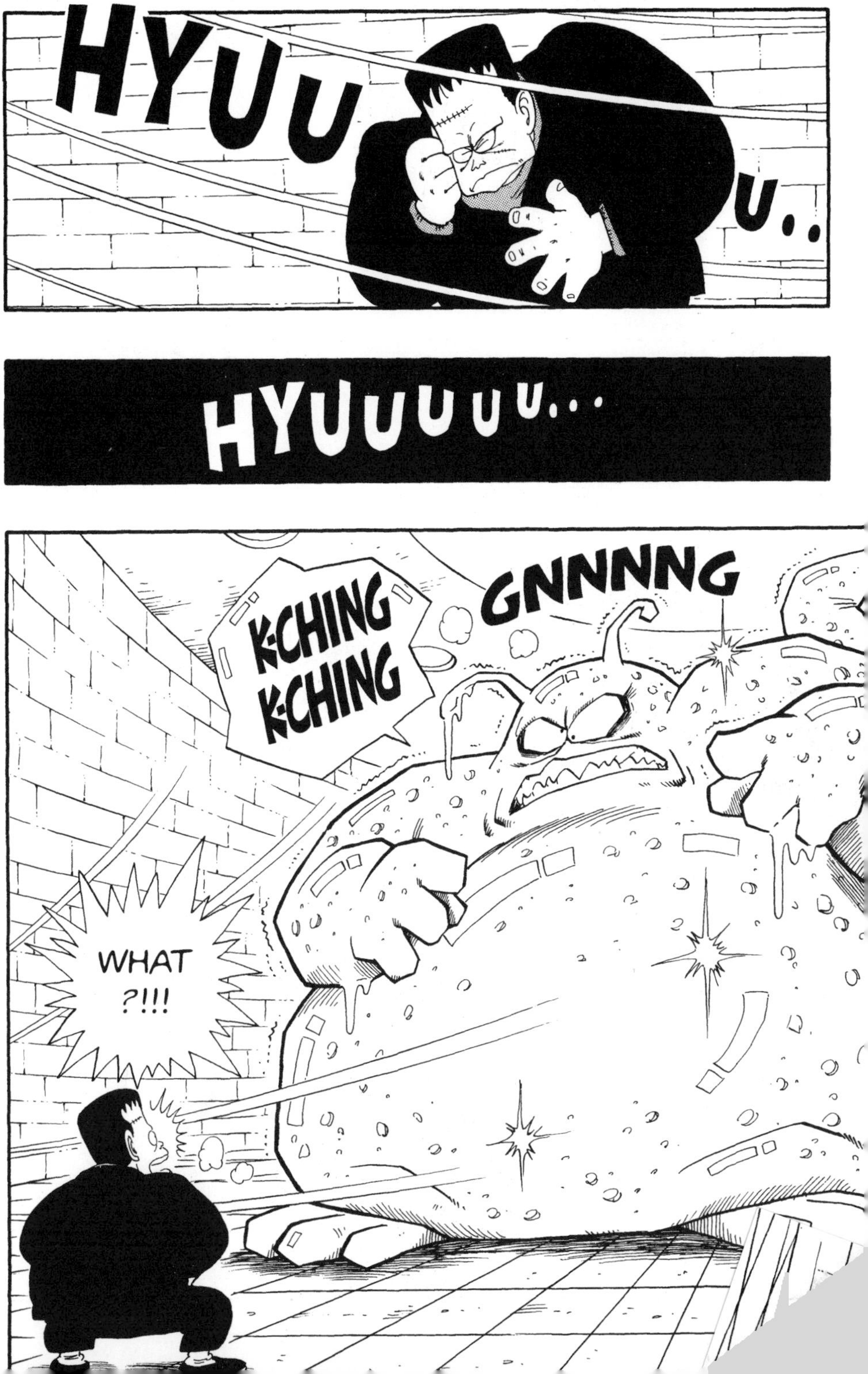
HYUUU
U..
HYUUUUU...
GNNNNG
K-CHING K-CHING
WHAT?!!!

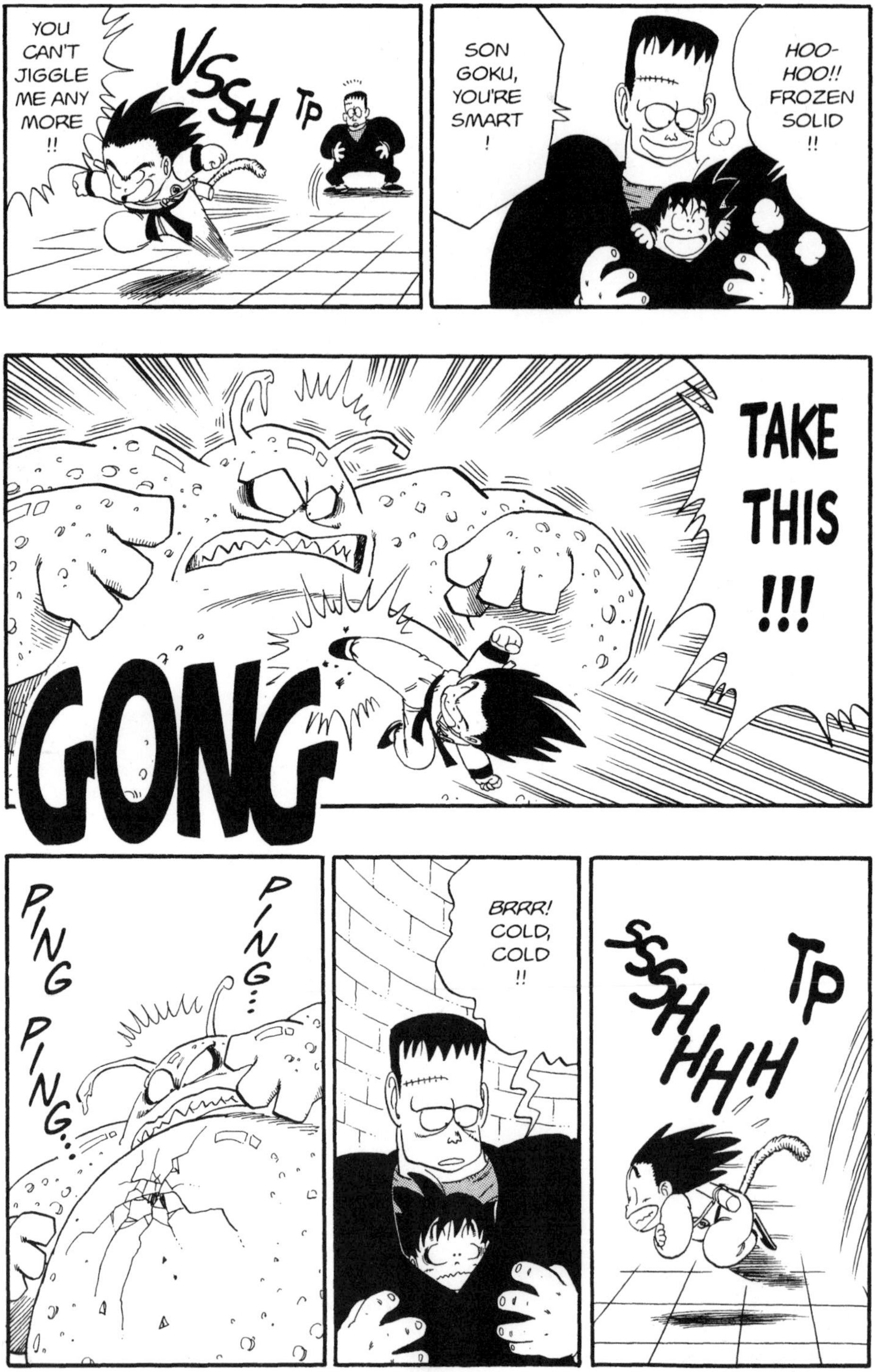
HOO-HOO!! FROZEN SOLID !!
SON GOKU, YOU'RE SMART !
YOU CAN'T JIGGLE ME ANY MORE !!
VSSH
TP
TAKE THIS !!!
GONG
TP
SSSHHHH
BRRR! COLD, COLD !!
PING...
PING PING PING...

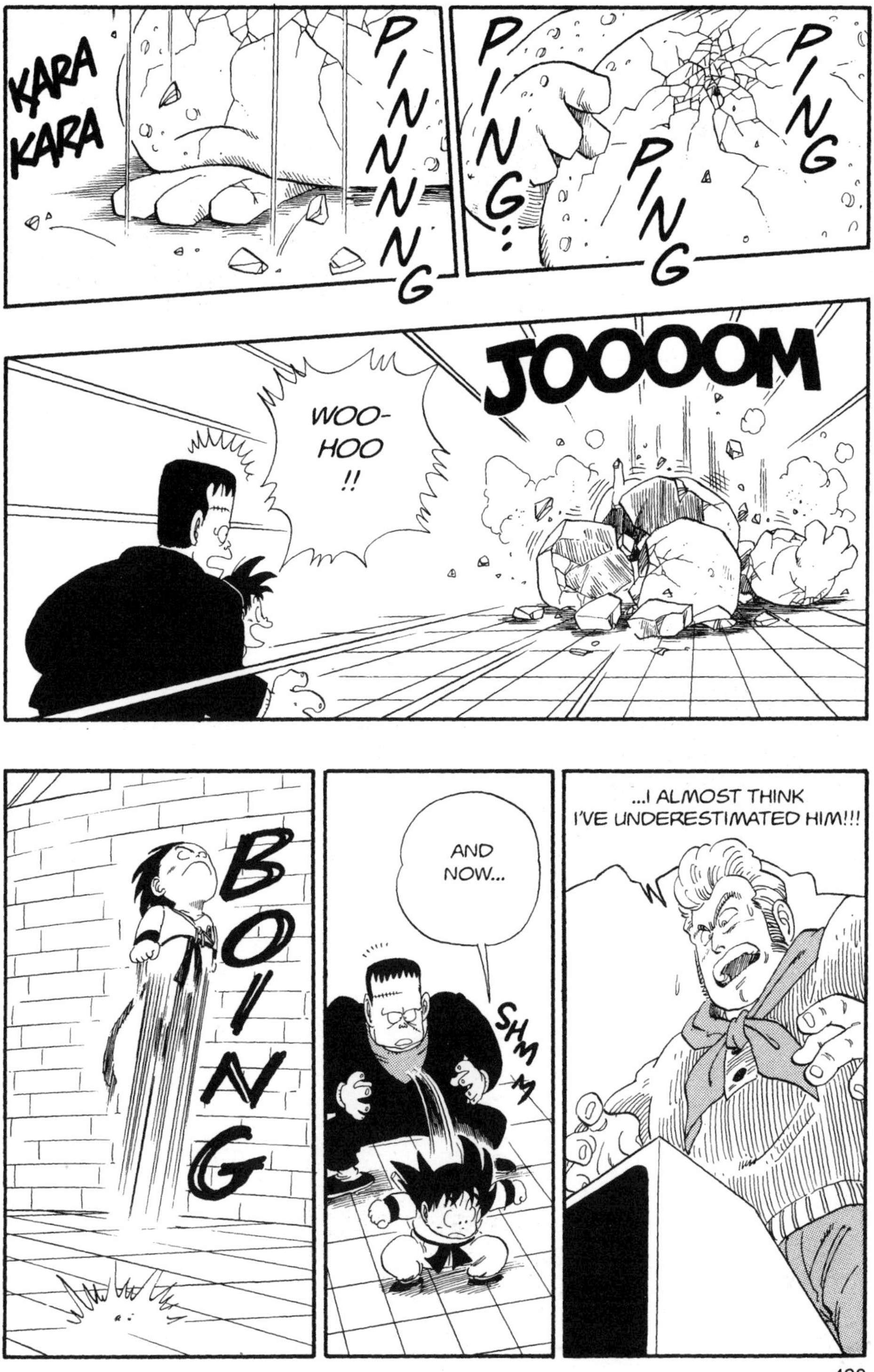
PING
PING
PING...
PINNNNG
KARA KARA
JOOOOM
WOO-HOO!!
...I ALMOST THINK I'VE UNDERESTIMATED HIM!!!
AND NOW...
SHMM
BOING

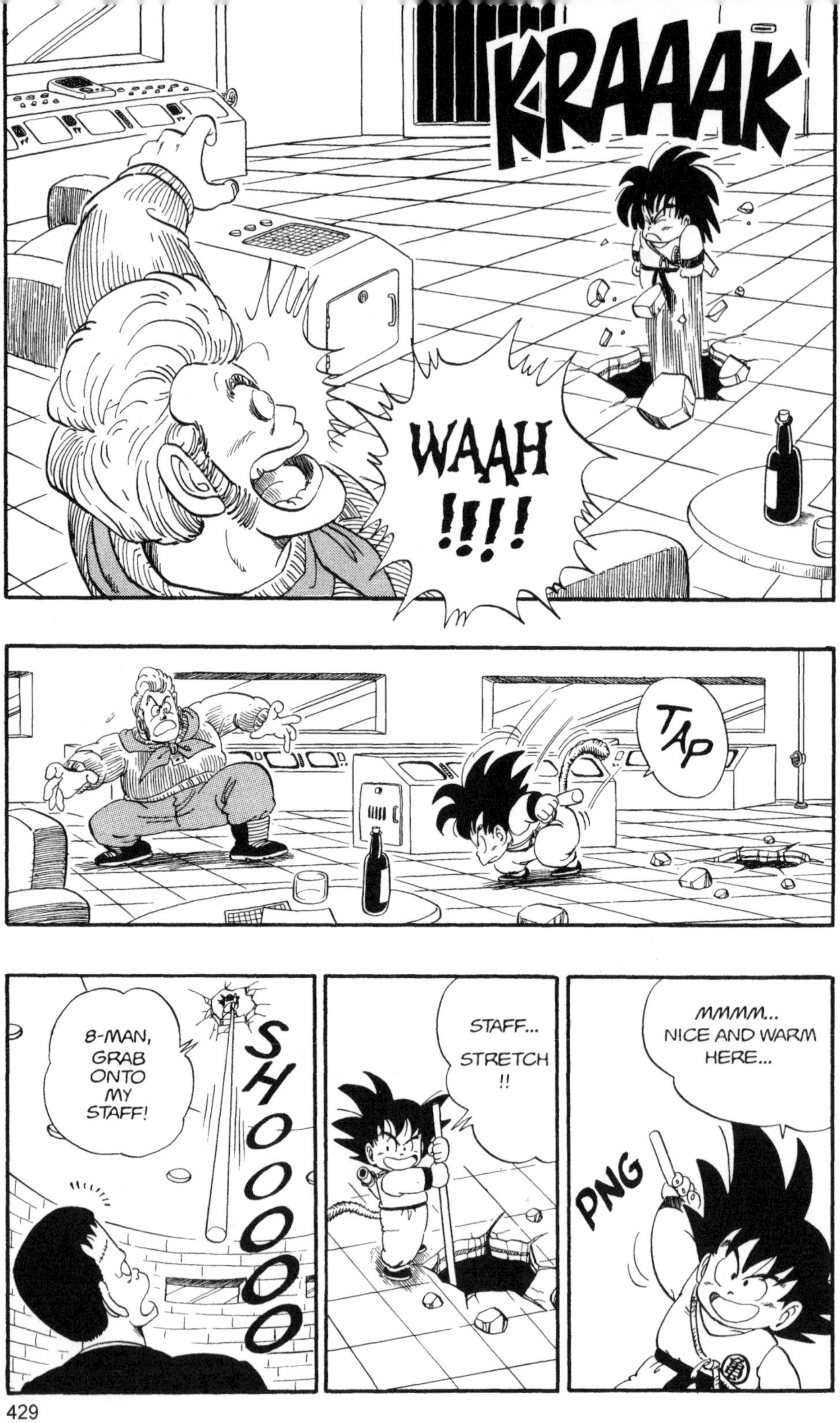
KRAAAK
WAAH !!!!
TAP
MMMM... NICE AND WARM HERE...
PNG
STAFF... STRETCH !!
8-MAN, GRAB ONTO MY STAFF!
SHOOOOO

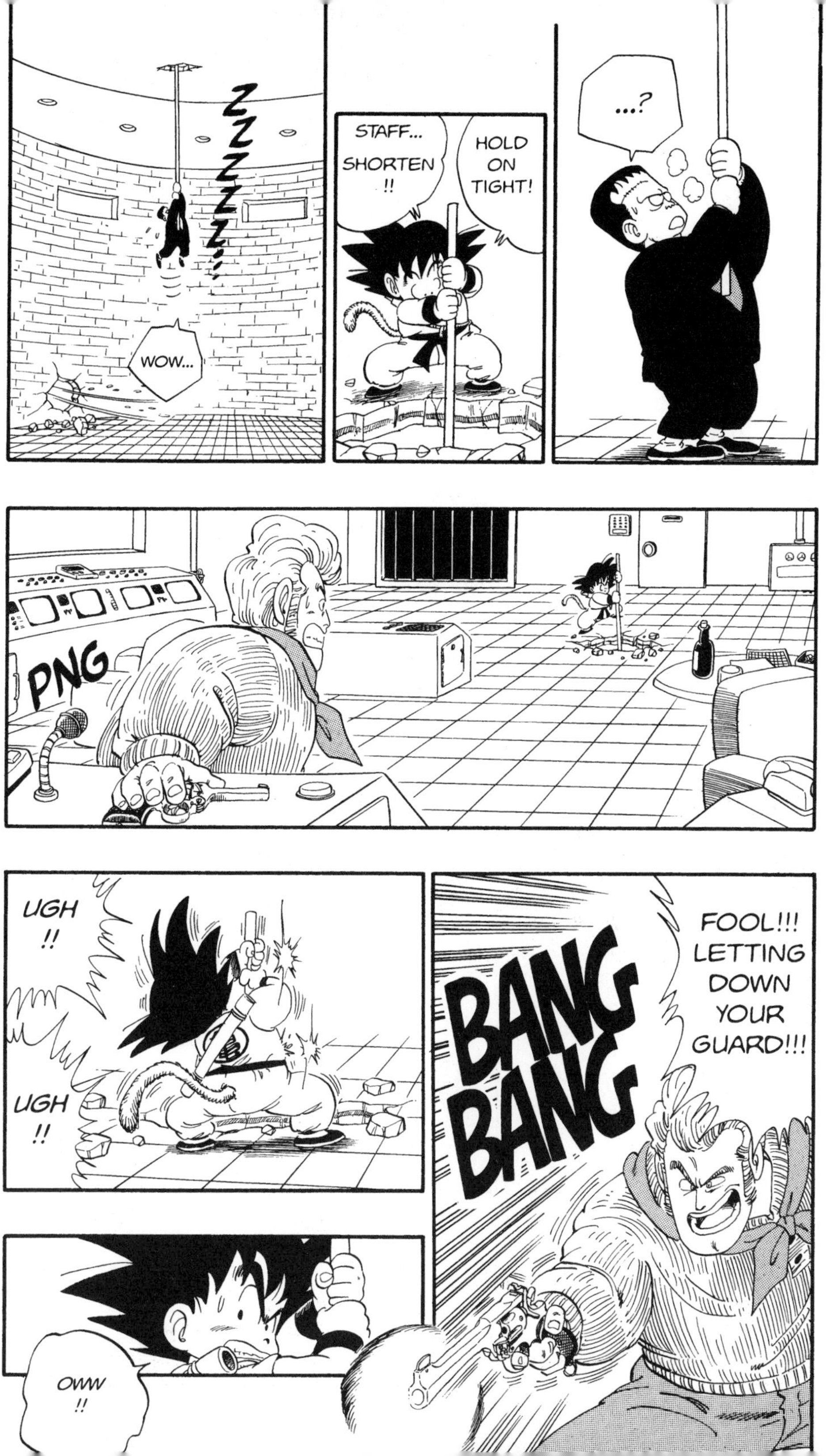
...?
HOLD ON TIGHT!
STAFF... SHORTEN !!
ZZZZZ...
WOW...
PNG
FOOL!!! LETTING DOWN YOUR GUARD!!!
BANG BANG
UGH !!
UGH !!
OWW !!

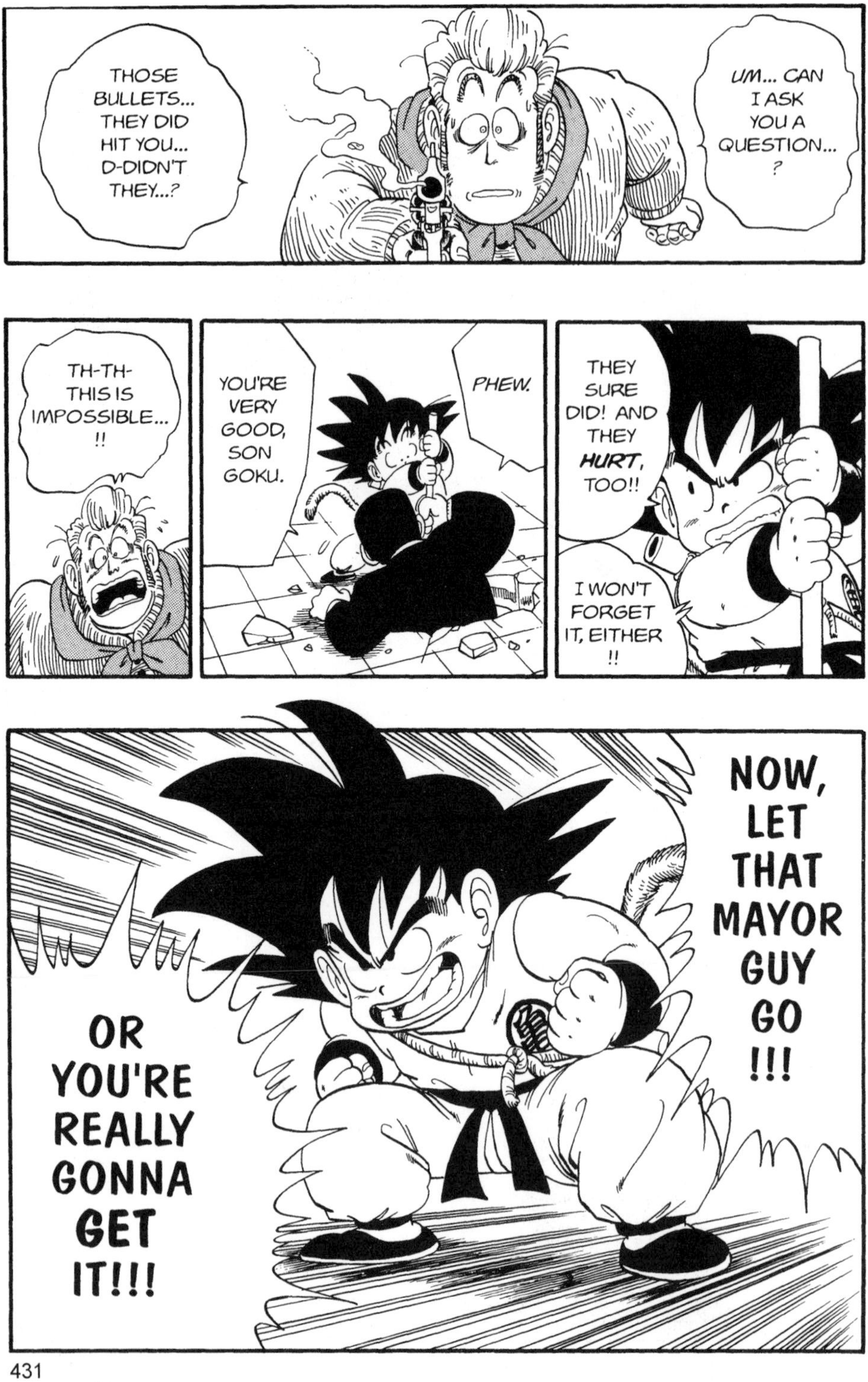
UM... CAN I ASK YOU A QUESTION... ?
THOSE BULLETS... THEY DID HIT YOU... D-DIDN'T THEY...?
THEY SURE DID! AND THEY **HURT**, TOO!!
I WON'T FORGET IT, EITHER !!
PHEW.
YOU'RE VERY GOOD, SON GOKU.
TH-TH-THIS IS IMPOSSIBLE... !!
NOW, LET THAT MAYOR GUY GO !!!
OR YOU'RE REALLY GONNA GET IT!!!

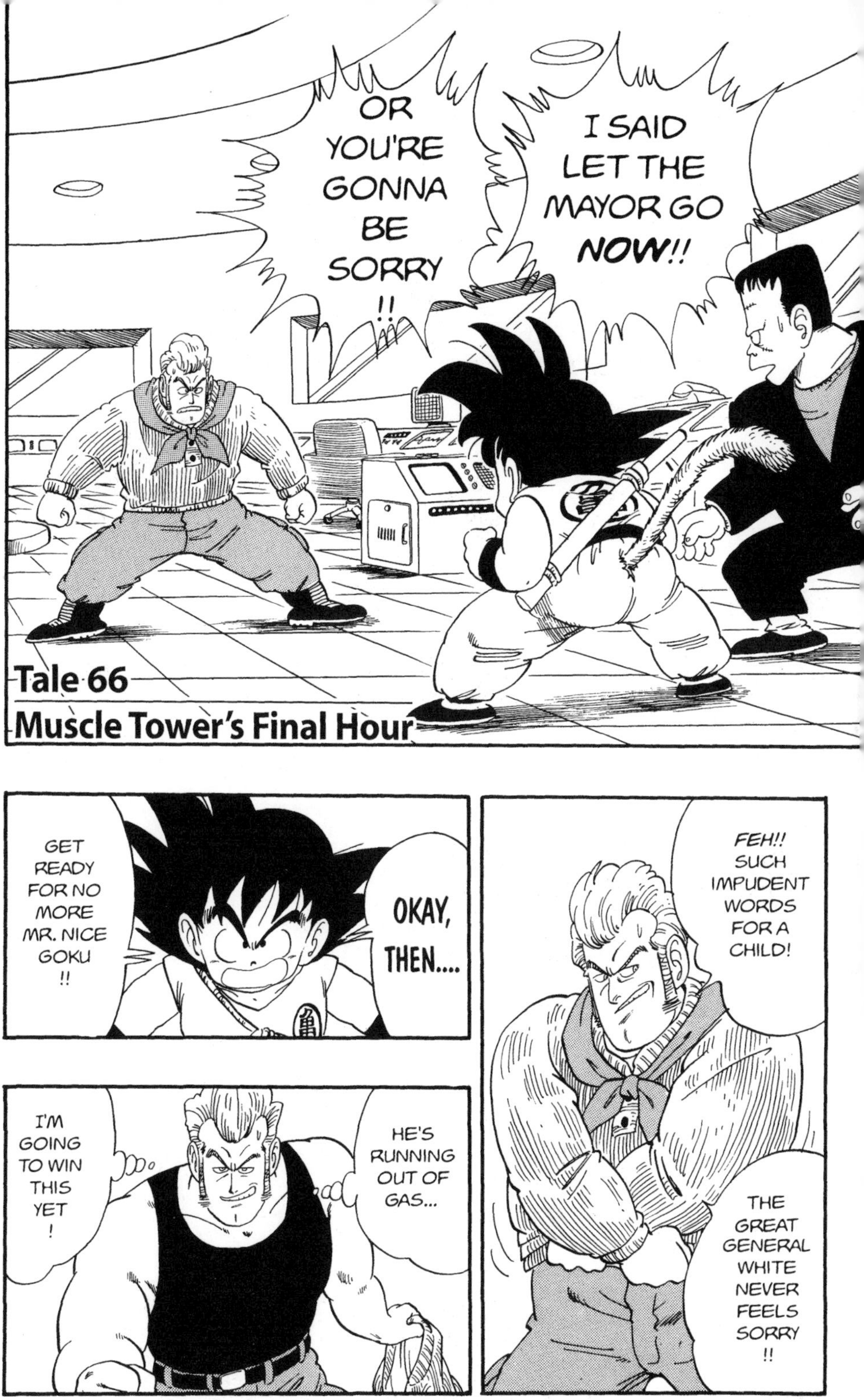
I SAID LET THE MAYOR GO NOW!!
OR YOU'RE GONNA BE SORRY!!
Tale 66
Muscle Tower's Final Hour
FEH!! SUCH IMPUDENT WORDS FOR A CHILD!
THE GREAT GENERAL WHITE NEVER FEELS SORRY!!
OKAY, THEN....
GET READY FOR NO MORE MR. NICE GOKU!!
HE'S RUNNING OUT OF GAS...
I'M GOING TO WIN THIS YET!

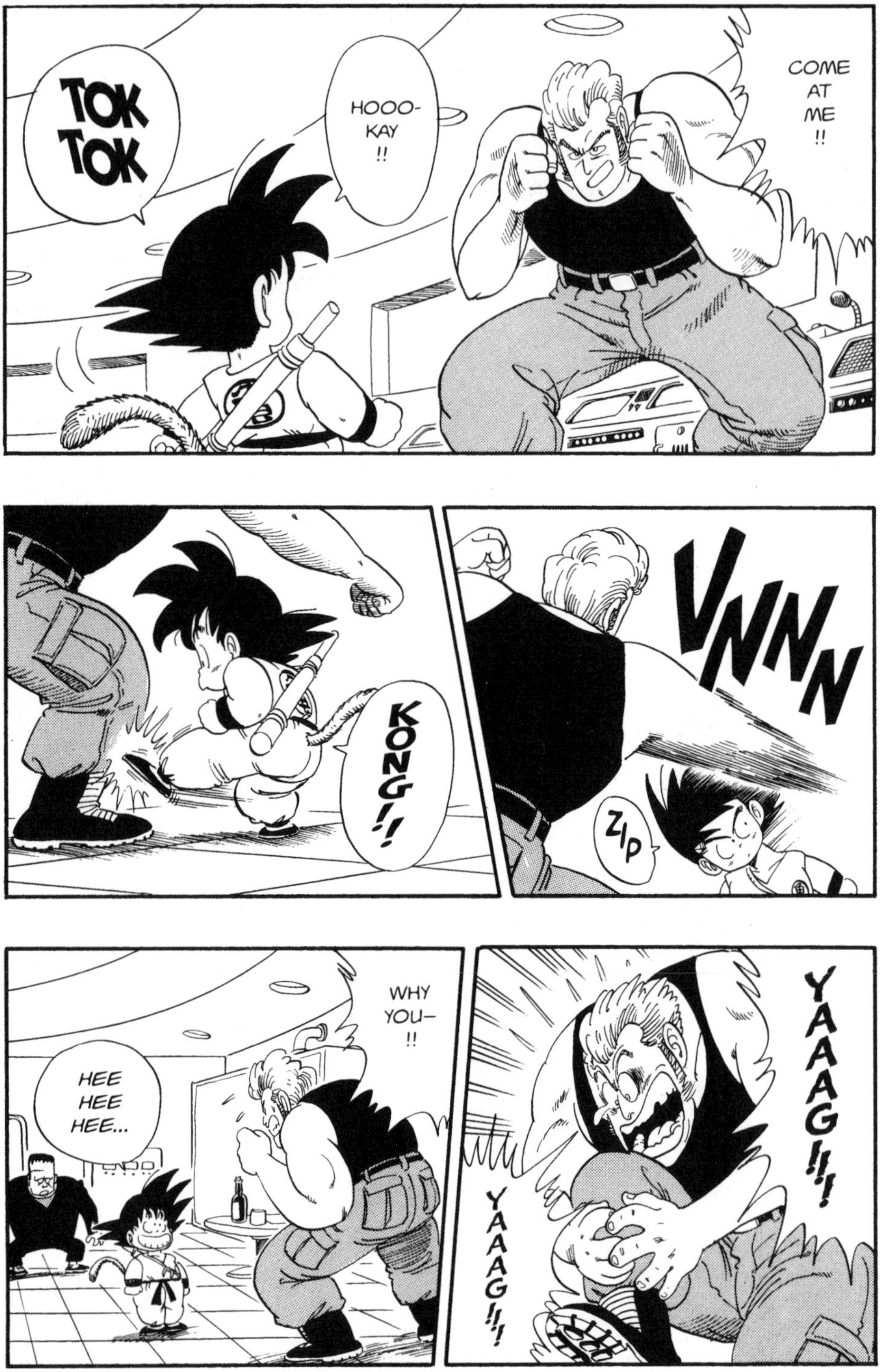

COME AT ME!!
HOOO-KAY!!
TOK TOK
VNNN
ZIP
KONG!!
YAAAG!!!
YAAAG!!!
WHY YOU—!!
HEE HEE HEE...

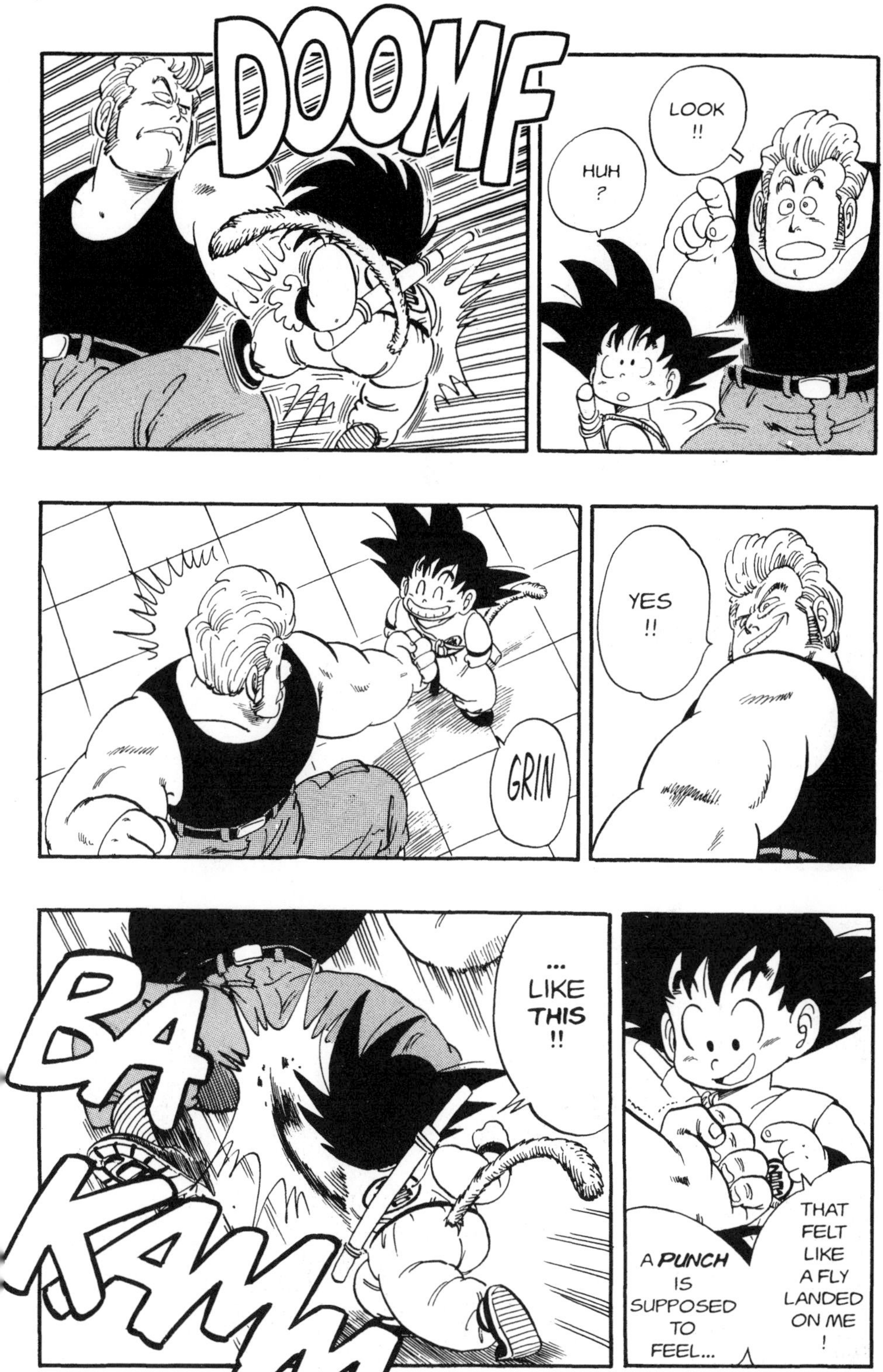
LOOK !!
HUH ?
DOOMF
YES !!
GRIN
THAT FELT LIKE A FLY LANDED ON ME !
A **PUNCH** IS SUPPOSED TO FEEL...
... LIKE **THIS** !!
BA KAMM

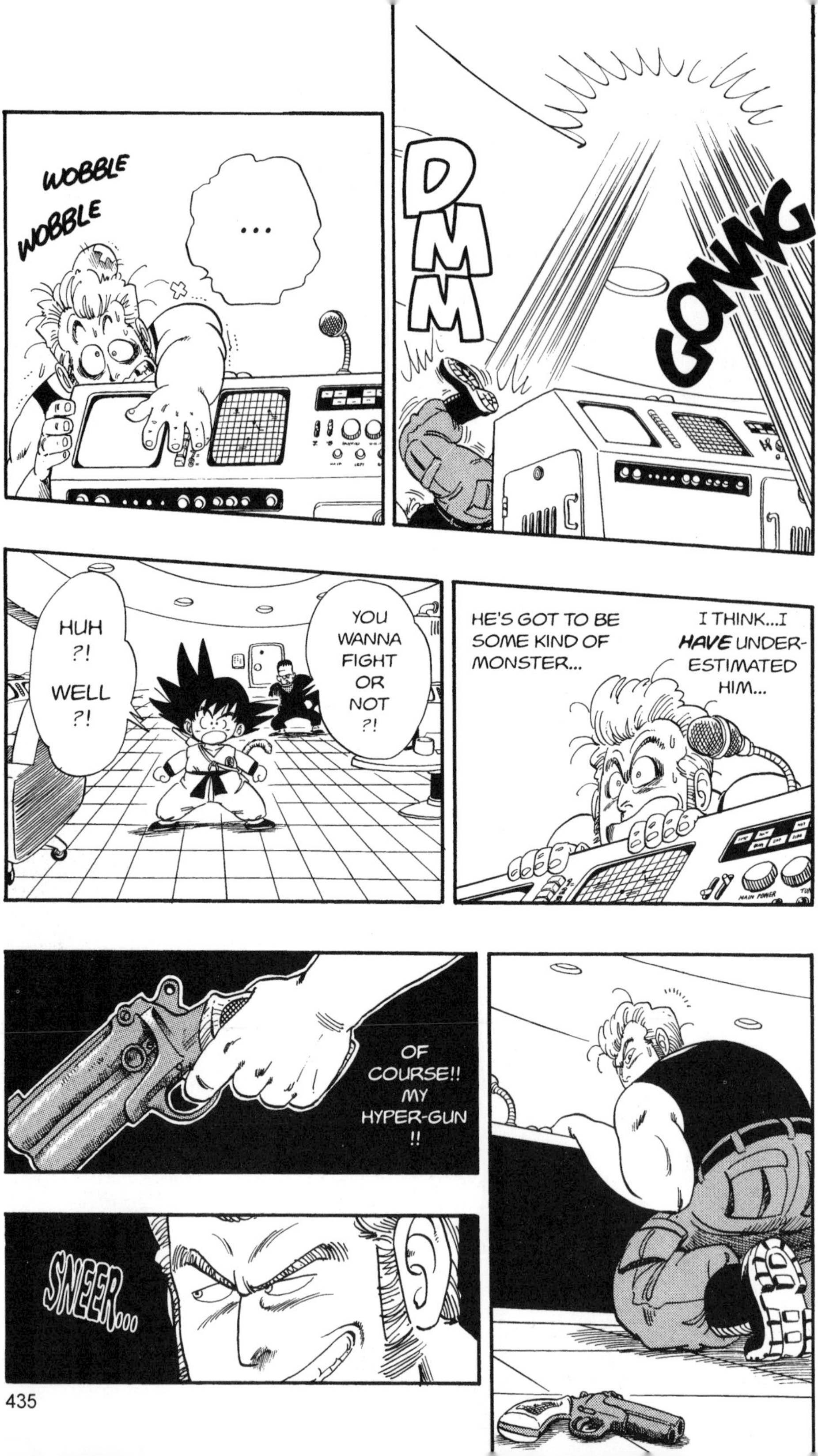
DMM
GONNG
WOBBLE WOBBLE
...
YOU WANNA FIGHT OR NOT ?!
HUH ?! WELL ?!
I THINK...I *HAVE* UNDER-ESTIMATED HIM...
HE'S GOT TO BE SOME KIND OF MONSTER...
MAIN POWER
OF COURSE!! MY HYPER-GUN !!
SNEER...

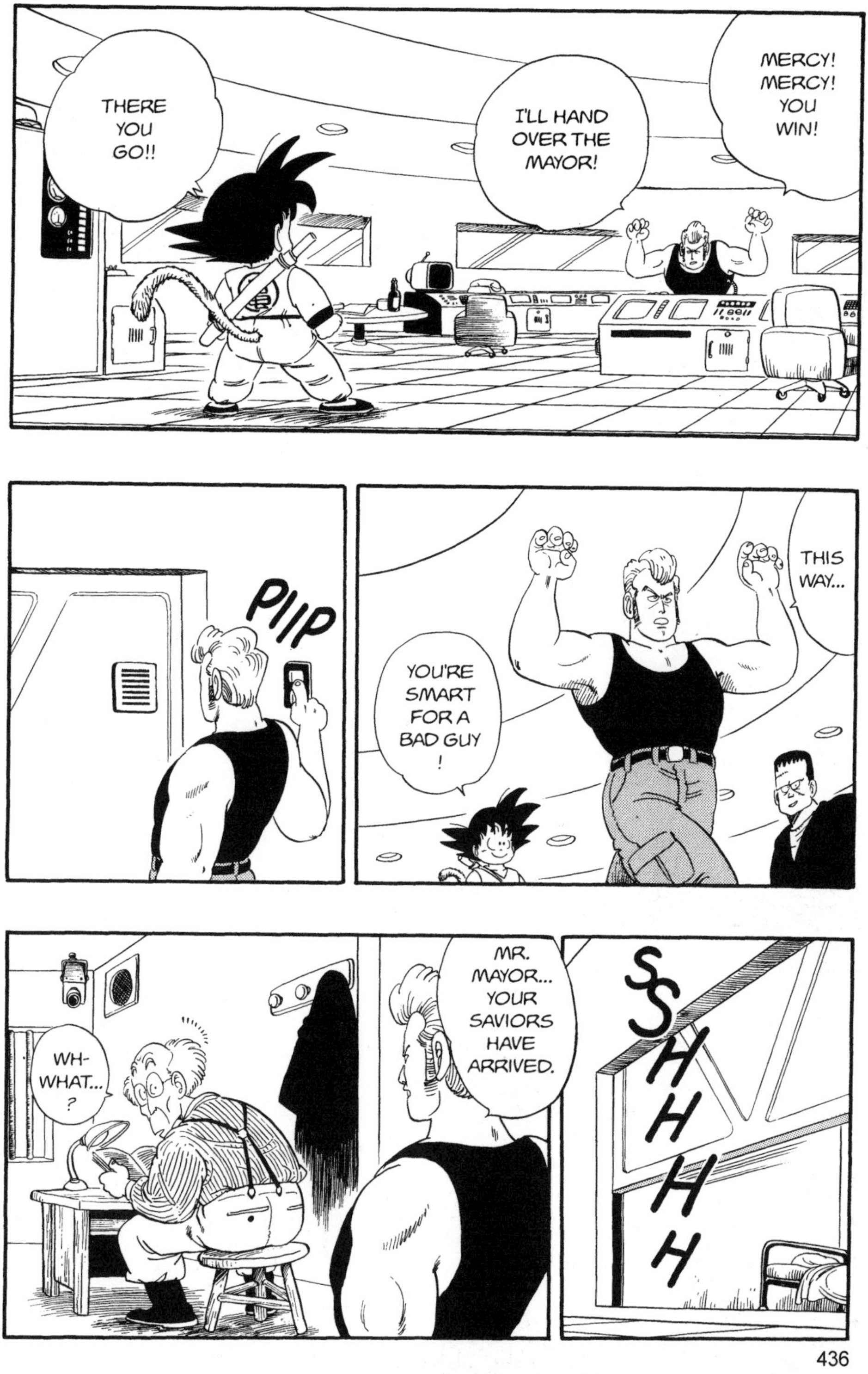
MERCY! MERCY! YOU WIN!
I'LL HAND OVER THE MAYOR!
THERE YOU GO!!
THIS WAY...
YOU'RE SMART FOR A BAD GUY!
PIIP
SSHHHH
MR. MAYOR... YOUR SAVIORS HAVE ARRIVED.
WH-WHAT...?

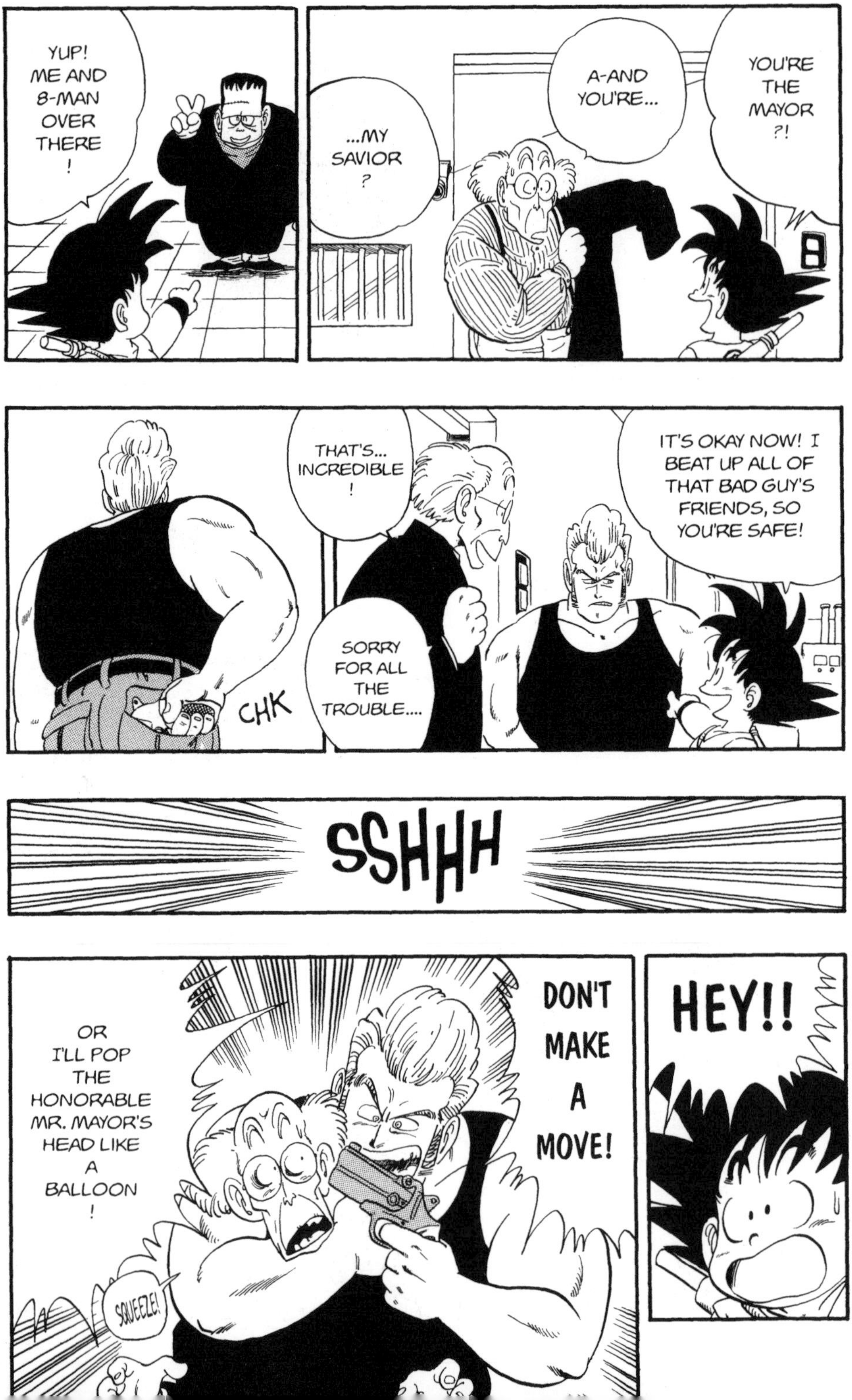
YOU'RE THE MAYOR ?!
A-AND YOU'RE...
...MY SAVIOR ?
YUP! ME AND 8-MAN OVER THERE !
IT'S OKAY NOW! I BEAT UP ALL OF THAT BAD GUY'S FRIENDS, SO YOU'RE SAFE!
THAT'S... INCREDIBLE !
SORRY FOR ALL THE TROUBLE....
CHK
SSHHH
HEY!!
DON'T MAKE A MOVE!
OR I'LL POP THE HONORABLE MR. MAYOR'S HEAD LIKE A BALLOON !
SQUEEZE!

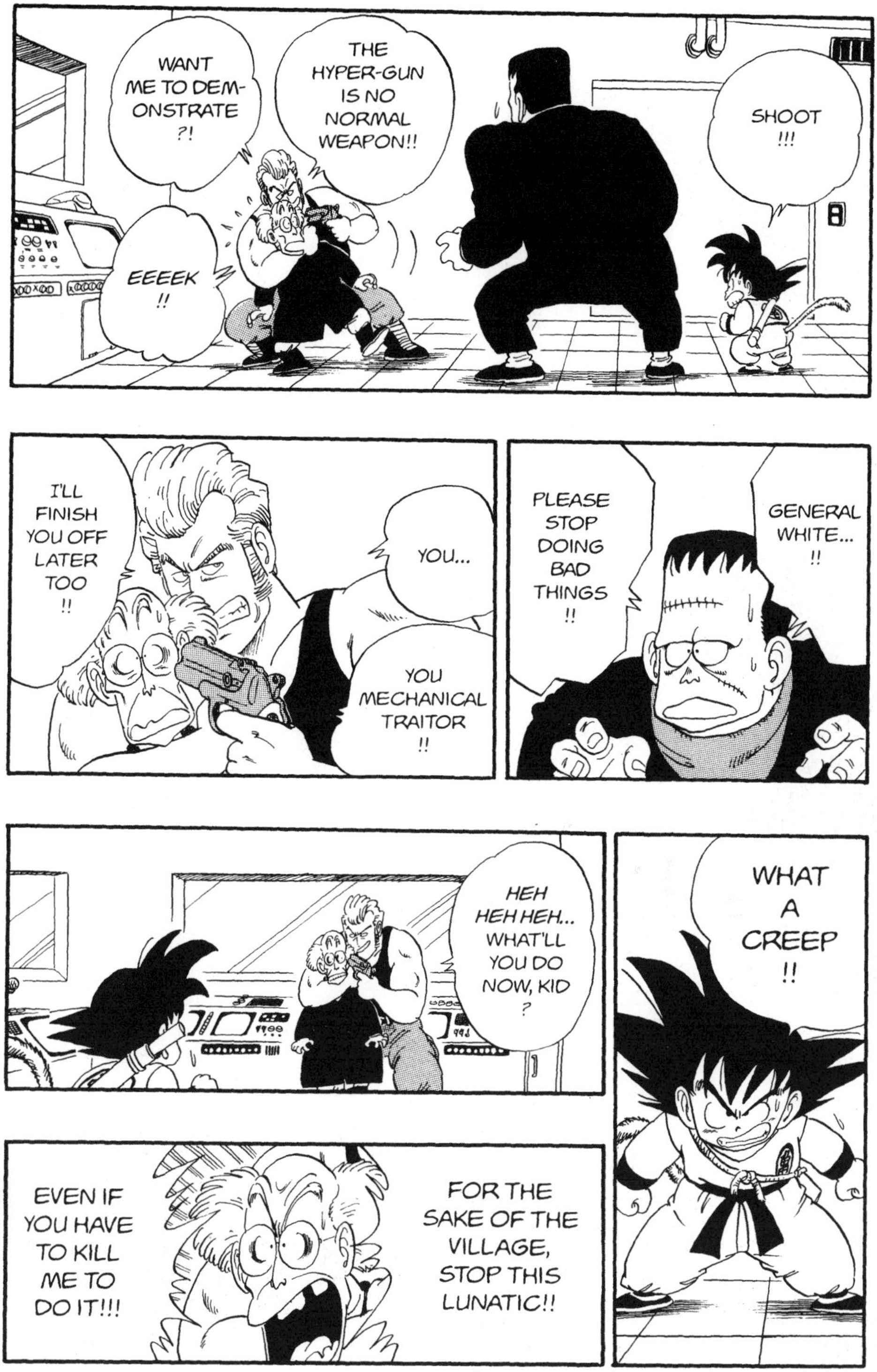
SHOOT !!!
THE HYPER-GUN IS NO NORMAL WEAPON!!
WANT ME TO DEMONSTRATE ?!
EEEEK !!
GENERAL WHITE... !!
PLEASE STOP DOING BAD THINGS !!
YOU...
YOU MECHANICAL TRAITOR !!
I'LL FINISH YOU OFF LATER TOO !!
WHAT A CREEP !!
HEH HEH HEH... WHAT'LL YOU DO NOW, KID ?
FOR THE SAKE OF THE VILLAGE, STOP THIS LUNATIC!!
EVEN IF YOU HAVE TO KILL ME TO DO IT!!!

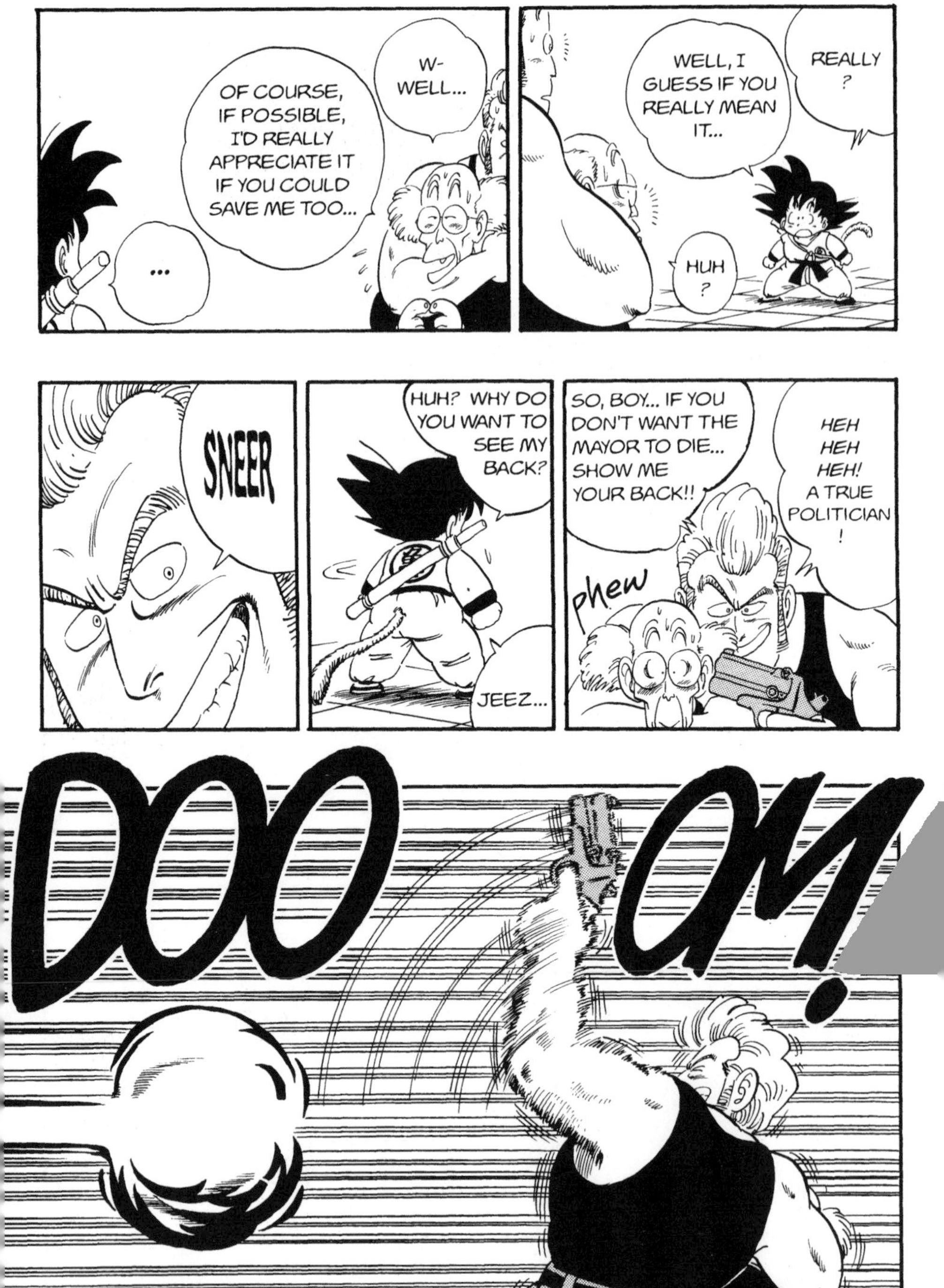
REALLY ?
WELL, I GUESS IF YOU REALLY MEAN IT...
HUH ?
W- WELL...
OF COURSE, IF POSSIBLE, I'D REALLY APPRECIATE IT IF YOU COULD SAVE ME TOO...
...
HEH HEH HEH! A TRUE POLITICIAN !
SO, BOY... IF YOU DON'T WANT THE MAYOR TO DIE... SHOW ME YOUR BACK!!
phew
HUH? WHY DO YOU WANT TO SEE MY BACK?
JEEZ...
SNEER
DOOOM!

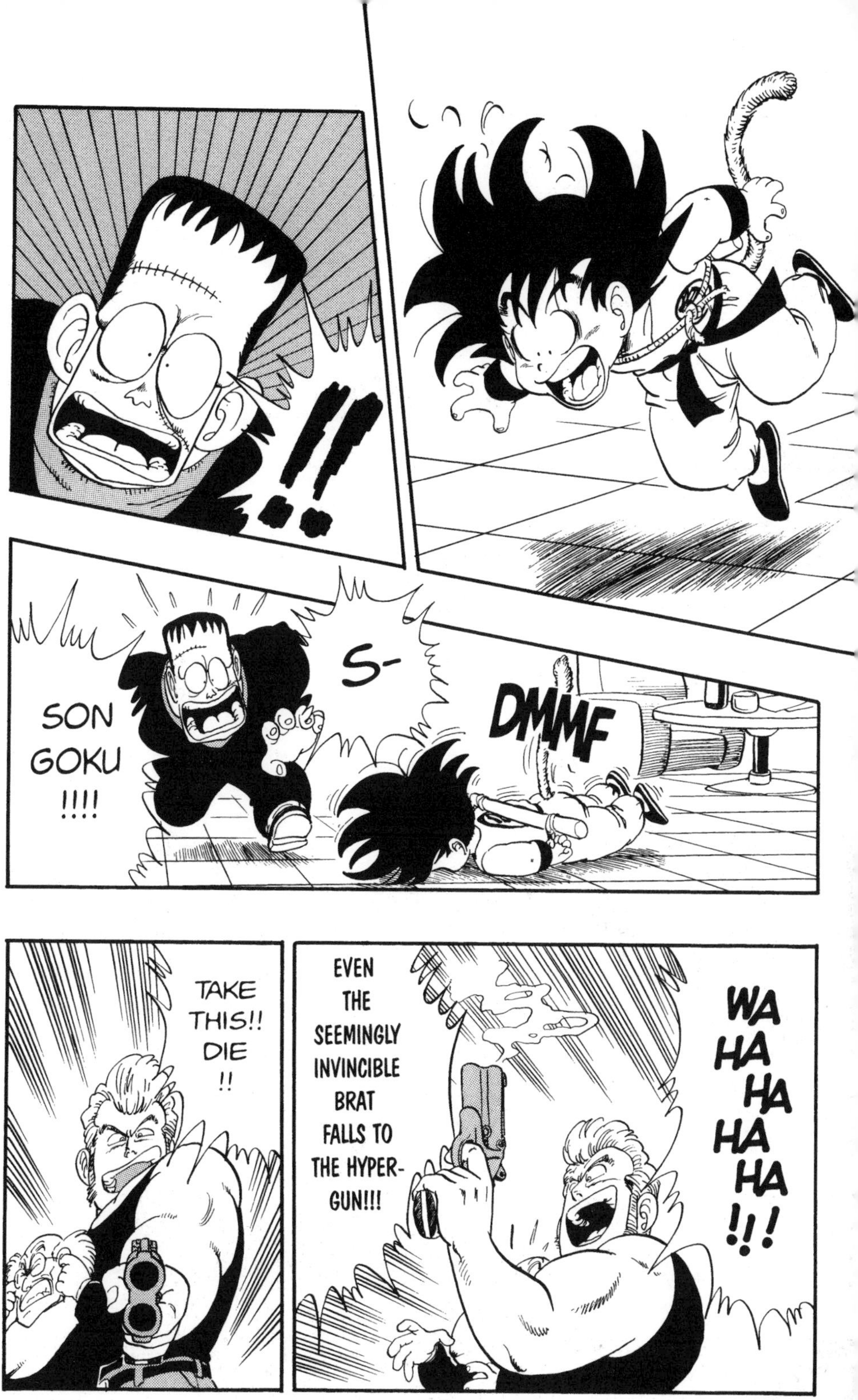
!!
DMMF
S-
SON GOKU !!!!
WA HA HA HA HA HA !!!
EVEN THE SEEMINGLY INVINCIBLE BRAT FALLS TO THE HYPER-GUN!!!
TAKE THIS!! DIE !!

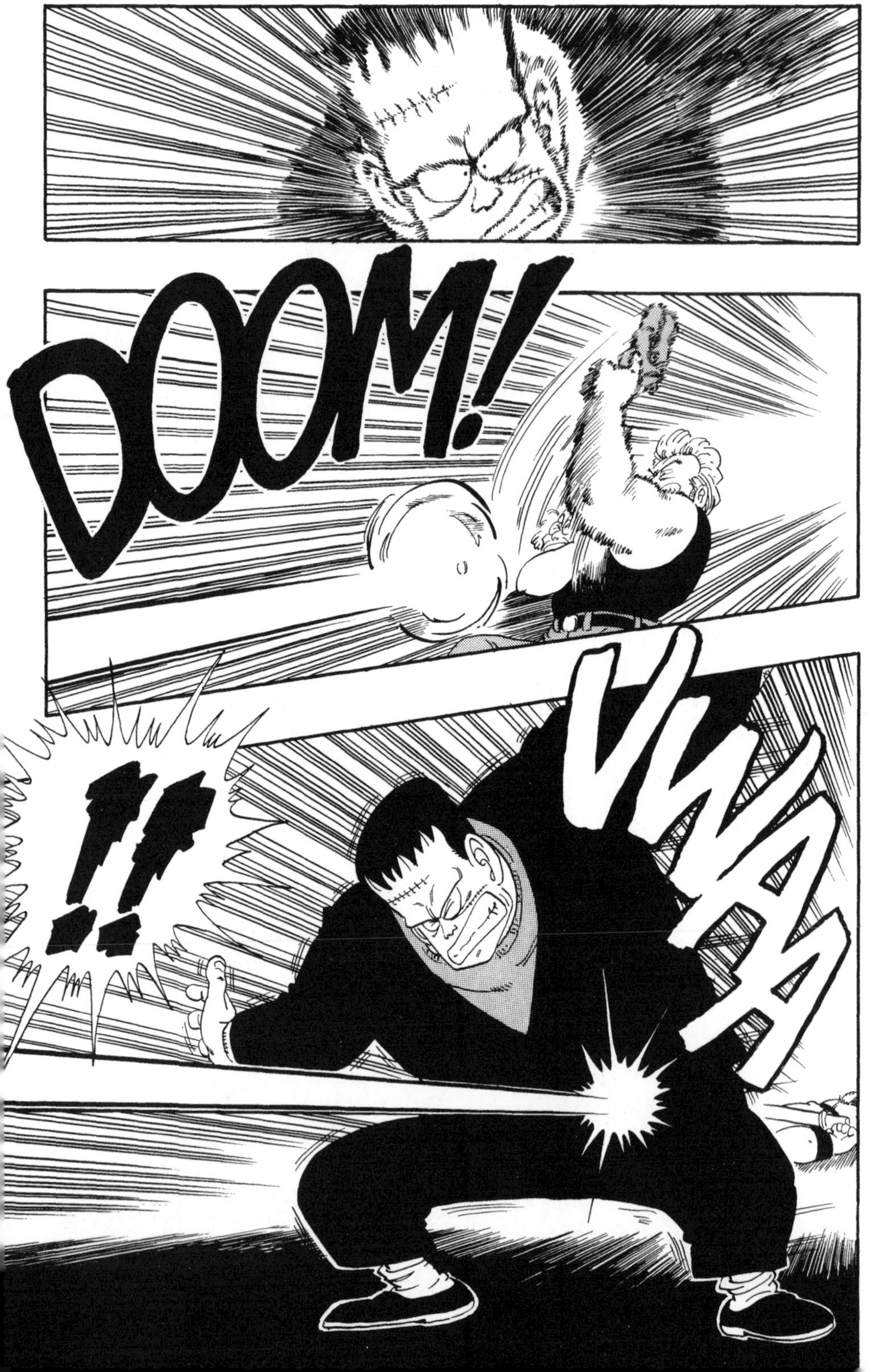
DOOM!
VWAA
!!

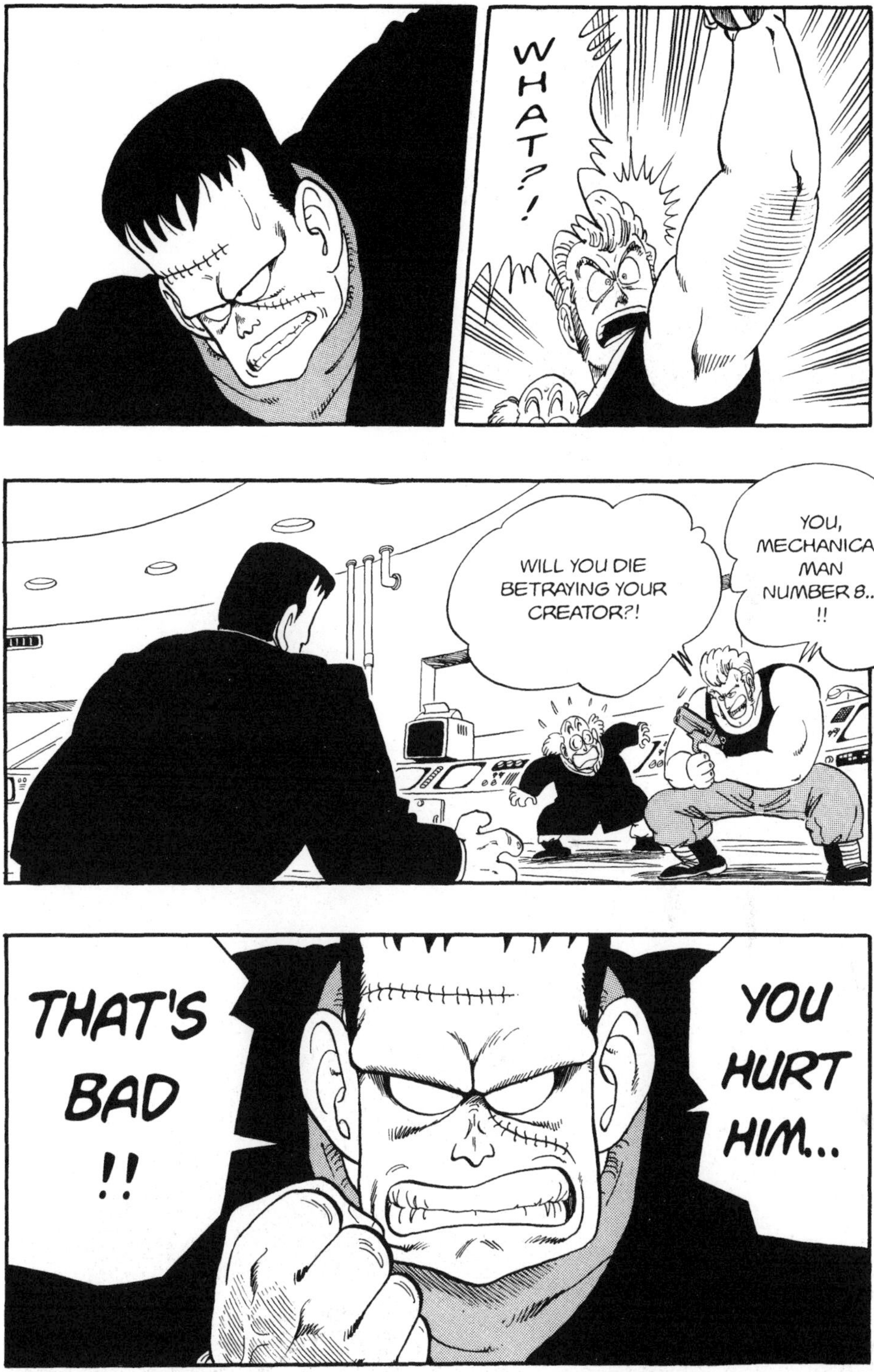
WHAT?!
YOU, MECHANICAL MAN NUMBER 8... !!
WILL YOU DIE BETRAYING YOUR CREATOR?!
YOU HURT HIM...
THAT'S BAD !!

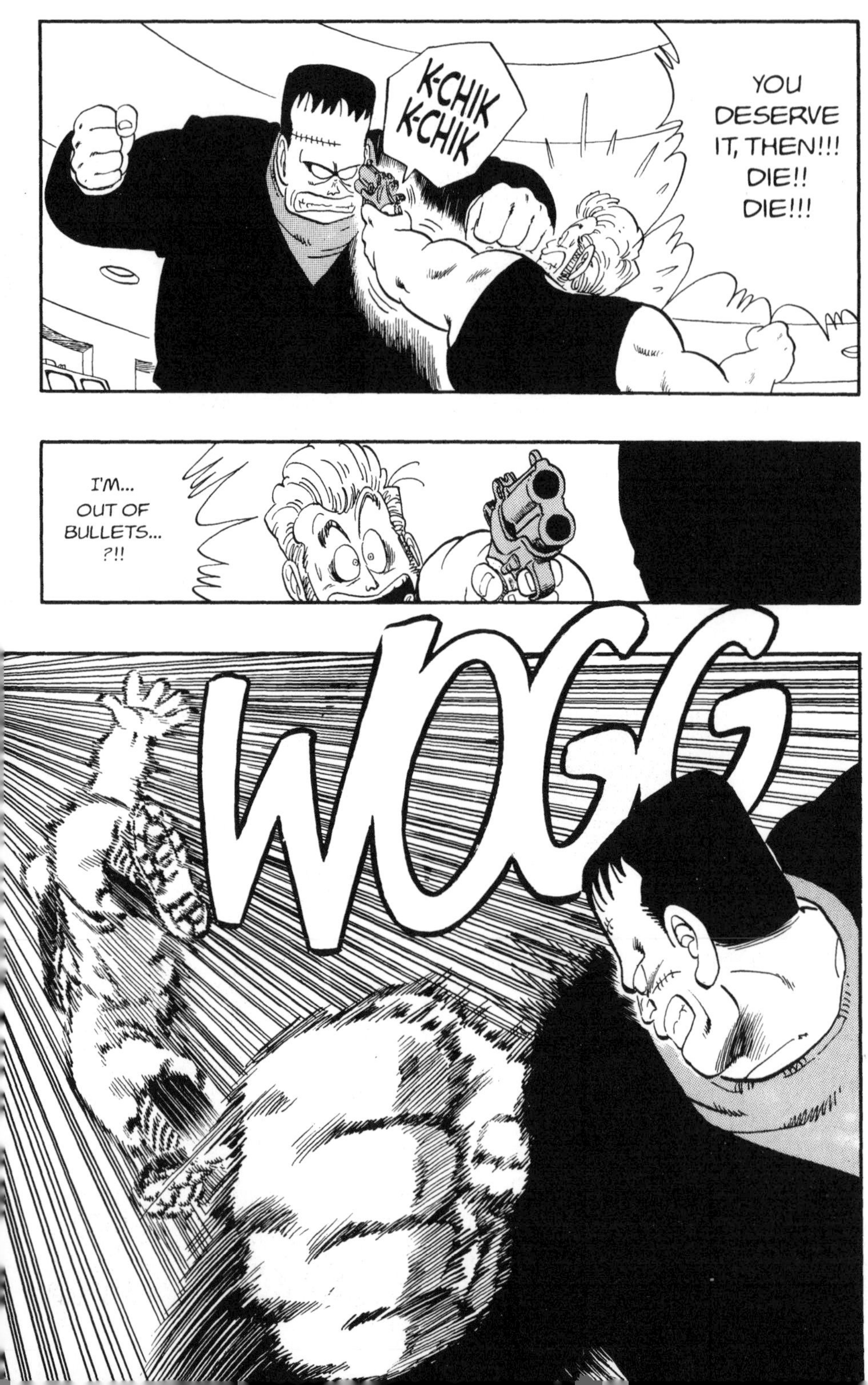
YOU DESERVE IT, THEN!!! DIE!! DIE!!!
K-CHIK K-CHIK
I'M... OUT OF BULLETS... ?!!
WOGG

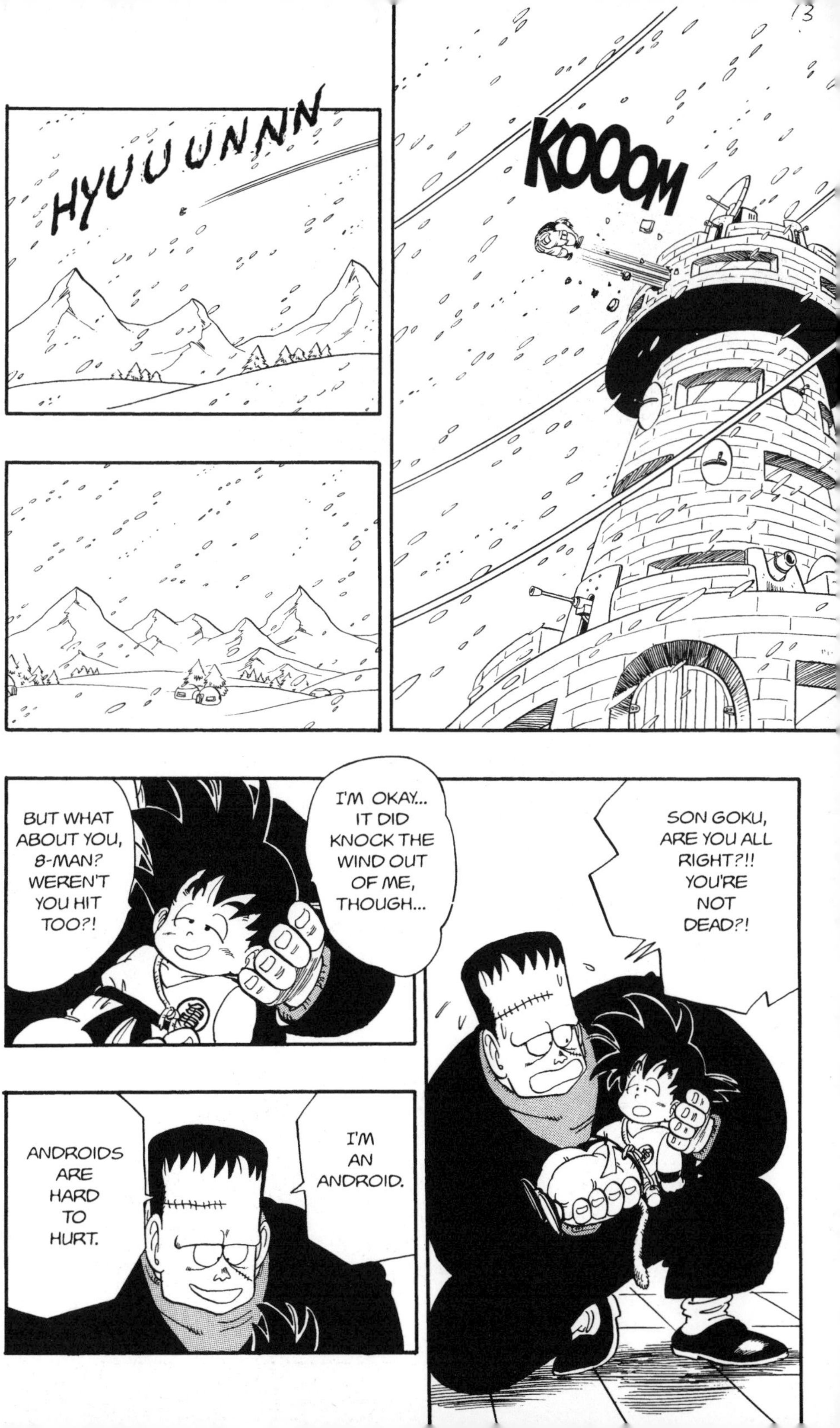
KOOOM
HYUUUNNN
SON GOKU, ARE YOU ALL RIGHT?!! YOU'RE NOT DEAD?!
I'M OKAY... IT DID KNOCK THE WIND OUT OF ME, THOUGH...
BUT WHAT ABOUT YOU, 8-MAN? WEREN'T YOU HIT TOO?!
I'M AN ANDROID.
ANDROIDS ARE HARD TO HURT.

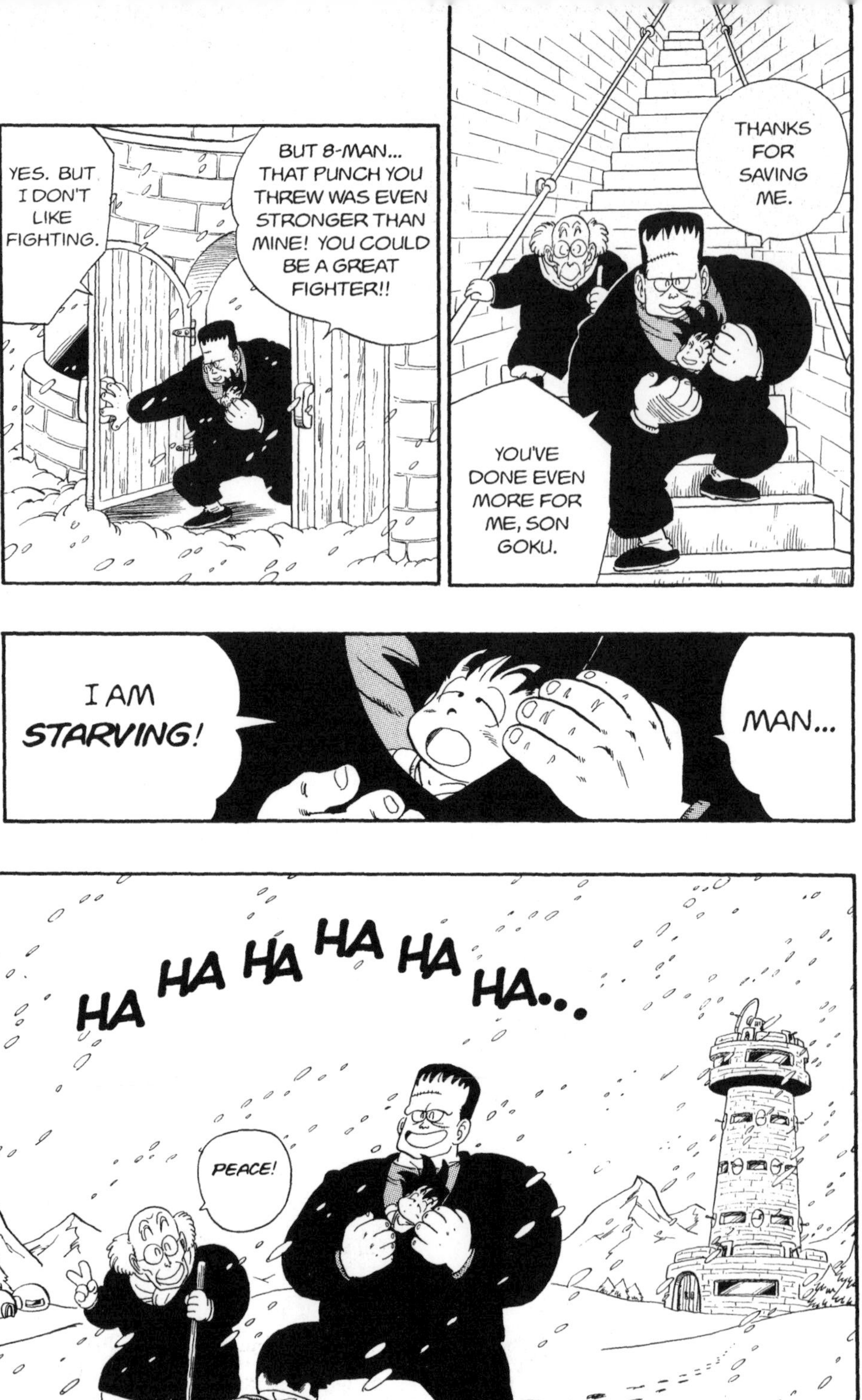
THANKS FOR SAVING ME.
YOU'VE DONE EVEN MORE FOR ME, SON GOKU.
BUT 8-MAN... THAT PUNCH YOU THREW WAS EVEN STRONGER THAN MINE! YOU COULD BE A GREAT FIGHTER!!
YES. BUT I DON'T LIKE FIGHTING.
MAN...
I AM *STARVING*!
HA HA HA HA HA HA...
PEACE!

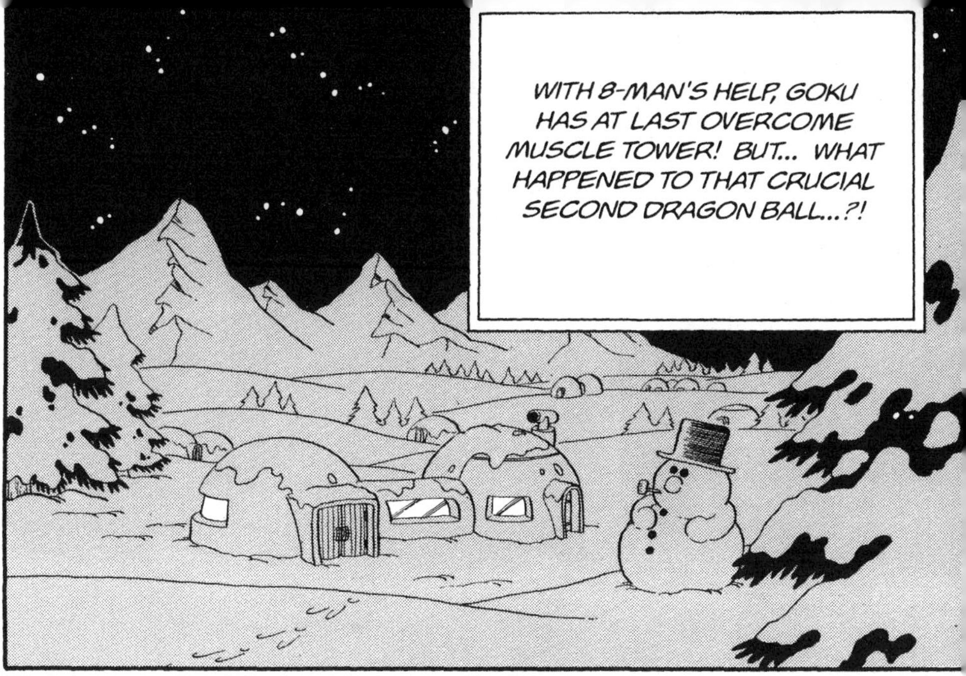
WITH 8-MAN'S HELP, GOKU HAS AT LAST OVERCOME MUSCLE TOWER! BUT... WHAT HAPPENED TO THAT CRUCIAL SECOND DRAGON BALL...?!

Tale 67 • Go West, Young Goku...

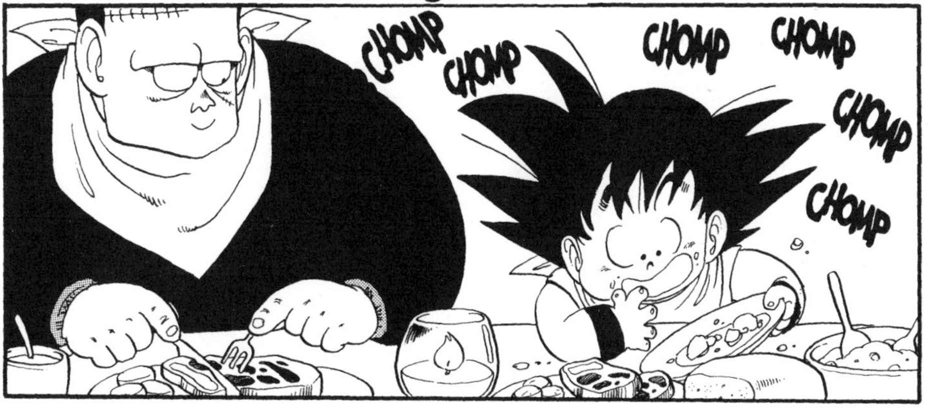
CHOMP
CHOMP
CHOMP
CHOMP
CHOMP
CHOMP

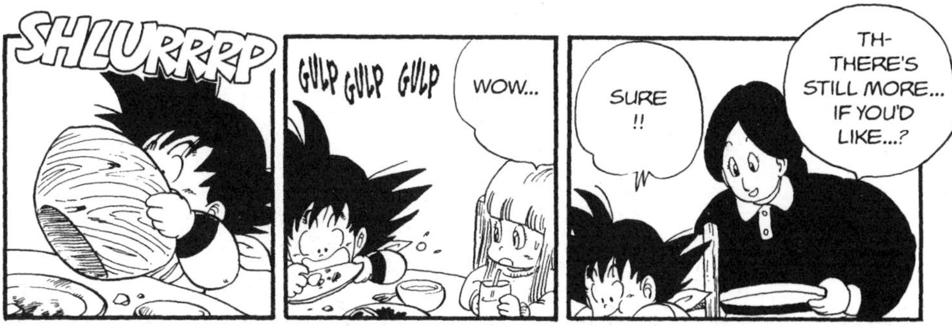
TH-THERE'S STILL MORE... IF YOU'D LIKE...?
SURE !!
WOW...
GULP GULP GULP
SHLURRRP

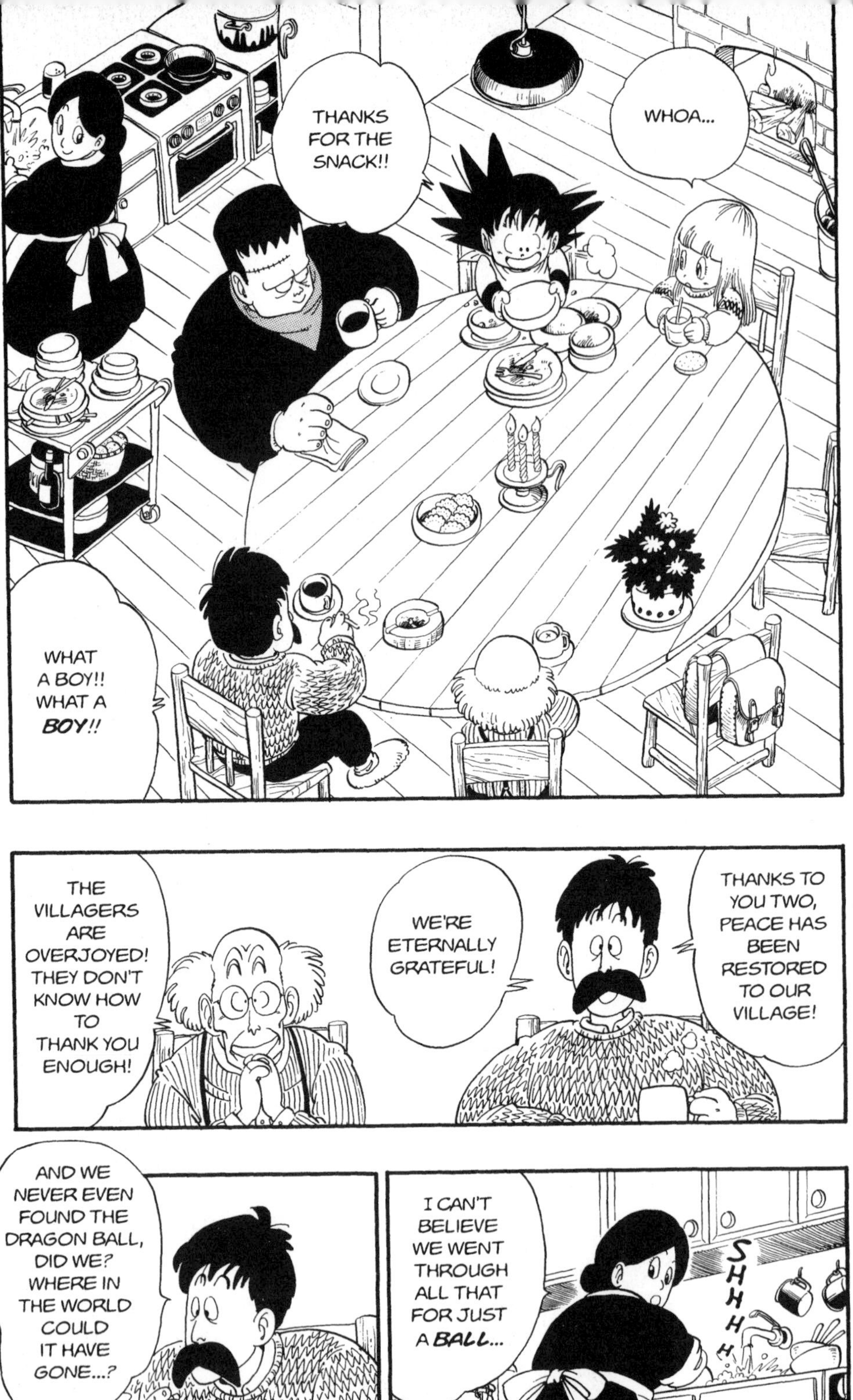
WHOA...
THANKS FOR THE SNACK!!
WHAT A BOY!! WHAT A BOY!!
THANKS TO YOU TWO, PEACE HAS BEEN RESTORED TO OUR VILLAGE!
WE'RE ETERNALLY GRATEFUL!
THE VILLAGERS ARE OVERJOYED! THEY DON'T KNOW HOW TO THANK YOU ENOUGH!
I CAN'T BELIEVE WE WENT THROUGH ALL THAT FOR JUST A BALL...
SHHHHH
AND WE NEVER EVEN FOUND THE DRAGON BALL, DID WE? WHERE IN THE WORLD COULD IT HAVE GONE...?

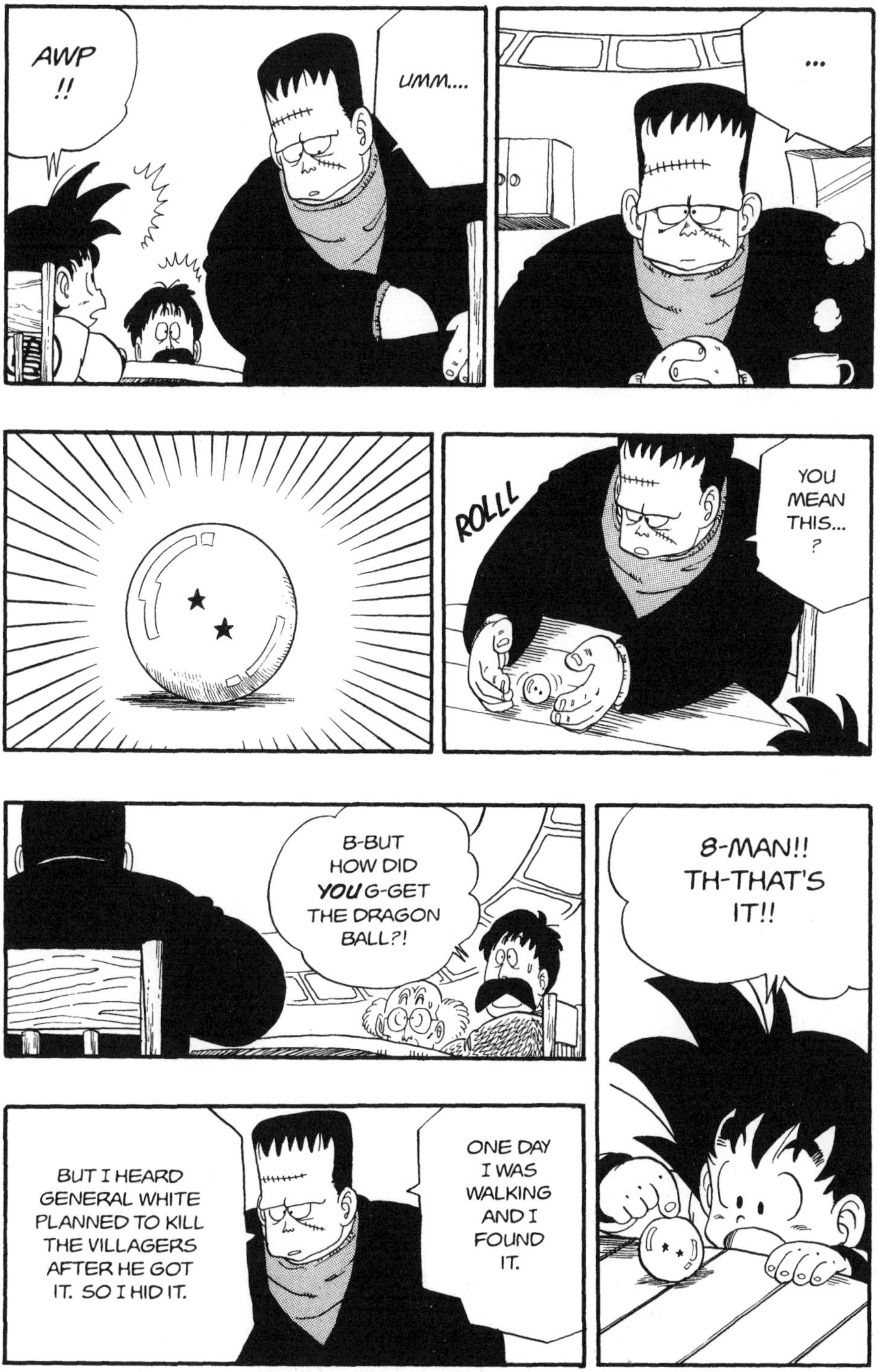
...
UMM....
AWP !!
YOU MEAN THIS... ?
ROLLL
8-MAN!! TH-THAT'S IT!!
B-BUT HOW DID **YOU** G-GET THE DRAGON BALL?!
ONE DAY I WAS WALKING AND I FOUND IT.
BUT I HEARD GENERAL WHITE PLANNED TO KILL THE VILLAGERS AFTER HE GOT IT. SO I HID IT.

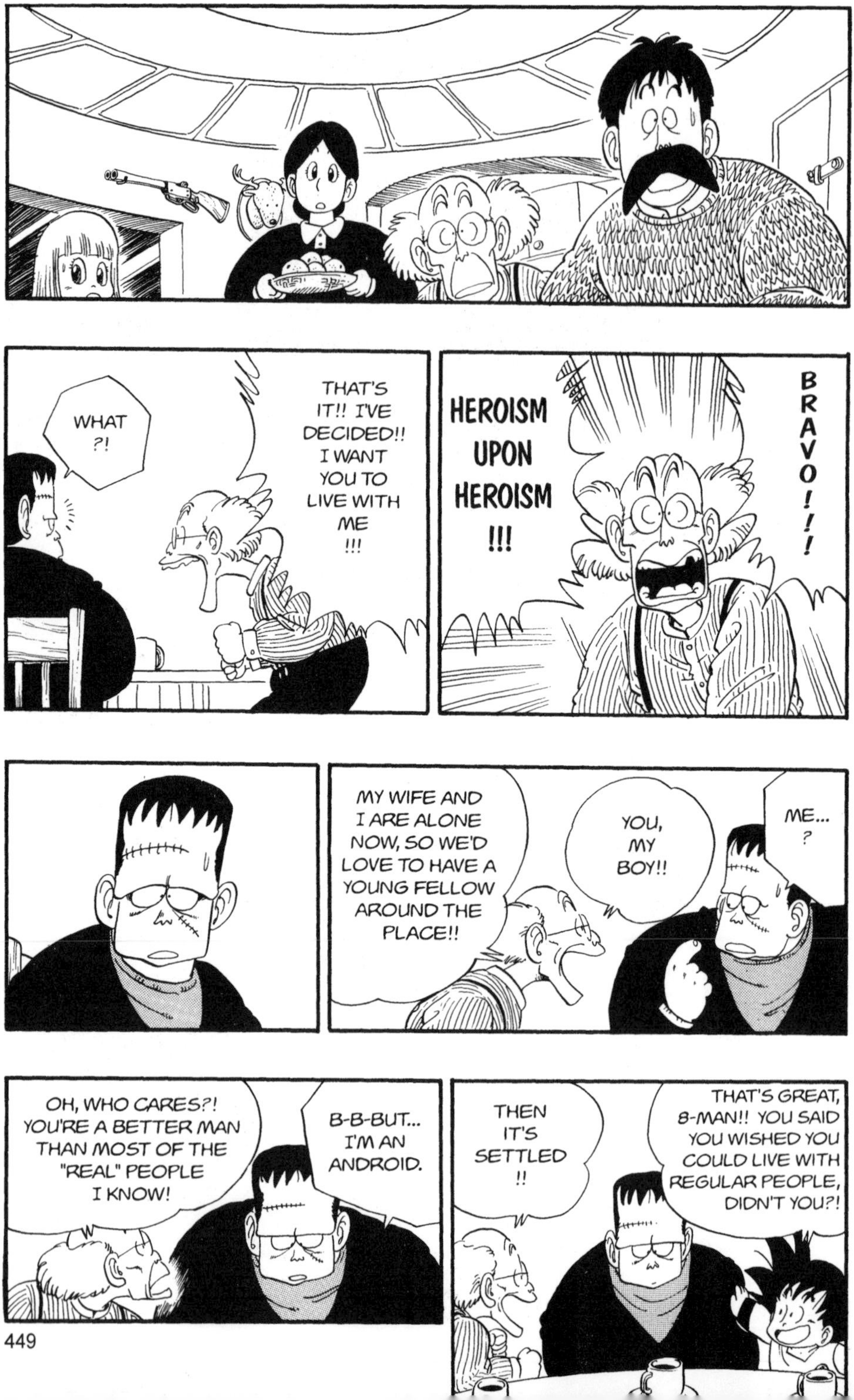
BRAVO!!!
HEROISM UPON HEROISM!!!
THAT'S IT!! I'VE DECIDED!! I WANT YOU TO LIVE WITH ME!!!
WHAT?!
ME...?
YOU, MY BOY!!
MY WIFE AND I ARE ALONE NOW, SO WE'D LOVE TO HAVE A YOUNG FELLOW AROUND THE PLACE!!
THAT'S GREAT, 8-MAN!! YOU SAID YOU WISHED YOU COULD LIVE WITH REGULAR PEOPLE, DIDN'T YOU?!
THEN IT'S SETTLED!!
B-B-BUT... I'M AN ANDROID.
OH, WHO CARES?! YOU'RE A BETTER MAN THAN MOST OF THE "REAL" PEOPLE I KNOW!

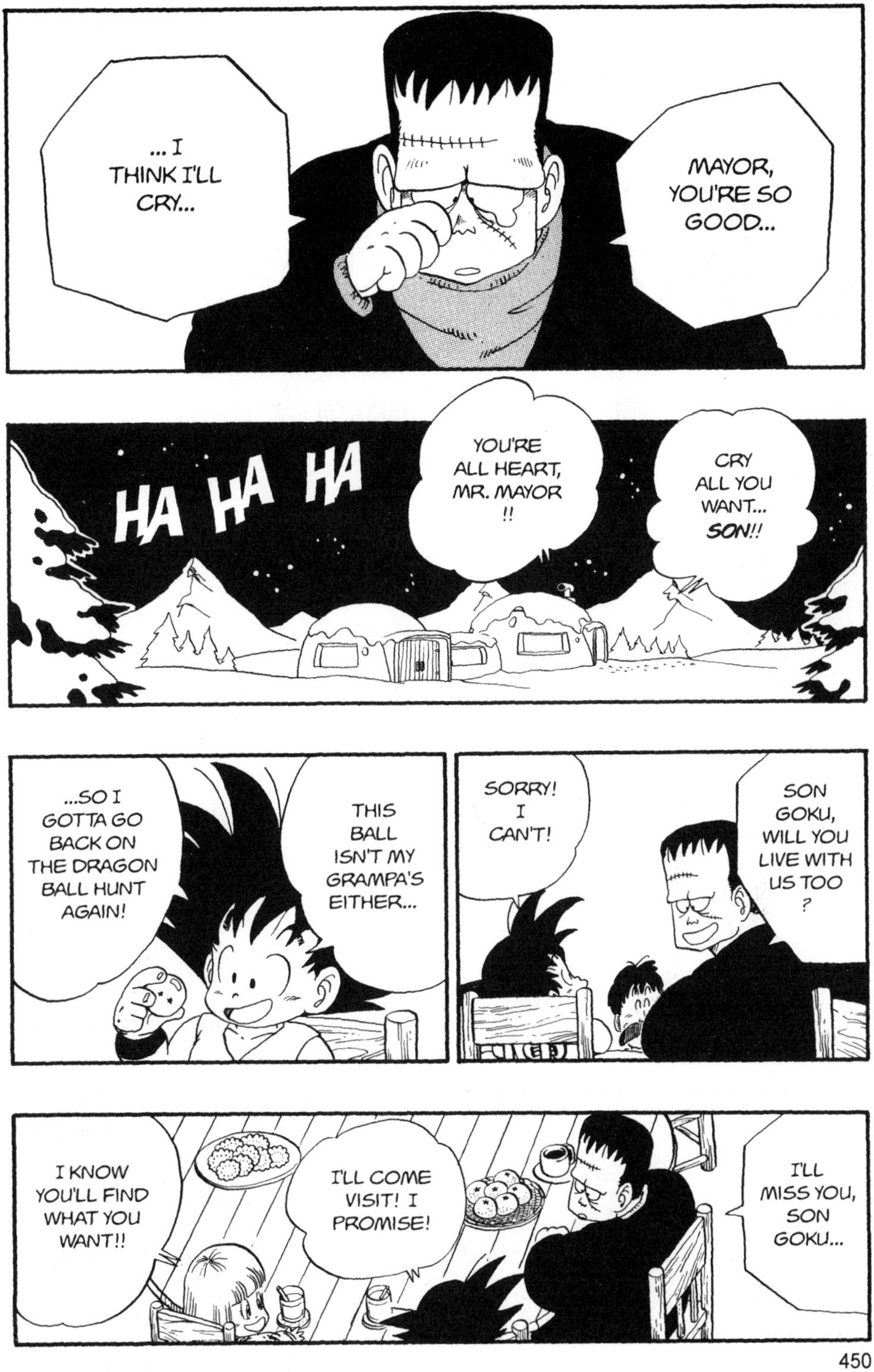
MAYOR, YOU'RE SO GOOD...
...I THINK I'LL CRY...
CRY ALL YOU WANT... SON!!
YOU'RE ALL HEART, MR. MAYOR !!
HA HA HA
SON GOKU, WILL YOU LIVE WITH US TOO ?
SORRY! I CAN'T!
THIS BALL ISN'T MY GRAMPA'S EITHER...
...SO I GOTTA GO BACK ON THE DRAGON BALL HUNT AGAIN!
I'LL MISS YOU, SON GOKU...
I'LL COME VISIT! I PROMISE!
I KNOW YOU'LL FIND WHAT YOU WANT!!

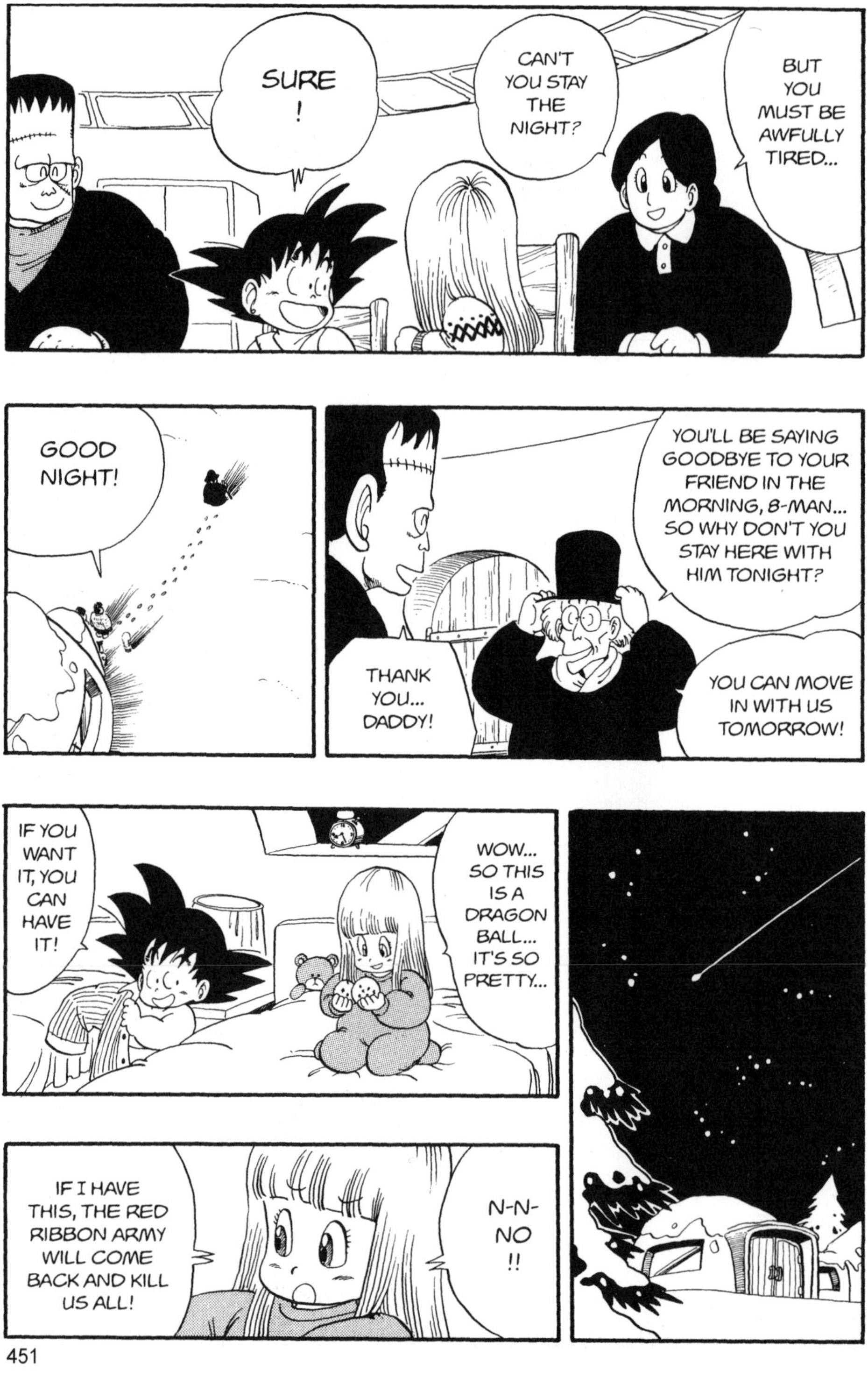
BUT YOU MUST BE AWFULLY TIRED...
CAN'T YOU STAY THE NIGHT?
SURE !
YOU'LL BE SAYING GOODBYE TO YOUR FRIEND IN THE MORNING, 8-MAN... SO WHY DON'T YOU STAY HERE WITH HIM TONIGHT?
YOU CAN MOVE IN WITH US TOMORROW!
THANK YOU... DADDY!
GOOD NIGHT!
WOW... SO THIS IS A DRAGON BALL... IT'S SO PRETTY...
IF YOU WANT IT, YOU CAN HAVE IT!
N-N-NO !!
IF I HAVE THIS, THE RED RIBBON ARMY WILL COME BACK AND KILL US ALL!

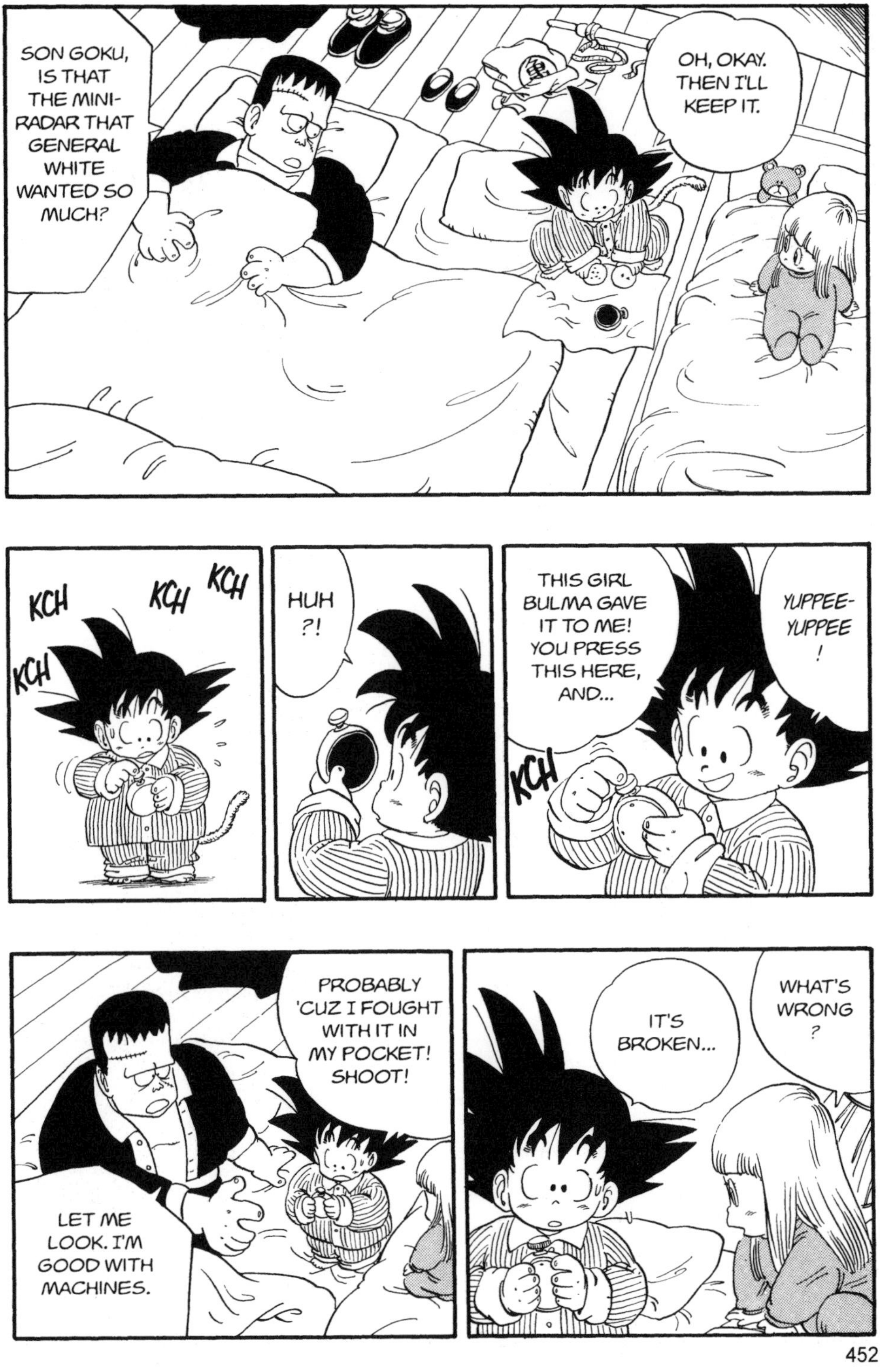
OH, OKAY. THEN I'LL KEEP IT.
SON GOKU, IS THAT THE MINI-RADAR THAT GENERAL WHITE WANTED SO MUCH?
YUPPEE-YUPPEE!
THIS GIRL BULMA GAVE IT TO ME! YOU PRESS THIS HERE, AND...
KCH
HUH ?!
KCH
KCH
KCH
KCH
WHAT'S WRONG?
IT'S BROKEN...
PROBABLY 'CUZ I FOUGHT WITH IT IN MY POCKET! SHOOT!
LET ME LOOK. I'M GOOD WITH MACHINES.

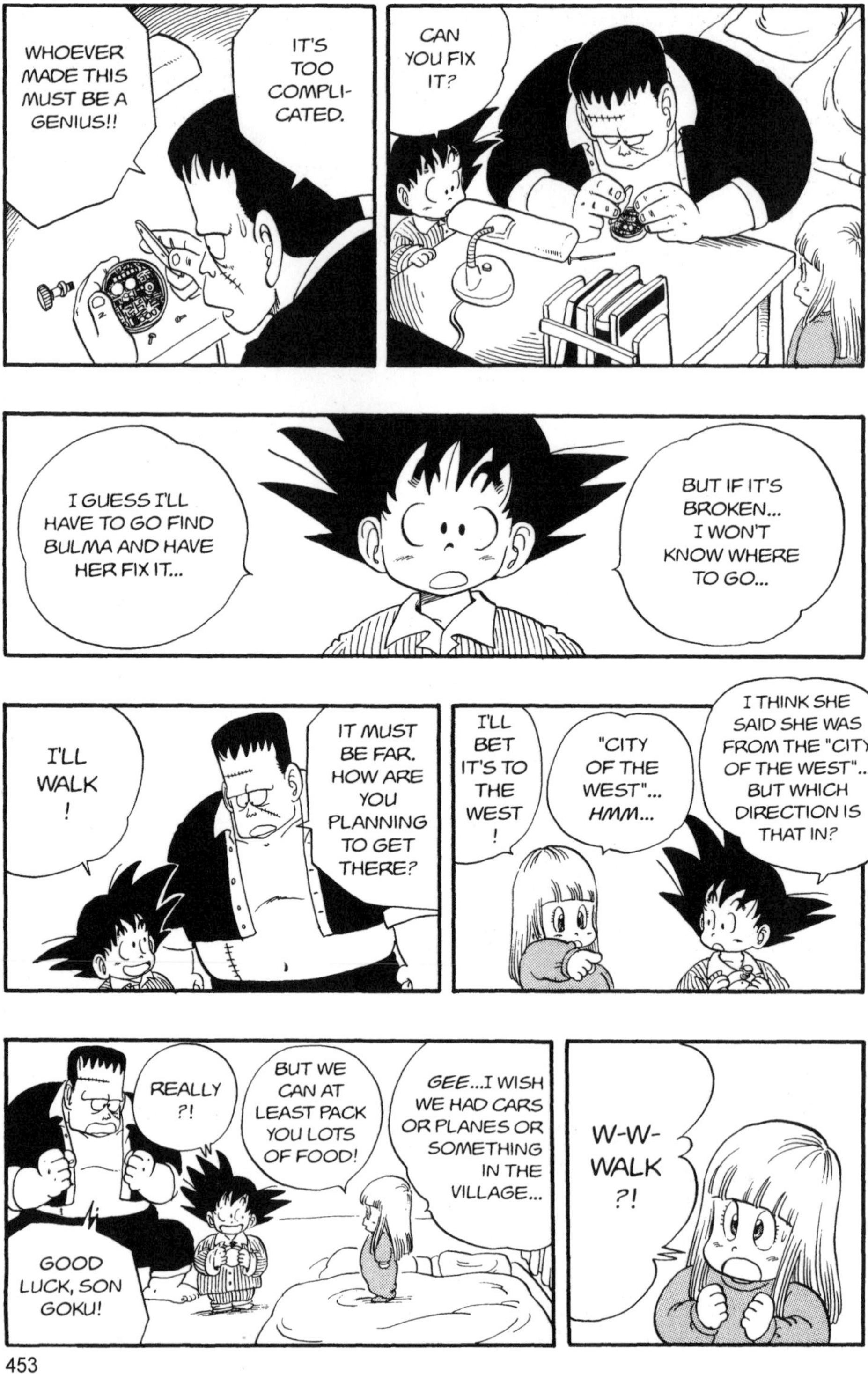
CAN YOU FIX IT?
IT'S TOO COMPLI-CATED.
WHOEVER MADE THIS MUST BE A GENIUS!!
BUT IF IT'S BROKEN... I WON'T KNOW WHERE TO GO...
I GUESS I'LL HAVE TO GO FIND BULMA AND HAVE HER FIX IT...
I THINK SHE SAID SHE WAS FROM THE "CITY OF THE WEST"... BUT WHICH DIRECTION IS THAT IN?
"CITY OF THE WEST"... *HMM*...
I'LL BET IT'S TO THE WEST!
IT MUST BE FAR. HOW ARE YOU PLANNING TO GET THERE?
I'LL WALK!
W-W-WALK?!
GEE...I WISH WE HAD CARS OR PLANES OR SOMETHING IN THE VILLAGE...
BUT WE CAN AT LEAST PACK YOU LOTS OF FOOD!
REALLY?!
GOOD LUCK, SON GOKU!

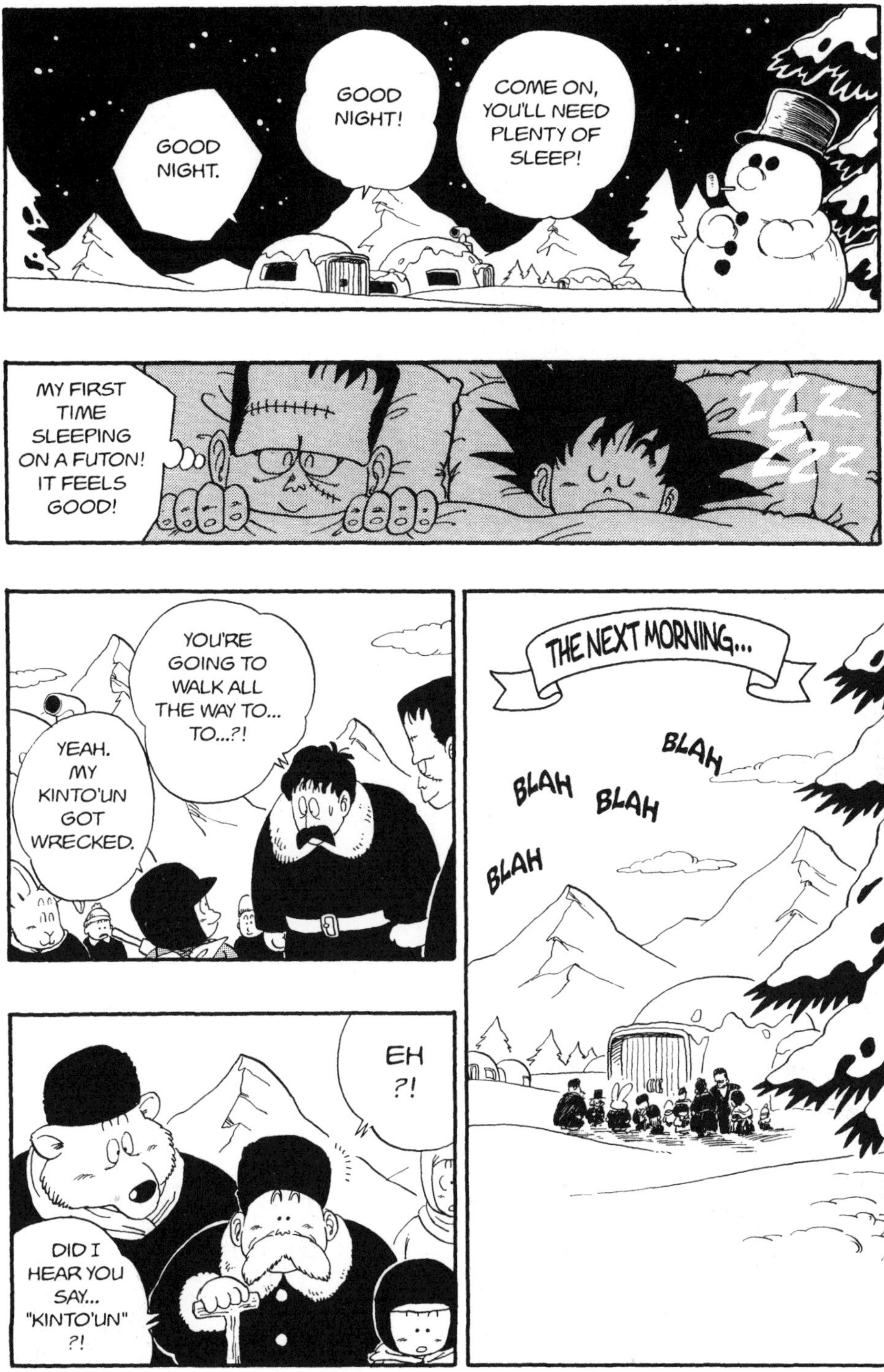
COME ON, YOU'LL NEED PLENTY OF SLEEP!
GOOD NIGHT!
GOOD NIGHT.
MY FIRST TIME SLEEPING ON A FUTON! IT FEELS GOOD!
THE NEXT MORNING...
BLAH
BLAH
BLAH
BLAH
YOU'RE GOING TO WALK ALL THE WAY TO... TO...?!
YEAH. MY KINTO'UN GOT WRECKED.
EH ?!
DID I HEAR YOU SAY... "KINTO'UN" ?!

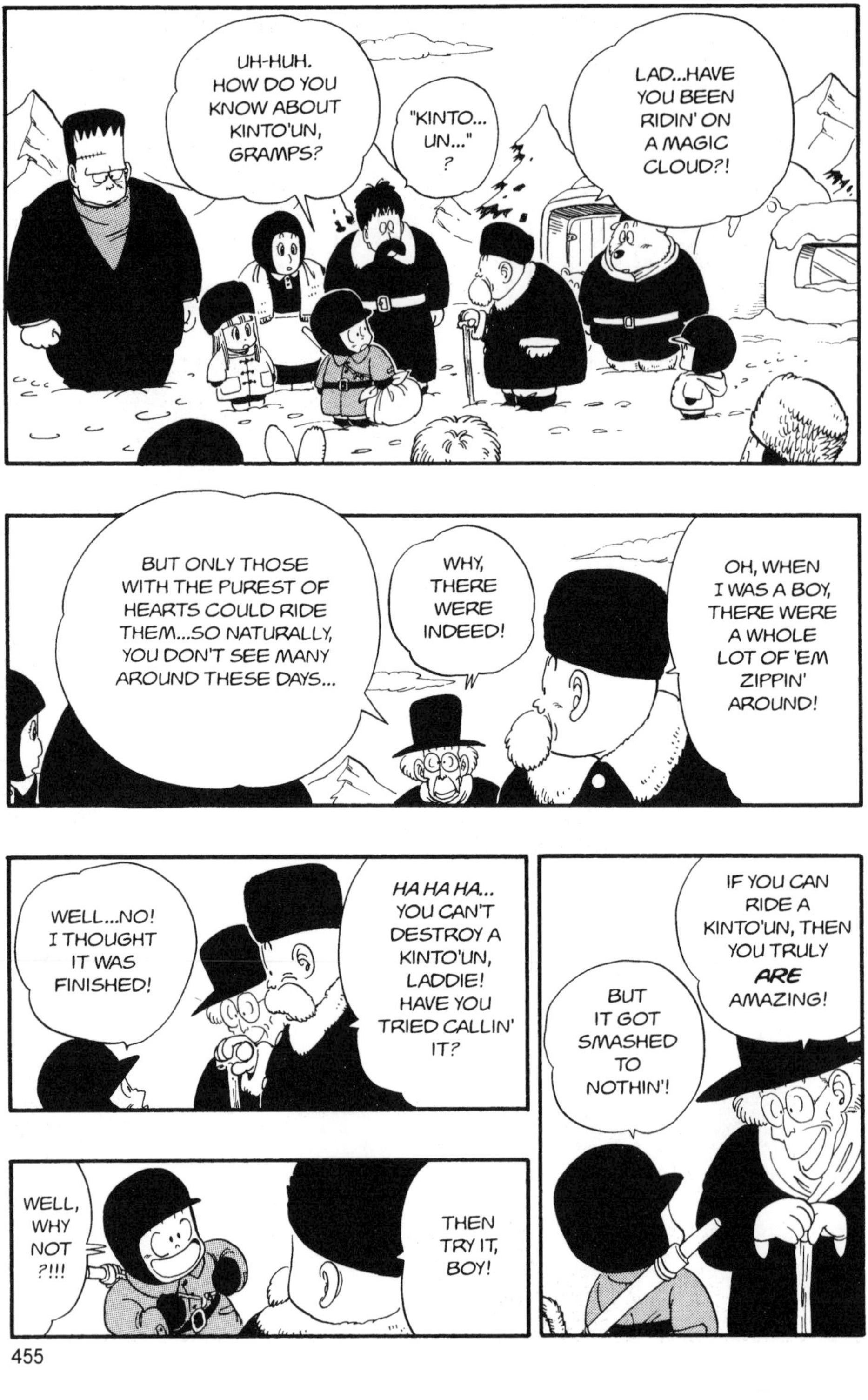
LAD...HAVE YOU BEEN RIDIN' ON A MAGIC CLOUD?!
"KINTO... UN..." ?
UH-HUH. HOW DO YOU KNOW ABOUT KINTO'UN, GRAMPS?
OH, WHEN I WAS A BOY, THERE WERE A WHOLE LOT OF 'EM ZIPPIN' AROUND!
WHY, THERE WERE INDEED!
BUT ONLY THOSE WITH THE PUREST OF HEARTS COULD RIDE THEM...SO NATURALLY, YOU DON'T SEE MANY AROUND THESE DAYS...
IF YOU CAN RIDE A KINTO'UN, THEN YOU TRULY **ARE** AMAZING!
BUT IT GOT SMASHED TO NOTHIN'!
HA HA HA... YOU CAN'T DESTROY A KINTO'UN, LADDIE! HAVE YOU TRIED CALLIN' IT?
WELL...NO! I THOUGHT IT WAS FINISHED!
THEN TRY IT, BOY!
WELL, WHY NOT ?!!!

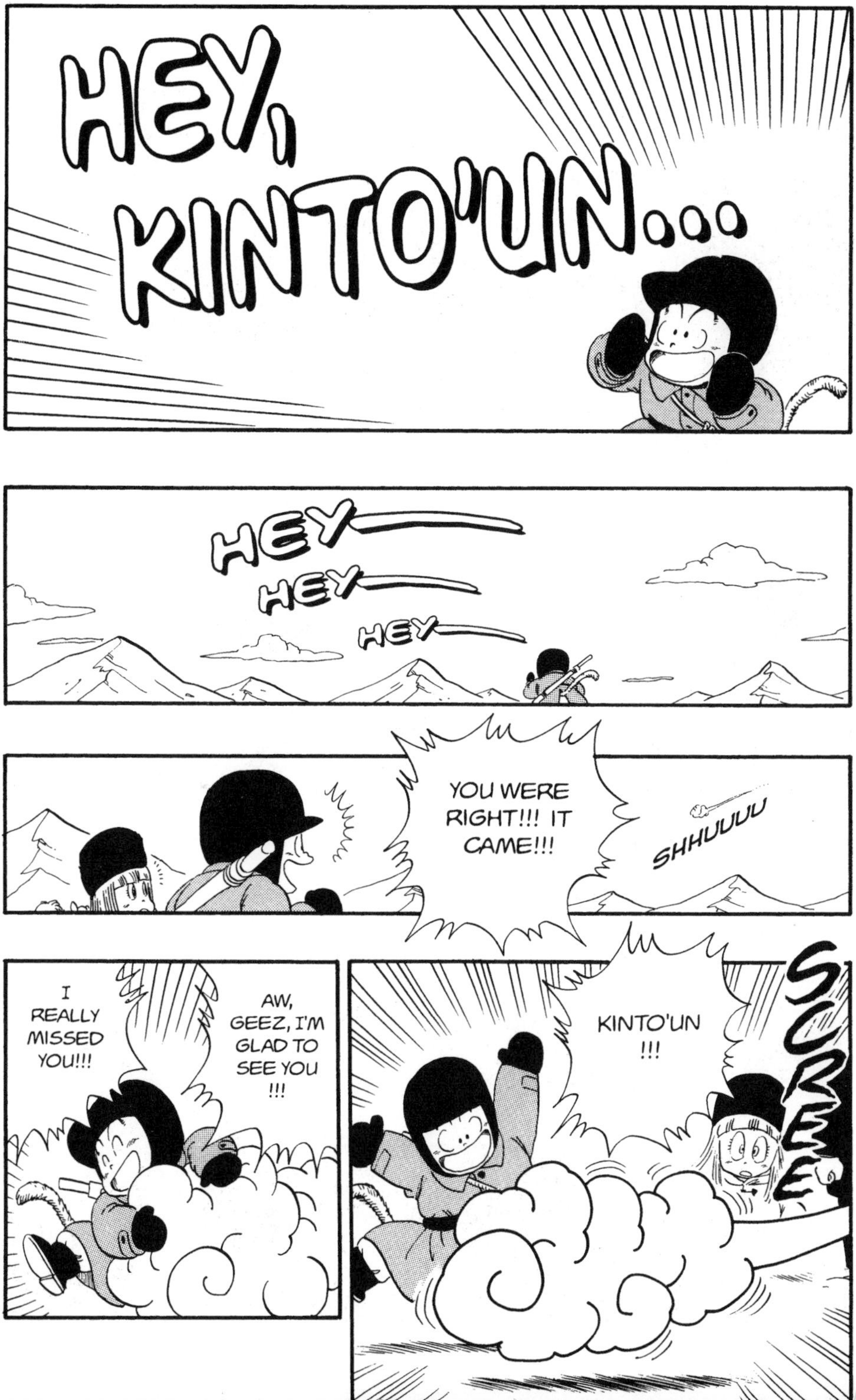
HEY, KINTO'UN...
HEY
HEY
HEY
SHHUUUU
YOU WERE RIGHT!!! IT CAME!!!
SCREEE
KINTO'UN !!!
AW, GEEZ, I'M GLAD TO SEE YOU !!!
I REALLY MISSED YOU!!!

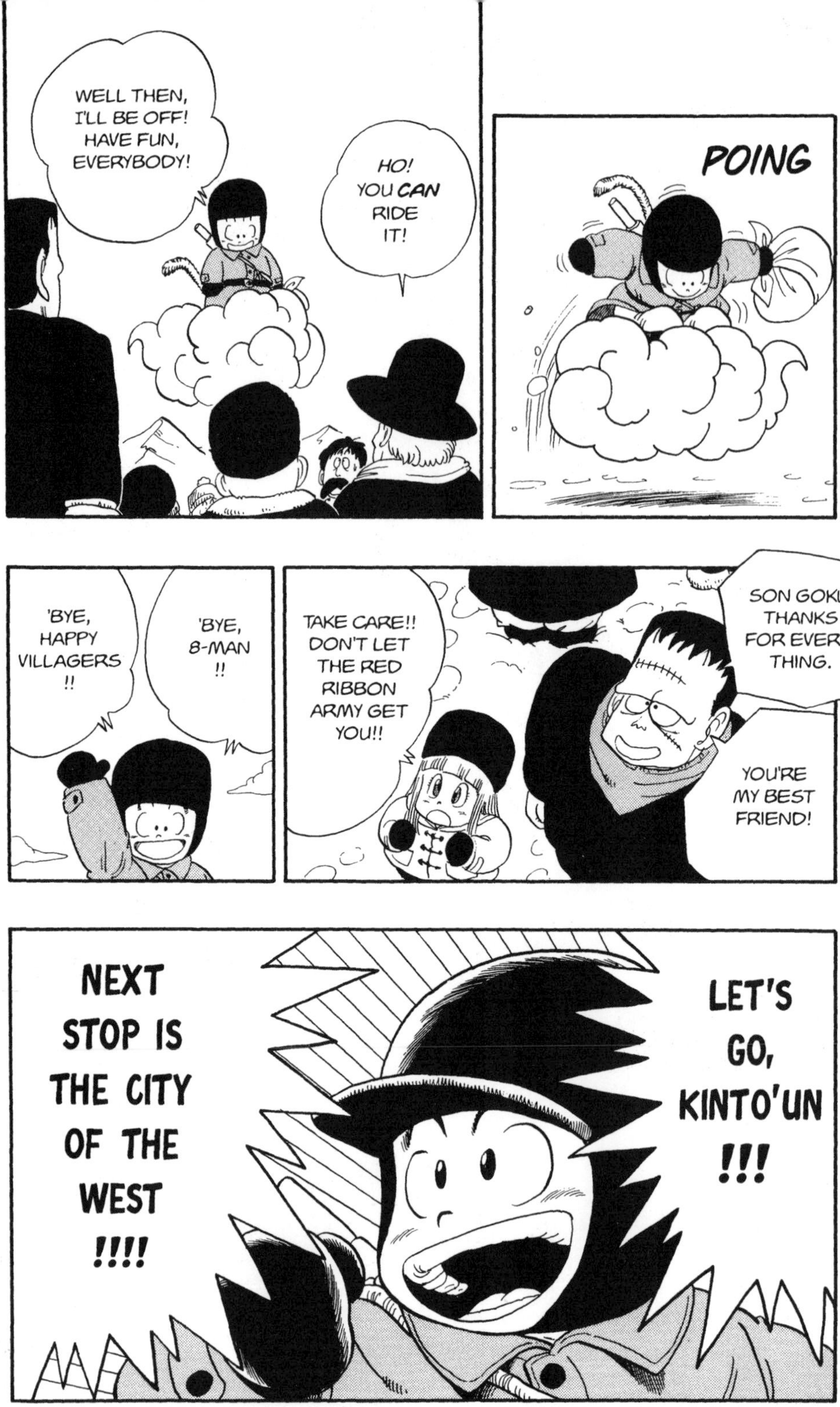
POING
HO! YOU CAN RIDE IT!
WELL THEN, I'LL BE OFF! HAVE FUN, EVERYBODY!
SON GOKU, THANKS FOR EVERY-THING.
YOU'RE MY BEST FRIEND!
TAKE CARE!! DON'T LET THE RED RIBBON ARMY GET YOU!!
'BYE, 8-MAN !!
'BYE, HAPPY VILLAGERS !!
LET'S GO, KINTO'UN !!!
NEXT STOP IS THE CITY OF THE WEST !!!!

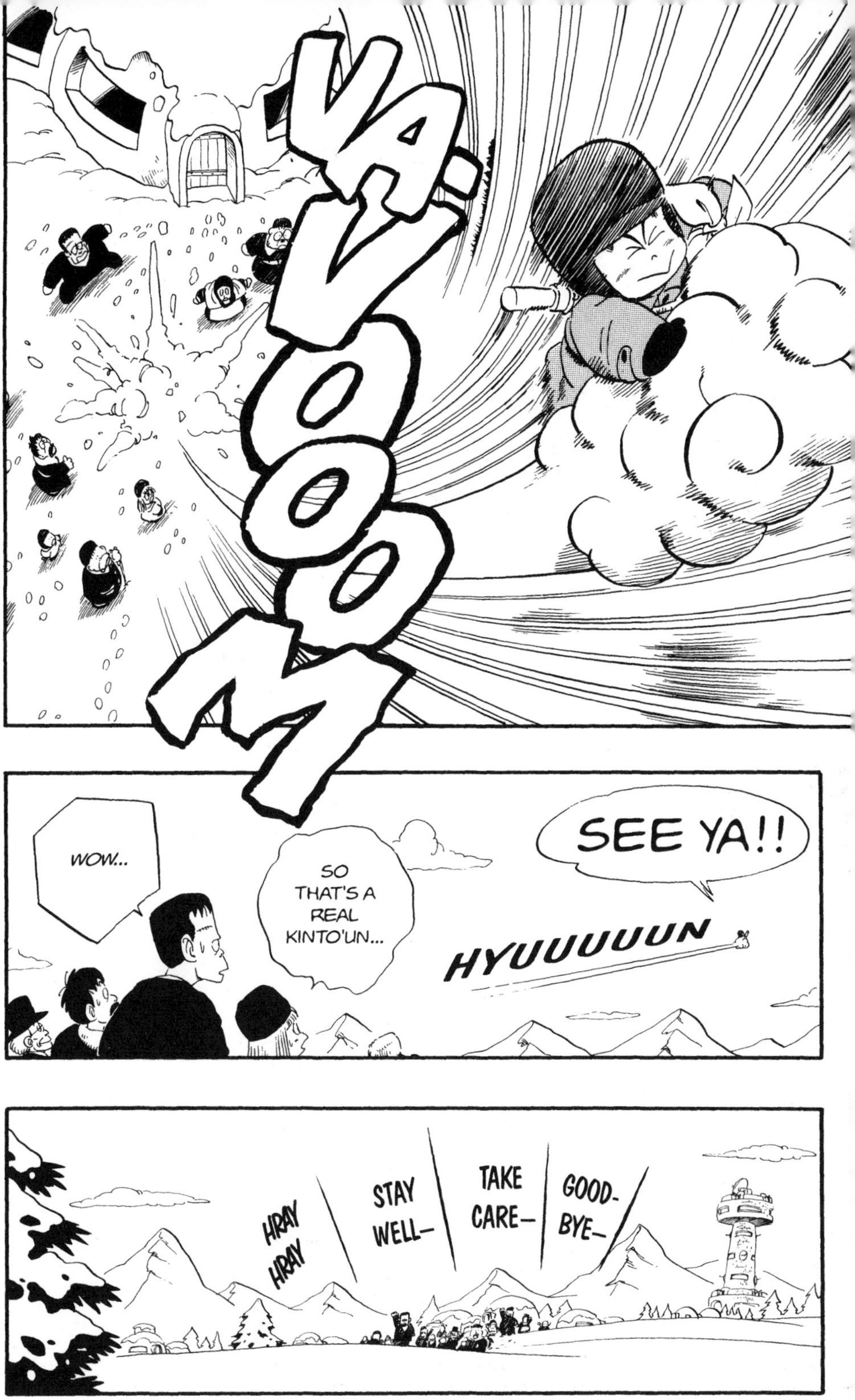
VAVOOOM
SEE YA!!
HYUUUUUN
SO THAT'S A REAL KINTO'UN...
WOW...
GOOD-BYE-
TAKE CARE-
STAY WELL-
HRAY HRAY

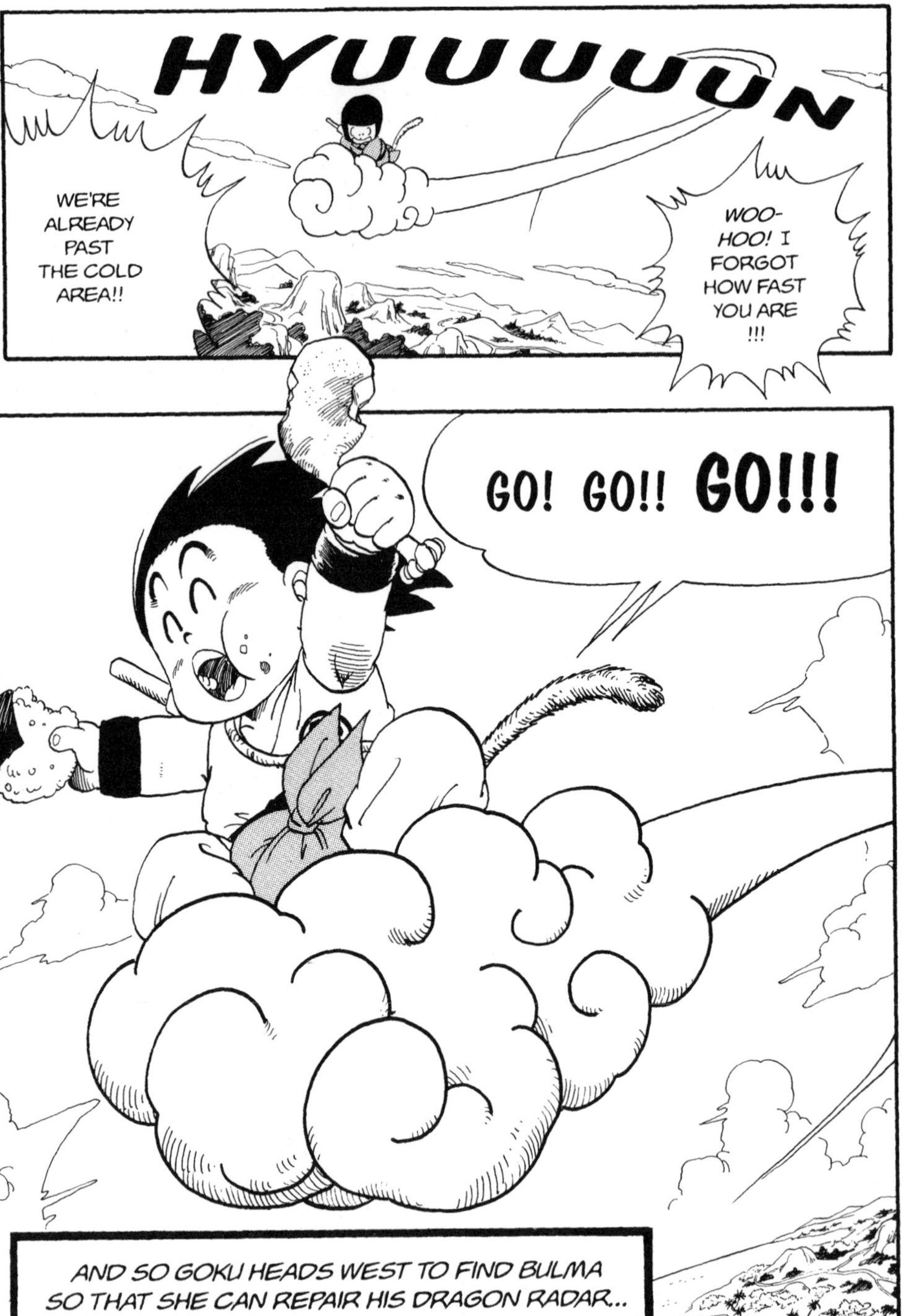
HYUUUUUUN
WOO-HOO! I FORGOT HOW FAST YOU ARE!!!
WE'RE ALREADY PAST THE COLD AREA!!
GO! GO!! GO!!!
AND SO GOKU HEADS WEST TO FIND BULMA SO THAT SHE CAN REPAIR HIS DRAGON RADAR... BUT YOU KNOW IT'LL NEVER BE THAT EASY...

Tale 68 • Monkey in the City

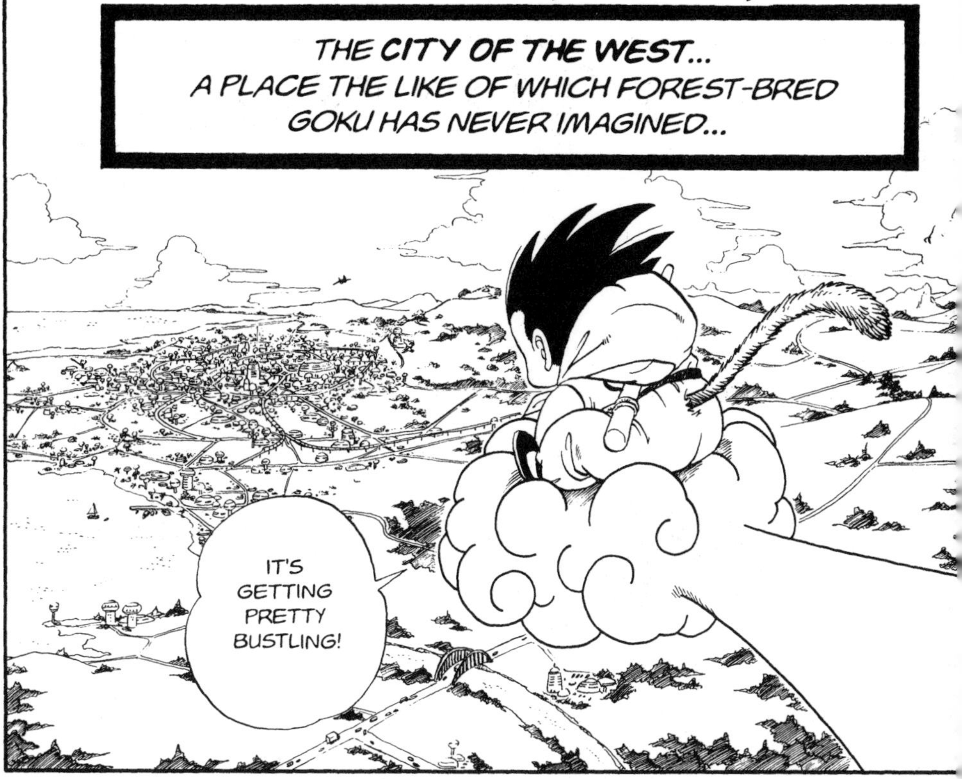
THE **CITY OF THE WEST**...
A PLACE THE LIKE OF WHICH FOREST-BRED GOKU HAS NEVER IMAGINED...
IT'S GETTING PRETTY BUSTLING!

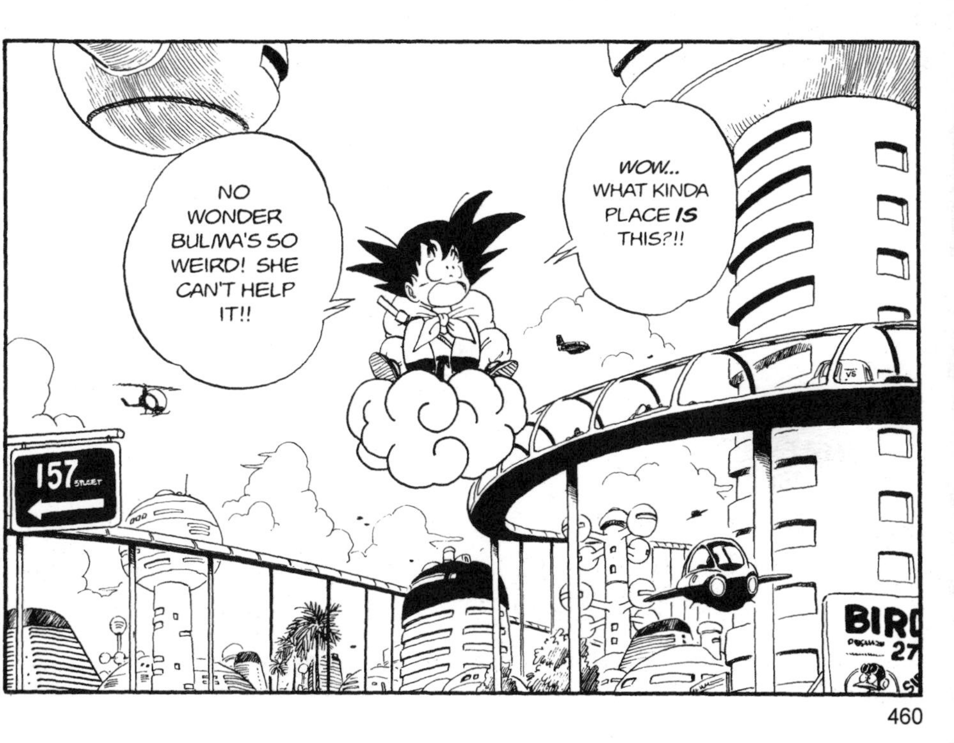
WOW... WHAT KINDA PLACE ***IS*** THIS?!!
NO WONDER BULMA'S SO WEIRD! SHE CAN'T HELP IT!!
157

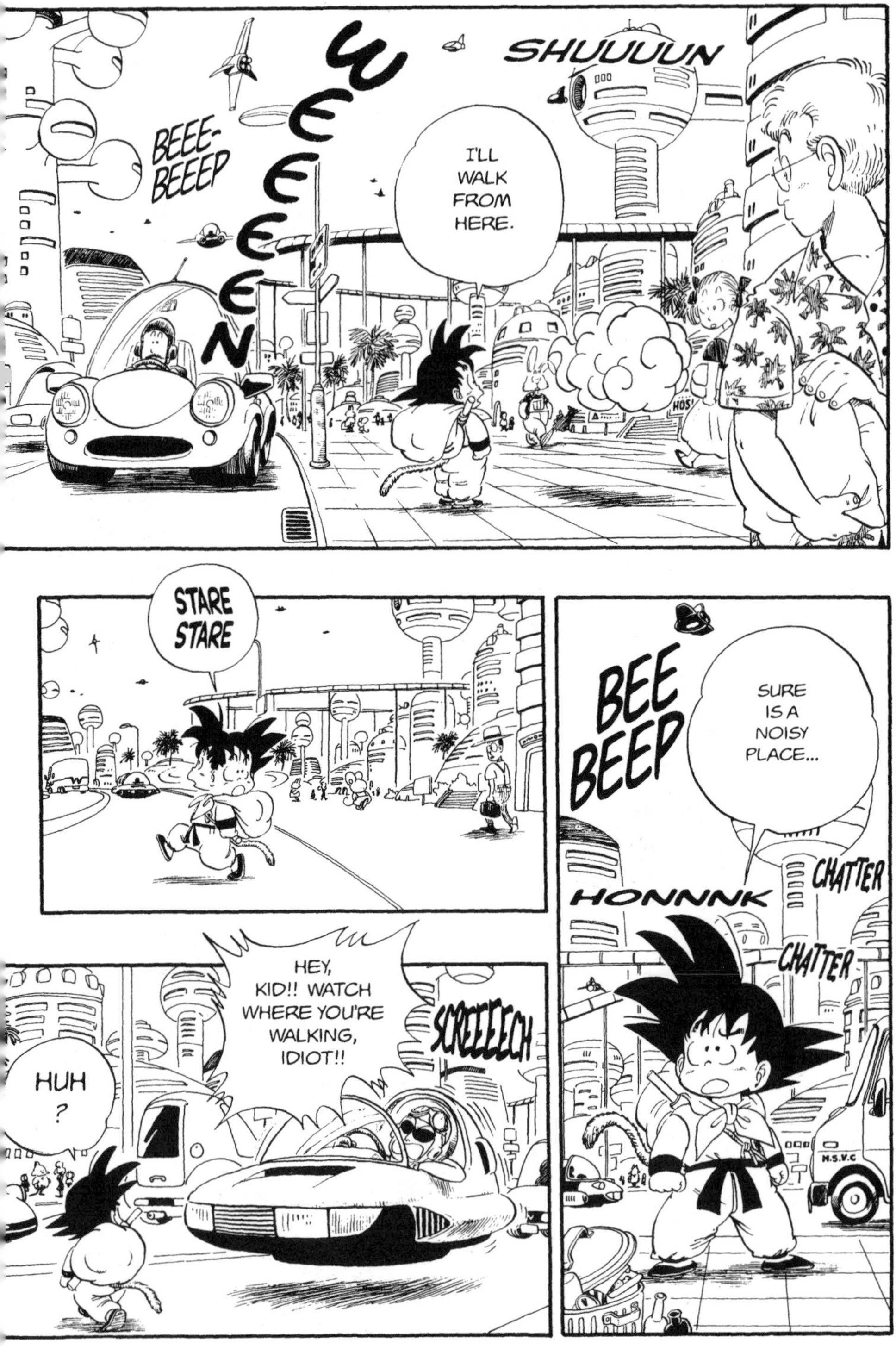
SHUUUUN
I'LL WALK FROM HERE.
WEEEEEEN
BEEE-BEEEP
BEE BEEP
SURE IS A NOISY PLACE...
CHATTER
HONNNK
CHATTER
STARE STARE
SCREEEECH
HEY, KID!! WATCH WHERE YOU'RE WALKING, IDIOT!!
HUH?

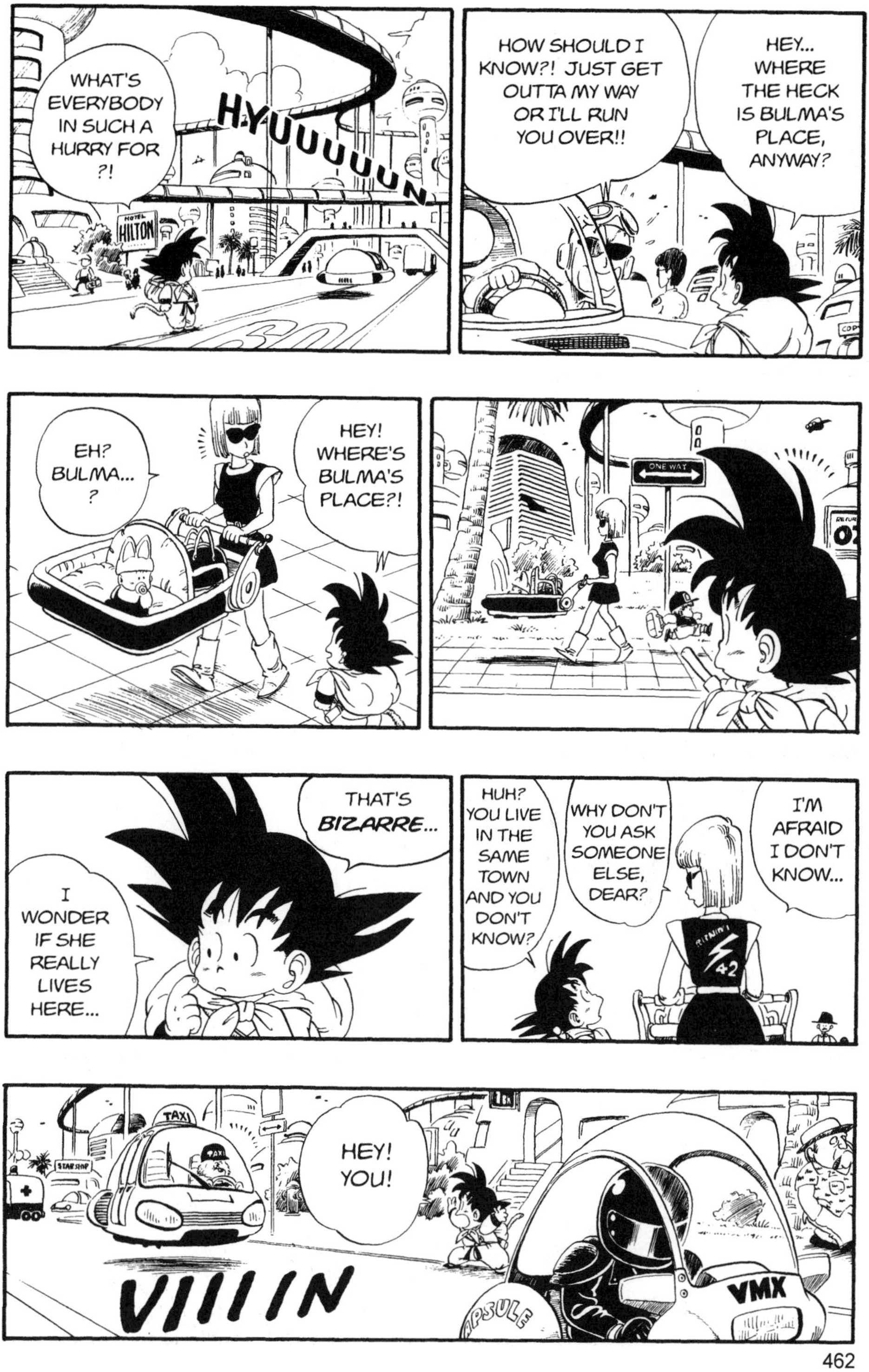
HEY... WHERE THE HECK IS BULMA'S PLACE, ANYWAY?
HOW SHOULD I KNOW?! JUST GET OUTTA MY WAY OR I'LL RUN YOU OVER!!
HYUUUUUUN
WHAT'S EVERYBODY IN SUCH A HURRY FOR?!
HOTEL HILTON
ONE WAY
HEY! WHERE'S BULMA'S PLACE?!
EH? BULMA...?
I'M AFRAID I DON'T KNOW...
WHY DON'T YOU ASK SOMEONE ELSE, DEAR?
HUH? YOU LIVE IN THE SAME TOWN AND YOU DON'T KNOW?
THAT'S *BIZARRE*...
I WONDER IF SHE REALLY LIVES HERE...
VMX
HEY! YOU!
TAXI
STAR SHOP
VIIIIN

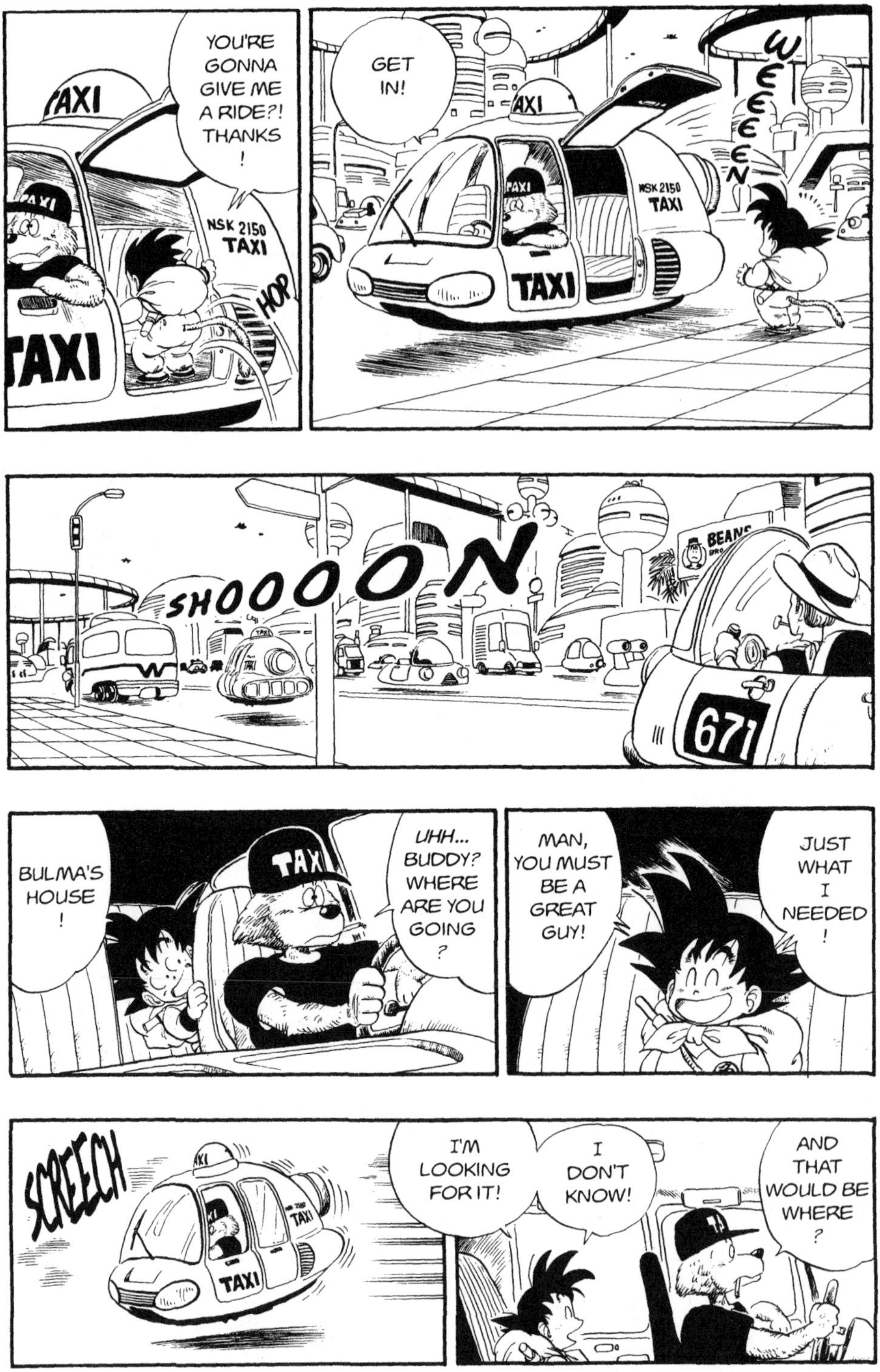
GET IN!
WEEEEEN
NSK 2150 TAXI
TAXI
YOU'RE GONNA GIVE ME A RIDE?! THANKS!
NSK 2150 TAXI
HOP
TAXI
SHOOOOON
BEANS
671
JUST WHAT I NEEDED!
MAN, YOU MUST BE A GREAT GUY!
UHH... BUDDY? WHERE ARE YOU GOING?
BULMA'S HOUSE!
AND THAT WOULD BE WHERE?
I DON'T KNOW!
I'M LOOKING FOR IT!
SCREECH
TAXI

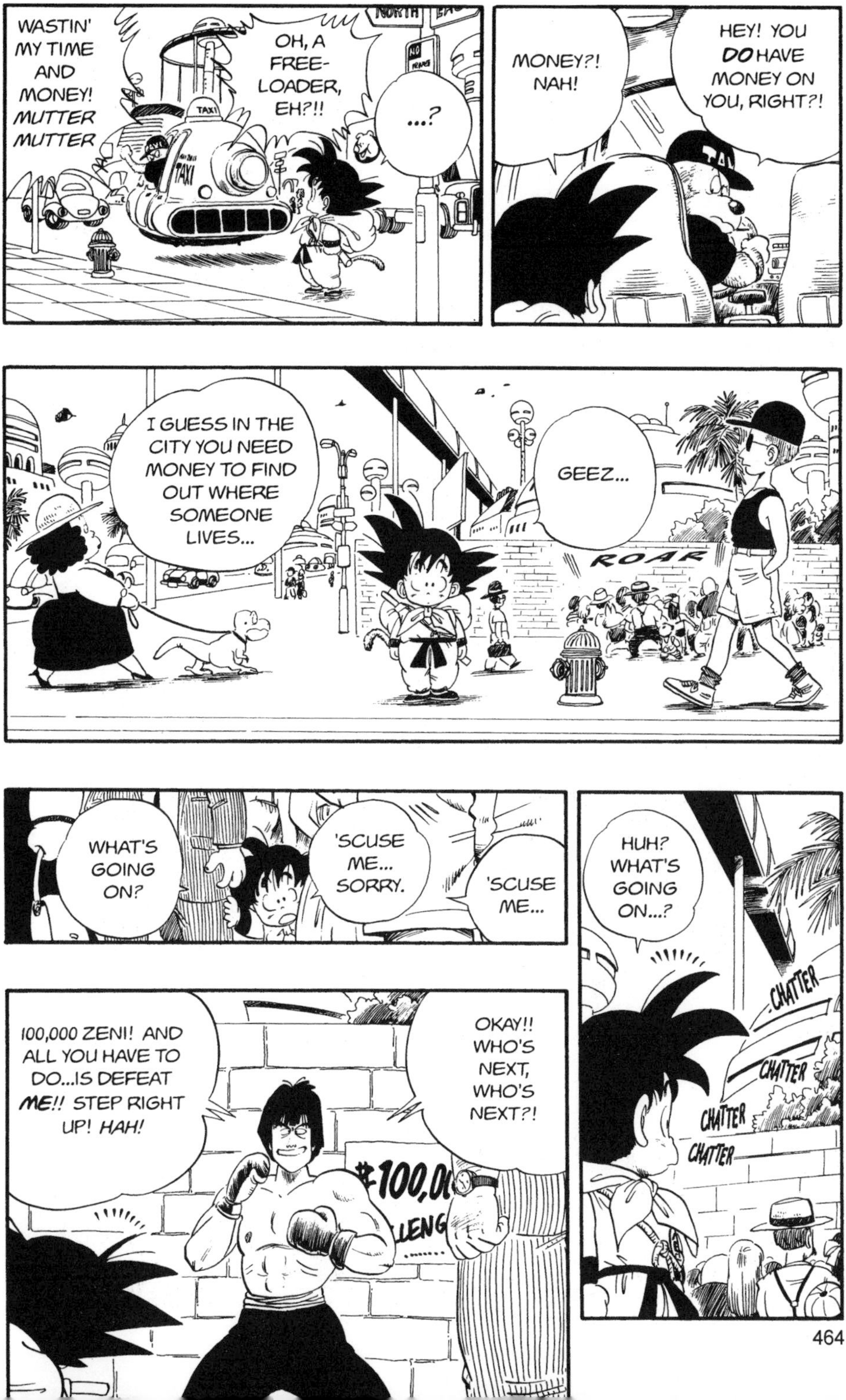
HEY! YOU **DO** HAVE MONEY ON YOU, RIGHT?!
MONEY?! NAH!
...?
OH, A FREE-LOADER, EH?!!
WASTIN' MY TIME AND MONEY! *MUTTER MUTTER*
GEEZ...
ROAR
I GUESS IN THE CITY YOU NEED MONEY TO FIND OUT WHERE SOMEONE LIVES...
HUH? WHAT'S GOING ON...?
CHATTER
CHATTER
CHATTER
CHATTER
'SCUSE ME...
'SCUSE ME... SORRY.
WHAT'S GOING ON?
OKAY!! WHO'S NEXT, WHO'S NEXT?!
100,000 ZENI! AND ALL YOU HAVE TO DO...IS DEFEAT ***ME!!*** STEP RIGHT UP! *HAH!*

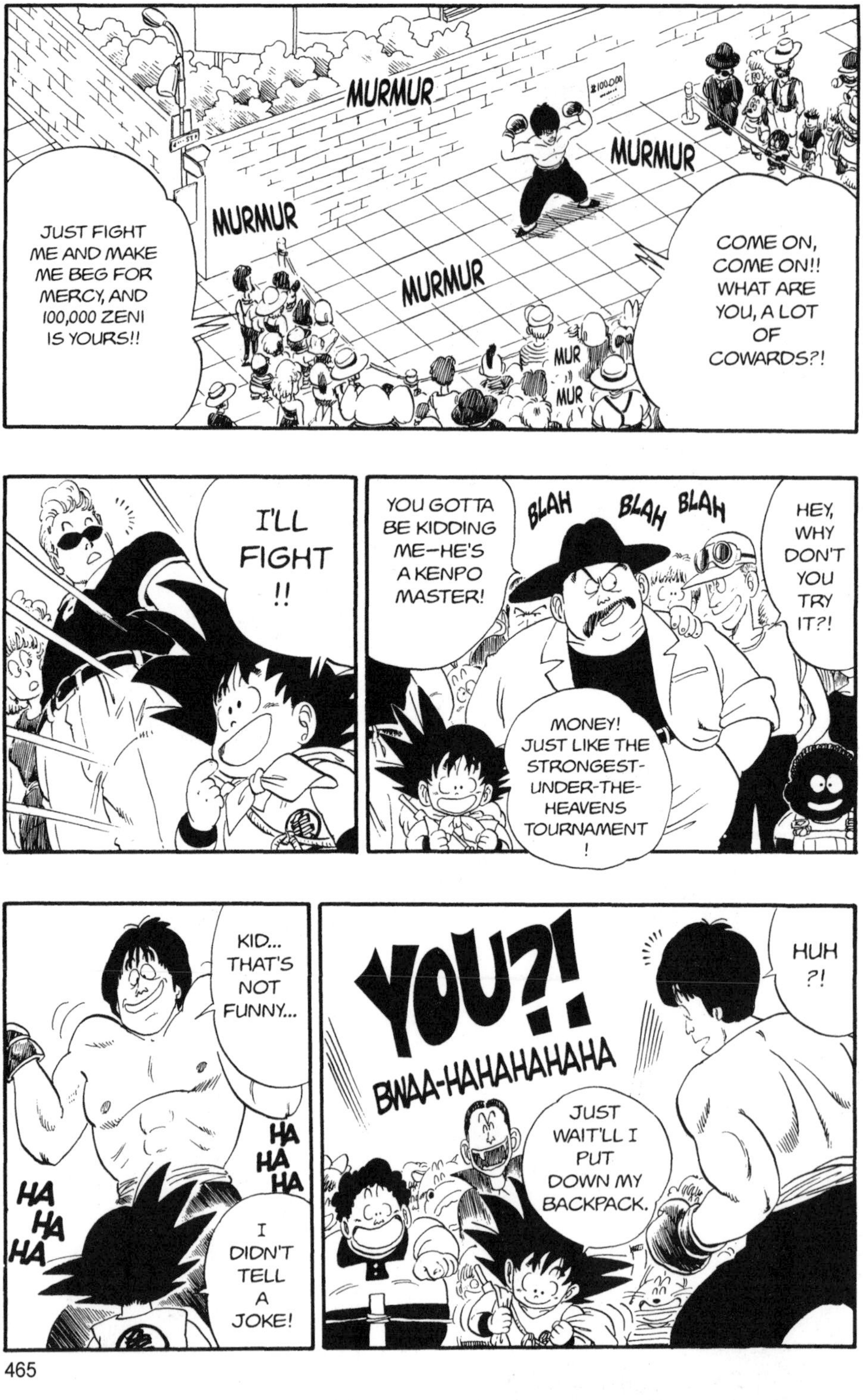
MURMUR
MURMUR
JUST FIGHT ME AND MAKE ME BEG FOR MERCY, AND 100,000 ZENI IS YOURS!!
COME ON, COME ON!! WHAT ARE YOU, A LOT OF COWARDS?!
MURMUR
MURMUR
MUR
MUR
HEY, WHY DON'T YOU TRY IT?!
BLAH BLAH BLAH
YOU GOTTA BE KIDDING ME—HE'S A KENPO MASTER!
MONEY! JUST LIKE THE STRONGEST-UNDER-THE-HEAVENS TOURNAMENT!
I'LL FIGHT!!
HUH?!
YOU?!
BWAA-HAHAHAHAHA
JUST WAIT'LL I PUT DOWN MY BACKPACK.
KID... THAT'S NOT FUNNY...
HA HA HA
HA HA HA
I DIDN'T TELL A JOKE!

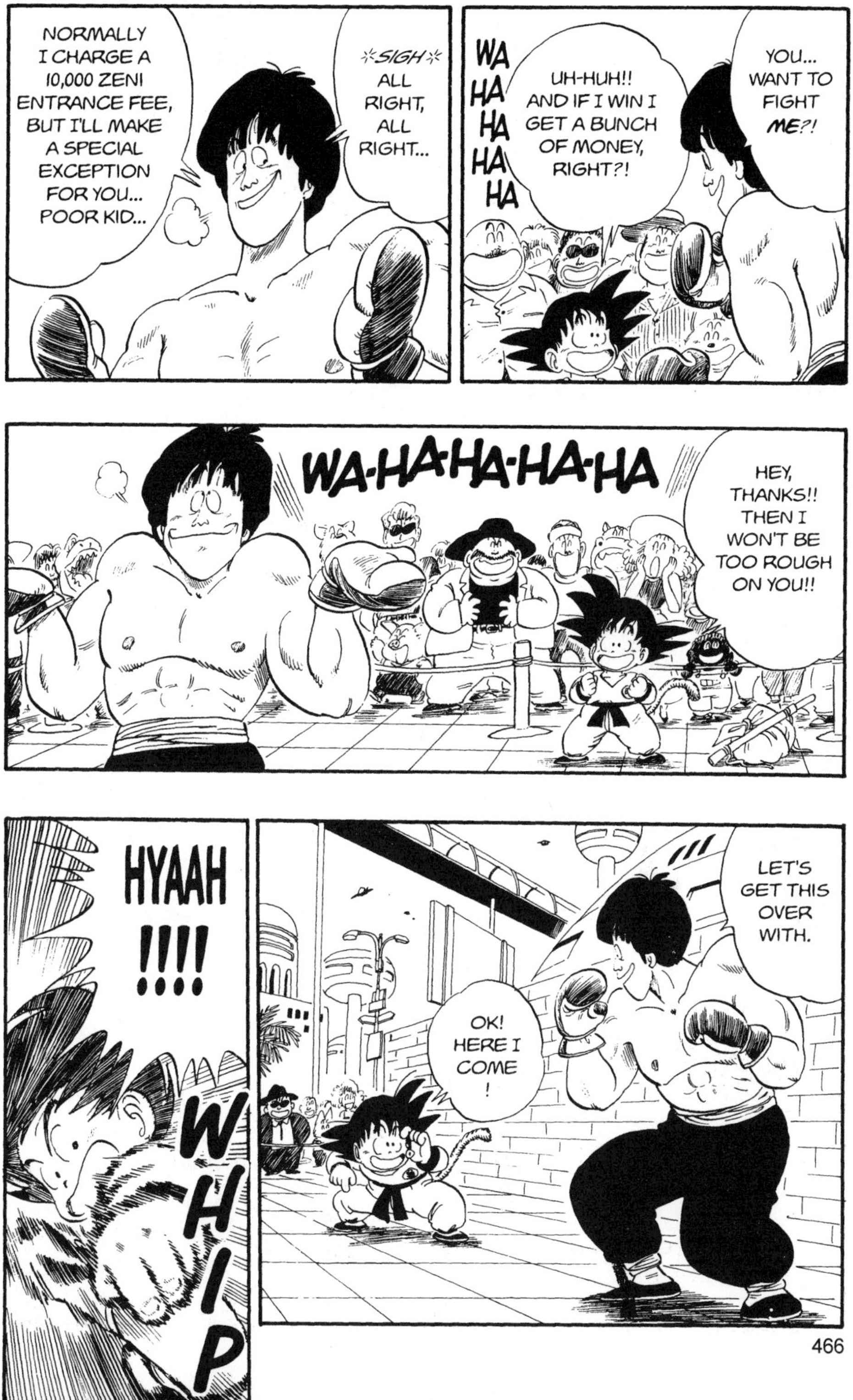
YOU... WANT TO FIGHT ME?!
UH-HUH!! AND IF I WIN I GET A BUNCH OF MONEY, RIGHT?!
WA HA HA HA HA
SIGH ALL RIGHT, ALL RIGHT...
NORMALLY I CHARGE A 10,000 ZENI ENTRANCE FEE, BUT I'LL MAKE A SPECIAL EXCEPTION FOR YOU... POOR KID...
HEY, THANKS!! THEN I WON'T BE TOO ROUGH ON YOU!!
WA-HA-HA-HA-HA
LET'S GET THIS OVER WITH.
OK! HERE I COME!
HYAAH!!!!
WHIP

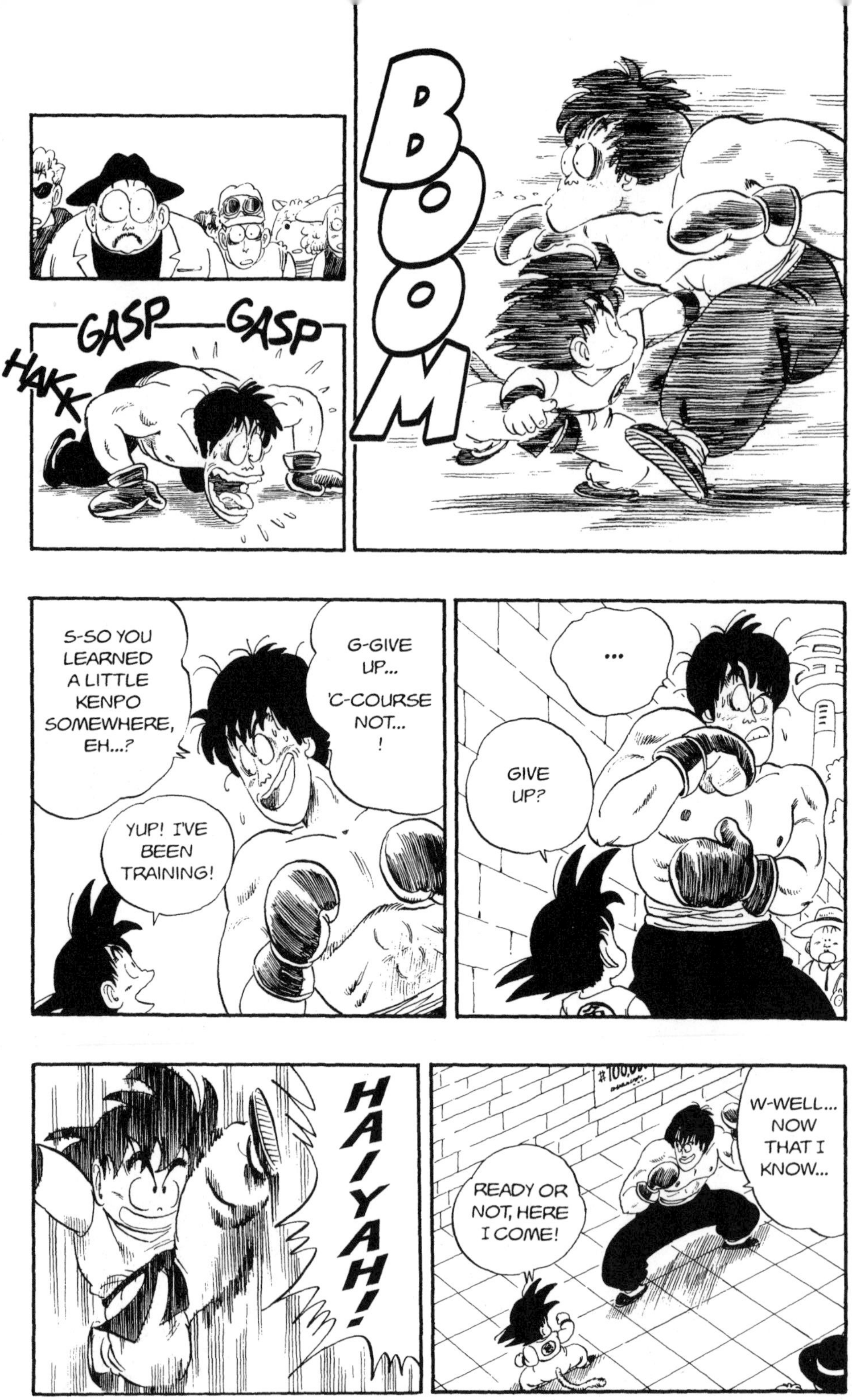
BOOM
GASP GASP
HAKK
...
GIVE UP?
G-GIVE UP... 'C-COURSE NOT... !
S-SO YOU LEARNED A LITTLE KENPO SOMEWHERE, EH...?
YUP! I'VE BEEN TRAINING!
W-WELL... NOW THAT I KNOW...
READY OR NOT, HERE I COME!
HAIYAH!

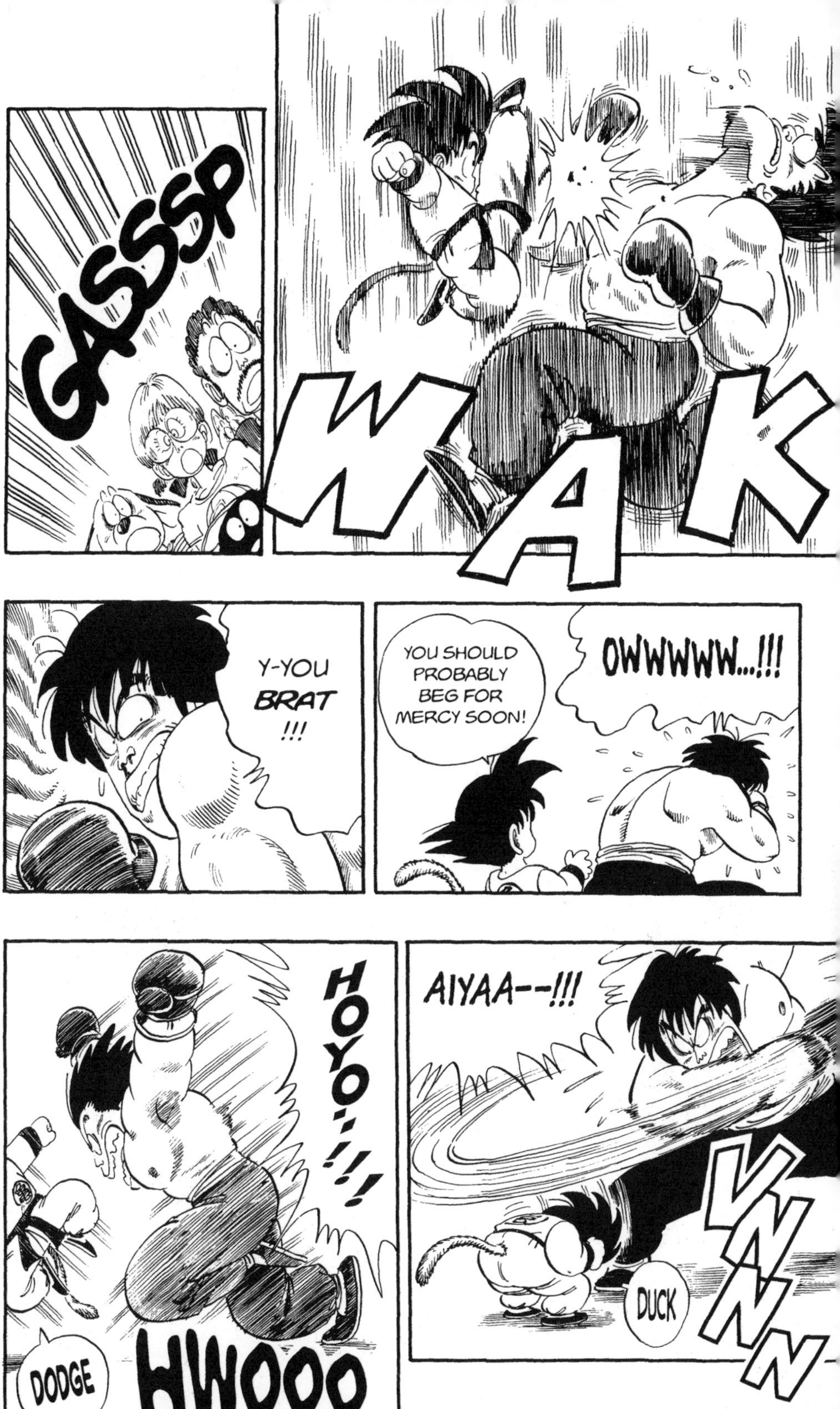
WAK
GASSSP
OWWWWW...!!!
YOU SHOULD PROBABLY BEG FOR MERCY SOON!
Y-YOU BRAT !!!
AIYAA--!!!
VNNNN
DUCK
HOYO--!!!
HWOOO
DODGE

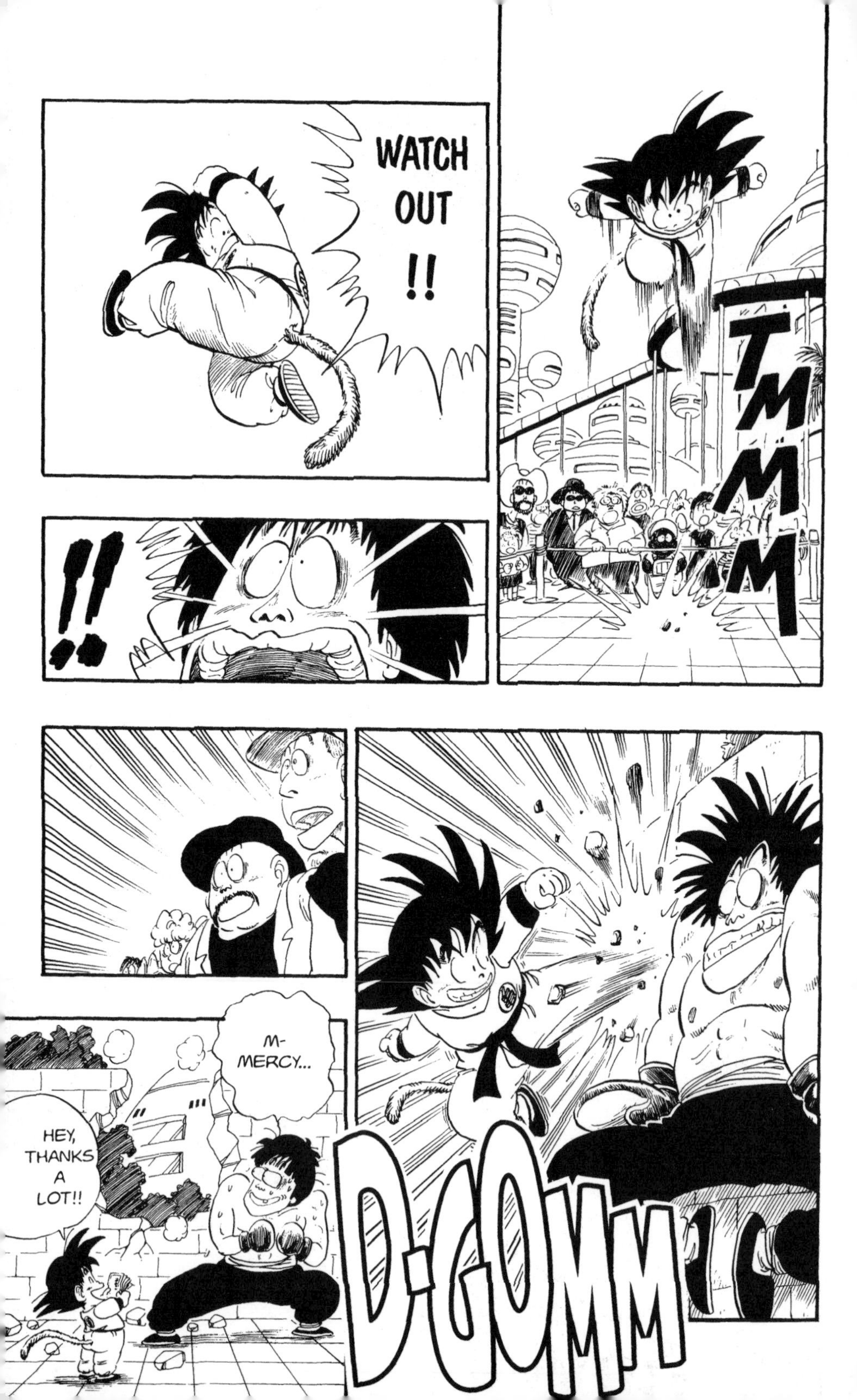
TMMM
WATCH OUT !!
!!
D-GOMM
M-MERCY...
HEY, THANKS A LOT!!

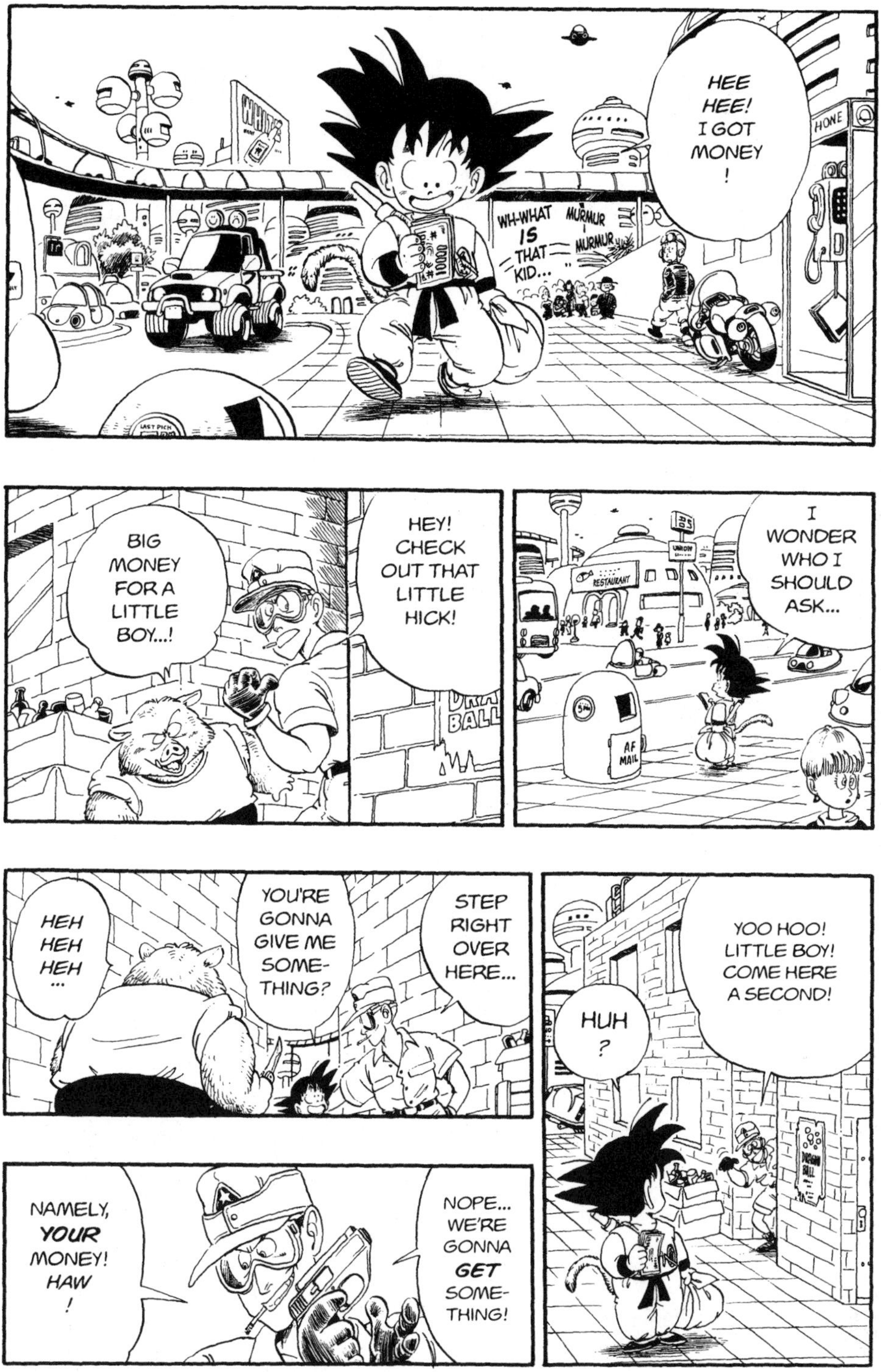
HEE HEE! I GOT MONEY!
WH-WHAT IS THAT KID...
MURMUR MURMUR
I WONDER WHO I SHOULD ASK...
RESTAURANT
AF MAIL
HEY! CHECK OUT THAT LITTLE HICK!
BIG MONEY FOR A LITTLE BOY...!
YOO HOO! LITTLE BOY! COME HERE A SECOND!
HUH?
STEP RIGHT OVER HERE...
YOU'RE GONNA GIVE ME SOMETHING?
HEH HEH HEH...
NOPE... WE'RE GONNA GET SOMETHING!
NAMELY, YOUR MONEY! HAW!

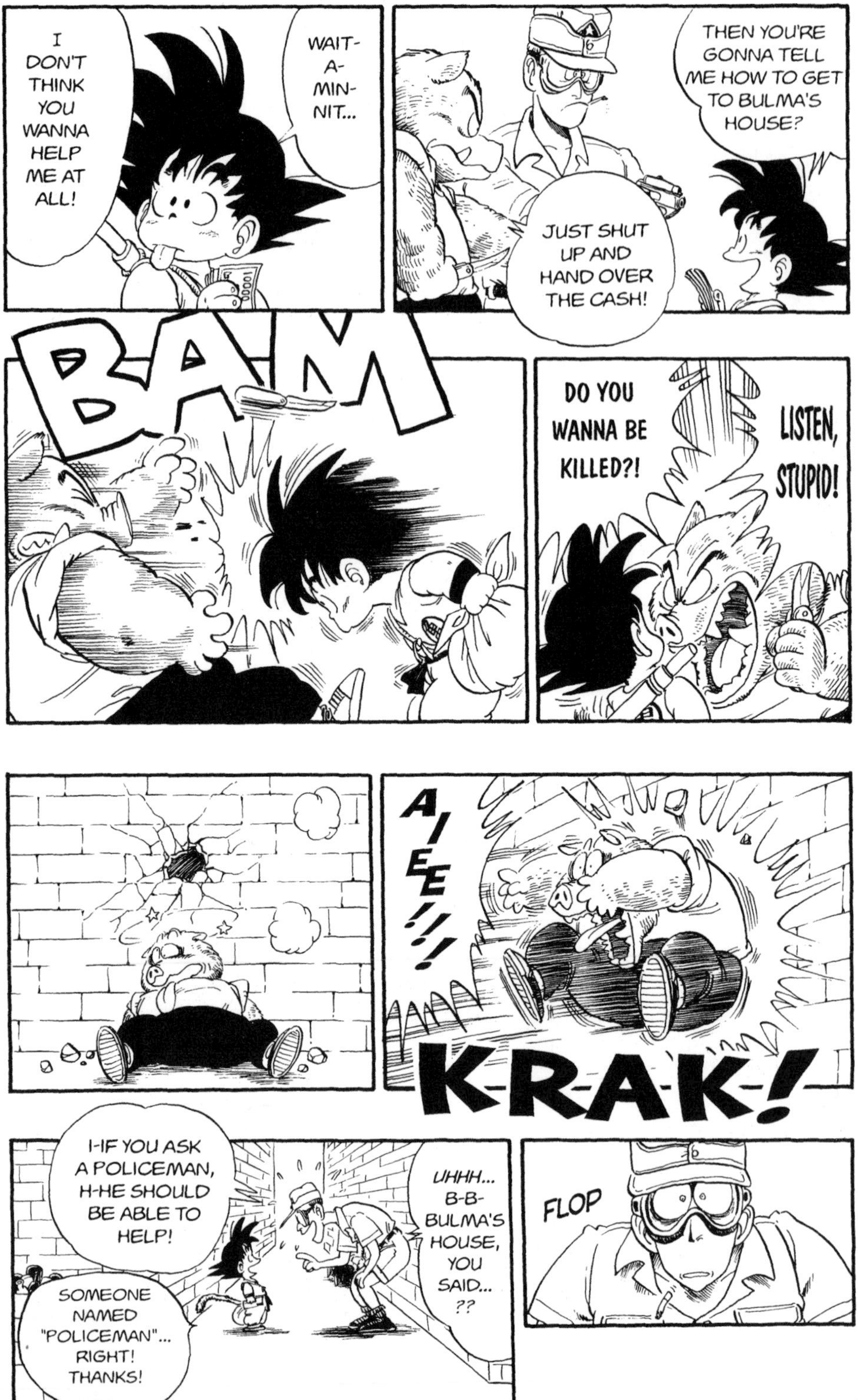
THEN YOU'RE GONNA TELL ME HOW TO GET TO BULMA'S HOUSE?
JUST SHUT UP AND HAND OVER THE CASH!
WAIT-A-MIN-NIT...
I DON'T THINK YOU WANNA HELP ME AT ALL!
LISTEN, STUPID!
DO YOU WANNA BE KILLED?!
BAM
AIEE!!!
K-R-A-K!
FLOP
UHHH... B-B-BULMA'S HOUSE, YOU SAID... ??
I-IF YOU ASK A POLICEMAN, H-HE SHOULD BE ABLE TO HELP!
SOMEONE NAMED "POLICEMAN"... RIGHT! THANKS!

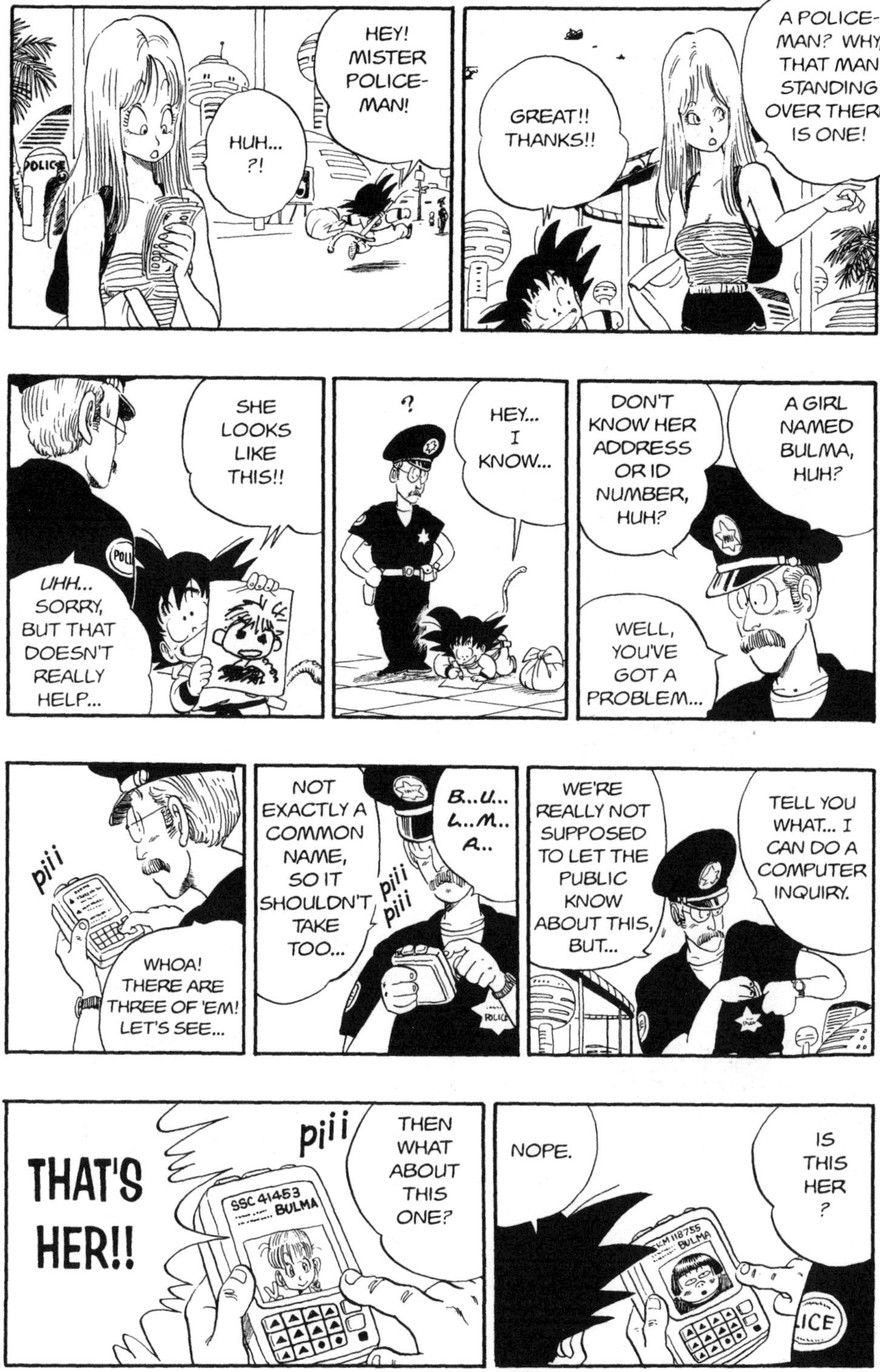
A POLICE-MAN? WHY, THAT MAN STANDING OVER THERE IS ONE!
GREAT!! THANKS!!
HEY! MISTER POLICE-MAN!
HUH... ?!
POLICE
A GIRL NAMED BULMA, HUH?
DON'T KNOW HER ADDRESS OR ID NUMBER, HUH?
WELL, YOU'VE GOT A PROBLEM...
HEY... I KNOW...
?
SHE LOOKS LIKE THIS!!
UHH... SORRY, BUT THAT DOESN'T REALLY HELP...
TELL YOU WHAT... I CAN DO A COMPUTER INQUIRY.
WE'RE REALLY NOT SUPPOSED TO LET THE PUBLIC KNOW ABOUT THIS, BUT...
B...U... L...M... A..
NOT EXACTLY A COMMON NAME, SO IT SHOULDN'T TAKE TOO...
piii piii
POLICE
piii
WHOA! THERE ARE THREE OF 'EM! LET'S SEE...
IS THIS HER?
NOPE.
KM 118755 BULMA
ICE
THEN WHAT ABOUT THIS ONE?
piii
SSC 41453 BULMA
THAT'S HER!!

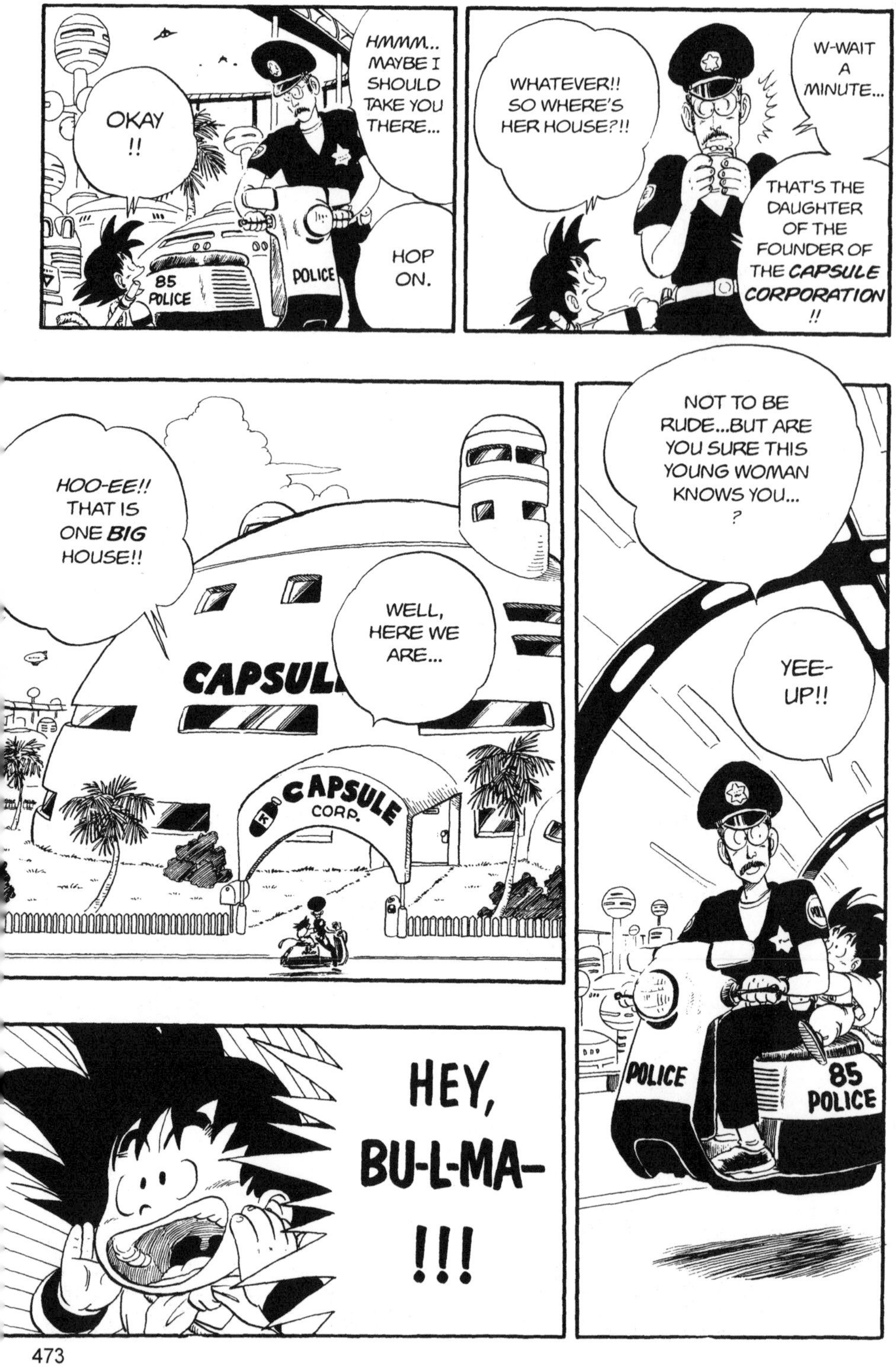
W-WAIT A MINUTE...
THAT'S THE DAUGHTER OF THE FOUNDER OF THE CAPSULE CORPORATION !!
WHATEVER!! SO WHERE'S HER HOUSE?!!
HMMM... MAYBE I SHOULD TAKE YOU THERE...
OKAY !!
HOP ON.
85 POLICE
POLICE
NOT TO BE RUDE...BUT ARE YOU SURE THIS YOUNG WOMAN KNOWS YOU... ?
YEE-UP!!
POLICE
85 POLICE
WELL, HERE WE ARE...
HOO-EE!! THAT IS ONE BIG HOUSE!!
CAPSULE CORP.
HEY, BU-L-MA-!!!

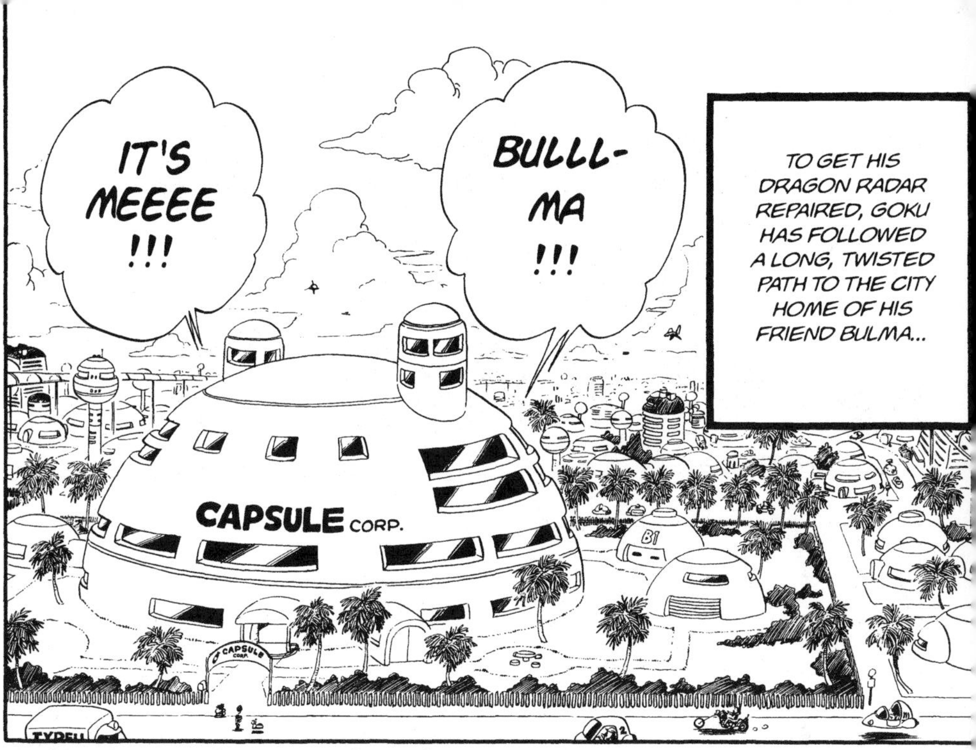
TO GET HIS DRAGON RADAR REPAIRED, GOKU HAS FOLLOWED A LONG, TWISTED PATH TO THE CITY HOME OF HIS FRIEND BULMA...
BULLL-MA !!!
IT'S MEEEE !!!
CAPSULE CORP.
B1

Tale 69 • Bulma and Goku

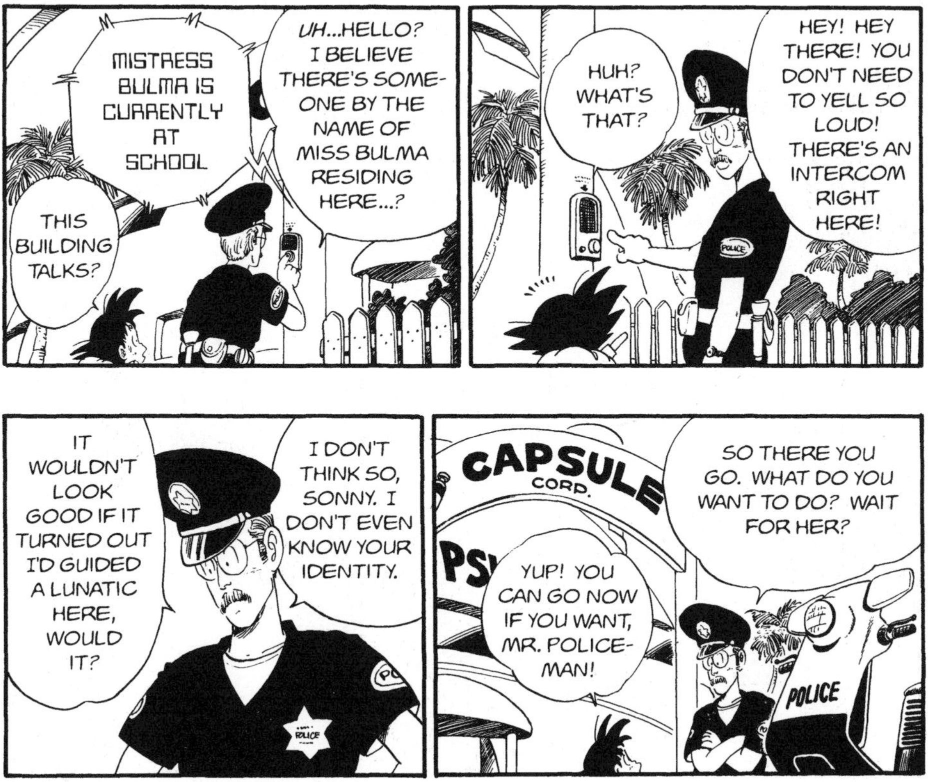
HEY! HEY THERE! YOU DON'T NEED TO YELL SO LOUD! THERE'S AN INTERCOM RIGHT HERE!
HUH? WHAT'S THAT?
UH...HELLO? I BELIEVE THERE'S SOME-ONE BY THE NAME OF MISS BULMA RESIDING HERE...?
MISTRESS BULMA IS CURRENTLY AT SCHOOL
THIS BUILDING TALKS?
SO THERE YOU GO. WHAT DO YOU WANT TO DO? WAIT FOR HER?
YUP! YOU CAN GO NOW IF YOU WANT, MR. POLICE-MAN!
CAPSULE CORP.
POLICE
I DON'T THINK SO, SONNY. I DON'T EVEN KNOW YOUR IDENTITY.
IT WOULDN'T LOOK GOOD IF IT TURNED OUT I'D GUIDED A LUNATIC HERE, WOULD IT?

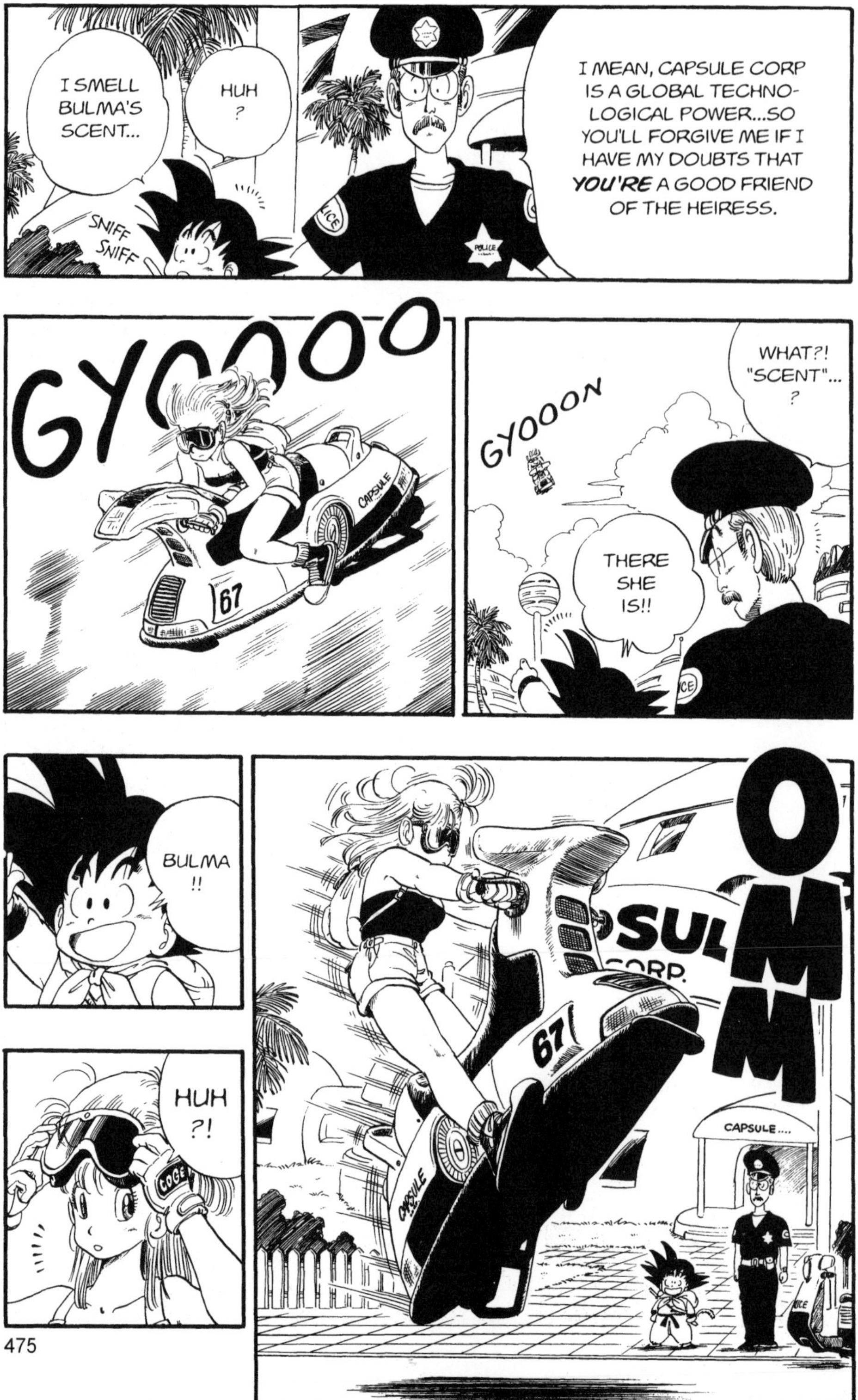
I MEAN, CAPSULE CORP IS A GLOBAL TECHNO-LOGICAL POWER...SO YOU'LL FORGIVE ME IF I HAVE MY DOUBTS THAT ***YOU'RE*** A GOOD FRIEND OF THE HEIRESS.
HUH ?
I SMELL BULMA'S SCENT...
SNIFF SNIFF
WHAT?! "SCENT"... ?
GYOOON
THERE SHE IS!!
GYOOOO
OMM
CAPSULE....
BULMA !!
HUH ?!

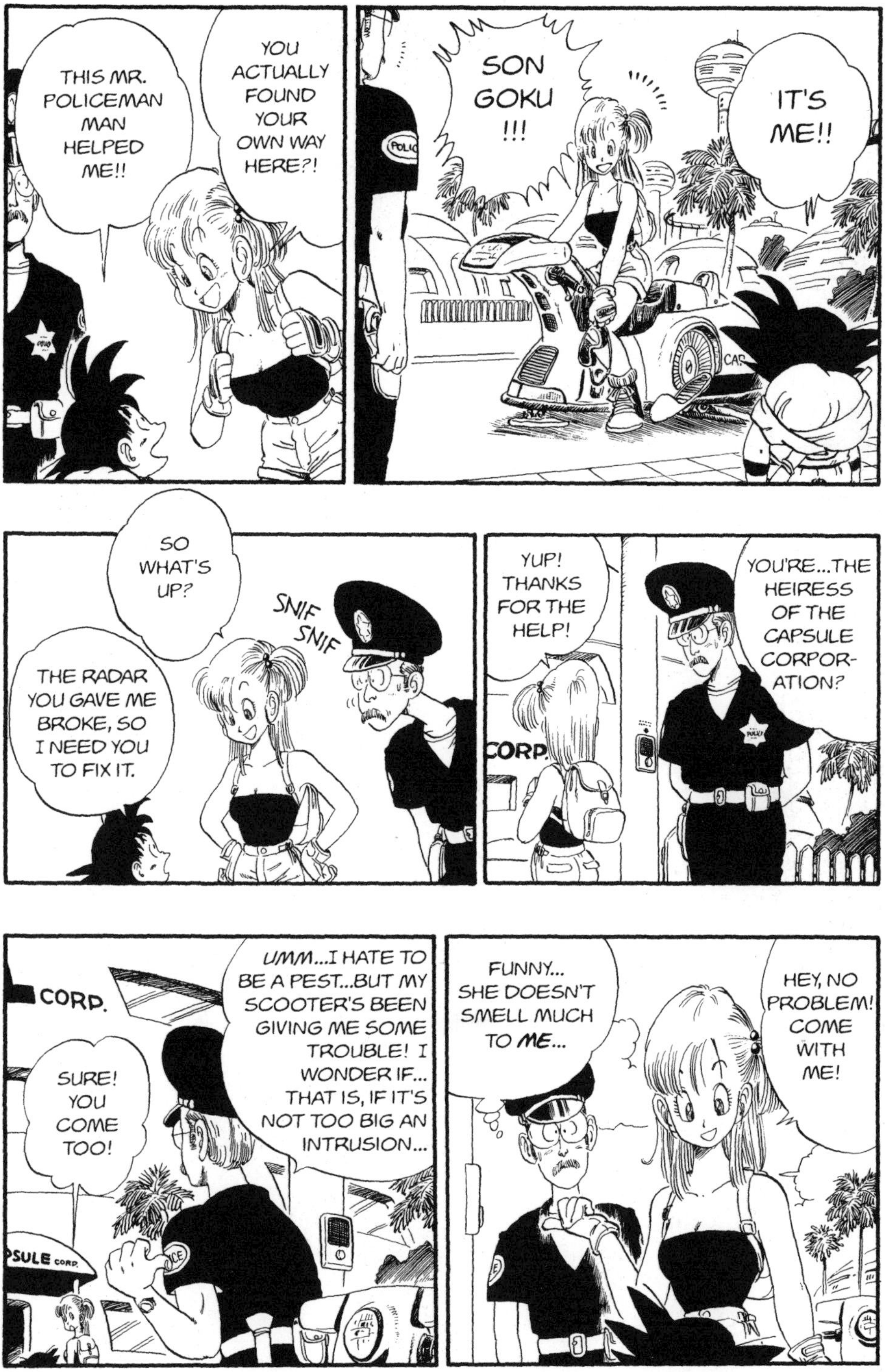
SON GOKU !!!
IT'S ME!!
YOU ACTUALLY FOUND YOUR OWN WAY HERE?!
THIS MR. POLICEMAN MAN HELPED ME!!
YOU'RE...THE HEIRESS OF THE CAPSULE CORPORATION?
YUP! THANKS FOR THE HELP!
CORP.
SO WHAT'S UP?
SNIF SNIF
THE RADAR YOU GAVE ME BROKE, SO I NEED YOU TO FIX IT.
HEY, NO PROBLEM! COME WITH ME!
FUNNY... SHE DOESN'T SMELL MUCH TO *ME*...
CORP.
UMM...I HATE TO BE A PEST...BUT MY SCOOTER'S BEEN GIVING ME SOME TROUBLE! I WONDER IF... THAT IS, IF IT'S NOT TOO BIG AN INTRUSION...
SURE! YOU COME TOO!
PSULE CORP.

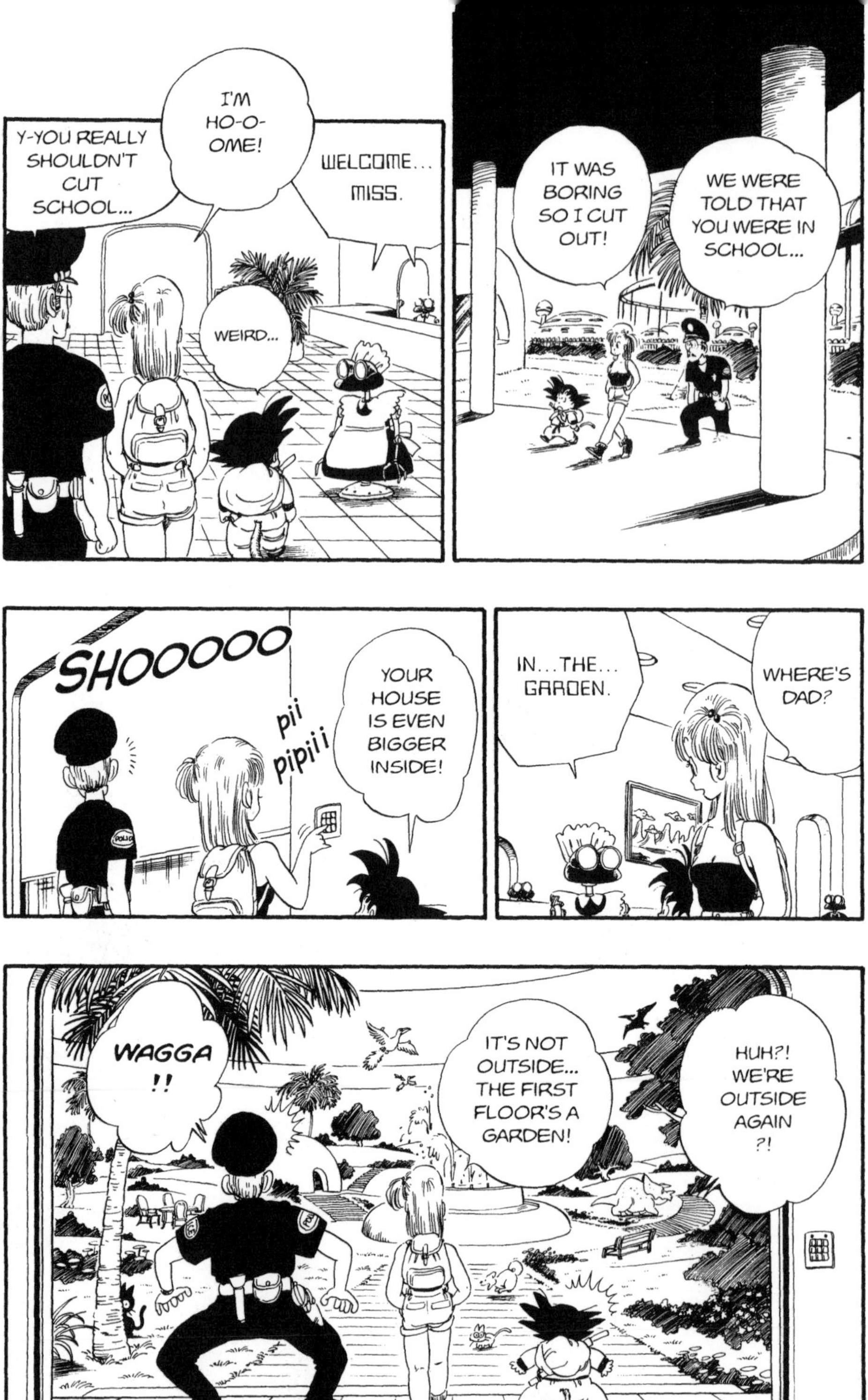
WE WERE TOLD THAT YOU WERE IN SCHOOL...
IT WAS BORING SO I CUT OUT!
I'M HO-O-OME!
WELCOME... MISS.
Y-YOU REALLY SHOULDN'T CUT SCHOOL...
WEIRD...
WHERE'S DAD?
IN... THE... GARDEN.
YOUR HOUSE IS EVEN BIGGER INSIDE!
pii pipiii
SHOOOOO
HUH?! WE'RE OUTSIDE AGAIN ?!
IT'S NOT OUTSIDE... THE FIRST FLOOR'S A GARDEN!
WAGGA !!

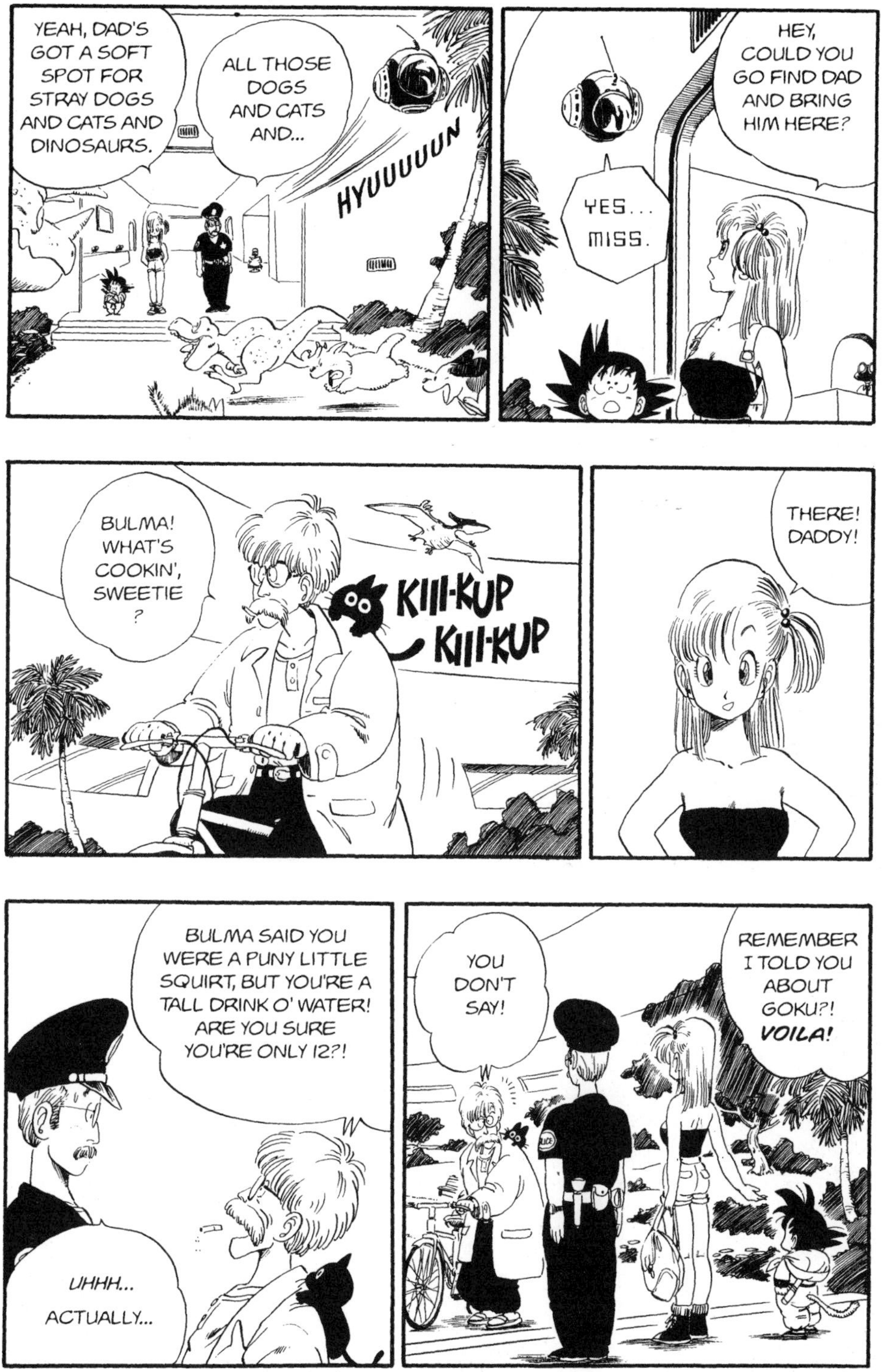
HEY, COULD YOU GO FIND DAD AND BRING HIM HERE?
YES... MISS.
ALL THOSE DOGS AND CATS AND...
YEAH, DAD'S GOT A SOFT SPOT FOR STRAY DOGS AND CATS AND DINOSAURS.
HYUUUUUN
THERE! DADDY!
BULMA! WHAT'S COOKIN', SWEETIE?
KIII-KUP
KIII-KUP
REMEMBER I TOLD YOU ABOUT GOKU?! *VOILA!*
YOU DON'T SAY!
BULMA SAID YOU WERE A PUNY LITTLE SQUIRT, BUT YOU'RE A TALL DRINK O' WATER! ARE YOU SURE YOU'RE ONLY 12?!
UHHH... ACTUALLY...

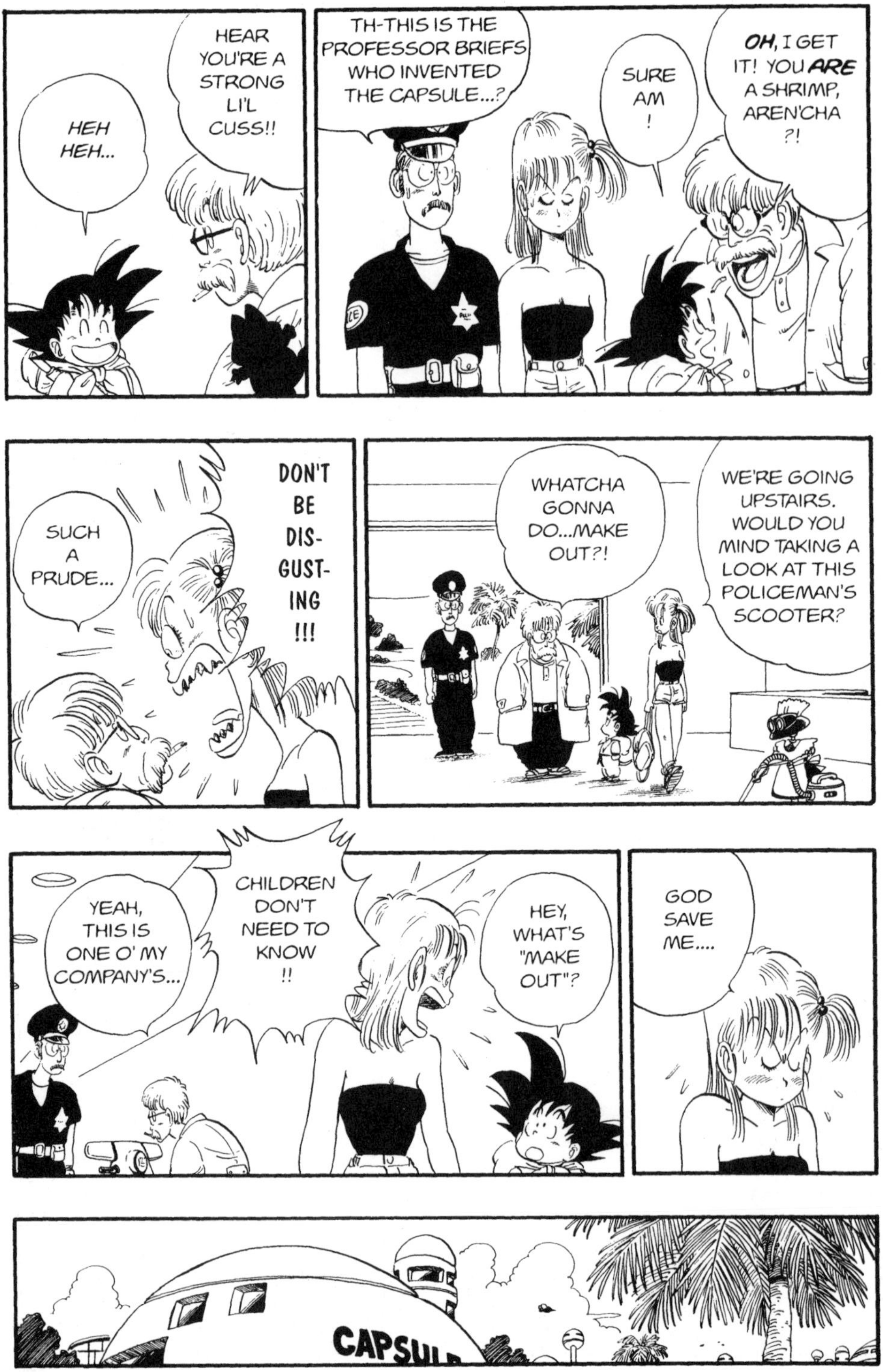

OH, I GET IT! YOU ARE A SHRIMP, AREN'CHA ?!
SURE AM !
TH-THIS IS THE PROFESSOR BRIEFS WHO INVENTED THE CAPSULE...?
HEAR YOU'RE A STRONG LI'L CUSS!!
HEH HEH...
WE'RE GOING UPSTAIRS. WOULD YOU MIND TAKING A LOOK AT THIS POLICEMAN'S SCOOTER?
WHATCHA GONNA DO...MAKE OUT?!
DON'T BE DIS-GUST-ING !!!
SUCH A PRUDE...
GOD SAVE ME....
HEY, WHAT'S "MAKE OUT"?
CHILDREN DON'T NEED TO KNOW !!
YEAH, THIS IS ONE O' MY COMPANY'S...
CAPSUL

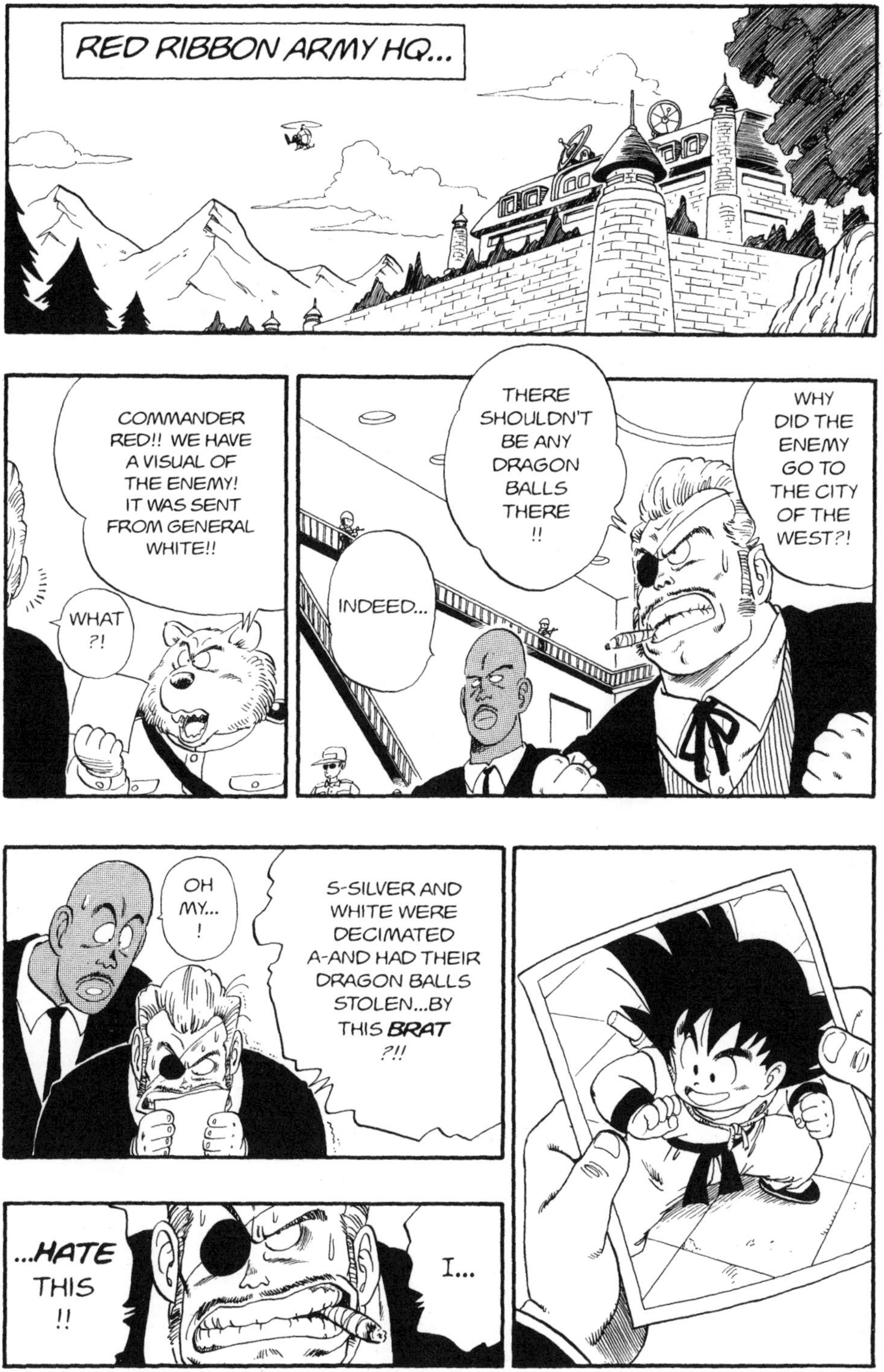
RED RIBBON ARMY HQ...
WHY DID THE ENEMY GO TO THE CITY OF THE WEST?!
THERE SHOULDN'T BE ANY DRAGON BALLS THERE !!
INDEED...
COMMANDER RED!! WE HAVE A VISUAL OF THE ENEMY! IT WAS SENT FROM GENERAL WHITE!!
WHAT ?!
S-SILVER AND WHITE WERE DECIMATED A-AND HAD THEIR DRAGON BALLS STOLEN...BY THIS ***BRAT*** ?!!
OH MY... !
I...
...***HATE*** THIS !!

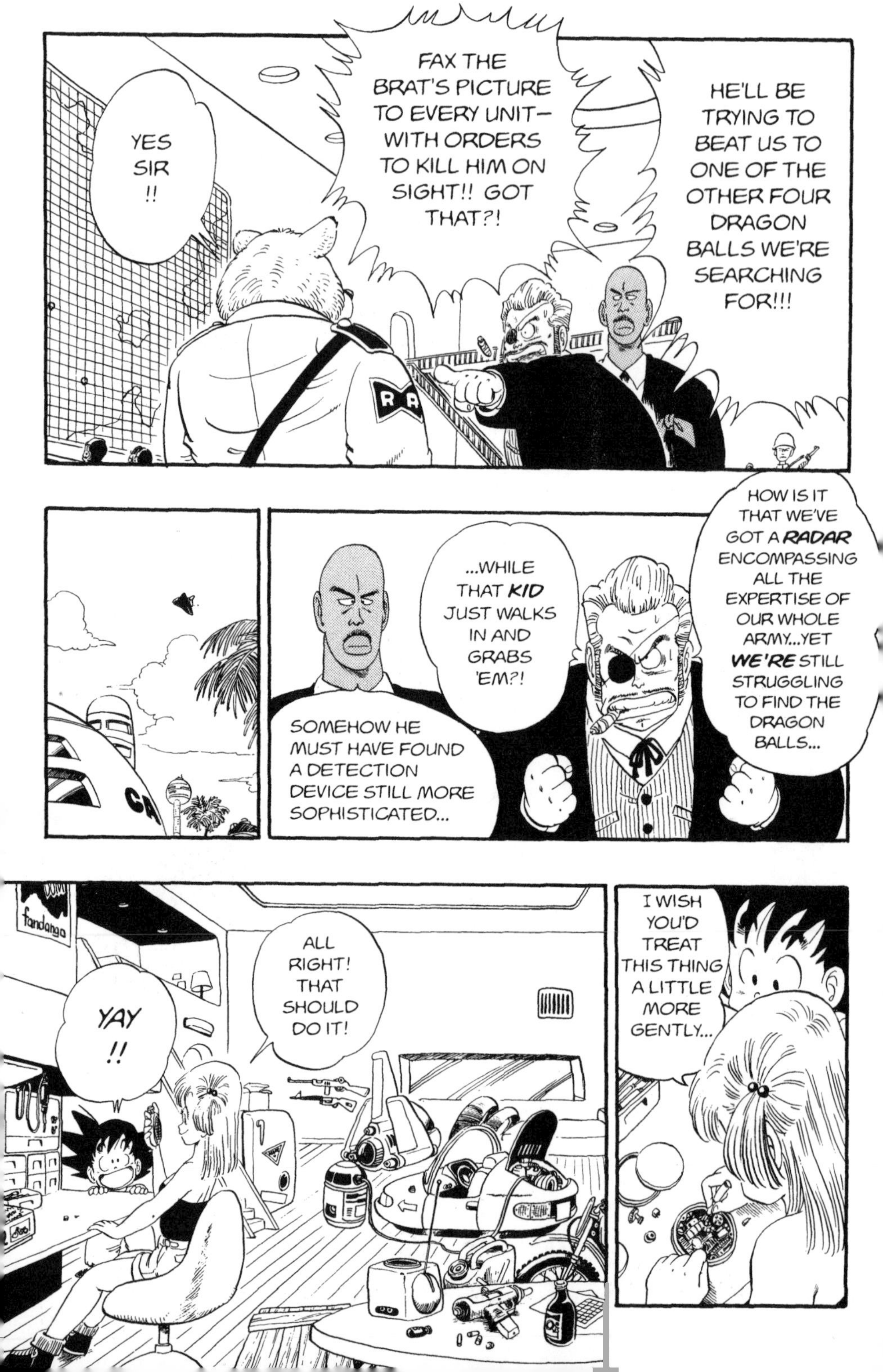
HE'LL BE TRYING TO BEAT US TO ONE OF THE OTHER FOUR DRAGON BALLS WE'RE SEARCHING FOR!!!
FAX THE BRAT'S PICTURE TO EVERY UNIT— WITH ORDERS TO KILL HIM ON SIGHT!! GOT THAT?!
YES SIR !!
HOW IS IT THAT WE'VE GOT A **RADAR** ENCOMPASSING ALL THE EXPERTISE OF OUR WHOLE ARMY...YET **WE'RE** STILL STRUGGLING TO FIND THE DRAGON BALLS...
...WHILE THAT **KID** JUST WALKS IN AND GRABS 'EM?!
SOMEHOW HE MUST HAVE FOUND A DETECTION DEVICE STILL MORE SOPHISTICATED...
I WISH YOU'D TREAT THIS THING A LITTLE MORE GENTLY...
ALL RIGHT! THAT SHOULD DO IT!
fandango
YAY !!

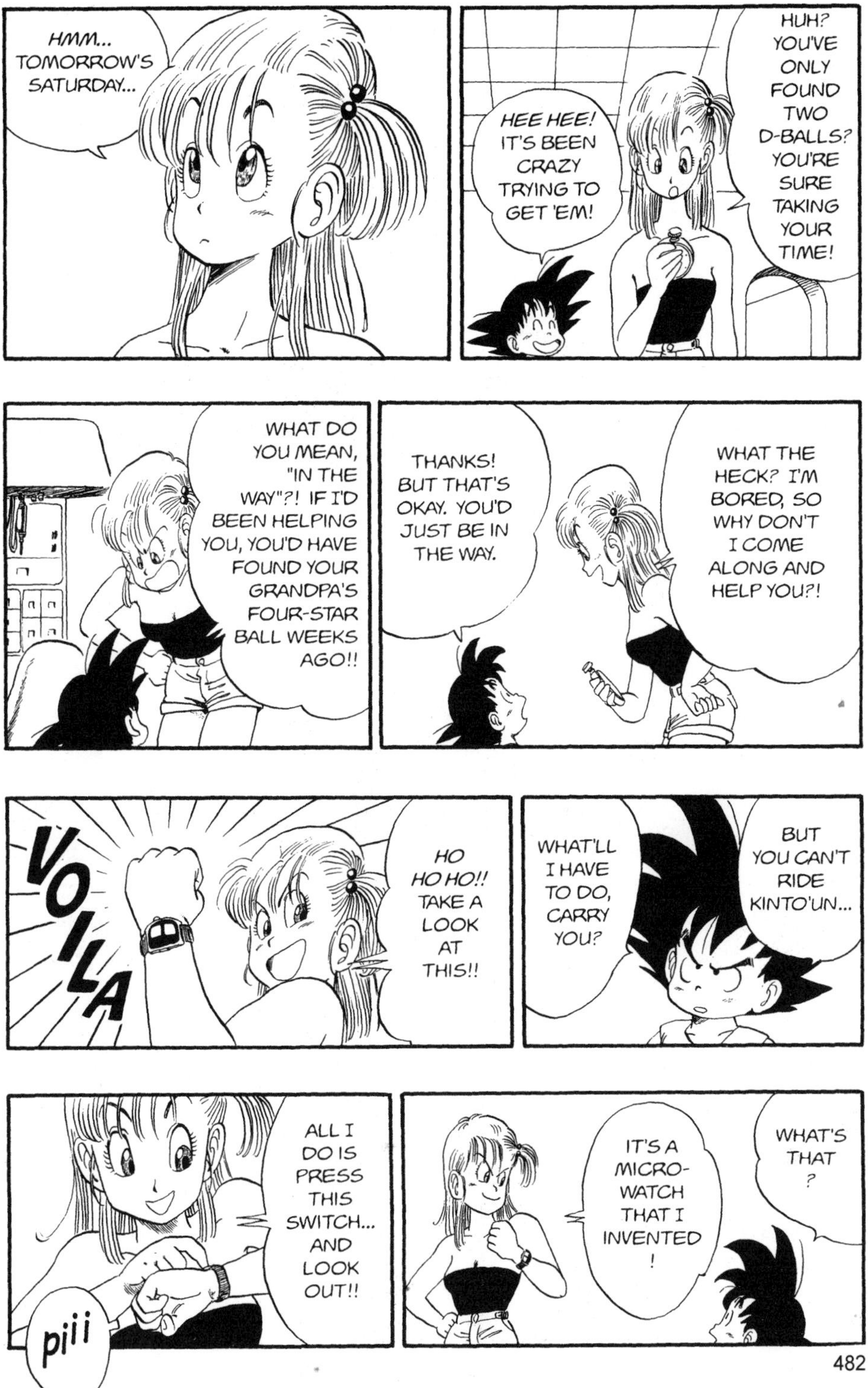
HUH? YOU'VE ONLY FOUND TWO D-BALLS? YOU'RE SURE TAKING YOUR TIME!
HEE HEE! IT'S BEEN CRAZY TRYING TO GET 'EM!
HMM... TOMORROW'S SATURDAY...
WHAT THE HECK? I'M BORED, SO WHY DON'T I COME ALONG AND HELP YOU?!
THANKS! BUT THAT'S OKAY. YOU'D JUST BE IN THE WAY.
WHAT DO YOU MEAN, "IN THE WAY"?! IF I'D BEEN HELPING YOU, YOU'D HAVE FOUND YOUR GRANDPA'S FOUR-STAR BALL WEEKS AGO!!
BUT YOU CAN'T RIDE KINTO'UN...
WHAT'LL I HAVE TO DO, CARRY YOU?
HO HO HO!! TAKE A LOOK AT THIS!!
VOILA
WHAT'S THAT?
IT'S A MICRO-WATCH THAT I INVENTED!
ALL I DO IS PRESS THIS SWITCH... AND LOOK OUT!!
piii

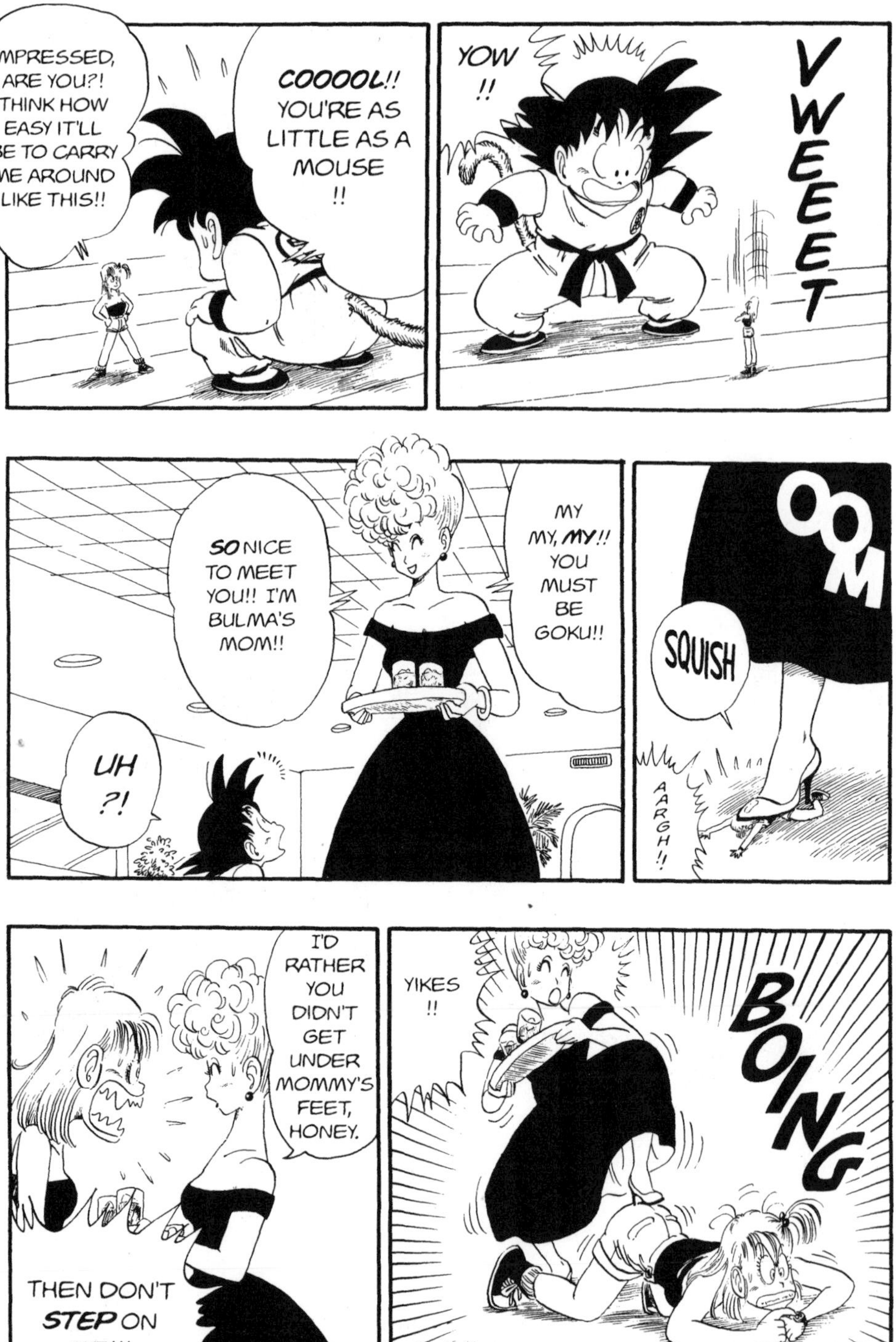

VWEEET
YOW!!
COOOOL!! YOU'RE AS LITTLE AS A MOUSE!!
IMPRESSED, ARE YOU?! THINK HOW EASY IT'LL BE TO CARRY ME AROUND LIKE THIS!!
OOM
SQUISH
AARGH!!
MY MY, MY!! YOU MUST BE GOKU!!
SO NICE TO MEET YOU!! I'M BULMA'S MOM!!
UH?!
BOING
YIKES!!
I'D RATHER YOU DIDN'T GET UNDER MOMMY'S FEET, HONEY.
THEN DON'T STEP ON ME!!!

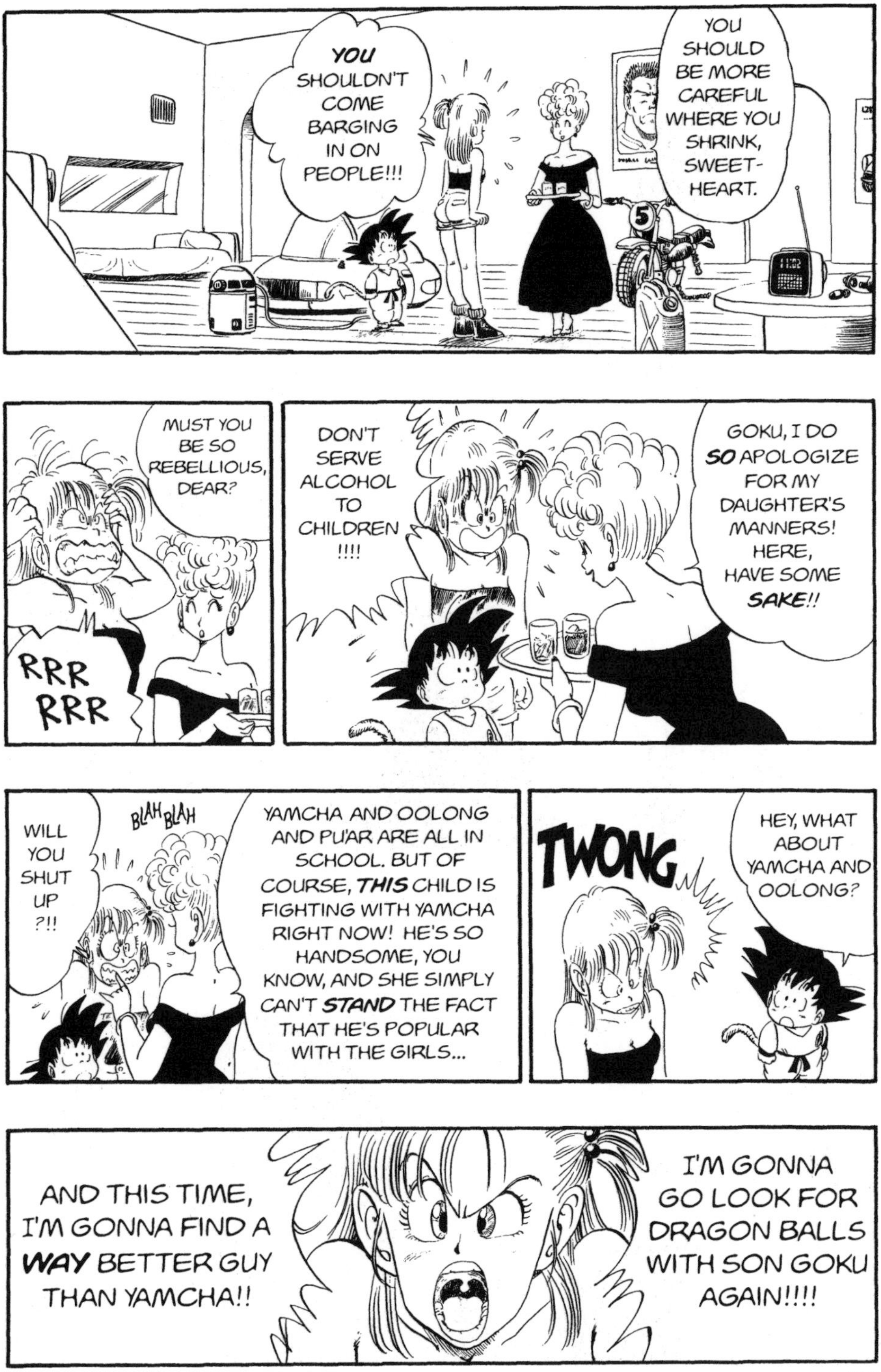
YOU SHOULD BE MORE CAREFUL WHERE YOU SHRINK, SWEET-HEART.
YOU SHOULDN'T COME BARGING IN ON PEOPLE!!!
GOKU, I DO SO APOLOGIZE FOR MY DAUGHTER'S MANNERS! HERE, HAVE SOME SAKE!!
DON'T SERVE ALCOHOL TO CHILDREN !!!!
MUST YOU BE SO REBELLIOUS, DEAR?
RRR RRR
HEY, WHAT ABOUT YAMCHA AND OOLONG?
TWONG
YAMCHA AND OOLONG AND PU'AR ARE ALL IN SCHOOL. BUT OF COURSE, THIS CHILD IS FIGHTING WITH YAMCHA RIGHT NOW! HE'S SO HANDSOME, YOU KNOW, AND SHE SIMPLY CAN'T STAND THE FACT THAT HE'S POPULAR WITH THE GIRLS...
BLAH BLAH
WILL YOU SHUT UP ?!!
I'M GONNA GO LOOK FOR DRAGON BALLS WITH SON GOKU AGAIN!!!!
AND THIS TIME, I'M GONNA FIND A WAY BETTER GUY THAN YAMCHA!!

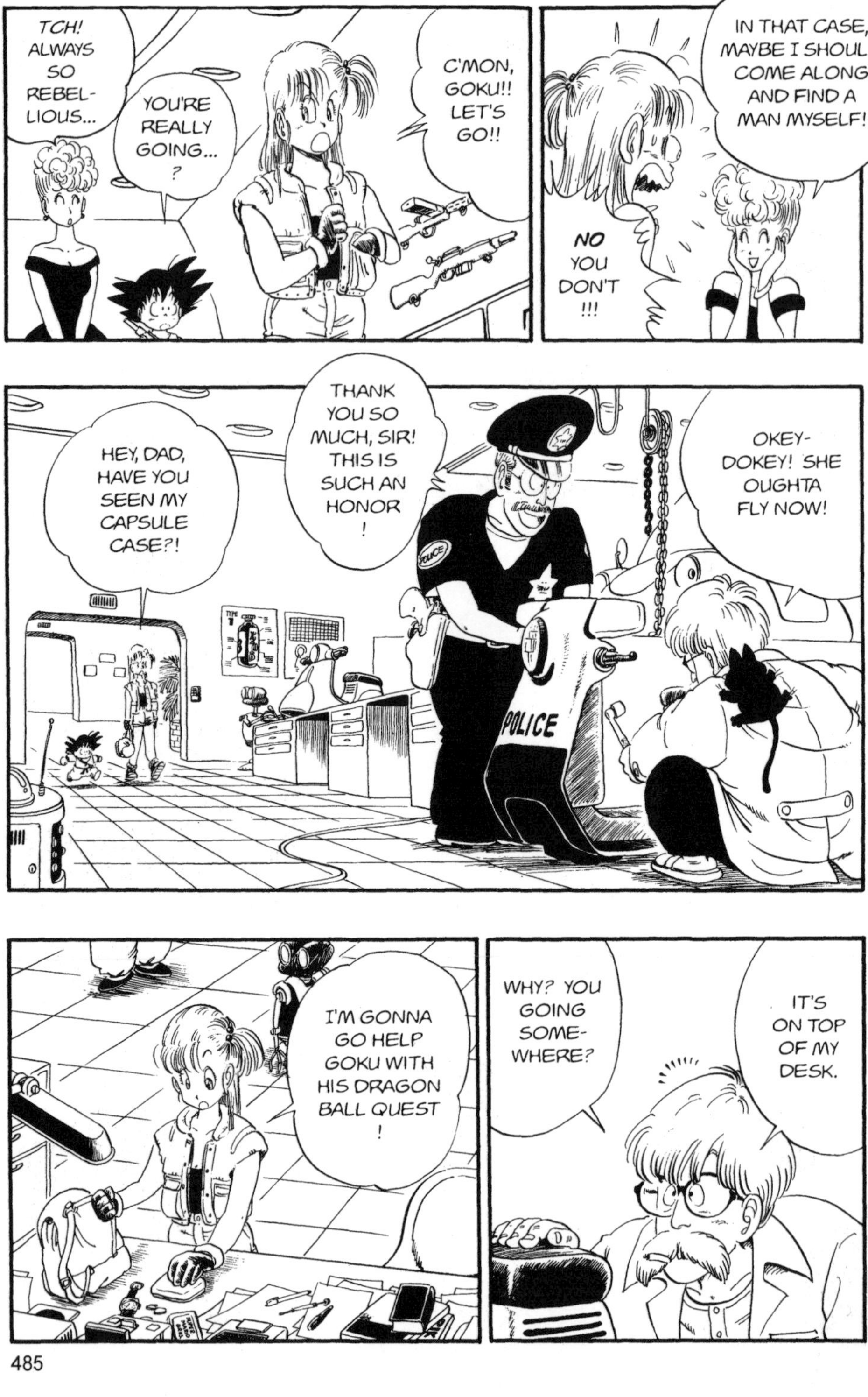
IN THAT CASE, MAYBE I SHOULD COME ALONG AND FIND A MAN MYSELF!
NO YOU DON'T !!!
C'MON, GOKU!! LET'S GO!!
YOU'RE REALLY GOING...?
TCH! ALWAYS SO REBEL-LIOUS...
OKEY-DOKEY! SHE OUGHTA FLY NOW!
THANK YOU SO MUCH, SIR! THIS IS SUCH AN HONOR!
HEY, DAD, HAVE YOU SEEN MY CAPSULE CASE?!
POLICE
IT'S ON TOP OF MY DESK.
WHY? YOU GOING SOME-WHERE?
I'M GONNA GO HELP GOKU WITH HIS DRAGON BALL QUEST!

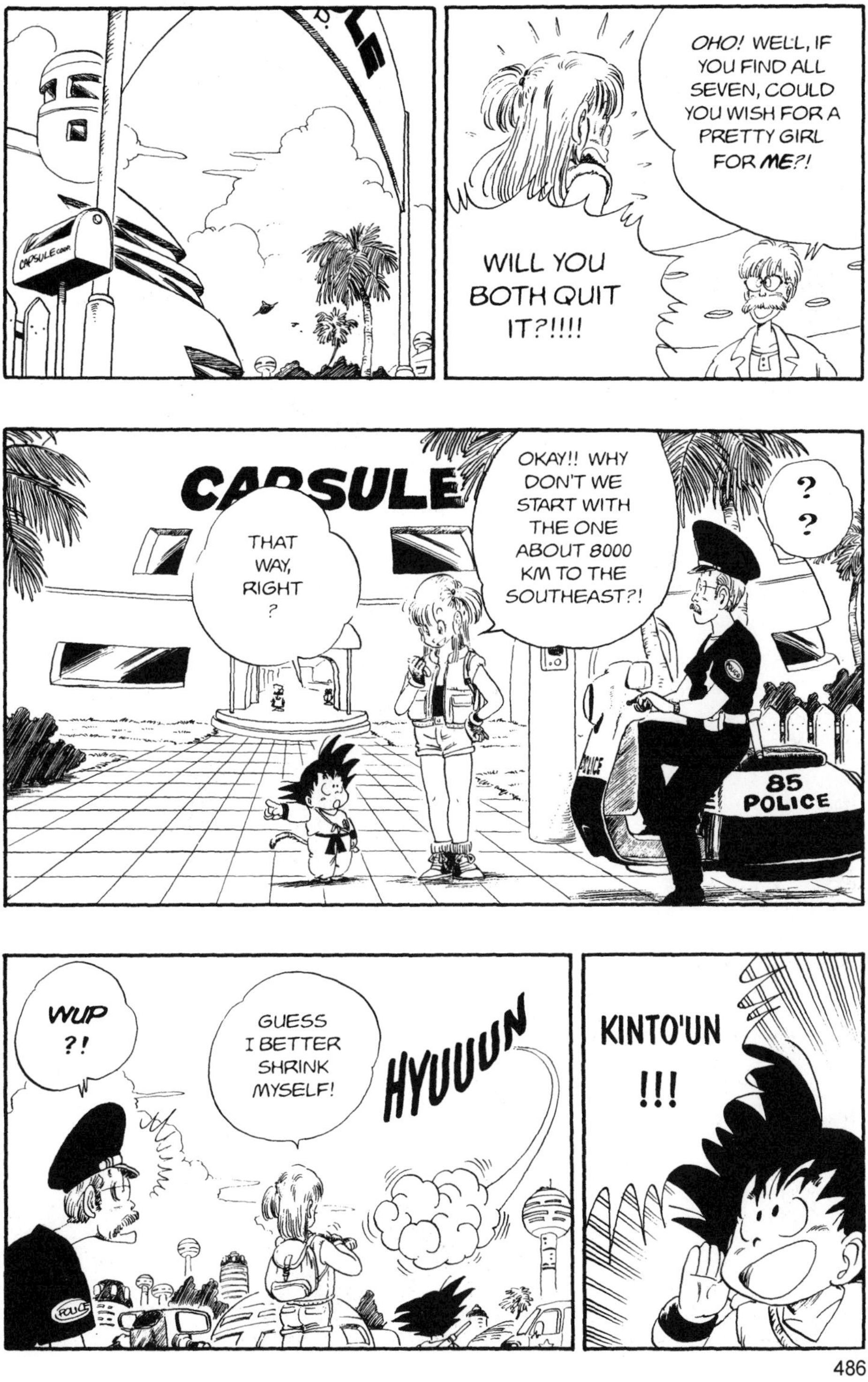
OHO! WELL, IF YOU FIND ALL SEVEN, COULD YOU WISH FOR A PRETTY GIRL FOR *ME*?!
WILL YOU BOTH QUIT IT?!!!!
CAPSULE CORP.
??
OKAY!! WHY DON'T WE START WITH THE ONE ABOUT 8000 KM TO THE SOUTHEAST?!
CAPSULE
THAT WAY, RIGHT?
85 POLICE
KINTO'UN !!!
HYUUUN
GUESS I BETTER SHRINK MYSELF!
WUP?!

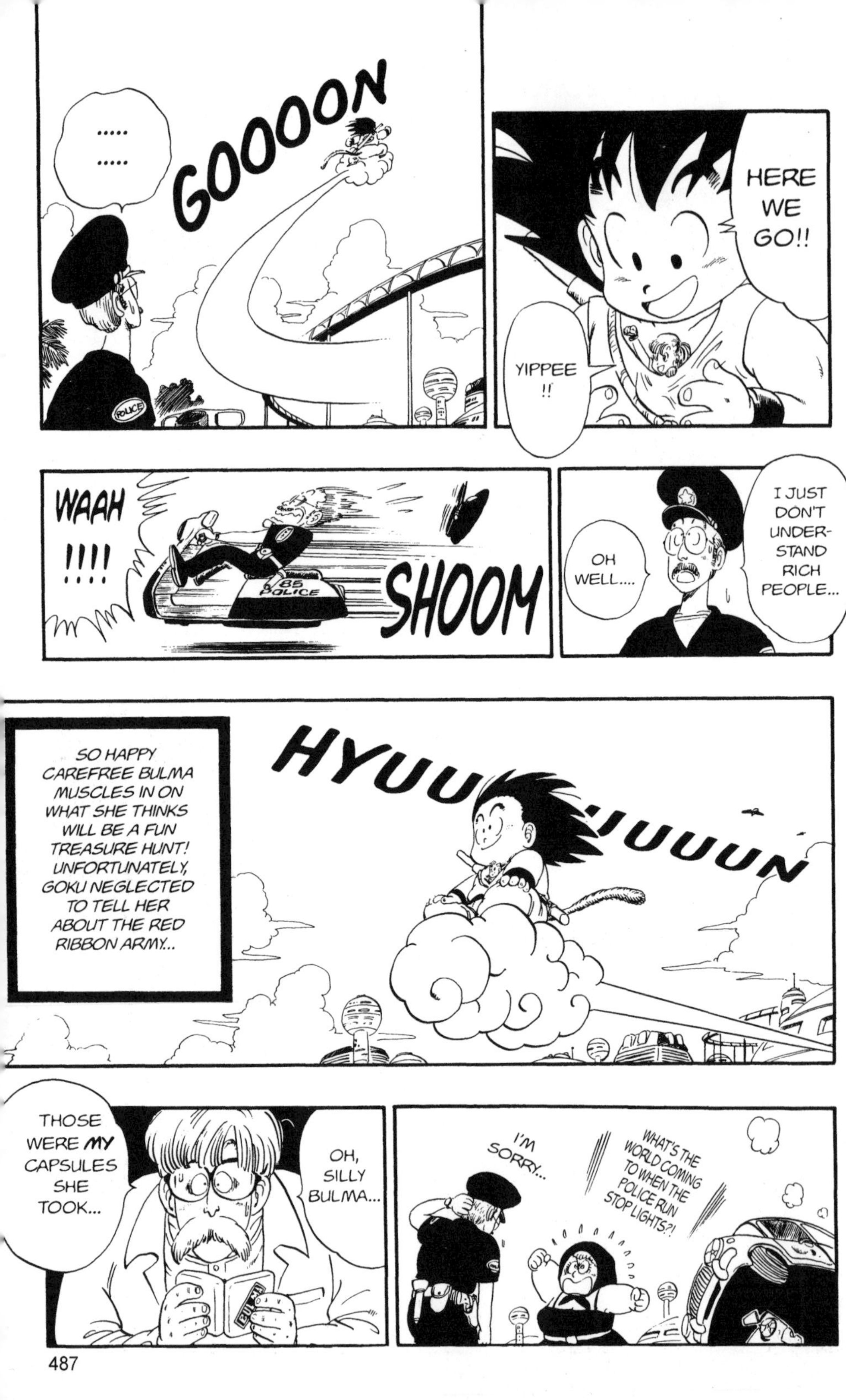
HERE WE GO!!
YIPPEE !!
.....
.....
GOOOON
I JUST DON'T UNDER-STAND RICH PEOPLE...
OH WELL....
WAAH !!!!
SHOOM
HYUUUUUUUN
SO HAPPY CAREFREE BULMA MUSCLES IN ON WHAT SHE THINKS WILL BE A FUN TREASURE HUNT! UNFORTUNATELY, GOKU NEGLECTED TO TELL HER ABOUT THE RED RIBBON ARMY...
WHAT'S THE WORLD COMING TO WHEN THE POLICE RUN STOP LIGHTS?!
I'M SORRY...
THOSE WERE MY CAPSULES SHE TOOK...
OH, SILLY BULMA...

Tale 70
Bulma's Big Mistake!!

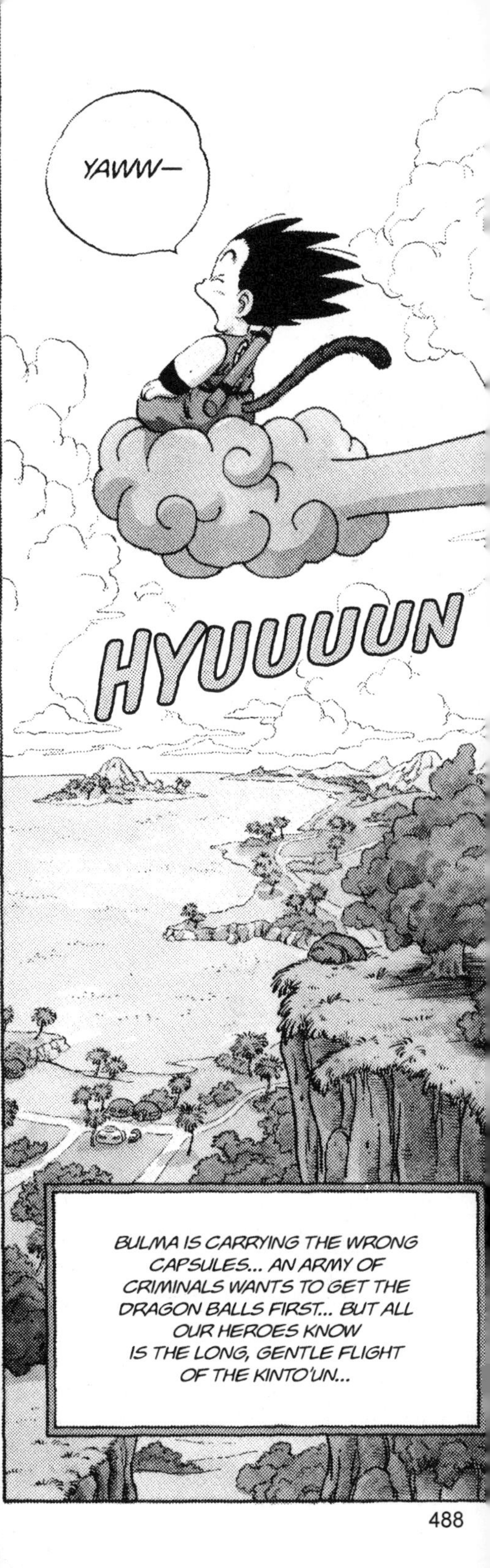
YAWW—
HYUUUUN
BULMA IS CARRYING THE WRONG CAPSULES... AN ARMY OF CRIMINALS WANTS TO GET THE DRAGON BALLS FIRST... BUT ALL OUR HEROES KNOW IS THE LONG, GENTLE FLIGHT OF THE KINTO'UN...

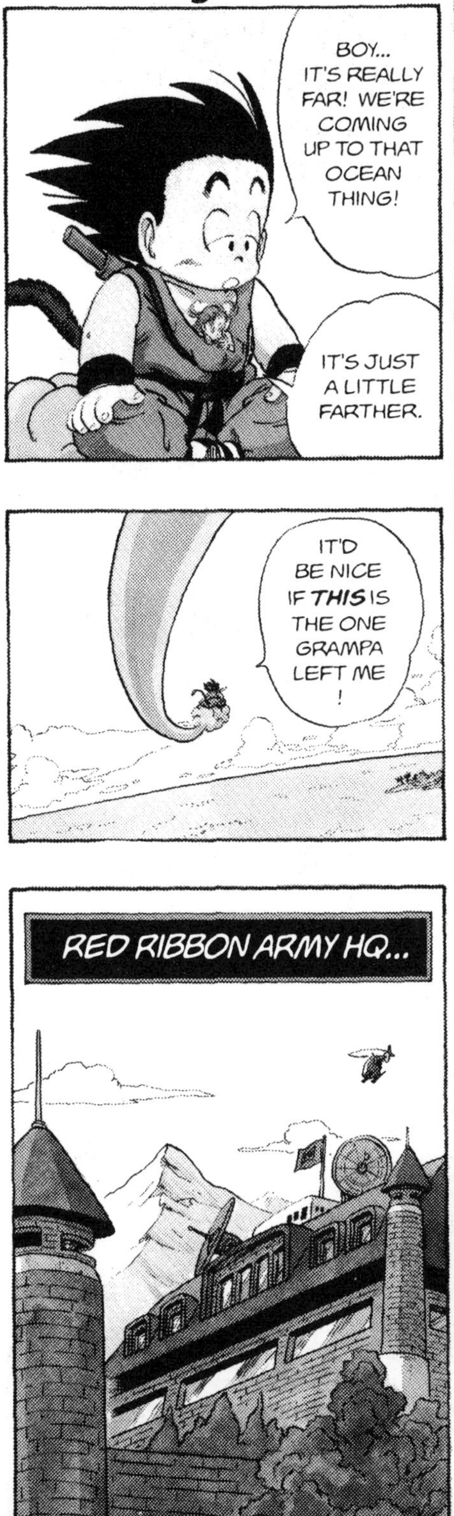
BOY... IT'S REALLY FAR! WE'RE COMING UP TO THAT OCEAN THING!
IT'S JUST A LITTLE FARTHER.
IT'D BE NICE IF ***THIS*** IS THE ONE GRAMPA LEFT ME!
RED RIBBON ARMY HQ...

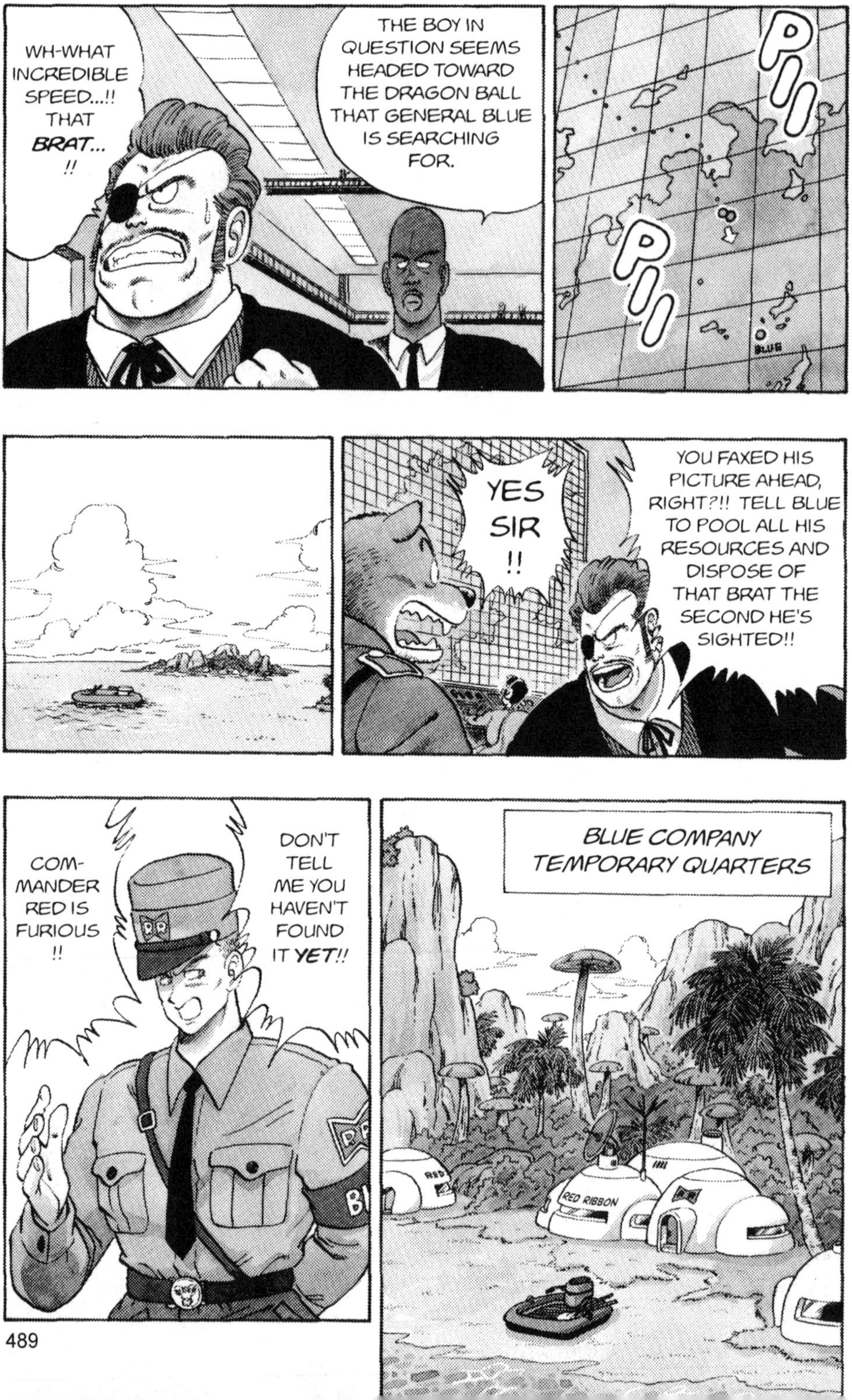
PII
PII
BLUE
THE BOY IN QUESTION SEEMS HEADED TOWARD THE DRAGON BALL THAT GENERAL BLUE IS SEARCHING FOR.
WH-WHAT INCREDIBLE SPEED...!! THAT *BRAT*...!!
YOU FAXED HIS PICTURE AHEAD, RIGHT?!! TELL BLUE TO POOL ALL HIS RESOURCES AND DISPOSE OF THAT BRAT THE SECOND HE'S SIGHTED!!
YES SIR!!
BLUE COMPANY TEMPORARY QUARTERS
RED RIBBON
RED
DON'T TELL ME YOU HAVEN'T FOUND IT *YET*!!
COM-MANDER RED IS FURIOUS!!

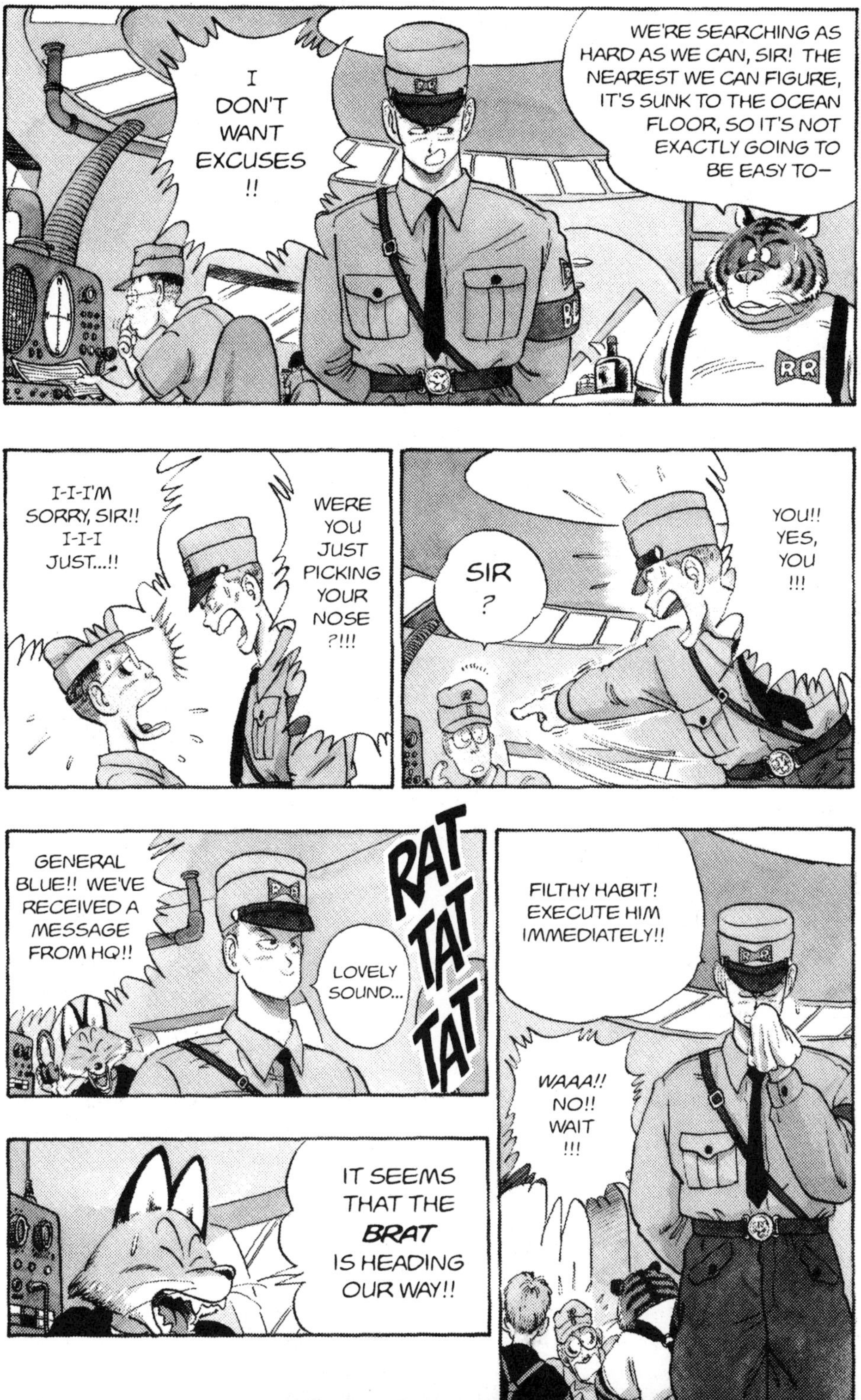
WE'RE SEARCHING AS HARD AS WE CAN, SIR! THE NEAREST WE CAN FIGURE, IT'S SUNK TO THE OCEAN FLOOR, SO IT'S NOT EXACTLY GOING TO BE EASY TO—
I DON'T WANT EXCUSES!!
YOU!! YES, YOU!!!
SIR?
WERE YOU JUST PICKING YOUR NOSE?!!!
I-I-I'M SORRY, SIR!! I-I-I JUST...!!
FILTHY HABIT! EXECUTE HIM IMMEDIATELY!!
WAAA!! NO!! WAIT!!!
RAT TAT TAT
LOVELY SOUND...
GENERAL BLUE!! WE'VE RECEIVED A MESSAGE FROM HQ!!
IT SEEMS THAT THE *BRAT* IS HEADING OUR WAY!!

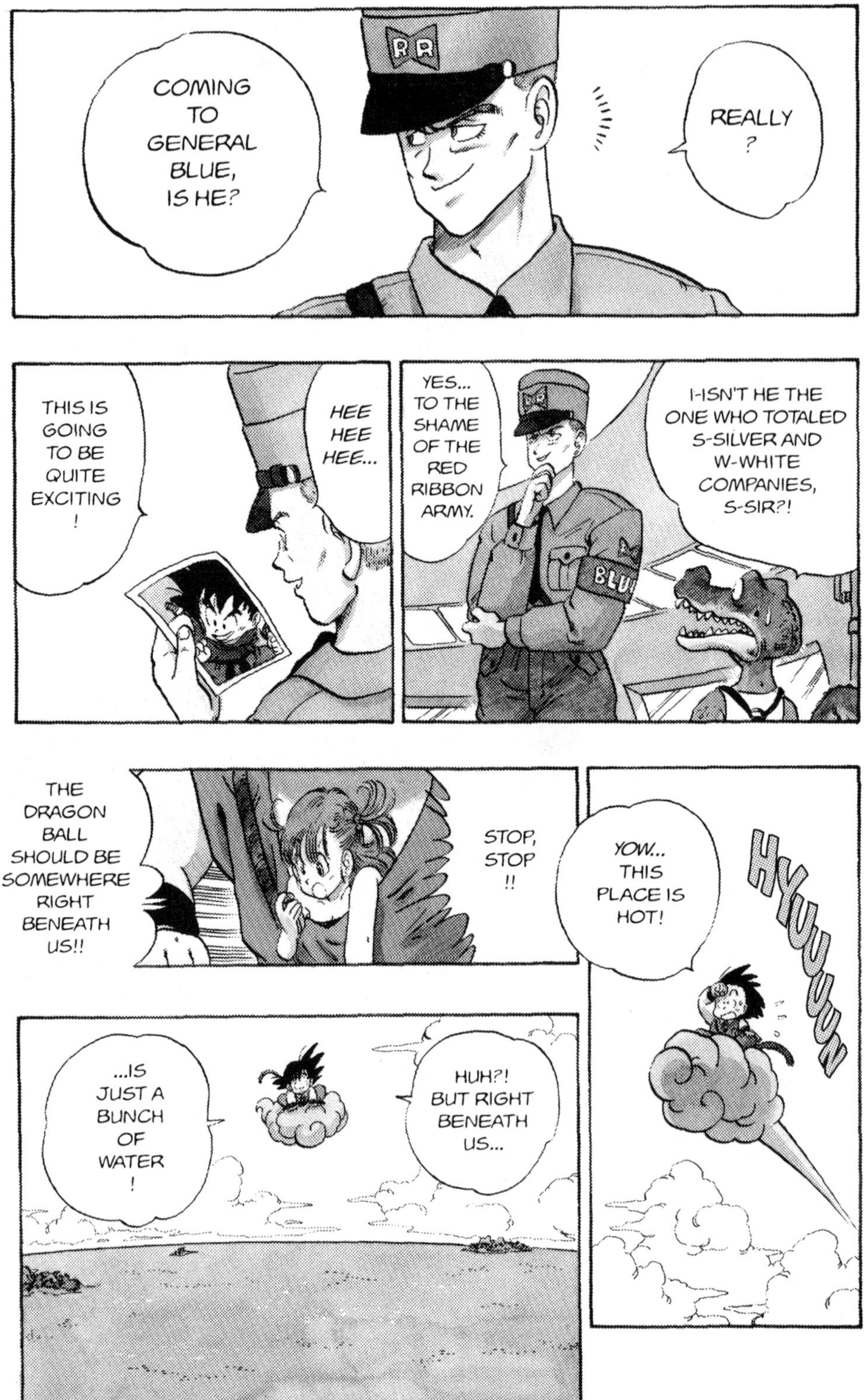
REALLY?
COMING TO GENERAL BLUE, IS HE?
I-ISN'T HE THE ONE WHO TOTALED S-SILVER AND W-WHITE COMPANIES, S-SIR?!
YES... TO THE SHAME OF THE RED RIBBON ARMY.
HEE HEE HEE...
THIS IS GOING TO BE QUITE EXCITING!
HYUUUUN
YOW... THIS PLACE IS HOT!
STOP, STOP!!
THE DRAGON BALL SHOULD BE SOMEWHERE RIGHT BENEATH US!!
HUH?! BUT RIGHT BENEATH US...
...IS JUST A BUNCH OF WATER!

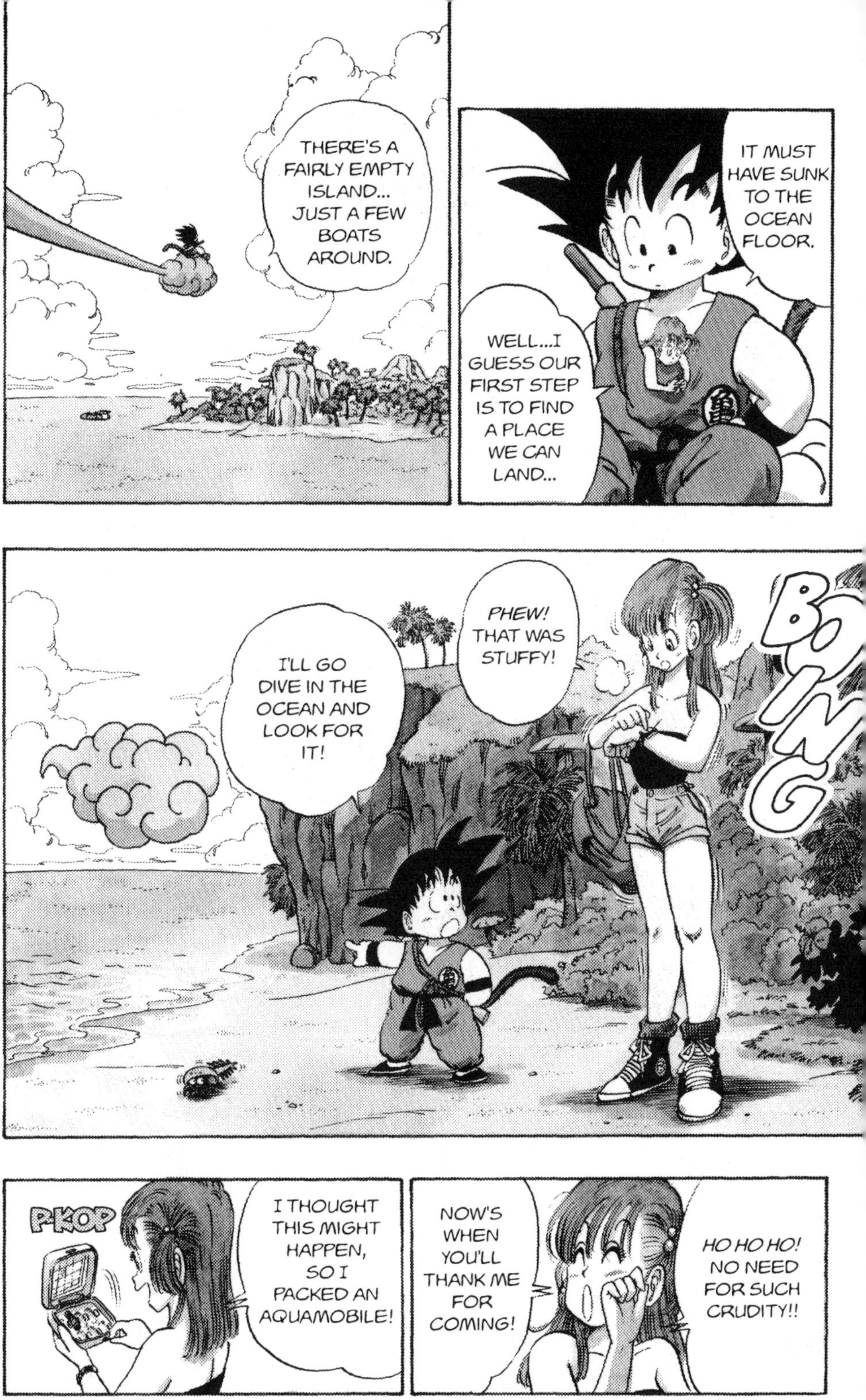
IT MUST HAVE SUNK TO THE OCEAN FLOOR.
WELL...I GUESS OUR FIRST STEP IS TO FIND A PLACE WE CAN LAND...
THERE'S A FAIRLY EMPTY ISLAND... JUST A FEW BOATS AROUND.
BOING
PHEW! THAT WAS STUFFY!
I'LL GO DIVE IN THE OCEAN AND LOOK FOR IT!
HO HO HO! NO NEED FOR SUCH CRUDITY!!
NOW'S WHEN YOU'LL THANK ME FOR COMING!
P-KOP
I THOUGHT THIS MIGHT HAPPEN, SO I PACKED AN AQUAMOBILE!

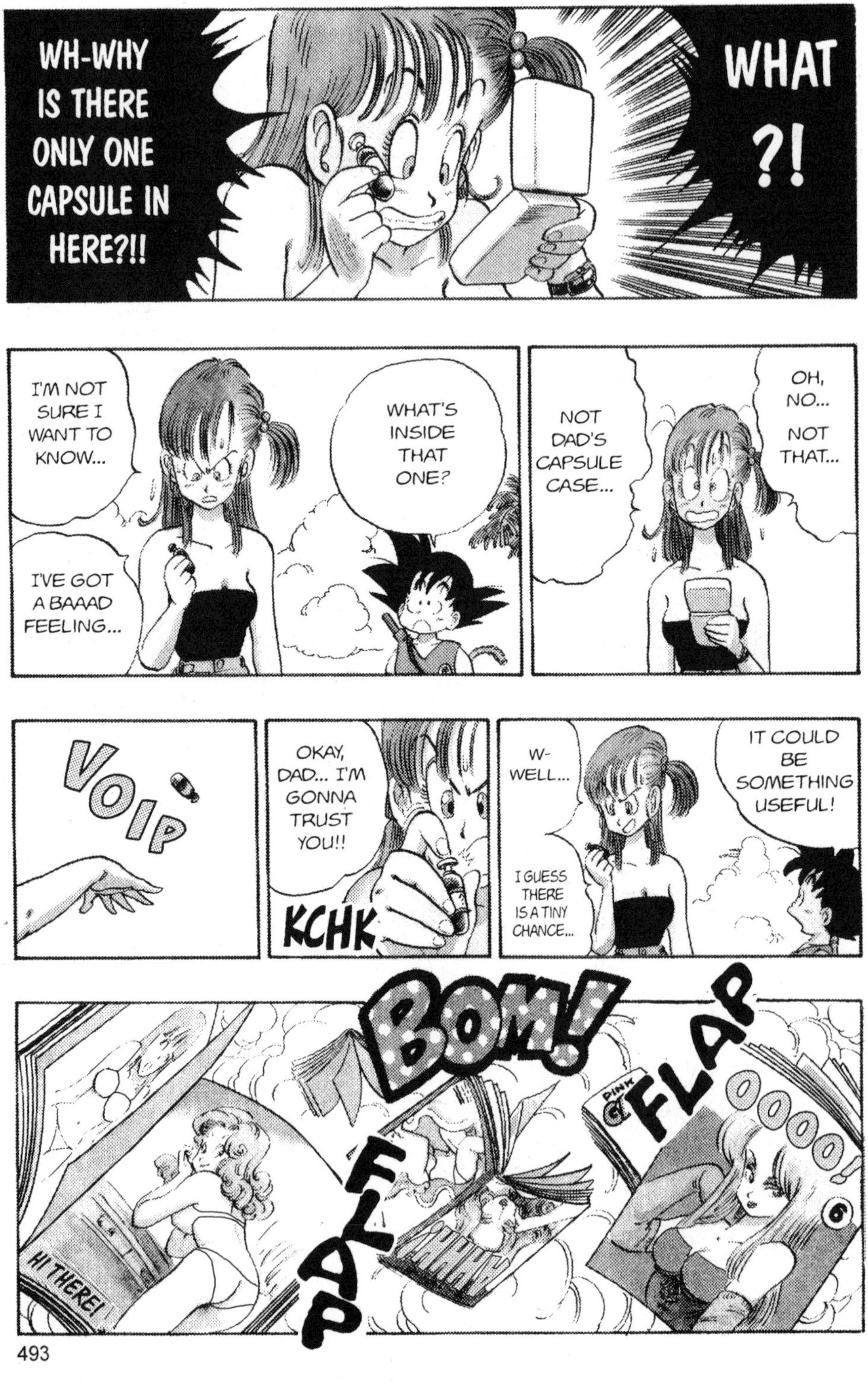
WHAT ?!
WH-WHY IS THERE ONLY ONE CAPSULE IN HERE?!!
OH, NO... NOT THAT...
NOT DAD'S CAPSULE CASE...
WHAT'S INSIDE THAT ONE?
I'M NOT SURE I WANT TO KNOW...
I'VE GOT A BAAAD FEELING...
IT COULD BE SOMETHING USEFUL!
W-WELL...
I GUESS THERE IS A TINY CHANCE...
OKAY, DAD... I'M GONNA TRUST YOU!!
KCHK
VOIP
BOM!
FLAP
OOOO!
PINK
FLAP
HI THERE!

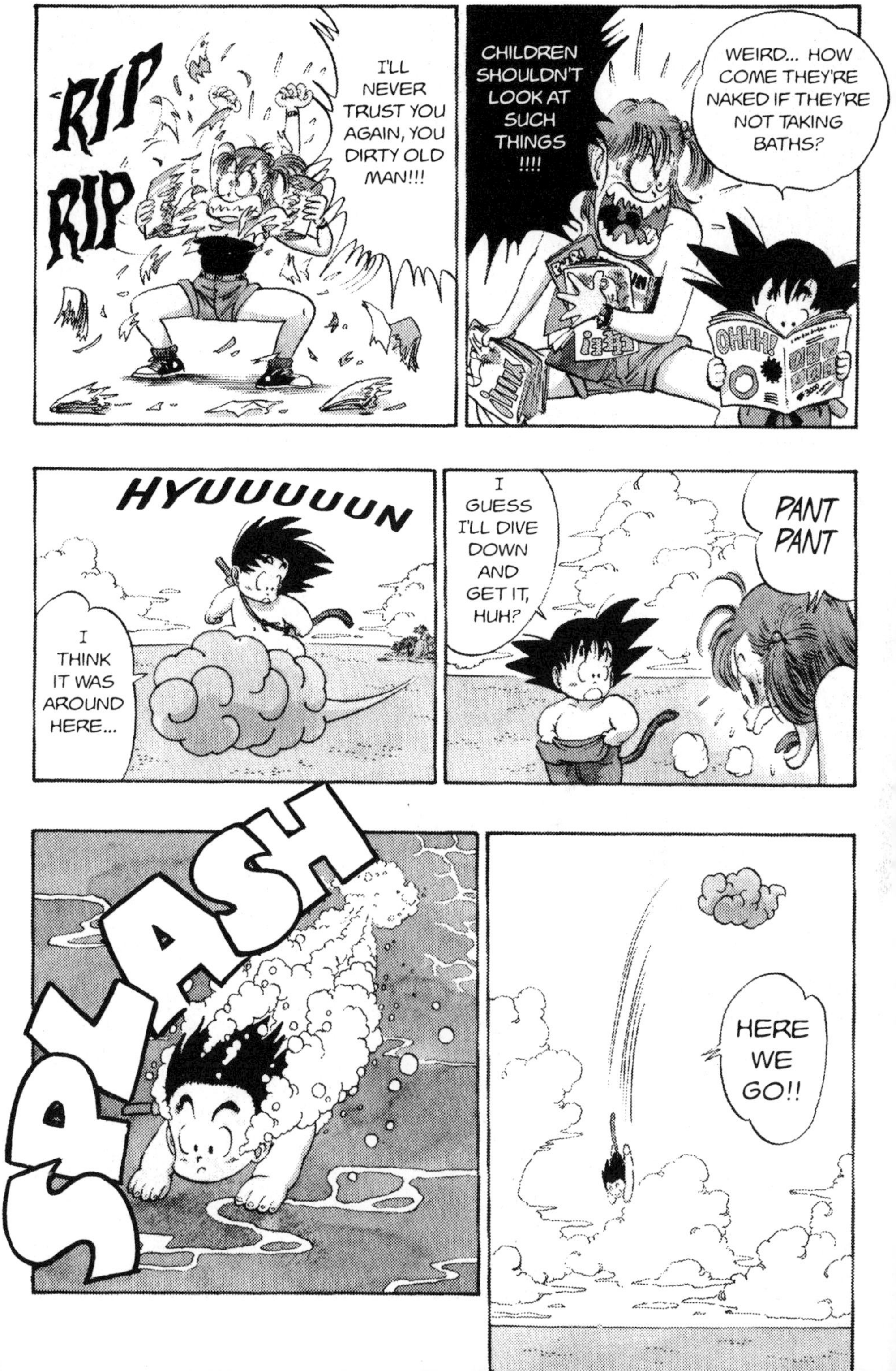
WEIRD... HOW COME THEY'RE NAKED IF THEY'RE NOT TAKING BATHS?
CHILDREN SHOULDN'T LOOK AT SUCH THINGS !!!!
OHHH!
I'LL NEVER TRUST YOU AGAIN, YOU DIRTY OLD MAN!!!
RIP RIP
PANT PANT
I GUESS I'LL DIVE DOWN AND GET IT, HUH?
HYUUUUUUN
I THINK IT WAS AROUND HERE...
HERE WE GO!!
SPLASH

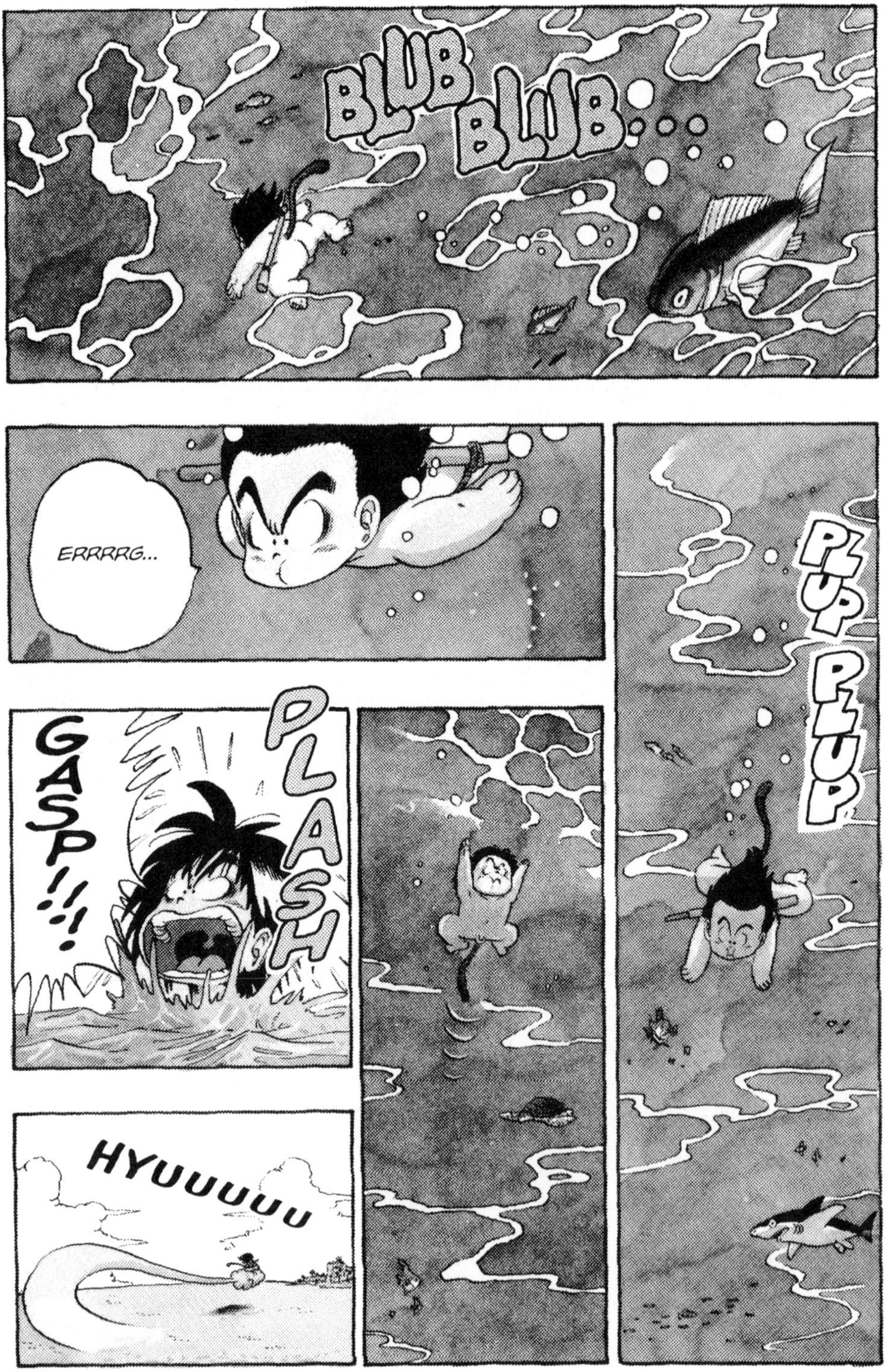
BLUB BLUB...
PLUP PLUP PLUP
ERRRRG...
PLASH
GASP!!!
HYUUUUUU

WE INTERRUPT THIS DULL STORY
FOR A THRILLING ANNOUNCEMENT!

GENERAL BLUE IS APPROACHING!!

WHAT WILL HAPPEN?! READ ON!!

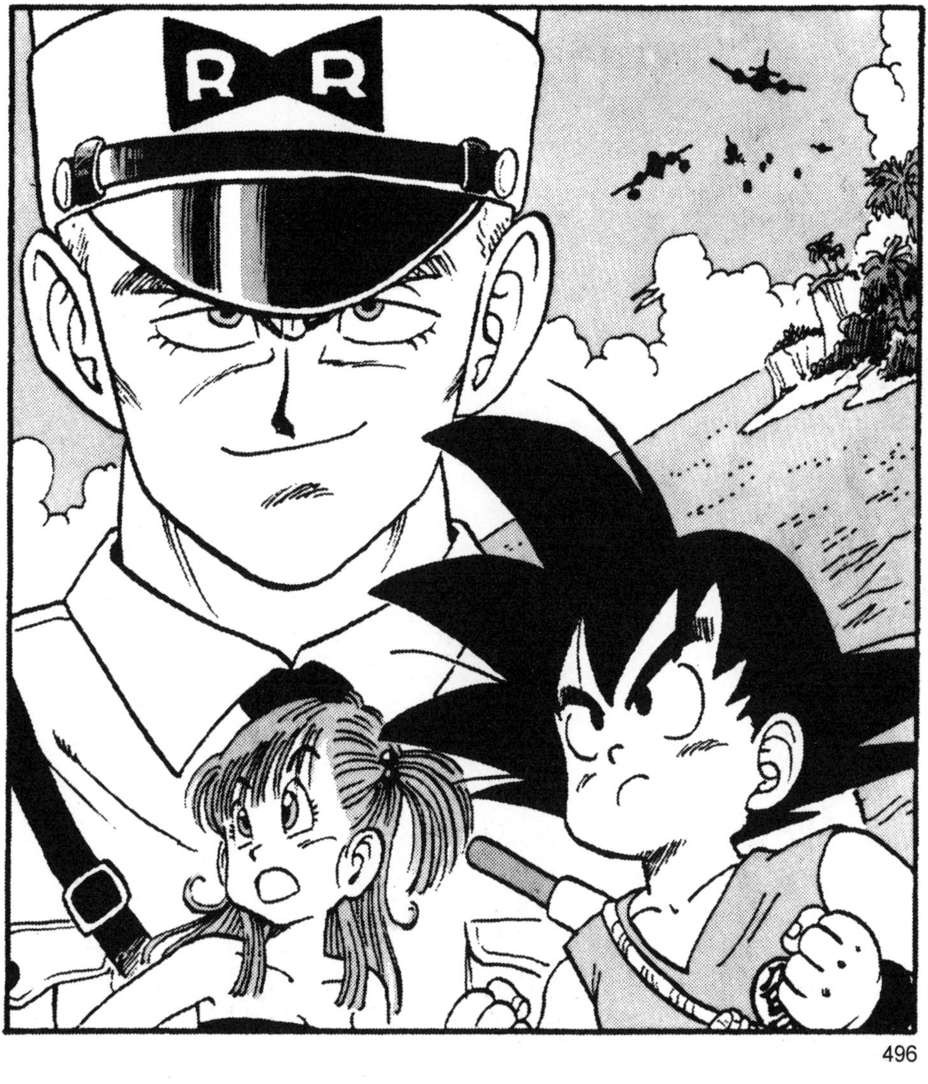
R R

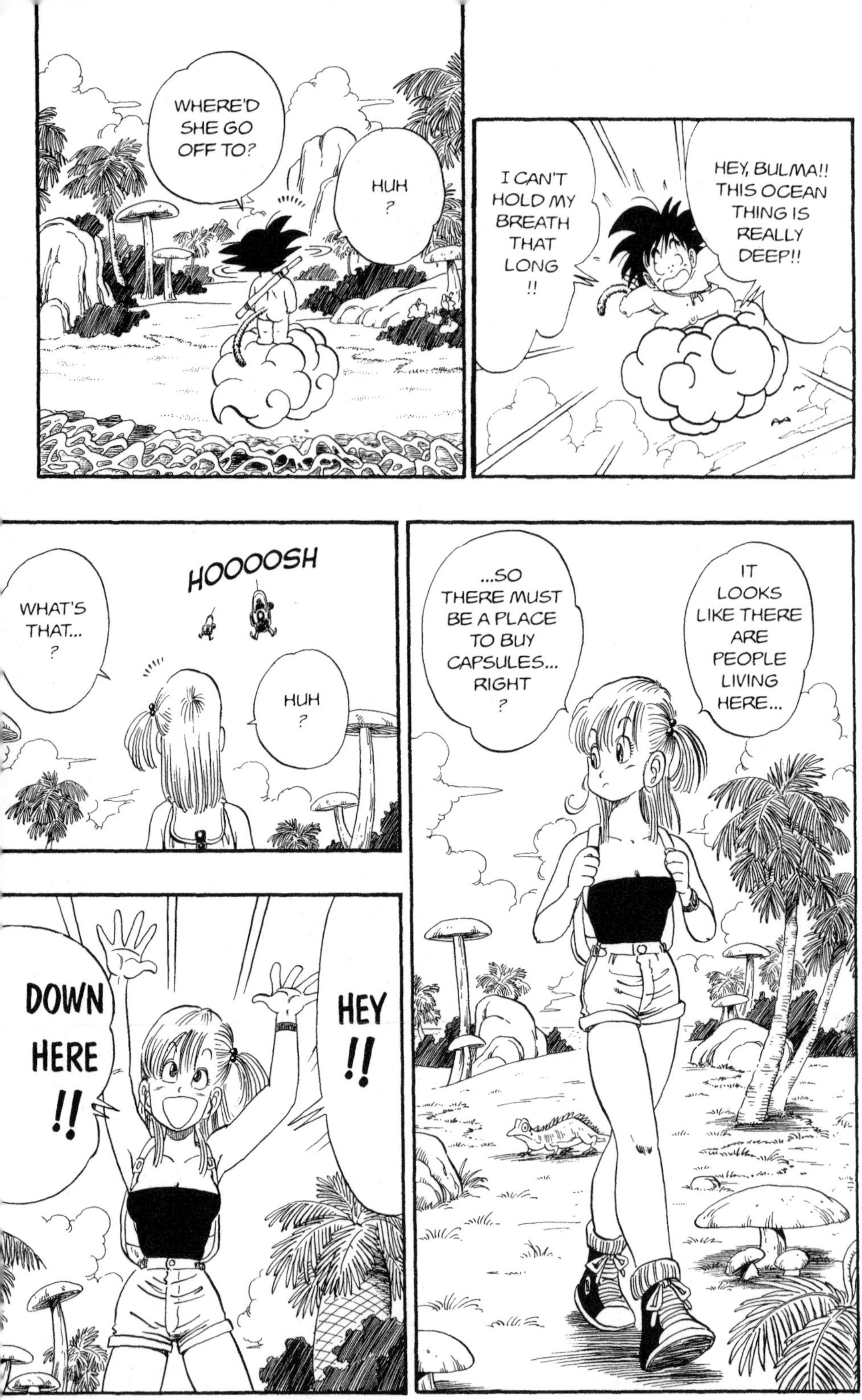
HEY, BULMA!! THIS OCEAN THING IS REALLY DEEP!!
I CAN'T HOLD MY BREATH THAT LONG !!
WHERE'D SHE GO OFF TO?
HUH ?
IT LOOKS LIKE THERE ARE PEOPLE LIVING HERE...
...SO THERE MUST BE A PLACE TO BUY CAPSULES... RIGHT ?
HOOOOSH
HUH ?
WHAT'S THAT... ?
HEY !!
DOWN HERE !!

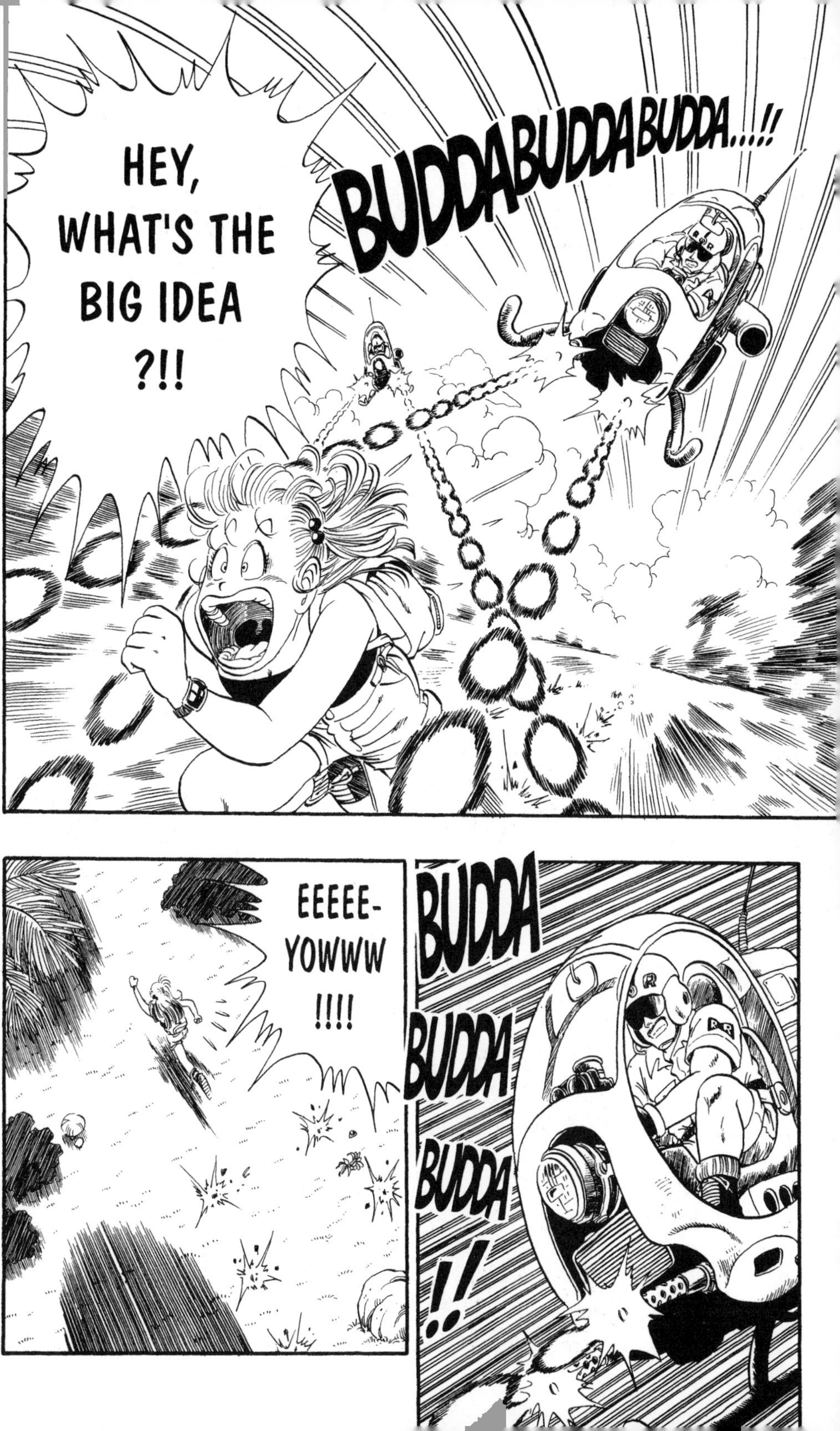
BUDDABUDDABUDDA...!!
HEY, WHAT'S THE BIG IDEA ?!!
BUDDA BUDDA BUDDA !!
EEEEE-YOWWW !!!!

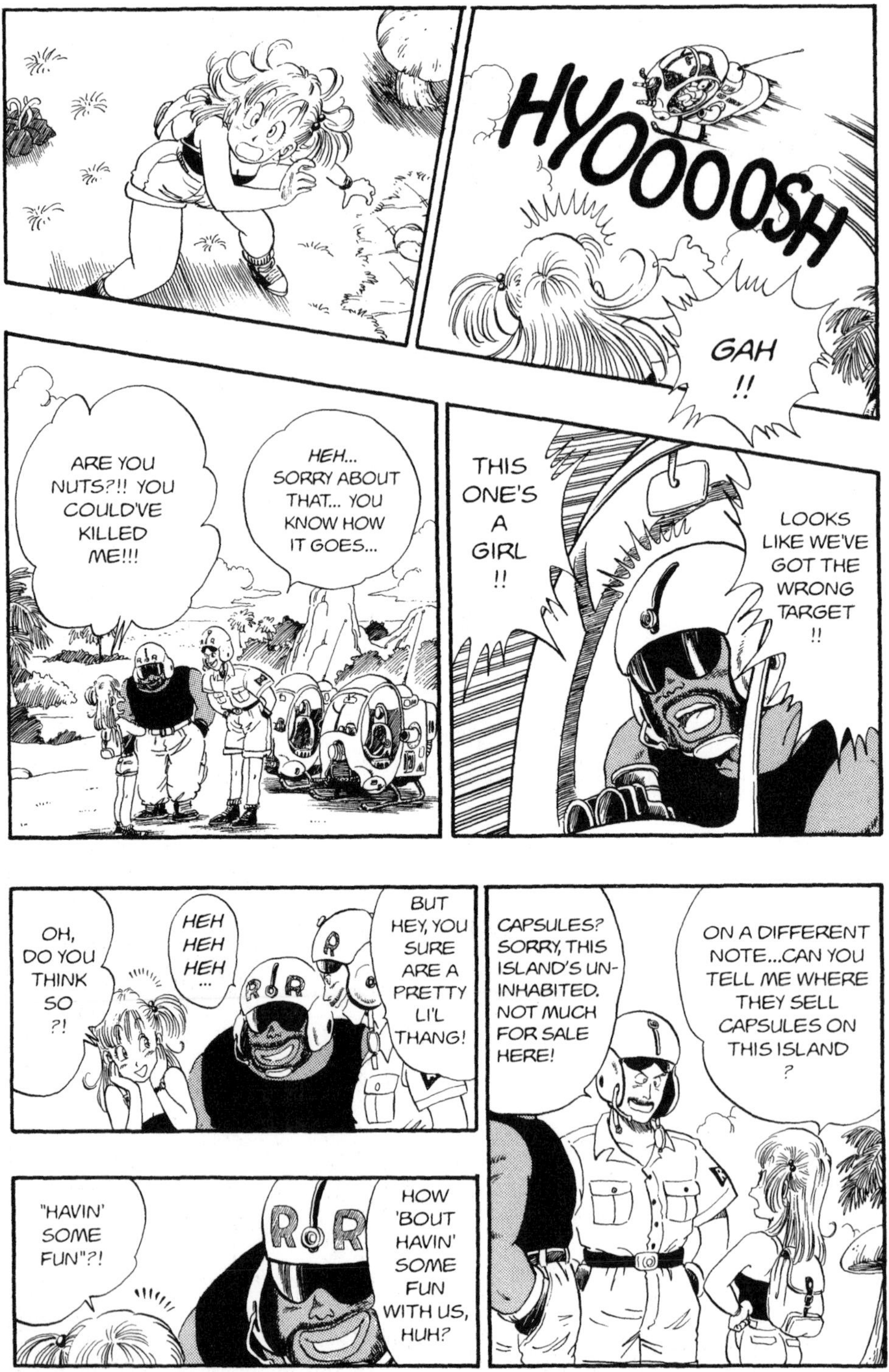
HYOOOOSH
GAH !!
LOOKS LIKE WE'VE GOT THE WRONG TARGET !!
THIS ONE'S A GIRL !!
ARE YOU NUTS?!! YOU COULD'VE KILLED ME!!!
HEH... SORRY ABOUT THAT... YOU KNOW HOW IT GOES...
ON A DIFFERENT NOTE...CAN YOU TELL ME WHERE THEY SELL CAPSULES ON THIS ISLAND ?
CAPSULES? SORRY, THIS ISLAND'S UN-INHABITED. NOT MUCH FOR SALE HERE!
BUT HEY, YOU SURE ARE A PRETTY LI'L THANG!
HEH HEH HEH ...
OH, DO YOU THINK SO ?!
HOW 'BOUT HAVIN' SOME FUN WITH US, HUH?
"HAVIN' SOME FUN"?!

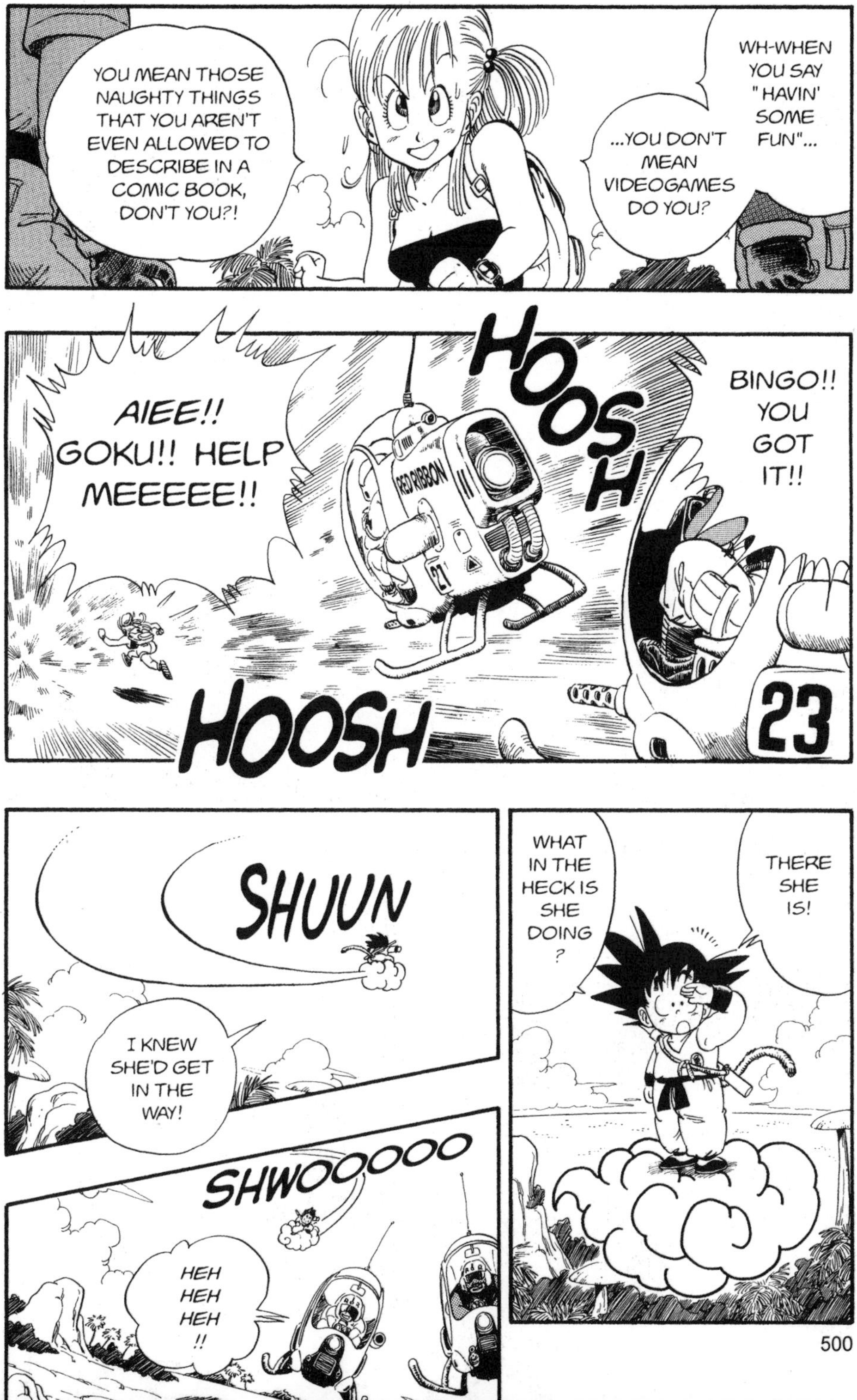
WH-WHEN YOU SAY "HAVIN' SOME FUN"...
...YOU DON'T MEAN VIDEOGAMES DO YOU?
YOU MEAN THOSE NAUGHTY THINGS THAT YOU AREN'T EVEN ALLOWED TO DESCRIBE IN A COMIC BOOK, DON'T YOU?!
BINGO!! YOU GOT IT!!
HOOSH
RED RIBBON
27
AIEE!! GOKU!! HELP MEEEEEE!!
HOOSH
23
THERE SHE IS!
WHAT IN THE HECK IS SHE DOING ?
SHUUN
I KNEW SHE'D GET IN THE WAY!
SHWOOOOO
HEH HEH HEH !!

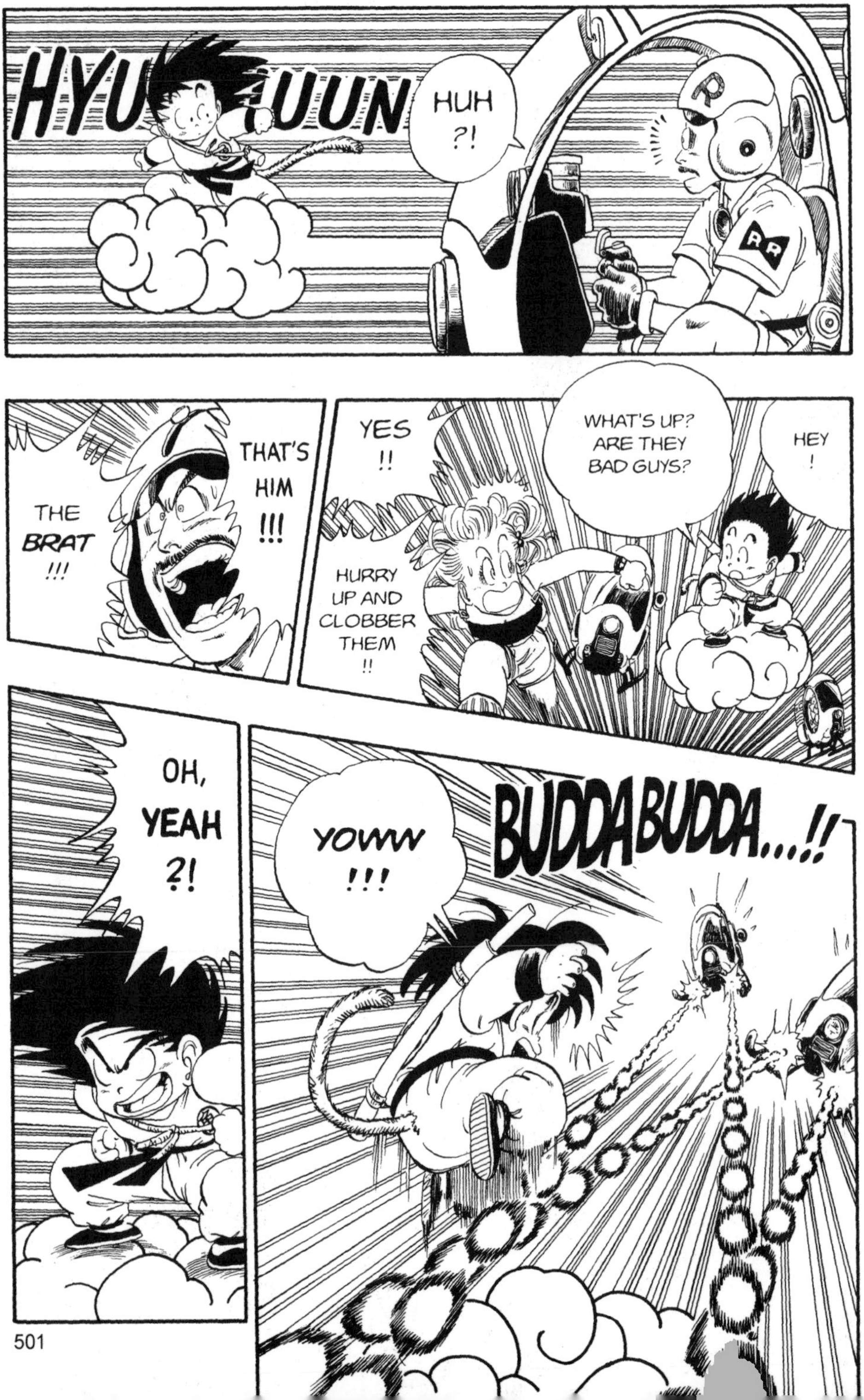
HUH ?!
HYU UUN
HEY !
WHAT'S UP? ARE THEY BAD GUYS?
YES !!
HURRY UP AND CLOBBER THEM !!
THAT'S HIM !!!
THE BRAT !!!
BUDDABUDDA...!!
YOWW !!!
OH, YEAH ?!

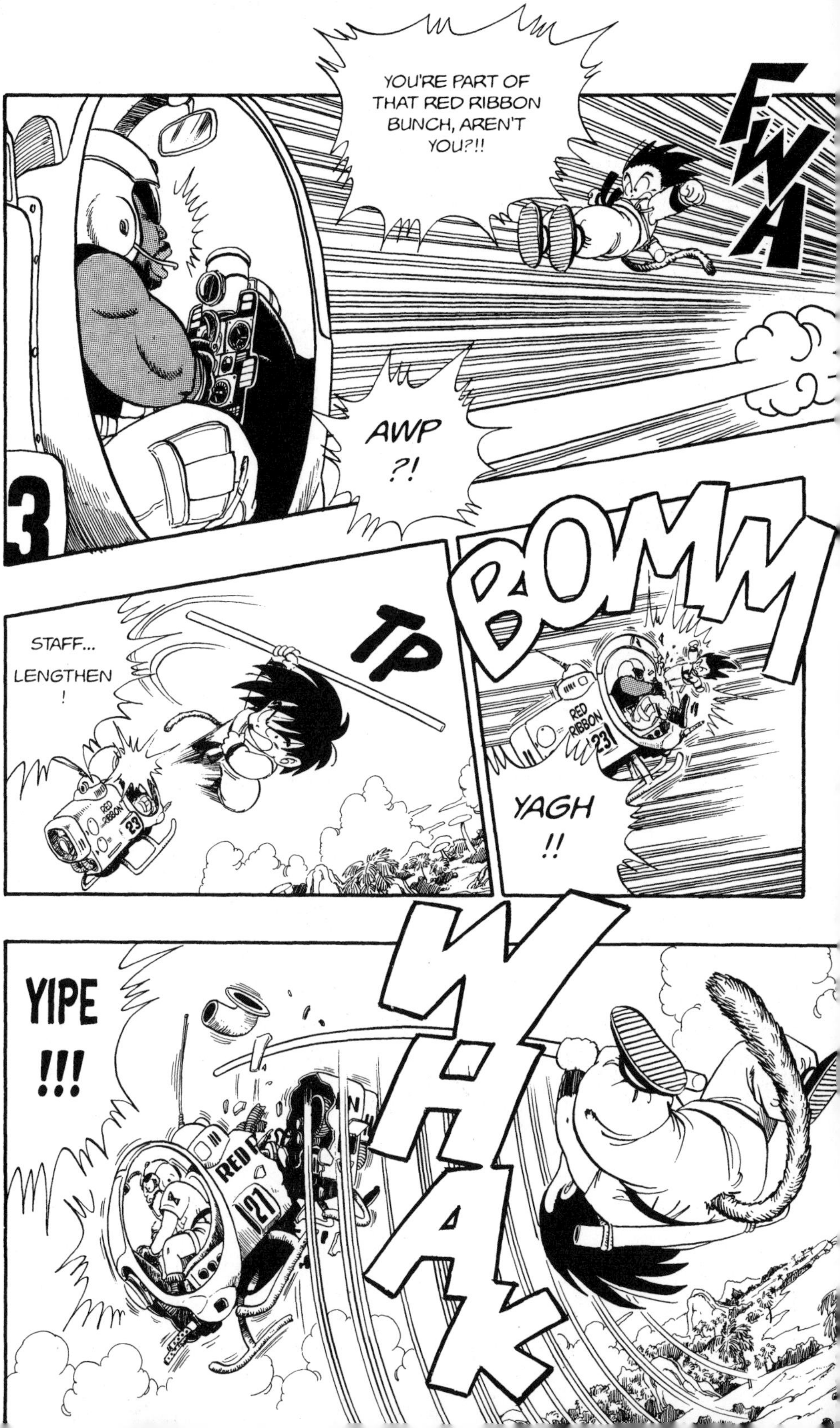
YOU'RE PART OF THAT RED RIBBON BUNCH, AREN'T YOU?!!
FWA
AWP ?!
BOMM
YAGH !!
TP
STAFF... LENGTHEN !
WHAK
YIPE !!!

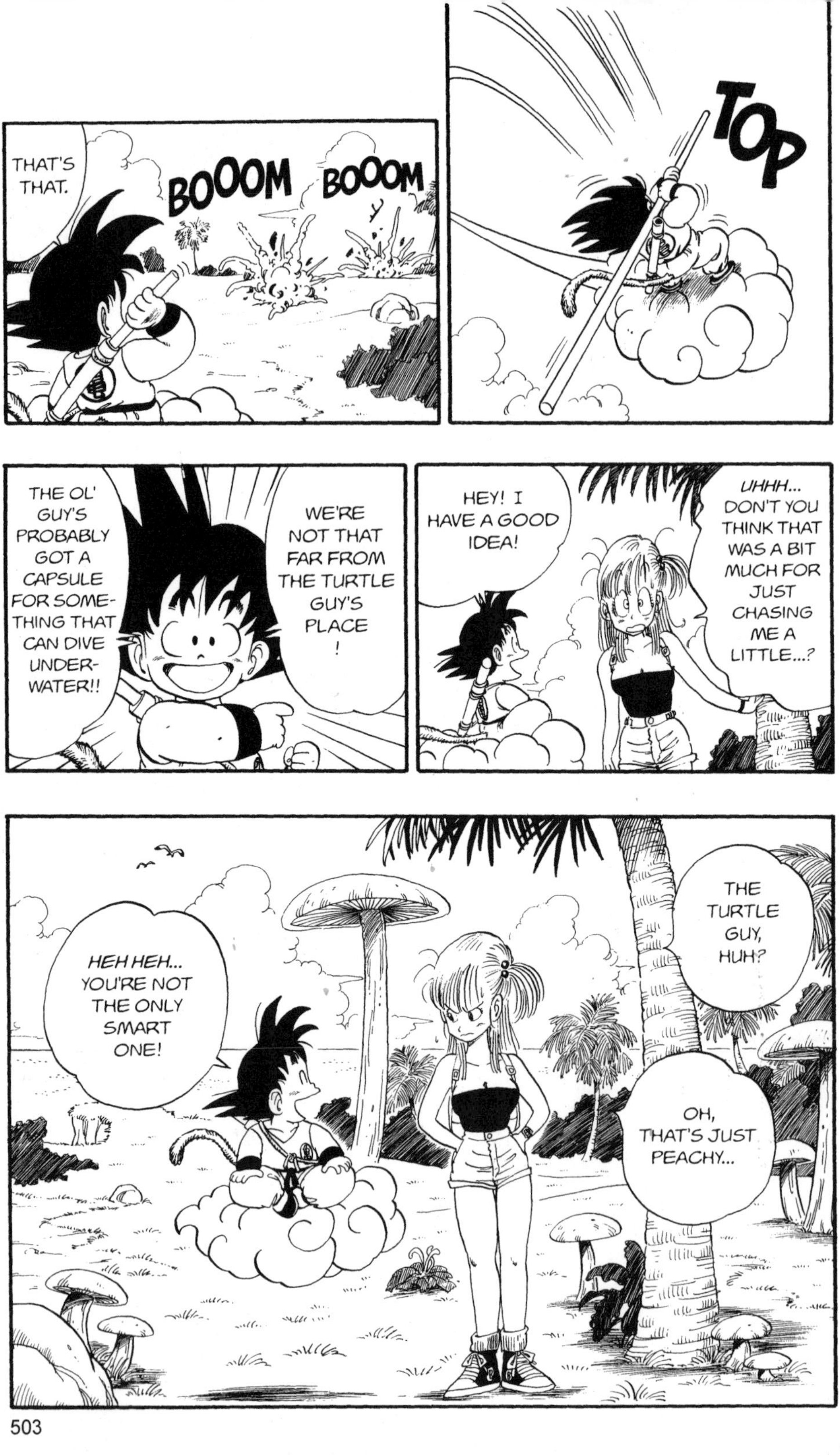
TOP
THAT'S THAT.
BOOOM BOOOM
UHHH... DON'T YOU THINK THAT WAS A BIT MUCH FOR JUST CHASING ME A LITTLE...?
HEY! I HAVE A GOOD IDEA!
WE'RE NOT THAT FAR FROM THE TURTLE GUY'S PLACE!
THE OL' GUY'S PROBABLY GOT A CAPSULE FOR SOMETHING THAT CAN DIVE UNDERWATER!!
THE TURTLE GUY, HUH?
HEH HEH... YOU'RE NOT THE ONLY SMART ONE!
OH, THAT'S JUST PEACHY...

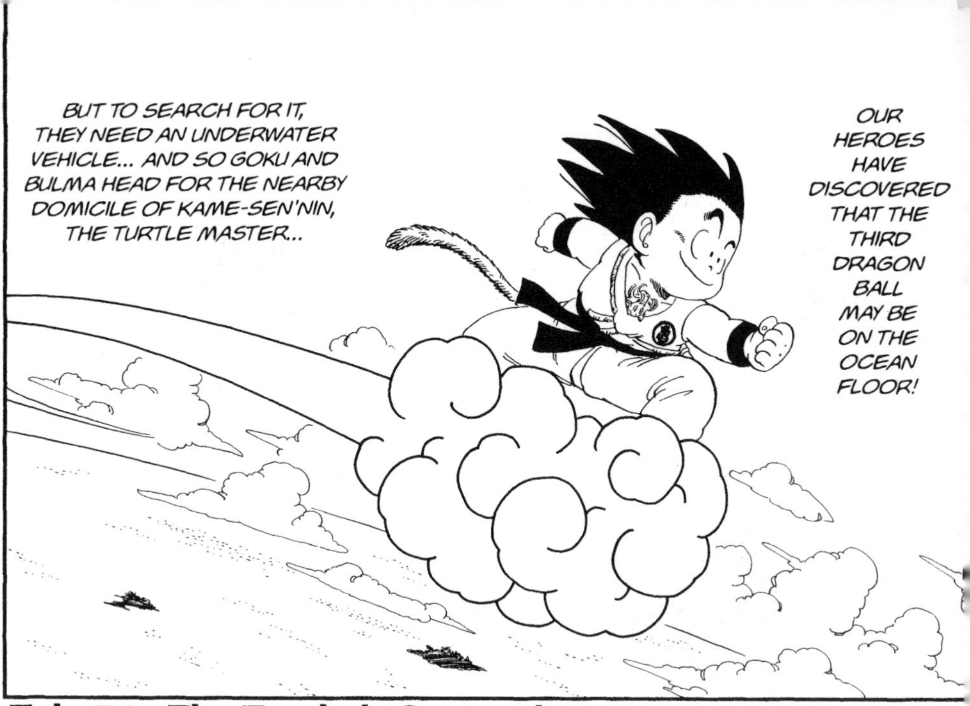
OUR HEROES HAVE DISCOVERED THAT THE THIRD DRAGON BALL MAY BE ON THE OCEAN FLOOR!
BUT TO SEARCH FOR IT, THEY NEED AN UNDERWATER VEHICLE... AND SO GOKU AND BULMA HEAD FOR THE NEARBY DOMICILE OF KAME-SEN'NIN, THE TURTLE MASTER...

Tale 71 • The Turtle Is Spotted!

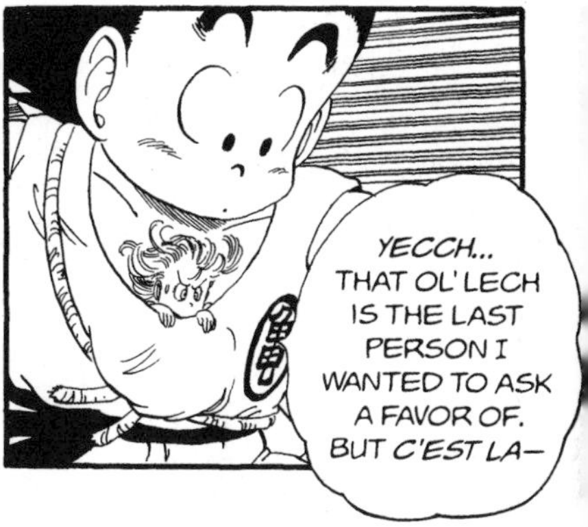
YECCH... THAT OL' LECH IS THE LAST PERSON I WANTED TO ASK A FAVOR OF. BUT C'EST LA–

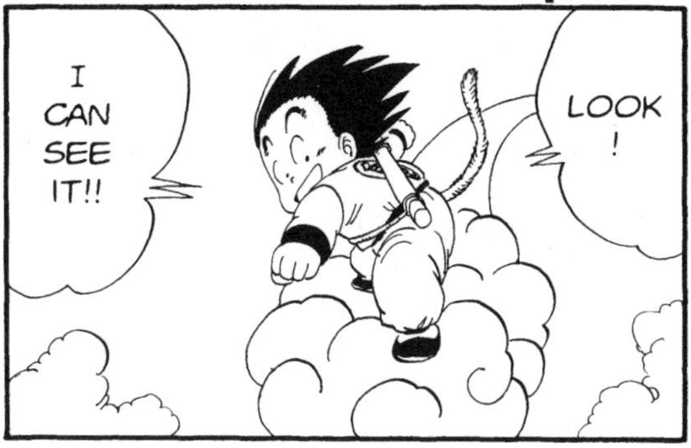
LOOK!
I CAN SEE IT!!

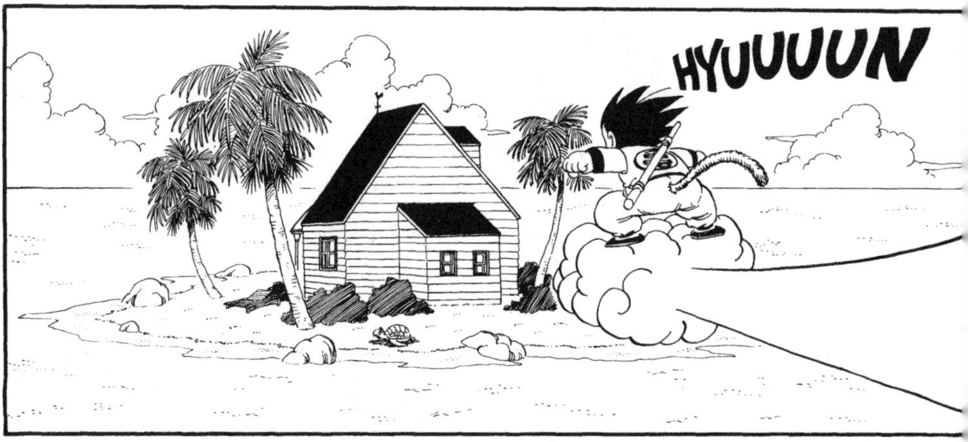
HYUUUUN

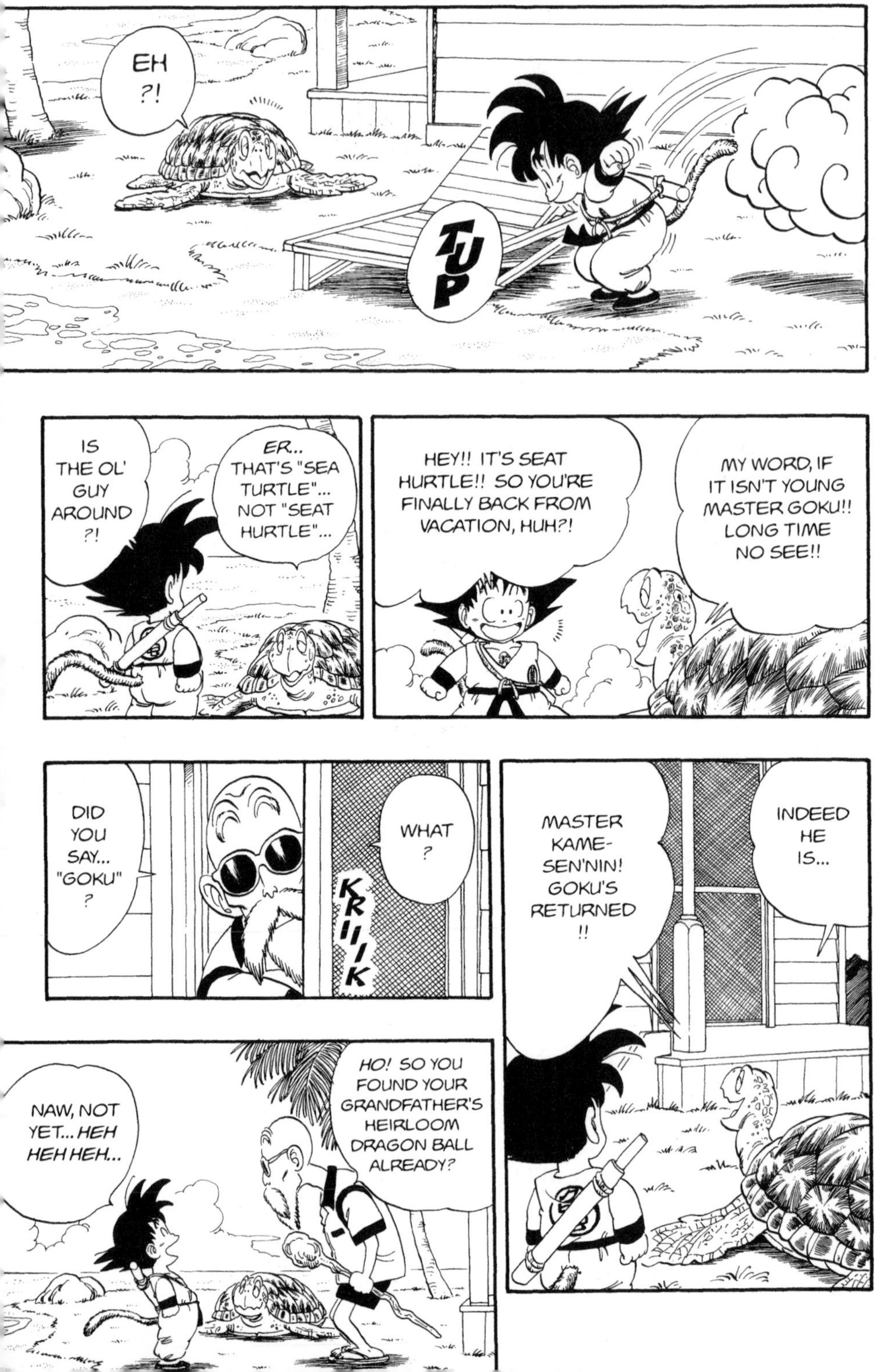
TUP
EH ?!
MY WORD, IF IT ISN'T YOUNG MASTER GOKU!! LONG TIME NO SEE!!
HEY!! IT'S SEAT HURTLE!! SO YOU'RE FINALLY BACK FROM VACATION, HUH?!
ER... THAT'S "SEA TURTLE"... NOT "SEAT HURTLE"...
IS THE OL' GUY AROUND ?!
INDEED HE IS...
MASTER KAME-SEN'NIN! GOKU'S RETURNED !!
WHAT ?
KRIIIK
DID YOU SAY... "GOKU" ?
HO! SO YOU FOUND YOUR GRANDFATHER'S HEIRLOOM DRAGON BALL ALREADY?
NAW, NOT YET... HEH HEH HEH...

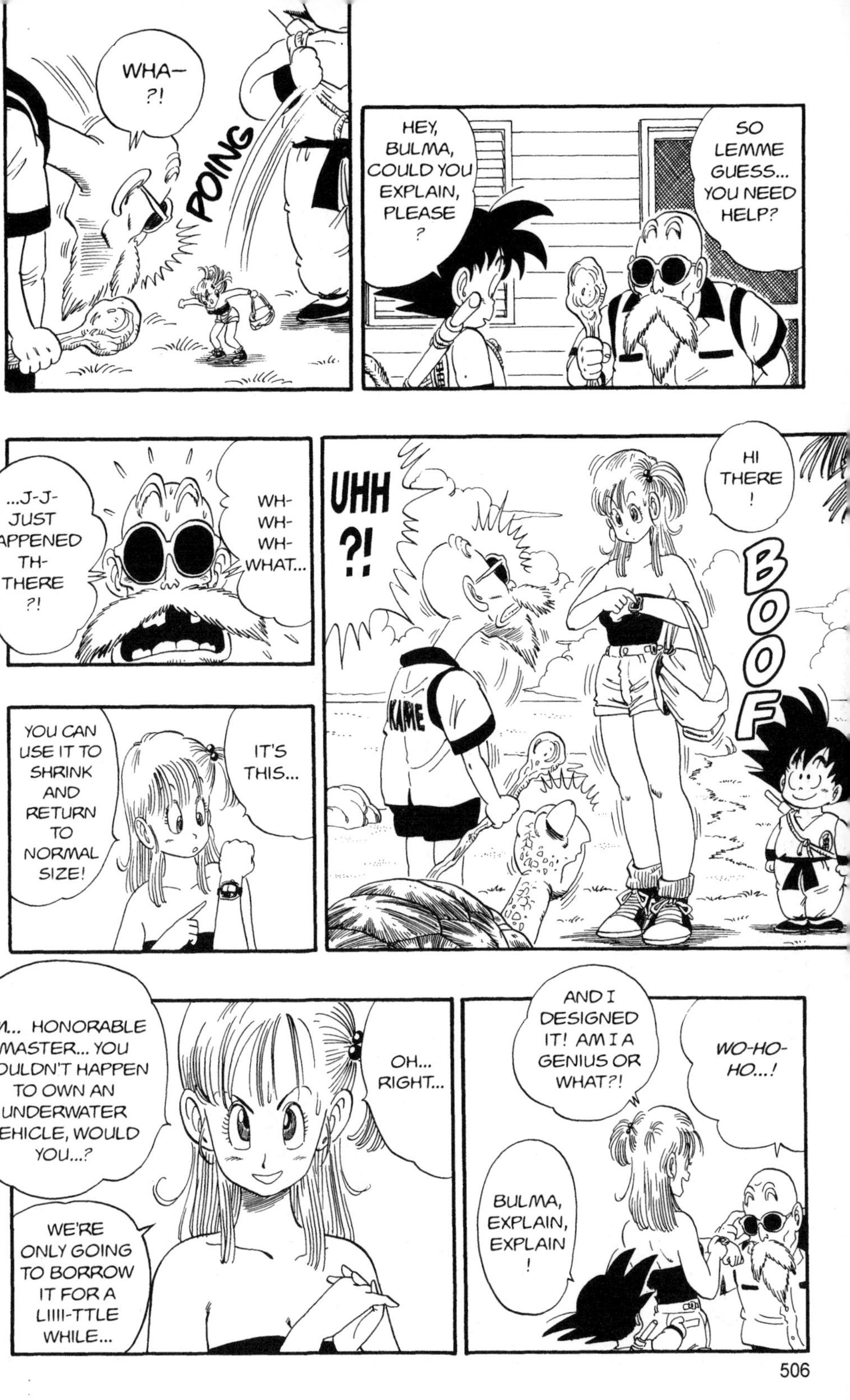
SO LEMME GUESS... YOU NEED HELP?
HEY, BULMA, COULD YOU EXPLAIN, PLEASE?
WHA— ?!
POING
HI THERE!
BOOOF
UHH ?!
WH-WH-WH-WHAT...
...J-J-JUST HAPPENED TH-THERE ?!
IT'S THIS...
YOU CAN USE IT TO SHRINK AND RETURN TO NORMAL SIZE!
WO-HO-HO...!
AND I DESIGNED IT! AM I A GENIUS OR WHAT?!
BULMA, EXPLAIN, EXPLAIN!
OH... RIGHT...
UM... HONORABLE MASTER... YOU WOULDN'T HAPPEN TO OWN AN UNDERWATER VEHICLE, WOULD YOU...?
WE'RE ONLY GOING TO BORROW IT FOR A LIIII-TTLE WHILE...

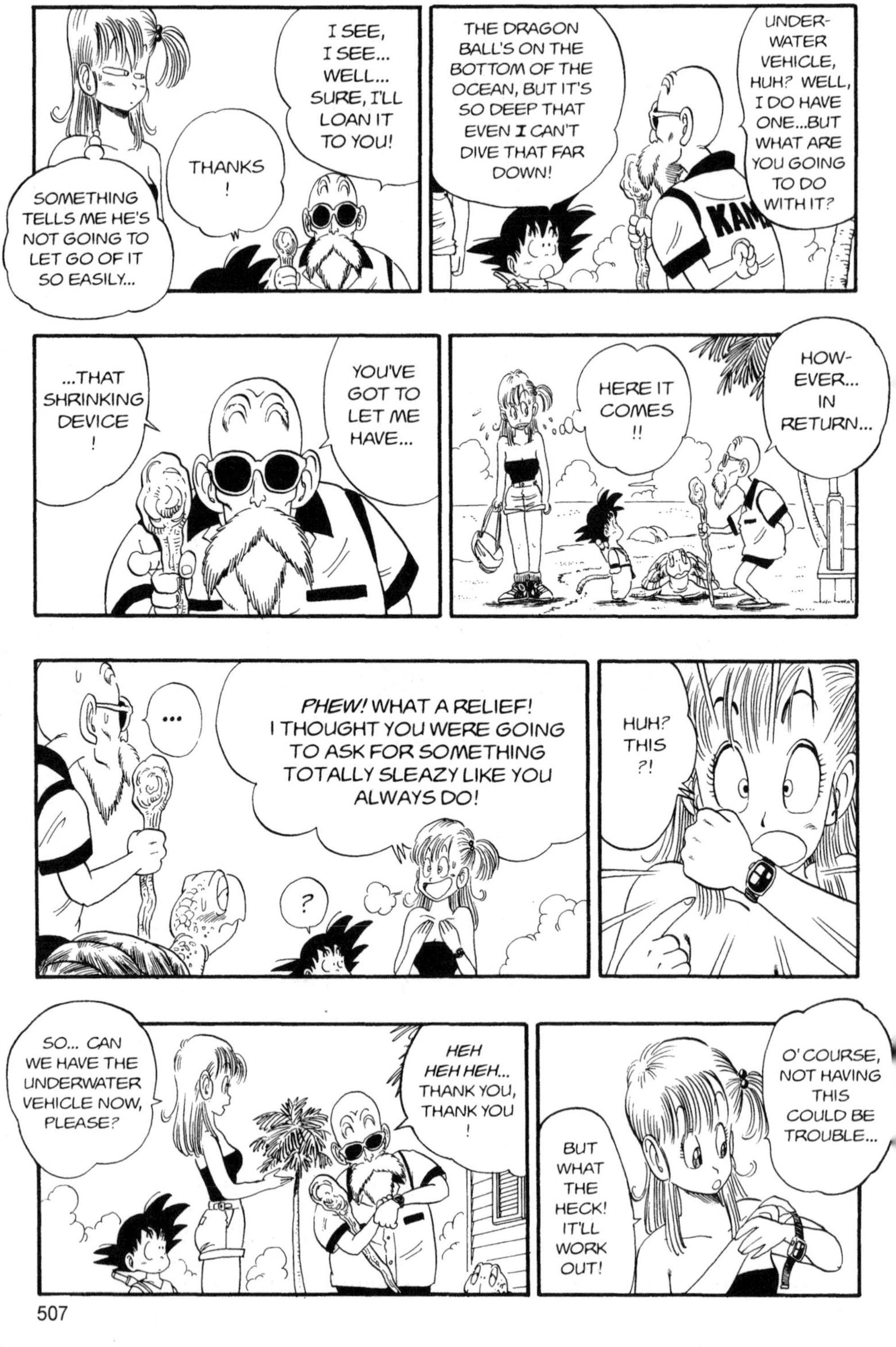
UNDER-WATER VEHICLE, HUH? WELL, I DO HAVE ONE...BUT WHAT ARE YOU GOING TO DO WITH IT?
THE DRAGON BALL'S ON THE BOTTOM OF THE OCEAN, BUT IT'S SO DEEP THAT EVEN I CAN'T DIVE THAT FAR DOWN!
I SEE, I SEE... WELL... SURE, I'LL LOAN IT TO YOU!
THANKS!
SOMETHING TELLS ME HE'S NOT GOING TO LET GO OF IT SO EASILY...
HOW-EVER... IN RETURN...
HERE IT COMES!!
YOU'VE GOT TO LET ME HAVE...
...THAT SHRINKING DEVICE!
HUH? THIS?!
PHEW! WHAT A RELIEF! I THOUGHT YOU WERE GOING TO ASK FOR SOMETHING TOTALLY SLEAZY LIKE YOU ALWAYS DO!
...
?
O' COURSE, NOT HAVING THIS COULD BE TROUBLE...
BUT WHAT THE HECK! IT'LL WORK OUT!
HEH HEH HEH... THANK YOU, THANK YOU!
SO... CAN WE HAVE THE UNDERWATER VEHICLE NOW, PLEASE?

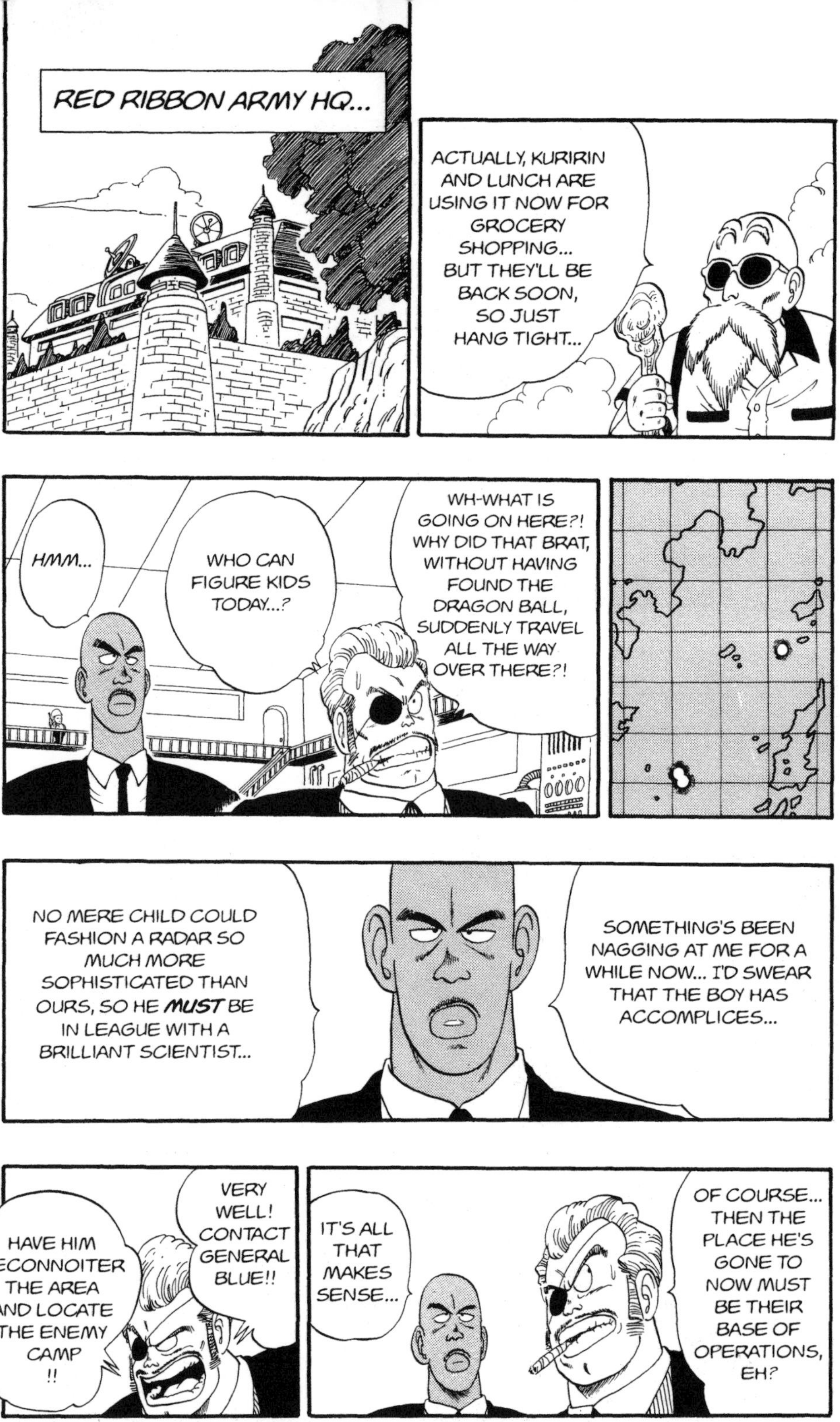
ACTUALLY, KURIRIN AND LUNCH ARE USING IT NOW FOR GROCERY SHOPPING... BUT THEY'LL BE BACK SOON, SO JUST HANG TIGHT...
RED RIBBON ARMY HQ...
WH-WHAT IS GOING ON HERE?! WHY DID THAT BRAT, WITHOUT HAVING FOUND THE DRAGON BALL, SUDDENLY TRAVEL ALL THE WAY OVER THERE?!
WHO CAN FIGURE KIDS TODAY...?
HMM...
SOMETHING'S BEEN NAGGING AT ME FOR A WHILE NOW... I'D SWEAR THAT THE BOY HAS ACCOMPLICES...
NO MERE CHILD COULD FASHION A RADAR SO MUCH MORE SOPHISTICATED THAN OURS, SO HE *MUST* BE IN LEAGUE WITH A BRILLIANT SCIENTIST...
OF COURSE... THEN THE PLACE HE'S GONE TO NOW MUST BE THEIR BASE OF OPERATIONS, EH?
IT'S ALL THAT MAKES SENSE...
VERY WELL! CONTACT GENERAL BLUE!!
HAVE HIM RECONNOITER THE AREA AND LOCATE THE ENEMY CAMP !!

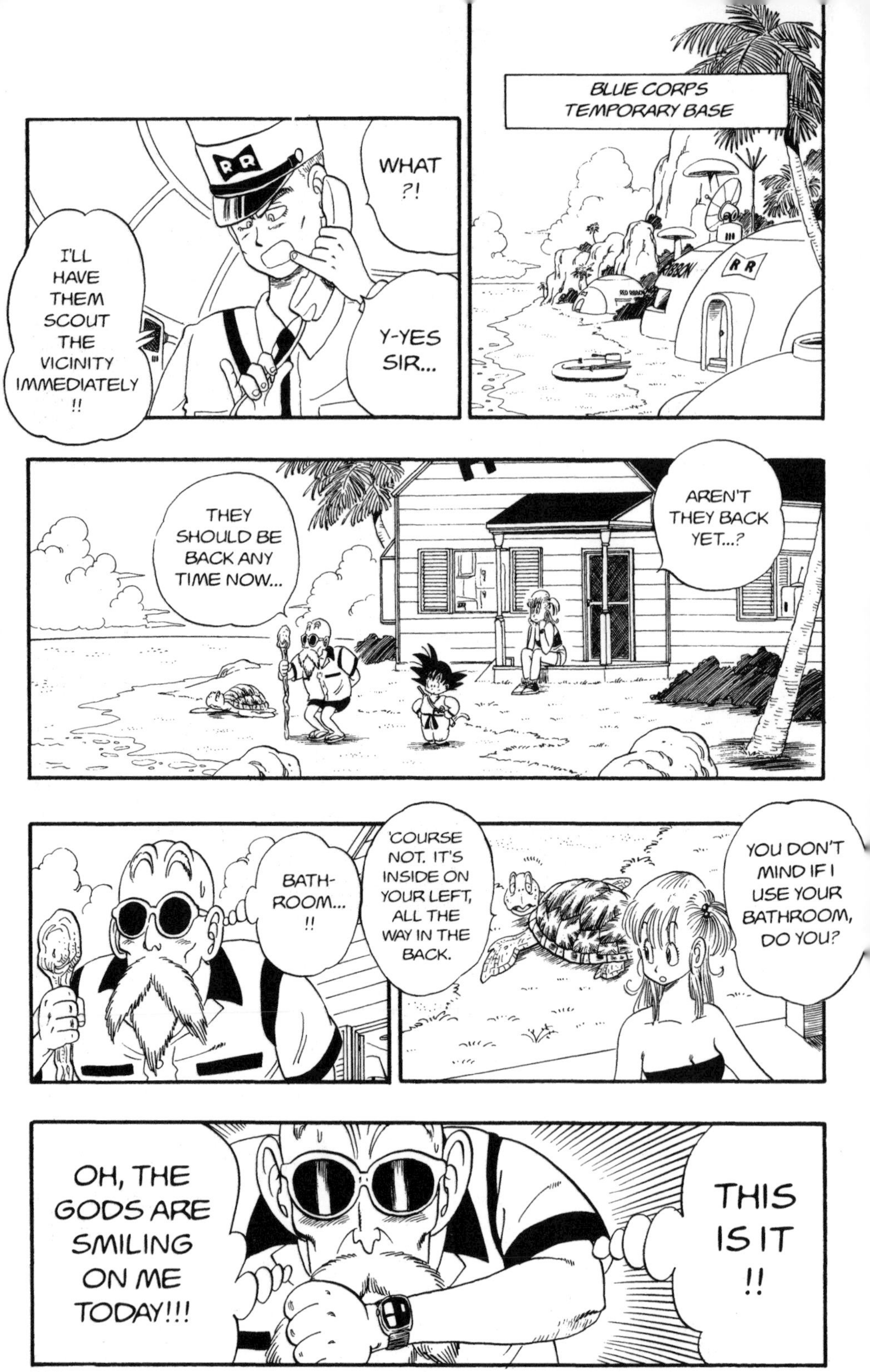
BLUE CORPS TEMPORARY BASE
WHAT ?!
Y-YES SIR...
I'LL HAVE THEM SCOUT THE VICINITY IMMEDIATELY !!
AREN'T THEY BACK YET...?
THEY SHOULD BE BACK ANY TIME NOW...
YOU DON'T MIND IF I USE YOUR BATHROOM, DO YOU?
'COURSE NOT. IT'S INSIDE ON YOUR LEFT, ALL THE WAY IN THE BACK.
BATH-ROOM... !!
THIS IS IT !!
OH, THE GODS ARE SMILING ON ME TODAY!!!

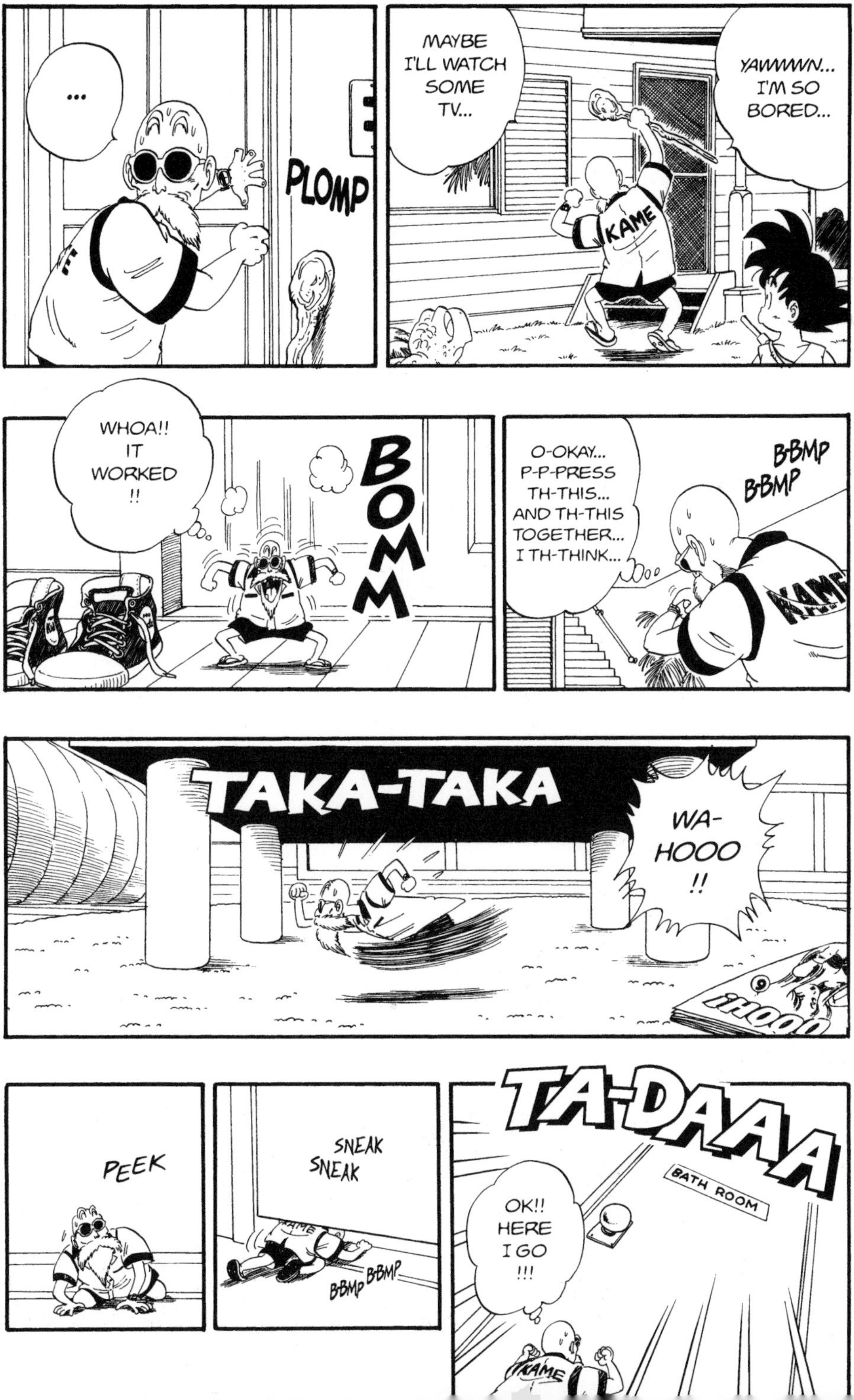
YAWWWN... I'M SO BORED...
MAYBE I'LL WATCH SOME TV...
...
PLOMP
B-BMP B-BMP
O-OKAY... P-P-PRESS TH-THIS... AND TH-THIS TOGETHER... I TH-THINK...
BOMM
WHOA!! IT WORKED !!
WA-HOOO !!
TAKA-TAKA
TA-DAAAA
BATH ROOM
OK!! HERE I GO !!!
SNEAK SNEAK
B-BMP B-BMP
PEEK

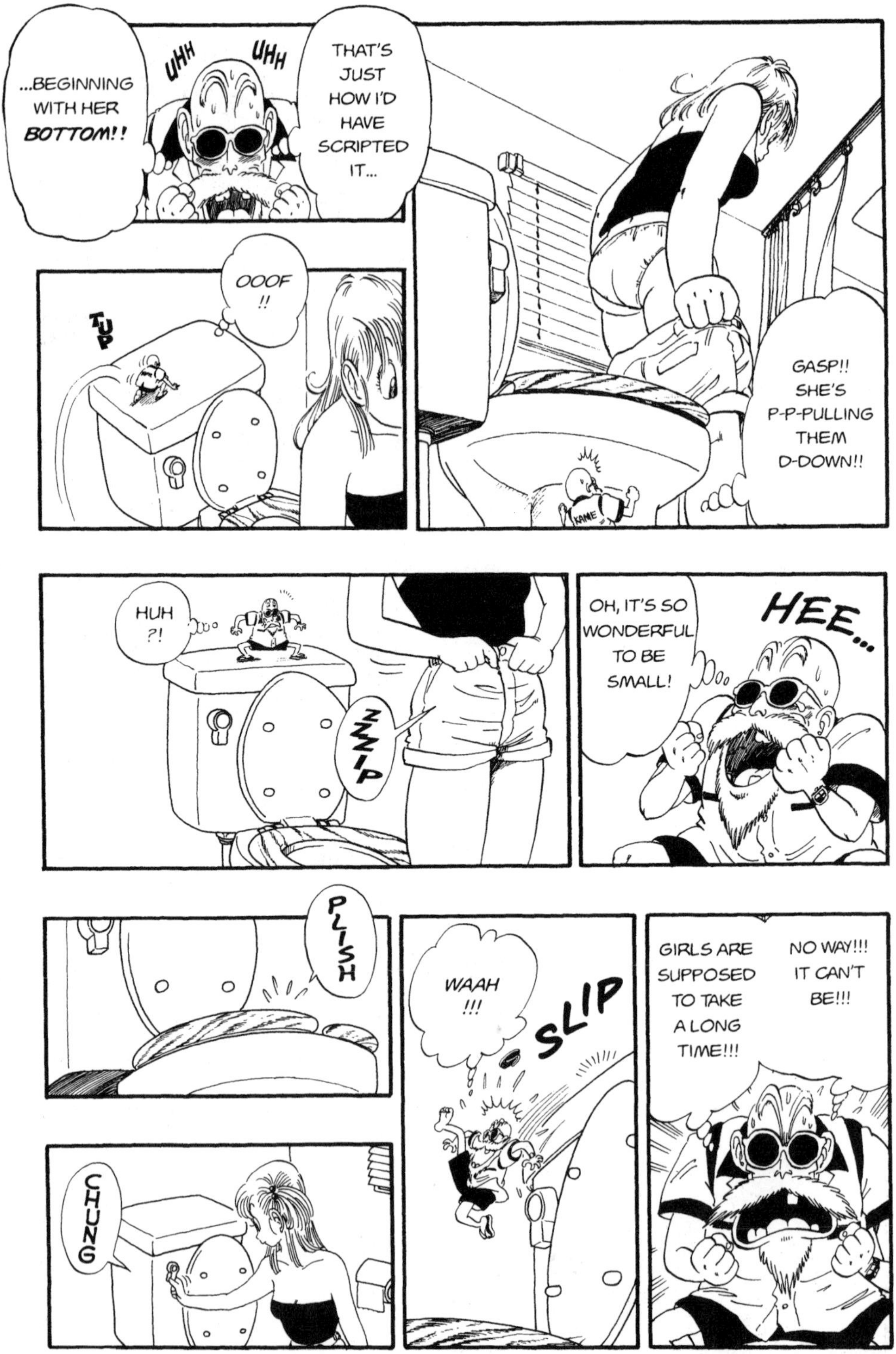
GASP!! SHE'S P-P-PULLING THEM D-DOWN!!
THAT'S JUST HOW I'D HAVE SCRIPTED IT...
UHH
UHH
...BEGINNING WITH HER BOTTOM!!
OOOF !!
TUP
HEE...
OH, IT'S SO WONDERFUL TO BE SMALL!
ZZZIP
HUH ?!
NO WAY!!! IT CAN'T BE!!!
GIRLS ARE SUPPOSED TO TAKE A LONG TIME!!!
SLIP
WAAH !!!
PLISH
CHUNG

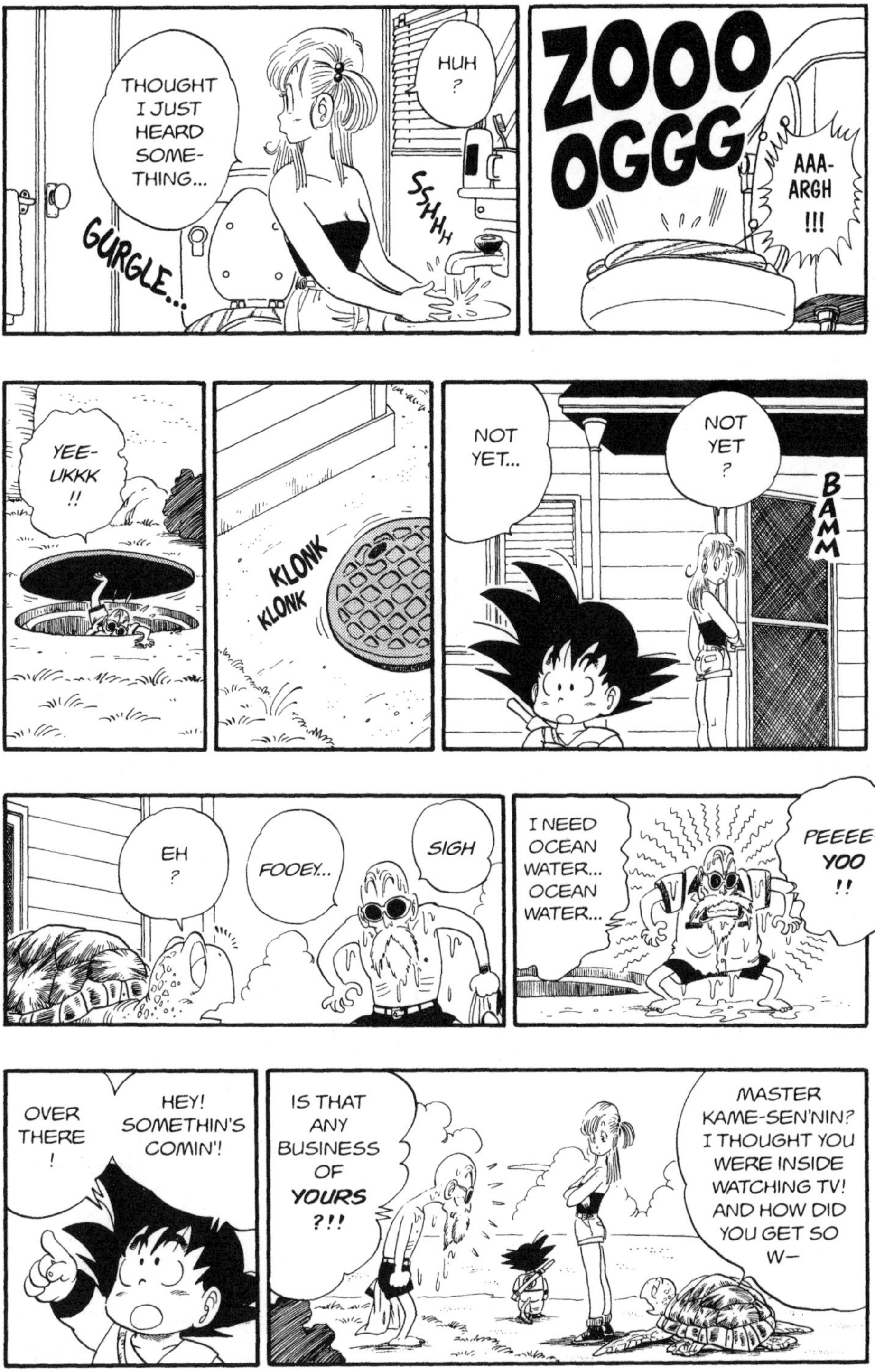
ZOOO OGGG
AAA-ARGH !!!
HUH ?
THOUGHT I JUST HEARD SOME-THING...
SSHHHH
GURGLE...
BAMM
NOT YET ?
NOT YET...
KLONK
KLONK
YEE-UKKK !!
PEEEE-YOO !!
I NEED OCEAN WATER... OCEAN WATER...
SIGH
FOOEY...
EH ?
MASTER KAME-SEN'NIN? I THOUGHT YOU WERE INSIDE WATCHING TV! AND HOW DID YOU GET SO W—
IS THAT ANY BUSINESS OF YOURS ?!!
HEY! SOMETHIN'S COMIN'!
OVER THERE !

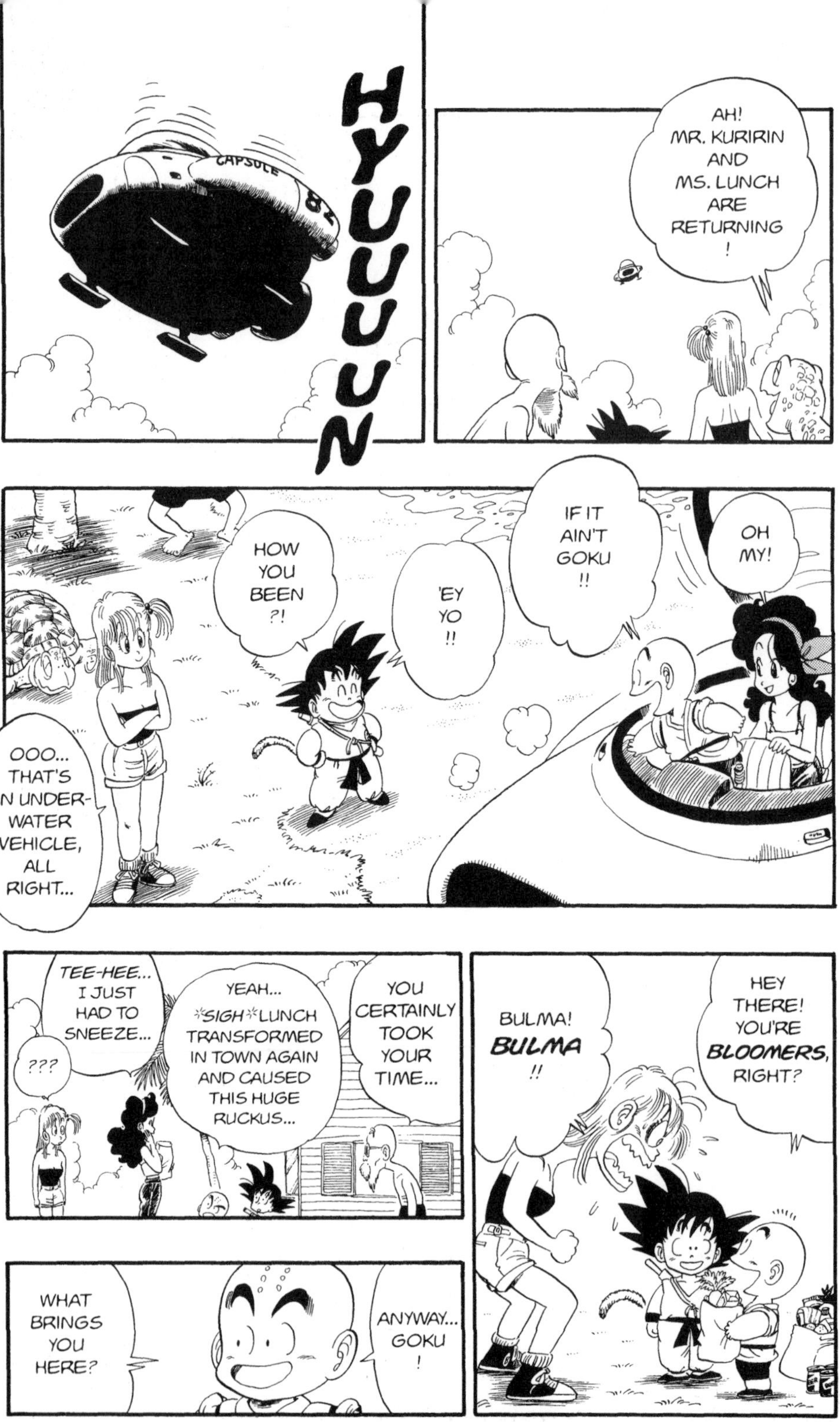
AH! MR. KURIRIN AND MS. LUNCH ARE RETURNING!
HYUUUUN
CAPSULE
82
OH MY!
IF IT AIN'T GOKU!!
'EY YO!!
HOW YOU BEEN?!
OOO... THAT'S AN UNDER-WATER VEHICLE, ALL RIGHT...
HEY THERE! YOU'RE **BLOOMERS**, RIGHT?
BULMA! **BULMA**!!
YOU CERTAINLY TOOK YOUR TIME...
YEAH... *SIGH* LUNCH TRANSFORMED IN TOWN AGAIN AND CAUSED THIS HUGE RUCKUS...
TEE-HEE... I JUST HAD TO SNEEZE...
???
ANYWAY... GOKU!
WHAT BRINGS YOU HERE?

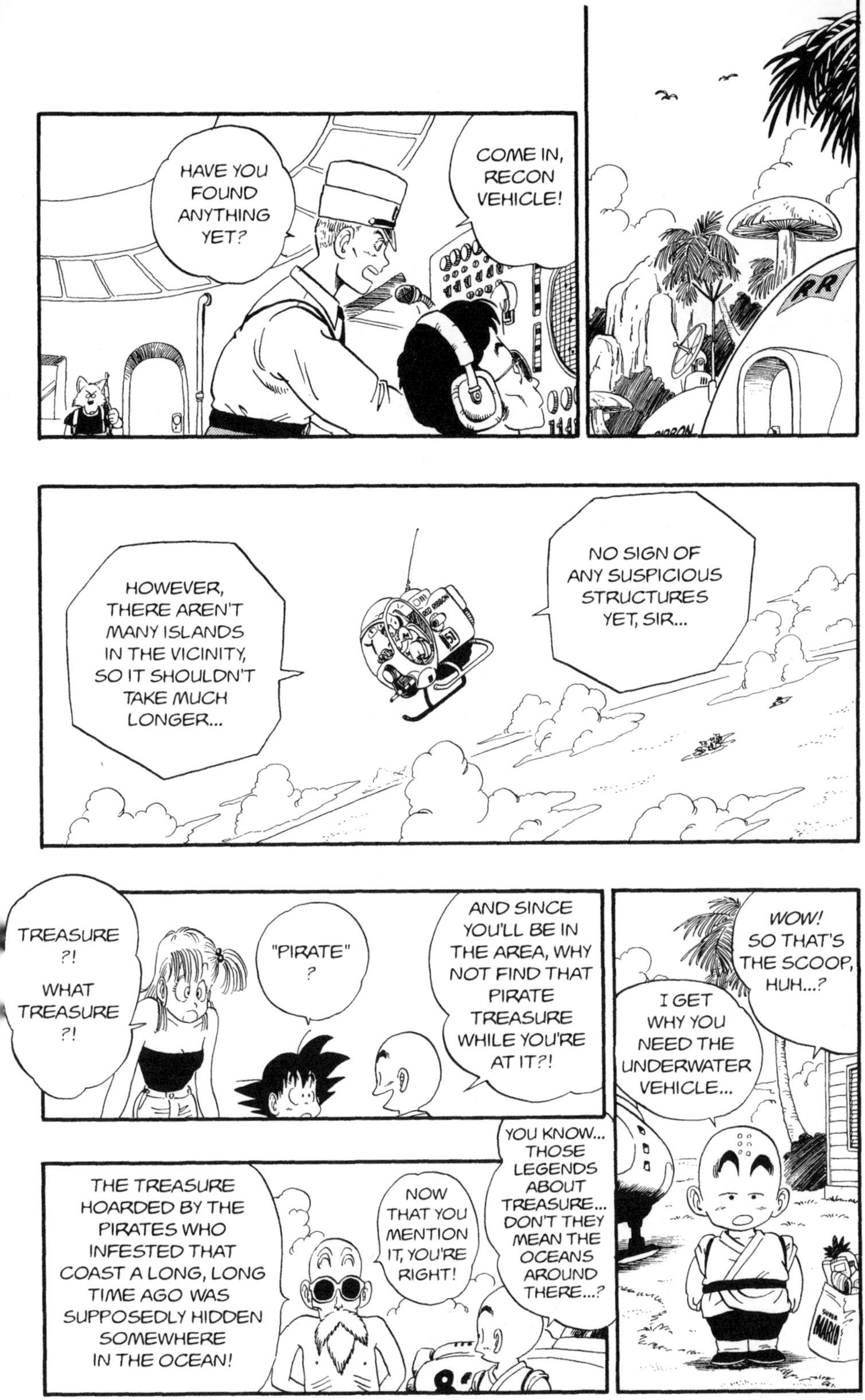
COME IN, RECON VEHICLE!
HAVE YOU FOUND ANYTHING YET?
NO SIGN OF ANY SUSPICIOUS STRUCTURES YET, SIR...
HOWEVER, THERE AREN'T MANY ISLANDS IN THE VICINITY, SO IT SHOULDN'T TAKE MUCH LONGER...
WOW! SO THAT'S THE SCOOP, HUH...?
I GET WHY YOU NEED THE UNDERWATER VEHICLE...
AND SINCE YOU'LL BE IN THE AREA, WHY NOT FIND THAT PIRATE TREASURE WHILE YOU'RE AT IT?!
"PIRATE" ?
TREASURE ?! WHAT TREASURE ?!
YOU KNOW... THOSE LEGENDS ABOUT TREASURE... DON'T THEY MEAN THE OCEANS AROUND THERE...?
NOW THAT YOU MENTION IT, YOU'RE RIGHT!
THE TREASURE HOARDED BY THE PIRATES WHO INFESTED THAT COAST A LONG, LONG TIME AGO WAS SUPPOSEDLY HIDDEN SOMEWHERE IN THE OCEAN!

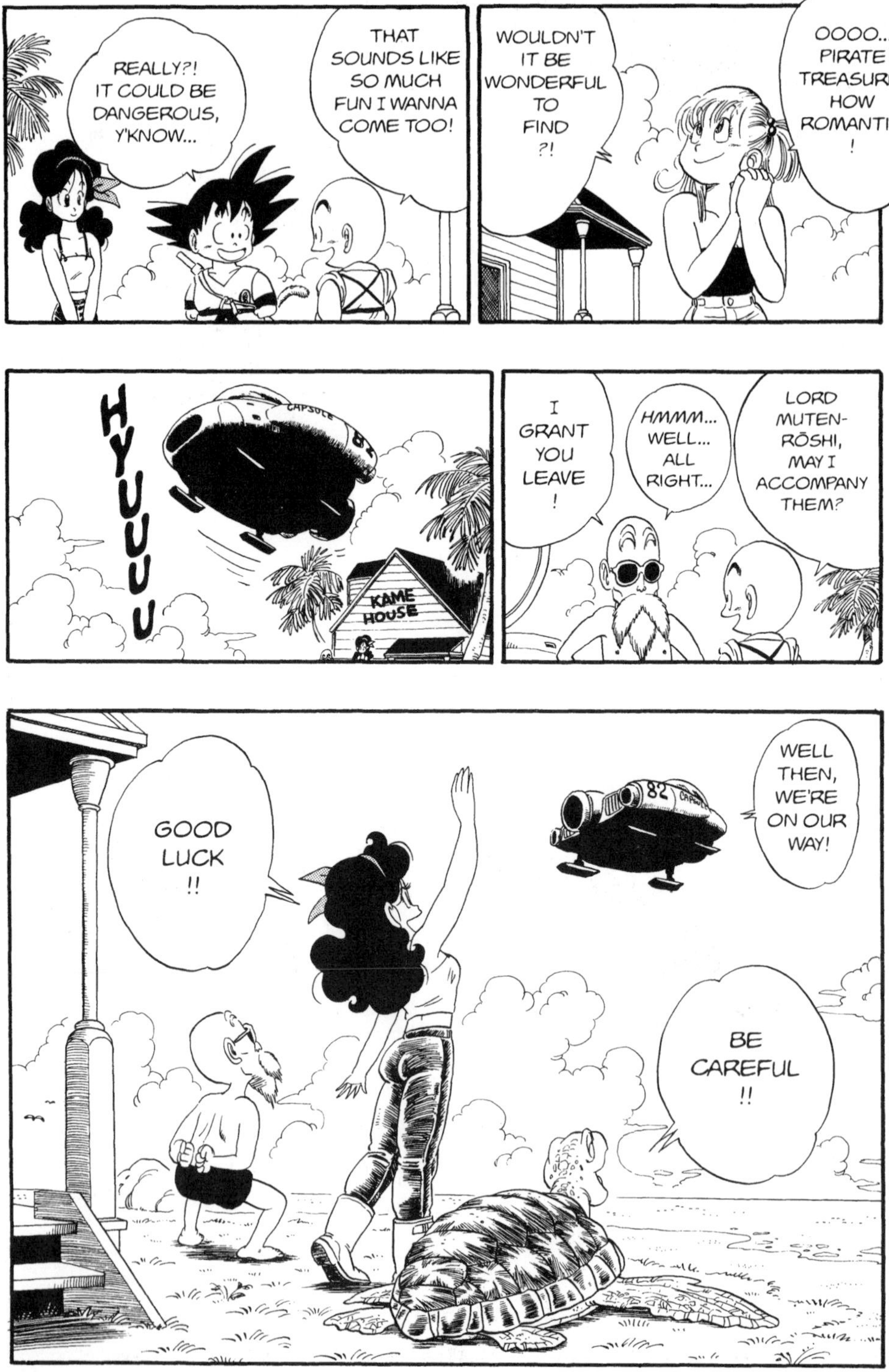
OOOO... PIRATE TREASURE! HOW ROMANTIC !
WOULDN'T IT BE WONDERFUL TO FIND ?!
THAT SOUNDS LIKE SO MUCH FUN I WANNA COME TOO!
REALLY?! IT COULD BE DANGEROUS, Y'KNOW...
LORD MUTEN-RŌSHI, MAY I ACCOMPANY THEM?
HMMM... WELL... ALL RIGHT...
I GRANT YOU LEAVE !
CAPSULE
KAME HOUSE
HYUUUU
WELL THEN, WE'RE ON OUR WAY!
82
GOOD LUCK !!
BE CAREFUL !!

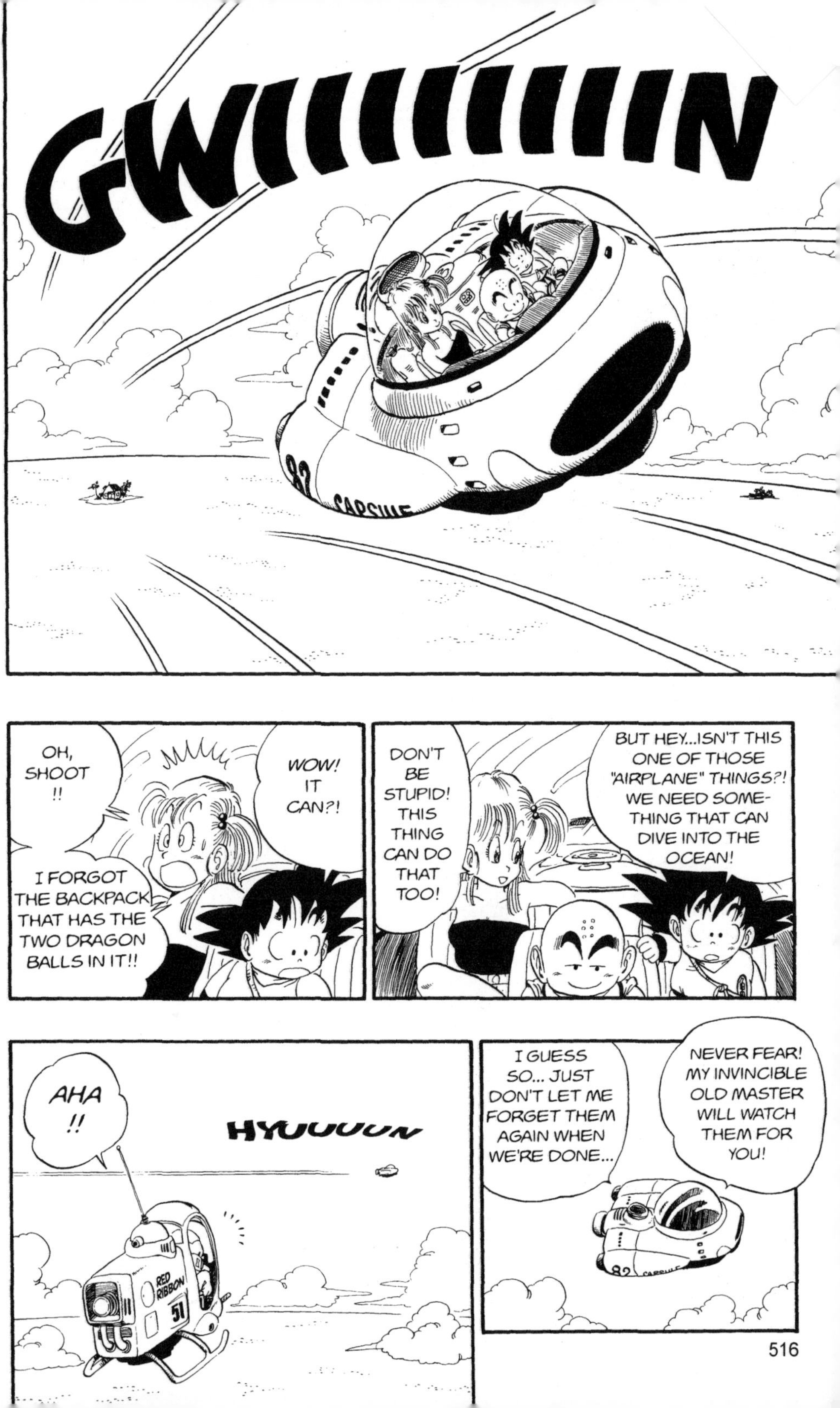
GWIIIIIIIIN
BUT HEY...ISN'T THIS ONE OF THOSE "AIRPLANE" THINGS?! WE NEED SOME-THING THAT CAN DIVE INTO THE OCEAN!
DON'T BE STUPID! THIS THING CAN DO THAT TOO!
WOW! IT CAN?!
OH, SHOOT!!
I FORGOT THE BACKPACK THAT HAS THE TWO DRAGON BALLS IN IT!!
NEVER FEAR! MY INVINCIBLE OLD MASTER WILL WATCH THEM FOR YOU!
I GUESS SO... JUST DON'T LET ME FORGET THEM AGAIN WHEN WE'RE DONE...
HYUUUUN
AHA!!

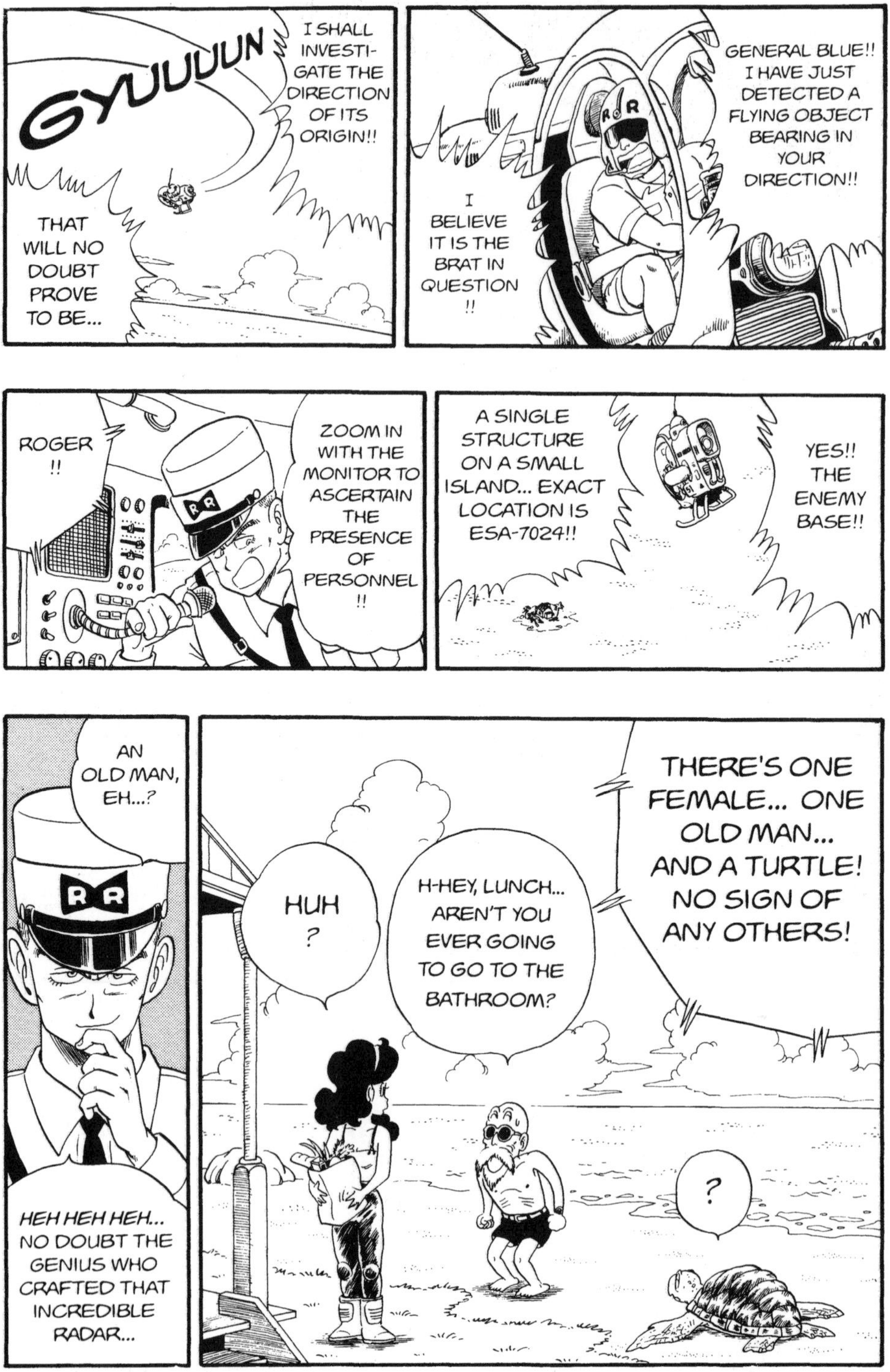
GENERAL BLUE!! I HAVE JUST DETECTED A FLYING OBJECT BEARING IN YOUR DIRECTION!!
I BELIEVE IT IS THE BRAT IN QUESTION!!
I SHALL INVESTIGATE THE DIRECTION OF ITS ORIGIN!!
GYUUUUN
THAT WILL NO DOUBT PROVE TO BE...
YES!! THE ENEMY BASE!!
A SINGLE STRUCTURE ON A SMALL ISLAND... EXACT LOCATION IS ESA-7024!!
ZOOM IN WITH THE MONITOR TO ASCERTAIN THE PRESENCE OF PERSONNEL!!
ROGER!!
THERE'S ONE FEMALE... ONE OLD MAN... AND A TURTLE! NO SIGN OF ANY OTHERS!
H-HEY, LUNCH... AREN'T YOU EVER GOING TO GO TO THE BATHROOM?
HUH?
?
AN OLD MAN, EH...?
HEH HEH HEH... NO DOUBT THE GENIUS WHO CRAFTED THAT INCREDIBLE RADAR...

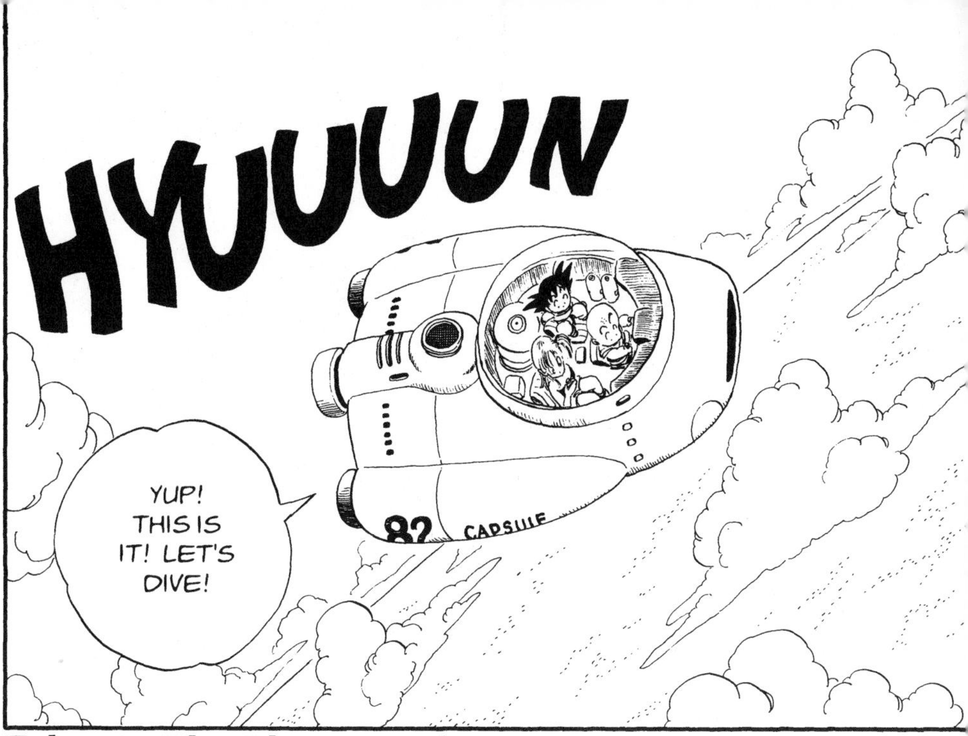
HYUUUUN
YUP! THIS IS IT! LET'S DIVE!
82 CAPSULE

Tale 72 • The Blue Meanies

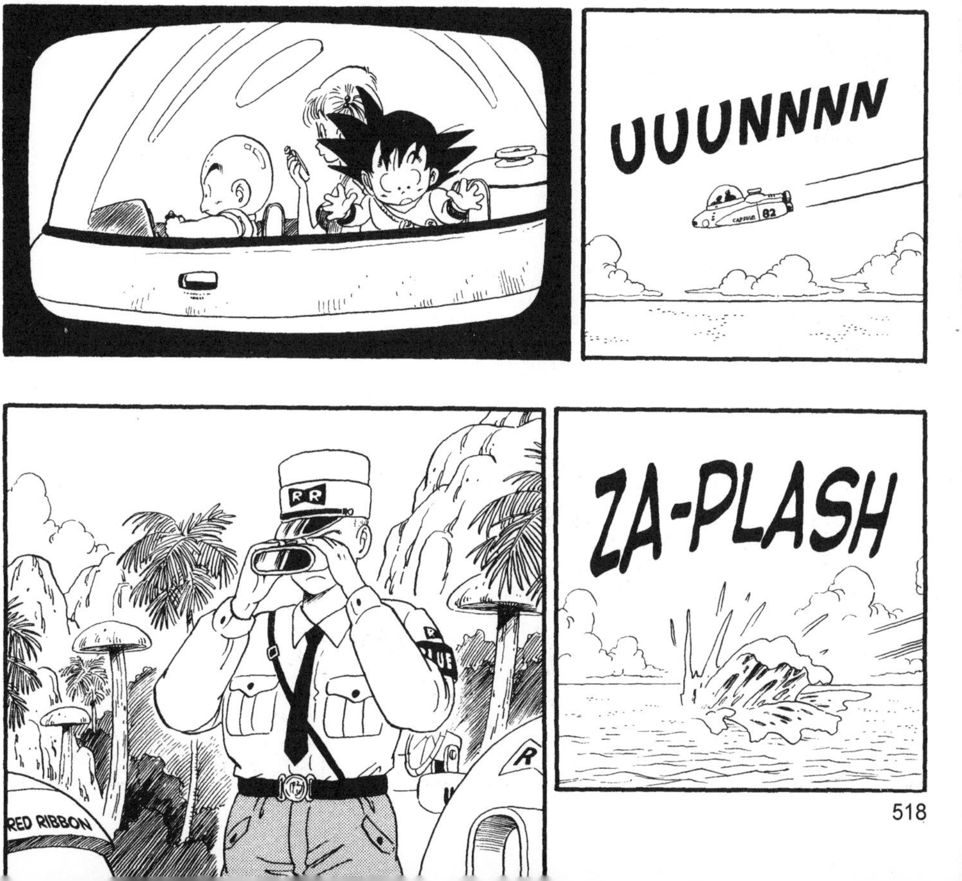
UUUNNNN
ZA-PLASH
RED RIBBON

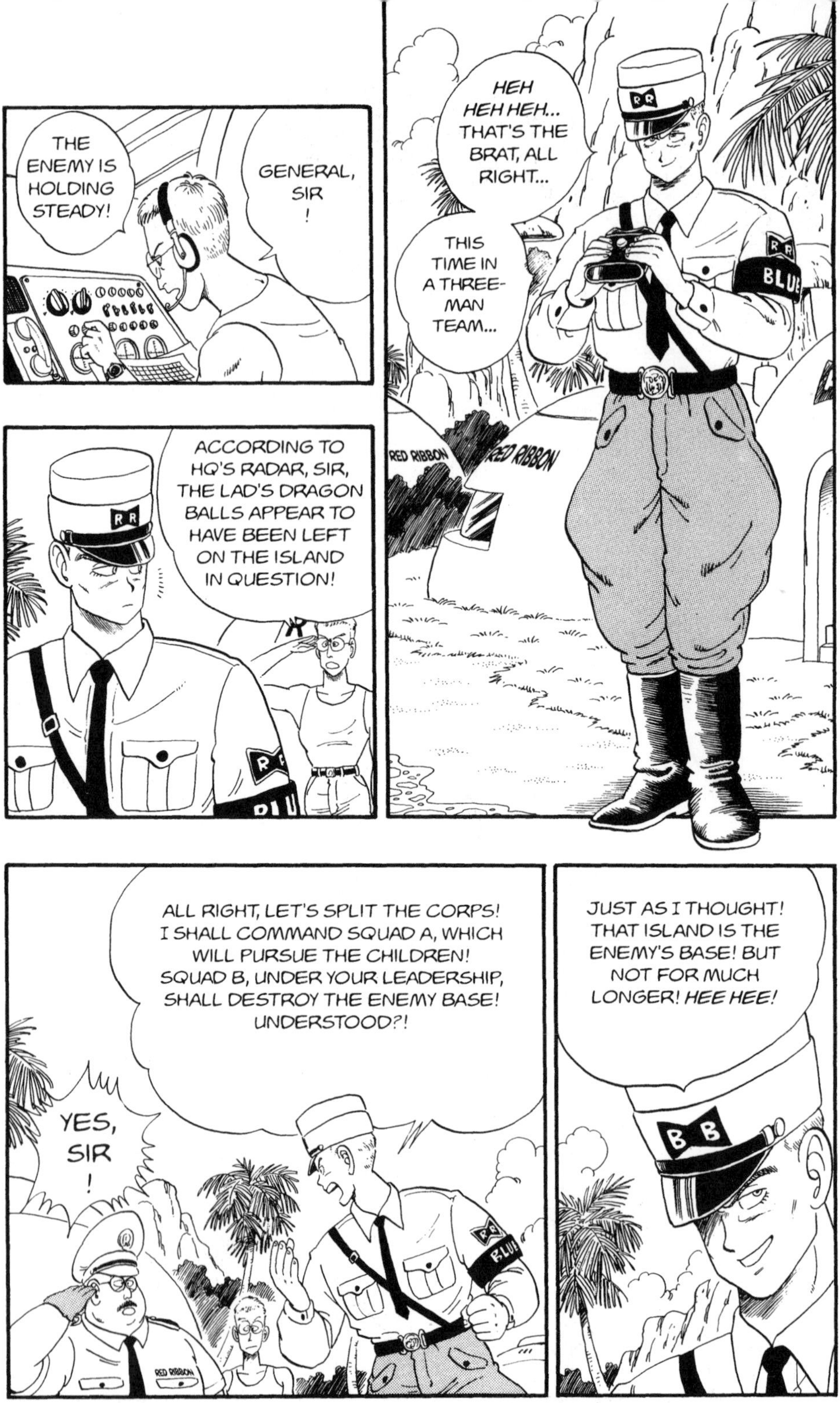
HEH HEH HEH... THAT'S THE BRAT, ALL RIGHT...
THIS TIME IN A THREE-MAN TEAM...
GENERAL, SIR!
THE ENEMY IS HOLDING STEADY!
ACCORDING TO HQ'S RADAR, SIR, THE LAD'S DRAGON BALLS APPEAR TO HAVE BEEN LEFT ON THE ISLAND IN QUESTION!
JUST AS I THOUGHT! THAT ISLAND IS THE ENEMY'S BASE! BUT NOT FOR MUCH LONGER! *HEE HEE!*
ALL RIGHT, LET'S SPLIT THE CORPS! I SHALL COMMAND SQUAD A, WHICH WILL PURSUE THE CHILDREN! SQUAD B, UNDER YOUR LEADERSHIP, SHALL DESTROY THE ENEMY BASE! UNDERSTOOD?!
YES, SIR!

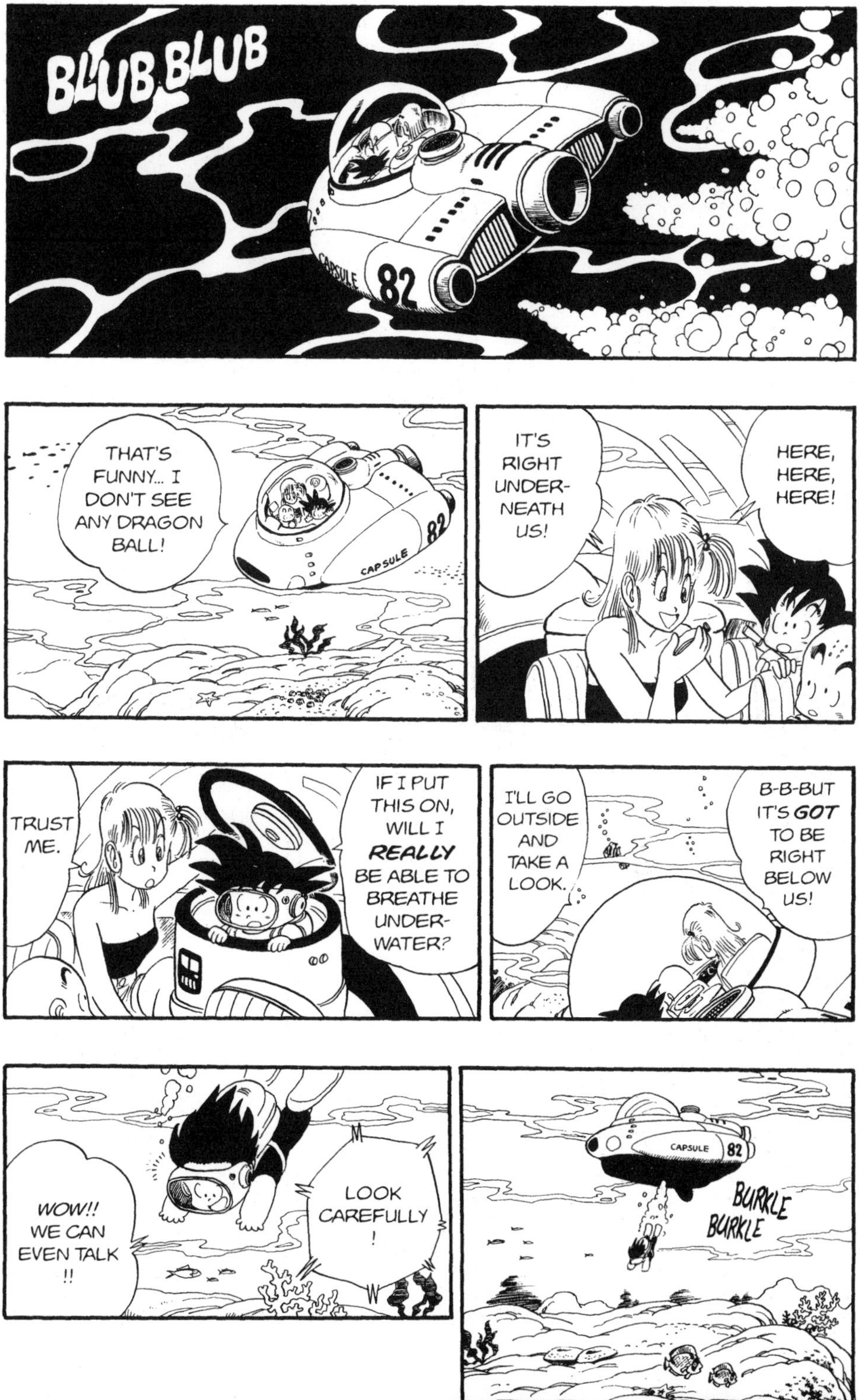
BLUB BLUB
HERE, HERE, HERE!
IT'S RIGHT UNDERNEATH US!
THAT'S FUNNY... I DON'T SEE ANY DRAGON BALL!
B-B-BUT IT'S ***GOT*** TO BE RIGHT BELOW US!
I'LL GO OUTSIDE AND TAKE A LOOK.
IF I PUT THIS ON, WILL I ***REALLY*** BE ABLE TO BREATHE UNDERWATER?
TRUST ME.
BURKLE BURKLE
LOOK CAREFULLY!
WOW!! WE CAN EVEN TALK!!

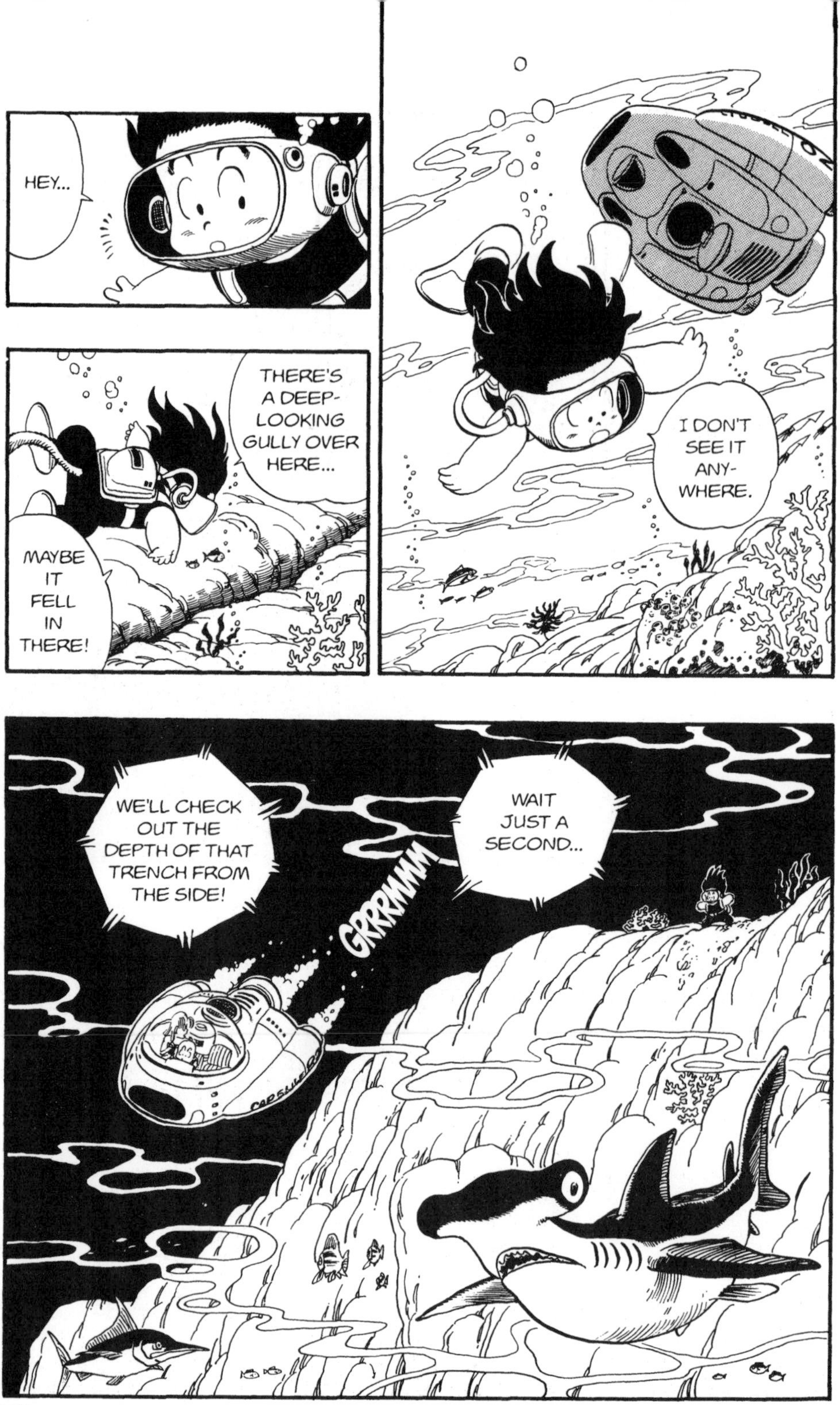
I DON'T SEE IT ANYWHERE.
HEY...
THERE'S A DEEP-LOOKING GULLY OVER HERE...
MAYBE IT FELL IN THERE!
WAIT JUST A SECOND...
WE'LL CHECK OUT THE DEPTH OF THAT TRENCH FROM THE SIDE!
GRRRMMM

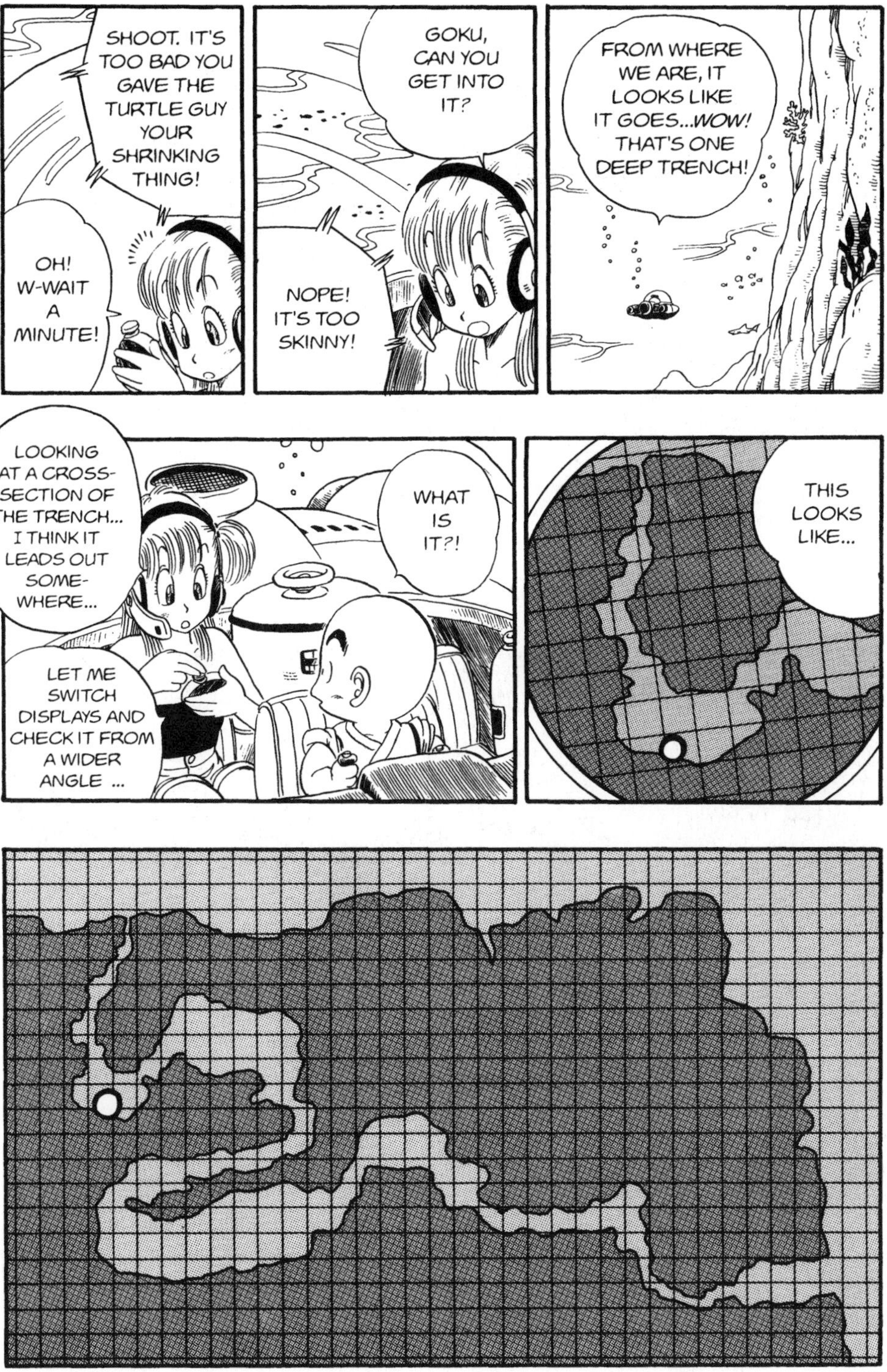
FROM WHERE WE ARE, IT LOOKS LIKE IT GOES...*WOW!* THAT'S ONE DEEP TRENCH!
GOKU, CAN YOU GET INTO IT?
NOPE! IT'S TOO SKINNY!
SHOOT. IT'S TOO BAD YOU GAVE THE TURTLE GUY YOUR SHRINKING THING!
OH! W-WAIT A MINUTE!
THIS LOOKS LIKE...
WHAT IS IT?!
LOOKING AT A CROSS-SECTION OF THE TRENCH... I THINK IT LEADS OUT SOME-WHERE...
LET ME SWITCH DISPLAYS AND CHECK IT FROM A WIDER ANGLE ...

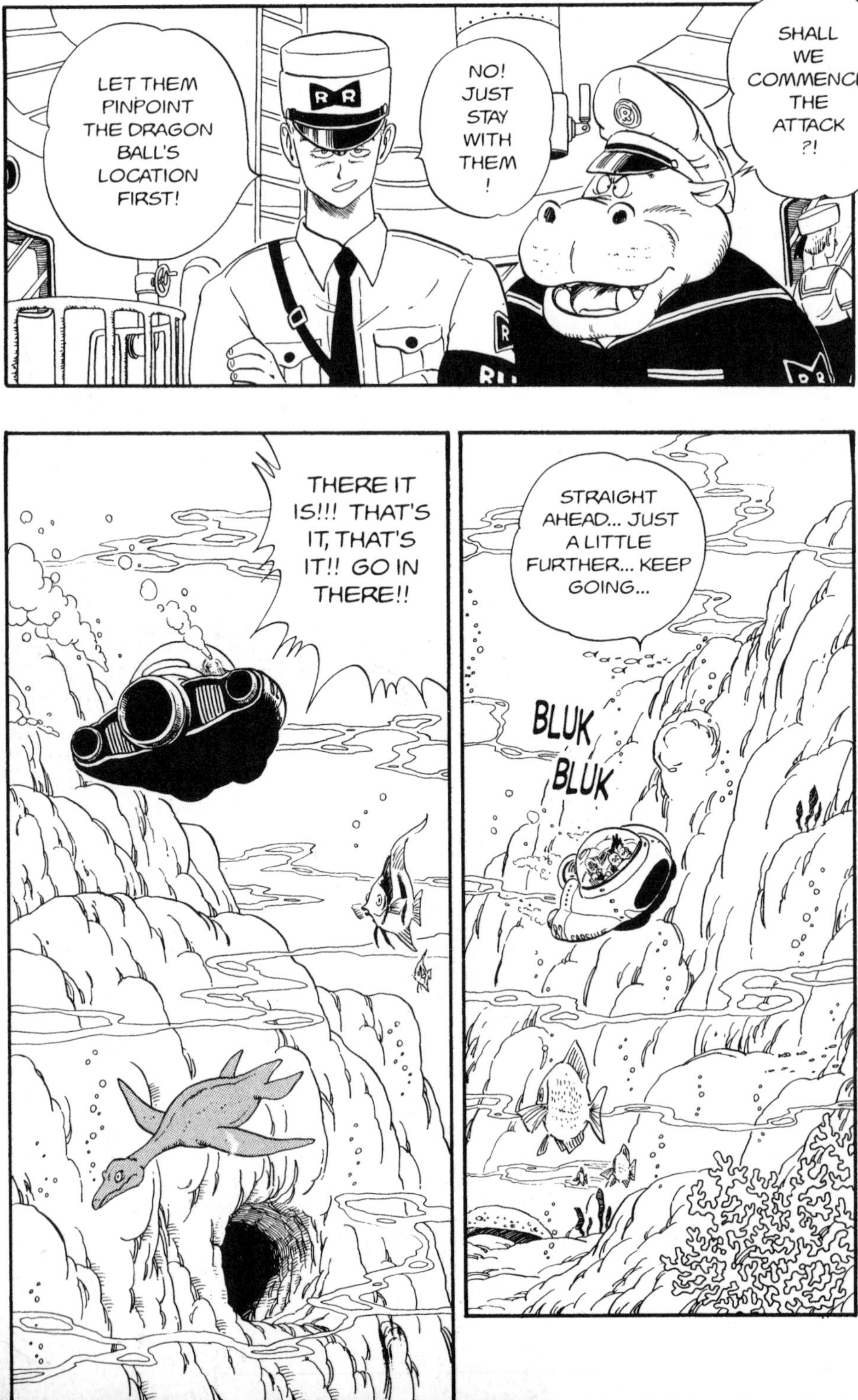
SHALL WE COMMENCE THE ATTACK ?!
NO! JUST STAY WITH THEM !
LET THEM PINPOINT THE DRAGON BALL'S LOCATION FIRST!
STRAIGHT AHEAD... JUST A LITTLE FURTHER... KEEP GOING...
BLUK BLUK
THERE IT IS!!! THAT'S IT, THAT'S IT!! GO IN THERE!!

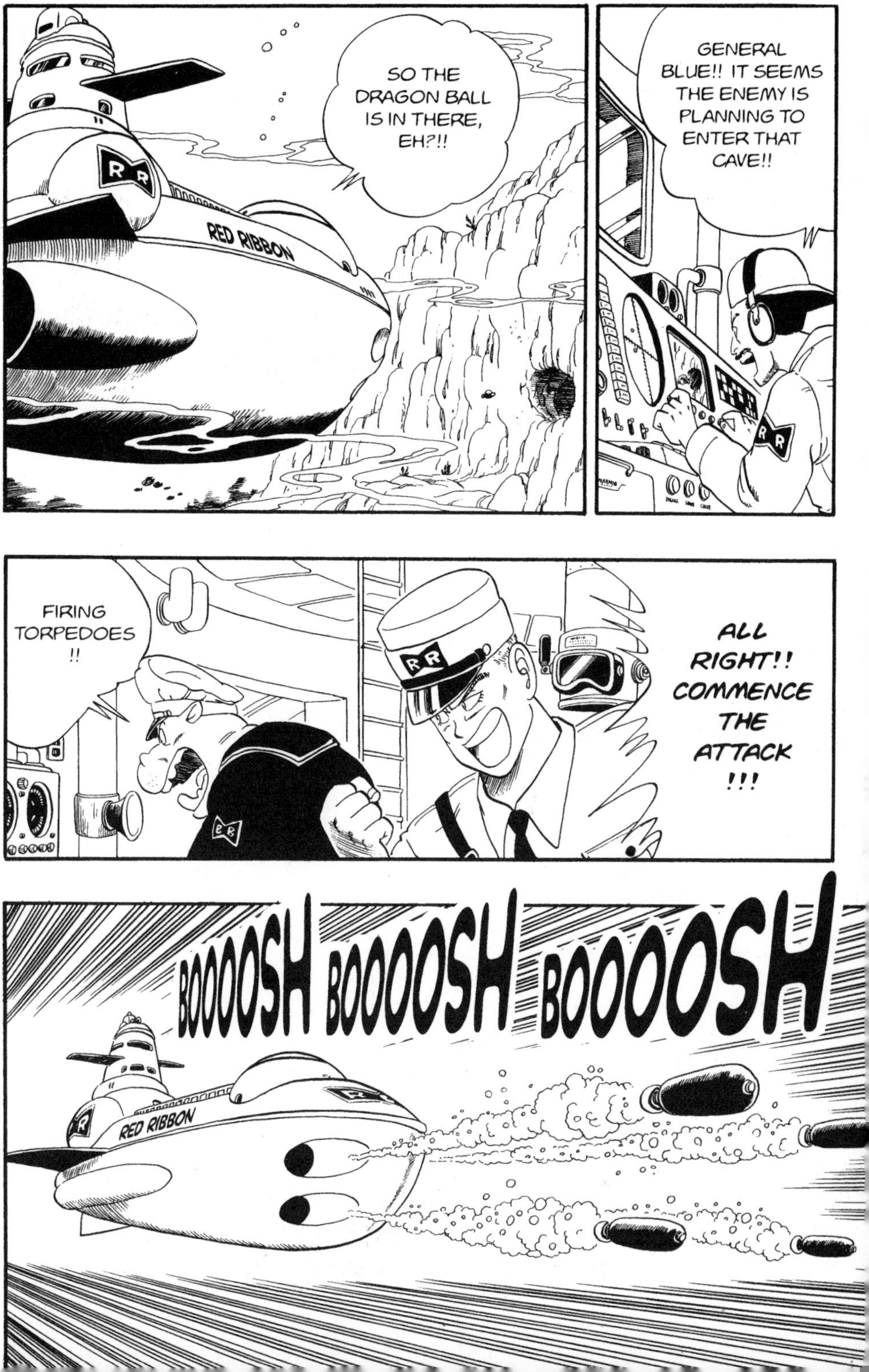
GENERAL BLUE!! IT SEEMS THE ENEMY IS PLANNING TO ENTER THAT CAVE!!
SO THE DRAGON BALL IS IN THERE, EH?!!
RED RIBBON
ALL RIGHT!! COMMENCE THE ATTACK !!!
FIRING TORPEDOES !!
BOOOOSH BOOOOSH BOOOOSH
RED RIBBON

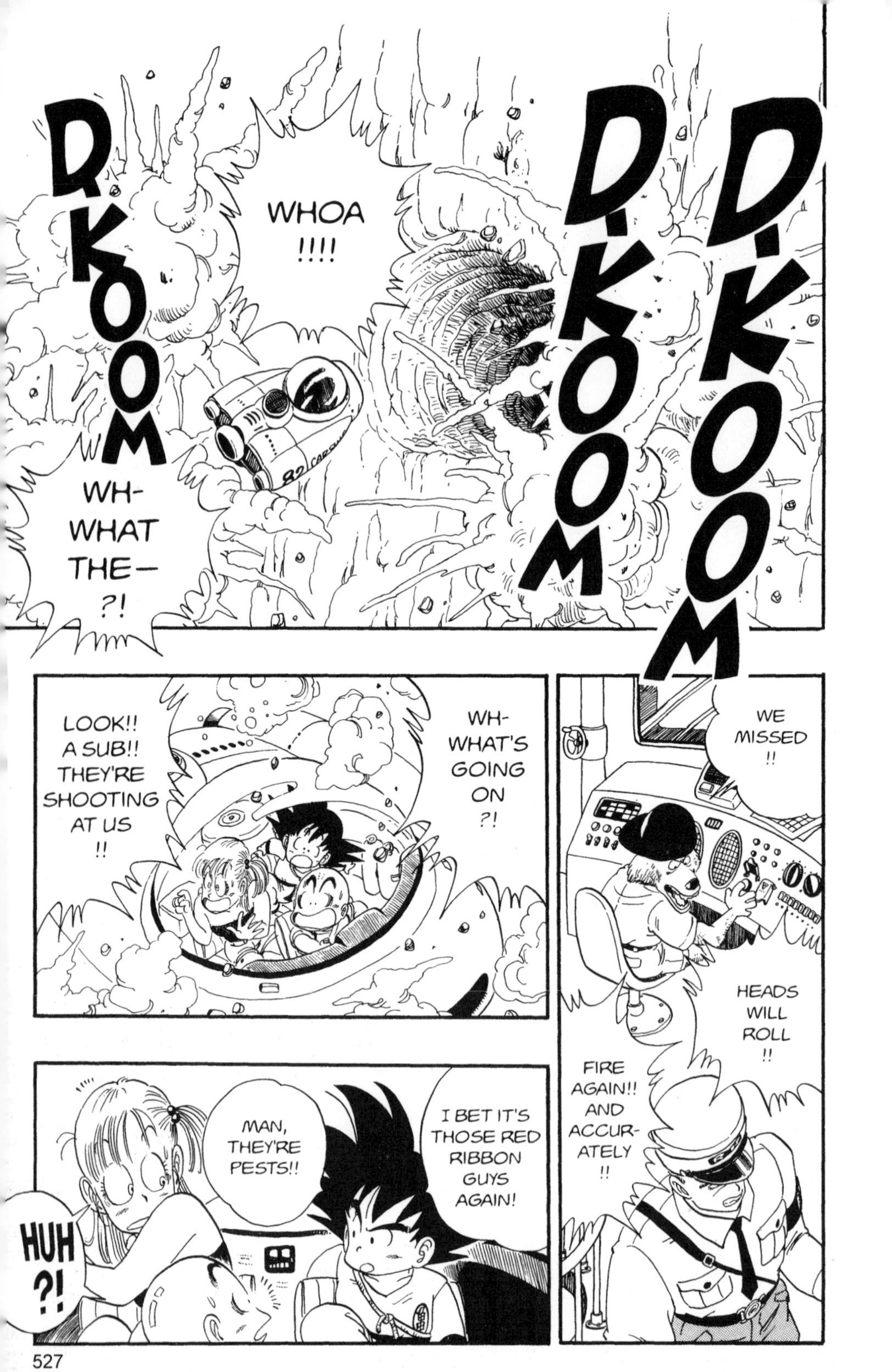
DKOOOM
DKOOM
WHOA !!!!
DKOOM
WH-WHAT THE—?!
WE MISSED !!
HEADS WILL ROLL !!
FIRE AGAIN!! AND ACCUR-ATELY !!
WH-WHAT'S GOING ON ?!
LOOK!! A SUB!! THEY'RE SHOOTING AT US !!
I BET IT'S THOSE RED RIBBON GUYS AGAIN!
MAN, THEY'RE PESTS!!
HUH ?!

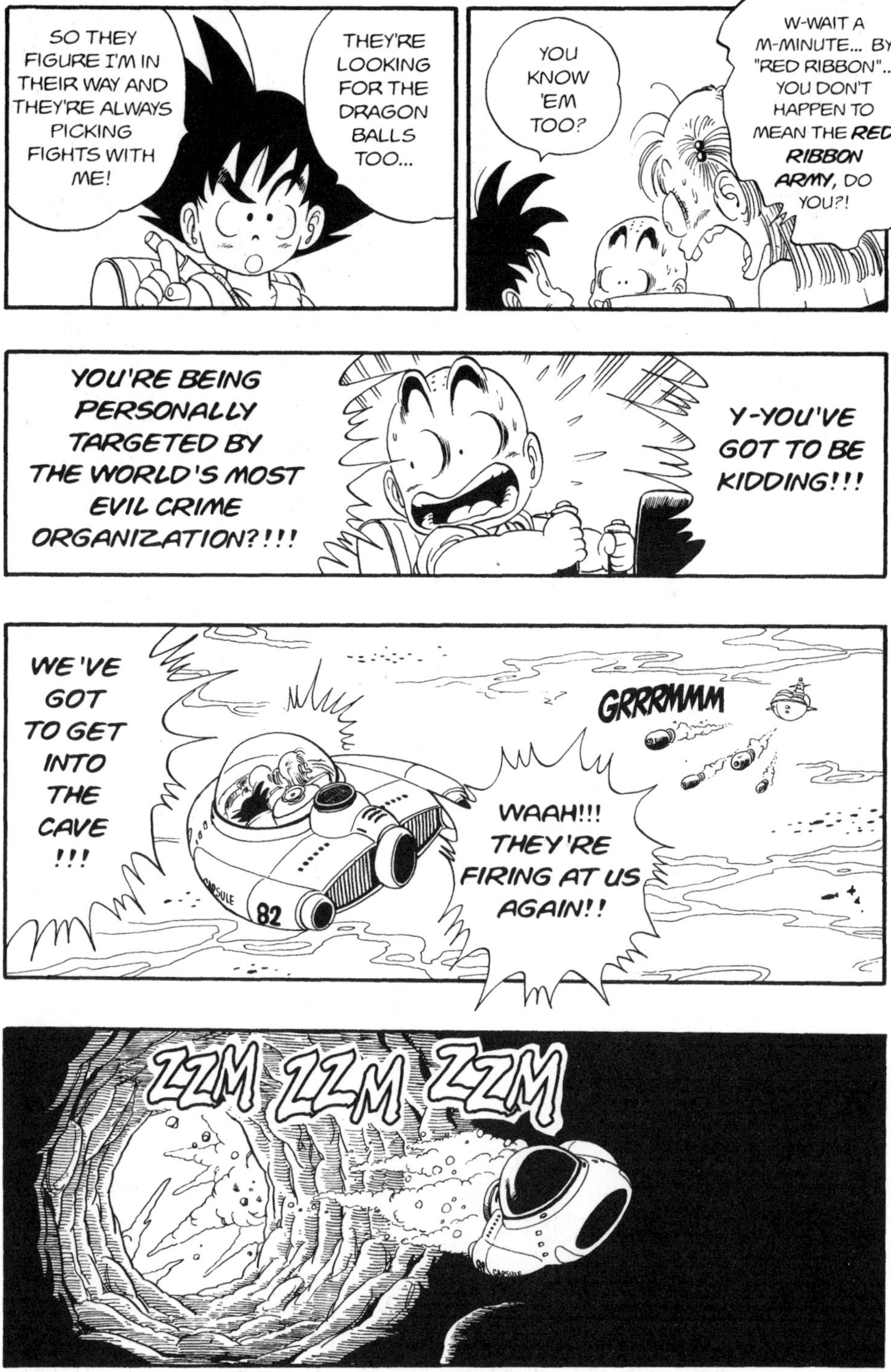

W-WAIT A M-MINUTE... BY "RED RIBBON"... YOU DON'T HAPPEN TO MEAN THE **RED RIBBON ARMY**, DO YOU?!
YOU KNOW 'EM TOO?
THEY'RE LOOKING FOR THE DRAGON BALLS TOO...
SO THEY FIGURE I'M IN THEIR WAY AND THEY'RE ALWAYS PICKING FIGHTS WITH ME!
Y-YOU'VE GOT TO BE KIDDING!!!
YOU'RE BEING PERSONALLY TARGETED BY THE WORLD'S MOST EVIL CRIME ORGANIZATION?!!!
GRRRMMM
WAAH!!! THEY'RE FIRING AT US AGAIN!!
WE'VE GOT TO GET INTO THE CAVE!!!
ZZM ZZM ZZM

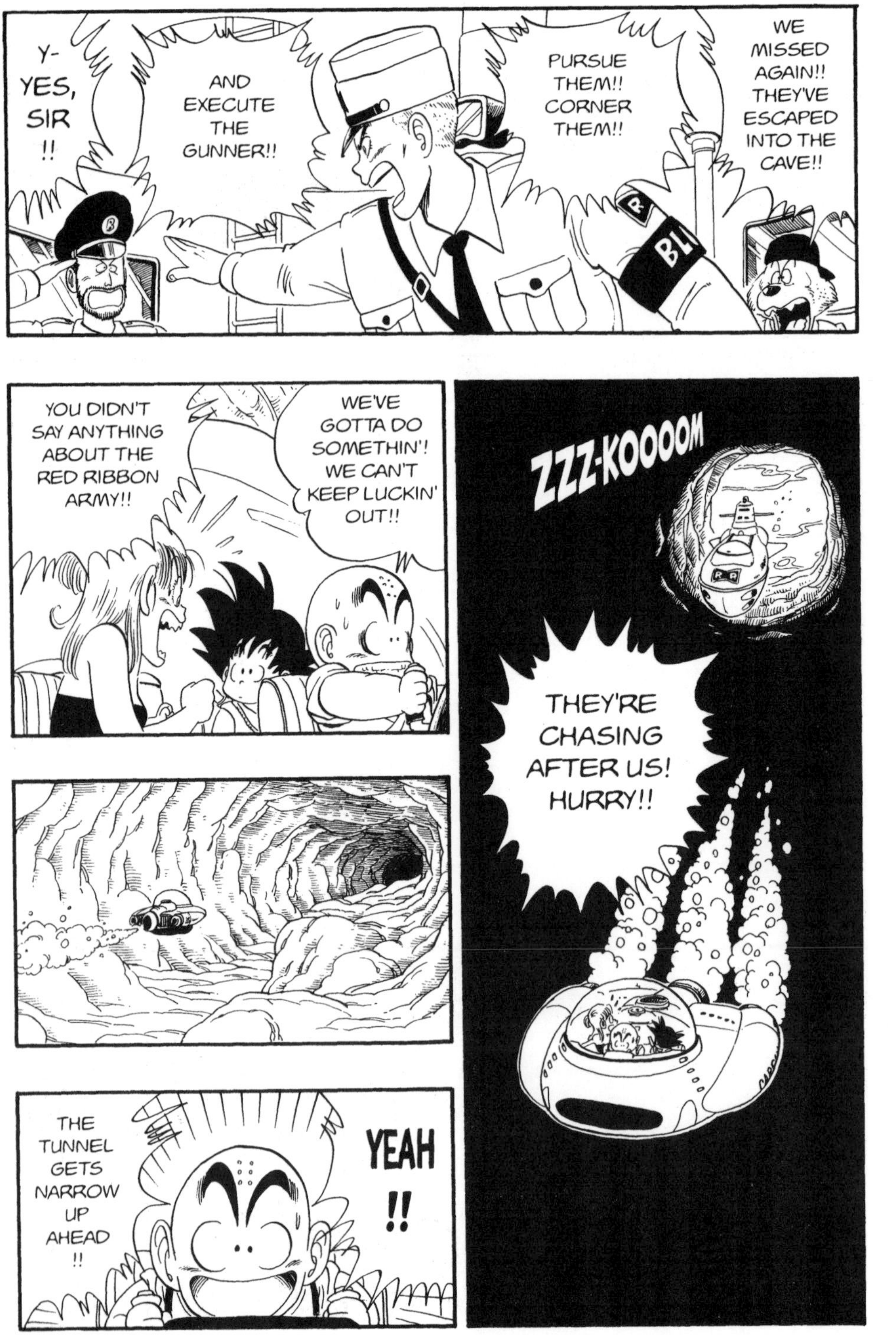
WE MISSED AGAIN!! THEY'VE ESCAPED INTO THE CAVE!!
PURSUE THEM!! CORNER THEM!!
AND EXECUTE THE GUNNER!!
Y-YES, SIR!!
ZZZ-KOOOOM
THEY'RE CHASING AFTER US! HURRY!!
WE'VE GOTTA DO SOMETHIN'! WE CAN'T KEEP LUCKIN' OUT!!
YOU DIDN'T SAY ANYTHING ABOUT THE RED RIBBON ARMY!!
YEAH!!
THE TUNNEL GETS NARROW UP AHEAD!!

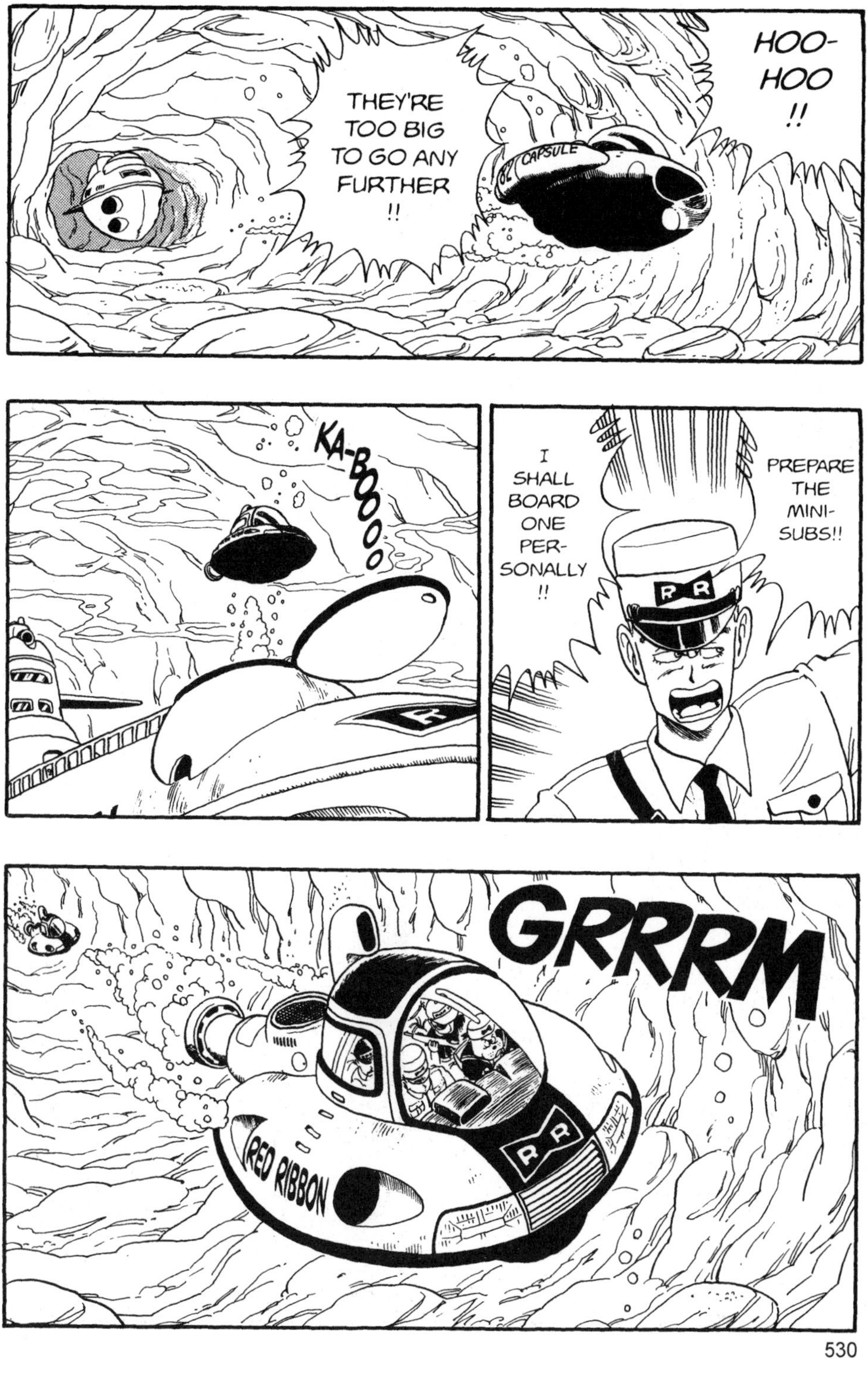
HOO-HOO !!
CAPSULE
THEY'RE TOO BIG TO GO ANY FURTHER !!
PREPARE THE MINI-SUBS!!
I SHALL BOARD ONE PER-SONALLY !!
KA-BOOOOO
GRRRM
RED RIBBON

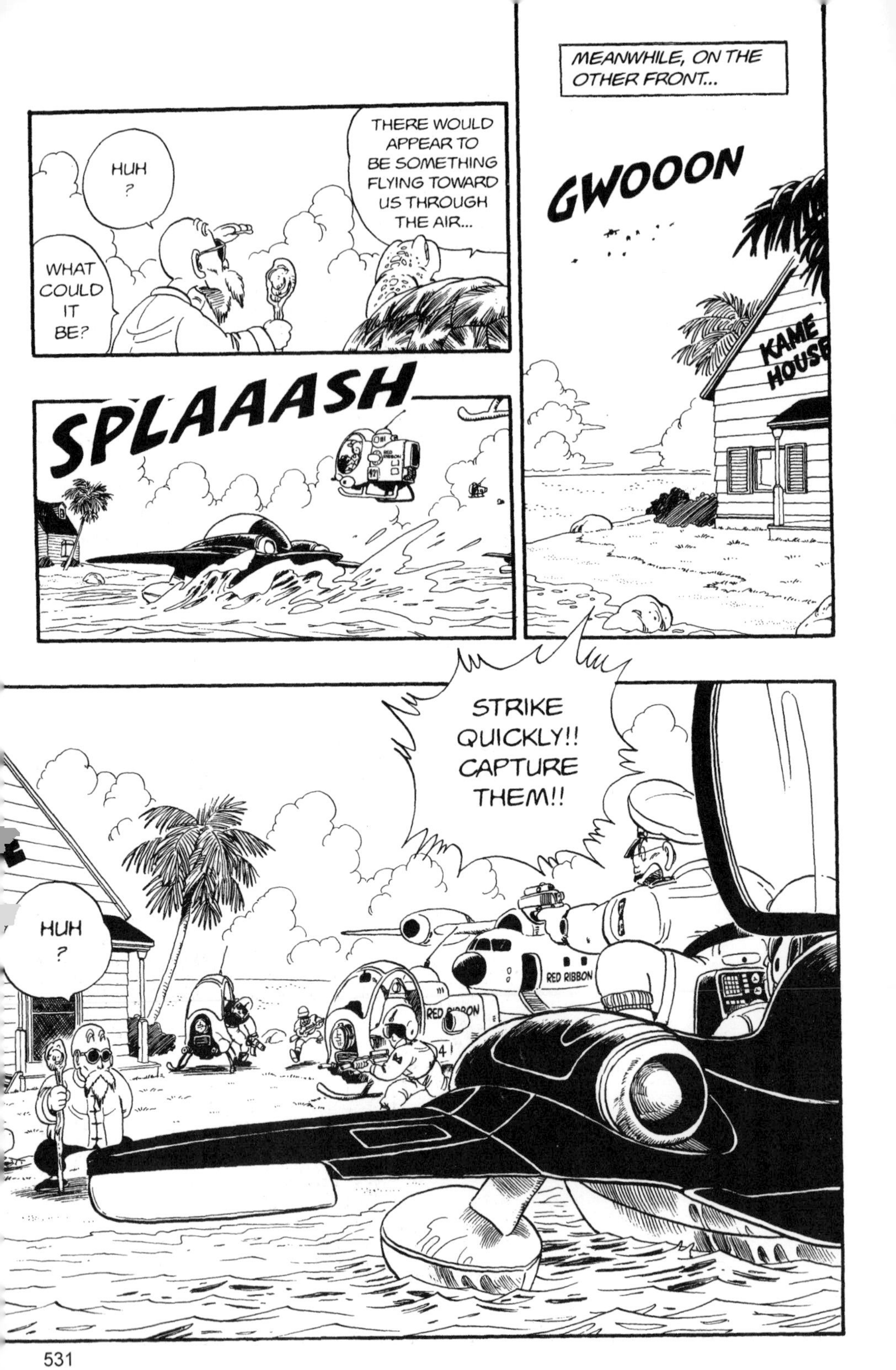
MEANWHILE, ON THE OTHER FRONT...
GWOOON
KAME HOUSE
THERE WOULD APPEAR TO BE SOMETHING FLYING TOWARD US THROUGH THE AIR...
HUH ?
WHAT COULD IT BE?
SPLAAASH
RED RIBBON
STRIKE QUICKLY!! CAPTURE THEM!!
RED RIBBON
RED RIBBON
HUH ?

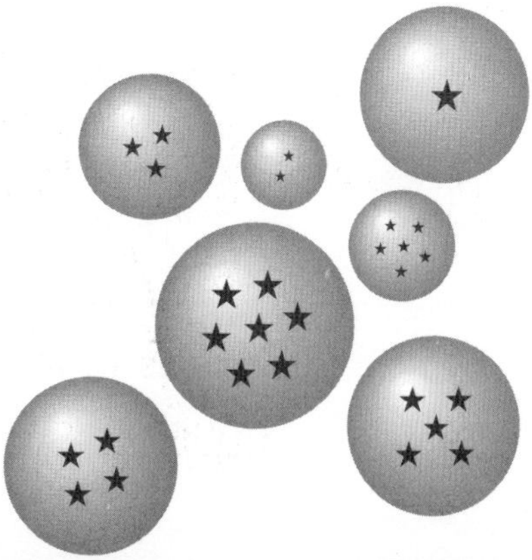

TITLE PAGE GALLERY

Following are the title pages for the individual chapters. Most of them are as they appeared during their original serialization in *Weekly Shonen Jump* magazine in Japan from 1984 to 1988.

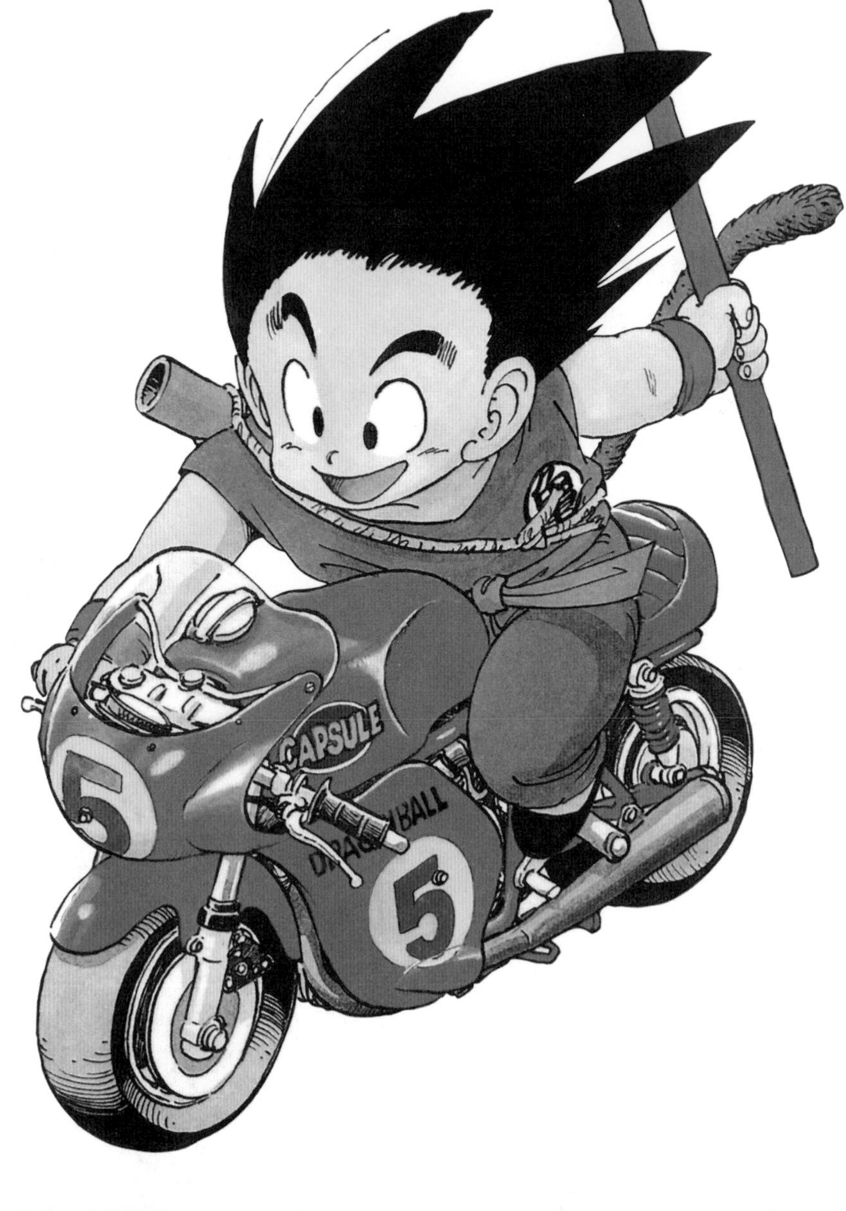
CAPSULE
5
5

ドラゴンボール

DRAGON BALL

Tale 37 • Match No. 2

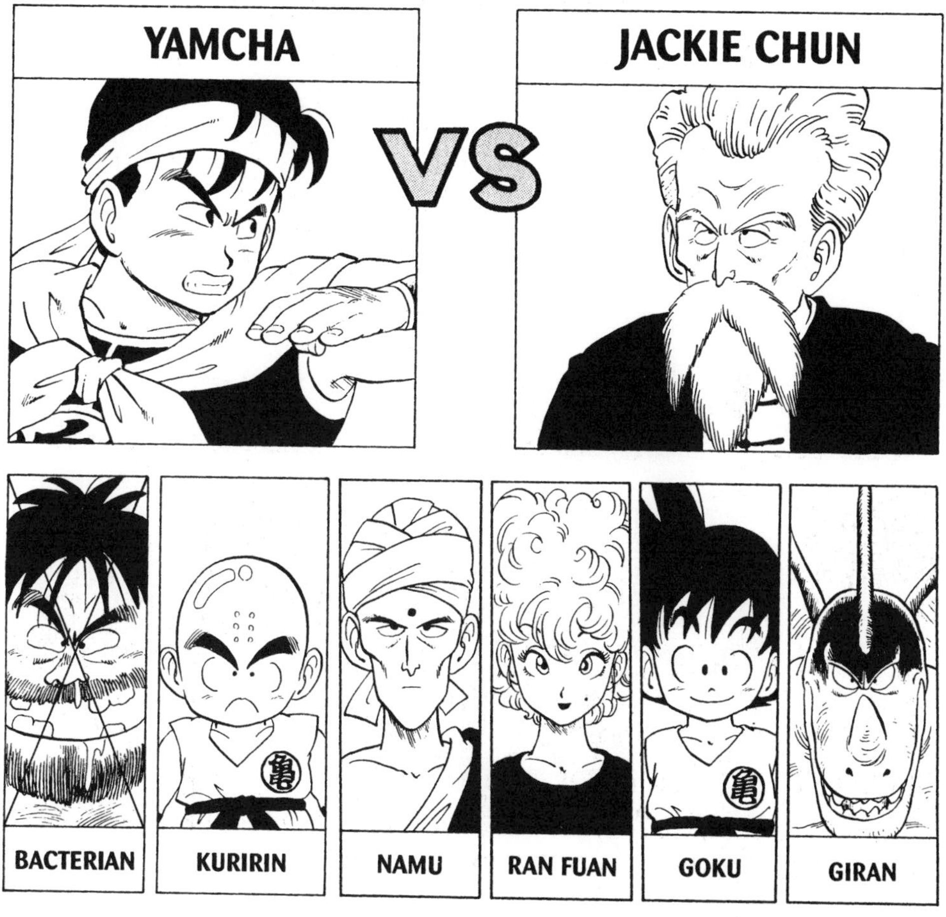
JACKIE CHUN
VS
YAMCHA
GIRAN
GOKU
RAN FUAN
NAMU
KURIRIN
BACTERIAN

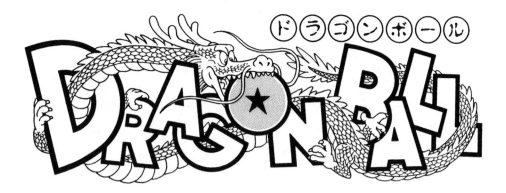

ドラゴンボール

DRAGON BALL

Tale 38 · Water and Cheesecake

NAMU
VS
RAN FUAN
BACTERIAN
KURIRIN
JACKIE CHUN
YAMCHA
GOKU
GIRAN

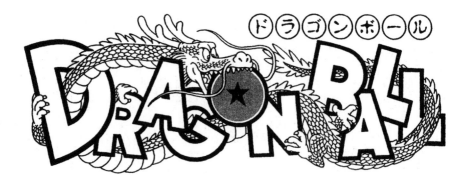

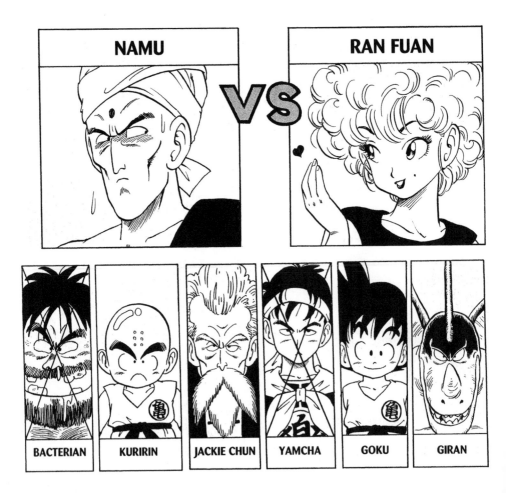

ドラゴンボール

Tale 39 · Monster Smash!

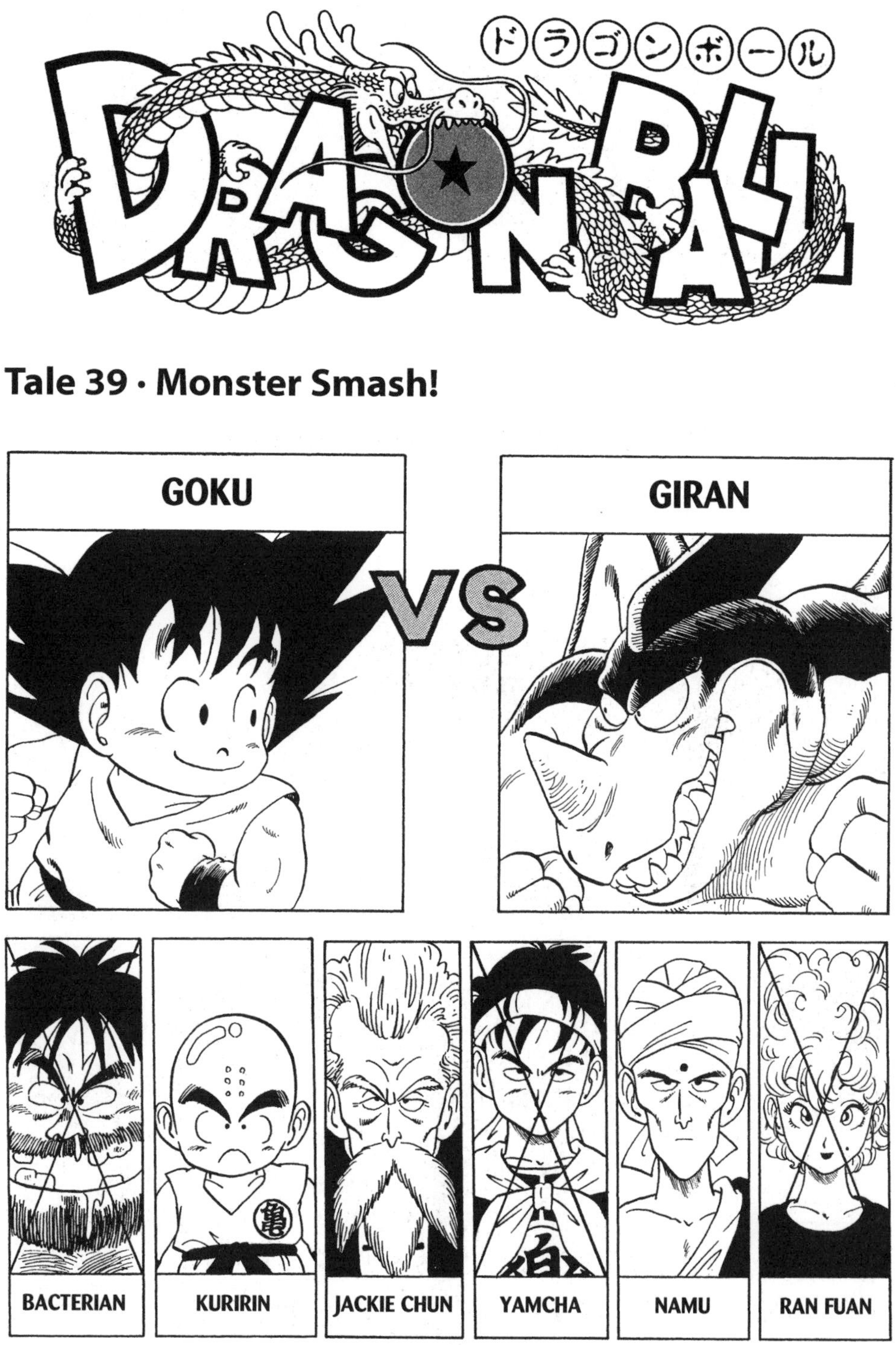
GIRAN
VS
GOKU
RAN FUAN
NAMU
YAMCHA
JACKIE CHUN
KURIRIN
BACTERIAN

ドラゴンボール

DRAGON BALL

Tale 40 • The Tail of Goku

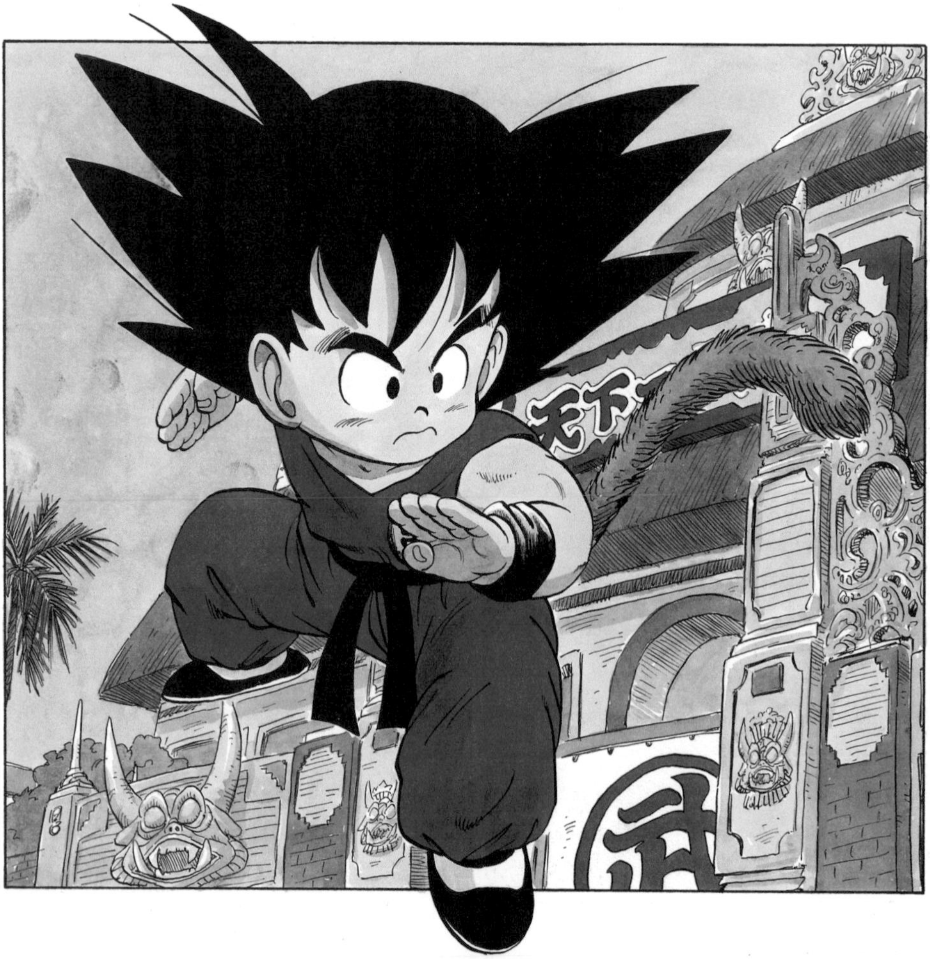
天下
武

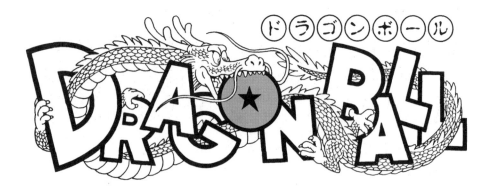

DRAGON BALL

ドラゴンボール

Tale 41
Kuririn vs. Jackie Chun

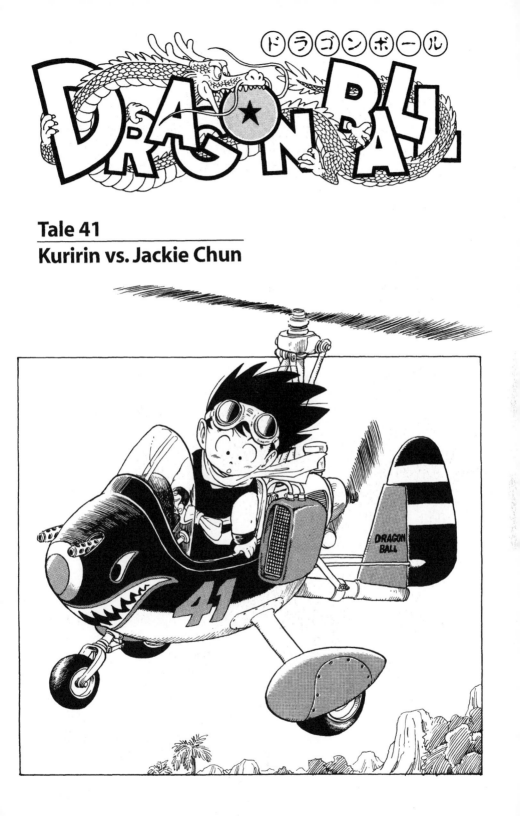

ドラゴンボール

Tale 42 · The Big Fight

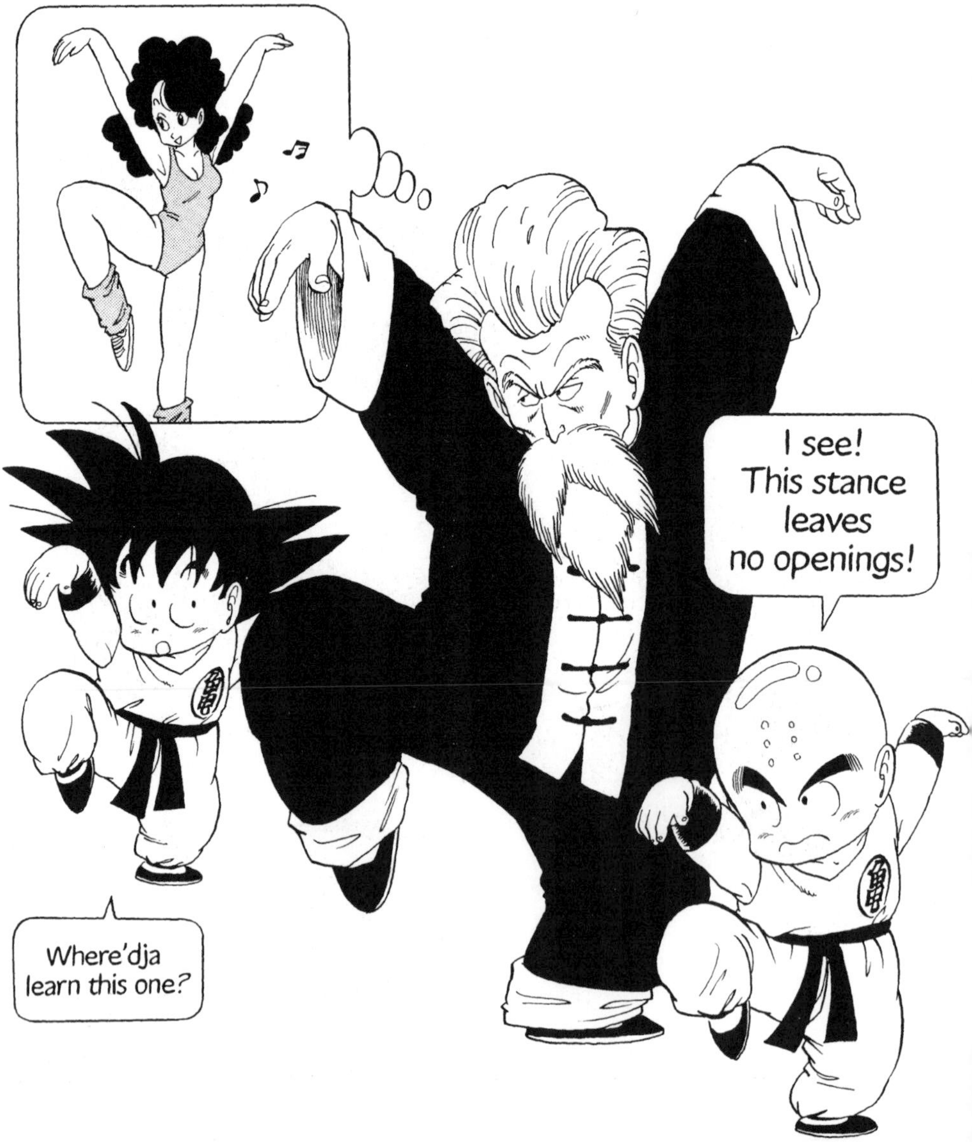
I see! This stance leaves no openings!
Where'dja learn this one?

ドラゴンボール

DRAGON BALL

Tale 43 • The Mysterious Jackie Chun

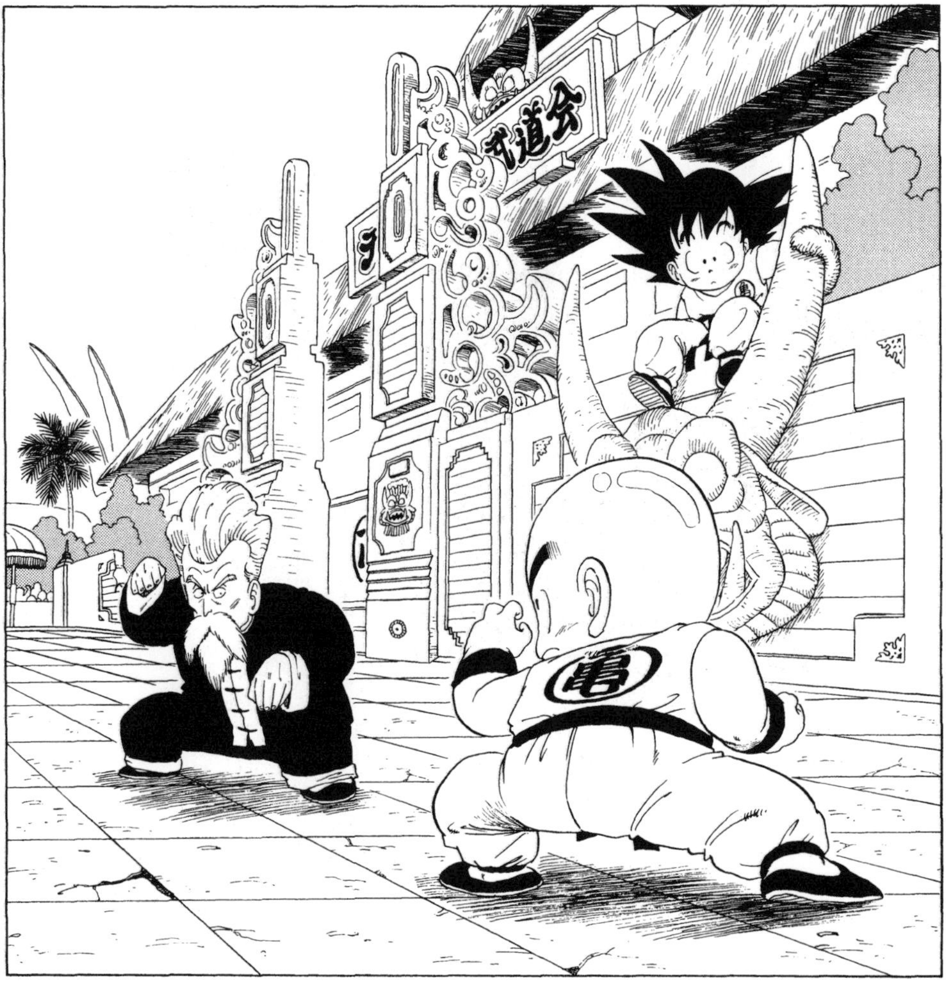
武道会

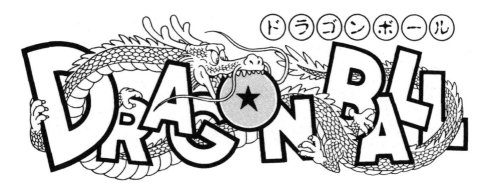

ドラゴンボール

DRAGON BALL

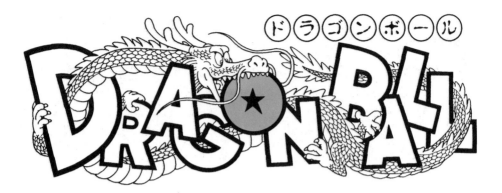

Tale 44 · The Name of the Game Is Namu

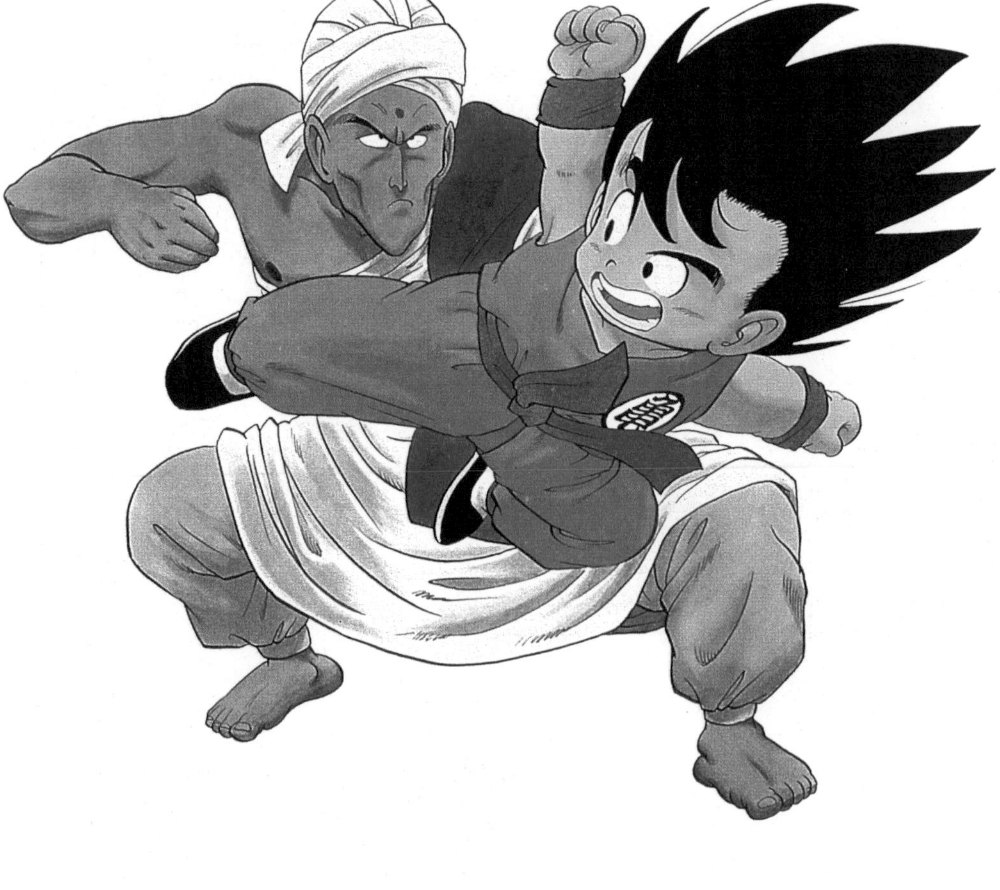

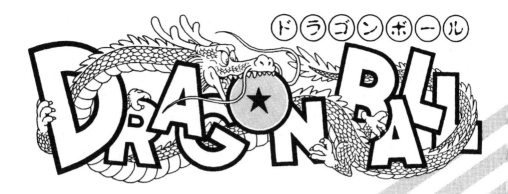

Tale 45 · Taking the Air

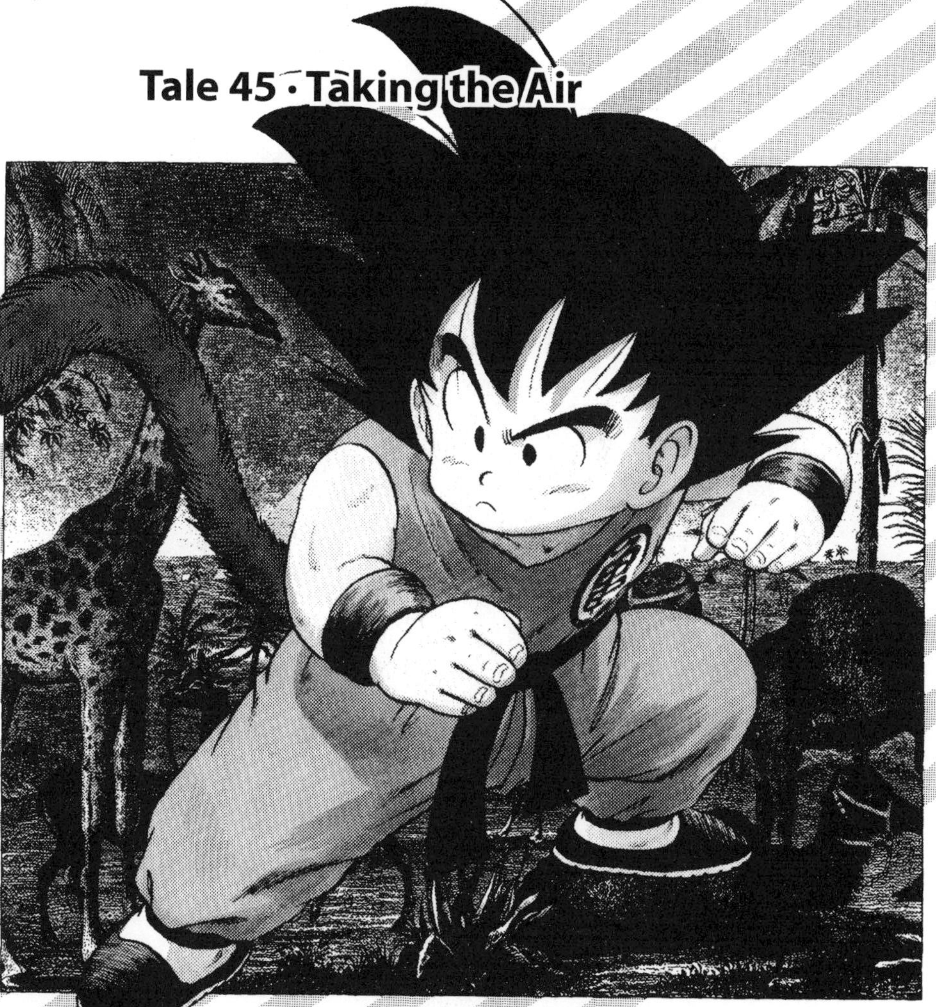

ドラゴンボール

DRAGON BALL

Tale 46
The Final Match

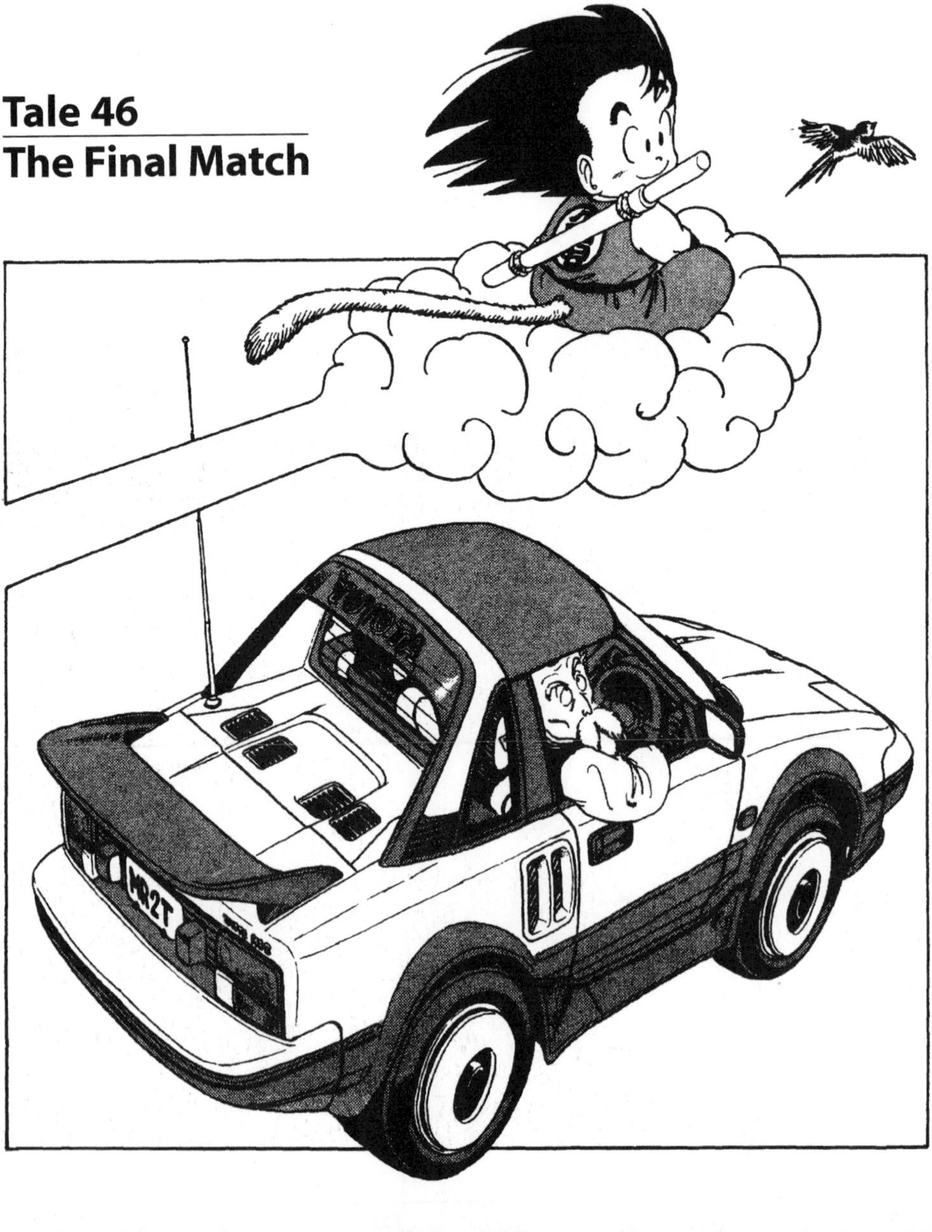
MR2T

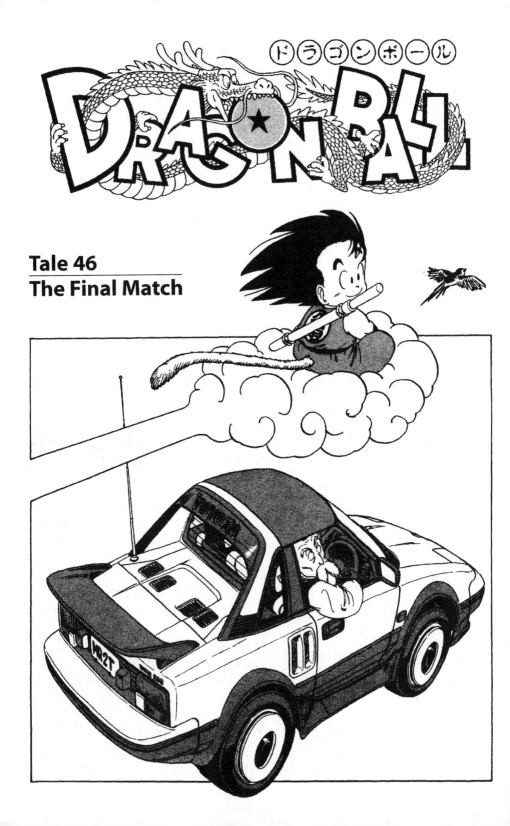

ドラゴンボール

DRAGON BALL

Tale 47 • The Kamehameha

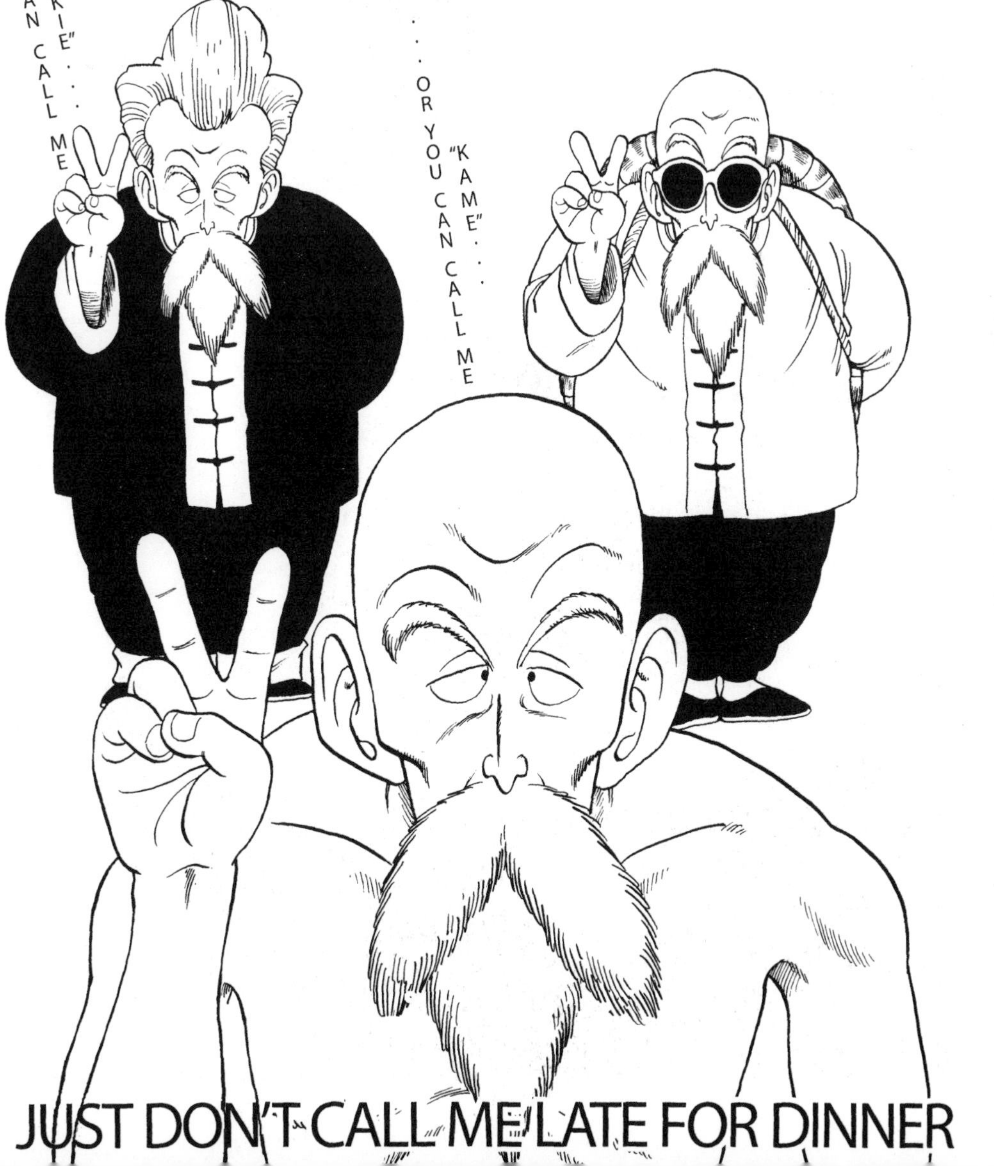
YOU CAN CALL ME "JACKIE"...
...OR YOU CAN CALL ME "KAME"...
JUST DON'T CALL ME LATE FOR DINNER

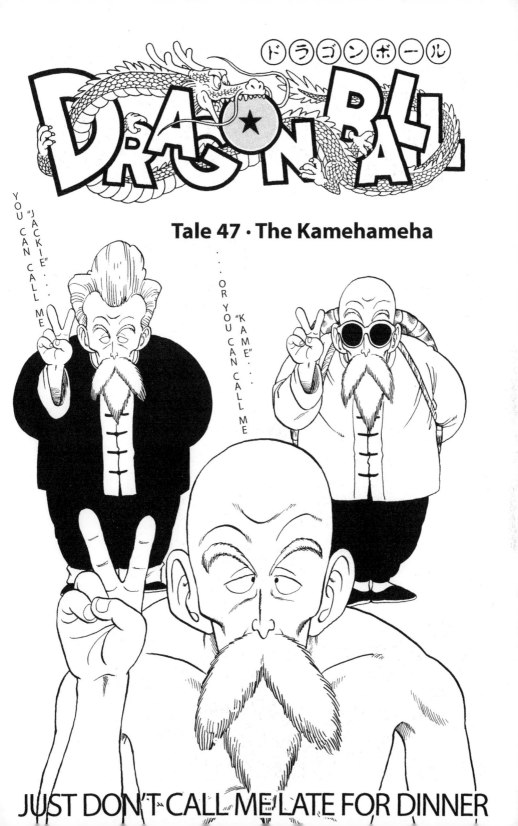

Tale 48 · One Lucky Monkey

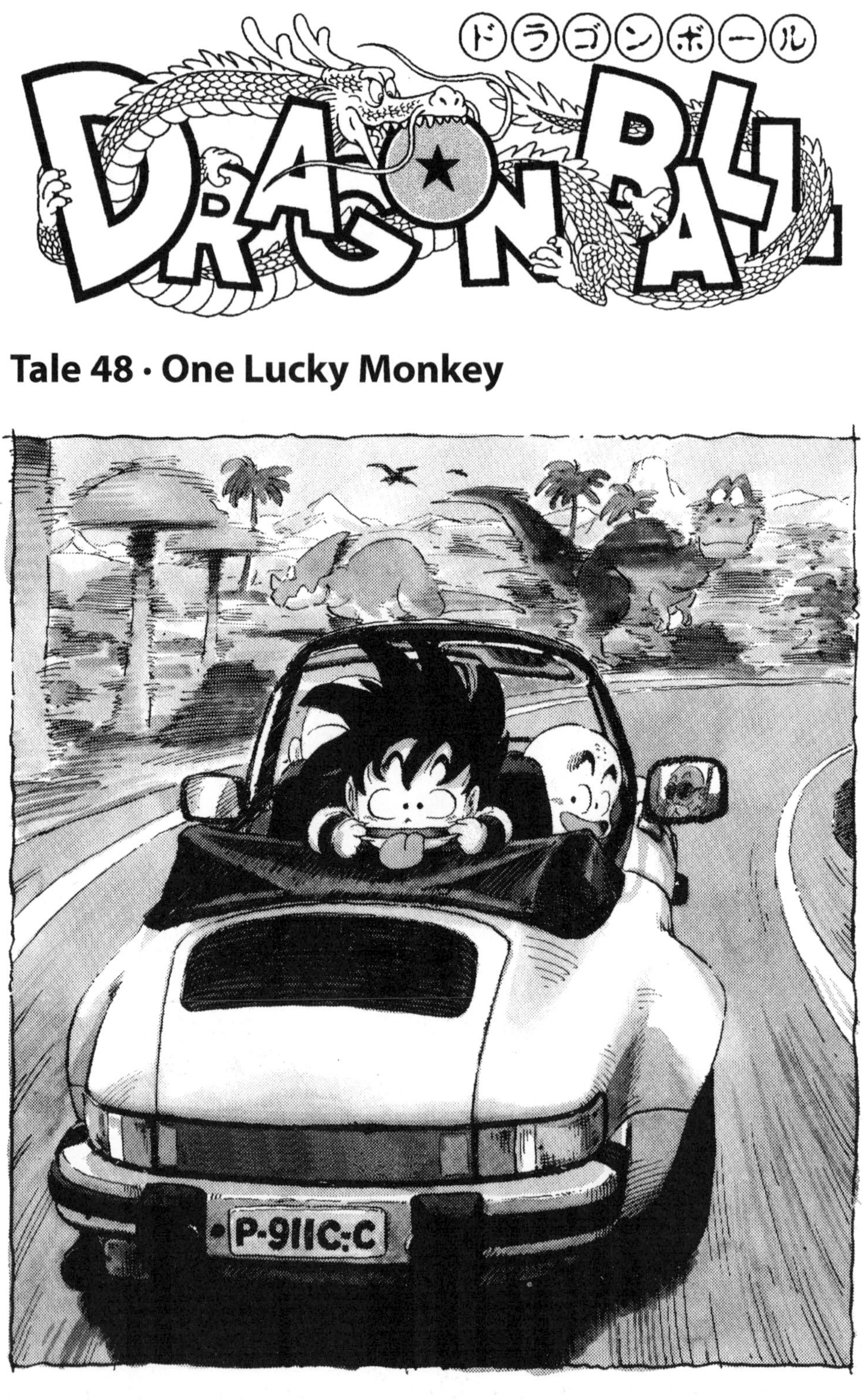
P-911C:C

ドラゴンボール

DRAGON BALL

Tale 49 • The Big Sleep

天下一
天下一

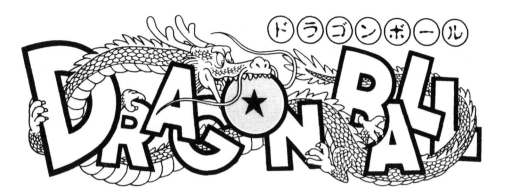

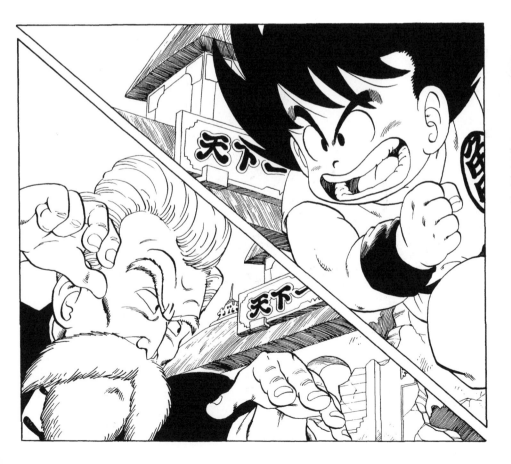

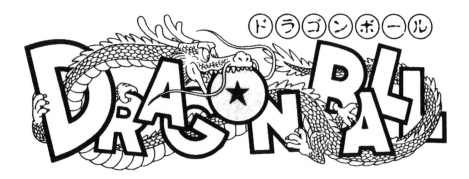

Tale 50 • Jackie's Shocking Secret

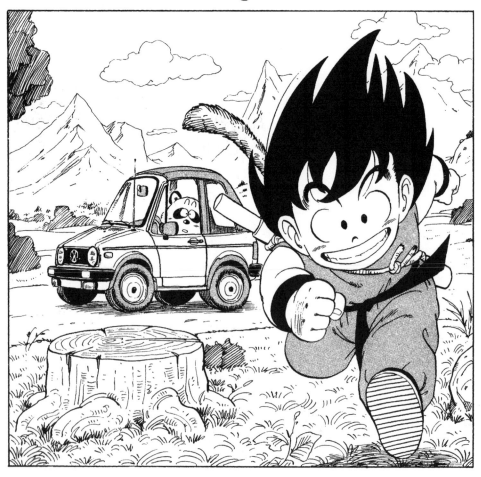

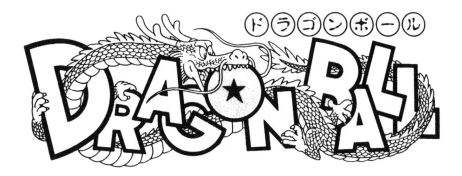

Tale 51 • And the Crowd Goes Wild!!!

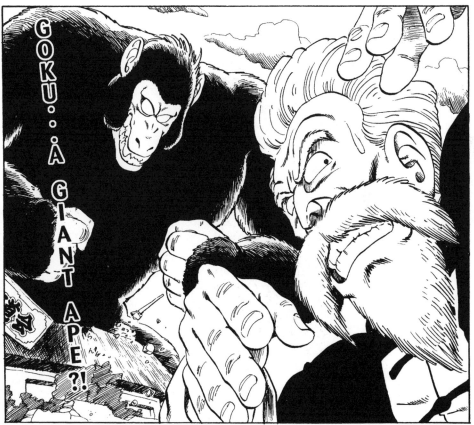

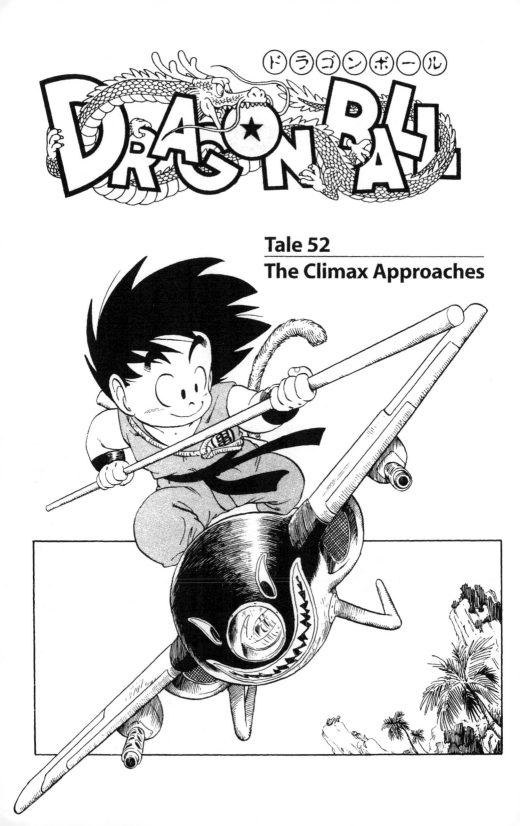

Tale 52
The Climax Approaches

Tale 53 • The Final Blow

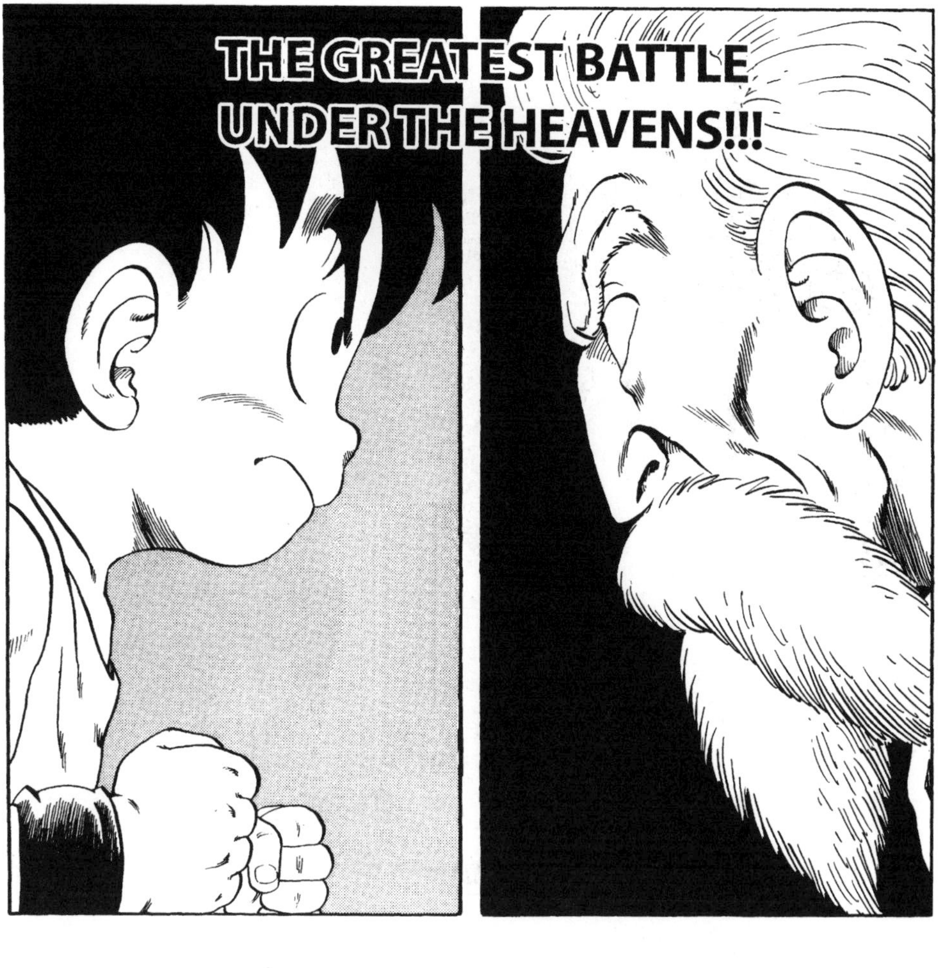
THE GREATEST BATTLE UNDER THE HEAVENS!!!

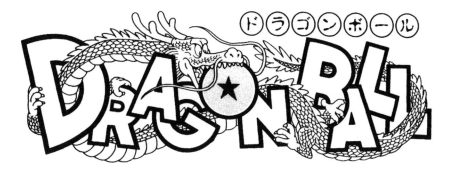

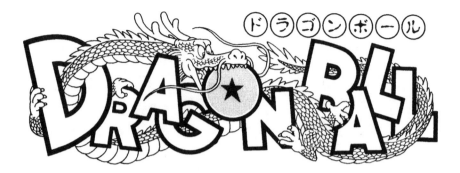

Tale 54 • On the Road Again

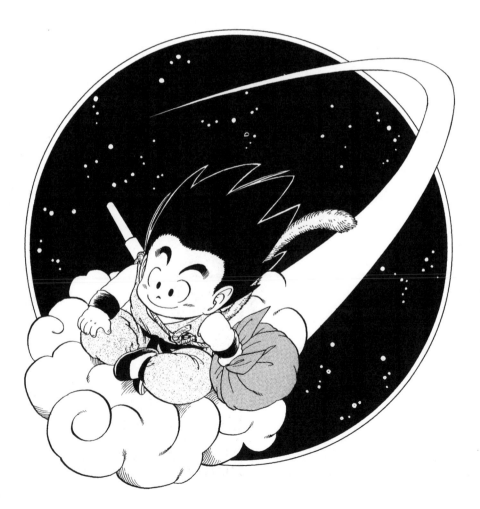

ドラゴンボール

DRAGON BALL

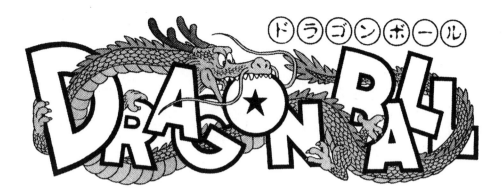

Tale 55 • The Red Ribbon

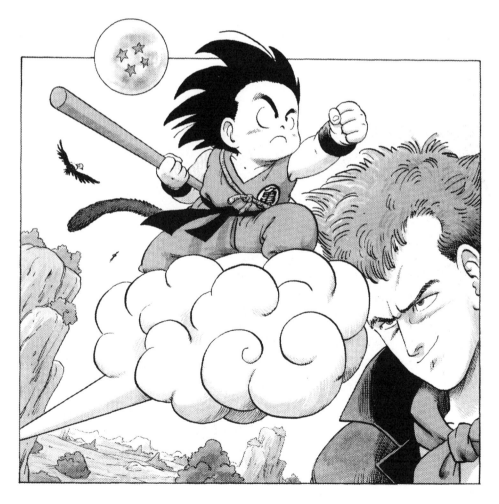

ドラゴンボール

DRAGON BALL

Tale 56 • The Dragon Ball Scramble

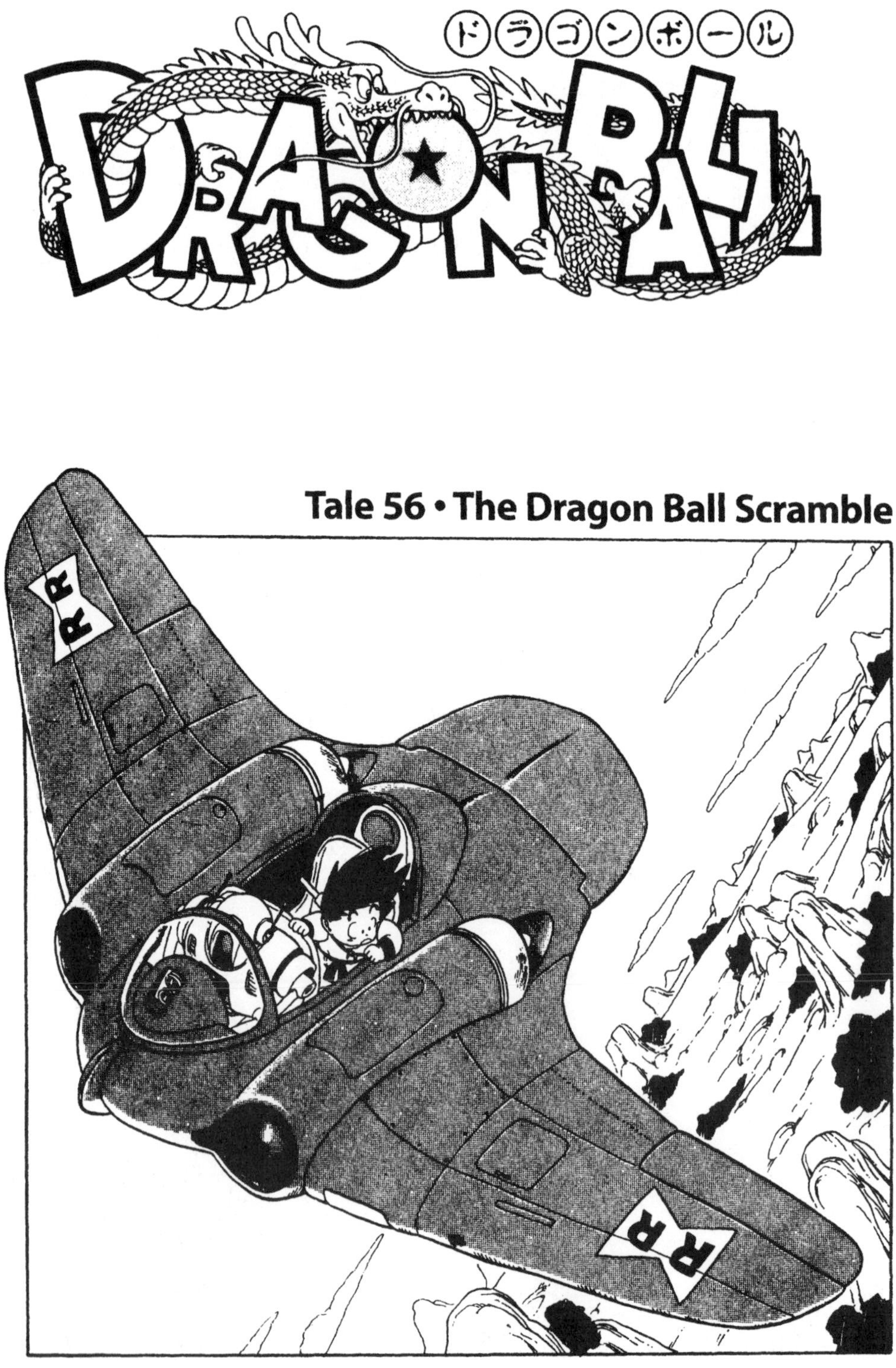

RR
RR

ドラゴンボール

DRAGON BALL

Tale 57 · The Storming of Muscle Tower

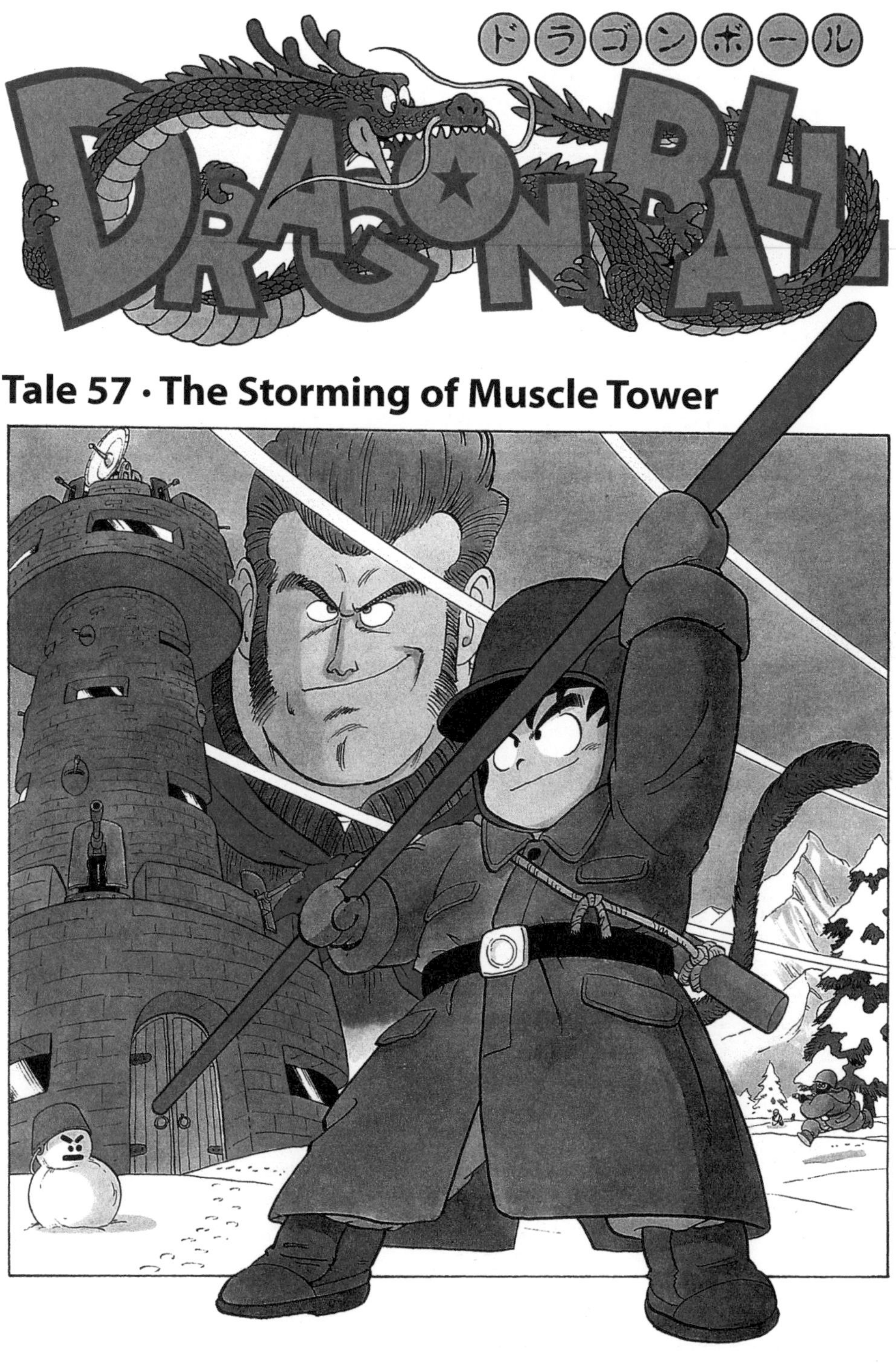

Tale 58 · The Flexing of Muscle Tower

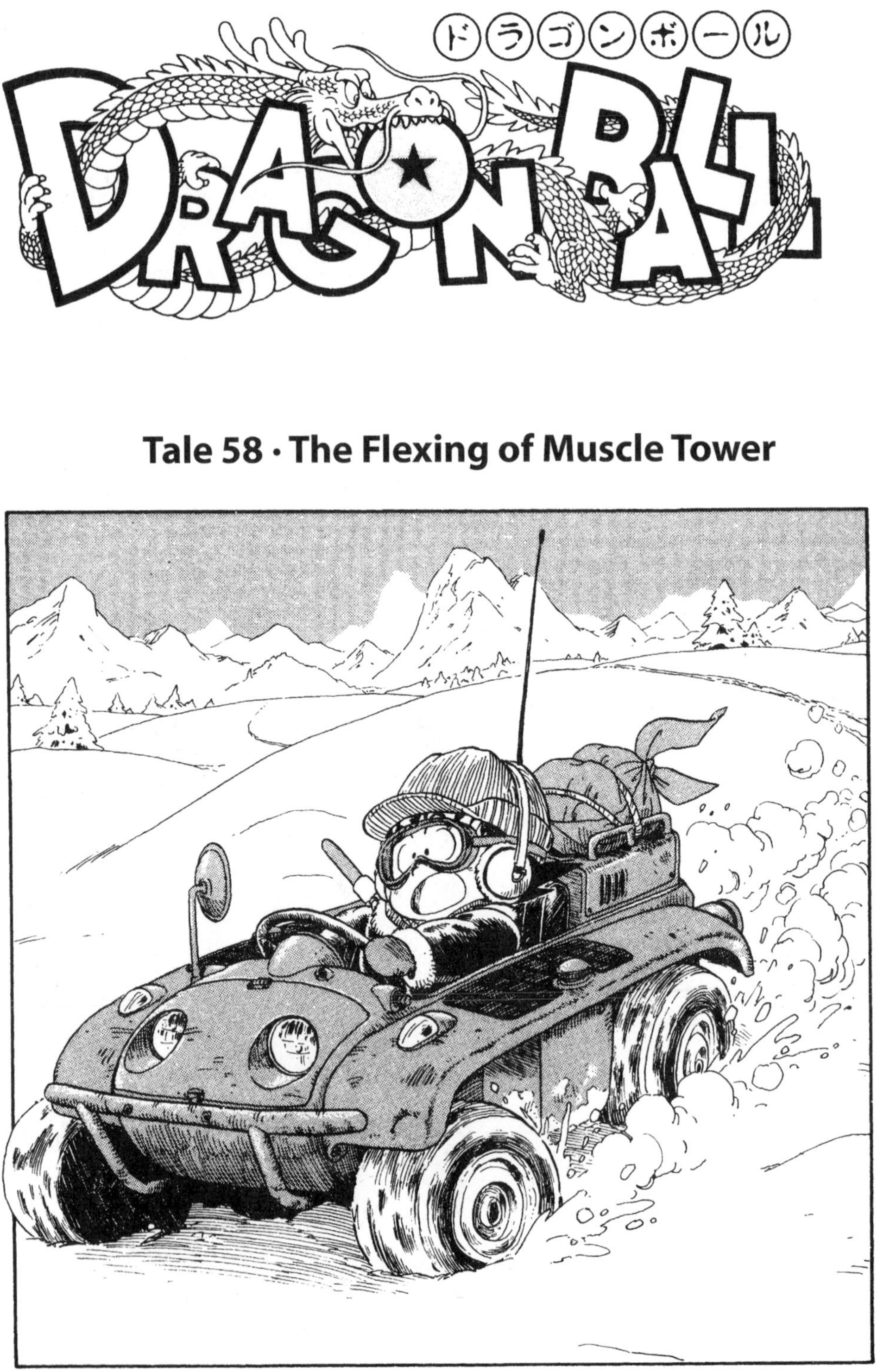

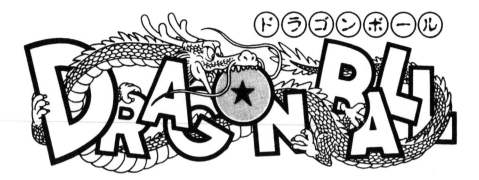

Tale 59 · Devil on the Third Floor

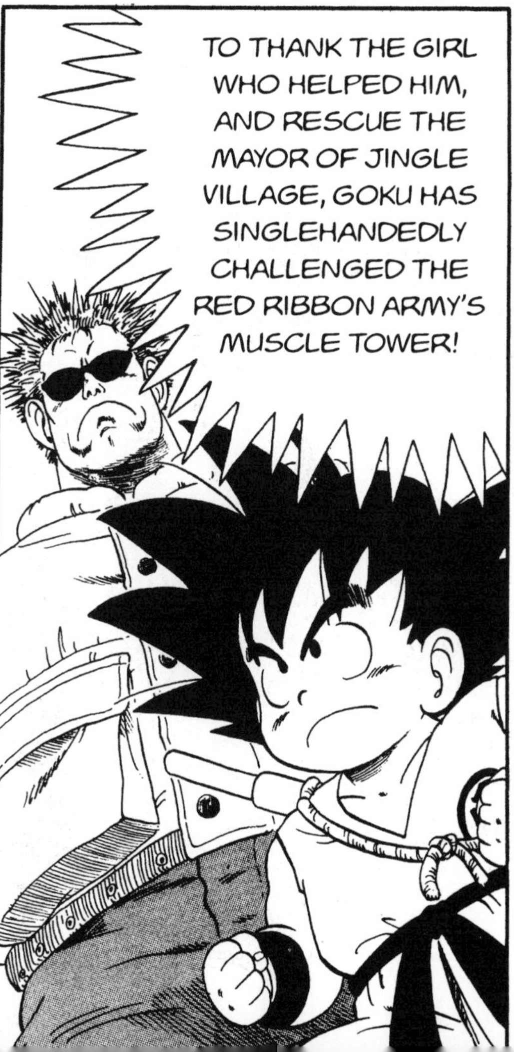
TO THANK THE GIRL WHO HELPED HIM, AND RESCUE THE MAYOR OF JINGLE VILLAGE, GOKU HAS SINGLEHANDEDLY CHALLENGED THE RED RIBBON ARMY'S MUSCLE TOWER!

This is the terrifying Muscle Tower!!!

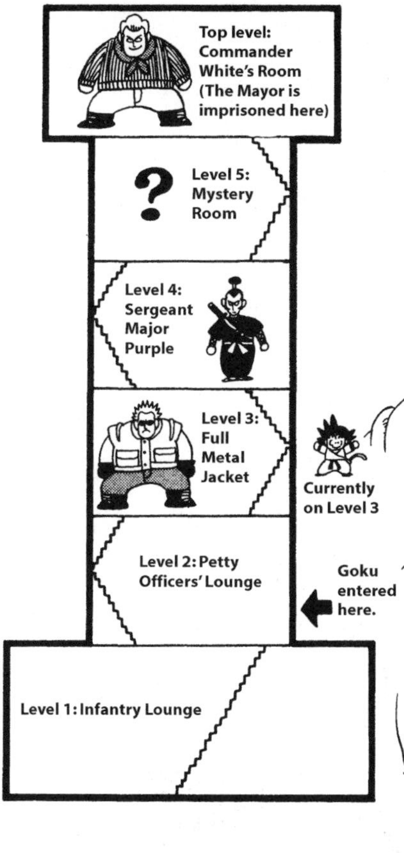
Top level: Commander White's Room (The Mayor is imprisoned here)
?
Level 5: Mystery Room
Level 4: Sergeant Major Purple
Level 3: Full Metal Jacket
Currently on Level 3
Level 2: Petty Officers' Lounge
Goku entered here.
Level 1: Infantry Lounge

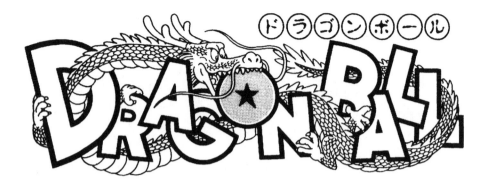

Tale 60 · Purple People Beater

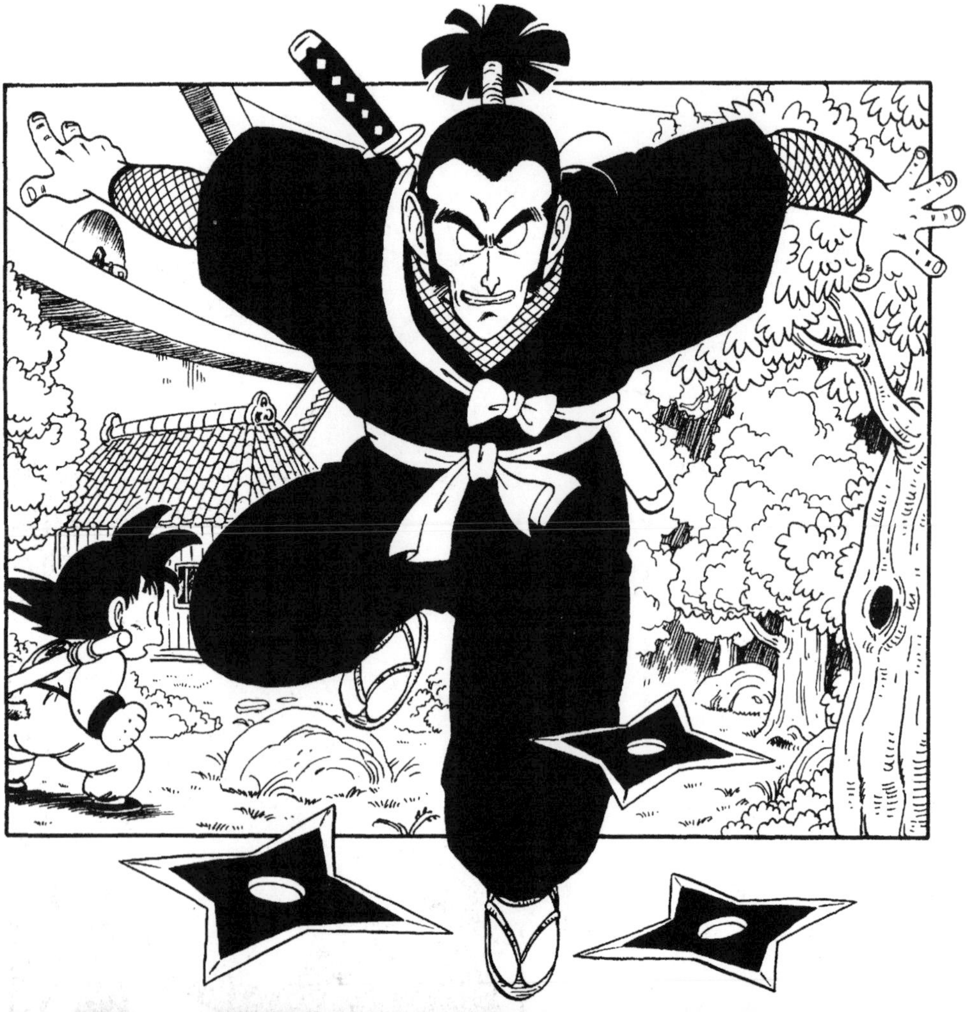

Tale 61 · The 4 ½ Tatami Mat Flip

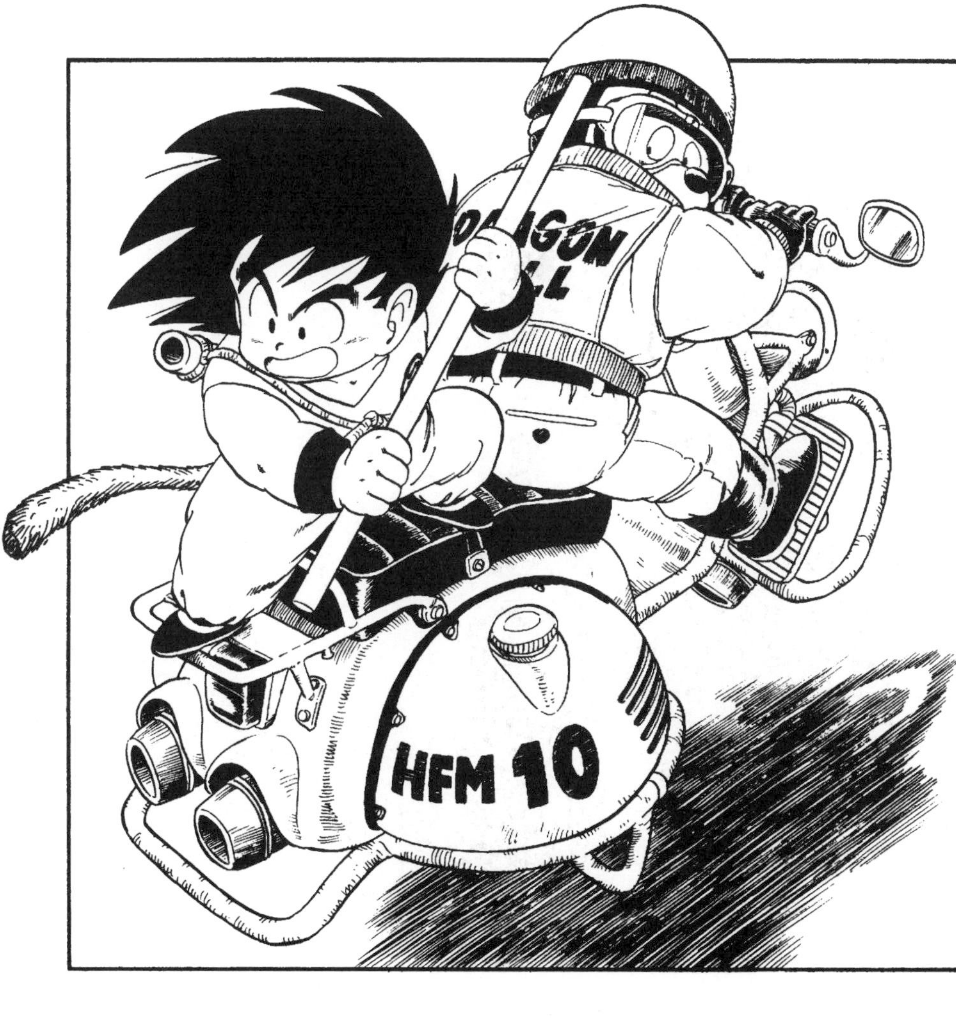
HFM 10

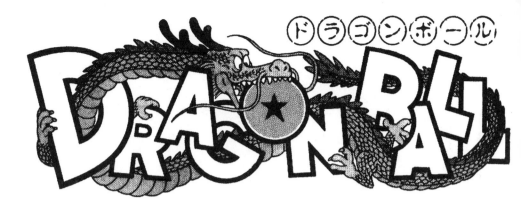

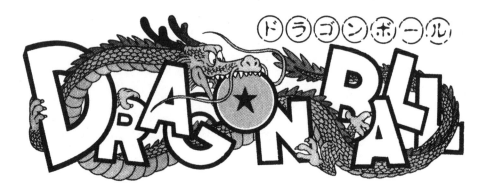

Tale 62 • The Ninja Split!

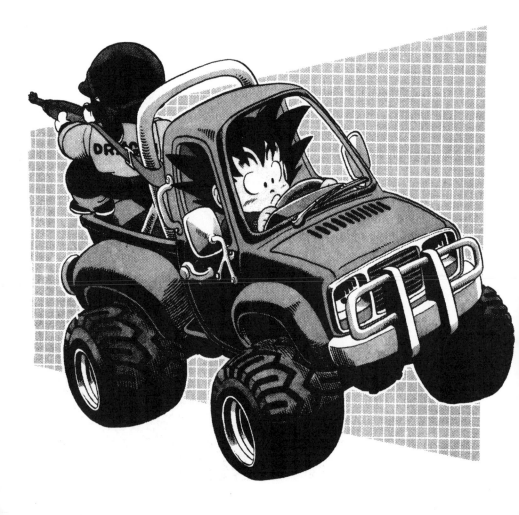

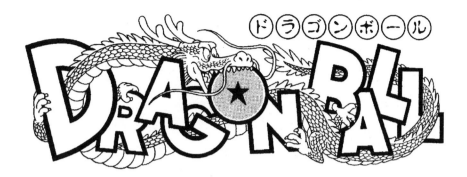

Tale 63 · Mechanical Man No.8

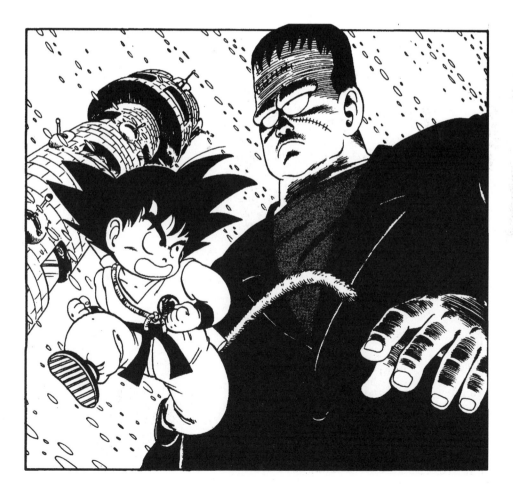

Tale 64 · The Horrible...Jiggler!

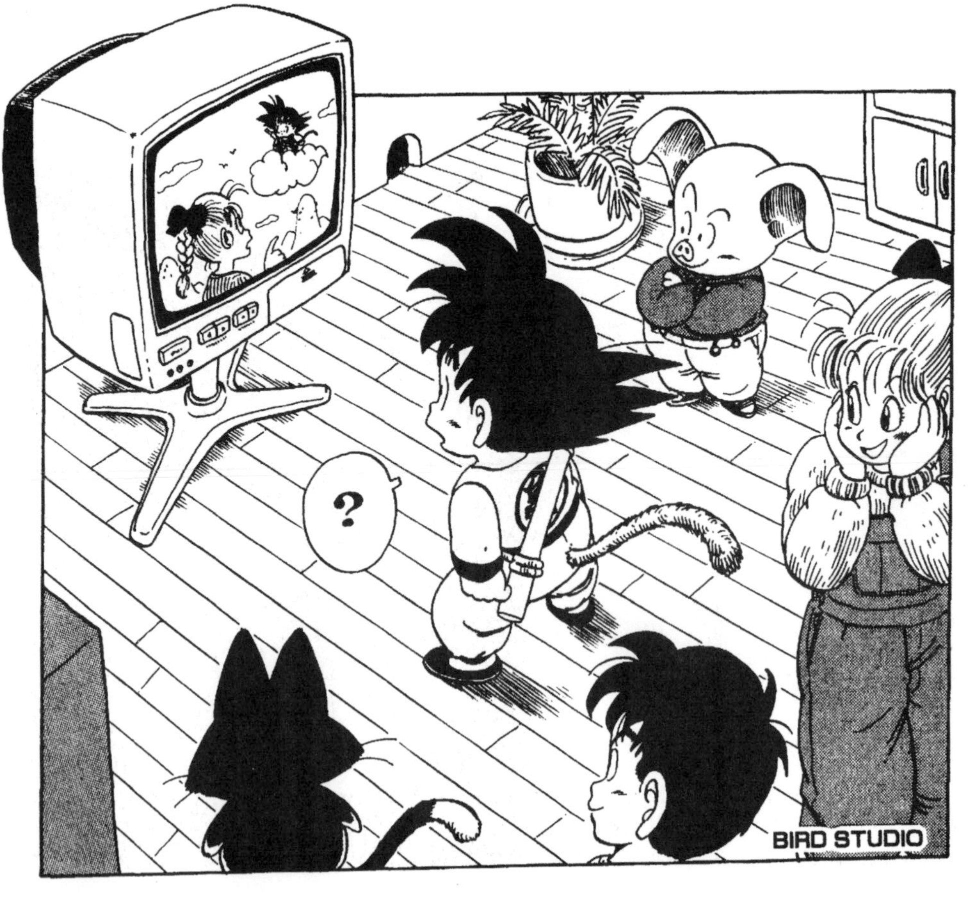
?
BIRD STUDIO

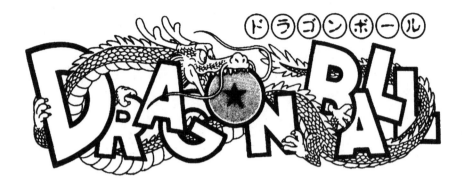

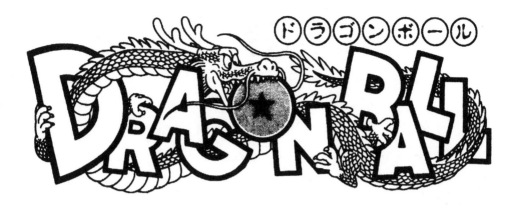

Tale 65 · How to Unjiggle a Jiggler

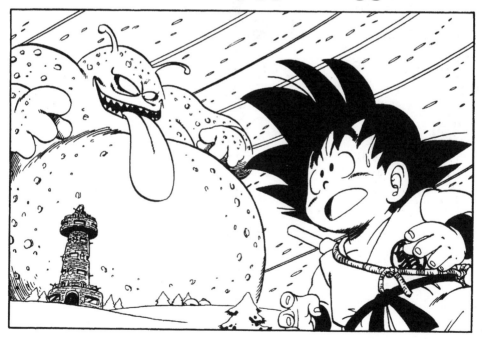

DRAGON BALL

ドラゴンボール

Tale 66
Muscle Tower's Final Hour

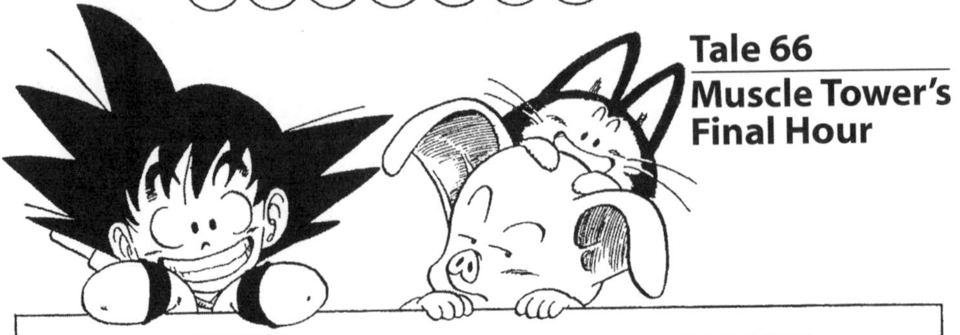

DRAGON BALL クイズスペシャルの答えだよ!

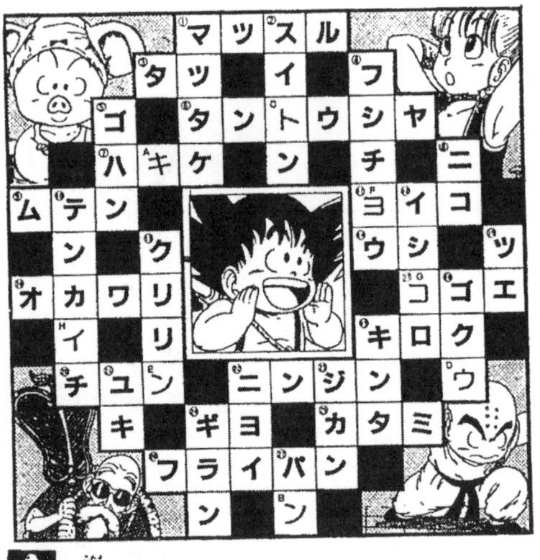
マツスル
タツ イ フ
ゴ タントウシヤ
ハキケ ン チ ニ
ムテン ヨイコ
ン ク ウシ ツ
オカワリ コ ゴエ
イ リ キロク
チユン ニンジン ウ
キ ギヨ カタミ
フライパン
ン ン

Ⓐの答：キントウンヨコイ

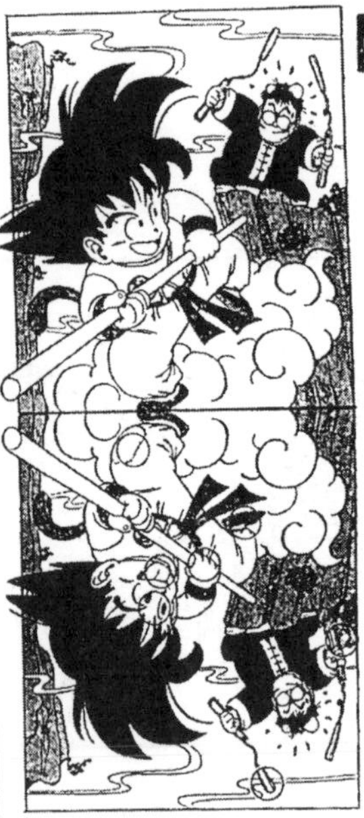

Ⓒの答：Ⓐ7つ

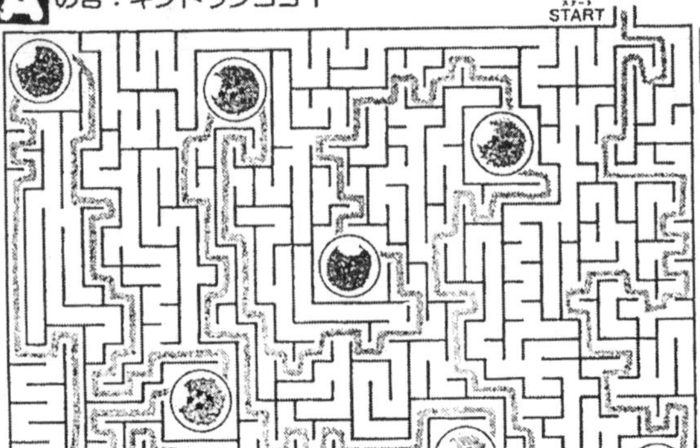
START
GOAL

Ⓑの答：3

Ⓓの答：ミンナガマツタアニメ

Ⓓの⑦悟空にバンバンされたのは何人 という設問については、「女の人で」という部分がぬけていましたので、(カ)4人(ン)3人(テ)2人、いずれも正解とします。

全部で4万2千通もの応募がありましたが正解者多数のため抽選で180名の方を当選とさせていただきました。328ページの発表をご覧ください。当選なさった方には、1カ月以内に賞品が届きますので、しばらくお待ちください。これからも応援よろしく。

※ This page was from the time **Dragon Ball** was serialized in the magazine in Japan.

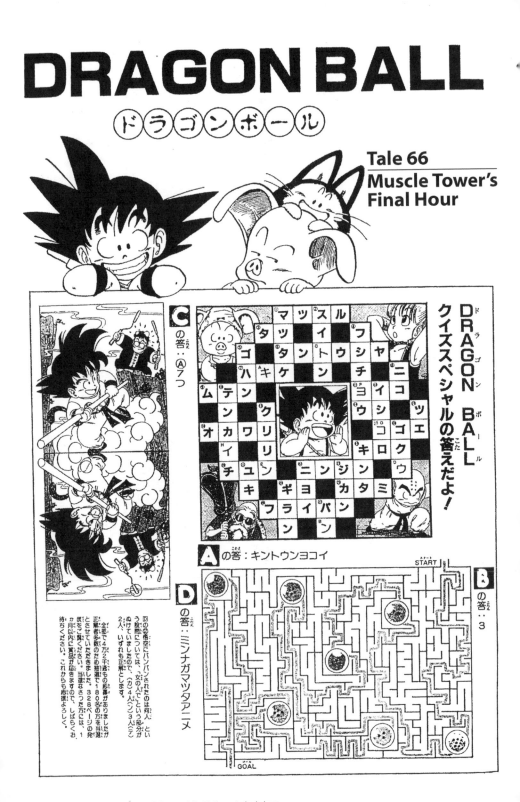

ドラゴンボール

DRAGON BALL

Tale 67 • Go West, Young Goku...

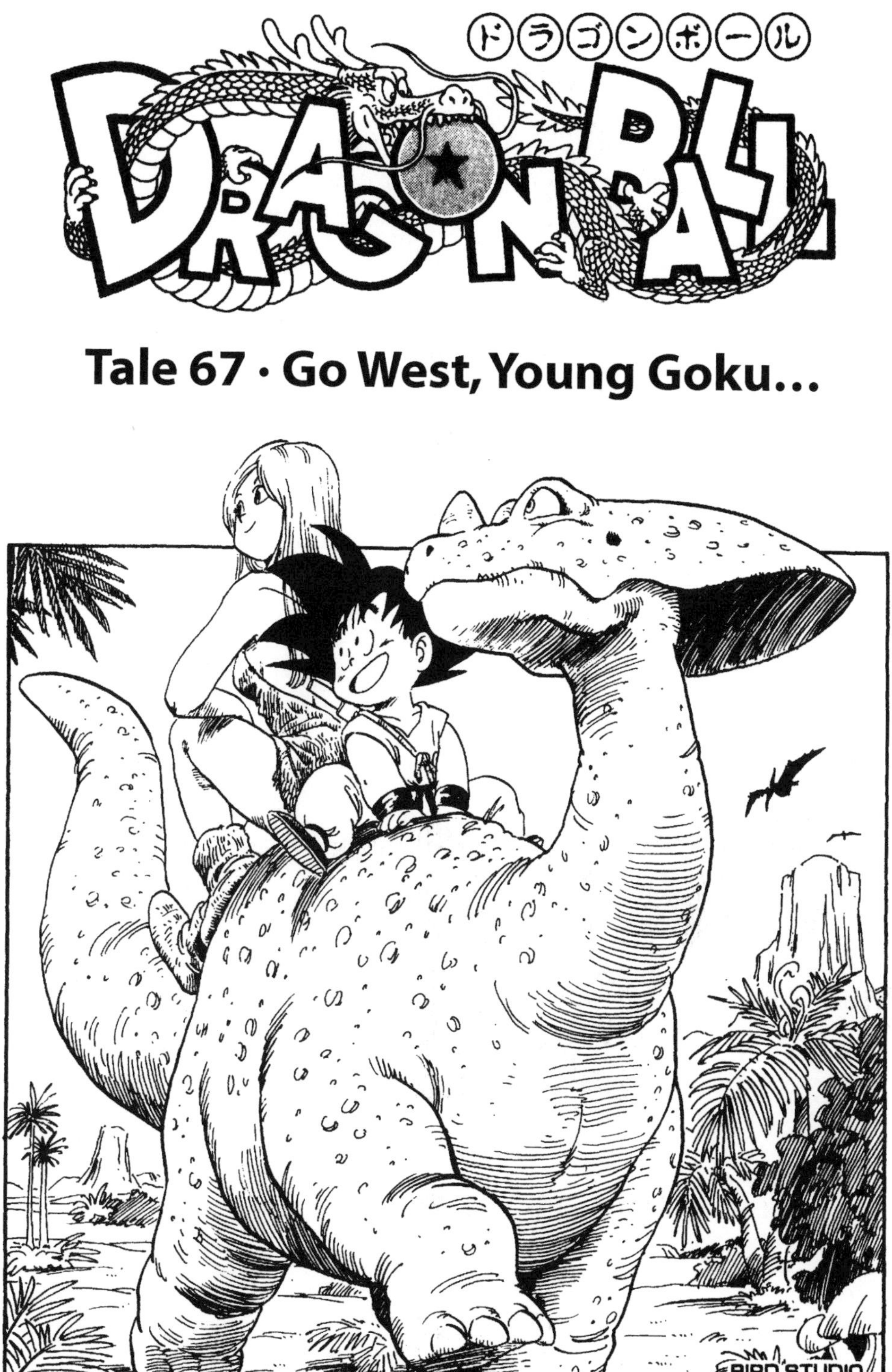
BIRD STUDIO

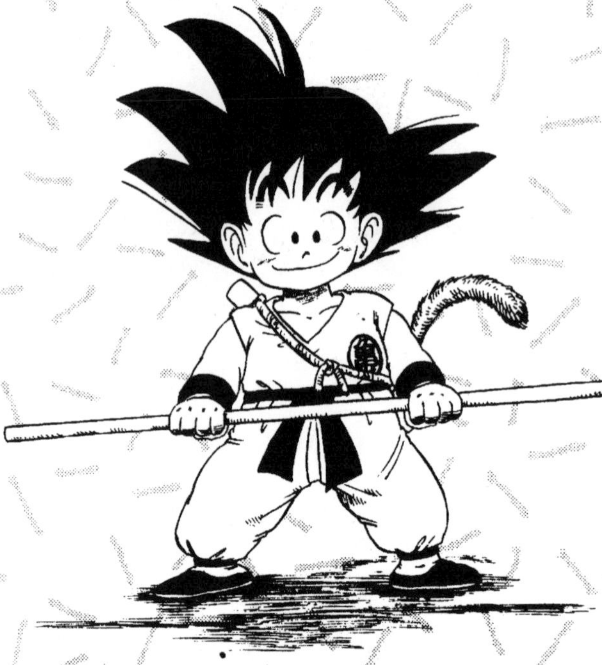

DRAGON BALL

Tale 68 • Monkey in the City

鳥山明
BIRD STUDIO

Tale 69 · Bulma and Goku

CAPSULE
CORP.
67

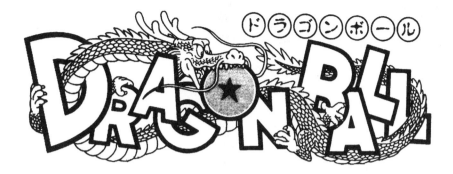

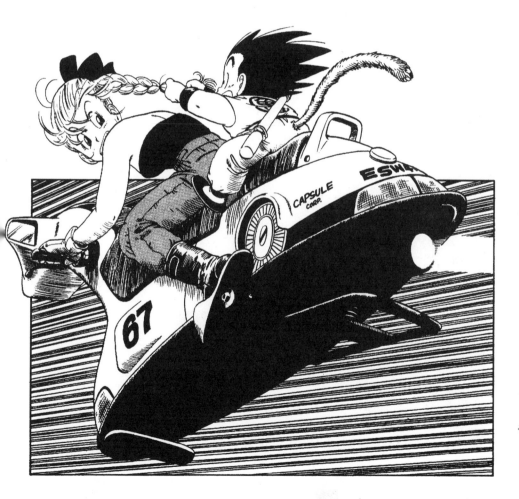

DRAGON BALL

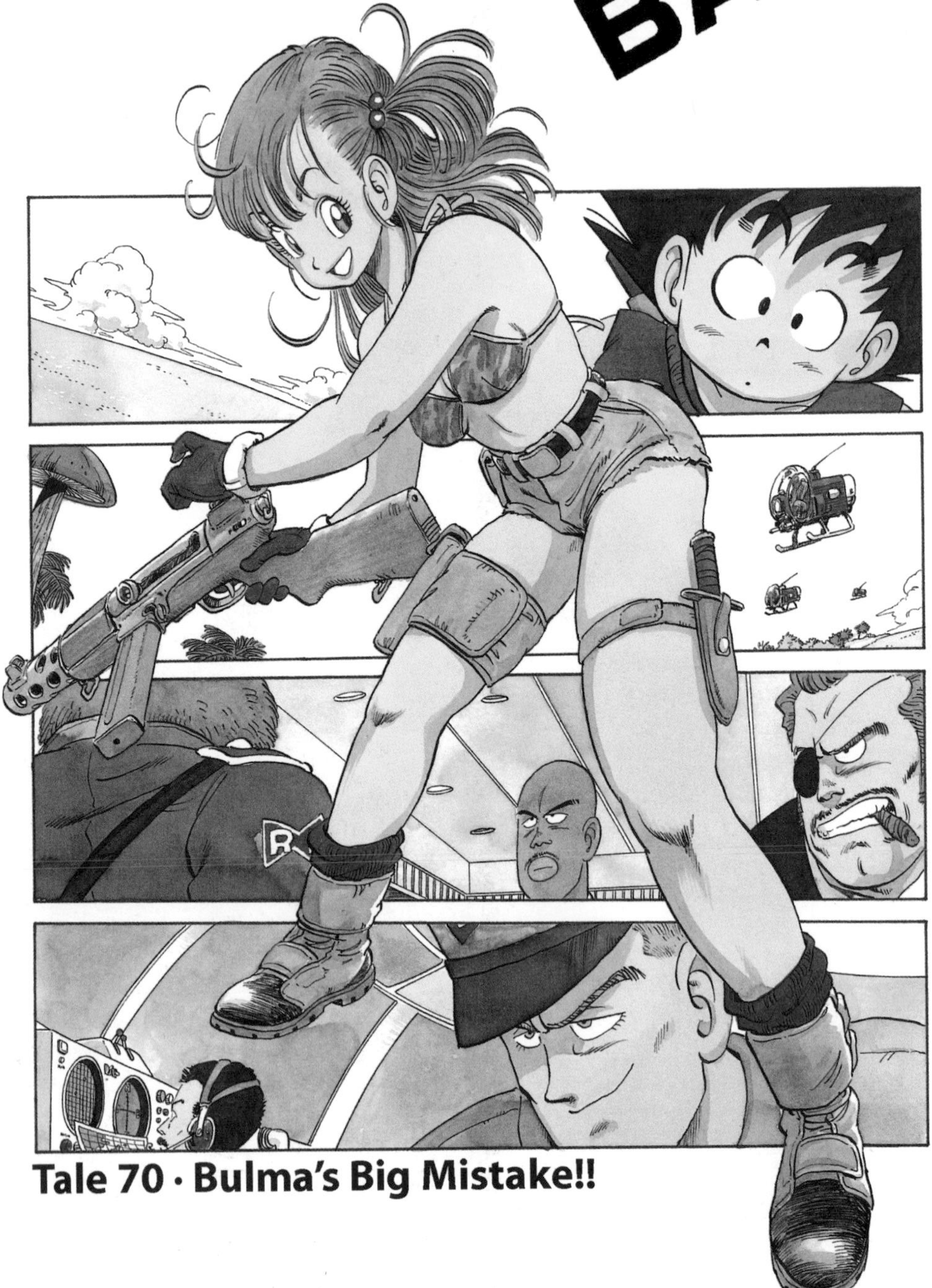

Tale 70 · Bulma's Big Mistake!!

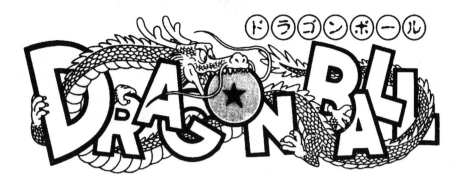

Tale 71 · The Turtle Is Spotted!

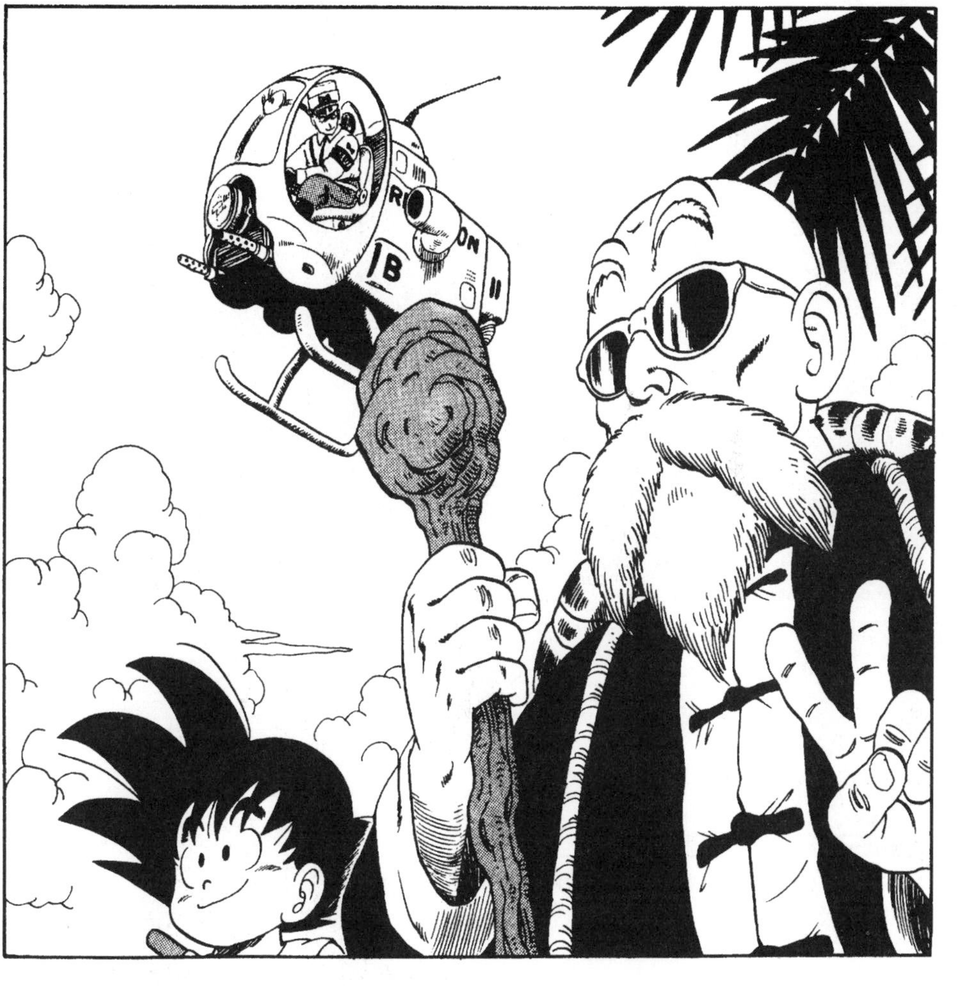

Tale 72 · The Blue Meanies

DRAGON BALL

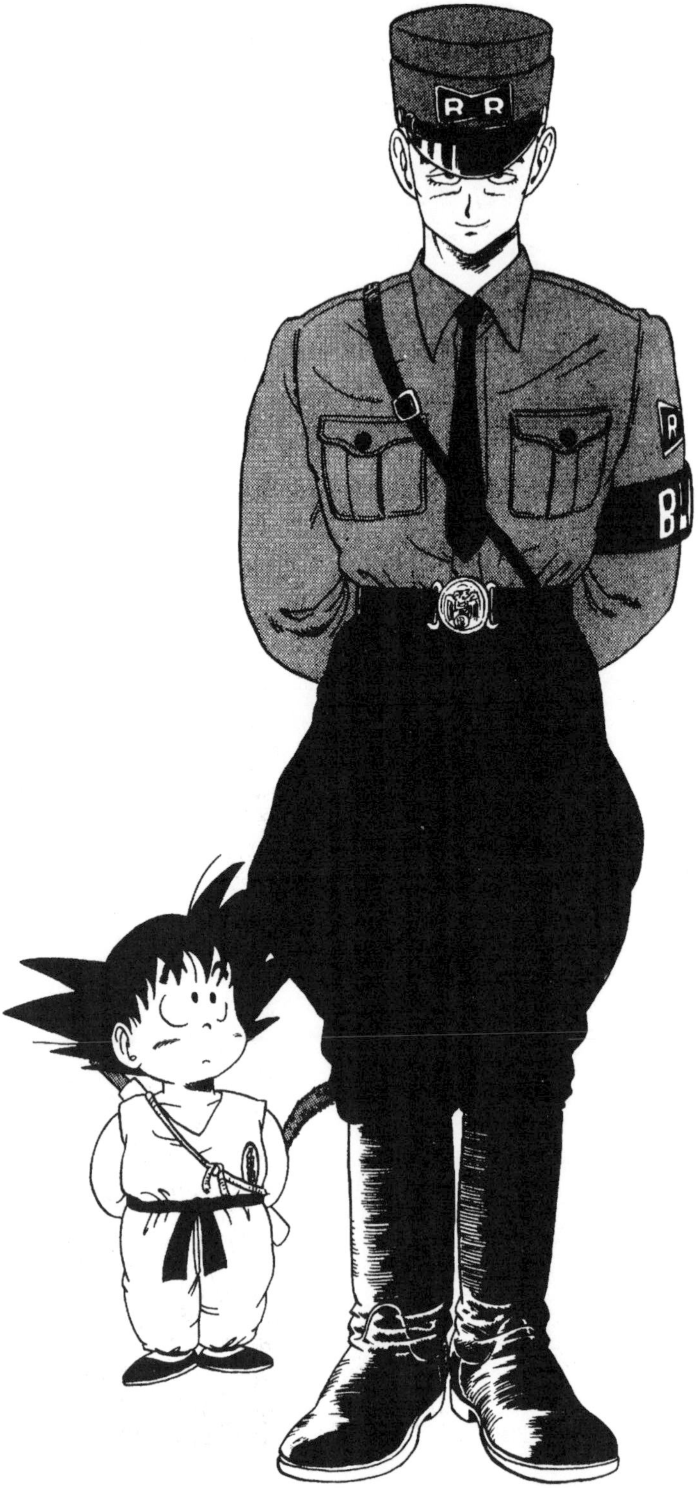
R R

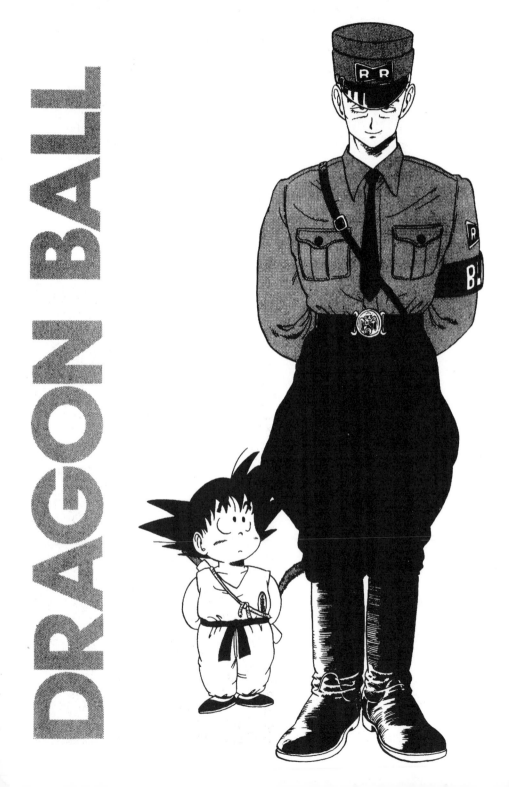

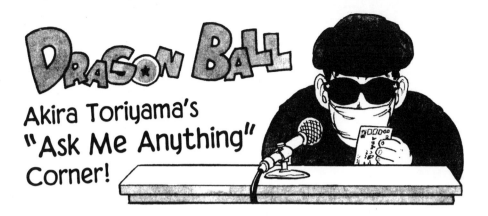

DRAGON BALL
Akira Toriyama's "Ask Me Anything" Corner!

Q. Hello Toriyama-sensei. I have a question. If you had one whole day of uninterrupted free time, what would you do?
–Naohiro Yonemoto, Tokushima Prefecture

A. Occasionally I do have a day of free time. [For *Dragon Ball*, Akira Toriyama drew an average of 15 pages every week for about 10 years—Ed.] I usually end up sleeping late and when I wake up I may go to the supermarket with my wife, or ride my bike, or see a movie, or work on a plastic model, or watch TV, or... I pretty much just putter away the day.

Q. Okay, I've figured it out... *Dragon Ball* is based on the old Chinese legend *Saiyūki* (Journey to the West). Even the characters are the same: Bulma is Sanzō Hōshi, Oolong is Hakkai, Yamcha is Sagojo, and Shen Long is Sanzō Hōshi's horse. Even the order that they appear in is the same. Am I wrong? I am a girl in my third year of middle school. [In Japan, junior high is always three years, and high school is always three years, so this is the same as being a 9th grader or a high school freshman—Ed.] I am afraid of the high school entrance exams!
–Masae O'ouchi, Ibaraki Prefecture

A. It's true, in the beginning I set out to create a modern-day version of *Saiyūki*. But soon it became difficult to remain true to the original, so I started ignoring it. So even though they have the same name, please consider my Son Goku and the monkey king Son Goku to be two different characters. However, I did get the Ox King story from *Saiyūki*. Good luck on your entrance exams!

The following contains selected questions and comments made by Japanese readers in volumes 4-6 of the original *Dragon Ball*, which were published in 1986-1987. Check out Akira Toriyama's answers to his fan mail!

Q. Since Son Goku and Kuririn both trained with Kame-Sen'nin, please have "Goku vs. Kuririn" be the final match at the Tenka'ichi Budōkai!
–Masayuki Katsumata, Osaka Prefecture

A. That's a very intriguing idea, but unfortunately it's too late for this tournament. The final match has already been set as Son Goku vs. Jackie Chun. But I think if there ever was a Goku vs. Kuririn match, Goku would win overwhelmingly.

Q. Just so you know, I really like Oolong tea and Pu'ar tea. By the way, in volume 1 where Son Goku meets Bulma, he says, "I never saw another human before!" Wasn't Goku's "grandpa" (the guy who raised him) a human?
–Yasuhiro Kubo, Nara Prefecture

A. W-Well...if you put it that way...yes. Oops...I made a mistake. Sorry, I apologize. You're also very smart to realize that I got the name "Pu'ar" from the name of the Chinese tea.

Q. I like Pu'ar. I told my brother that Pu'ar is a cat and he told me that Pu'ar is a mouse. Who is right?
–Nobukatsu Sekigawa, Kanagawa Prefecture

A. Actually, Pu'ar is neither a cat nor a mouse, but I draw him a little bit like a cat.

Q. The caricature that you draw of yourself in the comics looks like a dirty old man, so I thought that you probably looked like a dirty old man yourself. But I saw your photograph in Shonen Jump and you looked very handsome.
–Yasuhiro Ando, Aichi Prefecture

A. Ha ha ha! You think so? You're right! I do look good! You're a great guy! Unfortunately, I just can't get too excited about a guy complimenting me like this...

Q. What are those six marks on Kuririn's face? Is it a scar? Please tell me.
–Yasuto Tamagawa, Osaka Prefecture

A. Ah! You noticed it! The marks on Kuririn's forehead are incense burns. Sometimes you see these scars on Chinese monks in the movies. I thought I should add them because Kuririn's face is so plain.

Q. Often in the last page of your comic in Shonen Jump (the "free talk" page, where the artist answers letters from readers and talks about upcoming projects—Ed.), you write about how you have pet birds. I would like to become a manga artist, and I also love animals. I would love to draw manga and have a lot of pets.
–Koki Yasuda, Osaka Prefecture

A. I think it's a great thing to be an animal lover, although if you are going to have pets you should be responsible for them. In my household we have a bird, a cat, and a dog. Actually, if I could, I would love to also have a goat and a chicken.

Q. I always look at your manga and use them as a reference to draw my own manga. I really respect you. I have all of your manga including Dr. Slump, Dragon Ball, Hetappi Manga Kenkyujō (Lousy Manga Laboratory), and Toriyama Akira Marusaku Gekijō (Akira Toriyama's Insert-Adjective-Here Theater). I keep them to use as reference material. In particular, Hetappi Manga Kenkyujō greatly influenced the way I draw manga.
–Takeya Nakamura, Okinawa Prefecture

A. Thank you. You've complimented me so much I'm a bit embarrassed. Please keep up the hard work on drawing your own manga.

Q. I love Dragon Ball. I really like Bulma. Please continue to draw your great manga.
–Mami Sato, Ibaraki Prefecture

A. Surprisingly, there are a great number of girls that say they like Bulma. Perhaps it's because her personality is a bit like a boy's. Personally, I don't really like harsh, selfish girls like Bulma.

Q. I was really happy to see Kuririn appear in the manga. (Although he hasn't made an appearance in a while.) Kuririn looks exactly like my daughter who is about to turn one year old.
–Akina Deura (my daughter), Shizuoka Prefecture

A. Thank you. So, your daughter looks exactly like Kuririn... I don't know how to respond to that. But I'm sure your daughter is very cute. By the way, does she have a nose?

Q. On the spines of the Dragon Ball graphic novels, so far you've drawn a Dragon Ball with one star for every volume of the series. What will you do if the series goes over seven volumes?
–Tatsuhira Koike, Saitama Prefecture

A. You're right! The spines with the drawings of the dragon and the Dragon Balls will end after the seventh volume. I am wondering myself what to do from the eighth volume on.

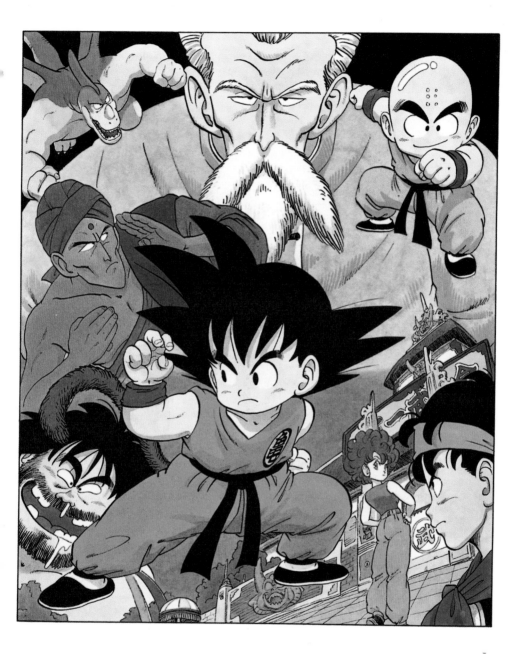

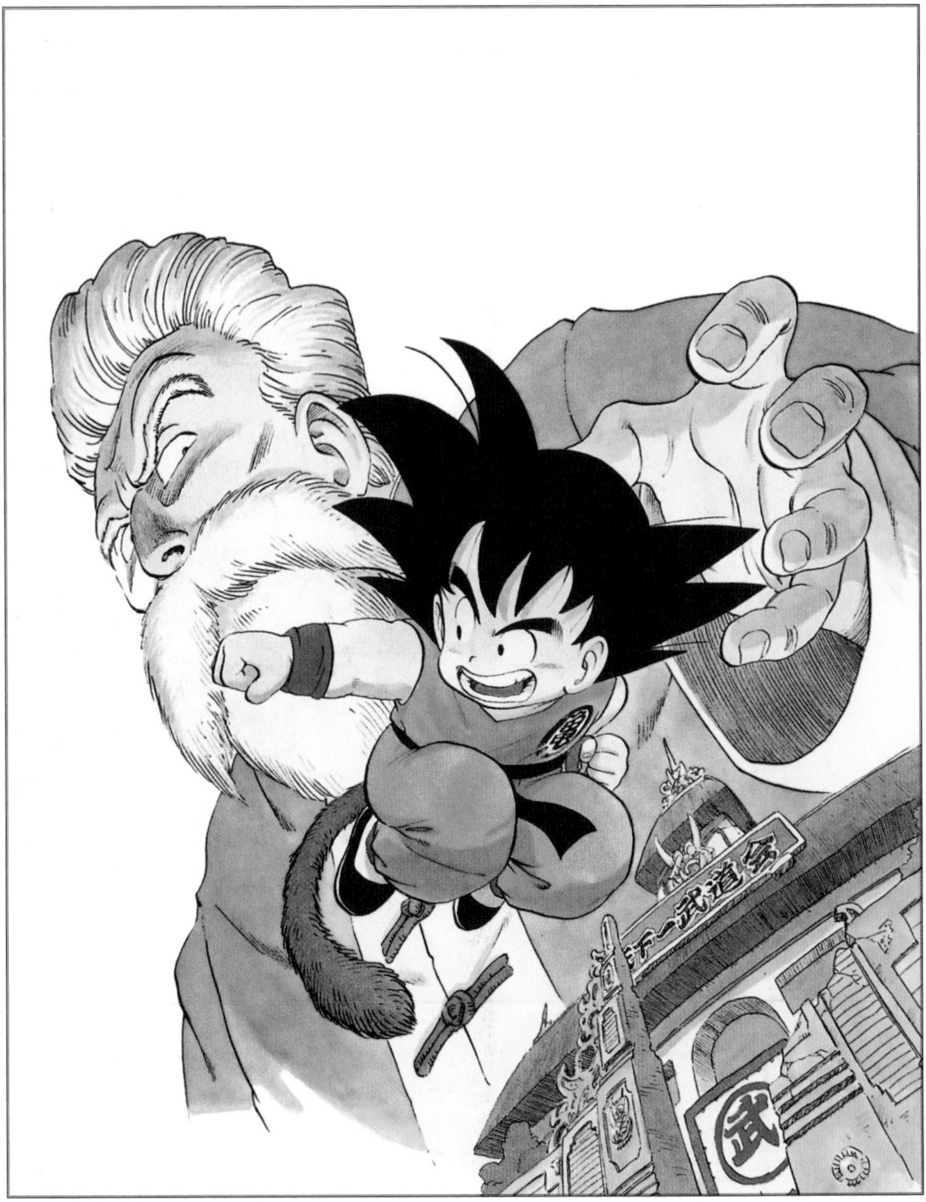
下一武道会
武

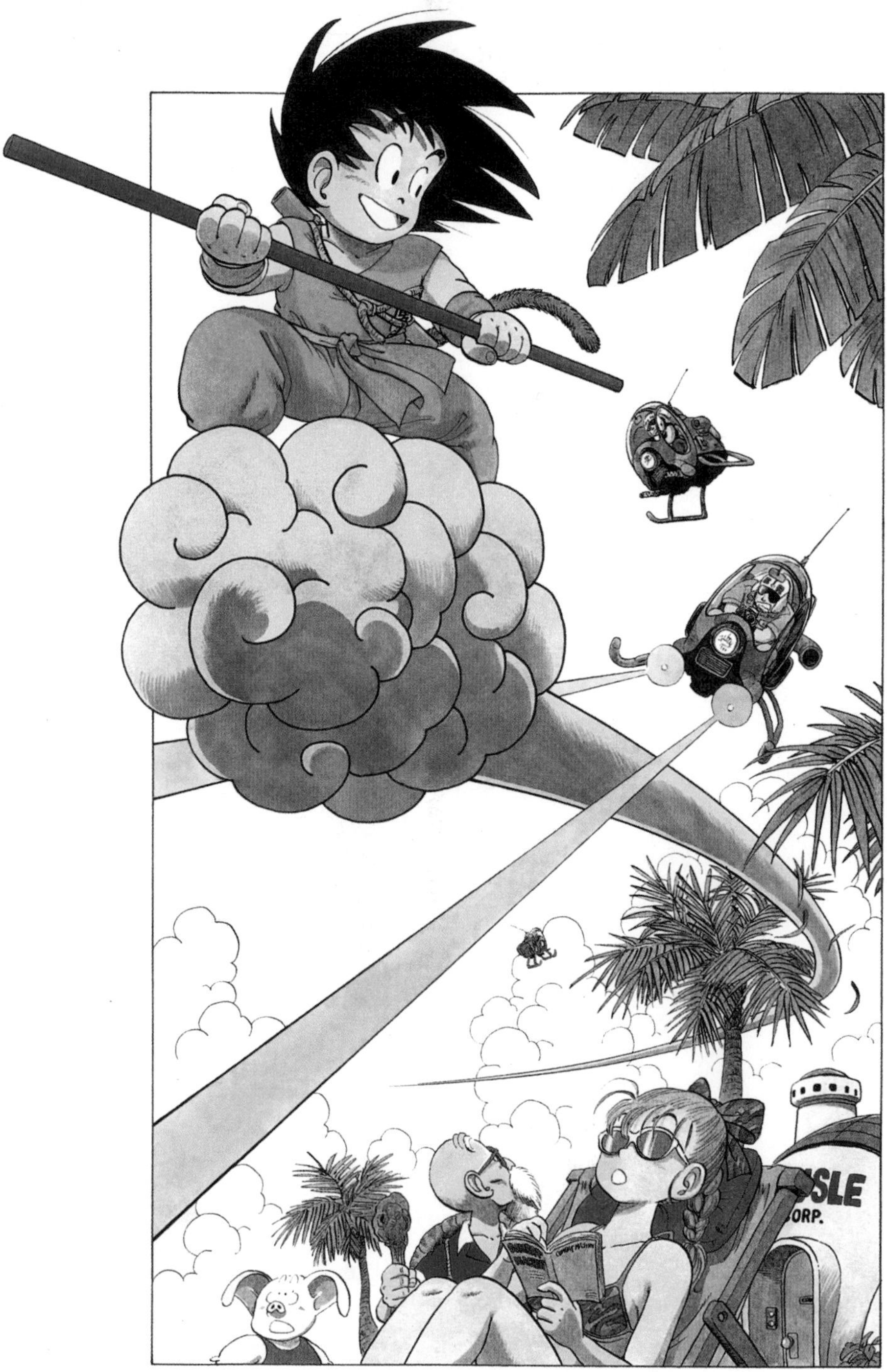
SLE
ORP.

AUTHOR NOTES

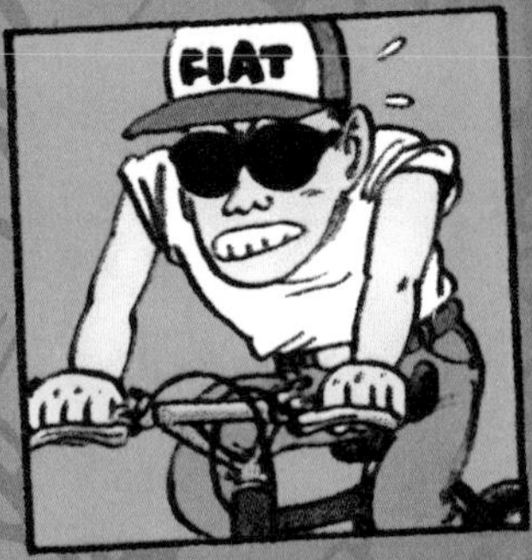
FIAT
1986

VOLUME 4

I've recently slacked off on my exercise routine, getting lazy and using the motorcycle or the car to run short errands. As a result, I now have a sizeable gut. I thought to myself, "This'll be bad if it goes on any longer!", so I made the decision that I'd at least *try* to get in shape by riding a bicycle. That was the theory anyway. In practice, I always end up looking at women along the way and riding slower than dirt. You couldn't really call it "exercise"...

VOLUME 5

I've mentioned this many times before, but I really hate the cold. If you turn on the heater, your head feels like it's in a daze, and if you turn it off, your hands get numb from the cold and you can't even hold your pen properly. When it gets cold I stop riding my bicycle and I only go places by car. Frankly, I'm just not that much of a cycling enthusiast. Oh, and I just want to hibernate! Spring, hurry up and get here! Every winter's day I long for you to come.

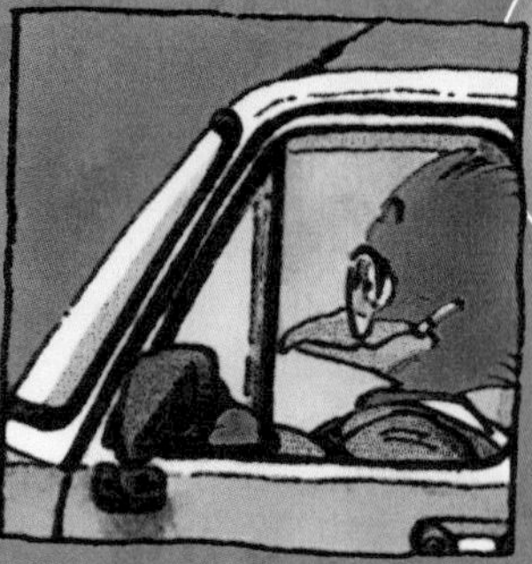
1987

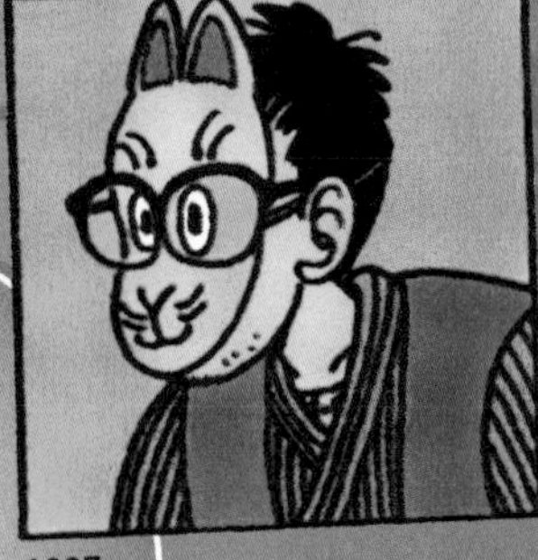
1987

VOLUME 6

Recently, the neighborhood where I live has started to get more developed, with new roads and shops being built. It's pretty convenient, but on the other hand, it's getting rarer and rarer to see weasels, pheasant or quail. The noise level has increased too. Being a country boy, I prefer a nice quiet lifestyle so I can really take it easy and reeeelax. I know it might be inconvenient in some ways, but I'd like to live way, way out in the country. This is the sort of thing that I end up thinking about.

IN THE NEXT VOLUME

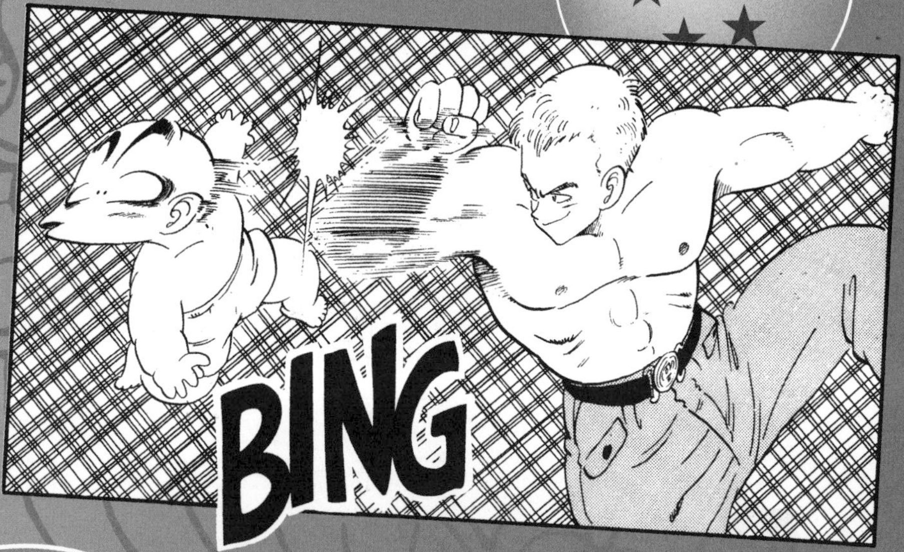
BING

The Red Ribbon Army is closing in on all sides! While Kame-Sen'nin fends off the troops that have infiltrated his island, Goku, Bulma and Kuririn try to outrun gun-toting bad guys underwater. The gang is in for a whole lot of trouble, especially when General Blue steps up with his mysterious power...

AVAILABLE NOW